1 MONTH OF
FREE
READING

at
www.ForgottenBooks.com

By purchasing this book you are eligible for one month membership to ForgottenBooks.com, giving you unlimited access to our entire collection of over 1,000,000 titles via our web site and mobile apps.

To claim your free month visit:
www.forgottenbooks.com/free228588

ISBN 978-0-266-21838-8
PIBN 10228588

This book is a reproduction of an important historical work. Forgotten Books uses
state-of-the-art technology to digitally reconstruct the work, preserving the original format
whilst repairing imperfections present in the aged copy. In rare cases, an imperfection in
the original, such as a blemish or missing page, may be replicated in our edition. We do,
however, repair the vast majority of imperfections successfully; any imperfections that
remain are intentionally left to preserve the state of such historical works.

SECOND REPORT

OF THE

Provost Marshal General

TO THE SECRETARY OF WAR

ON THE OPERATIONS OF THE SELECTIVE SERVICE SYSTEM TO DECEMBER 20, 1918

WASHINGTON
GOVERNMENT PRINTING OFFICE
1919

DECEMBER 20, 1918.

ɘ SECRETARY OF WAR.

IR: Herewith I submit my second report as Provost Marshal
eral. This report covers the operations of the selective draft
m May 18, 1917, the date of the selective service act, to the
sent date, with special reference to the operations since December
1917, the date of my first report.

Provost Marshal General.

III

CONTENTS.

CHAPTER I.

A SURVEY OF EVENTS AND POLICIES.

CHAPTER II.

REGISTRATION.

CHAPTER III.

THE PROCESS OF SELECTION.

VI CONTENTS.

Chapter V.

SPECIAL GROUPS OF REGISTRANTS.

Chapter IX.

Chapter X.

List of Text Tables.

CONTENTS.

List of Charts.

CHAPTER I.

(I) INTRODUCTION.

Nineteen months of war have brought to a successful conclusion our conflict with the Central Powers. Entering the struggle at a time when the prospect was decidedly dismal, we witnessed German success advance to an almost overwhelming allied defeat, until, throwing our hastily assembled forces into the balance, we saw impending catastrophe turn into brilliant and decisive victory.

We are now too close upon the events accurately to assess them. How great a part American Selective Service played in the drama of the world war, history alone can tell. That a new and untried scheme of selection could succeed at all was to many doubtful; that it should attain results beyond the fondest dreams of its most ardent supporters was unbelievable. To enroll for service over 24,000,000 men; to mobilize a selected Army of more than 2,800,000, a million of them within the space of 90 days; to have presently available for military duty 2,000,000 additional fighting men; to classify this vast group of man-power in the order of its military and industrial importance, so as to preserve the domestic and industrial life of the Nation, to speed up war-time activities, to maintain them in a status of maximum efficient production, and to pave the way to a speedy return to normal peacetime pursuits while recruiting the full fighting strength of the Nation—these are results which would be instantly rejected as impossible did not the actual facts stand as irrefutable testimonials of their accomplishment.

The registration.—In the first report submitted to you on December 20, 1917, it was stated that the classification of the first registration group which had been enrolled on June 5, 1917, and which then numbered 9,586,508, was just beginning. On June 5, 1918, by the registration of men who had attained the age of 21 since June 5, 1917, and whose enrollment was authorized by the Joint Resolution of May 20, 1918, 735,834 were enrolled. On August 24, 1918, the registration of youths attaining their majority since June 5, 1918, was accomplished, and increased the enrollment by 159,161 men. Finally, on September 12, 1918, under the provisions of the act of August 31, 1918, a final registration of all men between the ages of 18 and 45, both inclusive, who had not previously registered was accomplished, and 13,228,762 men were added to lists of those available for military service. Including interim accessions, a total of 24,234,021 men was enrolled and became subject to the terms of the Selective Service Law.

That this vast labor should have been accomplished without friction and without the slightest manifestation of antagonism on the part of any disturbing elements is in itself a complete vindication of the loyalty of the American people. The organization of each registration proceeded to a completion of its task with the smoothness and facility of the perfectly adjusted machine. In contrast to riots and bloodshed attendant upon the enrollment under the civil war draft act, the cheerful and eager submission of the nation to the assumption of its military obligation is a glorious monument to the unselfish spontaniety of its patriotism.

The classification.—The classification of man power thus enrolled so as instantly to disclose the relative importance to the military and industrial realms of its components was the next great task. Under the scheme outlined in my former report, all available man power was to be grouped into four classes in the inverse order of its industrial importance; the fifth class containing those exempted from all liability under the terms of the selective service law. Class I was to constitute the reservoir of man power, the drain of which for military duty would least disturb the domestic and economic life of the nation. The other classes were to contain the men whose domestic and industrial relations were such that their call to the colors should be deferred as long as the exigencies of the military situation would permit.

My report of December 20, 1917, carried the statement that—

It can be announced now as the policy and belief of this Office that in all probability it will be possible to fill our military needs without ever invading any class more deferred than Class I; and this is the promise, the standard and the goal. here for the first time announced, toward which every administrative effort of this Office shall be directed.

The promise has been fulfilled. Our fighting forces were supplied with men from Class I, and from Class I only. From the ordinary walks of civil life, 2,810,296 men were drawn and placed in the military service. But the deferred classes have remained intact. When hostilities closed, there remained in Class I a supply of fighting men sufficient to meet every military necessity.

The classification of the twenty-four million registrants proceeded rapidly. The first registration group of over nine million was disposed of in little more than 60 days, and the registrants of June 5 and August 24, 1918, were speedily classified. On September 18, 1918, the local boards began the task of classifying the registrants of September 12 between the ages of 19 and 36, both inclusive. By November 1, this labor had been substantially completed and the boards took up the work of classifying the remaining registrants, i. e., the 18-year-old men and those above the age of 36. Their efforts were well under way when the signing of the armistice on November 11, put a halt upon their work. On November 11, the local boards were, pursuant to your direction, ordered to complete the classification of the 18-year-old men and the men between the ages of 19 and 36 but to discontinue the classification of registrants above the age of 36. Their labors were completed before December 10, 1918, when their records were sealed and their activities ended.

With the accomplishment of this stupendous labor, the foundation and framework of the selective structure were erected. With a complete registration and classification effected, the whole field of available man-power turns, as if by magic touch, from a conglomerate mass of potential resource into a well-ordered, easily manipulated supply, capable of ready adjustment to any military or industrial emergency, making possible the facile control of the nicest military-industrial balance, the maintenance of which the selective organization necessarily assumed.

Economic necessities.—But with the classification completed by successive registration stages, and the separation made between those who should properly contribute their energies to the fighting forces in the theater of war and those who for industrial or domestic reasons should be retained in their civilian status, the task of selection was not completely accomplished.

War makes strange stern calls upon affected nations. It not only demands its armies but requires heroic adjustments in civil walks. New industries spring up and must be continued; the nonessential pursuits must be curtailed or abandoned and every energy bent toward a common purpose. As time goes on, the steady drain upon man-power for the battle front increases, industrial tension quickens, the factory and the mill must yield to the sterner call of wartime preparations. The supply of labor, skilled and unskilled, the proper maintenance and adjustment of industrial and agricultural production, the slow and careful combing of the nonfighting groups so as to yield the greatest military return with the least disturbance of civil activity, all these become matters of vital national importance. How to divert labor, skilled and unskilled, from the nonessential to the essential industries; how to prepare an easy transition from wartime activities to peace time conditions—such are typical of the broader problems with which selection concerned itself to the very end, each growing increasingly delicate as time went on. It is true that the selective draft act was primarily a means of raising armies. But there was not lacking in the minds of the proponents of the measure and of the Congress which enacted it, an appreciation of the broader aspects to which I have alluded. This was evidenced by the provisions of the bill, as proposed by the Department, looking toward liberal deferments and exemptions because of dependency and occupation. So it was that the act, and the regulations made in aid of its execution, looked both to a military and economic classification which would not only effect the deferment of the economically useful, but would also furnish a ready means for diverting their talents into civil pursuits most directly contributing to the efficient maintenance of the military establishment.

Great national issues have been affected by it. The one of ship-building was referred to in my first annual report. The war found us without the essential requirement to the conduct of an overseas campaign, namely, an immediately available merchant marine, and all the energies of our nation were exerted to the building of one. The genius of construction was ours, but labor, skilled and unskilled, was not at hand. The contributions of the selective draft of this labor and of the operative crews are statistically presented elsewhere in this report, and form one of its most interesting chapters.

But these tasks, indispensable to the preservation of our domestic and economic life, did not proceed in the quiet isolation of peace time conditions. The burning fact was always present, that the primary purpose of the selective service law was the raising of armies.

Mobilization.—On January 1, we had accomplished the mobilization of 516,000 men. On September 30, 1918, 2,552,173 selected men had been mobilized. In the first nine months of the current year, therefore, we put into the camps and cantonments over 2,000,000 men. In addition, when the Student's Army Training Corps was created, 145,000 youths were inducted into the service for military training during the continuance of their studies in some 500 colleges and universities throughout the country. On November 11, 1918, when your order directed the immediate discontinuance of all mobilization, we had produced a selective army of 2,810,296 men. Had mobilization lasted five days longer, the selective service organization would have placed with the colors more than 3,000,000 soldiers.

I call your attention to the fact that mobilization under the selective plan began on September 5, 1917. At the end of the first 14 months over 2,750,000 men were put in camp, and 14½ months of selective mobilization would have raised the total to more than 3,000,000 men.

Many difficulties were encountered growing out of the emergent demands upon the selective service organization. The accelerated program of the War Department came in the early summer, necessitating calls for men far in excess of the number that had theretofore been contemplated. During the months of May, June, and July we called to the colors 1,076,151 men. In the month of July alone 401,147 men were placed in camp. In the latter part of May an emergent call was made for the immediate mobilization of 50,000 men; we called and mobilized the full number within seven days after receipt of the requisition for them.

In the mobilization of these men, 1,708 separate calls were made, varying in sizes from calls for 1 man to 220,000 men. Men were sent to 283 mobilization points throughout the country. The average period of mobilization, that is, the time elapsing between the date of the demand upon this office and the date of the arrival of selected contingents at camp, was 20 days. Actual mobilization was accomplished in an average time of 5 days.

Every type of man desired by the Army, from the soldier qualified for full line service to the highly skilled specialist of limited physical qualifications only, was furnished. Of specially skilled men furnished, I mention only a few—bricklayers, expert timbermen, accountants, locomotive engineers, autogenous welders, draftsmen, butchers, cabinetmakers, meteorologists, chemists, veterinarians, and watch repairmen.

I have stated these facts in outline only. A full discussion of them appears later in this report.

State quotas.—The method of apportioning quotas was radically changed after my first report. The old rule of population, under which the first levy of 687,000 men was made, was abandoned, and, under authority of the joint resolution of May 16, 1918, Class I was made the basis of contribution among the States. The population rule early demonstrated its inequity, taking, as it did, no count of that part of the population which was exempted from draft and laying the burden of furnishing men for the Army without regard to actual availability. The population scheme was a blind rule of numerical equality only. Gross population included aliens, who under the terms of the law were exempted from draft. In districts with a large alien population, the population rule, therefore, resulted in a grossly disproportionate reduction of citizen population, which, in some instances, was little short of calamitous.

The adoption of the classification scheme carried with it as a necessary corollary, the basing of quotas upon availability for military service. Without such a rule, we would soon have been confronted with the intolerable situation of having one community furnishing its contingents from Class I while a neighboring locality would be drawing upon Class IV. The concurrent operation of the classification plan and the Class I quota basis obviated the injustice that would otherwise have ensued. Class I had to be exhausted nationally before a more deferred class could be made subject to military duty. Since Class I was the class the members of which were most easily spared from civil life, it followed that the end of the whole classification scheme, viz, the preservation of the domestic and industrial spheres, was thus, in a large measure, attained. The Class I quota basis regarded the Nation in war, not as 48 separate, jealous States, but as a firmly united whole, contributing to our fighting forces in a manner which would least disturb peace time normality, locally and nationally.

Voluntary enlistment.—But while the classification and mobilization under the selective service law were proceeding, the Army, the Navy, and the Marine Corps were recruiting under the old system of voluntary enlistment. Enlistment in the Army, as to registrants, was discontinued on December 15, 1917; but recruiting in the Navy and Marine Corps, as to registrants, and in the Army, as to nonregistrants, continued until August 8, 1918, when all voluntary enlistments were ordered discontinued.

Such recruiting played havoc for a time with the orderly process of selection. During the period in which enlistments were permitted, 1,300,000 men were withdrawn from the available source of supply, upon which the selective service organization relied. The volunteer plan took no heed of economic value; it received as readily the man indispensable to production as it did the industrially worthless. We were presented with the strange anomaly of a nation which had intrusted its man power to a selective organization, at the very breath turning over the same resources to an indiscriminate withdrawal by the agencies of recruitment. The task of accounting became highly difficult; an equitable or efficient apportionment of man power between the military and industrial realms was impossible. Recruitment disturbed every phase of the scientific administration of our task and impaired the efficiency of the whole organization.

These facts were readily cognizable by the summer of 1918, and all recruitment was discontinued. The act of August 31, relegated the Navy and Marine Corps to selective drafts in securing additional man power, and for the remainder of the war every branch of our fighting forces was supplied through the selective service organization.

It is not certain, however, that the country as a whole, thoroughly understood the imperative necessity of eliminating indiscriminate volunteering. The desire for its continuance persisted to the last, in infrequent requests that it be reopened, at least as to registrants in Class I. Experience showed that such a course, if widely adopted, would prove most unwise, as it would have led to uncertainty in mobilization and to substitution against which we could not guard too jealously, if the democratic ideals, to which we had pinned our faith, were to prevail to the end. To carry selection to its logical and efficient end, there could be no deviation from the rule that each registrant must await his time and perform his military obligation only when his call, in orderly process, came to him.

In brief outline, this is the story of the selective draft since the last report to you and up to the cessation of hostilities, the date upon which the selective organization halted its constructive efforts. Detailed and elaborate treatment will be found in the following pages.

I would be remiss in the performance of a public duty did I not, at this point, accord the credit which is so richly due to the war governors and their several State headquarters, the 155 district boards, the 4,648 local boards, the 1,319 medical advisory boards, the 3,646 legal advisory boards, as well as their auxiliary agencies of Government appeal agents, examining physicians, boards of instruction, and other civilian and enlisted assistants, upon whom has fallen the great strain of the task that has been accomplished. No labor has been so onerous and no demand so exacting but that it has been performed with a zeal and dispatch that are unparalleled in the history of free peoples. Without adequate compensation, often at great financial sacrifice, the members of the local administrative organizations have bent themselves to their tasks with a devotion that spells the imperishability of our democratic instititions.

I am certain that no great national undertaking was ever begun which depended so utterly upon faith in a people for its execution; and undoubtedly no faith has ever been more completely justified and no confidence more abundantly rewarded.

(II) SOME LESSONS OF EXPERIENCE.

Before casting a survey into the future, I turn aside to make one or two comments suggested by the administrative experience of the draft.

In the report of Brig. Gen. James Oakes, acting assistant provost marshal general for Illinois, in 1865, printed in the report of the Provost Marshal General of the United States for the Civil War (Final Report to the Secretary of War, 1866, Pt. II, p. 37), there is a remarkable passage, in which the writer of the report expresses the hope "that the great lessons of the war will not be lost upon the country," and predicts "that if these lessons are wisely improved, the Nation would embark in another war, whether foreign or domestic, with incomparably greater advantages for its successful prosecution than were possessed at the commencement of the late rebellion." The remarkable thing about the prediction thus made is that the hope expressed was verified in a degree so complete that it merits national thankfulness. The preceding few pages of that report commented on nearly a dozen features of the Civil War draft in which, it was pointed out, shortcomings had been developed. The principal recommendations made for the avoidance of these shortcomings in the future were as follows: (1) Registration by personal report of the citizen at a registration office, and not by a house-to-house census; (2) the determination of regional liability for man-power to be made by the place of residence of the citizen, and not by his casual place of registration; (3) the responsibility for furnishing quotas to be allotted to the several States, and not to the congressional districts, and the calculations of the quantities to be centralized at State headquarters; (4) substitutes to be forbidden; (5) bounties for volunteering to be forbidden; (6) short periods of service to be abandoned, and the duration of the war to be the uniform period of service; (7) State headquarters to have a supervising medical aide; and (8) State officials to have legal advisers on the administration of the law. It is a notable fact that every one of the lessons thus pointed out in 1865 was followed in the year 1917, either in the selective service act itself or in the regulations issued thereunder. And thus it happened that we entered upon the present war with all the advantages which the reporting officer, in his solemn warning of 1865, had hoped that we would possess "in another war, whether foreign or domestic."

Fortified as we thus were by the lessons of the Civil War, and profiting as we have done since the first six months of 1917 by our initial experience in the present system, there remains indeed no large scope for critical comment based on the experience of the last 10 months. Nevertheless, a few important topics suggest themselves, upon which it is desirable here to interpolate comments; these may serve to answer questions that have occurred to the minds of observers of the system during the present year.

Civilian administration.—The quickness with which the American people adapted themselves to the selective service law, and their ready cooperation in carrying out its provisions, were notable. Since the foundation of this Republic our people have inherited a deep-seated prejudice against anything akin to universal compulsory military service. This tradition, to be sure, was offset by the popular will to win the war—so imbued were they all with the determination to perpetuate democratic ideals—so impressed with the knowledge that not only was it necessary to raise an army but to raise it quickly. Nevertheless, such a stupendous undertaking could not have been accomplished through a system not in harmony with the National spirit. And the most influential feature in bringing about this harmony was the fact that the selective draft system was mainly placed in the hands of men taken from the people themselves—a civilian organization without previous experience except in the diverse civilian pursuits. The knowledge that the privilege and the responsibility belonged to them made the draft more popular with the citizenry than if it had been effected by purely military processes. It was their task, and its achievement was their reward. The system was peculiarly democratic in that it lodged the maximum of authority with the smallest unit practicable. It was essentially the people's institution, subjecting our form of government to the severest test and resulting in its triumphant vindication.

State agencies.—The use of the State officials in administering the draft has unquestionably brought about a closer union between the States and the Central Administration, thus welding more firmly the various parts of the Union. The governors of the States have become in a sense Federal officials, with a sense of responsibility to the National Government that did not theretofore exist. The significance of this feature of the system, and its lesson for the art of American Government, receive fuller comment in Chapter X of this report.

Since it became necessary to function with great rapidity under the selective service law, in order to place adequate armies in the field, speed was the controlling idea in perfecting the organization of the personnel of the various draft boards and officials throughout the country. Here it was necessary to rely upon the sound judgment and integrity of the various draft executives of the States in selecting the personnel. It would naturally have been expected, therefore, that in such a hastily constructed organization, many errors of judgment in making such recommendations would be committed, and that even in some instances evidence of political influence would appear. The result, however, bears out the conclusion that the executives of the various States were thoroughly imbued with the patriotic desire to create a war machine of maximum efficiency, and that they made efficiency their sole watchword. In consequence, maladministration in the performance of official duties was noticeably less than in the cases of officials constituted by the usual methods of election and appointment. The personnel of the Selective Service organization was perhaps its greatest possession, because upon it depended the success of every activity connected with the operation of the draft.

Deferred status as a means of evasion.—Not much difficulty was experienced by draft officials in determining the worth of a registrant to the Nation as affected by his industrial or domestic status prior to the initiation of the selective service system. But a just decision upon a status acquired by change of circumstances subsequent to the act was not always plain and simple of attainment. Some criticism developed, on the ground that there was a lack of uniformity throughout the country in the interpretation of the rules governing such cases. In the field of dependency, this was met by a ruling, issued from this office on June 13, 1918, prescribing the conditions under which claims based on recent marriages might be granted;

and the general opinion of draft officials was that this ruling brought about uniformity in the consideration of such cases. A similar ruling, governing a subsequently acquired industrial and occupational status, would probably have prevented a great many evasions of military service. It is beyond doubt that thousands of registrants succeeded in evading service, by removing to farms purchased by indulgent parents, and by other like means, undertaken subsequent to the passage of the act; and that, therefore, the system did not effectively prevent on the part of registrants the evasion of its requirements. But it is also true that, in the absence of an auxiliary system of conscription for industry, the classification of registrants according to their status at any fixed date would not have been practicable.

The selective service regulations, therefore, while not being proof against the wiles of the artful evader, at least effected one of two things: Either they placed such registrants in the military service, or they forced them, through fear of such service, to engage in a useful industrial or agricultural undertaking, thus probably preventing the necessity for legislation that would have signified labor conscription.

Jurisdiction of boards.—The statutory provision vesting in district boards the original jurisdiction in industrial and agricultural cases was of doubtful wisdom. In many instances, such boards were too far removed from the locality of the individual registrant to be able to know or to ascertain the actual economic conditions of his community. Many district boards followed substantially the cursory recommendations of local boards in occupational cases, while other boards ignored such recommendations, relying upon data which were often incomplete and artificial. The provision made in September, 1918, for the appointment of three industrial advisers for the respective district boards, went far toward remedying these conditions, though the cessation of hostilities and the resultant suspension of mobilization prevented a full test of the wisdom of this plan. On the whole, a more just and effective classification would have been secured, had original jurisdiction in all cases been vested in local boards, reserving to district boards a jurisdiction strictly of an appellate character. This would have effected a fairer coordination of industrial and dependency deferments, and a reviewing authority other than the President would have been provided for occupational cases.

Delinquents and deserters.—It must be admitted that the selective service system was not altogether successful in dealing with draft evaders, delinquents, and deserters. The fault lay not primarily in the law and regulations governing this phase of the draft. In a few regions, undoubtedly, registrants could with impunity refuse to obey the requirements of the law. The selective service officials possessed no police or penal authority of their own; and although the Department of Justice, and police officials generally, rendered valuable service in enforcing the draft, this division of responsibility naturally lessened their efficiency. By a very substantial enlargement of its field force, had that been possible, the Department of Justice could have handled the situation. But it is believed that a more effective method would have been to provide local boards with sufficient police assistance thoroughly to cover their respective territories. Moreover, net desertion lists would have been substantially reduced had a definite scheme been adopted of requiring the regular publication, through the press, of alphabetical lists of delinquents and deserters in the same manner as casualty lists are published.

Publicity.—The publicity incidentally brought about by the draft process has thrown light upon practically every problem in our social and economic life, and has formed an invaluable stimulus to the progress of the Nation. The reference is not to publicity in the sense of public knowledge of once private facts, but in the sense of a conscious stirring up of universal interest in the many aspects of community life. It has been the greatest educative process in the history of the country. Ignorance has been exposed, and with its exposure the necessity for greater educational facilities has been impressed upon all the people. Disease, heretofore hidden in holes and corners, has been uncovered. With all has come, in many quarters where it was needed, the conviction on the part of all intelligent citizens that there must be new methods and new efforts. The stimulus thus given to patriotic and disinterested organization for the purposes of the common welfare will be the means hereafter of saving an hundred times the lives lost in the war.

(III) THE FUTURE.

The war having now been brought to a successful conclusion, the activities of this office and of the whole selective machinery will soon come to an end. Perhaps it will not be without interest to outline the policies that were shaping and the plans that were developing when the close of the war was reached. If these matters are now no longer of present value, the consideration of them may not be without worth, if the Nation is, at some future time, again presented with an emergency such as that through which it has just passed. Nor am I uncertain but that, in the administration of selective service, we have evolved certain principles of national significance which can be applied as advantageously in times of peace as in time of war, and the successful execution of which was never contemplated until the impetus of war forced us to the test.

That selective service can raise expeditiously a fighting force limited in numbers only by the demands of the Army and Navy has been conclusively demonstrated. In 14 months little short of

3,000,000 selected men were mobilized, and an abundant supply still remained in Class I. If military necessity had ever become so dire that its demands could not have been met from the supplies of Class I, there existed a simple solution for the shortage, which, happily, never arose. The primary object of the selective service law—that is, the raising of a fighting force—was, therefore, fully attained.

But the task of selective service does not stop with the raising of armies; rather it becomes more intricate and more highly difficult.

The classification scheme sorted out from over 24,000,000 registrants and placed in Class I those whose withdrawal from domestic and industrial connections would create the least disturbing effect upon the current of our national life. But the remainder far outnumbered those who went to the fighting forces. The residue, the deferred classes, formed the great army behind the lines whose efforts had so to be directed as to contribute most effectively to the fighting forces. How to mold this vast group of man-power; how to weave its energies into the general pattern of national effectiveness, attaining a maximum of wartime production and a minimum of peacetime disturbance—these were the problems, herculean in magnitude, yet susceptible of only the most delicate treatment, to which the selective organization had to address itself.

From the wartime standpoint, occupations may be roughly grouped into three classes:

1. Those enterprises such as shipbuilding and the manufacture of munitions, which have a direct and immediate relation to the military problem.

2. Those enterprises contributing to the general good, without which the normal life of the Nation would be seriously affected and the continuance of which must be fostered to render a return to peacetime conditions easy.

3. The harmful and nonproductive employments.

For the man-power between the ages of 18 and 45 in each of these groups the selective system was responsible.

Let us examine each of these labor groups separately. First, however, it must be stated that the ultimate aim of the selective service system was to eliminate entirely useful man-power in the third, to comb the second to the minimum consistent with the preservation of the framework of normality, and to fill the first to the utmost possible limits. The whole scheme may be envisioned as an instantaneous destruction of the third group, a gradual compression of the second and a constant expansion of the first. To the accomplishment of these ends, the selective service law provided powerfully persuasive means, holding out the alternatives of productive employment on the one hand and enforced military service on the other.

1. THE NECESSARY INDUSTRIES.

Compulsory deferment.—The first task was to preserve intact the industrial group then employed in the war time industries, the so-called "necessary" industries, which have a direct relation to the military problem. Only when we have preserved the original group may we concern ourselves with the enlargement of it.

The regulations, promulgated in execution of the selective service law took abundant precaution to withhold from military duty the labor and directing talent necessary to the continuance of such industries. The regulations always contemplated the deferment of call to military service of men necessary to the continuance of them and their scope was extended from time to time. Deferment on the ground of employment alone was, therefore, the initial step in the solution of the problem. To attempt the enlargement of an industrial group and yet to take no precaution to preserve the original nucleus is to build with the one hand and to destroy with the other.

There was at first no safeguard thrown about the industrial type, which, though indispensable to production, sought to enter the military service. Fired with a patriotism which conceives the highest obligation as service in the fighting forces, large numbers of men whose energies were of infinitely more value in the industrial world than on the battle field, abandoned their productive labors for service in the Army or Navy. It was here that the pernicious system of volunteer recruitment, to which I have already referred, dealt its most vital blow. What selection sought to establish and protect, recruitment consistently disrupted and disorganized. The industrial expert voluntarily enlisting in the Army or Navy left vacant a place in the forces of production to occupy a place which he could not fill with equal effectiveness in the fighting forces. The industrial group, which selection had been zealously building, was thus subjected to a steady and alarming drain. When viewed from this standpoint, it is inconceivable that the advocates of voluntary enlistment should have continued to press their point. If patriotism is the desire to serve one's country, then the highest type is the desire to serve one's country best. If the industrial expert is of greater value in the factory than in the field, then it is unpatriotic for him to abandon his labors in the former to resume them in the latter. Fortunately, the evil of recruitment was finally abandoned definitely for the period of the emergency.

The evils of voluntary enlistment existed in a less degree in the opportunities offered to registrants in deferred industrial classes to secure voluntary induction into the service through the medium of the Selective Service organization. Originally, no restraint had been placed upon such voluntary induction and the hurtful effects of recruitment were modifiedly duplicated by it. The regulations promulgated in September, 1918, however, placed additional restraints upon the classes deferred on account of industrial usefulness. To waive industrial deferment for the purpose of securing induction into the Army was made more difficult of accomplishment. Great pains were taken to lay before the Nation the patriotic duty both of employers and employees to claim and establish the right to deferred classification for all those whose occupation was such that necessary industrial effectiveness would have been reduced by their withdrawal for military service.

Thus were established the partial means for protection of the "necessary" industries, both nuclei and accretions.

But before hostilities ceased, the time was rapidly approaching when we would have been compelled to take the final step in the process and to have denied absolutely to the registrants deferred upon industrial grounds, all rights to military service. We had almost reached the time when it would have been necessary to make it as impossible for the man deferred for industrial reasons to secure military service as it had been for the registrants in Class I to avoid it. This was the logical end to which we had been led and to which we had inevitably been tending.

When this final step had been taken we would have effectively accomplished the end which we had set out to attain.

Compulsory transfer.—But it is one matter to conserve labor in the "necessary" industries from withdrawals by the army, and another matter to augment labor in those industries to the desired scope. Both are equally important. We were not prepared to accept an industrial draft, and therefore had to look elsewhere for a solution.

Fortunately, the means for supplying the initial additions of labor in these industries were readily available. For two and one-half years prior to the declaration of war against Germany, our country had been serving the embattled nations of Europe. Labor had already thronged to the munition factories and the powder mills, and the rapidly rising wage scale accelerated the influx. The lure of the rising wage brought its full measure of returns. But wage competition became so keen, and in many instances its results were so little short of calamitous, that it was folly to believe that the ebb and flow of labor supply could or should be governed by such means alone. Indeed the efforts of other departments of the Government had long been devoted to the elimination of the indiscriminate competition and to the stabilization of all wage scales.

Here the selective service law furnished a powerful lever needed for forming into the "necessary" industries the needed additional supplies of labor. The operation of the "Work or fight" regulations is fully set forth in the later pages of this report. Demanding, as these regulations did, that continuance in a deferred class on the ground of dependency should be contingent upon employment in a productive occupation and that every man should become an effective producer or a soldier, the result of the regulations was to destroy idleness and to drive from the nonproductive pursuits all registrants whose deferment hinged upon a change of occupation.

The possibilities of this principle are practically limitless. They are as wide as the field of labor itself. The "Work or fight" principle had been only sparingly applied when the war ended, but it had already succeeded in cleaning out the idle class and the small group of occupations theretofore declared to be nonproductive. The labor thus diverted turned, perforce, to the field of necessary or productive industry. The shipyards, for example, were materially aided by the augmentation of labor in them. We had only to extend the scope of the "Work or fight" regulations to produce their added effectiveness. As time went on, more and more occupations were to be catalogued as nonproductive and the evacuation of labor from them would have been initiated. The labor thus affected turns for reemployment naturally to the fields of highest wages. Since the highest wage scale is found in the purely war time industries, the labor thus diverted turns almost as a unit to these very industries. Thus at one stroke is accomplished the elimination of the nonproducer and his transformation into the most effective producer.

In time of war, we have only to apply the "Work or Fight" principle understandingly and sympathetically to attain any desired adjustment of the labor supply. Cooperation with other departments of the Government to this end will prove helpful. When the war ended, the Department had under consideration the immediate extension of the scope of the "Work or Fight" regulations. It was considered that the study of this problem and the execution of the future policy in respect of it were among the most important tasks remaining for the Selective Service organization.

Group transfer.—The "Work or Fight" principle was effective in diverting labor from the nonproductive to the productive employments. But since its purpose was persuasive only, it did not go to the length of dictating to the nonproducer the exact field of employment to which he should turn his efforts upon abandoning his nonproductive occupation. It is true, the consideration of higher wages in the most essential labor fields, and the economic law of supply and demand in the several industries within these fields, must have an important bearing on the ultimate location of such labor. But, when the laborer has his choice between, say, the shipyard and the munition factory, he may choose either the one or the other. It is conceivable that situations may arise when it is possible to obtain abundant labor for the shipyard and insufficient labor for the munition factory, and when the "Work or Fight" doctrine will not adequately serve to divert the deficit of labor to the munition factory. We had, therefore, to seek some measure supplemental to the "Work or Fight" regulations which would solve the problem of diverting labor into definite branches of necessary occupations. The "Work or Fight" regulations served to turn labor from the nonproductive to the productive fields, but they did not serve to distribute productive labor among the various industries in the productive fields. How could this be accomplished when the ordinary law of supply and demand failed to produce the desired result?

There was abundant legal authority for calling into military service, through the selective service organization, any or all of a particular group of skilled industrials, regardless of their classification. It was quite feasible, therefore, to call for service all or any part of a group of skilled labor and to offer to the men thus called the options of remaining in the Army for military duty or accepting an indefinite furlough dependent, as to duration, upon the continuance of employment in a certain definite work. The industrial furlough had been, in a limited way, already employed in individual cases, but it had not been extended to an industrial group.

Assume that there should have arisen a shortage of labor in the longshore labor group, which could not have been adequately filled under any of the methods in operation. Under the law it was possible to call for military service all skilled longshoremen who were subject to the Selective Service Law. When these men had been inducted into the military service, they might each have been offered an industrial furlough upon the condition that they secure and retain employment in the loading of transports and supply ships. The result of such a method is easily visualized. The necessary labor would have been secured and the uncertain shifting of it that might otherwise have ensued would have been stabilized. The adoption of such a plan to meet emergent situations arising out of labor shortage in particular fields of necessary industries was not foreign to my thoughts when hostilities ceased.

Labor efficiency.—But after all precautions had been taken to protect the necessary industrial classes by granting deferred classification to the members thereof, and after these classes had been increased through the methods outlined, a complete solution of the problem had not yet been attained. While the "Work or Fight" regulations, for example, succeeded in diverting such labor from nonproductive to productive fields, they had not been sufficiently broad to insure a fair and honest return from the labor thus diverted. In other words, the bartender turned shipbuilder might or might not devote a decent effort to his new vocation. If he did not, there was no recourse for the selective organization to pursue, as his nominal employment in a productive field placed him beyond the purview of the existing "Work or Fight" regulations.

Many factors could and did exist which tended to slacken the efforts of labor in the necessary industries. Many of these were found in labor's conscious and willful avoidance of a full and fair measure of exertion. The habitual failure or refusal of a certain class of registrants employed in occupations not declared nonproductive, to devote a fair amount of time per week to their tasks gave rise to a distinct group which may be termed "industrial slackers." The elimination of this group was another task to which the selective organization had to bend its efforts.

The "Work or Fight" regulations had received instant popular approval. The public had been more than ready to accept the doctrine that the man who was industrially useless should lose the deferred classification which he would otherwise have continued to enjoy. But the criterion of industrial usefulness was made employment in a useful occupation. It is quite apparent, however, that a man may be as useless to production while nominally engaged in a productive industry as if engaged in a nonproductive one. Unless he devoted a fair and reasonable amount of time and energy to his work, no matter what that work may be, he is a slacker whose pernicious inactivity should be reached.

The remedy that suggested itself was simple. We had merely to class as a nonproducer, and make subject to the "Work or Fight" regulations, the registrant who, though employed in a useful occupation, did not devote a reasonable amount of time to his work. There is no difficulty in determining what a "reasonable amount of time" is. Labor has consistently insisted, and it is generally impliedly recognized, that eight hours is the reasonable working day. From such a premise it would not have been difficult to determine a "reasonable working week." Having determined a "reasonable working week," it would have been a mere matter of regulation to provide that the deferred classification of no registrant should be continued unless he devoted such reasonable length of time per week to the useful occupation in which he was employed. In other words, a minimum working week would have been established and the failure to observe it would have deprived the registrant of his deferment regardless of any other industrial or domestic connection.

Regulations putting into effect the principle described above had been prepared and submitted to you for approval when the signing of the armistice obviated the necessity for their promulgation.

97250°—19——2

2. THE NORMAL AND THE NONPRODUCTIVE EMPLOYMENTS.

The second industrial group is made up, as has been indicated, of those enterprises contributing to the general good without which the normal life of the Nation would be seriously affected and the continuance of which must be fostered to render the return to peace time conditions easy. These are the industries which constitute the framework of the normal economic life in times of peace. They must not be destroyed nor ruinously injured in time of war if the difficult return to peace is to be anything short of chaotic. We can never risk becoming a Nation without the means for supplying the ordinary necessities and the smaller comforts of civil life. Neither can the production of these things in a period of hostilities proceed along peace-time lines if war-time development is to be speeded.

The task in the war just ended was not to eliminate, but so to compress this group as to maintain its framework while at the same time producing the maximum of efficiency and production in the necessary wartime industries.

There were many outside influences at work which aided the selective organization in the accomplishment of its share in this particular task. The curtailment of production in many of these industries, made possible by the action of other departments of the Government, released supplies of labor for the necessary war industries and the higher regulated wage scales in the latter also attracted the labor which might not otherwise have been forthcoming.

But there were many occupations with abundant supplies of labor in them which could be reached only by the Selective Service organization. It was to these employments that the peculiar obligation of the administration of the Selective Service organization attached —for example, chauffeurs. This group consisted of well over one hundred thousand men engaged in all phases of the employment. Obviously, men thus employed could not be controlled by the agencies authorized to regulate production in the various industries, for they produce nothing. But it required only an extension of the "Work or Fight" regulations so as to include chauffeurs, or certain designated types of chauffeurs, in the nonproductive employments, to divert their labor to other channels.

Labor groups, similar to chauffeurs in their relation to the economic structure, are numerous and could be reached only through the selective organization. Regulations extending the scope of the "Work or fight" principle had been submitted to you when hostilities ceased and their approval became unnecessary.

The third group, to which reference has been made, is the nonproductive. The extent to which the "nonproductive" field has been defined by the "Work or fight" regulations when the war ended, has already been indicated. But it had been realized that the scope of those regulations would have to be enlarged in direct ratio to the exigencies of the situations as they developed. The primary purpose was not to destroy the nonproductive occupations, but to utilize the available man-power in them. The continuance of such occupations, in time of war, with the labor of women and the physically and legally disqualified is not only possible but actual.

3. THE LOCAL AND THE NATIONAL VIEWPOINTS.

In dealing with the broad questions of labor distribution by means of selective service, there is one important consideration that ought not be overlooked. It is true that all of the larger problems of a great war are national and must be solved with the end in view of obtaining the greatest national efficiency. But we can not afford to lose sight of the fact that all wars eventually come to an end, and that sooner or later the Nation must return to a peace-time basis. This Nation, at bottom, is one of local entities. It would be such for geographical reasons alone even were it not fundamentally so politically. The solidarity and the prosperity of the Nation are, under our peculiar organization, dependent upon the well-being of the local community. To disrupt the whole economic structure of the community for the single purpose of promoting the maximum of national production is not only a harsh rule, but, with the return of peace, a ruinous one. If the return to normal peace-time conditions is to be made anything less than impossible, we must take the steps while still at war successfully to accomplish the eventual readjustment.

We cannot afford absolutely to destroy local economic life except in the direst military necessity. We must leave in each community the framework of its normal economic structure. In this way alone is an easy readjustment possible. Yet, withal, the overwhelming consideration, during an emergency, is national and not local effectiveness. How to attain the greatest national good with the least local harm, therefore, becomes the nicest and most delicate problem which can present itself.

With this end in view the Selective Service administration consistently entrusted to local agencies the duty of determining the industrial usefulness of its registrants. The criterion was always national necessity, but no other attempt was ever made arbitrarily to define those necessities. The American people have always appreciated the fact that national well-being is inextricably bound up in local well-being; they are too patriotic to allow local interest to impede national success during an emergency. As a result, we secured a classification of skilled labor which kept local life going, while at the same time national industrial development proceeded at a rapid pace. Skilled labor was classified from a national viewpoint, so tempered by a local one that national development was unhampered while communities retained the roots of economic life; and these, now that peace has returned, will again blossom into pre-war fruition.

We should never permit ourselves to become so imbued with nationalistic ideas about labor during a period of war as to lose sight of the local economic life to be resuscitated when war ceases.

It is perhaps to be regretted that the selective service law as originally enacted did not provide for a classification of labor upon industrial grounds as broad as industry itself. Yet the haste in which the act of May 18, 1917, was prepared, and the lack of precedent available at the time, precluded the enactment of a more perfect measure. The act of March, 1863, the Civil War draft measure, contained no provision for industrial deferment. The British military service acts, complicated by antecedent war labor policies, succeeded so little in systematizing an industrial classification that the results by the spring of 1917 were confusion rather than an orderly scheme for military-industrial correlation. The original selective service law was therefore an experiment so far as the scope of industrial classification was concerned. The amendment of August 31, 1918, broadened the field to the proper limits.

That district boards should have been made the tribunals for the solution of industrial readjustment can no longer be doubted. The duty imposed upon them was likewise an experiment, the wisdom of which subsequent events fully justified. The evolution of selective service developed two antagonistic viewpoints respecting the proper distribution of war-time labor. On the one hand were those who would have made all labor questions matters of purely national significance; on the other hand, were those who would have tested each labor question in the light of local situations only. The district boards, standing between the two extremes, succeeded in accomplishing a distribution of labor from a viewpoint impossible alike to a national body or a purely local one.

4. AFTER THE WAR.

The end of the war leads one necessarily to a contemplation of the possible changes that may be brought about in our national life by the application, after the war, of the principles evolved in the operation of the selective service during the emergency. The feasibility of many theories, widely divergent from the pre-war conception of things, has been demonstrated. How far these principles should be projected after the war is a matter of vital national importance.

Before the war, it would have been considered highly improbable that a law requiring all persons within designated age limits voluntarily to present themselves at a given time for enrollment, would meet with any fair degree of success. Yet the enactment of such a law resulted in the enrollment of over 24,000,000 men—13,000,000 within a single day, and a total of over 24,000,000 in four days. Not alone was the enrollment accomplished, but a complete survey and classification as to the domestic and industrial status of those enrolled was made.

The machinery for enrollment has been once established, and there is no reason to suppose that it can not be reconstituted.

The taking of the decennial census has heretofore always proceeded upon the idea that no satisfactory results could be attained unless the desired information was sought out piecemeal and compiled. The possibility of having every man, woman and child report at a given place on a given day for enrollment and submitting to an examination as to domestic and industrial status, was considered remote, if indeed it was considered at all. The administration of selective service has demonstrated not only the practicability of such a scheme but the superiority of it in speed, accuracy, and completeness. What under the present census method is a matter of months, becomes under the selective procedure a matter of days. The machinery for the taking of the census by registration is established. To apply the selective plan to the census would not be an experiment but the extending of the application of a principle already established.

CHAPTER II.

REGISTRATION.

(I) FIRST REGISTRATION—AGES 21-30—JUNE 5, 1917.

Results of this registration.—The first registration, pursuant to the act of May 18, 1917, took place on June 5, 1917; an account of it was given in my first Report (December, 1917). The total number registered on that date (exclusive of the Territories), with accretions from tardy registrants and transferred cards up to November 12, 1917, was 9,586,508 (Report for 1917, Table 1). But new accessions filtered in throughout the intervening period; complete reports were received from the Territories; and the total number on the eve of the third registration (Sept. 11, 1918) was 9,925,751. After that date, any additional persons presenting themselves in the ages overdue to be registered in the first registration were required to be entered as of the third registration (Sept. 12, 1918).

(II) SECOND REGISTRATION—AGE 21—JUNE 5-AUGUST 24, 1918.

1. *Need for this registration.*—In the spring of 1918 it was apparent that the yield of effectives in the first registration would not suffice for the increasing demands of the military program; and a further registration for military service became necessary. On May 20, 1918, Congress passed a joint resolution (Pub. Res. No. 30, 65th Cong., S. J. Res. 124) requiring the registration of all males who had attained the age of 21 since June 5, 1917, on or before the day set by the President for their registration; and further authorizing the President to require the registration, at such intervals as he might prescribe, of all males attaining the age of 21 since the day of this second registration and on or before the next day set by him for such registration. This resolution made all such persons liable to military service under the act of May 18, 1917; but provided that they should be "placed at the bottom of the list of those liable to military service in the several classes to which they are assigned."

June 5, 1918, was fixed by presidential proclamation as the date for this second registration.

2. *Plan of registration.*—Anticipating the enactment of this legislation, a plan for conducting the registration was decided upon and communicated to the local boards three weeks in advance of the passage of the act. The registration organization was thus made ready in advance and was enabled to conduct the registration at an early date after the enactment of the law.

22

An experienced and fully equipped organization—the local boards—was in existence to accomplish the registration, and the vast machinery found to be necessary for the first registration would have been cumbersome as well as useless. It was therefore decided that every person subject to registration would be required to register under the supervision of the local board having jurisdiction of the area in which he permanently resided.

In the cities, normally, the office occupied by a local board was the place of registration. If this was deemed inadequate, the local board consulted with the adjutant general or draft executive of the State and obtained such additional rooms or offices as were authorized by him. In the rural districts the office of the local board, wherever practicable, was likewise the place of registration. It was realized that many such offices would be too small, and also, that in exceptional cases, registration offices should be established in cities and towns other than those in which the boards had their permanent offices. Whenever, in the opinion of a board, its office was too small or places for registration seemed to be necessary at other points, it consulted with the adjutant general or draft executive of the State and established such additional offices as he authorized. Of course, where the territory of a board was relatively large or travel therein was unusually difficult, registration offices were established at such points as were necessary successfully to accomplish the registration; but the fact that the board had jurisdiction over a rural district was not in itself sufficient to warrant their establishment. The determination of the necessity for additional offices depended upon the circumstances and conditions peculiar to the locality, and was a matter which was left largely to the discretion of the local boards. Offices in public buildings were procured wherever practicable, and rented buildings and rooms were not authorized unless other suitable offices were unavailable

A chief registrar had immediate supervision over each place of registration. Board members acted in the capacity of chief registrars. If there were more than three places of registration under the supervision of one board, or for any other reason a member of the board was not available to act as chief registrar, the board designated a thoroughly reliable registrar having familiarity with the regulations to act in the capacity of chief registrar. Generally speaking, the board members and salaried attachés of the board performed the duties of registrars; but, in the event additional registrars were needed, the board recommended to the adjutant general or draft executive of the State the appointment of such additional registrars, and, upon his approval of the recommendation, proceeded to make the appointment. The duties of registrars and chief registrars are explained in that part of the report relating to the registration held on September 12, 1918.

This second registration of June 5, 1918, added to the lists approximately 735,834 persons in all.

3. *Supplemental registration of August 24, 1918.*—But the rapid and unexpected increase in shipments of troops abroad, followed by equally large calls of new contingents to camp, soon made it plain that the authority of the President, given under the joint resolution of May 20, 1918, must again be exercised to require the registration of those who arrived at age 21 since the registration of June 5, 1918. Accordingly, on August 13, 1918, the President issued a proclamation requiring the registration on August 24 of all male persons (except those exempted by law from registration) who, since June 5, 1918, and on or before August 24, 1918, had attained their twenty-first birthday.

This registration was accomplished in the same general manner as that held on June 5, 1918; but, in view of the comparatively small number of persons to be registered, it was not necessary to provide as many registration places within the jurisdiction of the Local Boards as were provided for the registration held on June 5, 1918.

On this supplementary second registration approximately 159,161 young men of age 21 were registered.

Meantime additional tardy registrations were taking place of men due to have registered on June 5, 1918.

4. *Results of second registration.*—The total number of men of the new age 21, thus registering between June 5 and August 24, 1918, representing the entire second registration group, was 912,564.

(III) THIRD REGISTRATION. AGES 18–20, 32–45, SEPTEMBER 12, 1918.

1. *Necessity for extending the draft ages.*—The military situation, above alluded to, had begun to develop as early as March, 1918, when the great spring drive of the German Armies was started. The pressure of this drive on the allied forces made it apparent that the time had imperatively arrived for strengthening the defense at the earliest moment by the largest possible American contingent. Shipping was released for the purpose; the existing monthly program for deliveries overseas was more than doubled; and the calls upon the selective service for deliveries into camp were correspondingly increased. The list of inductions by months, given in Chapter VII, Table 79, shows the figures leaping up, from April onwards. At the same time, enlistments of men of draft age in the Navy and Marine Corps, and entries in the Emergency Fleet service, were rapidly increasing, due in part to the desire to enlist before being reached in the draft. The total of these and a few other important but unexpected items of depletion approximated 475,000 men. In other words, the 425,000

men originally scheduled by the program of early June as available for the October, November, and December calls, were found by the end of July to be more than offset by these 475,000 withdrawals. Thus it was apparent that, by September, the effectives available would number only 100,000, and perhaps less, after filling the calls indicated for July and August and making deductions for the unexpectedly heavy losses due to the rush in June and July to the Navy, Marine Corps, and Emergency Fleet. (Memorandum of the Provost Marshal General to the Chief of Staff, dated July 27, published in the Congressional Record, August 5, and printed here in Appendix B).

Class I, by the original program, would have sufficed until January, 1919. It now threatened to become exhausted in September, 1918. Even the increment from the newly registered youths of 21, on June 5–August 24, 1918, would be inadequate to replenish the gaps in Class I. Should the Nation now proceed to send into service its deferred Classes II, III, and IV, of the age 21–30 group, registered June 5, 1917? Or should it proceed to enlarge the age groups registered for service, and to call upon the Class I men obtainable from this additional registration?

In no quarter was any disposition apparent to adopt the former of these alternatives. The latter was therefore the obviously unavoidable one.

But the question then presented itself, How far was it necessary to go, in extending the ages, to obtain the necessary additions? In round numbers, 2,000,000 more men would be needed to fulfill the military program from October, 1918, to June, 1919. What combination of age groups would yield at least this number of men in effectives? A computation was made by this office (Appendix B). This computation presented the estimate in three studies, covering, respectively, the age groups 19–20, 32–40; 19–20, 32–45; and 18–20, 32–45; and the net estimated yield, based on the experience of the first registration, was, for the respective age combinations, 1,569,720, 1,722,870, and 2,398,845 effectives. Obviously, only the last and most extensive of these three combinations would suffice to meet the requirements of the military program.

2. *Legislative measures.*—A bill was therefore drafted, at the instance of the Secretary of War (S. 4856), and introduced in Congress on August 5, 1918, to enlarge the registration ages down to 18 and up to 45, inclusive, with a view to obtaining immediately the needed additions to military man power.

There was a natural reluctance on the part of many members of Congress to direct the taking of youths of minimum military age; and the debate on this subject is an illuminating record of the weighty considerations on both sides (Congressional Record, Aug. 5, 12, 21, 22, 23, and 24, 1918). But, in the face of the military necessity, the general policy became a matter of secondary consequence, and the bill was passed on August 31, 1918. Its provisions extended those of the Act of May 18, 1917, by subjecting to military service all male citizens and declarants "between the ages of 18 and 45, both inclusive." It further defined these persons as those "who shall have attained their eighteenth birthday and who shall not have attained their forty-sixth birthday on or before the day set for registration," and it provided for future expanding needs by authorizing the President to require at later intervals the registration of those who from time to time attained the age of 18.

On August 31, 1918, the same day of its passage, the President approved the act of Congress extending the draft ages to include all persons between 18 and 45 years of age. The date of September 12, 1918, was immediately set by the President as the registration day.

In anticipation of the enactment of the legislation, a communication was addressed on August 5, 1918, to the draft authorities of all States outlining the general plan for conducting the registration, if the then pending bill became a law. Consequently, all arrangements for the registration were practically completed before the passage of the act, and the registration could have been held as soon thereafter as was desired.

The law exempted from registration those who had previously registered, and also the following descriptions of persons: Officers and enlisted men of the Regular Army; officers commissioned in the Army of the United States, and men of the forces drafted under the provisions of the act approved May 18, 1917 (the selective service law); officers and enlisted men of the National Guard while in the service of the United States; officers of the Officers' Reserve Corps and enlisted men in the Enlisted Reserve Corps while in the service of the United States; officers and enlisted men of the Navy and Marine Corps; officers and enlisted and enrolled men of the Naval Reserve Force and Marine Corps Reserve while in the service of the United States; and diplomatic representatives, technical attachés of foreign embassies and legations, consuls general, consuls, vice consuls, and consular agents of foreign countries, residing in the United States, who were not citizens of the United States.

3. *Plan of registration.*—The Governors of all States and the Commissioners of the District of Columbia were called upon to supervise the execution of the registration in their respective States and the District of Columbia. The adjutant general or draft executive in each State, acting under the direction of the governor, was the central administrative authority of the registration system within the States. The local boards had immediate supervision and direction of the registration within their respective jurisdictions.

The actual registration was made in the customary voting precincts in the jurisdiction of each local board, and, generally speaking, at the place and in the manner ordinarily employed in the registration of voters. However, in exceptional cases, the boundaries of the voting precincts were disregarded, and registration booths were established by the local board in such places as seemed most desirable within its jurisdiction, after consultation with the adjutant general or draft executive of the State.

Each local board appointed a registrar or registrars for each voting precinct or place of registration within its jurisdiction. Where there was more than one registrar, one of them was designated by the local board as chief registrar; and where there was only one registrar, he performed the duties of chief registrar in addition to those of registrar. In each city and county or similar subdivision having more than one local board within its jurisdiction, this office urged that a central registration committee be organized from and by the membership of the local boards. Such committees were charged with the duty of coordinating and supervising generally the preparations for the registration and directing the activities looking toward a complete registration. County and city attorneys cooperated with the members of the legal advisory boards; marshals, deputy marshals, and police officers held themselves in readiness to render assistance in the execution of the law.

The responsibility for providing suitable places for registration rested upon the local boards, assisted by the Governor of the State, the mayor in cities of 30,000 population or over, the authorities of the county or similar subdivision (if they were not already serving on the local board), and the central registration committee in those jurisdictions where such a committee had been appointed. Registrars were charged in the first instance with making places ready for registration. This duty was performed under the direction of the local board. They were charged also with the duty of making the actual registration. The chief registrar, when not otherwise engaged, likewise made out registration cards, and held every person acting as registrar under him strictly accountable for the registration cards and certificates supplied to him. The chief registrar was likewise held accountable for the registration cards and certificates supplied to him by the local boards.

4. *Securing 100 per cent registration; publicity methods.*—The exhaustion of Class I under the first two registrations was impending. The new registration act had gone to the extreme age limits, recognized in our law for a century and a quarter past as the ages of liability for military service. And this extreme inclusion of man power was calculated to fulfill the military program up to June, 1919, only. It therefore behooved all concerned that the registration should

yield up, on the day of registration, the maximum man-power actually existing within those ages. In short, it became the task of the Provost Marshal General to insure a 100 per cent registration on September 12.

The problem was this: The estimates of male population for the new ages came to 13,200,000 (as set forth later in Table 65); from these must be deducted some 400,000 already enlisted in military or naval service and therefore not required by the law to register; leaving some 12,800,000 (estimated) due to register. It was necessary to register this entire mass, and then to classify those who were entitled to exemption or discharge. Though only about one in six or seven would ultimately find his way into a uniform, yet unless these 12,800,000 men all came forward, we should lose just so many proportionately for the Army. The registration was voluntary, in the sense that it could not be known who these men were, and that they must voluntarily and honestly come forward and identify themselves. If they shirked this duty, they would be lost to our registration, and we should never be able to find more than a few thousand of the shirkers. Therefore, the problem for the War Department was to make it psychologically a certainty that every one of those 12,800,000 men would hear of the need, would receive the President's message proclaiming his duty to register, and would honestly and frankly come forward and register. This was where the problem of publicity began—how to reach, in a startling, inspiring and universal appeal, every individual in those thirteen million. If they did not come forward under control of their own consciences, the loss would be substantially irreparable. We had to stake our whole result on the response of the men's consciences as citizens. The problem of publicity, therefore, divided itself into two: How to reach every individual so that he heard and knew of the call; and next, how to make him responsive to that call.

The President's proclamation (Appendix A), dated August 31, 1918, concluded with an eloquent and inspiring appeal calculated to evoke a loyal response to the call to register. Of this proclamation 700,000 copies were printed and distributed to all officials in the selective service system as well as to all postmasters. Governors and county and municipal officials were called upon to lend their assistance in organizing the registration.

But the time was short. Moreover, the selective service draft was now a well-worn theme to the public at large; they had been surfeited with announcements of its various phases. In May, 1917, the extraordinary event of our entry into the war, and the novelty of the draft, had a combined effect calculated to awaken every citizen to the knowledge of his duty to register. But in September, 1918, the situation was far otherwise. It was too likely that the extreme nature of the step thus taken by Congress would not be known or appreciated by a large proportion of our people, and that the registration would fail of its full harvest. We were attempting to do voluntarily in one day what the Prussian autocracy had been spending nearly 50 years to perfect. There was too much at risk to permit of sparing any effort that would insure against the risk. Accordingly it was decided to invoke the assistance of the two best organized official agencies that could be counted upon to reach every inhabitant of the country—every farm, every factory, every shop, and every home. These two agencies were the Council of National Defense, with its multiple State and local branches, and the Committee on Public Information, with its splendid organization for carrying publicity in every form. To the officials and staff of those two bodies particular gratitude is felt for the vigorous, unstinted, and effective assistance placed at the disposal of this office.

Among the various methods used for reaching and influencing all who were due to register, there were included the daily press (63 releases going to 4,000 newspapers), farm newspapers (bulletins to 150 farm weeklies), trade newspapers (bulletins to 500 trade weeklies), sundry newspapers (bulletins to 14,000 minor newspapers), foreign language press (reading matter and telegrams to 1,400 foreign language newspapers, covering 20 languages), chambers of commerce (25,000 bulletins sent through the United States Chamber of Commerce), manufacturers (bulletins sent to 15,000 manufacturers), labor unions (17,000 in all), libraries (9,000 in all), banks (32,000 in all), churches (125,000 ministers, priests, and rabbis), general stores (60,000 in all), Y. M. C. A. (3,500 branches in all), ad. clubs (bulletins to 8,000 advertising clubs and a similar number of Rotary clubs), postmasters (bulletins to 56,000 postmasters), railway station agents (bulletins to 55,000 station agents), painted signs (public billboards erected by 350 firms in as many cities), window display (35,000 posters distributed through 550 chairmen of local committees of the National War Service Committee on Window Display), street cars (50,000 advertising cards posted), drug stores (bulletins to 50,000 drug stores), and American Red Cross (100,000 bulletins to local committees). To reach the population in rural districts, 7,000,-000 leaflets were distributed by mail, one to every person on a rural free delivery or star route. In the meanwhile, several hundred cartoonists were supplied with material for cartoons in the newspapers. A film announcing the date, September 12, was furnished to 17,000 motion picture houses. For seven days before September 12 some 30,000 Four-minute Men spoke in all public places of resort. The Secretary of War and the Secretary of the Navy authorized commanding officers to loan all military bands for the day; and the

Council of National Defence notified mayors of all cities and towns of this opportunity to give patriotic emphasis to the occasion. So huge an effort at publicity, concentrated upon a single vital moment, had probably not before been made during the war.

And the gratifying feature was that virtually all of this publicity effort was contributed gratuitously by the persons who took part; down to the humblest worker in the cause this readiness to contribute service was notable. For example, in the Mailers' Union of New York City, numerous volunteers, after their day's labor elsewhere was done, came over at night to the office of the Committee on Public Information and took part in this work of the War Department. Including the donations of advertising space, the aggregate value of the total contributions amounted to several millions of dollars. The actual expense amounted to slightly over $20,000; and this covered some unavoidable expense in the preparation and distribution of printed matter and films.

As the day of registration arrived, it was apparent that every human being in the United States had been made fully aware of its meaning, and the occasion took on all the appearance of a public festival. The volunteer spirit prevailed over all. Every citizen seemed to feel that (in the words of the President's announcement for that day) "he owed it to himself and to his country to make the day a unanimous demonstration of loyalty, patriotism, and the will to win."

5. *Results of the third registration.*—The registration of September 12 was indeed America's final demonstration of military efficiency. The result showed that this registration, in the President's words, "was America's announcement to the world that we are ready to complete the task already begun with such emphatic success." The provisional figures of the returns received during September from the State headquarters showed a total of 12,966,594, or nearly 200,000 above the estimated male population due to register. The total, as finally shown by the official reports directly from the local boards, including the accessions during September and October, amounted to 13,395,706 (Table 1).

In so far as the excess was due to the difficulty of making correct actuarial estimates, this interesting phase is further discussed in Chapter V. But it may be supposed that a substantial portion of the excess is accounted for by the large numbers of men of ages 46 and 17 who found this opportunity to volunteer by declaring themselves within the ages for registration, as well as by the large numbers of delayed registrations from men of ages 21 to 30 who should have registered in the preceding year. Whatever the explanation, the tremendous fact remains that virtually every man due to register had done so; and the Nation could rest assured that it was mustering the entire man-power actually in existence within the new ages.

This complete national response to the call to duty could hardly have been effected without the assistance of the Committee on Public Information. Its superb organization, its efficient officers, and the vast network of influential agencies voluntarily contributing at its request, demonstrated it to have been one of the most powerful and beneficient agencies created for war service.

The total number of persons thus registered in all three registrations was 24,234,021. The ratio of each registration to the whole was as follows:

TABLE 1.—*Total registration.*

	Total registration.	Number.	Per cent of total.	Per cent of total.
1	Total of all three registrations.................	24,234,021	100.00	100.00
2	June 5, 1917–Sept. 11, 1918................	9,925,751	40.96	
3	June 5–Aug. 24, 1918.....................	912,564	3.77	
4	Sept. 12, 1918...........................	13,395,706	55.27	
5	Alaska, Hawaii, and Porto Rico (three series)..	325,445	....	1.34
6	United States without Territories (three series).	23,908,576	100.00	98.66
7	June 5, 1917–Sept. 11, 1918..............	9,780,535	40.91	
8	June 5–Aug. 24, 1918....................	899,279	3.76	
9	Sept. 12, 1918...........................	13,228,762	55.33	

6. *Ratio of registrants to male population.*—An important, if not a vital, question of military preparation is the ratio of the arms-bearing male population to the total male population. Much will some day be revealed of the extent to which the several nations of Europe have been able, during the present war, to count upon possessing man-power of given ages. For the United States (exclusive of the Territories) it appears that the ratio of its total registration—that is, of males registered for military service—to its total male population of all ages is 44 per cent.

TABLE 2.—*Ratio of males liable for military service to total male population.*

	Ratio of males liable for military service to total male population.	Number.	Per cent of population.	Per cent not registered but in service.
1	Total male population Sept. 12, 1918.............	54,340,000	100.00	....
2	Ages 18–45 registered June 5, 1917–Sept. 12, 1918.................................	23,908,576	44.00	....
3	Ages 18–45 not registered but in military service...............................	1,438,901	2.65	100.00
4	Ages 21–30 in military service June 5, 1917 (estimated)....................	364,298	....	25.32
5	Age 21 in military service June 5, 1918 (estimated)...........................	260,703	....	18.12
6	Ages 18–20, 32–45 in military service Sept. 12, 1918 (estimated)...........	813,900	....	56.56
7	Remainder not registered.................	28,992,523	53.35	....
8	Under 18 (67.3 per cent)...............	19,511,968	....	....
9	Over 45 (32.7 per cent)...............	9,480,555	....	....

The corresponding figures for Great Britain and France can not be obtained with accuracy to date. A rough estimate to serve merely for mass comparison is as follows:

TABLE 3.—*Ratio of males liable for military service to total male population in Great Britain and France.*

Ratio of males liable for military service to total male population in Great Britain and France.	United Kingdom.		France.	
	Number.	Per cent.	Number.	Per cent.
1 Total male population 1914......	22,827,261	100.00	19,700,000	100.00
2 Males 18–45..................	9,407,000	41.21	8,045,789	40.84
3 Remaining ages..............	13,420,261	....	11,654,211	....

A comparison of the figures for the United States and for our two principal cobelligerents on the Western Front reveals something of the relative national capácity for bearing the burden and duty of the struggle, had the destiny of nations required its prolongation beyond the present winter. The man-power of the given military ages in the United States was equal to the total combined man-power of both France and Great Britain plus almost half as much again. If the entire reservoir of man-power of both those countries, duplicated by an equal contribution from this country, had been drained, we should still have had had in reserve a quantity equaling two-thirds the man-power of either of them.

(IV) SPECIAL ARRANGEMENTS FOR REGISTRATION ON INDIAN RESERVATIONS, IN NATIONAL PARKS, IN THE TERRITORIES, AND IN FOREIGN COUNTRIES.

1. *Registration on Indian reservations.*—The registration of Indians and other persons residing on Indian Reservations was conducted under the direction of the Commissioner of Indian Affairs, whose duties approximated as closely as practicable those prescribed for the adjutants general of the several States. A registration board was established on each reservation and consisted of the superintendent of the agency, the chief clerk, and the physician. The Commissioner of Indian Affairs was notified that the rules for conducting the registration of Indians were not to be inflexible, and much was left to his discretion and judgment. The effective manner in which the Indian Bureau conducted the registration is additional evidence of the whole-hearted spirit of cooperation and zeal which was manifested by all agencies of the Government in the administration of the draft.

The registration cards of citizen Indians were allocated to local boards having jurisdiction of the area in which the reservations were located and such registrants were classified in the same manner as other citizens of the United States. The registration cards of noncitizen Indians, who were not under the law subject to military service, were retained by the registration boards on the Indian reservations.

2. *Registration in national parks and monuments.*—The registration of persons residing in Yellowstone, Glacier, and Mount Rainier National Parks was conducted under the supervision of the Director of National Park Service, which bureau exercises supervision over 16 national parks and 24 national monuments, covering an area of 10,591 square miles, in a number of States, principally in the West. His duties in connection with the registration approximated as closely as was practicable those prescribed for the draft executives of the several States. A registration board was established for each of the national parks named, and consisted of the supervisor, the commissioner, and a third member who was named by the Director of National Park Service. In effecting the second and third registrations, the registration boards consisted, so far as practicable, of persons constituting such boards on June 5, 1917, the date of the first registration. After the registration, the cards of all persons registered in the national parks were allocated to local boards adjoining and convenient to the parks.

The registration of persons residing in national monuments and in national parks, other than those above named, was accomplished by the registration machinery of the local boards having jurisdiction of the county or other subdivision in which the monuments or parks were located. If not located in any such subdivision, persons subject to registration residing therein were instructed by the Director of National Park Service to present themselves for registration at a place designated by a neighboring board.

In all, 220 registrations of persons residing in national parks were recorded.

3. *Registration in the Territories—Alaska, Hawaii, and Porto Rico.*—The registration in the Territories of Alaska, Hawaii, and Porto Rico was not conducted on the days prescribed for the registration in the several States and the District of Columbia. In view of the desirability of holding each registration as soon as possible after the enactment of the law authorizing it, there was not sufficient time for the transmission of registration cards and other necessary forms to the Territories before the day set for registration in the States.

First registration.—A separate proclamation was therefore issued for each registration in each Territory. In 1917, July 5, one month after the registration held in the States, was the date fixed for conducting the registration in Porto Rico. July 31 was the day prescribed for the registration in Hawaii. In Alaska, the period

97250°—19——3

of time between July 2 and September 2 was fixed by Presidential proclamation for the registration. A period of time rather than a single day was necessary because of the magnificent distances and difficulties of travel in Alaska. So much for the registration in the Territories in 1917.

Second registration.—In 1918, July 5 was the day fixed for the registration of the 21-year old registrants in Porto Rico; July 31 for such registration in Hawaii, and the period between July 2 and September 3 for such registration in Alaska. It will be noted that this registration in each Territory was held one year after the first registration, following the plan adopted in the States. September 3 was fixed as the end of the period of time for registration in Alaska, inasmuch as September 2, the end of the period of the first registration, fell on Sunday.

In the Territories there was no registration corresponding to that held in the States on August 24, the purpose of which was to obtain a sufficient number of registrants to fill September calls, and to bridge over the gap until the September, 1918, registrants were available. It will be remembered that legislation extending the draft ages was pending in Congress at the time of the August 24 registration.

Third registration.—The registration in the Territories of Hawaii and Porto Rico, corresponding to that conducted in the States on September 12, 1918, was held on October 26. In Alaska, the period between October 15 and December 16 was fixed as the time for the registration.

The dates for the entire series of registrations were thus as follows:

Porto Rico:
    First registration, July 5, 1917.
    Second registration, July 5, 1918.
    Third registration, October 26, 1918.
Hawaii:
    First registration, July 31, 1917.
    Second registration, July 31, 1918.
    Third registration, October 26, 1918.
Alaska:
    First registration, July 2 to September 2, 1917.
    Second registration, July 2 to September 3, 1918.
    Third registration, October 15 to December 16, 1918.

The registration in the Territories was conducted along the same lines as those prescribed for the States. The Governor of each Territory was called upon to supervise the execution of the registration. The adjutant general or draft executive was the central administrative authority for the registration system in each Territory, and the local boards in the Territories had immediate supervision and direction of the registration within their respective jurisdictions.

Owing to the territorial registrations being held at different times and under special circumstances, the returns for the various groups of registrants did not arrive in season for assimilation with the national tables given in the ensuing chapters. Such returns as have been received are therefore set forth separately, in their original form, in Appendix C.

4. *Registration in foreign countries.*—The registration of United States citizens and declarants residing abroad was at no time obligatory. Nevertheless many citizens in all parts of the world from time to time voluntarily chose to register, and thus patriotically placed themselves at the call of the Government.

To accomplish the registration of such persons, the assistance of United States consular representatives throughout the world was invoked. It was provided by regulation that a citizen or a declarant residing abroad and desiring to register should have his registration card filled out at the nearest American consulate and certified by an official or agent of the consulate. The card was then forwarded to a local board in the place in the United States designated by the registrant as his permanent home. In practice many such cards were transmitted through the State Department to the office of the Provost Marshal General and thence to State headquarters for distribution to the proper local boards. The registrant then received his registration certificate and became subject to the normal process of selection.

In appraising the patriotic response of Americans to the need for men, the share of these volunteer registrants, many of them in remote parts of the world, for whom a call to service meant more than the ordinary degree of sacrifice, should not be overlooked.

Great Britain and Canada.—The conclusion of the reciprocal military service conventions, which under certain conditions subjected American citizens in Great Britain and Canada to compulsory service in the British or Canadian forces, resulted in a great increase of registration under the selective service act by American citizens in those countries. These conventions, which became effective July 30, 1918, imposed liability on male citizens of the United States in Great Britain and Canada to the compulsory service laws and regulations from time to time in effect in such countries, provided they did not within certain limited periods enlist or enroll in the forces of the United States or return to the United States for service in such forces. The prescribed limit of time for the exercise of this option was 60 days, in the case of those immediately liable for service by the laws of Great Britain or Canada when the conventions became effective, and in other cases, 30 days from the time when such liability accrued.

The question at once arose as to the status in Great Britain or Canada of Americans registered under the selective service law of the United States. Was this an "enrollment in the forces of the United States," as provided in the convention? It was thereupon agreed by the three countries concerned that, within the meaning of the option provided by the conventions, registration for service in the United States forces should be regarded as enrollment in such forces. Therefore, any American citizen in Great Britain or Canada, who registered before a consular representative prior to the expiration of the 60 or 30 day period or who had previously registered in the United States, was thereby placed outside the operation of the conventions and could not be subjected to service in the British or Canadian forces. Any other course would have placed some Americans under obligation to respond to calls by both countries; and the object of the treaties was accomplished if such persons chose liability under the laws of their native country only. Thus it came about that many thousands of Americans in Great Britain and Canada registered before consular officers subsequent to July 30, 1918.

The convention also provided that the United States, through its diplomatic representatives, could grant to its citizens in Great Britain and Canada certificates of exemption from service in the armies of those countries. Such certificates were to be issued within the 60 or 30 day period above referred to. Accordingly, the ambassador to Great Britain and the consul general at Ottawa were authorized by the State Department to grant such exemptions on certain specified grounds.

In both Great Britain and Canada it became necessary to assure adequate publicity to all American citizens regarding their rights and liabilities under these treaties. The public press and other agencies could not be relied upon to the same extent as in the United States. The American consular representatives were, therefore, again called upon to accomplish this object. Regulations were prepared in cooperation with the State Department and promulgated by that department to all consulates and consular agents in Great Britain and Canada. These regulations defined the classes of Americans affected by the convention, described their privileges of enlisting or enrolling or returning to the United States, outlined the method of registration at the consulates, and stated the requisites for application for diplomatic exemption and the grounds on which such certificates could be granted. In order to protect Americans who had registered under the selective service act from overzealous British or Canadian draft officials, a form of certificate under the seal of the consul was provided for each registered person, attesting the fact of his registration.

Meantime authority was granted by General Pershing for the establishment of a recruiting service in Great Britain; and thereafter American registrants in Great Britain who were called for service by their local boards were allowed to enlist, thus obviating the necessity of their return to the United States for induction.

No complete statistics are available on the number of Americans who registered as a result of these conventions. Approximately 20,000 registration cards from Canada were transmitted through the office of the Provost Marshal General. It is believed that both in Great Britain and Canada a large majority of Americans of military age preferred registration under the Selective Service Act to the liability to service under the British flag. Conversely, it is probable (although no figures are available) that relatively few Americans actually entered the British or Canadian Armies through the operation of these conventions.

In both Great Britain and Canada authority of law for the drafting of alien Americans was provided by orders in council based on the general draft legislation already in force. These orders in council operated with the same effect as the provisions in the act of Congress approved July 9, 1918, subjecting to the draft in the United States the nationals of countries with which such reciprocal treaties were concluded. An interesting feature of the Canadian order in council, issued August 21, 1918, is that it required the registration in Canada of every American citizen residing in that country within 10 days from the expiration of the limited period within which he might be exempted by the United States. Heavy penalties for failure to register were provided, questionnaires were distributed, and Americans were required to allege and prove their prior enlistment or enrollment (registration) in the forces of the United States, as well as any other claim for relief from service allowed by the Canadian laws. After the conventions became effective, all registration certificates, questionnaires, and other communications from local boards were sent to the registrants in Great Britain and Canada through the consular officers before whom registration occurred. Consuls were called upon to assist registrants in filling out questionnaires; and in Canada authority was given for the organization, wherever needed, of volunteer advisory boards corresponding to the legal advisory boards in the United States. Much credit is due to the consular and diplomatic officers and other officials of the State Department for continued effective cooperation in the administration of the selective service law, not only in those countries where the draft conventions made the work especially important, but throughout the entire world wherever Americans responded by voluntary registration.

Other countries.—A reciprocal draft convention between the United States and France became effective November 8, 1918, and the ratifications of similar conventions with Italy and Greece were exchanged November 12, the day following the armistice. The provisions of these treaties were practically identical with those affecting Americans in Great Britain and Canada. Although corresponding regulations were prepared and transmitted by the State Department to the American diplomatic representatives in those countries, the prompt receipt of information from the governments of France, Italy, and Greece that no effort would be made to enroll Americans in their armies under the authority of the conventions rendered it unnecessary to put these instructions into actual operation.

CHAPTER III.

THE PROCESS OF SELECTION.

The process of selection for military service in 1918 departed in some essential respects from the process followed in 1917. It will, therefore, be worth while to call attention briefly to the specific differences. This will be done under the following heads: (1) Assignment of serial numbers; (2) drawing of order numbers; (3) determining and recording of order numbers; (4) the questionnaires and the classification system; (5) making and granting of claims for deferment and exemption; (6) permits for departure abroad; (7) noncombatants; (8) the emergency fleet classification list; and (9) the "work or fight" order.

(I) ASSIGNMENT OF SERIAL NUMBERS.

A primary measure, in any registration system designed to enable large masses of persons to be handled as individuals, must be to identify the individuals by serial numbers. Accordingly, the procedure followed, from the inception of the registration system, was to assign to each registrant a number, proceeding serially from one upwards, the series being separate and independent for each local board area. Thus each registrant could be identified by citing his local board name and his serial number.

In affixing these serial numbers, it was necessary to make the assignment in such a manner that there could be no tampering and no confusion of identity. The method employed in the registrations of June 5, August 24, and September 12, 1918, was not essentially different from that employed in the registration of June 5, 1917. But as the details of the method were not set forth in my first annual report, it is desirable to place them on record here, describing the method as enployed for the registration of September 12, 1918:

First and third registrations.—On the day following that set for registration, each local board caused to be numbered every registration card then in its possession, beginning with No. 1, and continuing consecutively until all registration cards were numbered. These numbers were known as "serial numbers" and were entered in red ink on each registration card in the space designated for such numbers. The registration cards were not alphabetically arranged for the purpose of assigning such serial numbers, but were consecutively numbered without regard to alphabetical or other arrangement. Additional registration cards of late registrants received by any local board were numbered consecutively in the order in which they were received.

The first of such additional cards received by a local board bore the serial number next following the last serial number placed upon a registration card theretofore received, and other or additional cards received bore the numbers next following this number in consecutive order.

Immediately after the numbering of registration cards, each local board caused to be prepared five identical lists of the names of all persons whose registration cards were in its possession. Such lists contained the names and serial numbers of all such persons, arranged in the order of their consecutive serial numbers. One copy of the list was retained for the records of the board; another copy was posted in a conspicuous place in the office of the local board; another copy was made accessible to the press with a request for publication; another copy was furnished to the State adjutant general or draft executive, and the remaining copy was transmitted to the Provost Marshal General. Each local board thereafter daily caused to be prepared in the same manner five identical lists of the names of all persons whose registration cards were thereafter received, and such additional lists were daily retained, posted, offered for publication, and transmitted to the State draft executive and the Provost Marshal General, respectively.

This procedure continued until and including September 21, 1918. Thereafter, under directions previously given, local boards were not permitted to assign serial numbers to additional registration cards or to cards which lacked serial numbers.

Second registration.—Registrants of the second registration (of June 5, 1918), who were known as the class of June, 1918, were assigned "registration" numbers corresponding to the "serial" numbers of the first registration. It was originally intended, in drafting registrants of the June, 1918, registration, to integrate them with those who had previously registered. However, before the enactment of the legislation authorizing their draft, an amendment was inserted in the bill providing that all persons registered pursuant to its terms were to be placed at the bottom of the list of those liable to military service in the several classes to which they were assigned. In view of this requirement of law, draft authorities were directed not to order into military service any registrant of the June, 1918, registration until those registrants of the first registration and of the corresponding class, who were available for general military service, had been ordered to report for duty.

The registration cards of persons registered on August 24, 1918, were treated as those of late registrants of the class of June, 1918, and were assigned registration and order numbers in the following manner: A copy of all registration cards and a list of the names of all registrants was forwarded by each local board to the adjutant general or draft executive of the State, together with the statement of the highest registration number on the list of persons in the class of June, 1918, whose registration cards were within the jurisdiction of the local board. Upon receipt of such registration cards and list of the names of registrants, the adjutant general or draft executive proceeded to assign registration numbers by lot, and then certified to the local boards lists showing the registration numbers so assigned. Upon receipt of such lists, the local boards entered the registration numbers on the original registration cards, and assigned the proper order numbers by consulting the master list of numbers drawn for the class of June, 1918. The registrants of the August, 1918, registration were in this manner integrated with the registrants of the class of June, 1918.

(II) DRAWING OF ORDER NUMBERS.

In order to designate impartially the sequence in which registrants qualified for military service should be called when needed, a single national drawing for all registrants of a given registration group was instituted. This method has been fully described in my report for 1917; and substantially the same method was followed in the drawings of numbers for the registration of June 5, 1918, and of September 12, 1918; the registrants of age 21 on August 24, 1918, being treated as late registrants of the group of June 5, 1918.

In brief, the method consisted in preparing a single set of numbers, beginning at one and including the highest serial number reached in the largest local board area; in inclosing the small squares of paper containing these printed numbers within a gelatin capsule; in placing the numbers in a large glass bowl, and then causing them to be drawn from the bowl at random by a blindfolded person in a public place. The place of drawing for the three registrations was the Senate Office Building. The day of the drawing was obliged to be some three or four weeks after the day of the registration; because it was necessary that every local board should have completed the assignment of serial numbers (as already described), and should have placed the duplicate list of such serial numbers in the mail for transmission to the Provost Marshal General's Office. Thus only could there be a guarantee against the possible alteration of a serial number, with a view to improper manipulation of the order of service, after public announcement of the order numbers.

The three national drawings took place, respectively, July 20, 1917, June 27, 1918, and September 30, 1918. At each of these drawings, personages of national importance were invited to draw the first few numbers. The names of those who drew the first few numbers in the several drawings, with the numbers drawn by them, were as follows:

First drawing.—Room No. 226, the public hearing room, of the Senate Office Building, was the scene of the first two drawings. In the first drawing, 10,500 numbers were drawn, the first capsule being taken from the glass bowl at 9.30 a. m., Friday, July 20, and the last at 2.16 a. m., Saturday, July 21, 1917; elapsed time, 16 hours 46 minutes. Those who drew the first few were:

Capsule.	Name.	Title.	Serial number drawn.
1	Newton D. Baker.........	The Secretary of War..................	258
2	George E. Chamberlain...	Senator from Oregon, Chairman, Senate Committee on Military Affairs.	2522
3	S. Hubert Dent, jr........	Representative from Alabama, Chairman, House Committee on Military Affairs.	9613
	Francis E. Warren........	Senator from Wyoming................	4532
	Julius Kahn..............	Representative from California.........	10218
6	Tasker H. Bliss...........	Major general, Chief of Staff, United States Army.	458
7	Enoch H. Crowder........	Provost Marshal General, United States Army.	3403
8	Henry P. McCain.........	The Adjutant General, United States Army.	10015

Second drawing.—In the second drawing 1,200 numbers were drawn, the first capsule being taken from the glass globe at 9.34 a. m., and the last at 11.38 a. m., Thursday, June 27, 1918; elapsed time 2 hours, 4 minutes. These officials participated:

Capsule.	Name.	Title.	Serial number drawn.
1	Newton D. Baker.........	The Secretary of War..................	246
2	George E. Chamberlain...	Senator from Oregon, Chairman, House Committee on Military Affairs.	1168
3	Francis E. Warren........	Senator from Wyoming.................	818
4	S. Hubert Dent, jr........	Representative from Alabama, Chairman, House Committee on Military Affairs.	1091
5	Julius Kahn..............	Representative from California, member of the same committee.	479
6	Peyton C. March.........	Major general, Acting Chief of Staff, United States Army.	469
7	Enoch H. Crowder........	Provost Marshal General, United States Army.	492
8	Charles B. Warren	Colonel, Judge Advocate, United States Army.	154
9	James S. Easby-Smith ...	.....do...............................	529
10	Harry C. Kramer.........	Major, Infantry, United States Army..	355

Third drawing.—The Caucus Room in the Senate Office Building was the scene of the third drawing. There were 17,000 numbers drawn, the first capsule being taken from the same glass bowl that had been used in the first drawing, at noon, Monday, September 30, and the last at 8 a. m., Tuesday, October 1, 1918; elapsed-time, 20 hours. Officials who participated were:

Capsule.	Name.	Title.	Serial number drawn.
1	Woodrow Wilson..........	The President of the United States....	322
2	Thomas R. Marshall......	Vice President of the United States....	7277
3	Willard Saulsbury........	Senator from Delaware, president pro tempore of the Senate.	6708
4	Champ Clark..............	Speaker of the House of Representatives.	1027
5	Josephus Daniels........	The Secretary of the Navy.............	16169
6	Benedict Crowell........	The Acting Secretary of War..........	8366
7	George E. Chamberlain...	Senator from Oregon. Chairman, Senate Committee on Military Affairs.	5366
8	Francis E. Warren........	Senator from Wyoming.................	1697
9	S. Hubert Dent, jr......	Representative from Alabama. Chairman, House Committee on Military Affairs.	7123
10	Julius Kahn.............	Representative from California. Member of the same committee.	2781
11	Peyton C. March.........	General, Chief of Staff, United States Army.	9283
12	William S. Benson......	Admiral, chief of operations, United States Navy.	6147
13	Samuel B. M. Young....	Lieutenant General, United States Army, retired, governor of United States Soldiers' Home.	10086
14	Enoch H. Crowder......	Provost Marshal General, United States Army.	438
15	Charles B. Warren.......	Colonel, Judge Advocate, United States Army.	904
16	James S. Easby-Smith...	.....do...............................	12368
17	John H. Wigmore........	.....do...............................	1523

(III) DETERMINING AND RECORDING OF ORDER NUMBERS.

The method employed for determining the result of the national drawing, in its application to the individual registrants, was as follows, for the registration group of September 12, 1918:

Master list.—A schedule or "master list" was prepared by this office, containing the numbers from 1 to 17,000, placed in the exact order in which they were drawn. The first number drawn was placed at the top of column 1 of the "master list," the second number drawn was placed next below in such list, and this order was followed until all the numbers were so placed in the "master list" in the exact order in which they were drawn. The number 17,000 was in excess of the total registration of the local board having the largest registration, the excess numbers being drawn to provide for persons registered after September 21.

Determining order numbers.—The method of determining the order numbers assigned to each of these registrants, who are known as the class of September, 1918, was as follows:

A second list of the names of the persons in this class of September, 1918, was made by each local board. The first name entered on the list prepared by each local board was the name of the person in the class of September, 1918, the serial number of whose registration card was first placed on the "master list" reading down from the top of the first column on the first page of the schedule and disregarding the numbers in the schedule which did not appear on any registration card in the possession of the local board. Before the name of the first person on each list was written the serial number of his registration card. The order number written on the list after the name of such first person was No. 1.

The next name to be entered on the list prepared by each local board was the name of the person in the class of September, 1918, whose serial number was next placed in such "master list," reading down the columns from the top thereof and disregarding the numbers in the schedule which did not appear on any registration card in the possession of the local board. The order number written on the list after the name of such person was No. 2.

The order in which the names of all remaining persons of the class of September, 1918, were entered on the list prepared by each local board was determined in the exact manner above described for determining the names of the first and second persons on each such list; and this method was pursued by each local board until the name of every person whose registration card was in its possession and had been given a serial number on or before September 21, 1918, had been entered upon the list.

Those registration cards received after September 21, 1918, were assigned serial numbers by lot under the supervision of the adjutant general or draft executive of each State. Directions were also given for the draft executive to determine the serial numbers to be assigned to any cards lacking serial numbers or improperly, erroneously, or illegibly serially numbered. Upon the assignment of serial numbers to such cards, the method above described was followed by the local boards in determining their proper order numbers. These precautions were taken, notwithstanding the experience of this office confirmed the opinion that they were unnecessary, in order to prevent, so far as possible, any element which might give rise to a baseless charge of fraud or favoritism in the assignment of serial and order numbers, and to dispel any doubt that they were not to be impartially assigned. By prohibiting the assignment of serial numbers by local boards a number of days in advance of the drawing, local boards were saved from the suspicion, however unjust, that they did not assign serial numbers to certain registration cards until after the drawing, and that the serial numbers then assigned gave favorable order numbers to the registrants involved.

(IV) THE QUESTIONNAIRES AND THE CLASSIFICATION SYSTEM

The further procedure necessary to complete the selection of individuals for military service departed essentially in 1918 from the method originally employed in 1917. That method (which may be denominated the method of calling and discharging or accepting), rested upon the general assumption that a specific number of men were known to be needed for military service at a given time, and that, therefore, enough régistrants should be called by each local board, in the sequence of the registrants' order numbers, and selected according to the terms of the Law and Regulations, until a number of qualified men had been obtained equal to that local board's share or quota of the entire specified number then needed.

This plan was adapted to the exigency of the early stage of the war, and was effective for the purpose. But experience showed that it was, in some respects, wasteful; that, in other respects it would begin to be ineffective in speed as the Army needs grew larger and more pressing; and that it did not sufficiently take account of certain equitable distinctions affecting the order of liability for military service. A new method, involving several essential alterations, was, therefore, prepared and received the sanction of the President for promulgation on November 8, 1917, to become effective December 15, 1917—at the time when the first call for 687,000 men had been more than filled by the local boards and an opportunity for change of plan was presented. This new method was announced in my First Report, which was dated December 20, 1917, before the new plan had been put into practical operation.

The essential changes were as follows: (1) The physical examination *followed, instead of preceding, the determination of the claim* for discharge or exemption. Under the original procedure, the first step after the giving of registration numbers and order numbers was the calling of registrants before the local boards (according to their order numbers) for physical examination. Those registrants found to be physically disqualified for general military service were given a certificate of discharge on that ground. Those who were found physically qualified for military service were given an opportunity to submit claims for exemption or discharge. At the conclusion of the hearings upon the claims, those men who had been found physically qualified for general military service and who failed to make claims for exemption or discharge, or whose claims were disallowed, were certified for service and subsequently were inducted according to the order numbers of men who had so been certified. This method required the calling for physical examination of more than 3,000,000 registrants and the actual physical examination of more than 2,500,000 registrants, of whom 1,780,000 were found physically qualified. Subsequent to this, 1,420,000 claims were filed, and a very large number of men found physically qualified failed to make any claim. As a net result of the actual physical examination of 2,500,000 men and the adjudication of 1,420,000 claims, there were certified for military service 1,057,000, of whom there had been actually inducted to December 15, 1917, slightly more than 500,000 men.

Under the new system the procedure was reversed. The registrant was first required to file answers to a questionnaire, the filing of which might include a claim for exemption or deferred classification. The failure to make claims, or the final adjudication rejecting or granting claims, resulted in the classification of the entire registration list, and it then became necessary to perform the labor of physical examination only in respect of the class liable to earliest call, viz, Class I.

Thus, under the first method there were actually called for physical examination more than 3,000,000 registrants, of whom 1,057,000 were certified for service; while under the new system not only was the total number physically examined of the first registration group but slightly larger (3,200,000) than had been examined under the first process (which resulted in the net induction of slightly over 500,000 men), but the relatively much smaller labor under the new system resulted in the net induction, between December 15, 1917, and November 11, 1918, of more than 2,000,000 men.

(2) Another improvement in the second plan was a greater flexibility in the equitable distinctions affecting the order of liability for military service. Under the original plan, the registrant was either accepted, on the one hand, or discharged or exempted on the other; whatever the varying degrees of equity in those cases, virtually there was only a choice between these two alternatives. It is true that all discharges were in form temporary or provisional, and were, therefore, revocable in case of need. Nevertheless, the method did not specifically point out any grades of distinction between the various ones thus discharged; and had it become necessary to revoke the discharges and to resort to this group for heavier drains for military purposes, the establishment of further discriminations would have been a cumbrous and tedious process.

The new plan established five groups, representing the equitable order of liability for military service, and thus made once for all an inventory of all registrants by placing them in one or another of these five groups. This made it possible to recognize, by differences in the order of liability for the different groups or classes, the equitable distinctions which might well obtain between the suitability of one or another group for earlier or later call. These several groups or classes were made by Presidential regulation, exercising the authority given by the Selective Service Act to discharge certain descriptions of persons, but assigning the different order of liabilities as between these different descriptions.

Nothing has done more than this measure to establish in popular conviction the equity of the whole draft system as established by the act of Congress. All the apprehension and unrest once involved in the popular idea of a military conscription has settled down into a firm national acceptance which would have seemed incredible two years ago.

(3) Another result of the classification system was that the Nation was ready from an early date in 1918 immediately to raise an army of practically any size that might be necessary. The whole registered man-power had been examined and was ready to be called in the order of availability. Even if the new legislation of August 31, 1918, increasing the draft ages, had not been enacted, we could nevertheless have proceeded in the order of availability, and after exhausting Class I, to call men of the first registration from Class II, III, and IV, with practically accurate knowledge that they were being called in direct order of their availability and in inverse order of their need for the social and economic life of the country. The classification system thus not only gave us an accurate inventory of the registered man-power, coupled with the knowledge of availibility of the several classes, so that if it was necessary to call the majority of the registrants they could have been called in the order of availibility; but the results undoubtedly furnished the only adequate basis for consideration by Congress in proceeding to extend the draft ages in August, 1918.

(4) A further advantage resulting from the classification system was that, for the first time, it enabled the respective contributions of men, due from the different areas, to be allotted in just proportion to the ability of each area to make that contribution. If Class I, throughout all boards, represented the reservoir of man power available equitably for the earliest call, then the quotas of each State and each board could be allotted, at the time of making each levy, in proportion to the size of that reservoir. And if it had become necessary to proceed into Class II, after exhausting Class I, then similarly the proportion of quotas could have been equitably made in ratio to the size of Class II in each State and in each board. In other words, the classification system furnished an opportunity for abandoning the inequities of the population basis for levying quotas— inequities which had given rise to complaint under the act as administered in 1917. In this respect, however, the change could not be made without amendatory legislation, which is elsewhere referred to in Chapter II and in Chapter VI of this report.

The classification system, as promulgated in the Selective Service Regulations effective December 15, 1917, amply withstood the test of experience throughout the year. It can be stated that, in spite of constant watchfulness with a view to detecting difficulties or inequities in their operation, these regulations have proceeded without a single essential change, in principle or procedure, since December, 1917, to the present date; and that no essential change would have been needed for any further operations of the selective draft in its application to the 13,000,000 registrants added to our list on September 12, 1918.

(V) MAKING AND GRANTING OF CLAIMS FOR DEFERMENT AND EXEMPTION.

1. *Method of making claims and appeals.*—The method of making claims for deferment or exemption was improved by the use of the questionnaire. Under the original plan, a registrant who made no claim for deferment or exemption placed no document on file, and the facts of his status appeared only upon the registration card. Under the new plan, an inventory was taken of every registrant. A questionnaire was filled out by every registrant without exception. Those who made the claims for exemption or deferment simply filled out the additional series of answers appropriate to their specific claims. There was thus on file for each registrant a single document containing all the facts and papers necessary to determine his status in liability for military service.

The questionnaire went through three editions; the first being used beginning December 15, 1917, for the remaining registrants of the first registration not already inducted; the second edition for the registrants of age 21, registered on June 5, 1918, and August 24, 1918; and the third edition for the registrants of September 12, 1918. No essential changes were found to be necessary in the questionnaires contained in these several editions; but the second and third edition contained a few improvements of detail, dictated by experience, together with some additional series of questions made necessary by the establishment of additional divisions in the several classes pursuant to new legislation affecting minor groups of persons.

In the method of making claims, an important change took place in that a claim for deferment as a necessary worker in industry or agriculture received a notation by the local board before transmission to the district board. The district board had sole jurisdiction to adjudicate under the act of Congress; but under the original method, by which the claim was filed directly with the district board, that board lost the benefit of the knowledge and judgment of the local board as to the merits of the claim; and the requirement that the local board should append a recommendation for or against the claim was undoubtedly of material assistance to the district board in passing upon the facts and the justice of the case.

In respect to appeals from the district board to the President, a material innovation (S. S. R., sec. 111) consisted in limiting the right of appeal to cases where there had been at least one dissenting vote in the district board and where one member of the local board and either the Government appeal agent or the adjutant general of the State recommended that the decision of the district board be reviewed. This innovation, with one or two minor additional details, was rendered advisable, in view of the fact disclosed by the appeals of 1917, that of the 13,000 appeals acted on up to December 19, 1917, less than 8 per cent had been granted, the fact indicating that the vast majority of appeals were not meritorious, and that measures should be taken to restrict them as nearly as possible to apparently meritorious cases. On the other hand, a contrary innovation was made by permitting an appeal to the President in claims for deferment on the ground of dependency, which under the original regulations had not been allowed; they were now made allowable when accompanied by a statement of one member of the local board and either the Government appeal agent or the adjutant general of the State certifying that the case was one of great and unusual hardship and recommending its reconsideration.

2. *Number of claims made and granted in local boards.*—The following Table 4 shows the total claims for deferment, made and granted, and their distribution:

TABLE 4.—*Deferment claims; ratio of claims made to claims granted.*

	Deferment claims; ratio of claims made to claims granted.	Number.	Per cent of claims made.	Per cent of claims granted.
1	Total claims made Dec. 15, 1917, to Sept. 11, 1918 (first and second registration)	10,085,296	100.00	
2	Total claims granted	7,681,176	76.16	100.00
3	Class II claims made	1,646,905	16.33	
4	Granted	1,329,582	....	17.31
5	Class III claims made	1,452,266	14.40	
6	Granted	803,373	....	10.46
7	Class IV claims made	4,450,266	44.13	
8	Granted	3,373,496	....	43.92
9	Class V claims made	2,535,859	25.14	
10	Granted	2,174,725	....	28.31
11	Industrial claims made	543,200	5.39	100.00
12	Granted	291,078	....	53.59
13	Agricultural claims made	1,051,679	10.43	100.00
14	Granted	544,665	....	51.79
15	Dependency claims made	4,968,237	49.26	100.00
16	Granted	3,744,399	....	75.37
17	Sundry claims made	3,522,180	34.92	100.00
18	Granted	3,101,034	....	88.04

(*a*) It appears from this table that the volume of business transacted by the local boards in the disposal of claims under the first and second registrations amounted to 10,085,296.

(b) It further appears that, as between the several classes, the claims for deferment in Class IV were nearly double those for any. other class.

(c) As to the several specific grounds for the claims represented by the divisions within the classes and distributed according to their nature as industrial, agricultural, or domestic, it appears that the domestic claims were very largely in the majority and that the industrial claims formed a small minority.

(d) In the method of calling used in 1917 it was possible to show the ratio of persons making claims to total registrants (first report, p. 48); but under the questionnaire system of 1918 the records did not permit this ratio to be computed, inasmuch as a single registrant • might make claims on several grounds.

The records permit some idea to be gained of the ratio of claims made by the several economic and domestic groups, i. e., what ratio of farmers or of nonfarmers or of married registrants made claims for deferment; this, however, can be shown only for the first registration, as the economic status of the registrants, as classified, was not ascertained for the second and the third registrations. The figures are as follows (Table 5):

TABLE 5.—*Deferment claims made; ratio to registrants.*

	Deferment claims made; ratio to registrants.	Number.	Per cent of registrants classified.	Per cent of claims made.
1	Total claims made in first registration since Dec. 15, 1917	9, 493, 328	....	100. 00
2	Industrial registrants classified	6, 068, 021	100. 00	....
3	Claims made on industrial grounds	497, 909	8. 21	5. 24
4	Agricultural registrants classified	2, 509, 698	100. 00	....
5	Claims made on agricultural grounds	956, 233	38. 10	10. 07
6	Married registrants classified	4, 631, 065	100. 00	....
7	Claims made for married dependency	4, 054, 233	87. 54	. 42. 71

(e) It is interesting to compare the years 1917 and 1918 with reference to the ratio of claims granted. There had been a belief, on the part of some, that after the first urgent rush of raising the first levy of 687,000 men, and in view of the popular superficial notion, prevailing early in 1918, that we had perhaps accomplished our part in man-power contribution, there would be seen a relaxation in the strictness in which claims were scrutinized and that the ratio of claims granted would decrease. But how little the Nation could afford to indulge in such relaxation, and how completely needed was the entire group of effectives obtainable from the first 10,000,000, was amply perceived later in the year, when our troops, from April onward, began to be rushed overseas in large numbers, and when our Class I of the first registration became exhausted. And so, in retrospect, it is interesting to observe (Table 5a) that in 1917

(Report for 1917, p. 48, Table 19) the ratio of total claims granted was greater than in 1918, as also the ratio for dependency claims granted; showing that there had been no relaxation of strictness by the boards. But the substantial increase in the 1918 ratio of industrial and agricultural claims granted (Table 5a) was precisely what might be expected and justified in view of the increasing necessity of preserving the economic operations of the country from impairment.

TABLE 5a.—*Claims granted, 1917 and 1918, compared.*

	Claims granted, 1917 and 1918, compared.	Per cent.
1	Percentage of all claims granted:	
2	1917	77. 86
3	1918	76. 16
4	Percentage of dependency and sundry claims granted—	
5	1917	81. 79
6	1918	80. 63
7	Percentage of agricultural claims granted—	
8	1917	35. 89
9	1918	51.79
10	Percentage of industrial claims granted—	
11	1917	42. 81
12	1918	53. 59

3. *Number of claims made and granted in district boards.*—The claims made before district boards were as follows:

TABLE 6.—*District board claims filed.*

	District board claims filed, Dec. 15, 1917–Sept. 11, 1918.	Number.	Per cent of registrants.	Per cent of claims.
1	Total registrants classified	9, 952, 735	100. 00	....
2	Total claims presented to district boards	2, 623, 835	26. 36	100. 00
3	Appeals from local boards filed	623, 335	....	23. 76
4	Claims filed on agricultural and industrial grounds	1, 989, 046	....	75. 81
5	Appeals filed as to physical qualifications	11, 454	....	.43

The disposition of these claims before the district boards was as follows:

TABLE 7.—*Disposition of district board cases.*

	Disposition of district board cases, Dec. 15, 1917, to Sept. 11, 1918.	Number.	Per cent of appeals.	Per cent of claims.
1	Total appeals from local boards	623, 335	100. 00	....
2	Placed in Class I	313, 451	50. 29	....
3	Placed in deferred classes	309, 884	49. 71	....
4	Total claims on agricultural and industrial grounds	1, 989, 046	....,....	100. 00
5	Placed in Class I	906, 425	....	45. 57
6	Placed in deferred classes	1, 082, 621	....	54. 43
7	Total appeals as to physical qualifications	11, 454	100. 00	....
8	Found fully qualified	6, 739	58. 84	....
9	Found disqualified	1, 777	15. 51	....
10	Found qualified for limited service	2, 938	25. 65	....

That the district boards performed a very necessary function is evident, this year as last year, in the number of appeals granted:

4. *Number of appeals to the President.*—At the time of going to press with my first report (Dec. 20, 1917), the appeals to the President, then pending, had been little more than half disposed of, owing to the fact that these appeals were more than 22,000 in number, and that even with the utmost dispatch the accumulation of the preceding few weeks could not be more rapidly disposed of with justice to the cases. It is, therefore, necessary here to replace my report of last year on this subject (Report for 1917, p. 63, Tables 40 and 41) by a new statement covering the entire mass of appeals as subsequently disposed of.

(a) *Appeals from district boards to the President under the regulations of June 30, 1917, effective to Dec. 15, 1917.*—In the report of the first draft, Table No. 40 showed that 8,496 appeals to the President were pending on December 19, 1917. Under the classification system, all registrants not in the Army became subject to classification and all previous discharges were revoked on December 15, 1917. Accordingly, the appeal records were returned without action in all cases in which no report of induction had been received. This disposed of a large majority of the pending appeals.

The final disposition of appeals to the President under rules and regulations of June 30, 1917, was as follows:

TABLE 8.—*Appeals to the President under regulations of 1917.*

	Appeals to the President under regulations of 1917.	Number.	Per cent of claims disallowed.	Per cent of appeals.
1	Total, industrial and agricultural claims disallowed by district boards.......................	85, 059	100. 00	....
2	Total appeals to President....................	22, 771	26. 77	100. 00
3	Denied................................	15, 368	....	67. 49
4	Granted................................	1, 324	....	5. 82
5	Withdrawn or dismissed for want of jurisdiction...............................	450	....	1. 97
6	Returned without action (registrants not inducted)...............................	5, 629	....	24. 72

The result of this action for the different kinds of claims was as follows:

TABLE 9.—*Presidential appeals of 1917, compared as to kind of claims.*

	Presidential appeals of 1917, compared as to kind of claims.	Number.	Per cent of claims disallowed.	Per cent of agricultural appeals.	Per cent of industrial appeals.
1	Total agricultural claims disallowed...	58,812	100.00		
2	Appeals to President...............	17,701	30.09	100.00	
3	Denied......................	11,604		65.56	
4	Granted....................	981		5.54	
5	Withdrawn or dismissed for want of jurisdiction.........	227		1.28	
6	Returned without action......	4,889		27.62	
7	Total industrial claims disallowed.....	26,247	100.00		
8	Appeals to President...............	5,006	19.07		100.00
9	Denied.....................	3,764			75.19
10	Granted....................	343			6.85
11	Withdrawn, or dismissed for want of jurisdiction.........	159			3.18
12	Returned without action......	740			14.78

(b) *Appeals to the President under the regulations in force since December 15, 1917·*—Although the total number of registrants classified under the new regulations of December, 1917 greatly exceeded the number of men examined and certified by the same boards under the first draft, the cases appealed to the President from classification by the district boards have been few, compared with the appeals arising under the former regulations. The chief reason for this shrinkage is found in the requirements of Section 111, Selective Service Regulations, limiting the right of appeal in the manner already described. Under the first draft, appeals were confined to industrial and agricultural claims denied by the district board. These appeals numbered 22,771 or more than 26 per cent of all such claims disallowed by the district board. The regulations of December, 1917 granted an appeal to the President also in dependency cases certified as of great and unusual hardship. Despite this extension of the jurisdiction, the procedure described in Section 111, Selective Service Regulations, has restricted the total appeals to 1,584, or only 0.13 per cent of the claims for deferred classification on industrial, agricultural, and dependency grounds denied by the district boards. In addition, the lack of one or more of the jurisdictional requirements specified by the regulations has necessitated the return of a large proportion of the records received, without action on the appeals.

Although the percentage of cases appealed to the President from the millions of classifications by the district boards is thus insignificant, each decided case represents a division of opinion in a district board, and the decisions rendered have doubtless promoted uniformity of classification in a larger number of doubtful cases, in which appeals were not perfected.

The *disposition* of Presidential appeal records, as a whole, was as follows:

TABLE 10.—*Presidential appeals of 1918; disposition.*

	Presidential appeals of 1918; disposition.	Number.	Per cent of rulings.	Per cent of total appeals.	Per cent of appeals acted on.
1	Total, rulings by district boards placing in Class I................	1,219,876	100.00	....	....
2	Total appeals to the President.	1,584	.13	100.00	....
3	Returned for want of jurisdiction, etc............	1,025	.08	64.71	....
4	Appeals acted on..	559	....	35.29	100.00
5	Appeals affirmed......... ...	452	....	28.54	80.86
6	Appeals modified.........	78	....	4.92	13.95
7	Appeals reversed..........	29	....	1.83	5.19

Appendix Table 10–A shows the distribution of these cases by States. The several results of this action, as to the kind of claim involved, were as follows:

TABLE 11.—*Presidential appeals of 1918; kinds of claims.*

	Presidential appeals of 1918; kinds of claims.	Total.	Affirmed.	Modified.	Reversed.
1	Appeals acted on.......................	559	452	78	29
2	Agricultural......................	197	171	19	7
3	Industrial.	137	122	10	5
4	Agricultural and industrial..........	8	7	....	1
5	Dependency.......................	181	129	41	11
6	Agricultural and dependency	13	11	1	1
7	Industrial and dependency..........	19	9	7	3
8	Work or fight order.................	4	3	....	1

There remain four special topics, involving changes in procedure instituted by the new regulations of December 15, 1917, two of them of minor importance and two of major importance.

(VI) PERMITS FOR DEPARTURES ABROAD.

By an act of Congress approved May 22, 1918, it was provided that, when the United States is at war, if the President shall find that the public safety requires that restrictions and prohibitions in addition to those provided otherwise than by this act be imposed upon the departure of persons from and their entry into the United States, and shall make public proclamation thereof, it shall be unlawful for any alien to depart from the United States except under such reasonable rules and regulations as the President shall prescribe, and for any citizen of the United States to depart from the country unless he bears a valid passport.

In a proclamation dated August 8, 1918, the President announced, pursuant to this act that he found and publicly proclaimed that the public safety required restrictions and prohibitions in addition to those provided by the act of May 22, 1918; and he issued certain orders to be carried out by the Secretary of State, with regard to the departure of citizens and aliens from the country. By an Executive order (August 8) it was provided (in sec. 12) that no person registered or enrolled or subject to registry or enrollment for military service in the United States should depart from the United States' without the consent of the Secretary of War or of such person or persons as he might appoint to give such consent, and that the Secretary of State should issue no passport or permit entitling such person to depart from the United States without satisfactory evidence of such consent. In accordance with these regulations, local boards were designated by the Secretary of War to issue permits to registrants to leave the country.

By section 156 of the Selective Service Regulations, rules were prescribed respecting the issuance of these permits by local boards. A registrant who desired to depart from the United States was required to apply to the local board with which he had registered. The board considered the application, and if the applicant was not likely to be called for service during the period of his proposed absence, or if the board was otherwise assured that the issuance of the permit would not result in evasion or interference with the execution of the Selective Service Law, the board took from the applicant a statement of his address while absent and an engagement to keep himself informed of any call that might be made on him and to return immediately on such call. Thereupon the board issued a permit.

It became unnecessary, after the signing of the armistice on November 11, that the regulations with regard to the departure from the United States of persons registered or enrolled or subject to registry or enrollment for military service in the United States should continue in force. Section 12 of the Executive order of August 8, 1918, was therefore revoked by the President by an order under date of November 22, and thereupon section 156 of the Selective Service Regulations was also rescinded.

The act of May 22, 1918, furnished a specific statutory authorization for executive regulations with regard to the departure of registrants from the United States. Prior to the enactment of this law, the Treasury Department, by virtue of authority conferred on it by an act approved June 15, 1917, over vessels in American waters had declined to permit persons of military age to sail from the United States unless they were in possession of evidence from officials vested with the execution of the Selective Service Law, that they had obtained permission to leave the country. And the Department of State issued passports to persons subject to draft only when their applications were accompanied by permits issued by these officials. Up to August 5, 1917, these permits were furnished to registrants directly from the office of the Provost Marshal General. After that date, the more practical plan was adopted (Selective Service Regulations, sec. 156) of causing the permits to be granted by local boards which were in possession of information respecting the status of registrants and this plan was continued until the executive regulations with regard to the departure of registrants from the country were revoked.

No figures are obtainable showing the number or kinds of persons, subject to military service, who obtained permits for departure on passport.

(VII) NONCOMBATANTS.

1. *Religious-creed members.*—The Selective Service Act provided that members in a well-recognized religious sect on May 18, 1917, whose creed forbade participation in war in any form, would be required to serve only in a capacity declared by the President to be noncombatant. Under the classification system, therefore, registrants claiming relief from noncombatant service under this provision (embodied in Selective Service Regulations, sec. 79, Rule XIV) were not placed in a deferred class on this claim alone; for a deferred class signified total or temporary withdrawal from military service. The registrant was classified as any other registrant, according as he claimed or did not claim some ground for deferment. His classification was entered in the records like that of any other registrant; but, for the purpose of designating him, if in Class I and when called for noncombatant service, his name was accompanied in all records by the insertion of a cipher.

The administration of this regulation was left to the decision of the local boards; i. e., no list was prepared of religious denominations recognized as existing on May 18, 1917, and professing a creed opposed to war in any form. To compile such a list was impracticable; and each board decided for itself on the facts of each claim. No report has ever been required of the boards showing the creeds thus recognized. But is is interesting, now that the war period has closed, to attempt to estimate the ratio of registrants in such creeds who claimed the noncombatant status. From materials gathered in the Census Bureau it appears that the principal creeds professing such a tenet are these:

Brethren in Christ: The Yorker, or Old Order Brethren, and the United Zion's Children belong to this group; they believe that inasmuch as Christ is Prince of Peace His kingdom is of peace and as his subjects they should abstain from the employment of carnal forces which involve the taking of human life; for this reason the doctrine of nonresistance is a prominent feature of their belief;

Christadelphians: Conscientious scruple as to serving in the Army in the Civil War was the occasion for the organization of the body under this name;

Amana Society: The members believe war to be contrary to the will of God and the teachings of Christ;

Churches of Christ: This body has no published creed, but a leading elder stated that the churches believe in "nonresistance";

Church of the Brethren (Conservative Dunkers): They hold that the bearing of arms is forbidden by the sixth commandment;

Old Order German Baptist Brethren: Denominational practice calls for nonconformity to the world in war, politics, secret societies, dress, and amusements;

Brethren Church (Progressive Dunkers): In doctrinal matters the Brethren Church is in general accord with the Church of the Brethren;

German Seventh Day Baptists: In general accord with other Dunkers;

Church of God (New Dunkers): A new body in general accord with other Dunkers;

Friends (four bodies): The official position of the Friends in regard to the war with Germany is practically the same as that taken by the Friends at the time of the American Revolution; they have simply reaffirmed their historic position in regard to all war.

Mennonites (16 bodies): "Christ has forbidden his followers the use of carnal force in resisting evil and the seeking of revenge for evil treatment. Love for enemies can not be shown by acts of hatred or revenge, but by deeds of love and good will." (from Summary of Articles of Faith.)

The total membership of the religious bodies reported to the Bureau of the Census as holding the doctrine of nonresistance is as follows:

TABLE 12.—*Religious denominations opposed to war.*

	Religious denominations opposed to war.	Total membership.	Membership reporting sex.	Males.
1	Brethren in Christ	3,805	3,805	1,541
2	The Yorker, or Old Order Brethren	432	432	174
3	United Zion's Children	1,152	1,145	478
4	Christadelphians	2,922	2,905	1,235
5	Amana Society	1,534	1,534	715
6	Churches of Christ	317,937	317,812	132,755
7	Church of the Brethren (Conservative Dunkers)	105,102	103,135	44,923
8	Old Order German Baptist Brethren	3,399	3,399	1,494
9	Brethren Church (Progressive Dunkers)	24,060	23,648	9,699
10	German Seventh Day Baptists	136	136	48
11	Church of God (New Dunkers)	929	676	261
12	Friends	112,982	105,161	47,864
13	Mennonites	79,363	77,294	35,656
	Total			276,843

Taking the total number of members of such creeds, estimating the males of ages 21 to 30 at 20 per cent, and comparing the numbers reported by the boards as claiming and receiving the noncombatant privilege, we reach the following result:

TABLE 13.—*Noncombatant religious creeds and conscientious objectors.*

	Noncombatant religious creeds and conscientious objectors.	Number.
1	Total registrants ages 21 to 30, June 5, 1917, to Sept. 11, 1918, professing noncombatant religious creeds	55,368
2	Total claims made for noncombatant classification	64,693
3	Total claims recognized	56,830

It appears that the entire body of registrant creed-members availed themselves of this privilege. The general experience of local boards with this exemption is temperately expressed in a passage from a local board report, printed as Appendix D.

The disposition of the Class I men whose noncombatant claims were denied, and who were later inducted into service, was merged with that of the other group now to be mentioned, viz:

2. *Conscientious objectors.*—The so-called conscientious objector was not recognized either in the law or in the Selective Service Regulations. But when Class I men were inducted and received in camp, the distinction between religious creed claimants and conscientious objectors was not in general given marked recognition. At this point the subject fell entirely within the authority of the camp commanders, acting under the direction of the President and of the Secretary of War.

The following regulations were issued by the President, March 20, 1918:

1. By virtue of authority contained in section 4 of the act approved May 18, 1917, entitled, "An act to authorize the President to increase temporarily the military establishment of the United States," whereby it is provided: "And nothing in this act contained shall be construed to require or compel any person to serve in any of the sorces herein provided for who is found to be a member of any well-recognized religious fect or organization at present organized and existing and whose existing creed or principles forbid its members to participate in war in any form and whose religious convictions are against war or participation therein in accordance with the creed or principles of said religious organizations; but no person so exempted shall be exempted from service in any capacity that the President shall declare to be noncombatant," I hereby declare that the following military service is noncombatant service:

(*a*) Service in the Medical Corps wherever performed. This includes service in the sanitary detachments attached to combatant units at the front; service in the divisional sanitary trains composed of ambulance companies and field hospital companies, on the line of communications, at the base in France, and with the troops and at hospitals in the United States; also the service of supply and repair in the Medical Department.

(*b*) Any service in the Quartermaster Corps in the United States may be treated as noncombatant. Also in rear of zone of operations, service in the following: Stevedore companies, labor companies, remount depots, veterinary hospitals, supply depots, bakery companies, the subsistence service, the bathing service, the laundry service, the salvage service, the clothing renovation service, the shoe-repair service, the transportation repair service, and motor-truck companies.

(*c*) Any engineer service in the United States may be treated as noncombatant service. Also, in rear of zone of operations, service as follows: Railroad building, operation, and repair; road building and repair; construction of rear line fortifications, auxiliary defenses, etc.; construction of docks, wharves, storehouses, and of such cantonments as may be built by the Corps of Engineers; topographical work; camouflage; map reproduction; supply depot service; repair service; hydraulic service, and forestry service.

2. Persons ordered to report for military service under the above act who have (*a*) been certified by their local boards to be members of a religious sect or organization as defined in section 4 of said act; or (*b*) who object to participating in war because

of conscientious scruples but have failed to receive certificates as members of a religious sect or organization from their local board, will be assigned to noncombatant military service as defined in paragraph 1 to the extent that such persons are able to accept service as aforesaid without violation of the religious or other conscientious scruples by them in good faith entertained.

Upon the promulgation of this order it shall be the duty of each division, camp, or post commander, through a tactful and considerate officer, to present to all such persons the provisions hereof with adequate explanation of the character of noncombatant service herein defined, and, upon such explanations, to secure acceptances of assignment to the several kinds of noncombatant service above enumerated; and whenever any person is assigned to noncombatant service by reason of his religious or other conscientious scruples, he shall be given a certificate stating the assignment and reason therefor, and such certificate shall thereafter be respected as preventing the transfer of such persons from such noncombatant to combatant service by any division, camp, post, or other commander under whom said person may thereafter be called to serve, but such certificate shall not prevent the assignment of such person to some other form of noncombatant service with his own consent. So far as may be found feasible by each division, camp, or post commander, future assignments of such persons to noncombatant military service will be restricted to the several detachments and units of the Medical Department in the absence of a request for assignment to some other branch of noncombatant service as defined in paragraph 1 hereof.

3. On the first day of April and thereafter monthly, each division, camp, or post commander shall report to The Adjutant General of the Army, for the information of the Chief of Staff and the Secretary of War, the names of all persons under their respective commands who profess religious or other conscientious scruples as above described and who have been unwilling to accept by reason of such scruples, assignment to noncombatant military service as above defined, and as to each such person so reported a brief, comprehensive statement as to the nature of the objection to the acceptance of such noncombatant military service entertained. The Secretary of War will from time to time classify the persons so reported and give further directions as to the disposition of them. Pending such directions from the Secretary of War, all such persons not accepting assignment to noncombatant service shall be segregated as far as practicable and placed under the command of a specially qualified officer of tact and judgment, who will be instructed to impose no punitive hardship of any kind upon them, but not to allow their objections to be made the basis of any favor or consideration beyond exemption from actual military service, which is not extended to any other soldier in the service of the United States.

4. With a view to maintaining discipline, it is pointd out that the discretion of courts-martial, so far as any shall be ordered to deal with the cases of persons who fail or refuse to comply with lawful orders by reason of alleged religious or other conscientious scruples, should be exercised, if feasible, so as to secure uniformity of penalties in the imposition of sentences under Articles of War 64 and 65, for the willful disobedience of a lawful order or command. It will be recognized that sentences imposed by such courts-martial, when not otherwise described by law, shall prescribe confinement in the United States Disciplinary Barracks or elsewhere, as the Secretary of War or the reviewing authority may direct, but not in a penitentiary; but this shall not apply to the cases of men who desert either before reporting for duty to the military authorities or subsequently thereto.

5. The Secretary of War will revise the sentences and findings of courts-martial heretofore held of persons who come within any of the classes herein described, and bring to the attention of the President for remedy, if any be needed, sentences and judgments found at variance with the provisions hereof.

WOODROW WILSON,

THE WHITE HOUSE, *March 20, 1918.*

Those drafted objectors who refused to accept noncombatant service under military authority, and were held in segregated units as provided in section 3 of the President's order, were dealt with in the following order of the Secretary of War, made public June 1, 1918:

1. By the terms of the presidential order of March 20, 1918, men reporting at the training camps under the provisions of the selective service law who profess conscientious scruples against warfare are given an opportunity to select forms of service designated by the President to be noncombatant in character. By direction of the Secretary of War dated April 22, 1918, instructions were issued by this office, April 27, 1918, to try by court-martial those declining to accept such noncombatant service; (a) whose attitude in camp is defiant; (b) whose sincerity is questioned; (c) who are active in propaganda.

2. All other men professing conscientious objections, now segregated in posts and camps, i. e., those who, while themselves refusing to obey military instructions on the ground of conscientious scruples, religious or other, have given no other cause of criticism in their conduct, and all who have been or may be acquitted by such court-martial, shall be transferred, upon orders issued by this office to camp and other commanders, to Fort Leavenworth, Kans. The commanding officer, Fort Leavenworth, will keep these men segregated, but not under arrest, pending further instructions from this office.

3. The same procedure shall be carried out as promptly as possible in the cases of men professing similar scruples who may report at posts or camps in the future.

4. Under no circumstances will conscientious objectors otherwise qualified to perform military duty be discharged from their responsibilities under the Selective Service Law, but the Secretary of War has constituted a board of inquiry, composed of a representative from the Judge Advocate General's office (Maj. R. C. Stoddard) chairman, Judge Julian W. Mack of the Federal court, and Dean H. F. Stone of the Columbia University law school. It will be the duty of this board to interrogate personally each man so transferred. Such men as may be determined by this board to be sincere in their attitude and desirous of serving their country in any way within the limits of their conscientious scruples may be furloughed by the commanding officer, Fort Leavenworth, without pay, for agricultural service, upon the voluntary application of the soldier, under the authority contained in the act of Congress of March 16, 1918, and the provisions of General Orders No. 31, War Department, 1918, provision being made:

(1) That monthly report as to the industry of each person so furloughed shall be received from disinterested sources, and that the furlough shall terminate automatically upon the receipt of report that he is not working to the best of his ability; and

(2) That no person shall be recommended for such furlough who does not voluntarily agree that he shall receive for his labor an amount no greater than a private's pay, plus an estimated sum for subsistence if such be not provided by the employer. It is suggested that any additional amount which may be offered for the service of such men be contributed to the Red Cross.

5. In exceptional cases the board may recommend furlough for service in France in the Friends' Reconstruction Unit.

6. If there shall be any instances in which the findings of courts-martial at camps or posts in cases involving conscientious objectors shall be disapproved by the Secretary of War, the men concerned shall also be transferred to Fort Leavenworth, and similarly examined and reported upon by the board of inquiry.

7. Any man who is not recommended for furlough by this board, or who being offered such furlough shall refuse to accept it, or whose furlough shall be terminated for the reasons indicated above. or for other reasons deemed sufficient by the Secre-

tary of War, shall be required to perform such noncombatant service as may be assigned to him and shall be held strictly accountable under the articles of war for the proper performance of such service and to strict obedience of all laws governing or applicable to soldiers employed in that status. In the event of disobedience of such laws or failure to perform such service, the offender shall be tried by court-martial, and if found guilty and sentenced to confinement shall be detained in the disciplinary barracks for the term of his sentence.

8. Pending the final decision in each case as to the disposal of these men, the directions as to their treatment issued from time to time by order of the Secretary of War remain in force. These may be summarized as follows:

As a matter of public health every man in camp, entirely apart from his military status, shall be expected to keep himself and his belongings and surroundings clean, and his body in good condition through appropriate exercise. Men declining to perform military duties shall be expected to prepare their own food.

If, however, any drafted man, upon his arrival at camp either through the presentation of a certificate from his local board, or by written statement addressed by himself to the commanding officer, shall record himself as a conscientious objector, he shall not, against his will, be required to wear a uniform or to bear arms; nor if, pending the final decision as to his status, he shall decline to perform, under military direction, duties which he states to be contrary to the dictates of his conscience, shall he receive punitive treatment for such conduct.

No man who fails to report at camp, in accordance with the instructions of his local board, or who, having reported, fails to make clear upon his arrival his decision to be regarded as a conscientious objector, is entitled to the treatment outlined above.

In the assignment of any soldier to duty, combatant, or noncombatant, the War Department recognizes no distinction between service in the United States and service abroad.

The board of inquiry named in the order of the Secretary of War, and consisting of one military officer and two civilians, visited the various camps between June and October, 1918, and inquired into the individual cases of recalcitrants, both religious creed claimants and conscientious objectors, and made recommendations for action of the President. Reports of this board show the following state of facts;

TABLE 14.—*Disposal of conscientious objectors.*

	Disposal of conscientious objectors.	Number.
1	Total cases of objectors inquired into	1,697
2	Found to be sincere entirely or in part	1,461
3	Found insincere	103
4	Remanded for further inquiry	88
5	Remanded for examination as to mental deficiency	7
6	Otherwise disposed of	38

3. *Court-martial trials of conscientious objectors.*—During the period extending from September, 1917, to the middle of November, 1918, the number of professed conscientious objectors (as reported from the Judge Advocate General's Office) who were tried by courts-martial, convicted, and sentenced to terms ranging from three months to 50 years, was 371.

Of this number, 80 per cent were charged with violations of the sixty-fourth article of war, the specification in nearly every instance being that the accused had disobeyed the order of a superior officer to perform work about camp, to drill, to submit to vaccination and innoculation, to sign the enlistment card, or to wear the uniform. The maximum sentence imposed on men convicted on this charge was 50 years; the average sentence was 10 years. In 95 cases, sentence of life imprisonment was mitigated to 25 years by the reviewing authority.

Approximately 12 per cent were accused and convicted of desertion. In these cases sentences averaged 15 to 20 years. In one instance the deserter was sentenced to life imprisonment, but the reviewing authority reduced the term to 25 years. Another deserter was sentenced to be shot; this sentence was changed by the reviewing authority to confinement for 25 years.

Violation of the ninety-sixth article of war was charged against 5 per cent of the total number convicted, the specifications being disloyal utterances and abusive language against the United States Government. The average sentence was 10 years imprisonment; three were sentenced to terms of 30 years, and in five cases sentences to life imprisonment were changed to 25 years.

The remaining 3 per cent were charged with disobedience, refusal to submit to physical examination, failure to report for guard duty, and similar offenses. The sentences averaged 10 years.

(VIII) THE EMERGENCY FLEET CLASSIFICATION LIST.

1. *Reasons for this measure.*—When the United States entered the World War, the most important problem with which our Government was confronted was that of raising and equipping a large army. The next most important problem was that of transporting to France this army and all necessary food, ammunition, and material for maintaining it in the field. This problem reduced itself to a question of ships.

For the purpose of mobilizing the man-power of the Nation and of raising the necessary army, Congress enacted the Selective Service Law. This law left the details of administration to presidential regulation, and the task of putting the law into execution was assigned to this office whose guiding principle has been and is "military effectiveness first." Military effectiveness is closely related to and dependent upon industrial and agricultural effectiveness. Therefore the industrial and agricultural needs of the Nation were strongly developed with reference to deferments under the first draft. But when a war is being waged on a battle field 3,000 miles from our coast line, military, industrial, and agricultural effectiveness are attainable only by attaining at the same time marine effectiveness, next in importance to military effectiveness. Thus it will be seen that this office was vitally interested in so adjusting the incidence of the military draft as to make it consistent with marine effectiveness.

. The shipping facilities of this country at that time were wholly inadequate to accomplish the great task of transporting the Army to France and maintaining it there. We did not have the ships. The shipping facilities of Great Britain, though very large, were already overtaxed with the great burdens of transporting, feeding, and maintaining the armies which Great Britain had placed in the field on all fronts and of transporting food from different parts of the world to England for the sustenance of the civilian population there. Moreover, the loss of shipping tonnage, sunk by German submarines, was extremely heavy and menacing. On April 12, 1917, in a speech at the American Luncheon Club, Premier Lloyd George sounded his clarion call to America for ships: "The road to victory, the guarantee of victory, the absolute assurance of victory, is to be found in one word—Ships. In a second word—Ships. In a third word—Ships. I see that America fully realizes this."

The American Government immediately formulated and put into process of execution an extensive shipbuilding program involving the vast enlargement of all existing shipyards, the building outright of many new shipyards, and the transforming of numerous established industrial enterprises into plants for the manufacture of fittings for ships.

Prior to the entrance of the United States into the war it is estimated approximately 47,000 men were engaged in the shipbuilding industry. The large national shipbuilding program now undertaken called for such tremendous extensions in this industry that the number of men trained and skilled in shipbuilding was totally inadequate. By October, 1917, it was estimated there were 112,000 men engaged in shipbuilding. But it soon appeared that even this number was not sufficient to carry the project forward. The problem presented was to secure labor for the shipbuilding industry, and, so far as consistent with the military necessities of the Nation, to protect the organization of that industry against continual disorganization and resultant ineffectiveness by the removal of its employees who were registrants, through induction into the military service under the Selective Service Law and regulations.

This office undertook to cooperate with and assist the shipbuilding industry so far as was possible by granting a special deferment of call into military service to all registrants engaged in the building and manning of ships under the supervision of the Navy Department, the United States Shipping Board Emergency Fleet Corporation, and the recruiting service of the United States Shipping Board.

For the foregoing reasons, provisions were made in November, 1917, in drafting sections 152 to 155¼ of the revised Selective Service Regulations for an Emergency Fleet Classification List. The purpose of these sections of the regulations was twofold: First, to defer and postpone the call for military service of all registrants placed thereon by reason of the fact that they were engaged in the building of ships or the manufacture of fittings therefor under the supervision of the Navy Department or the United States Shipping Board Emergency Fleet Corporation or were in training for or actually in service as mariners under the general supervision of the recruiting service of the United States Shipping Board; second, to encourage men to engage in the building and manning of ships. This special deferment obtained only so long as the registrants remained so engaged. To what extent these regulations proved to be effective will appear later.

2. *General plan—(a) Functions of the office of the Provost Marshal General.*—Under the general plan for Emergency Fleet classification listing of registrants, as provided for in the Selective Service Regulations, a registrant was placed on the Emergency Fleet classification list, and granted a special deferment of call for military service, at the request of an authorized official of the Navy Department, of the United States Shipping Board Emergency Fleet Corporation, or of the recruiting service of the United States Shipping Board.

The conditions precedent entitling a registrant to Emergency Fleet classification listing were: First, that he be actually employed and engaged in the building of ships or the manufacture of fittings there for, or be in training for or actually in service as a mariner; second that such employment be under the supervision of the Navy Department or the United States Shipping Board Emergency Fleet Corporation, or that such training for or service as a mariner be under the supervision of the recruiting service of the United States Shipping Board; and third, that a request for such listing be made and signed by one of the designated officials, as specifically set forth in the regulations, on the prescribed P. M. G. O. Form 1024.

Every local board maintained a special copy of the classification list, preceding the caption of which, in the box there provided, was written in bold characters the words "Emergency Fleet." The local board, upon the receipt of the above-mentioned Emergency Fleet request, if the same was received prior to the mailing to the registrant of an order to report for military service, forthwith entered the name of such registrant on the Emergency Fleet classification list and also entered in Column 29 of the original classification list, opposite the name of such registrant, the letters "E. F." in red ink. The classification of such registrant upon his questionnaire, and all process prescribed in the selective service regulations with respect to him, were not changed by placing him on the Emergency Fleet classification list, except that so long as he remained thereon he was to be regarded as not available for military service.

Under the Selective Service Regulations, first edition, effective December 15, 1917, all registrants, irrespective of their classification, whether in Class I, II, III, IV, or V, were eligible to be placed on the Emergency Fleet classification list. It was also provided that the official requesting the Emergency Fleet classification listing of a registrant should make a monthly report to the registrant's local board, stating that the registrant was still employed. Each local board was required to make a monthly check of its Emergency Fleet classification list; and in the event the monthly report was not received by the local board, at the specified time, the board was required to remove the registrant from the list. On June 25, 1918, local boards were instructed that these reports would be suspended for June and July; on July 20, 1918, these monthly reports were indefinitely suspended. (Sec. 154, note 1, S. S. R., 2d ed.) And on July 23, 1918, by a general telegram from this office, the placing of Class I men on the list by the Navy Department and the United States Shipping Board Emergency Fleet Corporation (though not by the Recruiting Service of the United States Shipping Board) was suspended. (Sec. 153, note 3, S. S. R., 2d ed.)

With exception of the removal of a registrant from the Emergency Fleet classification list by his local board upon failure to receive the monthly report (which exception no longer obtains) a registrant could not be removed from the Emergency Fleet classification list by his local board until the board received from the official who made the request for such listing in the first instance a notice, on specified P. M. G. O. Form 1025, that the registrant was no longer entitled to such listing and should be removed from the list. Upon the receipt of this notice the local board forthwith struck the registrant's name from the list, and he immediately became once more subject to call for military service in accordance with his original classification and order number.

The powers and functions of the Provost Marshal General's office with respect to the administration of the Selective Service Regulations relating to Emergency Fleet classification listing were supervisory and directory. The details of the operation of the general plan were left to the discretion and good judgment of the three shipbuilding agencies. They acted independently of each other, and adopted slightly different systems of operation to meet their different needs and conditions.

(b) *Plan of operation issued by the Navy Department.*—The Secretary of the Navy placed the administration of the Selective Service Regulations relating to Emergency Fleet classification listing of employees of navy yards and naval stations in the hands of the commandants of such yards and stations. The commandants selected those registrants employed by the Navy Department, under their supervision, to be placed on the Emergency Fleet classification list, and the requests on P. M. G. O. Form 1024, for the listing of such registrants were made by the commandant direct to the local boards without reference to the Navy Department.

The responsibility for the selection of men employed by private shipbuilding plants engaged on naval work to be placed on the Emergency Fleet classification list was lodged in the hands of the superintending constructors at such plants, and in these cases the requests were forwarded to the commandant of the naval district in which the plant was located and by him to the local boards.

In addition to the private shipbuilding plants actually engaged in building ships for the Navy Department there were several hundred private manufacturing plants throughout the country engaged in the manufacture of fittings for ships. In these cases action looking to the Emergency Fleet classification of his employees was initiated by the contractor in each case, who submitted a list of such employees to the Secretary of the Navy, through the naval inspector in charge of work at the plant, who was charged by the Secretary of the Navy with the duty of making careful investigation in each case of the necessity for Emergency Fleet classification. The list was passed upon by the Secretary or Assistant Secretary of the Navy, and, in the cases of those for whom Emergency Fleet classification was approved, the inspector forwarded P. M. G. O. Form 1024 to the commandant of the naval district in which the plant was located, who thereupon signed and forwarded it to the local board, retaining a duplicate in his files.

(c) *Plan of operation used by the United States Shipping Board Emergency Fleet Corporation.*—The United States Shipping Board Emergency Fleet Corporation, for purposes of administering the Selective Service Regulations relating to the Emergency Fleet classification list, designated the industrial relations division of the corporation as the administrative agency of its several divisions to deal with all matters pertaining to such listing. This division assigned the same to its draft classification and transfer branch of labor supply section—the branch which under different designations has handled this work since the initial publication of the regulations. Until June 1, 1918, the work was centered at the home office at Washington. Then it was decentralized, and there were established branch district offices.

The various shipyards and subcontractors, under the supervision of the United States Shipping Board Emergency Fleet Corporation, were assigned to the various district (or branch) offices in such a way as to bring each plant within the radius, by mail or otherwise, of a maximum of 24-hour personal service. These employers submitted to the yard representatives of the industrial relations division stationed at the shipyards, or inspectors or officers inspecting at the industrial plants, as the case might be, for forwarding to the proper district office all applications, requests, reports, etc., required by the Selective Service Regulations. All applications, requests, reports, etc., respecting Emergency Fleet classification listing prepared or compiled for forwarding to an office of the industrial relations division, or to the home office, as the case might be, were first submitted to the yard representative or inspector making inspections and examinations at the manufacturing plant. He indicated his approval, disapproval, comment, or suggestion, upon the face of such application, etc., or attached his separate memorandum to each copy thereof and forwarded the same to the district office of the territory in which such yard or plant was located. The district offices, if Emergency Fleet classification listing was deemed proper, then sent requests for such listing on P. M. G. O. Form 1024 to the registrants' local boards. The district offices likewise notified the local boards when the registrants' names should be removed from the Emergency Fleet classification list by sending a notice to that effect on P. M. G. O. Form 1025.

The home office had supervision of the work of the various district offices. It indicated and directed the policies to be followed, prepared and initially distributed all forms used, and handled all matters of correspondence relating to deferments. Regular inspections were made of the several shipyards, industrial plants, and establishments as to all matters connected with Emergency Fleet listing, and reports were transmitted to the home office for such action and further instruction as the facts justify and circumstances demand.

(d) *Plan of operation used by the recruiting service of the United States Shipping Board.*—The recruiting service of the United States Shipping Board, for administrative purposes, was divided into seven sections. Under the system which it used in connection with the administration of the Selective Service Regulations, each section chief, having supervision of the engineering and navigation schools in his section, mailed P. M. G. O. Form 1024, in behalf of the registrant, to his local board, upon his enrollment in any of these schools. Immediately upon the discharge or resignation of any registrant, the section chief immediately mailed P. M. G. O. Form 1025 to the local board. Upon graduation from any of these schools, the registrant reported to the agent of the nearest sea-service bureau, and was then placed in sea service. Each supervisor of sea training, having supervision of a training ship, mailed P. M. G. O. Form 1024, in behalf of any registrant to his local board, upon his acceptance.

aboard the training ship; and immediately upon his discharge from the service, P. M. G. O. Form 1025 was mailed to the local board. Upon the graduation of the registrant from the training ship, he was sent to the nearest agent of the sea-service bureau and placed in sea service. The recruiting service also placed on the Emergency Fleet list a small number of experienced mariners, most of whom were classified in Class I, and consequently were unable to ship unless they were reclassified in Class IV–B, or were placed on the Emergency fleet list. All these mariners signed a sea-service contract to serve for the duration of the war. Reports, registrations, and placements from the sea-service agents were sent in daily to headquarters at Boston.

In addition to being placed on the Emergency Fleet classification list, registrants under the supervision of the recruiting service were issued permits for passports by their local boards. When a registrant was discharged by the recruiting service his local board was so notified on P. M. G. O. Form 1025, and his permit for passport was returned to his local board.

3. *Shipbuilding labor-power obtained by this system.*—The numerical results of the system, as shown by reports received from the various shipbuilding agencies and compared with the reports received from the local boards, may now be examined (all of these figures being approximate only, because of the complex records involved).

The total number of registrants placed at various times on the Emergency Fleet classification list at the request of the various agencies was 202,849; the number of such registrants removed from the list at various times was 56,414; leaving a net total of registrants on the list on October 15, 1918, as 146,435. These original placements and subsequent cancellations were distributed among the three shipbuilding agencies as follows:

TABLE 15.—*Emergency Fleet deferments as reduced by later action.*

	Emergency Fleet deferments as reduced by later action.	Number.	Per cent of deferments.	Per cent of total cancellations.
1	Total Emergency Fleet deferments originally granted..................................	202,849	100.00	
2	Total cancellations....................	56,414	27.81	100.00
3	Navy Department—			
4	Total deferments......................	55,653	27.43	
5	Cancellations........................	12,749	6.28	22.60
6	Emergency Fleet Corporation—			
7	Total deferements....................	129,897	64.04	
8	Cancellations........................	42,291	20.85	74.97
9	Shipping Board Recruiting Service—			
10	Total deferments	17,299	8.53	
11	Cancellations........................	1,374	.68	2.43

The net total number of registrants on the Emergency Fleet Classification List, on October 15, 1918, was 146,435; distributed as shown in Table 16 among the three shipbuilding agencies; the same table shows also the total numbers of employees in the respective agencies:

TABLE 16.—*Emergency fleet (shipbuilding) entries—ratio to employees, by districts.*

	Emergency fleet (shipbuilding) entries—ratio to employees, by districts.	Number.	Per cent of total employees.	Per cent of total emergency fleet entries.
1	Total shipping employees	788, 755	100. 00	
2	Total Emergency Fleet entries in force Oct. 15, 1918	146, 435	18. 57	100. 00
3	Navy Department—			
4	Total employees	175, 000	22. 19	
5	Entered Emergency Fleet	42, 904	5. 44	29. 30
6	Shipping Board Recruiting Service—			
7	Total employees	15, 925	2. 02	
8	Entered Emergency Fleet	15, 925	2. 02	10. 88
9	Emergency Fleet Corporation—			
10	Total employees	597, 830	75. 79	
11	Entered Emergency Fleet	87, 606	11. 11	59. 82

Of these 146,435 registrants on the list on October 15, 1918, 48,374, or 33 per cent, were classified in Class I; the distribution among the three shipbuilding agencies being as shown in Table 17.

TABLE 17.—*Ratio of Emergency Fleet deferments to other grounds for deferment for shipbuilding registrants.*

	Ratio of Emergency Fleet deferments to other grounds for deferment for shipbuilding registrants.	Number.	Per cent of employees.	Per cent of Class I.
1	Total employees, ages 21–39 years (entered as Emergency Fleet)	146, 435	100. 00	....
2	Class I	48, 374	33. 03	100. 00
3	Deferred on other grounds	98, 061	66. 97	....
4	Navy Department—			
5	Total entered as Emergency Fleet	42, 904	100. 00	....
6	Class I	9, 297	21. 67	19. 22
7	Deferred on other grounds	33, 607	78. 33	....
8	Emergency Fleet Corporation—			
9	Total entered as Emergency Fleet	87, 606	100. 00	....
10	Class I	26, 337	30. 06	54. 44
11	Deferred on other grounds	61, 269	69. 94	....
12	Shipping Board—Recruiting Service—			
13	Total entered as Emergency Fleet	15, 925	100. 00	....
14	Class I	12, 740	80. 00	26. 34
15	Deferred on other grounds	3, 185	20. 00	....

4. *Operation of the system.*—(a) *Complaints.*—Before pointing out the effect of the general plan of the Emergency Fleet Classification List, it will be well to discuss briefly a number of complaints which arose

in connection with the administration of the Selective Service Regulations concerning the list.

Numerous complaints were made to this office by individuals and by local boards, and others appeared in the public press, with respect to a supposed abuse of the privilege extended under these regulations. The complaints, in the main, alleged that registrants in Class I sought employment in the shipbuilding industry, or training or service as mariners, for the avowed and express purpose of evading military service under the Selective Service Regulations; that the industrial establishments under the supervision of the privileged agencies used the Emergency Fleet Classification List to aid and assist personal friends, who were in Class I, to get this special deferment for the purpose of evading military service; and that registrants, who were professional baseball players, were placed on the list to exempt them from military service when called in the sequence of their class and order number. On the other hand, this office received complaints from the same official agencies, to the effect that local boards were not cooperating with them in the administration of these regulations, and arbitrarily refused to honor Emergency Fleet requests, or removed registrants from the Emergency Fleet Classification List without authority.

There is no doubt that there were some abuses of this privilege of being placed on the Emergency Fleet Classification List. Some registrants sought employment in the shipbuilding industry or training or service as mariners, intentionally and in such manner as to clearly demonstrate that they were actuated solely by their desire to evade military service. Some registrants were assisted in getting on the Emergency Fleet Classification List by personal friends, who were operating industrial plants under the supervision of the Navy Department or the Emergency Fleet Corporation, in order that they might in this manner avoid being drafted. An attempt, which from the newspaper reports seemed to be an organized plan, was made by some professional baseball players to get on the Emergency Fleet Classification List, in order to avoid being called for military service, and thus to continue to play ball.

How many cases of abuse of the foregoing character there were, it is impossible to state. However, every case in which a complaint of the foregoing nature was brought to the attention of this office was promptly and thoroughly investigated. Where the facts showed an abuse of the privilege of Emergency Fleet classification listing, the registrant was forthwith removed from the Emergency Fleet Classification List by the supervising agency.

With respect to the complaints of an organized attempt on the part of professional baseball players to be placed on the Emergency Fleet Classification List to evade military service, this office, immediately upon having the matter brought to its attention, made an investigation. The investigation showed that such individual attempts were being made, and that in a few instances baseball players had been placed on the list and were being permitted to continue to play baseball by their employers, who required them to do only a nominal amount of work in connection with the building of ships or the manufacture of fittings therefor. With the cooperation of the three agencies, this office promptly put an end to this practice. Where an abuse of this nature was found, the registrant was removed from the Emergency Fleet Classification List at once, thereupon automatically becoming subject to call for military service in the sequence of his class and order number.

The officials in authority in the three shipbuilding agencies, cooperated with and assisted this office, in every way in their power, by making investigations of all complaints and in removing registrants who were found to be improperly placed on the Emergency Fleet Classification List or were found to have abused this privilege.

How many such registrants sought employment in the shipbuilding industry, or training or service as mariners, for the purpose of obtaining the special deferment granted by the Selective Service Regulations governing the Emergency Fleet Classification List, can not be estimated with any degree of accuracy. But it must be noted that this motive in and of itself did not constitute an abuse of the special privilege. The regulations permitted this listing, and it was realized that many would avail themselves of it by seeking such employment. In fact, one of the purposes of these special regulations was to induce laborers to seek this essential employment. If any registrants did so from this motive, and if there were no elements of abuse (such as failing to report to local boards when ordered and then seeking this employment as a protection, or such as shirking in their work), and if they were placed on the Emergency Fleet Classification List in the prescribed way, and if they conscientiously performed their duty while so employed, they acted clearly within their rights. They performed work of immense value to the Government, and contributed materially and effectively to the winning of the war. And this office has no criticism to offer for such a course of action.

With reference to complaints made by the Navy Department, the Emergency Fleet Corporation, and the Recruiting Service that local boards failed to honor Emergency Fleet requests and removed registrants from the Emergency Fleet classification list, in some instances arbitrarily and without authority, it may be stated that, although there was cause for complaint in a number of cases, yet on the whole the local boards responded to and cooperated with these departments and this office in a splendid manner. The boards acted under trying conditions and were subject to great pressure in the matter of classifying registrants and filling quotas under the large calls which were being made upon them, and this in the face of the natural resentment aroused in some communities on account of individual cases of personal abuse of the regulations by registrants or their employers.   The large majority of cases in which it was alleged that local boards refused to honor requests proved upon investigation to be cases in which the requests failed to reach the boards because of incorrect or insufficient addresses used in mailing out the requests or because the cards were lost in the mails or because the requests reached the boards after they had mailed orders to the registrants to report for military service.   The number of cases where the boards arbitrarily declined to honor Emergency Fleet requests was almost negligible, and this office in such cases immediately took steps to correct any mistakes the boards might have made and pointed out to the boards their errors and the necessity of complying strictly with the provisions of the Selective Service Regulations.

(b) *General results of the measure.*—The interesting question now remains, whether or not the plan of the Emergency Fleet classification list accomplished the desired and expected results.

It may be stated that the Emergency Fleet Classification List, as a measure for the purpose of deferring and postponing the call for military service of all registrants placed thereon, was entirely effective and satisfactory.   Thus one of the expected results, though perhaps the least important, was accomplished.

With respect to the success of the plan as a means of assisting and forwarding the execution of the national shipbuilding program, we have to depend for an answer upon the figures given above and upon the opinions of the officials of the Navy Department, the Emergency Fleet Corporation, and the Recruiting Service.

On October 15, 1918, there were (Table 16) approximately 788,755 men engaged in the building of ships or the manufacture of fittings therefor or in training for service as mariners under the supervision of these three departments or agencies of the Government.   Of this total number about one-fifth, or to be exact 18.57 per cent, were on the Emergency Fleet classification list.   It would thus appear, at first impression, that the shipbuilding industry secured one-fifth of its present force, or, approximately, 146,435 men, through the assistance of the provisions of the Selective Service Regulations relating to the Emergency Fleet classification list.   If this is true, it can be said at once that the extent of the assistance thus rendered to the shipbuilding industry by the Emergency Fleet classification list regulations, relative to its general labor force, was large and material and that the plan was entirely successful.

When, however, the statistics given above are examined more closely, and other matters taken into consideration, it will become evident that it can not be said or assumed that all of the 146,435 registrants sought this employment by reason of desiring to be placed on the Emergency Fleet classification list. In addition to a desire for the special deferment, it must be remembered that at least two other motives actuated men who sought employment in the ship-building industry, to wit: A patriotic sense of duty to assist the Government in one of the most important undertakings assumed by the Government in connection with the waging of the war; and a desire to secure the high wages which were being paid employees in this industry. The further questions are, what percentage of the 146,435 registrants went into the shipbuilding industry by reason of a patriotic desire to aid the Government in this important work; what percentage sought this employment because of the high wages; and what percentage was actuated by a desire to secure the special deferment. The truth probably is that these men were actuated by mixed motives, so it is impossible to answer the foregoing questions with any degree of accuracy.

If we must rely entirely on the figures for our answer, then we should be compelled to say that of the 146,435 registrants on the Emergency Fleet classification list, the number who sought this listing for the purpose of getting a special deferment would be represented by the number of men on said list who are in Class I, and the number who sought this employment for other reasons would be represented by the number of men on said list who were in deferred classes on dependency or industrial grounds. If this is a correct basis for an answer to the question of the effectiveness of the Emergency Fleet Classification List regulations as a means of causing registrants to seek this character of employment, it would appear (Table 17) that the measure of success of this plan, in the number of men secured, is 48,374 men (the number of Class I men) or approximately one-twentieth—to be more exact, 6 per cent—of the total number of men employed in the shipbuilding industry.

Not all of the Class I men, however, sought this employment for the purpose of getting a deferment of call. So it must be admitted that the foregoing figures can not be taken as a true indication of the effectiveness of the Emergency Fleet Classification List regulations. If we relied solely upon the figures, we should be compelled to assume that the total number of men secured by the Emergency Fleet Classification regulations was only about 6 per cent of the total number of men employed. If this were true, it could be very easily said that the shipbuilding industry did not need the assistance of this office, and that the success and effectiveness of the Emergency Fleet Classification List plan was small and rather negligible.

But we must not rely solely upon the figures. It must be remembered that the need for large numbers of men in this industry was urgent. Great publicity was needed to place this urgent need before the country, and there was no more effective way to do it than to link the matter with the administration of the Selective Service law. By so doing, this urgent need was at once brought to the attention of the people in every section of the country. And it is a fact that immediately after the promulgation of the Emergency Fleet Classification List regulations, there was a rush of men to enter the employment of shipyards and industrial establishments engaged in the manufacture of fittings therefor. It is stated by the Navy Department, the United States Shipping Board Emergency Fleet Corporation, and its Recruiting Service, that in their opinion these regulations were entirely successful in aiding and assisting them to secure a sufficient number of men to carry forward the national shipbuilding program. This opinion is further substantiated by the fact that at the time, July 23, 1918, when this office suspended the regulations with respect to the placing of Class I men on the list by the Navy Department and the Emergency Fleet Corporation, they both objected, fearing that they could not secure the additional number of men they were needing and would need in the future without this special privilege.

Based on the figures at hand, we would have to say that the number of men secured by means of the Emergency Fleet Classification List regulations was somewhere between 48,374 men and 146,435 men. If we took the mean of these numbers, then it could be said that 97,405 men were secured, or 12 per cent of the total number employed. This perhaps is as nearly accurate an estimate as could be reached.

With respect to the success of the regulations in connection with the administration of the Recruiting Service of the United States Shipping Board, it will be noted (Table 17) that of the 15,925 registrants so listed 12,740, or 80 per cent, were in Class I. It will therefore appear at once that without the Emergency Fleet Classification List regulations the Recruiting Service would have been so badly crippled as to render it practically ineffective. In fact, it could not have operated at all.

It may be safely stated therefore, that the Emergency Fleet Classification List regulations accomplished the expected result of causing many registrants and other persons to seek employment in the ship building industry, and in this manner greatly assisted the Navy Department and the United States Shipping Board Emergency Fleet Corporation in the execution of the national shipbuilding program.

(IX) THE WORK OR FIGHT ORDER.

1. *Origin and purpose.*—On May 17, 1918, the so-called "Work or fight" order was promulgated; it was, in form, an amendment to Section 121 of the Selective Service Regulations. Its genesis was as follows:

The selective service draft was in itself a purely military measure. But inherent in its administration by the President was the necessity of so employing it as to minimize the disturbance to industry and agriculture, and to preserve the civic processes necessary to the military establishment and national welfare during the emergency. Constantly, therefore, it required a watchful adjustment to the issues thus developing in the industrial situation.

For some months before the date of promulgation, one aspect of these issues had been emphatically revealed by the experiences of the draft and by the comments reaching this office. The spectacle had been not infrequent of a contingent of selectives, taken by the incidence of the draft order-numbers from farms and factories, and marched for entrainment down the streets of their home town, past crowds of sturdy idlers and loafers standing at the street corners and contemplating placidly their own immunity. The spectacle was not a pleasing one to any right-minded citizen. It demanded direct measures. What gave those idlers that immunity? They were in Class I; but they chanced to receive high order numbers in the drawing, and thus became immune in their idleness, until their order numbers might be reached. The remedy for this was simple, viz, to let no man who was idle be deferred in the draft merely because his order number had not yet been reached; to require him to go promptly to work, or be inducted immediately into military service, his high order number being canceled. The Army and Navy were taking the men who were best able physically to do the fighting. But that was only one part of the national task imposed by the war. The other part, the part that fell on the other men, was to set free those men who were to do the fighting. Every man who helped to set free a fighting man was helping to fight and win the war.

And it was every man's duty to give that share of help. That duty to work, and to work effectively, was the foundation of the new measure. "Work or fight"; there was no other alternative.

Another class of fruitless immunes was represented by those who obtained deferment in Classes II, III or IV on grounds of dependency, but who were not engaged in productive industries. Those deferred classes were meant to protect domestic relations and also economic interests. But thousands, if not hundreds of thousands, of men thus deferred for dependency were in obviously noneffective occupations, and thus their deferment served no economic war purpose whatever. If they were to retain their immunity, they should transfer into useful and effective occupations, or else forfeit their immunity of deferment. The alternative was a fair one. The Nation should now force them to make their choice.

There was a popular demand for the organization of man power. With the information then available, however, no complete readjustment by transfer of individuals from one useful industry to another could be attempted. This would first require a determination of the grades of usefulness for all industries—a task as yet impracticable.

However, sheer idleness and obviously noneffective occupation must and could be reached. And a measure which would achieve this would receive instant welcome from our people everywhere, and would give substantial relief to existing needs.

2. *Method.*—How could this be done? The selective service system was the one agency of law as yet available for this vital purpose.

For some months past this office had been studying its possibilities; and the measure which finally received the approval of the Secretary of War and the President was this:

To idlers and to men not effectively employed was to be given the choice between military service and effective employment. Every man, within the draft age, at least, must now work or fight. "Work or fight" was to be the slogan from now onward.

Naturally this regulation must take account of all reasonable circumstances of excuses. Idleness, for example, would be, of course, excusable for men who are on vacations from regular work, or are ill, or can not at the time find employment suitable to their capacity, or temporarily unemployed because of strikes or lockouts or other industrial disputes. So, too, employment in a noneffective occupation would be excusable in view of personal circumstances which would not permit a change without disproportionate hardship to the dependents, or in view of the difficulty of finding an opening for effective employment in the home community.

But it was believed that these circumstances affecting individual cases could all be handled successfully by the knowledge and discretion of the local boards. The list of noneffective occupations was a small one, and represented only those open to little or no controversy. The superb work of the local and district boards in administering the law during the preceding year, their accurate knowledge of local conditions, their proved wisdom and impartiality, all combined to insure a fair and practical, as well as a vigorous, enforcement of the new regulation. The law, as well as the boards, would deal impartially with all registrants now as hitherto. Wealth and social position were to afford no immunity from its operation.

Work or fight—such was the fair alternative imposed alike upon all. Every assistance would be supplied for making this choice, if desired. The boards would be in cooperation with employment agencies, work bureaus, labor representatives, and employers of all kinds. An opportunity for work would be found if it existed. How extensive would be the additions to the military forces could not be foretold. But it was certain that a large, if not the largest, part of the result would be felt in industrial and agricultural activities. The moral and psychological effect would be seen in the choice that many or most would make to get promptly into the ranks of effective occupations.

3. *Provisions of the rules.*—In general the rules provided that any registrant in Class I, II, III, or IV, who after due notice and investigation, with opportunity to present evidence, was found by a local board to be an idler or to be engaged in a nonproductive occupation as designated and defined in the rules, without reasonable excuse, which finding was approved on review by the district board, should suffer the withdrawal of his deferred classification, if any, and of his order number, and should become immediately liable to induction into military service.

While the principle extended potentially to all nonproductive occupations, and while all registrants in deferred classes were explicitly urged to engage, if practicable, in some employment in which they could render effective assistance to the Nation, it was deemed advisable, at the outset, to confine the legal application of the rules to the following classes of registrants:

(*a*) Persons engaged in the serving of food and drink, or either, in public places, including hotels and social clubs.

This definition did not include managers, clerks, cooks, or other employees unless they were engaged in the serving of food and drink, or either, and did not apply to dining-car waiters.

(*b*) Passenger-elevator operators and attendants, and doormen, footmen, carriage openers, and other attendants in clubs, hotels, stores, apartment houses, office buildings, and bathhouses.

The words "other attendants" included bell boys, and also included porters unless such porters were engaged in heavy work.

(*c*) Persons, including ushers and other attendants, engaged and occupied in and in connection with games, sports, and amusements, excepting owners and managers, actual performers, including musicians, in legitimate concerts, operas, motion pictures, or theatrical performers and the skilled persons who are necessary to such productions, performances, or presentations.

This definition did not include public or private chauffeurs unless they were primarily engaged in other occupations or employments defined by these regulations as nonproductive.

(*d*) Sales clerks and other clerks employed in stores and other mercantile establishments.

This definition did not include store executives, managers, superintendents, nor the heads of such departments as accounting, financial, advertising, credit, purchasing, delivery, receiving, shipping, and other departments; did not include registered pharmacists, or registered drug clerks employed in wholesale and retail drug stores or establishments; and did not include traveling salesmen, buyers, delivery drivers, electricians, engineers, carpet-layers, upholsterers, nor any employees doing heavy work outside the usual duties of clerks.

The words "sales clerks and other clerks" included the clerical force in the office, and in all departments of stores and other mercantile establishments.

The words "stores and other mercantile establishments" included both wholesale and retail stores and mercantile establishments engaged in selling goods and wares.

Excuses.—The local and district boards were directed in the regulations to consider all cases with sympathy and common sense, and to accept the following as reasonable excuses for temporary idleness or for nonproductive occupation or employment:

(*a*) Sickness.

(*b*) Reasonable vacation.

(*c*) Lack of reasonable opportunity for employment in any occupation outside of those designated in the regulations as nonproductive.

(*d*) Temporary absences (not regular vacations) from regular employment, not to exceed one week, unless such temporary absences were habitual and frequent, were not to be considered as idleness.

(*e*) Where there were compelling domestic circumstances that would not permit change of employment by the registrant without disproportionate hardship to his dependents; or where a change from a nonproductive to a productive employment or occupation would necessitate the removal of the registrant from his place of residence, and such removal would, in the judgment of the board, cause unusual hardship to the registrant or his family; or when such change of employment would necessitate the night employment of women under circumstances deemed by the board unsuitable for such employment of women, boards were authorized to consider any or all of such circumstances as reasonable excuse for nonproductive employment.

(*f*) In addition to the cases where reasonable excuses might be accepted for temporary idleness or for being engaged in a nonproductive occupation or employment, local and district boards had authority under the regulations to withhold or postpone action for a reasonable time in cases where it appeared that the registrant, in good faith was, or had been, seeking productive employment, and that such reasonable postponement would have enabled him to secure such employment. Local boards were instructed to cooperate with the State directors of the United States Employment Service, or local agents of such service when advised of their appointment and location, in order that this agency of the Government might be enlisted to assist registrants engaged in nonproductive occupations or employments to obtain work of a productive character as soon as possible and with the least hardship or inconvenience.   To this end local boards were to furnish to such directors or agents the names and addresses of registrants to whom notice to appear was given; to furnish such directors or agents with the names and addresses of registrants who might inquire for information in respect of a change of employment, and to refer all registrants requesting such information to the directors or agents of the United States Employment Service.

4. *Enforcement of the rules.*—That the rules met with popular approval is amply proved by the volume of editorial commendation with which the press greeted their promulgation.   As was anticipated, the rules proved in large measure self-executing, the prompting of conscience and the pressure of public opinion causing thousands of men to seek productive employment without awaiting notice from their local boards.   For this reason the reports of the boards, summarized below, by no means show the full effect of the rules.

(a) *Formal action by boards.*—The figures showing the action of local . and district boards in enforcing the regulations are as follows:

TABLE 18.—*Work or fight order; cases disposed of.*

	Work or fight order; cases disposed of.	Number.	Per cent of notified to appear.	Per cent of certified to district boards.
1	Total registrants notified by local boards to appear	118,541	100.00	....
2	Registrants changing occupation without further action	54,313	45.82	....
3	Cases pending	50,451	42.56	....
4	Registrants failing to change and certified to district boards	13,777	11.62	100.00
5	Held to be nonproductive or idle	2,695	....	19.56
6	Held not to be nonproductive or idle	5,608	....	40.71
7	Not disposed of or not reported	5,474	....	39.73

(1) It thus appears that of 118,541 registrants who were notified to appear on account of idleness or nonproductive occupations, 45.82 per cent changed to productive occupations without further action by the boards, while 11.62 per cent were certified with the finding and recommendation of the local boards, to the district boards for final decision.

(2) The large number of registrants whose cases were reported as pending before the local boards, being 42.56 per cent of the total number notified to appear, is due in large measure to the provision in the regulations which authorizes the boards "to withhold or postpone action for a reasonable time in cases where it appears that the registrant, in good faith, is, or has been, seeking productive

employment, and that such reasonable postponement will enable him to secure such employment."

(3) It further appears that of the total number of cases certified to them, the district boards, on August 25, 1918, had disposed of 60.27 per cent.

(4) It further appears that of the registrants disposed of by the district boards, 19.56 per cent were held to be idle or nonproductively employed without reasonable excuses, while 40.71 per cent were held either to be productively employed or to have a reasonable excuse for idleness or nonproductive employment.

(5) Except in the few cases in which an appeal to the President was taken and a stay of induction pending such appeal was granted, the boards withdrew the deferred classification, if any, and the order number of the registrants who were held to be idle or nonproductively employed; and they became immediately liable to induction. The total number of appeals to the President in this class of cases was only 4.

(b) *Collateral evidence of the effect of the rules.*—Realizing that a large number of registrants must have sought productive employment without awaiting notice from the local boards, inquiry was made, through the United States Employment Service and the United States Shipping Board Emergency Fleet Corporation, as to the effect of the rules upon the volume of applications for productive employment. Accurate figures were not obtainable; but reports from the Employment Service in eight cities, viz, Boston, Chicago, Cleveland, Columbus, New Orleans, New York, San Francisco, and St. Louis, indicated that up to August 1, 1918, about 40,000 men had sought productive employment as a result of the regulations; and reports from the Emergency Fleet Corporation showed that in a majority of the yards and plants under its control there was, at least for a time, an average increase of more than 20 per cent in applications for employment.

In view of these reports, as well as of the reports of the local boards and of information received from other sources, it is believed to be a conservative estimate that the Work or Fight Rules have resulted in the movement of at least 137,255 men to productive occupation.

There is much testimony to the effect that the rules have been in large measure self-executing. A Chicago board says:

We estimate that the publicity given the Work or Fight Order caused 450 of our men to change occupations, and our interviews with the registrants added 35 to that number, making a total of 485 changes.

An Indiana board reports a similar experience, as follows:

The Work or Fight order has done wonders; in fact, it is one of the bright shining spots of the war. When the order was promulgated, we started out to enforce the law, but found that most of the people had anticipated our action; so we had little to do.

Many boards appear, indeed, to have relied on the moral effect of the rules, and to have made no great effort to enforce them by board action. A Kansas board, for instance, says:

> The Work or Fight order was not invoked by us. The slackers "beat us to it" and went to work. In our estimation, that order was of great importance, not so much on account of the men turned into the Army or into industry, but because of its effect on the country at large. It showed all the people that the Government was driving with a "tight rein" and was on the job with a thoroughness and determination which we had not, till then, understood.

Sometimes, indeed, the Work or Fight order anomalously came to be the one effective door of entrance for the fighting patriot, as the following incident illustrates:

> A young man in a certain town felt it his duty to fight for his country; but his wife absolutely refused to give her consent, and so informed the local board. The young fellow held a good position with a local concern, so he just quit his job, became a loafer, and the local board was compelled to send him to the Army under the Work or Fight rule. He sure outwitted her.

But even the potent Work or Fight order proved powerless to help this older patriot who sought to invoke its aid:

> I am writing you to inform you that I think your Work or Fight order is all right, only you have not put the age limit high enough. There are plenty of men past 50 who are better able to work than some who are younger. Now I want to be useful to the Government in this crisis, but as I am 53 years old they do not seem to want my help. I have tried several times to get in the Army, the same answer every time, "You are too old." Now please forget how old I said I was, and get me a good job; there is no work going on at this place, but my hat is in the ring. I am ready to work or fight provided the chance is given me.
>
> Yours for Victory.

The variety of situations, however, that developed under the Work or Fight order was endless; the following must suffice as a final illustration:

> We had one registrant who professed that it was against his religion to work. He certainly lived up to his religion, too. He was always loafing around on the streets or in the pool hall. His father was forced to support him or turn him out, and chose the former. His friends and relatives had tried to persuade him to go to work, but in vain. Finally the draft came along, the idle one was registered, and classified. One day the father came into the office and told us about the boy—which was quite unnecessary, as we were entirely familiar with the situation. He asked us if we could not help him out and try to get the boy to go to work. We told him that we would try. So the next day we served a notice on the boy, "You will either have to go to work or fight." He looked at us quite calmly, and said "D—— the work. I'll fight." Just then a call was issued; so we inducted him and sent him to fight. We later learned that he had developed into an excellent soldier.

(c) *Effect on different occupations.*—The several classes of occupations enumerated in the rules varied, of course, both in their numbers and in their relative amenability to the influence of the order. Just how widely the effect of the order varied as to the occupations covered can not be ascertained with entire accuracy; but the following table compiled from reports by local boards gives an adequate idea of the relative effect:

TABLE 19.—*Occupational distribution of work or fight rulings.*

	Occupational distribution of work or fight rulings.	Number.	Per cent notified to appear.	Per cent changing occupa- tions.
1	Total registrants notified by local boards to appear, by occupations.	118,541	100.00	....
2	(a) Food or drink service.	43,551	36.74	....
3	(b) Attendants at doors, etc.	9,745	8.22	....
4	(c) Amusements.	8,950	7.55	....
5	(d) Domestic service.	8,556	7.22	....
6	(e) Clerical service.	40,405	34.08	....
7	Idle.	7,334	6.19	....
8	Total registrants changing without further action.	54,313	....	100.00
9	(a) Food or drink service.	17,889	....	32.94
10	(b) Attendants at doors, etc.	4,725	....	8.70
11	(c) Amusements.	3,715	....	6.84
12	(d) Domestic service.	4,429	....	8.15
13	(e) Clerical service.	17,320	....	31.89
14	Idle.	6,235	....	11.48

(d) *Baseball.*—Following the promulgation of the rules, there was great popular interest in the status of professional baseball players and the effect of the rules upon organized baseball. In the case of Edward Ainsmith, which was appealed from the district board of the District of Columbia to the President, the Secretary of War announced on July 20, 1918 (Official Bulletin, July 20, 1918), that the decision of the district board, holding baseball to be a nonproductive occupation within the purview of the rules, was affirmed. The chief argument of the appellant was that the discontinuance of baseball, which afforded wholesome outdoor relaxation to such large numbers of the American people, "would work a social and industrial harm far out of proportion to the military loss involved." On this the Secretary of War commented in part as follows:

The stress of intensive occupation in industry and commerce in America, in normal times, is such as to give the highest importance and social value to outdoor recreation. It may well be that all of the persons who attend such outdoor sports are not in need of them; but certainly a very large preponderance of the audiences in these great national exhibitions are helped, physically and mentally, and made more efficient, industrially and socially, by the relaxation that they there enjoy. But the times are not normal; the demands of the Army and of the country are such that we must all make sacrifices, and the nonproductive employment of able-bodied persons, useful in the national defense, either as military men or in the industry and commerce of our country, can not be justified. The country will be best satisfied if the great selective process by which our Army is recruited makes no discriminations among men, except those upon which depend the preservation of the business and industries of the country essential to the successful prosecution of the war.

The officers of organized baseball immediately petitioned for an order extending to October 15, 1918, the period within which their players should be required to seek productive employment, alleging that the enforcement of the rules would cause the immediate cessation of baseball, and that they had not had sufficient notice to adapt themselves to the conditions resulting from the order in the Ainsmith case. A hearing was had before the Provost Marshal General, who reported to the Secretary of War that it was not clear to him that the game would have to be discontinued if the order were made immediately applicable; but the Secretary, on July 27, 1918, directed that, "in order that justice may be done to the persons involved," the application of the rules .to baseball players be postponed to September 1. (Official Bulletin, July 27, 1918.) Subsequently, the application of the order to players on the winning teams of the National and American leagues was further postponed to September 15, in order that the "world's series" of games might be played.

5. *Relation of the "Work or Fight" Order to the War Industries Board Priorities List.*—An erroneous impression became current, in September, 1918, that the "nonproductive" list of occupations contained in the "work or fight" regulation corresponded to the group of industries omitted from the "preference list" announced by the chairman of the War Industries Board on September 9. Because the former list was brief (only five classes of occupations), while the latter group was very large (including all industries except the 70 priority classes enumerated), and because the announcement of September 9 stated that the "preference list" was the "basis for industrial exemption from the draft," some persons formed the impression that the small list of five "nonproductive" occupations had suddenly been enlarged by the Provost Marshal General to include the extensive group of industries omitted by the chairman of the War Industries Board.

This impression that the "nonproductive" list had been enlarged at all, and particularly that it was identical with "nonpriority" industries, was erroneous and misleading. Selective service boards had been expressly directed, until further notice, to bring no other occupation under the "Work or Fight" order, except those expressly listed.

What, then, was the distinction between these two groups? The War Industries Board was charged with determining the principles upon which fuel, power transportation, materials, capital, and labor ought to be allocated to the several industries most essential to the war program. An industry omitted from that list was, therefore, in the position of not being entitled to a priority privilege. The relation of that list to the Selective Service System was that an industry included in it was thereby recommended to the district boards as being a "necessary" industry; and the district boards could take advantage of that recommendation in determining whether an indispensable man in such an industry should be placed in a deferred class on that ground.

But there were of course many scores, perhaps hundreds, of industries not positively essential to the war program nor to the maintenance of national interest during the emergency. In those industries were millions of registrants deferred on grounds of dependency, and many others in Class I without deferment. At this point the "Work or Fight" order came into play, but for only very few classes of occupations—five in all, expressly enumerated in that order—and for a relatively small number of individuals. Among this extensive and unlisted group of "nonpriority" industries, the "Work or Fight" order found very few which it designated as "nonproductive"; meaning, in general, those occupations in which the man power within draft age could better, during the emergency, be replaced by woman's work or by older men or boys. The policy involved was that those men of draft age would serve the country best by getting out of those occupations, either into the military forces or into some other occupation. Now this other occupation might be in a priority industry or in a nonpriority industry. The "Work or Fight" order did not prescribe any occupation for them to enter. There were plenty of nonpriority industries to enter; though naturally they could do well to seek out a priority industry, if one was available. But the "Work or Fight" order did not attempt to dictate on that point; it merely gave them the option of getting out of the "nonproductive" occupation, or of losing the benefit of their deferred classification or their high order number.

Thus the War Industries Board was concerned merely with strengthening the priority position of a limited number of industries located at the top of the scale, so to speak, in relation to war needs, while the Selective Service Regulations were concerned mainly with strengthening the Army by taking the registrants who chose to stay in a small number of occupations at the bottom of the scale. The whole range of occupations in between the two lists remained open to receive those who might leave the five occupations named in the "Work or Fight" order. Lawyers, for example, were not mentioned in the "preference" list; hence a lawyer could presumably not obtain a priority order for the transportation of a set of office furniture. Nor were lawyers mentioned in the "nonproductive" list; hence, a lawyer deferred on grounds of dependency did not have to give up his occupation in order to retain his deferment. On the other hand, pool rooms were not on the "preference" list while they did appear in the "nonproductive" list; hence a registrant pool-room keeper not only could not obtain a priority order-for the transportation of his pool-room furniture, but he must either go into some other occupation or lose his deferment, if any.

The two groups ("nonpriority" and "nonproductive"), therefore, not only were directed to different purposes, but they were not identical and presumably never would have become identical.

6. *Effect on compulsory work movement.*—Meanwhile, the problem of reaching those outside of the draft age who were idle in time of war was attracting special attention in other quarters. Public and legislative opinion had already begun to consider this problem actively. On August 20, 1917, became effective the Maryland "Compulsory work law," making it the duty of every able-bodied man between the ages of 18 and 50 to have some regular and continuous employment. This law was already operating with good results. New Jersey followed suit not long after, and on May 13, Gov. Whitman, of New York, signed an "anti-loafing bill" modeled on similar lines. In his memorandum accompanying this bill the governor referred to the circumstance that "many persons were coming into New York State from New Jersey in order to escape the operation of the law in the latter State." This showed that cooperation of all agencies, both State and Federal, was needed in order to effect complete results.

As a marked effect of the promulgation of the "Work or Fight" order a nation-wide drive now began. The one Federal agency possessing already the authority of law to reach the core of the problem with nation-wide effect was the Selective Service System. By this single measure it accomplished the double purpose of increasing the military forces and of stimulating the replenishment of the effective industrial ranks throughout all ages and all States. At least 10 other States—Delaware, Georgia, Kentucky, Louisiana, Massachusetts, New Jersey, New York, Rhode Island, South Dakota, and West Virginia—have since enacted legislation of like character to the Maryland law.

7. *Industrial conscription.*—What was the relation between the "work or fight" order and industrial conscription? The two were certainly not identical, either in scope or in purpose, for the former was in scope and purpose essentially a military measure and the latter would have been essentially an industrial one. Yet there was a definite and obvious relation, in that the "Work or Fight" order was calculated to supply the experimental foundation for a successful measure of pure industrial conscription had the necessity ever arrived. This larger aspect of the "Work or Fight" order has been already dwelt upon in Chapter I of this Report.

CHAPTER IV.

CLASSIFICATION PRINCIPLES AND RESULTS.

(I) ALIENAGE.

Introductory—(a)—Loyalty of aliens.—The problem of the alien was fraught with many intricacies. It was in this field that were encountered not only the subtle efforts of the Imperial German Government to insinuate its intrigues into our armed forces, but also (and this was the larger and infinitely the more complicated side) the diplomatic situations arising out of relations with our allies and the neutral nations.

Truly were we the melting pot of the world; and the cosmopolitan composition of our population was never more strikingly disclosed than by the recent events of the world war. Then the melting pot stood in the fierce fires of the national emergency; and its contents, heated in the flames, either fused into the compact mass or floated off as dross.

The great and inspiring revelation here has been that men of foreign and of native origin alike responded to the call to arms with a patriotic devotion that confounded the cynical plans of our arch enemy and surpassed our own highest expectations. No man can peruse the muster roll of one of our camps, or the casualty list from a battle field in France, without realizing that America has fulfilled one of its highest missions in breeding a spirit of common loyalty among all those who have shared the blessings of life on its free soil. No need to speculate how it has come about; the great fact is demonstrated that America makes Americans. In the diary of a German officer, found on the battle field, the following sentence, penned by one of the enemy whom these men went out to fight, speaks volumes: "Only a few of the troops are of pure American origin; the majority are of German, Dutch, and Italian parentage. But these semi-Americans— almost all of whom were born in America and never have been in Europe—fully feel themselves to be true-born sons of their country."

On the other hand, not the least valuable of the lessons of the draft is its disclosure that to-day there are certain portions of our population which either will not or can not unite in ideals with the rest. We have welcomed to our shores many who should be forever denied the right of American citizenship. The operation of the draft in respect to aliens is a great object lesson for the American people. While many declarant aliens completed their citizenship after they had been

86

inducted into the service, and fought loyally under the Stars and Stripes, yet many others refused to do so and were discharged under the order of April 11, 1918. Furthermore, thousands of nondeclarant aliens claimed and received exemption; and thousands of others who had failed to claim exemption sought and obtained their discharge from the service after they had been duly inducted. Many of these friendly and neutral aliens, who refused to aid their adopted country in time of need, had made the United States their home for many years, had acquired a comfortable livelihood, and had enjoyed to the fullest extent the benefits and protection of our country. But while millions of American boys gladly left their homes, and all that home means, to fight for high ideals and the preservation of all that is near and dear to a patriot, these men deliberately refused to make the sacrifice.

Confronted as we are with these revelations, we may join in the solemn warning, on the meaning of the oath of allegiance, voiced a few months ago by an eminent Federal judge in a charge to the jury on the trial under the espionage act of a citizen of German birth (U. S. *v.* Fontana, Amidon, J., U. S. District Court for North Dakota, Congressional Record, Oct. 3, 1918).

If you were set down in Prussia to-day, you would be in harmony with your environment. It would fit you just as a flower fits the leaf and stem of the plant on which it grows. You have influenced others who have been under your ministry to do the same thing. You said you would cease to cherish your German soul. That meant that you would begin the study of American life and history; that you would try to understand its ideals and purposes and love them; that you would try to build up inside of yourself a whole group of feelings for the United States the same as you felt toward the fatherland when you left Germany * * * I do not blame you and these men alone. I blame myself. I blame my country. We urged you to come. We welcomed you; we gave you opportunity; we gave you land; we conferred upon you the diadem of American citizenship, and then we left you. We paid no attention to what you have been doing. And now the world war has thrown a searchlight upon our national life, and what have we discovered? We find all over these United States, in groups, little Germanies, little Italies, little Austrias, little Norways, little Russias. These foreign people have thrown a circle about themselves, and, instead of keeping the oath they took that they would try to grow American souls inside of them, they have studiously striven to exclude everything American and to cherish everything foreign. A clever gentleman wrote a romance called "America, the Melting Pot." It appealed to our vanity, and through all these years we have been seeing romance instead of fact. That is the awful truth. The figure of my country stands beside you to-day. It says to me: "Do not blame this man alone. I am partly to blame. Teach him, and the like of him, and all those who have been misled by him and his like, that a change has come."

There must be an interpretation anew of the oath of allegiance. It has been in the past nothing but a formula of words. From this time on it must be translated into living characters incarnate in the life of every foreigner who has his dwelling place in our midst. If they have been cherishing foreign history, foreign ideals, foreign loyalty, it must be stopped, and they must begin at once, all over again, to cherish American thought, American history, American ideals. That means something that is to be done in your daily life. It does not mean simply that you will not take up arms against the United States. It goes deeper far than that. It means that you will live for the United States, and that you will cherish and grow American souls inside of you.

(b) *The legal status of aliens.*—Immediately after the declaration, on April 6, 1917, that a state of war existed between the United States and the Imperial Government of Germany, the question of the alien's liability to military service arose. It was realized that, from the point of view of international law, not all aliens stood on the same footing in this country. (a) An alien occupying a diplomatic post enjoys immunity from military service, as well as from many other burdens, for he is the representative of a foreign country present by consent and invitation, and is protected by a number of privileges not enjoyed by a private citizen. Diplomatic privileges do not extend to consuls, as they are not diplomatic officers, but merely representatives for commercial purposes. (b) A transitory alien friend can not be compelled to serve other than mere police duty, for otherwise commercial intercourse would be interrupted and the person might be required to aid a country in which he is a stranger. (c) An alien friend who is domiciled, that is to say, who is a permanent resident, can be compelled to serve, for otherwise he would receive the benefits of the Government without sharing the burdens. An alien's declaration of intention to become a citizen, though it does not make him a citizen, is conclusive evidence that he is properly to be considered a permanent resident. (d) An alien enemy can not be forced to serve, for otherwise he would be compelled to fight against his own country. (e) A national of a country with which the United States has a treaty containing appropriate provisions may enjoy exemption from compulsory military service. Some of our treaties exempt all of the citizens of each of the high contracting parties. Others exempt only certain designated classes.

Congress crystallized its view on this all-important question in the enactment of the Selective Service Law, approved May 18, 1917; the guiding principles of which are: (1) The draft "shall be based upon liability to military service of all male citizens, or male persons not alien enemies who have declared their intention to become citizens" between the designated ages; (2) certain designated classes of persons shall be exempt from the draft, the local and district boards having power to hear and determine all questions of exemption and the decisions of the district boards to be final, unless revised by the President; and (3) all persons registered "shall be and remain subject to draft into the forces hereby authorized, unless exempted or excused therefrom as in this Act provided".

(c) *Numbers of aliens.*—Before explaining the several problems raised by alienage under the selective service system, it is necessary to take note of the numbers involved, and of the distribution of those numbers among the various groups affected by the draft.

(1) The total number of aliens registered, and the relation of these totals to citizens registered, is shown in the following Table 20:

TABLE 20.

	Aliens and citizens, registration compared.	Number.	Per cent of aliens and citizens.	Per cent cf aliens registered.
1	Total aliens and citizens registered, June 5, 1917–Sept. 12, 1918	23, 908, 576	100. 00	....
2	Aliens	3, 877, 083	16. 22	100. 00
3	Citizens	20, 031, 493	83. 78	....
4	Registration, June 5, 1917	9, 780, 535	....	....
5	Aliens	1, 616, 812	....	41. 70
6	Citizens	8, 163, 723	....	....
7	Registration, June 5–Aug. 24, 1918	899, 279	....	....
8	Aliens	86, 194	....	2. 23
9	Citizens	813, 085	....	....
10	Registration, Sept. 12, 1918	13, 228, 762	....	....
11	Aliens	2, 174, 077	....	56. 07
12	Citizens	11, 054, 685	....	....

(2) The citizens registered were divided, as to native born and naturalized, in the following ratios (Table 21):

TABLE 21.

	Citizens registered.	Number.	Per cent of citizens registered.	Per cent of native born.
1	Total citizens registered	20, 031, 493	100. 00	....
2	Native born	18, 694, 526	93. 33	100. 00
3	Naturalized	1, 336, 967	6. 67	....
4	Registration June 5, 1917 (ages 21–30)	8, 163, 723	100. 00	....
5	Native born	7, 904, 253	96. 82	42. 28
6	Naturalized	259, 470	3. 18	....
7	Registration June 5–Aug. 24, 1918 (age 21)	813, 085	100. 00	....
8	Native born	801, 870	98. 62	4. 29
9	Naturalized	11, 215	1. 38	....
10	Registration Sept. 12, 1918 (ages 18–20, 32–45)	11, 054, 685	100. 00	....
11	Native born	9, 988, 703	90. 35	53. 43
12	Naturalized	1, 065, 982	9. 65	....

(3) The aliens were divided, as to declarants and nondeclarants, in the following ratios (Table 22):

TABLE 22.

	Aliens registered.	Number.	Per cent of total alien registration.	Per cent of aliens registered.
1	Total aliens registered	3, 877, 083	100. 00	100. 00
2	Declarants	1, 270, 182	....	32. 76
3	Nondeclarants	2, 606, 901	....	67. 24
4	Registered June 5, 1917 (ages 21–30)	1, 616, 812	41. 70	100. 00
5	Declarants	518, 216	....	32. 05
6	Nondeclarants	1, 098, 596	....	67. 95
7	Registered June 5–Aug. 24, 1918 (age 21)	86, 194	2. 23	100. 00
8	Declarants	20, 147	....	23. 37
9	Nondeclarants	66, 047	....	76. 63
10	Registered Sept. 12, 1918 (ages 18–20, 32–45)	2, 174, 077	56. 07	100. 00
11	Declarants	731, 819	....	33. 66
12	Nondeclarants	1, 442, 258	....	66. 34

(4) The war status of these aliens was as follows:

TABLE 23.

	Alien registration distributed as to war status.	Number.	Per cent of aliens registered.
1	Total aliens registered in all three registrations...........	3,877,083	100.00
2	Ages 21–31, June 5, 1917–Sept. 11, 1918..............	1,703,006	....
3	Ages 18–20, 32–45, Sept. 12, 1918...................	2,174,077	....
4	Cobelligerents..	2,228,980	57.49
5	Ages 21–31..	1,021,063	....
6	Ages 18–20, 32–45.................................	1,207,917	....
7	Neutrals...	636,601	16.42
8	Ages 21–31..	249,034	....
9	Ages 18–20, 32–45.................................	387,567	....
10	Enemy and allied enemy..............................	1,011,502	26.09
11	Ages 21–31..	432,909	....
12	Ages 18–20, 32–45.................................	578,593	....

Appendix Table 23–A shows the figures by States, and adds a comparison for German aliens with the figures of the registrations taken by the Department of Justice.

Appendix Table 23–B shows the distribution, by nationalities, for each of the three registrations.

(5) Upon proceeding to the classification of these aliens of the first and second registration (the classification under the third registration was stopped by the armistice of November 11, 1918), the results showing the contrast between aliens and citizens appear in the following Table 24; in this table, Class I is used as covering all registrants certified for service, including those prior to Dec. 15, 1917.

TABLE 24.

	Classification of aliens and citizens compared.	Number.	Per cent of aliens.	Per cent of citizens.
1	Total aliens registered June 5, 1917–Sept. 11, 1918.	1,703,006	100.00	....
2	Placed in Class I...........................	414,389	24.33	....
3	Placed in deferred classes.................	1,288,617	75.67	....
4	Total citizens registered June 5, 1917–Sept. 11, 1918.......................................	8,976,808	....	100.00
5	Placed in Class I...........................	3,292,155	....	36.67
6	Placed in deferred classes.................	5,684,653	....	63.33

(6) As between declarants and nondeclarants, the ratio for the deferred classes is naturally higher for the latter, as shown in Table 25:

TABLE 25.

	Classification of aliens in general.	Number.	Per cent of aliens registered.	Per cent of nondeclarants.	Per cent of declarants.
1	Total aliens registered June 5, 1917–Sept. 11, 1918	1,703,006	100.00	....	....
2	Declarants	538,363	31.61	....	100.00
3	Nondeclarants	1,164,643	68.39	100.00	....
4	Placed in Class I	414,389	24.33	....	....
5	Declarants	160,594	....	....	29.64
6	Nondeclarants	253,795	....	21.79	....
7	Placed in deferred classes	1,288,617	75.67	....	....
8	Declarants	377,769	....	....	71.36
9	Nondeclarants	910,848	....	78.21	....

(7) Among the three groups of aliens, viz, cobelligerent, neutral, and enemy, the classification showed the following contrasts:

TABLE 26.

	Classification of cobelligerent aliens.	Number.	Per cent of cobelligerents.
1	Total cobelligerents registered June 5, 1917–Sept. 11, 1918.	1,021,063	....
2	Placed in Class I	311,895	30.55
3	Declarants	117,842	....
4	Nondeclarants	194,053	....
5	Placed in deferred classes	709,168	69.45
6	Declarants	203,485	....
7	Nondeclarants	505,683	....

TABLE 27.

	Classification of neutral aliens.	Number.	Per cent of neutrals.
1	Total neutrals registered June 5, 1917–Sept. 11, 1918	249,034	100.00
2	Placed in Class I	61,942	24.87
3	Declarants	25,918	....
4	Nondeclarants	36,024	....
5	Placed in deferred classes	187,092	75.13
6	Declarants	51,726	....
7	Nondeclarants	135,366	....

It thus appears that the neutrals obtained deferred classification to a slightly greater extent than the cobelligerents, viz, 6 per cent. One would perhaps have assumed that the difference of sympathies would have shown a greater readiness than these figures indicate, on the part of cobelligerents, to waive deferment and enter the combat.

That the difference, such as it is, was mainly to be ascribed to nondeclarants, appears from Table 28.

TABLE 28.

	Nondeclarant cobelligerent and neutral deferments, compared.	Number.	Per cent of cobelligerents.	Per cent of neutrals.
1	Total, cobelligerent nondeclarant aliens registered June 5, 1917–Sept. 11, 1918............	699, 736	100. 00	....
2	Placed in Class I.........................	194, 053	27. 73	....
3	Placed in deferred classes................	505, 683	72. 27	....
4	Total neutral nondeclarant aliens registered June 5, 1917–Sept. 11, 1918................	171, 390	....	100. 00
5	Placed in Class I.........................	36, 024	....	21. 02
6	Placed in deferred classes................	135, 366	....	78. 98

(8) *Alien enemies and alien allies of the enemy* included, of course, a large share of anti-German aliens, belonging to other race stocks; these were usually enemies in a purely technical sense. How a certain number of them came to be placed in Class I is explained in a later paragraph of this chapter. The figures for deferments in line 8 of Table 29 show the deferments specifically made on the ground of enemy alienage; lines 6 and 7 include deferments on other grounds:

TABLE 29.

	Alien enemies and allied enemies classified.	Number.	Per cent of alien enemies.
1	Total alien enemies and allied enemies registered June 5, 1917–Sept. 11. 1918..........................	432, 909	100. 00
2	Placed in Class I................................	40, 552	9. 37
3	Declarants..........................	16, 834	....
4	Nondeclarants......................	23, 718	....
5	Placed in deferred classes........................	392, 357	90. 63
6	Declarants..........................	122, 558	....
7	Nondeclarants......................	269, 799	....
8	Class V-E of deferments (alien enemies).................	334, 949	....
9	Alien enemies reported as discharged at camp...........	5, 637	....

We are now in a position to understand the scope and bearing of the serious problems that arose in connection with alienage, and the solutions reached.

Those problems were, in the main, three: (1) The problem of alien numbers as affecting the quota basis; (2) the problem of neutral and cobelligerent alien liability to service, as involving diplomatic negotiations; and (3) the problem of enemy aliens in the armed forces.

1. *Alienage as disturbing the quota basis.*—The supposed inequity of the selective service act in requiring quotas to be based on population including aliens, while payments for quotas were obliged to be made

in natives and declarants only, led to great popular dissatisfaction. This situation existed as early as August, 1917, and was described in my First Report. Several remedies were proposed.

(a) *Alien nonliability to the draft.*—One remedy was to amend the law so as to make all aliens liable to the draft. This was the purport of several bills introduced in Congress. Besides its administrative difficulties, it involved opposition from diplomatic representatives, particularly of neutral treaty countries. In August, 1917, an acute situation was reached. At the request of the Department of State, the subject was temporarily withdrawn from consideration by Congress, pending the development of a second remedy, proposed by the Department of State, viz:

(b) *Reciprocal treaties of conscription with cobelligerents.*—This second remedy, then begun by negotiation, did not mature for almost a year; the resulting treaties are described later. The reason why this remedy, if immediately maturing, would have sufficed practically was that the cobelligerent countries represented some 700,000 of the nondeclarant aliens, while the neutrals represented a few more than 170,000, and therefore the effect of the latter element on the quota basis was relatively not important. The subjection of nondeclarant cobelligerent aliens to mutual conscription would have furnished a substantially complete relief to the complaints of inequity.

In the meanwhile, however, complete relief came about through a third remedy, adopted for other controlling reasons, viz:

(c) *The classification system.*—In December, 1917, the method of calling and examining registrants from time to time as needed to fill a requisition was replaced by the method of classifying all registrants in advance once for all (as already described in Chapter III). Of the five classes thus formed, nondeclarant aliens formed a division in Class V; and it was planned to apportion the quotas of the several States and subdivisions on the total numbers in Class I, respectively, as forming the most just basis for quotas. This method thus eliminated aliens in the computation and apportionment of quotas. The bill containing the necessary amendment to the law, though introduced in January, 1918, was not enacted until May (as described in Chapter VI); but from the time of the announcement of the plan no further complaint was heard as to the effect of alienage upon quotas. By this change of regulations nondeclarant aliens fell into Class V, and the quota basis was formed by Class I. This, therefore, reduced to an equitable basis the relative quotas of communities having large alien elements.

General satisfaction is expressed by the boards with the new quota system, as disposing finally of the discontent produced by the original statutory rule. But in answering the inquiry put to them on this point many boards eagerly seize the opportunity to express in the strongest terms the intense and widespread popular feeling that aliens, if otherwise qualified, should be compelled to serve in the Army; or, if this were impossible, that they should at least be prevented in some way (possibly by taxation) from turning their privilege of exemption to pecuniary profit. It is not too much to say that the spectacle of American boys, the finest in the community, going forth to fight for the liberty of the world while sturdy aliens—many of them born in the very countries which have been invaded by the enemy—stay at home and make money has been the one notable cause of dissatisfaction with the scheme of military service embodied in the selective service act.

2. *Treatment of aliens by the law and by the officials as a subject of diplomatic protest by foreign representatives*—(a) *Nondeclarant aliens.*—The acceptance of many nondeclarant aliens by the selective service officials, gave rise to diplomatic protest on the ground that nondeclarants, though exempt, were nevertheless made to serve. This involved both the law and procedure of the regulations, and the conduct of the officials administering them.

(1) In so far as the law itself was concerned, the two great principles embodied in the selective service regulations, viz., first, that exemption is an exception, and, secondly, that an alien claiming exemption must prove his case, were subsequently vindicated by the courts. At the outset, this office was of the opinion that the Congress intended to establish and did establish the presumption that every registrant is a citizen of the United States; that this presumption stands until the contrary is shown; and that every registrant, therefore, is and remains subject to be drafted into the military forces unless exempted or excused by a local or district board, or by the President on review. The selective service machinery, accordingly, was erected by Executive regulations, the foundation of which, in respect of enemy aliens and nondeclarant aliens, rested upon the proposition that the boards must exempt, upon their own initiative if necessary, every alien enemy, and that nondeclarant aliens, after registration, are not automatically exempt from further operation of the act and the rules and regulations.

The Federal courts throughout the country (with one exception only, so far as I am advised) have ruled to the same effect.[1] The courts reasoned that while alien enemies and nondeclarant aliens

---

[1] The leading cases are: United States ex rel. Bartalini v. Capt. Mitchell, 248 Fed. 997; United States ex rel. Joseph Koopowitz, alias Jacob Koopowitz, v. John P. Finley, 245 Fed. 871; United States ex rel. George Cubyluck v. J. Franklin Bell, 248 Fed. 995; United States ex rel. Giovanni Troiani v. John E. Heyburn, sheriff, 245 Fed. 360; James Summertime v. Local Board, 248 Fed. 832; Ella H. Tinkoff et al., petitioners, Department of Justice, Bulletin No. 57; Mathias Hutfils, petitioner, 245 Fed. 789; United States ex rel. Max Pascher v. Eugene Kinkead et al., 248 Fed. 141, affirmed on appeal by the United States Circuit Court of Appeals, 250 Fed. 692, 698, citing Arver v. United States, 245 U. S. 366; ex parte Kusweski, 251 Fed. 977; and ex parte Romano, 251 Fed. 762.

Contra: Ex parte Beck, 245 Fed. 967; John Napora, petitioner, v. James H. Rowe et al., United States District Court for the District of Montana, decided October 24, 1918, not yet reported.

are not subject to be drafted, it is clear that whether a particular person belongs to one or the other of these classes is a question of fact, exactly the same as whether a person is a duly ordained minister of religion or a student for the ministry in a recognized theological or divinity school; that the plain purpose of the act was that the fact should be ascertained by the administrative boards which the President was authorized to create; that it must be assumed that it was impossible for the local and district boards or any other governmental agencies independently to ascertain whether or not a registrant was a nondeclarent alien, because such an inquiry would involve a search of the records of the naturalization courts, Federal and State, throughout the entire country to ascertain a negative, viz, whether a person had not declared his intention ("an obviously impossible and absurd inquiry," as one judge has said); and that it was only when the action of the boards was without jurisdiction, or when, having jurisdiction, they failed to give the parties complaining a fair opportunity to be heard and present their evidence, that the action of such tribunals was subject to review by the civil courts.[1] The Federal courts further held that there is no conflict between the selective service law and the treaty stipulations in respect to nondeclarent aliens, because the act and the rules and regulations expressly give such aliens the right to claim and receive exemption from the draft.[2]

(2) In so far as the action of the local boards was concerned, the regulations and instructions required local and district boards to give every alien, as well as every other registrant, a full and fair hearing, or a full and fair opportunity to be heard, on any claim of exemption that he might have. While this office believed that, when such a full and fair opportunity was offered and no claim was made, or when a claim was made and after such a full and fair hearing the boards disallowed the claim, no one had a legal right to complain, authority was given to the boards to reopen any claim upon proper suggestion at any time before induction. Furthermore, local boards were authorized to inquire into the status of any registrant where they had reason to believe that the particular registrant was a nondeclarant alien and had failed through ignorance to claim exemption, and, if such were found to be the case, the boards were required to exempt him. •

---

[1] In ex parte Beck and in John Napora v. James H. Rowe et al., supra (the Napora case is pending on appeal in the United States Circuit Court of Appeals, Ninth Circuit), the United States District Court for the District-of Montana held that registrants who at the time of registration stated to the registrars that they were nondeclarent aliens and claimed exemption as such on their registration cards were automatically exempt from further operation of the act and rules and regulations, and that all rules and regulations to the contrary are void as being inconsistent with the terms of the act.

[2] Ex parte Dragutin Blazekovic, Department of Justice Bulletin No. 67, and Mathias Hutfils, petitioner, supra. Furthermore, the courts hold that if there be, in fact, an irreconcilable conflict between the act and any particular treaty stipulation in respect of declarent aliens, the act, the last in date, must control. Id.; id.

In order further to obviate the question which had arisen as to the advisability of acting upon implied waivers of aliens, the regulations promulgated on November 8, 1917, provided that no declarant should thereafter be inducted, the fact of such alienage having been established, unless and until he had expressly waived his right to exemption. At the same time legal advisory boards were established for the purpose of aiding registrants, and this measure thereafter eliminated almost entirely such misunderstanding as had heretofore prevailed anywhere among aliens.

There can be no doubt, from a perusal of the reports from local boards (summarized in my First Report, 1917, p. 53) that throughout the country, and with only occasional and local exceptions, the practice of the boards was in entire accord with the law and regulations. In the regions of large alien population, the personnel of the boards often included men of foreign race stock, fully aware of the conditions of alienage in their localities, as well as men of wide experience in social welfare work, deeply interested in the alien immigrant; these men took every pains to inform the ignorant and to protect the helpless.

Consuls were appealed to by draft officials in an effort to surround the alien with every opportunity to establish his foreign allegiance. It is a matter of record in the Naturalization Bureau that 53,346 cases were referred to it by local boards in the effort to establish in the case of aliens whether a declaration of intention had previously been filed.

Moreover, the mass of foreign-born residents were themselves permeated by the spirit of readiness to waive their exemptions and voluntarily accept the call to military service. Thousands of nondeclarant aliens of cobelligerent and even of neutral origin welcomed the opportunity to take up arms against the arch enemy of all; the records of correspondence in this office contain eloquent testimony to this spirit. The figures of alien classification already given (Tables 24 and 26) indicate this; and the local boards report explicitly that the number of nondeclarant aliens waiving their exemption was very large (191,491). And finally, the figures of naturalizations in camp since May, 1918 (given below in par. 3(b)) refute the notion that any appreciable number of those men had entered the service unwillingly. That the boards occasionally allowed themselves the patriot's privilege of pleading with the man who had not fully reflected on his duty is not to be doubted. An Italian was about to claim exemption on account of alien citizenship. "Are you sure you want to do this?" asked the chairman of the board. "Why not?" was the inquiry. "There are two reasons," said the official. "One is the United States, the other is Italy. Two flags call you to the colors. There's a double reason for you." "I'll go," he said. But that the boards should be disparaged for thus at times taking on the attitude of a recruiting officer no one would maintain.

Here, as in all other incidents of the draft, the situation varied somewhat in different localities; and without a doubt there were rare and sporadic local instances of carelessness and of bias which led to improper inductions. The zeal of some local boards, irritated by the slacker spirit of some classes of population, resulted occasionally in such improprieties. Moreover, in some regions, especially on the border States, many ignorant aliens, not appreciating their immunity, left the country for Mexico and Canada shortly after the first registration, without filing any claim for the exemption to which they were entitled; and they were thus carried on the books as delinquents and became liable to apprehension as deserters. Boards were authorized to reclassify them in proper cases, even in the absence of any formal claim for exemption; but this measure could not reach all such cases.

These various instances of induction of nondeclarant aliens, whether properly or improperly made, led to a number of diplomatic protests on their behalf by the representatives of foreign Governments. The number of these protests reaching this office from the Secretary of State was some 5,852 in all. A list by countries is given with Appendix Table 30–A.

(3) To allay this dissatisfaction on the part of the diplomatic representatives, however, certain administrative measures were applied.

One of these consisted in authorizing inquiry into the propriety of the induction of individual nondeclarant aliens on request of their diplomatic representatives. This involved an elaborate mechanism of inquiry on the part of the selective service officials and the camp commanders and the State adjutants general, and in the great majority of cases the complaints proved not to be well founded.

A second measure (circular letter of Apr. 27, 1918) consisted in authorizing the discharge from the Army, by The Adjutant General of the Army, of individual nondeclarant aliens already inducted, this discharge being directed at the mere request of the diplomatic representative and without regard to the merits of the induction. This measure, applied under the President's order of April 11, quoted below, was designed to apply only to individual cases that had been called to diplomatic attention spontaneously. During the months of December, 1917, and January, 1918, only one or two cases a week had been presented. But about that time the measure received an extraordinary extent of publicity in the newspapers. The result was that all over the camps there arose demands for discharge, stimulated by this publicity, on the part even of nondeclarant neutral aliens who had been voluntarily inducted and who had afterwards changed their minds. In consequence, the months, of February and March saw such claims presented at the rate of a hundred or more per week; by October a total of nearly 6,000 had been called to the attention of this office.

The method of remedy by discharge on diplomatic request became permanent, and was incorporated in certain changes in the selective service regulations as to classification. (S. S. R., 2d edition, sec. 79, (j).) The total number of discharges reported to this office from camp commanders, P. M. G. O. Form 1029–D, as having been made by reason of diplomatic request or the like, for aliens of neutral or cobelligerent nationalities, between February 10, 1918, and November 22, 1918, was 621. The local boards were directed by the regulations to classify such persons in Class V–J. The numbers so classified are reported as 1,344. The discrepancy between these two figures is, of course, due to the different manner of keeping the records; but the figures indicate sufficiently the extent of the action taken, which was found desirable in consequence of the diplomatic representations.

(b) *Declarants.*—The selective service act placed declarants expressly under liability for military service. This provision followed the tradition of the Civil War. But it led in two ways to negotiations with foreign Governments.

(1) In the first place, foreign treaty countries, i. e., those having treaties providing for exemption from military service, claimed that these treaties remained in force, and that the act violated the treaties. Naturally, this claim was made by neutral countries mainly.

Almost at the very beginning, the neutral nations' diplomatic representatives approached the State Department with numerous requests to relieve their nationals from the operation of the law, and many protests were filed against the induction of individual aliens into the military service, as being in violation of international law and treaty obligations. Frequently no distinction was made, in these requests of the diplomatic representatives, between declarants and nondeclarants. Desirous as this Government was to find a solution which should relieve the difficulty thus created, it was realized that the President as chief executive had no authority to go counter to the express terms of the law by declaring the nationals either of friendly or of neutral countries to be exempt from liability under the selective service law. But the extent of his authority as commander in chief of the armed forces in respect to such nationals after they had been inducted into the service was a distinct matter. The discussion was finally closed by the President, as commander in chief of the Army and Navy, promulgating his order of April 11,' 1918, wherein he directed, in respect to aliens drafted into the military service of the United States, that—

I. Both declarants and nondeclarants of treaty countries shall in all cases be promptly discharged upon request of the accredited diplomatic representatives of the countries of which they are citizens.

II. Nondeclarants of nontreaty countries shall be promptly discharged upon the request of the Secretary of State, and also when the War Department is satisfied that a discharge should be granted in cases where a full and fair hearing has not been given by the local board.

The first paragraph of this order, in its application to declarants, was directed to relieve the situation caused by the conflict between the selective service act and the treaties. The second paragraph, as well as the nondeclarant portion of the first paragraph, was directed to relieve the situation already described as to nondeclarants.

As to declarants, relief was finally given by Congress to neutrals (but without distinction as to treaty countries or nontreaty countries) by the act approved July 9, 1918, which provided that any citizen or subject of any neutral country, who has declared his intention to become a citizen, shall be relieved from liability to military service upon his making a declaration withdrawing such intention, which shall operate and be held to cancel his declaration, and he shall then forever be debarred from becoming a citizen of the United States. This provision was construed, so far as the Selective Service machinery was concerned, to apply only to declarant neutral aliens who had not already been inducted into the service. But for those already inducted, it was given practical effect by War Department General Orders No. 92, October 16, 1918, which authorized commanding officers to discharge such neutral declarant aliens upon application.

(2) The foregoing measures of relief applied virtually (though not literally) to neutral countries. For cobelligerent countries, the solution was reached by reciprocal treaties of conscription. The negotiations for these treaties had their inception in the situation already described in regard to the problem of including nondeclarant aliens in computing the quota basis. But as the negotiations progressed, the proposed measure was found to contribute also to the solution of these other problems concerning the liability of declarant aliens of cobelligerent nationality. So as early as July 19, 1917, the British Embassy suggested to the Department of State the conclusion of a convention respecting the military service of the nationals of Great Britain and of the United States residing in the United States and Great Britain, respectively, this convention to authorize the reciprocal drafting of such nationals both declarant and nondeclarant. On August 29, 1917, the Secretary of State submitted to the Secretary of War the draft of a convention which it was proposed to conclude with all the allied nations; and on September 17, 1917, the Secretary of State submitted to the British, French, Italian and Greek Embassies the draft of a convention for consideration by their respective govern-

ments, having for its purpose the reciprocal drafting of the nationals of each country. The proposed conventions provided that alien residents should be allowed an opportunity to enlist in the forces of their own governments, and that, failing to do so within a prescribed time, they should become subject to the selective draft regulations of the country in which they were residing. It was agreed that the convention with Great Britain should be finally concluded before those proposed to our other cobelligerents were proceeded with. Necessary modifications in the proposed draft of the convention with Great Britain caused long delay in its final ratification. The convention with Great Britain was signed on June 3, 1918; the Senate on June 24 advised its ratification, it was ratified on the 28th of June; and the ratifications were exchanged in Washington and London on July 30, 1918. The convention with the French Government was signed on September 3, 1918, ratified by the Senate on September 19 and by the President on September 26; the ratifications were exchanged and the convention became effective on November 8, 1918. The Greek convention was signed on August 30, 1918, ratified by the Senate on September 19 and by the President on October 21 and exchanged on November 12, 1918. The Italian convention was signed on August 24, 1918, ratified on October 24, and exchanged on November 12, 1918.

A further diplomatic situation, concerning cobelligerent declarants, particularly of the British Empire, arose in connection with those declarants who were being sought for enlistment by the recruiting missions authorized by the act of May 10, 1917, to be established in this country. Declarants who thus offered themselves for enlistment under the cobelligerent flag became a subtraction from the potential armed forces of the United States, if they were in Class I. This led to occasional local misunderstanding between cobelligerent recruiting officers and some of the local boards where the recruiting missions were stationed; negotiation between the State Department, the foreign embassies, and the Secretary of War was the result. This situation, however, was remedied by the completion, already referred to, of the British and Canadian treaties of reciprocal conscription, signed on June 3, 1918, which were given effect in the Army appropriation act, chapter 12. By section 79 (k) of the Selective Service Regulations (2d edition, October, 1918), a cobelligerent declarant thus enlisting in the forces of the cobelligerent country under one of these conventions was placed in Class V–K, by his local board, and thus was recorded as exempt from military service in the United States forces; but this provision did not come into effect in season to apply to registrants prior to September 12, 1918. Nondeclarant aliens who had claimed exemption from the draft in this country, and whose claims had been allowed, could of course, with propriety, be enlisted by the foreign missions. The hearty approval given by our Government to the efforts to secure them for their own governments, since they had been exempted from service in our forces, was exhibited in the act of Congress above cited.

(c) *Naturalization.*—Arising in part out of the foregoing last described situation and operating also as a remedial measure for both of the foregoing situations came the amendments to the naturalization laws, approved May 9, 1918, which removed many of the limitations of procedure and time in the process of naturalization, and were especially directed to facilitate the naturalization of aliens serving in the military or naval service of the United States. The effect of this statute was to make it possible for an alien, whether a declarant or nondeclarant who had been either enlisted or drafted into the service of the United States to change his status into that of a full citizen, thus enabling him to enter upon his military career without the handicap imposed upon him by his foreign nativity. This measure opened the way for the camp commanders, under the direction of The Adjutant General of the Army, to encourage naturalization on a large scale and resulted in the conversion of the "Foreign Legion" of the Army of the United States into a host of loyal American citizen-soldiers. By this act the number of those military persons as to whom any question could henceforth be raised, either on the ground of their proper induction as nondeclarant aliens or on the ground of their nonliability as declarant aliens of treaty countries or of neutral countries was substantially diminished.

3. *Effect of foregoing measures.*—As indicating the effect of the foregoing measures in relieving the several situations, it is worth while to note the figures obtainable as to alien discharges in camps, alien naturalization, and cobelligerent recruiting.

(a) *Discharges in camp.*—On October 5, 1918, The Adjutant General of the Army called for reports from the different camps as to the number and names of aliens who desired discharge or were suitable for dischgare. The reports thus far available cover only a single camp, but the proportions in the returns at hand are significant. Out of a total of 1,589 aliens in this camp in October, 1918, only 289 asked for discharge when the opportunity was thus offered, or less than 20 per cent. Of these aliens, 383 were technically enemy aliens, virtually all being either of Austro-Hungarian or Turkish allegiance; and 139, or a few more than 36 per cent, applied for discharge. Of the cobelligerent aliens, 1,006 in all, and composed almost entirely of British, Italians, and Russian subjects, only 24 applied for discharge, or a little more than 2 per cent. Of the neutral aliens, 200 in all, 84 applied for discharge, or 42 per cent. These contrasts between the several groups show just such cleavage as we might expect. The general figures indicate how slight was the disposition of these alien groups to withdraw from the opportunity of taking arms against the world foe.

Similarly, the returns from the local boards (though only partially covering the field) as to the neutral declarants who have availed themselves of the right, under the act of Congress above cited, to obtain exemption by withdrawing their declaration of intention to become citizens, are illuminating:

TABLE 30.

	Neutral declarants withdrawing from service.	Number.	Per cent of neutral declarants.	Per cent of Class I.
1	Total neutral alien declarants registered June 5, 1917–Sept. 11. 1918	77, 644	100. 00	....
2	Placed in deferred classes	51, 726	66. 62	....
3	Placed in Class I	25, 918	33. 38	100. 00
4	Exempted on withdrawal of declaration	818	1. 05	3. 16

(b) *Naturalizations in 1918.*—One test of the spirit of loyalty among aliens may be found in the number of naturalizations applied for and granted to registrants since the United States entered the war. Such action inspires a sentiment of admiration for their readiness to enter the war in the service of their adopted country. The Bureau of Naturalization reports that the total number of naturalizations in the United States between October 1, 1917, and September 30, 1918, was 179,816; and that since the passage of the act of May 8, 1918, above referred to, the number of naturalizations accomplished in camp, up to November 30, 1918, was 155,246. As there were only 414,389 aliens (Table 25) placed in Class I up to September 11, 1918 (including declarants and nondeclarants), and as a large portion of these must have gone overseas prior to June, 1918, it is plain that the opportunity for naturalization found a hearty response from the great majority of aliens to whom it was offered. Unfortunately, time has not sufficed to analyze the naturalization papers and thus discover the variances between the different nationalities in this demonstration of loyalty to their adoptive country.

(c) *Cobelligerent recruiting.*—The results of the recruiting missions of the cobelligerents are full of significance. Under the British flag were recruited about 48,000 men. The Polish Legion raised about 18,000. The Czecho-Slovaks also recruited a considerable number; and the Slavic Legion was in active inception when the armistice arrived.

(d) *Local boards.*—In summary of the alien attitude toward the draft, and as a main explanation of the relatively large percentage inducted from this exempt class, attention may be called to the testimony of the local boards. Apart from exceptions here and 'there for a particular region or a particular nationality, the general attitude is described in the following passage from a local board report:

I found patriotism in all our boys; not one instance can I recall where the yellow streak was shown. Many young men with German names, whose parents were citizens of the United States, seemed to be full of fight for their country. The Italians were full of ginger and wanted to get into the fight, many coming to the board and asking to be inducted before their turn, which we, of course, could not do. The American boys, of course, were all full of fight, and the Negro was just as anxious as any. So, from observation, I believe all nationalities registered by this board were eager to be of service to the United States Government and help win the glorious victory which finally came.

In spite of the indications of the figures (Table 28) that non-declarants were the least ready to go into the war, the general fact seems to be that the individual's attitude depended more on the nationality than on the legal status. A sentiment of reluctance in a particular race stock in any given community was as likely to be shared by the declarants, who were legally subject to draft, as by the nondeclarants, who were not subject.

Another important explanatory circumstance for the number of alien inductions is found in the gradual change of popular attitude. As the war went forward and the sentiment in support of the draft became marked, there was a progressive change in the attitude of men of foreign race stock. They caught the spirit and swung loyally into line. The following instance is typical:

That the feeling of the public toward the operation of the selective service law changed rapidly for the better as the months went by, there can be no doubt. Many, many instances came to our attention bearing out those facts. Probably one of the most significant examples of the change from slacker to patriot was shown in the case of the father of our registrant Z.

Z's father was a Russian Jew; he had been in this country probably 15 or 20 years. He had the Russian Jew's horror of war, and when his son's questionnaire was mailed he made haste to claim exemption for him on the ground that the son was his only support. Investigation, however, showed that there were two other boys, one close to 21, another about 19, and a sister some 22 or 23 years old, all of whom contributed toward the support of the parents. The claim for a deferred classification for Z was therefore denied, and he was sent to camp. After being in the service some two or three months, he was discharged for physical disability.. Upon his arrival home, on the strength of his discharge, he was placed in Class V–G, and a card to that effect mailed him; and some days later the father appeared, thanked the board for being, as he termed, "square with his boy," but a few days later he appeared again and stated that the boy liked the service and wanted to know if we couldn't examine him again and return him to camp. In the next two or three months both the father and the boy appeared before the board several times and made the same request; and finally, after an examination had shown us that the physical disability had disappeared, we again inducted the boy. He was sent to camp and is now in the service. In the meantime, passing the home of Z's father, we noticed, first, that a Red Cross appeared in the window, indicating that he had contributed to that fund. Later, we noticed that he had commenced contributing to the various Liberty loans. Finally, not long prior to the registration of September, 1918, the father appeared before the board and volunteered the use of his house for the September registration. At that registration, his two remaining sons were registered. They both filed questionnaires and waived all claim for exemption. The old man was proud to have his boys in the service.

The war made Z's father an American citizen. It took the war to open his eyes.

4. *Alien enemy subjects in the Army.*—(a) *Alien enemies as affected by the draft.*—The selective service act made only alien declarants subject to draft and by express statement made enemy alien declarants not subject to draft. This left the selective service regulations free to impose an absolute prohibition upon the local boards to accept for military service any enemy alien, declarant or nondeclarant, in spite of his waiver of nonliability.

While the field was thus cleared of all obstacles from a legal standpoint, the problem of the enemy alien in the practical administration of the law was fraught with many difficulties and called for constant vigilance and great discernment on the part of the local and district boards. Out of the registration of 9,586,508 men on June 5, 1917, some 41,000 were subjects of Germany. These were expressly excluded from admission into the draft, but not from the operation of the act for the purpose of ascertaining the fact of alienage. As the exclusion from the service of alien enemies was demanded by international law, by public policy, and by the effective operation of our forces, local boards were strictly charged with the duty of exempting every one of them from the draft.

Four peculiar situations arose, however.

(1) *Germany* was our first enemy. As early as the first draft, which had sent 500,000 men to camp by December 15, it was found that somewhat less than 1,000 German alien nondeclarants were reported by the boards as having been sent to camp; the number of German declarants sent to camps was also doubtless an appreciable one. It thus became necessary, through The Adjutant General, to direct camp commanders to make inquiry and to discharge such German aliens. This was a matter which did not come within the jurisdiction of the Provost Marshal General's office, except so far as it raised the question how the local boards could have permitted these men to have been inducted. There are various adequate explanations for this, but they need not be here elaborated. Suffice it to say that the President's power to discharge was so exercised as to dispose of all cases meriting such action.

(2) The second situation arose when *Austria-Hungary* became an enemy country, on November 11, 1917; this brought some 239,000 registrants into the status of enemy aliens. Up to that time, the prohibition against induction of enemy aliens had not applied to these nationals. The camps were thus found to contain thousands of Austro-Hungarian declarants, not deferred on ordinary grounds, and also a large number (probably about 9,000) of Austro-Hungarian

nondeclarants, who had waived their alienage exemption. The problem was how to discriminate in the discharge of these technical aliens. This also was a problem for The Adjutant General's office and not for the Provost Marshal General's office, the inductions presumably having been completely in accordance with law. By the letter of October 5, 1918, above cited, The Adjutant General called for a report on the numbers of such aliens in the various camps with a view to making discharges therefrom, but the reports thus far received do not afford any clear basis for ascertaining either the exact numbers of such persons or the action taken thereon. It is certain, however, that large numbers, in fact a great majority, of these men were of the oppressed races of Austria-Hungary and therefore sympathetic with the cause of the allies and ready to remain in camp. The camp reports above cited (par. 3 (a), p. 101), and also the local board reports in Table 29, show that the majority preferred to remain in the military service of the United States.

(3) The relation of *Turkey* and *Bulgaria* to the war presented a third situation. While our allies were at war with Turkey and Bulgaria, we had never declared war upon them. For all intents and purposes the registrant subjects of these two countries (some 43,000 in number) were alien enemies, although they were not in law enemies of the United States. This office was requested by the military authorities to instruct local boards to treat the subjects of Turkey and Bulgaria as enemy aliens and to classify them as such, but whether Turks and Bulgars could properly be classified as enemy aliens was a matter of original determination by the Department of State. Until the State Department ruled that the subjects of Turkey and Bulgaria were enemy aliens, the agencies of the draft were not authorized to treat them as such. The State Department finally held on October 24, 1918, that the subjects of Turkey and Bulgaria for the purposes of the draft were enemy aliens, but before instructions could be published carrying into effect the decision of the department, hostilities against Turkey and Bulgaria were suspended and the instructions were not promulgated.

(4) A fourth situation, equally anomalous but tending to an opposite result, arose in connection with the *oppressed races*, subjects of the Imperial Governments of Germany and Austria-Hungary. Jugo-Slavs, Czecho-Slovaks, and Ruthenians, subjects of Germany and Austria-Hungary, were technically enemy aliens, and as such must be excluded from the draft. Yet the known antipathy of these peoples to their sovereign Governments, and their eagerness to espouse the cause of the United States and our allies, brought us squarely into an inconsistency which produced the military ostracism of real patriots whose every interest was our own. No provision was made

for the removal of the technical barrier which prohibited their serving in our forces, until the act of Congress, approved July 19, 1918, authorized the formation of a Slavic Legion. This act provided that the Slavic Legion was to be recruited by enlistment, which necessitated the administration of an oath, rather than by the usual method of induction, which dispenses with the oath. Complete arrangements had been consummated whereby local boards were to act as recruiting agencies for enlistment into the Slavic Legion, when the cessation of hostilities on the western front caused the abandonment of the plan.

The case of *Alsace-Lorraine* was never thus provided for, by law or regulations. And the case of its sons was indeed a hard one. Many of them left this country for France to join that army. Many others, waiving deferment, were reluctantly rejected by the boards. But it may be supposed that many boards took the law into their own hands, and found a way to let these men fight in the American ranks for the restoration of the lost provinces:

A bright young man came from Alsace-Lorraine to Wisconsin, where he registered on June 5, 1917. Being a subject of Germany, the local board classified him as an alien enemy. He remonstrated, and told this story to the board: "It is true that I was born in Alsace-Lorraine, but my parents were French. When the order came that only German was to be spoken in my country, my father sent me to America, and the German Government confiscated our property and misused my father. In the face of all this, and the further fact that I have taken out my first papers, you call me an alien enemy and refuse to let me fight for my adopted country or help to right the wrongs that have been heaped upon my people." He found his way into the Army, and his record as a soldier is worthy of emulation.

A further problem was here presented by the desire of the representatives of the oppressed races of Central Europe to organize armed forces under their own commanders and to join immediately the allied forces in the battlefield. So far as these organizations solicited the enlistment of men without the draft age, no obstacle could arise as to the selective service law. But, so far as they solicited men within the draft age, they were subtracting from the potential armed forces of the United States. The group thus subtracted fell into three parts, of varying utility to the American armed forces. One of these was the technically enemy aliens, who could not be admitted to the American Army, and, therefore, might well be released to these foreign legions. The second part was those not technically enemy aliens (e. g., Russian Poles), who were in deferred or exempted classes on some claim of alienage or other ground of deferment; these were temporarily immune from the American draft, but, if they were willing to fight, they might as well fight in the American Army. The third part was those not technically enemy aliens who had been classified in Class I; these men would be distinct and immediate subtractions from the American armed forces, though if they were permitted to enlist in the foreign legions, they might go into the field earlier than if they waited for their order numbers to be reached.

The situation thus presented remained unsettled for some months. It was finally relieved in part by two measures. In the first place, the War Department conceded that aliens of the oppressed races who had already enlisted in the Polish foreign legion should not be required to be discharged and returned to the American draft; but that in future no such enlistment should be sanctioned. In the second place, the Army appropriation act authorized the organization of the Slavic legion above mentioned, into which could be enlisted aliens of the oppressed races—Czecho-Slovak, Jugo-Slav, and Ruthenian (omitting Polish), who were otherwise exempted or deferred under the draft. War Department General Orders, No. 90, October 5, 1918, gave effect to this statute. Computations made in this office, as well as by the statistician of the Carnegie Foundation, give estimates for the number of males of military age who would have been eligible for enlistment under this act ranging between 188,000 and 330,000.

(b) *Naturalization*.—The amendment to the naturalization law above mentioned operated here also to alleviate the situation by permitting alien enemy subjects enrolled in the military or naval service to obtain speedy naturalization, whether declarants or non-declarants, under certain conditions. The result of this is notable in many of the reports from camp commanders received in response to The Adjutant General's letter of October 5, 1918. The figures above set forth indicate that large numbers of technically alien enemies belonging to the oppressed races of Austria-Hungary or Germany had accepted the benefits of naturalization.

(c) *German race-stock*.—A final word must be added on behalf of those registrants of German stock who loyally stood by the American flag. There were thousands of them. A natural distrust at first attended them in public opinion; and the notorious intrigues of the German Government to secure their support have perhaps left in the public mind an emphasis on that feature. It is therefore worth while here to place on record the reassuring experience of the local boards, an experience which should preserve equally in our memory the other side of the picture. How large and loyal a share of genuine support was given to the draft by families of this race stock may be illustrated by the following typical letters from local boards:

But 24 hours were given us to fill a call for six men to go to one of the large universities for preliminary mechanical training. The chief clerk set out with an automobile in search of six registrants who could leave on short notice. At one house his ring was answered by one of those comfortably stout matrons whom we always associate with splendid culinary talents. She absent-mindedly greeted the clerk with "Guten morgen." He asked if Fred X was home, and was told he was out for the day.

He then stated his errand, and the mother went on to tell him how four others of her sons were already in the war. Drafted? Oh, no. Two of them had enlisted in the Canadian Army, another was in the Regulars, and only one had gone with a selective contingent. "Well, as long as your boy isn't here this morning, perhaps I had better hunt·up some one else." "Ach, nein, nein; he want to go. What time the train leave? I tell him. He been there already." And he was.

In this county we have had for our prosecuting attorney a young lawyer who was of German descent. In 1916 he was opposed for that office by another lawyer here who had two sons. The former candidate had a very narrow margin when the votes were counted, so his opponent thought it would be a good plan probably to try to stir up a little feeling against Germany and thus help his case in the next campaign, i. e. in 1918. He sat around the barber shops, hotel lobbies, and pool rooms, and bellowed for war with Germany. This he did all the winter of 1916–17. He said that we should go to war with Germany, and that the German in this country was all dabbed with the same stick as the German across the ocean. In due time war was declared against Germany. The American's two sons registered. One of them he knew could not pass the physical examination, so that did not concern him any. The other was a young man who was a very good sand-lot baseball player; in fact that was about all he was good for; but all in a night he became the best farmer who ever lived in this county. The father transferred to him all his property, which consisted of a set of abstracts and a farm which never raised a crop and was not big enough to turn around on. A claim was filed and denied by the district board. The case was appealed to the President and denied, and afterwards the son was inducted into the service. In the drives which followed in the way of Liberty loan, Y. M. C. A., K. of C., thrift stamps, etc., the county war board wanted all the help they could get, naturally, and in those campaigns this man never bought a Liberty bond, a thrift stamp, nor even made a speech for the board. On the other hand, the prosecuting attorney of German descent never missed a Liberty loan drive; he bought thrift stamps; he was chairman of the Four-Minute Men of the county, was chairman of the Y. M. C. A. committee in their drives, was chairman of the county committee in the drive in November, 1918, and his speeches rang throughout the county in any way he could see it would help beat the Kaiser. In 1918 he was elected over his opponent by 2 votes to 1.

(II) DEPENDENCY.

1. *Early rulings under the method ·of calling and discharging.*— Under the original Presidential Rules and Regulations of June 30, 1917, every registrant was either accepted for military service or excused from liability thereto. Accordingly, a claim for discharge on the ground of dependency was either entirely rejected and the claimant held for service, or it was granted and the claimant discharged. The object of the selective service agencies in the early period of the draft was the expeditious creation of an army. By reason of the urgency of their task, some boards overlooked meritorious dependency claims and held all married men for service unless there appeared a condition of total dependency; while other boards, less impressed by the seriousness of the emergency, were very liberal in discharging married registrants, releasing all such registrants in whose cases there was any degree of dependency. How variant was local sentiment may be seen from Appendix Table 22 in my report for 1917; for, although the national ratio of married persons accepted

to married persons discharged for dependency was 18 per cent of the total, yet in the several States it ranged between 6 per cent and 38 per cent.

Moreover, this variance of attitude led to requests for more detailed instructions to cover specific classes of cases commonly presented. The case of a wife able to obtain support either from her own labor or from the assistance of relatives of herself or her husband was a common one. As early as the end of July, 1917, this office ruled provisionally (Compiled Rulings, P. M. G. O., No. 6, par. (B), Aug. 8) that no dependency should be deemed to exist in the following cases:

1. Where the parents or other relatives of the wife or the husband are able, ready, and willing to provide adequate support for her (and children, if any) during the absence of the husband.

2. Where the wife owns land which has produced income by the husband's labor, but which could with reasonable certainty be rented during his absence to other persons so as to produce an adequate support.

3. Where there exists some arrangement by which the salary or wage of the husband is continued, in whole or in part, by third persons, being employers or insurers or others, and such portion of the salary or wage, either alone or with an allotment of his soldier's pay or with other definite income, will furnish a reasonably adequate support.

The matter having been presented to the President, the following were his orders thereon:.

We ought as far as practicable to raise this new National Army without creating the hardships necessarily entailed when the head of a family is taken and I hope that for the most part those accepted in the first call would be found to be men who had not yet assumed such relations. The selective service law makes the fact of dependents, rather than the fact of marriage, the basis for exemption, and there are undoubtedly, many cases within the age limits fixed by law, of men who are married and yet whose accumulations or other economic surroundings are such that no dependency of the wife exists in fact. Plainly, the law does not contemplate exemption for this class of men. The regulations promulgated on June 20, 1917, should be regarded as controlling in these cases, and the orders issued under that regulation directing exemption boards to establish the fact of dependents in addition to the fact of marriage ought not to be abrogated.

Accordingly, the following ruling was announced (Compiled Rulings, P. M. G. O., No. 10, par. i, Aug. 27):

Dependency—Other sources of support.—Paragraph B, Compiled Rulings of this Office, No. 6, addressed a state of affairs where the parents or other relatives of the wife or husband are able, ready, and willing adequately to support the wife and children, if any, during the absence of the husband. This ruling was responsive to a class of cases that had been brought to the attention of this office where claims of discharge had been made on the ground of dependency on a husband, who, as a matter of fact, was not dependent upon himself. The ruling directed the attention of local boards to the fact that scrutiny of cases of this kind might disclose that no discharge was advisable.

It was not intended that paragraph B, Compiled Rulings No. 6, should apply to the case of the head of a family whose family, at the time of his summons and prior thereto, were and had been mainly dependent upon his labor for support.

At the same time, for the specific case of a wife able to earn a livelihood by her own skill, it was announced that "where the wife and children were actually dependent on the applicant's labor for support, and where there are no other means of support, the wife should not be put to the necessity of going to work to support herself"; and that such claims should therefore be recognized "where in his absence they will be left without reasonably adequate support, after duly taking into consideration the soldier's wage, and support from relatives partially or totally previously extended to the applicant himself."

It was thus apparent that though the principle of dependency, as distinguished from marriage alone, was the fundamental characteristic of the law and the regulations, yet its application developed a number of well-defined intermediary cases of varying degrees of equity, upon which the local boards could not be expected to deal with uniformity to general satisfaction. The first system of selection, therefore, while well adapted to cases where the presence or the absence of dependency was unmistakable, was found to lack sufficient flexibility to cover satisfactorily the great mass of intermediary cases.

2. *The classification system.*—The experience of the first months of the draft had naturally suggested various modifications which would strengthen the system. The adoption of the classification system has been already described in Chapter III.

It was decided to create five general classes, in which all registrants would be placed for call to military service in the inverse order of their importance to the social and economic interests of the Nation. In three of these five classes (S. S. R., 2d ed., secs. 72–76), subdivisions were established for the listing of married registrants according to the degree of dependency (Classes I, II, and IV). Class I included those married registrants, without children, whose families were not dependent on their labor for support; as well as those whose presence with their families did not promote the domestic interests of the Nation, i. e., the married man who habitually failed to support his family, or who was dependent upon his wife for support, or whose family was not dependent upon his labor for support, provided the registrant was not usefully engaged. Class IV, the class of greatest deferment by reason of dependency, included those registrants with wives, or wives and children, or fathers of motherless children, mainly dependent upon them for support. The necessary finding of a board in this class of cases was that a registrant's claimed dependents were mainly dependent upon his labor for support; i. e., that his removal deprived them of reasonably adequate support.

Between these groups of married men—those in whose cases there was a total absence of dependency and those whose removal would deprive dependents of adequate support—there was a very large class of registrants, having wives, or wives and children, or mother-less children, not mainly but in some aspect dependent upon them for support. This intermediary group was placed in Class II under divisions A and. B.

3. *Class II–A.—Married registrants with children.*—Class II–A was provided for. the married registrant with both wife and children, or a father of motherless children, where such persons were not mainly dependent upon his labor for support for the reason that there were other reasonably certain sources of support available, such that the removal of the registrant would not deprive such dependents of reasonably adequate support. The question early arose as to the proper classification of the man, usefully em-ployed, whose wife and children or motherless children were in no degree dependent upon him for material support. Obviously he could not be classified with those registrants having persons mainly dependent upon them for support (Class IV, above); on the other hand, it was not thought that the head of a family of children, although his responsibility in providing for their livelihood was negligible, should be classified in Class I, so as to be liable for mili-tary service at the same time as was the man with no domestic obli-gations. Clearly he belonged in an intermediary class; the phrase "not mainly dependent" including the case of a married man with a wife and child or children or with motherless children where there was in fact no dependency whatever other than the natural respon-sibility which attaches to the status of the normal husband and father.

4. *Class II–B.—Married registrants without children.*—The fore-going Class II–A did not include married registrants without chil-dren; and it has been seen that married men without children whose wives were mainly dependent upon their labor for. support were properly placed in Class IV. The question arose what sort of defer-ment, if any, should be given married registrants, without children, where the induction of such registrants would not deprive their wives of reasonably adequate support.

In view of the demands of the Military Establishment, it was considered that the case presented sufficient distinction to justify a lower degree of classification than Class IV, the distinction thus drawn being based upon the added responsibility in the latter case attaching to the care and protection of children (S. S. R., 2d ed., sec. 74). Accordingly, it was ruled (Tel. A–1923, Dec. 29, 1917) that where a registrant had a wife, but no children, and there were such other sources of support available that the removal of the registrant would not deprive the wife of reasonably adequate support, he should be placed, not in Class II, but in Class I.

But, in determining whether or not there were "other sources of support available," could the wife's own labor be considered as an available source of support? This case did not seem to stand in the same degree with that of a wife (Class I, above) for whom other sources of support than her own labor were available. On the other hand, it was recognized that the wives of many registrants virtually supported themselves or were qualified by special skill so to do; and that in such a situation a wife without children could obviously spare her husband for military service with less hardship than could the wife with children who had been dependent upon her husband for support (Class IV). The argument for this view was forcibly stated in the following letter received from a Massachusetts mill town:

Perhaps I have no right to speak to you about this matter, and I realize I have nothing to say really about making laws concerning the Army. But did you ever stop and think of the poor, aged mothers that are giving up their boys, while next door are young married couples enjoying life to the fullest extent? That poor mother had to save and many times do without the necessaries of life to bring her boys to the age of manhood. Now, when she is old and slow and broken down in health, do you think it just right to take all her boys? There are in Class II right here men working every day demanding large salaries. Their wives also work in most cases, and the mills are paying well now. They go to the pictures, beaches, and enjoy life, while it really seems to me they could serve their country as well as young men in Class I. These mothers that I refer to, some of them have had to go to work; really it seems some laws are unjust. One young wife says "I won't work now; if I did they would take my husband in the Army." Surely she can work far more easily than those poor mothers. Now do you think it is a just law that allows these men and their lazy wives to stay at home while the poor old mother gives her three or four sons?

The object of the classification system being to establish degrees of dependency corresponding to well-defined differences, it was determined that this case should form a subdivision B of Class II, i. e., where the wife who was not mainly dependent upon the husband's labor for support for the reason that she was skilled in some class of work which she was physically able to perform and in which she was actually employed, or in which there was an immediate opening for her under conditions which would enable her to support herself decently and without suffering or hardship.

In no case were boards required to exercise sounder judgment than in the application of this rule; but it is believed to have received the substantial support of public sentiment. Judged by that standard it erred if at all on the side of liberality.

In applying it, boards were confronted with the questions: What constitutes skill in some special class of work? What shall be considered as an immediate opening for a married woman under favorable circumstances? Generally, what wife should be expected to assume employment outside her home duties, and what wife should be allowed

·to remain at home through the deferment of her husband on dependency grounds? The answer to these questions was left solely to the good sense and sympathy of the local and district boards; this office cautioning them that such cases could not be determined by a rule of thumb, but that each case must be determined upon its own merits, consideration on the one hand being given to the interests of the Government and on the other hand to the interests of the claimed dependents, and that the wife must have some actual and specific skill in some class of work before a board would be justified in causing her to seek employment. With the realization of the purpose of Division B of Class II, boards had no substantial difficulty in determining the cases meant to be therein comprehended.

5. *Class I–B, C.*—As to the remaining group of married men, viz, those who failed to support their families, or who were even supported by their wives or families, no doubt ever arose over their proper disposal in the classification, and naturally enough. The following incidents illustrate how they were often handled:

The humdrum of the everyday duties of the board members was broken by a woman appearing at headquarters leading a man. She asked for the chairman, and then to see the questionnaire. Turning to the "Waiver," she directed Jim to "sign here" and then attached her name below his signature. She then demanded physical examination blanks and the way to the examining room. The chairman at this juncture ventured to ask the reason; for Jim had a wife and two children. The answer came immediately: "My man sits around all day while I take in washing to support him and the kids. I'm getting tired of it, and he's going to war, where he will support himself." In 30 minutes she returned with the examination papers and Jim. His examination was "O. K." She then inquired when the next contingent left for camp. Upon being informed that it was the next day at 3 o'clock p. m., she departed, saying: "We'll be here." She and Jim were duly on hand; and Jim didn't get out of her sight until the train disappeared from view at the station. Her parting remark was: "Jim, don't you dare come back until the war is over!" Jim didn't.

An old negro mammy of "befo' de war" type overheard her son-in-law, who had deserted his wife, trying to get her to come in and make the oath as to dependency. The old mammy took charge of him and brought him up the next morning, and, with fire in her eyes, told the board: "Dis nigger is a liar, and I says it to his face, and I fotch him here to tell you. He haint gin my darter de rappin of your finger in two years, and las nite he come dar axin her to hep him, and I locked him up and fotched him here." He was asked what he had to say. He looked at his mother-in-law, and then thought of the German bullets; and with beads of perspiration on his face said that he would join the Army.

One feature of this class and division, however, was its frequent use by wives as a mode of remedying the domestic situation. There were innumerable instances of fluctuation in the classification of I–B; a man's wife would swear to his nonsupport, and he would go into Class I, then she would recant, and prove that he was resuming support, then he would backslide, and she would apply for a reversal of the ruling. In short, as a remedy for domestic delinquencies,

Class I–B proved an effective measure. The following is a typical instance:

> Mrs. X came to the local board to get some advice as to how she could get support from her husband. The first question asked her was, "How old is your husband?" "Thirty-five," she answered. "How long has he failed to contribute to your support?" "Two months." "Where is he at this time?" "He has gone to the city." "Do you hear from him?" "I heard one time." "What did he say?" "He said, he did not love me, as he had found so many good-looking women in the city." "Madam, I feel very sorry for you, and I will advise you to wait a short time; we are going to have a new registration; your husband will have to register somewhere; if he should come home to register, would you sign his supporting affidavit?" "No, sir; I would not." "Do you want us to send him to the Army so the Government will make him contribute to your support?" "I do." Mr. X came home to register. A questionnaire was sent to him. The poor woman forgot all she had said to the local board and now swore that he was supporting her. She was ordered to appear before the board. "Madam, I see that you have changed your mind about your husband; explain to us why you did so." "Well, he seems so good to me I don't want him sent to the Army." By unanimous vote of the board, the "good" husband drew Class I–B.

Sometimes, however, even the selective draft was not able to reach these shiftless husbands, where they were not physically fit, and the grim tragedy of domestic life went on without remedy. The following appealing letter reveals the pathos of these cases:

> I ask you in the name of God see that my husband is sent to the front to fight the Germans and not a defendless woman. I am writing this letter to you with the worst black eye that a woman could carry, one side of my face is as it always was but the other is a sight to look. This is the second beating in six months, the 7th of January, 1918, he beat me so that the judge gave him 5 hours to get out of New York. Since then he is living in Brooklyn but will not work but sends to me to come over and give him his bed money and his eat money which I can't not stand any longer. If I ant got it he calls me the worst names and tells me to get out amd make it with men on the street wich I will not do. Well, sir; I went to his board and the girl told me she done everythink to help me but the doctor says his back teeth are bad, but every other way he is healty, eat well, and sleeps well, but has no desire for work, only the desire he has is for rum and beating me. I dont want to have him arresseted as it is no use he is hardened to that; what I want is let him fight men not woman. He laughs at me when I tell him to enlist and says he will go when all the generals are sent a head of him. Now for God sake pleas help me in some way to send him over there.

6. *Board opinion as to the classification.*—With a view to obtaining the benefit of local board judgment on the wisest adjustment of these groups, the following inquiries were put:

> In your opinion, what should be done with Class II–A and B registrants in view of the expected need in camp for all of Class I new registration before the summer of 1919? (1) Should they be included in Class I? (2) Or, should they be called first after Class I, or before Classes II–C and D? (3) Or, should the whole of Class II, if finally reached, be called without discrimination? (4) And, in case you favor (1) or (2) above, should Class II–A and B of the old registration be given priority of call over Class II–A and B of the new registration?

The Boards' answers may be summarized as follows:

(1) A decisive majority of the boards—the ratio is nearly 4 to 1—were opposed to the inclusion of Class II–A and B registrants in Class I. Doubtless this view springs chiefly from a belief in the wisdom and fairness of the regulation in force.

(2) There was a substantially even division of opinion as to whether Class II–A and B registrants should be called first after Class I or indiscriminately with the other division of Class II—possibly there is a slight preponderance in favor of the former method. It should be noted in this connection that a number of boards believed that Class II–C and D should be called before Class II–A and B. As a New York City board put it, "All American life is built around the marriage status, and great effort should be made not to dissolve the home ties." It should also be noted that there was distinctly less sympathy for Class II–B than for Class II–A, some boards believing that Class II–B registrants should be placed in Class I; others that they should be called first after Class I. The opinion was not infrequently expressed that upon the exhaustion of Class I, as at present constituted, Class II should not be called, but there should be a recombing of Classes II, III, and IV, with the view of placing an additional number of men in Class I.

A very large majority of the boards—the ratio was 5 to 1— were in favor of calling Class II–A and B of the old registration in advance of Class II–A and B of the new registration.

7. *Third persons' claim.*—It appears plainly from the chronicles of the local boards that the dependency claims were by no means merely a matter of the registrant's own choice. Under the Regulations, the consent of the wife or other dependent was necessary for validating a waiver of such a claim; and this regulation was thoroughly availed of, both by the families and by the boards. So that the determination of a dependency claim became, in a real sense, just what the Regulations intended it to be, namely, a determination as to the best interests of the nation in the domestic relations. This much is said to dismiss the impression, if such should anywhere obtain, that the granting of a dependency claim signified the registrant's unwillingness to serve. It was often far otherwise; and the records are full of instances where the registrant was placed in the position of being held back by a legal obstacle which he could not overcome:

A young man, a registrant of this local board, was one of a family of three boys, two of whom were in the military service of the United States. Their father was dead, but he had served in the Union Army during the Civil War. The mother was very old, and lived on a large farm, and the only help she had at home was this son. This local board passed his order number under P. M. G. O. Telegram B–80, at the request of the superviser of the township. One day, shortly after this, the registrant appeared at the office of this local board and asked why he was not called for entrainment when his order number was reached. He was informed that many people had requested that he be allowed to stay on his mother's farm as long as possible, and that it was our desire that he raise and care for his mother's crop. He thereupon stated that his two brothers who were in the service were making his mother an allotment; that she was drawing a pension; and that it seemed peculiar to him why other people had their nose in his affairs. He said that, all there was to it, he was going to get into the service, and if Uncle Sam did not want him he would go to Canada, for they wanted men there. The registrant was inducted under the next call, and is now "doing his bit" in France.

A colored man who had been placed in a deferred class asked to be placed in Class I and sent to camp. He was told that his wife would have to agree. He went to see her, came back, and said she would not assent. A few days later he came again, and said he had succeeded in getting her to allow him to answer the call, asked that a release be drawn, which was done, and she signed it. A board member asked him why he wanted to go. His reply was that he wanted to go because his country needed him; that he was going into the war to kill Germans, and help win the fight or be killed.

8. *Results of the classification.*—We may now, in the light of the foregoing explanation of the development of these definitions for the several classes of dependency, observe the results of the boards' action in applying these distinctions.

(a) *Married men.*—The total deferments of married registrants on the ground of dependency of wife or children were as follows:

TABLE 31.

	Marriage dependency as ground for deferment.	Number.	Per cent of married registrants.	Per cent of deferred on all grounds.
1	Total married registrants June 5, 1917, to Sept. 11, 1918	4,883,213	100.00	....
2	Total married deferred on all grounds	4,394,676	90.00	100.00
3	Deferred on ground of dependency of wife or children	3,619,466	74.12	82.36

How a respectable percentage of married men came to figure in Class I may be easily understood from the following typical incidents:

Mr. H., a married man, had waived all claim for deferred classification in September, 1918. A member of the local board knew H. and his circumstances, and sending for him, he said: "If it is right that you should go into Class I, we'll put you there; but what is to become of your wife? You know, it is our business to look out for the needs of the individual just as well as for the needs of the Army." It, thereupon, leaked out that the man's son had been killed in action at Chateau Thierry on May 29, and that the wife was entitled to a small insurance; wherefore he felt he had no right to ask for deferment. Further inquiry developed the fact that there was absolutely no other means of support for the wife; whereupon the board put H. in Class II. No shirker was H.

Mr. F., a registrant, who made no claim whatsoever, was certified and received 164B. He came to the board after receiving same and gave change of address. Form 164C for October entrainment, 1917, was sent to the new address, but the card came back "not found." So we surmised that he would not answer the call. But when the roll was called Mr. F. answered and stepped in line and was entrained. That evening his wife, with her two children, came to the board to see the chairman and stated she understood her husband was sent away that morning. She was informed by the chairman that he had gone to camp. She stated he had received a colored card about a week ago, but he informed her it was simply a regular notice. We immediately proceeded to have husband recalled, which caused us considerable trouble. This registrant had in fact changed his address, so that the notice would not be seer. by his wife, so as he could leave her, he not caring for his wife and children. Mr. F. was returned to his wife in two weeks.

Appendix Table 31-A and Chart A show the details by States.

It is interesting to compare this ratio of the boards' action in 1918, under the classification system, with that of their action in 1917, under the earlier system:

TABLE 32.

	Marriage dependency, 1917 and 1918, compared.	Per cent.
1	Ratio of married men deferred to total married registrants, June 5, 1917–Sept. 11, 1918...	90. 00
2	Ratio June 5, 1917, to Nov. 12, 1917.................................	89. 13
3	Ratio of married men deferred for dependency to married men deferred on all grounds, June 5, 1917, to Sept. 11, 1918.......................	82. 36
4	Ratio June 5, 1917, to Nov. 12, 1917.................................	56. 00
5	Ratio of married men deferred for dependency to total married registrants, June 5, 1917, to Sept. 11, 1918.............................	74. 12
6	Ratio June 5, 1917, to Nov. 12, 1917.................................	49. 92

It should be noted, however, that the ratio (line 5) of married men deferred for dependency to total married registrants is perhaps hardly comparable as between 1917 and 1918, because the claims for dependency were disposed of prior to physical examination in 1918, instead of after it, as in 1917, and thus the claims for dependency in 1918 were relatively more numerous.

(b) *Classes II–A, II–B, IV–A.*—Taking up now the several divisions of the dependency classes above described (II–A, II–B, IV–A), the registrants thus classified were distributed as follows:

TABLE 33.

	Divisions of marriage dependency.	Number.	Per cent of deferred.	Per cent of Class II.
1	Total deferred for dependency of wife or children, June 5, 1917–Sept. 11, 1918..............	3, 619, 466	100. 00	....
2	Class II.................................	686, 991	18. 98	100. 00
3	Division A.................................	183, 770	....	26. 75
4	Division B.................................	503, 221	....	73. 25
5	Class IV, Division A........................	2, 932, 475	81. 02	....

No figures are obtainable to reveal the number classified into Class I whose wives were not dependent because of available sources of support other than their own work; such cases being merged into the general Class I without subdivision.

(c) *Single men.*—The contrast between single and married men, in respect to the dependency deferment being generally available for the latter but not for the former, is brought out in the following table:

TABLE 34.

	Married and single registrants compared as to classification.	Number.	Per cent of regis-trants.	Per cent of married or single.
1	Total registrants June 5, 1917–Sept. 11, 1918	10, 679, 814	100.00	....
2	Ages 21–30, June 5, 1917	9, 780, 535	91.58	....
3	Married	4, 712, 622	44.13	100.00
4	Class I	442, 592	4.14	9.39
5	Deferred classes	4, 270, 030	39.98	90.61
6	Single..................................	5, 067, 913	47.45	100.00
7	Class I	2, 741, 914	25.67	54.10
8	Deferred classes	2, 325, 999	21.78	45.90
9	Age 21, June 5–Sept. 11, 1918	899, 279	8.42	....
10	Married	170, 591	1.60	100.00
11	Class I	45, 945	.43	26.93
12	Deferred classes...................	124, 646	1.17	73.07
13	Single..................................	728, 688	6.82	100.00
14	Class I	476, 093	4.46	65.34
15	Deferred classes	252, 595	23.65	34.66
16	Total married.........	4, 883, 213	45.72	100.00
17	Total deferred	4, 394, 676	.41.15	90.00
18	Total single	5, 796, 601	54.28	100.00
19	Total deferred	2, 578, 594	24.14	44.48

These figures indicate the degree of correctness of the general assumption that single men form the group most available for seeking military effectives. It would have been useful, had the figures been available, to contrast this result with the record for organizations formed solely by voluntary enlistment.

So far as single men were entitled to any claim on the ground of dependency, the results were as follows:

TABLE 35.

	Single men deferred for dependency.	Number.	Per cent of single regis-trants.	Per cent of depen-dency de-ferments.	Per cent of single deferred.
1	Total single men registered...........	5, 796, 601	100.00	....	....
2	Total deferments for dependency, June 5, 1917–Sept. 11, 1918	3, 903, 733	67.35	100.00	....
3	Single men deferred for dependency..	284, 267	4.90	7.28	100.00
4	Class III, Division A (adopted chil-dren).....................	14, 816	.26	.39	5.21
5	Ratio June 5, 1917–Nov. 12, 1917..	....	....	....	....
6	Class III, Division B (parents)....	236, 553	4.08	6.05	83.22
7	Ratio June 5, 1917–Nov. 12, 1917, per cent...................	....	....	12.26	....
8	Class III, Division C (brothers or sisters).....................	32, 898	.57	.84	11.57
9	Ratio June 5, 1917–Nov. 12, 1917, per cent...................	....	....	.58	....

Three-fourths of the boards declared upon inquiry that nothing should be done in the way of transferring to less deferred classes any portion of the registrants in Classes III and IV on dependency grounds. But a few boards expressed the opinion that registrants with dependent aged or infirm parents or dependent helpless brothers or sisters, now in Class III, might well have been advanced into the same class as registrants with dependent wife or children. On the other hand, a number of boards declared that Class III, Divisions A, B, and C, is a "slackers' paradise;" "Many a young man," says one board, "supported his parents after June 5, 1917, who never did before." It would, however, do an injustice to allow that impression to attach to this class in any important degree. The conflict between national and parental duty was for many a severe one; and the sacrifice was often made in favor of the former:

Material being short for the July call, we gave a careful reclassification of men in Class III on ground of dependent father or mother, and immediately ordered them for physical examination. In one of these cases the registrant, living at a distance from local board headquarters, drove down, bringing his father and mother. Had he passed the examination without question, we would never have known the difference; but the local examiner, having some question about his physical qualifications, sent him up to local board headquarters to have his papers indorsed to the medical advisory board, and when the three stopped in front of the office we saw them. The young man came in and presented the papers for indorsement. We asked him who the people were with him, and he said they were his father and mother. We asked him to bring them in. The mother, somewhat crippled with rheumatism, led the totally blind father into the office, and then we began questioning the boy about the dependency, supposing that he would anxiously seize upon the opportunity. But he seemed to skillfully avoid the issue, while the old people maintained silence. So we asked the old gentleman if he would be able to get along without this only child. And he replied that he didn't know how they would be able to get along, but everyone must make a sacrifice and they would get along somehow. We persistently endeavored to have either party make a request for him to be put back in Class III, but without avail. Then we asked the old gentleman if he had any objection to the young man staying at home. He manifested genuine surprise. "Objection? Why, no; the Lord knows we need him badly enough, but if the country needs him more, we will find some way to get along." So we reclassified him in Class III-B.

9. *Recent marriages.*—In the whole field of the draft no subject has occasioned more general interest than the classification of recently married registrants. The rulings of the Provost Marshal General during the first draft and the pertinent section of the selective service regulations (Rule V, sec. 72), promulgated December 15, 1917, were designed to prevent the institution of marriage from becoming an aid to draft evaders. Local and district boards were cautioned to scrutinize carefully all claims based upon marriage entered into since May 18, 1917, bearing in mind the probability that many were contracted with the primary view of evading military service, and, in the event of an affirmative finding to that effect, to disregard the dependency resultant upon such marriage as a ground for deferment

It early became apparent that in so far as a deferred classification was granted to registrants on the ground of dependency arising from marriages entered into subsequent to the enactment of the selective service law, and even though some such marriages were not believed to have been contracted with a view to evading military service, the deferment thus obtained was extremely unpopular with the great majority of local and district boards as well as with the people at large. This condition was evidenced by an immense volume of complaint from individuals and from the various State headquarters. Undoubtedly more correspondence resulted from this rule than from any other single selective service regulation. Many boards were not disposed to release any man who had married since the enactment of the law and claimed deferment by reason of the resultant dependency. Obviously, there was difficulty in procuring evidence of a sufficiently definite character to establish the fact that a marriage was entered into with an intent to evade military service; in the majority of instances, conclusions were necessarily based largely upon inference. The natural consequence of this situation was an absence of uniformity in the disposition of this great class of cases.

This lack of uniformity existed not only between different States and sections of the country, but also between the boards of neighboring towns and cities. For instance, at one period of the administration, inquiry established that in Texas 11,000 out of 18,000 claimants, or 2.7 per cent of the entire registration of the State, were granted deferred classification because of dependency resulting from marriage entered into since May 18, 1917, while in Tennessee only 0.7 per cent of the registration were deferred on that ground. Again, in one of the largest cities of Tennessee, out of approximately 300 claims based on recent marriage, none was allowed, while in a neighboring county, every one of the 150 claims filed were granted.

During the spring of 1918, it became evident that Class I would be substantially smaller than had been estimated. Of the many causes responsible for this condition, one of the most conspicuous was the shelter from military service afforded by marriage contracted for the purpose. On May 1, 1918, an effort was made to ascertain as accurately as possible the number of registrants who had been lost to Class I because of marriage since May 18, 1917. A number of States, representative of the entire country from industrial and agricultural viewpoints, were requested to furnish data on the subject; figures were secured from 1,114 local boards. It appeared that an average of 69 registrants per local board had married since May 18, 1917; this average, carried throughout the country would have totaled 320,367 registrants, or 3.34 per cent of the entire registration of June 5, 1917. It further appeared that of registrants who had married subsequent to May 18, 1917, an average of 66 per local board claimed deferred classification because of dependency resulting from their marriages, making a total of 360,348 for the entire country, or 3.19 per cent of the total registration. Finally, it appeared that of those who so claimed deferment, an average of 36 per board were successful in being relieved from military service, making a total of 167,148 for the entire registration for the Nation; in other words 1.74 per cent of all registrants were granted deferred classification because of dependency resulting from marriage entered into since May 18, 1917. In order, therefore, to realize an approximation of Class I as it had originally been estimated, it was apparent that many dependency claims which had been granted must be reconsidered. Consequently it was felt that those registrants whose dependency status had been least definitely established, and in whose cases hardship would in the normal situation be most remote, should be the first to be taken from the great class of registrants having persons dependent upon them for support.

(a) *Change of rule.*—To correct as far as possible the irregularities resulting from Rule V, section 72 (above cited), and to render available for military service as many as possible of the approximately 175,000 registrants to whom deferment had been granted because of marriage contracted since May 18, 1917, the situation was, on June 7, 1918, laid before the Secretary of War, with the suggestion that the regulation be amended so as to provide that dependency resulting from a marriage contracted since May 18, 1917, should be disregarded as a ground for deferred classification, unless the dependent were a child of such marriage, born or unborn on or before a date to be designated. This suggestion was approved by the Secretary and confirmed by the President, and on June 13, the amendment in question was promulgated to all selective service officials. Inasmuch as in the meantime the registration of June 5, 1918, had been accomplished, provisions similar to the above and covering those registrants were included in the amendment.

The amendment provided in brief as follows: (1) In the case of registrants of the class of June 5, 1918, which included the registrants of August 24, 1918, dependency arising from marriage contracted since January 15, 1918 (the date of the introduction of the public resolution authorizing the registration of the above class), should be entirely disregarded as a ground for deferment; and dependency arising from marriage entered into since May 18, 1917, but prior to January 15, 1918, should also be disregarded, unless there was of such a marriage a child born or unborn on or before June 9, 1918, in which event, unless it had been found that a registrant had been placed in Class I with a finding that he had married with the primary view of evading military service, he was entitled to be placed in Class II. (2) In the case of registrants of the class of June 5, 1917, dependency arising from marriage entered into subsequent to that date should be disregarded as a ground for deferred classification, unless the dependent were a child of the marriage, born or unborn on or before June 9, 1918, when the registrant might be placed in Class II upon the same condition as stated for the foregoing class of cases.

This amendment to Rule V, section 72, of the regulations, was carried over into the second edition of the selective service regulations. A paragraph was added to govern particularly the classification of registrants of the new class of September, 1918, providing that the fact of dependency resulting from a marriage contracted subsequent to August 5, 1918, should not be considered as a ground for deferred classification.

This disposition of the cases met with general favor, and is regarded as having been a prudent measure, not only in that it substantially augmented Class I, but also that it produced a greater uniformity and equality of classification.

(b) *Results of change of rule.*—Reports from the local boards show that action was taken, pursuant to the foregoing change of rules, with the following results:

TABLE 36.

	Recent marriages.	Number.	Per cent of total recent marriages.
1	Total recent marriages......................................	344, 872	100. 00
2	In 1917 class, since May 18, 1917......................	217, 398	....
3	Reclassified into Class I...........................	91, 299	....
4	In 1918 class, since Jan. 15, 1918.....................	36, 630	....
5	Reclassified into Class I...........................	16, 324	....
6	In 1918 class before Jan. 15, 1918....................	90, 844	....
7	Reclassified into Class I...........................	14, 940	....
8	Recent marriages reclassified into Class I.................	122, 563	35. 54

But the complex nature of the recent marriage cases, and the injustice of regarding them as invariably evidence of evasion, is shown in the following typical incidents:

A young man, in the initial stages of the draft, waived all claim. The next day his mother appeared and said that he had been the main support of his brothers and sisters and herself, as the father was incapacitated for work. Later the boy stated that he had been taking care of the family for five years, was tired, and that he looked upon this draft law as an opportunity to relieve himself of his responsibilities. He was discharged. Later, when questionnaires were sent to all registrants, it developed that this registrant had since married; but he continued the claim of dependent parents. An anonymous communication was received, stating that he had married to evade the draft, that his wife was employed, etc. It was a late marriage. Investigation developed that the change in labor conditions brought about by the war had made it possible for the family to get along without his aid. The pathetic figure was the brave little wife, who came before the board and stated she was of the opinion that her husband should do his part in the world war, and that she was willing to give him up and undertake to care for herself. She had been an inmate of an orphan asylum, and had never had a home until the one they were building since their marriage. The board obtained employment for her, and sent him to camp.

A registrant in Class I, limited service, did not lease a farm for this year, as he expected to be called for service at any time. He used to call at the office frequently, asking for information as to when he might expect his call. But as month after month elasped, and no call came, he began to think he would not be needed, so he leased a residence in town, bought all his household furniture, and made all arrangements for his wedding. But just the day prior to the wedding a call did come, which included his order number, and he received notice to report for service. This was quite a surprise to him, and he immediately came to the office and asked for further time. The board granted him a delay of 48 hours, so the marriage was celebrated; but he took all his furniture back to the store and sent his wife back to her parents until his expected return. Happily he returned a few days ago.

(III) MILITARY OR NAVAL SERVICE.

The figures reported by the local boards for Class V, Division D, are 619,727. What does this signify?

1. *Significance of this classification.*—The act of May 18, 1917, exempted from the duty of registration all male persons who were on that date already in the military or naval service. This group of men therefore remained unrecorded. Again, when the new age 21 group registered on June 5, 1918, and August 24, 1918, and when finally the groups of ages 18–20, 32–45, registered on September 12, 1918, the same provision applied. So that the aggregate of men of these three groups who on those four dates had already entered service by enlistment in Army or Navy never entered into the classification. How large that aggregate was is indicated in Chapter V, in dealing with age groups.

Moreover, among the registrants of June 5, 1917, all those who by December 15, 1917, had already been inducted by selective draft (some 500,000 in all, as noted in Chapter VI, dealing with induction), were, of course, left out of the classification plan, which went into effect after that date; their names being struck out of the classification list by a red-ink line.

When, therefore, the boards came to classify the registrants after December 15, 1917, the men due to be entered in Class V, Division D ("person in the military or naval service of the United States"), the names of none of the two foregoing descriptions of persons would be due for entry in that class. In other words, the number of entries in Class V–D would not include unregistered soldiers and sailors enlisted or commissioned before any of the registration dates, nor registered soldiers inducted by draft before December 15, 1917. This much explanation is needful to avoid misinterpretation of the meaning of the figures of Class V–D.

In one further respect, also, they fall short of telling the whole story. The act of May 18, 1917, provided that "all persons in the military and naval service of the United States shall be exempt from the selective draft;" hence, the boards could not place a registrant in the exempt Class V–D on this ground unless they were satisfied of the facts in the usual manner. But the youths who thus precipitated themselves into service without waiting for the sequence of their order number in the draft were not always particular to report the fact to their local boards and to send home a proper certificate. They were in the service; that satisfied them; and the formality of a report to the boards either was forgotten or was neglected as a needless piece of red tape. The boards, of course, were able from local repute to establish the fact in many cases, and felt justified in making the entry. But in thousands of other cases the entry could not be made. The anomaly. was thus presented of registrants who were actually with the colors but were nominally recorded as deserters in the books of the local board. This anomaly is further considered in dealing with the figures of desertion (Chapter V). Finally, it appears that the Class V–D entries, conversely, were unduly increased by including men inducted, not enlisted; this misapplication of the regulations is revealed by the boards' reports.

The number recorded by the local boards in Class V–D signified nothing therefore as to the number of men actually in military or naval service, nor does it represent actual enlistments. It signifies only the number of registrants recorded by the boards as being known, by formal finding, to have been enlisted or commissioned after registering and before being called in the draft, together with a certain number who were inducted.

2· *Number classified in V–D.*—The figures representing the foregoing-described men in compared groups are as shown in Table 37, line 4; the excess of entries over estimated enlistments may be accounted for by the frequent error of entry above mentioned, viz, of men inducted, not enlisted.

TABLE 37.

	Persons in military or naval service.	Number.	Per cent in service.
1	Total ages, 21–30 in military or naval service (estimated).	3,579,805	100.00
2	Enlisted before registration (Table 2, line 4)........	364,298	10.18
3	Enlisted after registration (estimated)...............	548,640	15.33
4	Placed in Class V–D............................	619,727	....
5	Inducted......................................	2,666,867	74.49

(IV) SUNDRY SPECIFIED VOCATIONS.

1. *Exemptions and deferments in specified vocations.*—The selective service act directed that exemptions be granted to persons in certain vocations specifically named, as follows: Officers, legislative, judicial,

and executive, of the United States and of the several States; ministers of religion, and divinity students (as of May 18, 1917). The act further authorized the President to discharge from military service persons in certain other vocations specifically named, as follows: County or municipal officials, customhouse clerks, United States employees transmitting the mails, workmen in United States armories, arsenals, and navy yards; pilots, and mariners. By this authority the President might also designate any other persons employed in the service of the United States. The first-mentioned group above, being expressly entitled to an exemption by the terms of the act, were allotted to Class V in the classification system, as were also the pilots named in the second group. All the remainder of the second group were allotted between Classes III and IV in the classification system; that is, they occupied as a group the last place, or the next to the last place, in order of time for liability for military service. The clause giving authority to designate individuals in any other part of the Federal service was a flexible provision designed to protect indispensable positions of public service not covered by the group descriptions above mentioned.

All persons in the three described vocations entitled to exemption (Class V), viz, Federal and State officers, ministers, and divinity students, were, of course, entitled to obtain such exemption without any qualification; and the President's authority under the regulations gave an unqualified deferment to all pilots (S. S. R., sec. 79), to all county or municipal officials (sec. 77) and to all mariners actually employed in sea service (including the Great Lakes) of any citizen or merchant within the United States (sec. 78). But, exercising the same authority, the regulation qualified the discharge to be granted to persons in the remaining occupations, viz. customhouse clerks, United States employees transmitting mails, and United States workmen in armories, arsenals, and navy yards, by requiring that the individuals to be granted such discharges should be necessary employees, and should not be entitled to discharge by the mere fact of belonging to the described group. The same general qualification was, of course, applied also to the remaining described groups, viz, persons employed in the service of the United States; the restriction of these discharges to necessary individuals only was effected by requiring the filing of affidavits of necessity issued by the chief of the Government department in which the employee belonged (S. S. R. Part XIV).

Apart from the mere numbers of deferments and exemptions thus granted, it is interesting to observe the extent to which this group of deferments and exemptions were utilized to protect the necessary vocations, official and unofficial, specially recognized in the act. For this purpose is set forth in Table 38, first the estimated number of all persons within each vocation, and then the number of deferments or exemptions reported by the local boards to have been granted on the ground of such vocation. The estimates of the former numbers were made independently of the local board reports, and some of the resulting ratios are incongruous. Nevertheless, this approximation to the facts deserves study.

TABLE 38.

	Vocations specifically recognized.	Number.	Per cent of exempted or deferred to total persons.	Per cent of exemptions, etc., to total exemptions.
1	Total engaged in vocations specifically recognized, ages 21-30	129,337	100.00	....
2	Total exempted and deferred on vocational grounds	76,497	59.15	100.00
3	Federal and State officers (V-A)	6,700	100.00	....
4	Federal officers	4,000	....	....
5	State officers	2,700	....	....
6	Exempted	6,695	99.93	8.75
7	Ministers (V-B)	17,761	100.00	....
8	Exempted	18,067	101.72	23.62
9	Divinity and medical students (V-C)	19,600	100.00	....
10	Exempted	16,673	85.07	21.80
11	Pilots (V-I)	1,900	100.00	....
12	Exempted	1,705	89.74	2.23
13	Mariners (IV-B)	41,698	100.00	....
14	Deferred	16,128	38.68	21.08
15	County or municipal officers (III-D)	3,480	100.00	....
16	Deferred	2,767	79.51	3.62
17	Firemen and policemen (III-E)	19,273	100.00	....
18	Deferred	2,885	14.97	3.77
19	Customhouse clerks (III-F)	(¹)	....	....
20	Deferred	577	....	.75
21	Mailmen (III-G)	18,925	100.00	....
22	Deferred	6,381	33.72	8.34
23	Artificers in arsenals, etc. (III-H)	(¹)	....	....
24	Deferred	4,619	....	6.04
25	Other Federal employees subject to designation by the President (III-I)	(²)	....	....

¹ Not ascertainable.   ² See Table 39.

2. *Federal employees designated by the President.*—The clause above mentioned, viz, authorizing the discharge of "such other persons employed in the service of the United States as the President may designate," was of course vital for the maintenance of the Federal civil establishment. The Government could not have been conducted during the emergency if it had been subject to disruption by large depletion of civil servants all along the line.

Nevertheless, it was equally obvious that there must be, among the several hundred thousand Government employees, large numbers of registrants whose posts could be as well filled by other men not subject to military service or by women; and it was fair to assume that the chiefs of Government departments might well expect to exercise the same efforts at replacement that were obliged to be exercised by the managers of industry at large.   As early as July, 1917 (Executive Order of July 25, 1917), the President's direction established a method for enabling the chiefs of all departments to exercise the most careful scrutiny before approving claims for discharge based upon this ground; and in all departments the selective service administration received the most cordial and effective support by way of a strict limitation of these approvals for claims for discharge or deferment.   However, with such an enormous number of employees, scattered throughout the country and filling positions of such variety of necessity, it was natural that a wide variance of judgment would develop in the recommendations made by officials for the discharge or deferment of employees within their jurisdiction.   Occasional instances of what appeared to be an exaggerated sense of the importance of a particular employee led to some public discussion.

As the heavy calls to camp matured in the spring of 1918, and it seemed probable that the entire strength of Class I would be needed for the Army, the attention of Congress was directed to this supposed excessive use of the above clause by Government officials as a ground for deferment of their employees.   On June 3, 1918, Congressman Madden submitted to the House a series of resolutions requesting that various governmental departments report to the House of Representatives the number of men in the service of such departments who were on June 5, 1917, between the ages of 21 and 31 years, for whom requests for exemption from military duty or deferred classification had been asked and allowed.

Before the introduction of Mr. Madden's resolutions the possibility that deferred classification had been given Government employees who might readily be spared for military service had been discussed in this Office, and a subsequent telegram to the draft executives of all States, while not specifically designating Class III–I (necessary employees in service of United States), clearly contemplated that all cases in which deferred classification had been granted should be reopened and the registrants reclassified, if there appeared to be any question as to the propriety of the original classification.

Upon the publication in the Congressional Record of the reports called for by Mr. Madden's resolutions, this Office immediately communicated to the local boards concerned the names of certain of the registrants listed and requested prompt investigation and report of any action which might result therefrom.   Reports from local boards on cases to which attention had been called indicated that there had been no excessive use of certificates of necessity issued by the executives of Governmental departments, and it was considered therefore that no further action on the part of this Office was necessary. It is interesting to note from the report submitted to the House of Representatives that deferment had been asked for only 14 employees of the Post Office Department at Washington; that the Secretary of the Navy had already voluntarily withdrawn requests for the exemption of clerical employees, and that in many of the bureaus of governmental departments no civilians within the draft ages were employed. The fact was also brought out that registrants employed in a civil capacity in various branches of the War Department were constantly being released for military service, and that many branches of the civil Government had already been hampered by the loss of men who, at the call of war, had voluntarily abandoned their civil posts and enlisted in the Army.

The following Table 39 shows the deferments granted under this clause for the principal departments of the Federal Government:

TABLE 39.

	Federal employees designated by President.	Number.	Per cent of deferments to total male employees, ages 21-30.	Per cent of deferments to total deferments.
1	Total male Federal employees ages 21-30 in principal departments	32,380	100.00	
2	Deferred under Class III-I	3,478	10.74	100.00
3	State Department	390	100.00	
4	Deferred	176	45.13	5.06
5	Treasury Department	3,043	100.00	
6	Deferred	607	19.95	17.45
7	Department of Justice	245	100.00	
8	Deferred	71	28.98	2.04
9	War Department	12,825	100.00	
10	Deferred	642	5.01	18.46
11	Post Office Department	243	100.00	
12	Deferred	20	8.23	.58
13	Navy Department	523	100.00	
14	Deferred	345	65.97	9.92
15	Interior Department	2,757	100.00	
16	Deferred	309	11.21	8.88
17	Department of Agriculture	5,634	100.00	
18	Deferred	828	14.70	23.81
19	Commerce Department	1,639	100.00	
20	Deferred	446	27.21	12.82
21	Labor Department	1,080	100.00	
22	Deferred	(1)		
23	Food Commission	1,737	100.00	
24	Deferred	27	1.55	.78
25	Fuel Commission	2,177	100.00	
26	Deferred	6	.28	.17
27	War Industries Board	87	100.00	
28	Deferred	1	1.15	.03

1 No report.

3. *Divinity and medical students.*—Under the terms of the original act of May 18, 1917, an exemption was accorded to students "who at the time of the approval of this act are preparing for the ministry

in a recognized theological or divinity school." But by the original act no exemption or discharge was accorded to medical students; the necessity of protection to the training of medical students for military purposes was recognized late in the summer of 1917, by providing for their enlistment in the Enlisted Reserve Corps of the Medical Department. One year after the passage of the original act the act of May 20, 1918, provided that an exemption should be granted to "students who are preparing for the ministry in recognized theological or divinity schools and students who are preparing for the practice of medicine and surgery in recognized medical schools at the time of the approval of this act." Therefore, under the classification system as it proceeded during the spring of 1918 the exemption in force up to May 20, 1918, was applicable only to divinity students of May 18, 1917; but after May 20, 1918, it was applicable to the following larger group thus defined in Selective Service Regulations:

SEC. 79.—A student who on May 18, 1917, or on May 20, 1918. was preparing for the ministry in a recognized theological or divinity school, or who on May 20, 1918, was preparing for the practice of medicine and surgery in a recognized medical school.

The ascertainment of the ratio of medical and divinity students thus availing themselves of exemption becomes a difficult matter in view of these legislative changes in the composition of the group. The reports from the local boards, compared with the figures of total medical students (furnished by the Surgeon General's Office) and with the figures of total divinity students (obtained from the Bureau of Education and Industrial Index of this office), are as shown in Table 40; but some of the figures necessarily rest upon estimate only:

TABLE 40.

	Divinity and medical students.	Number.
1	Total divinity and medical students, ages 21–30, May 18, 1917, and May 20, 1918 (estimated)	19,600
2	Exempted (divinity and medical)	16,673
3	Reserved (medical)	6,194
4	Total divinity students, ages 21–30 (estimated)	9,900
5	On May 18,.1917, ages 21–30	5,387
6	On May 20, 1918, all ages	8,618
7	Exempted	5,161
8	Total medical students, ages 21–30 (estimated)	9,700
9	On May 18, 1917, ages 21–30	4,714
10	On May 20, 1918, all ages	7,984
11	Enlisted in Reserve Corps	6,194
12	Exempted as medical students	535

4. *Firemen and policemen.*—By the terms of the selective service act, no specific exemption was granted to firemen and policemen as a group. But under the clause of the act, authorizing the President to discharge county and municipal officials, authority existed to include this group specifically, and with limitations, in the Selective Service

Regulations providing for discharge or deferment.   During the latter part of the summer of 1917, the matter was urgently called to the attention of this office by the mayors of New York City and other cities; and in the new regulations, promulgated by the President on November 8, 1917, section 77, paragraph (e), provision was made for placing in Class III, Division E, "A fireman or policeman who is highly trained as such and has been continuously employed and compensated by the municipality which he is now serving for a period of at least three years, and who can not be replaced without substantial and material detriment to the public safety in the municipality in which he is serving."

In the spring of 1918, however, as the prospects increased for · heavier calls to camp and for the utilization of the entire Class I effectives, renewed requests for a modification of the regulations were received from several municipalities.   The prudence of acceding to this request depended, to some extent, upon the probable numbers that would thus be lost to military service on the one hand, or to the fire and police protection on the other hand, by establishing or refusing the deferment per se of all firemen and policemen.   The figures were found to be as follows, as shown by the Industrial Index of this Office (based on data of January–March, 1918):

TABLE 40a.

	Firemen and policemen deferred.	All ages.	Ages 21–30 classified in 1918.	Deferred on other grounds.	Class I.
1	Firemen	40,946	8,544	6,982	1,562
2	Policemen and constables	81,713	10,729	8,736	1,993

It was obvious from these figures that while blanket deferment of all firemen and policemen would not result in the loss of a serious number of Class I men, additional to those already lost by deferments on other grounds, nevertheless, the number that would be saved to the fire and police systems by such a deferment would be only a trifling percentage of their total force; and that this saving was not sufficient to justify a departure from the fixed policy of the selective service system to add no more blanket deferments by entire occupations than were already specifically designated in the act of Congress.

Nevertheless, as the exhaustion of Class I drew nearer and proposals were made in Congress to extend the draft ages upward and downward to include all men of 18 to 45 years, the demands from municipalities for protection of the fire and police system were renewed in the summer of 1918.

From New York City particularly the demand in this respect was especially strong, and representations for the exemption of the entire police and fire forces of that city were made by the mayor of the city, the police commissioner, representatives of the city and State in Congress, and members of the chamber of commerce and board of trade. It was contended that, when the military age was extended to 45 years, virtually every able-bodied policeman and fireman, sooner or later, would be taken into the Army, not only because of their desirability from the standpoint of physical fitness, but because it would be impossible for them to claim deferment on dependency grounds by reason of the fact that under the law of New York State the city would pay the difference between their salaries as municipal employees and their pay as soldiers. With respect to policemen, it was set forth also that should there be a further depletion of their ranks the city would face the possibility of grave consequences from internal disorder, due to labor unrest, the fomenting of disturbance by enemy alien elements, and a possible uprising against authority due to dissatisfaction with the war or the Government by reason of insufficient, improper or unacceptable food, or due to the high cost of food and clothing or increased burdens. Arguments of like nature, on behalf of firemen, dwelt upon the danger of disaster and loss from conflagrations should the fire-fighting forces be reduced by the induction of firemen into the military service. The mayor of New York, in a letter to the congressional representatives of that city and State, pointed out that at that time (Aug. 9, 1918) more than 700 policemen had been drafted, that before the end of the year at least 1,000 would be drafted, and that ultimately 3,000 or 28 per cent of the entire police force would be called into the military service.

In view of this circumstance, and of the special effect, to be expected under the new law extending draft ages, upon the body of municipal firemen and policemen, it was deemed prudent to extend a measure of relief by amending the existing regulations so as to omit the limitation to men who had served for three years. Selective Service Regulations, section 77, Rule X, paragraph (e) was, therefore, amended by omitting that clause, and by substituting the requirement that such fireman or policeman must have been a "compensated member of a regularly organized, permanent, compensated fire department or police department, which existed as such prior to May 18, 1917."

By this measure it was considered that adequate protection would be given to municipal interests, especially in view of the provisions of note 2, Rule I, section 72, Selective Service Regulations (second edition):

In considering claims for deferred classification on dependency grounds, local and district boards will disregard income provided by a State or municipality for the maintenance of dependent while the registrants upon whose labor these persons are dependent for support are in the military service of the United States.

The results of the reclassification of men of the first and second registrations, to September 11, 1918, made in view of the above amendment, were to place in Class III-E 2,885 firemen and policemen (Table 38).

5. *County and municipal officials.*—Considerable doubt as to whether certain registrants should properly be included in the term "a county or municipal official" resulted from Rule X, paragraph (d), section 77, as it appeared in the first edition of the Selective Service Regulations. Among the offices involved were those of justice of the peace and others of similar grade. The difficulty experienced by local and district boards in classifying these officials centered about that clause of the regulation which required that a county or municipal official, in order to merit classification in Class III-D, must be found: (1) "To have been elected to such office by popular vote,' and also (2) " where the office may not be filled by appointment for an unexpired term."

The purpose of this regulation was to limit deferment in Class III-D to elected officials—not to grant deferment to a municipal or county official, as such, but to avoid the creation of a vacancy which could not be filled without the delay and expense of a special election. It was meant to apply in cases where the call to the colors of a county or municipal official would leave the office vacant and thereby prevent its function being exercised for a substantial period of time. The question whether such an office could be filled by appointment had to be determined, of course, by the constitutions and statutes of the respective States. A less restrictive interpretation than that adopted would have resulted in withdrawing from liability to military service a substantial number of registrants who could not be deemed absolutely necessary to the adequate administration of the cities, counties, or the municipalities. This was especially apparent in the cases of notaries public and other offices of similar grade.

There was likewise the necessity in some States of differentiating between State officers and county and municipal officials. For example, in a certain middle-western State the judges and prosecuting attorneys of the circuit courts have a jurisdiction in certain cases inclusive of several counties. Taking into consideration the theory upon which State officers are granted greater deferment than county and municipal officials—namely, that the duties of the former presumably involve matters of greater importance to the people generally than do the duties of the latter, the rule was followed that the selective service boards, within States having political subdivisions of such character that the officials do not, under the court decisions of the respective States, clearly fall within any one of the three classes above mentioned, must determine which of the said classes should properly embrace those officers for the purposes of classification

With respect to county and municipal officials specifically, a case in point was that of the classification of justices of the peace in the State of Illinois. The attorney general of that State expressed the opinion that "the office of justice of the peace under the provisions of the constitution and statutes of this State, is a municipal office and a vacancy in said office can not be filled by an appointment, where the unexpired term is for a period exceeding one year." From this it appeared that, under certain conditions, a vacancy in the office of a justice of the peace in the State of Illinois may be filled by appointment. Likewise, in the case of New York State, it was ascertained from the attorney general of that State that a vacancy in the office of a justice of the peace in New York may be filled by appointment.

However, the evident doubt in the minds of draft executives in several of the States seemed to warrant a more explicit regulation, and paragraph (d), Rule X, section 77, in the second edition of Selective Service Regulations (October, 1918), was amended to read: "In Class III shall be placed any registrant found to be (d) A county or municipal official who has been elected to such office by popular vote where the vacancy may not be filled by appointment," the word "vacancy" having been substituted for the word "office," and the words "for an unexpired term" having been eliminated. Thus, the test then became: May the vacancy in a county or municipal office, where such official has been elected by popular vote, be filled by appointment?

The application of the rules governing the classification of such officers is indicated in the figures of Table 38.

6. *Federal and State officers.*—Section 4 of the selective service act provides "that * * * the officers, legislative, executive, or judicial, of the United States and of the several States * * * shall be exempt from the selective draft herein prescribed."

Under this provision (applied in Selective Service Regulations, second edition, section 79, Rule XII (a)) a specific list of Federal offices was prepared (first published in Bulletin No. 1, Compiled Rulings, and republished in subsequent editions of the Selective Service Regulations as Part XIII, with additions to include a few indispensable offices designated by the heads of the governmental departments as having an analogous status). The list was based on a simple canon, viz, all Federal offices which were elective or the appointment to which required confirmation by the Senate. This canon was formulated after an exhaustive study of the use of the term "office" in Federal legislation. The obvious purpose of Congress appeared to discriminate between the supreme and superior offices and the inferior offices, and to grant absolute exemption to the former only. This construction was corroborated by the circumstance that any broader definition would have granted absolute exemption to some hundreds of thousands of employees of all grades.

For State offices the same simple test could not serve, as the State constitutional provisions and administrative organization varied widely in the different Commonwealths. Nevertheless the distinction intended by Congress, i. e., between the supreme and superior offices and the inferior ones, applied with equal positiveness to State offices; for Congress certainly had no intention to be more liberal to State than to Federal officers. Moreover, the act of Congress also obviously emphasized the distinction between the State-wide officers and the local, i. e., county or municipal officials; the former being given an absolute exemption, and the latter only a discretionary discharge under authority of the President. A construction was therefore adopted which would incorporate these two important distinctions intended by Congress. A supreme or superior State office, to entitle the holder to exemption under the provisions of section 79, Rule XII (a), should fulfill the following requirements:

(a) If elective, it should be filled by electoral vote of a political subdivision.

(b) If appointive there should be no intermediate superior between it and the appointing power, i. e., the governor, the legislature, and the supreme court.

(c) The function or jurisdiction of the office in question must be coextensive with the boundaries of the State.

(d) Its duties must represent the principal occupation of the incumbent, requiring the substance of his daily work and time.

Action of this Office has been confined to the statement of general principles of interpretation and has rarely extended to the decision of particular cases. Obviously, it was necessary to refer to the laws of the particular State in order to find whether a particular State officer held his office on such conditions, subject to the general principles outlined above. In the case of certain States where the jurisdiction of an officer was inclusive of several counties, but not coextensive with the boundaries of the State, it was held by this Office that for purposes of classification, the question whether such an officer is a State officer or a county or municipal official, should be determined by the State Selective Service authorities, in the light of the relative importance of the office in question to the community.

It was estimated in 1917 that there were some 350,000 persons in Federal public service and in State public service about 450,000 persons; and that of the gross amount some 250,000 and upward were males of draft age. But it was also estimated that under the above construction of the term "officers," the Federal incumbents would amount to not more than 11,000 in all (9,000 of which were postmasters), and the State incumbents to not more than 25,000 in all, or a total of not more than 36,000. The returns received from the local boards, showing exemptions claimed and granted on this ground, have been given above in Table 38.   But it must be remembered that many thousand additional deferments of officials of various grades have also been granted on grounds of dependency or physical disqualifications; as to these, no returns are obtainable.

(V) NECESSARY AGRICULTURAL AND INDUSTRIAL WORKERS.

1. *Purpose of the deferment.*—Under the selective service act, the district boards were entrusted with a vital problem of the war—namely, the duty of selecting the individuals whose engagements in industry, including agriculture, were such as to require their continued service in civil life rather than in the Army.   The original presidential regulations, promulgated on June 30, 1917, provided for the issuance of a certificate of discharge by the district board, which certificate could be modified or withdrawn at any time the district board should determine a change of status had been effected.

On December 15, 1917, became effective the new classification system, under regulations promulgated by the President on November 8, 1917 (Chapter III, above).   The new regulations were intended to accomplish two principal things.   The first was to make a scientific and most complete inventory of our man-power, with a searching inquiry into the qualifications and the industrial and domestic circumstances of each man registered; with this at hand, the second was to make a scientific classification of their relative availability for military service and for all the war-time activities of the Nation.   It was to this capital purpose that the new system was addressed.   It provided for an immediate classification of all registrants into five classes, arranged in the inverse order of their availability for military service.

Registrants were classified in Classes I, II, III, or IV, according to the degree of their skill and the relative necessity and importance of such an individual to a particular enterprise.   In Class II was placed a registrant found by his district board to be a necessary skilled farm laborer in a necessary agricultural enterprise or a necessary skilled industrial laborer in a necessary industrial enterprise.   In Class III was placed a registrant found by his district board to be a necessary assistant, associate, or hired manager of a necessary agricultural or industrial enterprise; also a registrant found to be a necessary highly specialized technical or mechanical expert of a necessary industrial enterprise.   In Class IV was placed a registrant found by his district board to be a necessary sole managing, controlling, or directing head of a necessary agricultural or industrial enterprise.

Examining the system more closely, we find that it was designed to list in Class I, the names of those whose immediate induction into military service would least interfere with the industrial, economic, and agricultural life of the Nation.   It excluded from that class the key and pivotal men, whether they were managers or assistant managers of farms or mechanical or administrative experts in factories. The latter, it deferred into Classes III and IV, and in Class II it excluded from immediate liability to draft skilled labor in both industry and agriculture. Furthermore, by the dependency deferments and by the fact that fully 90 per cent of workers in any particular industry, necessary or non-necessary, were removed entirely from the operation of the draft (being either women or men under or over draftable age or deferred on account of dependency), the protection to non-necessary industry, while not nearly so effective as that offered to necessary industry, was sufficient to prevent destruction.

2. *Numerical results of the deferment system on industry and agriculture.*—(*a*) A noticeable feature must first be emphasized, viz, that the total inroad made by the draft upon agriculture and industry in 1918 up to June (as shown by the Industrial Index) was slightly over 6 per cent, as appears in Table 41.

TABLE 41.—*Effects of draft on industries and occupations for 1917 registrants, since Dec. 15, 1917.*

	All Occupations—Census Key Nos. 000-999.	Number.	Per cent of all ages.	Per cent of ages 21-30.
1	Workers of all ages................................	43,206,912	100.00	....
2	Ages 21-30 within selective service law as classified in 1918 to June.	8,577,719	19.85	100.00
3	Deferred classes within selective service law.	5,897,722	13.65	68.75
4	Class I within selective service law.........	2,679,997	6.20	31.25

To this should be added, for determining the grand total, something like 1.5 per cent for the inroad of 1917, and a little less (estimated) than that percentage for the inroad made by the age-21 group in June–August, 1918. But, on the other hand, in explanation of these, as well as of the following figures, it should be said that the final ratios of deferments in 1918 were actually somewhat larger than as shown here—probably 10 per cent larger, in round numbers; because the Industrial Index, from which the above figures are taken, was compiled during the spring of 1918, when the physical examinations were not completed; hence a small percentage of the men here shown for Class I were afterwards placed in Class V.

(*b*) In the next place, it is to be noted the deferments on other grounds (dependency, alienage, etc.) gave an ample protection to industry and agriculture, amounting to more than 65 per cent of the total registrants; so that the relatively small 3.5 per cent of registrants granted deferments solely on agricultural and industrial grounds was merely an addition to this protection. The relative figures, by classes and divisions (since Dec. 15, 1917, as computed from the Industrial Index, Interim Ledger, on Aug. 9, 1918), are shown in Table 42.

TABLE 42.—*National occupational summary, by classes, for 1917 registrants, since Dec. 15, 1917.*

	Class and division.	Nondefer-ments.	Agricultural and industrial deferments.	Other defer-ments, etc.	Totals by classes.	Per cent to total classified.
1	Class I................	2, 679, 997	....	....	2, 679, 997	31. 24
2	Class II:					
3	C and D..........	....	194, 972	............}	466, 938	5. 44
4	Except C and D...	....	....	271, 966 }		
5	Class III:					
6	J, K, and L.......	....	˙65, 213	............}	395, 961	4. 61
7	Except J, K, and L.	....	....	330, 748 }		
8	Class IV:					
9	C and D..........	....	39, 238	............}3, 628, 980		42. 31
10	Except C and D..	....	....	3, 589, 742 }		
11	Class V.............	....	....	1, 405, 843	1, 405, 843	16. 40
12	Total classified.	2, 679, 997	299, 423	˙5, 598, 299	8, 577, 719	100. 00
13	Per cent to total classi-fied................	31. 24	3. 49	65. 27	100. 00	....

˙(c) Comparing the two grand groups recognized in the Regulations, we ask, What proportion of agricultural and industrial workers were deferred under the system as applied to the first registration? For agriculture, the deferments are shown in Table 43.

TABLE 43.—*Agricultural workers deferred.*

	Agricultural workers deferred, for 1917 registrants, since Dec. 15, 1917.	Number.	Per cent of total engaged in agri-culture.	Per cent of classi-fied.
1	Total of all ages engaged in agriculture..........	13, 777, 454	100. 00	....
2	Males ages 21–30 classified in first registration.	2, 509, 698	18. 22	100. 00
3	Deferments as necessary workers (II–C, III–J, IV–C)......................	180, 363	....	7. 19
4	Deferments on other grounds...........	1, 575, 937	....	62. 79
5	Class I, 1918......................	753, 398	....	30. 02

For industries (other than agriculture) the deferments are shown in Table 44.

TABLE 44.—*Industrial workers deferred.*

	Industrial workers deferred, for 1917 registrants, since Dec. 15, 1917.	Number.	Per cent of total engaged in indus-tries.	Per cent of classi-fied.
1	Total of all ages engaged in industries other than agriculture...........................	29, 429, 458	100. 00	....
2	Males ages 21–30 classified in first registration.	6, 068, 021	20. 62	100. 00
3	Deferments as necessary workers (II–D, III–K, L, IV–D).....................	119, 060	....	1. 96
4	Deferments on other grounds...........	4, 022, 362	....	66. 29
5	Class I, 1918......................	1, 926, 599	....	31. 75

It appears, therefore, that while the total protection given by all deferments to each group was substantially the same, the protection given by the specific deferment of necessary workers was nearly four times as great for agriculture as for other industries averaged (Table 43, line 3, and Table 44, line 3).

(d) Furthermore, it will be seen, the protection given, by deferments on all grounds, to the several industries varied considerably; partly because the ratio of men of ages 21–30 to the total workers of all ages in each industry varied considerably, and also because the number of married men deferred for dependency was greater in those occupations which required greater experience and therefore were made up chiefly of men of the higher ages within the age group 21–30. A good illustration of this is seen in the railroad industry (Table 46), where the deferments for conductors and engineers reached 80 per cent (of all registrants), while the deferments for signalmen and mechanics reached only 63 per cent (of all registrants).

TABLE 46.—*Effects of draft on 11 skilled railroad employments to June, 1918.*

Census key No.	Occupation.	Total males of all ages.	Ages 21–30, first registration, within selective service law, as classified to June, 1918.		Deferred classes within selective service law.			Class I within selective service law.		
			Number.	Per cent of all ages.	Number.	Per cent of ages 21–30.	Per cent of all ages.	Number.	Per cent of ages 21–30.	Per cent of all ages.
2119	Railroad blacksmiths	12,000	2,581	21	2,285	88	19	296	12	2
2137–8	Railroad boiler makers	17,500	3,856	22	3,567	92	20	289	8	2
372	Car and railroad shop mechanics	54,500	16,412	33	10,359	63	19	6,053	36	11
527	Engine hostlers and boiler washers	12,000	1,966	16	1,293	65	10	673	33	6
529	Brakemen	105,000	42,361	40	29,853	68	28	12,508	29	11
530	Conductors	75,400	7,480	9	6,010	80	7	1,470	19	2
539	Engineers	110,700	11,356	10	8,876	78	8	2,480	21	2
540	Firemen	86,800	42,299	48	30,233	71	34	12,066	28	13
544	Officials and superintendents, including train dispatchers	22,800	1,480	6	1,218	82	5	262	17	1
547	Signalmen, switchmen, and flagmen	84,400	15,018	17	9,542	63	11	5,476	36	6
549	Yardmasters, yardmen	11,000	1,527	13	1,281	83	11	246	16	2
	Total	592,100	146,336	24	104,517	71	17	41,819	28	7
	Inductions before Dec. 15, 1917		6,910					6,910		
	Grand total		153,246	25	104,517	67	17	48,729	31.8	8.2

The Industrial Index (Appendix Table 42–A) compiled by this office throws a full light on the condition of each occupation and industry as affected by the draft since December 15, 1917, up to June, 1918, and a study of it will be of the greatest value in analyzing the effect of the war upon industry

3. *Blanket deferments of entire occupations.*—It is obvious that the classification system of the Selective Service Regulations based its deferments solely on the ground of the necessity of the individual within his necessary occupation and did not purport to grant any deferments in mass. The whole method of district board operations rested on this idea of discovering and deferring key or "pivotal" individuals. The only exception to the principle was found in the Emergency Fleet deferments, and even these were not in name deferments, but merely conditional suspensions of a call to military service. In my report for 1917. (Dec. 20, 1917, p. 35) were emphasized the risks involved, to the imperative needs of the Army, in establishing any mass deferments of entire occupations, and it was pointed out that whatever concessions might later become necessary, "the time has not yet come for this."

But as the war proceeded into the year 1918, and more and more men were required for the battle line, it became evident that certain industries vital to the war were no longer adequately manned in labor power. There was more than one cause to account for this, and more than one remedy might be the most appropriate and effective one. But a number of industries and governmental agencies, such as the Railroad Administration, the Food Administration, and especially the Fuel Administration and the coal producers, looked to the draft as the source of the depletion, and urged such action as would amount to a blanket deferment of their employees. It was foreseen in this office that mass deferments would cause serious complexities and embarrassment; would afford a convenient retreat for many who should be in the military service, and would result in taking the statutory power and authority from the district boards under the President and in placing it into the hands of various civil governmental agencies and representatives of the various industries throughout the United States.

Moreover, it was indubitable that the draft was not the sole, nor even the major cause of the depletion (as appears for the railway industry from the figures above given). Many industries had lost the services of a considerable number of their employees through voluntary enlistment in the Army and Navy during the early period of the war, while thousands of others had been attracted by higher wages offered in certain fields of employment, such as shipyards and munition plants. The operation of the selective service law, therefore, was not alone responsible—in fact, it was responsible to a very minor degree for the loss of employees to the railroads and the coal-mining industry.

(a) *Deferments: United States railway service.*—In the early part of August, 1918, the United States Railroad Administration, maintaining that certain cases of its employees were not being properly disposed of by district boards, presented a number of instances in which registrants whom it considered necessary and entitled to deferred classification had been placed in Class I. Further complaint was made that district boards did not consider the ever-changing and restricted conditions which were constantly enlarging the class of skilled labor; that certain classes of labor, regarded as unskilled a few years ago, were now well within the skilled class when regarded in the light of the difficulty of operating railroads in the present emergency; and that many district boards in dealing with the cases of railroad .operators and workmen were far from liberal, and, in fact, were extremely severe in their interpretations, constructions, and findings. Inquiry showed that some of the claims presented were meritorious. The importance of efficiently operating the rail-. roads was, of course, not questioned, and prompt measures were taken to afford relief. A general telegram to all local and district boards recommended that every Class I case of a railroad employee, not then inducted into the military service, be carefully reconsidered in the light of the statements submitted by the Railroad Administration. Local and district boards were advised as follows:

Applications for reconsideration of cases of railroad employees on industrial grounds, when presented to local boards, should be received up to the day and hour of induction into the military service, and promptly forwarded, together with the local board's recommendation, to the district board having jurisdiction; district boards may directly receive applications for reconsideration in cases over which they have original jurisdiction, and immediately request from the proper local board the entire record of the case, and these applications may be received up to the day and hour of induction into the military service; even though a registrant employed in railroad work has not claimed deferment on industrial grounds, his employers may make that claim either through the local board or directly to the district board at any time up to the day and hour of induction, and the district board may grant the deferred classification.

After this instruction, few complaints were made by the Railroad Administration; and in the majority of cases to which the attention of this Office was invited, it was found, upon investigation, that the registrants in question had been inducted into military service because claims for their deferred classification had not been properly filed with the local and district boards.

(b) *Deferments: United States Fuel Administration.*—In the spring of 1918 attention was frequently called to what appeared to be an alarming curtailment of coal production, which was attributed largely to the withdrawal of mine workers for military service through the operation of the selective service law. It was represented that the exemption of mine workers as an entire group would afford the only adequate relief in this situation. Following several conferences, an officer was detailed to make a thorough investigation, particularly in the anthracite regions of Pennsylvania and the bituminous fields of West Virginia. Careful inquiry developed every evidence of cooperation on the part of both operators and miners. The former had, in many instances, refrained from filing claims on behalf of their employees; the workers themselves were loath to claim deferment because of the patriotic sentiment that was found to prevail in their communities. In many cases miners were known to waive deferment and even to abandon their work in order to be inducted into the military service. As above stated, it was conclusively shown that the draft was a relatively small factor in the shortage of man-power at the mines. Table 47 gives the figures from the Industrial Index:

TABLE 47.—*Effect of draft on coal-mining industry.*

Census key No.	Occupation.	Ages 21–30, first registration, within selective service law as classified to June, 1918.			Deferred classes within selective service law.			Class I within selective service law.		
		Total persons of all ages.	Number.	Per cent of all ages.	Number.	Per cent of ages 21–30.	Per cent of all ages.	Number.	Per cent of ages 21–30.	Per cent of all ages.
122A	Coal-mine operatives in United States............	706,012	177,502	25.6	130,749	73.0	18.0	46,253	26.0	6.5
	Coal-mine operatives in Pennsylvania...........	328,081	77,120	23.8	46,597	60.4	14.2	30,523	39.5	9.3
	Anthracite operatives in Pennsylvania...........	159,860	37,789	23.6	22,832	60.4	14.2	14,956	39.5	9.2

In order to cooperate with the production program of the Fuel Administration, prompt action was taken. Local and district boards· in some cases had, in their zeal to achieve a scrupulous administration of the law and regulations, been too strict in their interpretation of the letter and spirit of the selective service law. Frequently local boards had failed to give the benefit of their recommendations to district boards. In some localities district boards had failed to take advantage of the discretion vested in them, and in some instances, drew too inflexible a line between skilled and unskilled labor. Conferences of local and district boards were called, at which the elasticity of the regulations was pointed out. The privileges of dependents to make claims on dependency grounds and the right of employers to claim deferred classification for their workers on industrial grounds were emphasized. District boards were advised that cases within their original jurisdiction might be reopened and reconsidered up to the day and hour of induction into the military service. Local boards were likewise enjoined to aid the district boards by recommendations in every case and by a full presentation of the facts within their knowledge with respect to every claim. The employers were urged to exercise great care in filing claims for deferred classification for their employees; to keep themselves fully informed as to their employees who had been deferred, and to inform local and district boards of those employees whose claims for deferment were without merit. As a result of the action taken when the situation of the Railroad Administration and the Fuel Administration was first presented, the two Governmental agencies are reported to have experienced slight difficulty in the cases of railroad employees and mine workers whose labor was necessary to these vital industries.

Although no instructions were issued by this Office applying to specific industries, the general principles governing classification with respect to engagement in industries (secs. 80–89, Selective Service Regulations, second edition), a gratifying uniformity of district boards' decisions obtained. It is interesting to note in Table 94 how closely the decisions of district boards as to the "necessity" of various industries agreed with the War Industries Board's priorities list, which included a large number of industries designated as "essential."

4. *Industrial advisers.*—The experience of the first year of the draft in these and other fields involving large industrial establishments, revealed the necessity of more systematic attention by the large employers to the deferment of necessary employees, and of more direct cooperation between them and the district boards. It was found that many employers, in their desire to conserve the interests of their own work, had treated these claims merely as individual cases of individual necessity, and had given little or no thought to the larger aspects of their establishment as an entirety, in its relation to the industry as a whole, to other industries, and to military necessities.

This Office found itself obliged to put certain material inquiries calculated to stimulate reflection on the part of representatives of industry: How many employers had hitherto taken pains to inform themselves systematically which of their employees are registrants and which are not? How many had studied carefully the required conditions for occupational deferment, as laid down in the President's regulations pursuant to the statute? How many had made it a point to survey their entire plant so as to single out the really indispensable individuals? With the oncoming of a more extensive registration, an even larger outlook was necessary. The general industrial conditions, the supply of skilled men in the industry at large, the possibilities of training substitutes, the availability of women workers— these were some of the considerations which bore directly on the need of occupational deferment as related to the need of the Army. Moreover, it was often forgotten that the selective draft was only one element in the depletion of a particular industry's man-power. A second and a large element was found in the voluntary withdrawals for enlistment; how large this was may be seen from the circumstance that the total inductions by draft reached some 2,800,000, while the total enlistments in the Army and the Navy amounted to more than 1,300,000—nearly one-half as many. A third element, very large, but unknown as to its precise extent, had been the transfer of labor power from one industry to another, i. e., into the distinctively war industries offering the inducement of higher wáges.

These other influences were, therefore, to be kept in mind by employers and others in weighing the question whether the best solution in the national interest was to ask for the deferment of individuals or groups of men. Such deferments would assist the immediate situation in the particular establishment, but they merely forced the Army and the Navy to seek elsewhere for the same number of men thus deferred. The quantitative needs of the military forces were known and imperative, and any given quantity of deferments would ultimately have to be made up by the depletion of some other occupation. Thus, it became the employer's duty to consider these largest aspects of deferment in seeking that solution of his own problems which would best comport with the national interests.

With a view, therefore, to handling the industrial situation with maximum intelligence and efficiency and in view of the new registration of 13,000,000 more men on September 12, provision was made, in a new regulation (sec. 80, Selective Service Regulations, second edition) published early in September, for assisting boards in rulings upon industrial claims for deferment. There were appointed by each district board three persons known as industrial advisers to the district board. These industrial advisers were to acquire full information as to the necessities of individual establishments; to keep informed as to the priority lists of industries and products as determined by the War Industries Board; to observe the general conditions of labor and industry; and to give to the district boards the benefit of their knowledge and judgment on these matters. One of the advisers was nominated by the Department of Labor, representing both employer and employee; one was nominated by the Department of Agriculture with similar relations representing agricultural employments; and one selected by the district board, whose function was to consider the remaining employments or occupations, such as education, newspapers, insurance, banking, etc.

Upon employers was urged the duty and responsibility of becoming well advised in all these matters; of equipping themselves with full information as to the extent to which their particular establishment was affected by the liability of registrants to military service; of observing the extent to which other influences of depletion had affected it and the degree in which other methods of supply could relieve that depletion; and of laying these facts and other pertinent ones before the industrial advisers now to be placed at each district board, to the end that those individuals or groups who were indispensable and irreplaceable would receive deferment, whether or not they had made claim for it, and that the Army and the Navy should not be deprived of its proper supply of man power by ill-considered deferments not absolutely demanded by the national interest.

The keynote of purpose was meant to be that wise and profoundly significant phrase in the act of Congress of May 18, 1917, "the maintenance of the Military Establishment, or the effective operation of the military forces, or the maintenance of national interest during the emergency."

A thorough test of the newly devised machinery was prevented by the suspension of the work of classification by district boards shortly after the signing of the armistice on November 11.

5. *Industrial and agricultural furloughs.*—Notwithstanding the fact that the classification regulations were drawn up with scrupulous regard to the necessity of raising an army with as little as possible interference with industry and agriculture, it was found in a few instances that registrants were selected for the Army when their services were in greater need, from a national standpoint, in industry or on the farm. Such cases arose principally in two ways: First, by the failure of the registrant or his employer to present the merits of his claim and to show the importance of his connection with some industrial or agricultural enterprise; second, by the overzealousness on the part of district boards to select an army with the utmost speed. Such boards permitted themselves to apply a too strict construction to the term "necessary enterprise," or were overcareful in finding a registrant not "necessary" to a "necessary enterprise," as these terms are used in the regulations. As a safeguard against such a practice on the part of district boards, if in fact such a practice existed to an appreciable degree, Congress passed what is popularly called "the furlough act." (Public, No. 105, 65th- Cong.) This act reads as follows:

> *Be it enacted by the Senate and House of Representatives of the United States of America in Congress assembled,* That whenever during the continuance of the present war in the opinion of the Secretary of War the interests of the service or the national security and defense render it necessary or desirable, the Secretary of War be, and he hereby is, authorized to grant furloughs to enlisted men of the Army of the United States, with or without pay and allowances or with partial pay and allowances, and, for such periods as he may designate, to permit such enlisted men to engage in civil occupations and pursuits: *Provided,* That such furloughs shall be granted only upon the voluntary application of such enlisted men under regulations to be prescribed by the Secretary of War.

The agricultural aspect of this law was immediately taken advantage of, and War Department General Orders, No. 31, was issued. This order recited that its purpose was to provide for furloughs of short duration "for the purpose of augmenting the agricultural production." Of course, restrictions had to be placed upon the granting of these furloughs, and consequently camp commanders who were authorized to grant the furloughs were directed to observe the following limitations:

(1) The interference to be caused in the program of military training and preparation must be reduced to a minimum; "therefore whenever the furloughing of an enlisted man substantially interferes with the training or preparation of the organization of which he is a member the application will be denied."

(2) "Furloughs granted under this order will be for short periods, largely for seeding and harvesting time."

(3) "Such furloughs will not be granted to enlisted men of or above the grade of first sergeant."

(4) " * * * nor will they be granted in an organization which has been ordered or is in transit from points of mobilization or training to a port of embarkation."

(5) "Furloughs granted under this order will be without pay and allowances, except that enough pay will be retained in each case to meet allotments in force on the date of this order, war risk insurance, and pledges on Liberty bonds."

The order provided for the granting of furloughs to individual soldiers whose applications showed that they were needed on some farm; to "specially qualified experts in agriculture needed in the service of the United States Department of Agriculture;" to experts "in the service of agricultural colleges established under Federal law and regularly receiving Federal funds * * *"; and they were granted en bloc upon requests of farmers, when the time to be consumed in traveling from the post to the places of labor did not exceed 24 hours.

Applications for furloughs were made upon a prescribed form· (P. M. G. O. Form 1035), which contained a series of questions directed to identify the soldier and the person who desired the services of the soldier, and to show the acreage of the farm, the crops grown, the number of horses, cattle, etc., thereon, the market value of the last year's production and the current year's anticipated production, the soldier's experience in farming, and the inability of the person operating the farm to obtain otherwise the necessary labor and assistance. The application was made to his local board, and if it was approved by the local board it was placed in the hands of a county agricultural agent for his concurrence or nonconcurrence in the recommendation of the local board. The application was then sent to the soldier's camp commander, who would finally pass upon it.

It is known that a great number of these agricultural furloughs were granted and that they served substantially to relieve the agricultural situation, especially during the different harvesting seasons.

A somewhat similar scheme for the protection of industry was recently adopted, late in the summer of 1918. There was established . in the office of The Adjutant General of the Army a section known as the Industrial Furlough Section. The primary purpose of this section was to return indispensable employees to plants, factories, and concerns that were operating under Government contracts for war supplies, and materials of all sorts.

97250°—19——10

When it appeared that either through enlistment or through the operation of the draft, skilled workmen had been taken from such industrial enterprises, the procedure by which it was possible for such men to be returned to their former employment was as follows: The plant or industrial enterprise would make its application through the Government department with which it had contracts; the application would show the skill and training of the soldier for whom application was being made, and the length of time he was employed by the plant prior to his entering the Army. Each Government department maintained a certifying officer, who, through his various district officers, would determine the merits of the application and if he approved the application, it would be transmitted to the Industrial Furlough Section. That section, in order to harmonize its action with that of local and district boards, and in order to make its investigation as searching and thorough as practicable, required in every application the production of the minute of the district board, entered in the questionnaire, which showed the board's reason for not granting deferred classification to the soldier. Having before it the evidence collected by the certifying officer and his recommendation thereon, and the minute of the district board, the furlough section would investigate the case, and would either approve or disapprove the application. If it was approved, and if the soldier was willing to accept it and if he was not a member of a military organization under orders for service overseas, The Adjutant General of the Army ordered the furlough. In this way, between 16,000 and 17,000 men were furloughed back to their former occupations.

6. *Statutory enlargement of "Industries" to include "Occupations and Employments."*—The selective service act of May 18, 1917, intrusted to district boards the exclusive original jurisdiction of claims for exclusion or discharge from the selective draft of persons engaged in industries, including agriculture, found to be necessary to the maintenance of the Military Establishment, or the effective operation of the military forces, or the maintenance of national interest during the emergency. Until September, 1918, the boards had almost invariably disclaimed authority to consider certain important occupations as "necessary" under this provision. The necessity to the national interest in many instances could not be questioned; but the occupations could not be termed "industries." Thus banking was held not to be an industry; claims of teachers, physicians, and individuals engaged in hospital work or care of the public health, and of those engaged in Red Cross or other welfare work, even though directly related to the Army, were barred because these registrants were held to be not engaged in industry; and commercial enterprises were distinguished from productive undertakings. Under the terms of the original act these rulings were manifestly proper and were generally approved.

The limitation thus imposed on industrial classifications was not so serious a matter while the draft ages remained at 21 to 30 years, inclusive. With the proposal to increase the age limit, however, came the realization that a recognition of other activities as necessary to the national welfare during the war was imperative. Congress therefore provided, in the act of August 31, 1918, which extended the age limits to 18 and 45, that the words "industries, including agriculture," wherever occurring in the original law, should read "industries, occupations, or employments, including agriculture." Under this amendment the district boards' jurisdiction and authority to consider claims for deferment based upon a registrant's occupation were very materially enlarged. Consequently, upon the approval of the act of August 31, 1918, district boards had full authority to determine in the broadest sense, whether or not any industry, occupation, or employment, including agriculture, was necessary in the national emergency, and, of course, whether or not any registrant connected therewith was necessary to it.

Local and district boards were promptly informed, by special bulletins, of the changes involved by the amendment, and simultaneously the presidential regulations were altered to enable the selective service agencies to classify all of the 13,000,000 registrants now becoming liable to military service, in accordance with the new provisions of the law. Sections 80 to 89 of the Selective Service Regulations were redrafted and a new provision incorporated therein providing for the appointment of three or more advisers to district boards, one of whom should have special charge of questions arising in this part of the field.

The relief given by this amended phrasing of the act was appreciated in all parts of the country, and served materially to strengthen the welcome given to this supreme legislative measure for the enlargement of military man power.

(VI) MORAL DISQUALIFICATION.

1. *Definition of moral disqualification.*—The act of May 18, 1917, authorized the President to "exclude or discharge from the selective draft those found to be physically or morally deficient."

Moral deficiency was never attempted to be completely defined in the President's regulations. The boards no doubt exercised their own judgment, in a few cases, by excluding registrants not covered by the definition given. But the only definition given in the regulations was restricted to persons convicted of serious crime. This followed the analogy of the general law forbidding the enlistment of such persons (U. S. Rev. Stat., sec. 1118).

The original regulation of June 30, 1917 (sec. 21) excluded "persons convicted and sentenced for felony in any court of record." But the scope of the term "felony" varies widely in the several States; nor was it possible to devise any term which would set any uniform moral standard. However, to remove in some degree the doubts of interpretation and to assist in reaching uniformity, the revised regulation (S. S. R., 2d ed., sec. 79 (h)) was thus phrased: "A person shown to have been convicted of any crime which under the law of the jurisdiction of its commission is treason, felony, or an infamous crime."

The traditions of the Regular Army look upon certain civil offenses as particularly intolerable in soldiers, and it was desirable to conform to these traditions. Moreover, it was unquestionable that, for the honor of the American Army, a firm stand must be taken to repudiate in the public mind the unhealthy view (not infrequently found among judges of criminal courts) that a civil offender might sometimes be released without punishment if he would enter the Army to expiate his offense. The Army was not to become a repository of scapegoats, and especially in a war inspired by the highest principles of honor and righteousness; this was an honorable cause to be fought by honorable men only. On the other hand the strictest Army traditions as to unforgiveable offenses had already begun to undergo reconsideration, in some respects, among division commanders and officers dealing with court-martial records in the Judge Advocate General's Department; for it was recognized that the problem of accepting and rapidly training for military service a large mass of men, selected indiscriminately from all walks of life, presented novel conditions, in which the educative force of military life might be trusted to inculcate and preserve the best Army traditions, and to permit the probative toleration of men whose offenses might under original conditions have been a ground for instant elimination. Moreover, local board sentiment (as set forth in my First Report, p. 59) could not be made to understand with accuracy the strict Army tradition; and the anomaly might be presented of admitting men in the draft who were known to have been guilty of offenses which would be sufficient ground for discharge if committed after entrance to the Army.

The foregoing definition, therefore, seemed most likely to harmonize the general public attitude represented by the local boards, on the one hand, and by the best Army traditions, on the other hand.

In the calls of 1917 the number discharged from draft by local boards for conviction of felony was 2,001. In the classification of 1918 the number placed in Class V–H under the revised regulation was 18,620; this, of course, included the former number, as every registrant discharged in 1917 was classified in 1918.

2. *Convicted and indicted persons entering the Army.*—How many registrants having a penitentiary record or a status virtually equivalent, nevertheless entered the Army by draft, for lack of any claim

by them for exemption and of any knowledge by the boards of their disqualification? This question can, of course, be answered only by estimate. A careful computation was made for this purpose by the National Association for Prison Labor; the computation being based on the total numbers of persons of ages 21–30 discharged from State and Federal penitentiaries during the last 10 years, with due allowance for deductions of various sorts. To this number should be added the number of registrants charged with serious offenses and released by courts on condition of being inducted (as reported by the local boards). Table 48 shows the results.

TABLE 48.—*Morally unfit.*

	Morally unfit, first and second registrations.	Number.	Per cent of total convicts.
1	Total convicts and ex-convicts, age 21–30................	26,520	100.00
2	Exempted (V–H)..	18,620	70.21
3	Presumably inducted or enlisted......................	7,900	29.79
4	Releases by courts for induction or enlistment...	5,969	....

It appears, therefore, that approximately 7,900 men who had been convicted or probably charged with serious offenses were inducted by the draft or enlisted and are serving in the ranks alongside of others whose civil record contained no such blot. Had it been possible to identify these men, a comparison of their Army records would have thrown interesting light on the problem of the reform of the convict.

The following instance will serve to illustrate one aspect of the problem, from the local boards' point of view:

He was a month out of State's prison, where he had served three years for one of a series of many burglaries. He had other black marks against him for forgery and other crimes. He came out of prison with a well-formed notion of changing his life, and he married a good girl and got a good job. But crimes continued to be committed in his city; and it was not long before he was being called into the office of the chief of police and questioned, in the old third-degree way, about every depredation that was committed. He knew that suspicion was pointing his way, and he knew that he was innocent.

He came with his story to our chief clerk. He said that he had tried to do his best, that he had been steadily employed at good wages, and that he and his wife were getting along "fine." He went on to say that he was being called away from his work so much by the busy police official that his employers were dissatisfied, and that he was going to lose his job. He wanted to get into the Army. He was known to be a good machinist and also a skilled printer and pressman. He belonged, of course, in Class V–H. A letter was sent to headquarters fully explaining the situation and the man's mechanical qualifications. An answer was returned that the regulations could not be waived, but that it was possible that the future might work a change in the rules.

A month later, after he had lost his job and was on the blacklist, he committed another burglary. Writing from prison, he was inclined to reproach the draft officials for keeping him out of the Army, for, as he said, "This never would have happened, but we had to have things to eat and to wear."

We are wondering, if another war should come with more selective service, whether V–H would still be one of the classifications.

(VII) PHYSICAL QUALIFICATIONS.

1. *Physical examination system.*—(a) There was organized in the office of the Provost Marshal General a Medical Division, whose functions were to coordinate the medical activities associated with the selective service, and to render · authoritative decisions upon technical points related to physical standards and medical examinations.

(b) To the staff of the governor of each State, an Army medical officer was assigned as medical aide. His duties consisted in the establishment of close relations with all examining physicians of his State; in meeting examiners for the purpose of discussing the medical · problems of the draft and for the clearing up of doubtful points; in visiting local and medical advisory boards, to observe their work and to advise their members; in recommending the replacement of weak examining physicians, arranging for additional examiners, and hastening the operations of physical examinations where such were delayed; in studying causes of rejections at camps with a view to the detection of inefficiency in examiners; in the performance of such other duties in connection with the physical examinations of drafted men, as might be required of him.

(c) Each local board had an examining physician. As originally constituted, this physician was a member of the board, and such continued to be the case with a majority of the boards. Frequently, the medical member did not take part in the classification of registrants, although he was competent so to do. His prime function was to perform the physical examinations of registrants, and to advise the board thereupon. If not a member, the report of the examining physician was advisory only.

To assist in the physical examinations of registrants, additional examining physicians were appointed as needed. The services of volunteer physicians were also utilized.

(d) Since doubt arose in many cases in which examining physicians for local boards would find it difficult to decide, medical advisory boards, consisting of a number of specialists were formed. These boards were carefully districted with due regard to ease of communication and to hospital facilities. Local boards or Government appeal agents referred doubtful cases to such boards (or to a member or members thereof) for opinions.

(e) Each district board numbered a physician among its members. This physician member did not make physical examinations, but acted as expert adviser upon the medical evidence presented with appeals to the board.

(f) On arrival at Army camps or other points of mobilization, registrants were reexamined by a team of Army medical officers. Each team was made up of specialists, so that every part of the body was gone over by one who had given special study to the physical abnormalities of such part.

2. *Physical standards of qualification.*—The physical standards adopted at first for the selective service were based on those used by the Army under the volunteer system, though differing therefrom in some particulars. It was soon found that these standards were too severe. In time of peace, when the supply of volunteers ordinarily exceeds the demand, a high physical standard may be exacted. When a necessity exists for great numbers, many minor physical defects must perforce be waived, in order to secure the requisite man-power.

On request of the Provost Marshal General, a committee was therefore appointed by the Surgeon General of the Army to formulate a new set of physical standards. This was completed and promulgated to draft boards in June, 1918. Unfortunately, it was not published to those making physical examinations at Army camps until considerably later. As a result, two standards prevailed, and much confusion resulted.

The demand for men for limited or special service, which at first was negligible, began to increase rapidly. Secondly, it was found that registrants in the deferred remediable group were practically as exempt from induction as though they were totally disqualified. Thirdly, the Selective Service was called upon to furnish men for the Navy and the Marine Corps, whose physical requirements differed in some particulars from those of the Army. It thus became necessary, in order to meet these conditions, again to revise the standards of physical examination. In this second edition, which constitutes the present P. M. G. O. Form 75 (published Sept. 27, 1918) the greater number of conditions under Group B (remediable defects) were transferred to Group C (special or limited service), while the needs of the Navy were met by provisions relative thereto. In order to insure consistency, The Adjutant General of the Army promulgated these physical standards to the Army as Special Regulations No. 65.

3. *The Four Physical Groups.*—The method of physical examinations, since December 15, 1917, was changed in two important respects.

In the first place, the physical examination followed the decision upon claims for deferment, i. e., only those who were placed provisionally in Class I because of making no claim for deferment or because their claim was denied, were subjected to physical examination, whereas by the earlier method all registrants were physically examined when called in their order number sequence and the claims for deferment were then made by those who had been physically accepted. Thus, by the new plan, the number of physical examinations was relatively much reduced per 1,000 inducted men, as already pointed out more particularly in Chapter III, section (IV).

In the second place, greater utilization of man-power was attained by establishing grades of physical qualifications. By the original plan, the registrant was either accepted or rejected for military service on the physical examination. But by the new plan four physical groups were provided; the registrants placed in any one of the first three of these groups were deemed to be accepted for military service in some capacity or other, while only those registrants placed in the fourth group were deemed to be unconditionally rejected for any form of military service. These four groups were defined for the local boards as follows (S. S. R. 2d ed., sec. 128½; Standards of Physical Examination, 2d ed., sec. 4):

(a) Registrants who on examination are found to present conditions which fall within the proper standards shall be unconditionally accepted for general military service (Group A).

(b) Registrants who on examination are found to suffer from remediable defects which fall within the proper standards may be accepted for general military service in the deferred remediable group (Group B).

(c) Registrants who on examination are found to present defects which fall within the proper standards may be accepted for special or limited military service (Group C).

(d) Registrants who on examination are found to present defects which fall within the proper standards shall be unconditionally rejected for all military service (Group D).

Group A was composed of men who are vigorous and without any physical defect which might interfere with the full performance of military duties. These men conformed to the requirements implied by the following words, quoted from the Standards of Physical Examination:

* * * to make a good soldier, the registrant must be able to see well; have comparatively good hearing; his heart must be able to stand the stress of physical exertion; he must be intelligent enough to understand and to execute military maneuvers, obey commands, and protect himself; and must be able to transport himself by walking as the exigencies of military life may demand.

Group B was made up of individuals who possessed certain physical defects, diseases, or abnormalities which rendered them unfit for service, but which conditions were capable of cure by treatment, surgical or otherwise, whereby the registrants might be fitted for general military service. Group B is therefore known as the "deferred remediable" group.

Group C contained those men who were physically substandard for full military duties, but who were capable of rendering services of value to the military establishment in vocations which did not impose too great strain.

Finally, Group D contained those who were found to have conditions which unfitted them for military service.

The results of the physical examinations up to December 15, 1917, were set forth in my First Report. The results of the physical examinations since that date are as follows, by groups:

TABLE 49.—*Physical groups compared.*

	Physical groups compared.	Number.	Per cent of registrants.	Per cent of examined.
1	Total registrants Dec. 15, 1917 to Sept,.11, 1918, due to be classified............................	9,952,735	100.00	....
2	Not physically examined....................	6,744,289	67.76	....
3	Examined physically Dec. 15, 1917–Sept. 11, 1918....................................	3,208,446	32.24	100.00
4	Fully qualified (Group A)..............:	2,259,027	....	70.41
5	Disqualified partly or totally...........	949,419	....	29.59
6	Placed in Group B..................	88,436	....	2.76
7	Placed in Group C..................	339,377	....	10.58
8	Placed in Group D (Class V–G)....	521,606	....	16.25

4. *Group A; Qualified for general military service.*—The total number of registrants examined was 3,208,446; the number placed by local boards in Group A, as physically fit for general military service, was 2,259,027, being 70.41 per cent of the total number examined.

Appendix Table 49-A shows the variances between the different States. It will be noticed the States occupying the two highest places in their ratio of men placed in Group A were Oklahoma and Arkansas, and the States occupying the two lowest places were Rhode Island and Arizona.

It is necessary to note that owing to the frequent placing of a registrant in Group D by inspection only, without physical examination (i. e., where the defects were obvious, such as the lack of a limb), the records of the boards for Group D do not always signify a physical examination, and hence the base used for the above percentage is to a certain extent approximate only.

5. *Group B; Remediables.*—The remediable group at first included, among others, those having bone and joint deformities, hernias, benign tumors, large hemorrhoids, varicoceles, hydroceles, and strictures. Although arrangements were made by hospital authorities and medical men in many States for having such defects corrected without expense to the registrant, comparatively few offered themselves. The group thus sheltered many who were capable of rendering immediate military service in a limited capacity, and general military service after the correction of their defects. It was proposed to induct these registrants, and to have their defects corrected at Army hospitals, but the Army hospitals lacked capacity for the purpose. Since the group constituted an important reservoir of

man-power, and since the presence of such individuals in communities proved to be local sources of discontent, the great majority of those in the group were made available, by the "Standards of Physical Examination" already referred to (P. M. G. O., Form 75, dated September 27, 1918), which directed that they be transferred to Group C. Thereafter, Group B was restricted to drug addicts, to those having deformities which might interfere with the wearing of a uniform, and to a few other special conditions.

Under the standards in force to the above date, this group comprised 88,436, being 2.76 per cent of the total number of registrants examined. As finally constituted, the group was small, and but few of its members could have been expected to become fit for military service of any kind.

6. *Group C; Qualified for special or limited service.*—Out of 3,208,446 registrants examined, 339,377 or 10.58 per cent were reported by local boards as placed in Group C, unfit for general military service, but suitable for special or limited service. Some of the types of disabilities which rendered registrants acceptable for this group were: Defects of eye, ear, nose, throat, teeth or skin, of somewhat greater degree than were permitted by the standards for unconditional acceptance; abnormalities of the extremities, such as loss of certain minor members or impairment of motion; operable hernias; small benign tumors; urethral strictures; nocturnal enuresis; stammering; temporary anemias and debilities.

(*a*) *Number called.*—By the summer of 1918, plans were perfected by the General Staff for making use of this group. The first calls issued during the month of June, 1918, and calls for such men proceeded until the President's order of November 11, discontinuing all inductions into the Army. During this period the total number of such men called was 108,355. In addition to this number, there were approximately 20,000 who entered the military service through the process of individual induction. The numbers called and accepted at camp are shown in the following Table 50:

TABLE 50.—*Military status of Group C men.*

	Military status of Group C men.	Number.	Per cent of Group C placed.	Per cent of Group C called.
1	Total Group C men Dec. 15, 1917, to Sept. 11, 1918.	339,377	100.00	....
2	Number not yet called by Sept. 11, 1918....	211,022	62.18	....
3	Number individually inducted.............	20,000	5.89	....
4	Number called to Sept. 11, 1918............	108,355	31.93	100.00
5	Accepted at camp......................	91,867	....	84.78
6	Rejected at camp......................	16,488	....	15.22

It will be observed that nearly two-thirds of this group were never inducted.

The limited service men, and indeed also the other groups of rejected men, often felt keen chagrin on learning of their incapacity. Many of them would besiege the offices of the boards, pleading for an opportunity to be used. There were places in the Army, they thought, where they could help, and thus set free a fighting man; and it was difficult to make them understand the necessity for having able-bodied men, of full physical qualifications, for noncombatant positions in the theater of war. The persistence of some of them in searching for an opening was a testimony to their spirit of loyalty; whether the man who wrote the following letter (and his name revealed a foreign nativity or ancestry) ever succeeded in his ambition does not appear:

DEAR SIR: I am in the draft, and am very anxious to go, and my board won't send me because I have a very slight hernia. I went down there nearly every day, and they asked me to write you a letter, and if you say yes, they will send me. Please when you answer my letter, please put in a piece of paper for my board, and tell them to send me. When I was examined by my board they didn't know I had hernia until I told them, because it is very slight; you can hardly notice it; I am going around that way for the last 14 years. If you want to do me a favor, please have the board send me to the camp, as I am very anxious to go. Please answer my letter; by doing so you will oblige a good American citizen.

The local boards found this type of registrant a frequent one, and they chronicle with intense sympathy the ceaseless efforts made to secure their indulgence:

He was slightly underweight, following an illness, and a trifle deaf; and if he had been half an inch shorter he would have been entirely without the regulations. He had been rejected by every branch of the service, military and naval, but when required to register in June, 1918, he was yet in hope. The examining physicians were reluctant to make a Class A man of him; but he was importunate, and they yielded. He went to a general service camp, and was promptly rejected. He returned home, and asked to be reclassified as a limited service man. This was done, and he was entrained and accepted at camp. Then came this letter: "I have been 'shot' three times for inoculation in the arm, and I have got my uniform. I thank you very much." Inside of two weeks he was dead from influenza and pneumonia.

(b) *Uses made.*—What specific uses were made in the Army of those inducted? They were of especial value in filling places in headquarters offices, at camps of mobilization, at supply bases, on lines of communication, etc., where they were enabled to replace able-bodied soldiers for service at the front. Many were technical experts, in occupations valuable to the Army. The corps assignments (omitting the 20,000 individual inductions, as to which no data are available) are shown in the following Table 51:

TABLE 51.—*Army disposition of Group C men accepted.*

	Army disposition of Group C men accepted.	Number.	Number assigned on original call.	By transfer.
1	Total Group C men called and inducted to Sept. 11, 1918	108,355		
2	Rejected, not yet reported or otherwise disposed of	32,733		
3	Assignments reported	75,622		
4	Aircraft production		864	460
5	Chemical warfare			4,068
6	Coast Artillery			2,804
7	Construction			1,355
8	Divisions			900
9	Engineers			1,521
10	Field Artillery			
11	Industrial furlough			931
12	Medical Corps		314	6,704
13	Military Aeronautics		333	1,940
14	Military Intelligence		20	
15	Miscellaneous			7,158
16	Motor Transport			1,822
17	Ordnance		200	4,871
18	Provost Marshal General		5,913	
19	Quartermaster General		650	13,869
20	Schools		1,448	
21	Spruce Production		13,800	
22	Signal Corps			676
23	Stenographers (general assignment)		2,000	
24	Tank			1
25	Navy		1,000	

7. *Group D; Disqualified for any military service.*—The registrants who possessed physical defects of such degree as to prevent them from rendering military service of any kind numbered 521,606 individuals, and constituted 16.25 per cent of the whole number examined. Such defects were, broadly, organic diseases of the internal organs; marked visual or aural defects; mental diseases and deficiencies; muscular paralyses; disfiguring or disabling deformities; physical underdevelopment.

At the time of our entrance into the world war, and for a considerable period before, the standard as to minimum of height for the United States Army had been 5 feet 4 inches. In order to include many thousands of vigorous individuals who were physically competent for military duty, this minimum was from time to time lowered, after April, 1917, until it reached 5 feet.

For the requirement as to weight, a minimum of 110 pounds was, after some changes, finally fixed upon, and registrants of less weight were rejected. The American soldier must carry a load of about 50 pounds, and a man of less weight than the minimum cited can not be expected to bear up under such a burden.

That the examinations by local board physicians were too liberal—i. e., that many more men should have been rejected into Group D—might seem to be the inference from the percentage of subsequent rejections at camp of men accepted by the boards. The data on this point are more fully examined in paragraph 13. On the other hand, it is certain that in some respects and in some places the local board examinations were too strict—i. e., that considerable numbers of individuals were erroneously placed in Group D (Class V–G) by local boards. A careful review of the reports of physical examinations in 8,166 such cases, by the medical aide of one State, indicated that 13.4 per cent were physically competent to perform military service. The medical aide of another State recalled and reexamined 645 Class V–G registrants. Among this number 8.18 per cent were found fit for general military service, and 26.8 per cent for limited service. Individuals having such defects as operable hernias, loss of teeth, moderate flat feet, etc., were largely suitable for limited military service and the regulations so provided. Nevertheless, very large numbers of such men were unconditionally rejected into Group D. These observations clearly indicate that, in case of need, a careful reexamination of all registrants placed in Group D would yield a very large number of men for military service.

An overwhelming majority of the boards—the ratio is seven to one—declare (in answer to specific inquiry) that the medical examinations, as of late conducted, reduced to a minimum the subsequent rejections at camp. The minority boards give various reasons for their dissent, among which are the following: Suitable quarters or adequate equipment for making physical examinations were lacking; medical members had not sufficient time to make thorough examinations and found it difficult to obtain assistance; the rules were differently interpreted at the boards and at camp. Medical advisory boards did not function as efficiently as they should. A constructive suggestion was that board physicians should be sent to camp for instruction and conference with the camp examiners.

It is possible that a considerable number of rejections at camp have been the result of a policy which is stated by a Pennsylvania board as follows:

Our rejections from the beginning to the end amounted to 7 per cent rejected at camp. This percentage would have been smaller had it not seemed expedient in many cases to send certain men, even though we felt satisfied that they would be rejected. This was done in a number of instances in order to satisfy a critical public, on the one hand, and in other instances in order to secure the men from any stigma; in other words, to give them a better discharge than a local board discharge would amount to in the eyes of the general public.

8. *Malingerers.*—Not every man to whom the privilege comes is desirous of discharging his debt to his country by rendering military

service.   Some magnify existing physical defects; others feign non-existent disabilities; still others purposely cause conditions which they hope may disqualify them.

Malingerers may be divided into three general groups:

(a) Real malingerers with nothing the matter with them, who injure themselves, or make allegations respecting diseases or such conditions as drug taking, or who counterfeit disease with full consciousness and responsibility; all for the purpose of evading military service.   Many of these have been coached.

(b) Psychoneurotics, who are natural complainers and try to get out of every disagreeable thing in life.   Perhaps only partially conscious of the nature or the seriousness of what they do and only partly responsible.   In many the motives are not persistent and many can be made into good soldiers.

(c) Confirmed psychoneurotics with long history of nervous breakdowns and illnesses who behave like class (a), but more persistently, and from whom not much can be expected in the way of reconstruction.

Men shoot or cut off their fingers or toes, practically always on the right side, to disqualify themselves for service.   Sometimes they put their hands under cars for this purpose.   Many men have their teeth pulled out.   Retention of urine is simulated.   Egg albumen is injected into the bladder or put in urine.   Glucose is added to urine. Digitalis, thyroid gland preparations, and strophanthus are taken to cause disturbance of the heart and cantharides to cause albuminuria.   The skin is irritated by various substances, which are also injected under it to create abscesses.   Various substances are taken to bring about purging.   An appearance of hemoptysis may be produced by adding blood, either human or that of animals, to the sputa.   Sometimes merely coloring matter is added.   Those who can vomit voluntarily what they swallow use the same means to create the appearance of hematemesis.   Similarly, coloring matters may be added to the stools.   Mechanical and chemical irritants are made use of to cause inflammation about practically all the body orifices.   Jaundice may be simulated by taking picric acid.   Crutches, spectacles, trusses, strappings, etc., are made use of to create the appearance of disability.

The surest means of detecting malingering is a thorough understanding by the examiner of the types of people who actually do it— and the way they behave.   It is only in the feigned diseases of the eye and ear that special tests are required.   Observation in hospital is necessary in difficult cases.   The vast bulk of malingerers are those who exaggerate some actual defect, and the problem for the medical examiner is to decide whether the defect complained of is sufficient cause for rejection for service.

It was found often necessary to accept individuals having certain defects which are ordinarily objectionable, for the reason that many purposely contracted diseases or habits or created defects in order to escape service. In such cases the registrants were inducted if not incapacitated; if rendered unfit for any military service, their cases were referred to the Department of Justice for legal action.

9. *Urban and rural physical rejections compared.*—Table 52 contrasts rejections in certain urban and rural communities. Urban communities were selected from boards in the cities of New York, Chicago, Philadelphia, Cleveland, Milwaukee, Seattle, St. Louis, Cincinnati, and New Orleans. Rural communities were taken from all States, using only boards having less than 1,200 registrants in the June 5, 1917, registration. The results are as follows:

TABLE 52.—*Rural and urban physical rejections compared.*

	Rural and urban physical rejections compared	Number.	Per cent of examined.
1	Total examined in 100 selected urban and rural regions...	200,000	....
2	Rejected in 100 selected urban and rural regions..	38,569	19.28
3	Examined in urban regions............................	100,000	....
4	Rejected in urban regions........................	21,675	21.68
5	Examined in rural regions.........................	100,000	....
6	Rejected in rural regions......:.................	16,894	16.89

For further study, Appendix Table 52–A gives a percentage comparison of rejections, by disqualifying defects, for eight urban and eight rural districts. In this table 45,000 rejects were studied, nearly equally divided between city and country.

The figures of both of these studies indicate that a considerable physical advantage accrues to the boy reared in the country.

10. *Colored and white physical rejections compared.*—In the three groups representing partial or total disqualification, a further feature revealed by the local boards' records is to be found in the comparison of rejections of colored and white registrants. It will be remembered that the Report of the Provost Marshal General for the Civil War contains an elaborate study on this subject. In the present war the records for rejections in the selective draft prior to December 15, 1917, are not yet available; but for the period between December 15, 1917, and September 11, 1918, the figures are as follows:

TABLE 53.—*Colored and white physical rejections compared.*

	Colored and white physical rejections compared.	Number.	Per cent of examined.	Per cent of partial disqualifications.
1	Total, colored and white examined Dec. 15, 1917, to Sept. 11, 1918	3,208,446	100.00	....
2	Group A	2,259,027	70.41	....
3	Disqualified partly or totally	949,419	....	100.00
4	Group B	88,436	2.76	9.31
5	Group C	339,377	10.58	35.75
6	Group D	521,606	16.25	54.94
7	Total, colored examined	458,838	100.00	....
8	Group A	342,277	74.60	....
9	Disqualified partly or totally	116,561	....	100.00
10	Group B	9,605	2.09	8.24
11	Group C	27,474	5.99	23.57
12	Group D	79,482	17.32	68.19
13	Total white examined	2,749,608	100.00	....
14	Group A	1,916,750	69.71	....
15	Disqualified partly or totally	832,858	....	100.00
16	Group B	78,831	2.87	9.47
17	Group C	311,903	11.34	37.45
18	Group D	442,124	16.08	53.08

11. *Alien and native physical rejections compared.*—For the purpose of comparing the physical qualifications of natives and aliens a comparison was made of the rejections in local boards composed dominantly of natives and aliens, respectively. Some 85,000 examinations were assembled from local boards in dominant alien wards of the cities of New York, Philadelphia, Chicago, Cleveland, Milwaukee, and Cincinnati, representing a registration of 300,000. Then some 100,000 examinations were similarly assembled from other than city boards in the States of Indiana, Iowa, Kansas, Kentucky, and Ohio, representing also a registration of 300,000. The results were as follows:

TABLE 54.—*Physical rejections in alien and native communities compared.*

	Alien and native physical rejections compared.	Number.	Per cent of examined.
1	Total number of records of examination compared in dominant alien and native communities	184,854	....
2	Rejected (group D)	28,184	15.25
3	Total compared, alien communities	84,723	....
4	Rejected (group D)	14,525	17.14
5	Total compared, native communities	100,131	....
6	Rejected (group D)	13,659	13.64

It is interesting to note that, as might be expected, this comparison is greatly to the advantage of the native Americans. In every 100,000 men the native born would yield 3,500 more (an additional regiment at war strength) for military service than would a like number of foreign born.

An additional light on this subject is thrown by a report from local board for division No. 129, New York City. This board, realizing a great opportunity, made careful anthropometric studies of about 600 registrants. The work was performed at the American Museum of Natural History, in whose building the board had its quarters. The anthropometric examination, supplementary to the physical, comprised observations under the following six heads: (1) Ancestry and nationality; (2) measurements and observation of the head and body; (3) examination of teeth and measurement of jaws; (4) foot imprint; (5) nervous history and condition; and (6) photographs. Twenty-eight measurements of the body were taken, including 12 of the head and face. A human figure plotted according to the average from these measurements would give the main outline type of a registrant. A special blank was employed, and by following the order given in the blank all measurements could be made in about four minutes per man.

Time has been lacking for a final study of the observed data. However, the figures seem to indicate that the foreign born registrants were markedly less fit for service than the native born, but that there is no marked difference between the native born of foreign parents and those of native American stock.

12. *Age–21 physical rejections.*—Had the armistice of November 11, 1918, not resulted in a cessation of the physical examinations (partly completed) for the September 12 registrants of ages 18–45, it would have been possible to present an exact account of the differences between the several ages as to physical qualifications. Such an account of this important phase will now only be possible when the local board records shall have been assembled and analyzed by the Surgeon General's Office.

Meanwhile, an important clue to the possible difference can be found by comparing the physical examinations of the age-21 group registering June 5–August 24, 1918, with the average for ages 21–30 registering June 5, 1917. The comparison results as follows:

TABLE 55.—*Age–21 physical rejections, compared with ages 21–30.*

	Age-21 physical rejections.	Ages 21–30, examined Dec. 15, 1917–June 5, 1918.		Age-21, examined June 5–Sept. 11, 1918.	
		Number.	Per cent.	Number.	Per cent.
1	Total registrants physically examined .	2,693,448	100.00	514,998	100.00
2	Fully qualified (Group A)........	1,863,047	69.17	395,980	76.89
3	Disqualified partly or totally....	830,401	30.83	119,018	23.11
4	Group B...................	75,120	2.79	13,316	2.59
5	Group C...................	284,824	10.57	54,553	10.59
6	Group D...................	470,457	17.47	51,149	9.93

13. *Camp surgeons' revision of local board physical examinations.*—An appreciable proportion of inducted men found by local boards

to be acceptable for military service were rejected for physical or mental defects by Army medical examiners at mobilization points. Several factors contributed to this result, namely, lack of uniformity between local board and Army standards (as already mentioned); inexperience or insufficient care on the part of examining physicians of local and medical advisory boards; errors and undue length of time elapsing between examination by local board and examination at camp, during which period changes occurred in physical conditions of registrants; particularity of Army examiners; and the varying human equation "when doctors disagree." Oddly enough, the camp rejections were largely for obvious defects, many of which, it would seem, might have been readily apparent to the examiners of local boards. Obvious defects accounted for over 50 per cent of camp rejections. Among these were deformities, flat feet, discharging ears, poor physique, defective mentality, hernias, loss of teeth, and varicose veins.

(a) The national figures and percentages are shown below in Table 56 for the period February 10, 1918, to October 31, 1918. This period is determined by the fact that the present system of reporting rejections only became effective as of the earlier date cited.

TABLE 56.—*Camp surgeons' revision of local board physical examinations.*

	Camp surgeons' physical rejections.	Number.	Per cent of camp examinations.
1	Total selectives placed in groups A and C by local boards and sent to camp Dec. 15, 1917–Oct. 15, 1918...........	2,124,293	100.00
2	Total rejected at camps...............................	172,000	8.10
3	Total accepted at camps............................	1,952,293	91.90

It thus appears that the national percentage of inducted men of Groups A and C afterwards rejected at camp was 8.10. The variances for the several States are shown in Appendix Table 56–A. The graphic representation for Appendix Table 56–A shows the comparison in another manner (Chart D).

(b) At this point, comparison must be made with the results in 1917, under the earlier plan of physical examination. The percentages of original rejections by local boards, and of subsequent rejections by camp surgeons of local board accepted men, were as follows:

TABLE 57.—*Comparison of 1917 and 1918 rejections.*

	Rejetions, 1917 and 1918, compared.	Per cent.
1	Percentage of rejections by local boards in 1917......................	29.11
2	Percentage in 1918, groups B, C, D (Table 49).....................	29.59
3	Percentage of camp rejections of local board acceptances, 1917........	5.80
4	Percentage in 1918 (Table 56)...............................	8.10

· It will be noted that the effect of the new physical group method was not to increase the ratio of rejections, but only to subdivide the old ratio into suitable grades.

(c) The possible explanations for this percentage of rejections at camp, and for the variances in different places, are numerous, as above stated. But they obviously fall under three general heads, viz, variances due to physical fitness of registrants in different localities, or variances due to different action by different local boards, or variances due to different action by different camp surgeons. It is highly desirable to determine, as closely as possible, which of these three influences was the most responsible. State pride is involved in discovering whether physical manhood is better developed in one region than another; and military administration is concerned with ascertaining whether local board physicians or camp surgeons came nearer the truth on the whole.

For this purpose, it is necessary to examine the rejections separately by States, then separately by principal camps, and then by a combination of camps and States covering an identical group of registrants.

The first of these analyses can be found in Appendix Table 56–A, already referred to, showing the percentage of camp rejections by States.

The second of these analyses is given in the following Table 58, showing the percentage of rejections for the principal camps:

TABLE 58.—*Physical rejections by camps compared.*

	Rejections by camps compared.	Number.	Per cent of examined.	Per cent of examined.
1	Total selectives received and examined at specified camps, Feb. 10, 1918, to Oct. 1, 1918..	326,784	100.00	....
2	Rejected...............................	25,731	7.87	....
3	Accepted...............................	301,053	92.13	....
4	Examined at Camp Custer...............	53,828	....	100.00
5	Rejected...............................	6,398	....	11.88
6	Accepted...............................	47,430	....	88.12
7	Examined at Camp Dodge...............	53,150	....	100.00
8	Rejected...............................	2,207	....	4.15
9	Accepted...............................	50,943	....	95.85
10	Examined at Camp Grant...............	71,266	....	100.00
11	Rejected...............................	6,880	....	9.65
12	Accepted...............................	64,386	....	90.35
13	Examined at Camp Lewis...............	59,233	....	100.00
14	Rejected...............................	5,175	....	8.74
15	Accepted...............................	54,058	....	91.26
16	Examined at Camp Riley...............	14,665	....	100.00
17	Rejected...............................	1,151	....	7.85
18	Accepted...............................	13,514	....	92.15
19	Examined at Camp Taylor...............	74,642	....	100.00
20	Rejected...............................	3,920	....	5.25
21	Accepted...............................	70,722	....	94.75

The third of these analyses takes an identical group of 242,642 inducted men rejected and compares them by States of origin and by camps of rejection; this reveals whether or not men from the same States and boards were differently treated at different camps, and whether or not the same camp surgeons varied in their rejections of men from different States and boards. The table is as follows:

TABLE 59.—*Physical rejections by camp surgeons, by selected coterminous camps and States, compared.*

		Total.	At Camp Custer.	At Camp Dodge.	At Camp Grant.	At Camp Taylor.
1	From eight States:					
2	Examined..........	242,642	50,725	52,419	70,056	69,442
3	Rejected..........	18,524	6,061	2,114	6,674	3,675
4	Percentage..........	7.63	11.95	4.03	9.53	5.29
5	From Illinois:					
6	Examined..........	47,564	2,000	4,522	30,690	10,352
7	Rejected:..........	3,726	225	371	2,637	493
8	Percentage..........	7.83	11.25	8.20	8.59	4.76
9	From Indiana:					
10	Examined..........	31,166	3,309	3,436	1,000	23,421
11	Rejected..........	1,929	451	341	149	988
12	Percentage..........	6.19	13.63	9.92	14.90	4.22
13	From Iowa:					
14	Examined..........	25,801	....	25,801	....	....
15	Rejected..........	885	....	885	....	....
16	Percentage..........	3.43	....	3.43	....	....
17	From Kentucky:					
18	Examined..........	35,669	....	....	....	35,669
19	Rejected..........	2,194	....	....	....	2,194
20	Percentage..........	6.15	....	....	....	6.15
21	From Michigan:					
22	Examined..........	42,204	42,204	....	....	....
23	Rejected..........	5,021	5,021	....	....	....
24	Percentage..........	11.90	11.90	....	....	....
25	From Minnesota:					
26	Examined..........	28,151	....	12,796	15,355	....
27	Rejected..........	1,764	....	280	1,484	....
28	Percentage..........	6.27	....	2.19	9.66	....
29	From North Dakota:					
30	Examined..........	5,864	....	5,864	....	....
31	Rejected..........	237	....	237	....	....
32	Percentage..........	4.04	....	4.04	....	....
33	From Wisconsin:					
34	Examined..........	26,223	3,212	....	23,011	....
35	Rejected..........	2,768	364	....	2,404	....
36	Percentage..........	10.56	11.33	....	10.45	....

It will be noticed by comparing each State for the several camps to which it contributed, and then comparing each camp for the contributing States, that some inferences can be drawn as to the correct explanation of a particular percentage of rejections, i. e., whether it was due to the peculiar standards of a specific camp, or whether it was in keeping with the general standard of physical condition contributed from that State.

14. *Specific causes of rejection.*—A most important revelation developing from the records of rejection is, of course, found in specific

causes forming the defects on which the rejections were based. A complete study of the records will, of course, not be feasible for some time to come. But the available records are on a large enough scale to justify generalization. Their value in all aspects of medical administration, and not least in that of the Army, can not be exaggerated. Not only do they represent the broadest basis ever available for such an inquiry, but they were made under such conditions of fair unformity, both as to time, as to area, and as to physical standards employed, that their scientific worth is unequaled by any statistics hitherto accessible.

Three series of examinations were here studied. The first series (Series X) covered some 255,000 records of rejection by local boards (P. M. G. O. Form 1010); these were forwarded by the boards to the Surgeon General's Office, and represent all of the records (arriving at random) that could be examined in the time available. The second series (Series Y) covered 172,000 records of rejection by camp surgeons of men accepted by local board physicians; these represent all of the records (P. M. G. O. Form 1029–B) forwarded from camps to this office between February 10 and October 31, 1918; they cover registrants of both Group A and Group C; but the former were greatly in the majority. The third series (Series Z) comprised discharges from the Army, after acceptance, of recently inducted registrants; the records of some 40,000 such individuals were available. These three series are shown, separately and in total, for each of the 20 physical causes of rejection, in the following Table 60:

TABLE 60.—*Varieties of defects disqualifying for military service, from Feb. 10, 1918, to Oct. 15, 1918.*

	Cause for rejection.	Total rejections by local boards and camp surgeons.		Rejected by local boards and placed in Group D (Series X).		Accepted by local boards for Groups A or C, but rejected by camp surgeons (Series Y).		Discharged from Army after acceptance by local boards and camp surgeons (Series Z).	
		Num-ber.	Per cent.	Num-ber.	Per cent.	Num-ber.	Per cent.	Num-ber.	Per cent.
1	Total for all causes	467,694	100.00	255,312	100.00	172,000	100.00	40,382	100.00
2	Alcohol and drugs.	2,007	.43	231	.09	1,238	.72	538	1.33
3	Bones and joints ..	57,744	12.35	33,283	13.04	19,623	11.41	4,838	11.98
4	Developmental defects (height weight, chest measurements, muscles)........	39,166	8.37	27,293	10.69	11,538	6.71	335	.83
5	Digestive system..	2,476	.53	1,586	.62	448	.26	442	1.09
6	Ears	20,465	4.38	12,100	4.74	6,455	3.75	1,910	4.73
7	Eyes	49,801	10.65	32,775	12.83	15,367	8.93	1,659	4.11
8	Flatfoot (pathological)	18,087	3.87	3,342	1.31	13,234	7.69	1,511	3.74
9	Genito-urinary (venereal).......	6,235	1.33	2,042	.81	2,744	1.60	1,449	3.59
10	Genito-urinary (non-venereal) ..	6,309	1.35	3,054	1.21	2,226	1.30	1,029	2.55

TABLE 60.—*Varieties of defects disqualifying for military service, from Feb. 10, 1918, to Oct. 15, 1918*—Continued.

Cause for rejection.	Total rejections by local boards and camp surgeons.		Rejected by local boards and placed in Group D (Series X).		Accepted by local boards for Groups A or C, but rejected by camp surgeons (Series Y).		Discharged from Army after acceptance by local boards and camp surgeons. (Series Z).	
	Number.	Per cent.	Number.	Per cent.	Number.	Per cent.	Number.	Per cent.
11 Heart and blood vessels..........	61,142	1.07	36,470	14.28	19,268	11.20	5,404	13.38
12 Hernia............	28,268	.04	8,473	3.32	18,353	10.67	1,442	3.57
13 Mental deficiency.	24,514	8.24	14,417	5.65	6,293	3.66	3,804	9.42
14 Nervous and mental disorders.....	23,728	5.07	10,945	4.29	7,319	4.26	5,464	13.53
15 Respiratory (tuberculous)......	40,533	8.67	27,559	10.77	10,792	6.27	2,182	5.40
16 Respiratory (nontuberculous)....	7,823	1.67	3,081	1.21	3,483	2.02	1,259	3.12
17 Skin	12,519	2.68	12,207	4.78	213	.12	99	.25
18 Teeth	14,793	3.16	4,314	1.69	9,952	5.79	527	1.31
19 Thyroid	8,215	1.76	3,151	1.23	3,697	2.15	1,367	3.38
20 Tuberculosis of parts other than respiratory......	4,136	.88	3,853	1.51	159	.09	124	.31
21 All other defects ..	14,314	3.06	12,671	4.96	1,373	.80	270	.67
22 Cause not given....	25,419	5.44	2,465	.97	18,225	10.60	4,729	11.71

The variances by States are shown in Appendix Table 60-A which takes the consolidated total for the three series, covering nearly half a million individuals.

In order to afford opportunity for a more careful study of the variance between localities in the recurrence of these several physical conditions, the first two series (X and Y) are set forth separately, by States and causes of rejection, in Appendix Table 60-B (local boards, P. M. G. O. Form 1010) and Appendix Table 60-C (camp surgeons, P. M. G. O. Form 1029-B). A more extended table for Series Y, showing the anatomical and pathological defects in greater detail, is given in Appendix Table 60-D.

Graphic representations, showing comparisons of causes of rejections for eight selected States, may be found in Charts E to L, inclusive. States were selected to contrast localities; New England, the Middle Atlantic, the South, the Central, the Mid-West, the Mexican border, and the Pacific sections each having a representative; Maryland is included as the State with the best record. The interesting fact is apparent that States differed widely in the principal defects for which inducted men were returned to them as rejected at camps. Thus, Texas and New York had highest rejection ratios for visual defects, Maryland for deformities, Massachusetts for dental abnormalties, Alabama for mental and nervous disorders, California and Colorado for tuberculosis, Illinois for hernia. These observations indicate either that the conditions cited were notably prevalent in the States named, or that an unusual number of failures in diagnosis occurred with respect to those conditions.

15. *Alcohol and drug addiction.*—In order to determine the degree to which these disabilities figured in physical examinations during the processes of the draft and in early Army service, a study was made of figures from three sources, namely, the above-mentioned rejections by local boards and rejections at camps and also discharges of recently inducted men from the Army (P. M. G. O. Form 1029–D). A total of 467,694 cases of such rejections and discharges were listed. In that number, only 2,007 rejections or discharges for the above-named conditions cited were found. As was to be expected, the largest percentage of these was found among those discharged from the Army. This, of course, resulted from the fact that better opportunity was afforded in the Army for observation for the detection of drunkards and addicts.

Since the physical standards in force for the local boards required that drug addicts be placed in Group B, as having defects to be regarded as remediable, and since few Group B men were sent to camp, it is probable that most of the registrants recognized by the local board physicians as such were so placed. However, only 88,436 individuals were placed in Group B for all causes, and but a moderate part of these could have been so included on account of drug addiction. Thus it is evident either that such cases went unrecognized, or that the condition is not so prevalent as some have thought.

A study of a selected group of 556 drug addicts by occupations gives the following data: Teamsters, drivers, and chauffeurs constituted 12.8 per cent of the whole number; men who called themselves laborers yielded 11.7 per cent; waiters and hotel servants were 8 per cent; bookkeepers and office assistants gave 7 per cent. Thus 40 per cent of the whole number were included within the occupations named. From this group of 556 addicts, 311 admitted that they were addicted to morphine; 118 cited heroin; 54 used two or more of the usual drugs; 72 did not state the drug; only one individual alleged cocaine addiction.

16. *Thyroid disease.*—As shown in the various tables pertaining to physical defects, diseases of the thyroid gland gave remarkably high figures in some States. This class of affections was responsible for 2.15 per cent of rejections in Series Y. The 3,697 cases were classified as follows: Simple goiter, 680; hyperthyroidism, 2,599; goiter with hyperthyroidism, 418.

The national average was high and the distribution of the condition peculiar. The District of Columbia led the country in its percentage of rejections for thyroid disease, which was responsible for 6.2 per cent of its total rejections. Wisconsin, which is known to have a high prevalence of thyroid abnormalities, was next with

6.1 per cent. Missouri had 5.3 per cent; West Virginia 4.8, per cent; Kansas, 4.3 per cent; and Virginia, 4 per cent.

17. *Mental deficiency and disorders.*—Analysis of the figures and percentages of men rejected on account of deficient mentality and because of mental and nervous disorders affords some interesting data. The figures in Appendix Table 60–E are derived from the three sources heretofore described, namely, rejections by local boards, rejections at camps, and discharges from the Army.

The first thing which is apparent is that most of the Southern States show high figures for the mentally deficient. This is perhaps explainable by reason of their large negro populations. Vermont, which stands nine on the list, is the only Northern State which appears among the first ten.

The next point is that, among the first ten, the Northern States mainly exhibit the higher figures for mental and nervous disorders. Alabama leads for the first-named condition, the District of Columbia for the other. Maryland stands high in both. The District of Columbia has the highest combined percentages, with Maryland a close second.

This table very strikingly exhibits the fact that, while comparatively few such cases were recognized in the hurried examinations made by local boards and camps, the opportunities for observation under service conditions promptly disclosed these types of disabilities. They formed nearly 23 per cent of the entire number of discharges from the Army of recently inducted registrants whose cases were available for study.

(VIII) DEFERMENTS AND EXEMPTIONS IN GENERAL.

1. *Ratio of different grounds for exemption and discharge.*—The foregoing several grounds of deferment and exemption, grouped together under their principal heads, show the relative extent to which each ground of exemption or deferment contributed to remove registrants from immediate liability to military service.

TABLE 61.—*Comparison of grounds of deferment.*

	Comparison of grounds of deferment.	Number.	Per cent of registrants.	Per cent of deferment, 1918.
1	Total registrants June 5, 1917–Sept. 11, 1918.....	10, 679, 814	100.00	....
2	Total deferments on all grounds.................	6, 973, 270	65.29	100.00
3	Physically disqualified....................	521, 606	....	7.48
4	Deferred on other grounds..................	6, 451, 664	....	92.52
5	Alienage..........................	1, 033, 406	....	14.82
6	Specific vocations....................	76, 497	....	1.10
7	Necessary agricultural and industrial vocations......................	364, 876	....	5.23
8	Dependency........................	3, 903, 733	....	55.98
9	Military and naval service.............	619, 727	....	8.89
10	Morally unfit......................	18, 620	....	.27
11	Undistributed in reports..............	434, 815	....	6.23

These figures, however, can be regarded as only approximate. Under the classification system, multiple claims on different grounds might be made by the same registrant, and only the most deferred ground became the effective one to place him in the class which operated to defer him. The scrutiny of the records, to disentangle with accuracy the effective claims granted from the noneffective claims granted, has not been feasible for the boards within the time limited for their reports. Nor must it be forgotten that the ground of a claim granted is not the most significant element in judging of the effects of the draft; e. g., an alien might be deferred on the ground of dependency, and a married man might be deferred on the ground of industrial necessity; and thus alienage or the married status were protected incidentally but effectually.

The above figures, therefore, represent only an approximate summary of the relative importance of the chief grounds for deferment. The result is useful merely as showing the relative effect of legislatively sanctioning one or another ground of deferment.

It would be natural to compare the results in 1918 with the results in 1917, for the specific grounds recognized in the law. Theoretically this might signify something of the difference between the classification system and the original method of calling and discharging or accepting. But in fact it has no significance, because of the reverse order, in 1917 and 1918, of the physical examinations and the filing of claims for deferment or exemption, already referred to in Chapter III. In 1918, claims for exemption or discharge were first granted or denied, and then physical examination followed for those not discharged or exempted; thus the ruling upon claims for exemption or discharge applied to a group of persons consisting of every registrant called up to a given date. But in 1917 the physical examination came first, and then those found qualified physically were given an opportunity to file claims for deferment or exemption; thus the rulings upon such claims covered a group of men consisting only of those physically qualified; so that in 1917 the ratio of physical disqualification to all grounds of discharge or exemption was 36.08 per cent, while in 1918 it was only 7.48 per cent. The comparison therefore has no significance.

2. *Ratio of different classes.*—Under the original plan practiced in 1917 there were but two classes of registrants; the first was those discharged or exempted, and the second was those accepted. But an important object of the classification system adopted for 1918 (as already pointed out in Chapter III) was to meet the equities of the situation by establishing as many as five classes, graded in the order of their equitable liability to immediate military service. It is, therefore, interesting to observe what was the total yield of each of these five classes, in their relation to the whole number of registrants.

One of the important questions arising in July, 1918, when the proposal for extending the draft ages to 18–45 was in contemplation, for the purpose of obtaining an additional 2,000,000 men or more, was whether this proposed course was preferable to that of going further into the original 10,000,000 registrants of ages 21–30, by taking in due sequence the higher deferred Classes II, III, and IV; and this question in turn depended somewhat on the probable yield of each of these higher classes; for, assuming that Class IV, containing chiefly registrants with dependent families, was not to be taken until a last resort, it might prove that Classes II and III, even if taken completely, would not furnish the necessary number required for the enlarged military program.   The following table now supplies the answer to this, as well as a number of other interesting questions:

TABLE 62.—*Deferments and exemptions in general.*

	Deferments and exemptions in general.	Number.	Per cent of total registrants.	Per cent of total exemptions.
1	Total registrants June 5, 1917–Sept. 11, 1918, classified since Dec. 15, 1917...............	9,952,735	100.00	....
2	Total deferments and exemptions on all grounds...............................	6,973,270	70.07	100.00
3	Class II...............................	989,568	....	14.18
4	Class III...............................	407,125	....	5.84
5	Class IV...............................	3,026,178	....	43.40
6	Class V...............................	2,123,825	....	30.46
7	Undistributed in reports..............	426,574	....	6.12
8	Placed in Class I.........................	2,979,465	29.93	....

One interesting feature of the above table is the revelation that Class IV was by far the largest of the deferred classes, and this, of course, by reason of its large element of dependency deferments. Class V's size was due chiefly to physical disqualifications, alienage, and military service.   Another important feature, not obvious from the mere figures, but patent in the administration of the system, was that Classes II and III served precisely the purpose, already mentioned, in establishing the system, viz, that of affording more elasticity and greater opportunity to recognize the several equitable grades in the order of liability for military service.   There can be no doubt that the administration of the system by the boards was made far more satisfactory in public ŏpinion by the recognition of these different grades; Classes II and III afforded an opportunity for recognizing the border-line groups of cases, which under the original system would have been disposed of either by an out-and-out acceptance or by an out-and-out discharge or exemption.

3. *Divisions within Classes.*—The several divisions within the classes, denoted on the first page of the questionnaire by letters and

brief description, represent the more specific grounds for ·deferment within each class. Appendix Table 62–A and Chart M show the figures in detail. Owing to the difficulty of compiling the tables from the records of the boards without expenditure of inordinate time and labor, these figures must be regarded as only approximate; they represent the records as footed up in November, 1918, although there were, of course, constant changes during the year due to reclassifications. Another approximate estimate, as of date February to April, 1918, is shown in the figures from the Industrial Index interim ledger given in Chapter IV, Table 42.

4. *Fluctuation of deferred classifications.*—It has been pointed out in Chapter III that multiple claims might be and were often made by or on behalf of a single registrant, and that more than one claim might thus be granted for the same registrant. So, too, a registrant might be reclassified from one class into another as circumstances changed and thousands were at various times thus reclassified, this process going on throughout the year and all over the country.

These two features of the classification system have made it difficult to ascertain the statistics of classification with exact accuracy as of a specific date. The boards' records themselves will show decisively the status of an individual registrant at a given time; but the process of tracing each case through the records for the purpose of ascertaining the total results for the year is a complex and tedious one, and any form of report necessarily increases in complexity and difficulty as it gains in accuracy and completeness. For these reasons it must be noted that the totals here shown for the various branches of the classification have not always been brought into consistency by the boards.

5. *Ratio of exemptions and deferments under the British system.*— By the British system of conscription (Appendix K) all men registered but not immediately called were "deemed to be enlisted" and were "posted to the Army Reserve." The selection of these men for the reserve was made by passing upon individual cases, much as in our system. The several grounds for such deferment, or "posting to the reserve," are summarized in Appendix K. The registration included all ages between 15 and 60; but the successive conscription acts extended, from time to time, the ages for immediate liability to military service, beginning at 18 to 40, thence going to 45, and upward, with varying qualifications.

The registration which took place August–September, 1915, covered some 5,000,000 men of ages 18 to 40, but did not include some 3,000,000 (estimated) who had already enlisted. The total men of military ages 18 to 45 numbered something more than 9,500,000, but the only available figures showing the deferments ("posting to the reserve") cover ages 18 to 43. Table 62a shows the result:

TABLE 62a.—*Deferments in British system.*

	British deferments, ages 18 to 43.	Number.	Per cent.	Per cent.
1	Total males, ages 18 to 43, Aug. 1914–May 1918.	9,452,000	100.00	....
2	Posted to the Army Reserve, Class B, since Aug. 15, 1915...........................	3,586,000	37.94	100.00
3	(1) Men, mainly of low categories, exempted on personal and domestic grounds...........................	250,000	....	6.97
4	(2) Men exempted on grounds of industrial necessity......................	2,028,000	....	56.55
5	(a) Fit men engaged on work of national importance............	670,000	....	....
6	(b) Fit men engaged on war work for Army or Navy..............	840,000	....	....
7	(c) Men engaged on war work for allies' armies or navies..........	119,000	....	....
8	(d) Fit men engaged in agriculture..	279,000	....	....
9	(e) Men engaged in mercantile marine.	120,000	....	....
10	(3) Men of lowest categories distributed among (b), (c), and (d)............	1,003,000	....	27.97
11	(4) Specific deferment not given.........	305,000	....	8.51

(1) It will be seen that the ratio of total deferments was virtually a little more than one-half of the American ratio. This is partly accounted for (just one-half) by our large alienage exemption. The remainder may perhaps be accounted for by our liberal method of grading the deferments into four classes.

(2) It will further be noted that among the deferments the ratio shown for dependency is relatively small (even including items (1) and (3) together, which seems proper). This indicates that the primary consideration was given, in the British system, to the determination of deferments on the grounds of war work and industrial necessity, while in the American system primary consideration was given to the dependency claims. The protection to war work and industrial necessity also resulted as an incident of the American system; but it was not attempted to be directly controlled to the same extent as in the British system; the adjustment being left in part to the general industrial trends and to the measures adopted by the War Industries Board and other agencies.

(IX) CLASS I.

1. *Nominal Class I.*—The selective service regulations, section 70, read: "Every registrant is to be considered as belonging in Class I until his status giving him the right of deferred classification is fully established." In other words, Class I represents those registrants that remain after all deferments or exemptions have been granted. "The effect of classification in Class I," says the regulation, "is to render every man so classified presently liable to military service in the order determined by the drawing."

The number of men classified into Class I fluctuated, of course, from time to time, not only because of additions from tardy registration, but mainly because of the reclassifications which took place constantly, because of change of status, or, in some instances, because of a change of law or regulation, or of a change of policy as to a specific ground of deferment. The numbers given in the ensuing tables represent the records as they stood in November, 1918, with such corrections as are necessary to account for known elements of change.

It will be noted that in a general sense Class I, speaking retroactively, included that body of men who were accepted and inducted into military service prior to December 15, 1917—i. e., some 500,000 men. But, technically, Class I included only those who were placed under that head after December 15, 1917, when the classification system came into effect. The registrants thus left out of the classification system included, first, all those who had already been inducted by December 15, 1917, and, secondly, all those who had already been reported as deserters and were thus obviously not safe to rely upon in future calculations of effectives, and, thirdly, a few small additional descriptions of persons, for example, those whose names had been canceled for death, for erroneous registration, or the like. In proceeding to the classification after December 15, 1917, therefore, all the foregoing body of registrants was eliminated. The remainder formed the registrants due to be classified, and out of this remainder were formed the several Classes I, II, III, IV, and V. Classes II to V, inclusive, comprehended, therefore, not only persons not called before December 15, 1917, but also every person who had been formally discharged or exempted up to December 15, 1917, for these persons came up again for classification and might be placed in any one of the five classes.

The total number thus placed in Class I between December 15, 1917, and November 1, 1918, is shown in Table 63.

TABLE 63.—*Nominal Class I.*

	Nominal Class I, since Dec. 15, 1917.	Number.	Per cent of total registrants.	Per cent of due to be classified.
1	Total registrants June 5, 1917–Sept. 11, 1918.....	10,679,814	100.00	....
2	Inductions, cancellations, and desertions prior to Dec. 15, 1917...................	727,079	6.81	....
3	Net due to be classified after Dec. 15, 1917..	9,952,735	93.19	100.00
4	Placed in Class I, as of records Nov. 1, 1918...........................	2,979,465	27.90	29.93
5	Deferments and exemptions............	6,973,270	.65.29	70.07

Thus the nominal Class I obtained since December 15, 1917, was 29.93 per cent of those remaining to be classified. But on adding the number already disposed of in 1917, it appears that the entire nominal Class I yielded by these two registrations was 34.71 per cent of the total registrants.

2. *Effective Class I.*—Class I, as thus nominally constituted, viz, "those presently liable to military service," included of course a number of noneffective elements, i. e., registrants who could not be depended upon for immediate use in ordinary general calls designed to deliver any specified numbers of men called for by requisitions from the General Staff. These elements of noneffectives were as follows:

(a) *Delinquents and deserters.*—The significance and extent of this body of registrants is fully explained in Chapter V.

(b) *Medical Groups B and C.*—These men were available either for limited service in certain capacities, or after defects had been remedied, and therefore not immediately nor generally; the extent of these groups has already been set forth in this chapter, section (VII).

(c) *Emergency fleet entries.*—These registrants were provisionally withdrawn from liability for immediate call, so long as they were carried on the books of the Government shipbuilding agencies; the conditions of this arrangement, and the extent of this body of men, have been fully set forth in Chapter III.

For the purposes, therefore, of filling the ordinary general calls, from time to time, the net effective Class I consisted of the nominal Class I with estimated deductions for the above three groups. On account of these fluctuations of Class I, from time to time, due to the causes above mentioned (and to other minor ones later described in Chapter VI), it is not possible to furnish exact figures of the net effective Class I at all times. The following Table 64 shows the net effective Class I for the first and second registration, as constituted on September 11, 1918, with the total deductions during the year for the various elements of noneffectives above mentioned:

TABLE 64.—*Effective Class I in 1918.*

	Effective Class I in 1918.	Number.	Per cent of nominal Class I.	Per cent of noneffectives.
1	Total nominally recorded in Class I, since Dec. 15, 1917, of registrants June 5, 1917–Sept. 11, 1918.	2,979,465	100.00	....
2	Deductions for noneffectives................	839,315	28.17	100.00
3	Reported delinquent.....................	324,137	....	38.62
4	Qualified physically for limited service only (Group C)......................	339,377	....	40.43
5	Qualified only after physical defects remedied (Group B)..................	88,436	....	10.54
6	Noncombatant creeds....................	38,991	....	4.65
7	Suspended in emergency fleet..........	48,374	....	5.76
8	Net effectives, Class I......................	2,140,150	71.83	....

Thus it appears that the effective Class I, compared with the nominal Class I, yielded a ratio of 72 in 100. Otherwise stated, a nominal Class I could be depended upon for a yield of about three quarters in effectives available immediately for full military service.

It will be noted that this effective Class I of 1918 represented 20.04 per cent of the total registration shown in Table 63; and that if there be added the 516,212 who went to camp in 1917, the combined effectives of the two groups represent 24.87 per cent of the total registrants in the first two registrations.

3. *Elements of complication in using Class I effectives.*—Even when the computation of Class I was thus reduced to its net effectives, there were at different times serious complications in relying upon the computations as a basis for placing the numbers called for on requisition from the General Staff. Among these elements of complications may be mentioned the following:

(a) Enlistments in the Army and Navy continued to be permitted for registrants within the selective draft through the year 1918, until August. But the numbers of enlistments fluctuated constantly, ranging in different months between 25,000 and 170,000, of whom a large and unknowable portion were registrants; moreover, these enlistments were often localized for one reason or another. It was impracticable to obtain prompt notice sufficient to identify either the amount or the locality of these enlistments; and thus they formed an ever uncertain element of depletion for Class I; so that the computation of Class I effectives, apparently valid for a given month might prove to be unreliable, and thus readjustments of the calls would become necessary. In Chapter VII, the changes of regulation, finally made necessary by this feature, are described.

(b) For the same reason, the entries in the Emergency Fleet proved an element of depletion from time to time, and introduced another complication, varying as they did by localities.

(c) Colored and white registrants were alike effectives for the purpose of the selective draft; but, for the purpose of completing specific organizations of the Army, colored registrants might not be serviceable at particular times; therefore, the computations of effectives in Class I had always to take account of distribution between colored and white, so that a general call which could not be filled by colored registrants had to be so levied as to include only white registrants. The complications from this cause were numerous and taxed the resourcefulness of the mobilization division.

(d) In the act of Congress of May 20, 1918 (already cited in Chapter II), it was provided that registrants becoming of age 21 since June 5, 1917, "shall be placed at the bottom of the list of those liable for military service in the several classes to which they are assigned." Thus the computation of effectives of Class I after June 5, 1918, was obliged to keep separate for each State the Class I registrants of the new age 21, so that in no State should a call include registrants of this new class until all other registrants of Class I available, for general service in that State had been exhausted.

These, as well as other complications, required constant watchfulness in the computation of the effectives of Class I. That which was simple in theory became far from simple in practice.

4. *Exhaustion of Class I.*—At the outset of the year 1918, when the announced military program looked only to the completion of the first call of the President for 687,000 men, and when Class I promised to hold about two and a half million nominal numbers and some two million effectives, the prospect of the exhaustion of Class I seemed too remote for practical contemplation at the time. But as the fortunes of the battlefield progressed and the military program was enlarged, and especially when the large shipments overseas marked the months of May and June and correspondingly increased requisitions were made upon the selective draft for deliveries to camp, it became apparent that Class I under the first registration was certain to be exhausted before long. Congress, by the act of May 20, 1918, had authorized the President to include for registration the new age—21 men—and the President had authorized their registration on June 5, 1918; but even this accession did not suffice to fill the camp needs then announced in the plans of the General Staff. It therefore became necessary either to consider the organization of an additional Class I or to call upon the deferred Classes II, III, or IV in the sequence of their liability. The result of this situation, viz, the congressional legislation enlarging the ages for registration, and thus enabling a new Class I, estimated at nearly two and a half million effectives, to be made available, has already been set forth in Chapter II.

5. *Class I in the registration of September 12, 1918.*—The date of the passage of the enabling act of August 31, 1918, extending the draft ages, left scanty time for the processes necessary to the replenishment of the almost exhausted Class I. Yet the enlarged military program made it absolutely necessary that a substantial portion of the new Class I should be ready at the earliest feasible date. There never had been a moment when the requisitions from the General Staff were not able to be filled by the selective service administration, and such a moment must not be allowed to arrive, or even to impend.

The responsibility for carrying the heavy labors now necessary would fall largely upon the local and district boards, the State executives, and the other field forces of the system. A letter was therefore addressed to the governors of all States on September 10, pointing out that the situation imposed an inevitable condition of promptness and celerity in disposing of the huge new task, and announcing that the entirety of the operation must be compressed into the space of 100 days.

Immediately after the registration day, September 12, the boards began the first stages of the operation of classification. By direction of the President on September 10, the new registrants were to be taken in two series, the first series including registrants between 19 and 36 years of age, inclusive, and the second series including the remainder; and the boards were directed to proceed first with the classification of the first group. In order to enable the several States and boards to proceed at a pace consistent with their powers, a system of telegraphic and mail communication was installed, by which each State and board together with this office were informed by daily bulletins of the progress of the classification work in all other States and boards. The loyal and devoted spirit of all of the officials without exception was exhibited in the zealous manner in which they proceeded to the dispatch of their task. By the first 10 days in November 6 States had reported the completion of the classification and physical examination of the first series of new registrants, viz, Utah, Nevada, Wisconsin, Iowa, Arkansas, and Oklahoma, in the order named. Of the remainder, all except 3 had completed the classification of the registrants (excluding the determination of district board cases); while among this remainder 16 had completed one-third of the physical examinations, and of these 9 had completed two-thirds of the physical examinations (Appendix Table 64–A). It is therefore apparent that, adding to the foregoing entire States the large numbers of individual boards which in other States had completed their classification and a part or a whole of their physical examinations, the selective service administration was in a position, by the first 10 days in November, to deliver on requisition approximately 270,000 effectives. Had not the wide prevalence of the influenza epidemic during October compelled a suspension of the physical examinations in many States, it is undoubted that the number of effectives ready for delivery on the 1st of November would have been twice as great.

Meanwhile the prevalence of the epidemic had likewise made it necessary to suspend calls to camp. When this obstacle had passed away, the date fixed for delivery to camp by entrainment of the men called under the first substantial requisition applicable to the new registrants was Monday, November 11, 1918. On that day were ready for entrainment at their local boards the total of 140,000 men of the new registration, as well as 130,000 more men not yet requisitioned, together with some 110,000 or more of those still available from the first and second registrations. It was on that very day that the armistice was signed, taking effect at 11 o'clock in the

97250°—19——12

morning; and by direction of the President the calls were canceled and the entrainment was abandoned.

The selective service administration, therefore, would have continued its unbroken record of providing an ample Class I to fill all requisitions called for by the general military program.

6. *Ratio of Class I in New Registration.*—What was the ratio of Class I, nominal and effective, that would have been developed from the newly registered 13,000,000 men? This question can never be answered with anything like accuracy. One reason is that the second series of registrants, viz, ages 18 and 37–45, had been brought into classification in only a minority of States at the time of the armistice and of the subsequent order of the Secretary of War directing the suspension of further classification of this series (with the exception of the 18-year group). Another reason is that the physical examination of the first series, viz, ages 19–36, had not been completed in all the boards on those ages. A further reason is that an accurate ascertainment of the several elements that contribute to reduce a nominal Class I to an effective Class I was impracticable.

Nevertheless, it is possible to make a fair estimate of the coefficient for the Nation, on the basis of such returns as have been available. It appears that the nominal strength of Class I was running to 29.7 per cent; while the effective strength of Class I was running to 17.4 per cent. Appendix Table 64–A shows the figures for the several States so far as reporting up to December 9, 1918. In Chapter VII (Induction), Table 81 shows an estimate of the total number of effectives to have been expected from the third registration.

CHAPTER V.

SPECIAL GROUPS OF REGISTRANTS.

(I) AGE GROUPS.

The classification of registrants was not directly affected by the registrant's age; that is, neither the registrant's place in one or the other class, nor the sequence of his call for military service within a class, was dependent on his age. In this respect the selective service system, as it was established and operated between May 18, 1917, and September 12, 1918, differed fundamentally from the universal compulsory military service systems of the Continent, which are based essentially on the annual call of each arriving age group of 18 or 19 years, in time of peace, and a special call, in time of war, of groups of reserves formed by uniting several age groups.

To the foregoing statement as to the selective service system there were, however, two exceptions; one of which affected the system in operation in July, 1918, and the other of which was just going into effect at the time of the armistice of November 11, 1918. The first exception was that registrants arriving at age 21 on June 5 and August 24, 1918, were placed "at the bottom of the list of those liable for military service, in the several classes to which they are assigned"; this was the explicit provision of the joint resolution approved May 20, 1918, already cited in Chapter II. The second exception was that, by direction of the President, a distinction of age groups was authorized for the new 13,000,000 registered on September 12, 1918. There had been considerable public discussion, both in and out of Congress, upon the propriety of postponing to the very last, in the call for military service, the youths of 18 who were then to be registered; and the same discussion also looked forward to a similar discrimination postponing the call of men of the oldest ages then to be registered. Without making at the outset a decision as to the relative order of call for the youngest and the oldest of these ages, the President's direction, made early in September, 1918, designated ages 19–20 and 32–36 as the groups subject to earliest call among the new registrants. The boards were, therefore, instructed to proceed first with the classification of these ages 19–20 and 32–36; the arrival of the armistice of November 11 cut short the process of classifying the remaining age groups; and the occasion never arose for deciding finally the order of liability of the highest and lowest ages.

The numbers of registrants, however, in the several age groups have several important practical aspects. In the first place, the

179

total numbers that might be expected in each age group to respond for registration go to determine the ultimate reservoir from which availables were to be drawn. Again, the number of effectives that could be counted upon as obtainable from each of these age groups is material in determining beforehand which of the age groups should be called, in view of the known military needs of the time. Further, the extent to which specific causes of deferment or exemption would affect particular age groups is important. And finally (though this was not a directly military aspect), it is desirable to test the reliability of the usual sources of information for estimating the numbers of male population within particular age groups.

1. *Estimates of size of age groups of males liable for military service—(a) Total for age groups 18–20, 32–45.*—At the time (July, 1918) of preparing for the enlargement, by legislation, of the draft ages to 18 and 45, it was necessary to make an estimate of the number of availables by the inclusion of various age groups. The estimate of July 27 furnished by this office (mentioned already in Chapter II; and printed in Appendix B of this report) indicated that the requisite number of at least 2,000,000 men for the period October, 1918, to June, 1919, could not be obtained without including the extreme ages 18 and 45 in the new registration. This estimate was based on the compared figures of insurance actuaries and the Census Bureau. The actual registration, upon September 12, now makes it possible to compare these estimates with the facts as developed on that registration.

The total number estimated for ages 18–20 and 32–45 was approximately 13,200,000; but, deducting the estimated number of more than 400,000 already in military or naval service, and therefore not due to register, there remained some 12,800,000 due to register. The actual registration, however (excluding the Territories, later registered), totaled more than 13,200,000. It is possible that this number is substantially less than the actual number of male population of those ages not already in military service; but it is not probable; because the publicity drive was so thorough that the number who failed to register, through ignorance or evasive intent, must have been trifling, certainly less than 50,000, and probably even smaller. On the other hand, it is certain that at least that number of registrants, viz, more than 13,200,000, did exist alive outside of military or naval service. Hence, the shortage found by the difference between this number and the highest actuarial or census estimate must represent an error of underestimation. It is interesting to note, therefore, that the total number of registered males of military age 18–20 and 32–45, i. e., 13,228,762 plus upwards of 400,000 estimated to be in military or naval service, or some 13,628,000 in all, amounts to between 300,000 and 400,000 more than even the highest actuarial or census estimate.   How to explain this excess must be left to further study by the experts of the Census Bureau and the actuarial departments.

The following Table 65 shows the summary of different combinations of ages.

TABLE 65.—*Registration, by age groups, compared with census and actuarial estimates.*

	Year.	Registration, by age groups, compared with census and actuarial estimates.		Estimates of male population.			
		Age group.	(1) Registration for continental United States.	(2) . Prudential Insurance (observed).	(3) Prudential Insurance, used by Provost Marshal General (graduated).	(4) Aetna Life Insurance (graduated).	(5) Census Bureau (graduated).
1	1918 ...	18–20	2, 458, 673	3, 129, 430	3, 171, 671	2, 817, 326	3, 131, 552
2	1918 ...	21	958, 739	1, 071, 261	1, 046, 598	951, 029	1, 056, 656
3	1917–18	21–30 22–31	9, 856, 647	9, 783, 681	9, 718, 981	9, 799, 797	9, 731, 062
4	1918 ...	32–36	3, 966, 584	4, 056, 533	4, 018, 205	4, 130, 427	4, 039, 891
5	1918 ...	32–45	10, 349, 650	10, 095, 239	10, 028, 973	10, 507, 763	10, 062, 856
6	1918 ...	37–45	6, 383, 066	6, 038, 706	6, 010, 768	6, 377, 336	6, 022, 965
7	1917–18	18–36	17, 240, 643	18, 040, 905	17, 955, 455	17, 698, 597	17, 959, 161
8	1917–18	18–40	20, 314, 407	21, 134, 034	20, 897, 782	20, 749, 483	20, 909, 406
9	1917–18	' 18–45	23, 908, 576	24, 079, 611	23, 966, 223	24, 075, 915	23, 982, 126
10	1918 ...	18–20 32–36	6, 425, 257	7, 185, 963	7, 189, 876	6, 947, 753	7, 171, 443
11	1918 ...	1 18–20 1 32–45	13, 093, 190	13, 224, 669	13, 200, 644	13, 325, 089	13, 194, 408

1 Includes excess of Form 101 (284,867): see par. (b).

(b) *Total for ages 21–30.*—The total for this age group, 9,856,647, is over 50,000 higher than any of the estimates; this is remarkable, inasmuch as probably 200,000 more should be added to the living males for men enlisted on June 5, 1917, and therefore not registered.

In explanation of the figures for the age group 21–30, it must further be pointed out that the returns from the local boards for the individual ages were furnished by separate tallying of the registration cards by each age, and that this computation was made during the month of September, 1918, while tardy registrations were still proceeding, but that the total registration figures already given in Table 1 were derived from the official registration lists (Form 101) arriving as late as the middle of November, and composed of lists of registrants by name but without the indication of age; and that the total of these later lists, accumulated through September and October, thus included some 300,000 tardy accessions to the registration list. So that the entire registration for September 12 included some 300,-000 of whose particular ages we have no report; we know only that they were somewhere between 18 and 45.   Hence, the total actual registration of ages 18–45, up to November, 1918, exceeds by some

300,000 the total formed by the addition of the above individual age groups in the reports of September, 1918. A small portion of these 300,000 belong presumably in the age 21–30 group.

Moreover, it must be noted (Table 66a) that, in the registration of September 12, 1918, although theoretically it included only ages 18–20 and 32–45 (ages 21–30 of 1917, or ages 22-32 of 1918, having been already registered on June 5, 1917), nevertheless as many as 67,000 persons representing themselves as of ages 21–30 came forward and were therefore explicitly included in the returns made by the boards for that registration; and that a similar addition, numbering 9,000, came forward on June 5–Sept. 11, 1918. These numbers have, therefore, been added into the figures for those ages (given in Tables 65 and 66).

(c) *Total for ages 18–20.*—The registration for the age group 18–20 fell short of the estimate used for male population by more than 700,000. Of this shortage 272,000 had already been foreseen and reckoned upon (Appendix B) as a deduction for prior enlistments. The remaining shortage of over 400,000 can in large part be attributed to enlistments, because between January and July, 1918, more than 200,000 enlisted in the Navy, and a considerable number of these were under 21. Nevertheless, of the total 1,314,000 enlistments (Table 79), nothing like 700,000 can have been under 21. Hence, the population estimates relied upon seem to have been overliberal; but one of the three estimates here given corresponds substantially with the actual registration minus the estimated enlistments.

(d) *Total for age group 32–45.*—For the age group 32–45 the actual registration was more than 300,000 in excess of the actuarial estimate used. It was, however, 158,000 less than the other actuarial estimate given. The estimated prior enlistments for these ages were 170,000 (Appendix B). Making all allowances, therefore, it is plain that the estimate used was as much too low for this age group as it was too high for the 18–20 age group.

(e) *Total for age group 18–45.*—The total for this entire age group, 23,908,576, is within 58,000 of the estimate used, which was the nearest of the three. But it must be remembered that a large number of men had already enlisted before the dates due for the registration of their age groups, and that all enlistments fell between ages 18–45 (except a small number, down to age 16, for the Navy); so that all such enlistments must be added to determine the actual number of living males of those ages. What that number is can only be calculated by a combination of estimates, as the enlistment records in The Adjutant General's Office can not at present be sorted by ages and enlistment dates so as to reveal the answer. This estimated number (already given in Table 2) is 1,438,901; added to the registered men, this would give 25,347,477 as the total actual males of those ages. This figure, however, is 1,250,000 in excess of the highest estimate, which seems disconcerting. The above given estimate of unregistered enlistments is therefore, doubtless, somewhat too high. Nevertheless it was based on the best available data. The dilemma therefore awaits a more convincing solution.

· (f) *Individual ages 18, 19, and 20.*—In Table 66. are shown the figures for the individual ages:

TABLE 66.—*Registration by individual ages.*

	Year.	Age.	Registration by individual ages.	Estimates of male population.			
			(1) Total for first, second, and third registrations.	(2) Prudential Insurance (observed).	(3) Prudential Insurance (graduated).[1]	(4) Ætna Life Insurance (graduated).	(5) Census Bureau (graduated).
1	Total....	....	23, 908, 576	24, 079, 611	23, 966, 223	24, 075, 915	23, 982, 126
2	1918........	18	939, 875	1, 085, 625	1, 065, 285	939, 301	1, 036, 959
3	1918........	19	761, 007	1, 015, 896	1, 056, 291	939, 737	1, 044, 177
4	1918........	20	757, 791	1, 027, 909	1, 050, 095	938, 288	1, 050, 416
5	1918........	21	958, 739	1, 071, 261	1, 046, 598	951, 029	1, 056, 656
6	1917–18....	21–22	1, 018, 407	1, 057, 420	1, 040, 202	983, 350	1, 056, 688
7	1917–18....	22–23	978, 975	1, 035, 483	1, 031, 708	1, 011, 166	1, 047, 175
8	1917–18....	23–24	1, 010, 287	1, 042, 273	1, 021, 315	1, 025, 536	1, 030, 761
9	1917–18....	24–25	997, 544	1, 049, 846	1, 007, 924	1, 028, 934	1, 014, 438
10	1917–18....	25–26	967, 576	993, 176	990, 236	1, 024, 289	998, 014
11	1917–18....	26–27	956, 494	935, 721	970, 849	1, 005, 533	976, 771
12	1917–18....	27–28	960, 460	1, 030, 782	949, 763	976, 507	949, 451
13	1917–18....	28–29	974, 555	840, 661	927, 278	945, 465	918, 569
14	1917–18....	29–30	948, 857	1, 112, 524	902, 994	916, 220	886, 821
15	1917–18....	30–31	1, 043, 492	685, 795	876, 712	882, 797	852, 374
16	1918........	32	499, 902	852, 151	851, 229	854, 168	825, 900
17	1918........	33	927, 968	758, 658	816, 452	834, 507	812, 573
18	1918........	34	920, 355	769, 626	802, 662	823, 500	807, 147
19	1918........	35	804, 778	929, 454	779, 577	813, 151	800, 051
20	1918........	36	813, 581	746, 644	768, 285	805, 101	794, 220
21	1918........	37	823, 150	682, 922	756, 093	794, 004	781, 019
22	1918........	38	836, 280	816, 112	743, 102	776, 512	755, 516
23	1918........	39	725, 416	672, 737	729, 011	752, 435	722, 416
24	1918........	40	688, 918	921, 358	714, 121	727, 953	691, 294
25	1918........	41	648, 599	508, 993	679, 544	702, 637	660, 160
26	1918........	42	693, 657	677, 699	645, 667	680, 824	632, 501
27	1918........	43	654, 915	553, 128	612, 789	663, 167	610, 997
28	1918........	44	624, 129	523, 095	580, 810	648, 070	593, 754
29	1918........	45	688, 002	682, 662	549, 631	631, 734	575, 308
30	Age not reported ...	....	284, 867	....	....	....	....

[1] Used by Provost Marshal General's Office.

For age 18, one of the estimates comes within 600 of the registration.

But it will be noted that the registering number for age 18 is largely in excess of both age 19 and age 20, although in all of the three estimates these three ages grade very close together. This peculiarity of the actual age 19 number must be ascribed in part to the circumstance that the War Department announcement of early September, restricting the first classification group to 19–36 and leaving the ages 18 and 36–45 for later classification and later call, presumably had the effect of inducing an appreciable number of less patriotic young men to postpone their calls, by representing themselves as of age 18 instead of age 19, their true age. In part, however, the excess in age 18 is due also to the effort of impetuous youngsters of 17 to get into the combat; for they were not eligible to enlistment in the Army, and the strict precautions required of recruiting officers made it less difficult to misrepresent successfully one's age to a registrar than to a recruiting officer.

On the whole, therefore, the patriots and the nonpatriots probably contributed equally to this excess. Moreover, as regards the patriotism of these age groups, it must be remembered that the enlistments for all of these ages were (as already pointed-out) probably many thousands more than had been expected. The following incidents are typical:

In a Connecticut town a colored citizen approached the chairman and said: "I'd like to get my nephew's name on that honor list," meaning the list of all the men gone into service from that board. The chairman replied, "Why, I didn't know F. was in the service. I thought he was too young. "Well," replied the other, "you see it is this way: He is only 16, and everybody here knows it, so he went to S., in Massachusetts, and swore that he was 18. He has been in France now for six months." F.'s name was posted.

One was 17 and the other 18, when in the autumn of 1917 they heard the call of the Marines. Not being twins, they had to increase their ages at the recruiting office, in order that the younger might be accepted. They trained at Paris Island and they came home for Christmas as fine soldiers as we ever saw. They honored their uniforms and they were in love with the service and anxious for action. They went to France with the first contingent of Marines, and in our attack at Belleau Wood their platoon was all but wiped out, for the Germans got their range. The older was killed instantly by a direct shell hit, and the other is back in a Hoboken hospital in a pitiable condition. The day after the elder one was reported dead, the father, only 42 years old, sought the recruiting station of the Marines. He interviewed, by lucky chance, the same officer who had enlisted the sons. He was accepted, and followed his sons to Paris Island. Although he is twice as old as any other man in the camp, he has qualified as a marksman and has made good in every way. He is the only man of our 4,000 in the class of September, 1918, who is marked for Class 5 D.

(g) *Individual ages 32, 33, etc., to 36.*—All these upper ages, individually, ran higher in actual registration than the estimates used, and this excess was notable up to age 38.

But the most interesting circumstance is that, in comparing the registered age numbers with the observed numbers, Table 66, the ages 35 and 40 do not show the expected artificial excesses. A well-known feature of census experience (1913 Census Report, Vol. I, Chap. IV, p. 291) is that an excessive number of persons, knowing their age only approximately, give it in figures ending in 5 or 0 ("concentration on multiples of 5"); hence, the actuarial custom is to seek accuracy by "smoothing" or "graduating" the observed figure, i. e., by distributing the excess over the nearest ages. This is illustrated in column 2 as contrasted with column 3 of Table 66; columns 3, 4, and 5 have been "graduated." But in the registration of September 12, 1918, this peculiar popular habit failed to exhibit itself, for the ages 35 and 40 proceeded downward in natural gradation with the adjacent ages. This singular result remains to be explained.

(*h*) *Age 45.*—The special upward turn at age 45, in the registered numbers, is apparently an exception to what has just been pointed out, and a reversion to the usual census experience. Yet it can more fairly be explained, as not an exception, but rather an indication of the desire of the older men to get into the fighting ranks. Beyond a doubt, many men over 45 misrepresented their age in a patriotic attempt to register for service in the draft.

X registered on September 12, 1918, and gave his age as 35 years. He was mailed a questionnaire and took it before the legal advisory board, intending to fill it out, but it appearing to the attorney before whom he went for assistance, that he was far beyond the draft age, he was refused assistance in filling out his questionnaire, and was told to report to his board. He did report to the board and admitted that he was 58 years old. On being questioned why he registered, he stated that he had made three attempts to get into the service and had been turned down. He hoped that this registration would open a way for him to get into the service. He begged the board member, with tears in his eyes, to put him down at not over 45. He offered, as proof of his physical fitness, to whip anyone in the house. Nevertheless, his registration was canceled.

(*i*) *Age 32.*—The noticeably low figure for age 32—in round numbers 500,000 instead of the 940,000 to be expected—calls for special attention. A portion of this 440,000 shortage is obviously due to the three months' difference between the registration dates of 1917 and 1918, i. e., June 5 and September 12; for the men who became 32 after June 5, 1918, and before September 13, 1918, had already registered in 1917, being then 30 years old; thus, the total for age 32 as registered on September 12, 1918, suffered a deduction which may be estimated at one-fourth of the actual number, i. e., one-fourth of about 940,000, or 235,000.

But this still leaves a shortage of some 200,000 to be accounted for. The high number for age 31 (age 30 in 1917), i. e., 1,040,000, might suggest that the same motive of patriotic misrepresentation of age had here operated to reduce age 32 (age 31 in 1917) and to raise age 31 (age 30 in 1917)—the same motive that undoubtedly affected the high numbers for ages 18 and 45. But this motive here fails. It could operate on September 12, 1918, for ages 18 and 45, because the avenue of enlistment was not open to men below or above those ages, and the avenue of the draft registration offered the opportunity;

but it could hardly have operated on June 5, 1917, when age 30 was registered, for enlistment was then free to all men of age 31; moreover, the patriotic readiness to enter by the draft—a readiness obvious enough in 1918—had hardly become noticeable as early as June 5, 1917. No explanation of this sort, therefore, suffices.

It seems probable that the phenomenon of "concentration on multiples of 5 or 0," above mentioned, is here the explanation for the missing 200,000; for ·the age immediately following a multiple of 5 or 0 is usually found to be correspondingly below its normal figure; and it will be noticed that the actuarial figures for "observed" (not "graduated") age 31 (age 32 in 1918), given in column 2 of Table 66, show a shortage more than enough to account·for the shortage here in question.

Nevertheless, after all hypotheses have been tried, the registration figures for age 32 remain an interesting field for speculation. As possibly bearing on the solution, it may be added that approximately the same ratio of shortage appears not only in every State but also in each local board area.

2. *Slackers and nonregistrants on June 5, 1917, and June 5, 1918.*— The foregoing figures give an opportunity for some hypotheses as to the possible extent of failures to register in the earlier two registrations.

(a) *June 5, 1917.*—It is evident that the 76,112 of ages 22–31, who came forward on June 5, August 24, and September 12, 1918, were overdue to register on June 5, 1917. Table 66a shows the distribution by ages.

TABLE 66a.—*Overdue registrants of ages 21–30, 1917, brought out by later registrations.*

	Age in 1918.	Total.	Arriving on June 5–Sept. 11, 1918.	Arriving on Sept. 12, 1918.
1	22–31	76,112	9,098	67,014
2	22	12,533	4,644	7,889
3	23	7,862	870	6,992
4	24	7,227	629	6,598
5	25	7,539	628	6,911
6	26	7,069	531	6,538
7	27	6,212	489	5,723
8	28	6,706	465	6,241
9	29	5,571	392	5,179
10	30	6,967	450	6,517
11	31	8,426		8,426

The local boards were asked this question in November, 1918:

How do you account for the fact that some 50,000 or more persons of those who registered on September 12 gave their ages as between 21 and 30, and, therefore, were apparently men who ought to have registered on June 5, 1917, and have gone unregistered ever since?

The answers to this question indicate that substantially all of the persons who, on September 12, 1918, gave their ages as between 21 and 30, fall within the following categories: (1) Persons who reached the age of 21 between August 24, 1918, the day of the last previous registration, and September 12, 1918; (2) persons who, on June 5, 1917, were either ignorant or neglectful of the requirements of the law, but who, largely as a result of the campaign of publicity which preceded the registration of September 12, 1918, were brought to a clear realization of the duty to register and of the consequences of default; (3) persons who were absent from the country on June 5, 1917, and who, because of ignorance or neglect, failed to register on their return; (4) persons who were in the military or naval service on June 5, 1917, and were subsequently discharged, but because of ignorance or neglect failed to register before September 12, 1918; (5) persons who evaded registration on June 5, 1917, on the pretense that they were over 30 years of age, but when the age limit was raised, realized that evasion was no longer possible and so registered on September 12, 1918, stating their age correctly; (6) aliens who immigrated to this country between June 5, 1917' and September 12, 1918; (7) persons who, on June 5, 1917, were inmates of prisons, asylums, and other institutions, but were not registered at that time because of the ignorance or neglect of the superintendent or other officer in charge.

The further inquiry remains, whether there is any reason to suppose that a still larger number, due to have registered on June 5, 1917, never did register, and exist still as an undiscovered residue. It will be noted that the highest advance estimate (Table 65) for all those age groups 21–30 was approximately 9,800,000 and that the lowest was 9,719,000; whereas the total registration returned from the boards in November, 1917, was 9,580,000; or a shortage of 145,000–214,000; while the final figures for the first registration (up to the last moment of September 11, 1918), were 9,780,535 (Table 2) or a shortage of 20,000 from the highest estimate and an excess of 60,000 over the lowest estimate. To this figure must be added, however, those who were not due to register, viz, those of ages 21–30 already in military service; the exact military and naval strength on April 1, 1917, was 378,619 (Table 80). Therefore, if as many as one-half of these were within ages 21–30, there was not a great shortage due to slackers in the first registration. But no figures are available to show exactly how many men of ages 21–30 were then in the military or naval forces. Hence, the answer to this question must remain for the present unsolved. We know only that at least some part of 76,000 men evaded registration at that time, but did come forward later. But the universal watchfulness for slackers in every community, and the practice of neighbors informing on each other (as noted in Chapter X), makes it certain that the actual loss was small. "The astounding thing about the registration" says one board, "was its unanimity. A few men tried to dodge the first one; but when the names of the registrants were published in the daily papers they were smoked out, and on one excuse or another came in to register."

(b) *June 5, 1918.*—Similarly, a question arises whether there was an extensive number of slackers in the registration of June 5, 1918, for men just arriving at age 21. The actual registration on June 5, 1918, was 735,834 (Chap. II), or some 300,000 short of the highest advance estimate, and 200,000 short of the lowest estimate. What was the explanation of this shortage? The war had then been going on more than a year, and the young men of age 21 had been among the first to enlist; so that this age group was undoubtedly depleted by a large number already in military service, and therefore not due to register. It is, however, impossible that this number amounted to 200,000 or 300,000; the grounds for this opinion are set forth in a note to the compilation of figures in Appendix B. It must be inferred therefore that there was a large shortage in that registration. This shortage can be attributed to the circumstance that the registration affected such a relatively small part of the population, and came amid such other absorbing matters, that the ordinary means of publicity for announcing the duty to register could not have been completely effective.

It was for this reason that, when the registration of September 12, 1918, approached, it was deemed indispensable (as described in Chap. II) to use a maximum effort to obtain a 100 per cent registration, and to place it beyond doubt that the Nation had obtained from this registration the maximum possible number of registrants that were humanly obtainable. In view of the fact, therefore, that the registration of June 5, 1917, fell nominally somewhat short of the advance estimates of male population, and that the registration of June 5, 1918, fell substantially short of the advance estimates, while the registration of September 12, 1918, reached some 400,000 in excess of the advance estimates, it must be concluded that the measures of publicity to secure this result were well advised.

It may be pointed out, finally, that inasmuch as registration is a voluntary act, in the sense that its complete success depends on the voluntary coming forward of the men who are due to register, any measures of the future, based fundamentally on an estimated number of expected registrants, must involve as a part of the problem the measures necessary to insure 100 per cent of the registration.

3. *Distribution of ages by States.*—The distribution of age groups by States (Appendix Table 65-A) has no particular significance in the

arrangements for military service, but will be of some value for various civic purposes.

4. *Effectives in the several age groups.*—One of the most elusive features to estimate, but at the same time one of the most important for military service, was the probable yield of effectives in each age group.

(a) *Ages 21–30.*—For ages 21–30 the first and second registrations supply illuminating data. Table 67 shows the results in Class I effectives for the 10 age groups thus classified. It will be noted that the youngest of the eleven ages yielded effectives in a ratio nearly three times as great as the oldest; and that the ratios descend in regular gradation.

TABLE 67.—*Ratio of effectives, by ages.*

	Ages.	Total registrants June 5, 1917–Sept. 11, 1918.	Placed in Class I.		Placed in deferred classes.	
			Number.	Per cent.	Number.	Per cent.
		10, 679, 814	3, 706, 544	34. 71	6, 973, 270	65. 29
1	1918. 21....................	890, 181	517, 787	58. 17	372, 394	41. 83
2	1917. 21....................	1, 010, 518	468, 294	46. 34	542, 224	53. 66
3	22....................	971, 983	424, 391	43. 66	547, 592	56. 34
4	23....................	1, 003, 689	392, 377	39. 09	611, 312	60. 91
5	24....................	990, 633	350, 835	35. 42	639, 798	64. 58
6	25....................	961, 038.	308, 258	32. 08	652, 780	67. 92
7	26....................	950, 771	280, 700	29. 52	670, 071	70. 48
8	27....................	954, 219	258, 015	27. 04	696, 204	72. 96
9	28....................	969, 376	256, 489	26. 46	712, 887	73. 54
10	29....................	942, 340	220, 369	23. 39	721, 971	76. 61
11	30....................	1, 035, 066	229, 029	22. 12	806, 037	77. 88

(b) *Ages 18–20, 32–36.*—In the estimates submitted by this office on July 27, 1918 (Appendix B), it will be noted that the estimate of effectives for the entire 14 age groups above 31 amounted to less than the estimate of effectives for the 3 age groups 18–20. Had the classification which the boards began in September been completed, we should have had an authentic basis for verifying these estimates for the different ages. But the armistice of November 11 and the consequent abandonment of the classification for ages 37–45 have made it impossible to obtain the expected data for those ages.

For the ages 18–20 and 32–36, which were under classification at the time of the armistice, November 11, no detailed report could be completed by the boards at the time of the preparation of this report. But it proved possible to obtain by telegram from State headquarters an estimate of the results of this classification based on results in 90 per cent of the boards; and these results (Table 68) offer a usable supplement to the more exact results already on record for ages 21–30.

TABLE 68.—*Effectives in age groups 18-20, 32-36.*

Ages.	Registrants, Sept. 12, 1918.	Reported gross Class I.	Effective Class I (71.83. per cent, as in Table 64).		Effectives as estimated July 28, 1918.
			Number.	Per cent of registrants.	
1	18-20.................	2, 458, 673	1, 897, 677	1, 363, 101	55. 44	1, 797, 609
2	18.....................	939, 875	828, 770	595, 305	63. 34	....
3	19.....................	761, 007	· 547, 658	393, 383	51. 69	....
4	20.....................	757, 791	521, 249	374, 413	49. 41	....
5	32-36.................	3, 966, 584	799, 979	574, 625	14. 49	240, 494
6	Total, 18-20, 32-36.	6, 425, 257	2, 697, 656	1, 937, 726	30. 16	2, 038, 103

This table is of the greatest value, because it offers a tangible clue to the man-power possibilities of the upper and the lower ages (i. e., outside the ages 21–30 of the first two registrations).

(1) The first notable feature is that the estimates for the effectives of the lower ages proved to be too high by about 25 per cent. This, of course, was chiefly due to the fact that the total registering number was itself lower than expected (Table 65); that variance has already been commented on in paragraph 1.

(2) The second notable feature is that the estimates for the effectives of the higher ages proved to be too low by nearly 140 per cent. In this case, however, the total registering number was virtually identical with the expected number—only 52,000 short (Table 65). Hence the excessive yield of effectives over estimate was due mainly to the unexpectedly low deductions for claims of deferment. Evidently the men of the upper ages do not need as large an allowance as expected for this item.

(3) The third notable feature is that these two variances from the estimate nearly counteracted each other for the combined ages; so that the result was a number of effectives only 100,000 short of the estimate. This result must, however, usually be expected in dealing with large masses; the errors of estimate on details tend to counteract each other.

(4) The wide difference between the percentage of effectives yielded for the upper and the lower ages (14.49 per cent for ages 32–36 and 55.44 per cent for ages 18–20) merely confirms the general assumption that the lower ages must always be deemed the most available as a reservoir of military man power.

(5) Finally, it must be pointed out that the 28 per cent discount from the reported gross Class I, here used from Table 64 (based on ages 21–30) to find the effective Class I, is perhaps not large enough for the ages 18–20, 32–36; the conditions attending the completion of

the process of classification after November 11 were peculiar. A footnote to Appendix Table 64–A explains the qualifications which should be considered.

(II) RACE AND COLOR GROUPS.

Color and race were, of course, not material under the law and the regulations for the purpose of the classification (except so far as noncitizen Indians were exempt from draft). But the organization of the Army placed colored soldiers in separate units; and the several calls for mobilization were, therefore, affected by this circumstance, in that no calls could be issued for colored registrants until the organizations were ready for them. In this and in some other aspects, therefore, it is worth while to note certain differences as to race and color groups.

1. *Colored and white registration compared.*—The colored and white registrants, for all three registrations, numbered as shown in Table 71 following:

TABLE 71.—*Colored and white registration compared.*

	Colored and white registration compared.	Number.	Per cent of total colored and white registration.	Per cent in each registration.
	Total colored and white registrants:			
1	June 5, 1917–Sept. 12, 1918..........	23,779,997	100.00	....
2	Colored.........................	2,290,527	9.63	....
3	White.........................	21,489,470	90.37	....
4	June 5, 1917–Sept. 11, 1918	10,640,846	....	100.00
5	Colored.........................	1,078,331	....	10.13
6	White.........................	9,562,515	....	89.87
7	Sept. 12, 1918.....................	13,139,151	....	100.00
8	Colored.........................	1,212,196	....	9.23
9	White.........................	11,926,955	....	90.77

In Appendix Table 71–A is shown the distribution by States. It need only be noted here that the total registration above given is not equal to the total registration set forth in Table 2, for the reason already mentioned elsewhere, viz, that the total in Table 2, taken from the final registration lists of September 12, 1918, arriving in November, 1918, did not show colored and white registrations separately and did include some 300,000 additional registrants during September and October, 1918, while the present figures are taken from earlier board reports of September, 1918, which showed colored and white registrants separately.

2. *Colored and white classification compared.*—The results of the classification of December 15, 1917, to September 11, 1918, in respect to colored and white registrants are shown in the following Table 72:

TABLE 72.—*Colored and white classification compared.*

	Color ed and white classification compared.	Number.	Per cent of total classified.	Per cent of classified.
1	Total colored and white registered:			
2	June 5, 1917, to Sept. 11, 1918	10' 640, 846	100. 00	....
3	Total colored registered	1, 078, 331	10. 13	100. 00
4	Class I	556, 917	....	51. 65
5	Deferred classes	521, 414	....	....
6	Total white registered	9, 562, 515	89. 87	100. 00
7	Class I	3, 110, 659	....	32. 53
8	Deferred classes	6, 451, 856	....	....
9	Percentage accepted for service on calls {Colored.	....	....	36. 23
10	before Dec. 15, 1917 (report for 1917). {White..	....	....	24. 75

In explanation of· the higher figures for colored registrants in Class I, three general considerations may here be pointed out.

In the first place, enlistments depleted the white Class I in the South of a large proportion of its eligibles, enlistment not being available for colored registrants except to a negligible degree (only 1.5 per cent of enlistments were of colored men); hence the colored Class I in the southern States, was certain to be large in relation to the white Class I, remaining for draft after enlistments. It is estimated that the white enlistments of ages 21–30 numbered 650,000, while the colored numbered 4,000; thus the former quantity represented a depletion of the white Class I.

In the second place, the ratio of colored delinquents in the South was ratably higher than that of white delinquents, and this served to increase the nominal Class I of colored registrants (delinquents being placed in Class I under the regulations). Labor conditions and other circumstances more fully mentioned in this chapter in the section on delinquency account for this higher ratio.

In the third place, social, agricultural, and industrial conditions, of course, lead to variant results of classification in different States and different groups of States. For example, the records of appeals from rulings on dependency show that in the South, as a whole, the average annual income of those making dependency claims is surprisingly low, and the average for the colored race is undoubtedly lower than for the whites. The result has been that many registrants both white and colored, have been put in Class I on the ground that their allotment and allowances while in the Army would furnish an equivalent support to their dependents.

The net result of the first two foregoing considerations would be to readjust the ratios of the colored and the white Class I, respectively, to approximately 42 and 35 per cent.

As a further indication of the closeness to which the two ratios approximate, after making all these special allowances, it should be noted that the numbers selected for full military service (Group A, as shown in Table 53) were respectively: Colored, 342,277; white, 1,916,750, and that these figures represent respectively 31.74 and 26.84 per cent of the total colored and the total white registrants (of the first two registrations), thus leaving them only 5 per cent apart. Now the same Table 53 shows that, for every 100 men examined physically, the ratio of colored men found qualified physically for general military service was substantially higher than the ratio for white men, by just 5 per cent, viz, 74.60 per cent as against 69.71 per cent; this difference in physical qualifications therefore accounts for this remaining excess (5 per cent) of colored registrants over white registrants accepted for full military service.

Only a careful scrutiny of these and other considerations, applicable under the law and regulations, will suffice in analyzing the final significance of these figures for the colored and white Class I ratio.

3. *Colored and white inductions compared.*—The numbers for colored and white registrants, respectively, depended of course upon the requisitions received at this office from the War Department for men composing the different units. And this was dependent more or less on the availability of colored men for the different units under organization. The following Table 73 shows the result of these calls; Appendix Table 73-A shows the distribution by States.

TABLE 73.—*Colored and white inductions compared.*

Colored and white inductions compared.	Number.	Per cent of inductions.
1 Total colored and white inductions, June 5, 1917–Nov. 11, 1918.	2, 810, 296	100. 00
2 Colored..	367, 710	13. 08
3 White..	2, 442, 586	86. 92
4 From registration of June 5, 1917–Sept. 11, 1918	2, 299, 157	....
5 From registration of Sept. 12, 1918.................	143, 429	....

4. *The negro in relation to the draft.*—The part that has been played by the negro in the great world drama upon which the curtain is now about to fall is but another proof of the complete unity of the various elements that go to make up this great Nation. Passing through the sad and rigorous experience of slavery; ushered into a sphere of civil and political activity where he was to match his endeavors with those of his former masters still embittered by defeat; gradually working his way toward the achievement of success that would enable both him and the world to justify his new life of freedom; surrounded for over half a century of his new life by the specter of that slavedom through which he had for centuries past laboriously

toiled; met continuously by the prejudices born of tradition; still the slave, to a large extent, of superstition fed by ignorance—in the light of this history, some doubt was felt and expressed, by the best friends of the negro, when the call came for a draft upon the man-power of the Nation, whether he would possess sufficient stamina to measure up to the full duty of citizenship, and would give to the Stars and Stripes, that had guaranteed for him the same liberty now sought for all nations and all races, the response that was its due. And, on the part of many of the leaders of the negro race, there was apprehension that the sense of fair play and fair dealing, which is so essentially an American characteristic, would not, nay could not, in a country of such diversified views, with sectional feeling still slumbering but not dead, be meted out to the members of the colored race.

How groundless such fears, how ill considered such doubts, may be seen from the statistical record of the draft with relation to the negro. His race furnished its quota, and uncomplainingly, yes, cheerfully. History, indeed, will be unable to record the fullness of his spirit in the war, for the reason that opportunities for enlistment were not opened to him to the same extent as to the whites. But enough can be gathered from the records to show that he was filled with the same feeling of patriotism, the same martial spirit, that fired his white fellow citizen in the cause for world freedom.

As a general rule, he was fair in his dealings with draft officials; and in the majority of cases, having the assistance of his white employers, he was able to present fairly such claims for deferment or discharge as he may have had, for the consideration of the various draft boards. In consequence, there appears to have been no racial discrimination made in the determination of his claims. Indeed, the proportion of claims granted to claims filed by members of the negro race compare favorably with the proportion of claims granted to members of the white race.

That the men of the colored race were as ready to serve as their white neighbors is amply proved by the reports from the local boards. A Pennsylvania board, remarking upon the eagerness of its colored registrants to be inducted, illustrated this by the action of one registrant, who, upon learning that his employer had had him placed upon the Emergency Fleet list, quit his job. Another registrant, who was believed by the board to be above draft age, insisted that he was not, and, in stating that he was not married, explained that he "wanted only one war at a time."

The following descriptions from Oklahoma and Arkansas boards are typical, the first serving to perpetuate one of the best epigrams of the war:

We tried to treat the negroes with exactly the same consideration as was shown the whites. We had the same speakers to address them. The Rotary Club presented them with small silk flags, as they did the whites. The band turned out to escort them to the train. And the negroes went to camp with as cheerful a spirit as did the white men. One of them when asked if he were going to France, said, "No, sir, I'se not gwine *to* France. I'se gwine *through* France."

In dealing with the negroes, the southern boards gained a richness of experience that is without parallel. No other class of citizens was more loyal to the Government, or more ready to answer the country's call. The only blot upon their military record was the great number of delinquents among the more ignorant; but in the majority of cases this was traced to an ignorance of the regulations, or to the withholding of mail by the landlord (often himself an aristocratic slacker) in order to retain the man's labor.

On October 1, 1917, in order that there might be no question of the full protection of the rights of the negroes, and that thorough examination might be made into all matters affecting their relation to the war and its many agencies, there was announced the appointment of Emmett J. Scott as special assistant to the Secretary of War. Having been for 18 years confidential secretary to the late Booker T. Washington, and being at the time of his appointment secretary of the Tuskegee Normal and Industrial Institute for negroes, he was peculiarly fitted to render necessary advice to the War Department with respect to the colored people of the various States, to look after all matters affecting the interests of negro selectives and enlisted men, and to inquire into the treatment accorded them by the various officials connected with the War Department. In the position occupied by him, the special assistant to the Secretary of War was thus enabled to obtain a proper perspective both of the attitude of selective service officials to the negro, and of the negro to the war, and especially to the draft. As the representative of his race, his expressions, therefore, have great weight. In a memorandum addressed to this office, on the subject of the relation of the negro to the war and especially to the draft, on December 12, 1918, he wrote:

The attitude of the negro to the war, and especially to the draft, was one of complete acceptance to the draft, in fact, of an eagerness to accept its terms. There was a deep resentment in many quarters that he was not permitted to *volunteer*, as white men, by the thousands, were permitted to do in connection with National Guard units and other branches of military service which were closed to colored men. One of the brightest chapters in the whole history of the war is the negro's eager acceptance of the draft and his splendid willingness to fight. His only resentment was due to the limited extent to which he was allowed to join and participate in combatant or "fighting" units. The number of colored draftees accepted for military duty, and the comparatively small number of them claiming exemptions, as compared with the total number of white and colored men called and drafted, presents an interesting study and reflects much credit upon this racial group.

Many influences were brought to bear upon the negro to evade his duty to the Government. Some effort in certain sections of the country was made to induce them not to register. That the attempt to spread German propaganda was a miserable failure may be seen from the statement of the Chief of the Bureau of Investigation of the Department of Justice to the United States Senate committee:

The negroes didn't take to these stories, however, as they were too loyal. Money spent in the South for propaganda was thrown away.

Then, too, these evil influences were more than offset by the various publicity and "promotion of morale" measures carried on through the office of the special assistant to the Secretary of War, and his assistants. Correspondence was kept up with influential negroes all over the country. Letters, circulars, and news items for the purpose of effecting and encouraging the continued loyalty of the negro citizens were regularly issued to the various papers comprising both the white and negro press. A special committee of 100 colored speakers was appointed to deliver public patriotic addresses all over the country, under the auspices of the Committee on Public Information, stating the war aims of the Government and seeking to keep unbroken the spirit of loyalty of colored American citizens. A special conference of negro editors was called to meet in Washington in June, 1918, under the auspices of the Committee on Public Information, in order to gather and disseminate the thought and public opinion of the various leaders of the negro race. Such has been only a part of the work of the department of the special assistant to the Secretary of War in the record of the marshaling of the man power of the American Nation.

The appreciation of this representative of the colored race for the cooperation shown by the Selective Service administration, especially as it affected members of the colored race, in reference to occasional complaints received, will appear from the following extract from a memorandum written to this office on September 12 by the special assistant to the Secretary of War:

Throughout my tenure here I have keenly appreciated the prompt and cordial cooperation of the Provost Marshal General's Office with that particular section of the office of the Secretary of War especially referred to herein. The Provost Marshal General's Office has carefully investigated and has furnished full and complete reports in each and every complaint or case referred to it for attention, involving discrimination, race prejudice, erroneous classification of draftees, etc., and has rectified these complaints whenever it was found, upon investigation, that there was just ground for the same. Especially in the matter of applying and carrying out the Selective Service Regulations, the Provost Marshal General's Office has kept a watchful eye upon certain local exemption boards which seemed disinclined to treat negro draftees on the same basis as other Americans subject to the draft law. It is an actual fact that in a number of instances, where flagrant violations have occurred in the application of the draft law to negro men in certain sections of the country, local exemption boards have been removed bodily and new boards have been appointed to supplant them. In several instances these new boards so appointed have been ordered by the Provost Marshal General to reclassify colored men who had been unlawfully conscripted into the Army or who had been wrongfully classified; as a result of this action hundreds of colored men have had their complaints remedied and have been properly reclassified.

It is also valuable to note the opinion of this representative of the colored race as to the results of the negroes' participation in the war:

In a word, I believe that the negro's participation in the war, his eagerness to serve, and his great courage and demonstrated valor across the seas, have given him a new idea of *Americanism* and likewise have given to the white people of our country a new idea of his citizenship, his real character and capabilities, and his 100 per cent Americanism. Incidentally the negro has been helped in many ways, physically and mentally and has been made into an even more satisfactory asset to the Nation.

5. *The Indian in relation to the draft.*—The registration of Indians presented at the outset some difficulties, owing mainly to the circumstance that noncitizen Indians were not liable to the selective draft, and that it was not always easy to ascertain the identity of the noncitizen Indians. These obstacles were, however, speedily overcome by inquiries and negotiations, particularly in the State of New York and in one or two Western States. The regulations (as already noted in Chapter II) provided that Indians domiciled in Government reservations should be registered with the Government agents and their registration returns forwarded through the Commissioner of Indian Affairs; the cards of citizen Indians being afterwards filed with the nearest local boards; for this reason, the September reports of race and color registration received from the local boards for the registration of September 12, 1918, were not able to indicate separately the number of Indians registered. These numbers have been obtained from the Commissioner of Indian Affairs; but they did not discriminate between the citizen and the noncitizen Indians; it may be assumed, however, that more than one-half of the registrants reported were citizen Indians.

In determining the citizenship of Indians, the rules laid down by the Bureau of Indian Affairs were followed. Generally speaking, an Indian born in the United States is a citizen if he, or his father or mother prior to his birth or before he attained the age of 21, was allotted land or received a patent in fee prior to May 8, 1906; or if he was allotted land subsequent to May 8, 1906, and received a patent in fee to his land; or if he was residing in the old Indian Territory on March 3, 1901; or if he has lived separate and apart from his tribe and has adopted the habits of civilized life.

It is beyond doubt that many Indians voluntarily registered, who were not bound to do so. Moreover, the report of the Commissioner of Indian Affairs for 1918 (dated Sept. 30, 1918), estimates that over 8,000 Indians entered some branch of the military service. He continues:

Of this number approximately 6,500 are in the Army, 1,000 in the Navy and 500 in other military work. It is also significant that fully 6,000 of these entered by enlistment. Moreover, it should go into the record that many Indians from our northern reservations enrolled in Canadian military organizations before the declaration of war by the United States. Their letters from cantonments or abroad are full of interest and in unpretentious language sound a note of steadfast courage, optimism, and a broadened view of the great events in which they mingle. Considering the large number of old and infirm Indians and others not acceptable under the draft, leaving about 33,000 of military eligibility, I regard their representation of 8,000 in camp and actual warfare as furnishing a ratio to population unsurpassed, if equaled, by any other race or nation. I am very proud of their part in this war.

The light here furnished, by the figures of the local board reports, upon the manner in which the members of the Indian race made their contribution to the raising of our armed forces, appears from the following Table 74:

TABLE 74.—*Ratio of Indian deferment claims and inductions.*

	Ratio of Indian deferment claims and inductions.	Number.	Per cent of Indian registrants.
1	Total Indians registered	17,313	....
2	First and second registration	11,803	100.00
3	June 5, 1917	10,464	88.66
4	June 5–Aug. 24, 1918	1,339	11.34
5	Third registration of Sept. 12, 1918	5,510	....
6	Indians claiming deferment prior to Sept. 11, 1918	228	1.93
7	Indians inducted prior to Sept. 11, 1918	6,509	55.15

Comparing these figures with the general averages (Tables 62 and 78), it will be seen that the ratio of Indians claiming deferment was negligible as compared with the average for all registrants; and that the ratio of Indian registrants inducted was more than twice as high as the average for all registrants.

As the raising of the Army proceeded, and the organizations entered upon their transit overseas, it was seen that the traditional aptitude of the Indian race for the military career was being verified, and that the men of this breed were nobly showing their zeal for the great cause. The story of their share in it will some day be told in full. The following item from the Field Army newspaper, Stars and Stripes, in the November issue, 1918, suggests something of the flavor imparted to the battle field by this band of red men:

It was the Prussian Guard against the American Indian on the morning of October 8 in the hills of Champagne. When it was all over, the Prussian Guards were farther on their way back toward the Aisne, and warriors of 13 Indian tribes looked down on the town of St. Etienne. The Indians—one company of them— were fighting with, the Thirty-sixth Division, made up of Texas and Oklahoma rangers and oil men, for the most part. "The Millionaire Company" was the title that had followed the Indians from Camp Bowie, Wyo., and there followed them also a legend of $1,000 checks cashed by Indian buck privates—of privates who used to spend their hours on pass in 12-cylinder motor cars—of a company football team that was full of Carlisle stars and had won a camp championship. Collectively, they owned many square miles of the richest oil and mineral lands of Oklahoma, and back home there were thousands of dollars in royalties piling up every day for the buying of Liberty bonds.

In the company were Creeks and Sioux, Seminoles, Apaches, Wyandottes, Choctaws, Iroquois, and Mohawks. It was a company with a roll of names that was the despair of the regimental paymaster, who never could keep track of Big Bear, Rainbow Blanket, Bacon Rind, Hohemanatubbe, and the 246 other original dialect nomenclature.

The Commissioner's concluding words may here be quoted:

I reluctantly withhold a detailed account of the many instances of tribal and personal patriotism and of individual valor and achievement by our Indian soldiers in the service of both Canada and the United States that came to my attention during the year, for no record here would seem fittingly impartial that did not include the hundreds of noteworthy and authenticated incidents on the reservation, in the camps, and in France that have been almost daily recounted in the public prints. The complete story would be a voluminous narration of scenes, episodes, eloquent appeal, stirring action, and glorious sacrifice that might better be written into a deathless epic by some master poet born out of the heroic travail of a world-embattled era.

(III.) DELINQUENTS, DESERTERS, AND RESISTANTS.

1. *Evasion of the draft; slackers, delinquents, and deserters; distinctions explained.*—Evasion of the draft was attempted by comparatively few persons. Nevertheless, to deal with these efforts proved to be one of the most difficult problems in the administration of the selective service law.

The would-be draft evaders were in general of three kinds: Those who failed to register, those who failed to submit themselves in the interim to the jurisdiction of the local board, and those who failed to obey the orders of the local board, or other competent authority, to report for military duty. These three groups came to be termed, respectively, slackers, delinquents, and deserters.

The term "slacker," meaning a person who had failed to do his part in the national defense, had come into general use by the time of the first registration on June 5, 1917. For that reason, usage of local boards came to apply that term to persons who failed to register, being the earliest stage of an attempt to evade military duty.

Of those who registered, a number subsequently failed to report to the local boards for physical examination, or failed to file questionnaires as required by the regulations; these were termed "delinquents."

Special orders were issued to delinquents by State adjutants general, directing them to report for military duty at a specified day and hour. Unless the order was rescinded upon the delinquent's reporting to the adjutant general, he was in the military service from and after the day and hour specified. If a delinquent failed to report, as directed, he was a "deserter." Other registrants became deserters by a different method. As the process of classification and selection proceeded, certain registrants were selected for service by their local boards and were ordered to report for military duty at a specified time; this process was termed "induction." A registrant who, upon being inducted into the military service, failed to report for military duty, was a deserter.

Briefly, then, a "slacker" was a person who failed to register; a "delinquent" was a registrant who failed to return the questionnaire or to report for physical examination; and a "deserter" was a registrant who failed to obey an order to report for military duty.

2. *Methods of detecting and apprehending slackers, delinquents, and deserters.*—The authority and duty of State and Federal police officers to apprehend slackers, delinquents, and deserters appears in the selective service law and regulations and other Federal statutes. Section 6 of the selective service act authorized the President to utilize the services of both State and Federal officers in the execution of the act. By the selective service regulations, section 49, it was made the duty of all State and Federal police officials to locate and take into custody, and to bring forthwith before local boards, all those who failed to return their questionnaires, to appear for physical examination, to report change of status, to report for any duty, or to perform any act required by the regulations or by proper direction of the local or district boards. The selective service regulations, section 57, provided that registrants must always keep in their possession, either the registration certificate, or, after classification, the final classification card, and must exhibit the same when called upon to do so by any local or district board member or police official.

Desertion is, of course, an offense by military law. State and Federal police officers are by statute authorized to arrest without warrant deserters from the Army and Navy of the United States, and a reward of $50 is payable for the apprehension and delivery to military control of each draft deserter who is physically qualified for military service and whose offense the local board finds to have been willful. In addition, failure to perform any duty imposed by the selective service act or the regulations made thereunder, is a mis- demeanor, punishable by fine and imprisonment. The Bureau of Investigation of the Department of Justice is charged by statute with the detection and prosecution of crimes against the United States.

Federal and State police officers alike have been very diligent in apprehending slackers, delinquents, and deserters. The agents of the Bureau of Investigation of the Department of Justice have been pioneers in this work. They have been ably assisted by State police officers, by the military and naval intelligence bureaus, by local and district board members, and by certain volunteer organizations, notably the American Protective League, working both in cooperation with the Department of Justice and independently. The United States attorneys have submitted reports to the Department of Justice showing that more than 10,000 prosecutions for failure to register had been instituted on or before June 30, 1918. It has been the policy of the Department of Justice to prosecute only when the failure to register appears to have been clearly willful. Up to that date the agents of the Bureau of Investigation of that department had made 220,747 investigations of failure to register and delinquency, resulting in the induction into military service of 23,495 persons.

Many of the persons whose cases have been investigated for failure to register have asserted that they were not within registration age. Effective investigation of such assertions was made by examination of public school records, life insurance records, birth and marriage records, immigration records, records of qualified voters, and records under the liquor laws of certain States (which require the affidavit of the person obtaining intoxicants from a common carrier that he has attained his twenty-first birthday). Thousands of letters have been received by the various authorities, reporting alleged instances of failure to register, of false statements submitted on questionnaires, and of failure to perform other duties under the selective service law. How keen the local communities were to aid the boards by informing on slackers is noted in Chapter X.

In addition to the general method of work on specific cases and running down complaints, as indicated in the preceding paragraph, this office made arrangements with manufacturers and other employers of labor to ask all applicants for employment to exhibit their registration and classification cards, and to advise the authorities of all persons who did not have them. Federal agents were stationed at large employment agencies, made visits from time to time to large lodging houses, and otherwise endeavored to attack the problem as systematically as practicable. Under the authority of section 57, Selective Service Regulations, State and Federal police officials have demanded of persons apparently of registration age the exhibition of registration certificates and certificates of final classification. From this practice developed the occasional so-called "slacker raids."

"Slacker raids."—At Pittsburgh, Pa., the agents of the Department of Justice, in March, 1918, arranged the first general canvass for draft evaders taking place in a specific locality. The agents of the Department of Justice, the police of the city of Pittsburgh, and the members of the American Protective League all cooperated in an effort to see that every man apparently within the draft age was called upon within a limited time, under authority of section 57 of the Selective Service Regulations, to exhibit a certificate showing his draft status, and that those who appeared to be delinquent were taken before the local boards for investigation. This canvass was successful and resulted in a large number of deserters being sent to mobilization camps and in many delinquents being reported to their local boards.

Subsequently this plan was tried by the Department of Justice in other localities with considerable success. In Chicago and Boston about 700 and 800 men, respectively, were found to be deserters and sent to camp.

The largest canvass arranged by the Department of Justice was conducted in New York City from September 3 to September 6, 1918, the report of that department showing that in New York, Brooklyn, and Jersey City 50,187 men were examined. About 15,000 of them were found to have become delinquents and were referred to their proper local boards; 1,505 were sent to camp as deserters, making a total of 16,505 draft evaders disposed of. The agencies employed in the raid were the marshals, deputy marshals, and special agents of the Department of Justice, police and detectives of the city of New York, members of the American Protective League, as well as some soldiers and sailors. It was not intended that the soldiers and sailors should make arrests, but that they should be used for the purpose of guarding prisoners and for disposing of men apprehended who were found to be deserters from the Army and Navy. Because of the various organizations involved, the large number of men engaged in the work, and the large number of men apprehended some confusion and lack of judgment in handling individual cases resulted. The methods followed were severely criticized by certain newspapers and by Senators on the floor of the Senate; the action taken was equally vigorously defended by certain other newspapers and Senators. This raid served not only to apprehend more than 16,000 delinquents and deserters, but the publicity given it caused many registrants who had been lax in keeping in touch with their local boards suddenly to realize the danger of that course and to communicate with their boards immediately for the purpose of putting their records in proper shape.

On a survey of this occurrence it now seems that the general purpose and scheme of the raid was meritorious, and that good results were obtained, but that in detail mistakes were made, which may be attributed to overzealousness on the part of officers who were making vigorous and effective efforts to accomplish the laudable purpose of apprehending draft evaders.

3. *Reported and net reported desertions.*—(a) *Reported desertions.*— The total number of registrants of the first and second registrations who have been reported by State adjutants general and local boards to The Adjutant General of the Army as deserters is 474,861 (Table 75). More than three-fourths of these registrants have become deserters because, having failed to return the questionnaire or to report for physical examination, and having been reported to the State adjutants general by the local boards as delinquent, they failed to obey the induction order mailed to them by that officer. The others acquired the status of desertion after classification and physical examination through failure to obey the local board's order to report for entrainment to camp. In other words, draft deserters became such because

they failed to perform a duty imposed on them by law, and not because they committed the affirmative act of absenting themselves from their post of duty. Generally speaking, they are passive deserters, as contrasted to active deserters, that is, to soldiers who desert after they have been mustered into the service and have acquired military training. The intent to evade military duty may be as strong in the first instance as in the second. Doubtless, however, many registrants have been charged with desertion who in fact had no intention to evade military service, but through ignorance permitted themselves to become delinquent. It is difficult to believe that men of military age in the United States could have remained wholly ignorant of the obligations imposed on them by the Selective Service Law and Regulations; but the experience of the draft officials shows that, whatever the cause, some persons did fail to comprehend them or were indifferent to their demands.

(b) *Net reported desertions.*—But the reports of desertions represent only the technical state of the record as made when the apparent default occurred. Table 75 shows the total number of desertions reported, and the net number of desertions remaining after deduction of those cases otherwise accounted for upon inquiry:

TABLE 75.—*Ratio of reported and outstanding desertions.*

	Ratio of reported and outstanding desertions.	Number.	Per cent of reported desertions.	Per cent of cancellations.	Per cent of net desertions.
1	Total reported desertions Jun. 5, 1917, to Sept. 11, 1918	474, 861	100. 00		
2	Otherwise accounted for as not desertions	111, 839	23. 55	100. 00	
3	Enlistments explicitly accounted for	74, 228		66. 36	
4	Deaths	2, 726		2. 44	
5	Foreign service	1, 778		1. 60	
6	Enemy aliens	33, 107		29. 60	
7	Net reported desertions	363, 022	76. 45		100. 00
8	Apprehended or otherwise disposed of	67, 838			18. 69
9	Net outstanding desertions	295, 184			81. 31

It thus appears that of the 474,861 reports of desertion that have been made, more than 111,839 have been found to be explainable, either by the prior enlistment of the person in the United States Army, Navy, or Marine Corps, by his entry into the army of a country at war with the enemy of the United States, by his death, or by his citizenship in an enemy nation.

(1) *Enlistments.*—From June 5, 1917, the first registration day, until December 15, 1917, registrants were permitted to enlist in the Army, with the result that a great many did so without informing their local boards. When the boards sent out questionnaires in December, 1917, many of these registrants, being already in the Army

and possibly feeling that it was unnecessary to return the questionnaire, failed to do so. The local board, not being advised of the enlistment and failing to receive the questionnaire, reported and advertised the registrant as delinquent. Similar conditions existed with respect to many registrants who entered the Navy or Marine Corps, enlistment in which was permitted under certain conditions until August 8, 1918. More than 74,228 such cases have been discovered. Up to this time it has been impracticable to compare the draft desertion records with the personnel records of the Army, Navy, and Marine Corps. When that is done, doubtless many thousand more names will be removed from the lists of reported draft deserters.

Furthermore, 1,778 deserters are found to have enlisted in the armies of nations associated with the United States in the present war. Under the authority of the act of May 7, 1917, the British have recruited about 48,000 men in the United States, the Poles have recruited about 18,000, and the Czecho-Slovaks have recruited a considerable number. It is also known that many registrants went to Canada and there enlisted. Doubtless, many such registrants failed to advise their boards of their enlistment or to return their questionnaires, and in consequence they are now carried as deserters.

(2) *Deaths.*—At least 2,726 reported deserters are found to have died and for that reason to have failed to return questionnaires, the local board at the time of making the reports not having been advised of such deaths. It is also probable that the death of other reported deserters has not been discovered.

(3) *Alien enemies.*—More than 33,107 persons who were alien enemies failed to return the questionnaire, or failed to submit to the local board any proof of German or Austrian citizenship. They too were reported as deserters; although the regulations, if the facts had been known at the time, required their exemption whether or not the questionnaire was returned.

The number of reported deserters is, therefore, too large by at least 111,839; the number of registrants who, at any time, have actually been in the status of desertion does not exceed 363,022. Enlistments in the Army, Navy, and Marine Corps, and in the armies of the allies, deaths, and alien enemy citizenship, yet to be discovered, will reduce this number still further.

(c) *Desertions disposed of.*—Of these 363,022 net reported deserters, 67,838 have been reported to have been apprehended or their cases otherwise to have been locally disposed of, leaving 295,184 deserters now at large and yet to be disposed of. The methods by which this large number of draft deserters have been apprehended are explained in the preceding paragraph 2. Although the figures are not available, it is known that the majority of those deserters who were apprehended and sent to camp were either restored to duty without trial;

having been able to show to the satisfaction of the commanding officer of the camp that their offense was not willful, or were discharged as physically disqualified. Only a comparatively small number have been brought before a court-martial.

4. *Reported desertions, by color, compared.*—Of the 474,861 reported deserters, 369,030 are white registrants, and 105,831 are colored registrants; the ratio of white reported deserters to white registrants being 3.86, and the ratio of colored reported deserters to colored registrants being 9.81. Table 76 shows the figures in detail; in Appendix Table 76–A, the variances in the several States are given.

TABLE 76.—*Reported desertions, by color, compared.*

	Reported desertions, by color, compared.	Number.	Per cent of total desertions.	Per cent of desertions by color.
1	Total colored and white registrants, June 5, 1917, to Sept. 11, 1918	10, 640, 846	100. 00	....
2	Total reported desertions	474, 861	4. 46	....
3	Total colored registrants	1, 078, 331	....	100. 00
4	Reported desertions	105, 831	. 99	9. 81
5	Total white registrants	9, 562, 515	....	100. 00
6	Reported desertions	369, 030	3. 47	3. 86

These figures of reported desertions, however, lose their significance when the facts behind them are studied. There is in the files of this office a series of letters from governors and draft executives of southern States, called forth by inquiry for an explanation of the large percentage of negroes among the reported deserters and delinquents. With striking unanimity the draft authorities replied that this was due to two causes; first, ignorance and illiteracy, especially in the rural regions, to which may be added a certain shiftlessness in ignoring civic obligations; and secondly, the tendency of the negroes to shift from place to place. The natural inclination to roam from one employment to another has been accentuated by unusual demands for labor incident to the war, resulting in a considerable flow of colored men to the North and to various munition centers. This shifting reached its height in the summer of 1917, shortly after the first registration, and resulted in the failure of many men to keep in touch with their local boards, so that questionnaires and notices to report did not reach them.

With equal unanimity the draft executives report that the amount of willful delinquency or desertion has been almost nil. Several describe the strenuous efforts of negroes to comply with the regulations, when the requirements were explained to them, many registrants traveling long distances to report in person to the adjutant general of the State. The conviction resulting from these reports is that the colored men as a whole responded readily and gladly to their military obligations once their duties were understood.

5. *Reported desertions, by nationality, compared.*—Of the 474,861 deserters reported, the registration cards of 185,081 state that they are aliens. Of this number 22,706 had declared their intention to become citizens, and were, therefore, subject to draft, while 129,268 had not declared such intention, and were, therefore, on proper proof of alienage, entitled to exemption. There were also 33,107 enemy aliens, who of course would not have been accepted in any event. Table 77 shows the figures for these groups; Appendix Table 77–A shows the variances for the several States.

TABLE 77.—*Reported desertions, by citizenship, compared.*

	Reported desertions, by citizenship, compared.	Number.	Per cent of registrants.	Per cent of desertions by nationality.
1	Total alien and citizen registrants June 5, 1917 to Sept. 11, 1918	10,679,814	100.00	....
2	Total desertions	474,861	4.45	....
3	Total alien registrants	1,703,006	....	100.00
4	Reported alien desertions	185,081	1.73	10.87
5	Total citizen registrants	8,976,808	....	100.00
6	Reported citizen desertions	289,780	2.71	3.23

There are two main reasons for the large proportion of alien deserters. The first is that many aliens, knowing that under the selective service law (and also, for many countries, by treaty) they were entitled to exemption, believed that, by stating on the registration cards that they were aliens, they had performed their full duty with respect to the draft; they ignored the regulations which required them to submit proof of alienage. The second is that many of them did not speak English, were ignorant of the laws and customs of this country, did not know that they were required to keep their local boards informed of their addresses, and failed to realize their obligations to this country under the selective service law. And the difficulty experienced by the local boards in reading and writing their names frequently caused the mail notices addressed to these registrants to go astray.

Apart from the foregoing explanations, however, which would suffice to show that such aliens did not desert in the ordinary sense; but merely failed to come forward to claim their exemption, there was undoubtedly a large exodus of aliens from some of the border States, and those near the seaboard, where the easiest course for these ignorant and misguided persons seemed to lie in a flight beyond the national boundaries. The percentages for the States of Arizona, Florida, New Mexico, Connecticut, and Massachusetts reveal this; and the same feature was pointed out in my report for 1917.

6. *Resistance to the draft.*—Resistance to the enforcement of the selective service law, while in some sections of the country finding expression in open violence, was from the national point of view negligible in amount; and it never obstructed or retarded in the slightest degree the raising of the new armies. There were, it is true, in a few scattered localities, some pitched battles between resisters and county and State forces, and possibly 15 or 20 persons were killed; but in 'every case the local authorities handled the situation without assistance from the National Government. And in every case it was found that the cause of the disturbance was due not to a lack of local patriotism, nor to the administrative methods of the draft, but rather to the pernicious influence of radicals charged with the spirit of anarchy and to ignorance and misinformation as to the purpose of the draft and the aims of this Nation in the war.

Texas: For several years prior to the entrance of the United States into the war there existed in Texas an organization known as the Farmers' and Laborers' Protective Association, the leaders of which were active radicals. Its announced purpose was the forming of a cooperative organization for the advancement and protection of farming and laboring men, and for the purchase of supplies of various kinds. Its members, of whom there were several thousand, were required to take a binding obligation to secrecy and to assist other members—even to death, if necessary. Little if anything of the cooperative program was accomplished, however, and the organization did not become active until the fall of 1916. Then, when the Nation was on the verge of war, the members were informed that the organization was opposed to war, and was pledged forcibly to resist war or military service.

When the United States declared war upon Germany, the agents of the organization increased their activities. Secret meetings were held in various sections of the State and forcible opposition to conscription was openly advocated and urged. On May 5, 1917, a State convention was held and the leaders strongly denounced the war, the President, the Congress, and the intention to raise an army by draft. Delegates were advised to return to their home lodges and urge every member of the order to obtain a high-powered rifle and 100 rounds of ammunition. Resolutions were also passed at this meeting looking toward amalgamation with the I. W. W. in Oklahoma and with the Working Class Union, an organization of similar character.

When the local delegates returned to their homes, many of the members became alarmed at the extent to which the thing was being carried, and communicated the facts to the county officials. It was learned that a committee had been appointed to kill one of the members who had given information to an officer, and that an attorney who had made a vigorous speech in favor of the draft was also marked for death. The situation became so acute that citizens armed themselves and patrolled the streets in localities where the agitation was most threatening.

At this point the Department of Justice was called upon to take action. In a few weeks the leaders of the organization were arrested, indicted by the grand jury, tried, and convicted on a charge of conspiracy. The Farmers' and Laborers' Protective Association thereupon disbanded. Thus was brought to an abrupt end an organization which for a time threatened to interfere most seriously with the operation of the draft.

Oklahoma: In August, 1917, the people of Oklahoma were astounded to learn that there was organized resistance to the orderly administration of the draft in portions of Seminole, Hughes, and Pontotoc Counties. These were adjoining counties, and the disturbance was really in but one community. It was very quickly put down by prompt action of the authorities of the three counties, resulting in the arrest of some 500 persons, the indictment of 184 of these men, and the conviction of 150, of whom 134 pleaded guilty. About half of the number convicted were given terms in the penitentiary, and the remainder jail sentences. The outstanding feature of this case was the appalling ignorance of practically all of the men involved, other than three or four leaders. The so-called "draft resisters" were the poorest and most densely ignorant tenant farmers of a poor and isolated section of the State.

The draft law was not the basic cause for this uprising; it was merely the excuse for the outbreak. The trouble started in what is commonly known as the Working Class Union.

This organization originated at Van Buren, Ark., on the western border of the State, in the fall of 1913, and spread into eastern Oklahoma. Its chief object, at the time of organization, was to secure more advantageous conditions from the landowners and better rates of interest from the country bankers and merchants who financed the tenants engaged in raising cotton. It was not an unusual thing, in the years prior to this organization of the association, for tenant farmers to pay from 20 to 60 per cent interest on money borrowed for the purpose of putting in crops. The situation became unbearable. These tenant farmers readily lent ear to the pleading of the men who organized the Working Class Union, some of whom were erratic demagogues of exceptional ability. The enactment of a law in this State preventing banks and merchants from charging exorbitant rates of interest reacted against the Working Class Union, and resulted in a majority of the local unions dying out of existence. It is a matter of common knowledge that the disturbance in August, 1917, in Seminole, Hughes, and Pontotoc Counties, led by the Working Class Union officials, was not so extensive nor so serious as the disturbance in 1914 and 1915, in the extreme eastern part of the State, centering

in Sequoyah County, where the Working Class Union practically captured the county seat and violently protested against conditions.
· In the Working Class Union an oath or initiation was provided, which bound the men to absolute obedience to their superiors, and not a few men, who declined to follow the leadership, were treated to severe punishment by members of the organization. After the selective service act was passed in 1917 the semi-monthly meetings of the unions became nightly meetings; agitators made violent speeches, telling their audiences that 6,000,000 men in America had organized, and would operate with them; that these men purposed to resist the draft; and that as a part of this scheme railroad communication would be cut and local authorities defied. In some communities Socialistic speakers and agitators then took charge of this union to spread their propaganda. This was especially true in the community wherein the draft disturbance occurred. For a good many weeks Socialistic leaders had been distributing literature and propaganda violently opposing the war.

There was practically no opposition to registration; but when the men were ordered to report for physical examination and the operation of the draft was in full swing, the leaders counseled open resistance, and as a part of this program seemed to have planned the assassination of county authorities. A number of bridges were burned, and members of the W. C. U. gathered at a point distant from any town and declared their intention of resisting the enforcement of the draft. The local authorities of Pontotoc, Hughes, and Seminole Counties at once took steps to suppress this lawlessness. There was some shooting, though not a great deal. There was no really organized resistance; and when armed parties went out into the hills to arrest the resisters, they readily gave up.

Men who accompanied the sheriff's posses, and whose judgment may be accepted, declared that not one out of a dozen of these men had the slightest idea of what it was all about. They had lived in a condition of unbelievable poverty, and had been denied the fruits of their own labor; and when agitators appeared on the scene and told them that there was a way to prevent this, they readily lent themselves to any plan presented.

The outbreak was a protest against local conditions, which were not only unbearable but which (as the officials of this State frankly admit) were a disgrace, and have since been corrected in some degree.

Montana; Open opposition to registration for the draft occurred in Butte, Mont., in the early part of June, 1917. Handbills, urging men not to register and advocating resistance to the draft law, were strewn about the streets. Several hundred men and women, all of whom seemed to be of foreign extraction, paraded the streets, shouting against the war and the draft. Policemen who attempted to break up the procession were attacked and several shots were fired, although no one was hurt. Citizens gathered in the path of the marchers, blocking their progress, and State troops who had been held in their armories were ordered to clear the streets. Several arrests were made and the crowd was dispersed.

Again in August, 1917, antidraft sentiment in Butte and in the neighboring county of Silver Bow came to the surface when the examination of registrants began. The situation in this quarter was aggravated and was closely related to labor troubles in the adjacent copper and zinc mines. As a whole the citizenship of the city was intensely patriotic, and there seemed to be no doubt that the difficulty was caused chiefly by the foreign element and radical agitators. In Chicago, in the spring of 1918, during the trial of 112 I. W. W. leaders, witnesses testified that the trouble in Butte was caused by I. W. W. agents who, by the use of force, terrorized the 15,000 miners in and about that city. To counteract the misinformation spread abroad by these men, the chairman of the Butte City board selected 50 leading business and professional men and assigned to each a list of delinquents. For a week these 50 loyal and patriotic citizens spent their time, day and night, hunting up the men on their lists and explaining to them thoroughly the meaning and purpose of the selective service law.

North Carolina: In North Carolina a condition of grave danger to the effective administration of the draft developed among the mountaineers of Mitchell and Ashe Counties in the summer of 1917. Through ignorance, many of the young men failed to register; others who had registered refused to answer the call to the colors. High up on the mountains they hid in caves or were concealed in the homes of relatives. Every trail was guarded, and the approach of the sheriffs was signaled back along the trails, so that every attempt to capture them failed. In Mitchell County there were also hidden in the mountains a number of deserters—drafted men who had been given furloughs from their camps and who had overstayed their leaves. The local authorities planned a roundup, by a great armed posse, that would encircle the mountains so that every cave and trail would be combed thoroughly.

It was never necessary, however, to put the plan into execution, for about that time a special agent of the Department of Justice, who was assigned to the case, rode alone up to Tar Heel Mountain. The rest of the story is best told by a journalist (Robert W. Hobbs), who afterwards chronicled the results:

Way back in the hills of Carolina, where runs undiluted the blood of the early English settlers, old Tar Heel Mountain rears its wooded crest. Tar Heel is loved by every Carolinian. Its name is inwoven in the history of his State. Such a great figure has it been, that the familiar State name of the Carolinian is "Tar Heel," as is the Indiana "Hoosier" and the Wisconsin "Badger."

The people of Tar Heel read no newspapers and have few schools. They know little of the war, and understand nothing of the necessity of "making the world safe for democracy." Many of their men are still voting for Andrew Jackson for President. They have seen telephone wires and a few have ridden on trains, but to most of them the fastest means of communication is horseback, when the woman still rides on a pillion behind her man; and the movement of freight is by oxen, yoked six and eight to a rough wooden cart, "geed" and "hawed" over the narrow corduroy roads by walking drivers brandishing long goads. Their language is a corruption from the old Elizabethan English; and to most of them the "outlander" is a "revenuer," or at least an object of suspicion.

Into this land came the draft, and with the draft came resentment that they should be taken from their homes to fight on alien soil. Many refused to register; others failed to respond when called to the colors; and it was only by the most diplomatic use of the mountain clan leaders that the Government here was enabled to make a showing in the National Army. Wonderful fighting men they were; reared from the cradle to use the rifle and knife; wonderful material for raiders in No Man's Land, when taught the self-restraint of discipline, but suspicious and resentful. The mountain and its people were a problem to the draft boards.

Gradually the men were won in, until but 9 were left who had refused to report to the draft boards. Hiding with these far out in the caves of the mountain, or concealed in the homes of their mountain kin, were 13 deserters, who had been called in the draft and sent to camp, whence they had fled.

The reward offered by the Government for deserters and the pride of the law officers stirred them to every effort at captures. But as they rode the mountain trails, their approach was signaled by the hooting of an owl or the call of the dove, closely imitated by the mountain sentinels. Every trail was guarded. There was no way of approach so that the fugitives could be taken by surprise. And when the sheriff's posse too closely pressed the fugitives, the whining of a bullet across the road in some dark patch of trail was warning that it was not well to push farther along that path. The mountain was made for ambuscades, and its people knew every art of guerilla warfare. Posse after posse came back empty handed. The mountain boasted that it held its own, and about the sheriff's office in the courthouse at Bakersville gloom fought, with tobacco smoke for the air. Local authorities, desperate, planned a huge roundup, an encircling movement of a grand armed posse on the mountain, to comb its trails and secret places until it had yielded up its all. The sheriff knew this meant a battle in which all the mountain men, armed and in ambush in the fastness they knew so well, would take bloody toll of the invaders.

Then came Handy. The attack was called off. Alone and unarmed he rode into the mountains to speed the story of the war and its lessons of patriotism. He met the mountain men and their women, always sending messages of patriotism and service to the outlaws. None of these did he ever see. But at times he felt certain that they were under the same roof with him, and that from behind half opened doors and rude lofts their sharp ears gathered each word he left as messages for them. The deserters began to talk among themselves and with the draft evaders, and their friends bore word to Handy.

He issued passes reading:

"To all officers of the United States and the Sheriff and his deputies, and all citizens of Mitchell County, greeting:

"You are directed not to arrest Bill L. Greene, and to allow him perfect freedom to come and go as he pleases till noon, June 9, 1918."

Passes for all the 22 were sent out into the mountain by trusted friends of the outlaws, and they were told to report at the courthouse in Bakersville, Saturday afternoon, June 8, at 4 o'clock.

It was just on the hour appointed that Handy walked into the courthouse. He found there grouped to meet him, in the jury box of the district court room, the 9 draft delinquents, while across the room, in tattered malion costumes of Army clothes and mountain homespun, were the 13 deserters from the Army. They glowered sullenly at him, for already, since their arrival in town, their minds had been poisoned by the tale that he had lured them into the hands of the law to arrest them and carry them to camp in chains.

Lifting his right-hand, palm forward, in the mountain gesture of peace, he addressed them: "Boys, if you believe that story, there is the door. Any of you who believe it, get out; and I promise you 24 hours to hide yourselves before any pursuit starts. Those who stay I keep my word to, and those who go I pledge that same word that they will be hunted down, if it takes years."

There was a round of hearty cheers, and all 22 broke for Handy to shake his hand, the binding of their bargain. Handy gave them leave to do as they might wish until 10.30 the next morning, when they were to report.

All were ready at the hour, and the occasion was celebrated by a parade through the city's streets. Leading, came the sheriff on horseback, carrying the United States flag. Then came Handy and John McBee, chairman of the local board, in a low-necked hack; then marched the deserters, followed by 50 men, women, and children from the mountain, their friends and kin. Out past the village they marched, 3½ miles to the nearest railroad station, Toscane, where they entrained for Spartanburg. The draft evaders in the meanwhile were left in Bakersville, to return to their homes and go through the regular selective service channels for induction into the Army.

When the deserters arrived at Camp Sevier, Handy redeemed every pledge he had made, backed up the pleas of McBee, and the men were sent to join their commands, which had preceded them on the way to France. Before they told Handy good-by each man insisted on reimbursing the Government agent for the car fare from Tar Heel Mountain back to camp. They had not understood the war; but now they did, and they wanted to start with a clean slate.

In Ashe County a similar method of inducing the delinquents to surrender was employed. The governor of the State rode through the county, addressing the people of the mountains, firing their patriotism, and promising that the draft officials would intercede for the men if they surrendered. Here, too, the method was effective; nearly every delinquent came down from the mountains and was sent to camp.

Other regions: Forcible resistance to the draft, but in negligible degree, was encountered also in other sections of the country, notably in the mountains of Georgia, Virginia, and West Virginia, and among the Indians in Utah, Arizona, and other Western States. In Arkansas small bands of resisters hid in the woods and several persons were killed when officers attacked them. An incipient rebellion among the Creek Indians in Utah was put down without bloodshed by a company of troops from Fort Douglas.

There can be little doubt that practically all of the opposition to the draft was directly traceable to the activities of radicals, whose fantastic dreams enchanted and seduced the ignorant and artless folk who came under their influence; while in the mountain regions the trouble seemed to be due principally to the ignorance and native suspicion of the mountaineers who could not at first comprehend the purpose of the draft.

CHAPTER VI.

QUOTA BASIS AND STATE QUOTAS.

1. *Quotas from September to December, 1917.*—For the purpose of describing the quota system for the year 1918, it is necessary first to review the quota situation for the year 1917.

The selective service act, after empowering the President to raise by draft certain military forces enumerated in the act, provides:

SEC. 2. * *. * Such draft * * * shall take place and be maintained under such regulations as the President may prescribe not inconsistent with the terms of this act. Quotas for the several States, Territories, and the District of Columbia, or subdivisions thereof, shall be determined in proportion to the population thereof, and credit shall be given to any State, Territory, district, or subdivision thereof, for the number of men who were in the military service of the United States as members of the National Guard on April first, nineteen hundred and seventeen, or who have since said date entered the military service of the United States from any such State, Territory, district, or subdivision, either as members of the Regular Army or the National Guard. * * *

SEC. 4. * * * Notwithstanding * * * exemptions * * * each State, Territory, and the District of Columbia shall be required to supply its quota in the porportion that its population bears to the total population of the United States.

The apportionment of quotas and credits (as fully explained in my first report) was determined in accordance with the regulations governing the apportionment of quotas and credits prescribed by the President on July 5, 1917, by virtue of authority vested in him by the terms of the selective service act (First Report of the Provost Marshal General, 1917, p. 15). For the purpose of apportioning quotas to the States and Territories and the District of Columbia, there was added to the total number of men 687,000, to be raised by the first draft under the selective service act, the further number of 465,985, by way of credits, thus composed: (*a*) 164,292 men who were in the military service of the United States as members of the National Guard on April 1, 1917; (*b*) 183,719 men who entered the military service of the United States as members of the National Guard during the period from April 2 to June 30, 1917, both dates inclusive; and (*c*) 117,974 men who entered the military service of the United States as members of the Regular Army during the period from April 2 to June 30, 1917, both dates inclusive. These four items made 1,152,985 in all. This levy was distributed among the several States in the ratio which the population of the respective States bore to the population of the Nation. The quotas under the first levy are set forth in Quota Sheet No. 1, Appendix Table 78–A.

213

Prior to December 31, 1917, there had been inducted, on this levy of 687,000, a total of 516,212 men; these men being called as follows, by months:

September... 296,678
October.. 163,493
November... 35,721
December... 20,320

2. *Quotas from January 1, 1918, to date of filling first levy of 687,000.* —On January 1, 1918, there was left uncalled, of the first levy of 687,000 men, a total of 170,788. This balance sufficed to cover the requisitions for the ensuing months, which were as follows:

January.. 23,283
February... 83,779

On requisition during the month of March all States completed their quotas of white men under the first levy. But the military program required additional white men. The procedure governing the calling of these men in excess of the first levy of 687,000 is hereafter described.

The last of the colored men remaining in the first quotas were called during the months of April and May. The delay in using these men was due to the inability of the Army to absorb into its organization the number of colored men available in the quota contingents, and also to the fact that southern negroes from States not having cantonments could not be sent North during the severe cold weather.

In the Territories of Alaska and Porto Rico, physical difficulties were encountered, which postponed the mobilization of the quotas from these Territories. The last of its quota under the first levy in Alaska was furnished on June 30, 1918, and in Porto Rico on June 20, 1918. Hawaii, having an excess of enlistments, had no net quota for the first levy.

Quota Sheet No. 1, Appendix Table 78-A, shows the quotas of each State under the first levy of 687,000, the numbers furnished by each to December 31, 1917, and the date when the remainder was furnished by each.

3. *Quotas from date of filling first levy of 687,000 to May 31, 1918.*— Meanwhile the classification method had been adopted; and on January 15, 1918, a joint resolution was introduced in Congress authorizing the President to apportion quotas, not by population, but by classes (as already set forth in Chapters III and IV), and omitting the requirement of deducting credits for enlistments. The terms of the resolution (as later enacted) were as follows:

That if under any regulations heretofore or hereafter prescribed by the President persons registered and liable for military service under the terms of the Act of Congress approved May eighteenth, nineteen hundred and seventeen, entitled "An Act to authorize the President to increase temporarily the Military Establishment of the

United States," are placed in classes for the purpose of determining their relative liability for military service, no provision of said Act shall prevent the President from calling for immediate military service under regulations heretofore or hereafter prescribed by the President all or part of the persons in any class or classes except those exempt from draft under the provisions of said Act, in proportion to the total number of persons placed in such class or classes in the various subdivisions of the States, Territories, and the District of Columbia designated by the President under the terms of said Act; or from calling into immediate military service persons classed as skilled experts in industry or agriculture, however classified or wherever residing.

The plan of apportioning quotas upon the number of men in Class I was the necessary corollary of the classification method. If it had not been adopted, we should have witnessed the spectacle of one State or local board furnishing its quota from Class IV while another board still had an ample Class I. This same result would have followed the continuance of the credit system. Moreover, the equity of the credit system was contained within the classification method itself, which gave credit for men who voluntarily enlisted in the military or naval service; for it placed them in Class V, and thus they form no part of the basis on which the quotas were computed.

Under this plan, all of Class I all over the United States was drawn upon coincidentally and exclusively, until its exhaustion, and Class II was not invaded except on special calls for skilled experts. The classification method was the scientific, equitable, logical, and practical method. No State and no local board, so long as it had on its lists an ample supply of men who were available for military service could be heard to insist that another State or another local board should send men who were admittedly, by the very terms of the classification, not available for military service. The rule of population was a rule of bare numerical equality regardless of merit and fact. The Class I rule was a rule of scientific and political soundness, which regarded this Nation in war as one Nation, and not as 48 independent States.

Meanwhile the military program called for a continuous supply of men to camps.

Section 2 of the selective service act provides as follows:

Organization of the forces herein provided for, except the Regular Army and divisions authorized in the seventh paragraph of Section one, shall, as far as the interests of the service permit, be composed of men who come, and officers who are appointed from, the same State or locality.

With this expression of Congress in mind, the calls under the next requisitions made for men in excess of the first levy, 687,000, were placed from localities adjacent to the camp. The United States had previously been divided into 16 regional divisions, each of which was contributory to a mobilization camp.

The first call was based on population, pursuant to the original method under the act of May 18, 1917. No credits for enlistments were computed; first, because the data were not available in the emergency, and secondly, because the impending adoption by Congress of the new proposed method would replace the credit system by another and simpler method of credits for enlistments. This call, based on population, and taken from the territory contributory to the several mobilization camps, produced unlevel percentages of men furnished in proportion to the population, running from 1 per cent to 9 per cent of the first gross quota of the respective States.

During the months of March and April, therefore, population without credits was used as a basis. In the latter part of April, inasmuch as the new proposed method was not yet enacted, a statement of credits for enlistments was secured from The Adjutant General of the Army, and these credits were immediately applied to the May quotas; so that the entire levy to date in excess of the first draft of 687,000 was equalized on the original basis of population with credits for enlistments. A quota sheet was published, dated May 1, 1918 (quota sheet No. 2, Appendix Table 78–B). This quota sheet provided for a net levy of 554,543 men. The credits applied totaled 481,503, which represented enlistments in the Regular Army, National Guard, and Enlisted Reserve from July 1, 1917, to March 31, 1918. The men produced by this levy were all entrained prior to May 31, 1918, with the exception of Alaska's quota of 542 men, Hawaii's quota of 71 men, and Porto Rico's quota of 12,007 men; these balances were carried forward into quota sheet No. 3, hereafter described.

It will be noted that quota sheet No. 2 charges Arizona with 2,016 men. This State, however, did not have that number of men in Class I; and in view of the pledges of this office, that Class II would not be invaded, and the further fact that the pending quota legislation was proposed to be retroactive, Arizona's quota was reduced to 1,784, or the actual number of men available in Class I in that State. Subsequent to compiling and promulgating this second quota sheet, an emergency requisition was received in this office for 50,000 men for delivery in seven days; the delivery on schedule time was absolutely necessary. This number was in excess of the number contained in the second quota sheet; the men thus called were included in the third quota sheet hereafter explained; their entrainment took place between May 20, 1918, and June 1, 1918.

4. *Quotas from June 1, 1918, to September 1, 1918.*—The joint resolution of Congress, above quoted, was approved May 16, 1918. It provided for the apportioning of State quotas upon the basis of Class I registrants.

In accordance with the resolution, the quota basis was on June 1, 1918, formally changed from that of population to that of the relative size of Class I in the respective States.

Subsequently, the act of Congress of July 9, 1918, further provided as follows:

" Method of determining quotas for military service: That in the determination of quotas for the several States, Territories, and the District of Columbia, or subdivisions thereof, to be raised for military service under the terms of the act entitled "An act to authorize the President to increase temporarily the Military Establishment of the United States," approved May eighteenth, nineteen hundred and seventeen, the provisions of the joint resolutions approved May sixteenth, nineteen hundred and eighteen, providing for the calling into military service of certain classes of persons registered and liable for military service under the said act shall apply to any or all forces heretofore or hereafter raised under the provisions of said act for any State, Territory, District, or subdivision thereof, from and after the time when such State, Territory, District, or subdivision thereof has completed or completes its quota of forces called and furnished under the President's proclamation dated July twelfth, nineteen hundred and seventeen.

This act made the apportionment on the Class I basis retroactive to the time of completion by each State of the first levy of 687,000 men. Quota sheet No. 2 was therefore cancelled; and quota sheet No. 3 (Appendix Table 78–C) was prepared on the Class I basis as it stood on June 1, 1918. This quota sheet No. 3 included in Class I all men then remaining classified in Class I and all Class I men already inducted since the filling of the first levy of 687,000 men. Each subsequent quota sheet cancelled the preceding sheet in the same manner, reverting back always, for each State, to the date of completing its quota under the first levy of 687,000 men. This was accomplished by adding the men remaining in Class I on June 1, 1918, or on each succeeding date, to the number previously inducted, thus securing a complete Class I basis.

The credits shown in column 6-b of quota sheets Nos. 3, 4, and 5 represent the number of men inducted and called for induction subsequent to the filling of the first levy of 687,000 men and prior to the date of promulgating each quota sheet. The credits do not quite equal the sum of column 3 (number inducted and called for induction since the date of completing quota on first levy) and column 4 (voluntary and individual inductions) for the reason that a few additional calls were made between the date of obtaining the reported strength of Class I from the respective States and the date of determining the quotas, and the sum of these calls had to be added to the sum of columns 3 and 4.

Up to the period in question, enlistment in the Navy and Marine Corps was open to Class I registrants. Large numbers monthly were thus enlisting. As more fully explained in Chapter VII, the effect of these enlistments upon the computations for calls under the draft was serious. They made it impossible to regard 100 per cent of Class I as the quota basis; for this would have resulted in certain States not having a sufficient number remaining in Class I to fill their quotas. It therefore became necessary to reduce this percentage to a safe estimate; and 80 per cent of Class I was therefore fixed upon as the quota basis. Careful computations had disclosed that such a percentage would produce a sufficient number of men to fill the then known requisitions, until such time as the new class of 21-year-old men would become available. Column 6-a therefore shows the quotas computed as 80 per cent of the quota basis.

The net current quotas shown in column 6-c of quota sheet No. 3 therefore sufficed to fill the calls for the month of June and a large portion of the month of July. It had originally been expected that the new quotas therein provided for would be able to take care of the July calls. An accelerated program was adopted by the War Department, however, and the inductions thus required exceeded by some 80,000 men the total of the 80 per cent quotas. In view of the fact that there was an ample reservoir in Class I to fill the July calls, the percentage figures for net quotas, calculated as 80 per cent of the quota basis, was increased to 89 per cent.

At this point, attention is directed to the variant elements affecting the interim computations of quotas based on Class I. Such an accounting was of course contingent upon the total registration, which was a constantly shifting mass of over 10,000,000. Registrants were constantly being reclassified in and out of Class I; deaths occurred; sickness was encountered; men were needed to replace rejections at camp; errors in telegraphic reports were found as well as occasional errors of computation by local boards and State headquarters. Until enlistments were suspended, on July 23, 1918, the rapidly fluctuating amount of enlistments figured largely in disturbing the accuracy of reports of effectives in Class I; thousands of men were enlisting daily; and a Class I report which was current one day was unreliable on the next. If this shifting had been uniform for all months and throughout the country, the problem would have been a simple one; but it was localized and sporadic. On July 20, 1918, a Class I report was called for, to be dated as of August 1, 1918. But at this time the registration of June 5, 1918, had not been classified entirely and physically examined; a rectification of the classification of the June 5, 1917, registration was in progress; entrainments were being made daily, a total of 401,147 men being called in July. Thus the July 20, 1918, Class I report was of value for provisional purposes only.

The situation received relief when, on July 23, 1918, a War Department order issued prohibiting releases from Class I for enlistment in the Navy and the Marine Corps. This order helped to stabilize the computation of the Class I quota basis. The general bearing of this order suspending enlistments is more fully described in Chapter VII.

The military program, however, now became so extensive that all Class I men of the first two registrations would be needed, and it was certain that all of Class I would be soon called. Hence no further percentage margin for safety was required. This same order therefore provided that 100 per cent of Class I should constitute the quotas for the respective States. As soon as men were reported available in Class I they were called, and all remaining men known to be in Class I were called during the month of August.

5. *Quotas in September.*—On August 15, 1918, a Class I report was called for as of September 1, and quota sheet No. 4 (Appendix Table 78–D) was prepared. Calls for September were levied on this basis. By this time the registration of June 5, 1918, had been entirely classified, and the rectification of the classification of the June 5, 1917, registration had been nearly accomplished.

6. *Quotas in October.*—On August 24, 1918, a registration was held of men who had become 21 years of age since June 5, 1918. It therefore became necessary to call for another Class I report as of October 1, 1918. From this report was compiled a quota sheet as of October 1 (quota sheet No. 5, Appendix Table 78–E). The net quotas represented, 58,133 men, were required, under the statute, to be completely called in each State before any State was required to furnish men from the registration of September 12, 1918. The latter group would thus form the basis for a new computation of quotas.

7. *Quotas in November.*—There remained on November 1, 1918, in the levy of October 1, 58,133 Class I registrants not inducted; but these men were all under call. The additional November calls described in Chapter VIII were made on a provisional computation based on 12 per cent of the registration of September 12, 1918. These calls were levied on the new group of ages 19 to 36; but they were canceled by the President's order of November 11, issued upon the signing of the armistice.

8. *Calls from Alaska, Hawaii, and Porto Rico, subsequent to the first levy of 687,000.*—Alaska, after filling its quota on the first levy, had 1,420 men in Class I; these men were all called.

Hawaii had no net quota on the first levy; but its Class I contained 5,420 men, and these were all called.

Porto Rico was called upon to furnish 2,900 men in excess of its first net quota; but complications of transport service and other physical obstacles delayed the calling of additional men from Porto Rico.

CHAPTER VII.

INDUCTION AND INCREMENTS RAISED BY SELECTIVE DRAFT.

1. *Enlistment and induction, distinguished.*—Enlistment and induction are two modes of entering military service. They differ in respect to the governmental agencies which control such entrance. Other modes of entrance to the Army are by commission as an officer and by appointment as an Army field clerk; these two modes are under the direction of The Adjutant General of the Army.

Enlistment in the Army is also under direction of The Adjutant General of the Army, and is accomplished on the terms prescribed by statute, by Army Regulations, and by General Orders. It is always voluntary—that is, upon application by the person desiring enlistment—though, for a given time, enlistment for one or more branches of the Army may be limited or suspended by the War Department.

Induction is under direction of the Provost Marshal General, and was accomplished on the terms prescribed by the selective service act and the regulations issued thereunder. It might be either voluntary—that is, upon application by the person desiring induction—or involuntary; that is, upon order from selective service officials, pursuant to instructions from the Provost Marshal General.

A person subject to registration under the selective service act might enter military service either by induction or by enlistment (so far as not forbidden by express rule); but a person not subject to the act could not enter by induction.

The foregoing contrasts and likenesses should be kept in mind in considering the sequence of events and the changes of rule, as the raising of the Army proceeded.

2. *Time of induction.*—The act of enlistment and the act of induction each mark the point of time when the person enters military service, i. e., passes from the civilian to the military status. Upon this change of status follows automatically a number of important consequences. Whether the person is subject to the jurisdiction of military courts; whether he has ceased to be subject to orders issued by the Provost Marshal General under the selective service act, and is thereafter subject to orders issued by The Adjutant General of the Army; whether he is guilty of desertion in failing to appear for duty; whether he is entitled to pay and allowances, or to the benefits of war-risk insurance, or is subject to the obligation of making a family allotment—these and other questions depend more or less upon the

220

determination of time of entrance into service by enlistment or by induction.

The act of enlistment is effected by the proper officer's acceptance of the applicant and by the applicant's taking the oath of enlistment.

Under the selective service act, no oath was provided for entrance into service by the selective draft. Hence, the point of time could not be determined by any act of taking the oath. But it was early held, in the administration of the act, that the decisive point of time was the time duly set by the local board (or the State adjutant general) for the registrant to report to the board for military duty, preliminary to entrainment for camp. The original regulation of August 8, 1917, read (P. M. G. O. Form 31, Mobilization Regulations, Sec. 5):

From the time specified for reporting to the local board for military duty, each man in respect of whom notice to report has been posted or mailed shall be in the military service of the United States.

The later editions of the regulations (S. S. R. 2d ed., secs. 133, 159–D) made only minor changes of phraseology in this rule.

The question of principle involved was a novel one; but the solution thus early adopted by this office was a logical consequence of the second article of war, and it was fully and consistently confirmed by the opinions of the Federal courts (Franke v. Murray, C. C. A., 248 Fed., 865) and of the Judge Advocate General of the Army (Opinions of Mar. 6, 1918; Mar. 26, 1918; May 1, 1918; July 5, 1918; July 29, 1918; printed in full in "Source Book of Military Law and War-Time Legislation[1].")

At the day and hour specified for reporting for duty, the local board formed the men in single rank, called the roll, appointed the party leader and the squad leaders, and read a short address, instructing them in the preparations to be made, and declaring them to be now "in the military service of the United States." This was the moment of induction. They were then dismissed until the second roll call, prior to entrainment.

That the crucial moment of induction often marked the transition from civil to military status in more than a merely technical sense, can be gathered from the following incidents:

A colored boy was called for service. When he appeared at headquarters he had a bottle of liniment in each pocket and was leaning heavily on a stout cane. The roll was called and he hobbled up to his place in line, complaining of his "rheumatics." The contingent was taken out for its preliminary drill and instructions. Willie lagged behind his squad. When the company returned for entrainment Willie was acting as right guide, with the bearing of a real soldier. While at drill he had thrown away his cane, destroyed his liniment bottles, and "caught the spirit."

One contingent of some 50 boys was about to be sent to camp and the leader was designated by the board chairman. One of the soldiers objected, claiming that they should have the right to elect their own leader. He was told that the regulation pro-

---

[1] St. Paul: West Publishing Company; 1918.

vided how the leaders should be selected, and that this was his first taste of Army life, in that he would have to obey orders. He still insisted that this was not democratic, and that they should have a right to select their own leaders. He was, of course, given to understand that there was no appeal in this case, and that he must submit to the regulations, and he was warned to be on his good behavior until he arrived at camp, where he would be reported by the leader and a proper reprimand meted out. Before leaving on the train he made apologies and promised to be good.

3. *Total inductions.*—Induction being the distinctive moment which marks the addition of a new unit of man-power to the military forces, we may now notice the results of the Selective Service process, in terms of man-power raised.

The total number of registrants inducted and accepted at camp between September 5, 1917, and November 11, 1918, was 2,810,296 (Table 79). Of these the total inducted from selectives of the first and second registrations was 2,666,867 (Table 79).

(a) *Ratio of inductions to registrants.*—For purposes of practical estimate of available man power in a given group of registrants the ratio of inducted men to registrants becomes important. This appears in the following table, covering the first and second registrations, of which the effective Class I man-power (with the exception of about 5 per cent, as noted in Chapter IV, par. (IX), had been virtually all utilized at the time of the armistice:

TABLE 78.—*Inductions; ratio to registrants.*

	Inductions; ratio to registrants.	Number.	Per cent of registrants.
1	Total registrants June 5, 1917, to Sept. 11, 1918, first and second registrations	10,679,814	100.00
2	Total registrants inducted by boards (and accepted at camp) Sept. 5, 1917, to Nov. 11, 1918	2,666,867	24.97

(b) *Induction totals by months.*—The numbers of inductions depended, of course, entirely on the requisitions for men, issued to the Provost Marshal General by the General Staff through The Adjutant General of the Army. The method of calls by the Provost Marshal General, directing local boards, through the State executive, to effect the inductions, is described in Chapter VIII (mobilization). It is here material to note that the first inductions were made in September, 1917, and that they proceeded, in quantities varying from month to month, until the date of the armistice. Table 79 shows the monthly figures.

TABLE 79.—*Enlistments and inductions, compared by months.*

Enlistments and inductions, compared by months.	Total increment by enlistment and induction.	Inductions.		Enlistments.					
		Total.	Per cent of increment.	Army.	Per cent of increment.	Navy and Reserves.	Per cent of increment.	Marine Corps and Reserves.	Per cent of increment.
1	Totals from Apr. 2, 1917, to Nov. 11, 1918....	4,178,172	2,810,296	67.26	877,458	21.00	437,527	10.47	52,891	1.27
	1917:									
2	April...................	113,633	....	....	86,405	76.04	24,593	21.64	2,635	2.32
3	May....................	146,868			119,470	81.35	22,174	15.10	5,224	3.55
4	June...................	150,249			95,818	63.77	50,502	33.61	3,929	2.62
5	July...................	85,838			73,887	86.08	8,698	10.13	3,253	3.79
6	August................	66,172			59,556	90.00	4,641	7.01	1,975	2.99
7	September.............	324,248	296,678	91.50	24,367	7.51	2,025	.63	1,178	.36
8	October...............	210,392	163,493	77.71	31,216	14.84	15,292	7.27	391	.18
9	November.............	90,395	35,721	39.52	45,699	50.55	8,458	9.36	517	.57
10	December.............	194,700	20,320	10.44	141,931	72.90	31,076	15.96	1,373	.70
	1918:									
11	January...............	93,522	23,288	24.90	41,225	44.08	26,860	28.72	2,149	2.30
12	February.............	121,693	83,779	68.84	26,197	21.53	10,258	8.43	1,459	1.20
13	March................	169,791	132,484	78.03	25,268	14.88	11,362	6.69	677	.40
14	April.................	220,079	174,377	79.23	23,155	10.52	19,921	9.05	2,626	1.20
15	May..................	428,466	373,063	87.07	25,794	6.02	24,537	5.73	5,072	1.18
16	June.................	431,582	301,941	69.96	27,583	6.39	97,158	22.51	4,900	1.14
17	July.................	452,417	401,147	88.67	19,028	4.21	23,732	5.24	8,510	1.88
18	August..............	346,924	282,898	81.54	10,859	3.13	48,137	13.88	5,030	1.45
19	September...........	273,080	262,984	96.30	....	....	8,103	2.97	1,993	.73
20	October.............	107,363	107,363	100.00	....	....	....	....	....	......
21	November...........	7,331	7,331	100.00	....	....	....	....	....	......
22	Total first and second registration...	....	2,666,867	......						
	1918: Third registration.									
23	October.............	141,822	141,822	100.00	....	....	....	....	....	......
24	November...........	1,607	1,607	100.00	....	....	....	....	....	......

Before comparing the results of induction and enlistment, as a source of man-power for the Army, it is necessary to note the effect of enlistments on Class I.

4. *Effect of enlistments on Class I.*—At the outset of the selective draft, enlistment, as a door for entrance to the Army or the Navy, was freely open to persons registered under the selective service act. By the new regulations, effective December 15, 1917 (sec. 151), a registrant was not permitted to enlist in the Army, except in certain branches (Surgeon General, Engineers, Signal, Quartermaster); but enlistment in the Navy or the Marine Corps was permitted to all registrants except those in class I whose order number brought them within the current quota due under a call. On July 27, 1918, a presidential direction prohibited further enlistments of Class I registrants in the Navy or the Marine Corps, and also prohibited entries of such registrants on the Emergency Fleet lists. On August 9, 1918, the Secretary of War announced (Official Bulletin, Aug. 9) that "the War Department to-day has suspended further volunteering;" and the Secretary of the Navy on August 9 made a similar announcement for the Navy and the Marine Corps. The second edition of the Selective Service Regulations (Sept. 16, 1918) embodied the

foregoing rules (with minor exceptions for reenlistments in Navy and Marine Corps, for American citizens abroad enlisting in the Army and for aliens enlisting in cobelligerent forces). This rule of prohibition, in its application to registrants, continued until the date of the armistice.

What was the reason for this sequence of orders gradually closing the door of enlistment to registrants? The reason was the reciprocal influence of the selective draft and voluntary enlistment upon each other.

(*a*) *Influence of the draft on enlistment.*—On the one hand, the selective draft, at certain stages, stimulated voluntary enlistment. A glance at Table 79 and Appendix Chart N will show that enlistments ran high in April, May, and June, 1917, and then gradually but emphatically dropped to 25 per cent of the highest figure, in the Navy in July and in the Army in September. In the Army this change was apparently influenced by the announcement of the order numbers of the draft in late July; for thereafter the certainty, implied by high order numbers, of not being liable to early call in the draft, removed for many persons the motive to enlist. Again in December the enlistment figures suddenly rise again, and to their maximum for the Army; and again one important influence was the classification system, promulgated on November 8, to be effective on December 15, 1917; for on that date all prior releases from the draft were to be canceled and no further Army enlistments of registrants were to be allowed, and an overwhelming rush of enlistments then marked the first half of December. As soon as the classification of January matured and the certainty began to arrive that a deferred classification would remove the registrant from immediate call the motive for enlistment in the Navy was once more lessened; and Navy enlistments dropped in February and March. Finally in May and June another upward rush of figures is found for the Navy (its high-water mark, in fact, totaling in June more than in the five months preceding); and this, too, was patently explainable by the sudden heavy increases in draft calls for May and June, which rapidly depleted Class I, thus placing the higher order numbers in unexpected prospect of early call and bringing into play the motive for enlistment.

In short, the selective draft, in the varying stages of its indirect compulsory influence, was an effective stimulant of enlistment. In spite of the general popularity of the selective service system as such, there persisted always—for many, at least—the desire to enter military service (if needs must) by enlistment rather than by draft— that is, to enter voluntarily in appearance at least. Thus, whenever the prospect of the draft call seemed near, enlistments received the benefit of the dilemma thus created. This indirect effect of a selective draft in stimulating enlistment must be reckoned as one of its powerful advantages.

(b) Influence of enlistment on the selective service mechanism.—On the other hand, the selective draft itself suffered seriously, in its administrative aspect, by these fluctuations of enlistment by registrants. The Army (or Navy) gained the man equally, it is true, by whichever door he entered. But if the maintenance of the open door of enlistment should impair the effective workings of the draft, it ceased to be a matter of indifference.

And such was the consequence when Class I came to be gradually depleted by reason of the heavy calls to camp in May, June, and July, 1918. Unless the numbers of Class I could be accurately known and located, the machinery for prompt and dependable deliveries of man power on requisition would lose its working efficiency. During May and June volunteering did not interfere materially with the operation of the draft, for Class I still contained a sufficient surplus of men to fill the calls for those months and also to permit of a considerable number of enlistments. But when the July and August calls were announced to the States, it became apparent that voluntary enlistment and the selective draft could not well operate coincidently. Telegrams from State headquarters disclosed the fact that it was impossible to administer the selective draft, due to the rush to volunteer before being called in the draft. A typical case is this: A State headquarters would call upon 20 local boards for 15 men each, advices of the previous week having stated that each of these local boards had 25 men remaining in Class I; but immediately the local boards would begin to report that their 25 men had enlisted, and that they therefore had no men remaining in Class I. These changes were so widespread and so large in quantity that it was impossible to ascertain seasonably where the Class I men were and how many they numbered. Hence the changes of rule already described.

Since the date of withdrawal from Class I registrants of the privilege of voluntary enlistment there occurred a slight increase (as might have been expected) in the number of voluntary individual inductions. The change was very slight, however, and the first appreciable increase was immediately after the September 12 registration, which brought a new 13,000,000 men under the selective draft. Voluntary individual inductions for the latter part of September and the month of October were heavy, due to the fact that the Navy, the Marine Corps, and certain staff corps of the Army were, for the time, permitted to secure their men of occupational skill in this manner during the period when the selective service administration was overwhelmed with the process of classification of the registrants of the Class of September, 1918, and this became the more convenient method of furnishing that type of man.

Such was the development of the successive steps above taken, in first restricting and finally suspending and closing the opportunity of enlistment to registrants subject to induction under the selective service system. A more detailed study of the story will reveal interesting conclusions of policy for the historian and the legislator.

5. *Extension of induction to supply Navy and Marine Corps.*—It was of course a logical consequence that, upon closing one of the doors of entrance, the other door should at any rate be kept open. In other words, if enlistment in Navy or Marine Corps should be forbidden for registrants subject to selective draft, the Navy and the Marine. Corps should not be thus deprived of opportunity to obtain such men, but should share the products of the draft. These two arms of the service would be benefitted as before, and the draft system would be under complete control. This radical step, forming an important addition to the scope of the selective service act, received the assent of the Secretary of the Navy, and the Secretary of War, but required new legislation. Accordingly Congress provided, in the act of August 31, 1918, enlarging the registration ages, that "all men rendered available for induction into military service of the United States through registration or draft * * * shall be liable to service in the Army or the Navy or the Marine Corps, and shall be allotted to the Army, the Navy, and the Marine Corps under regulations to be prescribed by the President"; the regulations thus made took effect on October 1, 1918.

The number of inductions for the Navy and the Marine Corps issued during the months of October and November was as follows:

TABLE 79a.—*Inductions, Navy and Marine Corps; Oct.-Nov., 1918.*

	Inductions; October-November, 1918.	Calls.	Individual inductions.	Total.
1	Navy	2, 100	1, 294	3, 394
2	Marine Corps		6, 529	6, 529

The application of the selective draft to the Navy and Marine Corps was of such short duration that it is difficult to state how satisfactory it would have been, as every change of this kind is attended with more or less experimentation. It is believed, however, that a continuation of the system would have resulted in complete satisfaction to the Navy and the Marine Corps, and at the same time would have enabled this office to keep that correct account of available man-power which is so necessary in the administration of the selective service law.

On October 1, 1918, the Students' Army Training Corps (Sec. A, or collegiate branch) was established, with an authorized strength of 200,000 men (open only, for Class I men, to the new registrants). As the colleges opened only 18 days subsequent to the date of the new registration, September 12, this office handled all inductions into that organization by the process of individual induction. The records show that 145,012 individual induction orders were issued on account of the Students' Army Training Corps to November 11, 1918.

6. *Total armed forces raised by induction and enlistment combined.*— The armed forces raised by induction and by enlistment combined represent the total armed forces raised, if we add the numbers entering directly by commission. The respective contributions of these three methods, and the relation between the original armed strength and the increment produced for the purposes of the war, can be observed from the following table:

TABLE 80.—*Total strength of Army, Navy, and Marine Corps compared as to original strength and increments.*

		Number.	Per cent of total forces.	Per cent of total military forces.	Per cent of military increment.
1	Total United States armed forces raised to Nov. 11, 1918...................	4,791,172	100.00	....	....
2	Total military forces......	4,185,220	87.35	100.00	....
3	Total naval forces..........	605,952	12.65	....	....
4	Existing strength Apr. 1, 1917.....	378,619	7.92	....	....
5	Military forces.................	291,880	....	6.97	....
6	Regular Army.............	127,588	....	....	....
7	National Guard...........	164,292	....	....	....
8	Naval forces...................	86,739	....	....	....
9	Navy	69,029	....	....	....
10	Marine Corps...............	13,599	....	....	....
11	Coast Guard...............	4,111	....	....	....
12	Increments to Nov. 11, 1918.......	4,412,553	92.08	....	....
13	Military forces.................	3,893,340	....	93.03	100.00
14	Commissioned	203,786	....	....	5.23
15	Inducted..................	2,810,296	....	67.15	72.18
16	Enlisted...................	877,458	....	....	22.54
17	Regular Army.........	390,874	....	....	10.04
18	National Guard.......	296,978	....	....	7.63
19	Reserve Corps and National Army......	189,606	....	....	4.87
20	United States Guards (commissioned and enlisted)[1].	1,800	....	....	.05
21	Naval forces...................	519,213	....	....	....
22	Navy	462,229	....	....	....
23	Commissioned........	24,702	....	....	....
24	Enlisted...............	437,527	....	....	....
25	Marine Corps...............	54,690	....	....	....
26	Commissioned........	1,799	....	....	....
27	Enlisted...............	52,891	....	....	....
28	Coast Guard...............	2,294	....	....	....

[1] While the strength of the United States Guards on Nov. 15, 1918, was 25,906, yet only 1,800 of those who were assigned to it prior to January, 1918, can be considered as an increment to the military forces, the later strength being supplied from inducted men assigned from the National Army.

(*a*) It will be noticed that the total increment raised for the present war was 4,412,553, or 1,165.43 per cent of the entire original strength; while the increment to military forces only was 3,893,340, or 1333.88 per cent of the original military strength.

(b) Of the total military forces, 2,810,296, or 67.15 per cent, was furnished by the selective draft; i. e., two men in every three now in the Army came in by induction.

(c) Of the total increment raised since the beginning of the war, the selective draft furnished 72.18 per cent, or nearly three-fourths.

(d) All of the foregoing totals should be slightly reduced by an amount representing the duplications under "commissioned." A large proportion of commissions were issued directly to men not already in service, but a portion were also granted to men already in service by enlistment or induction. The records of The Adjutant General's Office do not enable the distinction to be here made.

(e) The respective contributions of the several States are shown in Appendix Table 79-A. As between enlistment and draft, the three States furnishing by draft the highest percentage of their individual contributions were Alabama, South Carolina, and West Virginia; while the three States contributing the lowest percentage by draft were Oregon, Massachusetts, and Rhode Island. It would be interesting to pursue this comparative aspect of the contributions in various geographical or other combinations of States.

7. *Ratio of forces raised to males of military age and to total male population.*—This leads to a culminating inquiry, vital in any retrospect of the selective draft operations and any future contemplation of military policy, namely, the ratio of armed forces raised to males of ages 18-45 and to the male population of all ages. The figures are shown in the following Table 81:

TABLE 81.—*Ratio of military strength to males of ages 18-45 and to male population all ages.*

	Ratio of military strength to males of ages 18-45 and to male population all ages.	Number.	Per cent of male population.	Per cent of called and not called to males aged 18-45.	Per cent of effectives to males aged 18-45.
1	Total male population of all ages Sept. 12, 1918	54,340,000	100.00		
2	Total males ages 18-45 (registered, and not registered but in service)	25,347,477	46.65	100.00	100.00
3	Awaiting call to the colors Nov. 11, 1918	20,556,305	37.83	81.10	
4	Effective Class I (estimated)	2,340,000			9.23
5	Noneffectives (estimated) under present law and regulations	18,216,305			71.87
6	Already called to the colors, Nov. 11, 1918	4,791,172	8.82	18.90	18.90
7	In service Apr. 2, 1917	378,619			
8	Increment to Nov. 11, 1918	4,412,553			
9	Total present and prospective armed forces available from effectives under present law and regulations (estimated)	7,131,271			28.13

(a) It will be observed that the ratio, to total population, of the males of ages 18–45, forming the reservoir of males of military ages, was 46.65 per cent; the number being over 25,000,000.

(b) It will further be observed that, of this reservoir, 20,500,000 or 81.10 per cent, were still awaiting call to the colors on November 11, 1918, while nearly 5,000,000, or 8.82 per cent, were already called to the colors.

(c) Of the number awaiting call to the colors, it may be estimated (from Appendix Table 64–A) that the effective Class I strength that would have developed is at least 18 per cent of the new 13,000,000 registrants, giving in all 2,340,000, which represents 9.23 per cent of all males of military age.

(d) Finally, by combining lines 4 and 6 of the foregoing Table, it appears that the total armed forces which are and prospectively could have been made available in the year 1919, under the present law and regulations and without calling any of the deferred classes, would be 7,131,172. This would represent 28.13 per cent of the total males of military age; and it would leave more than twice as many still uncalled belonging to the lesser degrees of availability.

These figures may serve, to some extent, as a basis for estimate in future plans; and, in connection with the various ratios already given in Table 61, they will indicate the possible effect, plus or minus, that would be produced by changes of the law and regulations in one or another detail.

8. *Armed forces of Great Britain raised by enlistment and by conscription.*—The armed forces raised by the British Government from within the United Kingdom may serve as an interesting basis of comparison, with reference to the ratio of military man-power contributed. The following Table 81a is based on estimates only, but is as accurate as is feasible under the circumstances:

TABLE 81a.

	Ratio of United Kingdom forces raised to male ages 18–45 and to males all ages.	Number.	Per cent of males of all ages.	Per cent of males ages 18–45.
1	Total males, all ages, in 1918	[1] 22, 827, 261	100.00	....
2	Males, ages 18–45	[1] 9, 800, 000	42.93	100.00
3	Awaiting call to the colors, Nov., 1918	[1] 3, 945, 641	17.28	40.26
4	Already called to the colors	5, 854, 359	25.65	59.74
5	Remaining ages	13, 027, 261	57.07	....

[1] Estimated.

The notable feature is that by May, 1918, after nearly four years of war, the United Kingdom had contributed (line 4) to the armed forces one quarter of its males of all ages, or three-fifths of its males of military ages 18–45. Relatively, therefore, it had far exceeded the ratio of contribution in the United States.

What its total remaining available effectives would have amounted to can hardly become a subject of comparison, the law and regulations in the two countries being different in essential points.

· For the purpose of studying the comparative speed and product of voluntary enlistment and conscription, the increment of forces raised in the United Kingdom may be divided into two parts, taking October 31, 1915, as the dividing line. As set forth in Appendix K, the British registration of man-power, which served as the basis for the later conscription measures, was completed during August and September, 1915; canvassing under Lord Derby's attestation plan began on October 23, 1915; the conscription bill was introduced on January 5, 1916, passed on January 24, 1916 (first Military Service Act), and became effective February 10, 1916. The indirect compulsory effect of the registration marks the month of October as virtually the termination of the purely voluntary plan; all additions to the forces after that month, of ages 18–45, though termed "enlistments," were in effect not to be ascribed to a purely voluntary system. The figures, thus allotted before and after October 31, 1915, are as follows:

TABLE 81b.

| | Enlistment and conscription in the United Kingdom. | Number. | Per cent of— | |
			Military age.	Armed forces.
1	Total, military ages 18–45 (estimated)............	9,800,000	100.00	....
2	Armed forces raised in United Kingdom to Nov. 11, 1918...	5,854,359	59.74	100.00
3	Existing strength, Army and Navy, Aug. 1, 1914 (including reserves and territorials)....	883,457	....	15.09
4	Voluntary enlistments, Aug. 2, 1914, to Oct. 31, 1915..	2,289,774	23.37	39.11
5	Enlistments, Nov. 1, 1915, to Nov. 11, 1918...	2,681,128	....	45.80

It thus appears that in the United Kingdom, without conscription, and during the first 15 months of the war, the increment raised was 2,289,774. A reference to Table 79 will show that in the United States, during the 19 months of war, for more than 17 of which the draft system was in force, the increment raised was 4,178,172, and that of this increment 2,810,296 were raised by direct draft and 1,367,876 were raised by voluntary enlistment parallel with the draft (except for the first six weeks and the last three months). Any comparison, however, based on mere numbers or ratios is of relatively little significance, not only because of the different psychological conditions of the war in the two countries, but also because the reservoirs of military man-power differed in the two countries, because the military ages for draft and for enlistment varied in both countries at different times, and because the quantitative product was in both countries conditioned from time to time by the available equipment and quarters and by other circumstances.

The foregoing figures lend themselves to other aspects of comparative study, for which space does not here permit a digression. Suffice it to suggest, in general, that, as indicated by the facts set forth throughout this report, the superior efficiency of the draft as a method of raising armed forces, lies, on the one hand, in its ready and dependable supply of military man-power in quantities and at times when needed, and, on the other hand, in its adaptability to those industrial needs which affect war preparations and the national welfare.

CHAPTER VIII.

MOBILIZATION.

The process of mobilization, under the selective service administration, divides itself into three stages: The requisition, the call (including the order to report for duty), and the entrainment.

1. *Requisitions.*—The Provost Marshal General, in levying men by the selective draft, acted only by authority of the Secretary of War, upon requisition prepared by the General Staff, and issued through The Adjutant General of the Army, and specifying the number and the kinds of men needed; or (since Oct. 1 1918, as explained in Chap. VI) upon requisition from the Secretary of the Navy, issued through the Bureau of Navigation, Director of Mobilization. The only exception to this principle occurred in the case of individual inductions, which were issued on requisitions of the Chiefs of Staff Corps, or since October 1, 1918, of the Navy or the Marine Corps, the authority for these requisitions resting upon rules and arrangements otherwise existing between the General Staff and the Staff Corps; but these Staff Corps requisitions were all for individual inductions—that is, voluntary inductions; the involuntary inductions all rested upon the authority of a requisition from The Adjutant General.

Whenever the Army's need for additional men matured, this office received a preliminary notice by telephone from the General Staff, in order that preliminary computations and arrangements might be made; at the time of such notice the entrainment date, as well as other details, were specified. A formal requisition was later received from The Adjutant General of the Army. A sample form is given in Appendix E. To these requisitions were immediately assigned call numbers by this office. In appendix, Table 81–A, is given a list of all requisitions received from The Adjutant General of the Army from August 25, 1917, to November 7, 1918, both inclusive.

2. *Kinds of calls.*—During the year 1917 all requisitions and all calls were made for "the run of the draft;" that is, the specifications were for men physically qualified for general military service and for either white or colored men, as the need might be. The selection of men was made by calling them from the board list in sequence of order numbers, regardless of occupation or education. But during the year 1918, new conditions arose and more varieties of men were designated in requisitions. The requisitions now included specifications as to either physical, occupational or educational qualifications. Moreover, the number of mobilization camps to which men

232

could be sent was increased to include every camp, post, or station in the United States and in the territories of Alaska, Hawaii, and Porto Rico, as well as to include hundreds of stations at schools and colleges.

To meet these new conditions, it became necessary to devise new varieties of calls. Six brief designations were adopted for the several kinds of calls, viz: (a) General; (b) Voluntary; (c) Special; (d) Voluntary-special; (e) List; and (f) Individual.

Broadly speaking, these calls fell into three types: General, special, or individual. A general call signified a call for a quantity of men having certain physical qualifications. A special call signified a call for a quantity of men having specified occupational or educational qualifications. An individual call signified a call for an individual. There were also permitted, under the regulations, voluntary inductions of individuals ahead of time, without call, at the request of the registrant himself, as provided in the Selective Service Regulations (2d ed.), section 150; but these inductions, being wholly dependent on the wish of the individual to enter military service without waiting for the call applicable to himself, were, by their irregularity in quantities, a source of disturbance to the computations of men to be delivered at camp; and during the greater part of 1918 the regulation permitting this variety of individual induction was suspended.

Reverting to the six kinds of calls, their particular differences were as follows:

(a) The general call (S. S. R., 2d ed., sec.158A) was a call for men to be selected and inducted in sequence of class and order numbers; as to physical qualifications it might include men qualified for general military service or men physically qualified for special or limited military service only; and it might further specify color; for example, 1,000 white men qualified for general military service.

(b) Under the voluntary call (S. S. R., 2d ed., sec. 158B) volunteers were advertised for and were listed by the boards during a certain period; at the expiration of this period, allotments were made and the men inducted in the regular manner.

(c) The special call (S. S. R., 2d ed., sec. 158C) was a call for men possessing certain occupational or educational qualifications, and the selection under a special call was made by the appropriate occupational or educational qualifications. For example, if a special call were made upon a particular local board for 10 carpenters, the local board immediately proceeded to examine its list and to select the 10 carpenters, possessing the lowest order numbers, eliminating all registrants who were not carpenters.

(d) By the voluntary-special call (S. S. R., 2d ed., sec. 158D) a period was authorized during which registrants possessing the qualifications specified in the call might voluntarily present themselves to their local boards and be called. After the voluntary period had expired, and if a sufficient number of volunteers had not come forward, the local board proceeded to select a sufficient number of men to fill its quota, inducting them involuntarily in the sequence of their order numbers.

(e) The list call (S. S. R., 2d ed., sec. 158E) was a call for the induction of registrants known by this office to possess certain occupational or educational qualifications needed by the Army. This method of calling men was used in connection with the Industrial Index. For example, a requisition was received for all the white physicians who were physically qualified for special or limited military service only, classified in Class I; upon locating such men from the Industrial Index, calls issued for them, the State headquarters being notified of the local boards and the order and serial numbers of the men desired.

(f) The individual call (S. S. R., 2d ed., sec. 158F) was utilized when the chief of a staff corps or other department of the Army, or of the Navy or the Marine Corps, desired to obtain a particular individual, by reason of his special qualifications. A requisition naming this individual was made by the department chief upon the Provost Marshal General, who in turn directed the local board to induct the registrant for the special duty in question, provided the registrant consented to such induction.

In regard to these several kinds of calls, the most fundamental distinction, with reference to the availability of man-power material, was the difference between physical and other qualifications for general service and for limited service. The following Table 82 shows the total numbers inducted to November 11, 1918, grouped according to the most important practical distinctions:

TABLE 82.—*Mobilization, by kinds of calls issued.*

	Mobilization, by kinds of calls issued.	Number.	Per cent of inductions.
1	Total inductions to Nov. 11, 1918......................	2, 810, 296	100. 00
2	Qualified only as to physical conditions and color ("Run of the draft")............................	2, 384, 026	84. 83
3	Occupational qualifications also. ("Special lists").	54, 779	1. 95
4	Educational qualifications also. ("Schools").......	127, 943	4. 55
5	More specific qualifications ("Individual inductions")..	243, 548	8. 67

The disposition made of the limited service men thus called has been already shown in Table 51 (Chapter IV, Physical qualifications).

With reference to the further important distinction between voluntary and involuntary inductions, the following Table 83 shows their distribution.

TABLE 83.—*Inductions compared as to voluntary and involuntary.*

Inductions compared as to voluntary and involuntary.	Number.	Per cent of inductions.	Per cent of voluntary inductions.
1 Total inductions June 5, 1917 to Nov. 11, 1918.	2,810,296	100.00	....
2 Involuntary	2,365,752	84.18	....
3 Mixed	160,984	5.73	....
4 Voluntary	283,560	10.09	100.00
5 Individual	243,548	....	85.89
6 General	40,012	....	14.11

It thus appears that the number of men raised by involuntary induction in the draft was 2,365,752, leaving only a comparatively minor quantity to be credited to volunteering.

As to the branches of the Army whose needs gave rise to the several requisitions and calls, only a small minority of the requisitions and calls were based on specified needs of the several staff corps and departments. The vast majority were by the requisition destined directly to depot brigades, recruiting depots, or line organizations, the sorting out being done afterwards, and the assignment to the special needs of the staff corps and departments being made by transfers between camps. The following Table shows the distribution of the requisitions and calls between the different branches:

TABLE 84.—*Inductions, by branches of the Army, compared.*

Inductions, by branches of the Army, compared.	Number.	Per cent of inductions.	Per cent of staff corps inductions.
1 Total inductions to Nov. 11, 1918	2,810,296	100.00	....
2 Depot brigades, recruit depots, and line organizations (Army)	2,292,022	81.56	....
3 Marine Corps	6,529	.23	....
4 Navy	2,394	.08	....
5 Schools (Army)	269,693	9.60	....
6 Staff Corps (Army)	239,658	8.53	100.00
7 Aircraft Production	3,453	....	1.44
8 Chemical Warfare	550	....	.23
9 Coast Artillery	54,984	....	22.94
10 Engineers	37,195	....	15.52
11 Field Artillery	3,274	....	1.37
12 Medical	24,927	....	10.40
13 Military Aeronautics	22,214	....	9.27
14 Military Intelligence	78	....	.03
15 Motor Transport	4,304	....	1.80
16 Ordnance	7,112	....	2.97
17 Provost Marshal General	5,913	....	2.47
18 Quartermaster	12,074	....	5.04
19 Signal	41,247	....	17.21
20 Tank	9,296	....	3.88
21 Veterinary	1,600	....	.66
22 Sundries	11,437	....	4.77

3. *Mode of allocating a call.*—The total quantity of men specified in a requisition had, of course, to be apportioned among the States and the local boards for the purpose of distributing the levy in the proper shares, and this apportionment had to be made before the call issued. A requisition, immediately on its receipt, was assigned a series of call numbers, a separate call number being taken for each camp to which a separate contingent was directed to be sent. The several calls to be issued under a particular requisition were then allocated to the States which were to contribute to the levy.

In allocating a call many considerations had to be taken into account. Consideration, of course, was first given to the laws and regulations for apportionment of State quotas, as well as the quota situation for the time being; the condition of accounts showing how many men were due from the several States. This subject has been fully described in Chapter VI. The next step was to ascertain what States could furnish the particular type of men specified in the requisition; for example, what States could furnish an appreciable portion of 20,000 colored men. Then, in sequence, the following considerations were weighed: First, the matter of transportation; this was necessary in order to save the Government needless expense in railroad fares, as well as to insure a sufficient supply of railroad facilities to handle the number of men to be entrained; secondly, the mobilization orders already pending for the same period, since, to insure an orderly mobilization, it was desirable to avoid calling on a local board to send men to several posts or stations at the same time; thirdly, climatic conditions, for it would not, of course, have been advisable to send men from Southern States to northern camps during the winter; fourthly, local conditions, such as an epidemic in a particular State, making it necessary to relieve that State from sending men until the epidemic abated; and, fifthly, agricultural conditions, for example, the prudence of delaying a call upon a particular State until the end of the month, so that the crops might be gathered by the men who were to be taken.

The calls being allocated it then became necessary to issue induction telegrams calling on the respective States for the men to be entrained therefrom. The railroads were then consulted, the camp commanders were notified of the calls, the Surgeon General of the Army was notified (in order that proper medical officers might be in attendance upon the arrival of the men), and the Staff Corps, if any, for whom the men were needed was notified, as well as some eight or ten other bureaus of the War Department that might be concerned.

Immediately upon receipt of a call, each State headquarters proceeded to allocate the call for that State among the respective local boards, taking into account similar considerations to those affecting the apportionment of the national levy.

Effect of the influenza epidemic.—During the month of October, 1918, an epidemic of influenza swept the country. This epidemic interfered seriously with the mobilization of selected men. A call for 142,000 white men had been arranged for entrainment during the five-day period beginning October 7, 1918, but shortly prior to this date the epidemic became serious, and practically all of the camps to which the men were destined were quarantined, so that this entire call was canceled. Additional calls issued for entrainment during the remainder of October for some 163,946 men, but the entrainment of approximately 78,035 of these men had to be postponed until November. Of this number 5,731 had actually entrained in November prior to November 11, but the calls for the remaining 72,304 were canceled by the President's order of November 11, the date of signing of the armistice. Besides causing these cancellations the epidemic made it necessary to divert men from one camp to another. These cancellations, suspensions, and diversions, occurring daily, made it extremely difficult to keep an accurate check on the mobilization.

4. *Entrainment.*—The process of entrainment may be described under the heads of (a) assembly of selectives for entrainment, (b) railroad arrangements, (c) camp destinations, and (d) total mileage, with other general facts.

(a) *Assembly of selectives for entrainment.*—The time set for entrainment was generally made, by the local board, an occasion of formality and ceremony, and in most communities it took on the marks of a public festivity. The men were assembled at the office of the local board, which was sometimes the court room of the county seat, or at a large hall, a public school, or a municipal building. Where the contingent was a large one, it was drawn up in ranks in the street or public square. A photographer officiated, to preserve for the participants' families a pictured memento of the occasion. The chairman made an address, reminding them of the significance of the occasion, and calling attention to the various regulations to be observed in their progress from home to camp. Usually other short addresses were made, sometimes by the mayor of the town or by other notables. Friends were already waiting at the railroad station. Often, in the large cities, the entire contingent was transferred from the office of the board to the railroad station in automobiles, loaned for the purpose and gaily decorated. Where the contingent marched on foot to the station, the town band (if there was any) usually led the procession; crowds of friends and relatives, with mingled cheers, laughter, and tears, watched their passage; and a combined resonance of music, singing, shouting, and the din of horns announced the transit of the contingent through the streets. At the station, sometimes the whole of the town's citizenship would be found assembled to cheer the parting moments of "the boys." For the town felt that these men represented its own honor and patriotism; it looked proudly upon its contribution to the National defense; and it was keenly desirous to make them feel that they represented the honor of the town, the county, and the State, in the new service to which they were called.

This celebrative aspect of the day and moment of departure of the selectives became a notable feature of the system. It was in strong contrast with the casual and uncelebrated departure, now and then, of a single enlisted man—unnoticed except by his family. The departure en masse of a large contingent of selectives made it natural to focus publicly on this single moment the local patriotism for the war. And it is an undoubted fact that as the mobilization became more frequent and this feature became more and more noticeable, there were often heartburnings in the families of those other men who had enlisted, when they reflected upon the public applause that was given to the men called in the selective draft.

It was this public celebration on the day of entrainment which counted for a great deal in gradually accumulating the popularity of the draft; for the general sentiment of military patriotism came thus to be associated in an open and emphatic manner with the processes of the draft.

Because of the large numbers of men being mobilized, it became necessary, toward the summer of 1918, to inject several new features into the mobilization regulations. The kinds of calls were rearranged; the procedure at the local boards on the occasion of the first roll call and on the day of entrainment was simplified; and an order was issued which permitted the detailing of officers to accompany special trains of selected men to the camps.

Prior to July 31, 1918, serious damage had occasionally been done to railroad equipment by selectives en route from their local boards to mobilization camps, chiefly by contingents whose friends had unwisely supplied them with intoxicating liquor. On July 31, 1918, a change in the mobilization regulations was directed to the prevention of this. The first new feature was the providing of arm bands, or brassards, which were stitched on the sleeves of selected men at the time of their induction. Such arm bands or brassards were designated as the uniform of the United States Army from the time of induction into the military service until the arrival of the men at the mobilization camps. This uniform made unlawful (under sect. 12 of the selective service act) the sale of intoxicating liquors to selected men. The second feature was the appointment of leaders and assistant leaders of draft contingents as special police, with enlarged authority and responsibility under the selective service regulations. The third feature was the distribution of a form entitled "Regulations Governing Drafted Men en Route to Camp," containing instructions and full information upon the duties of inducted men. These changes in the mobilization regulations resulted in the substantial prevention of drunkenness and disorder, and of damage to railroad equipment and other property en route to the camps.

(b) *Railroad arrangements.*—The Nation-wide distribution of the camps to which the selectives were to be sent complicated the entrainment problem and required the most careful handling. Before a call could issue, the Railroad Administration required 14 days' notice. Eight days of this period were used for the compilation and printing of the train schedules for the movement of the selected men. The remaining six days were needed by the local boards to notify the registrants and to allow them sufficient time to arrange their affairs before leaving for camp. The entrainment schedules were all compiled and published by the United States Railroad Administration. In Appendix F is a sample entrainment schedule for a single call in a single State; it provides as carefully for a contingent of one man as for a contingent of one hundred. By thus working out every detail in advance, the mobilization proceeded in a smooth and orderly manner, so that few persons in the community at large realized the enormous task which was being performed.

It is a matter of duty and pleasure here to express admiration of the work of the United States Railway Administration in transporting selectives. No more difficult transportation problem could be conceived, involving as it did the simultaneous movement of small detachments in variant numbers from thousands of county seats and the concentration of their delivery at several hundred posts and stations. The arrangements for transporting and feeding these men were made by the railroads, and this work was so satisfactorily performed that less than a dozen complaints were received during the entire year. They have been called upon to handle as many as 50,000 selected men in one day; and to transport within a single month over 400,000 men for the selective service system alone. Their hearty cooperation at all times was one of the main assets of this office in the work of mobilization. Special attention is invited to their performance on November 11, 1918, the day on which the armistice was signed and hostilities ceased. Calls had issued and all arrangements had been made for some 250,000 men to be entrained during the five-day period beginning November 11. The United States Railway Administration was advised by telephone at 10.25 a. m. on Monday, November 11, of the cancellation of these calls by order of the Secretary of War. In 35 minutes they had notified all the railroads of the country; had stopped further entrainments; had reversed such contingents as were en route; and were restoring the men to the original points of entrainment. This achievement stands out as a marvel of efficiency, and is but an indication of the cooperation which they constantly tendered.

(c) *Camp destinations.*—During the year 1917, inducted men were sent to the 16 National Army camps only; but the military program for 1918 required that they be sent to every camp, post, and station in the United States and in the Territories of Alaska, Hawaii, and Porto Rico.

The following Table 85 shows the distribution of men forwarded the several camps:

TABLE 85.—*Mobilization by camps, compared.*

	Mobilization by camps, compared.	Number.
1	Total inductions to Nov. 11, 1918	2, 810, 296
2	Fort Armstrong (Hawaii)	5, 420
3	Camp Beauregard	14, 887
4	Camp Bowie	14, 524
5	Camp Cody	20, 852
6	Camp Custer	89, 146
7	Camp Devens	93, 819
8	Camp Dix	105, 528
9	Camp Dodge	111, 462
10	Camp Forrest	16, 532
11	Camp Fremont	8, 000
12	Camp Funston	122, 364
13	Camp Gordon	102, 603
14	Camp Grant	114, 140
15	Camp Greene	19, 423
16	Camp Greenleaf	39 664
17	Camp Hancock	15, 980
18	Camp Humphreys	17, 941
19	Camp Jackson	96, 704
20	Camp Johnston	4, 429
21	Camp Kearney	11, 000
22	Camp Las Casas (Porto Rico)	15, 733
23	Camp Lee	138, 349
24	Camp Lewis	112, 474
25	Camp Logan	4, 000
26	Camp MacArthur	11, 124
27	Camp McClellan	7, 805
28	Camp Meade	103, 305
29	Camp Pike	116, 236
30	Camp Sevier	14, 414
31	Camp Shelby	26, 673
32	Camp Sheridan	5, 224
33	Camp Sherman	103, 800
34	Camp Taylor	120, 522
35	Camp Travis	112, 357
36	Camp Upton	111, 737
37	Camp Wadsworth	55, 834
38	Camp Wheeler	31, 209
39	Fort Wm. Seward (Alaska)	1, 852
40	Coast Artillery Posts	47, 386
41	Recruit Depots	191, 084
42	Schools	269, 657
43	Miscellaneous	185, 103

(d) *Mileage.*—The number of men called, to October 31, 1918, was 2,801,358. Of this number 45,882 did not travel over railroads under the control of the United States Railway Administration, due to the fact that they reported at mobilization camps within the immediate vicinity of their local boards. The remaining number, 2,755,476 men, were handled by the United States Railway Administration. The average number of miles per man traveled to a mobilization camp was 388; the entire mobilization, therefore, involved the equivalent of 1,069,124,688 miles of travel by one passenger.

. The. relation of this mileage movement of selectives from local boards to camps, to the entire mileage for War Department troop movements of all kinds, and to the total passenger mileage in the United States for the same period, is shown by the following Table 86:

TABLE 86.—*Mobilization by mileage.*

	Mobilization, by mileage.	Number.	Per cent of total mileage.	Per cent of War Department mileage.
1	Total passenger mileage in United States, Sept. 1, 1917, to Nov. 1, 1918 (estimated)	51, 494, 683, 000	100. 00	....
2	For War Department troop movements of all kinds (estimated).....	4, 440, 000, 000	8. 62	100. 00
3	For movements from boards to camps (estimated)............	1, 069, 124, 688	....	· 24. 08
4	For movements intercamp and from camps to seaboard (estimated).......................	3, 370, 875, 312	....	75. 92

It thus appears that the movements required for mobilization under the selective draft represented about one-fourth of the entire troop movement for the War Department.

97250°—19——16

CHAPTER IX.

FISCAL ARRANGEMENTS.

1. *Compensation in general.*—The fiscal policy as described in chapter 8, page 28, of my report to the Secretary of War on the first draft under the selective service act, 1917, has been followed during the past year. This policy was, briefly, to offer an opportunity to all of those board members and clerks, who were financially able to do so, to render uncompensated services to the Government in the administration of the selective service law. This policy was set forth in the original regulations governing disbursements issued June 15, 1917, which the President stated.

The desire in all communities to render patriotic service to the Government has given rise to numerous assurances that civilian services required in connection with the registration, selection, and draft authorized by the selective service act will, in many cases, be rendered gratuitously. In order, however, that no person selected for such service may find himself compelled to decline to serve because the financial sacrifice involved is too great, compensation was authorized in cases in which the services referred to are not rendered gratuitously.

Changes in the regulations, however, governing compensation of board members and salaries of clerks of local boards were found to be necessary, for reasons hereinafter stated.

2. *Compensation of local board members.*—Several plans of compensation have been tried. In the beginning of the administration of the selective service law it was believed that the duties of board members would become comparatively light after a period of two or three months. Thousands of the members, with this idea in mind, offered their services without compensation. This form of service was encouraged by this office as being the ideal to be striven for.

At the same time it was realized that many of the board members whose patriotism was unquestioned would be unable to devote the necessary time to their duties without causing a serious drain upon their limited financial resources. In order to retain the services of these men, many of whom were in every way desirable as board members, provision was made in the first regulations governing disbursements, issued June 15, 1917, that "members of district and local boards may receive compensation at the rate of $4 per day for each day upon which the board is in session and the member claiming compensation present."

Experience proved that this plan was not thoroughly satisfactory. The daily basis of compensation left no choice to the board members

242

who were forced to claim compensation at the daily rate of $4, or none at all, regardless of whether they had been at the quarters of the board but a small portion of the day or not. It was then decided to place the plan of compensation on an hourly basis; and the Selective Service Regulations issued in November, 1917, provided pay at the rate of $1 per hour, with a maximum of $7.50 per day and $150 per month per member.

In December, 1917, the great problem of classification of questionnaires became acute. There was urgent necessity for speeding up the work of the boards in order to complete the huge tasks as expeditiously as possible. This emergency brought forth the plan of compensating board members at the rate of 30 cents for each questionnaire classified, which was to be equally divided among the members; upon the unanimous vote of the board, the moneys due could be paid in some other proportion, with the proviso that in no case could one member receive more than 15 cents of the allowance of 30 cents for each classification, and no two members more than 25 cents for each classification, to be distributed between them.

At that time it was believed that upon completion of classification there would be little work for board members beyond attending occasionally at the quarters of the board, and supervising the work of their clerk or clerks. This expectation, however, was overthrown by the course of military events. With the expansion of the military program demanding more men, and the numerous war industries, shipbuilding, and agriculture, each demanding protection and assistance, numerous modifications of the regulations and rulings thereon were unavoidable. It also became necessary to order a rectification of the classification lists, and to issue the "Work or fight" regulations. Each of these measures added heavily to the work of board members. Together with the steady flow of orders for induction, both of groups and of individuals, the necessary action demanded practically all of the board members' time. While their spirit and willingness to serve did not decrease to any material extent, appeals for financial relief reached the office from every part of the country. Finally these appeals for relief became so numerous and their insistence so strong, that a meeting of adjutants general and draft executives of 17 States, representing every section of the country, was called in Washington on July 9, 1918.

At this meeting the whole subject was discussed at length. It was agreed that a change from the plan of compensation on the questionnaire basis was necessary and that the members of boards should be paid for past uncompensated services after March 1 (the period when compensation for classification under the first registration had about ceased). Immediately upon the adjournment of the meeting above referred to, work upon a new plan of compensation was begun.

Several memoranda on the subject were prepared. The plan finally evolved was briefly this: To compensate the board members for past services from March 1 to August 31 on the basis of $3 to the board for each man inducted into the military service and accepted at camp from its jurisdiction, and, after September 1, upon the basis of $1 per hour with a daily maximum of $10, and a monthly maximum varying from $150 for the smaller boards, to $600 for the larger boards, to be divided among all of its members.

This was submitted in a memorandum to the Secretary of War under date of August 20, 1918, with the recommendation that the plan be adopted and that a request that the Provost Marshal General be authorized to request the necessary appropriations from Congress. This memorandum was approved by the Secretary on August 24.

3. *Clerical services for local boards.*—In the first disbursing regulations issued June 15, 1917, compensation of clerks was provided for at a rate of $2.50 per day. As was the case with the board members, many of the clerks performed their duties without compensation as a patriotic service, until it became apparent that the strain upon their resources would be too great.

The Selective Service Regulations adopted in November, 1917, in section 43, provided for one chief clerk for each board at not to exceed $100 per month, and for one additional clerk for each 1,500 registrants additional, or a fraction thereof exceeding 700; the first additional clerk was to receive $80 per month and all other additional clerks $60 per month. In December, 1917, after the period of mailing questionnaires had been completed, this office urged upon local boards having a registration of 3,000 or under to dispense with the services of all but the chief clerk, on the theory that one clerk would be ample to attend to all of the work of the board thereafter. But the actual conditions previously described as confronting board members, applied also to the clerks, and it was found in most cases that one clerk would be insufficient. Many objections arose in the various sections of the country relative to the rigidity of the regulations fixing the pay of clerks. The local boards in many sections of the country were in competition with other Government departments and war industries, which were able to and did pay larger salaries than those provided for in our regulations. It was found that in many cases it was impossible to obtain competent clerks at the rates provided, or to retain them at the old rates of pay. In some instances it was necessary to make special exceptions to the regulations to meet these abnormal conditions.

A careful study of the subject, and a consideration of suggestions made from various parts of the country, resulted in the adoption of a plan of compensation based upon the number of registrants under the jurisdiction of the board. This plan provided that all local boards should receive for the first 2,000 registrants or under, 7 cents per registrant per month on the board lists: *Provided, however,* That no local board should receive less than $100 per month; that each local board having more than 2,000 registrants should, in addition to the foregoing, receive for each additional registrant above 2,000 and up to and including 2,500, 6 cents per month per registrant on its lists; that each local board having more than 2,500 registrants should, in addition to all the foregoing, receive for each additional registrant above 2,500 and up to and including 3,000, 5 cents per month per registrant on its lists; that each local board having more than 3,000 registrants should, in addition to all the foregoing, receive for each additional registrant above 3,000 and up to and including 5,000, 4 cents per month per registrant on its lists; that each local board having more than 5,000 registrants should, in addition to all the foregoing, receive for each additional registrant above 5,000 and up to and including 8,000, 3 cents per month per registrant on its lists; that each local board having more than 8,000 registrants should, in addition to all the foregoing, receive for each additional registrant above 8,000, $2\frac{1}{2}$ cents per month per registrant on its lists. The plan further provided that the monthly allowance to a board should be regarded as a budget from which they were to compensate their clerks, paying the salaries necessary in their particular locality to obtain efficient services, subject to the proviso that $100 per month should not be paid to any individual except upon specific approval of the governor, or $150 except upon the recommendation of the governor and approval of this office. The new plan further differed from the old in that it was more flexible and permitted board members to carry forward to their credit from month to month, any balance from their monthly allowance that might not have been expended, and enabled them to use this balance at any time when the necessity arose for the employment of additional clerks, without being required to obtain specific authorization from this office through State headquarters, as had been previously required. This latter requirement had entailed a vast amount of correspondence on the part of the boards, State headquarters, and this office. This new plan involved practically no increase of expenditures over what would have been necessary under the new registration, had section 43, as promulgated in the regulations of November, 1917, been continued in operation after the registration of September 12.

A memorandum setting forth this plan was submitted to the Secretary of War on September 3, 1918, with recommendation that it be adopted, and was approved by the Acting Secretary of War, September 4.

This feature of the administration, however, was one in which it was virtually impracticable to devise a uniform method which would operate both equitably and economically in all regions, and would be acceptable to all types of members serving on the boards. In spite of all efforts made to profit by experience, the conflicting considerations could not be reconciled into a single fixed rule.

To ascertain the operation of the new rules in the period between their promulgation and the date of preparing this report, the boards were asked, "In your experience, how are the new rules for compensation working?" A large majority of the boards expressing an opinion replied that the new rules for compensation were satisfactory. Many of them, however, especially those whose members served gratuitously, declined to comment on the rules. And it can not be denied that criticism of the rules was both considerable in volume and vigorous in expression.

A number of boards declared that the basis of compensation of board members was unsound. Thus a New York City board, referring to the provisions of section 195, paragraphs B and C, expressed the view that any method of compensation based on the result of judicial action is vicious; "to give a member compensation according to the number of men he inducts, or the number of men he puts in a certain class, is as wrong as to give a magistrate compensation for every defendant whom he finds guilty." Referring to the provisions of section 195, paragraph A, a Detroit board says:

> The members of the board in all previous positions were never paid on an hourly basis, having been paid a stipulated amount for results accomplished rather than on the time employed. This ruling has had the effect of taking the joy out of the work; the zest displayed prior to this ruling has very much depreciated. The thought which can not be dispelled is that local board members can not be trusted.

A number of boards complained that the compensation of board members was inadequate; and a larger number expressed the opinion that the allowance for clerical assistance should have been more liberal. But the chief cause of dissatisfaction (though not always emphasized) lay not in the rules themselves, but in the difficulty that has been encountered in the proper preparation of vouchers and the consequent delay in the receipt of compensation. Many boards said in effect that they found it practically impossible to prepare their vouchers in a way satisfactory to the disbursing officers, and that as a result they did not receive any pay for many months.

Not a few boards favored a "straight salary" for board members; while others believed that their services should in every case be gratuitous. Says a Philadelphia board:

> One of the greatest aids to the impression that has long obtained in our district, that no man was sent through our board into the Army ahead of his time, was the fact, once it became generally known, that the majority of the members of our board had

declined to accept any pay for the work. We were of the impression at the beginning, and continue of that opinion, that with our country at war and our young men being called from their homes and from the useful and remunerative employments upon which a majority of them had just entered, to risk their lives at $30 a month, it ought to be possible for those of us called upon to help as members of draft boards to give such comparatively small service free.

4. *Appropriations.*—The total appropriations made by Congress for the administration of the selective service system amounted to $54,896,903 in all, divided among the following sums and dates:

TABLE 87.—*Appropriations for registration and selection for military service.*

	Appropriations for registration and selection for military service. (R. & S. for M. S.)	Number.	Per cent of total appropriations.
1	Total appropriations to date........................	$54,896,903.00	100.00
2	R. & S. for M. S. 1917–18, act of June 15, 1917....	2,658,413.00	....
3	R. & S. for M. S., 1918, act of Oct. 6, 1917.......	4,000,000.00	....
4	Urgent deficiency, 1918, act of Mar. 28, 1918.....	8,476,490.00	....
5	National Security and Defense, War Department; allotted by President, Apr. 15, 1918...........	4,000,000.00	....
6	R. & S. for M. S., 1919, act of July 9, 1918.......	15,762,000.00	....
7	Urgent deficiency, 1919, act of Nov. 4, 1918......	20,000,000.00	....
8	Total disbursements to Oct. 1, 1918..................	16,216,215.22	29.54
9	Unexpended Oct. 1, 1918............................	38,680,687.78	70.46

It will be noted that the sum of $35,762,000, forming the greater part of the total $55,000,000, was designed to cover the current fiscal year (July 1, 1918–July 1, 1919). Of this sum, the $15,762,000 of July 9, 1918, was based on the work then in prospect as needed to handle the 11,000,000 registrants of the first two registrations already classified; while the $20,000,000 of November 4, 1918, was provided for handling the additional 13,000,000 registrants brought in by the act of August 31, 1918, and registered on September 12, 1918. The heavy labor of classifying the new 13,000,000 registrants began immediately after September 12, and was proceeding, in a hundred-day drive, when the Armistice was signed; the completion of the classification for the age-groups 18–36 required until early December. Hence the monthly disbursements for September, October, and November, when finally liquidated, will much exceed those for July and August, the first months of the fiscal year for which the additional appropriations were made.

5. *Disbursements.*—The total disbursements from the several appropriations, as shown in Table 87 (line 8) above, amount to $16,216,215.22. To this sum should be added three items representing, respectively, the outlay for telegrams, the outlay for printing at the Government Printing Office, and the estimated sum, as yet unpaid, for increased compensation to board members from March 1 to August 31, 1918. (Appendix Table 87–A, columns 9, 10, and at the foot of column 1.) The first two of these items were expended

out of appropriations charged to other Government agencies; the third item has not yet been entirely closed, pending the receipt of complete statements of accounts from State headquarters. All three of these items should, of course, be included for the purpose of establishing a per capita cost; the aggregate thus becomes $20,174,652.53, representing the total expenses, estimated and actual, of the Selective Service System from June, 1917, to October 1, 1918. A detailed statement arranged by States and showing the distribution of this expense, will be found in Appendix Table 87–A.

These figures are taken to October 1, 1918, and exclude the third registration of September 12, 1918, because the work of classifying the new group of registrants had only just begun at the time when the latest accurate figures were available, and because the task of registration alone was the smallest part of the labor and expense required in the ultimate disposition of this additional thirteen millions of men. The amount expended to October 1, therefore, represents the cost of disposing of the men included in the first and second registrations, and of producing the effectives resulting therefrom up to October 1, 1918.

At this time it is practically impossible to furnish any further details than are shown in Appendix Table 87–A. It is proposed in the final report to show by tables the expenditures of each of the State headquarters, district and local boards, each table to contain a statement showing the amount of compensation drawn by each board member by name, as well as the names of those who have served throughout the entire time without receiving any compensation for their services.

6. *Per capita cost, National and State.*—(1) The per capita cost of the Selective Service System, nationally, from the beginning, in 1917, to October 1, 1918, is shown in the following Table 88, which presents two sets of figures, the one representing the per capita cost on the basis of disbursements from appropriations charged to this office, and the other representing the figures on the basis of total actual and estimated expenses of the system, regardless of the appropriation source.

TABLE 88.

	Per capita cost of draft.	Cost.
1	Total disbursements May 18, 1917, to Oct. 1, 1918	$16,216,215.22
	Per capita cost by disbursements from P. M. G. O. appropriations:	
2	Per registrant (10,838,315 total registration, June 5, 1917, to Sept. 11, 1918)	1.50
3	Per man inducted (2,552,173 to Oct. 1, 1918)	6.35
4	Total expenses, actual and estimated, for same period	20,174,652.53
	Per capita cost by expenses:	
5	Per registrant	1.86
6	Per man inducted	7.90

It thus appears that the cost per registrant (based on all expenses, regardless of the source of appropriations) was $1.86; and that the cost per man inducted was $7.90.

Of the two' costs shown, the second, viz, per man inducted, is obviously the most significant, being the real measure of the money expense for each man effectively obtained for service.

The first figure of cost, viz, per registrant, is important from the point of view of the individual States and boards.

(2) The per capita cost in the several States is shown in Appendix Table 88-A and Chart O. Part of the expense was proportionate to the number of registrants in a given area; that is, a board having 5,000 or 6,000 registrants necessarily incurred larger expenses than a board having 500 or 600 registrants, no matter how many men were inducted. The labor and time necessary to keep records, to answer inquiries, to pass upon claims for deferment and exemption, to search for delinquents, and to do a hundred other things were fairly proportionate to the number of registrants, even though the legitimate claims for deferment and exemption ultimately reduced the number of effectives inducted to a relatively small number. For these reasons, it is only just to the several States to set forth also the cost per registrant; and it appears that in some States having a relatively high cost per man inducted the cost per registrant was much more moderate; the same would be found true of various local boards.

Per man inducted, the cost in the several States ranged between $2.64 and $10.94. The lowest cost was in Florida and Oklahoma; and the highest cost was in Delaware and Arizona. The causes for this variance can not yet be stated with accuracy.

7. *Per capita cost in 1917 and 1918 compared.*—The foregoing figures cover the entire cost of the system from June, 1917.

But a comparison of the per capita cost in 1917 and in 1918 is worth while, because the classification system introduced in December, 1917, while far more efficient, speedy, and accurate than the method used up to that time, involved more labor on the part of the boards and seemed likely to import a higher per capita cost. For these two periods, viz, June, 1917, to December, 1917, and January, 1918, to August 31, 1918, corresponding to the two systems employed, the comparison results as shown in the following Table 89:

TABLE 89.

	Per capita cost 1917 and 1918 compared.	Cost.
1	Total disbursements May 18, 1917, to Dec. 1, 1917	$5, 211, 965. 38
2	Cost per man called for examination and hearing in 1917 (3,082,949)	1. 69
3	Total disbursements Dec. 1, 1917, to Oct. 1, 1918	11, 004, 249. 84
4	Cost per man classified in 1918 (9,952,735)	1. 11

It is therefore apparent that the classification method proved to be not more expensive, but less expensive, than the former method.

The per capita cost above compared, viz., per man called and per man classified, is the only comparable basis for the two years. The other two per capita costs shown in my Report for 1917, viz, per man certified and per man of quota allotted, are of little value for comparison; the latter, because the quotas allotted had not been entirely filled by induction on December 15, 1917; and the former, because the men certified and ready on December 15, 1917, were twice as many as those actually inducted by that date, hence the expense of the system had not then produced its full results in effectives; and there was no way of exactly allotting the cost of what had been effected.

8. *Per capita cost of induction and enlistment compared.*—A comparison between the per capita cost of enlistment under the voluntary recruiting system prior to April, 1917, and of induction under the selective draft, results as shown in Table 90:

TABLE 90.—*Per capita cost of induction and enlistment compared.*

	Per capita cost of induction and enlistment compared.	Cost.
1	Enlistments, per capita cost: For 1914	$24.48
2	For 1915	19.14
3	For 1916–17 (9 months)	28.95
4	Inductions, 1917–1918: Per capita cost	7.90

The details of the figures for cost of recruiting were set forth in my first Report (Appendix Tables F and G, 1917). It appears, this year as last year, that the Selective Service system, besides its advantages as a rational, equitable, and necessary method of raising a National Army, has the additional advantage of being a far more economical method than that of recruiting by voluntary enlistment.

9. *Per capita cost in the Civil War.*—A comparison with the Civil War expenses means little in absolute figures, because of the changed standards of money values. But the comparison is worth while in revealing the beneficent difference between a draft law of the Civil War type (Appendix J) and a draft law of the 1917 type; the former embodying as essential elements a bounty system and a federalized administrative force .. The entire forces raised in the Civil War, by the mixed system of draft and bounties for enlistment, numbered 2,690,401, at a combined per capita cost of at least $227.71, or over $600,000,000. The armed forces raised under the Selective Service Act of 1917 alone, during the first fourteen months of the war, numbered 2,552,173, at a per capita cost of only $7.90, or slightly over $20,000,000 in all.

CHAPTER X.

ORGANIZATION AND PERSONNEL OF THE SELECTIVE SERVICE SYSTEM.

National summary.—The administration of the selective service system under the Provost Marshal General was organized on the principle of "supervised decentralization." The terms of the act of May 18, 1917, lent themselves readily to this effective mode of linking the district and local boards (explicitly created by the act), through the State executives, with a small Federal directive agency, designated by the President through the Secretary of War and serving as a central source of instruction and guidance, to give uniformity, accuracy, and speed to the operations of the boards. Appurtenant to this main vertebral organization, there developed in course of time, at various points, a few additional agencies made necessary by the growth of the work and the dictates of experience.

The entire administrative system thus consisted of the following coordinated parts, operating regularly and almost constantly: (1) The Provost Marshal General; (2) the State governors and draft executives; (3) the district boards; (4) the industrial advisers; (5) the local boards; (6) the Government appeal agents; (7) the medical advisory boards; (8) the legal advisory boards; (9) the boards of instruction. To these should be added (10) civic associations casually contributing volunteer assistance.

The distribution of this personnel, and its numbers for each of the constituent parts, are shown in the following Table 91. The numbers of persons in these different branches for the several States are shown in Appendix Table 91–A.

TABLE 91.—*Personnel of selective service administration.*

Line.	Personnel of selective service administration.	Number.	Per cent of personnel.
1	Total personnel Oct. 31, 1918..........................	193,117	100.00
2	Governors...................................	54	.03
3	Military personnel............................	4,004	2.07
4	Commissioned officers.....................	192	.10
5	Enlisted men............................	3,812	1.97
6	Civilian personnel............................	189,059	97.90
7	Board members and other officials..........	57,104	29.57
8	Other civilians............................	131,955	68.33
9	Provost Marshal General's Office....................	429	..22
10	Commissioned officers..........................	45	....
11	National inspectors............................	12	....
12	Civilians.................................	343	....
13	Enlisted men............................	29	....

TABLE 91.—*Personnel of selective service administration*—Continued.

Line.	Personnel of selective service administration.	Number.	Per cent of personnel.
	Total personnel Oct. 31, 1918—Continued.		
14	State headquarters	999	**0. 52**
15	Governors [1]	54	....
16	Military officers	147	....
17	Civilians	624	....
18	Enlisted men	174	....
19	District boards	2, 539	**1. 31**
20	Members	1, 039	....
21	Industrial advisers	411	....
22	Other civilians	944	....
23	Enlisted men	145	....
24	Local boards	43, 579	. 22. 57
25	Members	14, 416	....
26	Government appeal agents	4, 679	....
27	Additional examining physicians	12, 039	....
28	Other civilians	9, 227	....
29	Enlisted men	3, 218	....
30	Medical advisory boards	10, 234	**5. 30**
31	Members	9, 577	....
32	Other civilians	411	....
33	Enlisted men	246	....
34	Legal advisory boards	119, 282	61. 77
35	Members	110, 915	....
36	Associate members	108, 367	....
37	Boards of instruction	16, 055	**8. 31**

[1] Includes the Commissioners of the District of Columbia.

The two notable features of the selective service organization, under the act of May 18, 1917, viz, the civilian quantity of its personnel, and its decentralization into the several States, are strikingly exhibited by these figures.

That the administration was essentially a civilian one is shown by the fact that the military officers were only 192, and the enlisted men (serving in clerical capacities, and coming into the system at the eleventh hour) were only 3,812; or a total of only 4,004, leaving a civilian force of 189,059. The spectacle is thus presented of the National Army being raised by the activities of a body of civilians. It is believed that in this respect the contrast of the system, not only with that of the Civil War in our own country, but also with the usual methods on the continent, is notable. The plan adopted by Congress one year and a half ago was without precedent, and was, therefore, an experiment made on faith; and that faith has been amply vindicated.

The other feature, viz, that of decentralization into the several States, is even more emphatically illustrated when we compare the personnel of the Provost Marshal General's Office, only 429 in number, with the aggregate personnel in the several States, 192,688 in all. This vast machinery was supervised from a headquarters of relatively insignificant size in Washington. Every one of the 192,688 workers in the several States owed his immediate duty to some State superior under the State executive. The contrast here is again remarkable. It illustrates not only the wisdom of resorting to State agencies in handling an operation which involved State pride and responsibility, but also the prudence of committing to the hands of local officials the administration of a law which so intimately affected the homes and livelihood of the people.

These figures only corroborate the great fact, already patent to all, that the Nation itself raised this National Army.

It is now necessary to give some particular description of the several parts of the system.

(I) THE PROVOST-MARSHAL GENERAL.

1. *Personnel.*—On May 22, 1917, the formal designation of a Provost Marshal General was made in the following Executive Order:

GENERAL ORDERS, }   WAR DEPARTMENT,
    No. 65. }   *Washington, May 22, 1917.*

By direction of the President, Brig. Gen. Enoch H. Crowder, Judge Advocate General, United States Army, is hereby detailed as Provost Marshal General, and vested with the execution, under the Secretary of War, of so much of the act of Congress entitled "An act to authorize the President to increase temporarily the Military Establishment of the United States," approved May 18, 1917, as relates to the registration and the selective draft.

By order of the Secretary of War:

                         TASKER H. BLISS,
                 Major General, Acting Chief of Staff.

Official:
    H. P. McCAIN,
        The Adjutant General.

Meanwhile (as already noted in my report for 1917), the task of preparing plans for the execution of the law, when enacted, had already been undertaken. On May 22, 1917, the date of the above order, four days after the passage of the act, the administrative staff consisted of 8 officers and a small clerical force. By November, 1917, the staff of officers had increased to 35 and the clerical force to about 150, and during November and December some 25 more officers were added temporarily as a Division of Appeals, to brief the voluminous mass of cases then coming up on appeal to the President; in this heavy task some 45 members of the District of Columbia Bar rendered volunteer assistance. During the spring of 1918, the compilation of the Industrial Index required a large accession to the clerical force; and this extra force was trained by a deputation of 20 experts, loaned for the same period by the Director of the Census. By November, 1918, the staff of officers numbered 45, the civilian and clerical force numbered 343, and the enlisted men 29.

A roster of the names of the military officers on duty here at various times and of the civilians holding positions of principal responsibility, is given in Appendix G.

From the decisive day of May 18, 1917, the dominant and emphatic note for every worker on the force was the vital need of speed and promptness. There was never a moment of anything less than anxious energy. The spectacle of the allied European armies, eagerly awaiting the arrival of our forces to make the turn of the tide, was daily present in the consciousness of all. Imagination saw our camps gradually peopled by the selective contingents produced through the ceaseless efforts of the boards; and each day's work, however tedious and technical, was seen to speed the arrival of the day when the selectives thus raised would join the ranks of the fighters. Nor night nor Sunday signified a cessation of labors; and no conventional office hours limited the zeal of the workers. Whenever emergencies required, the clerical force cheerfully responded to the call; and on many occasions women who had worked all through the day remained until midnight to complete the tasks for which their assistance was necessary. To all who gave thus their unstinted contribution of faithful toil, the appreciation and gratitude of the Department is amply due. It was a period of anxious and fervid zeal and effort which will live in the memory of all who shared its privilege.

It would seem invidious for me to call to your especial attention, in this place, particular officers who have been on duty in the Provost Marshal General's Office, for the reason that the enumeration of certain ones might appear to imply, by exclusion, that others have not performed a service as loyal and efficient. Such is not the case, for a complete acknowledgment of loyalty and efficiency would necessitate the mention of all who have been identified with the work in Washington, whether officers or civilians.

2. *Divisions of the office.*—As the work of classifying the 10,000,000 registrants proceeded, and the heavy calls of the spring of 1918 began, the operations of the office called for a separation into divisions, each division with its chief and subordinate officers and a special clerical force. These divisions, after several alterations, stood on October 28, 1918, as follows:

(1) Administration Division, having jurisdiction of the following:

All questions relating to the personnel of local and district boards, legal and medical advisory boards, Government appeal agents, and State headquarters, including complaints from official sources, resignations, removals, increased membership of boards, appointments, rank of Army officers detailed as disbursing agents, and board activities.

(2) Aliens Division, having jurisdiction of the following:

All questions relating to the classification and deferment of aliens, declarants, recruiting by foreign powers (other than those under treaties), citizenship, passports, and international law.

(3) **Appeals Division, having jurisdiction of the following:**
Recommendations for the decision of cases sent on appeal to the President.

(4) **Auxiliary Agencies and Statistics Division, having jurisdiction of the following:**
All matters connected with the Industrial Index, the Students' Army Training Corps, boards of instruction, and all statistical work (and all such other work as may be specially referred by the Provost Marshal General) for the yearly report.

(5) **Classification Division, having jurisdiction of the following:**
All questions relating to classification, reclassification, transfers, matters relating to the apprehension and disposition of delinquents and deserters, furloughs, Emergency Fleet list, and general questions relating to the status of registrants both before and after induction. In short, this division handled all questions arising from the time the Questionnaire was filed until the registrant acquired a military status or was undergoing civil punishment for delinquency, except those matters incident to induction and mobilization proper.

(6) **Finance Division, having jurisdiction of the following:**
All matters covered by Part IX (disbursement regulations) of the Selective Service Regulations.

(7) **Information Division, having jurisdiction of the following:**
All requests for general information, general correspondence not otherwise assigned, and the handling of personal calls upon the office.

(8) **Inspection and Investigation Division, having jurisdiction of the following:**
All information and material dealing with the activities of boards and coming from sources other than official (which were handled by the Administration Division), and investigation of complaints against boards, or draft executives, the execution in the field of speed-up programs, and handling of national inspectors.

(9) **Law Division, having jurisdiction of the following:**
All general questions of law other than those relating to citizenship, alienage, and international law. All matters involving amendments, changes, or interpretations of the Selective Service Regulations, and all matters relating to the jurisdiction, powers, and duties of boards and draft officers generally, including questions of procedure. This division also kept a record of general statutes of court decisions and the Judge Advocate General's opinions.

(10) **Medical Division, having jurisdiction of the following:**
All matters relating to rules and regulations covering physical requirements and examination of registrants, and, in connection with the Administration Division, all matters affecting medical aids and medical advisory boards.

(11) **Mobilization Division, having jurisdiction of the following:**
All matters relating to the allocation, making, and filling of calls and the accomplishment of individual inductions. All questions which, arising in the carrying out of the foregoing functions, dealt with the interpretation of the Selective Service Law and Regulations, or required change, modification, or suspension of the Selective Service Law and Regulations were referred to the appropriate division for action, but that division conferred with the Mobilization Division in making its determination.

(12) Publication Division, having jurisdiction of the following:

All matters having to do with the publication of forms and documents and their distribution to the Selective Service officials.

(13) Registration Division, having jurisdiction of the following:

All matters relating to registration, the giving of serial and order numbers, the making out and filing of Questionnaires and listing on the classification list; "Work or Fight" regulations; registration and classification under treaty provisions; matters of personnel of industrial advisers; matters affecting registrants up to and including the filing of Questionnaires.

3. *National inspectors.*—With the growth of the selective service system by reason of the added registrations of June 5, August 24, and September 12, 1918, the problems of the State draft executives became so great and so varied that I deemed it advisable to create a system of visitation and inspection, in order to establish a personal touch with each State headquarters. To secure suitable persons to be charged with this most important duty, inquiry was made of the governors and other selective service officials in various parts of the country. Thirteen men, skilled in the application of the selective service law, were chosen, and, after a careful course of instruction in Washington, were on September 3 assigned to different sections of the country. Since that date they have been on duty almost continuously. Every State headquarters has been visited by them, carrying the message of the national headquarters.

With scarcely an exception the results have justified the appointment. A quickened activity invariably followed the visit of a national draft inspector and the sense of personal contact which ensued was highly beneficial to the State and national headquarters. The national inspectors functioned in perfect harmony with the State draft executives. At the request of the latter, many visits were made to local boards which needed added incentive or a word of advice as to methods of classification or the keeping of records. Through the national inspectors a means of local inspection of the entire system was gradually being installed, with the assistance of State inspectors, and much good was accomplished.

In the completion of the records of the selective service system, their verification, and their final lodgment in Washington, much will devolve on the inspection force thus created.

4. *Correspondence with the field force.*—Early in the experience of the office, certain principles were developed to accord with the general plan of local administration, and to relieve national headquarters of an excessive burden of detail. These principles were later embodied in section 25 of the Selective Service Regulations, and were consistently adhered to. Reference to that section will show that correspondence with the Provost Marshal General by individuals or by the local and district boards relating to the draft

was required to be conducted only through the adjutants general of the States, who were expected to deal with such communications. No opinions or rulings in individual cases were given by the Provost Marshal General; and general rulings were communicated only through the State headquarters. Local and district boards were made the centers for all inquiries by individuals, to be referred by the boards to the State adjutant general, and thence to the Provost Marshal General, if necessary. Complaints against boards were to be addressed to State executives. The office of the Provost Marshal General undertook to answer all requests for information from State headquarters as expeditiously as possible. Accordingly, with every letter which according to these rules could not be answered from this office, there was inclosed a printed form explaining why the letter could not be answered, and quoting the pertinent parts of section 25 of the Selective Service Regulations.

The justification of this procedure was obvious. This office controlled, through a system of supervised decentralization, and the cooperation of the governors of the several States, Territories, and the District of Columbia, an administrative machine comprising nearly 4,600 local boards, 160 district boards, and 52 State, Territorial, or District headquarters. Under the administration of the system there were from the very outset 10,000,000 registrants, and more or less directly interested in the registrants were perhaps 50,000,000 people. It was obviously impracticable and impossible to attempt direct correspondence either with the local and district boards or with the individuals who were affected by the system. It would have been inefficient and impossible to attempt to do so.

There was another reason why this office could make no rulings and give no opinion directly to individuals concerning the circumstances of individual cases. The law placed the determination of individual cases within the exclusive jurisdiction of local and district boards. For this office to attempt to make rulings on individual cases, on ex parte statements, and in the absence of complete information that was accessible to the proper board, would have been subversive of the law, and would have been an invasion of the jurisdiction of boards. Such rulings, moreover, might have been used to embarrass the function of these boards. For these reasons direct answers to such inquiries were inadvisable and impracticable.

However, it was desired to render the execution of the Selective Service law uniform and consistent throughout the country, and further, it was the purpose of this office to disseminate in the promptest manner and to the widest possible extent information and rulings concerning this law. To this end it was desired to make each local and district board a center of information for the community over which it had jurisdiction, and to make each State headquarters a center of information for all the local and district boards within the State. To accomplish this purpose the rules were framed for the correspondence of this office, as indicated in section 25, Selective Service Regulations.

By this system questions arising either in individual cases or from boards, were answered far more promptly than they would have been under any system of direct correspondence; uniformity and consistency in the execution of the law were also secured; and boards became convenient centers of information, obviating the time and expense that would have been lost by individuals if any attempt had been made to carry on direct correspondence with this office. The system, moreover, has relieved this office from the labor. of writing an average of from 200 to 250 letters daily.

Through the same system of supervised decentralization, all instructions, rulings, information of a general nature, and amendments to the Selective Service Regulations, with few exceptions, have been transmitted to the draft executives of the various States and Territories, and by them communicated to the local and district boards. Whenever possible the mails were used. Often, however, the nature of the instructions made it necessary to use the telegraph, although frequently it was possible to communicate instructions to near-by States, and in some cases to all States east of the Mississippi River, by letter, using the telegraph for the remainder. To have attempted direct communication with the boards, rather than with the State executives, would have enormously increased the telegraph tolls of this office.

Subsequent to the promulgation by mail or telegraph of rulings on and amendments to the Selective Service Regulations, it was the practice of this office, at first, to print them in pamphlet form. Seven such pamphlets were issued after the reprinting of the Regulations in September, 1917, but since the reprint of September, 1918, in which all amendments and important rulings and changes were included, it has not been necessary to issue any pamphlets.

Volume of correspondence.—Since January 1, 1918, over 3,500,000 pieces of mail have been received in this office, and over 340,000 letters and 30,000 telegrams have been sent out. Table 92 shows by months the number of pieces of mail and telegrams received and sent by this office to November 15, of this year. The large increase in incoming letter mail, beginning with June, is chiefly due to the heavy mobilization which began in the latter part of May. The further heavy increase, beginning in August and continuing through October, was caused by the continued heavy mobilization, and to the preparations for the September 12th registration and the subsequent classification of registrants. The summary of outgoing mail and telegrams shows increases in about the same degree.

TABLE 92.—*Summary of mail to Nov. 15, 1918.*

INCOMING.

1918	Letters.	Telegrams.	Other mail.
January	14,612	2,307	25,139
February	18,059	2,445	50,940
March	17,100	2,394	142,488
April	19,494	2,046	214,950
May	19,938	2,604	286,230
June	25,020	3,270	359,082
July	23,010	2,448	464,226
August	40,968	4,902	630,264
September	49,416	5,700	423,546
October	90,864	6,246	478,536
November	15,456	2,472	128,880
	333,937	36,834	3,204,281
Grand total			3,575,052

OUTGOING.

1918	Letters.	Telegrams.	Other mail.
January [1]	14,334	2,263	(2)
February [1]	17,716	2,399	(2)
March [1]	16,775	2,349	(2)
April [1]	19,124	2,007	(2)
May	11,130	1,960	(2)
June	35,700	2,520	(2)
July	25,296	3,024	(2)
August	48,936	4,080	(2)
September	36,828	4,176	(2)
October	88,698	5,262	(2)
November	26,970	1,668	(2)
	341,507	31,708	(2)
Grand total			373,215

[1] Estimated.   [2] Handled by Publications Division; see paragraph 6.

Filing system.—The system of filing originally installed to care for the general records of the office was adapted from the numerical system, completely indexed. At all times it has been equal to the burden thrown upon it, and has proved entirely satisfactory.

5. *Information Division.*—Though the District of Columbia boards were the appropriate headquarters for inquiries by registrants within the District, this office early became the Mecca for a vast volume of miscellaneous inquiries by telephone and by personal visits. To give the necessary satisfaction, the Information Division was established; and this division became a national mirror, in miniature, for the infinite variety of matters on which the Selective Service system was supposed, rightly or wrongly, to be able to cast some light.

On many days the number of visitors ran as high as 250; and there were equally as many telephone calls daily. In the minds of all of the inquirers there seemed to be the dominant thought that information on any subject connected with the war could be obtained at the headquarters of the Provost Marshal General. The majority of the inquiries dealt with matters entirely beyond the jurisdiction of this office. The questions propounded covered the entire gamut of things military. The inventor of a body armor, the originator of a new method of measuring skulls for the purposes of identification, the discoverer of a high explosive, and all kinds of efficiency experts, came seeking the Provost Marshal General's Office.

The approach of any important event in connection with the draft—such as the registrations, the beginning of physical examinations, heavy entrainments, the discontinuance of voluntary enlistment, the mailing of questionnaires—always placed upon this division an exceptionally heavy burden. And always there was the steady, daily volume of visits of registrants, or their relatives, who sought to have this office arbitrate their differences with local boards. Without doubt, the most difficult phase of the work of the Information Division has been to counsel and to placate that class of visitors, large in number, who considered they had been unjustly treated. With but few exceptions, however, they were sent away calm and satisfied. This answer, sympathetically but firmly given, usually sufficed to close the interview: "There is probably some equity in your case, and it certainly deserves to be carefully considered by your local board, on which Congress and the President have conferred exclusive jurisdiction. Go back to your local authorities and abide by their decision, because under the law and the regulations the Provost Marshal General has nothing whatever to do with this case." The majority of cases were of necessity handled in this manner. The experience in this division is a new proof that the conferring of authority upon local civilian boards to pass upon these questions was the master stroke of the Selective Service act. It was simply the carrying over, to the raising of an Army, of the familiar Anglo-Saxon principle of a local jury trial. That principle was understood by the people, and therefore it was accepted by the people. Any reasonable and fair method of drafting an army, if based on this principle, would have succeeded.

Cases involving technical questions and interpretations of the law and regulations generally were turned over to an officer having jurisdiction in the matter. In this respect, the Information Division acted as a clearing house for the visitors, and the constant interruption of officers by those seeking general information was prevented.

The visits of limited service men and those who had been placed in Class V as being physically unfit for military service, created a problem of no mean importance, as both groups of men were bent upon finding a place in the Army where they could render service. Some of the latter class, the physically unfit, pleaded for assistance in getting into the service. In a number of cases in both groups, where the defects were not too serious, suggestions were offered which led to the placing of the men.

From the great volume of miscellaneous inquiries it was interesting to note, as the months went by, the turn of sentiment toward the draft. At first the question was : "How can I keep out of the Army?" Gradually that attitude changed, until finally the question became: "How can I get into the Army right away?"

6. *Publications.*—The operations of the Publications Division embraced the printing and distribution of all printed regulations, instructions, and draft forms for the Selective Service system. It is easily conceivable that the registration and classification of 24,000,000 persons and the mobilization of 2,800,000 men for the Army would require many millions of forms; but not until it is stated that the administration of the Selective Service act required the printing and distribution to draft boards of more than 500,000,000 separate pieces of printed matter is a full realization gained of the magnitude of the the undertaking. Table 93 shows the quantities of printed matter, separated as to registrations.

TABLE 93.—*Printed forms required for the Selective Service system.*

	Registrations.	Number.
1	Total	544,000,000
2	First registration, June, 1917–June, 1918	284,000,000
3	Second registration, June–August, 1918	27,000,000
4	Third registration, September–November, 1918	233,000,000

(a) *Printing.*—The printing of this quantity of forms was a task of such proportions as to tax to the utmost the Government Printing Office. This institution, however, responded admirably to the unprecedented demands made upon it, and some remarkable records were made. The most notable of these was the printing of forms of all kinds for the registration, classification, and mobilization of the registrants of September 12, 1918. This immense task was performed during a period of 50 days. Several records for quantity and speed made during this time deserve special mention. Fifteen million questionnaires were printed in 34 days. Fourteen and one-half millions of one-page leaflets were printed within 60 hours after the presses were started, at an average hourly production of 240,000 copies. Thirty-two and one-half million registration cards were turned out in 8 days; and numerous other achievements could be mentioned. Historians of the future, in recording the many wonderful deeds to the credit of the Nation during this war, should not overlook the assistance rendered by the Government Printing Office in raising the National Army; and this Report would not be complete without an acknowledgment of the manner in which that establishment performed its portion of the work.

For the purpose of enabling accurate reference in the future, by historians and other inquirers, to the literature of the selective service system, a list is given in Appendix H, of the principal printed forms issued from this office.

(b) *Distribution.*—The supplies were shipped to the various State headquarters and by them distributed to local boards. Under this decentralized plan, bulk shipments were made to 52 auxiliary depots at State headquarters for reshipment direct to nearly 5,000 boards. This resulted in marked economy and efficiency, without any resultant loss of control by this office. The responsibility for furnishing local boards with proper forms was thus placed squarely on the various State draft executives, who were in close touch with local conditions. The distribution of these supplies was based on the number of registrants in each State; by a simple system of recording, it was possible to arrange the shipments so that actual requirements were met and at the same time losses and wastage held to a minimum.

The shipment to local boards of all these millions of forms represented a distribution problem of huge proportions. Lacking the necessary printed forms, the local Selective Service machinery would have been like an army without guns and ammunition. But at no time was the machinery in danger of even a temporary stoppage due to lack of printed supplies.

(II) THE STATE EXECUTIVES.

1. *The governors.*—Section 6 of the Selective Service Act represented some of the deepest wisdom of its framers; for under this section it became possible to decentralize the administration, and to lay hold, for war purposes, of the time-honored traditions of local self-government which have been the bulwark of our national progress in times of peace. The act authorized the President "to utilize the services of any or all departments and any or all officers or agents of the States, Territories, and the District of Columbia," and required all persons so designated "to perform such duty as the President shall order or direct." It was obvious, from the outset, that for the vast task impending nothing less would suffice than the employment of the official energies of each State, already organized in the State

administrations. These 52 centers of power were ready at hand, and must be invoked.

The President's letter of April 23, 1917, to the governors (printed in full in my first Report, p. 7) referred to the "gratifying and evident eagerness of the States to do their utmost in aid of the Nation at this emergent moment," and expressed the conviction that State agencies "promise the swiftest and the most effective possible execution of the law." How promptly and effectively the governors responded to this preliminary call, in organizing the first registration of June 5, 1917, was told in my first report. But it has remained for the succeeding months to demonstrate that this initial response was but the forerunner of a steady and increasing contribution of organized mass energy which ensured the success of the Selective Service system.

During the Civil War there emerged half a dozen notable figures who have come down in the annals of history as "war governors"— men whose vigorous patriotism set a pace for public opinion, organized the war effort, and threw the whole strength of their States in support of the Federal Government war measures. But in the raising of the Army for the present war we have had, it may be said, 51 war governors. Accepting with ready hands the charge committed to them by the President under this act, they have turned the State and Territorial capitals into decentralized selective service agencies, and have labored unremittingly in the thousands of detailed tasks necessary for mustering the manhood of their several States into the service of the Nation.

In the report of Brig. Gen. James B. Fry, Acting Provost Marshal General, rendered at the close of the Civil War, bitter allusion is made to the stubborn and hostile attitude exhibited by some of the then governors to the President's requisitions in the early period of that conflict. From the governor of one State came this communication: "Your requisition is illegal, unconstitutional, revolutionary, inhuman, diabolical, and can not be complied with." From the governor of another this protest was received: "Your despatch is received; in answer, I say, emphatically, this State will furnish no troops for the wicked purpose of subduing her sister southern States." These States themselves were afterwards found contributing amply and generously of men to the armies of the North. They were misrepresented by their leaders; but these messages, and others of like tenor, brought dismay to those who bore the national burden at Washington. It seems scarcely credible, living at this day, that the Union could have succeeded in its war effort against the undermining influence exerted within its own ranks by State leaders holding such views in opposition to the raising of the Federal Army.

But, looking away from those dark days to the present, we may well be thankful a hundred times—nay, a thousand times—that the contrast stands revealed with such startling brightness.   There lies before me a typical telegram of 1918 from a State governor, sent to acknowledge receipt of a notice from this office outlining the measures needed for a new stage then approaching in the selective draft; it can not be read without emotion:

> I take pleasure in assuring you that the people of this State are unitedly and whole-heartedly in accord with these plans for the creation of an army that will bring victory soon and decisively, and that any call which you may see fit to make upon them will be enthusiastically answered.

The annals of our country will never yield a finer record of stanch and devoted cooperation by all State leaders in the common national cause.   It is this hearty cooperation by the governors with the Federal Executive that has made possible the success of the selective service system.

The phrase "supervised decentralization" has come to be a short term descriptive of this relation.   The task was a Federal one, but the agencies were the State administrations.   Though they acted under presidential guidance and direction, yet the responsibility for success or failure in carrying out these directions lay upon each one for his State, and they retained the fullest measure of their inherent authority within their own jurisdiction.   But it was never doubted that the States would respond to the call; and this faith was vindicated.

The relation was an anomalous and a novel one.   It lay between the extremes of voluntary independent State action, on the one hand, and local multiplication of direct Federal agencies on the other hand: the only two types hitherto recognized in our political system. But it proved efficient, amply efficient, and in a cause where inefficiency would have been fatal.   Perhaps some lessons in the field of American government can hereafter be drawn from this experience.

2. *The draft executives.*—It was inevitable that the President's call upon the governors of the several States and the Board of Commissioners of the District of Columbia, to supervise the execution of the Selective Service Law and Regulations in their respective jurisdictions, should add enormously to the labors, burdens, and responsibilities of the governors.   The suggestion was therefore made at an early date that each governor charge his adjutant general with the duty of administering the details of the system, and generally to delegate to his adjutant general so much of his authority as he saw fit.   This course was adopted, and all State headquarters were without delay authorized to obtain the necessary clerical assistants.

As time went on, and the intricacies and problems of the decentralized system became more numerous and multifarious, it became apparent that each State adjutant general was in need of an assistant executive officer, who could give his entire time to draft activities. It was decided that this assistant should be paid by the Federal Government. Accordingly, the governors were called upon to recommend for appointment, as commissioned officers, men who had been connected with the execution of the Selective Service Law, and had disclosed the greatest qualifications for the accurate, fair, and expeditious execution of the selective service processes. It also become necessary to place at the disposal of State headquarters a medical officer. Consequently, each governor was asked to recommend for appointment, as an Army officer, a physician and surgeon who possessed particular skill and training in his profession and who could immediately acquaint himself with the Army physical examination regulations, so that he might become the adviser of the governor along those lines, and thereby secure a uniform application of the rules for physical examinations. From those recommended as requested, one medical aide and one military aide for each State were appointed and assigned to duty to assist the governor and his adjutant general.

In this way a most dependable and efficient organization was developed for each State. These organizations owed immediate accountability to the respective governors and were under their direct supervision. The governors accepted the grave responsibility tendered them. Gladly and unselfishly becoming a vital part of the draft machinery, they continuously, promptly, and effectively gave their whole cooperation to this office.

Notwithstanding the fact that each governor has retained in himself authority to pass finally upon any question that might arise in relation to the draft, in a substantial number of the States the actual administration has practically been placed in the hands of the adjutant general or his commissioned assistant. As evidence of this fact, the governors of some States have designated either their adjutants general, or the Army officers assigned to State headquarters, as their draft executives, and have requested this office to address all communications dealing with draft matters to such draft executives.

3. *Duties of State headquarters.*—The functions and tasks of State selective service headquarters are epitomized in section 27, Selective Service Regulations, which reads as follows:

The governors shall be charged with general supervision over all matters arising in the execution of the selective draft within their States. The determination of questions of exemptions and deferred classifications is within the exclusive jurisdiction of local and district boards, subject only to review by the President; but all other functions and duties of boards, departments, officers, agents, and persons within the State, except departments, officers, and agents of the United States not appointed, designated, or detailed under authority of the selective service law, shall be under the direction and supervision of the governor.

Perhaps the most fundamental of the duties of the State headquarters was the creation, establishment, and maintenance of registration, selection, and auxiliary boards; under the selective service act the President appointed the members of these boards, but the actual selection of personnel was made by the governors; for appointments, removals, and substitutions were made only upon the recommendations of the governors. Besides this primary task, however, they bore a heavy burden of miscellaneous work, which may be thus summarized: (1) The handling of delinquency cases as required by Selective Service Regulations (2d ed.), sections 132–139; (2) the purchase and distribution of supplies, the checking of vouchers, the payment of accounts, and the performance of all other duties required by the disbursement regulations; (3) the apportionment of quotas, the allotment of calls, the ·routing and entrainment of registrants, and the performance· of other duties relating to induction and mobilization; (4) the conduct of a heavy correspondence, not only with the various selective service boards, but with other Government officials, with representatives of all kinds of organizations, and with individuals; (5) the assignment of serial numbers to late registrants, and the cancellation of registrations; (6) the general supervision and direction of the work of the selective service, boards, including medical advisory boards, frequently involving trips of inspection and meetings for conference and exchange of views; (7) the interpretation of the regulations, involving correspondence with this office and with the boards; (8) the selection and nomination of members of all the various selective service boards, the investigation of charges against boards or members thereof, and the maintenance of a sound morale throughout the system; (9) the preparation of reports called for, from time to time, by this office; (10) the preparation and distribution of bulletins or circular letters for the information of the boards; (11) the organization and supervision of boards of instruction; (12) the performance of all duties required of them as commanders of the force of enlisted men assigned to headquarters and to the offices of the various boards; (13) cooperation with State councils of defense, the War Risk Insurance Bureau, and other organizations or bureaus in war work of all kinds.

4. *State inspectors.*—When each of these State systems is envisioned in its decentralization—the headquarters at the State capital; the local boards and the legal advisory boards and Government appeal

agents attached to them, scattered throughout the State; the medical advisory boards located at convenient points and each serving several local boards; and the district board established in each Federal judicial district—the question naturally arises, How was it possible to maintain effective State supervision over so many instrumentalities? It is apparent that the few officers on duty at State headquarters could not frequently leave their posts to advise with boards or members thereof. Yet experience had taught that, because of the intricacies of the selective service system, the changing presidential regulations, and the complexity of the domestic, industrial, and military conditions of this country, the best results were obtained, both from a national and individual standpoint, by conferences between the trained experts and board members. In order to provide for these conferences, to maintain closer contact, and to augment uniformity of decision, the governors were authorized to employ a limited number of State inspectors. The inspection, advisory, and checking system thus created has worked efficaciously and satisfactorily.

5. *Clerical force.*—In the early stages of the classification method there developed a class of registrants disqualified by physical condition for actual combatant service but qualified for noncombatant service. The uses made of these group C men, in general, have been pointed out in Chapter IV. One of these uses was that of clerical service in War Department offices. The War Department accordingly, in the summer of 1918, authorized commanding officers of divisions, bureaus, branches, and departments, including that of the Provost Marshal General, to make requisitions for such men as could be used to advantage in such positions. By virtue of this authority, some 4,000 limited service men were brought into use as clerks, assistants, stenographers, etc., by local and district boards and State headquarters. The Army officer assigned as aid to the governor, or as assistant to the adjutant general in each State, was the commanding officer of such enlisted men in the State. The adoption of this expedient greatly relieved the clerical difficulties, and was an important factor in enabling the production of accurate, valuable, and enduring draft records.

6. *Supervision and control.*—The foregoing outline indicates the vital part that the State organizations formed in the selective service mechanism. It should be emphasized that the system which has proven so successful is essentially one of *National* supervision but of *State* control. In the light of the accomplishments that stand out, and with the knowledge of the problems that have arisen, it is fair to indulge the opinion that the demands of this war for man-power could have not been met under a system controlled and supervised in every respect by one central office.

(III) DISTRICT BOARDS.

1. *Number and personnel.*—To the ordinary citizen the selective service law was personified by the local board engaged in dispatching to the camps his friends and neighbors. In the mind of every registrant the memories of the draft will be centered in that local board with which he registered, to which he mailed his questionnaire, and upon whose summons the whole course of his life, perhaps life itself, depended. While the local boards were thus vividly brought into the foreground of the war drama, winning the credit which will justly be theirs, the rôle of the district boards contributed scarcely less to the successful raising of our selective forces.

Any account of the personnel of the district boards should therefore begin and end by recalling the importance of the functions intrusted to them by the selective service act. Their duties were twofold: First, to review the decisions of local boards upon appeal; second, to hear and determine as courts of first instance all questions of accepting or excluding from the draft persons engaged in necessary industries, including agriculture, or other necessary occupations or employments. Thus in their capacity as appellate tribunals they provided a check on irregularities by local boards, promoted uniformity in the application of the law, and assured to every registrant the opportunity of a rehearing before a court removed from local prejudice and influence. In the exercise of their original jurisdiction, they became not only agents of selection for the Army, but guardians of the industrial and agricultural interests of the Nation. These responsible and burdensome obligations demanded the selection of members not only representative of the leading divisions of our population, but possessed of experience, breadth of view, and executive ability.

The normal board consisted originally of five members appointed by the President on the recommendation of the governors. The instructions calling for such nominations required that the composition of the boards should be as follows:

One member who is in close touch with the agricultural situation of the district, one member who is in close touch with the industrial situation of the district, one member who is in close touch with labor, one physician, one lawyer.

The result was the enlistment in 155 boards of 780 men of recognized achievements and integrity, many of them possessing a national reputation. As the magnitude of the task of selection increased, their number was augmented from time to time until it reached a total of 1,039. Appendix Table 91–A shows their distribution by States.

The immediate infusion into the selective service system of this group of able and highly patriotic civilians went far in itself to vindicate the wisdom of intrusting to local agencies the raising of our armies. No such cooperation from proved leaders of our people could possibly have been secured by any centralized or militarized organization devised for the purpose.

2. *Scope of work.*—On the average the district board had within its jurisdiction 30 local boards, each of these with an aggregate average registration of 5,000. Appendix I shows the jurisdiction of the respective district boards. It was important to establish successful working relations with these local boards. At the start, the appeals from local boards on behalf of both the Government and of the registrants assumed enormous proportions. All the boards were new at the work, the regulations allowed some elasticity, hence lack of uniformity was the rule rather than the exception, especially in the important field of dependency and the selection of married men. To reconcile the decisions of 30 lower tribunals, numerous reversals were made by the district boards, the reason for which was not always fully understood by the local boards concerned. Very often also the district boards did not follow the recommendations of local boards with respect to industrial and agricultural claims. A local board striving honestly to apply the regulations often felt aggrieved when repeatedly overruled by the district board which, with a broader field of action, read the rules from a slightly different angle. But, in the main, cordial and helpful relations were maintained, uniformity increased, and a constantly lessening number of cases were appealed to the district board.

As the appellate work of the district boards diminished, the importance of their position as arbiters between industry and the Army steadily grew. The withdrawal of the first 687,000 men from the economic life of the nation did not impose a serious handicap on any activity which could in any wise be classed as necessary. But as the draft mounted into the millions, the problem became more serious. The rôle of the district boards commanded attentive study by all large employers of labor and became of vital interest to the farmer as the supply of labor waned. It was then that the caliber of the district boards received its severest test, and that its members performed their most valuable service to the country.

Finally Congress, while enlarging the draft ages, opened a still broader field to the district boards, by giving them added jurisdiction of all claims based on engagement in necessary occupations or employments. With a body of 13,000,000 new registrants, the majority of them upward of 31 years of age, with the already great depletion of man-power and with the uncertainty attending the definition of a necessary occupation or employment, the task facing the district boards at the termination of hostilities imposed still more responsible and arduous duties. With rare exceptions, the district boards performed their duties with great fidelity and success.

3. *Necessary industries.*—Among these numerous groups of able men, accustomed to independent thought and action, uniformity of interpretation was not to be expected. Some confined their definition of a necessary industry to agriculture and enterprises directly engaged in productive war work, hesitating at first to include even transportation operations. Others adopted a wider view and included undertakings of a commercial nature or those upon which communities were so dependent as to require protection.

Through administrative suggestion and experience such variations were gradually narrowed. The idea was frequently advanced from many sources that a list or classification of necessary industries and occupations should be promulgated for the guidance of district boards, but such action was wisely avoided except as to the Emergency Fleet list. Nevertheless much popular misunderstanding and confusion arose, as already noted in Chapters III and IV, from the priorities list of the War Industries Board, and even from the group of nonproductive occupations enumerated in the "Work or Fight" regulations. There can be no doubt that the elasticity gained by the untrammeled exercise of judgment by each board on the problem of protection for industry overbalanced the loss of any apparent uniformity that would have arisen from a classification of preferred activities. Congress obviously intended the district boards to settle this problem. An enterprise properly regarded as necessary in one part of the country might not require similar protection elsewhere. Lack of national uniformity, therefore, was not necessarily objectionable.

Nevertheless, to ascertain how far in actual practice the rulings of the district boards, based on their own knowledge and judgment, did coincide with the national recommendations formulated in September, 1918, by the War Industries Board, in its priorities list, this list was submitted to the district boards in November, 1918 (without disclosing to them its origin), and they were asked to mark those industries and products which they had treated as "necessary," in the administration of the selective service act during 1917 and 1918. The results are shown in Table 94, and will repay study. Appendix Table 94–A shows the variance by States.

TABLE 94.—*Essential industries (priorities list) found "necessary" by district boards.*

Key No.	Industry.	Rating of War Industries Board priorities.	Number of district boards ruling the industry to be necessary.
	Agricultural implements. (See Farm implements.)		
1	Aircraft: Plants engaged principally in manufacturing aircraft or aircraft supplies and equipment..................	I	132
2	Ammunition: Plants engaged principally in manufacturing same for the United States Government and the allies......	I	138
3	Army and Navy: Arsenals and navy yards.................	I	134
4	Army and Navy: Cantonments and camps..................	I	118
5	Arms (small): Plants engaged principally in manufacturing same for the United States Government and the allies......	I	130
6	Bags: Hemp, jute, and cotton—plants engaged principally in manufacturing same...:	IV	68
7	Blast furnaces (producing pig iron).........................	I	104
8	Boots and shoes: Plants engaged exclusively in manufacturing same..	IV	89
9	Brass and copper: Plants engaged principally in rolling and drawing copper, brass, and other copper alloys in the form of sheets, rods, wire, and tubes............................	II	97
	Buildings. (See Public institutions and buildings.)		
10	Chain: Plants engaged principally in manufacturing iron and steel chain.....................................	III	78
11	Chemicals: Plants engaged principally in manufacturing chemicals for the production of military and naval explosives, ammunition, and aircraft, and use in chemical warfare..	I	137
12	Chemicals: Plants, not otherwise classified and listed, engaged principally in manufacturing chemicals.............	IV	79
13	Coke: Plants engaged principally in producing metallurgical coke and by-products, including toluol..................	I	111
14	Coke: Plants, not otherwise classified and listed, producing same...	II	74
	Copper and brass. (See Brass and copper.)		
15	Cotton: Plants engaged in the compression of cotton........	IV	56
	Cotton textiles. (See Textiles.)		
16	Cranes: Plants engaged principally in manufacturing locomotive cranes...	II	77
17	Cranes: Plants engaged principally in manufacturing traveling cranes...	II	77
18	Domestic consumers: Fuel and electric energy for residential consumption, including homes, apartment houses, residential flats, restaurants, and hotels......................	I	93
19	Domestic consumers: Fuel and electric energy not otherwise specifically listed.................................	III	65
20	Drugs: Medicines and medical and surgical supplies, plants engaged principally in manufacturing same...............	IV	104
21	Electrical equipment: Plants engaged principally in manufacturing same..	III	103
22	Explosives: Plants engaged principally in manufacturing same for military and naval purposes for the United States Government and the allies.................................	I	134
23	Explosives: Plants not otherwise classified or listed, engaged principally in manufacturing same..................	III	105
24	Farm implements: Plants engaged principally in manufacturing agricultural implements and farm-operating equipment..	IV	107
25	Feed: Plants engaged principally in preparing or manufacturing feed for live stock and poultry....................	I	77

TABLE 94.—*Essential industries (priorities list) found "necessary" by district boards—*
Continued.

Key No.	Industry.	Rating of War Industries Board priorities.	Number of district boards ruling the industry to be necessary.
26	Ferro alloys: Plants engaged principally in producing ferrochrome, ferromanganese, ferromolybdenum, ferrosilicon, ferrotungsten, ferrouranium, ferrovanadium, and ferrozirconium.	II	79
27	Fertilizers: Plants engaged principally in producing same.	IV	77
28	Fire brick: Plants engaged principally in manufacturing same.	IV	69
29	Foods: Plants engaged principally in producing, milling, refining, preserving, refrigerating, or storing food for human consumption embraced within the following description: All cereals and cereal products, meats (including poultry), fish, vegetables, fruit, sugar, sirups, glucose, butter, eggs, cheese, milk and cream, lard, lard compounds, oleomargarine and other substitutes for butter or lard, vegetable oils, beans, salt, coffee, baking powder, soda, and yeast; also ammonia for refrigeration.	I	128
30	Foods: Plants engaged principally in producing, milling, preparing, re ning, preserving, refrigerating, or storing food for human consumption not otherwise specifically listed, excepting herefrom plants producing confectionery, soft drinks, and chewing gum.	III	103
31	Food containers: Plants engaged principally in manufacturing same.	IV	95
32	Foundries (iron): Plants engaged principally in the manufacture of gray iron and malleable iron castings.	IV	119
	Fungicides. (See Insecticides and fungicides.)		
	Gas. (See Oil and gas; also Public utilities.)		
33	Guns (large): Plants engaged principally in manufacturing same for the United States Government and the allies.	I	127
	Hospitals. (See Public institutions and buildings.)		
34	Ice: Plants engaged principally in manufacturing same.	III	75
35	Insecticides and fungicides: Plants engaged principally in manufacturing same.	IV	45
36	Laundries.	IV	37
37	Machine tools: Plants engaged principally in manufacturing same.	II	115
	Medicines. (See Drugs and medicines.)		
38	Mines: Coal.	I	113
39	Mines: Producing metals and ferro-alloy minerals.	II	104
40	Mines: Plants engaged principally in manufacturing mining tools or equipment.	III	93
	Navy. (See Army and Navy.)		
	Navy Department. (See War and Navy Departments.)		
41	Newspapers and periodicals: Plants engaged principally in printing newspapers or periodicals which are entered at the post office as second-class mail matter.	IV	77
42	Oil and gas: Plants engaged principally in producing oil or natural gas for fuel or for mechanical purposes, including refining or manufacturing oil for fuel or for mechanical purposes.	I	102
43	Oil and gas: Pipe lines and pumping stations engaged in transporting oil or natural gas.	I	85

TABLE 94.—*Essential industries (priorities list) found "necessary" by district boards—*
Continued.

Key No.	Industry.	Rating of War Industries Board priorities.	Number of district boards ruling the industry to be necessary.
44	Oil and gas: Plants engaged principally in manufacturing equipment or supplies for producing or transporting oil or natural gas or for refining and manufacturing oil for fuel or for mechanical purposes	III	81
	Paper and pulp. (See Pulp and paper.)		
	Periodicals. (See Newspapers and periodicals.)		
45	Public institutions and buildings (maintenance and operation of) other than hospitals and sanitariums	III	51
46	Public institutions and buildings (maintenance and operation of) used as hospitals or sanitariums	I	109
47	Public utilities: Gas plants producing toluol	I	103
48	Public utilities: Street railways, electric lighting and power companies, gas plants not otherwise classified, telephone and telegraph companies, water-supply companies, and like general utilities	II	129
49	Public utilities: Plants engaged principally in manufacturing equipment for railways or other public utilities	II	109
50	Pulp and paper: Plants engaged exclusively in manufacturing same	IV	88
51	Railways: Operated by United States Railroad Administration	I	141
52	Railways: Not operated by United States Railroad Administration (excluding those operated as plant facilities)	II	116
	Railways (street). (See Public utilities.)		
	Rope. (See Twine and rope.)		
	Rope wire. (See Wire rope.)		
	Sanitariums. (See Public institutions and buildings.)		
53	Ships (maintenance and operation of): Excluding pleasure craft not common carriers	I	120
54	Ships: Plants engaged principally in building ships, excluding (a) pleasure craft not common carriers, (b) ships not built for the United States Government or the allies nor under license from United States Shipping Board	I	108
55	Soap: Plants engaged principally in manufacturing same	IV	72
56	Steel-making furnaces: Plants engaged solely in manufacturing ingots and steel castings by the open-hearth, Bessemer, crucible, or electric-furnace process, including blooming mills, billet mills, and slabbing mills for same	I	106
57	Steel-plate mills	I	99
58	Steel-rail mills: Rolling rails, 50 or more pounds per yard	II	96
59	Steel: All plants operating steel rolling and drawing mills exclusive of those taking higher classification	III	107
	Surgical supplies. (See Drugs and medicines.)		
60	Tanners: Plants engaged principally in tanning leather	IV	90
61	Tanning: Plants engaged principally in manufacturing tanning extracts	IV	73
62	Textiles: Plants engaged principally in manufacturing cotton textiles, including spinning, weaving, and finishing	IV	90
63	Textiles: Plants engaged principally in manufacturing woolen textiles, including spinners, top makers, and weavers	IV	97
64	Textiles: Plants engaged principally in manufacturing cotton or woolen knit goods	IV	93
65	Textiles: Plants engaged principally in manufacturing textile machinery	IV	77

TABLE 94.—*Essential industries (priorities list) found "necessary" by district boards*—Continued.

Key No.	Industry	Rating of War Industries Board priorities.	Number of district boards ruling the industry to be necessary.
66	Tin plates: Plants engaged principally in manufacturing same...	III	73
67	Tobacco: Only for preserving, drying, curing, packing, and storing same—not for manufacturing and marketing........	IV	57
	Toluol. (See Coke; also Public utilities.)		
68	Tools: Plants engaged principally in manufacturing small or hand tools for working wood or metal....................	III	93
69	Twine (binder and rope): Plants engaged principally in manufacturing same..................................	IV	80
70	War and Navy Departments: Construction work conducted by either the War Department or the Navy Department of the United States in embarkation ports, harbors, fortified places, flood-protection operations, docks, locks, channels, inland waterways, and in the maintenance and repair of same.......	II	130
71	Wire rope and rope wire: Plants engaged principally in manufacturing same.................................	II	89
	Woolen textiles. (See Textiles.)		

NOTE.—The term "principally" means 75 per cent of the products mentioned.

4. *Methods of work.*—Methods of work naturally varied also. A practice widely followed, when the questionnaires were received, was to assign the cases to the several members; the agricultural representative taking the claims of farmers, the industrial member the claims based on industry, and perhaps the labor member the dependency claims, and the lawyer the alienage cases. A majority of the claims could thus be disposed of on the recommendation of one member, while only the difficult minority required more extended consideration. The largest board in the country, that of New York City, comprising 30 members, operated in this way with a fully developed system of committees.

At times, and often for extended periods, all of the boards worked under high pressure and for long hours, giving the best that in them lay, to hold the balance equitably between the demands of the Army and the necessities of the Nation's home and economic life. Numerous members served without compensation. In a few instances the entire board declined to receive pay; and it is estimated that about one-fifth of the total personnel labored without monetary recompense.

Under the original regulations of June 30, 1917, appeals to the President were allowed without restriction to those whose industrial or agricultural claims were denied by the district boards. These rules required a minute of the reasons for the decision in each case.

Many of such notations forwarded with the records on appeal amounted to careful legal opinions, sometimes accompanied with dissenting views, and conclusively showing the intelligent and painstaking efforts of the boards to be just to both the Government and the registrant. It was perhaps unfortunate that the restricted space provided on the questionnaire for a minute of the action by the boards curtailed a similar expression of recorded opinion.

Not infrequently a case of local or even national notoriety arose in which great pressure was exerted for the discharge of a registrant. The record became voluminous, with affidavits pro and con, and occasionally the board patiently received extensive oral testimony. It is safe to say that in nearly all such cases the final decision received the approval of intelligent public opinion.

The majority of the boards were liberal in the matter of reopening a decided case upon the presentation of new evidence. All were jealous of their independence of action and imbued with a desire to carry through to a successful conclusion this novel and drastic application of democratic principles.

All classification by district boards ceased on November 16, 1918, when they were in the midst of a flood of cases arising from the September 12th registration. Thus their work continued about 16 months. During this period their members gave the strongest possible indorsement to the principles embodied in the selective service system. With unselfish patriotism they made, for the winning of the war, an unobtrusive contribution of far greater worth than has yet been generally recognized.

(IV) INDUSTRIAL ADVISERS.

It became necessary (as already explained in Chapter IV), after the amendment of the selective service act on August 31, 1918, to give special assistance to the district boards for obtaining complete data upon occupational claims for deferment. It was directed that each district board should appoint three persons, to be known as industrial advisers to the board; one to be nominated by the Department of Labor, one by the Department of Agriculture, and one by each district board.

These advisers were to confer with the managers and heads of various industries and those familiar with the needs in other occupations, including agriculture; to instruct such persons as to their right to file claims for deferred classification for registrants in their employ; and to furnish to the district boards all information in their possession which might be of use in the work of classification. Any adviser was authorized to initiate a claim for deferred classification on any ground within the jurisdiction of the district board, although no claim had previously been made for the registrant; and this right could be exer-cised up to the day and hour fixed for the registrant to report for military duty.

On the date of the armistice 126 out of the total of 155 district boards in the whole country had reported the appointment of the full quota of their advisers. But the cessation of military activities and of the further operations of the selective draft brought to an early end the work of the industrial advisers. There can be no doubt that their work would have increased greatly the efficiency of the system of deferment of registrants necessary for retention in civil occupations.

(V) LOCAL BOARDS.

The term "local board" occupies a unique place in the thought of the Nation and in the hearts of the people. It has acquired a distinct individuality. Long after the selective service machinery will have been dismantled, and the processes of the draft will have faded from memory, the term "local board" will hold its place in our speech as the typical mark of the system that lifted America from the most peaceful of Nations to a place of first magnitude among military powers. That mobilization of man power was chiefly accomplished, not by military officers, nor even by civilians peculiarly trained for such service, but by laymen from each community, chosen only for their unquestioned patriotism, fair-mindedness, and integrity, and impelled solely by the motive of patriotic self-sacrifice.

1. *Character of membership.*—In framing the selective service act Congress definitely decided to entrust the draft directly to the people, and to enlist their full confidence by placing upon them the fullest responsibility. Thus was the draft, by the very terms of the act, made neither Federal nor military, but civilian and local. To effectu-ate the ideal of localizing the draft, it seemed necessary to have it administered by committees of men intimately acquainted with the lives and circumstances of the people of their communities. This intimate knowledge was reckoned to be physically possible only in a community not exceeding 30,000 inhabitants. The total number of boards has fluctuated slightly, owing to changes in county organiza-tion; but it finally stood at 4,648 (including the Territories), with a total roster of 14,416 members. Appendix Table 91–A shows the composition in the respective States.

It was further realized that board members should be chosen from the standpoint of environment rather than with reference to their professions or calling. Neither legal nor governmental train-ing was the essential qualification. An intimate knowledge and appreciation of all varieties of local conditions being necessary, a composite board of capable, reputable, and representative men, having different careers and experiences, would be the best judges of the equities of the law in its application to their neighbors. Local boards were constituted on the principle of their peerage with the men whose cases they were to decide. That the boards were genuinely representative of their communities is demonstrated by the wide range of their occupations, given in Table 95.

TABLE 95.—*Occupations of local board members.*

	Occupations of local board members.	Number.
1	Total, personnel, Oct. 1, 1918, reporting as to occupations	13,564
2	Medicine	4,246
3	Public office	2,841
4	Law	1,517
5	Agriculture	982
6	Commerce	975
7	Banking	379
8	Manufacturing	313
9	Education	142
10	Labor	121
11	Transportation	102
12	Clergy	74
13	Other occupations	1,872

How vital to the system was this feature of the local board composition, viz, the local character of their membership, has already been dwelt on in Chapter I. But it is here appropriate to note some practical consequences, due apparently to this feature.

(a) One was that they became the buffers between the individual citizen and the Federal Government; and thus they attracted and diverted, like local grounding wires in an electric coil, such resentment or discontent as might have proved a serious obstacle to war measures, had it been focussed on the central authorities. Its diversion and grounding at 5,000 local points dissipated its force, and enabled the central war machine to function smoothly without the disturbance that might have been caused by the concentrated total of dissatisfaction. A disappointed claimant for exemption met a board member one day on the street, and burst out: "Your ruling was rank and damnable." The board member replied: "We did our duty in the light of the facts." "All the same," replied the irate citizen, "you went wrong. And if I only took the time and trouble to appeal to Washington, they would tell you that you were wrong, and I would get justice. They would never stand for such a ruling. They know what's right, and they would soon see that you were made to do the right thing. But I am not going to appeal. Only I want you to know what I think of your board." This was typical of the board's function as a buffer—a decentralizer of individual discontent with the enforcement of the law. The war value of this function was enormous, and it is a demonstration of one of the virtues of a decentralized administration.

But the boards became the bearers of this burden; they, and they only, were the sufferers; while the Government was the gainer, and was all the freer to achieve its war measures. This feature must be counted, therefore, in footing up the national bill of gratitude to the devoted men who bore uncomplainingly the slings and arrows of such discontent.

(b) Another feature, developing from the responsibility placed on local leaders, was the conscientious and fearless persistence shown in following up the technical draft register—rich and poor alike, powerful as well as humble. To the genuine pleadings of a meritorious claimant, they were considerate and patient. But to the quibbling expedients of the man who sought to evade his obvious duty, they were relentless, especially when he sought the aid of legal technicalities. In such cases, they exhibited the qualities of the sleuthhound which never leaves the trail until the quarry is run down. Their official responsibility for raising the Army was touched to the quick; their personal efficiency was at stake; and they made it their business to persist in that man's case till the end, and to demonstrate to him and to the public that the national claim on him was inexorable and immutable, and that neither fear nor favor would relax their enforcement of that duty. In this attitude they found ample support in the public sentiment of their community.

In two or three instances of national notoriety the aid of the Department of Justice had finally to be invoked to fortify the efforts of the boards. But the following letter, from an Atlantic local board, exhibits the board relying sturdily upon its own pluck to cope with the problem, in the form of a whole family of technical evaders:

SEPTEMBER 2, 1918.

DEAR SIR: Our chief clerk says that you telephoned for a report on the X cases, which were in the United States district court. We would have written sooner but we were in the United States court Friday from 10 a. m. till 4.30 p. m.; also on Saturday the board was there till 1 p. m., after which we had 42 hearings for the evening, which we finished at 11 p. m.; these cases involved the questions as to whether the condition occurred according to the new rulings as mentioned in the seventy-fourth section of the two hundred and eleventh amendment as embodied on the second page of the one hundred and ninth Bulletin; if we heard these cases the way they do in the United States court, we wouldn't have finished them in 26 years.

John X's case was dismissed by the court in our favor at 1 p. m. Friday, August 23; John was inducted at 7 a. m. August 26; he failed to report, and the same afternoon was reported to the police as a deserter; at 9 p. m. we were served with a writ to show cause, etc., and stop further proceedings and come down to the Federal Building in the morning. We went down the next morning, and the United States court said to withdraw the order of arrest as John was not a deserter. We said he was. The court said he wasn't. We said he was and the United States attorney said he was, Capt. A.

said he was, and Inspector B. from The Adjutant General's Office said he was; so we .
telegraphed to Washington for instructions. John was given into our custody in the
courtroom Saturday at 1 p. m. We still held he was a deserter, and took him right up
to your office. Capt. C. held that it was up to the board whether he was a real deserter
or a nonwillful delinquent. Neither Capt. C. nor Capt. A. offered to feed him, and the
Government has given us no allowance for meals (or for anything else since last
February). So we took John over to Main Street at 1.15, and paroled him in his own
custody so he could buy his own dinner. He reported back to the board at 5 p. m.
(These fellows are big eaters). John is now at Camp Gordon, Ga.

James X was previously brought down from Fort Blank by a lieutenant. His case
was dismissed in our favor at 4.30 p. m. on Friday, and he is now back at Fort Blank.

Jim's case was a haebus corpus. John had a certiorari. Joseph X, the last member
of the family, has now taken out some new kind of a writ, which we argued some on
Saturday morning, but don't quite understand. The United States court reserved
decision in this case, but we think it will be finished to-morrow, Tuesday, so that
Joseph can go with the band on Wednesday when the 240 boys go to Camp. This
wipes out our class I.

·P. S.—These writs are getting the board all balled up. We are taking a course in
"writs" now, so we can do our bit and help make the world safe for democracy.

(c) One further consequence of the method adopted in the selection of local board members remains to be mentioned. In making
the selection of some 14,000 individual officials from the local citizenship, it was inherent that an even standard of excellence could
not be attained. Weaknesses in personnel occasionally developed;
but this, it is believed, must be regarded as an inseparable incident
in the prompt organization of any body of public servants of equal
size, destined for an exacting task novel to the present generation.
Time developed the necessity for the removal of only a very limited
number of members. In a few instances this action was called forth
by the discovery of irregularities either in connection with compensation or in dealings with registrants. Occasionally a member was
found to lack the requisite administrative capacity. In other
scattered instances, neglect of duty required removal. The aggregate of these cases, however, was so negligible from a national standpoint that the efficiency of the draft administration was never
threatened, and the high average quality of public service rendered
by the boards was not appreciably lowered.

2. *Duties.*—The duty of the local board was to mobilize the selectives as directed. But in this concise statement is comprised the
entire gamut of a hundred complex processes. Except for the
initial registration of June 5, 1917, the local boards had charge of
every one of the steps in the transit from home to camp.

The registration was the first main stage of the process. Then
came the determination of serial and order numbers. The classification was the next and largest stage. And finally came the call
and the entrainment. But each of these parts became itself a center
for many minor processes, and each of these in turn for others.

Moreover, each individual case had its own variety of peculiarity, and led to special inquiries and deliberations. Add to this, that records must accurately be kept of each act done in every part of every registrant's case. And, besides the attention necessary merely for reaching an official decision, there was added the time and labor demanded in almost every case for a cluster of tentative and informal inquiries appurtenant to matters coming before the board. The regulations composed a thick volume, numbering 250 sections and 433 pages, with more than 100 important forms; and these must be mastered for daily and instant use.

In short, the duties of the local boards, even when considered merely in the dry enumeration of their several details, constituted a complete and intricate administrative system. It would be idle here to set them forth in detail; suffice it to say that there is scarcely a page in the entire volume of regulations which does not contain a half dozen times, in endless variety, that most familiar phrase of duty, "*The local board shall proceed*" to do this or that.

But even these interminable duties of the selective service system were by no means the measure of the boards' task. For it soon came about that the community identified the board as the sole local agent and embodiment of affairs military; and there was ever-increasing resort to it for information on all subjects related to the war. A literally endless stream of inquiries submerged them, at all hours of day and night. Nothing in the broad range of national or local affairs was deemed unlikely to be known by the board, or to be unworthy of their attention. Solomon himself would have been jealous of the wisdom and judgment attributed to them.

This addition to their burden was an exhausting one, in time and energy. It brought some compensations, no doubt, in the gratification naturally to be gained from popular attribution of semi-omniscience and semi-omnipotence. But whatever the balance of burden or compensation, the boards accepted and discharged this additional portion of their duty with the same steady and genial devotion which marked all of their work.

The annals of every board, no doubt, here run much the same. But the following letter to a State adjutant general, with its frank but good-humored repartee and its revelation of dogged perseverance under a hopeless overload, may be taken as typical of the cheerful and manly American spirit which helped the boards to carry their heavy duties; the letter was written in response to a request for an immediate report of progress due to be made in the classification of registrants of September 12, 1918:

SIR: Because this board and its meager staff is so busy
    Counseling registrants—
    Reconciling mothers—

Patiently answering dozens of inquiries by mail, telephone, and telegraph—
Issuing permits for passports—
Writing to transfer boards and telling them what to do with Form 2008–A—
Making out induction papers for S. A. T. C. registrants—
Copying our 4,439 registration cards—
Writing up cover sheets—
Hunting up questionnaires without order numbers in order to append additional
   late arrival affidavits of the X. Y. Z. Co. for deferred industrial classi-
   fication in Class II of aliens (who are sure to be in Class V)—
Preparing routings and transportation requests for individual inductants under
   competent orders, who are to be entrained for Kelly Field, San Antonio, Tex.,
   or Carlstrom Field, Arcadia, Fla.—
Counseling the poor innocents as to how many "suits of underwear shall I take?"—
Advising them firmly though with kindness that while requests for tourist sleep-
   ing-car accommodations will be issued to them, our experience is that there
   will be no tourist cars available, and that they will sleep on the floor—
Preparing seven meal tickets, three copies for each man—
Issuing new registration cards and new final classification cards to men who have
   "had their pocketbooks stolen" (?) and are afraid of being rounded up—
Issuing certificates of immunity to 46-year old men who present proofs of birth
   date so that *they* won't be rounded up—
Advising colored ladies (to their manifest satisfaction) as to prospective Government allotments and allowances to come from their casual spouses when in
   the service—
Telling anxious Y. M. C. A. recruits how they can apply to have their cases reopened and claims for occupational exemption considered—
Advising by mail the assistant district attorney of ——— county, who desires to
   prosecute a registrant for not supporting his wife—
Trying to keep several thousand questionnaires and registration cards, minus
   order numbers as yet, out of irremediable chaos due to lack of filing cabinets
   or other facilities—
Reconciling our hardworking limited service man to writing up his "daily morning reports" on a form adapted for a full company of men, including mules—
Conducting voluminous correspondence with perturbed mustering-in officers at
   distant cantonments about registrants who have been picked up without Form
   1007 in their possession and shot into camp without proper induction papers in
   order that some yap deputy sheriff can get the $50 reward because he needed
   the money—
Futilely registering ex-soldiers and sailors discharged for physical disability—
Getting into a corner occasionally and going crazy trying to study out an abstruse
   legal problem from an interesting 433 page textbook called Selective Service
   Regulations, second edition, Form 999–A—
Classifying questionnaires—
Engaging, for physical examinations of several hundred men, doctors who are
   already bereft of their wits on account of the Spanish influenza—
Preparing dozens and dozens and dozens of Form 1010 for these examinations,
   three copies of each—
Postponing the examinations after all, because the doctors simply can't come,
   and redating all the Forms 1010—
Doing dozens more things daily and nightly and Sundays and holidays, of which
   the foregoing are mere samples—
Because, I say, the board and its meager staff are so busy with a number of such
matters, I beg to report

That, though probably about half the questionnaires of the "First series, registrants of September, 1918," have been classified, we haven't time or inclination or energy to count them, even approximately; about half the physical examinations have been concluded, and on Sunday we are going to try to catch up with our correspondence, if the master list doesn't come, which we presume it will, however, in which event, we hope to have four volunteer typists pound out five copies of Form 102 (the churches are all closed, so it won't matter),—and, anyhow, we lost the "Progress chart" the very day it arrived. And it is our opinion, if we may be permitted the liberty to express it, that what the Government wants (or ought to want in the present urgency) is men, not classifications, and we firmly believe that the boys on the firing line in France don't care a whoop in hades how many registrants Local Board No. 3 of Union County classifies in Class V or in Class IV, Division A, so we called out every man who made no claim or who waived all claims, or who had a manifestly insufficient claim, classified him at once, and called him for physical examination; if it were not for the blasted epidemic, we should be ready to report practically full completion of physical examinations now; but we shall be in any event, within a week, even if we explode in the attempt and incapacitate for all time the few remaining distraught doctors that are still available to cajolery and patriotic urging; in the meantime, we shall classify now and then, when we can, an alien or two, to swell our general list of classifications.

The fact is, we have been wanting to write this letter since we were appointed in May, 1917; so excuse it, please. Furthermore—and we say this in no mood of rancor or in undue pride of spirit—we don't care if you do send it to the Provost Marshal General. In fact, we wish you would. No more benevolent attention could accrue to members of local boards than the gentle joys of court-martial and cool retirement somewhere in nice quiet cells, fed and cared for, during the period of the balance of the Emergency.

And further deponent sayeth not (because his wife has just telephoned as to why the deuce he doesn't come home, he'll surely be sick), and will now quench the midnight shining bulb and go, and try to get around early in the morning and endeavor to find that lost "Progress chart" (drat it!)"

One of the remarkable and unexpected results of this congeries of responsibilities was that often the boards, incidentally to their military decisions, became also, and perforce, a beneficent welfare agency for the community. Obliged by their duties to gain acquaintance with the intimate facts of the family life of their neighbors, they constantly assisted in the placation of domestic difficulties and the lightening of family burdens:

John married a widow with a child, after May 18, 1917, and so was called for a hearing. The three of them appeared, accompanied by his 60-year-old mother. The neatly attired wife acted disdainfully intolerant of the old woman, who was bareheaded and shrouded in a well-worn shawl; but the trembling mother was too anxious about the welfare of her son to mind that. John earned $100 a month and contributed $6 a month to his mother, who did washing for a living, although suffering from rheumatism. The young wife was angry, and John was uneasy, when we upbraided him for deserting in her old age the woman who had given birth to him, his best friend who had lovingly cared for him in his sickness, fed, clothed, and educated him; leaving her in an enfeebled condition, the only time she had ever needed his comfort and support. He was denied exemption on the dependency created by marriage, but was told that if he provided properly for his mother his claim would receive favorable consideration. The result was a written agreement, signed by the son, wife, and mother, that John would give the old woman $20 a month, and that failure in a single month would mean his induction into the Army. Half a year later John was called in on the "Work or Fight" order. The whole family appeared. The old mother was comfortably dressed and wore a feathered hat. The wife acted in a kindly and considerate manner toward the mother.

In one case an affidavit in support of a claim for deferred classification, which the wife had originally signed, was subsequently withdrawn by the wife. In the ensuing investigation it developed that both the man and wife were apparently persons of little moral character. There was present in the case the appalling feature of a fine little boy, perhaps 5 years of age, who was living in an environment that promised nothing short of his absolute ruin if he were not placed in the hands of responsible and reputable persons. The final outcome of the case was that the man was certified for service and sent to an Army camp, a position was obtained for the woman, and through the instrumentality of the board, the little boy was placed in a home where he would have an opportunity to develop properly.

3. *Moral responsibility for the selective draft.*—But to the strictly technical and administrative part of the boards' task, laborious as it proved, was added the momentous moral responsibility of making the selective draft a success in its human and patriotic aspect. The boards were the outer point of official contact, local and national, between the civilian life and the Army life. The task was theirs of so administering the system, in spirit and in conduct, as to reconcile the people to its drastic requirements while effectively and speedily raising the Army. To assist in keeping this great objective ever before their conscience, the following letter was addressed to members of local boards on July 26, 1917, at the moment when they were to issue their first call to registrants to appear for examination:

You are entering on a difficult task, the gravity of which is beyond anything that can be said in the way of discussion. You realize the significance of what you are to do, and you know that a responsibility heavier perhaps than any you have ever faced, is upon you.

War demands individual sacrifice to the common cause. No people ever approached war with a calmer appreciation of that sacrifice or a firmer resolve to bear it and to present themselves "to be classified for service in the place to which it shall best serve the common good to call them." This calm determination could not exist were it not for the confidence of the Nation in its institutions. In this public confidence is found the very spirit of the selective service law. The most sacred rights of country, home, and family are entrusted for adjudication to local citizens and officials, nominated by State governors and appointed by the President. The most equitable rules that could be devised have been prescribed for guidance, and the administration of these rules and the sacrifice that is offered by your neighbors is entrusted to your hands.

From every one is demanded a sacrifice. But there is one thought to be kept always in your mind. *The selected man offers his life.* There is no greater giving than this; and that thought should guide you always. There may be a few who will urge upon you claims for exemption or discharge that, whatever may be your inclinations of sympathy or affection, you will know ought not to be granted. It will strengthen you to remember that *for every exemption or discharge that is made for individual convenience, or to escape personal loss of money or property, or for favor or affection, some other man, whose time would not otherwise have come, must incur the risk of losing his life.* There can be no room for hesitation in such a case.

Another fundamental thought is this:

You are not a court for the adjustment of differences between two persons in controversy. You are agents of the Government, engaged in *selecting* men for the Government and there is no controversy. You, acting for the Government, are to investigate each case *in the interests of the Nation, and never in the interests of an individual.* There is not one exemption or discharge in the law or regulations that is put there for the benefit of any individual. All are there for the benefit of the Nation and to the end that "the whole Nation may be a team in which each man shall play the part for which he is best fitted."

There should be no rules like those of court procedure, no technical rules of evidence. You should proceed to investigate cases about which you are not satisfied exactly as you, as an individual, would proceed to inform yourself of any fact about which you are in doubt.

Last of all, it is important to say a word about your own sacrifice. The place to which you have been called is one which no man would seek save in the performance of one of the highest of patriotic duties. There is not, in any real sense, any remuneration. Because thousands of citizens urged that members of local boards should not be placed in a position of performing their grave duties for pay, the regulations provide that, ordinarily, the service shall be uncompensated. Beacuse it was not desired that any man be prevented from rendering the service by the necessity for earning his daily bread, a small remuneration was provided.

The Nation needs men, and needs them quickly. The hours will then be long and the work absorbing. The duty is always to take and never to give, and human nature is such that there will be little praise and some blame. The sacrifice of many of those whose cases are to be decided is no greater than that of the men who are to decide them; and your only reward must be the knowledge that, at great personal sacrifice, you are rendering your country an indispensable service in a matter of the utmost moment.

It will be seen that the responsibility of local boards was staggering. Men hitherto safe from the turmoil of life were being withdrawn from sheltered homes, to be thrown into the maw of a military machine. The course of lives was being radically and violently turned. Most of the selectives were severing family ties. All were called for the supreme sacrifice of their lives. Any other than a democratic government would have scouted the idea of intrusting to civilians, in most cases untrained in administrative capacities, such an enormous and complex task. The tremendous menace of the German military machine was never more obvious than at the time America took up arms. Many wise men of our own Government doubted the feasibility of creating an army entirely through civilian agencies. It is an irrefutable proof of the high capacity of our people for self-government, and an everlasting vindication of true democracy, that a system so intimately affecting the lives of our people should have been intrusted to untrained representatives of the local community and that it should have been so well executed.

4. *Popular support.*—A law directly affecting, and with sacrificial burden, the mass of citizens in their daily life, to be successful must be supported by popular sentiment. That the boards did achieve that success is undoubted. What were the reasons?

(a) One reason undoubtedly is that the law itself and the regulations framed to apply it were essentially fair and reasonable. This is apparent, in theory at least, to all who have studied them. But the test of these qualities was in the practical application; and if this test had failed, the board members themselves would have been the most sensitive to perceive the shortcomings of the system which their duty obliged them to enforce. Yet their testimony is unanimous that amidst all the complexities of local variety of conditions the law and the regulations emerged as thoroughly fitted to the task.

A typical letter from a board member in the State of New York says: "The rules were so eminently fair and so perfectly adaptable to every case that there remained small room for debate. Personally I believe I have many more friends in this district than before the work began; and there was indeed not a little apprehension in the beginning as to how a Protestant Episcopal rector would get on with a population 90 per cent of which is composed of Russians, Austrians, and Roumanian Jews. The S. S. R. has made it all possible." A midwestern member, with rational appreciation of the difficulty of reconciling a uniform system to local conditions, thus expresses a general sentiment: "Things which might not appear to work the best with us we realized were probably better than some other suggestion might prove in actual practice; and the rule which might not exactly fit one locality was probably fitting better the country over than a different one." "All of our registrants," says another board in Philadelphia, "are satisfied, whether at home or in the Army; for even if they do have to go to camp they leave with a feeling of having gotten the best treatment possible. I can honestly say that this system devised by the War Department meted out justice to all, regardless of religion, local standing, or color."

"The selective service system," says another, "is the leveler of barriers between the classes and the masses; it is the only method which overcomes the often repeated complaint that 'the poor fight the battles of the rich.' It is the only fair method of recruiting an army." And a Missouri board formally places on record the following conclusion: "We have no hesitancy in saying that in our official judgment the Selective Service Law is the greatest scheme ever conceived in the minds of men for raising an army. It is fair, just, equitable, humane, and admirable, even to its minutest detail. In our judgment a sufficient army could not have been raised without the comprehensive draft system."

To the fairness and reasonableness of the law and the regulations must be ascribed a large part of the satisfaction with the system.

(b) But the boards themselves must also be fair and reasonable if the law were to have its perfect working. It was necessary that the personal element in its administration be wise and impartial. Upon the boards rested the task of developing confidence in the well-devised system of the draft. Many persons were at first pessimistic at the prospect of its administration. But the impression early gained ground that the system was and would be a fair one. As time went on, and the care, devotion, fairness, and sacrifice of board members became obvious, the confidence of the people grew steadily and surely. Those within its operation demanded nothing more than that it be impartially administered; this fact once obvious, even those least moved by the impulse of sacrifice awaited their turn philosophically. And as the war proceeded, and America's part became a more important one and the boards' qualities of strength and wisdom became more and more obvious throughout all classes of the community, the tide of approval for the selective draft rose higher and higher, and the dominant sentiment finally became a readiness and even an eagerness to enter the draft without waiting for a call. In short, the spirit of volunteering had been bred within the draft.

The boards' letters chronicle this spirit abundantly. A few of these characteristic passages must be quoted:

We thought it would interest you to hear with what fine patriotic spirit 99 per cent of the qualified registrants received the information that they had been selected to serve their country. Here are some of the things they said when so informed: "Good," "I am glad," "Thank you," "I am very proud," "That just suits me," "Fine," "No objections," "Tickled to death;" and some of them seemed so pleased that nothing short of a hearty handshake would satisfy them. Many of them who were rejected showed signs of disappointment; one man went away with tears in his eyes. To show further the spirit animating the men, we must tell you that we had several married men, who not only made no claim for deferred classification, but also signed the waiver and got their wives to do likewise. One of such men, an Italian, who has been in this country 11 years, was rejected, as he thought, for underweight. He was so disappointed that the day after his examination he visited the office of the chairman of the board and requested that he be given some medicine to build him up so that he might gain the weight necessary to enable him to qualify. When asked why he did not claim deferred classification on the ground of having a dependent wife and child, he answered with the wisdom of a simple mind, "If everybody claims exemption, who is going to do the fighting?"

The youths of the land became more and more eager, and the younger they were, the more impatient were they to get away. This board had on the list to be advanced in their call at least 50 of the late registrants under 21 years of age. At such times as they could not be called in advance of their order, we were compelled to listen to their censures; but such censures were indeed music to our souls. A great change began to manifest itself among those who had been persistent in claims for deferred classification; and we observed a strong tendency among married men without children to have their classification changed. Wives were beginning to take a different view, perhaps beginning to feel somewhat envious of their married friend whose husband was in the service.

Whatever other influences helped to this beneficient result, it must never be forgotten that a main cause was the solid popular confidence built up for the system by the conduct and spirit of the local boards.

It can all be summed up in the concise phrase of one of the board members:

We realized that we were expected to raise the Army with (as near as could be) exact justice to everybody. We tried to play the game squarely, and to do the business in man fashion.

(c) The result was that, virtually everywhere and notably in the small towns, the entire community was transformed into a unanimous unofficial body of assistants to the boards. Everyone was interested; everyone was in favor of the system; and everyone was ready and eager to help. At the lift of the hand the boards could commandeer all varieties of contributions, to do honor to the town's contingent and to make the selective draft a success.

The following description of this support, from an Oklahoma board, would probably be true for most others, and its concluding sentence expresses an important political truth:

The public stood behind the local and district boards in their administration of the Selective Service law. The members of the board served without pay, and the assistance here mentioned was all rendered without monetary recompense.

The newspapers devoted columns of space to these boards. They published the serial and order number lists and the lists of the men called for examination or induction and gave publicity to whatever notices the board wanted to get before its registrants or the public.

The lawyers served on the legal advisory boards and assisted the registrants in filling out their questionnaires.

. The doctors served on the local examining and medical advisory boards and examined the men to see if they were qualified.

The banks and industrial concerns loaned us their clerks and accountants to assist in the clerical work.

The school-teachers prepared the industrial cards for the War Department and rendered other valuable assistance to our clerks.

The Council of Defense and Red Cross assisted in making investigations, and the latter looked after the dependents of inducted men.

Taxi companies, individuals, and corporations loaned their automobiles to aid in canvassing the county when that was necessary, in carrying through the registrations or in investigating cases, and furnished trucks to carry the men's baggage to the depot.

The photographers came and took the pictures of the boys before they left and the band turned out to accompany them to the station.

The home guards and the police officers aided in maintaining order and managing the crowds.

We had the undivided support of the entire community behind us. And the men sent to camp went cheerfully, and the families they left behind made very little complaint.

The American public is easy to get along with when reasonable explanation is made of what is expected from them and why.

(d) In a still deeper sense this support of public sentiment became potent, for it supplied that solid drive of public opinion without which the law alone remains often a barren record and a mere technical command. The community sentiment was present in the consciousness of every registrant; he knew that it was judging him; and it fairly drove him to do the honest and right thing. The sanction of law was multiplied a hundredfold, and public opinion reached consciences which the law alone could never have probed.

How potent was this force in supplementing the boards' action is well described in the following letter:

Public opinion is kind and cruel, lenient and severe, just and unjust, but never corrupt. It passes sentence after hearing only one side of a case, but nevertheless in most cases it enforces its decree. It was public opinion that enforced the draft law. The local boards simply administered it.

The entire population volunteered. Congress merely designated the method of selection, local boards determined who should be exempted and the order in which the selected men should go, and public opinion attended to all cases of opposition to the law.

A was married late. He was inducted and later discharged. Public opinion declared that A married to evade service, and decreed that he should return to the Army. A stood out for a while. If it had not been for his family obligations he would have preferred to be in the service. Finally he could stand it no longer; he waived the deferred classification he had received and was inducted.

Another instance. When B was examined the doctors disagreed regarding his physical qualifications; some said he was fit, and others said he was not. We sent him to another medical advisory board, where he was disqualified. But public opinion was not satisfied. I can still hear the rumblings of its dissatisfaction. And that man will never be able to forget that he has defied public opinion's decree.

I have seen men who looked haunted because of the moral conflict raging within their breasts, between the duties they owed their country, their families, their business, or themselves. I know of cases where it took moral courage to enlist and others where it took more courage to stay out. I know of cases where men displayed a lack of courage when they joined the colors, and of others where they showed a lack of courage because they did not. But in this emergency public opinion condemned no man who donned the uniform. It concerned itself only with those who did not.

(e) This concentration of public opinion on the registrants will explain why we may well assume (as noted in Chapter V) that the successful slackers were few. The selective draft went into nearly every home; and thus every citizen, feeling its incidence in his own family, was determined that others also should do their full duty. Every registrant's case became the subject of observation and discussion; his action, in claiming or not claiming deferment was well known; the neighbors knew the truth about his circumstances even if the board members might not, and the boards were surfeited with information—by visit and by letter, signed and unsigned. The most efficient detective force that the War Department could have organized would not have been more productive of information than were the neighbors in their scrutiny of the registrants.

5. *Spirit of the boards.*—The members of the local boards had need of all the manhood and courage that was in them, thus to "play the game squarely;" for the moral and mental burden was one to tax their endurance. The physical labors were enormous and exhausting; but the added strain of maintaining their moral hold on the community, while deciding these heavy matters of life and death, was one which none but those who passed through it can appreciate. "Chastened

in spirit, and calloused in body, but buoyant in the knowledge that they were serving to win the war," such is the description, by one of them, of the effect of their toil. Another board thus sums up, in 'fitting terms, the dominant spirit:

The work, in many instances, has been disagreeable, and our way beset with thorns and thistles which pricked deep, and made the smarting, at times, almost unbearable. But deep down in our hearts we felt and we knew that we were serving our country and helping to fight its battles as effectively as the boys across the sea, and that the smarting of the thistles and the pricking of the thorns was only our part of the disagreeable features of war. In many respects, financial loss has been sustained, friends have been sacrificed, social standing forfeited, hopes and plans blasted. But all this is only a part of the sacrifice we have been called to make for Liberty, Freedom, and Democracy. And our star of sacrifice is very dim compared with the sacrifice which the performance of our duties has-compelled fathers and mothers to make in giving their sons to the cause; many of whom have already been required to make the supreme sacrifice.

, And those who could take this largest view of their task were broadened and enlivened by the new views of human nature unrolled before them, and especially by the revelation of solid character and unpretentious patriotism among the plain people of our land. One of the local board members (now the draft executive for his State) has already faithfully depicted, with the genial and classic art of a Charles Lamb, the intimate drama of life as it was presented in the office of the boards.[1] · The reports of the boards are full of acknowledgment of the inspiration gained from their experiences, and, taken all in all, their revelations renew our faith in human nature and American character: "My work on this board," says one, "has been the greatest experience of my life. To have come into such close contact with the men of this community, their families and friends, during this crisis, has increased my respect and admiration for their unselfish loyalty and patriotism. The mean and cowardly have been so few in number as to be a negligible factor; their cases will soon be forgotten." "We came," says another, "into most intimate contact with all classes of people, learned of their trials and tribulations, their fears and hopes, their opinions, prejudices, and feelings, and their histories, sometimes containing faults and crimes carefully concealed from the world. While most was commonplace, there was also much that was sad and pathetic, much that was noble, as well as much that was amusing. There was very little that was base or cowardly. The patriotism which displays itself in frothy enthusiasm was the exception; the quiet, grim patriotism, based upon a sense of duty and a real regard for country, was the rule. This dominant feeling on the part of the registrants and their dependents was of the enduring character that lasts to the end; and it made the draft a wonderful success."

---

[1] "Reflections of a Draft Official," by Gordon Snow, Boston, Houghton Mifflin & Co., 1918.

But it is idle to attempt to put into words here the full story of what the local boards achieved. Every military man must recognize what they did for the Nation's Army; and every civilian must recognize what they did for the Nation's liberty and welfare. And every American is proud of them. Whatever of credit is accorded to other agencies of the selective service law, the local boards must be deemed the corner-stone of the system.

(VI) GOVERNMENT APPEAL AGENTS.

1. *Appointment under original regulations.*—Local and district boards had exclusive authority to pass upon questions vitally affecting the interests of the individual and the Government. But there is fallibility in all bodies exercising judicial functions; and it was early foreseen that, whatever the character and ability of the personnel of such boards, errors of judgment would undoubtedly creep in. These occurrences, unless an ample opportunity was given to correct them, would tend to raise doubt in the mind of the American public as to the fairness of the execution of the law relied upon to produce our armies. Provision was therefore made at the outset by which individuals were given adequate means, in cases affecting their interest, to make their appeal from the boards of original jurisdiction to appellate tribunals. But it would have been manifestly unwise to provide such safeguards for individuals and yet to neglect to make similar provisions for the full protection of the interest of the Government. In consequence, the rules and regulations prescribed by the President, of date June 30, 1917, and the compiled rulings amendatory thereto, provided for the automatic appeal of all cases of discharge on account of dependency, and for discretionary authority to appeal in other cases. Governors of the various States were authorized to appoint representatives of the Government to take these appeals.

In the majority of instances, county and city attorneys were appointed to perform these duties. There was at first no specific designation of title, but generally speaking, the appeals were taken in the name of the United States Government under the signature of the person so appointed. In all cases, except in the case under which automatic appeals were provided, the person so designated was required to keep himself informed of the action of the local boards; and, on his own initiative, or from information brought to his attention by other persons, he was required to take appeal to the appellate tribunal when, in his opinion, the best interests of the Government and justice to other registrants made such an appeal desirable.

At the close of the first draft, and before the preparation of the Selective Service Regulations published November 8, 1917, it was fully realized that the work to be performed was one of magnitude, and that the agents·constituted one of the mainstays to the selective service system. That their services might be made more available in the proper selection of registrants under the new scheme of classification, provision was made for the enlargement of their duties and of authority. Even under the first draft it had been seen that Government appeal representatives were called upon to perform arduous tasks beyond the scope of their regularly prescribed duties. No provision had been made under the first draft for the legal advisory boards and other assistants to render advice to the local boards, district boards, and other draft officials and registrants; and the person so designated to represent the Government was called upon to advise the various board members, clerks, and other assistants upon any and all questions relating to the performance of their work under the selective service law; to formulate, for presentation to the higher draft officials, questions relating to the interpretations of the law which could not be easily answered. They were expected to familiarize themselves thoroughly with local conditions and with the circumstances surrounding each individual case passed upon by the local board, in order to determine whether or not the rights of the Government had been protected and whether injustice had been done to registrants. They were relied upon by the various district boards of the country to render exhaustive reports where the records forwarded to the district boards failed to disclose sufficient facts to enable the boards to reach a proper conclusion. Thus, because of their known familiarity with the draft law and the local administration of it, they became practically centers of information, and registrants resorted to them at all hours of the day either to make inquiry or discuss claims.

2. *Under the regulations of December, 1917.*—Under the Selective Service Regulations effective December 15, 1917, the governors of the various States were authorized to designate for each local board one or more persons to take appeals for and on behalf of the United States. There were 4,679 in all. Appendix Table 91–A shows their distribution by States.

It was expected, and it resulted, that the persons heretofore acting as representatives of the Government for the purpose of taking appeals were designated by the various draft executives in this capacity as Government appeal agents. Thus, there was no upsetting of the organization already perfected. Their duties, however, were so enlarged that they were now required to appeal, from deferred classifications by a local board, rulings which in the opinion of the appeal agent were erroneous; to care for the interests of ignorant registrants; to inform them of their rights, where the decision of the local board was against the interests of such persons, or where it appeared that such persons would not take appeals, due to their nonculpable ignorance, and to assist them to enter appeals to the district board; to investigate and report upon matters submitted for such purpose by local or district boards; to suggest a reopening of any case where the interests of justice might require; to impart to the local board any information which in the opinion of the appeal agent ought to be investigated; to furnish suggestions and information to the district boards; to instruct local boards to take additional proof; to receive information from interested persons affecting any case under the jurisdiction of the boards where such interested persons did not desire to make a personal disclosure to the boards; and to prepare appeals in any cases, whether by the registrant or by the Government, where he considered appeals to be to the interest of the Government. In these various capacities the Government appeal agent was authorized to administer oaths; and, in fact, a large proportion of the time of the appeal agents was taken up in assisting with the probate of questionnaires.

3. *Performance of their duties.*—It can thus be seen that Government appeal agents were faced with a heavy task. To perform this task to a degree satisfactory to the Government, it was inevitable in a large proportion of the cases that the private livelihoods and business interests of these men would materially suffer. It was a task that meant unlimited sacrifice; and the records of this office show that the duties were fully realized, and that they were adequately performed.

It was, of course, virtually necessary that the appeal agents should be selected from the members of the legal profession. In the further draft that was made upon the legal profession at the same time by the appointment of members of legal advisory boards and their associates, it can readily be seen that the practice of the law for these officials, during the administration of the draft, became merely a secondary interest. In a large number of instances, such Government appeal agents served in the dual capacity of appeal agent and member or associate member of a legal advisory board. Numbers of instances were found where such officials pactically abandoned their own private offices, and stayed on continuous duty at the office of the local boards, in order that they might effectively keep in touch with the decisions rendered by such boards, and be in a position to to protect better the interests of the registrants and of the Government.

It was not intended, nor did they interpret their duty to be, that they should be partisan representatives of the Government for the purpose, if possible, of placing every registrant in military service, as would normally be the case of a prosecuting attorney trying his docket. They properly conceived their duty to be that of representing the Government, by seeing that the selective principle of the selective service law was applied—that no man escaped who owed the duty to go, and that the Government was not put to the expense of sending to the camps men who were better fitted to preserve the necessary industries at home and to protect the family integrity. Their province was to see that substantial fairness was observed; and the relative fewness of discharges at camps, of men finally accepted for service, is ample proof of the admirable manner in which that duty was performed. The outstanding fact that this duty was performed uncomplainingly and without any compensation whatever, places them in the enviable position of the patriot who is unrewarded, save in the consciousness of duty well performed, and in the knowledge that both the Government and the people composing it proudly acknowledge a debt which can not be liquidated.

Such devotion to duty can only be described by the thought that these men were putting into their part of the great fight the conscience of the American people.

(VII) MEDICAL ADVISORY BOARDS.

When the Selective Service Regulations were promulgated, provision was made for the creation and organization of medical advisory boards. Their functions were to examine physically those registrants whose cases had been appealed to them by a registrant, by a Government appeal agent, or on motion of a local board. Each board consisted of three or more members. The desired minimum consisted of one each of the following specialists: Internist; eye, ear, nose, and throat specialist; orthopedist; surgeon; psychiatrist; radiographer, and dentist. To these boards were referred doubtful cases of registrants who had obscure physical defects. By means of this highly trained technical agency, many obscure physical defects in registrants were detected, thereby materially assisting the local boards, which were not equipped to conduct an exhaustive examination, to reduce materially the number of rejections at mobilization camps and also to detect malingerers. Originally these boards could pass finally on cases in a formal meeting only, at which a quorum was present; but as their duties became heavier, it became necessary to consider cases in the most expeditious manner, and provision was made for the examination and consideration of cases by one or more of their members.

The members of these boards were nominated by the governors of their respective States, and appointed by the President. There were 1,319 boards, with a total membership of 9,577. Appendix Table 91–A shows their distribution by States.

At this point a tribute is due to the American Medical Association. From this association came the suggestion for medical advisory boards and cordial assistance in their selection. The Journal of the American Medical Association, with a circulation of 66,000 copies, has been a valuable medium of information between this office and the medical men who discharged the duties of the profession to the Government through the draft.. The medical profession has responded and served in a devoted manner that has received universally favorable comment. It is gratifying to note the part which the association has taken in thus assisting to raise our great Army, as well as its valuable contribution to the war generally.

Medical advisory members served without compensation. The exacting details incident to the examination of tens of thousands of registrants, drawn from every precinct of the United States, have been accomplished with a patient, prompt precision that impels me to express my personal appreciation for their loyal services to our Government, through their cooperation with this office. It is keenly appreciated that their duties were an additional burden to busy lives, and were not publicly recognized either by uniform, or rank, or the applause of the multitude. They continued at their tasks unflinchingly, often far into the night, with only conscience as their commander, and with stern duty as their censor. To them, whose services were so cheerfully, assiduously, and efficiently rendered, the Nation owes a debt of gratitude.

(VIII) LEGAL ADVISORY BOARDS.

1. *Need for these officials.*—The legal adage that "Ignorance of the law is no excuse" could not, as a practical proposition, be applied to the administration of the selective service law. After a very few months of the draft it was recognized that a law which applied alike to the literate and the illiterate, and the success of which depended upon the prompt compliance of registrants, could be successfully enforced only by careful instruction of the people as to its requirements and by assisting them in meeting those requirements.

Some ready and competent means of bringing the selective service system to registrants of every description and of assisting them in discharging the duties imposed by the draft, were obviously necessary. The selective service law and regulations contained many technical requirements which people not versed in legal matters might find confusing. In searching the field for an agency which might meet the situation, the legal profession was naturally resorted to as the institution best fitted for the service.

2. *Resort to the legal profession.*—No doubt was ever entertained as to the willingness of the lawyers of the country to contribute their services. The idea of utilizing their services had barely been conceived before plans for mobilizing the strength of the profession were

formulated. A formal call to men of the legal profession, to offer their services for the purpose of instructing registrants concerning their rights and obligations under the selective service law, and of assisting them in the preparation of their answers to their question-naires, was made on November 8, 1917, by the President in his Foreword to the Selective Service Regulations.

The response of the profession at large was magnificent. Indeed, promptly upon the publication of the President's call, and before they learned of the definite plans of organization, attorneys became so impatient to respond to the call that meetings for preliminary organization were held throughout the length and breadth of the land; meetings attended by hundreds and sometimes by thousands. With such splendid spirit to build upon, the success of the plan depended largely upon the organization of this willingness to serve.

3. *Organization of the boards.*—The fullest success of the plan for availing the selective service system of the services of attorneys, and of other citizens in a position to assist registrants, could be attained only by the utilization of the maximum number of attorneys. It was, however, realized that greater efficiency would be had by constituting small committees. These could be held to strict accountability. For the assistance of those committees, as many other attorneys and other public spirited citizens as possible would be associated. Pursuant to this plan, there was constituted for each local board a legal advisory board, composed of three reputable attorneys, whose duties were to see "that there should always be a competent force of lawyers or laymen available to * * * registrants at any time during which the local or district boards within such district are open for business." To legal advisory boards fell the task of mobilizing assistant advisers for their districts and of distributing as evenly as possible the work to be exacted of them. These latter advisers were called associate legal advisers.

4. *Appointment of the members.*—In accordance with the decentralized plan under which the selective service system was administered, the governors of the several States were assigned the task of constituting legal advisory boards in such numbers and within such districts as would be convenient to every registrant. The governors were further charged with the duty of nominating, for the appointment of the President, legal advisory board members. Associate legal advisory members were appointed by the permanent legal advisers.

The selection of the legal personnel, while most essential, was in many States a large undertaking. Yet promptness was of the utmost importance. To expedite that end, the Provost Marshal General on November 13, 1917, appealed to the good offices of the American Bar Association, and suggested for each State the assignment of the vice president and the State member of the general council of that association, the President of the State Bar Association, and the attorney general of the State, as a central committee to assist their governor in the organization of legal advisory boards.

The response of the American Bar Association was most encouraging. So promptly did its officers organize central committees and select and nominate the legal advisory boards attached to each local board, and so spontaneously did the members of the legal profession throughout the whole country respond to the call of duty, that one week later, nearly a month in advance of the time when the legal advisory boards would be required to begin their actual labors, I.was able to write to the Secretary of the American Bar Association as follows:

By reason of the valuable services rendered by you and by the national officers of the association and by the vice presidents and members of the general council in the respective States, and by the prompt and almost universal response of the members of . the association generally, legal advisory boards have been fully organized in many of the States and are being rapidly organized in the others; and I have no doubt whatever that the aid to be rendered by them during the classification of registrants, which will begin about December 15, will make the accomplishment of the classification completely successful.

The members of legal advisory boards numbered in all 10,915, and the associate members 108,367. There were 3,646 boards in all; Appendix Table 91–A shows their distribution by States.

5. *Method of work.*—Wide publicity was given the existence of legal advisory boards and their purposes, every effort being made to bring to the attention of registrants the fact that gratuitous professional advice might be had upon the requirements of the selective service law. Letters of instruction were issued along with questionnaires to registrants, showing exactly where free legal assistance might be secured from legal advisory members in filling out questionnaires, as well as any other information concerning the operation of the selective service law and corollary acts.

The question of compensation was early considered by the American Bar Association and by this office, and it was unanimously decided that men leaving their homes and offering their lives for their country should not be charged fees in connection with the filling out of papers required by the Selective Service Regulations. Comparatively little difficulty was encountered in this respect. Wherever it was found that an attorney had charged a fee for assisting a registrant, he was, by his bar association or by the State legal advisory board, requested to discontinue such practice and return the fees collected. In practically every instance the reasonableness of this demand was seen, and compliance ensued. A very few scattered prosecutions against members of legal advisory boards for charging fees were instituted; and where the practice was clearly established, convictions were secured.

The following quotation from a report of one of the States illustrates the devoted industry of legal advisers in serving registrants:

It will be remembered that the latter part of December and early January (1917–18) witnessed the coldest and worst weather this section of the country has suffered in many years; the ground was covered with snow 6 to 12 inches deep, and the thermometer frequently went below zero for days at a time, rendering the roads almost impassable and travel exceedingly difficult, especially in the rural and mountain districts. To meet this situation the legal advisory boards in the mountain districts arranged to organize branch boards in various parts of the county, so that the distance necessary to be traveled by the registrants was greatly reduced. In some of the mountain counties as many as four branches would be acting; and in the lowlands, where the roads were almost impassable, greater numbers were organized, so that the registrants could leave home, taking their dependents with them, and answer the questionnaires and make necessary affidavits and return home within the period of the day. Where registrants were ill, and could not come, members of the board would go to them, often traveling 10 to 20 miles through the snow and over the mountains, to render this service.

The splendid services of legal advisers was greatly helped by the patriotic attitude taken by the various courts. Realizing that it would be impossible for legal advisers to render efficient service if the courts continued in regular session, the judiciary of many States, during the first part of December, 1917, adjourned court for a number of weeks, or until the completion of questionnaires. The result was that courts practically ceased operation during the period the questionnaires were being answered, and many of the members of the judiciaries lent their assistance to the legal advisory board nearest to them. Justices of the peace and city magistrates, when requested, followed the example of the higher courts.

6. *Scope of the work.*—Legal advisory members were constantly consulted with reference to legislation cognate to the selective service act. Particularly was this so in the case of the soldiers and sailors' civil rights act and the war risk insurance act. Some boards published articles explanatory of the above statutes and did everything in their power to secure to drafted men the benefits thereof. Many patriotic organizations, such as the Council of National Defense, the War Service Leagues, the American Protective League, etc., found willing assistance from legal advisory members.

The task of legal advisers lasted for the duration of the war. When it became apparent that Class I was not as large as had been reckoned upon, and that a general rectification was necessary, legal advisory board members were asked in May of 1918 to cooperate with local boards in accomplishing that reclassification. With this request there was a most hearty compliance. Again, in September, 1918, the new registration laid upon the selective service officials a task equivalent to all that they had previously accomplished, and legal advisory boards were again called upon to help meet the situation. Willingly and promptly they reconvened, and placed themselves at the disposal of the new registrants, as they had done with respect to the old. Again the courts lent their assistance to the occasion, and adjourned entirely, or to such extent as to eliminate any delay in the work of assisting registrants.

7. *Results.*—A large volume would not suffice to record the names of the lawyers of the country who lent their aid to the draft, and could contain but a bare summary of the labor and achievements. A brief citation of the figures of one State alone, and this not the largest, shows that there were organized within two weeks 850 permanent members and 3,000 associate members of legal advisory boards; that during the months of December and January these boards held more than 4,000 meetings and devoted more than 3,000,000 hours in aiding and advising more than 400,000 registrants. In the greatest city of the Nation, where half a million registrants were required to respond to the questionnaire, the permanent and associate members exceeded 3,000 in number.

There is no brighter chapter in the history of the draft than that of the services rendered by the lawyers of the country. Legal advisers richly deserve the credit for upholding the tradition of American fairness in the administration of her laws. Not only did the expert advice accorded by the lawyers of the country contribute toward the expeditious creation of an army; but the impression of equity engendered by their services was of inestimable value in developing and in maintaining a healthy morale in the body politic. On the honor list of the war must be numbered the thousands of lawyers and other public-spirited citizens who, without emolument and without the glory of the battlefield, served their country by supporting and aiding in the administration of the most drastic legislation of the last half century.

(IX) BOARDS OF INSTRUCTION.

In a letter from this office dated July 4, 1918, local boards were advised to select and organize boards of instruction, one for each local board.

The measure had its origin in suggestions made to the Secretary of War personally, and by him transmitted with approval to this office in June, 1918. The suggestions originated with a group of Cleveland men, whose experience in dealing with some 35,000 selectives sent to camp from that region, had developed available methods of pre-induction preparation in military morale. In many other regions local boards had taken various measures for the better preparation of the young men in their jurisdiction who were to become soldiers. But the peculiar efficacy of the Cleveland method was that it approached the young men as individuals, secured their confidence, and was thus enabled to exercise a stronger influence on their views and their conduct.

1. *Object.*—The general object, in the appointment of boards of instruction, was concisely stated as follows:

To put the selective service men into camp willing, loyal, intelligent, clean, and sober, and thus to fit them better for rapid progress in becoming good soldiers.

And to accomplish this by systematic personal instruction given beforehand to each selective by members of a local committee of reputable citizens in each board area acting under the auspices of the local board.

Very few selectives had seen any military training before reaching camp. A larger number had some intelligent idea of what awaited them and why they were to go. A still larger number were loyally, though ignorantly, willing to go. But, after all these allowances, there remained many men, represented in every local board area, who were neither willing, nor intelligent, nor loyal, nor fit, in the proper degree. Moreover, the family surroundings often tended to emphasize this condition; family sentiments affected the drafted man, and might make him less ready to go. All this was especially true in the cities where foreign-born populations abound. Further, camp surgeons reported that the man's mental attitude affected his physical condition. Any one of a score of small ailments might develop into a cause for discharge, if nurtured by a wrong mental attitude, or might become negligible, if the man had the will and the motive to overcome them.

Thus the efficiency of the national Army was affected by the mental condition of the individual after selection in Class I and before arrival in camp. Moreover, the existence of these conditions among drafted men had entailed immense additional labor for the selective service boards in overcoming them.

The foregoing elements of inefficiency could be largely removed by personal instruction. Experience had demonstrated this conclusively. To send a contingent of men who had been put into fit condition mentally and morally was to gain at least a month, and often more, in time, for the readiness of the division to leave for the battle field of human freedom.

For this reason the work of such instruction required to be organized, and on a large scale. To accomplish this, in the existing peculiar conditions cited, required a group of men that would devote themselves unselfishly and unreservedly to the immediate elimination of the obstacles, and to the presentation of the patriotic inducement in terms such as all types of American youth could comprehend. Recognizing that not numbers alone but also the morale of the American Army was a conquering factor, this group of men, by using their personal influence on the mental and moral make-up of the selectives, would be able to evoke and strengthen that fundamental patriotic impulse which every true man possesses. The proven methods by which the results could be accomplished called for the most patriotic devotion by men whose only compensation would be the consciousness that they were contributing to that spirit in the American soldier which was to win the war.

2. *Organization: local board of instruction in every area.*—The general plan of operation was to use local boards of instruction; the members to be appointed by the local selective service board. As the final result was to depend upon personal sympathetic contact with registrants, the members would be individually selected with reference to their local repute and standing; their character and human experience; ardor to help win the war; willingness to serve without compensation or exploitation; appreciation of the possibilities of the plan; intelligent conception of the kind of soldiers the Nation needed; ability to analyze young men's difficulties, and to inspire in them a patriotic desire to serve.

Wherever one or more existing agencies had already undertaken some part of this work, sanction was to be given by the local board, if it approved the kind of work and the personnel in charge. The work already organized and under way in many communities would receive as ample recognition as possible. But it would rest with the local board to organize the personnel of the board of instruction in such manner as to insure conformity to the purposes and methods outlined, and to emphasize rigorously the main object of preparing the men to be better soldiers when the time came for their call to the colors.

3. *Methods.*—The following methods were suggested in outline:

(a) At the time of the medical examination the registrants would be assembled in small groups, for a personal interview, and particular information be given by individual members of the boards of instruction, perplexities cleared, and encouraging suggestions made as to the personal value of military training, the chances for promotion, etc.; and the aid and friendly support of the Red Cross, the Army K. of C., the Y. M. C. A., the Hebrew Welfare Board, the Commission on Training Camp Activities, would be mentioned. This personal interview would establish a relation of immense initial importance between the board member and the drafted men; he would be a friend, the one encouraging personality in a system which to many of them represents only compulsion. The power of this man to influence their estimates of the service and their patriotic ideals could not be overestimated.

(b) During the pre-induction period the selected men would be called together once or twice at which time they would be met in groups for instruction as follows: (1) The provision which the Government had made for the protection and welfare of disabled soldiers and, in event of death, of their families or dependents, through its War Risk Insurance Bureau; this information would assist in neutralizing the family opposition due to ignorance of such safeguard.   (2) The Government provision for allowances and allotments to soldiers' dependents; this information would relieve apprehension in the soldier's home and inspire respect for all the Government's demands.   (3) Discussion of these topics: Why America Entered the War; Why America Must Win the War; The Necessary Character of the American Soldier; Sexual Restraint and the Avoidance of Liquor as a Patriotic Obligation; Camp Life.   Free discussion of these subjects would develop the principles of American democracy, personal character, conduct, personal habits, patriotic abstemiousness, and soldierly ideals and obligations.

(c) Preliminary military drill would be encouraged where feasible, to familiarize the men with first principles.   Wherever local militia reserve organizations already existed, the selectives would be advised to join them for training during the period of waiting.

(d) Each phase of this instruction was to supplement and not to duplicate any similar effort which already was or might be authorized by the Government.

The labor required from the selective service boards themselves, after appointing the boards of instruction, was to be confined to the issuance of two or three board orders, for the purpose of securing interviews with the men.

4. *Publications.*—The boards of instruction naturally needed and sought more ample information than was possessed by many of them, for the purpose of answering inquiries of the selectives and of instructing them on the various necessary subjects.   It had been recommended to the boards that every member should pay a visit to the nearest Army camp and to spend a day or so there observing the methods and incidents of camp life; for this experience would give them a greater assurance of statement, and would add much to the confidence that would be placed in them by the men.   But so widespread were the inquiries for additional information on special subjects that a number of bulletins were prepared, with the assistance of other agencies; and during August, September, and October these bulletins were distributed to the boards.

They were as follows:

Bulletin No. 3, August 22—"Home Reading Course for Citizen Soldiers," a pamphlet prepared by the War Department and published by the Committee on Public Information in October, 1917, as War Information Series No. 9; this pamphlet is undoubtedly the most valuable concise account of the facts about the Army as the civilian and intending soldier needs to know them.

Bulletin No. 4—"War Aims; How to Conduct a Course of Talks on that Subject for Young American Soldiers," prepared by Frank Aydelotte, Assistant Educational Director, War Department, Committee on Education and Special Training.

Bulletin No. 5—"How the Selectives Are Treated by Uncle Sam in Camp," prepared by Julius R. Kline, Lieutenant Colonel, Illinois National Guard.

Bulletin No. 6—"Teaching English to nonspeaking Selectives," a vocabulary and phrase book employing words and phrases used in Army life, prepared by Capt. Emery Bryan, Cantonment Intelligence Officer at Camp Upton, New York, and approved by the Military Morale Section of the General Staff, and used also by the Bureau of Education, Department for the Interior.

Bulletin No. 7—two pamphlets, one entitled "Before you Go," prepared by the Home Service Section of the American Red Cross, and the other entitled "Commissions on Training Camp Activities, War and Navy Departments" prepared by those commissions.

Bulletin No. 8—entitled "Hygiene," which announced a plan of the U. S. Public Health Service for lectures at the various local boards, and was accompanied by a pamphlet prepared by the Public Health Service, entitled "Come Clean."

These bulletins could be distributed only in limited numbers, and the demand far outran the supply.

5. *Work of the boards.*—The proposal to appoint boards of instruction received a hearty response in a large majority of the States and local boards. Representatives of the Cleveland Committee traveled throughout the country, gratuitously contributing their patriotic service, and attended meetings called for the purpose, either by the State adjutant general or by board members in various localities, or by the selective service associations in some of the larger cities. The boards appointed numbered 2,952, representing a personnel of more than 16,000 men (as shown by States in Appendix Table 91–A). The most representative citizens of the community were found on the boards. And not the least of the benefits secured was the welcome opportunity thus afforded to many older men to take a direct part in helping to make a better Army. The gratitude of these men for this privilege of rendering effective service has been notable; and their appreciation of its value to the young men is testified by the frequent suggestion, received since the armistice, that a similar work could be conducted voluntarily for civic purposes.

The activities of the boards were in general those recommended by the original letter of July 4, 1918; although the boards differed widely in the attention given to one or another of these forms of service. In some States or boards the greatest interest was displayed in the instruction in patriotism, or in Army methods, or in camp life. In others, different topics received emphasis. In still others, military drill was the subject of most interest; but in virtually all such cases the activities of the boards consisted chiefly in encouraging the selectives to join one of the State organizations of reserve militia or home guards, or one of the drill companies already initiated by private effort. A remarkable disclosure, in the correspondence on this subject, was the great number of cities, all over the country, in which military drill companies of one sort or another had already sprung up spontaneously. Many thousands of young men were. already voluntarily studying and practicing the manual of arms in preparation for their future military service. The value of this work in fitting them to become good soldiers more rapidly is shown by the numerous reports from the boards of instruction, relating with satisfaction that a large number of their men who had taken this training were made noncommissioned officers within a short time after arrival at camp.

Had the war continued, and had the new registrants of ages 18–45 been called into the military service, there can be no doubt that the work of the boards of instruction would have been a most effective means of improving the pre-induction morale of the selectives, and thus of making more effective the organized Army.

(X) CIVIC COOPERATING AGENCIES.

Over and above the personnel recorded in the roster of boards having a direct official duty under the selective service act and regulations, this office received a great amount of organized assistance from civic associations, as well as from Government departments, at various times and for special purposes. These agencies lent their personnel, on request, for the work desired, or undertook special work of their own to assist some purpose of this office.

Some of these agencies have been already expressly alluded to, with a description of their work and acknowledgment of their cooperation, in earlier parts of this report. The work of the Government Printing Office, in printing and distributing the forms and announcements, has been already described in the present chapter. The work of the American Railway Association, in assisting the mobilization of selectives to camps, was described in Chapter VIII. What was there said in acknowledgment of the achievement of the United States Railway Administration applies equally to the American Railway Association, which had charge of rail movements prior to the taking over of the railways by the Government. The Committee on Public Information, as already set forth in Chapter II, made possible the attainment of a complete registration on September 12, 1918. The agencies of the Department of Justice, in tracing and finding deserters, have been acknowledged in Chapter V. The Post Office Department extended invaluable assistance in securing the delivery of the vast number of mail notices addressed to registrants, as already noted in Chapters II and III. The Bureau of the Census, in the Department of Commerce, generously lent a large force of experts in the compilation of the Industrial Index; and from time to time furnished this office with computations on technical topics of many sorts. The Council of National Defense, as already mentioned in Chapter II, devoted its extensive machinery to the stimulation of the registration of September 12, 1918; and from time to time used its State and local committees to secure popular response to many administrative measures promulgated from this office.

Of the many civic bodies which gladly came forward to assist in securing the smooth operation of the selective service system, it is impracticable to mention more than a few of the principal ones. The American Red Cross, for example, in order to make comfortable the transit of the selectives to camp, furnished canteen service at the various railroad stations and distributed to local boards a list of these stations, for the information of the selectives en route; this ministered to the young men in the period between their departure from home and their arrival in camp—a period when they were most in need of encouragement and friendly attention. The American Protective League placed its entire membership at the disposal of the Department of Justice and of local boards, in order to locate delinquents and to furnish other useful information; and they formed an investigative body of extreme value. The representatives of the press gave freely of their time and their printed space, in order to bring home to every registrant and every family the duties required under the selective service act, and the stages of business reached by local boards from time to time; nearly every local paper in the United States has carried a daily column of selective service information; and the extraordinary contribution of the press in the publicity measures for the registration of September 12, 1918, has already been described in Chapter II.

The hearty and invaluable cooperation of the legal profession, especially represented by the American Bar Association and affiliated bodies, and the medical profession, especially represented by the American Medical Association and affiliated bodies, has been duly described in the present chapter. The work of the dental profession, especially represented by the National Dental Association, can not be passed over without a particular expression of admiration. The Preparedness League of American Dentists, organized February 27, 1916, was reorganized and expanded, for the purposes of the war, on December 6, 1917. The purpose of the league was to furnish dental assistance to all persons in the military and naval service, and particularly to the selectives; it pledged each member of the league to give one hour of free service. Its report for October 31, 1918, shows that it had enrolled 17,160 members; that it had examined 170,933 selectives and others in the military and naval service; and that it had performed a total of 613,285 operations.

Under the guidance of the Bureau of Education, Department of the Interior, virtually the entire body of school-teachers in the United States, including college professors, volunteered in the early months of 1918 to assist in transcribing 9,000,000 occupational cards for the Industrial Index; and the chronicles of the labors and sacrifices made for that urgent occasion would alone fill many chapters

---

It is true that the raising of the Army by the selective draft was a measure which touched every home, every shop, every factory, and every farm in the country; and, therefore, there was a natural and universal popular interest in the processes of the draft. Nevertheless, this popular interest might have been that of mere curiosity, or it might have been one of sullen distrust or resistant hostility. In fact, it was one of active sympathy and desire to help. The obvious fairness of the system; its direct relation to the raising of the Army, and therefore to the winning of the war; and the opportunity for service which it presented to those who were not qualified to give direct help to the fighting forces in other ways—these features enabled the system to rely upon the voluntary assistance of thousands upon thousands of men and women who gladly "did their bit" to help raise the Army.

As one surveys the ever widening circles of citizens who thus contributed in the work of the system, the boundaries become more indefinite between the various groups of persons who gave their help for a longer or shorter time, until finally the numbers become countless. The closing impression left upon the mind is one of profound gratitude and satisfaction—gratitude for the destiny which has given us an entire people united in hearty support of the war, and satisfaction in the revelation that a peaceful Nation, ambitious only for its own prosperity and happiness, can none the less be relied upon in time of national danger to devote itself to the task of raising a defensive Army.

97250°—19——20

Provost Marshal General

APPENDIXES.

APPENDIX A.

THE PRESIDENT'S PROCLAMATION OF AUGUST 31, 1918.

BY THE PRESIDENT OF THE UNITED STATES OF AMERICA.

A PROCLAMATION.

Whereas Congress has enacted and the President has, on the thirty-first day of August, one thousand nine hundred and eighteen, approved an act amending the act approved May eighteen, one thousand nine hundred and seventeen.

And whereas said act, as amended, contains the following provisions:

"SEC. 5. That all male persons between the ages of eighteen and forty-five, both inclusive, shall be subject to registration in accordance with regulations to be prescribed by the President, and upon proclamation by the President or other public notice given by him or by his direction stating the time or times and place or places of any such registration, it shall be the duty of all persons of the designated ages, except officers and enlisted men of the Regular Army; officers and enlisted men of the National Guard while in the service of the United States; officers of the Officers' Reserve Corps and enlisted men in the Enlisted Reserve Corps while in the service of the United States; officers and enlisted men of the Navy and Marine Corps; officers and enlisted and enrolled men of the Naval Reserve Force and Marine Corps Reserve while in the service of the United States; officers commissioned in the Army of the United States under the provisions of this act; persons who, prior to any day set for registration by the President hereunder, have registered under the terms of this act or under the terms of the resolution entitled "Joint resolution providing for the registration for military service of all male persons citizens of the United States and all male persons residing in the United States who have, since the fifth day of June, nineteen hundred and seventeen, and on or before the day set for the registration by proclamation by the President, attained the age of twenty-one years, in accordance with such rules and regulations as the President may prescribe under the terms of the act approved May eighteenth, nineteen hundred and seventeen, entitled 'An act to authorize the President to increase temporarily the Military Establishment of the United States,'" approved May twentieth, nineteen hundred and eighteen, whether called for service or not; and diplomatic representatives, technical attachés of foreign embassies and legations, consuls general, consuls, vice consuls, and consular agents of foreign countries, residing in the United States, who are not citizens of the United States, to present themselves for and submit to registration under the provisions of this act; and every such person shall be deemed to have notice of the requirements of this act upon the publication of any such proclamation or any such other public notice as aforesaid given by the President or by his direction; and any person who shall willfully fail or refuse to present himself for registration or to submit thereto as herein provided shall be guilty of a misdemeanor and shall, upon conviction in a district court of the United States having jurisdiction thereof, be punished by imprisonment for not more than one year and shall thereupon be duly registered: *Provided*, That in the call of the docket precedence shall be given, in courts trying the same, to the trial of criminal proceedings under this act: *Provided further*, That persons shall be subject to registration as herein provided who shall have attained their eighteenth birthday and who shall not have attained their forty-sixth birthday on or before the day set for the registration in any such proclamation by the President or any such other public notice given by him or by his direction, and all persons so registered shall be and remain subject to draft into the forces hereby authorized unless exempted or excused therefrom as in this act provided: *Provided further*, That the President may at such intervals as he may desire from time to time require all male persons who have attained the age of eighteen years since the last preceding date of registration and on or before the next date set for registration by proclamation by the President, except such persons as are exempt from registration hereunder, to register in the same manner and subject to the same requirements and liabilities as those previously registered under the terms hereof: *And provided further*, That in the case of temporary absence from actual place of legal residence of any person liable to registration as provided herein, such registration may be made by mail under regulations to be prescribed by the President. * * *

"SEC. 6. That the President is hereby authorized to utilize the service of any or all departments and any or all officers or agents of the United States and of the several States, Territories, and the District of Columbia, and subdivisions thereof, in the execution of this act, and all officers and agents of the United States and of the several States, Territories, and subdivisions thereof, and of the District of Columbia, and all persons designated or appointed under regulations prescribed by the President, whether such appointments are made by the President himself or by the governor or other officer of any State or Territory, to perform any duty in the execution of this act are hereby required to perform such duty as the President shall order or direct, and all such officers and agents and persons so designated or appointed shall hereby have full authority for all acts done by them in the execution of this act by the direction of the President. Correspondence in the execution of this act may be carried in penalty envelopes bearing the frank of the War Department. Any person charged as herein provided with the duty of carrying into effect any of the provisions of this act or the regulations made or directions given thereunder who shall fail or neglect to perform such duty, and any person charged with such duty or having and exercising any authority under said act, regulations, or directions who shall knowingly make or be a party to the making of any false or incorrect registration, physical examination, exemption, enlistment, enrollment, or muster; and any person who shall make or be a party to the making of any false statement or certificate as to the fitness or liability of himself or any other person for service under the provisions of this act, or regulations made by the President thereunder, or otherwise evades or aids another to evade the requirements of this act or of said regulations, or who, in any manner, shall fail or neglect fully to perform any duty required of him in the execution of this act, shall, if not subject to military law, be guilty of a misdemeanor, and upon conviction in the district court of the United States having jurisdiction thereof, be punished by imprisonment for not more than one year, or, if subject to military law, shall be tried by court-martial and suffer such punishment as a court-martial may direct.''

Now, therefore, I, Woodrow Wilson, President of the United States, do call upon the Governor of each of the several States and Territories, the Board of Commissioners of the District of Columbia, and all members of Local Boards and agents thereof appointed under the provisions of said act of Congress approved May eighteenth, one thousand nine hundred and seventeen, and all officers and agents of the several States and Territories, of the District of Columbia, and of the counties and municipalities therein, to perform certain duties in the execution of the foregoing law, which duties will be communicated to them directly in regulations of even date herewith.

And I do further proclaim and give notice to every person subject to registration in the several States and in the District of Columbia, in accordance with the above law, that the time and place of such registration shall be between seven a. m. and nine p. m. on Thursday, the twelfth day of September, one thousand nine hundred and eighteen, at a registration place in the precinct wherein he then has his permanent home or at such other place as shall be designated by public notice by the Local Board having jurisdiction of the area wherein he then has his permanent home. All male persons in the United States who shall have attained their eighteenth birthday and who shall not have attained their forty-sixth birthday on or before Thursday, the twelfth day of September, one thousand nine hundred and eighteen, the day herein named for registration, are required to register: *Provided, however,* That the following persons are hereby exempted from registration, to wit: Persons who, prior to the day herein set for registration, have registered under the terms of the Act approved May 18, 1917, or under the terms of the Public Resolution of Congress approved May 20, 1918, whether called for service or not; officers and enlisted men of the Regular Army; officers commissioned in the Army of the United States, and men of the forces drafted, under the provisions of the Act approved May 18, 1917; officers and enlisted men of the National Guard while in the service of the United States; officers of the Officers' Reserve Corps and enlisted men in the Enlisted Reserve Corps while in the service of the United States; officers and enlisted men of the Navy and Marine Corps; officers and enlisted and enrolled men of the Naval Reserve Force and Marine Corps Reserve while in the service of the United States; and diplomatic representatives, technical attachés of foreign embassies and legations, consuls general, consuls, vice consuls, and consular agents of foreign countries, residing in the United States, who are not citizens of the United States.

A day or days for registration in the Territories of Alaska, Hawaii, and Porto Rico will be named in later proclamations.

As required by the regulations, every Local Board having jurisdiction in a city of 30,000 population or over will promptly cause the mayor thereof to be notified of the place or places designated for registration; every Local Board having jurisdiction in a county, parish, or similar unit will promptly cause the clerk thereof to be notified of the place or places designated for registration, and every Local Board having jurisdiction in a State or Territory the area of which is divided into divisions for the administration of the Act approved May 18, 1917, will promptly cause the clerks of the townships within its division to be notified of the place or places designated for registration.

And I do call upon every mayor, county clerk, or township clerk receiving such notification to have a list of said places of registration posted, and do charge him with the duty of having all persons making inquiry informed of the place or places

Any person who, on account of sickness, will be unable to present himself for registration may apply on or before the day of registration at the office of any Local Board for instructions as to how he may register by agent.

Any person who expects to be absent on the day designated for registration from the jurisdiction of the board in which he then permanently resides may register by mail, but his registration card must reach the Local Board having jurisdiction of the area wherein he then permanently resides by the day herein named for registration. Any such person should apply as soon as practicable at the office of a Local Board for instructions as to how he may register by mail.

Any person who has no permanent residence must register at the place designated for registration by the Local Board having jurisdiction of the area wherein he may be on the day herein named for registration.

Any person who, on account of absence at sea, or on account of absence without the territorial limits of the United States, may be unable to comply with the regulations pertaining to absentees, shall, within five days after reaching the United States, register with his proper Local Board or as provided in the regulations for other absentees.

Fifteen months ago the men of the country from twenty-one to thirty years of age were registered. Three months ago, and again this month, those who had just reached the age of twenty-one were added. It now remains to include all men between the ages of eighteen and forty-five.

This is not a new policy. A century and a quarter ago it was deliberately ordained by those who were then responsible for the safety and defense of the Nation that the duty of military service should rest upon all able-bodied men between the ages of eighteen and forty-five. We now accept and fulfill the obligation which they established, an obligation expressed in our national statutes from that time until now. We solemnly purpose a decisive victory of arms and deliberately to devote the larger part of the military manpower of the Nation to the accomplishment of that purpose.

The younger men have from the first been ready to go. They have furnished voluntary enlistments out of all proportion to their numbers. Our military authorities regard them as having the highest combatant qualities. Their youthful enthusiasm, their virile eagerness, their gallant spirit of daring make them the admiration of all who see them in action. They covet not only the distinction of serving in this great war but also the inspiring memories which hundreds of thousands of them will cherish through the years to come of a great day and a great service for their country and for mankind.

By the men of the older group now called upon, the opportunity now opened to them will be accepted with the calm resolution of those who realize to the full the deep and solemn significance of what they do. Having made a place for themselves in their respective communities, having assumed at home the graver responsibilities of life in many spheres, looking back upon honorable records in civil and industrial life, they will realize as perhaps no others could, how entirely their own fortunes and the fortunes of all whom they love are put at stake in this war for right, and will know that the very records they have made render this new duty the commanding duty of their lives. They know how surely this is the Nation's war, how imperatively it demands the mobilization and massing of all our resources of every kind. They will regard this call as the supreme call of their day and will answer it accordingly.

Only a portion of those who register will be called upon to bear arms. Those who are not physically fit will be excused; those exempted by alien allegiance; those who should not be relieved of their present responsibilities; above all, those who can not be spared from the civil and industrial tasks at home upon which the success of our armies depends as much as upon the fighting at the front. But all must be registered in order that the selection for military service may be made intelligently and with full information. This will be our final demonstration of loyalty, democracy, and the will to win, our solemn notice to all the world that we stand absolutely together in a common resolution and purpose. It is the call to duty to which every true man in the country will respond with pride and with the consciousness that in doing so he plays his part in vindication of a great cause at whose summons every true heart offers its supreme service.

In witness whereof, I have hereunto set my hand and caused the seal of the United States to be affixed.

Done in the District of Columbia this thirty-first day of August in the year of our Lord one thousand nine hundred and eighteen and of the independence of the United States of America, the one hundred and forty-third.

WOODROW WILSON.

By the President:
    ROBERT LANSING,
        Secretary of State.

APPENDIX B.

ESTIMATES OF MAN-POWER; AGES 18–20, 32–45.

WAR DEPARTMENT,
OFFICE OF THE PROVOST MARSHAL GENERAL,
Washington, July 27, 1918.

From: The Provost Marshal General.
To: The Chief of Staff, War Department, Washington, D. C.
Subject: Changes of draft age.

1. Pursuant to your memorandum of July 24, transmitting a copy (secret) of the approved military program for 1918–19, and calling for the draft of a proposed bill lowering the draft age to 19 and raising it to 40, I transmit herewith estimates of the effectives obtainable by the enlargement of the draft ages, in the shape of three studies covering age groups 32–40 combined with 19–20, 32–45 combined with 19–20, and 32–45 combined with 18–20, and showing the estimated effectives for each combination.

2. These figures were made by a careful calculation in this office, checking the calculations at various points with experience in the several items represented; the basic figures, viz, the total males of the respective age groups, were ascertained by comparison of reliable insurance actuarial figures with census tables projected to date.

This explanation is made because the totals shown are considerably below what might have been supposed to be the ample size of the reservoir in the higher ages. The combination ages 32–40 and 19–20 (see Study No. 1) designated in your memorandum would yield only a little over a million and a half men (or half a million less than the total amount called for by the program for the nine months October, 1918–June, 1919). By including age 45 at the top, the second combination (see Study No. 2) would yield only a million and three-quarters effectives. By taking the extreme step and adding age 18 at the bottom and including age 45 at the top (see Study No. 3) something over two million and one-quarter effectives would be obtained.

3. This seems to indicate that the bill as drafted should at least provide authority to call into service the extreme age of 45 at the top and 18 at the bottom; and it is accordingly recommended that the draft of a bill be prepared with those ages as the limits.

4. Furthermore, the authority to draw upon this new reservoir must be obtained immediately. The estimated number of class I men under the present ages (and including the class of 1918, age 21, that has been registered under the President's proclamation) will be only about 100,000 men (and may fall below that figure) on September 1, 1918, after filling the calls indicated for July and August, and making deductions for the unexpected heavy losses due to a rush in June and July to the Navy, Marine Corps, and Emergency Fleet.

* * * *   *   *

E. H. CROWDER,
Provost Marshal General.

Estimate of effectives obtainable by enlargements of draft ages—Summary of Studies 1, 2, and 3.

ESTIMATED NUMBERS F EFFECTIVES FOR EACH AGE GROUP.

I. Ages 32–40	448,086	III. Ages 19–20	1,121,634
II. Ages 32–45	601,236	IV. Ages 18–20	1,797,609

NUMBERS FOR COMBINATIONS OF AGE GROUPS.

Study No. 1:
By combining ages 32–40 and 19–20—

Ages 32–40	448,086
Ages 19–20	1,121,634
Total	1,569,720

Study No. 2:
    By combining ages 32–45 and 19–20—
        Ages 32–45... 601,236
        Ages 19–20... 1,121,634

        Total.. 1,722,870
Study No. 3:
    By combining ages 32–45 and 18–20—
        Ages 32–45... 601,236
        Ages 18–20.. 1,797,609

        Total.. 2,398,845

STUDY NO. 1.

Ages 32–40 (inclusive)... 448,086
Ages 19–20 (inclusive)... 1,121,634

    Combined ages.. 1,569,720

Ages 32–40.		*Source of figures.*
1. Total males................................... 6,960,532		1. Insurance tables.
2. Less married (deferred)................... 5,311,952		2. Insurance tables.
3. Less deferred solely for industry and agriculture........................ 278,421		3. 4 per cent of line 1.
4. Less other deferments.................. 139,210		4. 2 per cent of line 1.
5. Less delinquents......................... 208,815		5. 3 per cent of line 1.
	5,938,398	
6. Remainder (gross class I)................ 1,022,134		
7. Less enlistments...................... 150,000		7. Special estimate.
8. Less aliens........................... 91,992		8. 9 per cent of line 6.
9. Less Emergency Fleet................. 50,000		9. Special estimate.
	291,992	
10. Remainder............................... 730,142		
11. Less physical rejects............................... 292,056		
(a) Groups B, C..................... 73,014		(a) 10 per cent of line 10.
(b) Group D........................ 219,042		(b) 30 per cent of line 10.
12. Net effectives............................ 448,086		

EXPLANATION.

1. Line 1 is taken from Prudential Insurance Actuarial Tables of July, 1918, compared with census tables projected in this office. The actuarial tables are brought down to date by the actuaries, and the census tables thus brought down at the bureau are not yet available.

2. Line 2 is taken from same source as line 1.

3. Line 3 is taken from Industrial Index Ledger Sheets for occupational registrants; the ratios there shown are: Class I, 31 per cent; classes II to IV, deferred for industry and agriculture only, 4 per cent.

The percentage here taken is the same as for ages 21–30 classification. This is too large, in that many more such men in ages 32–40 would get their exemption on dependency grounds, without invoking industrial or agricultural necessity. But it is too small, in that a larger proportion of men in ages 30–40 would be entitled to such deferment. Hence, these two differences may be estimated to set off each other.

4. Line 4 represents the corresponding figure for the 1917 draft. This is too low, if anything, as the numbers of State officials, etc., increases in the higher ages.

5. Line 5 is taken from reports in this office on delinquents, figuring 3.9 per cent of total registration. This would be too high because the total delinquents include at least some portion of the married; hence, 3 per cent is a safer figure.

7. Line 7 is thus figured: Total enlistments (Army and Navy) to date 1,400,000; of which, those about 30 are estimated at 10 per cent, or 140,000; of these, 120,000 may be estimated to be within ages 32–40; deduct 20,000 married, leaving 100,000 now enlisted; add 50,000 more probable enlistments before liability accrues in the new draft, equals 150,000.

8. Line 8 is found thus: In the first registration, 13 per cent were aliens; and the census report shows that the percentage of aliens ages 20–30 and 30–40 or 45 is not

substantially different. But many aliens have left the country, and 12 per cent is a safe figure. Of these, one-quarter are subjects of Great Britain and Italy, who will presumably become liable and largely available; hence, the deduction should be corrected to 9 per cent. This might seem too large, by a considerable factor, because in the 1917 draft only 50 per cent of called aliens obtained exemption on that ground, another 33 per cent obtaining it on other grounds, while 17 per cent of all aliens were certified for service; this would seem to show that in any given number of aliens the net number to be deducted on that ground is nearer 50 per cent. But as the 33 per cent who were exempted on other grounds are already included under the deferments already deducted, and as the 17 per cent volunteers are likely not to reappear (partly because of the Slavic and Polish legions, etc.), there should be no reduction of the 9 per cent, which is the figure here taken on line 7.

Declarants are not deducted; the neutrals being a negligible amount.

9. Line 9 is based on recent reports in this office.

11. Line 11 (a) is based on the returns of classification of 1918, showing 10 per cent. Line 11 (b) is based on similar figures, which show not quite 20 per cent, including camp rejections. To this must be added 10 per cent for ages 32–40, according to advices from the Surgeon General's office. This gives 30 per cent in all.

Ages 19 and 20.			Source of figures.
1. Total males		2,106,386	1. Insurance tables.
2. Less married (deferred)	163,812		2. Insurance tables.
3. Less deferred solely for industry or agriculture	10,532		3. ½ of 1 per cent of line 1.
4. Less other deferments	2,106		4. 1⁄10 of 1 per cent of line 1.
5. Less delinquents	63,191		5. 3 per cent of line 1
		239,641	
6. Remainder (gross class I)		1,866,745	
7. Less enlistments	207,777		7. Special estimate.
8. Less aliens	56,634		8. 3 per cent of line 6.
9. Less Emergency Fleet			9. Not allowed.
		264,411	
10. Remainder		1,602,334	
11. Less physical rejects		480,700	
(a) Groups B, C	160,233		11. (a) 10 per cent of line 10.
(b) Group D	320,467		11. (b) 20 per cent of line 10.
12. Net effective		1,121,634	

EXPLANATION

Lines 1 and 2 are taken from the same tables as for ages 32–40.

Line 3 obviously here can not use the same 4 per cent as for ages 21–30; the ratio one-half of 1 per cent is here taken.

Line 4 similarly is taken at a negligible figure of one-tenth of 1 per cent.

Line 5 is reckoned as for ages 32–40.

Line 7 is based upon reports of July 26, 1918, from The Adjutant General's Office, as set forth later in study No. 3.

Line 8 is based upon census figures showing that the numbers of aliens of ages 15 to 19 are less than one-half the number for the next 5-year period, while the native born are 10 to 20 per cent more numerous than in the higher age period. Thus the 9 per cent for ages 21–30 should here be reduced to 3 per cent.

Line 9. Emergency Fleet withdrawals for these age years should not be allowed.

Line 11 is based on the percentage for ages 21–30. Three officers of the Surgeon General's Office agree in believing that the ages 19–20 or 18–20 do not permit of any lower percentage than for ages 21–30.

STUDY NO. 2.

Ages 32–45 (inclusive).. 601, 236
Ages 19–20 (inclusive).. 1, 121, 634

Combined ages... 1, 722, 870

Ages 32-45.		Sources of figures
1. Total males......................... 10,028,973		1. Insurance tables.
2. Less married (deferred)............... 7,734,482		2. Insurance tables.
3. Less deferred solely for industry and 401,159		3. 4 per cent of line 1.
agriculture.		
4. Less other deferments................. 200,579		4. 2 per cent of line 1.
5. Less delinquents...................... 300,869		5. 3 per cent of line 1.
	8,637,089	
6. Remainder (gross class I)................. 1,391,884		
7. Less enlistments....................... 170,000		7. Special estimate.
8. Less aliens.............................. 125,270		8. 9 per cent of line 6.
9. Less Emergency Fleet................. 60,000		9. Special estimate.
	355,270	
10. Remainder............................. 1,036,614		
11. Less physical rejects.................... 435,378		
(a) Groups B, C.................. 103,661		(a) 10 per cent of line 10.
(b) Group D..................... 331,717		(b) 32 per cent of line 10.
12. Net effectives........................ 601,236		

EXPLANATION.

Lines 1 to 6 are reckoned as for ages 32–40 in study No. 1.

Line 7 is thus reckoned: Enlistments above age 30=140,000; deduct 30,000 married, leaving 110,000; add 60,000 more probable anticipatory enlistments, making 170,000 in all.

Line 8 is reckoned as for ages 32–40 in study No. 1.

Line 9 is based on reports in this office.

Line 11 is reckoned as for ages 32–40, but adding 5 per cent more for ages 40–45 (as recommended by the Surgeon General's Office) making 15 per cent; or an average of 12 per cent added for 32–45; or 32 per cent in all.

Ages 19 and 20.		Source of figures.
1. Total males......................... 2,106,386		1. Insurance tables.
2. Less married (deferred)............... 163,812		2. Insurance tables.
3. Less deferred solely for industry or agri- 10,532		3. $\frac{1}{2}$ of 1 per cent of line 1.
culture.		
4. Less other deferments................. 2,106		4. $\frac{1}{10}$ of 1 per cent of line 1.
5. Less delinquents....................... 63,191		5. 3 per cent of line 1.
	239,641	
6. Remainder (gross class I)................. 1,866,745		
7. Less enlistments....................... 207,777		7. Special estimate.
8. Less aliens.............................. 56,634		8. 3 per cent of line 6.
9. Less Emergency Fleet..................		9. Not allowed.
	264,411	
10. Remainder............................. 1,602,334		
11. Less physical rejects.................... 480,700		
(a) Groups B, C.................. 160,233		11. (a) 10 per cent of line 10.
(b) Group D..................... 320,467		11. (b) 20 per cent of line 10.
12. Net effectives........................ 1,121,634		

EXPLANATION.

Lines 1 and 2 are taken from the same tables as for ages 32–40.

Line 3 obviously here can not use the same 4 per cent as for ages 21–30; the ratio one-half of 1 per cent is here taken.

Line 4 similarly is taken at a negligible figure of one-tenth of 1 per cent.

Line 5 is reckoned as for ages 32–40.

Line 7 is based upon reports of July 26, 1918, from The Adjutant General's Office, as set forth later, in study No. 3.

Line 8 is based upon census figures showing that the numbers of aliens of ages 15 to 19 are less than one-half the number for the next 5-year period, while the native born are 10 to 20 per cent more numerous than in the highest-age period. Thus the 9 per cent for ages 21-30 should here be reduced to 3 per cent.

Line 9. Emergency Fleet withdrawals for these age years should not be allowed.

Line 11 is based on the percentage for ages 21-30. Three officers of the Surgeon General's Office agree in believing that the ages 19-20 do not permit of any lower percentage than for ages 21-30.

STUDY NO. 3.

Ages 32-45 (inclusive)... 601,236
Ages 18-20 (inclusive)... 1,797,609

　　　Combined ages... 2,398,845

Ages 32-45.			*Sources of figures.*
1. Total males..		10,028,973	1. Insurance tables.
2. Less married (deferred).....................	7,734,482		2. Insurance tables.
3. Less deferred solely for industry and agriculture.	401,159		3. 4 per cent of line 1.
4. Less other deferments......................	200,579		4. 2 per cent of line 1.
5. Less delinquents.............................	300,869		5. 3 per cent of line 1.
		8,637,089	
6.　　Remainder (gross class I).................		1,391,884	
7. Less enlistments.............................	170,000		7. Special estimate.
8. Less aliens....................................	125,270		8. 9 per cent of line 6.
9. Less Emergency Fleet......................	60,000		9. Special estimate.
		355,270	
10.　　Remainder..............................		1,036,614	
11. Less physical rejects.....................		435,378	
(*a*) Groups B, C.....................	103,661		(*a*) 10 per cent of line 10.
(*b*) Group D...........................	331,717		(*b*) 32 per cent of line 10.
12.　　Net effectives.........................		601,236	

EXPLANATION.

Lines 1 to 6 are reckoned as for ages 32-40 in study No. 1.

Line 7 is thus reckoned: Enlistments above age 30=140,000; deduct 30,000 **married**, leaving 110,000; add 60,000 more probable anticipatory enlistments, making **170,000** in all.

Line 8 is reckoned as for ages 32-40 in study No. 1.

Line 9 is based on reports in this office.

Line 11 is reckoned as for ages 32-40, but adding 5 per cent more for ages 40-45 (as recommended by the Surgeon General's Office), making 15 per cent; or an average of 12 per cent added for 32-45, or 32 per cent in all.

Ages 18-20.			*Sources of figures.*
1. Total males..................................		3,171,671	1. Insurance tables.
2. Less married (deferred)...................	158,175		2. Insurance tables.
3. Less deferred solely for industry and agri-	15,858		3. One-half of 1 per cent of line 1.
culture.			
4. Less other deferments....................	3,171		4. One-tenth of 1 per cent of line 1.
5. Less delinquents...........................	95,150		5. Three per cent of line 1.
		272,354	
6.　　Remainder (gross class I).............		2,899,317	
7. Less enlistments...........................	244,326		7. Special estimate.
8. Less aliens..................................	86,979		8. Three per cent of line 6.
9. Less Emergency Fleet...................			9. Not allowed.
		331,305	
10.　　Remainder............................		2,568,012	
11. Less physical rejects...................		770,403	
(*a*) Groups B, C...................	256,801		11. (*a*) 10 per cent of line 10.
(*b*) Group D.........................	513,602		11. (*b*) 20 per cent of line 10.
12.　　Net effectives.......................		1,797,609	

EXPLANATION.

Lines 1–5, 8, and 11 are obtained as for ages 19–20, in study No. 1.
Line 9, Emergency Fleet withdrawals for these ages should not be allowed.
Line 11 is reckoned as for ages 19–20, in study No. 1.
Line 7 is based on The Adjutant General's Office estimates of July 26, 1918, as follows:
1. On account of the present arrangement of records in the several offices it would require the services of some hundred clerks for months to obtain an accurate count of the number of men in the military service of the United States between the ages of 18 and 20. An accurate count can only be had from a study of all enlistment papers in The Adjutant General's Office, the Navy Department, and the Marine Corps. An estimate may be made from the actual number of enlistments since January 1, 1917, and the number in this age group in service at the present time is 244,326; of which number 36,549 are estimated to be under 19, and 207,777 are estimated to be of ages 19–20.
2. This estimate has been arrived at in the following manner:
(a) *Enlisted men in the Régular Army and National Guard between 18 and 20.*—The chief clerk of the recruiting department of The Adjutant General's Office makes the statement that ''due to the Selective Service Regulations practically all enlistments in the Regular Army and National Guard since January 1, 1918, represent men outside of the draft age and of these about 70 per cent are under the age.'' This estimate was verified by his assistant, who thought that possibly the reenlistments of older men might place as many as 75 per cent below the draft age. Another assistant in the department, at First and B Streets, estimated between 60 and 70 per cent, so that the average estimate of 70 per cent has been used in this computation. An actual count of current enlistment papers selected at-random revealed 80 out of 115 to be below the draft age. The total number of enlistments in the Regular Army during this period was 113,794, which figure it is estimated is about 90 per cent of the combined figures for the Regular Army and National Guard. Therefore, the total enlistments in the above would be approximately 126,436. But this figure includes men registered on June 5, 1918, the percentage of which is estimated to be 45. The net figure then for the age group 18–20 is estimated at 69,540. Of these 15 per cent, or 10,430, are under the age of 19. For the years 1916 and 1917 an average estimate by the same experts divides the enlistments into three age groups by percentages, as follows:

	Per cent.
Under 21	27
21–30	57
Over 30	16

On the basis of the 235,000 enlistments for 1916–17, exclusive of the National Guard, 63,450 would be between 18 and 20. Assuming that as many of those attained age 21 by June 5, 1918, as were enlisted during 1916 under age, it is estimated that this figure, 63,450, would be approximately the number of men now in the service enlisted prior to January 1, 1918. No figures for the National Guard are available. Hence, the total strength of the Regular Army between 18 and 20 is approximately at 133,000, and under 19 at 19,950.
(b) *Navy.*—The approximate strength of the Navy and Naval Reserve forces at this time is 400,000 enlisted men, or a little over about half in each. Of the 200,000 men in the Navy proper, very close to 50 per cent are between the ages 21–30. Of the 100,000 men outside of these ages it is estimated that 75 per cent are under and 25 per cent over. In the Navy, then, 75,000 are to-day under 21. Of the 200.000 in the Naval Reserves, between 80 and 88 per cent are within the ages 21–30. Assuming 170,000 to be a fair figure, 30,000 remain, which are equally divided into two age groups—those over 30 and those under 21. Hence, the number of men in the naval forces under 21 is approximately 97,500. Of these it is estimated that 15 per cent, or 14,625, are under the age of 19. The above estimates are furnished by the clerk of the enlisted·personnel of the Navy.
(c) *Marine Corps.*—Total minors enlisted since April 1, 1917, 13,826, or applying 15 per cent, 1,974 are under 19.
3. Summarized estimate:

	18 to 20.	Under 19.	19 and 20.
Army	133,000	19,950	113,050
Navy	97,500	14,625	82,875
Marine Corps	13,826	1,974	11,852
Total	244,326	36,549	207,777

APPENDIX C.

TERRITORIAL RETURNS.

I. ALASKA.

[From a report on the operation of the selective service law in Alaska, from July, 1917, to Sept. 30, 1918 submitted to the governor of Alaska by Capt. J. J. Finnegan, executive officer, Sept. 29, 1918.]

By proclamation dated June 30, 1917, the President set the period between July 2 and September 2, 1917, inclusive, as the time for registration in the Territory under the act of May 18, 1917.

To accomplish the purpose of the act, 21 local and 4 district boards (one in each judicial division of the Territory) were created. Local board No. 15 at Chena was abolished in 1917. Local board No. 22 at St. Michael was created in 1918. Their jurisdiction extended over an area which is one-fifth that of the United States proper and is handicapped with inadequate and, at times, primitive means of transportation. In the greater portion an unsatisfactory and intermittent mail service prevails. In many instances three months elapse before replies to communications are received. These conditions have forced the omission herefrom of compiled data relative to many interesting features in connection with the effect of the draft on industries, particularly those of mining and fishing.

Eleven thousand seventy-one persons were registered at a cost of $380.90, or 3.2 cents per registrant, as compared to the national average of 54 cents in 1917. Thirty-eight per cent of the above were aliens, of whom approximately 1,000 were alien enemies, 326 being Germans. One hundred eighteen were colored persons. No Indians were registered.

Under orders from the Provost Marshal General those registrants who claimed residence in other States or Territories or who gave permanent addresses therein were transferred to their respective jurisdictions. Local boards state that these transferred cases have caused nearly as much work, investigation, and trouble as those remaining. Transferred cases numbered 4,496, leaving our net registrants at 6,575. Exceedingly few cards of Alaskans who registered in the States were transmitted to the Territory, although their number was considerable.

The registration of July–September, 1917, and the inductions to November, 1918, are as follows:

Local board.	Registration July, 1917.	Accepted at camp.	Local board.	Registration July, 1917.	Accepted at camp.
Anchorage	1,739	461	Nenana	210	98
Cordova	412	118	Nome	243	62
Chena		1	Petersburg	135	35
Douglas	189	43	Ruby	67	31
Eagle	21	9	St. Michael		
Fairbanks	445	186	Seward	477	100
Haines	28	8	Sitka	155	54
Iditarod	122	35	Skagway	92	30
Juneau	801	210	Tanana	33	16
Ketchikan	796	222	Valdez	293	77
McCarthy	256	64	Wrangell	96	37

On September 1, 1918, the report of registrants in class I disclosed the following:

Remaining, finally classified in class I and examined physically and accepted

for general military service	849
Limited military service	278
Remedial defective group	34
Emergency Fleet	120
Delinquents	837
Not physically examined	223
Inducted and called for induction	295

Total 2,636

To this number should be added the following:

Inducted under call 193	696
Credits for enlistments, voluntary inductions, etc	164

Grand total 3,496

It will thus be seen that 0.532 per cent of our registrants have been classified in class I.

The 837 delinquents and the 223 not physically examined constitute 16 per cent of the number registered. This high ratio is due primarily to the following causes, listed in the order of their importance: (1) The high percentage of illiterate and non-English-speaking aliens in the Territory. (2) Vast extent of the Territory. Some registrants are from 500 to 1,000 miles distant from the nearest local board. (3) Infrequent mail service to remote points and consequent failure to receive orders within the allotted time. (4) The absence of physicians in many localities. Many registrants are located several hundred miles from the nearest medical examiner. Many have traveled hundreds of miles at their own expense for purposes of examination and induction.

By October 1, 1918, 2,200 registrants (or $33\frac{1}{2}$ per cent of the gross number) will have been inducted. In addition thereto many hundreds, impatient for action, enlisted prior to the registration period or joined the British and Canadian forces. Alaska has furnished at least 3,000 men to the colors, or approximately 12 per cent of its present total white population.

The expense of accomplishing the draft for the first 15 months will not exceed $12,000, or $5.45 per man inducted. The national average for 1917 was $4.93.

Incomplete returns disclose that 118 men were physically rejected out of 1,220 examined by local boards, an average of 10 per cent, as compared to the national average of 29 per cent. Of those examined by local boards and accepted, who were again examined at mobilization camps, available data at this time discloses that 18 out of 681 were rejected by the camp surgeons, a ratio of 2.66 per cent as compared to the national ratio of 5.8 per cent. When this data is complete it will furnish a most interesting medical and sociological study.

Under the provisions of the act of May, 1918, persons who attained the age of 21 years since September 2, 1917, were registered in the period between July 2 and September 3, 1918. Returns thereof are yet incomplete. It is estimated the number will not exceed 250, including Indians.

By proclamation on September 18, 1918, the President set the period between October 15 and December 16, 1918, inclusive, as the time for registration in Alaska, under the act of August 31, 1918. Indians will be included.

To the members of the local boards too much credit can not be extended for their intelligent and loyal efforts. Their labors have been intense and, heretofore, uncompensated. The district boards, medical and legal advisory boards, and their associates, have performed a great work with efficiency and fidelity and deserve the gratitude of the country.

It is estimated that the total registration between October 15 and December 16, 1918, was approximately 9,800. Incomplete returns from all but three boards show the registration of—

Citizens	4, 238
Declarant aliens	1, 500
Nondeclarant aliens	1, 483
Total	7, 221
Whites	6, 585
Negroes	26
Orientals and Indians (estimated)	610
Total	7, 221

II. HAWAII.

1. REGISTRATION.

First registration (July 31, 1917)	28, 851
Second registration (July 31, 1918)	2, 349
Third registration (Oct. 26, 1918)	41, 541
Total	72, 741
Transfers	176
First registration (net)	28, 675

2. MARRIED AND SINGLE.

First registration	28, 675
Married	12, 752
Single	15, 923

3. AGE.

Age.	First registration.	Third registration.	Age.	First registration.	Third registration.
18		2,090	32		1,258
19		1,921	33		2,415
20		2,300	34		2,465
21	2,713	591	35		2,514
22	2,774	173	36		2,492
23	2,504	119	37		2,411
24	2,262	103	38		2,642
25	2,423	102	39		2,340
26	2,246	86	40		2,473
27	4,035	83	41		2,366
28	3,184	77	42		2,684
29	3,186	79	43		2,580
30	3,348	106	44		2,469
31		126	45		2,386

4. CLASSIFICATION (FIRST REGISTRATION).

Class I 7,028
Class II 1,839
Class III 473
Class IV 2,284
Class V 12,617

5. PHYSICAL EXAMINATION OF CLASS I (FIRST REGISTRATION).

Failed to appear 1,374
Qualified for general service 4,733
Qualified for limited service 793
Remediable defects 74
Examination postponed 54

6. INDUCTIONS.

Called 5,464
Inducted 5,529
Rejected at camp 583

7. ACCEPTED AT CAMP.

Local board:
    Hawaii County No. 1 1,759
    Hawaii County No. 2 516
    Honolulu County and city No. 1 452
    Honolulu County and city No. 2 1,164
    Kauai County 450
    Mauii County 753

8. NATIONALITY OF MEN QUALIFIED FOR MILITARY DUTY.

Per cent.

American 11.39
Japanese 11.08
Chinese 4.56
Hawaiian 13.08
Filipino 48.79
Portuguese 8.08
Spanish .... .70
Korean 1.48
Porto Rican .... .83
Colored American .... .01

III. PORTO RICO.

1. REGISTRATION.

First registration (July 5, 1917).. 109,706
Second registration (July 5, 1918)....................................... 10,744
Third registration (Oct. 26, 1918)....................................... 116,403

Total.. 236,853

2. PHYSICAL EXAMINATIONS.

First registration:
    Called for examination.. 58,209
        Failed to appear... 2,910
        Accepted... 38,932
        Rejected... 16,367

3. INDUCTIONS.

First registration:
    Ordered to report at camp.. 17,855
        Failed to report... 139
        Rejected at camp... 2,733

4. CLAIMS AND EXEMPTIONS.

First registration:
    Claims made for exemption or discharge........................... 7,573
        Claims allowed... 2,546
        Claims disallowed.. 5,027

5. MARRIED AND SINGLE.

First registration:
    Married registrants called and accepted 18
    Single registrants called and accepted........................... 26,381

6. CITIZENS AND ALIENS.

First registration:
    Citizens... 107,486
        Called and accepted.. 39,688
    Aliens... 2,220
        Called and accepted.. 165
Third registration:
    Citizens... 114,330
    Aliens... 2,073
        Declarants... 136
        Nondeclarants.. 1,937

7. COLOR.

First registration:
    White.. 80,551
    Colored.. 25,627
Third registration:
    White.. 89,773
    Colored.. 26,611

8. AGE.

(FIRST REGISTRATION.)

Age.	Number.	Age.	Number.
21	16,333	26	7,974
22	16,030	27	7,159
23	16,357	28	8,407
24	11,791	29	6,920
25	9,710	30	12,025

9. REGISTRATION JULY, 1917, AND INDUCTIONS TO NOVEMBER 11, 1918, BY LOCAL BOARDS.

Local board.	Registration July, 1917.	Accepted at camp.	Local board.	Registration July, 1917.	Accepted at camp.
Adjuntas	1,514	146	Lajas	855	93
Aguada	1,164	99	Lares	1,857	173
Aguadilla	1,980	157	Las Marias	758	22
Aguas Buenas	766	80	Las Peidras	786	57
Aibonito	1,028	90	Loiza	1,160	122
Anasco	1,298	123	Luguillo	553	51
Arecibo	4,497	511	Manati	1,719	150
Arroyo	595	57	Maricao	561	52
Barceloneta	436	143	Maunabo	534	40
Barranquitas	828	69	Mayaguez	4,159	497
Barros	1,143	109	Moca	1,194	169
Bayamon	2,960	278	Mororis	1,093	102
Cabo Rojo	1,727	174	Naguabo	1,408	134
Caguas	3,447	373	Naranjito	717	85
Camuy	1,072	131	Patillas	1,098	118
Carolina	1,156	98	Penuelas	997	108
Cayey	2,211	169	Ponce	6,607	745
Ceiba	484	25	Quebradillas	669	54
Ciales	1,407	154	Rincon	714	46
Cidra	1,128	106	Rio Grande	965	84
Coamo	1,368	138	Rio Piedras	1,901	169
Comerio	1,138	119	Sabana Grande	939	86
Corozal	1,039	113	Salinas	1,481	157
Culebra	37	1	San German	1,788	156
Dorado	567	50	San Juan	7,793	839
Fajardo	1,270	125	San Lorenzo	1,259	137
Guanica	747	81	San Sebastian	1,595	164
Guayama	1,942	192	Santa Isabel	822	77
Guayanilla	927	85	Toa Alta	732	84
Guaynabo	603	63	Toa Baja	529	71
Guarabo	1,066	111	Trujillo Alto	776	10
Hatillo	1,046	98	Utnado	2,637	254
Hormigueros	425	50	Vega Alta	880	57
Humaco	1,799	160	Vega Baja	1,263	107
Isabella	1,377	118	Vieques	1,040	97
Jayuga	970	92	Villalba	1,006	92
Juana Diaz	1,722	175	Yabucoa	1,459	146
Juncos	1,090	89	Yauco	2,286	256

APPENDIX D.

CONSCIENTIOUS OBJECTORS—A LOCAL BOARD VIEW.

"This board began its work of classification with the conscientious feeling that the selective service law had the right name, in that, as far as could be noted, it was wholly impartial in its treatment of the registrants, and that none was discriminated against intentionally nor unjustly impressed into active soldier life.

"Our impression was that the framers of the law had been marvelously wise, honestly intent and soundly just in their considerations of what the Government should provide as right and reasonable requirements of a citizen in taking up the cause of his country against a belligerent nation.

"With these convictions we entered upon our onerous work, prompted and encouraged by the realization that we were to serve the department loyally and without the restraint of any scruples of violating the principles of brotherhood, fraternity, and Christian dealing with our fellow men.

"We had progressed very little ere we found an obstacle that proved to us that there was a flaw in the legal enactment that made an open question of the just application of the conscription method of procuring fighting man-power.

"We refer to the status given by the law to the so-called noncombatant class, who receive special classification because of religious objection to warfare or the taking up of arms.

"We found many physically fit beyond their fellows in the examination classes, intelligent beyond compare, and in every way constituted to develop into splendid fighting men.

"Simply because they had espoused a certain religious faith, confession, or creed, whether in Christian sincerity or not, according as our private opinion may have been formed, we were compelled to deprive Uncle Sam of a fit soldier, grant the examinee his freedom, and impress into the service some other man, who in sincerity and truth worshipped the Almighty equally as acceptably in the Divine sight, yet not trammeled nor held back by an article of faith that said in so many words, 'Thou shalt not kill.'

"We remonstrated with our consciences before we freely acquiesced in their right to plead for discrimination, but were compelled to succumb to the legal force of the argument they produced, based upon the point in the selective law.

"Having had personal contact and touch with supporters of the church notions of the Dunkards, Amish, Quakers, Menonites, etc., since boyhood days, we know whereof we spake when we demurred and reluctantly complied with the draft loophole that gave these professed religionists 'a way out of it.' In our immediate neighborhood we had tacit knowledge that these people refrained from taking part in any of the war activities. They refused to buy bonds, stamps, or contribute to the Red Cross, Y. M. C. A., or any patriotic movement that meant for the winning of the war. Substantial proof stared us in the face, showing that they even withheld their crops from the market with the thought of prospective future higher prices.

"We also noted that the young men who were trained in this school of faith attended church services since the war started, as never before, as a camouflage to justify their plea for exemption or special rating.

"That they were 'Sayers of the Word, and not doers,' we know by association with them, for they are of the world, worldly, even as those of other church affiliations are inconsistent in religious living, and in our opinion, for them to take up arms would not lower them in the sight of their heavenly Father as much as would their hypocritical actions, just to escape the military service.

"Fortified as they were additionally by the assurance from our President that exoneration was theirs, they practically demanded the full granting of every minute protection, and thereby handicapped us more fully in our endeavors to seek a way by which we could get them to do their duty from our viewpoint.

"These few reasons, gained from practical experience, prompt us to point out this section of the law as being pernicious, unjust, and in all respects a mistake, if not a blunder.

"Had the lawmakers considered that once a nation is at war it is very difficult for dissenting opinion to make itself known or felt, the regulation would have been made more just, we opine. 'My country! may she ever be right; but right or wrong, My country!' is a sentiment strong in America and in many other nations as well. It evidences faith in and loyalty to government that may be misguided, as far as the Scriptures are concerned, but, nevertheless, praiseworthy and laudable.

"Nowhere is there much patience with the 'conscientious objector' to the policies of the government in time of war, and our experience convinces us that disregard for his scruples would have made the law definite as to its general application and free from criticism.''

APPENDIX E.

SAMPLE FORM OF REQUISITION FOR REGISTRANTS TO BE MOBILIZED.

From: The Adjutant General of the Army.
To: The Provost Marshal General.
Subject: General call of the draft (white).

1. The Secretary of War directs that requisition be made on you for the calling into the service on October 21, 1918, of the following number of white drafted men classified for general military service, at the camps and stations as indicated below:

Camps and stations.	Number of men to report.	Camps and stations.	Number of men to report.
Camp McClellan, Ala	5,000	Fort Howard, Md	421
Camp Travis, Tex	8000	Fort Washington, Md	651
Camp Greenleaf, Ga	15,000	Fort Monroe, Va	1,226
Camp McArthur, Tex	10,000	Fort Caswell, N. C	1,485
Camp Kearny, Cal	6,000	Camp Eustis, Va	2,000
Camp Cody, N. Mex	6,000	Fort Moultrie, S. C	312
Camp Wadsworth, S. C	12,000	Fort Screven, Ga	2,110
Camp Wheeler, Ga	5,000	Key West Barracks, Fla	154
Camp Shelby Miss	5,000	Fort Dade, Fla	425
Camp Bowie, Tex	5,000	Fort Barrancas, Fla	55
Camp Forrest, Ga	5,000	Fort Morgan, Ala	222
Fort Williams, Me	1,897	Jackson Barracks, La	2,142
Fort Constitution, N. H	569	Fort Crockett, Tex	1,202
Fort Warren, Mass	877	Fort Rosecrans, Cal	1,531
Fort Rodman, Mass	295	Fort McArthur, Cal	2,233
Fort H. G. Wright, N. Y	774	Fort Winfield Scott, Cal	3,950
Fort Totten, N. Y	987	Fort Stevens, Oreg	236
Fort Hamilton, N. Y	2,117	Fort Worden, Wash	2,204
Fort Hancock, N. J	1,714		
Fort Du Pont, Del	606	Total	114,395

(Signed)   PAUL GIDDINGS,
Adjutant General.

324

APPENDIX F.

SPECIMEN ENTRAINMENT SCHEDULE.

CALL No. 1121.

Movement of National Army, August 22–24, 1918, from Arkansas to Camp Pike (Little Rock), Ark. (Negroes only).

(Index—See key.)

(Page 1.)

County	County seat and entraining station	Number of men	Schedule No.	Page No.
Arkansas	Stuttgart	25	14	4
Ashley	Hamburg	3	6	3
Baxter	Mountain Home. (Entrain Cotter.)	None.		
Benton	Bentonville	None.		
Boone	Harrison	None.		
Bradley	Warren	21	6	3
Calhoun	Hampton	9	17	5
Carroll	Berryville	None.		
Chicot	Lake Village	37	6	3
Clark	Arkadelphia	35	4	2
Clay	Piggott	None.		
Cleburne	Heber Springs	None.		
Cleveland	Rison	33	17	5
Columbia	Magnolia	2	16	4
Conway	Morrilton	12	7	3
Craighead	Jonesboro	22	18	5
Crawford	Van Buren	7	7	2
Crittenden	Marion	90	12	4
Cross	Wynne	31	8	3
Dallas	Fordyce	None.		
Desha	Arkansas City	12	6	3
Drew	Monticello	23	6	3
Faulkner	Conway	12	7	3
Franklin	Ozark	4	7	3
Fulton	Salem (entrain Mammoth Spring)	1	10	4
Garland	Hot Springs	8	3	2
Grant	Sheridan	4	3	2
Greene	Paragould	None.		
Hempstead	Hope	3	4	2
Hot Springs	Malvern	9	4	2
Howard	Nashville	None.		
Independence	Batesville	11	2	2
Izard	Melbourne. (Entrain Guion.)	None.		
Jackson	Newport	11	2	2
Jefferson: Board No. 1	Pine Bluff	None.	12	3
Board No. 2	....do....	None.	12	3
Johnson	Clarksville	1	7	3
Lafayette	Lewisville	8	17	5
Lawrence	Walnut Ridge	8	2	2
Lee	Marianna	8	1	2
Lincoln	Star City. (Entrain Gould.)	30	6	3
Little River	Ashdown	14	4	2
Little Rock City	(See Pulaski County.)			
Logan	Paris	None.		
Lonoke	Lonoke	16	13	4
Madison	Huntsville. (Entrain Springdale.)	None.		
Marion	Yellville	None.		
Miller	Texarkana	28	4	2
Mississippi	Osceola. (Entrain Blytheville.)	40	12	4
Monroe	Clarendon	13	18	5
Montgomery	Mount Ida. (Entrain Womble.)	3	4	2
Nevada	Prescott	None.		
Newton	Jasper. (Entrain Harrison.)	1	9	3
Ouachita	Camden	38	11	4
Perry	Perryville. (Entrain Perry.)	21	15	4

CALL No. 1121—Continued.

Movement of National Army, August 22-24, 1918, from Arkansas to Camp Pike (Little Rock), Ark. (Negroes only)—Continued.

County.	County seat and entraining station.	Number of men.	Schedule No.	Page No.
Phillips	Helena	3	1	2
Pike	Murfreesboro	5	5	2
Poinsett	Harrisburg	48	8	3
Polk	Mena	None.		
Pope	Russellville	1	7	3
Prairie	Des Arc. (Entrain Devalls Bluff.)	6	13	4
Pulaski:				
Board No. 1	Little Rock	None.		
Board No. 2	do	16	19	5
City Board 1	do	9	19	5
City Board 2	do	3	19	5
Randolph	Pocahontas	None.		
Saline	Benton	3	3	2
Scott	Waldron	None.		
Searcy	Marshall	None.		
Sebastian:				
Board No. 1	Fort Smith	50	7	3
Board No. 2	Good	3	7	3
Sevier	De Queen	None.		
Sharp	Evening Shade. (Entrain Hardey.)	None.		
St. Francis	Forrest City	12	1	2
Stone	Min View (Min Sylamore.)	None.		
Union	El Dado	45	11	4
Van Buren	Clinton (Min Shirley.)	1	9	3
White	Fayetteville	2	7	3
Woodruff	Searcy. (Entrain New Augusta.)	3	9	3
Yell	Danville	18	8	3
Total		882		

KEY.

To ascertain routing and time of departure, refer to page and schedule numbers as above. Departure is invariably made from county seat or headquarters shown in column 2, pages 2 to 5. For time of departure from desired points, see column 6.

EXAMPLE: Phillips County, page 2, schedule 1, shows that three men move from Helena via Mo. Pac. to Camp Pike, leaving Helena (column 6, line 1) on Mo. Pac. train No. 308 at 5.15 p. m. August 22.

The same course is followed in locating routes and schedules from points not located on any railroad. Thus, Prairie County, page 4, schedule 13, county seat Des Arc (not located on a railroad), entrain at Devalls Bluff (see column 6, line 1, schedule 13); six men in this movement via C. R. I. & P. to Little Rock, thence Mo. Pac. to Camp Pike.

From Arkansas to Camp Pike (Little Rock), Ark., routes and schedules.

(Page 2.)

SCHEDULE No. 1.—ENTRAIN AUGUST 22, 1918.

1	2	3	4	5	6
			Route.		
County.	County seat or headquarters.	Number of men.	Road.	Junction.	TRAIN SCHEDULE.
Phillips	Helena	3	Mo. Pac.	Camp Pike	Meals will be provided as follows:
Lee	Marianna	8			Breakfast between 6.30 a. m. and 8.30 a. m.
St. Francis	Forrest City	12			Luncheon between 11.30 a. m. and 1.30 p. m.
					Dinner between 5.30 p. m. and 8 p. m.
Total		23			

AUGUST 22.

1. Lv. Helena..........5.15 p. m. Mo. Pac., No. 308.
2. Lv. Marianna........6.25 p. m. Mo. Pac., No. 308.
3. Lv. Forrest City.....7.14 p. m. Mo. Pac., No. 308.
4. Ar. Wynne..........7.50 p. m. Mo. Pac., No. 308.
5. Lv. Wynne..........11.48 p. m. Mo. Pac., No. 201.

AUGUST 23.

6. Ar. Little Rock........3 a. m. Mo. Pac., No. 201.
7. Mo. Pac. switch to Camp Pike.

SCHEDULE No. 2.—ENTRAIN AUGUST 22, 1918.

1	2	3	4	5	6
Lawrence	Walnut Ridge	8	Mo. Pac.	Camp Pike	Dinner before departure.
Independence	Batesville	11			1. Lv. Walnut Ridge.......5.43 p. m. Mo. Pac. No. 33.
Jackson	Newport	11	Mo. Pac.	Camp Pike	2. Lv. Batesville.......5.50 p. m. Mo. Pac. No. 205.
					3. Ar. Newport.......7.30 p. m. Mo. Pac. No. 205.
					4. Lv. Newport.......7.45 p. m. Mo. Pac. No. 33.
Total		30			

5. Ar. Argenta.........10.50 p. m. Mo. Pac. No. 33.
6. Mo. Pac. switch to Camp Pike.

From Arkansas to Camp Pike (Little Rock), Ark., routes and schedules—Continued.

SCHEDULE No. 3.—ENTRAIN AUGUST 22, 1918.

1	2	3	4	5	6
County.	County seat or headquarters.	Number of men.	Road.	Junction.	TRAIN SCHEDULE.
			Route.		Meals will be provided as follows: Breakfast between 6.30 a. m. and 8.30 a. m. Luncheon between 11.30 a. m. and 1.30 p. m. Dinner between 5.30 p. m. and 8 p. m.
Garland	Hot Springs	8	Mo. Pac	Camp Pike	Dinner before departure. 1. Lv. Hot Springs..........5.30 p. m. Mo. Pac. No. 18.
Grant	Sheridan	4			2. Lv. Sheridan............5.30 p. m. Mo. Pac. No. 847.
Saline	Benton	3			3. Ar. Benton.............6.30 p. m. Mo. Pac. No. 847.
Total		15			4. Lv. Benton.............6.45 p. m. Mo. Pac. No. 18. 5. Ar. Little Rock..........7.30 p. m. Mo. Pac. No. 18. 6. Mo. Pac. switch to Camp Pike.

SCHEDULE No. 4.—ENTRAIN AUGUST 22, 1918.

1	2	3	4	5	6
Little River	Ashdown	14	K. C. Sou. Mo. Pac	Texarkana. Camp Pike.	1. Lv. Ashdown..........6.15 a. m. K. C. Sou. No. 1. 2. Ar. Texarkana........6.55 a. m. K. C. Sou. No. 1. Breakfast Texarkana.
Miller	Texarkana	28	Mo. Pac	Camp Pike	3. Lv. Texarkana.........7.15 a. m. Mo. Pac. No. 36.
Hempstead	Washington. (Entrain at Hope.)	3			4. Lv. Nashville..........7.15 a. m. Mo. Pac. No. 845. 5. Ar. Hope.............8.20 a. m. Mo. Pac. No. 845.
Clark	Arkadelphia	35	Mo. Pac	Camp Pike	6. Lv. Hope.............8.40 a. m. Mo. Pac. No. 36.
Hot Springs	Malvern	9			7. Lv. Womble...........6.50 a. m. Mo. Pac. No. 835.
Montgomery	Mount Ida. (Entrain at Womble.)	3			8. Ar. Gurdon...........9.50 a. m. Mo. Pac. No. 835.
Total		92			9. Lv. Gurdon..........10.25 a. m. Mo. Pac. No. 36. 10. Lv. Arkadelphia......11.00 a. m. Mo. Pac. No. 36. 11. Lv. Malvern.........11.45 a. m. Mo. Pac. No. 36. 12. Ar. Little Rock........1.25 p. m. Mo. Pac. No. 36. Luncheon at Little Rock. 13. Mo. Pac. switch to Camp Pike.

(Page 3.)

SCHEDULE No. 5.—ENTRAIN AUGUST 22, 1918:

Pike...	Murfreesboro...	5	M. D. & G. ...	Hot Springs...
			Mo. Pac. ...	Camp Pike...

1. Lv. Murfreesboro............11.45 a. m. M. D. & G. No. 2.
2. Ar. Hot Springs............5.30 p. m. M. D. & G. No. 2.
3. Lv. Hot Springs............5.30 p. m. Mo. Pac. No. 18.
4. Ar. Little Rock............7.30 p. m. Mo. Pac. No. 18.
   Dinner at Little Rock.
5. Mo. Pac. switch to Camp Pike.

SCHEDULE No. 6.—ENTRAIN AUGUST 23, 1918.

Chicot...	37		
Ashley...	3		
Bradley...	21		
Drew...	23		
Desha...	12		
Lincoln...	30	Lake Village...	Camp Pike...
(Entrain at Gould.)		Hamburg...	Mo. Pac. ...
Total...	126	Warren...	
		Monticello...	
		Arkansas City...	
		Star City...	

1. Lv. Lake Village............12:50 p. m. Mo. Pac. No. 851.
2. Ar. Montrose............1:50 p. m. Mo. Pac. No. 851.
3. Lv. Hamburg............8:00 a. m. Mo. Pac. No. 852.
4. Ar. Montrose............9:50 a. m. Mo. Pac. No. 852.
   Luncheon at Montrose.
5. Lv. Montrose............1:53 p. m. Mo. Pac. No. 106.
6. Ar. Dermott............2:30 p. m. Mo. Pac. No. 106.
7. Lv. Warren............9:40 a. m. Mo. Pac. No. 840.
8. Lv. Monticello............10:23 a. m. Mo. Pac. No. 840.
9. Ar. Dermott............11:30 a. m. Mo. Pac. No. 840.
   Luncheon at Dermott.
10. Lv. Dermott............2:30 p. m. Mo. Pac. No. 106.
11. Ar. McGehee............2:45 p. m. Mo. Pac. No. 106.
12. Lv. Arkansas City............12:30 p. m. Mo. Pac. No. 840.
13. Ar. McGehee............1:10 p. m. Mo. Pac. No. 840.
14. Lv. McGehee............2:55 p. m. Mo. Pac. No. 106.
15. Lv. Gould............3:52 p. m. Mo. Pac. No. 106.
16. Ar. Little Rock............7:10 p. m. Mo. Pac. No. 106.
    Dinner at Little Rock.
17. Mo. Pac. switch to Camp Pike.

From Arkansas to Camp Pike (Little Rock), Ark., routes and schedules—Continued.

SCHEDULE No. 7.—ENTRAIN AUGUST 23, 1918.

1	2	3	4	5	6
County.	County seat or headquarters.	Number of men.	Route.		TRAIN SCHEDULE.
			Road.	Junction.	Meals will be provided as follows: Breakfast between 6:30 a. m. and 8:30 a. m. Luncheon between 11:30 a. m. and 1:30 p. m. Dinner between 5:30 p. m. and 8:00 p. m.
Sebastian	Greenwood. (Board No. 2.)	3	Mo. Pac.	Camp Pike	1. Lv. Greenwood..........9:15 a. m. Mo. Pac. No. 752. 2. Ar. Fort Smith. Luncheon at Fort Smith..........10:15 a. m. Mo. Pac. No. 752.
Washington	Fayetteville.	2	Frisco. Mo. Pac.	Fort Smith. Camp Pike.	3. Lv. Fayetteville..........7:32 a. m. Frisco No. 5. 4. Ar. Fort Smith..........9:35 a. m. Frisco No. 5.
Sebastian	Fort Smith. (Board No. 1.)	50	Mo. Pac.	Camp Pike.	5. Lv. Fort Smith..........12:47 p. m. Mo. Pac. No. 103. 6. Lv. Van Buren..........1:25 p. m. Mo. Pac. No. 03. 7. Lv. Ozark..........2:45 p. m. Mo. Pac. No. 103. 8. Lv. Clarksville..........3:55 p. m. Mo. Pac. No. 103. 9. Lv. Russellville..........5:05 p. m. Mo. Pac. No. 03. 10. Lv. Morrilton..........6:10 p. m. Mo. Pac. No. 103. 11. Lv. Conway..........6:52 p. m. Mo. Pac. No. 103. 12. Ar. Little Rock..........8:00 p. m. Mo. Pac. No. 103. Dinner at Little Rock. 13. Mo. Pac. switch to Camp Pike.
Crawford	Van Buren.	7			
Franklin	Ozark.	4			
Johnson	Clarksville.	1			
Pope	Russellville.	1			
Conway	Morrilton.	12			
Faulkner	Conway.	12			
Total		92			

SCHEDULE No. 8.—ENTRAIN AUGUST 24, 1918.

1	2	3	4	5	6
Poinsett	Harrisburg.	48	Mo. Pac.	Camp Pike.	1. Lv. Hamburg..........5:10 a. m. Mo. Pac. No. 305. 2. Ar. Wynne..........6:00 a. m. Mo. Pac. No. 305. Breakfast at Wynne. 3. Lv. Wynne..........8:57 a. m. Mo. Pac. No. 283. 4. Lv. New Augusta..........10:13 a. m. Mo. Pac. No. 283. 5. Ar. Little Rock..........1:00 p. m. Mo. Pac. No. 283. Luncheon at Little Rock. 6. Mo. Pac. switch to Camp Pike.
Cross	Wynne.	31			
*Woodruff	Augusta. (Entrain at New Augusta.)	18			
Total		97			

(Page 4.)

SCHEDULE No. 9.—ENTRAIN AUGUST 22, 1918.

Newton............... (Entrain at Harrison.)			
Van Buren............ (Entrain at Shirley.)			
White................	M. & N. A.........	1	Kensett...........
	Mo. Pac...........	1	Camp Pike.........
	....	3	
Total...............		5	

1. Lv. Harrison........... 1:05 p. m. M. & N. A. No. 201.
2. Lv. Shirley........... 4:54 p. m. M. & N. A. No. 201.
   Dinner at Heber Springs.
3. Lv. Searcy............ 7:41 p. m. M. & N. A. No. 201.
4. Ar. Kensett........... 7:51 p. m. M. & N. A. No. 201.
5. Lv. Kensett........... 9:05 p. m. Mo. Pac. No. 33.
6. Ar. Little Rock....... 11:00 p. m. Mo. Pac. No. 33.
7. Mo. Pac. shuttle train to Camp Pike.

SCHEDULE No. 10.—ENTRAIN AUGUST 22, 1918.

Fulton............... (Entrain at Mammoth springs.)	Salem.............	1	Hoxie.............
	Frisco............		Camp Pike.........
	Mo. Pac...........		

1. Lv. Mammoth Springs.... 1:21 p. m. Frisco No. 101.
2. Ar. Hoxie............. 3:18 p. m. Frisco No. 101.
   Dinner at Hoxie.
3. Lv. Hoxie............. 5:55 p. m. Mo. Pac. No. 33.
4. Ar. Little Rock....... 11:00 p. m. Mo. Pac. No. 33.
5. Mo. Pac. shuttle train to Camp Pike.

SCHEDULE No. 11.—ENTRAIN AUGUST 22, 1918.

Union................	El Dorado.........	45	Camp Pike.........
Ouachita.............	Camden............	38	
	Mo. Pac...........		
Total...............		83	

1. Lv. El Dorado.......... 9:55 a. m. Mo. Pac. No. 836.
2. Lv. Camden............ 11:25 a. m. Mo. Pac. No. 836.
3. Ar. Gurdon............ 1:00 p. m. Mo. Pac. No. 836.
   Luncheon at Gurdon.
4. Lv. Gurdon............ 3:05 p. m. Mo. Pac. No. 8.
5. Ar. Little Rock....... 6:30 p. m. Mo. Pac. No. 8.
   Dinner at Little Rock.
6. Mo. Pac. switch to Camp Pike.

SCHEDULE No. 12.—ENTRAIN AUGUST 22, 1918.

Mississippi.......... (Entrain at Blytheville.)	Osceola...........	40	Bridge Junction...
	Frisco............		Little Rock.......
	C. R. I. & P......		Camp Pike.........
	Mo. Pac...........		
Crittenden...........	Marion............	90	Bridge Junction...
	C. R. I. & P......		Little Rock.......
	Mo. Pac...........		Camp Pike.........
Total...............		130	

1. Lv. Blytheville........ 7:13 a. m. Frisco No. 821.
2. Lv. Marion............ 9:46 a. m. Frisco No. 821.
3. Ar. Bridge Junction.... 10:00 a. m. Frisco No. 821.
4. Lv. Bridge Junction.... 9:40 a. m. C. R. I. & P. No. 45.
5. Ar. Little Rock....... 1:00 p. m. C. R. I. & P. No. 45.
6. Mo. Pac. switch to Camp Pike.
   a C. R. I. & P. to hold train No. 45 for connection.

From Arkansas to Camp Pike (Little Rock), Ark., routes and schedules—Continued.

Schedule No. 13.—Entrain August 22, 1918.

County.	County seat or headquarters.	Number of men.	Route.		Train Schedule.
			Road.	Junction.	
Prairie (Entrain at De Valls Bluff.)	Des Arc	6	C. R. I. & P.	Little Rock	Meals will be provided as follows: Breakfast between 6:30 a. m. and 8:30 a. m. Luncheon between 11:30 a. m. and 1:30 p. m. Dinner between 5:30 p. m. and 8:00 p. m.
Lonoke	Lonoke	16	Mo. Pac.	Camp Pike	1. Lv. De Valls Bluff.......10:30 a. m. C. R. I. & P. No. 601. 2. Lv. Lonoke............11:40 a. m. C. R. I. & P. No. 601. 3. Ar. Little Rock........12:30 noon C. R. I. & P. No. 601. Luncheon.
Total		22			4. Mo. Pac. switch to Camp Pike.

Schedule No. 14.—Entrain August 22, 1918.

Arkansas	Stuttgart	25	St. L. S. W.	N. Little Rock Camp Pike	1. Lv. Stuttgart...........7:25 a. m. St. L. S. W. No. 436. 2. Ar. N. Little Rock....10:15 a. m. St. L. S. W. No. 436. 3. Mo. Pac. shuttle train to Camp Pike.

Schedule No. 15.—Entrain August 22, 1918.

Perry (Entrain at Perry.)	Perryville	21	C. R. I. & P. Mo. Pac.	Little Rock Camp Pike	1. Lv. Perry............9:40 a. m. C. R. I. & P. No. 42. 2. Ar. Little Rock......11:55 a. m. C. R. I. & P. No. 42. Luncheon. 3. Mo. Pac. shuttle train to Camp Pike.

(Page 5.)

SCHEDULE NO. 16.—ENTRAIN AUGUST 22, 1918.

| Columbia....... | Magnolia....... | L. & N. W....... / St. L. S. W....... / Mo. Pac....... | 2 | McNeil....... / N. Little Rock....... / Camp Pike....... |

AUGUST 22.
1. Lv. Magnolia........ 6:30 p. m. L. & N. W. No. 10.
2. Ar. McNeil........ 7:00 p. m. L. & N. W. No. 10.
3. Lv. McNeil........ 8:26 p. m. St. L. S. W. No. 4.

AUGUST 23.
4. Ar. Pine Bluff........ 12:42 a. m. St. L. S. W. No. 4.
5. Lv. Pine Bluff........ 7:35 a. m. St. L. S. W. No. 436.
6. Ar. N. Little Rock....... 10:15 a. m. St. L. S. W. No. 436.
7. Mo. Pac. shuttle train to Camp Pike.

SCHEDULE NO. 17.—ENTRAIN AUGUST 22, 1918.

La Fayette........	Lewisville........	St. L. S. W........ / Mo. Pac........	8	N. Little Rock........ / Camp Pike........
Cleveland........	Rison........	St. L. S. W........ / Mo. Pac........	33	N. Little Rock........ / Camp Pike........
Calhoun........ (Entrain at Thornton.)	Hampton........	St. L. S. W........ / Mo. Pac........	9	N. Little Rock........ / Camp Pike........
	Total........		50	

1. Lv. Lewisville........ 8:50 a. m. St. L. S. W. No. 2.
2. Lv. Thornton........ 11:42 a. m. St. L. S. W. No. 2.
3. Lv. Rison........ 12:39 p. m. St. L. S. W. No. 2.
Luncheon in diner.
4. Ar. Pine Bluff........ 1:42 p. m. St. L. S. W. No. 432.
5. Lv. Pine Bluff........ 3:10 p. m. St. L. S. W. No. 432.
6. Ar. N. Little Rock........ 6:00 p. m. St. L. S. W. No. 432.
7. Mo. Pac. shuttle train to Camp Pike.

NOTE.—Lewisville contingent will secure luncheon at Pine Bluff. Rison contingent will secure luncheon before departure.

SCHEDULE NO. 18.—ENTRAIN AUGUST 22, 1918.

Craighead........	Jonesboro........	St. L. S. W........ / Mo. Pac........	22	N. Little Rock........ / Camp Pike........
Monroe........	Clarendon........	St. L. S. W........ / Mo. Pac........	13	N. Little Rock........ / Camp Pike........
	Total........		35	

1. Lv. Jonesboro........ 9:05 a. m. St. L. S. W. No. 1.
2. Lv. Clarendon........ 1:04 p. m. St. L. S. W. No. 1.
3. Ar. Altheimer........ 2:49 p. m. St. L. S. W. No. 1.
4. Lv. Altheimer........ 4:05 p. m. St. L. S. W. No. 432.
5. Ar. N. Little Rock........ 6:00 p. m. St. L. S. W. No. 432.
6. Mo. Pac. shuttle train to Camp Pike.

From Arkansas to Camp Pike (Little Rock), Ark., routes and schedules—Continued.

SCHEDULE NO. 19.—ENTRAIN AUGUST 22, 1918

1	2	3	4	5	6
			Route.		TRAIN SCHEDULE.
County.	County seat or headquarters.	Number of men.	Road.	Junction.	Meals will be provided as follows: Breakfast between 6:30 a. m. and 8:30 a. m. Luncheon between 11:30 a. m. and 1:30 p. m. Dinner between 5:30 p. m. and 8:00 p. m.
Pulaski. City (Board No. 1.)	Little Rock	9			1. Use Mo. Pac. shuttle train service to Camp Pike.
Pulaski. City (Board No. 2.)	Little Rock	3	Mo. Pac.	Camp Pike	
Pulaski. County (Board No. 2.)	Little Rock	16			
	Total	28			

APPENDIX G.

OFFICERS ON DUTY IN OFFICE OF PROVOST MARSHAL GENERAL, 1917-18.

Officer.	Reported.	Relieved.
Maj. Gen. ENOCH H. CROWDER, Provost Marshal General..................	Apr. 26, 1917	
Maj. Gen. CARROLL A. DEVOL, retired.....................................	June 14, 1917	Sept. 8, 1917
Col. HUGH S. JOHNSON, Deputy Provost Marshal General................	Apr. 26, 1917	Mar. 31, 1918
Col. CHARLES B. WARREN, judge advocate..............................	Apr. 27, 1917	
Col. JOHN H. WIGMORE, judge advocate	July 15, 1917	
Col. JAMES S. EASBY-SMITH, judge advocate..........................	Sept. 20, 1917	
Col. FRANK R. KEEFER, Medical Corps.................................	Aug. 2, 1918	
Lieut. Col. CASSIUS M. DOWELL, judge advocate..........................	Apr. 26, 1917	Sept. 3, 1917
Lieut. Col. EDWARD A. KREGER, United States Military Academy........	May 2, 1917	Mar. 8, 1918
Lieut. Col. ALLEN W. GULLION, judge advocate.........................	May 4, 1917	Mar. 26, 1918
Lieut. Col. ROSCOE S. CONKLING, judge advocate	Sept. 21, 1917	Dec. 4, 1918
Lieut. Col. HARRY C. KRAMER, judge advocate............................	Oct. 4, 1917	
Lieut. Col. JOSEPH FAIRBANKS, judge advocate..........................	Oct. 7, 1917	
Lieut. Col. GRANT T. TRENT, judge advocate.............................	Nov. 19, 1917	
Lieut. Col. HUBERT WORK, Medical Corps................................	Mar. 22, 1918	Dec. 12, 1918
Maj. EDWIN W. FULLAM, Adjutant General.............................	Apr. 26, 1917	Apr. 15, 1918
Maj. WILLIAM C. McCHORD, Cavalry...................................	May 5, 1917	Dec. 4, 1917
Maj. HENRY L. WATSON, Cavalry.....................................	May 7, 1917	Mar. 7, 1918
Maj. JAMES B. SCOTT, judge advocate................................	May 15, 1917	Feb. 7, 1918
Maj. GEORGE P. WHITSETT, judge advocate............................	May 28, 1917	Aug. 23, 1917
Maj. REDMOND C. STEWART, judge advocate...........................	July 20, 1917	Nov. 8, 1917
Maj. MALCOLM A. COLES, judge advocate.............................	July 28, 1917	Feb. 10, 1918
Maj. JAMES C. FOX, judge advocate.................................	Sept. 14, 1917	Nov. 8, 1917
Maj. WILLIAM O. GILBERT, judge advocate............................	.....do........	Sept. 20, 1917
Maj. GUY D. GOFF, judge advocate...................................	.....do	Do.
Maj. EDWARD J. BROUGHTON, judge advocate	Sept. 17, 1917	Nov. 9, 1917
Maj. JASPER YEATES BRINTON, judge advocate........................	Sept. 18, 1917	Mar. 20, 1918
Maj. HOWARD W. ADAMS, judge advocate............................	Sept. 19, 1917	Aug. 29, 1918
Maj. RICHARD R. KENNEY, judge advocate............................	Oct. 6, 1917	Dec. 29, 1917
Maj. DURAND WHIPPLE, judge advocate	Oct. 9, 1917	Dec. 7, 1917
Maj. JOHN A. ELMORE, judge advocate....:	.....do	Nov. 9, 1917
Maj. ALEXANDER JOHNSTON, Infantry	Oct. 11, 1917	Mar. 2, 1918
. ALFRED M. CRAVEN, judge advocate	Oct. 15, 1917	Dec. 29, 1917
Maj. THOMAS FINLEY, judge advocate	.....do	Dec. 22, 1917
Maj. VICTOR E. RUEHL, judge advocate..............................	Oct. 16, 1917	Dec. 30, 1917
Maj. NEAL POWER, judge advocate	Oct. 24, 1917	Feb. 25, 1918
. SCOTT HENDRICKS, judge advocate	Nov. 15, 1917	Dec. 17, 1917
. GIST BLAIR, judge advocate.......................................	.....do	May 1, 1918
. TIMOTHY J. MAHONEY, judge advocate	Nov. 16, 1917	Sept. 16, 1918
. GEORGE T. WEITZEL, judge advocate...............................	Nov. 17, 1917	Jan. 3, 1918
. REGINALD S. HUIDEKOPER, judge advocate..........................	Nov. 19, 1917	Mar. 25, 1918
. CHARLES B. PARKHILL, judge advocate.............................	.....do	Feb. 12, 1918
. HENRY B. SHAW, judge advocate	Nov. 20, 1917	
. AUGUSTUS R. BRINDLEY, judge advocate	Nov. 23, 1917	Do.
Maj. EDWARD S. THURSTON, judge advocate..........................	Nov. 25, 1917	Jan. 24, 1918
Maj. IRA K. WELLS, judge advocate.................................	Dec. 5, 1917	Feb. 20, 1918

Officer.	Reported.	Relieved.
Maj. FREDERIC C. WOODWARD, judge advocate	Dec. 8, 1917	
Maj. HAROLD E. STEPHENSON, Infantry	Jan. 14, 1918	
Maj. LOUIS L. KORN, judge advocate	Jan. 18, 1918	May 16, 1918
Maj. FRANK BILLINGS, Medical Corps	Feb. 1, 1918	Mar. 14, 1918
Maj. JAMES BERRY KING, judge advocate	Feb. 5, 1918	Sept. 30, 1918
Maj. WINFIELD S. PRICE, Infantry	Apr. 26, 1918	
Maj. EDWARD M. BAINTER, Ordnance	....do.......	
Maj. DAVID CHESTER BROWN, Medical Corps	July 27, 1918	Dec. 12, 1918
Maj. JOSHUA REUBEN CLARK, jr., judge advocate	Aug. 1, 1918	Dec. 18, 1918
Maj. CHARLES T. HENDLER, judge advocate	Aug. 7, 1918	
Maj. PEYTON GORDON, judge advocate	Sept. 6, 1918	
Maj. JOHN D. LANGSTON, Infantry	....do.......	
Maj. FRED K. NIELSEN, judge advocate	Sept. 12, 1918	
Capt. PERRIN L. SMITH, Infantry	May 25, 1917	June 12, 1917
Capt. DAVID L. ROSCOE, Cavalry	Apr. 28, 1917	Aug. 14, 1917
Capt. EDWARD W. CHATTERTON, Quartermaster Corps	Apr. 30, 1917	Mar. 26, 1918
Capt. ROYAL G. JENKS, Quartermaster Corps	May 26, 1917	Mar. 23, 1918
Capt. CHARLES R. MORRIS, Quartermaster Corps	Aug. 22, 1917	Apr. 15, 1918
Capt. DOUGLAS D. FELIX, Infantry	Oct. 3, 1917	
Capt. CLAUDE A. HOPE	....do.......	
Capt. ROBERT E. MCCORMICK	Oct. 5, 1917	
Capt. LUCIUS B. BARBOUR, Infantry	Nov. 6, 1917	
Capt. RICHARD H. HILL, Coast Artillery Corps	Dec. 14, 1917	
Capt. JESSE I. MILLER	Jan. 18, 1918	
Capt. JAMES H. HUGHES, Infantry	Jan. 23, 1918	
Capt. DORRANCE D. SNAPP	Feb. 6, 1918	
Capt. ROY L. DEAL	Feb. 11, 1918	
Capt. DAVID A. PINE	Mar. 6, 1918	
Capt. CARTER D. STAMPER	Mar. 10, 1918	
Capt. WEBSTER W. HOLLOWAY, judge advocate	Apr. 2, 1918	
Capt. RAYMOND O. WILMARTH, Infantry, adjutant	Apr. 5, 1918	
Capt. WILLIAM G. DE ROSSET	June 10, 1918	
Capt. BRECKINRIDGE JONES, Infantry	June 17, 1918	
Capt. JOHN EVANS, Infantry	Oct. 11, 1918	Dec. 5, 1918
First Lieut. JOSEPH J. MACKAY, jr., Infantry	Oct. 17, 1917	July 29, 1918
First Lieut. WALTER B. WHITE, Infantry	Jan. 1, 1918	
First Lieut. MALCOLM H. LAUCHHEIMER, Coast Artillery Corps	Feb. 6, 1918	Sept. 7, 1918
First Lieut. CAREW F. MARTINDALE	May 24, 1918	
First Lieut. HENRY G. STEPHENS	Mar. 15, 1918	May 28, 1918
First Lieut. STANLEY H. UDY	Mar. 29, 1918	
First Lieut. WILLIAM K. GILMORE	May 6, 1918	
First Lieut. CHARLES SCOTT MILLER, Medical Corps	Aug. 31, 1918	
First Lieut. CHARLES S. DOUGLAS, judge advocate	Oct. 1, 1918	
First Lieut. DUDLEY B. SNOWDEN	Nov. 9, 1918	
Second Lieut. BUZ M. WALKER, jr	Mar. 11, 1918	

CIVILIANS IN CHARGE OF SECTIONS.

Mr. G. Lyle Hughes, chief clerk.
Mr. William E. Mattingly, assistant chief clerk.
Miss Elmear C. Chinn, senior clerk, Personnel of Boards Section.
Miss Katherine E. Cowan, senior clerk, Appeals Division.
Mr. Clifton F. Balch, statistician, Statistics and Auxiliary Agencies Division.
Mr. Howard E. Marker, senior clerk, Statistics and Auxiliary Agencies Division.
Mr. Samuel R. Hinwood, senior clerk, Delinquency and Deserters Section, Classification Division.

S. Crow, senior clerk, Finance Division.
llborn, senior clerk, Information Division.
cott, senior clerk, Quota Records Section, Mobilization Division.
N. Crymes, senior clerk, Individual Induction Section, Mobilization

. Skinner, senior clerk, Statistical Section, Mobilization Division.
. Noland, senior clerk, Publications Division.
T. Cunningham, senior clerk, Mail Section.
. Reynolds, senior clerk, Stenographic Section.
. Dimond, senior clerk, Record Section.
C. Vaughan, supply clerk.
Campbell, civilian personnel clerk.

APPENDIX H.

LIST OF THE PRINCIPAL FORMS PRINTED FOR THE PROVOST MARSHAL GENERAL'S OFFICE.

Form No.	Title.
1	Registration card.
2	Summarization blank (first registration).
3	Telegraphic report of board of registration to governor (first registration).
4	Telegraphic report of governor to Provost Marshal General (first registration).
5	Mailing label.
8	Registrar's oath (first registration).
10	Telegraphic report of readiness (first registration).
11	Regulations governing physical examination.
11	Regulations governing physical examination (modified to Aug. 27, 1917).
12	Report of registration board.
13	Rules and regulations prescribed by the President for local and district boards.
14	Physical examination under the selective service act of May 18, 1917.
15	Regulations governing disbursements incident to the registration and selective draft.
17	Instructions to local boards.
18	Estimates of population.
19	Suggestions to local boards.
20	Amendments to Regulations, Form 13.
21	Information for persons registered.
22	Compiled Rulings No. 1.
23	Letter to members of local boards, July 26, 1917.
24	Compiled Rulings No. 2.
25	Supplemental Rules and Regulations, No. 1. (The disposition of persons called for examination who fail to report for or submit to examination.)
26	Compiled Rulings No. 3.
27	Letter answering inquiries, used in office of Provost Marshal General.
27-A	Letter answering inquiries, used in office of Provost Marshal General.
28	Compiled Rulings No. 4.
29	Manual governing the use of records by local and district boards.
30	Compiled Rulings No. 5.
31	Mobilization regulations.
32	Compiled Rulings No. 6.
33	Distribution sheet (used when moving men to national camps).
34	Compiled Rulings No. 7.
35	Letter of Provost Marshal General to accompany marked copy of bulletins.
36	Compiled Rulings No. 8.
37	Supplement to bulletin of information concerning appeals for discharge of persons engaged in industries, including agriculture.
38	Compiled Rulings No. 9.
39	Letter by the President relative to operation of the selective service law, with particular reference to its effect on agriculture.
40	Compiled Rulings No. 10.
41	Statement of gratuitous service.
42	Compiled Rulings No. 11.
43	Extracts from Selective Service Regulations, relative to organization of legal advisory boards.
44	Compiled Rulings No. 12.
45	Letter of Provost Marshal General to members of the American Bar Association, relative to new classification system.
47	Extracts from Selective Service Regulations, relative to organization of medical advisory boards.
49	Letter of Provost Marshal General to physicians of the United States, relative to the new system of medical examinations.
51	Letter of Provost Marshal General to superintendents and principals of public schools, relative to the new classification system.
53	Important instructions to boards, relative to the Selective Service Regulations.
57	Extracts from selective service regulations, relative to clerical assistance to medical and legal advisory boards.
59	Suggested rules of procedure for medical advisory boards.
59-B	Docket of examinations of medical advisory boards.
61	Instructions for the preparation and use of Forms 1029 (new), 1029-A-B, and 1029-C-D.
62	Letter of Provost Marshal General to members of all local boards, relative to the soldiers' and sailors' civil relief act.
62-A	Letter of secretary of the American Bar Association to members of the American Bar Association and to all judges of superior courts, relative to the soldiers' and sailors' civil relief act.
62-B	Relief of soldiers and sailors.
62-C	Insurance placards.
63	Occupational list, indicating kind of men desired in the branches of service mentioned.
64	Manual of instructions for Medical advisory boards.
64-A	Amendment to Manual of Instructions for medical advisory boards.
65	Correspondence post card.
65-A	Inquiry as to address of registrants.
66	General Orders, No. 31, relative to applications for farm furloughs.

Form No.	Title.
66	Notice of intended requisitions for men.
66–A	Requisition for men classified by occupation.
66–B	Requisition for men unclassified.
67	Registration Regulations No. 2.
68	Registration certificate.
69	Placard of instructions on how to answer questions (second registration).
69–A	Placard of instructions on how to answer questions (for second registration in Alaska).
69–B	Placard of instructions on how to answer questions (for second registration in Hawaii).
70	Telegraphic report of readiness to Adjutant General (second registration).
71	Telegraphic report of local board to Adjutant General (second registration).
72	Mail report on age 21 registration (summarization blank, second registration).
73	Telegraphic report from Adjutant General to Provost Marshal General (second registration).
74	Rules and regulations prescribed by the President for determining the order of liability (master list No. 2, second registration).
75	Standards of physical examination (first and second editions).
76	Boards of instruction to be appointed by selective service boards.
77	Address to Class I selective service men.
78	Physical examination chart.
79	Standard accepted measurements.
80	Telegraphic report of readiness to Adjutant General (third registration).
81	Registrar's oath (third registration).
82	Telegraphic report of local board to Adjutant General (third registration).
83	Telegraphic report from Adjutant General to Provost Marshal General (third registration).
84	Summarization blank (third registration).
85	Registration Regulations No. 3.
86	Circular to medical examiners relative to physcial examination of registrants.
87	Letter of Provost Marshal General to members of all selective service boards relative to the classification of September, 1918, registrants.
88	Local board progress chart.
89	State progress chart.
90	Rules and regulations prescribed by the President for determining the order of liability (master list No. 3, third registration).
90–A	Index to master list No. 3.
91	Letter of Provost Marshal General to employers and other representatives of industry relative to classification.
92	A manual for legal advisory boards.
93	Letter of Provost Marshal General to local boards relative to allotments and allowances of selectives.
94	Chronicles of the selective draft.
95	Receipt for records delivered to The Adjutant General of the Army.
100	Appendix to rules and regulations (Form 13).
101	List of names of persons whose registration cards are in possession of a local board (first registration).
101	List of names of persons whose registration cards are in possession of a local board (second and third registrations).
102	List of registrants in order of liability (first and third registrations).
102–A	List of registrants in order of liability (second registration).
103	Notice of call and to appear for physical examination.
103–A	List of persons ordered to appear for physical examination.
104	Bulletin to local boards, "What To Do Next."
107	Certificate of discharge because physically deficient.
108	Certificate of postponement of physical examination because of temporary physical deficiency.
110	Claim of exemption from military service when filed by person claiming exemption.
111	Claim of exemption from military service when filed by person other than person sought to be exempted.
112 to 144	Affidavits, certificates, and claims for exemption.
145	Certificate of discharge from military service.
146	List of persons called into the service of the United States not exempted or discharged.
146–A	List of persons called by local board who failed to report and submit to examination.
146–B	List of persons who are in military service and who have failed to report for duty.
146–C	Report of persons ordered to report to local boards for military duty who have failed to report.
147	List of persons exempted or discharged from the service of the United States.
148	Notice of certification to district boards when claim of exemption or discharge has been denied.
149	Notice of certification to district board when claim of exemption or discharge made in respect of another has been denied.
150	Notice of certification to district board when no claim of exemption or discharge has been made.
151	Notice of claim of appeal by person certified to district board.
152	Notice of claim of appeal by person other than person certified.
153	Claim of appeal by person certified to district board.
154	Claim of appeal by another in respect of person certified.
155	Notice of extension of time for filing claim and notice of appeal.
156	Record of the first and organization meeting of the district board.
157	Notice of decision of district board on claim of appeal filed by person called.
158	Notice of decision of district board on claim of appeal filed in respect of another.
159	Certificate of exemption issued by district board on appeal.
159–A	Certificate of discharge issued by district board on appeal.
160	Notice to local board of decision of district board on claim of appeal filed by Provost Marshal General.
161	Claim for discharge filed with district board by person certified.
161–A	Claim for discharge of person certified to district board made by another.
162	Certificate of discharge because engaged in a necessary industrial or agricultural enterprise.
163	Claim of appeal to the President by person certified or by another on his behalf.
164	Partial list of men selected for military service.

Form No.	Title.
164–A	List of persons ordered to report to the local board for military service.
164–B	Postal card (notification of selection for military service).
164–C	Postal card (notification date to report for departure for mobilization camp).
165	Revocation of certificate of exemption by local board.
166	Notice of revocation of certificate of exemption by local board.
167	Revocation of certificate of discharge by local board.
168	Notice of revocation of certificate of discharge by local board.
169	Revocation of certificate of exemption or discharge by district board.
170	Notice of revocation of certificate of exemption or discharge by district board.
171	Revocation of certificate of discharge granted by district board to person engaged in necessary industrial or agricultural enterprise
172	Notice of revocation of certificate of discharge to person engaged in a necessary industrial or agricultural enterprise.
173	Notice of denial of claim for discharge.
174	Certificate to person claiming exemption under subdivision (i) of section 20 of the rules and regulations.
175	Form prepared by Provost Marshal General that may be used for application to be filed for an order that another local board be designated to make physical examination and hear and determine any claim for exemption or discharge filed by or in respect for a person, under section 29 of rules and regulations of June 30, 1917.
176	Form of notice prepared by Provost Marshal General that may be used under terms of section 29 of rules and regulations of June 30, 1917.
177	Form of notice prepared by Provost Marshal General that may be used under section 29 of rules and regulations of June 30, 1917, for designation of another local board to make physical examination and to hear and determine any claim for exemption or discharge.
178	Docket for local board.
179	Claim of appeal by person authorized under section 27, rules and regulations June 30, 1917, by the Provost Marshal General to take an appeal from the decision of a local board.
180	Notice of claim of appeal by person authorized under section 27, rules and regulations June 30, 1917, by the Provost Marshal General to take an appeal from the decision of a local board.
181	Notice to local board of decision of district board on claim of discharge filed by or in respect of person certified to the district board by local board.
182	Notice to local board of exemption or discharge granted on appeal from local board.
183	Notice to local board of decision of district board, in accordance with the mandate of the President, on claim of discharge filed by or in respect of person certified to the district board by local board.
184	Day book for local board.
185	Docket book for district board.
186	Day book for district board.
187	Account of quotas.
187–A	Report of accounts of quotas by local board.
187–B	Report of accounts of quotas in camp.
200	Oath of office.
201	Acceptance of appointment by the President as a member of the local board.
202	Notification of appointment as member of local board.
203	Telegram for reporting organization of local boards to governor.
204	Letter to member of local board directing organization.
205	Record of first and organization meeting of local board (sheriff member).
205–A	Record of first and organization meeting of local board (sheriff not member).
300	Regulations governing the apportionment of quotas and credits.
301	Quota form.
301–A	Record of State apportionment of quota.
301–B	Record of county or city apportionment of quota.
302	Notice of governor to local boards of apportionment of quota.
500	Rules and regulations prescribed by the President for determining the order of liability (master list No. 1, first registration).
999	Selective Service Regulations (edition of Nov. 8, 1917):
	Changes No. 1.
	Changes No. 2.
	Changes No. 3.
	Changes No. 4.
	Changes No. 5.
	Changes No. 6.
	Changes No. 7.
999–A	Selective Service Regulations (second edition).
1000	Classification list.
1001	Questionnaire.
1001–A	Duplicate of first page of questionnaire.
1001–B	Cover sheet of questionnaire.
1001–C	Duplicate of cover sheet of questionnaire.
1001–D	Key list of occupations.
1001–E	Explanatory memorandum for questionnaire.
1002	Important notice to registrants and public.
1003	Subpœna to witnesses to appear before district and local boards.
1004	Minute book of district and local boards.
1005	Notice of classification.
1006	Docket book of district board.
1007	Notice of final classification.
1008	Notice of exemption from combatant service.
1009	Notice to appear for physical examination.
1010	Report of physical examination.
1011	Notice of decision on physical examination.
1012	List of delinquents reported to local police authority.
1013	List of persons who failed to report for physical examination or submit questionnaires.
1013–A	Delinquent classification list.

Form No.	Title.
1014	Notice to delinquents to report to A. G. O. S.
1015	Order to delinquent to report to local board.
1016	Report to A. G. O. S. on appearance of delinquent ordered to report to local board.
1017	Notice from Adjutant General suspending order inducting delinquent into military service.
1018	Report of deserters to A. G. A.
1019	Order to delinquent to report to local board for entrainment.
1020	Report by State Adjutant General to Adjutant General of the Army of appearance of deserter.
1021	Certificate for police official apprehending a willful deserter.
1021-A-B	Report of disposition of deserters.
1022	Order to report to Medical Advisory Board for examination.
1022-A	Request to Medical Advisory Board to conduct examination.
1023	Notice of transfer for classification.
1024	Request for transfer of registrant to E. F. C. list.
1025	Report on registrant transferred to E. F. C. list.
1026	Application for passport permit.
1027	Permit for passport.
1028	Order of induction into the military service of the United States.
1028 and	
1028-A	Order of induction into the military service of the United States.
1028-A	Notice to men ordered to report for military duty.
1029	List of men ordered to report for military duty: Jacket sheet: Insert sheet.
1029 New	List of men ordered to report for military duty.
1029-A-B	Notice of acceptance or rejection for military service
1029-C-D	Notice of discharge from military service.
1029-E	Request for additional occupational information.
1029-F	Notice of change of classification.
1030	Order authorizing employment of clerical assistants.
1031	Travel order to be issued by governors.
1032	Travel order to be issued by district boards.
1033	Oath of office.
1034	Estimate of expenses.
1035	Application for furlough (agriculture).
1036	Notice to appear for reclassification on account of nonuseful occupation.
1037	Important notice to registrant and public regarding classification on account of nonuseful occupation.
1038	Certification in case of registrant claimed not to be engaged in a productive occupation or employment.
1039	Notice of reclassification on account of nonuseful occupation.
1040	Report of registrants whose deferred classification or order numbers have been withdrawn.
1041	Withdrawal of notices to become a citizen of the United States.
1042	Notice to neutral declarants.
1043	Property list.
1044	Supporting affidavit for Federal, State, and Municipal employees.
1045	Certificate for reenlistment in Navy or Marine Corps (printed copies not furnished).
1045	Monthly report of local boards.
1046	Monthly report of district boards.
1050	Family status report on inducted men.
2000	Regulations governing the apportionment of quotas.
2001	Report of classification.
2002-A	Local board report of Class I.
2002-B	State report of Class I.
2003	Quota sheet.
2004	Notice of quota.
2005	Quota ledger sheet.
2006	Request for individual induction.
2006 New	Request for individual induction.
2007	Competent order for induction.
2007 New	Competent order for induction.
2007-A	Competent order for induction.
2008	Report of action on competent order.
2008-A	Report of action on competent order.
2009	Regulations governing drafted men en route to mobilization camps.
2010	Warrant of leader or assistant leader and special police officer.
2011	Requests for release of registrant to volunteer in naval service for training as an officer.
2012	Order to release registrant for enlistment in Navy for training as an officer.
2013	Report of entrainment.
2014	Application for voluntary induction.
2015	Permit for transfer of entrainment.
2017	Statement of final account.
3006	Occupational list of registrants.
	Annual Report (1918), Statistical Data Forms:
3050	General instructions for preparing summary cards, 1918.
3051	Tally sheet No. 1, first registration.
3051-A	Tally sheet No. 1, second and third registrations.
3052	Tally sheet No. 2, first registration.
3052-A	Tally sheet No. 2, second and third registrations.
3053	Tally sheet No. 3, first registration.
3053-A	Tally sheet No. 3, second and third registrations.
3054	Summary card No. 1, first registration.
3054-A	Summary card No. 1, second and third registrations.
3055	Summary card No. 2, first registration.
3055-A	Summary card No. 2, second and third registrations.
3056	Summary card No. 3, first registration.
3056-A	Summary card No. 3, second and third registrations.
3057	Summary card No. 4, first, second, and third registrations.

Form No.	Title.
3058	Notice of mailing summary cards.
3059	Reminder post card No. 1.
3060	Reminder post card No. 2.
3061	District board summary card A (first registration).
3061–A	District board summary card A (second and third registrations).
3062	District board summary card B (first registration).
3062–A	District board summary card B (second and third registrations).
3063	Emergency fleet data card.
3064	Letter from Provost Marshal General to local boards relative to Emergency Fleet data cards.
4000	Regulations governing the disposition of records of district, local, and medical advisory boards.
4001	Tags for district, local, and medical advisory board records
4002	Inventory of records of district, local, and medical advisory boards.
4003	List of registrants recorded as delinquents or deserters.
4004	Dummy cover sheet.
	Bulletin A of May 24, 1917, relative to persons required to register.
	Boards of instruction:
	Letter of the Provost Marshal General to local boards relative to organization. (July 4, 1918.)
	Letter of the Provost Marshal General to local boards relative to class of June 5, 1918. (July 10, 1918.)
	Bulletin No. I (see Form 76).
	Bulletin No. II (see Form 77).
	Bulletin No. III.
	Bulletin No. IV, War Aims.
	Bulletin No. V, How Selectives Are Treated in Camp.
	Bulletin No. VI, Teaching English.
	Bulletin No. VII.
	Bulletin No. VIII, Hygiene.
	Letter of Provost Marshal General to members of local boards relative to disposition of registration cards. (June 26, 1917.)
	Occupational card.
	Conventions providing for reciprocal military service with Great Britain and Canada.
	Convention providing for reciprocal military service with France.
	Report of the Provost Marshal General to the Secretary of War on the first draft.
	Information for male persons of military age desiring to leave the United States.
	Instructions No. 1, for preparing voucher for personal service.
	Instructions No. 2, for preparing voucher for services and duties other than personal.
	Instructions No. 3, for preparation of vouchers.
	List of district boards.
	List of district and local boards.
	Poster, "The New American Plan of Selective Draft and Service."
	Registration regulations, first registration.
	Placard of instructions on "How to Answer Questions" (first and third registrations).
	Roster, Provost Marshal General's Office.
	The selective service system, its aims and accomplishments—its future.
	President's foreword to the selective service regulations.
	Circular of information relative to deferred classification of Government employees.
	Extracts from the revised selective-service regulations relative to classification with respect to engagement in industries, occupations or employment, including agriculture.
	Eye-test charts "B" and "E."
	Powers of the Congress and of the President over the land forces.
	President's letter relative to gratuitous services.
	Governor's letter relative to gratuitous services.
	The Nation's Want Column.
	Bulletin of information concerning appeals for discharge of persons engaged in industries including agriculture. (Sept. 24, 1917.)
	Letter of Provost Marshal General to local boards on classification of December, 1917. (Nov. 6, 1917.)
	Letter of Provost Marshal General to governors relative to selection of men for special training. (May 22, 1918.)
	Letter of Provost Marshal General to local boards relative to handling individual inductions. (June 14, 1918.)
	Letter of Provost Marshal General to draft executives relative to compensation of local board members. (Aug. 31, 1918.)
	Letter of Provost Marshal General to draft executives relative to individual induction of registrants into the Students' Army Training Corps. (Sept. 5, 1918.)
	Letter of Provost Marshal General to governors relative to classification of registrants of class of September, 1918. (Sept. 10, 1918.)
	Letter of Provost Marshal General to governors re advancement of classification and physical examination of certain registrants of class of September, 1918. (Sept. 25, 1918.)
	Letter of Provost Marshal General to members of district boards relative to classification of registrants of class of September, 1918. (Oct. 7, 1918.)
	Letter of Provost Marshal General to State draft executives relative to monthly reports of local boards. (Nov. 2, 1918.)
	Letter of Provost Marshal General to boards of instruction relative to their activities. (Nov. 20, 1918.)
	Letter of Provost Marshal General to local boards relative to statement of final account. (Nov. 25, 1918.)

APPENDIX I.

LIST OF DISTRICT BOARDS, SHOWING LOCATION AND JURISDICTION.

ALABAMA.

NORTHERN DISTRICT, DIVISION No. 1.

Headquarters.—Jefferson County Bank Building, Birmingham, Ala.

Jurisdiction—Counties.

Bibb.	Clay.	Jefferson.	Sumter.
Blount.	Cleburne.	Pickens.	Talladega.
Calhoun.	Greene.	Shelby.	Tuscaloosa.

NORTHERN DISTRICT, DIVISION No. 2.
Headquarters.—Federal Court Building, Huntsville, Ala.

Jurisdiction—Counties.

Cherokee.	Fayette.	Làuderdale.	Morgan.
Colbert.	Franklin.	Limestone.	St. Clair.
Cullman.	Jackson.	Madison.	Walker.
Dekalb.	Lamar.	Marion.	Winston.
Etowah.	Lawrence.	Marshall.	

MIDDLE DISTRICT.

Headquarters.—709 First National Bank Building, Montgomery, Ala.

Jurisdiction—Counties.

Autauga.	Coffee.	Geneva.	Montgomery.
Barbour.	Coosa.	Henry.	Pike.
Bullock.	Covington.	Houston.	Randolph.
Butler.	Crenshaw.	Lee.	Russell.
Chambers.	Dale.	Lowndes.	Tallapoosa.
Chilton.	Elmore.	Macon.	

SOUTHERN DISTRICT.
Headquarters.—Federal Building, Mobile, Ala.

Jurisdiction—Counties.

Baldwin,	Dallas,	Mobile.	Wilcox.
Choctaw.	Escambia.	Monroè.	
Clarke.	Hale.	Perry.	
Conecuh.	Marengo.	Washington.	

ARIZONA.

DIVISION No. 1.
Headquarters.—Room 2, County Courthouse, Phoenix, Ariz.

Jurisdiction—Counties.

Apache.	Maricopa.	Navajo.	Yavapai.
Coconino.	Mohave.	Pinal.	Yuma.

DIVISION No. 2.
Headquarters.—Tucson, Ariz.

Jurisdiction—Counties.

Cochise.	Graham.	Pima.
Gila.	Greenlee.	Santa Cruz

ARKANSAS.

EASTERN DISTRICT.
Headquarters.—Pulaski County Courthouse, Little Rock, Ark.

Jurisdiction—Counties.

Arkansas.	Dallas.	Jefferson.	Prairie.
Ashley.	Desha.	Lawrence.	Pulaski.
Bradley.	Drew.	Lee.	Randolph.
Chicot.	Faulkner.	Lincoln.	Saline.
Clark.	Fulton.	Lonoke.	Sharp.
Clay.	Garland.	Mississippi.	Stone.
Cleburne.	Grant.	Monroe.	St. Francis.
Cleveland.	Greene.	Mongomery.	Van Buren.
Conway.	Hot Spring.	Perry.	White.
Craighead.	Independence.	Phillips.	Woodruff.
Crittenden.	Izard.	Poinsett.	Yell.
Cross.	Jackson.	Pope.	

WESTERN DISTRICT.
Headquarters.—Fort Smith, Ark.

Jurisdiction—Counties.

Baxter.	Franklin.	Madison.	Polk.
Benton.	Hempstead.	Marion.	Searcy.
Boone.	Howard.	Miller.	Scott.
Calhoun.	Johnson.	Nevada.	Sebastian.
Carroll.	Lafayette.	Newton.	Sevier.
Columbia.	Little River.	Ouachita.	Union.
Crawford.	Logan.	Pike.	Washington.

CALIFORNIA.

NORTHERN DISTRICT, DIVISION No. 1.
Headquarters.—400 City Hall, San Francisco, Cal.

Jurisdiction—Counties.

San Francisco and Alameda.

NORTHERN DISTRICT, DIVISION No. 2.
Headquarters.—704 Fourth Street, San Rafael, Cal.

Jurisdiction—Counties.

Contra Costa.	Marin.	San Benito.	Solano.
Del Norte.	Mendocino.	Santa Clara.	Sonoma.
Humboldt.	Monterey.	Santa Cruz.	
Lake.	Napa.	San Mateo.	

NORTHERN DISTRICT, DIVISION No. 3.
Headquarters.—State Capitol Building, Sacramento, Cal.

Jurisdiction—Counties.

Alpine.	Lassen.	Sacramento.	Trinity.
Amador.	Modoc.	Shasta.	Tuolumne.
Butte.	Mono.	Sierra.	Yolo.
Calaveras.	Nevada.	Siskiyou.	Yuba.
Colusa.	Placer.	Stanislaus.	
Eldorado.	Plumas.	Sutter.	
Glenn.	San Joaquin.	Tehama.	

SOUTHERN DISTRICT, DIVISION No. 1.
Headquarters.—Room F, Chamber of Commerce Building, 100 South Broadway, Los Angeles, Cal.
Jurisdiction—Counties.

Los Angeles.	Orange.	San Diego.

SOUTHERN DISTRICT, DIVISION No. 2.
Headquarters.—Courthouse, Bakersfield, Cal.

Jurisdiction—Counties.

Fresno.	Kings.	Riverside.	Tulare.
Imperial.	Madera.	San Bernardino.	Ventura.
Inyo.	Mariposa.	San Luis Obispo.	
Kern.	Merced.	Santa Barbara.	

COLORADO.

DIVISION No. 1.
Headquarters.—Room 19, Courthouse, Pueblo, Colo.

Jurisdiction—Counties.

Alamosa.	Dolores.	La Plata.	Pueblo.
Archuleta.	Eagle.	Las Animas.	Rio Blanco.
Baca.	El Paso.	Mesa.	Rio Grande.
Bent.	Fremont.	Mineral.	Saguache.
Chaffee.	Garfield.	Montezuma.	San Juan.
Conejos.	Gunnison.	Montrose.	San Miguel
Costilla.	Hinsdale.	Otero.	Teller.
Crowley.	Huerfano.	Ouray.	
Custer.	Kiowa.	Pitkin.	
Delta.	Lake.	Prowers.	

DIFISION No. 2.
Headquarters.—244 Capitol Building, Denver, Colo.

Jurisdiction—Counties.

Adams.	Elbert.	Lincoln.	Sedgwick.
Arapahoe.	Gilpin.	Logan.	Summit.
Boulder.	Grand.	Moffat.	Washington.
Cheyenne.	Jackson.	Morgan.	Weld.
Clear Creek.	Jefferson.	Park.	Yuma.
Denver.	Kit Carson.	Phillips.	
Douglas.	Larimer.	Routt.	

CONNECTICUT.

DIVISION No. 1
Headquarters.—18 Asylum Street, Hartford, Conn.

Jurisdiction—Counties.

Hartfield.	Litchfield.	Tolland.	Windham.

DIVISION No. 2.
Headquarters.—County Courthouse, Waterbury, Conn.

Jurisdiction—Counties.

Miidlesex.   New London.
 New Haven, except the towns of Ansonia, Beacon Falls, Derby, Middlebury, Milford, Orange, Oxford, Seymour, Middlesex, New London, and Southbury.

DIVISION No. 3.
Headquarters.—County Courthouse, Bridgeport, Conn.

Jurisdiction—Fairfield County and that part of New Haven County embracing the towns of Ansonia, Beacon Falls, Derby, Middlebury, Milford, Orange, Oxford, Seymour, and Southbury.

DELAWARE.

DISTRICT BOARD FOR THE STATE OF DELAWARE.

Headquarters.—State Capitol, Dover, Del.
Jurisdiction.—Entire State.

DISTRICT OF COLUMBIA.

DISTRICT BOARD FOR THE DISTRICT OF COLUMBIA.

Headquarters.—Room 513, District Building, Washington, D. C.
Jurisdiction.—District of Columbia.

FLORIDA.

NORTHERN DISTRICT.

Headquarters.—Pensacola, Fla.

Jurisdiction—Counties.

Alachua Bay.	Holmes.	Liberty.	Walton.
Calhoun.	Jefferson.	Leon.	Washington.
Escambia.	Jackson.	Okaloosa.	Wakulla.
Franklin.	Lafayette.	Santa Rosa.	
Gadsden.	Levy.	Taylor.	

SOUTHERN DISTRICT.

Headquarters.—Tampa, Fla.

Jurisdiction—Counties.

Baker.	Duval.	Marion.	Pasco.
Bradford.	Flagler.	Monroe.	Putnam.
Brevard.	Hamilton.	Nassau.	St. Johns.
Broward.	Hernando.	Okeechobee.	St. Lucie.
Citrus.	Hillsborough.	Orange.	Seminole.
Clay.	Lake.	Osceola.	Sumter.
Columbia.	Lee.	Palm Beach.	Suwannee.
Dade.	Madison.	Pinellas.	Volusia.
De Soto.	Manatee.	Polk.	

GEORGIA.

NORTHERN DISTRICT.

Headquarters.—Fulton County Courthouse, Atlanta, Ga.

Jurisdiction—Counties.

Banks.	Early.	Henry.	Randolph.
Barrow.	Elbert.	Jackson.	Rockdale.
Bartow.	Fannin.	Lumpkin.	Schley.
Campbell.	Fayette.	Madison.	Spalding.
Carroll.	Floyd.	Marion.	Stephens.
Catoosa.	Forsyth.	Meriwether.	Stewart.
Chattahoochee.	Franklin.	Milton.	Talbot.
Chattooga.	Fulton.	Morgan.	Taylor.
Cherokee.	Gilmer.	Murray.	Terrell.
Clarke.	Gordon.	Muscogee.	Towns.
Clay.	Greene.	Newton.	Troup.
Clayton.	Gwinnett.	Oconee.	Union.
Cobb.	Habersham.	Oglethorpe.	Walker.
Coweta.	Hall.	Paulding.	Walton.
Dade.	Haralson.	Pickens.	Webster.
Dawson.	Harris.	Polk.	White.
Dekalb.	Hart.	Quitman.	Whitfield.
Douglas.	Heard.	Rabun.	

SOUTHERN DISTRICT, DIVISION No. 1.

Headquarters.—Savannah Fire Insurance Building, Savannah, Ga.

Jurisdiction—Counties.

Appling.	Chatham.	Grady.	Screven.
Bacon.	Clinch.	Irwin.	Tattnall.
Baker.	Coffee.	Jeff Davis.	Thomas.
Ben Hill.	Colquitt.	Jenkins.	Tift.
Berrien.	Crisp.	Lee.	Toombs.
Brooks.	Decatur.	Liberty.	Turner.
Bryan.	Dougherty.	Lowndes.	Ware.
Bulloch.	Echols.	McIntosh.	Wayne.
Calhoun.	Effingham.	Miller.	Worth.
Camden.	Emanuel.	Mitchell.	
Candler.	Evans.	Montgomery.	
Charlton.	Glynn.	Pierce.	

SOUTHERN DISTRICT, DIVISION No. 2.

Headquarters.—Public Utility Building, Macon, Ga.

Jurisdiction—Counties.

Baldwin.	Glascock.	Macon.	Telfair.
Bibb.	Hancock.	McDuffie.	Twiggs.
Bleckley.	Houston.	Monroe.	Upson.
Burke.	Jasper.	Pike.	Warren.
Butts.	Jefferson.	Pulaski.	Washington.
Columbia.	Johnson.	Putnam.	Wheeler.
Crawford.	Jones.	Richmond.	Wilcox.
Dodge.	Laurens.	Sumter.	Wilkes.
Dooly.	Lincoln.	Taliaferro.	Wilkinson.

IDAHO.

DIVISION No. 1.

Headquarters.—Sandpoint, Idaho.

Jurisdiction—Counties.

Benewah.	Clearwater.	Latah.	Shoshone.
Bonner.	Idaho.	Lewis.	
Boundary.	Kootenai.	Nez Perce.	

DIVISION No. 2.

Headquarters.—Boise, Idaho.

Jurisdiction—Counties.

Ada.	Butte.	Gem.	Owyhee.
Adams.	Camas.	Gooding.	Payette.
Bannock.	Canyon.	Jefferson.	Power.
Bear Lake.	Cassia.	Lemhi.	Teton.
Bingham.	Custer.	Lincoln.	Twin Falls.
Blaine.	Elmore.	Madison.	Valley.
Boise.	Franklin.	Minidoka.	Washington.
Bonneville.	Fremont.	Oneida.	

ILLINOIS.

NORTHERN DISTRICT, DIVISION No. 1.

Headquarters.—112 West Adams Street, Chicago.
Jurisdiction.—Local Boards Nos. 1-28, inclusive; 44, 45, 67-77, inclusive; 81, 82, and 83 of the city of Chicago.

NORTHERN DISTRICT, DIVISION No. 2.

Headquarters.—Room 1122, 112 West Adams Street, Chicago.
Jurisdiction.—Local Boards Nos. 29-43, inclusive; 46-66, inclusive; 78-80, inclusive; 84-86, inclusive, of the city of Chicago.

NORTHERN DISTRICT, DIVISION No. 3:

Headquarters.—Room 721, 112 West Adams Street, Chicago.
Jurisdiction.—Local Boards Nos. 1-9, inclusive, of Cook County outside of Chicago; and the counties of Boone, Dekalb, Dupage, Grundy, Kane, Kendall, Lake, La Salle, McHenry, and Will.

NORTHERN DISTRICT, DIVISION No. 4.

Headquarters.—Room 8, Fry's Block, Freeport, Ill.

Jurisdiction—Counties.

Carroll.	Lee.	Stephenson.	Winnebago.
Jo Daviess.	Ogle.	Whiteside.	

SOUTHERN DISTRICT, DIVISION No. 1.

Headquarters.—Room 601, Lehman Building, Peoria, Ill.

Jurisdiction—Counties.

Bureau.	Knox.	Mercer.	Stark.
Fulton.	Livingston.	Peoria.	Tazewell.
Henderson.	Marshall.	Putnam.	Warren.
Henry.	McDonough.	Rock Island.	Woodford.

SOUTHERN DISTRICT, DIVISION No. 2.

Headquarters.—State arsenal, Springfield, Ill.

Jurisdiction—Counties.

Adams.	Dewitt.	Macoupin.	Morgan.
Bond.	Greene.	Madison.	Pike.
Brown.	Hancock.	Mason.	Sangamon.
Calhoun.	Jersey.	McLean.	Schuyler.
Cass.	Logan.	Menard.	Scott.
Christian.	Macon.	Montgomery.	

EASTERN DISTRICT, DIVISION No. 1.

Headquarters.—Mount Vernon, Ill.

Jurisdiction—Counties.

Alexander.	Jackson.	Perry.	Union.
Clinton.	Jefferson.	Pope.	Washington.
Franklin.	Johnson.	Pulaski.	White.
Gallatin.	Marion.	Randolph.	Williamson.
Hamilton.	Massac.	St. Clair.	
Hardin.	Monroe.	Saline.	

EASTERN DISTRICT, DIVISION No. 2.

Headquarters.—Robeson Building, Champaign, Ill.

Jurisdiction—Counties.

Champaign.	Douglas.	Iroquois.	Richland.
Clark.	Edgar.	Jasper.	Shelby.
Clay.	Edwards.	Kankakee.	Vermilion.
Coles.	Effingham.	Lawrence.	Wabash.
Crawford.	Fayette.	Moultrie.	Wayne.
Cumberland.	Ford.	Piatt.	

INDIANA.

DIVISION No. 1.

Headquarters.—Laporte, Ind.

Jurisdiction—Counties.

Benton.	Howard.	Newton.	Tippecanoe.
Carroll.	Jasper.	Porter.	Warren.
Cass.	Lake.	Pulaski.	White.
Clinton.	Laporte.	St. Joseph.	
Fountain.	Marshall.	Starke.	
Fulton.	Miami.	Tipton.	

DIVISION No. 2.

Headquarters.—Physician's Defense Building, Fort Wayne, Ind.

Jurisdiction—Counties.

Adams.	Fayette.	Kosciusko.	Steuben.
Allen.	Franklin.	Lagrange.	Union.
Blackford.	Grant.	Madison.	Wabash.
Dekalb.	Henry.	Noble.	Wayne.
Delaware.	Huntington.	Randolph.	Wells.
Elkhart.	Jay.	Rush.	Whitley.

DIVISION No. 3.

Headquarters.—State house, Indianapolis.

Jurisdiction—Counties.

Bartholomew.	Hamilton.	Montgomery.	Shelby.
Boone.	Hancock.	Morgan.	Switzerland.
Clark.	Handricks.	Ohio.	Vermilion.
Clay.	Jefferson.	Parke.	Vigo.
Dearborn.	Jennings.	Putnam.	
Decatur.	Johnson.	Ripley.	
Floyd.	Marion.	Scott.	

DIVISION No. 4.

Headquarters.—Oliphant Building, Vincennes, Ind.

Jurisdiction—Counties.

Brown.	Harrison.	Orange.	Sullivan.
Crawford.	Jackson.	Owen.	Vanderburg.
Daviess.	Knox.	Perry.	Warrick.
Dubois.	Lawrence.	Pike.	Washington.
Gibson.	Martin.	Posey.	
Greene.	Monroe.	Spencer.	

IOWA.

NORTHERN DISTRICT.

Headquarters.—Marsh Place Building, Waterloo, Iowa.

Jurisdiction—Counties.

Allamakee.	Clay.	Howard.	Palo Alto.
Benton.	Clayton.	Humboldt.	Pocahontas.
Blackhawk.	Delaware.	Ida.	Plymouth.
Bremer.	Dickinson.	Iowa.	Sac.
Buchanan.	Dubuque.	Jackson.	Sioux.
Buena Vista.	Emmet.	Jones.	Tama.
Butler.	Fayette.	Kossuth.	Webster.
Calhoun.	Floyd.	Linn.	Winnebago.
Carroll.	Franklin.	Lyon.	Winneshiek.
Cedar.	Grundy.	Mitchell.	Woodbury.
Cerro Gordo.	Hamilton.	Monona.	Worth.
Cherokee.	Hancock.	O'Brien.	Wright.
Chickasaw.	Hardin.	Osceola.	

SOUTHERN DISTRICT.
Headquarters.—Statehouse, Des Moines, Iowa.

Jurisdiction—Counties.

Adair.	Des Moines.	Lucas.	Poweshiek.
Adams.	Fremont.	Madison.	Scott.
Appanoose.	Greene.	Mahaska.	Shelby.
Audubon.	Guthrie.	Marion.	Story.
Boone.	Harrison.	Marshall.	Taylor.
Cass.	Henry.	Mills.	Union.
Clarke.	Jasper.	Monroe.	Van Buren.
Clinton.	Jefferson.	Montgomery.	Ringgold.
Crawford.	Johnson.	Muscatine.	Wapello.
Dallas.	Keokuk.	Page.	Warren.
Davis.	Lee.	Polk.	Washington.
Decatur.	Louisa.	Pottawattamie.	Wayne.

KANSAS.

DIVISION No. 1.
Headquarters.—Statehouse, Topeka, Kans.

Jurisdiction.—Counties.

Allen.	Cowley.	Johnson.	Nemaha.
Anderson.	Crawford.	Labette.	Neosho.
Atchison.	Doniphan.	Leavenworth.	Osage.
Bourbon.	Douglas.	Linn.	Pottawatomie.
Brown.	Elk.	Lyon.	Shawnee.
Chase.	Franklin.	Marion.	Wabaunsee.
Chautauqua.	Greenwood.	Miami.	Wilson.
Cherokee.	Jackson.	Morris.	Woodson.
Coffey.	Jefferson.	Montgomery.	Wyandotte.

DIVISION No. 2.
Headquarters.—Federal Building, Wichita.

Jurisdiction—Counties.

Barber.	Grant.	Mitchell.	Scott.
Barton.	Gray.	Morton.	Sedgwick.
Butler.	Greeley.	Ness.	Seward.
Cheyenne.	Hamilton.	Norton.	Sheridan.
Clark.	Harper.	Osborne.	Sherman.
Clay.	Harvey.	Ottawa.	Smith.
Cloud.	Haskell.	Pawnee.	Stafford.
Comanche.	Hodgeman.	Phillips.	Stanton.
Decatur.	Jewell.	Pratt.	Stevens.
Dickinson.	Kearny.	Rawlins.	Sumner.
Edwards.	Kingman.	Reno.	Thomas.
Ellis.	Kiowa.	Republic.	Trego.
Ellsworth.	Lane.	Rice.	Wallace.
Finney.	Lincoln.	Riley.	Washington.
Ford.	Logan.	Rooks.	Wichita.
Geary.	McPherson.	Rush.	
Gove.	Marshall.	Russell.	
Graham.	Meade.	Saline.	

KENTUCKY.

EASTERN DISTRICT.

Headquarters.—Phoenix Hotel, Lexington, Ky.

Jurisdiction—Counties.

Anderson.	Fleming.	Lawrence.	Owsley.
Bath.	Floyd.	Lee.	Perry.
Bell.	Franklin.	Leslie.	Pendleton.
Boone.	Gallatin.	Letcher.	Pike.
Bourbon.	Garrard.	Lewis.	Powell.
Boyle.	Grant.	Lincoln.	Pulaski.
Boyd.	Greenup.	McCreary.	Robertson.
Bracken.	Harlan.	Madison.	Rockcastle.
Breathitt.	Harrison.	Mason.	Rowan.
Campbell.	Henry.	Magoffin.	Scott.
Carroll.	Jackson.	Martin.	Shelby.
Carter.	Jessamine.	Mercer.	Trimble.
Clark.	Johnson.	Menifee.	Wayne.
Clay.	Kenton.	Morgan.	Whitley.
Elliott.	Knott.	Montgomery.	Wolfe.
Estill.	Knox.	Nicholas.	Woodford.
Fayette.	Laurel.	Owen.	

WESTERN DISTRICT, DIVISION No. 1.
Headquarters.—Federal Building, Louisville, Ky.

Jurisdiction—Counties.

Adair.	Edmonson.	Larue.	Oldham.
Barren.	Grayson.	Marion.	Russell.
Breckenridge.	Green.	Meade.	Spencer.
Bullitt.	Hardin.	Metcalfe.	Taylor.
Clinton.	Hart.	Monroe.	Washington.
Cumberland.	Jefferson.	Nelson.	

WESTERN DISTRICT, DIVISION No. 2.
Headquarters.—Madisonville, Ky.

Jurisdiction—Counties.

Allen.	Crittenden.	Livingston.	Simpson.
Ballard.	Daviess.	Logan.	Todd.
Butler.	Fulton.	Lyon.	Trigg.
Caldwell.	Graves.	McCracken.	Union.
Calloway.	Hancock.	McLean.	Warren.
Carlisle.	Henderson.	Marshall.	Webster.
Casey.	Hickman.	Muhlenberg.	
Christian.	Hopkins.	Ohio.	

LOUISIANA.

EASTERN DISTRICT, DIVISION No. 1.
Headquarters.—Room 300, Federal Building, New Orleans, La.

Jurisdiction—Parishes.

Jefferson.	Plaquemines.	St. Charles.
Orleans.	St. Bernard.	St. John the Baptist.

EASTERN DISTRICT, DIVISION No. 2.
Headquarters.—The capitol, Baton Rouge, La.

Jurisdiction—Parishes.

Ascension.	Iberville.	St. James.	Washington.
Assumption.	Lafourche.	St. Mary.	West Baton Rouge.
East Baton Rouge.	Livingston.	St. Tammany.	West Feliciana.
East Feliciana.	Pointe Coupee.	Tangipahoa.	
Iberia.	St. Helena.	Terrebonne.	

WESTERN DISTRICT.
    Headquarters.—City National Bank Building, Shreveport, La.

Jurisdiction—Parishes

Allen.	Claiborne.	La Salle.	St. Landry.
Avoyelles.	Calcasieu.	Lincoln.	St. Martin.
Acadia.	Cameron.	Lafayette.	Sabine.
Beauregard.	De Soto.	Madison.	Tensas.
Bossier.	East Carroll.	Morehouse.	Union.
Bienville.	Evangeline.	Natchitoches.	Vermilion.
Catahoula.	Franklin.	Ouachita.	Vernon.
Caldwell.	Grant.	Rapides.	Winn.
Concordia.	Jackson.	Richland.	West Carroll.
Caddo.	Jefferson Davis.	Red River.	Webster.

MAINE.

DIVISION No. 1.
    Headquarters.—State house, Augusta, Me.

Jurisdiction—Counties.

Androscoggin.	Franklin.	Oxford.	York.
Cumberland.	Kennebec.	Sagadahoc.	

DIVISION No. 2.
    Headquarters.—Federal Building, Bangor, Me.

Jurisdiction—Counties.

Aroostook.	Lincoln.	Piscataquis.	Waldo.
Hancock.	Penobscot.	Somerset.	Washington.
Knox.			

MARYLAND.

DIVISION.No. 1.
    Headquarters.—American Building, Baltimore, Md.
    Jurisdiction.—Baltimore city.

DIVISION No. 2.
    Headquarters.—Annapolis, Md.

Jurisdiction—Counties.

Allegany.	Carroll.	Harford.	St. Marys.
Anne Arundel.	Charles.	Howard.	Washington.
Baltimore.	Frederick.	Montgomery.	
Calvert.	Garrett.	Prince Georges.	

DIVISION No. 3.
    Headquarters.—Denton, Md.

Jurisdiction—Counties.

Caroline.	Kent.	Somerset.	Wicomico.
Cecil.	Queen Annes.	Talbot.	Worcester.
Dorchester			

MASSACHUSETTS.

DIVISION No. 1.
    Headquarters.—31 Elm Street, Springfield, Mass.
    Jurisdiction.—Chicopee, Holyoke, Pittsfield, Springfield, and Divisions No. 1, 2,
    3, 4, 5, 6, 7, 8, and 9 or the State of Massachusetts.
DIVISION No. 2.
    Headquarters.—1029 Slater Building, Worcester, Mass.
    Jurisdiction.—Fitchburg, Worcester, and Divisions No. 10, 11, 12, 13, 14, 15, 16,
    17, 18, 32, 33, and 34 of the State of Massachusetts.
DIVISION No. 3.
    Headquarters.—Essex County courthouse, Lawrence, Mass.
    Jurisdiction.—Haverhill, Lawrence, Lowell, Malden, Medford, Waltham, and
    Divisions No. 19, 20, 21, 22, 24, 26, 27, 28, 29, and 30 of the State of Massachusetts.

DIVISION No. 4.
>   *Headquarters.*—514 Tremont Building, Boston, Mass.
>   *Jurisdiction.*—Boston.

DIVISION No. 5.
>   *Headquarters.*—702 Tremont Building, Boston, Mass.
>   *Jurisdiction.*—Brookline, Cambridge, Chelsea, Everett, Lynn, Newton, Salem,
>   Somerville, and Divisions No. 23, 25, and 31 of the State of Massachusetts.

DIVISION No. 6.
>   *Headquarters.*—County courthouse, Taunton, Mass.
>   *Jurisdiction.*—Brockton, Fall River, New Bedford, Quincy, Taunton, and
>   Divisions No. 35, 36, 37, 38, 39, 40, 41, 42, and 43 of the State of Massachusetts.

MICHIGAN.

EASTERN DISTRICT, DIVISION No. 1.
>   *Headquarters.*—Municipal Courts Building, St. Antoine and Clinton, Detroit,
>   Mich.
>   *Jurisdiction.*—City of Detroit, village of Highland Park.

EASTERN DISTRICT, DIVISION No. 2.
>   *Headquarters.*—2130 Penobscot Building, Detroit, Mich.

Jurisdiction—Counties.

Lapeer.	Macomb.	Oakland.	Washtenaw.
Lenawee.	Monroe.	St. Clair.	Wayne. [1]

EASTERN DISTRICT, DIVISION No. 3.
>   *Headquarters.*—Post office, Lansing, Mich.

Jurisdiction—Counties.

Branch.	Genesee.	Ingham.	Saginaw.
Calhoun.	Gratiot.	Jackson.	Shiawassee.
Clinton.	Hillsdale.	Livingston.	

EASTERN DISTRICT, DIVISION No. 4.
>   *Headquarters.*—City Hall, Bay City, Mich.

Jurisdiction—Counties.

Alcona.	Clare.	Isabella.	Otsego.
Alpena.	Crawford.	Midland.	Presque Isle.
Arenac.	Gladwin.	Montmorency.	Roscommon.
Bay.	Huron.	Ogemaw.	Sanilac.
Cheboygan.	Iosco.	Oscoda.	Tuscola.

WESTERN DISTRICT, DIVISION No. 1.
>   *Headquarters.*—409 Peck Building, Kalamazoo, Mich.

Jurisdiction—Counties.

Allegan.	Berrien.	Eaton.	St. Joseph.
Barry.	Cass.	Kalamazoo.	Van Buren.

WESTERN DISTRICT, DIVISION No. 2.
>   *Headquarters.*—City Hall, Grand Rapids, Mich.

Jurisdiction—Counties.

Antrim.	Kalkaska.	Mecosta.	Osceola.
Benzie.	Kent.	Missaukee.	Ottowa.
Charlevoix.	Lake.	Montcalm.	Wexford.
Emmet.	Leelanau.	Muskegon.	
Grand Traverse.	Manistee.	Newaygo.	
Ionia.	Mason.	Oceana.	

---

[1] Exclusive of Detroit and Highland Park.

354 APPENDIXES.

WESTERN DISTRICT, DIVISION No. 3.
    Headquarters.—Michigan College of Mines, Houghton, Mich.

Jurisdiction—Counties.

Alger.	Dickinson.	Keweenaw.	Menominee.
Baraga.	Gogebec.	Luce.	Ontonagon.
Chippewa.	Houghton.	Mackinac.	Schoolcraft.
Delta.	Iron.	Marquette.	

MINNESOTA.

DIVISION No. 1.
    Headquarters.—Federal building, Mankato, Minn.

Jurisdiction—Counties.

Blue Earth.	Houston.	Murray.	Scott.
Brown.	Jackson.	Nicollet.	Sibley.
Cottonwood.	Lac qui Parle.	Nobles.	Steele.
Dodge.	Le Sueur.	Olmsted.	Waseca.
Faribault.	Lincoln.	Pipestone.	Wabasha.
Fillmore.	Lyon.	Redwood.	Watonwan.
Freeborn.	Martin.	Rice.	Winona.
Goodhue.	Mower.	Rock.	Yellow Medicine.

DIVISION No. 2.
    Headquarters.—Federal office building, Minneapolis, Minn.

Jurisdiction—Counties

Anoka.	Minneapolis City.	Meeker.	Wright.
Carver.	Isanti.	Renville.	
Chippewa.	Kandiyohi.	Sherburne.	
Hennepin.	McLeod.	Swift.	

DIVISION No. 3.
    Headquarters.—Fourth floor new post-office building, St. Paul, Minn.

Jurisdiction—Counties.

Benton.	Grant.	Pine.	Stevens.
Big Stone.	Kanabec.	Pope.	Todd.
Chisago.	Mille Lacs.	Ramsey.	Traverse.
Dakota.	Morrison.	St. Paul City.	Washington.
Douglas.	Otter Tail.	Stearns.	Wilkin.

DIVISION No. 4.[1]
    Headquarters.—Duluth.

Jurisdiction—Counties.

Aitkin.	Cook.	Itasca.	Lake.
Cass.	Crow Wing.	Koochiching.	St. Louis.
Carlton.			

DIVISION No. 5.[2]

    Headquarters.—Crookston.

Jurisdiction—Counties.

Becker.	Hubbard.	Norman.	Roseau.
Beltrami.	Kittson.	Pennington.	Wadena.
Clay.	Marshall.	Polk.	
Clearwater.	Mahnomen.	Red Lake.	

[1] Board No. 4 was created October 2, 1918, prior to which date Board No. 4 with headquarters at Duluth, had jurisdiction of the entire territorial area now under Boards Nos. 4 and 5.
[2] Board No. 5 was created Oct. 2, 1918, prior to which date Board No. 4, with headquarters at Duluth, had jurisdiction of the entire territorial area now under Boards Nos. 4 and 5.

MISSISSIPPI.

NORTHERN DISTRICT.

Headquarters.—Professional Building, Tupelo, Miss.

Jurisdiction—Counties.

Alcorn.	Coahoma.	Monroe.	Tate.
Attala.	De Soto.	Montgomery.	Tippah.
Benton.	Grenada.	Oktibbeha.	Tishomingo.
Bolivar.	Itawamba.	Panola.	Tunica.
Calhoun.	Lafayette.	Pontotoc.	Union.
Carroll.	Lee.	Prentiss.	Webster.
Chickasaw.	Leflore.	Quitman.	Winston.
Choctaw.	Lowndes.	Sunflower.	Yalobusha.
Clay.	Marshall.	Tallahatchie.	

SOUTHERN DISTRICT.

Headquarters.—Government Building, Vicksburg, Miss.

Jurisdiction—Counties.

Adams.	Hinds.	Lawrence.	Scott.
Amite.	Holmes.	Leake.	Sharkey.
Claiborne.	Humphreys.	Lincoln.	Simpson.
Clarke.	Issaquena.	Madison.	Smith.
Copiah.	Jackson.	Marion.	Stone.
Covington.	Jasper.	Neshoba.	Walthall.
Forrest.	Jefferson.	Newton.	Warren.
Franklin.	Jeff Davis.	Noxubee.	Washington.
George.	Jones.	Pearl River.	Wayne.
Greene.	Kemper.	Perry.	Wilkinson.
Hancock.	Lamar.	Pike.	Yazoo.
Harrison.	Lauderdale.	Rankin.	

MISSOURI.

EASTERN DISTRICT, DIVISION No. 1.

Headquarters.—Boatmen's Bank Building, St. Louis, Mo.

Jurisdiction.

St. Louis County. St. Louis city.

EASTERN DISTRICT, DIVISION No. 2.

Headquarters.—Canton, Mo.

Jurisdiction—Counties.

Adair.	Lewis.	Monroe.	St. Charles.
Audrain.	Lincoln.	Montgomery.	Schuyler.
Chariton.	Linn.	Pike.	Scotland.
Clark.	Macon.	Ralls.	Shelby.
Knox.	Marion.	Randolph.	Warren.

EASTERN DISTRICT, DIVISION No. 3

Headquarters.—Poplar Bluff, Mo.

Jurisdiction—Counties.

Butler.	Franklin.	New Madrid.	Ste. Genevieve.
Bollinger.	Gasconade.	Pemiscot.	Scott.
Cape Girardeau.	Iron.	Perry.	Shannon.
Carter.	Jefferson.	Phelps.	Stoddard.
Crawford.	Madison.	Reynolds.	Washington.
Dent.	Maries.	Ripley.	Wayne.
Dunklin.	Mississippi.	St. Francois.	

WESTERN DISTRICT, DIVISION No. 1.

Headquarters.—201 Railway Exchange Building, Kansas City, Mo.

Jurisdiction—Counties.

Andrew.	Clinton.	Jackson.	Ray.
Atchison.	Daviess.	Johnson.	St. Clair.
Bates.	Dekalb.	Lafayette.	Saline.
Buchanan.	Gentry.	Livingston.	Sullivan.
Caldwell.	Grundy.	Mercer.	Worth.
Carroll.	Harrison.	Nodaway.	
Cass.	Henry.	Platte.	
Clay.	Holt.	Putnam.	

WESTERN DISTRICT, DIVISION No. 2.

Headquarters.—Federal Building, Jefferson City, Mo.

Jurisdiction—Counties.

Barry.	Dade.	McDonald.	Pulaski.
Barton.	Dallas.	Miller.	Stone.
Benton.	Douglas.	Monitau.	Taney.
Boone.	Greene.	Morgan.	Texas.
Callaway.	Hickory.	Newton.	Vernon.
Camden.	Howard.	Oregon.	Webster.
Cedar.	Howell.	Osage.	Wright.
Christian.	Jasper.	Ozark.	
Cole.	Laclede.	Pettis.	
Cooper.	Lawrence.	Polk.	

MONTANA.

DIVISION No. 1.

Headquarters.—State Capitol, Helena, Mont.

Jurisdiction—Counties.

Beaverhead.	Fallon.	Missoula.	Silver Bow.
Big Horn.	Gallatin.	Park.	Stillwater.
Broadwater.	Granite.	Powell.	Sweet Grass.
Carbon.	Jefferson.	Prairie.	Wibaux.
Custer.	Lewis and Clark.	Ravalli.	
Dawson.	Madison.	Rosebud.	
Deer Lodge.	Mineral.	Sanders.	

DIVISION No. 2.

Headquarters.—Great Falls, Mont.

Jurisdiction—Counties.

Blaine.	Hill.	Richland.	Wheatland.
Cascade.	Lincoln.	Sheridan.	Yellowstone.
Chouteau.	Meagher.	Teton.	
Ferges.	Musselshell.	Toole.	
Flathead.	Phillips.	Valley.	

NEBRASKA.

DIVISION NO. 1.

Headquarters.—Courthouse, Omaha, Nebr.

Jurisdiction—Counties.

Antelope.	Cuming.	Howard.	Platte.
Arthur.	Custer.	Keith.	Rock.
Banner.	Dakota.	Keyapaha.	Sarpy.
Blaine.	Dawes.	Kimball.	Scotts Bluff.
Boone.	Dawson.	Knox.	Sheridan.
Box Butte.	Deuel.	Lincoln.	Sherman.
Boyd.	Dixon.	Logan.	Sioux.
Brown.	Dodge.	Loup.	Stanton.
Buffalo.	Garden.	Madison.	Thomas.
Burt.	Garfield.	McPherson.	Thurston.
Cedar.	Grant.	Merrick.	Valley.
Cherry.	Greeley.	Morrill.	Washington.
Cheyenne.	Holt.	Nance.	Wayne.
Colfax.	Hooker.	Pierce.	Wheeler.

DIVISION NO. 2.

Headquarters.—Federal Building, Lincoln, Nebr.

Jurisdiction—Counties.

Adams.	Furnas.	Johnson.	Polk.
Butler.	Gage.	Kearney.	Red Willow.
Cass.	Gosper	Lancaster.	Richardson.
Chase.	Hall.	Nemaha.	Saline.
Clay.	Hamilton.	Nuckolls.	Saunders.
Dundy.	Harlan.	Otoe.	Seward.
Fillmore.	Hayes.	Pawnee.	Thayer.
Frontier.	Hitchcock.	Perkins.	Webster.
Franklin.	Jefferson.	Phelps.	York.

NEVADA.

DISTRICT BOARD FOR STATE OF NEVADA.

Headquarters.—Law library, county courthouse, **Reno, Nev.**
Jurisdiction.—Entire State.

NEW HAMPSHIRE.

DISTRICT BOARD FOR STATE OF NEW HAMPSHIRE.

Headquarters.—State House, Concord, N. H.
Jurisdiction.—Entire State.

NEW JERSEY.

DIVISION NO. 1.

Headquarters.—City Hall, Jersey City, N. J.

Jurisdiction—Counties.

Bergen.	Hudson.	Passaic.

DIVISION NO. 2.

Headquarters.—Mutual Benefit Building, 752 Broad Street, Newark.

Jurisdiction—Counties.

Essex.	Somerset.	Union.	Warren.
Morris.	Sussex.		

Division No. 3.
Headquarters.—119 West State Street, Trenton, N. J.

Jurisdiction—Counties.

Atlantic.	Cape May.	Huntingdon	Monmouth
Burlington.	Camden.	Mercer.	Ocean.
Cumberland.	Gloucester.	Middlesex.	Salem.

NEW MEXICO.

District for the State of New Mexico.[1]
Headquarters.—Santa Fe, N. Mex.
Jurisdiction.—Entire State.

NEW YORK.

Northern District, Division No. 1.
Headquarters.—Malone, N. Y.

Jurisdiction—Counties.

Clinton.	Fulton.	St. Lawrence.	Warren.
Essex.	Hamilton.	Saratoga.	Washington.
Franklin.	Herkimer.		

Northern District, Division No. 2.
Headquarters.—Special term room, county courthouse, Albany, N. Y.

Jurisdiction—Counties.

Albany.	Montgomery.	Rensselaer.	Schoharie.
Delaware.	Otsego.	Schenectady.	

Northern District, Division No. 3.
Headquarters.—Room 311, county courthouse, Syracuse, N. Y.

Jurisdiction—Counties.

Broome.	Cortland.	Madison.	Oswego.
Cayuga.	Jefferson.	Oneida.	Tioga.
Chenango.	Lewis.	Onondaga.	Tompkins.

Western District, Division No. 1.
Headquarters.—Glen Springs Hotel, Watkins, N. Y

Jurisdiction—Counties.

Allegany.	Chautauqua.	Schuyler.	Yates.
Cattaraugus.	Chemung.	Steuben.	

Western District, Division No. 2.
Headquarters.—Grand jury room, county courthouse, Rochester, N. Y.

Jurisdiction—Counties.

Livingston.	Ontario.	Seneca.	Wayne.
Monroe.			

---

[1] District Boards Nos. 1 and 2 for the State of New Mexico, with headquarters at Santa Fe and Roswell, respectively, formerly had jurisdiction over the area now covered by this board. The two former boards were consolidated Sept. 25, 1918, into the District Board for the State of New Mexico.

WESTERN DISTRICT, DIVISION NO. 3.
Headquarters.—804 Iroquois Building, Buffalo, N. Y.

Jurisdiction—Counties.

Erie.	Niagara.	Orleans.	Wyoming.
Genesee.			

SOUTHERN DISTRICT.
Headquarters.—Room 200, courthouse, White Plains, N. Y.

Jurisdiction—Counties.

Columbia.	Orange.	Rockland.	Ulster.
Dutchess.	Putnam.	Sullivan.	Westchester.
Greene.			

EASTERN DISTRICT.
Headquarters.—Nassau County Trust Co. Building, Mineola, N. Y.

Jurisdiction—Counties.

Nassau.	Suffolk.

DISTRICT BOARD FOR THE CITY OF NEW YORK.
Headquarters.—Room 411, Federal building, New York City. (Old post-office building.)
Jurisdiction.—New York City.

NORTH CAROLINA.

EASTERN DISTRICT.
Headquarters.—Goldsboro, N. C.

Jurisdiction—Counties.

Beaufort.	Duplin.	Jones.	Person.
Bertie.	Durham.	Lee.	Pitt.
Bladen.	Edgecombe.	Lenoir.	Richmond.
Brunswick.	Franklin.	Martin.	Robeson.
Camden.	Gates.	Moore.	Sampson.
Carteret.	Granville.	Nash.	Scotland.
Chatham.	Greene.	New Hanover.	Tyrrell.
Chowan.	Halifax.	Northampton.	Vance.
Columbus.	Harnett.	Onslow.	Wake.
Craven.	Hertford.	Pamlico.	Warren.
Cumberland.	Hyde.	Pasquotank.	Washington.
Currituck.	Hoke.	Pender.	Wayne.
Dare.	Johnston.	Perquimans.	Wilson.

WESTERN DISTRICT.
Headquarters.—Statesville, N. C.

Jurisdiction.—Counties.

Alamance.	Cherokee.	Jackson.	Rowan.
Alexander.	Clay.	Lincoln.	Rutherford.
Alleghany.	Cleveland.	Macon.	Stanly.
Anson.	Davidson.	Madison.	Stokes.
Ashe.	Davie.	McDowell.	Surry.
Avery.	Forsyth.	Mecklenburg.	Swain.
Buncombe.	Gaston.	Mitchell.	Transylvania.
Burke.	Graham.	Montgomery.	Union.
Cabarrus.	Guilford.	Orange.	Watauga.
Caldwell.	Haywood.	Polk.	Wilkes.
Caswell.	Henderson.	Randolph.	Yadkin.
Catawba.	Iredell.	Rockingham.	Yancey.

NORTH DAKOTA.

DISTRICT BOARD FOR THE STATE OF NORTH DAKOTA.
  Headquarters.—Federal building, Bismarck, N. Dak.
  Jurisdiction.—Entire State.

OHIO.

NORTHERN DISTRICT, DIVISION No. 1.
  Headquarters.—Post office, Canton, Ohio.

Jurisdiction—Counties.

Carroll.	Mahoning.	Summitt.	Tuscarawas.
Columbiana.	Portage.	Trumbull.	Wayne.
Holmes.	Stark.		

NORTHERN DISTRICT, DIVISION No. 2.
  Headquarters.—Old courthouse, Cleveland, Ohio.

Jurisdiction—Counties.

Ashland.	Erie.	Lake.	Media.
Ashtabula.	Geauga·	Lorain.	Richland.
Cuyahoga.	Huron.		

NORTHERN DISTRICT, DIVISION No. 3.
  Headquarters.—Courthouse, Findlay, Ohio.

Jurisdiction—Counties.

Allen.	Hancock.	Mercer.	Seneca.
Auglaize.	Hardin.	Ottawa.	Van Wert.
Crawford.	Henry.	Paulding.	Williams.
Defiance.	Lucas.	Putnam.	Wood.
Fulton.	Marion.	Sandusky.	Wyandot.

SOUTHERN DISTRICT, DIVISION No. 1.
  Headquarters.—Post-office building, Cambridge, Ohio

Jurisdiction—Counties.

Belmont.	Harrison.	Morgan.	Noble.
Coshocton.	Jefferson.	Muskingum.	Washington.
Guernsey.	Monroe.		

SOUTHERN DISTRICT, DIVISION No. 2.
  Headquarters.—Room 15, Federal building, Columbus, Ohio.

Jurisdiction—Counties.

Athens.	Franklin.	Licking.	Pickaway.
Champaign.	Gallia.	Logan.	Pike.
Clark.	Hocking.	Madison.	Ross.
Delaware.	Jackson.	Meigs.	Scioto.
Fairfield.	Knox.	Morrow.	Union.
Fayette.	Lawrence.	Perry.	Vinton.

SOUTHERN DISTRICT, DIVISION No. 3.
  Headquarters.—Room 710, Neave Building, Fourth and Race Streets, Cincinnati, Ohio.

Jurisdiction—Counties.

Adams.	Clinton.	Highland.	Preble.
Brown.	Darke.	Miami.	Shelby.
Butler.	Greene.	Montgomery	Warren.
Clermont.	Hamilton.		

OKLAHOMA.

EASTERN DISTRICT, DIVISION No. 1.
Headquarters.—Muskogee, Okla.

Jurisdiction—Counties.

Adair.	Craig.	McCurtain.	Ottawa.
Atoka.	Delaware.	McIntosh.	Pittsburg.
Bryan.	Haskell.	Marshall.	Pushmataka.
Cherokee.	Latimer.	Mayes.	Sequoyah.
Choctaw.	Le Flore.	Muskogee.	Wagoner.

EASTERN DISTRICT, DIVISION No. 2.
Headquarters.—Tulsa, Okla.

Jurisdiction—Counties.

Carter.	Jefferson.	Nowata.	Seminole.
Coal.	Johnston.	Okfuskee.	Stephens.
Creek.	Love.	Okmulgee.	Tulsa.
Garvin.	McClain.	Pontotoc.	Washington.
Hughes.	Murray.	Rogers.	

WESTERN DISTRICT.
Headquarters.—Oklahoma City, Okla.

Jurisdiction—Counties.

Alfalfa.	Cotton.	Jackson.	Osage.
Beaver.	Custer.	Kay.	Pawnee.
Beckham.	Dewey.	Kingfisher.	Pottawatomie.
Blaine.	Ellis.	Kiowa.	Roger Mills.
Caddo.	Garfield.	Lincoln.	Texas.
Canadian.	Grant.	Logan.	Tillman.
Cimarron.	Greer.	Major.	Washita.
Cleveland.	Harmon.	Noble.	Woods.
Comanche.	Harper.	Oklahoma.	Woodward.

OREGON.

DIVISION No. 1.
Headquarters.—Courthouse, Portland, Oreg.

Jurisdiction—Counties.

Clackamas.	Deschutes.	Marion.	Wasco.
Clatsop.	Hood River.	Multnomah.	Washington.
Columbia.	Jefferson.	Tillamook.	Yamhill.

DIVISION No. 2.
Headquarters.—Eugene, Oreg.

Jurisdiction—Counties.

Benton.	Douglas.	Klamath.	Lincoln.
Coos.	Jackson.	Lake.	Linn.
Curry.	Josephine.	Lane.	Polk.

DIVISION No. 3.
Headquarters.—La Grande, Oreg.

Jurisdiction—Counties.

Baker.	Grant.	Morrow.	Union.
Crook.	Harney.	Sherman.	Wallowa.
Gilliam.	Malheur.	Umatilla.	Wheeler.

PENNSYLVANIA.

CITY AND COUNTY OF PHILADELPHIA (EASTERN JUDICIAL DISTRICT).[1]
Headquarters.—401 Chestnut Street, Philadelphia.
Jurisdiction.—City and county of Philadelphia.

EASTERN DISTRICT, DIVISION NO. 3.
Headquarters.—Lehigh County courthouse, Allentown, Pa.

Jurisdiction—Counties.

Berks.	Lehigh.	Northampton.	Schuylkill.
Bucks.			

EASTERN DISTRICT, DIVISION NO. 4.
Headquarters.—Courthouse, Lancaster, Pa.

Jurisdiction—Counties.

Chester.	Delaware.	Lancaster.	Montgomery.

WESTERN DISTRICT, DIVISION NO. 1.
Headquarters.—Allegheny County courthouse, Pittsburgh, Pa.,
Jurisdiction.—Allegheny County.

WESTERN DISTRICT, DIVISION NO. 2.
Headquarters.—Erie, Pa.

Jurisdiction—Counties.

Armstrong.	Clearfield.	Forest.	McKean.
Beaver.	Crawford.	Indiana.	Mercer.
Butler.	Elk.	Jefferson.	Venango.
Clarion.	Erie.	Lawrence.	Warren.

WESTER DISTRICT, DIVISION NO. 3.
Headquarters.—Courthouse, Greensburg, Pa.

Jurisdiction—Counties.

Bedford.	Cambria.	Greene.	Washington.
Blair.	Fayette.	Somerset.	Westmoreland.

MIDDLE DISTRICT, DIVISION NO. 1.
Headquarters.—Federal Building, Scranton, Pa.

Jurisdiction—Counties.

Bradford.	Lackawanna.	Pike.	Tioga.
Cameron.	Luzerne.	Potter.	Wayne.
Carbon.	Lycoming.	Sullivan.	Wyoming.
Clinton.	Monroe.	Susquehanna.	

MIDDLE DISTRICT, DIVISION NO. 2.
Headquarters.—State Capitol Building, Harrisburg, Pa.

Jurisdiction—Counties.

Adams.	Franklin.	Lebanon.	Perry.
Center.	Fulton.	Mifflin.	Snyder.
Columbia.	Huntington.	Montour.	Union.
Cumberland.	Juniata.	Northumberland.	York.
Dauphin.			

---

[1] District Boards Nos. 1 and 2 of the eastern judicial district of Pennsylvania formerly had jurisdiction of the area now covered by this board. These two divisions were consolidated Sept. 4, 1918, into the District Board for the city and county of Philadelphia, eastern judicial district of Pennsylvania.

RHODE ISLAND.

DIVISION No. 1.

Headquarters.—103 Smith Street, Providence, R. I.
Jurisdiction.—Local Boards for Divisions Nos. 1, 2, 4, 5, 6, 7, 8, 9, 10 of the city of Providence; Divisions Nos. 5 and 6, State of Rhode Island, and the city of Newport.

DIVISION No. 2.

Headquarters.—103 Smith Street, Providence, R. I.
Jurisdiction.—Local Boards for Divisions Nos. 1, 2, 3, 4, 7, 8 of the State of Rhode Island; Local Board for Divisions Nos. 1 and 2, city of Pawtucket; Local Board for Division No. 3, city of Providence; and Local Board for the city of Woonsocket.

SOUTH CAROLINA.

EASTERN DISTRICT.

Headquarters.—Union Bank Building, Columbia, S. C.

Jurisdiction—Counties.

Aiken.	Chesterfield.	Georgetown.	Marion.
Bamberg.	Clarendon.	Hampton.	Marlboro.
Barnwell.	Colleton.	Horry.	Orangeburg.
Beaufort.	Darlington.	Jasper.	Richland.
Berkeley.	Dillon.	Kershaw.	Sumter.
Calhoun.	Dorchester.	Lee.	Williamsburg.
Charleston.	Florence.	Lexington.	

WESTERN DISTRICT.

Headquarters.—Greenwood, S. C.

Jurisdiction—Counties.

Abbeville.	Fairfield.	McCormick.	Saluda.
Anderson.	Greenville.	Newberry.	Spartanburg.
Cherokee.	Greenwood.	Oconee.	Union.
Chester.	Lancaster.	Pickens.	York.
Edgefield.	Laurens.		

SOUTH DAKOTA.

DISTRICT BOARD FOR STATE OF SOUTH DAKOTA.

Headquarters.—Sioux Falls, S. Dak.
Jurisdiction.—Entire State.

TENNESSEE.

MIDDLE DISTRICT.

Headquarters.—First National Bank Building, Nashville, Tenn.

Jurisdiction—Counties.

Bedford.	Franklin.	Macon.	Smith.
Cannon.	Giles.	Marshall.	Stewart.
Cheatham.	Grundy.	Maury.	Sumner.
Clay.	Hickman.	Montgomery.	Trousdale.
Coffee.	Houston.	Moore.	Van Buren.
Cumberland.	Humphreys.	Overton.	Warren.
Davidson.	Jackson.	Pickett.	Wayne.
Dekalb.	Lawrence.	Putnam.	White.
Dickson.	Lewis.	Robertson.	Williamson.
Fentress.	Lincoln	Rutherford.	Wilson.

EASTERN DISTRICT.

Headquarters.—Federal Building, Knoxville, Tenn.

Jurisdiction—Counties.

Anderson.	Greene.	Loudon.	Roane.
Bledsoe.	Hamblen.	McMinn.	Scott.
Blount.	Hamilton.	Marion.	Sequatchie.
Bradley.	Hancock.	Meigs.	Sevier.
Campbell.	Hawkins.	Monroe.	Sullivan.
Carter.	James.	Morgan.	Unicoi.
Claiborne.	Jefferson.	Polk.	Union.
Cocke.	Johnson.	Rhea.	Washington.
Grainger.	Knox.		

WESTERN DISTRICT.

Headquarters.—Y. M. C. A. Building, Memphis, Tenn.

Jurisdiction—Counties.

Benton.	Fayette.	Henry.	Obion.
Carroll.	Gibson.	Lake.	Perry.
Chester.	Hardeman.	Lauderdale.	Shelby.
Crockett.	Hardin.	McNairy.	Tipton.
Decatur.	Haywood.	Madison.	Weakley.
Dyer.	Henderson.		

TEXAS.

NORTHERN DISTRICT.

Headquarters.—Fort Worth, Tex.

Jurisdiction—Counties.

Armstrong.	Eastland.	Kaufman.	Reagan.
Archer.	Ellis.	Kent.	Roberts.
Baylor.	Erath.	King.	Rockwall.
Borden.	Fisher.	Knox.	Runnels.
Briscoe.	Floyd.	Lamb.	Schleicher.
Brown.	Foard.	Lipscomb.	Scurry.
Callahan.	Garza.	Lubbock.	Schackelford.
Carson.	Glasscock.	Lynn.	Sherman.
Castro.	Gray.	Menard.	Stephens.
Childress.	Hale.	Mills.	Sterling.
Clay.	Hall.	Mitchell.	Stonewall.
Coke.	Hansford.	Montague.	Sutton.
Coleman.	Hardeman.	Moore.	Swisher.
Collingsworth.	Hartley.	Motley.	Tarrant.
Comanche.	Haskell.	Navarro.	Taylor.
Concho.	Hemphill.	Nolan.	Terry.
Cottle.	Hood.	Ochiltree.	Throckmorton.
Crockett.	Howard.	Oldham.	Tom Green.
Crosby.	Hunt.	Palo Pinto.	Wheeler.
Dallam.	Hutchinson.	Parker.	Wichita.
Dallas.	Irion.	Parmer.	Wilbarger.
Dawson.	Jack.	Potter.	Wise.
Deaf Smith.	Johnson.	Randall.	Yoakum.
Dickens.	Jones.	Real.	Young.
Donley.			

SOUTHERN DISTRICT.
Headquarters.—Room 622, Binz Building, Houston, Tex.—

Jurisdiction—Counties.

Aransas.	Duval.	Kleberg.	San Jacinto.
Austin.	Fayette.	La Salle.	San Patricio.
Bee.	Fort Bend.	Lavaca.	Starr.
Brazos.	Galveston.	Live Oak.	Trinity.
Brazoria.	Goliad.	McMullen.	Vitoria.
Brooks.	Grimes.	Madison.	Walker.
Calhoun.	Harris.	Matagorda.	Webb.
Cameron.	Hidalgo.	Montgomery.	Wharton.
Chambers.	Jackson.	Nueces.	Willacy.
Colorado.	Jim Hogg.	Polk.	Zapata.
De Witt.	Jim Wells.	Refugio.	

EASTERN DISTRICT.
Headquarters.—Federal Building, Tyler, Tex.:

Jurisdiction—Counties.

Anderson.	Franklin.	Lamar.	Rusk.
Angelina.	Grayson.	Liberty.	Sabine.
Bowie.	Gregg.	Marion.	San Augustine.
Camp.	Hardin.	Morris.	Shelby.
Cass.	Harrison.	Nacogdoches.	Smith.
Cherokee.	Henderson.	Newton.	Titus.
Collin.	Hopkins.	Orange.	Tyler.
Cooke.	Houston.	Panola.	Upshur.
Delta.	Jasper.	Rains.	Van Zandt.
Denton.	Jefferson.	Red River.	Wood.
Fannin.			

WESTERN DISTRICT.
Headquarters.—Federal Building, Austin, Tex.—

Jurisdiction—Counties.

Andrews.	Edwards.	Kinney.	Presidio.
Atascosa.	El Paso.	Jeff Davis.	Reeves.
Bandera.	Falls.	Lampasas.	Robertson.
Bastrop.	Freestone.	Lee.	San Saba.
Bell.	Frio.	Leon.	Somervell.
Bexar.	Gaines.	Llano.	Terrell.
Blanco.	Gillespie.	Limestone.	Travis.
Bosque.	Gonzales.	McCulloch.	Upton.
Burleson.	Guadalupe.	McLennan.	Uvalde.
Brewster.	Hamilton.	Martin.	Valverde.
Burnett.	Hays.	Mason.	Ward.
Caldwell.	Hill.	Maverick.	Washington.
Comas.	Hudspeth.	Medina.	Williamson.
Coryell.	Karnes.	Midland.	Wilson.
Culberson.	Kendall.	Milam.	Winkler.
Dimmit.	Kerr.	Pecos.	Zavalla.
Ector.	Kimble.		

UTAH.

DISTRICT BOARD FOR THE STATE OF UTAH.
Headquarters.—Room 207, Federal Building, Salt Lake City, Utah.
Jurisdiction.—Entire State.

VERMONT.

DISTRICT BOARD FOR THE STATE OF VERMONT.
Headquarters.—Statehouse, Montpelier, Vt.
Jurisdiction.—Entire State.

VIRGINIA.

EASTERN DISTRICT.
  Headquarters.—Richmond, Va.

Jurisdiction—Counties.

Accomac.	Gloucester.	Lunenburg.	Prince George.
Alexandria.	Goochland.	Mathews.	Prince William.
Amelia.	Greenesville.	Mecklenburg.	Princess Anne.
Brunswick.	Hanover.	Middlesex.	Richmond.
Caroline.	Henrico.	Nansemond.	Southampton.
Charles City.	Isle of Wight.	New Kent.	Spotsylvania.
Chesterfield.	James City.	Norfolk.	Stafford.
Culpeper.	King and Queen.	Northampton.	Surry.
Dinwiddie.	King George.	Northumberland.	Sussex.
Elizabeth City.	King William.	Nottoway.	Warwick.
Essex.	Lancaster.	Orange.	Westmoreland.
Fairfax.	Loudoun.	Powhatan.	York.
Fauquier.	Louisa.	Prince Edward.	

WESTERN DISTRICT.
  Headquarters.—Roanoake, Va.

Jurisdiction—Counties.

Albemarle.	Charlotte.	Halifax.	Roanoke.
Alleghany.	Clarke.	Henry.	Rockbridge.
Amherst.	Craig.	Highland.	Rockingham.
Appomattox.	Cumberland.	Lee.	Russell.
Augusta.	Dickenson.	Madison.	Scott.
Bath.	Floyd.	Montgomery.	Shenandoah.
Bedford.	Fluvanna.	Nelson.	Smyth.
Bland.	Franklin.	Page.	Tazewell.
Botetourt.	Frederick.	Patrick.	Warren.
Buchanan.	Giles.	Pulaski.	Washington.
Buckingham.	Grayson.	Pittsylvania.	Wise.
Campbell.	Greene.	Rappahannock.	Wythe.
Carroll.			

WASHINGTON.

EASTERN DISTRICT, DIVISION No. 1.
  Headquarters.—Room 208, Federal Building, Spokane, Wash.

Jurisdiction—Counties.

Chelan.	Grant.	Okanogan.	Spokane.
Douglas.	Lincoln.	Pend Oreille.	Stevens.
Ferry.			

EASTERN DISTRICT, DIVISION No. 2.
  Headquarters.—Yakima, Wash.

Jurisdiction—Counties.

Adams.	Columbia.	Kittitas.	Walla Walla.
Asotin.	Franklin.	Klickitat.	Whitman.
Benton.	Garfield.	Yakima.	

WESTERN DISTRICT, DIVISION No. 1.
  Headquarters.—Room 118, Public Safety Building, Seattle, Wash.

Jurisdiction—Counties.

Clallam.	King.	San Juan.	Snohomish.
Island.	Kitsap.	Skagit.	Whatcom.
Jefferson.			

WESTERN DISTRICT, DIVISION No. 2.

Headquarters.—1607 National Realty Building, Tacoma, Wash.

Jurisdiction—Counties.

Clarke.	Lewis.	Pierce.	Thurston.
Cowlitz.	Mason.	Skamania.	Wahkiakum.
Grays Harbor.	Pacific.		

WEST VIRGINIA.

NORTHERN DISTRICT.

Headquarters.—Federal Building, Clarksburg, W. Va.

Jurisdiction—Counties.

Barbour.	Hancock.	Monongahelia.	Taylor.
Berkeley.	Hardy.	Morgan.	Tucker.
Brooke.	Harrison.	Ohio.	Tyler.
Calhoun.	Jefferson.	Pendleton.	Upshur.
Doddridge.	Lewis.	Pleasants.	Wetzel.
Gilmer.	Marion.	Preston.	Wirt.
Grant.	Marshall.	Randolph.	Wood.
Hampshire.	Mineral.	Ritchie.	

SOUTHERN DISTRICT.

Headquarters.—Federal Building, Charleston, W. Va.

Jurisdiction—Counties.

Braxton.	Jackson.	McDowell.	Raleigh.
Boone.	Kanawha.	Mingo.	Roane.
Clay.	Lincoln.	Monroe.	Summers.
Cabell.	Logan.	Nicholas.	Wayne.
Fayette.	Mason.	Pocahontas.	Webster.
Greenbrier.	Mercer.	Putnam.	Wyoming.

WISCONSIN.

WESTERN DISTRICT, DIVISION No. 1.

Headquarters.—State Capitol, Madison, Wis.

Jurisdiction—Counties.

Adams.	Green.	La Crosse.	Rock.
Buffalo.	Iowa.	Lafayette.	Sauk.
Columbia.	Jackson.	Monroe.	Trempealeau.
Crawford.	Jefferson.	Portage.	Vernon.
Dane.	Juneau.	Richland.	Wood.
Grant.			

WESTERN DISTRICT, DIVISION No. 2.

Headquarters.—United States Government Building, Eau Claire, Wis.

Jurisdiction—Counties.

Ashland.	Douglas.	Oneida.	St. Croix.
Barron.	Dunn.	Pepin.	Sawyer.
Bayfield.	Eau Claire.	Pierce.	Taylor.
Burnett.	Iron.	Polk.	Vilas.
Chippewa.	Lincoln.	Price.	Washburn.
Clark.	Marathon.	Rusk.	

EASTERN DISTRICT, DIVISION No. 1.

Headquarters.—United States Government Building, Milwaukee, Wis.
Jurisdiction.—County of Milwaukee.

368 APPENDIXES.

EASTERN DISTRICT, DIVISION No. 2.
Headquarters.—County Courthouse, Racine, Wis.

Jurisdiction—Counties.

Dodge.	Kenosha.	Racine.	Washington.
Fond du Lac.	Marquette.	Sheboygan.	Waukesha.
Green Lake.	Ozaukee.	Walworth.	

EASTERN DISTRICT, DIVISION No. 3.
Headquarters.—City Hall, Oshkosh, Wis.

Jurisdiction—Counties.

Brown.	Forest.	Marinette.	Waupaca.
Calumet.	Kewaunee.	Oconto.	Waushara.
Door.	Langlade.	Outagamie.	Winnebago.
Florence.	Manitowoc.	Shawano.	

WYOMING.

DISTRICT BOARD FOR STATE OF WYOMING.
Headquarters.—State Capitol, Cheyenne, Wyo.
Jurisdiction.—Entire State.

ALASKA.

DIVISION No. 1.
Headquarters.—Juneau, Alaska.

Jurisdiction—Local Boards.

Douglas.	Juneau.	Petersburg.	Sitka.
Haines.	Ketchikan.	Skagway.	Wrangell.

DIVISION No. 2.
Headquarters.—Nome, Alaska.

Jurisdiction—Local Boards.

Nome.	St. Michael.

DIVISION No. 3.
Headquarters.—Valdez, Alaska.

Jurisdiction—Local Boards.

Anchorage.	McCarthy.	Valdez.
Cordova.	Seward.	

DIVISION No. 4.
Headquarters.—Fairbanks, Alaska.

Jurisdiction—Local Boards.

Chena.	Fairbanks.	Nenana.	Tanana.
Eagle.	Iditarod.	Ruby.	

HAWAII.

The District Board of Hawaii has jurisdiction over the territory of Hawaii.
Headquarters.—Executive Building, Honolulu, Hawaii.

PORTO RICO.

The District Board of Porto Rico has jurisdiction over the territory of Porto Rico.
Headquarters.—Allen No. 86, San Juan, P. R.

APPENDIX J.

A SUMMARY OF THE CIVIL WAR DRAFT.[1]

1. PRE-CONSCRIPTION ACTIVITIES.

When the forces of the Confederacy fired on Fort Sumter, the total strength of the Union Army was 16,402 officers and men. On April 15, 1861, President Lincoln, under authority of the act of March 3, 1803, issued a call for 75,000 militia to serve for a period of three months. This number was promptly forthcoming, but before they could be properly organized their enlistment terms began to expire. The disastrous engagement at Bull Run constituted their only service of military importance.

On May 3, 1861, the President issued a second call for 39 regiments of volunteer infantry and 1 regiment of volunteer cavalry, totaling 42,034 men, for three years' service. At the same time a call was made for 22,714 volunteers to recruit 8 additional Regular regiments and for 18,000 seamen. No quotas were assigned to the loyal States, but more than the required number were quickly offered. Few men were obtained for the Regular Army regiments, but 71 volunteer regiments of infantry, 1 volunteer battery of heavy artillery, and 10 volunteer batteries of light artillery were secured. The behavior of these then untrained units at the first battle of Bull Run is notorious.

Following the initial reverses of the Union forces in the spring of 1861, on July 22 and 25, 1861, Congress, in several acts, authorized the President to accept not more than 1,000,000 volunteers for terms of enlistment not less than six months nor more than 3 years. To the call for 500,000 men made pursuant to this authority there was a ready and eager response. Regiments and individual companies were organized and accepted through the States, although in many instances acceptance of units by the Federal Government was made without reference to the State authorities.

By virtue of the foregoing acts and the calls detailed above, 807,557 men were secured for the service. However, a large number of these men had enlisted for short terms only, and included 18,000 seamen. As a result, in the spring of 1862 there were in the field 637,126 men, which was deemed a sufficient number for the expeditious subjugation of the southern forces. Therefore, on April 3, 1862, by general order, volunteer recruiting was discontinued. But the unfavorable events of the next two months, which included the disastrous peninsular campaign, depleted the armies in the field and necessitated a revival of the recruiting services. On June 5, 1862, the order of April 3 was rescinded, and active recruiting was again commenced. But the unfavorable outcome of military operations in the interval of two months exercised a most discouraging effect upon prospective recruits and impeded seriously the progress of recruiting.

Up to this time, calls had been made upon the loyal States at large, and no effort had been made to distribute equally the burden of contribution. As a result, the initial strength of the Union armies was made up of contributions by the several States with no equalizing results and with the further effect that some States contributed much more than their just share and other States exceedingly less. Since it had become apparent in June, 1862, that the progress of volunteering had reached a stage where ready response to calls was no longer to be had, it became necessary to issue calls with a view to equalizing the contributions of the several States. Hence, on July 2, 1862, the President called for an additional 300,000 men and made his demands upon the States to furnish quotas in proportion to their respective populations. Population was employed as the basis of contribution at this time for the reason that the act of July 22, 1861, which authorized the enlistment of 1,000,000 volunteers, provided that they be furnished by the several States in proportion to population. This was the only guide to be had at the time, and the call of July 2, 1862, was, therefore, made upon a population basis.

---

[1] Based on the "Final Report by the Provost Marshal General of the Operations of the Bureau of the Provost Marshal General of the United States," from Mar. 17, 1863, to Mar. 17, 1866. (Washington, 1866.)

2. Draft of the State Militia.

On August 4, 1862, it became apparent that the call of July 2 would not be filled, and that if a portion of the number called was furnished it would be made up largely of new organizations rather than of individual recruits for replacements in old units, to fill which the call had been made. The President, therefore, on August 4 directed a draft of 300,000 militia to serve for nine months, and ordered the governor of each State to fill his quota with volunteers, but if the quota of the State was not filled on or before August 15 by this method, to fill the deficiencies existing by a special draft from the militia forces. This was the first effort of the Federal Government to resort to compulsory methods in its efforts to secure troops.

On September 3, 1862, the draft under the call of August 4 was commenced. Of the 300,000 men called for, about 87,000 men were credited as having been drafted. Of this number, however, so many desertions and discharges for various reasons occurred that only a very small and negligible number ever joined the Army. This constituted the first and last effort of the Government to raise men by draft prior to the organization of the conscription system in the following spring.

It should be noted that while more than half a million volunteers were in the field in the spring of 1862 their enlistments had been accomplished, in a large measure, by the offer and pay of bounties. During this period the Federal Government paid a bounty of $100 to every volunteer who enlisted for a period of two years. After the enactment of the draft act as later detailed, bounties were materially increased by the Federal Government and a system of State and local bounties incorporated into the general scheme. The whole subject of bounties, however, will be more fully discussed hereinafter, and at this point nothing further need be said upon this point.

3. The Draft Act of March 3, 1863.

With the failure of the call of July 2, 1862, and the call and draft of August 4 and September 3, 1862, it was apparent that the volunteer system had collapsed and was incapable of furnishing further recruits even though the dire necessity of the Nation made the raising of large numbers of men immediately imperative. It should be remembered that the failure of the volunteer system occurred at the very time when the cause of the Confederacy was in the ascendency and when the military reverses of the Union had been of the most appalling and disastrous nature.

Since it had become apparent that the necessary number of troops could not be raised by volunteering, and since it was essential that the armies in the field be replenished immediately and that means for keeping them recruited to full strength be employed, the enrollment, or draft, act was passed by Congress on March 3, 1863.

Its purposes were threefold. First, to hold liable for military service all citizens' between the ages of 20 and 45 capable of bearing arms and not exempted therefrom by its provisions; second, to call out the national forces by draft; and, third, to arrest deserters and return them to their respective commands. On March 17, 1863, Col. J. B. Fry was appointed Provost Marshal General pursuant to the terms of said act, which imposed upon him the duty of raising troops by draft. However, on May 1 an order was issued giving to the Provost Marshal General the supervision of the entire volunteer recruiting service to be operated in connection with the draft organization.

At this point it may be well to examine briefly the salient features of the act of March 3. After declaring in section 1 that all males between the ages of 20 and 45, except as therein exempted, constituted the national forces and became liable to perform military duty in the service of the United States when called out by the President for that purpose, the act provided for exemption to seven classes of persons upon the grounds of dependency and employment in official capacities.

Section 3 provided as follows:

"That the national forces of the United States not now in the military service, enrolled under this act, shall be divided into two classes, the first of which shall comprise all persons subject to military duty between the ages of 20 and 35 and all unmarried persons subject to military duty above the age of 35 and under the age of 45; the second class shall comprise all other persons subject to do military duty, and they shall not, in any district, be called into the service of the United States until those of the first class shall have been called."

It therefore appears that registrants under the act of March 3, 1863, were divided into two classes, and that members of the second class could not be called for service in any district until the first class in that district had been exhausted. This provision was later rescinded by the amendment of February 24, 1864, which made members of both classes equally liable for service.

Section 12 of the act provided as follows:

"That whenever it may be necessary to call out the national forces for military service, the President is hereby authorized to assign to each district the number of men to be furnished by said district; and thereupon the enrolling board shall, under the direction of the President, make a draft of the required number, and 50 per cent in addition, and shall make an exact and complete roll of the names of the persons so drawn and of the order in which they are drawn, so that the first drawn may stand first upon the said roll and the second may stand second, and so on. And the persons so drawn shall be notified of the same within 10 days thereafter by written or printed notice to be served personally or by leaving a copy at the last place of residence requiring them to appear at a designated rendezvous to report for duty. In assigning to districts the number of men to be furnished therefrom the President shall take into consideration the number of volunteers and militia furnished by the several States in which such districts are situated and the period of their service since the commencement of the present rebellion, and shall so make said assignment as to equalize the numbers among the districts of the said States, considering and allowing for the numbers already furnished as aforesaid and the time of their service."

It has been noted that all calls prior to August, 1862, had been made upon the Nation as a whole, and that no effort had been made to equalize the number furnished by each State. The act of March 3, therefore, provided that in alloting quotas under calls made pursuant thereto, the whole progress of the volunteer system should be reviewed and subsequent quotas assigned with an eye to the equalization of all contributions from the commencement of hostilities in April, 1861. In other words, draft calls were to take into consideration all volunteers and militia furnished by the several States since the commencement of the war. The situation was further complicated by the provision quoted above that in making the equalization among the States the President was to make allowances not only for the number of men already furnished, but also for the time of their respective services. It will be noted that volunteers had been called for and furnished for terms of enlistment varying from three months to three years, and the act made it mandatory that the equalization be accomplished only after taking into consideration wide discrepancies in enlistment periods. The act of March 3 made no provision for allowing credits for naval enlistments, but credit for such enlistments was later authorized by the amendment of February 24, 1864.

Section 13 of said act provided as follows:

"That any person drafted and notified to appear as aforesaid may on or before the day fixed for his appearance, furnish an acceptable substitute to take his place in the draft; or he may pay to such person as the Secretary of War shall authorize to receive it, such sum, not exceeding $300, as the Secretary of War may determine for the procuration of such substitute, which sum shall be fixed at a uniform rate by a general order made at the time of ordering a draft of any State or Territory, and thereupon such persons so furnishing a substitute, or paying money, shall be discharged from further liability from that draft."

It will be noted that section 13 prescribed three options, any one of which might be exercised by the registrant called for service, i. e., (1) he might appear and, having been accepted, contribute his personal services to the Army; (2) having been accepted he might procure a substitute to serve in his place and thereby escape personal service otherwise made requisite; or, (3) he might pay a sum of money not to exceed $300 ($300 was fixed as the sum to be paid for commutation) and thereby be discharged from any further liability to the draft under which he had been called.

Construing the sections quoted together, the general scheme employed in the allocation and filling of quotas by the several States was as follows: The number of men required under the call was distributed among the several States in proportion to the population of the States. This rule was later changed so that the distribution of quotas was made upon the basis of men enrolled; that is, upon the basis of those within the States who were liable for military service. The adoption of the latter plan followed bitter complaint on the part of certain localities whose enrollment was proportionately greater in respect of population than the enrollment of other jurisdictions. After much discussion the equitable rule was stated by the Provost Marshal General to be:

"That the number of men to be taken at any one time from a community, whether they go voluntarily or be drafted, shall be in proportion to the number of men liable to military duty in that community and not to the number of its residents, including men, women, and children."

After quotas had been assigned to the several States they were then allocated by the draft executives within the States to the various subdivisions thereof. Quotas were first credited with the number of prior voluntary enlistments. After quotas had been announced they were required to be filled on or before a certain day by volunteers. If the full number of volunteers had not come forward on or before the day set, then a draft was held for the purpose of securing the deficit.

It is evident that the basic principle employed in the execution of the draft was to secure the filling of allotments by volunteering and to resort to conscription only in the event a quota could not be otherwise filled. Conscription was used as a spur to voluntary enlistment. Local communities immediately upon the announcement of a quota began the most vigorous efforts to fill their allotments with volunteers and to escape what was conceived to be the stigma of conscription. In order to fill their quotas by volunteers large sums of money were raised by the communities and offered as bounties in addition to the bounties paid by the Federal Government for volunteers. Bounties offered by the Federal Government varied from $100 to $400 according to the character and term of enlistment. Bounties offered by the States and subdivisions varied greatly and in some States exceeded $500 per man. It is apparent, therefore, that a man enrolled and liable for draft, upon the announcement of a call, had several options, any one of which he might elect to take. First, he might offer himself as a volunteer and thus escape threat of conscription and in addition secure the Federal, State, and local bounties offered for those volunteering. Second, he might refuse the opportunity to volunteer and await the result of conscription. If drawn as a selected man and accepted for service, he might either furnish a substitute or might by the payment of $300 avoid entirely his military obligations. Failing to exercise any of the foregoing options, he would be held for personal service.

It is apparent therefore that the man liable to military service had the choice either of volunteering and receiving a bounty or of being conscripted and receiving nothing. Naturally by far the largest portion of men raised under the operation of the act of March 3, 1863, consisted of volunteers, so called.

On May 25, 1863, the enrollment of all men between the ages of 20 and 45 was begun and was completed as rapidly as possible in the several States. However, since the enrollment progressed at varying rates of speed in the different jurisdictions, it was impossible on July 2 to determine the number of men who would be finally enrolled. Therefore, on that day a call was made by the President upon the States to furnish 20 per cent of the enrollment completed on that date.

4. THE CALL OF JULY 2, 1863.

No quotas were allotted to the States under this call; neither were credits contemplated under the call, since it was not for a definite number of men, but was merely for a drawing of 20 per cent of the enrollment. Credits and adjustments under this call were subsequently accounted for under the draft of March 14, 1864.

Accordingly, on July 7, the first drawing was made and 292,441 names were taken from the wheel, from which number the States were to produce whatever number they could. The results of the drawing were as follows:

Number of names drawn		292, 441
Failed to report	39, 417	
Discharged	460	
		39, 877
Number examined		252, 564
Number exempted		164, 394
Number found liable for duty		88, 170
Paid commutation		52, 288
Remaining liable for service		35, 882
Found substitutes		26, 002
Held to personal service		9, 880

It will be noted that from the drawing of 292,441 names only 9,880 men were actually held for personal service. The number who furnished substitutes and paid commutation were treated as a credit under subsequent drafts and adjusted under the draft of March 14, 1864, together with the 9,880 men who had been held for personal service.

Fifty-two thousand two hundred and eighty-eight men secured exemption by the payment of $300 each. Under the act of March 3, the money thus collected was to be used in the procuration of substitutes, which was done under the call of October 17, 1863.

· The weakness of the law, disclosed by the first draft, was apparent, yet the Nation was awakened to the fact that the Government was at last committed to a determined effort to reinforce its armies by measures as stringent as were necessary to the securing of the requisite numbers. While the first draft thus produced but meager returns in men, it furnished the basis for stimulating volunteering, which had up to that time been practically at an end.

· Having applied the draft in the call of July, 1863, and having increased bounties materially, the Government on October 17, 1863, issued a call for 300,000 volunteers.

5. THE CALL OF OCTOBER 17, 1863.

It has been noted that the call of July, 1863, was a draft of 20 per cent of the enrollment and that no quotas were assigned in pursuance of its execution. However, the call of October, 1863, was a call for volunteers amounting to 300,000 men with the proviso that if the call was not filled on or before January 5, 1864, the deficiencies, if any, were to be supplied by conscription. Under this call was credited the number of men secured under the call of July, 1863; that is, those who had been held to personal service, those furnishing substitutes, and those paying commutation, amounting in all to 88,170. Under the draft of July, 1863, over $15,000,000 had been secured from the 52,288 men paying commutation. Under the law this sum was to be employed in the procuration of substitutes, and the men so secured were to be applied as a further credit under the call of October, 1863.

The anxiety of towns and cities to fill their quotas without conscription became great, and large sums of money were raised in all communities to induce the voluntary enlistment of men prior to the time set for drafting. Contrary to the system employed by the Federal Government, which contemplated the payment of only a portion of the bounty upon enlistment and the remainder upon discharge, the cities and towns in their anxiety to secure volunteers paid the entire bounty upon enlistment not only under this call but under subsequent calls. As a result, an unlimited field for fraud and collusion was opened up. The procuring of volunteers and substitutes became a regular business among certain elements, and it is reported that many men volunteered and collected bounties many times over, deserting upon receiving their bounty money and employing a portion of it to travel elsewhere for reenlistment. It is reported that one bounty jumper enlisted 32 times within a short period.

As a result of the increased bounty and the dread of conscription on the part of citizens, the call of October 17 had progressed so well on January 5, 1864, the date set for the draft, that the drawing was postponed and on February 1 an additional call for 200,000 men was ordered, making a total called under the calls of October 17, 1863, and February 1, 1864, of 500,000 men.

6. THE CALL OF FEBRUARY 1, 1864.

This call was treated as a combination of the draft of July, 1863, the call of October, 1863, and the call of February 1, 1864, and the total quotas were 500,000 men. Against this levy were credited the men raised under the draft of July, 1863, and under the call of October, 1863. On February 24, 1864, the act of March 3, 1863, was amended. In addition to the changes noted, it was further provided that quotas were to be credited by naval enlistments accomplished prior and subsequent to the call. The amendment also rescinded the provision of the original act permitting the payment of commutation in lieu of personal service. However, it continued in effect the privilege of hiring substitutes to perform personal military service required of the drafted man.

Before the draft was resorted to under this combination call of February an additional call was made on March 14, 1864.

7. THE CALL OF MARCH 14, 1864.

Under the authority of the amendment of February 24, 1864, which authorized the President to raise a number of men limited only by military necessity, the calls of October, 1863, and February 1, 1864, were increased by 200,000 men, making a total of 700,000 men to be raised. This increase was made in order to secure a sufficient number of men for the army after allowing for naval enlistments prescribed in the amendment of February 24 and in order to create a substantial and available reserve force. The call of March 14 directed that quotas amounting, as stated above, to 700,000 were to be filled on or before April 15, 1864, by volunteers, but unless quotas were filled on or before such date the deficiencies were to be raised by conscription.

In order to raise the largest possible number by volunteering without resort to the draft, bounties were raised and the increase authorized until April 1, 1864, after which date only bounties of $100 were to be paid by the Federal Government to one-year volunteers. On April 15 drafting was begun to fill deficiencies under these calls. The results of the calls which are treated collectively as a joint call for 700,000 men were as follows:

Number called for		700,000
Reduced by reduction in quotas after distribution among the States	45,274	
Reduced by credits on account of excess over all quotas previously assigned	[1] 162,901	
Reduced by number who paid commutation	[2] 84,733	
		292,908
Balance to be obtained		407,092
Volunteers (white)	325,366	
Volunteers (colored)	11,378	
Veteran volunteers	136,507	
Regulars	7,776	
Seamen	7,697	
Marines	738	
Total volunteer credits		489,462
Number held to personal service	13,296	
Number substitutes for drafted men	34,913	
Total drafted		48,209
Total secured		537,671
Number required		407,092
Excess		130,579

It will be noted that under these calls there was an excess of contribution amounting to 130,579, which was credited on the next call, made on July 18, 1864.

8. THE CALL OF JULY 18, 1864.

This call was for 500,000 men, to serve for terms varying from one to three years. The levy of 500,000 was to be reduced by authorized credits for naval enlistments and by the excess of 130,579 men under the preceding call. The results of this call, which was filled partly by volunteers and the deficiency by conscription, were as follows:

Number called		500,000
Reduced by excess on former calls	130,579	
Reduced by correction of enrollment	22,675	
Reduced by naval credits	64,882	
Reduced by veterans not before allowed	11,869	
Reduced by credits allowed by adjustment	35,290	
Paid commutation	378	
Total reductions		265,673
Number to be obtained		234,327
Volunteers (white)	146,392	
Volunteers (colored)	15,961	
Regulars	6,339	
Seamen	17,606	
Marine Corps	1,874	
		188,172

---

[1] Includes excess on all calls previously made since April, 1861.
[2] Includes call of July, 1863.

```
Number held to personal service.........................................:   26, 205
Number of substitutes for drafted men...........................     28, 502
Number of substitutes for enrolled men.........................     29, 584
                                                                   ————————
    Total drafted.............................................................     84, 291

    Total secured.............................................................   272, 463
Number required...............................................................   234, 327
                                                                   ————————
    Excess..........................................................................     38, 136
```

Conscientious objectors only were allowed to purchase commutation under amendment of February 24, 1864.

It will be noted that under this call there was an excess of 38,136 men.

9. THE CALL OF DECEMBER 19, 1864.

This call was for 300,000 men net. Since there was an excess, the excess was added to the number to be furnished, making a gross quota to be furnished by the Nation. From this gross quota, as distributed, was deducted the excess of credits under the previous call, and the remainder, amounting to 300,000, was required to be furnished by the several States as allotted. The results of this call, which, as in all previous calls, was credited with volunteers up to a certain date and thereafter filled by draft, were as follows:

```
Net number desired....................................................      300, 000
Volunteers (white)....................................................   130, 620
Volunteers (colored)..................................................    10, 055
Regulars..............................................................     6, 958
Seamen................................................................     9, 106
Marine Corps..........................................................       319
                                                                    ————————
    Total volunteers......................................................      157, 058
Number held to personal service...................................  ¹ 12, 566
Number substitutes for drafted men................................    12, 014
Number substitutes for enrolled men...............................    12, 997
                                                                    ————————
Number drafted..........................................................       37, 577

Number secured.........................................................      194, 635
Number desired........................................................      300, 000
                                                                    ————————
Deficiency............................................................... ² 105, 365
```

It will be noted that the only credits for volunteers allowed under this call against the net quota of the State were those volunteers who entered the service after the call had been announced. In other words, this call differed from preceding calls in that it did not reduce the number to be furnished by reason of excess enlistment credits created prior to the date of call.

10. RESULT OF THE SEVERAL DRAFT CALLS.

It appears that the aggregate calls from April 16, 1861, to April 14, 1865, were for 2,759,049 men; that the number placed in the Army, Navy, and Marine Corps was 2,690,401, leaving a deficiency of 68,648 when recruiting and drafting were ordered discontinued owing to the cessation of hostilities.

The entire operation of the Civil War draft may be accurately and concisely shown by the following four tables:

TABLE I.—*Source of armed forces.*

```
1. Number of men secured for the fighting forces April, 1861–April, 1865..   2, 690, 401
2. Number who entered the service by volunteering prior to March 3,
     1863...........................................................  ³ 1, 358, 470

3. Number claimed as furnished by Provost Marshal General (subtract line
     2 from line 1)..................................................    1, 331, 931
```

---

¹ 1,404 of this number were not sent to the service on account of the termination of hostilities.
² No effort was made to fill this deficiency due to cessation of hostilities.
³ Many of this number were short-term who reenlisted one or more times and are therefore included more than once in this number.

4. Number secured as volunteers March 17, 1863–April, 1865 [1] 1,076,558

5. Number drafted (subtract line 4 from line 3)........................ 255,373
6. Number paid commutation.. [1] 86,724

7. Number whose personal services were demanded (subtract line 6 from line 5)... 168,649
8. Furnished substitutes... 117,986

9. Remainder, being number whose personal services were actually conscripted... [2] 50,663

TABLE II.—*Distribution of "volunteers" after passage of the conscription act, March 3, 1863, as shown in line 4 of Table I.*

Call of October, 1863, and February and March, 1864...................... 489,462
Call of July 18, 1864.. 188,172
Call of December 19, 1864.. 157,058

Actual number of volunteers.. 834,692
Credits for naval enlistments and excesses on quotas under calls prior to March 3, 1863.. 241,866

Total credits for volunteers under act of March 3, 1863.............. 1,076,558

[1] None of this number ever served, but commuters were counted as credits in furnishing quotas.
[2] Of this number only 46,347 men were actually delivered to the Army.

TABLE III.—*Disposition of men "drafted," as shown in line 5 of Table I.*

Call of—	Number held to personal service.	Furnished substitutes.	Total number furnishing personal service.	Paid commutation.
July, 1863..	9,880	26,002	35,882	52,288
October, 1863; February and March, 1864.................	3,416	8,887	12,303	32,678
July, 1864..	26,205	[1] 58,086	84,291	1,298
December, 1864...	[2] 11,162	[1] 25,011	36,173	460
Total..	[3] 50,663	117,986	168,649	86,724

[1] Includes substitutes for enrolled men as well as substitutes for drafted men.
[2] Of this number only 6,845 were delivered, due to termination of hostilities.
[3] Of this number only 46,347 were actually delivered to the Army for duty.

TABLE IV.—*Results of the several drafts which secured men appearing in Table III.*

Call.	Number drawn.	Failed to report.	Discharged, quota full.	Discharged per order.	Exempted.	Held to personal service.	Furnished substitutes.	Paid commutation.
July, 1863............	292,441	39,415	447	13	164,395	9,881	26,002	52,288
March, 1864...........	113,446	27,193	1,227	69	39,952	3,416	[1] 8,911	32,678
July, 1864............	231,918	66,159	26,416	807	82,531	26,205	28,502	1,298
December, 1864.......	139,024	28,477	18,011	46,408	28,631	6,845	10,192	460
Total............	776,829	161,244	46,101	47,297	315,509	46,347	[2] 73,607	86,724

[1] This figure, taken from Provost Marshal General's report is 27 greater than the corresponding item appearing elsewhere in the report.
[2] In addition to these men who were furnished as substitutes for drafted men, 44,379 men were furnished as substitutes for enrolled men.

11. Summary of Results.

It appears, therefore, that the total forces raised by the Union during the Civil War were 2,690,401, and that of this number 1,358,470 entered the service as volunteers prior to March 3, 1863, and that 1,076,558 entered as volunteers after that date. In other words, the total fighting forces included 2,435,028 volunteers. The remainder, 255,373 men, can be properly credited as conscripted. Of this last number 86,724 avoided military service by payment of commutation, leaving 168,649 actually drafted. Of this number, however, 117,986 were substitutes for drafted men or enrolled men, leaving a balance of 50,653 whose personal service in the military establishment was conscripted. But of this number, only 46,347 men actually entered the ranks of the Army. Therefore, it is apparent that while the total effectives were 2,690,401, conscription secured directly the personal service of only 46,347 men or less than 2 per cent of the total fighting forces.

12. Bounties.

Any discussion of the draft act of 1863 would be incomplete without a reference to the enormous cost entailed in the effort to secure volunteers by the payment of bounties. Casual reference to this subject has been made in the preceding pages but it is now proposed to deal with it more fully.

As has been seen, prior to March 3, 1863, the Government depended solely upon voluntary enlistment for the recruitment of its armies. It was soon found necessary to stimulate recruiting by offering to recruits inducements intended to compare favorably with the price of ordinary labor and at the same time to provide some support for the dependents of the volunteer. With this object in view bounties were allowed by the Federal Government from time to time as follows:

(1) From the commencement of the war to July 18, 1864, a bounty of $100 was allowed to all volunteers who served a period of two years or during the war, $25 of which was paid upon muster in and the remainder upon discharge.

(2) From June 25, 1863, to April 1, 1864, a bounty of $400 was paid to all veterans reenlisting for three years of the war, $25 being paid upon muster in and $75 at the expiration of three years' service, and the remainder distributed during the interval of service in $50 amounts.

(3) From October 24 to April 1, 1864, a bounty of $300 was paid to all recruits enlisting for three years in old organizations, $60 being paid upon muster in, $40 at the expiration of three years' service and the remainder distributed in sums of $40 during the interval of service.

(4) From December 24 to April 1, 1863, a bounty of $300 was paid to new recruits enlisting for three years in organizations already in service.

(5) From July 19, 1864, to the end of the war $100, $200, and $300 was paid to recruits enlisting for one, two or three years respectively. One-third of this bounty was paid on muster in, one third after the expiration of one-half the term of service and the remaining one-third upon discharge or expiration of the period of enlistment.

(6) On November 28, 1864, a special bounty of $300 from the draft and substitute funds was paid to men enlisting in the first Army Corps upon being mustered into the service. This bounty was in addition to the bounties already authorized. It will be noted that the Federal bounties were distributed over a period of enlistment and that a substantial portion thereof was paid only after the completion of the enlistment period.

On the other hand, while the Government distributed bounties over the whole period of enlistment, local authorities almost uniformly paid in advance. It should be remembered that the bounties paid by the local authorities were in addition to the sums paid by the Government and that the sums paid by the former were at least equal to and more often in excess of the sums offered and paid by the Federal Government. The payment of large sums was prompted by the nervous desire on the part of communities to fill their quotas completely before the arrival of the date for draft. Under the pressure of conscription, local authorities did not take into consideration the encouragement which large cash bounties offered to desertion. The only object in mind was the securing of recruits and the fact that the payment of large sums of money in advance offered easy means of escape from the locality in which a recruit had pledged his enlistment was entirely overlooked. In many districts exorbitant bounties were paid, while neighboring districts, unable to pay large sums, frequently lost men of their own districts who volunteered in other localities. The enormous profits which the system of local bounties yielded to those engaged in it soon produced a class of persons known as substitute brokers who sprang up in the various towns and cities and who finally monopolized the business of finding volun-

teers and substitutes.   The corrupt practice of many of those agents constituted one
of the most vicious outgrowths of the draft system.

Taken as a whole, the Federal Government expended in bounties, prior to the
enactment of the act of March 3, 1863, $90,586,900 and from October 17, 1863, to the
end of the war, expended $209,636,600 for the same purposes.   In other words, the
total expended by the United States during the period of the war for bounties alone
amounted to the enormous sum of $300,233,500.

In addition to this, the State and local bounties during the same period of time
amounted to $285,941,028.   It is thus seen that during the period of the Civil War
there was expended by the loyal States and the Federal Government for bounties
to secure the voluntary enlistment of recruits $586,164,528.

The total number of men raised during the period of the war was 2,690,401.   It
follows that the per capita cost for bounties alone was $217.87.

In his report (p. 2), Acting Provost Marshal General Fry states that the per capita
cost of recruitment under the act of March 3, 1863, was $9.84, exclusive of bounties.
However, when there is added to the per capita cost as estimated by the Provost
Marshal General, the per capita cost of $217.87 for bounty, the result does not argue
well for the methods of economy employed in recruiting under the volunteer-
conscription system then in operation.

It is interesting to note that during the Civil War period 2,690,401 men were secured,
with an expenditure in bounties alone of $586,164,528, and that during the first 14
months of actual operation under the present selective service law, 2,552,173 men
had been furnished the Army at a cost of approximately $20,175,000.

13. CONCLUSION.

A consideration of the foregoing discloses that conscription, as utilized in the Civil
War period, produced in personal service of draftees less than 2 per cent of the total
Union forces, and that primarily the draft act was mainly employed, in connection
with the expenditure of enormous sums of bounty money, to coerce so-called voluntary enlistments in the fighting forces.

APPENDIX K.

A STUDY OF CONSCRIPTION IN THE UNITED KINGDOM, 1914-1918.

I. The British Legislation on Conscription.

By CHALLEN. B. ELLIS, of the District of Columbia Bar.

The striking characteristic of British conscription, in contrast to the American, is that it was at first bound up with the idea that the war must be carried on by those who were willing to serve. The need for controlling and regulating entry into military service, so as to preserve the industries essential to maintaining the military establishment and to adjust the demands of the army to the demands of industry, was not apparent until the indiscriminate volunteering from all lines of business threatened disruption of the industrial structure. The recognition of the necessity for compelling all to serve, leaving to the State the selection of those who should be first used for the army, came even more slowly. Conscription, passed by Parliament nearly a year and a half after the war began, was brought about, not because considered wise or essential for its own sake, but because of its relation to voluntary enlistment; and the first conscription act, limited to single men of military age, was supported because it was merely the redemption of the pledge to married men given in the previous recruiting campaign, that if the single men did not enlist they would be compelled. So the extension of the military service act to all men of military age, married or single, was supported rather on the ground of fairness to those who had enlisted than on the ground that bringing to the service of the State all men capable of serving would be the wisest way to utilize the man-power resources of the country.

1. COMPOSITION OF THE ARMY IN AUGUST, 1914.

At the outbreak of the war the British Army consisted of some 700,000 men made up of the first line, composed of the regular army, the army reserve, and the special reserve; and the second line, composed of the territorial force. The professional soldiers making up the regular army were men enlisted for 12 years, part of the time with the colors and the remainder in the reserve. The period with the colors varied according to the arm of the service and was generally 7 years. The age limit for enlistment was from 18 to 25 and, in some cases, from 18 to 30, depending also upon the branch in which enlistment was made.

The army reserve consisted of trained regular soldiers who had returned to civil life after service in the army and who remained liable to be called out. It was composed of those volunteering to serve when called to complete units, those liable to be called only on general mobilization, and those who enlisted for a further 4 years after 12 years' service, and who were to be called only after the other reserves mentioned had been called.

The special reserve consisted of a fixed number of battalions constituting reserve battalions trained by the regular establishment, whose function was to act as a feeder to battalions in the field and to assist in the work of coast defense.

The territorial force was a body for home service only (although at the outbreak of the war practically all the force agreed to foreign service). Enlistment in the territorial force was for 4 years and the age limit was 17 to 35 years, inclusive.

As shown by the records, the British pre-war strength was 247,434 regulars, 214,834 in the army reserve and the special reserve, and 271,189 in the territorial force; or 733,457 in all.

In the navy there was at the outbreak of the war approximately 150,000 men.

2. VOLUNTARY ENLISTMENT, 1914-15.

In the first few days of the war there was an enthusiastic rush to the colors, much greater than the facilities for dealing with recruits could take care of. On August 6 Lord Kitchener was appointed secretary of state for war, and the next day he made his first call for 100,000 men. As set forth in the notice in the press, enlistment was asked for a period of three years or for the duration of the war, and the age limit was

379

stated to be between 19 and 30 years, with the provision that those having previous service in the army would be accepted up to the age of 42. Although not at first clearly indicated, it was later apparent that this additional force was not merely to increase the size of the regular army, but was to be a body in new formations called service battalions. Members of the territorial force were asked to transfer to the new army and for this purpose county associations were urged to cooperate in making a division of the territorial force into those who were able and willing to serve abroad and those who were precluded "on account of their affairs" from volunteering. Many of the territorials did join the new army, and by August 26, 69 whole battalions had volunteered for service abroad.

There was no adequate provision for taking care of the great number of men who enlisted. The war office, accustomed to dealing under the old system with about 30,000 recruits per year, was suddenly confronted with the task of taking care of many thousands per day, and the recruiting force was totally insufficient for the task. Civilian volunteers were called on to help, but even with their assistance the situation merely of enrolling the men with the formalities required under the army act could not be met, not to speak of the provisions for taking care of men in camps. There was no organization for distributing the food; there were no barracks, and not even sufficient tents to take care of the men.

On August 25 Lord Kitchener stated in the House of Lords that the first hundred thousand recruits had been practically secured. On August 28 Lord Kitchener called for another hundred thousand men. This time the age limit was raised, and enlistments were asked of those from 19 to 35 years and of all ex-soldiers up to 45 and of certain selected noncommissioned officers up to 50. Enlistment was required for the period of the war. Then began a more organized effort to stimulate recruiting. Mr. Asquith, in a communication to the lord mayor of London and others, proposed that meetings should be held throughout the United Kingdom for explaining the "justice of our cause" and "the duty of every man to do his part." There followed recruiting rallies in all parts of Great Britain and Ireland. A parliamentary committee took charge of this campaign and representatives of all opposing factions joined in supplying speakers and in the organized efforts to reach prospective recruits. Political organizations in every county, city, and village assisted in the campaign and the voters were canvassed very much as in a political campaign except that all parties united in the same appeal. A canvass by mail was conducted, and it was said that some 8,000,000 letters were sent out to men of military age. The work of speaking at rallies and individual canvassing was supplemented by advertising posters urging men to join the army, and the moving picture theaters were made use of to display advertisements.

In a little over a month after the beginning of the war (September 10), it was announced by the prime minister that over 438,000 men had joined the new army, exclusive of those who had enlisted in the territorial force, which had been recruiting up to its maximum strength and replacing men who had enlisted in the new army. But the time had not come when recruiting efforts could safely be relaxed. Although the new recruits could not be adequately taken care of, and the facilities for handling the men were being blocked, yet the prime minister stated, "We shall need more rather than less; let us get the men." He added, however, that thereafter the men who enlisted would not be required to go at once to the training fields but would be permitted to return to their homes until needed and sufficient accommodations could be found. But the authorities were still "blocked" with recruits and on September 11 the standard for enlistment was raised by requiring a height of 5 feet 6 inches. The moral effect of this doubtless was to suggest that more men were being received than were needed. At any rate toward the end of October recruiting had considerably fallen off. A general appeal was issued by the recruiting committee stating that the standard had again been lowered and that the age limit had been raised to 38 and, in the case of ex-soldiers, to 45. The efforts of the parliamentary committee were supplemented meanwhile by the action of municipalities and private individuals in raising local battalions, for which the municipalities and individuals assumed responsibility for clothing, eating, housing, and early training, to be afterwards reimbursed by the war office. This plan was sanctioned by Lord Kitchener and numerous units of this character were raised.

Various expedients were resorted to in the succeeding months to stimulate recruiting. In addition to an extensive advertising campaign with every conceivable form of poster there was a direct appeal, signed by Mr. Asquith and later by the parliamentary committee, sent to every householder in the country requesting a reply stating the number of members of the household who would be willing to enlist. It is said that by the middle of December some 4,400,000 of such appeals had been sent out and 2,500,000 replies had been received, of which 225,000 contained promises to enlist. About the middle of November the prime minister stated in the House of Commons that no less than 700,000 recruits had been received, not including those in the territorial force.   On March 1, 1915, the prime minister declared the Government had no reason to be dissatisfied with the progress of recruiting and in the latter part of April, Lord Derby, in a speech at Manchester, declared the Government might be satisfied for the moment, but the time would come soon when there would have to be additional and redoubled efforts.   On May 18 Lord Kitchener appealed for 300,000 more recruits, and the next day the age limit was raised to 40 years and the height standard reduced to 5 feet 2 inches.   Toward the end of June it was realized by the Government, as had been frequently urged before, that the best way to utilize the resources of the country was to take an inventory of the man power so as to ascertain what men were available.   This suggestion culminated in the introduction in Parliament of a bill for the registration of all males and females between the ages of 15 and 65.

Almost from the beginning of the recruiting campaigns, suggestions had been made that conscription ought to be introduced; but the war office announced from time to time during the progress of recruiting that the question of compulsion was not under consideration and conscription would not be necessary.   On August 25 Lord Kitchener stated in the House of Lords, "While other countries engaged in this war have, under a system of compulsory service, brought their full resources of men into the field, we, under our national system, have not done so.   I can not at this stage say what will be the limit of the forces required or what measures may eventually be necessary to supply and maintain them."   On August 26 the prime minister, in answer to a question in the House of Commons as to whether some measure of compulsory service should not be brought into force, answered in the negative.   In a manifesto issued September 3 by the parliamentary committee of the Trade Union Congress, it was stated: "In the event of the voluntary system of military service failing the country in its time of need, the demand for a national system of compulsory military service will not only be made with redoubled vigor, but may prove, too, so persistent and strong as to become irresistible."   On January 8 it was declared in the House of Lords by Lord Haldane that, while the Government saw no reason to anticipate the breakdown of the voluntary system, "compulsory service was not foreign to the constitution, and it might become necessary to resort to it."   On April 27 Lord Derby, in his speech before referred to, stated that in a short time there would be an appeal which none could resist, and that compulsory demand of the services of the country would be brought about.   On May 18 Lord Haldane said in the House of Lords, "Although we may think, under ordinary conditions in a time of peace, that the voluntary system is a system from which it will be most difficult for us to depart, yet we may find that we have to reconsider the situation in the light of the tremendous necessities of the nation.   We are not face to face with the problem at present, but I think that the time may come."   On the following day it was stated in the debates in Parliament that "the problem is here now" and that it was time "to take stock of what we have got in the way of men in this country and the manner in which they may be most usefully applied."

3. The Registration of August, 1915.

A national registration act was passed July 15, 1915.   It provided that "a register shall be formed of all persons, male and female, between the ages of 16 and 65 (not being members of His Majesty's naval force or of His Majesty's regular or territorial forces)."   It provided that the registrar general should be the central registration authority in England and the common council of the city of London and the councils of the metropolitan and municipal boroughs and of the urban and rural districts and the councils of the Scilly Islands should be local registration authorities for their respective areas; that each area should be a registration district; that the registrar general for Scotland should be the registrar general and the councils of counties and town councils of parliamentary burghs should be local registration authorities for their respective areas.   The act did not apply to Ireland, except as it was made to apply to certain small areas by order of the lord lieutenant.   It required that the local registration authorities should cause to be distributed to every household, forms prepared by the registrar general showing the name, residence, age, married state, dependents, occupation, employer, skill in other employment, and nationality, if not British, of every person of the ages mentioned, and should cause such forms to be collected and filed and registration certificates issued to the persons registering.   Under authority of regulations issued by the local government board and the secretary of Scotland, registration was begun as of August 15, 1915.   Enumerators were appointed in each registration district to distribute the cards about a week before August 15 and to collect the cards within a week or 10 days after August 15, and thereafter to check them and tabulate the result.   It is said that approximately

150,000 voluntary workers were engaged in this task. The forms received from the registrants were subsequently sorted and divided into groups according to occupations, and the men's groups divided also between the married and single. The men's occupations were divided into 46 groups and the women's occupations divided into 30 groups and a code number assigned to each group, which number was shown also on the registration certificates.

As to the military purpose of this national registration, Lord Kitchener said, on July 9, of the proposal to pass such an act: "When this registration is completed, we shall be able to know the men between the ages of 19 and 40 not required for munitions or other necessary industrial work, and therefore available, if physically fit, for the fighting line. Steps will then be taken to' approach, with a view to enlistment, all possible candidates for the army—unmarried men to be preferred to married men as far as may be."

Carrying out this idea, after the national registration was completed, the cards of all men between the ages of 19 and 41 (that is, those who had become 19 but had not attained 41 on August 15) were copied upon so-called "pink forms" for the use of the military authorities. Meanwhile, during the checking and tabulation of the registration, organized efforts were made· to decide upon the comparative needs of the army and of industry. Various committees were appointed to determine essential industries and the requirements of men in munition work, agriculture, and other occupations. Lists of trades were prepared in the order of their national importance and were classified as "reserved occupations." With these suggestions as to necessary industries and industrial requirements before them the registration authorities examined the list of men of military age for the purpose of making tentative allocations of the men necessary for industry and the men who were available for military service. The cards of those considered necessary for industry were marked or "starred." This was to indicate that such men were to be, at least for the present, exempt from recruitment. This process of starring was slow and tedious. Further, the number of reserved occupations and starred trades was changed from time to time and largely increased. Generally speaking, starring was brought about by the reservation of various trades as a whole, followed by the starring of all men engaged in such trades.

For the month or more during which registration and tabulation was proceeding there had been a decided lull in recruiting. When copies of the "pink forms" were ready to be turned over to the recruiting staffs there began a very intensive effort to induce all men of military age who were in the unstarred class to enlist. The parliamentary recruiting committee, by means of its organizations in every county, undertook to canvass systematically all the available men of military age who were now definitely known by the national registration and the process of starring. The advertising campaign began with renewed vigor. Recruiting marches, parades, and a series of meetings were held to call the attention of the men to the needs of the army. Enlistments, however, did not greatly increase and the results were disappointing. The total number of enlistments, however, since August 2, 1914, had probably been over 2,000,000. On September 30 the war office directed all recruiting officers to take whatever steps were considered most effective to induce unstarred men to join the army and to report the number of those who refused. Subsequently, upon the public announcement of this order, the drastic method of recruiting the unwilling was abandoned.

4. LORD DERBY'S AGE-GROUP ATTESTATION PLAN.

On October 5, 1915, Lord Derby was appointed director of recruiting. Shortly after his appointment he proposed an innovation in the method of securing enlistments for the army. His proposal was, in brief, that all men of military age should be divided into classes according to age and whether married or single—that is, unmarried men from 18 to 41 would be divided into 23 groups, and the married men from 18 to 41 into another 23 groups, a group for each age—and that all men were to be given an opportunity to "attest," that is, signify their willingness to serve if needed. It was understood that men so attesting would not be called up for service until the age group in which they were placed was called, and that the single men and unstarred men would be called before the married men. He also proposed that tribunals be appointed and set up in each registration district before whom any man about to be called up for service could appear and consideration would be given and determination reached as to his postponement to a later group if considered desirable. He explained that his system contemplated that recruiting should in the future be done by civilians instead of by the military authorities aided by civilians, and that in every registration district recruiting would be conducted by the parliamentary recruiting committee and the joint labor recruiting committee and their agents, and a direct appeal would be sent by mail to every unstarred man. In a letter to the press on November 3, Lord Derby said: "I hope by the present scheme not only to ascertain what is each man's right position, but to induce him voluntarily to take it. But before this can be done a man must actually enlist, not merely promise to do so. By enlisting men in groups, only to come up when called upon, and allowing them before actually joining to appeal to local tribunals to be put in later groups for reasons which can be specially urged, we shall· be able to allot proper places to all men in the 'unstarred' list. Then we must carefully examine the whole of the 'starred' list, and where we find a man wrongly placed in that list, or a man who, though rightly placed in it, can be spared from his industry, that man must be placed in the 'unstarred' list and dealt with accordingly. * * * There is no necessity under this scheme for a man when he enlists to join his regiment immediately. He can do so if he wishes; but if he prefers to be placed in such a group as his age and condition—i. e., married or single—entitled him to enter, and only come to the colors when his group is called up for service, he can request the recruiting officer to do this. He has this assurance: Groups will be called up strictly in their order, the younger unmarried men before the older men, and all unmarried men, except those who may be proved to be indispensable to their businesses, before any of the married men. The recruiting officer will inform the recruit of the number of his group, which is determined, as stated above, by age and whether married or single. Be it understood, however, that any man who has married since the date of registration will be placed in a group as if unmarried." No man was to be called up, however, until he attained the age of 19.

In short, under the Derby scheme the men of military age had the option either of joining the army at once for immediate training or service, or of attesting and being placed in the group appropriate to their age and condition (whether married or unmarried). In the latter case they would be "posted to the army reserve, section B," would receive pay for one day's "service" and would be immediately returned to their civilian occupations, to be called up, upon reasonable notice, when the group in which they belonged because of age and condition or in which they had been placed by action of the local tribunals was called. The men so attesting under the group system were in an anomalous position. Though theoretically in the reserve, their civilian status was in all respects preserved, they received no army pay, could apply to tribunals to be excused from being called up or postponed to later groups, and their actual military status did not begin until they were called up, had not been exempted or postponed, and the time to report arrived.

The plan did not apply to Ireland.

Canvassing under Lord Derby's scheme began October 23. The previous day an army order was issued publishing the royal warrant necessary before the plan could be carried out of having men enlisted in the army transferred to the reserve with their consent and without pay while theoretically in "service."

Canvassers had been appointed by local subcommittees of the parliamentary recruiting committee and the joint labor recruiting committee. The canvassing was carried out to a large extent by volunteer civilians, both men and women. Public halls, offices, and schools were used as district headquarters. The information on the "pink forms" was copied on blue and white cards—the blue cards for the use of the canvassers and the white, on which results were recorded, for filing. The canvassers were instructed to canvass for the regular army, the new army, the special reserve, or the territorials; to call personally upon each man listed on the card given them, to "put before him plainly and politely the need of the country," to record his reasons if he hesitated or refused and to report results daily at the district headquarters.

The rush of recruits came even before the plan could be put into full operation. Some uncertainty existed in the beginning, however, regarding the Government's intent as to the order in which the men would actually be called for service and whether the married men were to be really deferred, as suggested by Lord Derby. On November 2 the prime minister stated in Parliament that "the obligation of the married men to serve ought not to be enforced or held binding unless and until—I hope by voluntary effort, if it be needed in the last resort by other means, the unmarried men are dealt with." On November 12, in a formal announcement by Lord Derby, this was interpreted as a definite pledge of the Government that if single men (afterwards stated to mean the "vast majority") not indispensable to industry of national importance did not come forward to serve, compulsion would be used before the married men would be called upon to fulfill their engagement to serve. And it was added that whether the men attesting were indispensable for industry would be decided by local tribunals which were being set up.

The request for the appointment of the local tribunals referred to was made in a circular of the local government board about October 27. Such tribunals were to be appointed by town councils, metropolitan borough councils, and urban and rural district councils. On November 16 the composition of the tribunals was definitely decided on. The members were to be five in number, three chosen from the council and two from outside, one of whom should be a representative of labor. Subsequently regulations for procedure before these tribunals were issued and a central appeal tribunal to sit in London was decided upon and its members appointed.

At first, attesting was confined to the "unstarred" men on the national register, but later the "starred" men and those wearing badges showing they were in government work were asked to attest. As decided shortly after the campaign began, armlets bearing the royal crown were issued to all men who attested, but they were not at first generally worn.

Medical examination of all the men presenting themselves was not possible, and although examination was attempted and to some extent carried out, hundreds of thousands were attested without any examination at all.

When the group plan of recruiting began, it was announced that a time limit would be fixed for the campaign. This time was originally set for November 30, but was subsequently extended to December 12.

During the progress of recruiting under the Derby plan, enlistments directly in the army continued and some 215,400 men were taken for immediate training and service.

Lord Derby's complete report on the results of the group recruiting system was submitted December 20, 1915, but was not made public until several days later. It showed that the number of men of military age, 18-40, on the national register as of August 15 (exclusive of those already enlisted and those enlisting directly in the army between that date and October 23) was 5,011,441 (2,179,231 single, 2,832,210 married). Of these it was reported that 2,184,979 men (840,000 single and 1,344,979 married) had attested under the Derby plan up to the formal close of the campaign. This did not include 61,651 men whose attestations were received after the tabulation was made up. In addition, 428,853 men offered to attest but were rejected on physical examination. Inasmuch as only a part of the men attesting had been physically examined and such examination as was made was not considered final or complete, and as large numbers of the men taken were in "reserved occupations" or would likely be held "indispensable" to vital industries, the number reported did not represent the men really available for call to military service. Lord Derby estimated that out of the total, after making allowance for probable future rejections on physical grounds and exemptions on industrial grounds, about 831,062 men (343,386 single, 487,676 married) would be actually available to be called up.

On December 20 there was issued a proclamation calling up groups 2, 3, 4, and 5—that is, unmarried men between the ages of 19 and 23, inclusive. The men of 18 were to be postponed until they were older. The men called were required to report in batches, beginning January 20, 1916. Between the time of the call and the time to report the men were given the opportunity to present claims for postponement to later groups or for exemption from call. Regulations governing procedure for such claims had been prepared and sent out. Claims had to be presented on printed forms and before January 20. Men who were "starred" on the national register by reason of their occupation, men authorized to wear a government badge showing they were engaged on essential work and men engaged in any one of the "reserved occupations," lists of which had been published, were not to be called with their groups (unless it was decided in the future that their employment in civil life was no longer necessary), and such men could apply to the tribunals for certificates of temporary exemption. Such men remained in the age groups to which they belonged but were for the time exempt from call. Men could also apply for postponement to later groups upon grounds of domestic or business hardship, but postponement would be for not more than 10 groups.

The local tribunals which were to pass upon such claims had no legal sanction, but were unofficial committees appointed by local governmental bodies at the suggestion of the local government board. It was arranged with the military authorities, however, that the men whose claims for exemption or deferment were allowed would not be called for military service. As both "starred" and "unstarred" men had attested, these local tribunals were to be called upon to do over again, largely, the work that had been attempted at the time the national register was completed.

As shown by Lord Derby's report, of the 5,011,441 men of military age on the national register, 2,182,178 had neither attested, enlisted directly, or been rejected—1,029,231 of these, single men. Lord Derby said in his report: "I am very distinctly of the opinion that it will not be possible to hold married men to their attestation unless and until the services of the single men have been obtained by other means, the present system having failed to bring them to the colors."

5. THE CONSCRIPTION MEASURES.

.On December 27 and 28 the cabinet debated Lord Derby's report and the question of redeeming the pledge to married men. On January 4, 1916, the prime minister stated in the House of Commons that a measure which it was proposed to introduce, providing for compulsory enlistment of single men, could be "sincerely supported by those who either on principle, or * * * on grounds of expediency, are opposed to what is commonly called conscription." This bill, he said, was "confined to a specific purpose—the redemption of a promise publicly given by me in the House in the early days of Lord Derby's campaign." The bill referred to was introduced January 5, 1916, and was passed and received the royal assent January 27. It was provided to come into operation on such day as should be.fixed by royal proclamation. After its passage and before it became operative, the groups, under the Derby scheme, were reopened, and many additional men attested or enlisted directly. The new act became operative February 10—just about a year and a half after Great Britain's entrance into the war.

In this period of a year and a half before compulsory service became law there had been a tremendous increase of the military forces through voluntary enlistments. But though there had been various kinds of designations of men as free from the attentions of the recruiting officers, there had not been developed and put in practice any systematic plan for surveying the entire man-power of the nation and making the necessary allocations to the respective needs of the army and the vital industries.

. (a) The first act of 1916.—The first conscription law in Great Britain, known as the "military service act," was passed January 24, 1916, and became operative by royal proclamation February 10, 1916. It applied to single men between the ages of 18 and 41—that is, men who had attained 18 August 15, 1915, but had not attained 41 at the appointed date. The law made such men liable to military service by providing that they should be "deemed from the appointed date to have been duly enlisted in His Majesty's regular forces for general service or in the reserve and to have been forthwith transferred to the reserve." The appointed date was fixed on the twenty-first day after the act came into operation, which made it March 2, 1916.

It should, therefore, be remembered that the term "enlistment" was applied equally to those drafted under this act and to those already voluntarily entered. "Enlistment" signified merely the act of entering military service.

The law provided for exemptions by application to local tribunals, which were established for each registration district as defined in the national registration act of 1915. Exemptions were allowed on four grounds: (1) Expediency in national interest, of retention in present work, or other work desired, or continuation of education or training; (2) hardship, because of "business obligations" or "domestic position"; (3) physical disability; and (4) conscientious objection.

Exemption was allowed to be granted also by "any government department" to men or classes or bodies of men in the service of the department, or "employed or qualified for employment in any work certified by the department to be work of national importance." Certificates of exemption were provided to be given to the men. Such certificates were to provide for absolute, conditional, or temporary exemption, as the authority granting them might think best; and there were also to be certificates of exemption from combatant service only, for conscientious objectors. All certificates issued on the ground of exceptional financial or business obligations or domestic position or on the ground of continuance of education, were to be conditional or temporary only. No certificate should be conditioned on continuance in the employ of any specified employer or establishment. Provision was made for withdrawal of certificates on account of change of status, etc., and also for renewal of temporary certificates. •

Local tribunals were to be appointed by the registration authority of each district under the national registration act. Each local tribunal consisted of from 5 to 25 members.

Appeal tribunals were to be appointed by the king (for such areas as might be designated), to which appeals would lie from decisions of the local tribunals. A central tribunal for Great Britain, appointed by the king, was also provided for to which appeals would lie from the appeal tribunals. Appeals could be taken either by the individual aggrieved or by a government agent authorized by the army council. Regulations governing the constitution, functions, and procedure of the local tribunals, appeal tribunals, and the central tribunals were authorized to be made by order in council.

As a matter of practice both men who had attested under Lord Derby's scheme and men who were conscripted by virtue of the military service act were dealt with by these tribunals. The procedure relating to the former was governed by "instructions" to the tribunals and procedure relating to the latter by the "regulations" made by the local government board. The "instructions" were modifications of the former rules made for the old unofficial tribunals acting under the Derby scheme.

In strictness men who had attested under the Derby scheme were not within the provisions of the military service act (as being already in the reserve), and therefore were not authorized to make claims before the tribunals set up by the act. It was arranged, however, that applications of such men would be received and certificates granted to them were recognized as valid.

The instructions for cases of attested men and the regulations for those conscripted in the act, did not materially differ. The regulations (and the instructions) provided for the appointment of the local tribunals by the local registration authorities as required by the act. Applications for exemption were to be made to the local tribunals by mail or delivery at the office of the clerk; all applications were to be heard in public; except that under certain circumstances the public might be excluded. Disposition of applications upon papers submitted was the exception and not the rule; in ordinary cases oral hearings were to be conducted; a military representative had the right to appear as a party to every application; applications to any tribunal were confined to those persons within the jurisdiction of such tribunal, with certain exceptions in the case of employers within the jurisdiction having employees both within and without the jurisdiction. Notice of hearing was sent to the applicant and to the military representatives; the applicant had the right to be represented by counsel and cross-examination could be conducted by a representative of a government department interested; decision was to be communicated to the applicant and to the military representative immediately after the hearing; record of the decision was entered on the form of application and a register of applications and decisions kept. The hearing on appeal was very similar to the hearing before the local tribunal, and the appeal tribunal was authorized either to grant or refuse exemption direct or return the papers to the local tribunal for such action as was required. One of the important features was the withdrawal from the jurisdiction of the local tribunals of all cases of men employed in coal mines and men engaged in certain prescribed occupations otherwise dealt with. No general rules were laid down to govern the tribunals in determining what business was in the national interest, what employee of such business was necessary, or whether the continuation of education or training of any man was necessary in the national interest or what would be considered a hardship because of exceptional financial and business obligations or domestic position, except that in the last case it was suggested that the ground of hardship would apply to the case of a man who was the sole proprietor of a business upon which the support of his family mainly depended. Provisions were made for proceedings with reference to applications for withdrawal or variation of certificates of exemption, and somewhat the same procedure was followed in disposing of such cases.

The instructions and regulations were varied from time to time by circulars, orders, etc.

In the appointment of the local tribunals established by the act, there was a continuation largely of the former unofficial tribunals erected under Lord Derby's scheme. There were about 1,400 such bodies in Great Britain. Applications to the local tribunals were required to be made between the effective date of the law and the "appointed date," with power to allow later applications in exceptional cases.

Much dissatisfaction with the action of the tribunals in various instances was voiced in Parliament.

On April 25, 1916, the prime minister gave in Parliament the proposals of the government with reference to further plans for recruiting. He reviewed the expansion of the army from the beginning of the war, the various inquiries which had been conducted, and the number of men who could be safely spared from industry for military purposes, and the effect of calling out these numbers. It was shown that the results obtained to date had fallen short of the requirements; that this was not due to an overestimate of the number of men available, but to the length of time involved in settling individual cases. To meet the situation, the government proposed to continue the service of time expired men, to transfer men enlisted for territorial battalions to other units, to render exempted men liable for service immediately upon the expiration of the certificate of exemption, and to bring under the terms of the military service act all men who had attained military age as such age was attained. Further, the government proposed an immediate effort to obtain more men by voluntary enlistment from among the unattested married men, promising that, if at the end of four weeks 50,000 men had not been secured, the government would ask for compulsory powers. It was still not proposed to apply the military service act to Ireland.

(b) *The second Act of 1916.*—On May 2, 1916, the prime minister in proposing a second military service bill, stated:

"There is the immense advantage of getting rid of the piece-meal treatment to which so much objection was taken in all quarters of the house and of the temporary injustice and inequality which that mode of treatment is apt to engender."

The second military service act was passed May 16, 1916, and became a law May 25, 1916.

The new act provided that every male British subject resident in Great Britain who had attained the age of 18 years and had not attained the age of 41 years (except men resident temporarily for education, those already in service, ministers, men discharged from service, and men holding certificates of exemption) should be deemed after thirty days to be "enlisted in His Majesty's regular forces for general service with the colors or in the reserve for the period of the war and to have been transferred forthwith to the reserve." The act contained a provision that steps should be taken to prevent so far as possible sending men to serve abroad before they had attained the age of 19.

In addition the act extended the time of men in service, recalled to service time expired men under 41, required a review of medical certificates of those rejected since August 14, 1915, required a review of exemption certificates, required the transfer of the territorials into other corps or to the regulars without their consent and provided that the army council could transfer to the reserve any member of the regular forces or temporarily demobilize any member of the territorials in any case where the transfer or demobilization should appear expedient in the national interest.

(c) *The acts of 1917.*—The next military service act was the "review of exceptions" act, passed about a year later, April 5, 1917. That was an act "to enable the exemption from military service of men exempted on the ground of previous rejection or the previous relinquishment of or discharge from military or naval service or unsuitability for foreign service to be reviewed." The act provided that the army council might by written notice require any man who was a member of the territorial forces, as not suited for foreign service, a man discharged from service for ill health, or a man rejected on any grounds, either after attesting or after becoming subject to the military service acts; to present himself for reexamination. There were excepted from the act men engaged in agriculture, certified as necessary, and men discharged from the service because of wounds. The effect of the notice to appear for reexamination was to make the man to whom the notice was sent come within the operation of the previous military service acts, and procedure with reference to him then took place as though no previous action had been taken.

The next act was that relating to conventions with allied States, effective July 10, 1917. This act provided in brief that after order in council signifying that a convention had been made with the allied country imposing mutual liability to military service, subjects of the allied country with which convention had been made, should within 21 days after the convention be liable to service under the military service acts in the same manner as British subjects. There were certain modifications not necessary to be noted.

The next act of importance was the ministry of national service act, effective March 28, 1917. This provided that "for the purpose of making the best use of all persons, whether men or women, able to work in any industry, occupation, or service" there should be appointed a minister of national service with the title of director general of national service. He should have certain powers and duties theretofore conferred upon various Government departments.

The work of the ministry was divided among eight departments—recruiting, medical, registration, labor supply, trade exemptions, statistics, finance, and women's corps. For administrative purposes, the country was divided into 11 regions and each region into a number of areas. In each region, and, to some extent, in each area, the organization of the ministry was reproduced in miniature. For each administrative department there was created an advisory board of representative men in touch with professional and industrial organizations.

By order in council, as authorized by the act, certain powers theretofore exercised by the army council and the secretary of state were formally conferred upon the director general of national service, including powers with reference to recruiting, enlistment of aliens, certificates of exemption, etc.

In the war cabinet report for 1917 it is said of the establishment of the ministry of national service: "Henceforth a single agency will be responsible at once for providing the army with approved complement of fighting men for home and foreign service and at the same time for meeting—to the limits of what is possible—the essential demands of vital industries."

It is said in the same report that, up to the end of 1917, not far from 5,000,000 men, excluding those already serving in the navy and army at the outbreak of hostilities in August, 1914, had been raised in the United Kingdom for military service in the pending war. A further 2,797,000 were engaged in the latter part of 1917 on work in connection with the production of munitions and other war supplies. The number of enlistments in 1917 was 820,646.

(d) *The acts of 1918.*—The first military service act of 1918 was passed February 6. Its purpose was to secure greater equality and greater speed. It withdrew certain privileges which had attached to certificates of exemption, repealing the sections of the previous acts of 1916 authorizing renewal of certificates. The effect of this was to prevent a renewal of certificates on occupational grounds. It further authorized the director general of national service to withdraw, by order, certificates of exemption from military service, whether granted by a tribunal or by a Government department, where the certificate was granted or renewed on occupational grounds. The order of the director general of national service could either withdraw an individual certificate or withdraw certificates of any class or body of men and could, as to such class or body of men, specify particular ages as to which the withdrawal of certificates of exemption would apply. This still left to local tribunals the power to decide exemptions on grounds other than occupational.

The power of the director general was widely used, but statistics showing the extent to which certificates were withdrawn are not available. Two "de-certification orders" were issued by the director general of national service on April 9 and June 6, 1918, by which the policy of withdrawing men from industry by age blocks was applied to a large number of industries.

During the same period when the certificates of exemption were being withdrawn by age blocks, men were also being withdrawn from the army to be put into industry. For example, on February 14, 1918, it was announced in Parliament that arrangements had been made whereby men in the army, whose services could be utilized for ship-building purposes, could be transferred to the reserve and sent to shipyards, which could use them. Under this plan 20,000 men were to be released at the rate of 1,000 a week.

The second military service act of 1918 was passed April 18, 1918, after the opening of the German offensive of March. It conferred further and more drastic powers than any of the previous acts. The principal features were: (1) To raise the age limit to 51 years and to 56 years in the case of medical practitioners, with the power to raise to 56 in all cases by order in council; (2) to render men liable to be called immediately upon attaining military age instead of thirty days later as theretofore; (3) to authorize by royal proclamation declaring a national emergency to exist, the withdrawal of certificates of exemption held on any specified grounds; (4) to authorize by order in council the extension of the military service act to Ireland; and (5) to empower the local government board and the Scottish office (as to Scotland) to make the necessary variation in the constitution and procedure of local and appeal tribunals. The act further provided that any man holding a certificate of exemption which had been withdrawn or had expired should transmit the certificate to the local office of the ministry of national service. It further required that every person to whom a certificate of exemption should be granted after April 30 should be liable to attend such drill, and undergo such training, and perform such military duty as a member of the "voluntary forces" as might be prescribed by order in council. It also repealed the "review of exceptions act" of 1917. Subject to the military exigencies, it was proposed by the war office to assign the older men to the home defense infantry and garrison battalions, and to certain auxiliary services, at home and abroad. Several proclamations were issued under the act declaring a national emergency and withdrawing certain certificates of exemption held by men of certain ages.

6. SUMMARY OF RESULTS.

The results of the various methods resorted to in Great Britain to expand the armed forces of the nation for the requirements of the world war are best viewed by dividing the epoch into two periods. The first, extending from the beginning of the war to the institution of Lord Derby's scheme, may be considered the period of the voluntary system, carried out under the stimulus of extensive recruiting campaigns but without the certainty of conscription, and relying upon the traditional method of raising armies. During this time, comprising the first year and a quarter of the war, Great Britain added to her armed forces, by enlistments in the army and navy, 2,289,774 men. The second period, comprising the remainder of the war, was that during which compulsion, either as a pledge or as existing law, was the dominant factor in recruiting. While the first conscription act did not become a law until February, 1916, yet some form of compulsion had become a practical certainty during the early part of Lord Derby's scheme. Further, during the progress of that plan, the machinery of local and appeal tribunals, for selecting from those within military age the men deemed necessary for the army, and exempting those deemed necessary for industry, had been set up. During this second period, that is, from the last of October until November 11, 1918, the number of enlistments totaled 2,681,128.

Out of the total increment of 4,970,902 to the British army since the outbreak of hostilities, nearly half had been raised under the voluntary system and before the pressure of conscription had been effectively used.

II. THE INDUSTRIAL MAN-POWER SITUATION, 1917–18.

[From a memorandum by Sir A. C. GEDDES, minister of national service, June 17, 1918.]

On August 1, 1917, it was decided to transfer the functions of recruiting from the war office to a civil department of state which, under the war cabinet, should be generally responsible for the man-power policy of Great Britain. The exact status and the functions of the reorganized ministry of national service were settled on October 8, 1917.

In November, 1917, the director general of national service presented to the war cabinet a review of the man-power situation. This stated in detail the demands of the armed forces for recruits in 1918, amounting to no less than 1,250,000 men, and the labor reinforcement asked for by the principal war industries, and submitted recommendations as to legislative and administrative measures to meet these requirements so far as was possible. This report formed the subject of prolonged investigation by the war cabinet in the course of a series of meetings attended by representatives of the war office, the ministry of national service, and by the ministers representing other departments during such parts of the discussion as affected their interests.

In spite of difficulties with trade-unions, and of steady resistance during the winter months to recruiting on the part of certain sections of the community, much has been done. The following numbers of men have been raised as recruits month by month:

Year and month.	Army.	Navy.	Royal air force.[1]	Total.
1917.				
May	88,494	4,502	....	92,996
June	81,714	5,371	....	88,085
July	60,367	5,724	....	66,091
August	49,359	5,565	....	54,924
September	37,342	5,368	....	42,710
October	36,543	4,711	....	41,254
November	30,823	4,162	....	34,985
December	24,923	3,986	....	28,909
1918.				
January	35,150	2,021	....	37,171
February	33,722	10,074	....	43,796
March	30,197	7,832	....	38,029
April	78,298	5,296	4,647	88,241
May	84,019	7,443	9,228	100,690
June 1–13	32,340	2,531	5,591	40,462
Total	703,291	74,586	19,466	798,343

[1] The royal air force as a separate service dates from Apr. 1, 1918. The figures of the army and the navy prior to that date include the figures of the royal flying corps and the royal naval air service, respectively.

Simultaneously the home production of commodities formerly imported has been expanded. Timber, ore, and food production have each demanded large numbers of men. The output of new mercantile tonnage has been developed. The material equipment for the air service has been largely increased. The output of munitions of all sorts, of clothing and equipment for the armies and the allies, has not been permitted to decline.

By administrative action heavy quotas have been and are being levied from among the men engaged in vital industries. The nicety of the adjustments required to secure such levies without disorganizing the industries on which they are imposed is a matter requiring the most careful review of the whole position of an industry. To enable such reviews to be carried out the ministry of national service has constructed and maintains a register of all males of military age in civil life. Some of the administrative arrangements whereby the man-power requirements for these industries have been met and the numbers being withdrawn from them for military service are detailed in Appendix IV, under heading "Essential industries and special quotas."

New legislative powers have also been obtained by the passage of the first and second military service acts of 1918, and extended use is being made of the powers thereby conferred. (Appendix V.)

The position disclosed by the complete review of man-power which the director general of national service has been able to obtain makes it clear that if the flow of recruits to the forces is to be maintained without serious dislocation of the civil side of the national war effort, it is necessary that far greater control must be exercised over the choice by men in civil life of the place and the nature of their employment than has been attempted in the past. Steps have been taken to secure this. (Appendix VI.) Apart from such control over civilians it has been found necessary to employ a certain amount of military labor on civil work. The Canadian Forestry Corps is an example of this type of organization. Comparable British organizations exist in the docks and transport works, units with an aggregate strength of 17,000, and in the agricultural companies with an aggregate strength of 66,345.

In circumstances like these of to-day prophecy is idle, and even carefully considered forecasts are not infrequently falsified by the event. But, looking forward, it seems not unreasonable to hope that during 1918, as in 1917, Britain will be able, provided there is no overwhelming disaster, to produce sufficient recruits to prevent a decline in the aggregate personnel of the forces raised within her borders. How those recruits after they have been raised are apportioned between arms of the service is a matter with which the ministry of national service is not concerned.

    *   *   *   *   *   *

Appendix IV.—Essential Industries and Special Quotas.

The effort which Great Britain has made in recruiting has to a large extent exhausted the reservoir of the less essential industries, and the great bulk of the men, of what may be called the old military age, who are still in civil life, are to be found in the essential industries which contribute directly to the war effort of the country. The following levies have accordingly been authorized by the Government and are being raised from these industries at the present time:

(a) Admiralty and munitions work................................... 108,500
(b) Coal mines.. 75,000
(c) Railways and transport.. 18,000
(d) Agriculture... 35,500

(a) *Admiralty and munitions work* (108,500).—Shipbuilding, admiralty and munitions work together retain in civil life a larger number of young and fit men than any other group of essential industries. In the department of ship construction and repair it has been found necessary to protect all the skilled men employed. This has been done in view of the absolute necessity of safeguarding the food supply of the country and of providing the maximum of tonnage both for this purpose and for the transport of American troops. In March it was decided to release skilled men from the navy and army to reinforce the shipyards. The process of releasing the men has been continued as and when possible. Up to the present date upwards of 10,000 men have been returned to shipyard work. The bulk of the men to be withdrawn from this group must therefore be provided from munitions factories and every endeavor is made by careful administrative arrangements to secure that the necessary supplies shall not be affected by their removal.

The basis of the withdrawal of men from the munitions industries is one of occupation conditioned by age. In May, 1917, when the present system was inaugurated, a schedule of the various occupations was drawn up showing the ages in each occupation above which skilled men should not be taken for the forces. These ages were revised in February, 1918. From the unskilled men and the skilled men below the ages in the schedule the men who are fit for general service are chosen, whom the expert officials of the Admiralty and the Ministry of Munitions consider can best be spared. Even after such selection, the men called up have a right to appeal to special committees, known as the enlistment complaints committees, in addition to their ordinary tribunal rights. No right of exemption is conferred by the schedule; it is merely a safeguard against the depletion of occupations necessitating a certain degree of skill in the interests of production. From this it follows that no man can be retained upon work which can be performed by women or by males not fit for general service or over the military age. Similarly a man who is a bad timekeeper forfeits all right to protection. The demands for skilled men for the artificer corps are met for the most part from this type of recruit.

(b) *Coal* (75,000).—The release of men from the coal-mining industry is conditioned by the heavy liabilities of the country in respect of production. For its own purposes it has to provide for the coaling of the fleet and mercantile marine, for the supplies necessary for munition making and other industries, and for the domestic needs of the civil population. Among the allies Italy is almost entirely, and France to a great extent, dependent on the produce of British mines. The German occupation of the industrial districts of France has cut off a great part of the French home supply; and the difficulties of the position have recently been aggravated by the threat to the Pas de Calais coal fields, the loss of which would further seriously diminish the remaining French output. In addition to these vital requirements the British Government has in the allied interest undertaken obligations to supply coal to certain neutrals in return for material and political advantages.   For example, the Swedish Government, in consideration of the delivery of a certain quantity of coal, has agreed to place shipping at our disposal.

Production can not be maintained at a sufficient level to meet all these claims without severe economies and the strictest rationing of coal for both industrial and domestic requirements; and these are being carried to a point which will involve discomfort and even hardship to the civil population in the coming winter.   But in spite of all difficulties a further quota of 75,000 miners is being withdrawn, all of whom have already been called to the colors.

(c) *Railways and transport* (18,000).—Very large drafts have been made on the personnel of our railways system since the beginning of the war, both by way of general enlistment and in the shape of railway troops, for use in making and maintaining the gigantic system of communications necessary to our armies in France.   The strain on the home railways has also been exceedingly severe; and the demands on them for the transport of troops and munitions are not likely to diminish while the war lasts.   Severe restrictions have been placed on all ordinary traffic, both of passengers and goods.

The pressure on the docks owing to the submarine campaign and the consequent adoption of the convoy system has been equally great and at the same time irregular. To meet the difficulties experienced by a depleted staff in dealing with recurring periods of stress, specially constituted battalions of the Home Defense Forces are drawn upon for assistance in any locality when it is found impossible to provide sufficient emergency dock labor from civilian sources.

In the circumstances, the quota of 18,000 men is the utmost that can now be taken from these sources consistently with the efficiency of the transport services which are vital to the successful conduct of the war.

(d) *Agriculture* (35,500).—In the earlier phase of the war the recruitment of men engaged in agriculture followed a normal course; but the greatly increased production necessitated by the submarine campaign created a demand for such additional labor, and special measures had to be taken to preserve a large and permanent body of skilled workers on the land and in the auxiliary industries on which agriculture depends, and also to meet seasonal demands by temporary assistance.

These needs are met from various sources.   Men of low category, surplus to immediate army requirements, are formed into companies and distributed according to the needs of the county agricultural committees.   The nucleus of these companies consists of men with previous training on the land, the numbers being made up by men whom it is thought would benefit physically by occupation in the open air and by those whom it is hoped will readily acquire a certain degree of skill.   The maximum of elasticity is maintained in this form of permanent reinforcement.   The men are employed in every occupation of the agricultural industry, and not only are the benefits of organized parties obtained but men are employed singly where necessary.

There are now at work on the land over 250,000 women who have for the most part been engaged through the employment exchanges, the war agricultural committees, and the Women's Land Army.   The majority of the members of the Women's Land Army, whose strength is now over 12,000, have been specially trained, not only for the form of work which it is intended that they should take up, but also wherever possible in the locality in which they will be employed.   Considerable opposition to this form of labor was at first shown by farmers in some districts; but the experiment has been so successful that pressing applications are now being received for a very large number of recruits.

Prisoners of war have been extensively used for certain forms of agricultural work for which it was found difficult to obtain labor or which were of a more arduous nature than can be satisfactorily performed by women.   The use of prisoners has been found particularly successful in the cases of work requiring large organized bodies of men, both because labor is thereby economized and because the administration and guarding of workers of this kind is simplified when they can be concentrated in a relatively small area.   In all, about 12,000 prisoners of war have been actually placed on agricultutal work, and a further 8,000 have been allocated.   Those who have had previous experience of a particular form of employment have, if possible, been put to similar work.

A further military reenforcement is obtained by the release of individual soldiers from the colors in order, for the most part, that they may return to the occupations in which they were employed before the war.   Throughout the year, but particularly for the harvest, soldiers are also sent on agricultural furlough.   Very considerable assistance has been given to agriculture by the release of men from the troops of the dominions.   Men from these sources have not only been employed for prolonged periods, but times of emergency have been tided over by the loan of highly skilled farmer-soldiers used to undertaking work on the largest scale.

·The special seasonal calls of the·industry are met by volunteers of all sorts and by the holiday labor of schoolboys and students. Both for this seasonal work and for general assistance throughout the year the organization of part-time workers has been found to produce excellent results, particularly in the neighborhood of great centers of population, from which large groups of workers can be conveniently transported to work on the land.

The permanent nucleus of skilled labor and its distribution throughout the country have been carefully considered and regulated with a view to the release of the maximum number of young and fit men for the armed forces. · The control of agricultural exemptions by tribunals did not in practice work smoothly or uniformly, and there was some danger of a surplus of agricultural laborers being left in some districts while others were disproportionately depleted. When, therefore, the quota of 35,500 men to be released for military service in May and June had been agreed upon with the boards of agriculture in England and Scotland, a decertification order under the military service act, 1918 (see Appendix V), was made withdrawing all exemptioning of men engaged in agriculture and collateral industries and the retention in civil life of indispensable men is now controlled administratively by committees appointed by the board of agriculture in England and in Scotland by the Scottish office. These committees operate in each county to which a proportionate share of the total quota is assigned, and, subject to this share of the men required being secured, the committees are empowered to protect such men as are shown to be indispensable for work on the land which is necessary in the national interest.

(e) *The civil service.*—The increase in the civil service which has been found necessary in order to meet the enormous development of its work since the outbreak of war has been met by the increased employment of women. At the present time the number of men employed is less by 57,000 than in August, 1914. In spite of very numerous voluntary enlistments in the early stages of the war, and consequent depletion of the skilled staff, the civil service, by direction of the war cabinet, provided a further quota of 2,000 grades 1 and 2 men during 1917. It is not at present proposed to fix a further quota of men to be released from the civil service, but all exemptions held by men of the old military age are at present being reviewed by military service committees appointed by the minister of national service.

APPENDIX V.—THE MILITARY SERVICE ACTS OF 1918.

The object of the first military service act of 1918, which became law on **February 6,** was to equalize the incidence of recruiting, and to accelerate procedure. · It withdrew certain ·privileges which attached to certificates of exemption held by particular classes of men, and placed all men in the same position in respect of tribunal rights. It further conferred upon the minister of national service the power by decertification order to cancel certificates of exemption granted by tribunals on occupational grounds. This power, which has already been widely used, is of great value in standardizing the policy on which occupational exemptions can be granted in the national interest, while reserving to tribunals the power to use their special knowledge of local conditions in cases in which exemption is sought on personal grounds.

By two decertification orders issued on April 9 and June 6, the policy of taking men by age blocks according to occupations has been applied to a very wide range of industries, which, while not essentially and directly connected with the conduct of the war, are required even under war conditions for the maintenance of the fabric of the nation. The selection of the industries and the adjustment of the ages of the men affected by the orders has been a highly intricate and complicated task in which the ministry of national service has been in long and close consultation with the Government departments responsible for the interests of the industries affected and with representative associations of the industries themselves. Both in London and in the provinces the close cooperation of the chambers of commerce and trade is of the greatest assistance in the administration of the orders.

The military service (No. 2) act, 1918, was passed after the opening of the German offensive on March 21, when it became apparent that a rapid acceleration of the reinforcement of the armies in France would be necessary and that the further and more drastic powers foreshadowed in the debates on the previous act would immediately be required in order that measures might be taken to deal with the crisis.

Its principal provisions are (1) to render all·men liable to be called to the colors on attaining the age of 18 instead of 30 days later as heretofore, to raise the military age to 51, and in the case of medical practitioners to 56, with power to raise by order in council to 56 in all cases; (2) by royal proclamation to withdraw certificates of exemption held on any specified grounds; (3) to apply the provisions of the military service acts to·Ireland; (4) to empower the local government board and the Scottish office to make necessary variation in the constitution and procedure of tribunals.

Special consideration had previously been given by administrative concession to men discharged from the armed forces by reason of wounds or disability in respect to immunity from further service. Statutory force was given to this by definite provisions in the act, which under certain conditions excepted such men from its operation.

Two proclamations, dated respectively April 20 and June 4, have been made under the act, the effect of which is to make it impossible for any man in the higher medical categories between the ages of 18 and 23 to obtain a tribunal exemption except on very narrow personal grounds. By an instruction of the war cabinet the same principle has been extended to practically all men fit for general service of the same ages in the munitions industries, who are in possession of any form of administrative protection granted by a Government department.

Meanwhile the process of bringing the older men to the colors under the provisions of the act is already advanced. Men up to 51 have been summoned for medical examination, and the calling up of the earlier years of the new military age has already begun.

Special arrangements have been made for the medical examination of the older men to insure that the examination may be carried out with the greatest consideration and tact and that they may be fairly and scientifically graded, having regard to their age and relative fitness for service.

It has been decided that, subject to military exigencies, the corps to which the war office will post the older men are as follows: (a) Combatant service; home defence infantry and garrison battalions at home and abroad; royal field artillery and royal garrison artillery at home. (b) Auxiliary services at home and abroad, such as royal army medical corps, army service corps, e. g., motor and horse transport, remounts, supplies, etc., army ordnance corps, army veterinary corps, inland water transport and dock, railway troops, roads, and quarries.

Such men will also be posted to the air force for duty with the squadrons.

APPENDIX VI.—ECONOMY AND MOBILITY OF LABOR.

The need of the army for men and the measures which have been taken to meet it have created a shortage of skilled labor at a time when it is of paramount importance to maintain and even to increase the production of ships, munitions, and food, and to keep up the other essential national industries. The situation demands that the skilled labor which remains in the country should be available for diversion to those industries or firms whose needs are for the moment imperative. It is no longer possible to allow a skilled men to find himself employment where he pleases without any reference to the claims of his country; still less to allow an employer to keep in his works a man whose skill is not being fully utilized, or who is surplus to the minimum requirements of his business.

The government has therefore decided to take steps (a) to increase the supply of mobile labor by every possible means; and (b) to restrict the freedom of the employer to engage labor as and when he pleases.

With a view to securing the economic use of labor employed on essential work, instructions have been given to the responsible departments to make careful investigation into the labor conditions in munitions and other firms and that, when in the opinion of the investigating officers, men are surplus to requirements, or their skill is being inadequately used, they should be transferred where their services are required.

There are already in existence two main schemes for transferring workmen in this way. These are the war munition volunteer scheme. The former scheme applies to skilled men of certain trades and was started in 1916 by the ministry of munitions, both in order to create a mobile body of skilled labor, and also to form a reservoir which would be drawn upon when the need arose in any locality. The latter scheme provides for workmen not qualified to become war munition volunteers and was brought into operation by the ministry of national service in October, 1917. Under either scheme men receive subsistence and traveling allowances where necessary, and as compensation for removal, any loss of wages is, within certain limits, made up to them.

When, after inspection, it is decided that certain men are available for transfer elsewhere, such men, if not already enrolled, will be asked to enroll as war munition volunteers or war work volunteers, and so place their services at the disposal of the government for transfer, or alternatively, to satisfy the local enlistments complaints committee that such enrollment would in their particular case involve great personal hardship or that there are adequate reasons why they should not be transferred to a distance from their homes. In cases where a man who is of an age and grade which is being called up for the army refuses to enroll and fails to satisfy the enlistments complaints committee that he has no real ground for the refusal, the protection from recruiting, which he holds merely because he is indispensable to the work on which he is engaged, will be withdrawn.

It should be carefully noted that every possible protection is given under this scheme to the individual workmen against victimization. No man will be asked to move until (a) a responsible officer of the department concerned has decided that on technical grounds his skill would be better employed elsewhere; (b) a special enrollment officer has put the case clearly before him and appealed to him to enroll; (c) the enlistment complaints committee has had an opportunity of deciding on any contention the man may wish to put forward that he should not be required to enroll.

As regards employers, it is the intention of the government to use the powers they possess under the defense of the realm regulations to regulate and restrict the employment of any men or classes of men in any firm engaged upon war work. This will mean that instructions will be issued to firms forbidding them to engage labor without a license from the department of state by which they are controlled. In this way firms will be prevented from accumulating labor, and it will be possible to control the diversion of labor to the national purposes for which it is from time to time most required.

The government is not unaware of the difficulties it may encounter in carrying out this scheme or of the strain which it may necessarily impose both on employers and workmen. The exigencies of the situation, however, not only entitle but compel them to make a demand on the patriotism of the country which, after all, must be regarded as moderate, at a time when so large a proportion of the male population is being called up for service in the army.

NDIX TABLES
AND
CHARTS.

APPENDIX TABLE 1-A—*Total registration.*

	Total registration.	Registration of June 5, 1917.	Registration of June 5, and Aug. 24, 1918.	Registration of Sept. 12, 1918.
United States and Territories	24,234,021	9,925,751	912,564	13,395,706
Alabama	444,842	187,063	19,185	238,594
Arizona	94,310	38,308	2,209	53,793
Arkansas	365,904	152,216	16,086	197,602
California	839,614	310,123	22,470	507,021
Colorado	216,820	84,223	7,590	125,007
Connecticut	374,400	162,472	12,554	199,874
Delaware	55,277	22,322	2,241	30,714
District of Columbia	90,361	33,472	3,269	53,620
Florida	209,248	87,390	7,402	114,456
Georgia	549,235	238,184	22,112	288,939
Idaho	105,337	42,325	3,657	59,355
Illinois	1,574,877	653,587	54,375	866,915
Indiana	639,834	259,837	24,006	355,991
Iowa	524,456	219,297	21,637	283,522
Kansas	382,065	152,064	15,422	214,579
Kentucky	486,739	193,988	21,948	270,803
Louisiana	392,316	163,062	17,164	212,090
Maine	159,631	62,176	6,038	91,417
Maryland	313,489	124,068	12,484	176,937
Massachusetts	886,728	368,064	30,300	488,364
Michigan	873,383	380,752	30,844	461,787
Minnesota	541,607	227,600	22,337	291,670
Mississippi	344,724	143,030	14,577	187,117
Missouri	765,045	304,400	30,612	430,033
Montana	201,256	92,555	5,207	103,494
Nebraska	287,414	120,811	11,647	154,956
Nevada	30,808	12,319	725	17,764
New Hampshire	95,158	38,355	3,388	53,415
New Jersey	762,485	307,998	24,897	429,590
New Mexico	81,013	34,652	2,648	45,713
New York	2,511,046	1,034,599	85,733	1,390,714
North Carolina	482,463	208,430	20,414	253,619
North Dakota	160,292	67,238	6,103	86,951
Ohio	1,389,474	564,834	52,537	772,103
Oklahoma	435,668	173,744	19,492	242,432
Oregon	179,436	64,905	5,644	108,887
Pennsylvania	2,069,407	826,187	76,809	1,166,411
Rhode Island	134,515	54,254	4,805	75,456
South Carolina	307,350	131,643	13,058	162,649
South Dakota	145,706	60,121	6,068	79,517
Tennessee	474,347	191,726	21,701	260,920
Texas	990,522	418,160	42,166	530,196
Utah	103,052	43,214	3,687	56,151
Vermont	71,484	28,003	2,881	40,600
Virginia	465,439	187,711	18,479	259,249
Washington	328,466	116,113	9,595	202,758
West Virginia	325,266	127,994	14,180	183,092
Wisconsin	586,290	241,658	25,033	319,599
Wyoming	59,977	23,288	1,863	34,826
United States	23,908,576	9,780,535	899,279	13,228,762
Alaska	15,851	6,659	192	[1] 9,000
Hawaii	72,741	28,851	2,349	41,541
Porto Rico	236,853	109,706	10,744	116,403

[1] Telegram of Dec. 25, 1918, estimates this figure at 9,800.

APPENDIX TABLE 10-A—*Presidential appeals to Dec. 20, 1918.*

	Appeals received.	Appeals affirmed.	Appeals reversed.	Appeals modified.	Returned without action.
Total, United States	1,584	452	29	78	1,025
Alabama	96	29	2	3	62
Arizona	1	1			
Arkansas	20	5			15
California	23	2	2		19
Colorado	10	3			7
Connecticut	6	2		1	3
Delaware					
District of Columbia	2	2			
Florida	19	7			12
Georgia	97	25	4	6	62
Idaho	6				6
Illinois	46	5	1	1	39
Indiana	95	41		15	39
Iowa	24				24
Kansas	32	8			24
Kentucky	37	7	2	1	27
Louisiana	18	1			17
Maine	6	3			3
Maryland	27	3			24
Massachusetts	5	2			3
Michigan	11	3			8
Minnesota	24	5			19
Mississippi	23	4			19
Missouri	198	81	6	6	105
Montana	50	1			49
Nebraska	161	49		2	110
Nevada	2				2
New Hampshire	3				3
New Jersey	14	4			10
New Mexico					
New York	211	89	6	33	83
North Carolina	9	1			8
North Dakota	41	1	1		39
Ohio	47	20		2	25
Oklahoma	14	1			4
Oregon	8	3		1	13
Pennsylvania	31	5	2		24
Rhode Island	1				1
South Carolina	5	1			4
South Dakota	3			1	2
Tennessee	9	1			8
Texas	36	2			34
Utah	6	1	2		3
Vermont					
Virginia	49	22		1	26
Washington	7	2	1		4
West Virginia	21	7		3	11
Wisconsin	8	2		1	5
Wyoming	20				20
Alaska	1	1			
Hawaii	1			1	
Porto Rico					

APPENDIX TABLE 23–A.—*Registration of aliens and enemy aliens, by States.*

	Total regis-trants June 5, 1917, to Sept. 12, 1918.	Alien regis-trants June 5, 1917, to Sept. 11, 1918.	Alien regis-trants Sept. 12, 1918.	Total alien regis-trants	Per cent of aliens to total regis-tration.	German males (ages 18–45) reg-istered June 5, 1917, to Sept. 12, 1918.	Depart-ment of Justice registra-tions of German males (ages 14 upward).
United States..............	23,908,576	1,703,006	2,174,077	3,877,083	16.22	158,809	257,578
Alabama..................	444,842	1,558	2,812	4,370	.98	189	457
Arizona..................	94,310	15,283	22,326	37,609	39.87	357	459
Arkansas.................	365,904	652	1,583	2,235	.61	329	932
California................	839,614	86,954	144,326	231,280	27.55	7,735	12,205
Colorado.................	216,820	10,144	18,946	29,090	13.42	841	1,277
Connecticut..............	374,400	64,924	74,396	139,320	37.21	2,558	3,178
Delaware.................	55,277	3,892	4,283	8,175	14.79	184	256
District of Columbia......	90,361	1,590	3,515	5,105	5.65	108	89
Florida..................	209,248	4,543	8,061	12,604	6.02	326	648
Georgia..................	549,235	1,383	2,131	3,514	.64	177	355
Idaho...................	105,337	4,622	7,071	11,693	11.10	433	594
Illinois..................	1,574,877	143,299	174,740	318,039	20.19	14,801	20,811
Indiana..................	639,834	22,751	30,202	52,953	8.28	3,212	10,849
Iowa....................	524,456	16,847	18,278	35,125	6.70	4,450	5,964
Kansas..................	382,065	5,441	13,079	18,520	4.85	1,447	3,225
Kentucky................	483,739	1,256	2,713	3,969	.82	323	1,020
Louisiana................	392,316	2,829	7,113	9,942	2.53	437	1,021
Maine...................	159,631	9,413	15,072	24,485	15.34	148	324
Maryland................	313,489	9,546	13,921	23,467	7.49	1,963	3,334
Massachusetts............	886,728	139,766	152,521	292,287	32.96	2,799	3,836
Michigan................	873,383	106,830	104,275	211,105	24.17	10,675	16,875
Minnesota...............	541,007	40,260	46,225	86,485	15.97	4,887	7,859
Mississippi..............	344,724	572	1,180	1,752	.49	69	160
Missouri.................	765,045	11,719	22,367	34,086	4.46	3,044	5,890
Montana................	201,256	19,793	19,943	39,736	19.74	1,335	1,498
Nebraska................	287,414	8,897	13,923	22,820	7.94	3,500	7,167
Nevada..................	30,808	4,030	5,500	9,530	30.93	218	326
New Hampshire...........	95,158	10,896	12,429	23,325	24.51	183	238
New Jersey..............	762,485	80,932	126,772	207,704	27.24	11,936	16,226
New Mexico.............	81,013	4,364	7,288	11,652	14.38	141	253
New York...............	2,511,046	374,308	410,131	784,439	31.24	36,609	50,467
North Carolina...........	482,463	597	2,103	2,700	.56	47	139
North Dakota............	160,292	9,245	11,503	20,748	12.94	1,124	1,141
Ohio....................	1,389,474	113,000	139,964	252,964	18.21	7,446	9,259
Oklahoma...............	435,668	2,684	6,330	9,014	2.07	449	778
Oregon..................	179,436	11,048	17,337	28,385	15.82	1,133	2,227
Pennsylvania.............	2,069,407	215,070	280,167	495,237	23.93	10,713	14,620
Rhode Island............	134,515	20,037	21,580	41,617	30.94	429	412
South Carolina...........	307,350	654	2,704	3,358	1.09	92	221
South Dakota............	145,706	4,532	6,787	11,319	7.77	1,458	1,814
Tennessee...............	474,347	745	2,239	2,984	.63	141	385
Texas...................	990,522	35,437	52,431	87,868	8.87	2,799	6,290
Utah....................	103,052	7,502	10,627	18,129	17.59	527	725
Vermont................	71,484	2,472	4,991	7,463	10.44	100	122
Virginia.................	465,439	2,500	6,031	8,531	1.83	256	473
Washington..............	328,466	19,287	46,049	65,336	19.89	2,125	3,441
West Virginia............	325,266	10,744	18,574	29,318	9.01	646	386
Wisconsin...............	586,290	35,068	50,901	85,969	14.66	13,558	32,899
Wyoming................	59,977	3,090	6,637	9,727	18.37	343	392
Alaska..................							313
Hawaii..................							207
Porto Rico..............							75
Not allocated............							3,482

APPENDIX TABLE 23-B.—*Registration of aliens, by nationalities.*

	Total aliens registered.	Per cent of total aliens registered.	Aliens registered June 5, 1917.	Aliens registered June and August, 1918.	Aliens registered Sept. 12, 1918.
Total..........................	3,877,083	100.00	1,616,812	86,194	2,174,077
Cobelligerents......................	2,228,980	57.49	966,754	54,309	1,207,917
Belgium......................	16,701	.43	6,684	309	9,708
China......................	23,599	.61	7,815	979	14,805
France......................	18,314	.47	6,178	368	11,768
Canada......................	151,691	3.91	63,970	3,486	84,235
England......................	138,979	3.58	46,704	1,867	90,348
Ireland......................	98,800	2.55	44,656	1,166	52,978
New Zealand......................	1,186	.03	834	35	317
Scotland......................	28,408	.73	12,830	394	15,184
Wales......................	5,672	.15	2,503	74	3,095
Other British......................	42,732	1.10	16,137	1,047	25,548
Greece......................	88,831	2.30	84,949	3,882	....
Italy......................	652,971	16.84	230,352	20,682	401,937
Japan......................	56,697	1.46	13,647	935	42,115
Portugal......................	62,434	1.61	24,081	1,444	36,909
Roumania......................	18,428	.48	8,935	593	8,900
Russia......................	808,503	20.85	389,896	16,670	401,937
Serbia......................	13,386	.35	5,062	191	8,133
United States Indians (non-citizen)........	1,648	.04	1,461	187	....
Neutrals......................	636,601	16.42	235,746	13,288	387,567
Central and South America...............	11,386	.29	4,474	541	6,371
Denmark......................	33,457	.86	16,149	804	16,504
Mexico......................	192,617	4.97	72,723	3,698	116,196
Netherlands......................	27,190	.70	12,007	785	14,398
Norway......................	62,656	1.62	29,876	1,426	31,354
Spain......................	44,320	1.14	18,629	1,405	24,286
Sweden......................	99,995	2.58	44,251	2,622	53,122
Switzerland......................	21,888	.57	8,090	322	13,476
All other......................	143,092	3.69	29,547	1,685	111,860
Enemy......................	1,011,502	26.09	414,312	18,597	578,593
Austria-Hungary......................	751,212	19.38	307,400	13,342	430,470
Bulgaria......................	19,873	.52	7,065	650	12,158
Germany......................	158,809	4.09	58,479	2,794	97,536
Turkey......................	81,608	2.10	41,368	1,811	38,429

APPENDIX TABLE 26–A.—*Classification of aliens, by nationalities.*

	Aliens registered June 5, 1917, to September 11, 1918.	Class I aliens.	Percentage of total aliens.	Nondeclarants, Class I.	Percentage of Class I aliens.	Deferred classes, aliens.	Nondeclarants, deferred.	Percentage deferred classes, aliens.
Total....................	1,703,006	414,389	24.33	253,795	61.25	1,288,617	910,848	70.68
Cobelligerents............	1,021,063	311,895	30.55	194,053	62.22	709,168	505,683	71.31
Belgium.................	6,993	2,500	35.75	1,256	50.24	4,493	2,617	58.25
China...................	8,794	1,313	14.76	1,015	77.30	7,481	7,079	94.63
France..................	6,546	2,081	31.79	1,174	56.42	4,465	2,660	59.57
Canada.................	67,456	24,077	35.69	16,944	70.37	43,379	30,919	71.28
England................	48,631	15,693	32.27	8,875	56.55	32,938	18,472	56.08
Ireland.................	45,822	20,639	45.04	8,704	42.17	25,183	11,901	47.26
New Zealand............	869	378	43.50	157	41.53	491	288	58.46
Scotland................	13,224	4,714	35.64	2,486	52.74	8,510	4,415	51.88
Wales..................	2,577	943	36.59	501	53.13	1,634	1,007	61.63
Other British...........	17,184	5,540	32.24	4,149	74.89	11,644	9,517	61.73
Greece.................	88,831	22,090	24.87	13,123	59.41	66,741	56,933	85.30
Italy...................	251,034	104,358	41.57	69,028	66.15	146,676	89,591	61.08
Japan..................	14,582	983	67.41	751	76.40	13,599	12,114	89.08
Portugal................	25,825	3,391	13.29	2,543	74.99	22,134	19,847	89.67
Roumania..............	9,528	2,430	25.50	1,185	48.77	7,098	4,420	62.27
Russia.................	406,566	98,473	24.22	60,700	61.64	308,093	230,215	74.72
Serbia.................	5,253	1,802	34.30	1,121	62.21	3,451	2,746	79.57
United States Indians (non-citizen).........	1,648	490	29.73	341	69.51	1,158	942	81.35
Neutrals................	249,034	61,942	24.87	25,918	41.84	187,092	135,366	72.35
Central and South America.....................	5,015	1,093	21.79	804	73.56	3,922	3,307	84.32
Denmark...............	16,953	6,561	38.70	3,019	46.01	10,392	5,775	55.57
Mexico.................	76,421	10,129	13.25	8,477	83.69	66,292	50,784	76.61
Netherlands............	12,792	3,307	25.85	1,529	46.24	9,485	5,794	61.09
Norway................	31,302	10,897	34.81	4,826	44.29	20,405	12,446	60.99
Spain..................	20,034	3,455	17.25	2,621	75.86	16,579	15,112	91.15
Sweden................	46,873	15,113	32.24	6,382	42.22	31,760	19,811	62.38
Switzerland............	8,412	2,138	25.42	956	44.71	6,274	3,993	54.08
All other...............	31,232	9,249	29.61	7,410	80.12	21,983	18,344	83.45
Enemy..................	432,909	40,552	9.37	23,718	58.49	392,357	269,799	68.76
Austria-Hungary........	320,742	23,596	7.36	14,383	60.96	297,146	208,265	70.09
Bulgaria...............	7,715	1,256	16.28	870	69.27	6,459	5,819	90.09
Germany...............	61,273	5,278	8.61	2,727	51.67	55,995	29,469	52.63
Turkey.................	43,179	10,422	24.14	5,738	55.06	32,757	26,246	80.12

APPENDIX TABLE 30–A.—*Number of diplomatic requests received for discharge of aliens, by countries.*

Argentina..............	5	Germany................	8	Peru...................	4
Austria................	62	Great Britain...........	22	Portugal...............	65
Belgium...............	5	Greece.................	119	Russia.................	1,433
Brazil.................	12	Guatemala.............	3	Santo Domingo.........	1
Bulgaria...............	304	Honduras..............	2	Siam..................	2
Chile..................	2	Italy...................	166	Spain..................	592
China.................	5	Japan..................	13	Sweden................	216
Colombia..............	7	Mexico.................	109	Switzerland............	995
Cuba..................	23	Netherlands............	85	Turkey................	971
Denmark...............	241	Norway................	404	Venezuela..............	4
Ecuador...............	4	Panama................	4		
France................	3	Persia..................	61	Total............	5,852

APPENDIX TABLE 31-A.—*Married registered, deferred, and deferred for dependency.*

	Total registrants June 5, 1917, to Sept. 11, 1918.	Total married.	Percentage of total registrants.	Total married deferred.	Percentage of total married.	Total married deferred for dependency.	Percentage of total married deferred.
United States.........	10,679,814	4,883,213	45.72	4,394,676	90.00	3,619,466	82.36
Alabama............	206,248	111,886	54.26	93,786	83.82	80,629	85.97
Arizona............	40,517	15,776	38.93	14,499	91.90	7,963	54.92
Arkansas...........	168,302	92,188	54.78	76,925	83.44	74,049	96.26
California..........	332,593	126,364	37.99	112,758	89.23	91,440	81.09
Colorado...........	91,813	40,369	43.97	37,240	92.25	31,067	83.42
Connecticut........	175,026	70,251	40.14	65,354	93.03	40,273	61.62
Delaware...........	24,563	11,227	45.71	10,005	89.12	7,364	73.60
District of Columbia....	36,741	16,358	44.52	13,533	82.73	10,188	75.28
Florida.............	94,792	47,362	49.96	38,988	82.32	30,501	78.23
Georgia............	260,296	144,090	55.36	122,468	84.99	111,311	90.89
Idaho..............	45,982	18,555	40.35	17,077	92.03	14,993	87.80
Illinois............	707,962	314,150	44.37	286,200	91.10	220,777	77.14
Indiana............	283,843	146,342	51.57	133,981	91.55	113,096	84.41
Iowa...............	240,934	106,873	44.36	98,227	91.91	88,388	89.98
Kansas............	167,486	79,660	47.56	73,162	91.84	63,162	86.33
Kentucky...........	215,936	114,548	53.06	97,088	84.76	91,707	94.55
Louisiana..........	180,226	88,789	49.27	74,289	83.67	70,751	95.24
Maine..............	68,214	30,405	44.57	28,211	92.78	25,129	89.08
Maryland...........	136,552	65,485	47.94	59,987	91.60	49,176	81.98
Massachusetts......	398,364	158,988	39.91	145,906	91.77	104,270	71.46
Michigan...........	411,596	185,485	45.06	168,913	91.06	134,116	79.40
Minnesota..........	249,937	85,537	34.23	79,337	92.75	69,019	86.99
Mississippi.........	157,607	82,544	52.38	70,376	85.26	64,659	91.88
Missouri...........	335,012	163,191	48.71	145,495	89.16	121,209	83.31
Montana...........	97,762	31,721	32.45	28,816	90.84	25,766	89.41
Nebraska..........	132,458	57,246	43.20	52,205	91.19	44,903	86.01
Nevada............	13,044	3,588	27.52	2,977	82.97	2,346	78.80
New Hampshire......	41,743	17,860	42.79	16,404	91.85	12,923	78.77
New Jersey.........	332,895	152,770	45.89	141,685	92.74	107,397	75.80
New Mexico.........	37,300	17,547	47.04	14,628	83.36	11,615	79.40
New York..........	1,120,332	459,176	40.99	421,933	91.89	328,496	77.86
North Carolina......	228,844	122,922	53.72	111,554	90.75	101,147	90.67
North Dakota........	73,341	24,970	34.05	23,917	95.78	20,600	86.13
Ohio..............:	617,371	289,997	46.97	265,731	91.63	211,644	79.65
Oklahoma..........	193,236	104,831	54.26	90,953	86.76	83,291	91.58
Oregon.............	70,549	28,383	40.23	25,905	91.27	22,683	87.56
Pennsylvania........	902,996	412,581	45.69	380,832	92.30	298,139	78.29
Rhode Island........	59,059	25,452	43.10	23,774	93.41	18,708	78.94
South Carolina......	144,701	78,968	54.57	66,232	83.87	56,153	84.78
South Dakota........	66,189	24,625	37.20	23,220	94.29	19,001	81.83
Tennessee..........	213,427	115,654	54.20	102,151	88.32	94,845	92.85
Texas..............	460,326	238,276	51.77	211,485	88.76	161,768	76.49
Utah...............	46,901	21,470	45.78	19,905	92.71	17,819	89.52
Vermont...........	30,884	14,912	48.29	12,819	85.96	10,978	85.64
Virginia............	206,190	95,596	44.22	85,852	89.81	75,136	87.52
Washington.........	125,708	47,313	36.64	41,569	87.86	34,815	83.75
West Virginia........	142,174	69,841	49.11	63,253	90.57	56,421	89.20
Wisconsin..........	266,691	101,912	38.21	94,876	93.10	80,636	84.99
Wyoming...........	25,151	9,179	36.50	8,195	89.27	6,849	83.58

97250°—19——26

402

APPENDIX TABLES.

Chart A.—PER CENT OF MARRIED REGISTRANTS TO TOTAL REGISTRANTS

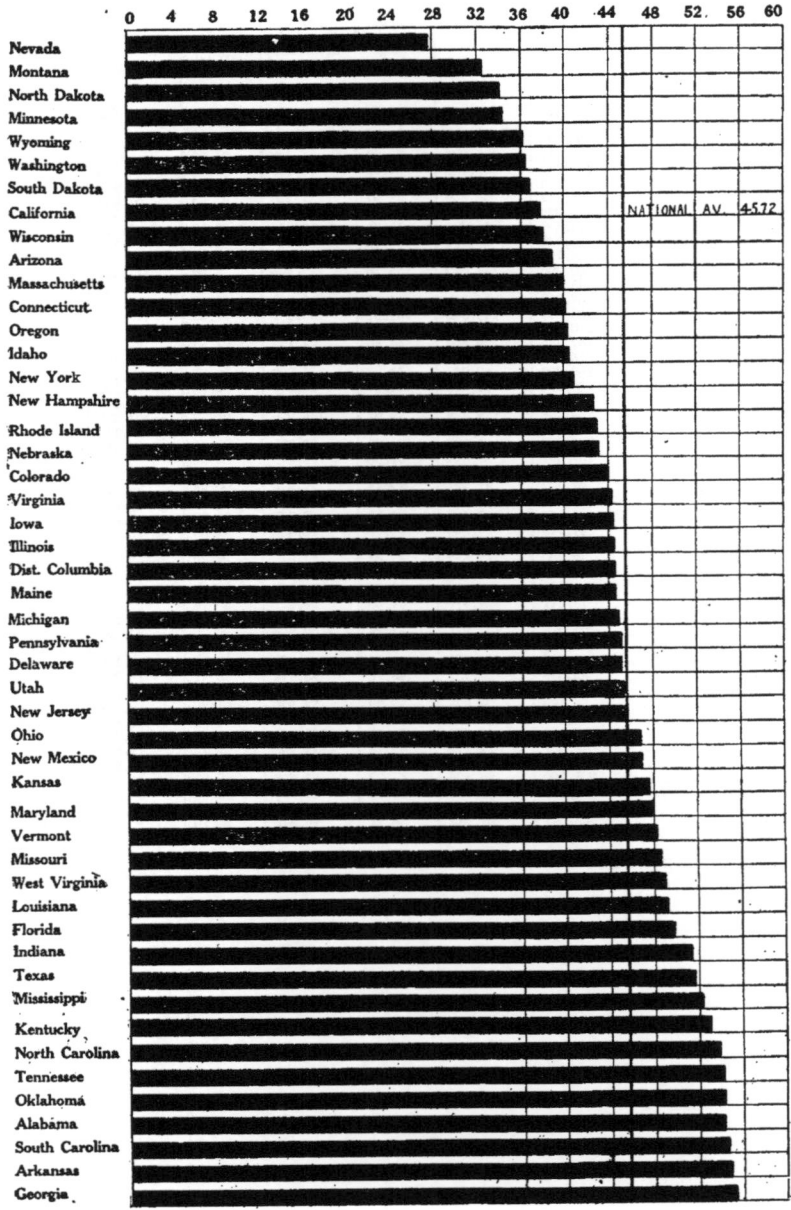

PER CENT

Chart B.—RATIO OF DEPENDENCY DEFERMENTS AND DEFERMENTS ON OTHER GROUNDS TO TOTAL MARRIED

PER CENT

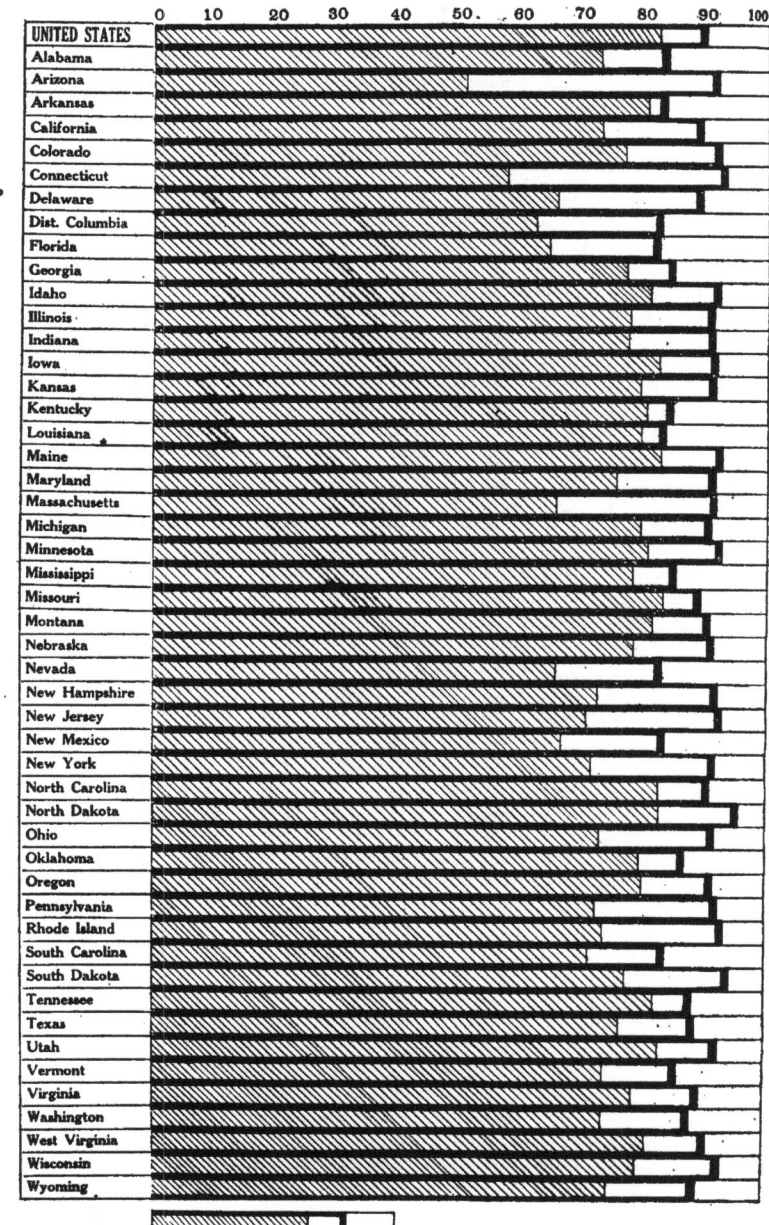

APPENDIX TABLE 36–A.—*Single men registered, deferred for dependency, and recent marriages.*

	Total registrants June 5, 1917, to Sept. 11, 1918.	Single registrants.	Percentage of total registrants.	Single deferred for dependency.	Percentage of single registrants.	Recent marriages.	Percentage of total registrants.	Reclassified to Class I.	Percentage of recent marriages.
United States	10,679,814	5,796,601	54.28	284,267	4.90	344,872	3.23	122,563	35.54
Alabama	206,248	94,362	45.76	5,018	5.32	10,223	4.96	3,851	37.67
Arizona	40,517	24,741	61.06	692	2.79	1,040	2.57	293	28.18
Arkansas	168,302	76,114	45.23	3,500	4.60	9,858	5.85	2,475	25.11
California	332,593	206,229	62.01	11,257	5.46	8,059	2.42	3,136	38.91
Colorado	91,813	51,444	56.03	3,212	6.24	2,540	2.77	1,059	41.69
Connecticut	175,026	104,775	59.87	4,694	4.48	3,140	1.79	1,076	34.27
Delaware	24,563	13,336	54.30	495	3.71	851	3.46	229	26.91
District of Columbia	36,741	20,383	55.48	834	4.09	1,390	3.78	732	52.66
Florida	94,792	47,430	50.04	2,630	5.55	2,128	2.24	751	35.29
Georgia	260,296	116,206	44.64	6,788	5.84	10,828	4.16	7,650	70.65
Idaho	45,982	27,427	59.65	762	2.78	1,565	3.40	576	36.81
Illinois	707,962	393,812	55.62	20,127	5.11	18,749	2.65	7,452	39.75
Indiana	283,843	137,501	48.45	5,352	3.89	9,379	3.30	2,976	31.73
Iowa	240,934	134,061	55.65	3,265	2.44	8,982	3.73	2,891	32.19
Kansas	167,486	87,826	52.43	3,348	3.81	7,695	4.59	2,153	27.98
Kentucky	215,936	101,388	46.96	5,283	5.21	9,563	4.43	4,941	51.67
Louisiana	180,226	91,437	50.74	5,001	5.47	6,871	3.81	2,658	38.68
Maine	68,214	37,809	55.43	1,470	3.89	1,646	2.41	760	46.17
Maryland	136,552	71,067	52.03	3,525	4.96	4,881	3.57	2,694	44.71
Massachusetts	398,364	239,376	60.08	11,326	4.73	9,027	2.27	4,037	44.72
Michigan	411,596	226,111	54.93	9,443	4.18	11,118	2.70	4,089	36.78
Minnesota	249,937	164,400	65.79	5,991	3.64	6,872	2.75	2,625	38.20
Mississippi	157,607	75,063	47.63	2,977	3.97	6,268	3.98	2,466	39.34
Missouri	335,012	171,821	51.29	10,440	6.08	12,395	3.70	1,096	8.84
Montana	97,762	66,041	67.55	2,334	3.53	2,373	2.43	972	40.96
Nebraska	132,458	75,212	56.76	1,754	2.33	4,641	3.50	1,335	28.77
Nevada	13,044	9,456	72.52	288	3.05	231	1.77	88	38.10
New Hampshire	41,743	23,883	57.23	1,118	4.68	937	2.24	424	45.25
New Jersey	332,895	180,125	54.11	10,241	5.69	7,556	2.27	2,752	36.42
New Mexico	37,300	19,753	52.96	702	3.55	1,093	2.93	537	49.13
New York	1,120,332	661,156	59.03	44,999	6.81	27,893	2.49	9,744	34.93
North Carolina	228,844	105,922	46.29	5,844	5.52	7,552	3.30	2,540	33.63
North Dakota	73,341	48,371	65.95	1,061	2.19	1,501	2.05	482	32.11
Ohio	617,371	327,374	53.02	17,526	5.35	24,490	3.97	7,349	30.01
Oklahoma	193,236	88,405	45.76	3,277	3.71	8,588	4.45	2,710	31.56
Oregon	70,549	42,166	59.77	1,168	2.77	2,148	3.04	846	39.39
Pennsylvania	902,996	490,415	54.31	24,153	4.93	25,148	2.78	8,558	34.03
Rhode Island	59,059	33,607	56.90	2,164	6.44	1,179	2.00	432	36.64
South Carolina	144,701	65,733	45.43	2,946	4.48	4,572	3.16	1,707	37.34
South Dakota	66,189	41,564	62.79	832	2.00	2,017	3.05	933	46.26
Tennessee	213,427	97,773	45.82	6,044	6.18	13,449	6.30	2,848	21.18
Texas	460,326	222,050	48.24	12,397	5.58	18,753	4.07	7,853	41.88
Utah	46,901	25,431	54.22	883	3.47	2,165	4.62	838	38.71
Vermont	30,884	15,972	51.72	479	3.00	577	1.87	157	27.21
Virginia	206,190	110,594	53.63	6,443	5.83	7,224	3.50	2,090	28.93
Washington	125,708	78,395	62.37	2,464	3.14	3,978	3.16	1,536	38.61
West Virginia	142,174	72,333	50.87	2,617	3.62	5,154	3.62	1,362	26.43
Wisconsin	266,691	164,779	61.78	4,860	2.95	6,033	2.26	2,647	43.88
Wyoming	25,151	15,972	63.51	243	1.52	552	2.19	157	28.44

APPENDIX TABLE 42–A.—INDUSTRIAL INDEX—STATISTICAL SUMMARY OF OCCUPA-
TIONS, BY CLASSES.

1. The following table (Appendix Table 42–A) shows the occupational distribution of registrants, as between Class I and the deferred classes, by totals for each
occupation; there is also shown, for each of the occupations represented, the total
number of persons of all ages and both sexes; this was obtained by projection from
the thirteenth census, 1910, Volume IV, "Population; Occupation Statistics."
These three series of figures will exhibit the ratio of the entire body of registrants to
persons of all ages, within each occupation, and also the ratio of Class I, for each
occupation, both to the total number of registrants and to the total number of persons of all ages.

The registration represented is only the first registration, viz, that of June 5, 1917,
covering ages 21–30, beginning with December 15, 1917, and thus excluding all those
who before that date were sent to camps, deceased, deserters, etc.; the second registration, covering ages 21 on June 5, 1918, and the third registration, covering ages
18–20 and 32–45, on September 12, 1918, are not represented.

2. The first line of the Table shows the above figures and ratio for the total of all
occupations. In this line, as in all the specific occupations, it must be noted that
Class I exceeds in numbers the actual facts, by about 10 per cent. This is because
the cards for the industrial index were transcribed between January and April, 1918,
and during that period the physical examinations in various regions had not been
completed; therefore, assuming that one-half of the Class I men thus carded had
not been physically examined, and taking 25 per cent as the probable figure for
physical rejections from Class I to Class V, Class I figures are not less than 10 per cent
and probably 12 per cent too high. This will bring it down to a figure consonant
with the final classification figures shown in the text of this report. The number
thus discounted from Class I should be transferred to Class V, thereby increasing
correspondingly the total in the column for deferred classes.

3. The industrial index was compiled for four main purposes. The first was to
assist in the individual selection, by local boards, under directions from the Provost
Marshal General's Office, of registrants qualified by occupational experience to meet
the needs of the several staff corps and also, to a limited extent, of the line divisions.
The second main purpose was to enable the selective service officials to defer the
calling of specific occupational groups, whenever either the Army needs required
them to be held in reserve for future calls or the industrial needs required them to be
deferred permanently. The third main purpose was to enable the local quotas, levied
upon the principle of the joint resolution of May 16, 1918 ("to call into immediate
military service persons classed as skilled experts in industry or agriculture however
classified and wherever residing") to be so equitably adjusted, if the need arose, as to
interfere least with the variant industrial conditions. The fourth main purpose was
to provide an accurate survey of the effect of the war upon industries and occupations
for whatever purpose of policy might prove important.

The industrial index was used to only a small extent for the first two of these purposes, partly because it could not be made completely ready in season, but mainly
because the special requisitions, issuing from the General Staff, for registrants of
occupational skill proved to be comparatively small in number (as shown in Chapter
VIII of this report), and also because the industrial situation never reached such a
point when measures of temporary or permanent deferment of specific occupational
groups proved to be necessary. The index was not used for the third-named purpose,
because the rapidity with which the large levies of May, June, July and August were
raised, and the consequent impossibility of sparing any numbers of Class I from military service, made any such allotment of quotas useless; nor did the industrial situation call for such allowances.

For the fourth-named purpose the industrial index is now given publicity. How far the historian, the economist, and other investigators may find a use for it can not be foretold. But as it represents the only existing calculation of its kind for the United States, it seems necessary to place it here at the disposal of all the persons who may have use for it.,

4. The data on which the industrial index was based were contained in the questionnaires filed by the registrants; from those questionnaires were extracted the facts as to age, education, occupation, etc., and these were transcribed onto an occupational card, so-called, at the respective local boards. These cards were forwarded to the Provost Marshal General's Office, and were there assembled by occupations.

5. For the classification of occupations the Census "Index of Occupations, Alphabetical and Classified," 1915, was used. The key numbers given in the following statistical summary correspond to the key numbers in the census index; and the totals given in column 3 (persons of all ages and sexes) are made up from the figures given in Volume IV ("Population; Occupation Statistics") of the thirteenth census. Thus, and thus only, was it possible to establish correct ratios between the registrants in a given occupation to the total persons of all ages in that occupation, forming the basis of the percentage. No compilation of statistics as to the effect of the draft on industry can be of reliable service (certainly not for the entire national body of occupations), unless the classification employed is identical with the Census Bureau classification; and this was the reason for adopting and adhering exclusively to this system of classification.

In the actual filing of the occupational cards the respective occupations were further subdivided, by adding a fourth digit, so as to make possible the accurate location of persons possessing the requisite kind of detailed skill; for example, under "machinists" it was possible within a few hours to locate 200 automatic screw machine operators for the purposes of an ordnance factory. In any practical use of an index like this one, such a further subdivision by a fourth digit would be necessary. The possibilities of the system are extensive; but it requires necessarily a coordination with the classification employed by any other agency whose needs are to be served. The committee on classification of personnel, in the Office of The Adjutant General of the Army, did not employ the census classification, and coordination with their work was, therefore, impracticable.

The key number lines bearing the suffix A (122A, etc.) represent special combinations of partial occupational groups prepared for certain purposes, and do not enter into the national total for each column.

For the precise meaning and scope of the occupational descriptive names used, reference should be made to the census index above cited. For the study of the results for an entire industry, it is indispensable to refer to that index.

6. The occupational cards were placed in the files first by occupations, and then within each occupation by States and by local boards; the entire mass, however, being first divided into two parts, one representing Class I and the few deferred classes which, under the law, were liable to call irrespective of deferment (Pile 1), and the second part representing the remainder of the deferred classes (Pile 2). The national totals represented in the ensuing table were made up by adding the totals for each of these two parts or "piles." The totals for these separate piles were carried in a statistical summary known as the "interim ledger;" the combined totals for the two piles were carried in the "final ledger." The figures given in the ensuing table reproduce the final ledger. The occupational cards forming the industrial index will be retained in the custody of The Adjutant General of the Army.

APPENDIX TABLE 42-A.—*Industrial index—Statistical summary of occupations, by classes.*

Key No.	Occupation.	Male employees of all ages.	Ages 21-30 within selective service law as classified, 1918.		Deferred classes within selective service law.			Class I within selective service law.		
			Number.	Per cent of all ages.	Number.	Per cent of ages 21-30.	Per cent of all ages.	Number.	Per cent of ages 21-30.	Per cent of all ages.
(1)	(2)	(3)	(4)	(5)	(6)	(7)	(8)	(9)	(10)	(11)
	All occupations............	43,206,912	8,577,719	20	5,897,722	69	14	2,679,997	31	6
[1]000	Unknown..................	(2)	277,121	......	185,527	67	......	91,594	33	......
010	Dairy farmers, foremen and laborers.............	112,603	26,362	23	19,647	75	17	6,715	25	6
022	Farmers............:....	13,633,161	2,478,802	18	1,734,729	70	13	744,073	30	5
023	Turpentine farmers and laborers.................	31,690	4,534	14	1,924	42	6	2,610	58	8
035	Foresters.................	4,982	1,312	26	883	67	18	429	33	8
[3]043	Fruit growers, florists, orchard men...........	314,497	21,004	7	14,570	69	5	6,434	31	2
045	Landscape gardeners and architects...............	4,360	689	16	414	60	9	275	40	6
066	Lumbermen and raftsmen.	168,164	42,358	25	26,363	62	16	15,995	38	9
075	Owners and managers of timber and log camps...	9,120	261	2.9	206	79	2.3	55	21	.6
[4]079	Stock raisers..............	132,820	31,258	24	19,643	63	15	11,615	37	9
085	Apiarists.................	2,467	147	6	25	17	1	122	83	5
086	Corn shellers, hay balers, grain thrashers.........	6,460	1,112	17	678	61	10	434	39	7
087	Farm ditchers.............	17,477	1,247	7	665	53	4	582	47	3
088	Poultry raisers and poultry yard laborers............	17,692	2,341	13	1,503	64	8	838	36	5
[5]089	Pigeon fanciers and persons n. o. s.	(2)	808	......	429	53	......	379	47	......
100	Foremen mines, oil and gas wells, salt works....	25,463	2,213	9	1,786	80	7	427	20	2
101	Inspectors, mine, quarry..	1,375	219	16	143	65	10	76	35	6
110	Managers, mine...........	11,268	1,359	12	1,055	78	9	304	22	3
111	Officials, mine...........	1,321	104	8	79	76	6	25	24	2
112	Operators, mine...........	16,430	472	2.8	337	71	2	135	29	.8
[6]122	Coal mine operatives......	706,012	58,472	8	35,768	61	5	22,704	39	3
[7]133	Copper mine operatives...	45,160	2,468	5	1,495	60	.3	973	40	2
[8]144	Gold and silver mine operatives..............	63,751	899	1.4	479	53	.8	420	47	.6
[9]155	Iron mine operatives......	57,043	4,117	7	2,810	68	5	1,307	32	2
[10]160	Coal mine repairmen......	(2)	356	......	284	80	......	72	20	......
[6]122A	All coal mine operatives..	706,012	199,148	28	147,004	74	21	52,144	26	7
[7]133A	All copper mine operatives	45,160	11,109	24	8,328	75	18	2,781	25	6
[8]144A	All gold and silver miners.	63,751	13,075	20	10,107	77	15	2,968	23	5
[9]155A	Iron miners..............	57,043	15,115	26	11,506	76	20	3,609	24	6
[11]166	Lead and zinc operatives..	22,409	928	4	390	42	2	538	58	2
[12]167	Mines not otherwise specified.	31,930	8,023	25	1,606	20	5	6,417	80	20
188	Oil and gas well operatives.	29,396	6,951	24	4,546	65	16	2,405	35	8
189	Salt wells and works operatives..................	5,020	672	13	508	76	10	164	24	3
[13]190	Crusher operators.........	(2)	173	......	143	82	......	30	18	......

[1] No census figure given.
[2] No data.
[3] Includes 027, 028, 042, 044, 054, 055, 056, and 057.
[4] Includes 077.
[5] Cards were combed from 088 and 089 (Census title "Other and not specified pursuits").
[6] To obtain 122A (all coal mine operatives) enter in columns 4, 6, and 9, the I. L. items of Key No. 122 plus 71½ per cent of the I. L. totals of the corresponding items of Key Nos. 190-199, inclusive, plus the corresponding items of Key No. 160.
[7] To obtain 133A (all copper mine operatives) enter in columns 4, 6, and 9, the I. L. items of Key No. 133 plus 4.4 per cent of the I. L. totals of the corresponding items of Key Nos. 190-199, inclusive.
[8] To obtain 144A (all gold and silver operatives) enter in columns 4, 6, and 9, the I. L. items of Key No. 144 plus 6.2 per cent of the I. L. totals of the corresponding items of Key Nos. 190-199, inclusive.
[9] To obtain 155A (all iron mine operatives) enter in columns 4, 6, and 9, the I. L. items of Key No. 155 plus 5.6 per cent of the I. L. totals of the corresponding items of Key Nos. 190-199, inclusive.
[10] Combed from Key No. 122.
[11] To obtain 166A (all lead and zinc mine operatives) enter in columns 4, 6, and 9, the I. L. items of Key No. 166 plus 2.2 per cent of the I. L. totals of the corresponding items of Key Nos. 190-199, inclusive.
[12] To obtain 167A (all other mine operators) enter in columns 4, 6, and 9, the I. L. items of Key No. 167 plus 3.1 per cent of the I. L. totals of the corresponding items of Key Nos. 190-199, inclusive.
[13] Combed from 122, 133, 144, 155, 166, and 177.

Appendix Table 42–A.—*Industrial index—Statistical summary of occupations, by classes*—Continued.

Key No.	Occupation.	Male employees of all ages.	Ages 21–30 within selective service law as classified, 1918.		Deferred classes within selective service law.			Class I within selective service law.		
			Number.	Per cent of all ages.	Number.	Per cent of ages 21–30.	Per cent of all ages.	Number.	Per cent of ages 21–30.	Per cent of all ages.
(1)	(2)	(3)	(4)	(5)	(6)	(7)	(8)	(9)	(10)	(11)
[1] 166A	All lead and zinc miners...	22,409	5,249	23	3,807	72	17	1,442	28	6
[2] 167A	All other mine operatives..	31,930	14,111	44	6,420	45	20	7,691	55	24
191	Diggers and muckers......	[3]	54,024	......	37,105	69	......	16,919	31	......
192	Drill runners.............	[2]	7,696	......	6,407	83	......	1,289	17	......
193	Blasters, demolition, and powder men.............	[3]	1,982	......	1,191	60	......	791	40	......
194	Laborers.................	[3]	26,371	......	22,922	87	......	3,449	13	......
195	Miners...................	[3]	92,787	......	78,462	85	......	14,325	15	......
196	Quarrymen...............	92,966	5,597	6	3,678	65	4	1,919	35	2
197	Timbermen...............	[3]	4,556	......	3,378	74	......	1,178	26	......
198	Topmen..................	[3]	486	......	259	53	......	227	47	......
199	Tracklayers..............	[2]	2,723	......	1,746	64	......	977	36	......
202	Apprentices to building and hand trades.........	90,760	1,023	1.1	129	12	.2	894	88	.9
[4] 203–311	Machinists	550,604	251,933	46	190,379	75	35	61,554	25	11
[5] 209–511	Auto and gas engine mechanics..............	[3]	95,466	......	58,571	61	......	36,895	39	......
210	Bakers...................	102,960	40,479	29	29,546	73	29	10,933	27	10
211	Blacksmiths	267,736	47,727	18	35,908	75	13	11,817	25	5
212	Forgemen................	8,660	6,991	80	5,471	78	63	1,520	22	17
213	Boilermakers.............	51,475	25,264	49	18,522	73	36	6,742	27	13
214	Brick or stone masons....	194,812	33,279	18	23,176	70	12	10,103	30	6
215	Builder and building contractors	200,585	8,699	4	6,441	74	3	2,258	26	1
216	Butchers.................	18,803	2,275	12	926	41	4	1,349	59	8
217	Cabinetmakers...........	48,175	19,675	40	14,670	74	30	5,005	26	10
218	Carpenters...............	939,688	144,794	15	101,206	70	10	43,588	30	5
219	Printers.................	146,727	47,370	32	31,200	66	21	16,170	34	11
220	Coopers.................	29,094	5,221	18	3,651	70	13	1,570	30	5
221	Dressmakers and milliners (not in factory).........	516,743	176	.03	146	83	.02	30	17	.01
222	Dyers...................	16,157	3,007	19	2,273	75	14	734	25	5
[6] 223	Electricians.............	......	72,287	......	50,148	69	......	22,139	31	......
[6] 229	Electrical engineers......	......	8,300	......	6,352	77	......	1,948	23	......
[6] 223, 229	Electricians and electrical engineers.................	155,847	80,587	52	56,500	70	36	24,087	30	16
224	Electrotypers............	5,023	2,206	44	1,443	65	28	763	35	16
225	Lithographers............	9,358	2,494	27	1,626	65	17	868	35	10
226	Mechanical engineers......	16,691	7,818	47	6,363	81	38	1,455	19	9
227	Enginemen..............	265,697	46,383	17	32,851	70	12	13,532	30	5
228	Engravers...............	16,062	4,600	28	3,354	72	21	1,246	28	7
230	Buffers and polishers (metal).................	35,070	9,013	26	8,921	99	25	92	1	2
231	Filers (metal).............	11,771	2,459	21	1,779	72	16	680	28	.5
232	Grinders................	10,112	4,094	40	2,719	66	27	1,375	34	13
233	Firemen.................	127,935	40,526	32	27,070	67	21	13,456	33	11
234	Construction foremen.....	201,362	28,971	14	23,434	81	11	5,537	19	3
235, 238, 322, 325	Molders, casters, puddlers, heaters, etc.............	180,714	69,720	39	54,224	78	30	15,496	22	9
239	Glass blowers............	17,898	2,773	15	1,999	72	11	774	28	4
240	Goldsmiths and silversmiths.................	6,620	991	15	664	67	10	327	33	5
241	Jewelers and lapidaries (factory)...............	12,225	2,355	19	1,674	71	14	681	29	5
242	Jewelers and watchmakers (not in factory).........	18,614	7,835	42	5,090	65	27	2,745	35	15

[1] To obtain 166A (all lead and zinc mine operatives) enter in columns 4, 6, and 9, the I. L. items of Key No. 166 plus 2.2 per cent of the I. L. totals of the corresponding items of Key Nos. 190–199, inclusive.
[2] To obtain 167A (all other mine operators) enter in columns 4, 6, and 9, the I. L. items of Key No. 167 plus 3.1 per cent of the I. L. total of the corresponding items of Key Nos. 190–199, inclusive.
[3] No data.
[4] Combed from 202,311, and 318.
[5] Census figure not given.
[6] In census 223 and 229 are given as one group. For statistical purposes they have been combined in Provost Marshal General's index. In census index, 229 appears as a newly created number.

APPENDIX TABLE 42–A.—*Industrial index—Statistical summary of occupations, by classes*—Continued.

Key No.	Occupation.	Male employees of all ages.	Ages 21-30 within selective service law as classified, 1918.		Deferred classes within selective service law.			Class I within selective service law.		
			Number.	Per cent of all ages.	Number.	Per cent of ages 21-30.	Per cent of all ages.	Number.	Per cent of ages 21-30.	Per cent of all ages.
(1)	(2)	(3)	(4)	(5)	(6)	(7)	(8)	(9)	(10)	(11)
243	General and not specified laborers..................	999,899	214,117	21	122,081	57	12	92,036	43	9
244	Building and hand trades, laborers and helpers.....	72,245	12,852	17	5,621	44	7	7,231	56	10
245	Fertilizer factories (laborers)...................	11,324	2,004	18	975	49	9	1,029	51	9
255	Automobile factories (laborers).................	18,150	7,561	42	5,979	79	33	1,582	21	9
256	Blast furnaces and rolling mills (laborers)..........	232,750	53,975	23	41,017	76	18	12,958	24	5
257	Car and railroad shop (laborers).................	55,593	3,685	7	2,776	75	5	909	25	2
258	Wagon and carriage factory (laborers)..........	14,250	894	6	609	68	4	285	32	2
259	(Laborers) other iron and steel factories.............	234,638	55,153	24	40,825	74	17	14,328	26	7
263	(Laborers) brass mills.....	12,517	4,441	35	2,938	66	23	1,503	34	12
264	(Laborers) copper factories	13,324	3,328	25	2,791	84	21	537	16	4
265	(Laborers) lead and zinc factories................	9,136	1,814	20	1,444	80	16	370	20	4
266	(Laborers) tin and enamel ware factory............	8,725	2,497	29	1,854	74	21	643	26	8
270	(Laborers) furniture, piano, organ factories.....	32,288	3,547	11	2,386	67	7	1,161	33	4
271	(Laborers) saw and planing mills.................	299,163	35,996	12	18,221	51	6	17,775	49	6
275	(Laborers) cotton mills....	41,974	8,576	20	5,945	69	14	2,631	31	6
276	(Laborers) silk mills.......	4,367	921	21	585	64	13	336	36	8
277	(Laborers) woolen and worsted mills...........	14,133	2,411	17	2,054	85	15	357	15	2
278	(Laborers) other textile mills...................	38,242	6,878	18	4,973	72	13	1,905	28	5
280	(Laborers) charcoal and coke works.............	13,163	1,148	9	827	72	6	321	28	3
281	(Laborers) cigar and tobacco factories...........	18,850	3,385	18	1,692	50	9	1,693	50	9
282	(Laborers) clothing industries..................	11,776	896	8	543	61	5	353	39	3
283	(Laborers) electric light and power plants........	9,402	2,267	24	1,443	63	15	824	37	9
284	(Laborers) electrical supply factories............	13,149	4,644	35	3,471	75	26	1,178	25	9
290	(Laborers) bakeries.......	5,186	1,440	27	939	65	18	501	35	9
291	(Laborers) butter and cheese factories..........	5,538	823	15	561	68	10	262	32	5
292	(Laborers) fish curing and packing..............	5,600	252	5	145	57	3	107	43	2
293	(Laborers) flour and grain mills...................	10,629	1,994	19	1,376	69	13	618	31	6
294	(Laborers) fruit and vegetable, canning, etc.....	5,370	711	13	461	65	9	250	35	4
295	(Laborers) slaughter and packing houses.........	38,988	11,714	30	8,409	72	22	3,305	28	8
296	(Laborers) sugar factories and refineries...........	10,068	2,960	29	2,108	71	21	852	29	8
297	(Laborers) other food factories.................	12,935	3,664	28	2,392	65	18	1,272	35	10
300	(Laborers) gas works......	17,881	2,592	14	1,948	75	11	644	25	3
301	(Laborers) liquor and beverage industries.........	21,685	2,916	13	1,883	65	9	1,033	35	4
302	(Laborers) oil refineries....	12,897	6,205	48	4,103	66	32	2,102	34	16
305	(Laborers) rubber factories.	15,578	7,517	48	5,451	73	35	2,066	27	13
309	(Laborers) other factories..	172,899	22,258	13	14,239	64	8	8,019	36	5
310	Loom fixers...............	15,242	2,584	17	2,139	83	14	445	17	3
312	Tool makers and die sinkers...................	10,652	18,388	......	13,500	73	......	4,888	27	......
313	Managers and superintendents, manufacturing	119,841	22,901	19	18,191	79	15	4,710	21	4

410 APPENDIX TABLES.

APPENDIX TABLE 42-A.—*Industrial index—Statistical summary of occupations, by classes*—Continued.

Key No.	Occupation.	Male employees of all ages.	Ages 21-30 within selective service law as classified, 1918.		Deferred classes within selective service law.			Class I within selective service law.		
			Number.	Per cent of all ages.	Number.	Per cent of ages 21-30.	Per cent of all ages.	Number.	Per cent of ages 21-30.	Per cent of all ages.
(1)	(2)	(3)	(4)	(5)	(6)	(7)	(8)	(9)	(10)	(11)
314	Manufacturers	270,373	8,120	3	6,169	76	2.3	1,951	24	.7
315	Manufacturing officials	24,706	1,840	7	1,476	80	6	364	20	1
316	Gunsmiths	3,738	2,050	54	1,452	71	38	598	29	16
317	Wheelwrights	4,292	1,097	25	764	70	18	333	30	7
¹318	Miscellaneous mechanics	31,974	32,118	.....	21,908	68	.....	10,210	32	.....
²319	Millwrights	No data.	8,287	.....	6,511	78	.....	1,776	22	.....
320	Miller, grain, flour, feed, etc	26,624	3,386	13	2,623	77	10	763	22	3
321	Milliners and millinery dealers	6,277	761	12	615	81	10	146	19	2
326	Oilers of machinery	16,115	5,594	35	3,927	70	24	1,667	30	11
327	Enamelers, lacquerers, and japanners	3,449	1,026	29	798	78	23	228	22	6
³328	Painters	384,509	78,268	20	53,680	69	14	24,588	31	6
330	Paper hangers	29,423	3,660	12	2,403	66	8	1,257	34	4
331	Pattern and model makers, wood and metal	27,093	7,870	29	6,081	77	22	1,789	23	6
332	Plasterers	54,834	10,061	18	6,954	69	12	3,107	31	6
333	Plumbers, gas and steam fitters	170,549	72,034	42	48,585	67	28	23,449	33	14
334	Pressmen, printing	23,096	8,328	36	5,564	67	24	2,764	33	12
335	Roller and roll hands	21,168	7,880	37	6,494	82	31	1,386	18	6
336	Roofer and slaters	16,189	2,793	17	1,761	63	11	1,032	37	6
337	Sawyers	49,767	7,855	15	5,310	68	10	2,545	32	5
340	(Semiskilled) paint factory	4,508	1,390	31	1,003	72	22	387	28	9
341	(Semiskilled) powder, car-cartridge, etc., factory	6,052	14,946	.....	9,879	66	.....	5,067	34	.....
342	(Semiskilled) other chemical factories	24,750	15,136	61	11,544	76	46	3,592	24	15
344	(Semiskilled) cigar and tobacco factory	174,247	16,747	9	11,761	71	6	4,986	29	3
345	(Semiskilled) brick, tile, or terra-cotta factory	15,428	14,261	92	9,821	69	63	4,440	31	29
346	(Semiskilled) glass factory	48,158	20,088	41	13,539	67	28	6,549	33	13
347	(Semiskilled) lime, cement, gypsum factory	9,828	6,637	67	5,022	75	51	1,615	25	16
348	(Semiskilled) marble and stone yards	9,820	2,222	23	1,740	78	18	482	22	5
349	(Semiskilled) potteries	18,698	5,515	29	3,885	70	21	1,630	30	8
355	(Semiskilled) hat factory	30,561	6,227	20	4,802	77	16	1,425	23	4
356	(Semiskilled) suit, coat, cloak, overall factory	62,342	4,840	8	3,645	75	6	1,195	25	2
357	(Semiskilled) other clothing factories	73,394	10,718	15	8,086	75	11	2,632	25	4
360	(Semiskilled) bakery	10,278	870	8	408	47	4	462	53	4
361	(Semiskilled) butter and cheese factory	13,337	5,809	44	4,316	74	32	1,493	26	12
362	(Semiskilled) confectioner	35,584	6,204	17	4,254	69	12	1,950	31	50
363	(Semiskilled) flour and grain mills	4,590	1,203	26	689	57	15	514	43	11
364	(Semiskilled) fruit and vegetable canning, etc	6,083	727	12	482	66	8	245	34	4
365	(Semiskilled) slaughter and packing houses	10,865	3,164	29	2,276	72	21	888	28	8
366	(Semiskilled) other food factories	21,118	5,733	27	3,979	69	19	1,754	31	8
⁴368	(Semiskilled) gas makers	(⁵)	2,093	.....	1,792	86	.....	301	14	.....
369	(Semiskilled) leather-workers	26,047	5,684	22	3,966	70	15	1,718	30	7
370	(Semiskilled) automobile factory	24,037	11,259	47	9,527	84	40	1,732	16	7

¹ Census figures lower than classified men of 1918.
² Combed from 311 and 318.
³ In census code book, 328 and 329 were combined under 328. Hence the combination of building and factory painters above.
⁴ Combed from 463 and 750.
⁵ No data.

APPENDIX TABLE 42–A.—*Industrial index—Statistical summary of occupations, by classes*—Continued.

Key No.	Occupation.	Male employees of all ages.	Ages 21-30 within selective service law as classified, 1918.		Deferred classes within selective service law.			Class I within selective service law.		
			Number.	Per cent of all ages.	Number.	Per cent of ages 21-30.	Per cent of all ages.	Number.	Per cent of ages 21-30.	Per cent of all ages.
(1)	(2)	(3)	(4)	(5)	(6)	(7)	(8)	(9)	(10)	(11)
371	(Semiskilled) blast furnaces and rolling mills...	80,649	28,826	35	23,575	81	29	5,251	19	6
372	(Semiskilled) machinists or mechanics	54,836	26,718	48	19,754	74	36	6,964	26	12
373	(Semiskilled) wagon and carriage factory	25,509	2,166	8	1,695	78	6	471	22	2
1375	(Semiskilled) airplane mechanics	(²)	2,300	......	1,674	73	......	626	27	......
380	(Semiskilled) metal finishers, brass mills	19,417	3,642	19	2,766	76	14	876	24	5
381	(Semiskilled) clock and watch factory	17,972	2,483	14	2,051	83	12	432	17	2
382	(Semiskilled) gold and silver and jewelry factory	19,148	2,886	15	1,979	69	10	907	31	5
383	(Semiskilled) lead and zinc factory	2,143	732	34	608	83	28	124	17	6
384	(Semiskilled) tin and enamel ware factory	12,202	2,850	23	1,819	64	15	1,031	36	8
385	(Semiskilled) metal finishers	9,327	8,233	88	4,549	55	48	3,684	45	40
390	(Semiskilled) breweries	25,104	3,859	15	2,814	73	11	1,045	27	4
391	(Semiskilled) distilleries	3,960	387	10	264	68	7	123	32	3
392	(Semiskilled) other liquor and beverage factories	7,163	2,610	36	1,732	66	24	878	34	12
394	(Semiskilled) furniture, piano, organ factories	72,233	13,660	19	9,808	72	14	2,852	28	5
395	(Semiskilled) saw and planing mills	75,969	37,431	49	23,418	63	31	14,013	37	......
396	(Semiskilled) other woodworking factories	44,410	15,162	34	10,217	67	23	4,945	33	11
400	(Semiskilled) paper and pulp mills	41,840	19,127	46	13,888	73	33	5,239	27	13
401	(Semiskilled) printing and publishing	77,589	10,565	14	7,358	70	9	3,207	30	5
402	(Semiskilled) shoe factory	208,161	42,542	20	28,786	68	14	13,756	32	6
403	(Semiskilled) tanneries	38,566	10,705	28	7,964	74	21	2,741	26	7
408	(Semiskilled) beamers, workers, slashers	19,197	1,901	10	1,368	72	7	533	28	3
413	(Semiskilled) bobbinboys, doffers, carriers	25,891	1,320	5	969	73	4	351	27	1
418	(Semiskilled) textile mills, carders, doffers, lappers	28,549	2,537	9	2,028	80	7	509	20	2
423	(Semiskilled) drawers, rovers, and twisters	34,494	2,335	7	1,836	78	5	499	22	2
428	(Semiskilled) spinners	85,513	7,366	8	5,453	74	6	1,913	26	2
433	(Semiskilled) weavers	234,275	28,597	12	21,997	77	9	6,600	23	3
438	(Semiskilled) winders, reelers, spoolers	73,983	639	.8	438	69	.6	203	31	.2
443	(Semiskilled) other occupations	247,240	47,111	19	38,057	81	16	9,054	19	3
³445	(Semiskilled) canvas workers	(²)	1,276	......	881	69	......	395	31	......
⁴446	(Semiskilled) cordage workers	(²)	828	......	668	81	......	160	19	......
460	(Semiskilled) electrical supply factory	28,378	9,438	33	6,823	73	24	2,615	27	9
461	(Semiskilled) paper box factory	20,580	2,431	12	1,737	71	8	694	29	4
462	(Semiskilled) rubber workers	34,825	18,627	53	13,256	71	38	5,371	29	15
463	(Semiskilled) other factories	271,416	54,387	20	39,823	73	15	14,564	27	5
⁵464	(Semiskilled) instrument makers or repairers	(⁴)	5,275	......	4,492	85	......	783	15	......

1 Census figure not given.
2 No data.
3 Combed from 443, 470, and 790.
4 Combed from 443.
5 Combed from 312 and 463.

APPENDIX TABLE 42-A.—*Industrial index—Statistical summary of occupations, by classes*—Continued.

Key No.	Occupation.	Male employees of all ages.	Ages 21–30 within selective service law as classified, 1918.		Deferred classes within selective service law.			Class I within selective service law.		
			Number.	Per cent of all ages.	Number.	Per cent of ages 21–30.	Per cent of all ages.	Number.	Per cent of ages 21–30.	Per cent of all ages.
(1)	(2)	(3)	(4)	(5)	(6)	(7)	(8)	(9)	(10)	(11)
470	(Semiskilled) sewers and sewing machine operators	334,890	15,647	5	13,463	86	4	2,184	14	1
471	Shoemakers and cobblers..	80,005	27,042	34	20,400	75	25	6,642	25	9
472	Skilled annealers and temperers (metal)	2,186	966	44	760	79	35	206	21	90
473	Skilled piano and organ tuners	7,628	1,496	19	1,129	75	14	367	25	5
474	Skilled wood carvers	6,173	506	8	395	78	6	111	22	2
475	Other skilled occupations..	3,342	1,869	56	1,419	76	43	450	24	13
480	Stonecutters	41,090	5,321	12	3,908	73	9	1,413	27	3
[1]481	Structural steel workers	13,141	13,802	......	9,545	69	......	4,257	31	......
482	Tailors	235,299	72,265	30	55,801	77	23	16,464	23	7
483	Coppersmiths	3,921	2,056	52	1,609	78	41	447	22	11
484	Tinsmiths	64,886	15,858	24	10,678	67	16	5,180	33	8
485	Upholsterers	23,254	6,575	28	4,720	72	20	1,855	38	8
[2]486	Sheet-metal workers	([3])	15,964	......	13,123	82	......	2,841	18	......
[4]487	Crane operators	([5])	15,435	......	12,389	80	......	3,046	20	......
[5]488	Tire repairers	([3])	839	......	487	58	......	352	42	......
[6]489	Vulcanizers	([3])	1,998	......	1,328	66	......	670	34	......
[7]490	Welders (cutters)	([3])	4,218	......	3,088	73	......	1,130	27	......
[8]491	Instrument makers and repairers	([3])	746	......	614	82	......	131	18	......
[9]492	Skilled riggers	([3])	5,036	......	3,759	75	......	1,277	25	......
500	Boatmen, canal men, and lock keepers	6,099	1,962	32	1,054	54	17	908	46	15
502	Mariners or boatmen, master officers	27,878	3,447	12	2,858	83	10	590	17	2
504	Stevedores (cargo handlers)	72,285	12,829	18	7,776	61	11	5,053	39	7
506	Mariners or boatmen	53,486	38,251	71	26,355	69	49	11,896	31	22
5065 374	(Semiskilled) other iron and steel workers, mariners, boatmen, calkers..	238,531	74,860	31	55,318	74	23	19,542	26	8
508	Carriage and hack drivers.	40,682	1,058	2	571	54	1	487	46	1
510	Chauffeurs or auto drivers..	52,652	152,253	......	89,610	59	......	62,643	41	......
512 514	Foremen, teamsters, draymen	469,739	161,503	34	96,803	60	20	64,700	40	14
516	Garage keepers and managers	6,070	4,565	75	3,368	74	55	1,197	26	20
518	Horsemen, hostlers, stablemen	72,896	10,283	14	5,062	49	7	5,221	51	7
520	Livery stable keepers and managers	40,014	840	2	637	76	1.5	203	24	.5
522	Proprietors and managers of transfer companies	17,937	736	4	551	75	3	185	25	1
524	Baggagemen	14,114	1,829	13	1,250	68	8	579	32	5
525	Freight agents	5,474	938	17	726	78	13	212	22	4
527	Boiler washers and engine hostlers	11,970	2,462	20	2,093	85	17	369	15	3
529	Brakemen, railroad	106,457	49,409	46	35,904	73	33	13,505	27	13
530	Conductors, steam railroad	75,444	8,967	12	7,491	84	10	1,476	16	2
532	Conductors, street railway.	65,471	17,777	27	13,376	75	20	4,401	25	7
534	Foremen and overseers, railroad	80,423	9,934	12	8,105	82	10	1,829	18	2
536	Laborers, steam railroad construction, maintenance	624,643	83,221	13	66,577	80	11	16,644	20	2
537	Laborers, street railway	31,978	28,872	90	4,580	16	14	24,292	84	76
539	Locomotive engineers	110,663	15,975	14	13,213	83	12	2,762	17	2
540	Locomotive firemen	87,838	48,462	55	35,123	72	40	13,339	28	15
542	Motormen	67,855	15,777	23	11,432	72	17	4,345	28	6
544	Officials and superintendents, steam railroads	22,773	2,305	10	1,960	85	9	345	15	1

[1] Census figure less than classified men.
[2] Combed from 371, 374, and 484.
[3] No data.
[4] Combed from 227, 371, 374, 577, and 585.
[5] Combed from 370, 387, and 482..

[6] Combed from 370, 387, and 462.
[7] Combed from 312.
[8] Combed from 374.
[9] Combed from 374, 463, and 481.

APPENDIX TABLE 42–A.—*Industrial index—Statistical summary of occupations, by classes*—Continued.

Key No.	Occupation.	Male employees of all ages.	Ages 21–30 within selective service law as classified, 1918.		Deferred classes within selective service law.			Class I within selective service law.		
			Number.	Per cent of all ages.	Number.	Per cent of ages 21–30.	Per cent of all ages.	Number.	Per cent of ages 21–30.	Per cent of all ages.
(1)	(2)	(3)	(4)	(5)	(6)	(7)	(8)	(9)	(10)	(11)
545	Officials and superintendents, street railroad.....	2,798	163	6	118	72	4	45	28	2
547	Switchmen, steam railroad....................	84,431	19,580	23	14,628	75	17	4,952	25	6
548	Switchmen and flagmen, street railway...........	2,476	399	16	307	77	12	92	23	4
549	Yardmen, steam railroad..	11,011	2,122	19	1,701	80	15	421	20	4
550	Ticket and station agents.	27,758	4,830	17	4,025	83	15	805	17	2
552	Agents(express company).	6,756	1,122	17	845	75	11	277	25	6
554	Messengers (express)......	7,768	2,500	32	1,690	68	22	810	32	10
555	Railway mail clerks.......	17,526	3,598	21	3,295	92	19	303	8	2
557	Mail carriers...............	92,779	15,327	17	11,251	73	12	4,076	27	5
559	Linemen...................	32,602	26,267	81	18,302	70	56	7,965	30	25
560	Telegraph messengers.....	10,524	725	7	344	47	3	381	53	4
562	Telegraph and wireless operators................	80,445	30,035	37	23,068	77	29	6,967	23	8
564	Telephone men............	112,577	5,677	5	2,943	52	3	2,734	48	2
566	Construction foremen.....	8,123	649	8	351	54	4	298	46	4
567	Foremen and overseers, telegraph and telephone companies.	4,419	518	12	409	79	9	109	21	3
568	Foremen and overseers, water transportation.	3,468	184	5	109	66	3	55	34	2
569	Foremen and overseers, other transportation.	937	374	39	267	71	28	107	29	11
570	Steam railroad inspectors	31,810	6,891	22	5,272	76	16	1,619	24	6
571	Street railroad inspectors.	2,640	366	13	281	77	10	85	23	3
572	Other transportation, inspectors................	3,804	2,178	57	1,983	91	52	195	9	5
575	Road and street building..	207,538	16,896	8	9,353	55	4	7,543	45	4
576	Street cleaning, laborers...	11,438	639	5	438	69	4	201	31	1
577	Other transportation, laborers..................	35,676	6,686	19	3,085	46	9	3,601	54	10
578	Steam shovel men.........	(1)	2,425	......	1,787	74	......	637	26	......
579	Well drivers..............	(1)	4,908	......	3,548	72	......	1,360	28	......
580	Proprietors and officials, telephone and telegraph.	11,602	1,372	12	1,157	84	10	215	16	2
581	Proprietors and officials, other transportation....	5,472	873	15	680	77	12	193	23	3
585	Steam railroad (semiskilled).................	28,091	36,930	......	26,264	71	......	10,666	29	......
586	Street railroad (semiskilled)	5,965	2,638	44	1,852	70	31	786	30	13
587	Other transportation pursuits (semiskilled).	10,500	5,161	49	3,442	66	33	1,719	34	16
588	Bridge workers...........	(1)	676	......	408	60	......	268	40	......
990	Chauffeurs or autodrivers, motorcycle...........	(1)	122	......	65	53	......	57	47	......
[2]591	Auto mechanics, motorcycle repairmen........	(1)	1,716	......	1,073	62	......	643	38	......
600	Bankers and bank officials.	64,467	7,717	12	5,703	74	9	2,014	26	3
601	Commercial brokers.......	27,610	794	3	569	71	2	225	29	1
602	Loan broker and loan company officials	2,427	126	5	103	82	4	23	18	1
603	Pawnbrokers	1,416	79	5	48	61	3	31	39	2
604	Stockbrokers	15,788	639	4	445	69	3	194	31	1
605	Brokers and promoters....	9,963	802	8	559	69	5	243	31	3
611	Clerks in store	445,260	68,873	15	41,057	60	9	27,816	40	6
613	Commercial travelers.....	188,163	8,400	4	5,919	70	3	2,481	30	1
615	Decorators, drapers, window dressers	6,142	1,932	31	1,288	66	21	644	34	10
[3]622	Deliverymen, bakery, laundry, and store....	264,061	26,792	10	17,797	66	6	8,995	34	4
624	Floorwalkers and foremen in stores...............	20,638	1,323	6	961	73	5	362	27	1

[1] No data.   [2] Combed from 318 and 374.   [3] Key No. 620 included above.

APPENDIX TABLE 42–A.—*Industrial index—Statistical summary of occupations, by classes*—Continued.

Key No.	Occupation.	Male employees of all ages.	Ages 21–30 within selective service law as classified, 1918.		Deferred classes within selective service law.			Class I within selective service law.		
			Number.	Per cent of all ages.	Number.	Per cent of ages 21–30.	Per cent of all ages.	Number.	Per cent of ages 21–30.	Per cent of all ages.
(1)	(2)	(3)	(4)	(5)	(6)	(7)	(8)	(9)	(10)	(11)
625	Foremen (warehouse, stockyards, etc.)........	3,194	582	18	419	72	13	163	28	5
627	Inspectors, gaugers, and samplers..............	15.463	3,930	25	2,690	68	16	1,240	32	9
630	Insurance agents..........	101,732	12,982	13	9,884	66	10	3,098	24	3
631	Officials of insurance company.................	10,926	666	6	519	78	5	147	22	1
633	Coal yard laborers........	19,162	4,208	22	2,801	67	15	1,407	33	7
634	Elevator laborers..........	7,298	956	13	653	68	9	303	32	4
635	Lumberyard laborers.....	49,907	3,771	8	2,373	63	5	1,398	37	3
636	Stockyard laborers........	6,897	1,786	26	1,163	65	17	623	35	9
637	Warehouse laborers.......	10,025	2,468	25	1,553	63	15	915	37	10
640	Laborers, porters, and helpers in stores........	117,683	12,705	11	7,448	59	6	5,257	41	5
642	Newsboys................	34,164	1,709	5	969	57	3	740	43	2
644	Employment office keepers	2,599	851	33	644	76	25	207	24	8
645 646 647	Proprietors...............	23,116	2,586	11	2,085	81	9	501	19	2
650	Real estate agents and officials...............	144,741	4,438	3	2,996	68	2	1,442	32	1
1 652	Refrigeration operating men...................	(2)	230	.....	145	63	.....	85	37	.....
655	Retail and wholesale dealers, exports and imports.	1,432,988	134,720	9	95,411	71	7	39,309	29	2
3 657	Pharmacists.............	(3)	18,289	.....	13,930	76	.....	4,359	24	.....
663	Auctioneers..............	4,588	260	6	191	73	4	69	27	2
664	Demonstrators...........	5,037	329	7	186	56	4	143	44	3
665	Sales agents.............	40,830	436	11	311	71	8	125	29	3
666	Salesmen in store........	1,008,823	224,874	22	150,931	67	15	73,943	33	7
668	Undertakers.............	23,844	5,288	22	3,512	66	15	1,776	34	7
686	Fruit graders and packers.	5,422	1,036	19	686	66	13	350	34	6
687	Butchers.................	17,715	50,936	.....	39,499	78	.....	11,437	22	.....
688	Other trade occupations...	24,748	1,180	4	641	54	2	539	46	2
1 690	Packers (shipping and warehouse).............	(2)	9,638	.....	7,293	75	.....	2,345	25	.....
700	Fire department men.....	40,946	8,544	21	6,982	82	17	1,562	18	4
702	Guards, watchmen, and doorkeepers............	90,011	4,308	5	2,700	63	3	1,608	37	2
706	Garbage men and scavengers..................	4,861	469	9	332	71	7	137	29	2
707	Other public service laborers..................	72,458	8,968	12	5,390	60	8	3,578	40	4
710	Detectives..............	7,301	2,379	33	1,551	65	22	828	35	11
711	Marshals and constables..	10,434	315	3	251	80	2.4	64	20	.6
712	Probation and truant officers.................	1,199	70	6	47	67	4	23	23	2
713	Sheriffs.................	8,204	535	7	392	73	5	143	27	2
715	Officials and inspectors, city...................	38,191	1,446	4	1,076	74	3	370	26	1
716	Officials and inspectors, county.................	21,900	1,429	6	1,130	79	5	299	21	1
720	Officials and inspectors, State.................	8,282	613	7	430	70	5	183	30	2
721	Officials and inspectors, United States...........	52,582	3,768	7	3,032	81	6	736	19	1
725	Policemen...............	71,279	10,314	14	8,385	81	11	1,929	19	3
727	Soldiers, sailors, and marines.................	88,726	419	.4	222	53	.2	197	47	.2
730	Life savers...............	2,481	94	3.7	66	70	2.6	28	30	1.1
731	Lighthouse keepers.......	1,832	126	6	100	79	5	26	21	1
732	Other public service occupations...............	7,494	2,486	33	2,081	84	28	405	16	5
740	Actors..................	32,541	5,743	17	2,998	52	9	2,745	48	8
742	Architects...............	19,105	1,646	8	1,182	72	6	464	28	2
744	Artists, sculptors, and teachers of art..........	38,219	6,761	17	3,765	55	10	2,996	45	7

1 Combed from 688.   2 No data.   3 Combed from 655 and 666.

APPENDIX TABLE 42–A.—*Industrial index—Statistical summary of occupations, by classes*—Continued.

Key No.	Occupation.	Male employees of all ages.	Ages 21–30 within selective service law as classified, 1918.		Deferred classes within selective service law.			Class I within selective service law.		
			Number.	Per cent of all ages.	Number.	Per cent of ages 21–30.	Per cent of all ages.	Number.	Per cent of ages 21–30.	Per cent of all ages.
(1)	(2)	(3)	(4)	(5)	(6)	(7)	(8)	(9)	(10)	(11)
746	Authors.................	5,023	355	7	208	59	4	147	41	3
747	Editors.................	39,539	7,011	18	4,520	64	11	2,491	36	7
750	Chemists or chemical workers.................	18,714	12,764	68	9,092	71	48	3,672	29	20
1752	Surveyors and civil engineers.................	59,838	15,069	25	10,934	72	18	4,135	28	7
753	Mining engineers..........	7,969	2,238	28	1,818	81	22	420	19	6
754	Surveyors................	(2)	4,117	......	1,587	39	......	2,530	61	......
755	Clergymen................	135,720	17,761	14	17,014	96	13	747	4	1
757	College presidents and professors.................	18,018	3,838	21	2,443	64	14	1,395	36	7
759	Dentists.................	45,996	10,980	24	7,860	72	17	3,120	28	7
760	Designers................	13,556	3,569	26	2,729	76	20	840	24	6
761	Draftsmen................	38,311	26,626	70	19,065	72	50	7,561	28	20
762	Inventors................	2,699	116	4	62	53	2	54	47	2
764	Lawyers, judges, and justices.................	131,909	17,218	13	11,509	67	9	5,709	33	4
766	Musicians and teachers (music).................	160,206	16,945	11	10,262	61	7	6,683	39	4
767	Musicians................	(2)	4,713	......	2,591	55	......	2,122	45	......
768	Photographers............	36,541	7,593	21	4,905	64	14	2,688	36	7
770	Physicians and surgeons..	173,801	12,826	7	9,401	73	5	3,425	27	2
772	Showmen.................	23,110	10,091	44	7,021	70	31	3,070	30	13
774	Teachers of athletics, dancing, etc...........	4,520	1,999	44	1,167	59	26	832	41	19
775	Teachers (school)........	684,602	44,448	6	26,271	59	4	18,177	41	2
777	Nurses or masseurs.......	94,676	2,066	2	725	35	6	1,341	65	1.4
779	Veterinarians or farriers....	13,399	3,196	24	2,397	75	18	799	25	6
780	Other professional pursuits.................	18,028	5,306	29	3,698	70	21	1,608	30	8
781	Abstractors, notaries, and justices of peace.......	8,561	737	9	542	74	7	195	26	2
782	Fortune tellers, hypnotists, and spiritualists ..	1,840	6	.3	5	83	.2	1	17	.1
783	Healers (except physicians and surgeons).....	7,859	329	4	305	93	3.7	24	7	.3
784	Keepers of charitable and penal institutions.......	8,614	167	1.9	120	71	1.3	47	29	.6
785	Officials of lodges, societies, etc.................	9,447	433	4	299	69	3	134	31	1
786	Religious and charity workers.................	18,365	2,130	11	1,402	66	7	728	34	4
787	Theatrical owners, managers and officers.........	13,020	2,418	18	1,625	67	12	793	33	6
788	Other semi-professional pursuits.................	6,956	698	10	292	42	4	406	58	6
790	Attendants and helpers...	21,391	2,945	14	1,641	56	8	1,304	44	6
4792	Statisticians.............	(2)	714	......	451	63	......	263	37	......
800	Barbers.................	224,566	59,768	27	42,300	71	19	17,468	29	8
802	Bartenders..............	116,419	14,375	12	8,992	63	8	5,383	37	4
804	Billiard and poolroom keepers............	15,917	1,673	11	1,112	66	7	561	34	4
805	Dance hall, skating rink, etc., keepers...........	3,337	298	9	170	57	5	128	43	4
5811	Boarding and lodging house keepers...........	190,269	200	.1	136	68	.07	64	32	.03
813	Bootblacks..............	16,123	4,827	30	2,998	62	19	1,829	38	11
5820	Charwomen and cleaners..	39,139	2,150	5	1,758	82	4	392	......	1
822	Elevator tenders........	28,790	10,259	36	5,807	57	21	4,452	43	15
830	Hotel keepers and managers.................	74,179	2,429	3	1,696	69	2	733	30	1

1 The census total includes surveyors, key No. 754. The Provost Marshal General's code numbers should be combined for comparison with census.
2 No data.
3 Combed from 766.
4 Combed from 780.
5 Females included in above figure.

Appendix Table 42-A.—*Industrial index—Statistical summary of occupations, by classes*—Continued.

Key No.	Occupation.	Male employees of all ages.	Ages 21-30 within selective service law as classified, 1918.		Deferred classes within selective service law.			Class I within selective service law.		
			Number.	Per cent of all ages.	Number.	Per cent of ages 21-30.	Per cent of all ages.	Number.	Per cent of ages 21-30.	Per cent of all ages.
(1)	(2)	(3)	(4)	(5)	(6)	(7)	(8)	(9)	(10)	(11)
[1] 833	Housekeepers and stewards	217,664	3,449	1.5	2,165	63	1	1,284	37	.5
835	Sextons	130,043	9,294	7	6,070	65	5	3,224	35	2
842	Laborers, domestic and professional service	61,502	6,164	10	3,565	57	6	2,509	43	4
846	Laundrymen	742,415	11,437	15	7,818	68	10	3,619	32	5
848	Laundry owners, officials and managers	20,749	820	4	611	75	3	209	25	1
[2] 855	Nurses or masseurs (not trained)	145,863	4,019	3	2,008	50	1	2,011	50	2
866	Porters (except in stores)	96,747	27,455	28	13,071	48	14	14,384	52	14
868	Restaurant and cafe keepers	69,956	7,024	10	5,038	72	7	1,986	28	3
870	Saloon keepers	78,447	1,953	3	1,505	77	2	448	23	1
873	Bell boys, shore boys, etc.	21,078	4,622	22	1,964	42	9	2,658	58	13
874	Chambermaids	187	(3)	.....	(3)	.....	.....	(3)	.....	.....
875	Coachmen and footmen	29,517	410	1	226	55	.5	184	45	.5
876	Cook	518,006	59,106	11	32,736	55	6	26,370	45	5
877	Other servants	1,193,700	13,927	1	7,502	54	.5	6,425	46	.5
888	Waiters	216,537	42,285	20	25,097	59	12	17,188	41	8
895	Bathhouse keeper and attendants	5,284	148	3	89	60	2	59	40	1
896	Cemetery keepers	5,568	145	3	105	72	2	40	28	1
897	Clothing cleaners	17,089	11,287	66	7,752	69	45	3,535	31	21
898	Umbrella menders and scissor grinders	1,211	72	6	44	61	4	28	39	2
899	Other domestic and personal-service pursuits	4,968	546	11	339	60	7	216	40	4
900	Students	(3)	41,306	.....	24,612	60	.....	16,694	40	.....
[4] 955	Agents, purchasing	(3)	10,867	.....	7,575	70	.....	3,292	30	.....
956	Canvassers	21,384	1,193	6	806	68	4	387	32	2
957	Collectors	41,109	4,257	10	2,892	68	7	1,365	32	3
966	Cashiers and accountants	559,705	139,728	25	87,899	63	16	51,829	37	9
976	Clerical workers—shipping clerks	92,406	28,566	31	18,417	64	20	10,149	36	11
977	Other clerks	736,166	293,763	39	188,136	64	26	105,627	36	13
[5] 978	Stock clerks (store or factory)	(3)	20,948	.....	12,449	59	.....	8,499	41	.....
987	Bundle and cash boys	12,496	248	19	121	49	9	127	51	10
988	Messengers, errand, and office boys	111,444	4,379	4	2,263	52	2	2,116	48	2
[6] 998 999	}Typists and stenographers	364,196	44,886	12	25,045	56	7	19,841	44	5

[1] Females probably included in above census figure.
[2] Females included in above.
[3] No data.
[4] Combed from 955.
[5] Combed from 611 and 977.
[6] No data on 998 in census index; combed from 999.

APPENDIX TABLE 49-A.—*Physical groups by States.*

	Total examined physically.	Physically qualified, Group A.	Per cent of examined.	Remediable Group B.	Per cent of examined.	Limited service Group C.	Per cent of examined.	Physically disqualified, Group D.	Per cent of examined.
United States.........	3,208,446	2,259,027	70.41	88,436	2.76	339,377	10.58	521,606	16.25
Alabama....'............	69,284	53,717	77.53	1,363	1.97	4,814	6.95	9,390	13.55
Arizona...............	8,979	4,941	55.03	166	1.85	738	8.22	3,134	34.90
Arkansas.............	58,928	46,560	79.02	929	1.57	3,732	6.33	7,707	13.08
California..............	67,772	41,135	60.70	1,375	2.03	10,578	15.61	14,684	21.66
Colorado	30,087	17,769	59.06	587	1.95	5,131	17.05	6,600	21.94
Connecticut...........	38,631	22,721	58.82	1,700	4.40	6,411	16.00	7,799	20.79
Delaware.............	7,003	4,599	65.67	25	.36	1,473	21.03	906	12.94
District of Columbia.....	12,538	9,069	72.32	490	3.91	1,530	12.21	1,449	11.56
Florida.................	32,780	24,659	75.23	573	1.75	2,794	8.52	4,754	14.50
Georgia...............	84,191	61,527	73.08	1,705	2.02	7,362	8.74	13,597	16.16
Idaho.................	15,871	11,250	70.89	762	4.80	1,566	9.87	2,293	14.44
Illinois................	225,127	163,507	72.63	5,727	2.54	21,334	9.48	34,559	15.35
Indiana...............	74,356	53,811	72.37	1,604	2.15	7,576	10.19	11,365	15.29
Iowa.................	78,272	60,364	77.13	1,797	2.29	5,181	6.62	10,930	13.96
Kansas...............	48,669	38,148	78.38	1,215	2.50	3,287	6.75	6,019	12.37
Kentucky.............	75,024	58,356	77.78	1,208	1.61	4,478	5.97	10,982	14.64
Louisiana.............	66,142	50,571	76.46	1,464	2.21	4,888	7.39	9,219	13.94
Maine.................	22,646	14,765	65.19	617	2.73	3,378	14.92	3,886	17.16
Maryland.............	38,392	26,237	68.35	943	2.45	4,197	10.93	7,015	18.27
Massachusetts........	108,356	62,216	57.42	3,747	3.46	22,192	20.48	20,201	18.64
Michigan.............	115,412	70,726	61.28	4,089	3.54	13,844	12.00	26,753	23.18
Minnesota............	81,862	62,199	75.98	1,155	1.41	5,930	7.24	12,578	15.37
Mississippi...........	55,615	43,376	77.99	951	1.71	3,467	6.24	7,821	14.06
Missouri..............	115,030	83,949	72.99	2,742	2.38	9,319	8.10	19,020	16.53
Montana..............	31,547	23,159	73.40	727	2.33	3,657	11.59	4,004	12.68
Nebraska.............	41,646	32,555	78.18	850	2.04	2,864	6.87	5,377	12.91
Nevada...............	3,482	2,407	69.13	143	4.11	435	12.49	497	14.27
New Hampshire........	12,258	7,793	63.57	247	2.02	2,552	20.82	1,666	13.59
New Jersey............	93,964	62,489	66.50	2,458	2.62	14,151	15.06	14,866	15.82
New Mexico...........	11,983	9,296	77.59	239	1.99	723	6.03	1,725	14.39
New York.............	315,536	192,311	60.95	12,631	4.00	49,670	15.74	60,924	19.31
North Carolina........	75,498	55,215	73.14	1,393	1.84	7,051	9.34	11,839	15.68
North Dakota.........	25,151	19,498	77.52	256	1.02	1,648	6.55	3,749	14.91
Ohio..................	166,177	120,142	72.29	4,925	2.96	18,176	10.94	22,934	13.81
Oklahoma.............	65,374	54,145	82.82	1,249	1.91	3,588	5.49	6,392	9.78
Oregon...............	23,996	16,582	69.10	657	2.74	3,243	13.51	3,514	14.65
Pennsylvania.........	246,884	171,101	69.30	10,833	4.39	27,632	11.19	37,318	15.12
Rhode Island.........	15,395	8,264	53.68	574	3.73	2,143	13.92	4,414	28.67
South Carolina........	40,197	28,091	69.88	1,478	3.68	3,696	9.20	6,932	17.24
South Dakota.........	25,806	19,718	76.41	1,183	4.58	1,775	6.88	3,130	12.13
Tennessee............	70,367	51,319	72.93	1,459	2.07	5,826	8.28	11,763	16.72
Texas.................	131,586	101,862	77.41	2,276	1.73	7,334	5.57	20,114	15.29
Utah.................	13,844	9,752	70.45	375	2.71	1,721	12.42	1,996	14.42
Vermont..............	10,761	6,056	56.28	364	3.38	1,914	17.79	2,427	22.55
Virginia..............	68,177	49,146	72.08	1,160	1.70	5,390	7.91	12,481	18.31
Washington...........	37,581	20,800	55.35	1,022	2.72	7,179	19.10	8,580	22.83
West Virginia.........	51,473	40,047	77.81	710	1.37	3,242	6.30	7,474	14.52
Wisconsin.............	90,517	64,579	71.35	4,158	4.59	7,974	8.81	13,806	15.25
Wyoming.............	8,279	6,528	78.85	135	1.63	593	7.16	1,023	12.36

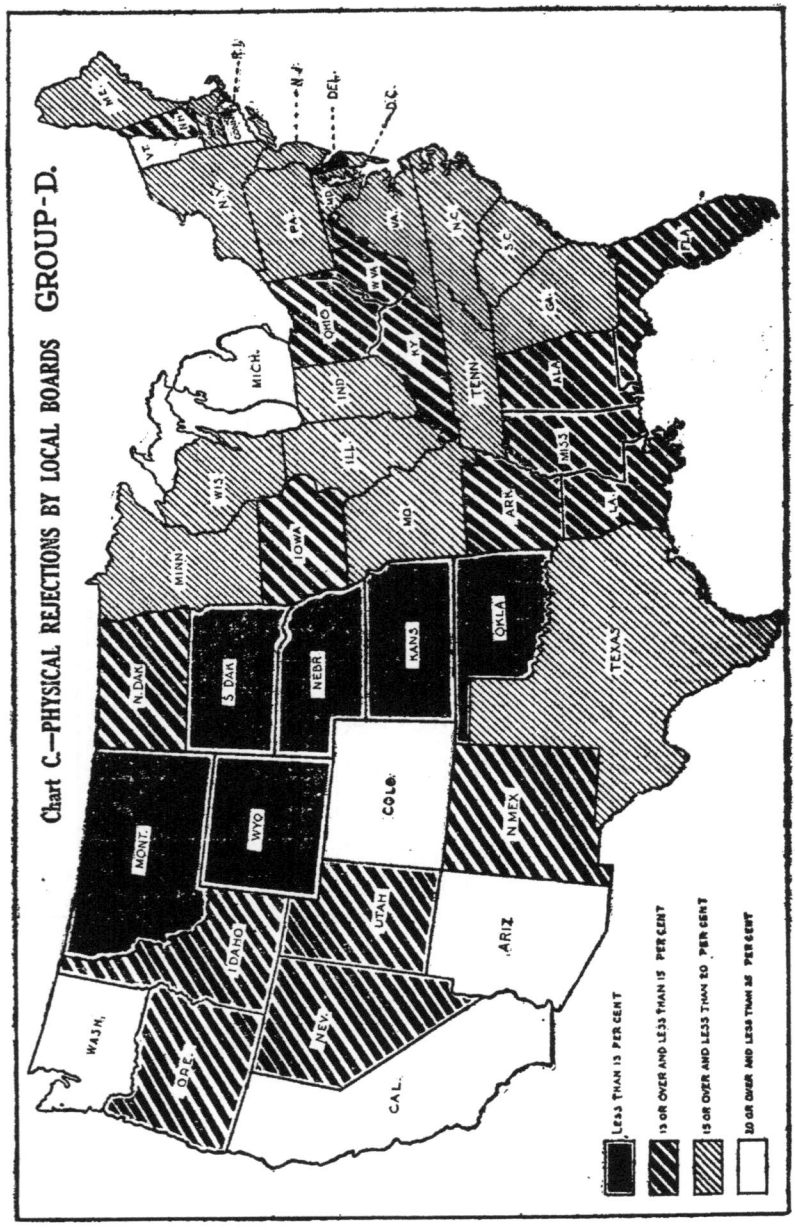

Chart C.—PHYSICAL REJECTIONS BY LOCAL BOARDS   GROUP-D.

APPENDIX TABLE 52–A.—*Causes for physical rejections in urban and rural districts, compared.*

URBAN DISTRICTS.

Disqualifying defects.	Average.	Md.	Mass.	Ill.	Ohio.	N. Y.	E. Pa.	W. Pa.	Mo.
Total	100	100	100	100	100	100	100	100	100
1. Alcohol and drugs	1.9	1.0	2.3	1.8	1.0	2.3	1.9	0.3	1.4
2. Bones and joints	8.9	15.2	7.4	8.9	12.6	8.1	9.1	11.2	8.3
3. Developmental	9.7	3.6	16.7	4.2	16.2	10.4	14.7	6.7	1.8
4. Digestive system	.2	.3	.2	.4	.3	.2	.2	.4	.3
5. Ears	5.8	7.5	4.0	4.0	3.1	5.7	8.6	8.7	3.4
6. Eyes	10.9	14.3	5.4	8.7	5.1	13.6	9.1	10.8	8.9
7. Flat foot	9.3	9.3	9.7	8.0	8.1	10.6	6.3	7.6	12.8
8. Genito-urinary (venereal)	1.4	1.6	.4	3.3	1.1	.9	1.0	1.7	2.5
9. Genito-urinary (nonvenereal)	1.2	.7	1.4	1.5	.9	1.3	1.1	.6	.8
10. Heart and blood vessels	8.9	10.4	11.3	7.1	7.7	7.9	10.7	13.1	10.0
11. Hernia	10.1	7.8	8.2	9.2	10.0	10.4	9.1	12.3	12.9
12. Mental deficiency	1.5	2.7	1.8	2.0	1.5	1.1	1.8	1.2	2.0
13. Nervous and mental disorders	4.6	4.7	2.9	5.2	5.0	4.8	3.7	4.1	5.7
14. Respiratory (tuberculous)	5.6	9.8	4.3	5.3	3.5	4.9	5.7	4.3	11.7
15. Respiratory (nontuberculous)	1.8	2.1	.6	.1.1	2.3	1.3	2.6	4.7	2.7
16. Skin	.1	.0	.1	.2	.0	.2	.1	.2	.2
17. Teeth	5.9	2.2	14.6	3.9	7.3	6.8	3.9	6.5	2.1
18. Thyroid	2.0	.6	.1	2.9	2.7	1.2	2.1	2.2	6.5
19. Tuberculous (nonrespiratory)	.1	.0	.0	.2	.4	.2	.1	.1	.0
20. Other defects	.7	1.0	.5	.4	.2	1.0	.5	.3	.8
21. Defects not stated	9.2	5.0	8.3	21.5	11.1	7.1	7.9	3.0	5.1

RURAL DISTRICTS.

Disqualifying defects.	Average.	Md.	Mass.	Ill.	Ohio.	N. Y.	E. Pa.	W. Pa.	Mo.
Total	100	100	100	100	100	100	100	100	100
1. Alcohol and drugs	0.6	0.2	0.6	1.1	0.9	0.8	0.1	0.1	0.5
2. Bones and joints	10.9	14.5	6.5	11.3	12.6	9.4	12.1	13.8	9.5
3. Developmental	6.3	1.4	14.3	6.6	9.0	8.2	5.0	2.9	.4
4. Digestive system	.3	.3	.2	.2	.2	.2	.4	.3	.2
5. Ears	4.4	6.4	3.8	3.3	2.5	3.8	7.7	5.7	2.7
6. Eyes	9.0	11.4	4.4	9.2	5.7	8.8	9.9	9.3	10.6
7. Flat foot	7.4	8.3	9.1	8.3	5.2	9.0	4.9	4.4	6.7
8. Genito-urinary (venereal)	1.1	1.2	.7	1.8	.6	1.1	.6	.6	.9
9. Genito-urinary (nonvenereal)	1.5	1.6	2.5	1.3	.4	2.1	1.1	1.0	.9
10. Heart and blood vessels	10.4	10.1	12.1	9.1	6.1	7.4	14.9	15.3	13.0
11. Hernia	9.6	9.0	9.5	11.8	10.4	9.2	7.5	8.5	10.6
12. Mental deficiency	3.9	11.7	3.5	3.4	2.4	1.9	5.6	2.9	7.9
13. Nervous and mental disorders	4.2	5.1	2.0	4.7	4.9	4.2	2.9	4.8	5.2
14. Respiratory (tuberculous)	5.3	6.2	4.0	6.4	4.7	3.1	4.9	3.9	14.3
15. Respiratory (nontuberculous)	2.4	3.9	2.5	1.4	3.9	1.3	4.1	3.9	2.2
16. Skin	.2			.3	.1	.2	.1	.1	.1
17. Teeth	6.7	3.9	10.2	4.8	- 8.1	7.2	8.6	8.1	1.9
18. Thyroid	3.4	2.8	.4	3.1	4.9	2.1	5.0	5.2	5.2
19. Tuberculous (nonrespiratory)	.1	.2		.1		.1	.1	.1	.2
20. Other defects	.5	.6	.9	.8	.2	.6	.3	.4	.5
21. Defects not stated	11.9	1.2	12.7	10.9	17.2	19.2	4.3	8.6	6.4

APPENDIX TABLE 56-A.—*Physical rejections at camp, compared by States (Feb. 10 to Nov. 1, 1918).*

States.	Total inducted.	Total rejected.	Per cent rejected.
United States................................	2,124,293	172,000	8.10
Alabama..........................	50,779	7,189	14.16
Arizona...........................	4,799	272	5.67
Arkansas..........................	41,178	3,056	7.42
California.........................	43,147	2,842	6.59
Colorado..........................	17,752	1,092	6.15
Connecticut.......................	23,631	1,178	5.11
Delaware..........................	3,815	342	8.96
District of Columbia..............	8,430	480	5.69
Florida...........................	23,729	2,068	8.72
Georgia...........................	56,534	7,041	12.45
Idaho.............................	9,592	855	8.91
Illinois..........................	145,063	9,368	6.46
Indiana...........................	58,418	3,047	5.22
Iowa..............................	61,889	3,346	5.41
Kansas............................	37,572	2,844	7.57
Kentucky..........................	49,350	3,235	6.56
Louisiana.........................	43,116	4,476	10.38
Maine.............................	14,114	1,336	9.47
Maryland..........................	26,678	1,318	4.94
Massachusetts.....................	60,178	4,953	8.23
Michigan..........................	72,899	6,287	8.62
Minnesota.........................	61,109	3,566	5.84
Mississippi.......................	38,546	4,060	10.53
Missouri..........................	74,595	8,055	10.80
Montana...........................	19,671	1,445	7.35
Nebraska..........................	24,130	1,471	6.10
Nevada............................	1,928	134	6.95
New Hampshire.....................	6,755	494	7.31
New Jersey........................	58,864	4,563	7.75
New Mexico........................	6,900	463	6.71
New York..........................	193,237	17,194	8.90
North Carolina....................	51,690	4,517	8.74
North Dakota......................	16,114	1,028	6.38
Ohio..............................	112,114	6,551	5.84
Oklahoma..........................	50,636	3,520	6.95
Oregon............................	15,184	1,451	9.56
Pennsylvania......................	154,930	14,996	9.68
Rhode Island......................	9,086	673	7.41
South Carolina....................	37,104	3,653	9.85
South Dakota......................	18,715	1,269	6.78
Tennessee.........................	45,861	4,825	10.52
Texas.............................	94,694	4,851	5.12
Utah..............................	8,035	525	6.53
Vermont...........................	5,291	492	9.30
Virginia..........................	43,791	5,667	12.94
Washington........................	20,202	1,425	7.05
West Virginia.....................	37,079	3,755	10.13
Wisconsin.........................	58,852	4,273	7.26
Wyoming...........................	7,117	459	6.45

Chart D.—PHYSICAL REJECTIONS OF INDUCTED MEN AT CAMP, BY STATES

PER CENT

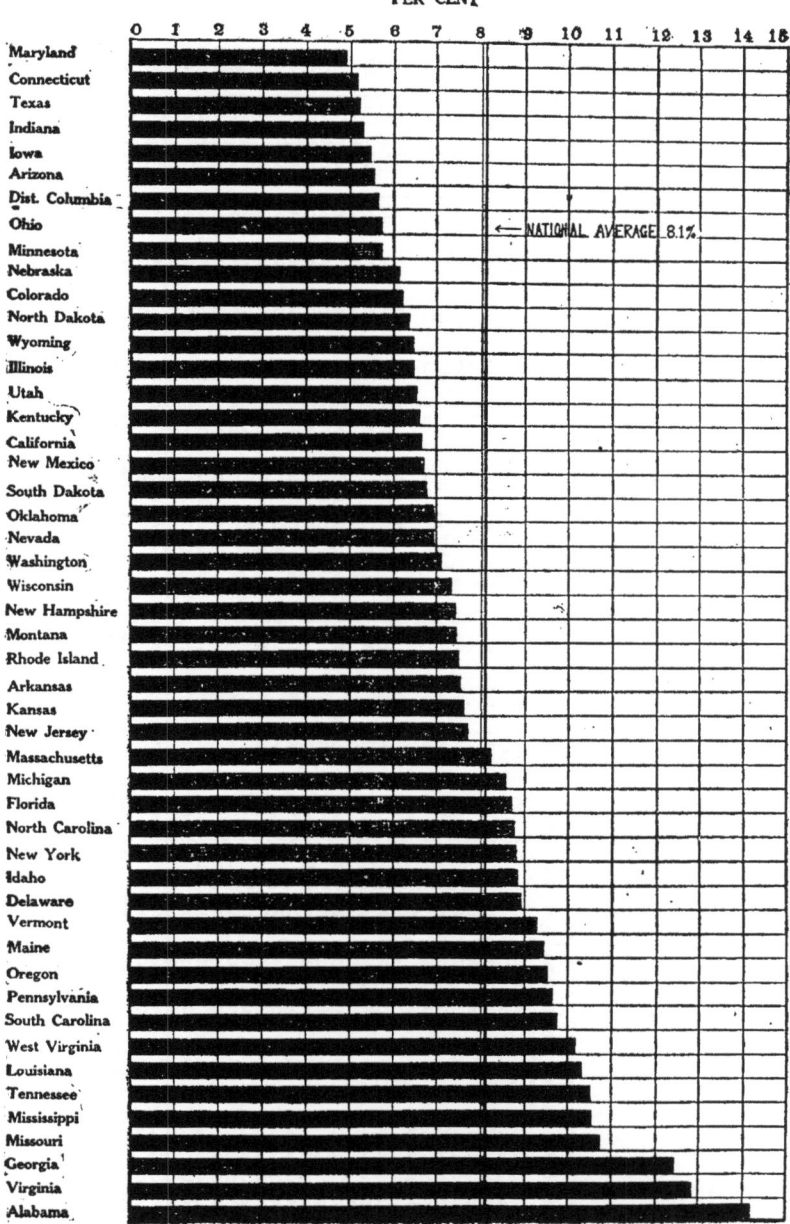

APPENDIX TABLE 60-A.—*Combined figures and percentages for causes of rejections by local boards and camp surgeons, and for discharges from the Army of recently inducted men (Series X, Y, Z) (Feb. 10 to Nov. 1, 1918).*

I. FIGURES.

	Total	Alcohol and drugs	Bones and joints	Developmental defects	Digestive system	Ears	Eyes	Flat foot	Genitourinary (venereal)	Genitourinary (nonvenereal)	Heart and blood vessels	Hernia	Mental deficiency	Nervous and mental disorders	Respiratory (tuberculous)	Respiratory (nontuberculous)	Skin	Teeth	Thyroid	Tuberculosis (nonrespiratory)	Other defects	Defects not stated
United States	467,094	2,007	57,744	39,166	2,476	20,465	49,801	18,087	6,235	6,309	61,142	28,263	24,514	23,728	40,533	7,823	12,519	14,793	8,215	4,136	14,314	25,419
Alabama	13,372	13	1,678	1,076	42	224	963	531	136	168	1,938	790	1,164	604	919	171	156	375	50	76	347	1,942
Arizona	1,703	18	171	61	12	68	134	36	22	13	168	30	30	51	593	27	36	22	7	20	139	71
Arkansas	9,903	15	1,387	845	44	322	1,034	574	173	66	1,320	600	739	469	888	175	491	84	26	87	290	261
California	4,196	63	359	123	14	133	240	236	85	27	465	238	119	232	480	35	17	139	73	8	28	1,058
Colorado	5,132	8	579	444	21	269	434	172	39	23	620	181	181	219	1,036	144	111	82	73	78	172	68
Connecticut	9,427	32	858	901	46	652	1,611	229	41	137	1,394	292	411	508	950	180	310	154	73	138	280	230
Delaware	435	22	53	31	2	23	36	42	9	8	39	30	17	21	28	11		24	8		1	30
District of Columbia	698	10	68	45	4	35	65	28	28	8	90	46	36	69	31	22	4	41	32	1	10	35
Florida	4,780	10	618	374	19	85	376	127	135	46	492	356	161	198	301	83	207	112	11	21	206	782
Georgia	19,140	28	2,989	2,803	80	422	1,627	581	296	150	2,755	964	983	774	1,492	211	819	888	113	203	490	476
Idaho	1,124		151	52	6	56	92	123	10	6	139	91	28	41	48	6	17	64	45	4	38	104
Illinois	28,999	200	3,358	1,927	179	1,663	3,942	1,113	600	393	3,522	1,755	1,216	1,046	2,020	387	317	620	777	206	831	1,617
Indiana	14,465	8	1,816	1,342	99	634	1,391	328	188	109	1,696	1,009	777	776	1,686	257	721	311	243	208	396	540
Iowa	14,670	28	1,911	1,427	121	653	1,547	554	66	121	2,084	625	859	570	993	215	750	457	254	126	737	315
Kansas	8,155	28	1,048	178	59	280	768	289	104	92	985	677	446	409	802	203	609	104	172	44	731	169
Kentucky	9,628	43	1,015	902	58	346	908	126	134	85	822	547	812	501	1,467	192	559	248	91	103	207	252
Louisiana	10,514	15	1,436	756	58	261	953	310	625	134	1,344	733	733	532	1,142	108	184	588	56	41	276	305
Maine	1,911	6	197	175	9	66	97	96	25	42	269	158	137	93	69	47	24	108	61	8	20	110
Maryland	6,026	12	486	406	31	380	918	146	53	48	983	152	152	379	692	89	48	104	88	71	252	185
Massachusetts	22,425	123	1,909	3,079	101	1,297	3,139	743	100	285	3,344	804	840	893	1,742	349	714	946	83	235	986	677
Michigan	20,045	43	2,213	1,126	104	1,001	2,093	632	175	274	2,205	1,041	1,022	949	1,583	249	210	843	59	144	608	281
Minnesota	16,008	87	2,222	1,251	87	653	1,351	532	109	217	1,284	1,271	900	729	1,133	183	864	774	351	217	625	468
Mississippi	11,146	19	2,705	691	95	239	770	966	559	213	1,617	840	836	542	1,039	125	473	357	58	97	382	244
Missouri	14,595	163	1,688	691	79	662	1,728	155	301	213	1,617	591	793	854	1,637	273	100	209	572	99	201	688
Montana	3,456	17	440	189	17	109	393	165	19	30	591	249	189	115	371	70	39	221	77	37	125	237
Nebraska	4,835	17	673	208	41	167	583	220	51	74	643	328	249	246	195	68	99	112	58	43	319	217
Nevada	633	2	73	41	2	33	66	18	6	8	75	44	44	10	68	8	39	20	77	4	46	52
New Hampshire	1,384	1	138	165	6	77	164	80	7	32	178	68	59	76	101	28	7	76	58	24	31	64
New Jersey	6,050	72	639	763	26	428	567	348	23	21	442	561	164	286	447	84	27	581	101	6	55	567
New Mexico	1,499	19	111	148	77	57	163	32	16	21	144	59	50	62	378	31	37	15	14	13	34	38
New York	24,970	436	2,178	2,109	77	1,475	2,921	1,948	245	389	2,850	1,970	645	1,613	1,378	365	254	1,200	458	83	367	2,259
North Carolina	15,708	5	1,943	1,483	57	274	1,276	312	194	74	1,774	522	522	701	1,637	382	442	258	14	104	532	2,450
North Dakota	4,090	1	641	363	31	281	440	128	10	43	598	220	246	190	247	73	45	235	90	61	147	130

Ohio	19,562	96	2,814	1,530	91	798	1,565	727	199	833	1,889	958	1,014	1,448	1,694	431	571	449	527	215	479	1,269
Oklahoma	9,706	62	1,376	680	54	438	1,233	287	158	92	1,022	743	566	466	773	148	457	98	56	84	214	694
Oregon	3,942	6	465	333	24	378	246	157	31	53	583	176	104	170	309	63	76	152	102	39	108	267
Pennsylvania	29,574	123	3,687	2,236	131	2,043	3,367	1,076	252	299	4,204	1,843	1,354	1,654	2,023	734	282	1,209	883	182	573	1,412
Rhode Island	2,853	26	213	435	12	161	381	194	12	21	286	153	101	120	225	44	55	140	13	25	87	149
South Carolina	9,023	12	1,008	1,044	43	199	665	236	92	62	875	304	504	427	521	112	75	157	61	58	302	2,176
South Dakota	1,488	3	272	23	10	30	152	115	10	15	191	121	56	67	110	44	4	97	52	4	13	99
Tennessee	13,310	43	1,802	1,427	95	324	1,200	699	131	134	1,467	686	1,032	622	1,225	204	651	251	129	140	378	670
Texas	21,114	45	2,987	2,232	161	871	3,220	436	275	211	2,305	1,469	961	1,051	2,180	332	471	362	68	200	673	514
Utah	2,614	11	366	205	13	128	250	117	14	35	566	127	72	110	128	24	29	114	53	37	97	113
Vermont	966	1	106	35	5	23	109	80	10	33	106	82	32	83	20	32	25	36	18		32	78
Virginia	11,624	12	1,627	702	40	296	1,229	412	213	149	1,929	680	873	609	1,094	349	124	356	325	121	277	277
Washington	4,983	17	651	379	29	274	437	271	21	48	1,054	217	144	207	382	54	20	162	159	58	141	248
West Virginia	9,082	17	1,506	512	40	384	1,048	224	116	104	1,180	647	543	429	615	270	411	225	331	70	198	210
Wisconsin	14,893	34	1,764	1,112	83	741	1,506	397	105	296	2,102	966	780	788	1,249	208	435	440	688	179	739	262
Wyoming	1,132	9	136	72	4	53	87	69	19	11	125	99	35	48	69	14	52	37	20	8	45	130
State not specified	726	1	104	105	5	22	86	11	3	7	88	19	40	30	71	14	51	6	11	14	29	9

APPENDIX TABLE 60-A.—*Combined figures and percentages for causes of rejections by local boards and camp surgeons, and for discharges from the Army of recently inducted men (Series X, Y, Z) (Feb. 10 to Nov. 1, 1918)—Continued.*

II. PERCENTAGES.

State.	Total.	Alcohol and drugs.	Bones and joints.	Developmental defects.	Digestive system, diseases of.	Ears, disease of.	Eyes, disease of.	Flat foot (pathological).	Genito-urinary (venereal).	Genito-urinary (non-venereal).	Heart and blood vessels.	Hernia.	Mental deficiency.	Nervous and mental disorders.	Respiratory (tuberculous).	Respiratory (non-tuberculous).	Skin, disease of.	Teeth.	Disease of thyroid.	Tuberculosis (non-respiratory).	All other defects.	Cause not given.
United States	467,694	0.4	12.3	8.4	0.5	4.4	10.6	3.8	1.3	1.3	13.1	6.0	5.2	5.1	8.7	1.7	2.7	3.1	1.8	0.9	3.1	5.4
Alabama	13,372	.1	12.5	8.0	.3	1.7	7.2	4.0	1.0	1.3	14.5	6.0	8.7	4.5	6.9	1.3	1.2	2.8	.4	.6	2.6	14.5
Arizona	1,703	.3	10.0	3.4	.7	4.0	7.9	2.1	1.3	.7	9.9	8.2	1.0	3.0	34.8	1.6	2.2	1.3	.4	1.2	8.2	4.2
Arkansas	9,953	.3	13.9	8.4	.4	3.2	10.4	4.8	1.7	.7	13.3	6.6	7.4	4.7	8.9	1.8	4.9	4.6	.3	.9	2.9	2.6
California	4,196	1.5	8.6	2.9	.3	3.2	5.7	6.8	2.0	.6	11.1	5.7	2.8	5.5	11.4	.8	.4	3.8	1.4	1.5	.7	25.2
Colorado	5,132	.2	11.3	8.7	.4	5.2	8.5	3.4	.4	1.5	12.2	3.1	3.5	4.9	20.2	2.8	2.2	1.6	1.8	1.5	3.4	1.3
Connecticut	9,427	.3	9.1	9.6	.5	6.2	17.1	2.4	.4	1.5	14.8	3.1	3.9	5.4	6.4	1.9	3.3	1.6	1.8	1.5	3.0	2.4
Delaware	435	5.0	12.2	7.1	.5	6.3	8.3	9.7	2.1	1.8	9.0	6.9	3.9	4.8	10.4	2.5	3.3	6.5	1.8	1.5	3.2	6.9
District of Columbia	698		9.7	6.4	.6	5.0	9.3	4.0	4.0	1.1	12.9	6.6	5.2	9.9	4.4	3.2	.6	5.9	4.6	.1	1.4	5.0
Florida	4,780	.2	12.9	7.8	.4	1.8	7.9	2.7	2.8	1.0	10.3	7.4	3.4	4.1	7.6	1.7	4.3	2.3	.8	.4	4.3	16.4
Georgia	19,140	.2	15.4	14.6	.4	2.2	8.5	3.0	1.5	.8	14.4	6.8	5.1	4.0	7.8	1.1	1.5	4.6	.3	1.1	2.6	2.5
Idaho	1,124	.1	13.4	4.6	.4	5.0	8.2	10.9	1.5	.8	12.4	8.1	2.5	3.6	4.3	.5	1.5	5.7	4.0	.4	3.4	9.3
Illinois	28,999	.7	11.6	6.3	.5	5.7	13.6	4.0	2.1	.8	11.7	7.0	4.2	5.7	9.0	1.3	5.0	2.1	1.7	1.4	2.9	5.6
Indiana	14,495	.1	12.5	9.3	.7	4.4	10.5	2.3	.4	1.2	14.2	6.0	5.9	5.4	10.9	1.8	5.0	3.1	1.7	.9	2.7	3.7
Iowa	14,670	.2	13.0	9.7	.8	4.5	10.1	3.8	1.3	.8	14.2	6.0	5.5	3.9	6.8	1.5	7.5	1.3	2.1	.9	5.0	2.1
Kansas	8,155	.2	12.9	2.2	.7	3.4	10.4	1.3	.4	.8	12.2	6.0	5.4	5.0	8.8	2.5	5.8	2.6	2.1	.9	9.0	2.1
Kentucky	9,628	.4	10.5	9.4	.6	3.6	10.4	2.9	1.8	.9	8.5	7.0	8.4	5.2	15.2	2.0	5.8	5.5	.8	1.1	2.1	2.6
Louisiana	10,514	.1	13.7	7.2	.6	2.5	9.1	1.3	1.3	.9	12.8	7.0	7.0	5.1	3.6	1.9	5.8	5.5	.6	.6	2.6	2.9
Maine	1,911	.3	10.3	9.2	.5	5.5	5.1	2.9	5.9	2.8	14.1	8.3	7.2	4.9	10.9	2.5	1.3	5.5	.1	.6	1.0	5.8
Maryland	6,025	.3	8.1	6.7	.5	5.5	5.1	13.1	.9	2.8	16.3	3.6	8.9	6.3	11.5	1.5	3.2	1.7	1.4	1.2	4.2	3.1
Massachusetts	22,425	.5	8.8	13.7	.5	5.8	14.0	2.4	1.0	2.6	16.3	3.6	3.7	4.0	7.8	1.6	3.2	4.2	1.4	1.0	4.4	3.0
Michigan	20,045	.2	11.4	7.8	.9	4.1	8.4	3.3	.9	1.3	14.9	7.1	5.6	4.7	7.6	1.2	1.0	4.8	.7	.7	3.0	1.4
Minnesota	16,008	.2	13.9	5.9	.9	2.1	6.9	3.3	.7	1.7	22.8	6.5	7.5	4.9	9.3	1.1	5.4	3.2	2.2	1.4	3.9	2.9
Mississippi	11,146	1.1	16.1	4.7	.8	2.1	6.9	4.8	5.0	1.5	13.8	8.7	7.5	5.9	11.2	1.1	.7	1.4	2.5	.5	1.4	4.0
Missouri	14,585	.5	10.9	5.5	.5	4.5	11.8	5.4	2.1	.9	11.1	8.7	2.0	3.4	5.6	1.0	4.7	6.4	3.9	.9	1.4	6.9
Montana	3,456	.5	13.0	6.6	.8	3.5	12.1	4.7	1.1	1.5	17.1	7.2	2.0	5.1	7.7	1.4	2.0	2.3	2.2	.9	6.6	4.5
Nebraska	4,835	.3	13.9	7.2	.5	3.5	12.1	2.8	1.1	1.1	13.3	6.9	1.6	5.1	7.7	.9	2.5	2.3	2.2	.9	6.6	4.5
Nevada	638	.3	11.4	7.2	.3	5.6	10.3	2.8	.9	.9	11.7	4.9	1.6	3.8	10.7	1.3	6.1	3.1	.3	.6	7.2	8.2
New Hampshire	1,384	.3	10.6	11.9	.4	5.6	12.1	5.8	.4	2.3	12.7	4.9	2.7	3.5	7.3	2.0	.4	5.5	.3	1.7	1.0	4.6
New Jersey	6,050	1.2	12.6	7.4	.3	7.1	9.4	5.6	.5	2.0	7.3	4.1	2.7	4.7	3.3	1.4	2.5	9.6	.9	.1	2.3	9.4
New Mexico	1,499	.2	9.9	4.9	.3	3.8	10.9	2.1	.4	2.0	9.6	9.1	2.1	3.9	29.8	2.1	.4	9.6	.9	.3	1.5	2.5
New York	24,970	1.7	8.7	9.4	.4	1.7	11.7	7.8	1.1	1.6	10.1	7.9	2.6	6.5	5.5	1.4	1.0	5.2	1.7	.3	3.4	9.0
North Carolina	15,708	.03	12.5	9.4	.4	1.7	11.7	2.0	1.2	1.4	11.3	3.3	7.1	4.5	10.4	1.5	2.8	1.6	1.0	1.0	3.4	15.6
North Dakota	4,086	.02	13.2	6.6	.8	5.7	13.6	3.1	.2	1.1	14.6	5.4	6.0	4.7	6.0	1.8	1.1	5.8	2.0	1.2	3.6	3.7

State	Population																					
Ohio	19,562	6.5	2.4	1.1	2.7	2.3	2.9	2.2	8.7	7.4	5.2	4.9	9.4	4.3	1.0	3.7	8.1	4.1	.5	7.8	14.4	.5
Oklahoma	9,706	7.2	2.8	.9	.6	1.0	4.7	1.5	8.0	4.8	5.8	7.7	10.5	.9	1.6	3.0	12.8	4.5	.6	7.0	14.2	.6
Oregon	3,842	6.9	1.9	1.0	2.7	4.0	2.0	1.6	8.0	4.4	4.2	4.6	15.2	1.4	.8	4.1	6.4	9.8	.4	8.7	12.1	.2
Pennsylvania	29,574	4.8	3.0	.6	3.0	4.1	1.0	2.5	6.8	5.6	4.6	6.4	14.2	1.0	.9	3.6	11.4	6.9	.4	7.6	12.5	.4
Rhode Island	2,853	5.2	3.3	.9	.5	4.9	1.9	1.5	6.8	4.4	3.5	5.4	10.0	.7	.4	6.8	13.4	5.6	.5	15.2	7.5	.9
South Carolina	9,023	24.1	.9	.6	.7	1.7	.8	1.2	7.9	4.7	5.6	3.4	9.7	.7	1.0	2.6	7.4	2.2	.7	11.6	12.2	.1
South Dakota	1,488	6.7	2.8	.3	3.5	6.5	.3	3.0	5.8	4.5	3.8	8.1	12.8	1.0	.7	7.7	10.2	2.0	.7	1.5	18.3	.2
Tennessee	13,310	5.0	3.2	1.1	1.0	1.9	4.9	1.5	9.2	4.7	7.8	5.2	11.0	1.0	1.0	5.3	9.3	2.4	.8	10.7	13.5	.3
Texas	21,114	5.0	3.7	.9	.3	1.7	2.2	1.6	7.4	5.0	4.6	7.0	11.3	1.0	1.3	2.0	15.3	4.1	.5	10.6	14.1	.2
Utah	2,614	2.4	3.3	1.4	2.2	4.4	2.1	.9	10.3	4.2	2.8	4.9	21.7	3.4	.5	4.5	9.6	4.9	.3	7.8	14.0	.4
Vermont	966	4.3	2.4		1.9	5.8	2.6	3.3	4.9	8.6	3.3	8.5	11.0	1.3	1.0	8.3	11.3	2.4	.6	3.7	11.0	.1
Virginia	11,624	8.1	2.2	1.0	2.8	3.1	1.1	3.0	2.1	5.2	7.5	5.8	16.6	1.3	1.8	5.4	10.6	2.5	.4	6.2	14.0	.1
Washington	4,983	2.4	2.8	1.2	3.2	3.3	1.4	1.1	8.8	4.0	2.9	4.4	21.4	1.0	.4	5.5	8.7	5.5	.6	7.6	13.1	.3
West Virginia	9,082	5.0	2.2	.8	3.6	2.5	4.5	3.4	7.7	4.7	6.2	6.5	13.0	1.1	1.3	2.5	11.5	4.2	.4	5.6	16.6	.2
Wisconsin	14,893	2.3	5.1	2.2	4.6	3.3	2.9	1.2	6.8	5.3	5.1	8.7	14.1	2.0	.7	2.7	10.1	5.0	.7	7.5	11.8	.2
Wyoming	1,132	11.5	4.0	.7	1.8	3.3	4.6	1.9	8.4	4.2	3.1	2.6	11.0	1.0	1.7	5.2	7.7	4.7	.4	6.4	12.0	.8
State not specified	726	1.2	4.0	1.9	1.5	.8	7.0		9.8	4.1	5.5		12.1	1.0	.4	1.5	11.8	3.0	.7	14.5	14.3	.1

APPENDIX TABLE 60-B.—*Causes of physical rejections by local boards, compared by States (Series X).*

I. FIGURES.

State.	Total.	Alcohol and drugs.	Bones and joints.	Developmental defects.[1]	Digestive system, diseases of.	Ears, disease of.	Eyes, disease of.	Flat foot (pathological).	Genito-urinary (venereal).	Genito-urinary (non-venereal).	Heart and blood vessels.	Hernia.	Mental deficiency.	Nervous and mental disorders.	Respiratory (tuberculous).	Respiratory (non-tuberculous).	Skin, disease of.	Teeth.	Disease of thyroid.	Tuberculosis (non-respiratory).	All other defects.	Cause not given.
United States[2]	255,312	231	33,283	27,293	1,586	12,100	32,775	3,342	2,042	3,054	36,470	8,473	14,417	10,945	27,559	3,081	12,207	4,314	3,151	3,853	12,671	2,465
Alabama	4,420	...	632	563	32	94	519	59	51	32	599	132	358	205	416	53	153	105	3	71	258	80
Arizona	1,297	1	119	61	10	40	94	8	11	9	121	24	24	19	556	17	35	...	4	20	136	5
Arkansas	6,099	2	910	770	31	201	677	126	102	44	652	293	361	291	604	54	487	47	4	85	267	82
California	311	...	21	28	...	12	34	2	2	...	41	14	14	9	79	6	16	4	...	5	11	15
Colorado	3,823	9	403	370	20	175	346	73	24	54	500	154	110	150	903	111	109	32	35	78	144	23
Connecticut	7,841	11	705	817	41	542	1,492	122	22	103	1,215	135	298	395	860	130	308	121	42	136	274	72
Delaware																						
District of Columbia	77	...	17	13	2	1	7	1	4	20	5	...	3	4	4	...	4	...	...	1	5	...
Florida	2,311	4	286	303	15	53	213	33	74	86	304	118	101	47	226	24	206	36	3	21	177	38
Georgia	11,212	8	1,431	1,403	61	266	1,035	134	167	91	2,105	396	636	386	1,151	116	810	232	62	198	437	112
Idaho	179	...	24	6	3	11	31	4	1	2	13	3	3	7	20	...	16	1	1	2	30	...
Illinois	16,278	16	1,978	1,345	94	1,075	2,882	223	99	167	2,402	577	735	686	1,823	179	270	168	378	242	747	192
Indiana	10,509	2	1,427	1,196	80	467	1,130	159	125	104	1,454	501	594	505	1,141	115	717	147	185	203	358	131
Iowa	10,772	7	1,454	1,278	84	481	1,169	198	40	96	629	450	714	304	768	123	743	296	142	120	711	120
Kansas	4,919	1	562	140	46	181	489	63	36	46	528	165	348	210	491	54	599	44	42	40	696	66
Kentucky	5,825	4	659	754	41	203	646	50	62	51	661	232	369	227	668	66	555	51	22	97	174	37
Louisiana	4,865	2	692	572	23	168	645	50	99	1	528	149	318	181	620	45	173	102	11	60	190	53
Maine	333	...	64	69	3	33	38	15	19	26	28	39	8	14	5	3	20	8	...	...	13	...
Maryland	3,960	2	246	371	19	234	722	17	51	169	674	276	281	214	567	25	47	57	39	68	238	45
Massachusetts	16,317	21	1,492	2,298	78	986	2,849	245	65	91	2,529	557	625	534	1,474	238	704	403	34	231	955	127
Michigan	12,594	11	1,507	1,002	59	671	1,528	168	48	138	2,714	665	710	557	1,291	153	195	289	440	129	555	108
Minnesota	11,855	16	1,734	986	61	510	1,104	173	133	89	1,770	289	701	466	964	139	856	385	184	210	597	129
Mississippi	6,910	5	985	564	66	134	423	77	19	39	789	68	467	212	582	57	468	211	14	90	321	43
Missouri	4,520	3	472	535	24	263	713	72	5	15	667	68	257	203	435	45	78	46	48	59	150	30
Montana	1,763	2	223	130	10	104	283	21	30	49	361	116	144	58	138	25	39	43	34	34	113	13
Nebraska	8,092	5	419	281	27	131	443	68	4	...	431	28	6	152	247	31	95	53	25	40	302	13
Nevada	460	1	56	36	3	28	60	2	...	10	47	10	31	38	88	7	4	15	...	3	43	4
New Hampshire	766	...	87	117	3	57	141	8	7	...	100	8	43	38	88	7	17	19	3	9	30	6
New Jersey	475	...	64	35	4	49	77	6	12	8	58	28	143	26	376	21	37	13	...	5	26	7
New Mexico	980	...	72	72	16	25	92	63	30	98	81	72	530	173	45	45	221	2	1	12	195	21
New York	4,076	6	363	398	42	355	690	138	6	51	1,503	391	530	460	1,317	141	438	45	44	102	436	110
North Carolina	10,305	8	1,000	1,228	34	339	1,005	56	...	...	403	90	188	127	189	47	44	103	51	47	137	81
North Dakota	2,963	...	404	282	...	178	469	...	...	...	...	...	...	...	...	...	...	70	53	...	...	...

Ohio	10,543	11	1,564	1,103	54	493	1,138	115	66	705	987	118	587	716	1,217	128
Oklahoma	5,278	6	889	484	45	205	758	58	51	44	502	289	297	253	514	41
Oregon	2,235	1	315	227	20	317	142	45	14	38	368	77	74	92	207	47
Pennsylvania	11,165	10	1,646	1,123	56	719	1,711	86	55	97	1,599	303	691	498	1,177	111
Rhode Island	1,921	10	143	387	10	106	311	43	8	12	231	55	54	59	165	23
South Carolina	5,099	6	812	885	33	171	500	117	78	42	710	09	412	286	406	64
South Dakota	57		2	11	1		4			1	14		1	2	2	
Tennessee	7,509	4	1,032	879	68	231	809	105	48	54	915	208	549	329	886	69
Texas	15,055	12	2,195	1,800	117	657	2,308	137	179	118	1,634	813	791	655	1,794	174
Utah	1,983	3	289	175	7	106	216	29	8	31	49	80	65	81	110	18
Vermont	352	1	49	4	4	11	81	18		6	13	47	3	41		15
Virginia	4,840	4	698	489	27	152	580	33	62	71	637	134	354	262	691	61
Washington	3,322	4	482	319	24	213	359	56	9	41	792	64	104	137	315	61
West Virginia	4,565	2	822	428	32	189	602	43	24	53	471	190	251	110	399	45
Wisconsin	9,715	13	1,235	890	48	543	1,087		33	110	1,583	179	565	438	1,073	58
Wyoming	569	1	79	45	3	25	46	14	5	7	74	33	17	14	46	5
Not allocated	726	1	104	105	5	22	86	11	3	7	58	19	40	30	71	14

1 Height, weight, chest measurement, muscles.
2 These figures do not represent full returns from States, but only those for which the records were available.

APPENDIX TABLE 60-B.—*Causes of physical rejections by local boards, compared by States (Series X)—Continued.*

II. PERCENTAGES.

State	Total	Alcohol and drugs	Bones and joints	Developmental defects	Digestive system, diseases of	Ears, disease of	Eyes, disease of	Flat foot (pathological)	Genito-urinary (venereal)	Genito-urinary (non-venereal)	Heart and blood vessels	Hernia	Mental deficiency	Nervous and mental disorders	Respiratory (tuberculous)	Respiratory (non-tuberculous)	Skin, disease of	Teeth	Disease of thyroid	Tuberculosis (non-respiratory)	All other defects	Cause not given
United States	255,312	0.1	13.1	10.7	0.6	4.7	12.8	1.3	0.8	1.2	14.2	3.3	5.6	4.2	10.7	1.2	4.8	1.7	1.2	1.5	4.9	0.9
Alabama	4,420		14.3	12.8	.7	2.1	11.7	1.3	1.2	.7	13.5	2.9	8.1	4.6	9.4	1.2	3.5	2.4	.1	1.6	5.8	1.8
Arizona	1,297	.1	12.4	13.9	.8	2.7	7.2	2.1	1.2	.7	9.3	1.9	.8	1.5	42.9	1.3	2.7	.6	.1	1.5	10.5	1.6
Arkansas	6,099	.1	15.1	12.6	.5	3.3	11.1	2.1	1.7	.7	10.7	4.8	5.9	4.8	9.9	.9	8.0	.7	.1	1.4	4.3	1.3
California	311		6.8	6.8		3.8	11.0	1.9	1.7		13.3	4.5	2.9	2.9	25.4	1.9	5.1	1.3		1.6	3.8	1.3
Colorado	3,823	.2	10.5	9.7	.5	4.6	9.1	1.9	.6	1.4	13.1	4.0	2.9	3.9	23.6	2.9	2.9	.8	.9	1.8	3.8	4.8
Connecticut	7,841	.1	9.0	10.4	.5	6.9	19.0	1.6	.2	1.3	13.5	1.7	3.8	5.0	11.0	1.6	3.9	1.5	.5	1.7	3.5	.9
Delaware																						
District of Columbia	77		22.1	16.8	2.5	1.2	9.2	1.2	5.2		6.5	7.8	3.9	5.2	5.2	1.0	5.2	1.6	1.3	1.2	6.5	
Florida	2,311	.17	12.4	13.1	.6	2.3	9.2	1.4	3.2	1.3	13.3	5.1	4.4	2.4	9.8	1.0	8.9	2.1	.5	.9	5.7	1.6
Georgia	11,212	.07	12.7	12.5	.9	2.4	17.3	2.2	2.5	.8	18.7	3.5	5.6	3.4	10.2	1.0	7.2	.6	1.1	1.8	5.0	
Idaho	179		13.4	3.4	1.7	6.2	17.6	2.2	1.5	1.1	7.3	1.1	1.7	4.1	11.1	1.1	8.9	1.4	2.3	1.7	16.7	1.2
Illinois	16,278	.09	12.1	8.2	.5	6.8	10.7	1.4	.6	1.0	14.6	3.4	4.4	2.8	10.8	1.0	6.8	1.0	1.8	1.5	4.6	1.2
Indiana	10,509	.01	13.5	11.3	.8	4.4	10.8	1.5	1.2	1.0	11.6	4.7	5.7	4.1	7.1	.8	6.9	2.7	1.3	1.1	3.4	1.1
Iowa	10,772	.06	13.4	13.4	.8	4.5	10.8	1.3	.4	1.0	13.5	3.4	6.6	2.8	9.9	1.2	12.1	.9	1.3	1.1	3.6	.8
Kansas	4,919	.02	11.4	2.8	.9	3.6	11.6	1.8	.8	.9	12.8	3.4	7.1	4.2	9.9	.8	3.0	.9	.8	.8	14.1	.6
Kentucky	5,525	.07	11.9	8.9	.7	3.5	13.3	1.0	1.8	1.3	9.6	3.1	6.7	3.7	12.1	.9	10.5	2.0	.39	1.8	3.9	1.2
Louisiana	4,865	.04	14.2	11.8	.5	3.5	11.4	4.5	2.0	1.3	13.6	4.0	6.5	3.7	12.7	.6	6.0	2.4		1.2	3.9	1.1
Maine	333		19.2	20.7	.5	10.0	18.3	4.5	.5	1.0	8.4	.9	3.3	5.4	14.3	1.5	1.1	1.4	.9	1.7	6.0	1.1
Maryland	3,950	.05	9.1	14.0	.5	5.9	17.4	.4	.3	.7	17.0	1.6	7.1	3.2	9.0	1.2	4.3	2.3	.9	1.4	5.8	.9
Massachusetts	16,317	.12	9.1	14.0	.5	6.3	15.0	1.5	.3	1.0	15.4	1.6	3.8	3.4	10.2	1.5	7.2	2.3	3.4	1.0	4.4	.9
Michigan	12,594	.08	11.9	8.3	.5	6.3	6.0	1.3	2.2	1.1	21.5	2.8	5.9	3.5	8.1	1.2	7.9	3.6	1.5	1.3	5.4	1.0
Minnesota	11,536	.13	14.6	9.5	1.1	4.3	9.3	1.3	2.2	.5	14.9	4.9	5.9	3.9	9.8	1.9	1.7	3.3	.2	1.5	5.0	.7
Mississippi	5,910	.08	15.8	9.5	1.1	2.3	7.2	1.7	2.2	.8	13.4	4.9	7.9	3.5	10.3	1.1	2.2	1.5	.2	1.5	5.4	.7
Missouri	4,220	.07	11.1	7.3	.8	5.9	16.8	1.7	.28	.8	15.8	1.6	6.1	4.9	7.4	1.4	3.1	1.7	1.9	1.9	6.4	.7
Montana	1,763	.11	12.6	9.1	.4	6.2	16.0	2.2	.9	.7	20.4	3.8	2.5	2.4	7.9	.9	2.2	2.5	.7	1.9	6.4	.7
Nebraska	3,992	.16	13.5	7.8	.6	4.2	14.3	2.2	.9	1.5	13.9	3.8	4.6	6.7	13.0	1.5	3.1	3.3	.7	1.3	9.3	.09
Nevada	460	.2	12.1	9.1	.4	4.4	13.0	1.0	.5	.8	10.3	3.0	4.0	5.0	10.8	.9	8.5	3.3	1.9	1.2	9.3	2.8
New Hampshire	765		11.4	15.3	.4	7.4	18.4	1.3	.3	1.3	13.1	1.3	8.4	2.4	8.0	.4	3.6	2.5		1.1	3.9	.5
New Jersey	476		11.4	7.7	.6	10.3	7.0	1.3	.8	.9	12.1	3.0	2.3	4.9	40.4	2.3	4.0	1.0	.1	1.0	4.2	1.3
New Mexico	630		8.3	7.7	.4	2.7	9.9	1.3	.8	.9	8.7	2.8	3.7	4.5	10.0	1.4	5.3	1.0	1.0	1.1	4.7	.4
New York	4,076	.1	8.8	9.6	.4	8.8	16.9	1.3	.8	.9	17.8	3.0	9.0	4.4	12.8	1.6	1.5	2.4	1.0	1.6	4.7	1.1
North Carolina	10,305	.01	14.1	11.9	.4	2.0	16.0	1.3	.8	.9	14.5	3.2	6.4	4.5	10.8	1.4	4.3	1.8	.5	1.6	4.7	1.1
North Dakota	2,883		14.1	8.1	.8	6.1	16.0	2.0	.2	1.0	14.1	3.2	6.4	4.4	8.6	1.6	1.5	2.4	1.8	1.6	4.8	2.8

Ohio	10,543	.1	14.8	10.5	.5	4.7	11.0	1.1	.6	6.7	9.4	1.2	5.6	6.8	10.5	1.2	4.4	.5	2.7	1.9	4.2	.3
Oklahoma	5,278	.1	16.8	9.2	.9	3.9	14.3	1.1	.1	.8	10.0	5.5	5.6	4.8	9.7	.8	8.6	1.0	.3	1.3	3.4	1.2
Oregon	2,295	.04	13.7	9.9	.9	13.8	6.2	2.0	.6	1.7	16.0	3.4	3.1	4.0	9.0	2.0	3.3	1.4	2.1	1.6	4.5	.4
Pennsylvania	11,153	.08	14.8	10.0	.5	6.4	15.3	.8	.5	.9	14.3	2.6	6.1	4.5	10.5	.9	2.2	1.0	1.3	1.4	4.2	1.0
Rhode Island	1,021	.5	7.4	20.1	.5	6.5	16.2	2.2	.4	.6	12.1	2.8	2.8	2.9	8.7	1.2	2.2	5.6		1.2	4.2	1.7
South Carolina	5,099	.1	15.9	17.0	.6	3.4	9.8	2.3	1.5	.8	13.9	2.1	8.1	5.2	7.9	1.3	1.5	1.3	.2	1.1	5.2	.3
South Dakota	57		3.5	19.2	1.7	1.7	7.0	3.5		1.7	24.5		1.7	3.5	3.5		8.5		12.2	1.7	12.2	
Tennessee	7,509	.05	13.7	11.7	.9	3.1	10.7	1.4	.6	.7	12.1	2.8	7.3	4.3	11.5	.9	3.0	1.7	.7	1.7	4.2	.9
Texas	15,055	.07	14.5	12.0	.8	4.3	15.2	.9	1.1	.8	10.8	5.3	5.3	4.1	11.8	1.2	1.5	1.4	.2	1.2	4.3	.9
Utah	1,983	.1	14.6	8.8	.4	5.3	10.9	1.5	.4	1.6	25.1	4.0	3.3	4.1	5.5	4.3	7.1	2.8	2.4	1.5	4.7	.5
Vermont	352	.2	13.9	1.1	1.1	3.1	23.0	5.1		1.5	3.7	13.3	.9	11.6		1.3	2.5		2.3		7.1	.2
Virginia	4,840	.08	14.1	10.1	.6	6.4	12.0	1.7	1.3	1.2	13.2	2.8	7.3	5.4	14.3	1.4	.6	1.7	.6	2.5	4.0	.8
Washington	3,322	.1	14.5	9.6	.7	4.1	10.8	1.7	.5	1.2	23.8	1.9	3.1	4.1	9.4	1.3	8.8	.6	3.4	1.6	4.2	.3
West Virginia	4,565	.04	18.0	9.4	.7	5.6	13.1	.9	.3	1.1	10.3	4.2	5.5	5.2	8.7	1.3	4.3	.9	1.4	1.4	4.0	1.8
Wisconsin	9,715	.1	12.7	9.2	.5	5.6	11.1		.9	1.1	16.3	1.8	5.8	4.5	12.0	1.3	9.1	.1	3.6	1.8	7.3	.4
Wyoming	569	.1	13.9	7.9	.5	4.4	8.1	2.5		1.1	13.0	5.8	3.0	2.5	8.1	.9	7.0	2.8	1.8	1.8	7.6	4.7
Not allocated	726	.1	14.3	14.5	.7	3.0	11.8	1.5	.4	1.0	12.1	2.6	5.5	4.1	9.8	1.9		.8	1.5	1.9	4.0	1.2

APPENDIX TABLE 60-C.—*Causes of physical rejections by camp surgeons, compared by States (series Y).*

I. FIGURES.

Disqualifying defects.	Total.	Ala.	Ariz.	Ark.	Cal.	Colo.	Conn.	Del.	D. C.	Fla.
Total	172,000	7,189	272	3,056	2,842	1,092	1,178	342	480	2,668
1. Alcohol and drugs	1,238	9	2	16	45	10	15	16	0	4
2. Bones and joints	19,623	833	39	308	262	136	108	47	38	261
3. Developmental defects	11,538	504	9	73	75	73	79	31	31	66
4. Digestive system	448	0	0	10	6	0	3	1	1	0
5. Ears	6,455	108	15	71	76	85	78	17	31	28
6. Eyes	15,367	417	34	328	159	83	97	35	51	140
7. Flat foot	13,234	409	20	419	263	88	94	38	24	72
8. Genito-urinary (venereal)	2,744	64	5	27	58	7	14	6	19	47
9. Genito-urinary (non-venereal)	2,226	112	1	11	12	7	26	8	4	16
10. Heart and blood vessels	19,288	729	33	573	328	105	140	23	62	150
11. Hernia	18,353	651	6	359	216	112	136	20	30	22
12. Mental deficiency	6,293	614	4	297	81	55	49	11	10	70
13. Nervous and mental disorders	7,319	285	18	98	149	72	53	13	43	82
14. Respiratory (tuberculous)	10,792	396	26	233	341	116	69	17	25	129
15. Respiratory (nontuberculous)	3,483	68	5	90	17	23	38	8	19	1
16. Skin	213	1	1	3	0	2	0	0	0	1
17. Teeth	9,952	254	12	37	150	47	32	22	39	75
18. Thyroid	3,697	37	2	19	14	29	23	5	30	6
19. Tuberculosis (nonrespiratory)	159	0	0	2	3	0	2	0	0	25
20. Other defects	1,373	84	3	16	16	27	4	0	4	25
21. Defects not stated	18,225	1,614	37	66	571	15	118	24	19	604

II. PERCENTAGES.

Disqualifying defects.	Total.	Ala.	Ariz.	Ark.	Cal.	Colo.	Conn.	Del.	D. C.	Fla.
Total	100	100	100	100	100	100	100	100	100	100
1. Alcohol and drugs	0.72	0.1	0.7	0.5	1.6	0.9	1.3	4.7	0.0	0.2
2. Bones and joints	11.41	11.6	14.3	10.1	9.2	12.5	9.2	13.7	7.9	12.6
3. Developmental defects	6.71	7.0	3.3	2.4	2.6	6.7	6.7	9.1	6.5	3.3
4. Digestive system	.26	.0	.0	.3	.2	.0	.3	.3	.2	.0
5. Ears	3.75	1.5	5.5	2.3	2.7	7.8	6.6	5.0	6.5	1.1
6. Eyes	8.93	5.8	12.5	10.7	5.6	7.6	8.2	10.2	10.6	7.1
7. Flat foot	7.69	5.7	7.4	13.7	9.3	8.1	8.0	11.1	5.0	3.5
8. Genito-urinary (venereal)	1.60	.9	1.8	.9	2.0	.6	1.2	1.8	4.0	2.3
9. Genito-urinary (non-venereal)	1.30	1.6	.4	.4	.4	.6	2.2	2.3	.8	.6
10. Heart and blood vessels	11.20	10.1	12.1	18.7	11.5	9.6	11.9	6.7	12.9	6.3
11. Hernia	10.67	9.1	2.2	11.7	7.6	10.3	11.5	5.8	6.2	11.1
12. Mental deficiency	3.66	8.5	1.5	9.7	2.9	5.0	4.2	3.2	2.1	1.4
13. Nervous and mental disorders	4.26	4.0	6.6	3.2	5.2	6.6	4.5	3.8	9.0	4.0
14. Respiratory (tuberculous)	6.27	5.5	9.6	7.6	12.0	10.6	5.9	5.0	5.2	5.8
15. Respiratory (nontuberculous)	2.02	.9	1.8	2.9	.6	2.1	3.2	2.3	4.0	1.2
16. Skin	.12	.01	.4	.1	.0	.2	.0	.0	.0	.05
17. Teeth	5.79	3.5	4.4	1.2	5.3	4.3	2.7	6.4	8.1	3.6
18. Thyroid	2.15	.5	.7	.6	.5	2.7	2.0	1.5	6.2	.3
19. Tuberculosis (nonrespiratory)	.09	.0	.0	.07	.1	.0	.2	.0	.0	.2
20. Other defects	.80	1.2	1.1	.5	.6	2.5	.3	.0	.8	1.3
21. Defects not stated	10.60	22.5	13.6	2.3	20.1	1.4	10.0	7.0	4.0	32.6

APPENDIX TABLE 60–C.—*Causes of physical rejections by camp surgeons, compared by States (series Y)*—Continued.

I. FIGURES.

Disqualifying defects.	Ga.	Idaho.	Ill.	Ind.	Iowa.	Kans.	Ky.	La.	Me.	Md.
Total....................	7,041	855	9,368	3,047	3,346	2,844	3,235	4,476	1,336	1,318
1. Alcohol and drugs................	13	0	110	5	13	23	32	10	2	8
2. Bones and joints................	1,388	123	996	344	411	428	267	471	117	196
3. Developmental defects..............	1,390	46	561	146	147	37	146	183	100	33
4. Digestive system.................	22	1	41	5	10	10	7	23	2	4
5. Ears...........................	128	42	339	134	149	78	99	81	14	92
6. Eyes..........................	545	59	850	210	361	264	302	290	51	170
7. Flat foot......................	425	116	805	156	339	198	60	223	227	116
8. Genito-urinary (venereal).......	94	8	242	42	15	46	69	308	12	19
9. Genito-urinary (nonvenereal).....	49	7	135	36	17	31	22	68	35	15
10. Heart and blood vessels...........	538	117	809	356	518	323	209	579	219	135
11. Hernia........................	561	88	1,014	435	416	446	377	387	140	111
12. Mental deficiency................	222	23	278	103	108	71	323	246	84	93
13. Nervous and mental disorders.....	291	18	495	118	188	141	199	205	43	65
14. Respiratory (tuberculous).........	276	26	591	400	177	286	768	476	51	106
15. Respiratory (nontuberculous).....	72	4	125	85	70	138	60	129	35	39
16. Skin..........................	8	0	29	3	5	10	3	9	3	0
17. Teeth.........................	646	63	410	106	156	59	111	478	99	39
18. Thyroid.......................	42	38	252	40	79	123	48	30	4	23
19. Tuberculosis (nonrespiratory).....	0	1	15	1	5	1	5	0	0	1
20. Other defects...................	52	8	55	33	16	33	27	82	7	11
21. Defects not stated...............	279	67	1,216	289	146	98	101	198	91	42

II. PERCENTAGES.·

Disqualifying effects.	Ga.	Idaho.	Ill.	Ind.	Iowa.	Kans.	Ky.	La.	Me.	Md.
Total....................	100	100	100	100	100	100	100	100	100	100
1. Alcohol and drugs................	0.2	0.0	1.2	0.2	0.4	0.8	1.0	0.2	0.1	0.6
2. Bones and joints................	19.7	14.4	10.6	11.3	12.3	15.0	8.3	10.5	8.8	14.9
3. Developmental defects..............	19.7	5.4	6.0	4.8	4.4	1.3	4.5	4.1	7.5	2.5
4. Digestive system.................	.3	..1	.4	.2	.3	.3	.2	.6	.1	.3
5. Ears...........................	1.8	4.9	3.6	4.4	4.5	2.8	3.1	1.8	1.0	7.0
6. Eyes..........................	7.7	6.9	9.1	6.9	10.8	9.3	9.3	6.5	3.8	12.9
7. Flat foot......................	6.0	13.6	8.6	5.1	10.1	7.0	1.9	5.0	17.0	8.8
8. Genito-urinary (venereal).......	1.3	.9	2.6	1.4	.4	1.6	2.1	6.9	.9	1.4
9. Genito-urinary (nonvenereal).....	.7	.8	1.4	1.2	.5	1.1	.7	1.5	2.6	1.1
10. Heart and blood vessels...........	7.6	13.7	8.6	11.7	15.5	11.3	6.5	12.9	16.4	10.2
11. Hernia........................	8.0	10.2	10.8	14.3	12.4	15.7	11.7	8.6	10.5	8.4
12. Mental deficiency................	3.2	2.7	3.0	3.4	3.2	2.5	10.0	5.5	6.3	7.0
13. Nervous and mental disorders.....	4.1	2.1	5.3	3.9	5.6	5.0	6.2	4.6	3.2	5.0
14. Respiratory (tuberculous).........	3.9	3.0	6.3	13.1	5.3	10.1	23.7	10.6	3.8	8.0
15. Respiratory (nontuberculous).....	1.0	.5	1.3	2.8	2.1	4.9	1.9	2.9	2.6	3.0
16. Skin..........................	.1	.0	.3	.1	.1	.4	.1	.2	.2	.0
17. Teeth.........................	9.2	7.4	4.4	3.5	4.7	2.1	3.4	10.7	7.4	3.0
18. Thyroid.......................	.6	4.4	2.7	1.3	2.4	4.3	1.5	.7	.3	1.7
19. Tuberculosis (nonrespiratory).....	.0	.1	.2	.03	.1	.04	.2	.0	.0	.08
20. Other defects...................	.7	.9	.6	1.1	.5	1.2	.8	1.8	.5	.8
21. Defects not stated...............	4.0	7.8	13.0	9.4	4.4	3.4	3.1	4.4	6.8	3.2

APPENDIX TABLE 60–C.—*Causes of physical rejections by camp surgeons, compared by States (series Y)*—Continued.

I. FIGURES.

Disqualifying defects.	Mass.	Mich.	Minn.	Miss.	Mo.	Mont.	Nebr.	Nev.	N. H.	N. J.
Total	4,953	6,287	3,566	4,060	8,055	1,445	1,471	134	494	4,563
1. Alcohol and drugs	60	24	19	10	119	11	10	1	1	30
2. Bones and joints	404	561	435	525	815	204	205	13	40	484
3. Developmental defects	741	121	260	85	130	59	26	10	45	716
4. Digestive system	9	23	8	19	33	0	8	0	0	13
5. Ears	197	283	115	70	271	59	30	5	8	285
6. Eyes	261	515	229	339	851	103	133	6	20	457
7. Flat foot	458	430	335	395	767	159	126	15	69	319
8. Genito-urinary (venereal)	30	89	53	299	213	8	16	1	2	10
9. Genito-urinary (nonvenereal)	75	90	115	50	76	9	15	1	17	95
10. Heart and blood vessels	681	1,595	344	425	763	205	172	24	60	255
11. Hernia	450	1,042	358	543	1,047	178	204	15	52	495
12. Mental deficiency	117	170	112	261	335	15	31	2	15	39
13. Nervous and mental disorders	141	218	205	219	438	31	68	6	18	101
14. Respiratory (tuberculous)	204	220	127	423	994	49	115	6	11	90
15. Respiratory (nontuberculous)	84	65	33	40	175	3	34	0	16	38
16. Skin	4	9	7	5	12	0	3	0	1	7
17. Teeth	526	553	387	142	151	174	56	5	55	564
18. Thyroid	13	121	127	30	425	33	28	1	1	57
19. Tuberculosis (nonrespiratory)	2	9	3	0	4	1	3	0	15	1
20. Other defects	26	49	24	56	33	9	11	2	1	25
21. Defects not stated	470	100	270	124	403	135	177	21	47	482

II. PERCENTAGES.

Disqualifying defects.	Mass.	Mich.	Minn.	Miss.	Mo.	Mont.	Nebr.	Nev.	N.H.	N. J.
Total	100	100	100	100	100	100	100	100	100	100
1. Alcohol and drugs	1.2	0.4	0.5	0.2	1.5	0.8	0.7	0.7	0.2	0.7
2. Bones and joints	8.2	9.0	12.2	12.9	10.1	14.1	13.9	9.7	8.1	10.6
3. Developmental defects	15.0	1.9	7.3	2.1	1.6	4.1	1.8	7.5	9.1	15.7
4. Digestive system	.2	.04	.2	.5	.4	.0	.5	.0	.0	.3
5. Ears	4.0	4.5	3.2	1.7	3.4	4.1	2.0	3.7	1.6	6.2
6. Eyes	5.3	8.2	6.4	8.3	10.6	7.1	9.0	4.5	4.0	10.0
7. Flat foot	9.2	6.8	9.4	9.7	9.5	11.0	8.6	11.2	14.0	7.0
8. Genito-urinary (venereal)	.6	1.4	1.5	7.4	2.6	.6	1.1	.7	.4	.2
9. Genito-urinary (nonvenereal)	1.5	1.4	3.2	1.2	.9	.6	1.0	.7	3.5	2.1
10. Heart and blood vessels	13.7	25.4	9.6	10.5	9.5	14.2	11.7	17.9	12.2	5.6
11. Hernia	9.1	16.6	10.0	13.4	13.0	12.3	13.9	11.2	10.5	10.8
12. Mental deficiency	2.4	2.7	3.1	6.4	4.2	1.0	2.1	1.5	3.0	.9
13. Nervous and mental disorders	2.8	3.5	5.7	5.4	5.4	2.1	4.6	4.5	3.6	2.2
14. Respiratory (tuberculous)	4.1	3.5	3.6	10.4	12.3	3.4	7.8	4.5	2.2	2.0
15. Respiratory (nontuberculous)	1.7	1.0	.9	1.0	2.2	.2	2.3	.0	3.2	.8
16. Skin	.08	.1	.2	.1	.1	.0	.2	.0	.2	.2
17. Teeth	10.6	8.8	10.9	3.5	1.9	12.0	3.8	3.7	11.1	12.4
18. Thyroid	.3	1.9	3.6	.7	5.3	2.3	1.9	.7	.2	1.2
19. Tuberculosis (nonrespiratory)	.04	.1	.08	.0	.05	.1	.2	.0	3.0	.02
20. Other defects	.5	.8	.7	1.4	.4	.6	.7	1.5	.2	.5
21. Defects not stated	9.5	1.6	7.6	3.1	5.0	9.3	12.0	15.7	9.5	10.6

Appendix Table 60–C.—*Causes of physical rejections by camp surgeons, compared by States (series Y)*—Continued.

I. FIGURES.

Disqualifying defects.	N. Mex.	N. Y.	N. C.	N. Dak.	Ohio.	Okla.	Oreg.	Pa.	R. I.	S. C.
Total	463	17,194	4,517	1,028	6,551	3,520	1,451	14,996	673	3,653
1. Alcohol and drugs	3	307	2	0	54	35	4	94	8	6
2. Bones and joints	58	1,476	361	114	933	375	145	1,692	53	259
3. Developmental defects	38	1,648	254	31	417	190	106	1,085	38	175
4. Digestive system	0	27	5	0	15	7	3	44	1	6
5. Ears	27	865	54	50	226	203	56	1,129	39	20
6. Eyes	62	2,046	247	87	365	439	100	1,485	65	157
7. Flat foot	19	1,727	160	69	480	198	111	833	146	115
8. Genito-urinary (venereal)	7	170	16	4	87	57	15	139	3	9
9. Genito-urinary (nonvenereal)	11	270	35	10	79	30	13	145	7	20
10. Heart and blood vessels	55	1,335	202	159	569	397	205	2,056	40	144
11. Hernia	34	1,717	204	123	756	424	96	1,385	85	194
12. Mental deficiency	24	240	104	43	124	182	26	412	11	46
13. Nervous and mental disorders	19	794	133	42	282	112	61	685	24	106
14. Respiratory (tuberculous)	61	735	288	42	352	189	94	728	45	101
15. Respiratory (nontuberculous)	6	216	62	17	206	73	13	542	17	41
16. Skin	0	28	1	1	5	2	0	16	2	1
17. Teeth	12	1,202	88	164	338	44	117	1,031	31	92
18. Thyroid	6	267	54	22	183	28	46	538	3	23
19. Tuberculosis (nonrespiratory)	1	26	0	3	11	11	1	18	0	0
20. Other defects	6	142	39	7	40	26	5	75	4	34
21. Defects not stated	14	1,956	2,208	40	1,029	498	234	864	51	2,104

II. PERCENTAGES.

Disqualifying defects.	N. Mex.	N. Y.	N. C.	N. Dak.	Ohio.	Okla.	Oreg.	Pa.	R. I.	S. C.
Total	100	100	100	100	100	100	100	100	100	100
1. Alcohol and drugs	0.6	1.8	0.04	0.0	0.8	1.0	0.3	0.6	1.2	0.2
2. Bones and joints	12.5	8.6	8.0	11.1	14.2	10.7	10.0	11.3	7.9	7.1
3. Developmental defects	8.2	9.6	5.6	3.0	6.4	5.4	7.3	7.2	5.6	4.8
4. Digestive system	.0	.1	.1	.0	.2	.2	.2	.3	.1	.2
5. Ears	5.8	5.0	1.2	4.9	3.4	5.8	3.9	7.5	5.8	.5
6. Eyes	13.4	11.9	5.5	8.5	5.6	12.5	6.9	10.0	9.7	4.3
7. Flat foot	4.1	10.0	3.5	6.7	7.3	5.6	7.6	5.6	21.7	3.1
8. Genito-urinary (venereal)	1.5	1.0	.4	.4	1.3	1.6	1.0	.9	.4	.2
9. Genito-urinary (nonvenereal)	2.4	1.6	.8	1.0	1.2	.9	.9	1.0	1.0	.5
10. Heart and blood vessels	11.9	7.8	4.5	15.5	8.7	11.3	14.1	13.7	5.9	4.0
11. Hernia	7.3	10.0	4.5	12.0	11.5	12.0	6.6	9.2	12.6	5.3
12. Mental deficiency	5.2	1.4	2.3	4.2	1.9	5.2	1.8	2.7	1.6	1.3
13. Nervous and mental disorders	4.1	4.6	2.9	4.1	4.3	3.2	4.2	4.6	3.6	3.0
14. Respiratory (tuberculous)	13.2	4.3	6.4	4.1	5.4	5.4	6.5	4.9	6.7	2.8
15. Respiratory (nontuberculous)	1.3	1.2	1.4	1.6	3.1	2.1	.9	3.6	2.5	1.1
16. Skin	.0	.2	.02	.1	.08	.06	.0	.1	.3	.03
17. Teeth	2.6	7.0	1.9	16.0	5.2	1.3	8.1	6.9	4.6	2.5
18. Thyroid	1.3	1.5	1.2	2.1	2.8	.8	3.2	3.6	.4	.6
19. Tuberculosis (nonrespiratory)	.2	.1	.0	.3	.2	.3	.07	.1	.0	.0
20. Other defects	1.3	.8	.9	.7	.6	.7	.3	.5	.6	.9
21. Defects not stated	3.0	11.4	48.9	3.9	15.7	14.1	16.1	5.8	7.6	57.6

APPENDIX TABLE 60–C.—*Causes of physical rejections by camp surgeons, compared by States (series Y)*—Continued.

I. FIGURES.

Disqualifying defects.	S. Dak.	Tenn.	Tex.	Utah.	Vt.	Va.	Wash.	W. Va.	Wis.	Wyo.
Total	1,269	4,825	4,851	525	492	5,667	1,425	3,755	4,273	459
1. Alcohol and drugs	1	33	16	5	0	7	9	10	19	7
2. Bones and joints	247	663	659	68	41	801	149	580	445	44
3. Developmental defects	11	544	428	27	26	210	60	83	216	26
4. Digestive system	4	12	32	5	1	7	3	1	15	1
5. Ears	26	78	169	19	3	126	51	174	136	21
6. Eyes	141	346	857	29	19	631	74	421	394	35
7. Flat foot	100	568	272	86	59	355	209	164	358	40
8. Genito-urinary (venereal)	9	60	62	4	6	122	9	71	61	10
9. Genito-urinary (nonvenereal)	14	68	78	3	22	68	4	33	158	3
10. Heart and blood vessels	147	445	610	59	82	1,032	253	578	411	44
11. Hernia	119	470	648	46	32	538	152	436	725	51
12. Mental deficiency	42	373	79	4	16	374	21	224	136	14
13. Nervous and mental disorders	45	99	191	16	23	230	52	136	223	25
14. Respiratory (tuberculous)	101	271	301	18	16	298	57	193	144	19
15. Respiratory (nontuberculous)	35	103	78	3	16	250	6	190	48	8
16. Skin	3	4	4	0	0	4	0	3	13	0
17. Teeth	95	119	145	57	53	273	140	180	303	20
18. Thyroid	42	62	19	9	6	228	35	179	259	8
19. Tuberculosis (nonrespiratory)	2	0	9	1	0	0	2	0	0	0
20. Other defects	6	50	27	2	3	76	2	47	41	2
21. Defects not stated	79	457	167	64	68	37	137	57	167	80

II. PERCENTAGES.

Disqualifying defects.	S. Dak.	Tenn.	Tex.	Utah.	Vt.	Va.	Wash.	W. Va.	Wis.	Wyo.
Total	100	100	100	100	100	100	100	100	100	100
1. Alcohol and drugs	0.1	0.7	0.3	1.0	0.0	0.1	0.6	0.3	0.4	1.5
2. Bones and joints	19.5	13.7	13.6	13.0	8.3	14.1	10.5	15.4	10.4	9.6
3. Developmental defects	.9	11.3	8.8	5.1	5.3	3.7	4.2	2.2	5.1	5.7
4. Digestive system	.3	.2	.7	1.0	.2	.1	.2	.02	.4	.2
5. Ears	2.0	1.6	3.5	3.6	.6	2.2	3.6	4.6	3.2	4.6
6. Eyes	11.1	7.2	17.7	5.5	3.7	11.1	5.2	11.2	9.2	7.8
7. Flat foot	7.9	11.8	5.6	16.4	12.0	6.3	14.7	4.4	8.4	8.7
8. Genito-urinary (venereal)	.7	1.2	1.3	.8	1.2	2.2	.6	1.9	1.4	2.2
9. Genito-urinary (nonvenereal)	1.1	1.4	1.6	.6	4.5	1.2	.3	.9	3.7	.7
10. Heart and blood vessels	11.6	9.2	12.6	11.2	16.7	18.2	17.8	15.3	9.6	9.6
11. Hernia	9.4	9.7	13.4	8.8	6.5	9.5	10.7	11.6	17.0	11.1
12. Mental deficiency	3.3	7.7	1.6	.8	3.3	6.6	1.5	6.0	3.2	3.1
13. Nervous and mental disorders	3.5	2.1	3.9	3.0	4.7	4.1	3.6	3.6	5.2	5.4
14. Respiratory (tuberculous)	8.0	5.6	6.2	3.4	3.3	5.3	4.0	5.1	3.4	4.1
15. Respiratory (nontuberculous)	2.8	2.1	1.6	.6	3.3	4.4	.4	5.1	1.1	1.7
16. Skin	.2	.1	.1	.0	.0	.07	.0	.1	.3	.0
17. Teeth	7.5	2.5	3.0	10.9	10.8	4.8	9.8	4.8	7.1	4.4
18. Thyroid	3.3	1.3	.4	1.7	1.2	4.0	2.5	4.8	6.1	1.7
19. Tuberculosis (nonrespiratory)	.2	.0	.2	.2	.0	.0	.1	.0	.0	.0
20. Other defects	.5	1.0	.6	.4	.6	1.3	.1	1.3	1.0	.4
21. Defects not stated	6.2	9.5	3.4	12.2	13.8	.6	9.6	1.5	3.9	17.4

APPENDIX TABLE 60-D.—*Physical rejections at camp, showing anatomical and pathological defects in detail (series Y).*

Disqualifying defects.	Total.	Ala.	Ariz.	Ark.	Cal.	Colo.	Conn.	Del.	D.C.	Fla.
Total	172,000	7,189	272	3,056	2,842	1,092	1,178	342	480	2,063
Bones:										
Amputation	2,259	84	56	58	32	26	12	5	2	29
Deformity	3,848	150	9	71	49	19	21	14	11	64
Disease	1,547	103	2	12	5	20	4	1	1	31
Fracture	2,554	116	10	45	53	10	19	7	2	27
Joints:										
Ankylosis	3,489		9	74	52		27	5	6	
Disease	3,259	303		21	28	49	9	4	6	89
Dislocation	334		1	4	9		2	1	2	
Spine	2,333	77	1	23	34	12	14	10	8	21
Tuberculosis, other than lungs	159			2	3		2			
Pes cavus	2,528	80	8	100	44	28	7	5	3	13
Pes planus	9,667	297	9	299	180	53	68	30	20	59
Hallux valgus	1,039	23	3	20	39	7	19	3	1	
Ear:										
Deafness	852	29	2	9	8	10	4	6	2	14
Otitis media (purulent)	5,309	78	12	55	43	59	74	11	29	9
Eyes:										
Vision	12,549	334	26	203	149	72	92	27	33	135
Nystagmus	98			14	2					
Trachoma	1,063	21	8	40	6	9	2	1	3	2
Teeth, deficient	9,952	254	12	37	150	47	32	22	39	75
Height	1,500	17		3	17	19	12	2		7
Weight:										
Over weight	899	1	1	2	4	2	16	2		1
Under weight	9,088	486	8	68	54	52	50	27	30	60
Chest measurements	51						1		1	
Varicose veins	2,176	31	2	29	24	5	22	4	1	14
Phlebitis	136				3		1		1	
Mental deficiency	6,293	614	4	297	81	55	49	11	10	29
Mental and nervous disorders:										
Paralysis	1,029	43	3	23	15	5	11	4	2	10
Stammering	694	13	2	4	10	2	3	2	2	5
Skin	213	1	1	3		2				1
Pellagra	55	3		3						1
Goiter	680	5		1	3	4	2	1	20	1
Goiter with hyperthyroidism	418		1	4	4				2	
Hernia:										
Inguinal	9,973		5	312	191		134	10	18	
Umbilical	587			20	3		2	3		
Not classified	7,793	651	1	27	22	112		7	12	229
Fistula	317			4	1		2	1	1	
Prolapse with hemorrhoids	476		1	12		2	1		1	
Venereal diseases:										
Syphilis	1,987	55	4	22	30	7	12	5	15	18
Gonorrhea	473	4	1	4	23			1	2	28
Other	284	5		1	5		2		2	1
Genito-urinary (nonvenereal):										
Hydrocele	359	12		2	3	1	3	2	1	3
Varicocele	463	14		2	3			5		2
Testis in canal	914	8	1	5	6	6	16		2	6
Other	307	20		2			2	1		2
Tachycardia, persistent	2,420	124	1	23			12	4	14	30
Eye defects	1,657	62		71	2	2	3	7	12	9
Ear:										
Perforated drum	253	1	1	4	25	16				
Other disease	41			3						
Respiratory system:										
Asthma	1,917	58	5	80	9	17	18	5	6	35
Chronic bronchitis	560	10		3	8	4	7	1		5
Sinusitis	693			2	4	2	5	2	11	
Pleurisy	313			5	1		8		2	
Tuberculosis	10,792	396	26	233	341	116	69	17	25	120
Heart and blood vessels:										
Heart, disease of	11,820	440	28	284	297	76	102	17	42	67
Hypertension	532			12	1	5	6		1	8
Other disease	1,708	134	1	213	3	5	4	2	2	5
Hyperthyroidism	2,599	32	1	14	7	25	21	4	8	5
Nervous system:										
Epilepsy	1,379	59	3	34	32	21	9	1	6	32
Neurasthenia	470	1	1	8	12	3	7	1	7	1
Hysteria	313		1	11	24		1			
Psychoneurosis	3,434	169	8	18	56	41	22	5	26	34
Alcoholism	377	1		1	9	6	6	1		
Drug addict	861	8	2	15	36	4	9	15		4
Diabetes	20	1					2		1	1
Nephritis	158	57					3			2
Digestive system	131			6	5		1			
Dyspituitarism	121				1					
Other defects	1,197	81	3	13	15	27	4		4	24
Not stated	18,225	1,614	37	66	571	15	118	24	19	694

APPENDIX TABLE 60-D.—*Physical rejections at camp, showing anatomical and pathological defects in detail (series Y)*—Continued.

Disqualifying defects.	Ga.	Idaho.	Ill.	Ind.	Iowa.	Kans.	Ky.	La.	Me.	Md.
Total	7,041	855	9,368	3,047	3,346	2,842	3,233	4,476	1,336	1,318
Bones:										
Amputation	95	17	115	57	68	64	31	61	12	17
Deformity	116	11	239	70	120	76	63	66	28	35
Disease	104	6	35	29	- 11	28	8	79	7	5
Fracture	104	15	118	39	46	98	24	45	7	12
Joints:										
Ankylosis	415	32	294	89	95	69	76	33	25	28
Disease	} 408	{ 14	74	20	42	48	11	} 160	17	13
Dislocation		2	26	6	6	10	3		3	3
Spine	146	26	95	34	23	35	51	27	18	83
Tuberculosis, other than lungs		1	15	1	5	1	5			1
Pes ca us	39	26	73	40	49	10	19	63	53	18
Pes planus	355	83	681	91	265	177	39	149	147	88
Hallux valgus	31	7	51	25	25	11	2	11	27	10
Ear:										
Deafness	39	1	51	7	69	11	9	34	1	1
Otitis media (purulent)	76	29	286	125	80	52	89	44	13	87
Eyes:										
Vision	530	55	717	132	336	218	139	219	48	141
Nystagmus			5	1	4		3			3
Trachoma	5	3	77	41	5	13	143	25	1	5
Teeth, deficient	646	63	410	106	156	59	111	478	99	39
Height	21	21	35	8	4	7	1	5	6	1
Weight:										
Over weight	40		88	7	21	5	8	5	15	6
Under weight	1,329	24	435	129	121	25	136	173	78	26
Chest measurements		1	3	2	1		1		1	
Varicose veins	72	8	198	37	18	18	13	33	25	7
Phlebitis	10	1	8	1	7		2	1		1
Mental deficiency	222	23	278	103	108	71	323	246	84	93
Mental and nervous disorders:										
Paralysis	30	1	45	22	34	32	18	19	8	11
Stammering	28	1	43	16	9	6	33	18	10	8
Skin	8		29	3	5	10	3	9	3	
Pellagra	4							2		
Goiter	19	30	81	7	6	8	1	6		1
Goiter with hyperthyroidism		3	24	6	22	15	4			
Hernia:										
Inguinal		79	530	260	348	414	253		87	73
Umbilical			27	70	2	3	41			14
Not classified	561	9	457	105	66	29	83	387	53	24
Fistula	22		32	1	6	6	6	23	2	3
Prolapse with hemorrhoids	35		43	3	8	7	3	18	6	4
Venereal diseases:										
Syphilis	58	3	158	36	13	44	64	192	7	17
Gonorrhea	32	3	53	5	2	1	1	42	4	
Other	4	2	31	1		1	4	74	1	2
Genito-urinary (nonvenereal):										
Hydrocele	4	2	29	5		4	3	8	12	5
Varicocele	9	2	33	5	6	1	3	16	4	3
Testis in canal	12	2	51	19	7	15	5	22	18	5
Other	15	1	12	6	4	11	4	20	1	1
Tachycardia, persistent	130	3	70	32	22	97	10	138	13	28
Eye defects	10	1	51	36	16	33	17	46	2	21
Ear:										
Perforated drum	13	12	1			15		3		1
Other disease			1	2			1			3
Respiratory system:										
Asthma	35	1	93	49	55	28	53	119	21	19
Chronic bronchitis	36		16	28	9	19	2	9	9	15
Sinusitis	1	2	6	7	2	3	4	1	2	3
Pleurisy		1	10	1	4	88	1		3	2
Tuberculosis	276	26	591	400	177	286	768	476	51	106
Heart and blood vessels:										
Heart, disease of	246	105	437	246	398	189	152	327	165	60
Hypertension	27		22	14	4	5	9	14	10	1
Other disease	18		31	23	61	7	20	48		34
Hyperthyroidism	23	5	147	27	51	100	43	24	4	22
Nervous system:										
Epilepsy	54	4	77	21	16	16	44	103	10	7
Neurasthenia	8	1	55	3	7	11	4	7	1	7
Hysteria		1	17	3	9	11	11			3
Psychoneurosis	171	10	258	53	113	65	89	58	11	29
Alcoholism	1		82	3	1	4	22		1	3
Drug addict	12		28	2	12	19	10	10	1	5
Diabetes			1							1
Nephritis	9		9	1		4	7	2		
Digestive system		1	9	4	4	4	● 1			1
Dyspituitarism		1	11	6	2	15	6			
Other defects	48	7	44	27	14	18	21	80	7	11
Not stated	279	67	1,216	289	146	98	101	198	91	42

Appendix Table 60–D.—*Physical rejections at camp, showing anatomical and pathological defects in detail (series Y)*—Continued.

Disqualifying defects.	Mass.	Mich.	Minn.	Miss.	Mo.	Mont.	Nebr.	Nev.	N.H.	N.J.	N. Mex.
Total	4,953	6,287	3,566	4,060	8,055	1,445	1,471	134	494	4,563	463
Bones:											
Amputation	26	38	86	63	85	21	21	1	5	44	4
Deformity	85	192	71	80	239	40	48	3	4	138	18
Disease	25	38	16	88	62	5	8	1	2	11	
Fracture	62	85	85	28	146	22	29	4	6	44	14
Joints:											
Ankylosis	95	116	76	23	90	72	48	3	10	88	9
Disease	28	40	33	210	97	27	21		87	31	8
Dislocation	14	14	26		9	5	6		1	5	2
Spine	69	38	42	33	87	12	24	1	5	123	3
Tuberculosis, other than lungs	2	9	3		4	1	3		15	1	1
Pes cavus	24	125	25	113	78	41	18	1	15	13	11
Pes planus	415	264	280	271	658	103	103	14	39	280	6
Hallux valgus	19	41	30	11	31	15	5		15	26	2
Ear:											
Deafness	26	28	16	32	27	7	6			63	2
Otitis media (purulent)	169	253	96	37	238	31	23	1	8	196	21
Eyes:											
Vision	253	442	209	248	636	91	122	6	20	380	51
Nystagmus		10			13	1	1			2	1
Trachoma	4	14	3	7	77	2	2			13	6
Teeth, deficient	526	553	387	142	151	174	56	5	55	564	12
Height	240	12	37	6	15	26	2	5	4	361	2
Weight:											
Over weight	55	24	45	2	11		1		9	80	3
Under weight	439	75	177	77	104	33	22	5	32	275	33
Chest measurements	7	10	1				1				
Varicose veins	110	121	126	39	47	19	9	2	12	61	2
Phlebitis	1	1	1	1			1			1	
Mental deficiency	117	170	112	261	335	15	31	2	15	39	24
Mental and nervous disorders:											
Paralysis	7	25	26	28	50	6	11		3	20	5
Stammering	14	20	17	25	25	7	10		3	7	
Skin	4	9	7	5	12		3		1	7	
Pellagra				2	1						
Goiter	5	34	42	3	21	12	3	1		1	
Goiter with hyperthyroidism		39	6		100	10	7			2	4
Hernia:											
Inguinal	265	798	60		949	161	175	10	30	182	28
Umbilical	10	131	2		29		5	1		5	
Not classified	175	113	296	543	69	17	24	4	22	308	6
Fistula	5	16	4	19	24		2			8	
Prolapse with hemorrhoids	17	7	1	13	20	2	1			8	2
Venereal diseases—											
Syphilis	19	73	39	147	179	5	14		2	5	5
Gonorrhea	4	12	4	113	32	3	1	1		1	1
Other	7	4	10	39	2		1			4	1
Genito-urinary (nonvenereal):											
Hydrocele	10	7	17	6	17	3	1		2	15	
Varicocele	57	8	34	5	24	2	2	1	2	42	
Testis in canal	2	63	56	12	16	3	9		11	22	9
Other	5	9	6	22	16		2		1	15	2
Tachycardia, persistent	36	165	8	93	203	1	26		5	27	3
Eye defects	4	49	17	84	125	9	8			62	4
Ear:											
Perforated drum	1	2	1	1	3	10	1	4		23	4
Other disease	1		2		3	11				3	
Respiratory system:											
Asthma	47	41	24	28	102		29		2	15	2
Chronic bronchitis	20	8	4	10	26				12	11	
Sinusitis	9	9	1	2	8	1	1			7	4
Pleurisy	8	7	4		39	2	4		2	5	
Tuberculosis	204	220	127	423	994	49	115	6	11	90	61
Heart and blood vessels:											
Heart, disease of	475	1,017	195	260	417	175	115	21	41	127	44
Hypertension	13	19	7	11	17		3		1	6	1
Other disease	29	265	6	8	59	8	17	1	1	25	3
Hyperthyroidism	8	48	79	27	304	11	18		1	54	2
Nervous system:											
Epilepsy	29	40	22	85	53	4	9	2	4	25	5
Neurasthenia	18	3	20	5	81		3	1	1	7	1
Hysteria	7	4	4		47	1	5		1	6	2
Psychoneurosis	66	126	116	76	182	13	30	3	6	36	6
Alcoholism	39	8	4		46	3	2	1		6	1
Drug addict	21	16	15	10	73	8	8		1	24	2
Diabetes				1							
Nephritis	1	3	2	4	3	1	1		1	1	
Digestive system	4	7	4		9		6			5	
Dyspituitarism		6		2	8		6			1	3
Other defects	26	43	24	52	24	9	5	2	1	24	3
Not stated	470	100	270	124	403	135	177	21	47	482	14

APPENDIX TABLE 60–D.—*Physical rejections at camp, showing anatomical and pathological defects in detail (series Y)*—Continued.

Disqualifying defects.	N.Y.	N.C.	N. Dak.	Ohio.	Okla.	Oreg.	Pa.	R.I.	S.C.	S. Dak.	Tenn.
Total	17,194	4,517	1,028	6,551	3,520	1,451	14,996	673	3,653	1,269	4,825
Bones:											
Amputation	156	34	13	146	46	19	155	10	23	26	30
Deformity	368	65	41	229	75	16	260	9	50	62	88
Disease	55	55	2	29	11	6	155	1	43	12	127
Fracture	171	24	13	148	59	14	366	10	35	53	45
Joints:											
Ankylosis	249	36	27	190	98	52	305	11	14	35	72
Disease	186 }	97	9	77	50	7	173	3	} 75	32 }	188
Dislocation	25		4	44	4	5	57			2	
Spine	266	50	5	70	32	26	221	9	19	25	63
Tuberculosis, other than lungs	26		3	11	11	1	18			2	
Pes cavus	319	30	18	148	28	106	188	33	16	10	133
Pes planus	1,274	100	45	303	154	5	533	103	89	74	303
Hallux valgus	134	30	6	29	16		112	10	16	16	42
Ear:											
Deafness	98	14	8	15	18	5	38	2	11	3	15
Otitis media (purulent)	750	33	38	209	150	35	1,087	37	9	18	63
Eyes:											
Vision	1,791	212	71	292	282	93	1,225	45	105	118	272
Nystagmus	10		1	4	4		10	1			
Trachoma	158	4	6	13	97	5	36	18	15	7	10
Teeth, deficient	1,202	88	164	338	44	117	1,031	31	92	95	119
Height	137	19	2	9	27	41	202		14	1	3
Weight:											
Over weight	219	5	2	38	15	2	47	5	2		14
Under weight	1,291	230	27	370	146	62	830	33	150	10	527
Chest measurements	1				2	1	6				
Varicose veins	258	19	18	139	26	15	198	8	17	7	40
Phlebitis	5	7		3	2		34		1		6
Mental deficiency	240	104	43	124	182	26	412	11	46	42	123
Mental and nervous disorders:											
Paralysis	105	25	3	45	30	5	104	5	11	14	39
Stammering	81	9	5	26	7	2	63		12	5	15
Skin	28	1	1	5	2		16	2	1	3	4
Pellagra	1	4		1	2				3		
Goiter	23	5	2	32	2	16	14			7	3
Goiter with hyperthyroidism	58		5	36	6	21	13			1	
Hernia:											
Inguinal	1,132		97	616	355	86	935	74		96	
Umbilical	12		8	57	18	1	113				
Not classified	573	204	18	83	51	9	337	11	194	21	470
Fistula	16	5		11	5		21		6	1	13
Prolapse with hemorrhoids	33	6	1	11	10		54	1	7	2	23
Venereal diseases:											
Syphilis	149	12	4	73	46	3	111	2	7	8	53
Gonorrhea	9	4		9	8	12	13	1		1	5
Other	12			5	3		15		2		2
Genito-urinary (nonvenereal):											
Hydrocele	22	5	4	7	4	3	34	2	2	2	8
Varicocele	96	8	3	9	5	3	18	1		1	3
Testis in canal	107	19	3	52	15	2	63	3	14	7	33
Other	24	3		6	5	3	20		4	4	11
Tachycardia, persistent	150	40	4	73	44	9	203	2	26	45	60
Eye defects	87	31	9	56	56	2	214	1	37	16	44
Ear:											
Perforated drum	14	7	4		34	16	3			3	
Other disease	3			2	1		1			2	
Respiratory system:											
Asthma	115	36	10	152	45	5	198	13	34	32	48
Chronic bronchitis	28	17		40	9	1	42	3	7	1	54
Sinusitis	38	9	4	7	5	5	278				1
Pleurisy	35		3	7	14	2	24	1		2	
Tuberculosis	735	288	42	352	189	94	728	45	101	101	271
Heart and blood vessels:											
Heart, disease of	773	100	111	315	220	179	1,455	20	48	77	283
Hypertension	21	11	8	16	22	1	102	2	30	8	12
Other disease	95	19	17	12	73	1	10	7	13	8	13
Hyperthyroidism	186	49	15	115	20	9	511	3	28	34	80
Nervous system:											
Epilepsy	130	32	7	61	23	11	75	5	13	3	20
Neurasthenia	43	4	1	9	1	4	48	3	3	3	12
Hysteria	58		2	16	6	1	34	3		3	
Psychoneurosis	377	63	24	125	45	38	361	8	67	16	13
Alcoholism	51	2		19	2		24	4	3		8
Drug addict	256			35	33	4	70	4	3	1	1
Diabetes	4					2	3				12
Nephritis	17			5	1		7	1			
Digestive system	11			4	2	3	23	1		3	
Dyspituitarism	12	1		1	4		17	1		3	
Other defects	129	34	7	38	20	5	58	3	30	3	40
Not stated	1,956	2,208	40	1,020	498	234	864	51	2,104	79	437

APPENDIX TABLE 60-D.—*Physical rejections at camp, showing anatomical and pathological defects in detail (series Y)*—Continued.

Disqualifying defects.	Tex.	Utah.	Vt.	Va.	Wash.	W. Va.	Wis.	Wyo.	Alaska.	Hawaii.	Porto Rico.
Total	4,851	525	492	5,667	1,427	3,755	4,273	459	74	581	694
Bones:											
Amputation	87	4	5	85	24	72	83	6	2		
Deformity	135	6	6	110	26	52	95	5			
Disease	21	1	1	129	7	133	11	1	1		
Fracture	114	11	7	49	13	26	65	9			
Joints:											
Ankylosis	167	18	6	53	42	55	88	12	4		
Disease	71	8	4	} 263	{ 12	} 142	39	4	3		
Dislocation	19	2	3		2		4	3		1	
Spine	45	18	9	112	23	100	61	4		1	
Tuberculosis, other than lungs	9	1			2						
Pes cavus	69	14	9	99	49	54	50	4	3		
Pes planus	174	59	50	218	119	93	295	33	7	1	
Hallux valgus	29	13		38	11	17	13	3			
Ear:											
Deafness	37	1	1	25	4	9	33	1	1		
Otitis media (purulent)	127	16	2	100	31	163	101	16		1	
Eyes:											
Vision	755	26	18	444	69	271	365	28	3		1
Nystagmus	5						2	1			
Trachoma	64	2		13	1	69	4	3	2		
Teeth, deficient	145	57	53	273	140	180	303	20	12	1	1
Height	50	8	10	10	31	22	9	9			
Weight:											
Over weight	46		3	17	1	6	23				
Under weight	330	18	13	183	28	55	177	16	1		
Chest measurements	2	1					7	1			
Varicose veins	61	4	12	68	31	50	89	7			1
Phlebitis	8	1		19		6		2			
Mental deficiency	79	4	16	374	21	224	136	14	1		
Mental and nervous disorders:											
Paralysis	36	2	8	29	2	12	32	3	1		
Stammering	11	1	2	64	4	17	26	1			
Skin	4			4		3	13				
Pellagra	4						24				
Goiter		4	2	8	24	51	167	2			
Goiter with hyperthyroidism	6	1	1		7		10		1		
Hernia:											
Inguinal	603	39	17		129		381	39	2	2	1
Umbilical	4	2			1		1	2			
Not classified	41	5	15	538	22	436	343	10	1		
Fistula	28	4	1	7	1	1	10				
Prolapse with hemorrhoids	47	2	4	43	1	6	10	1			
Venereal diseases:											
Syphilis	49	3	3	98	5	64	41	8	1		
Gonorrhea	4	1	3	6	3	4	11	1			
Other	9			18	1	3	9	1			
Genito-urinary (nonvenereal):											
Hydrocele	16		4	26	2	17	24				
Varicocele	8		7	6			64	1			
Testis in canal	44	3	5	◆15		12	56	2		1	
Other	8		5	18	1	3	12				
Tachycardia, persistent	60	1	2	239	6	92	24	5	1		
Eye defects	33	1	1	174	4	81	23	4	1		
Ear:											
Perforated drum	4	2		1	16	2	1	4	1		
Other disease	1						1				
Respiratory system:											
Asthma	43	2	13	90	2	47	34	2			
Chronic bronchitis	17		1	24		46	3				
Sinusitis	6			136	1	97	3	2			
Pleurisy	12	1	2		3		8	4			
Tuberculosis	301	18	16	298	57	193	144	19	12	1	
Heart and blood vessels:											
Heart, disease of	225	50	59	508	213	315	278	26	8		1
Hypertension	3		2	52	1	18	4	2			
Other disease	206		3	103	1	86	6	1			
Hyperthyroidism	13	4	3	220	4	128	82	6			
Nervous system:											
Epilepsy	66	5	5	26	8	22	34	6			
Neurasthenia	4			10	3	2	33	1			
Hysteria	4	2	1		3		8	1			
Psychoneurosis	70	6	6	101	32	83	90	13	1		
Alcoholism							14	4			
Drug addict	16	5		7	9	10	5	3	2		
Diabetes							2				
Nephritis	2		1	3	1	1					
Digestive system	4	1			2		5	1	1		
Dyspituitarism	2			4			5				
Other defects	21	2	3	72	2	46	12	2		1	
Not stated	167	64	68	37	137	57	167	80	1	573	689

Chart E.—COMPARISON OF CAUSES OF PHYSICAL REJECTIONS OF INDUCTED MEN FROM CAMP
(FEBRUARY 10 TO NOVEMBER 1, 1918)
FOR THE STATE OF MARYLAND
PER CENT

	0 1 2 3 4 5 6 7 8 9 10 11 12 13 14 15
Amputation	
Bone Disease	
Fracture	
Joint Disease	
Spine	
GROUP TOTAL	
Pes Cavus	
Pes Planus	
Hallux Valgus	
GROUP TOTAL	
Height	
Overweight	
Underweight	
Chest Measurements	
GROUP TOTAL	
Hearing, Defects of	
Otitis Media, Chronic	
Perforated Drum	
GROUP TOTAL	
Visual Defects	
Trachoma	
Other Disease of Eye	
GROUP TOTAL	
Mental Deficiency	
Epilepsy	
Psychoneurosis	
Paralysis	
Stammering	
Alcoholism	
Drug Addiction	
GROUP TOTAL	
Goitre	
Hyperthyroidism	
GROUP TOTAL	
Heart Disease, Organic	
Hypertension	
Tachycardia	
Phlebitis	
Varicose Veins	
Other Card.-Vasc. Disease	
GROUP TOTAL	
Asthma	
Bronchitis, Chronic	
Pleurisy	
Sinusitis	
GROUP TOTAL	
Tuberculosis of Lung	
Tuberculosis, Other Parts	
GROUP TOTAL	
Teeth	
Digestive Disorders	
Fistula in Ano	
Hemorrhoids with Prolapse	
GROUP TOTAL	
Hernia	
Skin	
Syphilis	
Gonorrhea	
Chancroidal Disease	
GROUP TOTAL	
Nephritis	
Testis in Canal	
Varicocele and Hydrocele	
Other G.-U. Diseases (Non-Ven.)	
GROUP TOTAL	
All other Causes	

Chart F.—COMPARISON OF CAUSES OF PHYSICAL REJECTIONS OF INDUCTED MEN FROM CAMP
(FEBRUARY 10 TO NOVEMBER 1, 1918)
FOR THE STATE OF MASSACHUSETTS
PER CENT

| 0 | 1 | 2 | 3 | 4 | 5 | 6 | 7 | 8 | 9 | 10 | 11 | 12 | 13 | 14 | 15 |

Chart G.—COMPARISON OF CAUSES OF PHYSICAL REJECTIONS OF INDUCTED MEN FROM CAMP.

(FEBRUARY 10 TO NOVEMBER 1, 1918)

FOR THE STATE OF NEW YORK

PER CENT

	0	1	2	3	4	5	6	7	8	9	10	11	12

Amputation
Bone Disease
Fracture
Joint Disease
Spine
GROUP TOTAL
Pes Cavus
Pes Planus
Hallux Valgus
GROUP TOTAL
Height
Overweight
Underweight
Chest Measurements
GROUP TOTAL
Hearing, Defects of
Otitis Media, Chronic
Perforated Drum
GROUP TOTAL
Visual Defects
Trachoma
Other Disease of Eye
GROUP TOTAL
Mental Deficiency
Epilepsy
Psychoneurosis
Paralysis
Stammering
Alcoholism
Drug Addiction
GROUP TOTAL
Goitre
Hyperthyroidism
GROUP TOTAL
Heart Disease, Organic
Hypertension
Tachycardia
Phlebitis
Varicose Veins
Other Card.-Vasc. Disease
GROUP TOTAL
Asthma
Bronchitis, Chronic
Pleurisy
Sinusitis
GROUP TOTAL
Tuberculosis of Lung
Tuberculosis, Other Parts
GROUP TOTAL
Teeth
Digestive Disorders
Fistula in Ano
Hemorrhoids with Prolapse
GROUP TOTAL
Hernia
Skin
Syphilis
Gonorrhea
Chancroidal Disease
GROUP TOTAL
Nephritis
Testis in Canal
Varicocele and Hydrocele
Other G.-U. Diseases (Non-Ven.)
GROUP TOTAL
All other Causes

Chart H.—COMPARISON OF CAUSES OF PHYSICAL REJECTIONS OF INDUCTED MEN FROM CAMP
(FEBRUARY 19 TO NOVEMBER 1, 1918)
FOR THE STATE OF ALABAMA
PER CENT.

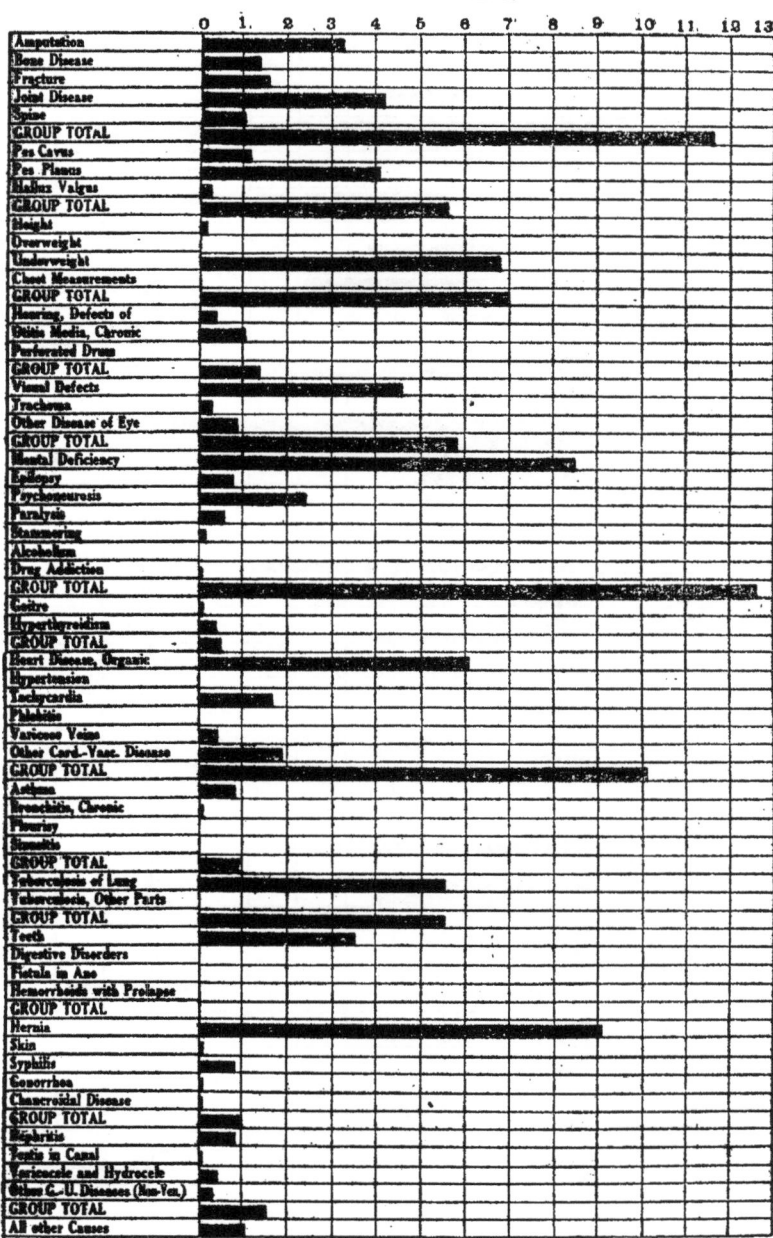

Chart L—COMPARISON OF CAUSES OF PHYSICAL REJECTIONS OF INDUCTED MEN FROM CAMP
(FEBRUARY 10 TO NOVEMBER 1, 1918)
FOR THE STATE OF ILLINOIS

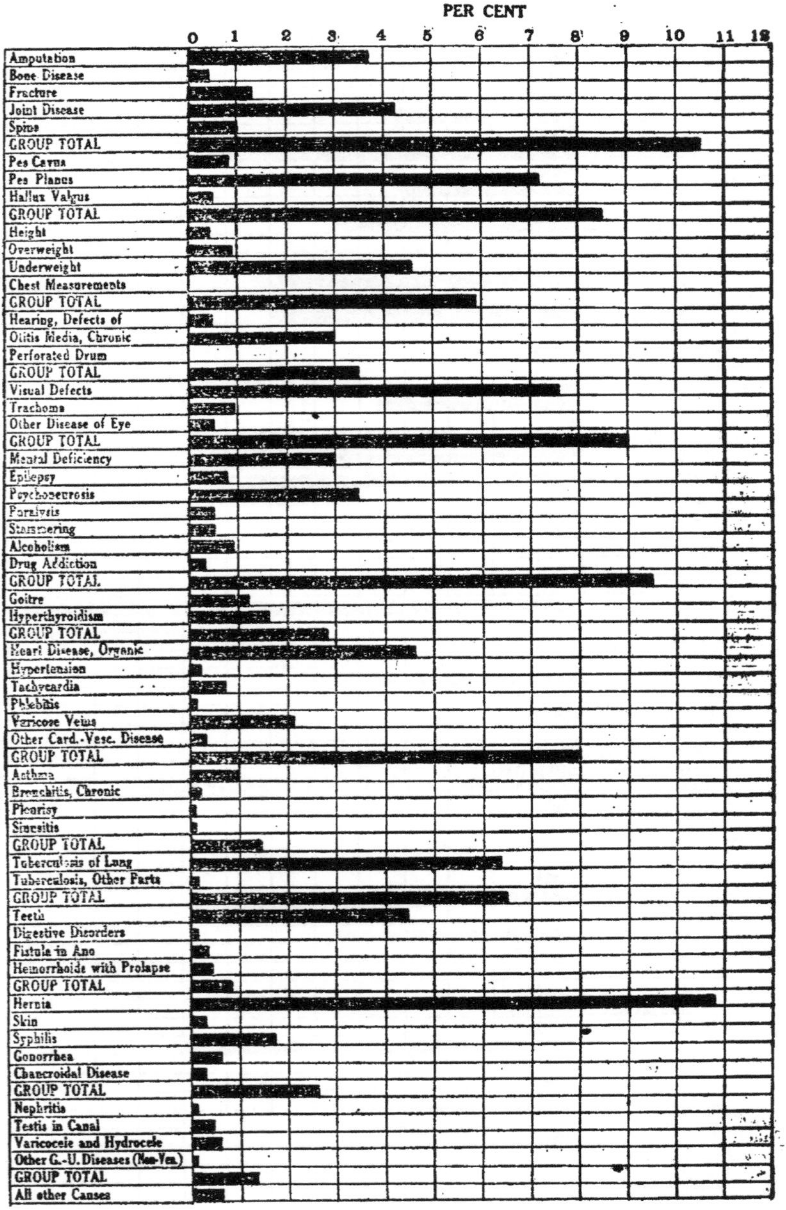

PER CENT

	0	1	2	3	4	5	6	7	8	9	10	11	12

Amputation
Bone Disease
Fracture
Joint Disease
Spine
GROUP TOTAL
Pes Cavus
Pes Planus
Hallux Valgus
GROUP TOTAL
Height
Overweight
Underweight
Chest Measurements
GROUP TOTAL
Hearing, Defects of
Otitis Media, Chronic
Perforated Drum
GROUP TOTAL
Visual Defects
Trachoma
Other Disease of Eye
GROUP TOTAL
Mental Deficiency
Epilepsy
Psychoneurosis
Paralysis
Stammering
Alcoholism
Drug Addiction
GROUP TOTAL
Goitre
Hyperthyroidism
GROUP TOTAL
Heart Disease, Organic
Hypertension
Tachycardia
Phlebitis
Varicose Veins
Other Card.-Vasc. Disease
GROUP TOTAL
Asthma
Bronchitis, Chronic
Pleurisy
Sinusitis
GROUP TOTAL
Tuberculosis of Lung
Tuberculosis, Other Parts
GROUP TOTAL
Teeth
Digestive Disorders
Fistula in Ano
Hemorrhoids with Prolapse
GROUP TOTAL
Hernia
Skin
Syphilis
Gonorrhea
Chancroidal Disease
GROUP TOTAL
Nephritis
Testis in Canal
Varicocele and Hydrocele
Other G.-U. Diseases (Non-Ven.)
GROUP TOTAL
All other Causes

Chart J.—COMPARISON OF CAUSES OF PHYSICAL REJECTIONS OF INDUCTED MEN FROM CAMP
(FEBRUARY 10 TO NOVEMBER 1, 1918)
FOR THE STATE OF COLORADO

PER CENT

0 1 2 3 4 5 6 7 8 9 10 11 12 13

Amputation
Bone Disease
Fracture
Joint Disease
Spine
GROUP TOTAL
Pes Cavus
Pes Planus
Hallux Valgus
GROUP TOTAL
Height
Overweight
Underweight
Chest Measurements
GROUP TOTAL
Hearing, Defects of
Otitis Media, Chronic
Perforated Drum
GROUP TOTAL
Visual Defects
Trachoma
Other Disease of Eye
GROUP TOTAL
Mental Deficiency
Epilepsy
Psychoneurosis
Paralysis
Stammering
Alcoholism
Drug Addiction
GROUP TOTAL
Goitre
Hyperthyroidism
GROUP TOTAL
Heart Disease, Organic
Hypertension
Tachycardia
Phlebitis
Varicose Veins
Other Card.-Vasc. Disease
GROUP TOTAL
Asthma
Bronchitis, Chronic
Pleurisy
Sinusitis
GROUP TOTAL
Tuberculosis of Lung
Tuberculosis, Other Parts
GROUP TOTAL
Teeth
Digestive Disorders
Fistula in Ano
Hemorrhoids with Prolapse
GROUP TOTAL
Hernia
Skin
Syphilis
Gonorrhea
Chancroidal Disease
GROUP TOTAL
Nephritis
Testis in Canal
Varicocele and Hydrocele
Other G.-U. Diseases (Non-Ven.)
GROUP TOTAL
All other Causes

445

Chart K.—COMPARISON OF CAUSES OF PHYSICAL REJECTIONS OF INDUCTED MEN FROM CAMP)
(FEBRUARY 10 TO NOVEMBER 1, 1918)

FOR THE STATE OF TEXAS

PER CENT

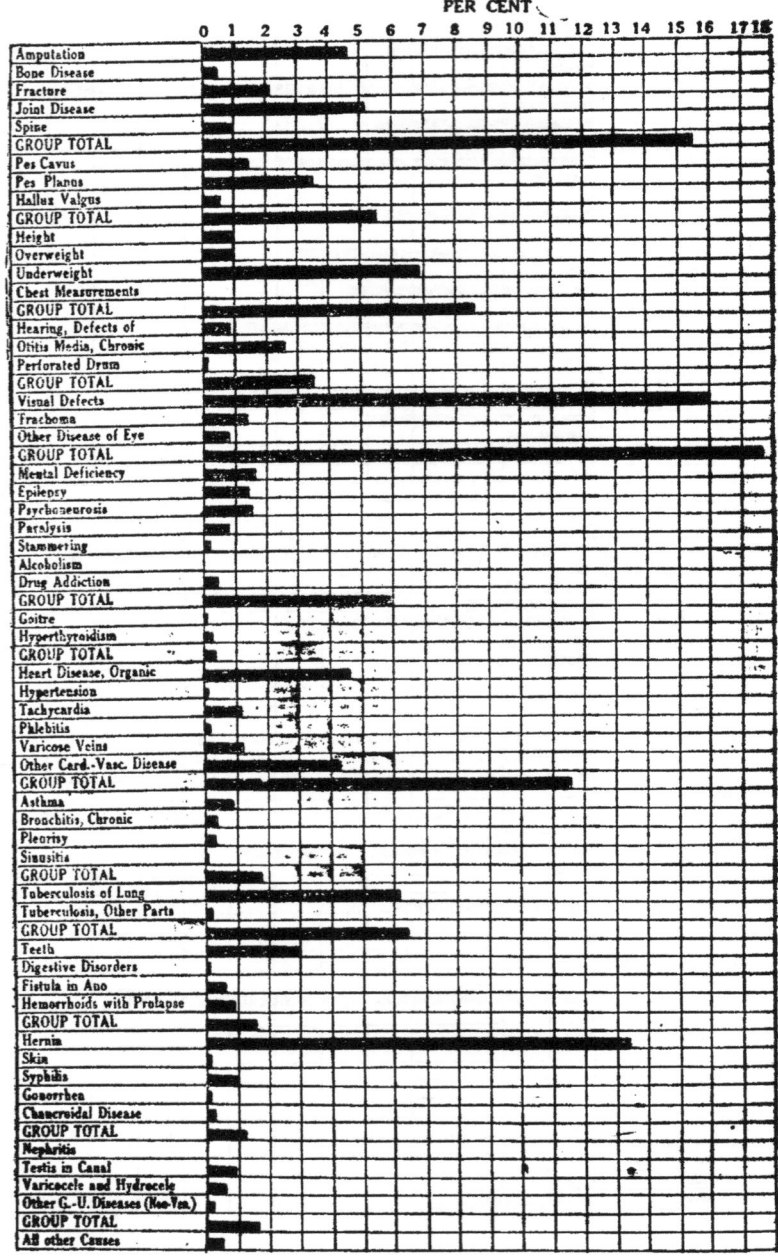

Chart L.—COMPARISON OF CAUSES OF PHYSICAL REJECTIONS OF INDUCTED MEN FROM CAMP
(FEBRUARY 10 TO NOVEMBER 1, 1918)
FOR THE STATE OF CALIFORNIA

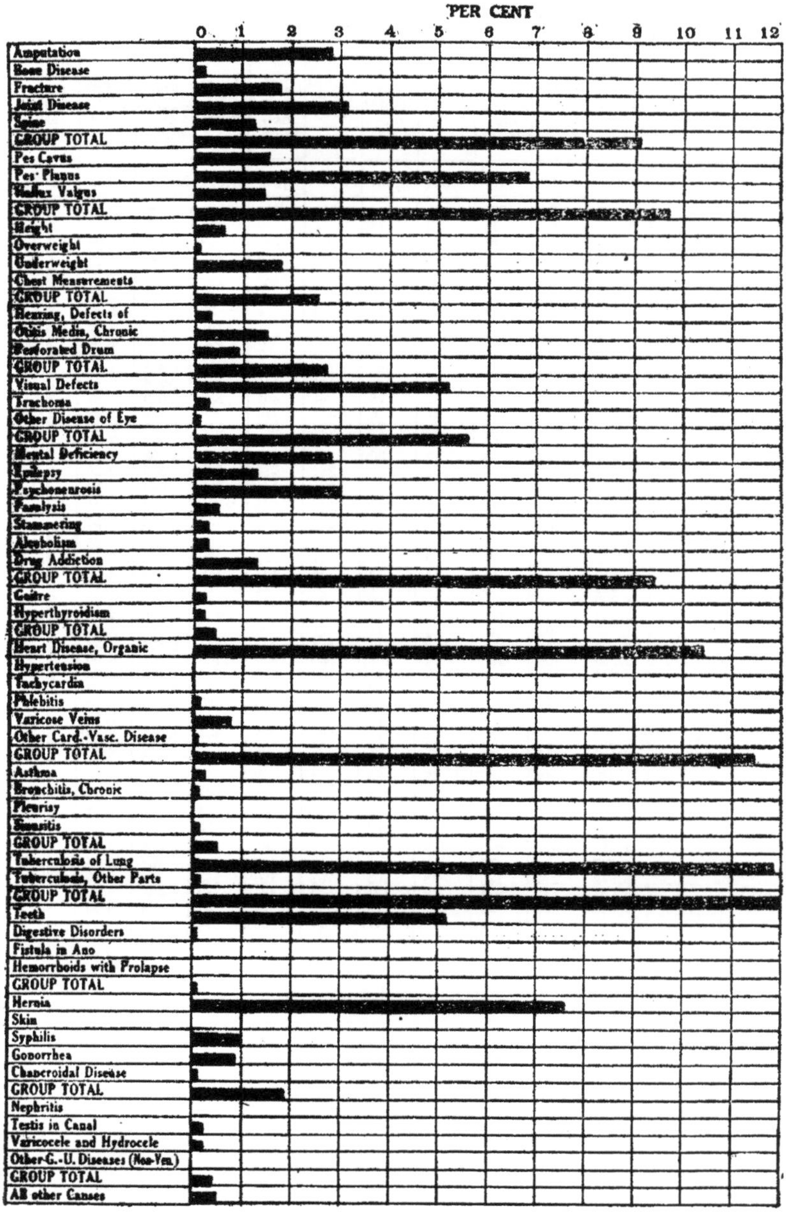

PER CENT

Cause	0	1	2	3	4	5	6	7	8	9	10	11	12
Amputation													
Bone Disease													
Fracture													
Joint Disease													
Spine													
GROUP TOTAL													
Pes Cavus													
Pes Planus													
Hallux Valgus													
GROUP TOTAL													
Height													
Overweight													
Underweight													
Chest Measurements													
GROUP TOTAL													
Hearing, Defects of													
Otitis Media, Chronic													
Perforated Drum													
GROUP TOTAL													
Visual Defects													
Trachoma													
Other Disease of Eye													
GROUP TOTAL													
Mental Deficiency													
Epilepsy													
Psychoneurosis													
Paralysis													
Stammering													
Alcoholism													
Drug Addiction													
GROUP TOTAL													
Goitre													
Hyperthyroidism													
GROUP TOTAL													
Heart Disease, Organic													
Hypertension													
Tachycardia													
Phlebitis													
Varicose Veins													
Other Card.-Vasc. Disease													
GROUP TOTAL													
Asthma													
Bronchitis, Chronic													
Pleurisy													
Sinusitis													
GROUP TOTAL													
Tuberculosis of Lung													
Tuberculosis, Other Parts													
GROUP TOTAL													
Teeth													
Digestive Disorders													
Fistula in Ano													
Hemorrhoids with Prolapse													
GROUP TOTAL													
Hernia													
Skin													
Syphilis													
Gonorrhea													
Chancroidal Disease													
GROUP TOTAL													
Nephritis													
Testis in Canal													
Varicocele and Hydrocele													
Other-G.-U. Diseases (Non-Ven.)													
GROUP TOTAL													
All other Causes													

APPENDIX TABLE 60-E.—*Mental and nervous disorders as cause for rejection by local boards and camp surgeons, and for discharge from the Army.*

	Total rejections for stated causes.	Local board.		Camps.		Army.		Totals.		Per cent of stated causes.	
		Mental deficiency.	Nervous and mental disorders.	Mental deficiency	Nervous and mental disorders.	Mental deficiency	Nervous and mental disorders.	Mental deficiency.	Nervous and mental disorders.	Mental deficiency.	Nervous and mental disorders.
United States	442,275	6,293	7,319	3,804	5,464	14,417	10,945	24,514	23,728	5.54	
Alabama	11,430	614	285	192	114	358	205	1,164	600	10.18	
Arizona	1,632	4	18	2	14	11	19	17	51	1.04	
Arkansas	9,692	297	98	81	80	361	291	739	469	7.62	
California	3,138	81	149	29	74	9	9	119	232	3.79	
Colorado	5,064	55	72	16	27	110	150	181	249	3.58	
Connecticut	9,197	49	53	64	60	298	395	411	508	4.47	
Delaware	405	11	13	6	8	....	....	17	21	4.20	
District of Columbia	663	10	43	23	22	3	4	36	69	5.43	
Florida	3,998	29	82	31	69	101	47	161	198	4.03	
Georgia	18,664	222	291	125	117	636	366	983	774	5.27	
Idaho	1,020	23	18	2	16	3	7	28	41	2.75	
Illinois	27,382	278	495	203	465	735	686	1,216	1,646	4.44	
Indiana	13,955	103	118	80	153	594	505	777	776	5.57	
Iowa	14,355	108	188	37	78	714	304	859	570	5.98	
Kansas	7,984	71	141	27	58	348	210	446	409	5.50	
Kentucky	9,376	323	199	120	75	369	227	812	501	8.66	
Louisiana	10,279	246	205	169	146	318	181	733	532	7.13	
Maine	1,801	84	43	42	36	11	14	137	93	7.61	
Maryland	5,840	93	65	163	100	281	214	537	379	9.20	
Massachusetts	21,749	117	141	98	218	625	534	840	893	3.86	
Michigan	19,764	170	218	142	174	710	557	1,022	949	5.17	
Minnesota	15,540	112	205	87	58	701	466	900	729	5.79	
Mississippi	10,902	261	219	108	111	467	212	836	542	7.67	
Missouri	14,007	335	438	201	213	257	203	793	854	5.66	
Montana	3,219	15	31	9	26	44	58	68	115	2.11	
Nebraska	4,618	31	68	14	26	144	152	189	246	4.09	
Nevada	586	2	6	2	7	6	11	10	24	1.71	
New Hampshire	1,320	15	18	13	20	31	38	59	76	4.47	
New Jersey	5,483	39	101	85	153	40	32	164	286	2.99	
New Mexico	1,461	24	19	5	14	21	26	50	59	3.42	
New York	22,711	240	794	262	647	143	172	645	1,613	2.44	
North Carolina	13,258	104	133	74	108	930	460	1,108	701	8.36	
North Dakota	3,936	43	42	20	21	183	127	246	190	6.25	
Ohio	18,293	124	282	303	450	587	716	1,014	1,448	5.54	
Oklahoma	9,012	182	112	87	101	297	253	566	466	6.28	
Oregon	3,575	26	61	4	17	74	92	104	170	2.91	
Pennsylvania	28,162	412	685	251	471	691	498	1,354	1,654	4.81	
Rhode Island	2,704	11	24	36	37	54	59	101	120	3.74	
South Carolina	6,847	46	106	46	55	412	266	504	427	7.36	
South Dakota	1,389	42	45	13	20	1	2	56	67	4.03	
Tennessee	12,640	373	99	110	194	549	329	1,032	622	8.16	
Texas	20,600	79	191	91	205	791	655	961	1,051	4.18	
Utah	2,501	4	16	3	13	65	81	72	110	2.88	
Vermont	888	16	23	13	19	3	41	32	83	3.60	
Virginia	11,317	374	230	145	117	354	262	873	609	7.72	
Washington	4,737	21	52	19	18	104	137	144	207	3.04	
West Virginia	8,872	224	136	68	103	251	190	543	429	6.12	
Wisconsin	14,631	136	223	79	127	565	438	780	788	5.33	
Wyoming	1,002	14	25	4	9	17	14	35	48	3.49	
Not allocated	....	....	....	....	....	40	30	40	30	....	....

APPENDIX TABLE 62-A.—*Deferments and exemptions in general, by States.*

	Registrants June 5, 1917, to Sept. 11, 1918.	Reported exemptions and deferments.	Per cent of registrants.	Class II.	Class III.	Class IV.	Class V.
United States.............	10,679,814	6,973,270	65.29	1,093,515	649,317	3,106,613	2,123,825
Alabama...................	206,248	120,067	58.21	20,850	8,630	72,685	17,902
Arizona...................	40,517	30,332	74.86	2,165	1,470	7,734	18,963
Arkansas..................	168,302	97,237	57.78	12,919	5,083	65,209	14,026
California.................	332,593	229,113	68.89	13,177	13,595	88,736	113,605
Colorado..................	91,813	61,595	67.09	6,591	4,603	29,386	21,015
Connecticut...............	175,026	127,019	72.57	17,808	10,572	38,837	59,802
Delaware..................	24,563	17,439	71.00	4,946	1,614	6,365	4,514
District of Columbia.......	36,741	22,676	61.72	4,540	3,270	9,339	5,527
Florida....................	94,792	54,021	56.99	4,525	3,681	29,917	15,898
Georgia...................	260,296	157,196	60.39	18,205	10,542	103,181	25,268
Idaho.....................	45,982	28,901	62.85	3,621	2,023	15,147	8,110
Illinois....................	707,962	469,675	66.34	122,609	70,567	120,358	156,141
Indiana...................	283,843	190,242	67.02	21,798	12,794	111,228	44,422
Iowa......................	240,934	152,863	63.45	26,563	10,447	82,071	33,782
Kansas....................	167,486	111,794	66.75	13,695	8,804	63,454	25,841
Kentucky.................	215,936	129,654	60.04	13,978	8,079	85,932	21,665
Louisiana.................	180,226	97,541	54.12	5,619	5,750	68,004	18,168
Maine.....................	68,214	45,415	66.58	9,543	3,468	20,609	11,795
Maryland.................	136,552	91,390	66.93	18,123	8,110	45,558	19,599
Massachusetts............	398,364	276,994	69.53	31,330	21,153	99,644	124,867
Michigan.................	411,556	280,972	68.26	84,601	47,051	43,256	106,064
Minnesota................	249,937	154,448	61.79	22,257	17,132	69,985	45,074
Mississippi...............	157,607	92,659	58.79	15,497	5,894	56,466	14,802
Missouri..................	335,012	211,745	63.21	89,289	47,530	23,953	50,973
Montana..................	97,762	58,205	59.54	8,582	4,694	26,539	18,390
Nebraska.................	132,458	85,599	64.62	14,649	7,866	43,715	19,369
Nevada...................	13,044	7,663	58.75	609	446	2,154	4,454
New Hampshire...........	41,743	29,112	69.74	4,898	2,726	11,744	9,744
New Jersey...............	332,895	231,735	69.61	23,905	17,222	103,049	87,559
New Mexico...............	37,300	22,865	61.30	2,832	1,388	10,799	7,846
New York.................	1,120,332	765,301	68.31	74,715	69,796	316,831	303,959
North Carolina...........	228,844	145,186	63.44	20,799	10,189	91,822	22,376
North Dakota.............	73,341	47,213	64.37	8,882	4,374	21,880	12,077
Ohio......................	617,371	418,557	67.80	47,467	33,724	209,582	127,784
Oklahoma.................	193,236	112,817	58.38	11,312	4,278	76,330	20,897
Oregon...................	70,549	46,162	65.43	8,024	3,278	21,117	13,743
Pennsylvania.............	902,996	618,048	68.44	79,794	47,306	283,168	207,780
Rhode Island.............	59,059	44,354	75.10	4,853	3,769	17,584	18,148
South Carolina...........	144,701	85,728	59.24	23,462	6,718	42,783	12,765
South Dakota.............	66,189	38,541	58.23	3,736	3,652	21,623	9,530
Tennessee................	213,427	132,482	62.07	11,920	8,553	90,349	21,630
Texas.....................	460,326	294,428	63.96	88,550	50,533	84,832	70,513
Utah......................	46,901	32,467	69.22	2,448	1,496	17,054	11,469
Vermont..................	30,884	21,145	68.47	3,608	1,211	9,932	6,394
Virginia..................	206,190	127,665	61.92	18,687	10,830	71,533	26,615
Washington...............	125,708	80,988	64.48	9,227	4,276	34,016	33,469
West Virginia.............	142,174	85,707	60.28	9,902	4,021	52,025	19,759
Wisconsin................	266,691	176,884	66.33	24,393	14,359	83,220	54,912
Wyoming.................	25,151	13,430	53.40	2,012	720	5,878	4,820

Chart M.—DISTRIBUTION OF REGISTRANTS, BY CLASSES

PER CENT

	0	10	20	30	40	50	60	70	80	90	100
UNITED STATES											
Alabama											
Arizona											
Arkansas											
California											
Colorado											
Connecticut											
Delaware											
Dist. Columbia											
Florida											
Georgia											
Idaho											
Illinois											
Indiana											
Iowa											
Kansas											
Kentucky											
Louisiana											
Maine											
Maryland											
Massachusetts											
Michigan											
Minnesota											
Mississippi											
Missouri											
Montana											
Nebraska											
Nevada											
New Hampshire											
New Jersey											
New Mexico											
New York											
North Carolina											
North Dakota											
Ohio											
Oklahoma											
Oregon											
Pennsylvania											
Rhode Island											
South Carolina											
South Dakota											
Tennessee											
Texas											
Utah											
Vermont											
Virginia											
Washington											
West Virginia											
Wisconsin											
Wyoming											

CLASS I   CLASS II   CLASS III   CLASS IV   CLASS V.

APPENDIX TABLE 62–B.—*Deferments and exemptions in general, by divisions.*

Total deferments and exemptions 6,973,270

CLASS II.

Division.

A. Married man with children, or father of motherless children, where such wife or children or such motherless children are not mainly dependent upon his labor for support for reason that there are other reasonably certain sources of adequate support (excluding earnings or possible earnings from labor of wife) available, and that the removal of registrant will not deprive such dependents of support.. 183,770

B. Married man, without children, whose wife, although registrant is engaged in a useful occupation, is not mainly dependent upon his labor for support, for the reason that the wife is skilled in some special class of work which she is physically able to perform and in which she is employed, or in which there is an immediate opening for her under conditions that will enable her to support herself decently and without suffering or hardship 503,221

C. Necessary skilled farm laborer in necessary agricultural enterprise.... 138,487

D. Necessary skilled industrial laborer in necessary industrial enterprise . 122,542

X. Recent marriages, etc 37,955

O. Noncombatants.. 3,593

Division not reported 103,947

CLASS III.

A. Man with dependent children (not his own), but toward whom he stands in relation of parent.. 14,816

B. Man with dependent aged or infirm parent......................... 236,553

C. Man with dependent helpless brothers or sisters 32,898

D. County or municipal officer...................................... 2,767

E. Highly trained fireman or policeman in service of municipality....... 2,885

F. Necessary customhouse clerk..................................... 577

G. Necessary employee of United States in transmission of the mails..... 6,381

H. Necessary artificer or workman in United States armory or arsenal 4,619

I. Necessary employee in service of United States...................... 9,857

J. Necessary assistant, associate; or hired manager of necessary agricultural enterprise... 67,018

K. Necessary highly specialized technical or mechanical expert of necessary industrial enterprise....................................... 20,424

L. Necessary assistant or associate manager of necessary industrial enterprise.. 6,042

O. Noncombatants.. 2,282

Division not reported 242,192

CLASS IV.

A. Man whose wife or children are mainly dependent on his labor for support... 2,932,475

B. Mariner actually employed in sea service of citizen or merchant in the United States... 16,128

C. Necessary sole managing, controlling, or directing head of necessary agricultural enterprise... 61,482

D. Necessary sole managing, controlling, or directing head of necessary industrial enterprise... 6,283

O. Noncombatants.. 9,410

Division not reported 80,435

APPENDIX TABLE 62–B.—*Deferments and exemptions in general, by divisions*—Contd.

CLASS V.

A. Officer—legislative, executive, or judicial of the United States or of
State, Territory, or District of Columbia........................... 6, 695
B. Regularly or duly ordained minister of religion...................... 18, 067
C. Student who on May 18, 1917, or on May 20, 1918, or since May 20, 1918,
was preparing for ministry in recognized theological or divinity
school, or who on May 20, 1918, or since May 20, 1918, was preparing
for practice of medicine and surgery in recognized medical school.. 16, 673
D. Person in military or naval service of United States.................. 619, 727
E. Alien enemy... 334, 949
F. Resident alien (not an enemy) who claims exemption................ 580, 003
G. Person totally and permanently physically or mentally unfit for mili-
tary service... 521, 606
H. Person morally unfit to be a soldier of the United States............. 18, 620
I. Licensed pilot actually employed in the pursuit of his vocation........ 1, 705
J. Person discharged from the Army on the ground of alienage or upon
diplomatic request.. 1, 344
K. Subject or citizen of cobelligerent country who has enlisted or enrolled
in the forces of such country under the terms of a treaty between
such country and the Unitd States providing for reciprocal military
service of their respective citizens and subjects................... 1, 064
L. Subject or citizen of neutral country who has declared his intention to
become a citizen of the United States and has withdrawn such intention under the provisions of act of Congress approved July 9, 1918,
and Selective Service Regulations............................... 818
O. Noncombatants... 2, 554

APPENDIX TABLE 64–A.—*Class I, nominal and effective strength, September, 1918, registration, ages 19–20; 32–36.*

	Total number boards in State.	Total from whom data were received by Dec. 19, 1918.	Total registrants Sept. 12, 1918, reported.	Total registrants ages 19–20; 32–36, reported.	Reported number classified Class I.	Percent Class I to registrants 19–20; 32–36; reported.	Total Group A reported.	Per cent Group A reported to registrants 19–20; 32–36.
United States.........	4,544	1,424	3,602,589	1,551,191	461,491	29.7	270,314	17.4
Alabama...............	78	7	19,101	8,500	3,222	37.9	1,903	22.3
Arizona...............	14	7	40,175	20,961	3,979	18.9	2,008	9.5
Arkansas..............	80	11	22,147	10,133	3,427	33.8	2,211	21.8
California.............	125	13	37,704	16,188	5,843	36.0	2,856	17.6
Colorado..............	75	38	60,006	26,564	6,602	24.8	2,263	8.5
Connecticut...........	44	9	36,927	15,965	3,478	21.7	1,413	8.8
Delaware..............	7	2	8,180	3,799	1,048	27.5	591	15.5
District of Columbia..	11							20.0
Florida...............	59							
Georgia...............	165	31	36,924	16,076	5,511	34.2	3,241	20.1
Idaho.................	42	6	5,193	2,243	732	32.6	438	19.5
Illinois...............	227	140	548,461	237,725	71,777	30.1	42,971	18.0
Indiana...............	124	88	239,332	103,357	31,187	30.1	18,940	18.3
Iowa.................	112	110	279,659	121,455	37,983	31.2	26,382	21.7
Kansas...............	115	56	89,356	39,538	10,525	26.6	6,131	15.5
Kentucky.............	131							
Louisiana.............	78	5		3,693	1,443	39.0	924	25.0
Maine................	24	3	11,757	5,110	1,260	24.6	297	5.8
Maryland.............	53	3	5,445	2,248	666	29.6	332	14.7
Massachusetts........	122	44	154,315	67,141	20,753	30.9	9,130	13.5
Michigan.............	136	55	167,617	73,741	18,594	25.2	7,924	10.7
Minnesota............	121	5		6,366	1,553	24.3	1,104	17.3
Mississippi...........	86	55	184,690	47,981	16,328	34.0	10,746	22.3
Missouri..............	166	61	157,927	64,329	21,095	32.7	12,715	19.7
Montana..............	44							
Nebraska.............	100	56	74,477	33,829	13,285	39.2	5,887	17.4
Nevada...............	16							17.5
New Hampshire.......	16							
New Jersey...........	106							
New Mexico..........	22	1	1,318	588	156	26.5	144	24.4
New York............	354	59	229,581	98,738	24,656	24.9	12,761	12.9
North Carolina.......	109	74	148,633	62,982	20,843	33.0	12,325	19.5
North Dakota.........	53							
Ohio.................	155	34	139,460	59,509	14,526	24.4	8,480	14.2
Oklahoma.............	85	70	190,348	83,682	27,332	32.6	18,579	22.2
Oregon...............	47	22	42,180	17,911	5,515	30.7	2,891	16.1
Pennsylvania.........	282							
Rhode Island.........	22	11	35,703	14,479	3,978	27.4	1,647	11.3
South Carolina.......	66	4		3,573	1,452	40.6	824	23.0
South Dakota.........	65	38	46,514	21,192	7,240	34.1	3,991	18.8
Tennessee............	113	42	88,139	38,416	11,070	28.8	5,950	15.4
Texas................	279	69	86,890	46,015	11,817	29.5	8,625	21.5
Utah.................	34	32	54,700	24,689	6,522	26.4	4,799	19.4
Vermont..............	15							
Virginia..............	113	58	118,369	51,782	16,230	31.3	8,891	17.1
Washington...........	66	41	63,352	27,963	7,837	28.0	4,631	16.5
West Virginia.........	65	18	53,721	23,975	6,921	28.8	4,199	17.5
Wisconsin............	104	42	116,834	51,293	14,013	27.3	10,468	20.4
Wyoming.............	21	4	7,454	3,462	1,092	31.5	702	20.2

NOTE.—It will be noticed that the net effectives here average 58.59 per cent of the nominal Class I, instead of 71.83 per cent, as in Table 64 in the text. Table 64 represents the percentage as found in the entire first and second registrations, i. e., ages 21–30, while the present Table represents ages 19–20, 32–36, as reported from one third of the boards for the third registration.

It will also be noticed that the percentage of effectives to total registrants here averages only 17.4 per cent, as against the average of 30.16 per cent shown in Table 68 of the text. The difference is due to two circumstances. In the first place, Table 68 includes age 18, whose effectives number much larger, both absolutely and in percentage, than any other age: hence the inclusion of that age would have raised considerably the lower figure of Table 64–A. In the second place, Table 68 was obtained in November, from State headquarters, for the purpose of ascertaining the results by ages, and furnished only the estimated gross Class I, the ratio of effectives being computed in this office: while Table 64–A was obtained from the local boards, in early December (just before going to press, too late for use in Table 68) and showed the results of the physical examinations, but without discrimination of ages. Thus, Table 64–A, for the age group covered, represents a closer approximation to the probable final result of the classification.

APPENDIX TABLE 66-A.—*Registration; age-distribution by States.*

	Total registration June 5, 1917, to Sept. 12, 1918.	Age 18.	Age 19.	Age 20.	Age 21.	Age 22.	Age 23.
United States	23,908,576	939,875	761,007	757,791	958,739	1,018,407	978,975
Alabama	444,842	27,084	17,802	16,738	20,750	24,379	21,999
Arizona	94,310	2,026	1,675	2,002	2,881	3,936	4,282
Arkansas	365,904	19,638	14,147	14,074	17,505	18,198	16,454
California	839,614	21,259	18,651	19,499	24,840	26,019	27,941
Colorado	216,820	7,790	6,642	6,503	8,164	7,283	8,746
Connecticut	374,400	11,304	9,807	10,107	13,271	15,685	15,909
Delaware	55,277	2,188	1,816	1,893	2,369	2,382	2,436
District of Columbia	90,361	3,620	2,757	3,091	3,482	3,180	3,153
Florida	209,248	9,949	6,628	6,701	8,076	10,540	9,500
Georgia	549,235	33,594	21,311	20,108	23,354	39,795	28,614
Idaho	105,337	3,731	3,149	3,005	3,977	4,094	3,901
Illinois	1,574,877	50,618	44,137	44,291	57,597	62,200	60,743
Indiana	639,834	23,798	20,955	20,381	23,965	25,666	25,247
Iowa	524,456	20,247	18,538	17,818	22,622	22,159	21,606
Kansas	382,065	15,578	13,355	13,153	16,536	15,985	15,890
Kentucky	486,739	25,309	19,402	18,816	23,234	21,186	20,966
Louisiana	392,316	20,549	14,887	15,274	18,746	19,154	18,223
Maine	159,631	5,740	5,191	4,948	6,392	7,259	5,972
Maryland	313,489	13,552	10,707	11,347	13,457	12,368	12,904
Massachusetts	886,728	27,384	23,914	23,611	31,948	35,268	35,255
Michigan	873,383	27,370	24,444	24,866	32,459	32,656	35,454
Minnesota	541,607	20,102	18,541	18,231	23,300	21,520	21,514
Mississippi	344,724	21,594	13,555	13,266	16,444	22,037	14,537
Missouri	765,045	29,971	25,774	25,802	32,217	30,346	30,141
Montana	201,256	4,130	3,572	3,682	5,443	8,707	7,515
Nebraska	287,414	11,309	10,158	9,877	12,258	13,210	12,155
Nevada	30,808	532	477	566	819	910	1,007
New Hampshire	95,158	3,476	3,140	2,014	3,549	4,052	3,459
New Jersey	762,485	25,292	20,930	21,616	26,268	27,399	28,390
New Mexico	81,013	3,279	2,701	2,561	3,025	3,624	3,852
New York	2,511,046	79,931	69,420	70,542	90,712	86,456	97,438
North Carolina	482,463	29,392	19,172	17,731	21,983	32,585	22,570
North Dakota	160,292	5,931	5,512	5,257	6,483	6,706	6,700
Ohio	1,389,474	44,984	40,817	41,311	55,569	52,787	53,996
Oklahoma	435,668	20,982	16,594	16,499	20,741	18,827	18,404
Oregon	179,436	5,581	4,827	4,805	5,969	5,590	5,595
Pennsylvania	2,069,407	73,531	62,613	64,414	82,097	79,432	80,534
Rhode Island	134,515	4,557	3,916	4,107	5,106	5,068	5,204
South Carolina	307,350	20,615	12,078	10,868	14,405	23,490	16,051
South Dakota	145,706	5,642	5,251	5,226	6,462	6,758	5,948
Tennessee	474,347	26,611	18,834	18,615	23,196	23,216	21,300
Texas	990,522	47,956	37,474	36,897	46,680	50,007	46,144
Utah	103,052	3,816	3,326	3,286	3,905	4,091	4,054
Vermont	71,484	2,819	2,565	2,490	3,065	3,248	2,988
Virginia	465,439	27,232	17,596	16,694	20,006	27,541	21,894
Washington	328,466	9,140	8,024	8,042	10,151	9,980	10,354
West Virginia	325,266	15,183	12,054	12,229	15,107	14,513	13,415
Wisconsin	586,290	22,335	20,773	20,402	26,137	25,050	23,935
Wyoming	59,977	1,624	1,398	1,575	2,017	1,865	2,131

APPENDIX TABLE .66–A.—*Registration; age-distribution by States*—Continued.

	Age 24.	Age 25.	Age 26.	Age 27.	Age 28.	Age 29.	Age 30.
United States	1,010,287	997,544	967,576	956,494	960,460	974,555	948,857
Alabama	21,397	19,472	17,825	17,227	16,726	16,880	15,149
Arizona	4,301	4,224	4,259	4,092	4,181	4,171	4,092
Arkansas	16,168	15,869	15,334	14,388	14,517	14,469	13,291
California	30,007	30,294	30,755	31,305	32,947	34,173	34,904
Colorado	8,856	8,718	8,756	8,595	8,583	8,715	8,690
Connecticut	16,804	17,034	15,952	16,322	15,795	16,471	16,036
Delaware	2,476	2,277	2,276	2,070	2,256	2,106	2,048
District of Columbia	3,569	3,857	3,633	3,263	3,357	3,256	3,284
Florida	9,246	9,239	8,601	8,598	8,140	8,238	7,885
Georgia	25,690	24,246	22,235	21,667	20,371	20,430	18,000
Idaho	4,193	4,384	4,288	4,047	4,296	4,383	4,514
Illinois	64,802	66,082	64,800	64,474	66,147	66,858	67,050
Indiana	26,468	26,403	26,273	25,294	27,698	25,738	25,506
Iowa	22,787	22,219	22,390	21,997	21,770	21,795	20,629
Kansas	16,265	15,784	15,421	15,117	15,281	15,269	14,722
Kentucky	20,821	20,376	19,109	18,804	18,987	18,399	17,152
Louisiana	17,755	17,370	16,296	16,184	14,939	15,213	14,986
Maine	6,209	6,205	6,208	6,062	5,970	6,146	6,067
Maryland	13,162	12,889	12,164	12,165	12,026	12,458	11,736
Massachusetts	36,266	36,453	36,806	37,585	36,323	37,295	37,136
Michigan	38,738	39,557	38,497	38,792	39,193	39,256	38,703
Minnesota	23,254	23,548	22,777	22,658	22,662	22,847	22,825
Mississippi	13,208	14,903	13,425	12,421	13,008	12,721	11,472
Missouri	31,542	30,394	30,493	30,337	29,417	30,545	29,635
Montana	8,254	8,840	9,365	9,415	9,938	10,277	9,866
Nebraska	12,557	12,199	11,876	11,957	11,886	11,864	11,606
Nevada	1,143	1,183	1,331	1,208	1,352	1,441	1,404
New Hampshire	3,988	3,876	3,694	3,889	3,778	3,698	3,670
New Jersey	31,105	30,974	29,763	30,400	30,982	31,870	32,813
New Mexico	3,891	3,801	3,661	3,390	3,339	3,366	3,361
New York	104,626	104,911	101,648	103,051	104,490	107,720	107,697
North Carolina	21,775	20,638	19,172	18,384	18,486	18,804	16,737
North Dakota	7,235	6,941	6,753	6,381	6,587	6,597	6,623
Ohio	58,059	56,828	56,813	55,438	56,682	57,971	55,242
Oklahoma	18,801	18,257	17,658	17,165	16,635	16,768	15,840
Oregon	6,100	6,291	6,259	6,561	6,702	7,284	7,154
Pennsylvania	84,625	83,554	80,659	80,590	81,502	85,152	84,168
Rhode Island	5,673	5,553	5,351	5,395	5,473	5,558	5,554
South Carolina	14,745	13,337	11,608	10,997	10,653	10,606	9,201
South Dakota	5,993	6,018	5,999	5,809	5,995	5,913	5,777
Tennessee	20,975	19,733	19,034	18,128	17,861	17,722	15,930
Texas	46,610	44,833	43,262	41,051	39,482	39,283	37,544
Utah	4,386	4,400	4,397	4,143	4,147	4,519	4,505
Vermont	2,903	2,751	2,691	2,790	2,659	2,639	2,741
Virginia	20,750	19,158	17,559	17,067	16,658	16,555	15,262
Washington	11,184	11,447	11,343	11,634	12,190	12,416	12,443
West Virginia	13,781	13,146	12,630	12,034	12,317	12,276	11,666
Wisconsin	24,737	24,604	24,018	23,879	23,617	23,926	24,034
Wyoming	2,347	2,474	2,449	2,274	2,460	2,498	2,507

APPENDIX TABLE 66–A.—*Registration; age–distribution by States*—Continued.

	Age 31.	Age 32.	Age 33.	Age 34.	Age 35.	Age 36.	Age 37.	Age 38.
United States	1,043,492	499,902	927,968	920,355	804,778	813,581	823,150	836,280
Alabama	17,025	7,546	15,580	15,649	13,454	14,268	15,057	15,154
Arizona	4,290	1,762	3,527	3,888	3,392	3,458	3,108	3,459
Arkansas	13,927	6,292	13,085	13,631	11,129	12,607	12,667	12,983
California	38,460	19,454	36,010	35,050	31,417	31,931	31,693	32,718
Colorado	9,010	5,151	9,471	8,975	7,918	7,785	7,548	7,807
Connecticut	17,614	7,981	15,075	14,496	12,799	12,660	12,542	12,657
Delaware	2,158	1,115	2,147	2,115	1,903	1,769	1,825	1,964
District of Columbia	3,226	1,956	3,702	3,589	3,047	3,020	3,616	3,801
Florida	8,287	3,595	7,997	7,952	6,497	6,883	7,415	7,733
Georgia	18,908	8,465	18,506	18,672	15,822	16,490	18,398	18,557
Idaho	4,649	2,506	4,511	4,363	3,763	3,846	3,535	3,751
Illinois	72,712	34,958	63,071	62,993	54,478	54,108	54,007	54,430
Indiana	27,520	14,094	24,498	25,028	22,528	22,568	22,199	22,824
Iowa	22,463	12,081	19,379	19,050	17,398	16,956	16,831	17,005
Kansas	15,854	8,531	13,719	14,267	12,694	12,721	12,619	12,757
Kentucky	18,731	9,353	17,486	17,846	15,133	15,786	16,789	16,784
Louisiana	14,055	6,530	13,993	14,624	12,243	13,536	13,418	13,461
Maine	6,418	3,297	5,809	5,794	5,177	5,325	5,436	5,661
Maryland	13,225	6,324	11,950	12,131	10,252	10,362	10,620	11,108
Massachusetts	41,226	18,446	34,001	33,565	29,382	29,757	29,999	30,969
Michigan	40,736	19,770	35,989	34,244	30,325	29,645	29,624	29,557
Minnesota	24,609	13,270	21,798	20,679	18,125	17,756	17,208	17,195
Mississippi	15,713	4,819	11,862	12,204	10,646	11,909	11,794	12,480
Missouri	33,089	16,216	29,346	29,313	25,518	25,704	27,279	26,589
Montana	10,643	4,595	8,028	7,740	6,710	6,348	6,164	6,048
Nebraska	12,151	6,739	10,999	10,654	9,849	9,450	9,311	9,207
Nevada	1,524	750	1,540	1,334	1,229	1,277	1,142	1,188
New Hampshire	3,957	2,121	3,548	3,121	2,748	2,857	2,967	3,103
New Jersey	35,961	16,087	31,702	31,251	27,506	27,323	27,432	27,577
New Mexico	3,767	1,823	3,570	3,243	2,798	2,637	2,389	2,537
New York	127,930	54,822	97,944	99,022	87,357	85,952	87,696	89,088
North Carolina	19,252	7,552	15,231	15,904	13,887	14,373	15,223	15,282
North Dakota	6,903	3,794	6,585	6,310	5,455	5,512	5,279	5,369
Ohio	62,760	29,793	56,493	55,632	48,625	47,985	48,675	49,393
Oklahoma	16,470	8,433	16,617	16,476	13,870	14,537	14,929	15,285
Oregon	7,659	4,759	8,037	8,062	7,129	7,394	7,217	7,172
Pennsylvania	91,041	44,104	84,589	82,954	73,538	74,195	74,252	75,599
Rhode Island	5,846	3,039	5,148	5,110	4,491	4,728	4,635	4,580
South Carolina	11,485	4,399	9,714	10,038	8,907	9,216	10,389	10,153
South Dakota	6,322	3,552	6,016	5,678	5,077	4,941	5,025	4,883
Tennessee	18,607	8,572	17,509	17,122	14,511	15,396	16,071	16,534
Texas	39,133	19,393	35,650	35,586	30,422	32,240	31,188	32,513
Utah	4,893	2,471	4,195	4,021	3,626	3,596	3,493	3,517
Vermont	2,912	1,505	2,540	2,509	2,408	2,419	2,416	2,555
Virginia	16,358	7,782	16,300	16,526	13,929	14,581	16,693	16,539
Washington	13,987	8,159	14,515	14,136	12,265	12,651	12,410	12,490
West Virginia	12,976	6,438	12,778	13,074	10,649	11,188	11,597	11,514
Wisconsin	24,390	14,090	23,040	21,748	20,325	19,437	19,044	20,327
Wyoming	2,660	1,615	3,168	2,986	2,427	2,498	2,286	2,404

APPENDIX TABLE 66–A.—*Registration; age-distribution by States*—Continued.

	Age 39.	Age 40.	Age 41.	Age 42.	Age 43.	Age 44.	Age 45.	Age not reported.
United States	725,416	688,918	648,599	693,657	654,915	624,129	688,002	284,867
Alabama	12,296	11,181	9,603	9,990	9,122	9,233	13,527	2,729
Arizona	2,557	3,270	2,350	3,075	2,407	2,041	3,051	2,553
Arkansas	10,436	9,700	8,530	8,632	8,455	8,127	10,783	848
California	29,104	27,354	26,462	27,942	25,361	24,466	26,027	33,571
Colorado	6,933	6,467	6,326	6,944	6,289	5,921	6,333	2,400
Connecticut	11,232	10,662	10,183	11,131	10,514	10,009	10,942	3,343
Delaware	1,649	1,513	1,454	1,672	1,562	1,465	1,651	691
District of Columbia	3,084	2,798	2,898	3,001	2,723	2,470	3,006	922
Florida	5,955	5,466	5,097	5,580	5,131	4,865	6,632	2,822
Georgia	14,448	14,006	11,808	12,505	11,836	11,125	14,562	5,712
Idaho	3,331	3,202	3,115	3,185	2,965	2,859	2,820	974
Illinois	47,406	45,331	42,208	45,477	43,165	41,186	42,520	37,028
Indiana	20,360	19,313	18,267	19,781	19,231	18,444	19,291	496
Iowa	15,323	14,816	14,558	15,505	14,662	14,086	14,658	3,025
Kansas	11,303	11,211	10,608	11,296	11,183	10,534	10,968	3,444
Kentucky	14,012	14,061	13,144	13,534	13,448	12,211	14,458	1,403
Louisiana	11,804	10,331	8,909	9,427	8,800	8,459	10,144	2,906
Maine	4,960	4,928	4,722	4,991	5,112	4,733	5,100	3,739
Maryland	9,561	9,021	8,623	9,607	9,158	8,828	9,590	2,194
Massachusetts	27,816	26,203	24,933	27,593	26,676	26,034	27,220	17,654
Michigan	25,796	24,259	23,278	25,376	22,978	22,239	23,583	5,989
Minnesota	15,435	14,795	14,223	14,851	14,122	13,738	14,330	5,395
Mississippi	9,327	9,122	7,452	7,688	7,312	6,986	8,926	3,593
Missouri	23,425	22,744	21,611	23,002	22,515	20,973	22,716	8,331
Montana	5,339	4,673	4,599	4,754	4,501	4,274	4,293	13,543
Nebraska	8,141	8,097	7,556	8,018	7,704	7,355	7,445	1,826
Nevada	1,146	1,079	988	1,070	970	877	940	381
New Hampshire	2,776	2,772	2,700	2,924	2,767	2,743	2,822	3,549
New Jersey	24,609	23,583	22,325	24,826	22,682	22,074	24,513	4,762
New Mexico	1,955	2,053	1,971	1,982	1,931	1,751	1,853	902
New York	80,039	74,842	71,831	77,760	74,035	70,853	76,737	27,506
North Carolina	13,504	12,918	11,495	11,853	11,356	10,687	12,256	3,261
North Dakota	4,868	4,327	4,223	4,519	4,221	4,016	4,085	1,105
Ohio	42,953	41,635	38,790	42,481	40,095	37,744	39,955	19,962
Oklahoma	12,574	12,233	11,460	11,705	11,779	10,730	12,287	2,972
Oregon	6,316	6,103	5,962	6,250	5,731	5,557	5,706	1,664
Pennsylvania	66,064	61,547	59,641	64,652	60,006	58,756	63,046	12,253
Rhode Island	4,230	4,092	4,048	4,229	4,106	3,997	4,171	1,541
South Carolina	8,126	7,703	6,708	7,553	6,403	6,340	8,660	2,902
South Dakota	4,410	4,030	3,996	4,038	3,844	3,645	3,734	[1]176
Tennessee	13,652	13,295	11,991	11,768	11,487	10,568	13,546	2,563
Texas	26,670	25,505	23,381	24,478	23,338	20,921	24,678	8,203
Utah	3,237	3,003	2,589	2,935	2,583	2,422	2,508	928
Vermont	2,452	2,331	2,234	2,418	2,296	2,161	2,360	[1]261
Virginia	13,380	12,905	12,250	12,752	12,053	10,957	13,444	5,016
Washington	11,128	10,617	10,135	10,808	9,686	9,323	9,699	18,100
West Virginia	9,671	9,347	8,812	9,010	8,815	8,116	9,136	1,794
Wisconsin	18,554	16,623	16,878	17,192	16,168	15,614	16,563	[1]1,150
Wyoming	2,069	1,851	1,674	1,897	1,631	1,566	1,667	[1]41

[1] The age returns from this State show an apparent excess in age distribution over the total registration reported.

Appendix Table 71-A.—*Colored and white registration, compared by States.*

	Total colored and white registrants.	Colored registrants, June 5, 1917, to Sept. 11, 1918.	Colored registrants, Sept. 12, 1918.	Total colored registrants.	Per cent of total registrants.	White registrants, June 5, 1917, to Sept. 11, 1918.	White registrants, Sept. 12, 1918.	Total white registrants.	Per cent of total registrants.
United States.......	23,779,997	1,078,331	1,212,196	2,290,527	9.63	9,562,515	11,926,955	21,489,470	90.37
Alabama............	444,692	81,963	81,410	163,373	36.74	124,247	157,072	281,319	63.26
Arizona............	93,078	295	680	975	1.05	39,884	52,219	92,103	98.95
Arkansas...........	365,754	51,176	53,659	104,835	28.66	117,111	143,808	260,919	71.34
California..........	787,676	3,308	6,404	9,712	1.23	312,994	464,970	777,964	98.77
Colorado...........	215,178	1,103	1,867	2,970	1.38	90,453	121,755	212,208	98.62
Connecticut........	373,676	3,524	4,659	8,183	2.19	171,296	194,197	365,493	97.81
Delaware...........	55,215	3,798	4,448	8,246	14.93	20,761	26,208	46,969	85.07
District of Columbia	89,898	11,045	15,433	26,478	29.45	25,625	37,795	63,420	70.55
Florida.............	208,931	39,013	43,019	82,032	39.26	55,572	71,327	126,899	60.74
Georgia............	549,020	112,593	108,188	220,781	40.22	147,604	180,635	328,239	59.78
Idaho..............	103,740	254	255	509	.49	45,224	58,007	103,231	99.51
Illinois............	1,571,717	21,816	35,597	57,413	3.65	685,254	829,050	1,514,304	96.35
Indiana............	639,431	11,289	16,549	27,838	4.35	272,442	339,151	611,593	95.65
Iowa...............	523,957	2,959	3,022	5,981	1.14	237,744	280,232	517,976	98.86
Kansas.............	381,316	5,575	7,448	13,023	3.41	161,691	206,602	368,293	96.59
Kentucky..........	486,599	25,850	30,182	56,032	11.52	190,060	240,507	430,567	88.48
Louisiana..........	391,664	76,223	82,256	158,479	40.46	103,718	129,467	233,185	59.54
Maine..............	159,350	163	179	342	.22	67,941	91,067	159,008	99.78
Maryland...........	313,255	26,435	32,736	59,171	18.89	110,066	144,018	254,084	81.11
Massachusetts.....	884,030	6,044	8,056	14,100	1.60	391,654	478,276	869,930	98.40
Michigan...........	871,410	6,979	8,950	15,929	1.83	404,040	451,441	855,481	98.17
Minnesota..........	540,003	1,541	1,809	3,350	.62	247,750	288,903	536,653	99.38
Mississippi.........	344,506	81,548	91,534	173,082	50.24	75,977	95,447	171,424	49.76
Missouri...........	764,428	22,796	31,524	54,320	7.11	372,106	338,002	710,108	92.89
Montana...........	198,999	320	494	814	.41	96,753	101,432	198,185	99.59
Nebraska..........	286,147	1,614	2,417	4,031	1.42	130,493	151,623	282,116	98.58
Nevada............	29,465	59	113	172	.58	12,581	16,712	29,293	99.42
New Hampshire.....	95,035	77	98	175	.18	41,617	53,243	94,860	99.82
New Jersey........	761,236	14,056	19,340	33,396	4.39	318,615	409,225	727,840	95.61
New Mexico........	80,158	235	360	595	.74	36,776	42,787	79,563	99.26
New York..........	2,503,290	25,974	35,299	61,273	2.44	1,092,061	1,349,956	2,442,017	97.56
North Carolina....	480,901	73,357	69,168	142,525	29.63	155,102	183,274	338,376	70.37
North Dakota......	159,391	65	165	230	.15	72,837	86,324	159,161	99.85
Ohio...............	1,387,830	28,831	35,156	63,987	4.61	588,170	735,673	1,323,843	95.39
Oklahoma..........	423,864	14,305	23,258	37,563	8.86	173,851	212,450	386,301	91.14
Oregon............	176,010	144	534	678	.38	69,376	105,956	175,332	99.62
Pennsylvania......	2,067,023	39,363	51,111	90,474	4.38	863,106	1,113,443	1,976,549	95.62
Rhode Island......	134,232	1,573	1,913	3,486	2.59	57,433	73,313	130,746	97.41
South Carolina....	307,229	74,265	74,912	149,177	48.56	70,395	87,657	158,052	51.44
South Dakota.....	142,783	144	171	315	.23	64,896	77,572	142,468	99.77
Tennessee........	474,253	43,735	51,059	94,794	19.99	169,674	209,785	379,459	80.01
Texas.............	989,571	83,671	82,775	166,446	16.82	376,385	446,740	823,125	83.18
Utah...............	100,038	169	392	561	.56	45,930	53,547	99,477	99.44
Vermont...........	71,464	63	89	152	.21	30,819	40,493	71,312	99.79
Virginia...........	464,903	64,358	75,816	140,174	30.15	141,714	183,015	324,729	69.85
Washington........	319,337	373	1,353	1,726	.54	123,752	193,859	317,611	99.46
West Virginia.....	324,975	13,292	14,652	27,944	8.60	128,852	168,179	297,031	91.40
Wisconsin.........	584,639	718	1,117	1,835	.31	265,501	317,303	582,804	99.69
Wyoming..........	58,700	280	570	850	1.45	24,612	33,238	57,850	98.55

APPENDIX TABLE 73–A.—*Colored and white inductions, compared by States.*

	Total colored and white registrants, June 5, 1917, to Sept. 11, 1918.	Colored registrants, June 5, 1917, to Sept. 11, 1918.	Percentage of colored and white registrants.	Colored inducted, June 5, 1917, to Nov. 11, 1918.	Per cent of colored registrants.	White registrants, June 5, 1917, to Sept. 11, 1918.	Per cent of colored and white registrants.	White inductions, June 5, 1917, to Nov. 11, 1918.	Per cent of white registrants.
United States.......	10,640,846	1,078,331	10.13	367,710	34.10	9,562,515	89.87	2,299,157	24.04
Alabama............	206,210	81,963	39.75	25,874	31.57	124,247	60.25	33,881	27.27
Arizona............	40,179	295	.73	77	26.10	39,884	99.27	8,036	20.15
Arkansas...........	168,287	51,176	30.41	17,544	34.28	117,111	69.59	31,768	27.13
California..........	316,302	3,308	1.05	919	27.78	312,994	98.95	66,148	21.13
Colorado...........	91,556	1,103	1.20	317	28.74	90,453	98.80	22,487	24.86
Connecticut........	174,820	3,524	2.02	941	26.70	171,296	97.98	31,598	18.45
Delaware...........	24,559	3,798	15.46	1,365	35.93	20,761	84.54	3,628	17.48
District of Columbia.	36,670	11,045	30.12	4,000	36.22	25,625	69.88	5,631	21.97
Florida............	94,585	39,013	41.25	12,904	33.08	55,572	58.75	12,012	21.62
Georgia............	260,197	112,593	43.27	34,303	30.47	147,604	56.73	32,538	32.04
Idaho.............	45,478	254	.56	95	37.40	45,224	99.44	12,471	27.58
Illinois............	707,070	21,816	3.09	8,754	40.13	685,254	96.91	168,729	24.62
Indiana............	283,731	11,289	3.98	4,579	40.56	272,442	96.02	65,170	23.92
Iowa..............	240,703	2,959	1.23	929	31.40	237,744	98.77	65,935	27.73
Kansas............	167,266	5,575	3.33	2,127	38.15	161,691	96.67	39,778	24.60
Kentucky..........	215,910	25,850	11.98	11,320	43.79	190,060	88.02	47,010	24.66
Louisiana..........	179,941	76,223	42.36	28,711	37.67	103,718	57.64	27,494	26.51
Maine.............	68,104	163	.24	50	30.67	67,941	99.76	15,216	22.40
Maryland..........	136,501	26,435	19.37	9,212	34.85	110,066	80.63	24,655	22.40
Massachusetts......	397,698	6,044	1.52	1,200	19.85	391,654	98.48	75,367	19.24
Michigan...........	411,019	6,979	1.70	2,395	34.32	404,040	98.30	94,085	23.29
Minnesota..........	249,291	1,541	.62	511	53.16	247,750	99.38	73,169	29.53
Mississippi.........	157,525	81,548	51.77	24,066	29.51	75,977	48.23	19,296	25.40
Missouri...........	334,902	22,796	6.81	9,219	40.44	312,106	93.19	83,624	26.79
Montana...........	97,073	320	.33	198	61.87	96,753	99.67	27,142	28.05
Nebraska...........	132,107	1,614	1.22	642	39.78	130,493	98.78	29,165	22.35
Nevada............	12,640	59	.47	26	44.07	12,581	99.53	3,138	24.94
New Hampshire.....	41,694	77	.18	27	35.07	41,617	99.82	8,377	20.13
New Jersey.........	332,671	14,056	4.23	4,863	34.60	318,615	95.77	66,527	20.88
New Mexico........	37,011	235	.63	51	21.70	36,776	99.37	8,811	23.96
New York..........	1,118,035	25,974	2.32	6,193	23.84	1,092,061	97.68	247,396	22.65
North Carolina......	228,459	73,357	32.11	20,082	27.38	155,102	67.89	38,359	24.73
North Dakota.......	72,902	65	.09	87	....	72,837	99.91	18,508	25.41
Ohio..............	617,001	28,831	4.67	7,861	27.27	588,170	95.33	130,287	22.15
Oklahoma..........	188,156	14,305	7.60	5,694	39.80	173,851	92.40	59,247	34.08
Oregon............	69,520	144	.21	68	47.22	69,376	99.79	16,090	23.19
Pennsylvania.......	902,469	39,363	4.36	15,392	39.10	863,106	95.64	185,819	21.53
Rhode Island.......	59,006	1,573	2.67	291	18.50	57,433	97.33	10,885	18.95
South Carolina......	144,660	74,265	51.34	25,798	34.74	70,395	48.66	18,261	25.94
South Dakota.......	65,040	144	.22	62	43.06	64,896	99.78	21,193	32.66
Tennessee..........	213,409	43,735	20.59	17,774	40.64	169,674	79.51	42,104	24.81
Texas.............	460,056	83,671	18.19	31,506	37.65	376,385	81.81	85,889	22.82
Utah..............	46,099	169	.37	77	45.56	45,930	99.63	10,711	23.32
Vermont...........	30,882	63	.20	22	34.92	30,819	99.80	6,607	21.44
Virginia...........	206,072	64,358	31.23	23,541	36.57	141,714	68.77	34,796	24.55
Washington........	124,125	373	.30	173	46.38	123,752	99.70	28,513	23.04
West Virginia.......	142,144	13,292	9.35	5,492	41.32	128,852	90.65	39,863	30.94
Wisconsin..........	266,219	718	.27	224	31.20	265,501	99.73	70,758	26.65
Wyoming...........	24,892	280	1.12	95	23.93	24,612	98.88	7,828	31.81
Alaska.............	....	....	....	5	....	....	....	1,957	....
Hawaii............	....	....	....	....	....	....	....	5,466	....
Porto Rico.........	....	....	....	....	....	....	....	15,734	....

APPENDIX TABLE 75-A.—*Desertions: Reported and outstanding.*

	Total registrants, June 5, 1917, to Sept. 11, 1918.	Total reported desertions.	Percentage of registrants.	Accounted for as not deserters.	Net reported desertions.	Percentage of registrants.	Apprehended or cases disposed of.	Outstanding desertions.	Percentage of registrants.
United States	10,679,814	474,861	4.45	111,839	363,022	3.40	67,838	295,184	2.76
Alabama	206,248	14,507	7.04	2,850	11,657	5.65	1,532	10,125	4.91
Arizona	40,517	7,003	17.28	1,780	5,223	12.90	1,023	4,200	10.37
Arkansas	168,302	7,246	4.31	2,151	5,095	3.03	1,294	3,801	2.26
California	332,593	15,591	4.69	2,420	13,171	3.96	1,748	11,423	3.43
Colorado	91,813	5,001	5.45	1,583	3,418	3.72	549	2,869	3.12
Connecticut	175,026	13,098	7.48	3,375	9,723	5.56	2,248	7,475	4.27
Delaware	24,563	989	4.03	310	679	2.76	....	679	2.76
District of Columbia	36,741	1,006	2.73	174	832	2.26	159	673	1.83
Florida	94,792	10,142	10.70	1,839	8,303	8.76	475	7,828	8.26
Georgia	260,296	13,468	5.18	3,106	10,362	3.98	1,079	9,283	3.57
Idaho	45,982	2,350	5.11	775	1,575	3.43	346	1,229	2.67
Illinois	707,962	24,589	3.47	4,904	19,685	2.78	3,977	15,708	2.22
Indiana	283,843	6,451	2.27	2,271	4,180	1.47	1,551	2,629	.98
Iowa	240,934	5,779	2.40	1,933	3,846	1.60	854	2,992	1.24
Kansas	167,486	3,427	2.05	1,007	2,420	1.44	419	2,001	1.19
Kentucky	215,936	3,854	1.79	551	3,303	1.53	1,004	2,299	1.06
Louisiana	180,226	8,212	4.55	221	7,991	4.43	428	7,563	4.20
Maine	68,214	2,582	3.79	876	1,706	2.50	450	1,456	2.13
Maryland	136,552	6,241	4.57	1,417	4,824	3.53	593	4,231	3.10
Massachusetts	398,364	20,506	6.87	6,139	14,367	4.81	2,661	11,706	3.92
Michigan	411,596	18,237	4.43	6,619	11,618	2.82	2,921	8,697	2.11
Minnesota	249,937	10,729	4.29	3,059	7,670	3.06	1,859	5,811	2.33
Mississippi	157,607	9,825	6.23	1,873	7,952	5.05	1,689	6,263	3.97
Missouri	335,012	12,340	3.68	1,909	10,431	3.11	1,296	9,135	2.73
Montana	97,762	8,009	8.19	1,297	6,712	6.87	1,748	4,964	5.08
Nebraska	132,458	2,537	2.14	592	2,245	1.69	255	1,990	1.50
Nevada	13,044	1,395	10.70	399	996	7.64	204	792	6.07
New Hampshire	41,743	1,431	3.43	490	941	2.25	91	850	2.02
New Jersey	332,895	16,649	5.00	4,880	11,769	3.54	3,122	8,647	2.60
New Mexico	37,300	3,257	8.73	778	2,479	6.69	474	2,005	5.38
New York	1,120,332	61,083	5.45	14,716	46,367	4.14	13,860	32,507	2.90
North Carolina	228,844	6,112	2.67	292	5,820	2.54	595	5,225	2.28
North Dakota	73,341	2,539	3.46	947	1,592	2.17	226	1,366	1.86
Ohio	617,371	26,894	4.36	6,494	20,400	3.30	2,370	18,030	2.92
Oklahoma	193,236	7,083	3.67	1,493	5,590	2.89	444	5,146	2.66
Oregon	70,549	2,041	2.89	381	1,660	2.35	336	1,324	1.88
Pennsylvania	902,996	38,338	4.25	8,874	29,464	3.26	3,131	26,333	2.92
Rhode Island	59,059	2,591	4.39	304	2,287	3.87	111	2,176	3.68
South Carolina	144,701	5,696	3.94	949	4,747	3.28	2,445	2,302	1.59
South Dakota	66,189	1,270	1.92	584	686	1.04	94	592	.89
Tennessee	213,427	7,953	3.73	2,014	5,939	2.78	448	5,491	2.57
Texas	460,326	24,597	5.34	2,856	21,741	4.72	4,209	17,532	3.81
Utah	46,901	1,746	3.72	575	1,171	2.50	348	823	1.75
Vermont	30,884	694	2.25	286	408	1.32	107	301	.97
Virginia	206,190	8,025	3.89	2,324	5,701	2.76	1,295	4,406	2.14
Washington	125,708	7,291	5.80	3,049	4,242	3.37	233	4,009	3.19
West Virginia	142,174	6,816	4.79	2,435	4,381	3.08	671	3,710	2.61
Wisconsin	266,691	4,736	1.78	1,385	3,351	1.26	796	2,555	.96
Wyoming	25,151	1,797	7.15	223	1,574	6.26	70	1,504	5.98
Alaska	....	609	....	80	529	....	....	529	....
Hawaii	....	184	....	....	184	....	....	184	....
Porto Rico	....	15	....	....	15	....	....	15	....

APPENDIX TABLE 76-A.—*Reported desertions by color, compared by States.*

	Total white and colored registrants, June 5, 1917, to Sept. 11, 1918.	Total white registrants.	Reported desertions, white.	Per cent of total registrants.	Per cent of white registrants.	Total colored registrants.	Reported desertions, colored.	Per cent of total registrants.	Per cent of colored registrants.
United States	10,640,846	9,562,515	369,030	3.47	3.86	1,078,331	105,831	.99	9.81
Alabama	206,210	124,247	3,672	1.78	2.96	81,963	10,835	5.25	13.22
Arizona	40,179	39,884	6,939	17.36	17.40	295	64	.16	21.69
Arkansas	168,287	117,111	2,476	1.47	2.11	51,176	4,770	2.83	9.32
California	316,302	312,994	15,323	4.84	4.90	3,308	268	.08	8.10
Colorado	91,556	90,453	4,910	5.36	5.43	1,103	91	.10	8.25
Connecticut	174,820	171,296	12,416	7.10	7.25	3,524	682	.39	19.35
Delaware	24,559	20,761	686	2.79	3.30	3,798	303	1.23	7.98
District of Columbia	36,670	25,625	390	1.06	1.52	11,045	616	1.68	5.58
Florida	94,585	55,572	1,823	1.93	3.28	39,013	8,319	8.71	21.32
Georgia	260,197	147,604	4,499	1.73	3.05	112,593	8,969	3.45	7.97
Idaho	45,478	45,224	2,242	4.93	4.96	254	108	.23	42.51
Illinois	707,070	685,254	21,678	3.07	3.16	21,816	2,911	.41	13.34
Indiana	283,731	272,442	5,252	1.85	1.93	11,289	1,199	.42	10.62
Iowa	240,703	237,744	5,262	2.19	2.21	2,959	517	.21	17.47
Kansas	167,266	161,691	3,172	1.90	1.96	5,575	255	.15	4.57
Kentucky	215,910	190,060	2,330	1.08	1.23	25,850	1,524	.71	5.90
Louisiana	179,941	103,718	2,250	1.25	2.17	76,223	5,962	3.31	7.82
Maine	68,104	67,941	2,553	3.74	3.76	163	29	.04	17.79
Maryland	136,501	110,066	3,831	2.81	3.48	26,435	2,410	1.77	9.12
Massachusetts	397,698	391,654	19,841	4.99	5.07	6,044	665	1.67	11.00
Michigan	411,019	404,040	17,222	4.19	4.26	6,979	1,015	.25	14.54
Minnesota	249,291	247,750	10,108	4.05	4.08	1,541	621	.25	40.30
Mississippi	157,525	75,977	1,713	1.09	2.25	81,548	8,112	5.15	9.95
Missouri	334,902	312,106	10,549	3.14	3.38	22,796	1,791	.53	7.86
Montana	97,073	96,753	7,895	8.13	8.16	320	114	.12	35.63
Nebraska	132,107	130,493	2,608	1.97	2.00	1,614	229	.17	14.19
Nevada	12,640	12,581	1,392	1.10	11.06	59	3	.02	5.08
New Hampshire	41,694	41,617	1,428	3.42	3.43	77	3	.01	3.90
New Jersey	332,671	318,615	15,114	4.54	4.74	14,056	1,535	.46	10.92
New Mexico	37,011	36,776	3,217	8.69	8.75	235	40	.11	17.02
New York	1,118,035	1,092,061	57,021	5.10	5.22	25,974	4,062	.36	15.64
North Carolina	228,459	155,102	1,175	5.14	.76	73,357	4,937	2.16	6.73
North Dakota	72,902	72,837	2,520	3.46	3.46	65	19	.03	29.23
Ohio	617,001	588,170	22,846	3.70	3.88	28,831	4,048	.66	14.04
Oklahoma	188,156	173,851	5,860	3.11	3.37	14,305	1,223	.65	8.56
Oregon	69,520	69,376	2,023	2.91	2.92	144	18	.03	12.50
Pennsylvania	902,469	863,106	31,739	3.52	3.68	39,363	6,599	.73	16.76
Rhode Island	59,006	57,433	2,340	3.97	4.07	1,573	251	.43	15.96
South Carolina	144,660	70,395	1,107	.77	1.57	74,265	4,589	3.14	6.18
South Dakota	65,040	64,896	1,243	1.91	1.92	144	27	.04	18.75
Tennessee	213,409	169,674	4,380	2.05	2.58	43,735	3,573	1.67	8.17
Texas	460,056	376,385	19,209	4.18	5.10	83,671	5,388	1.17	6.44
Utah	46,099	45,930	1,735	3.76	3.78	169	11	.02	6.51
Vermont	30,882	30,819	690	2.23	2.71	63	4	.01	6.35
Virginia	206,072	141,714	3,090	1.50	2.18	64,358	4,935	2.39	7.67
Washington	124,125	123,752	7,261	5.85	5.87	373	30	.02	8.04
West Virginia	142,144	128,852	4,803	3.38	3.73	13,292	2,013	1.41	15.14
Wisconsin	266,219	265,501	4,663	1.75	1.76	718	73	.03	10.17
Wyoming	24,892	24,612	1,734	6.96	7.05	280	63	.25	22.50
Alaska			601						
Hawaii			184						
Porto Rico			15						

APPENDIX TABLE 77-A.—*Reported desertions by citizenship, compared by States.*

	Total registrants June 5, 1917–Sept. 11, 1918.	Total alien registrants.	Reported desertions, alien.	Per cent of total registrants.	Per cent of alien registrants.	Total citizen registrants.	Reported desertions, citizen.	Per cent of total registrants.	Per cent of citizen registrants.
United States	10,679,814	1,703,006	185,081	1.73	10.87	8,976,808	289,780	2.71	3.23
Alabama	206,248	1,558	179	.09	11.49	204,690	14,328	6.95	7.00
Arizona	40,517	15,283	4,388	10.83	28.71	25,234	2,615	6.45	10.36
Arkansas	168,302	652	40	.02	6.13	167,650	7,206	4.28	4.30
California	332,593	86,954	8,713	2.62	10.02	245,639	6,878	2.07	2.80
Colorado	91,813	10,144	2,179	2.37	21.48	81,699	2,822	3.07	3.46
Connecticut	175,026	64,924	9,239	5.28	14.23	110,102	3,859	2.20	3.50
Delaware	24,563	3,892	407	1.66	10.46	20,671	582	2.37	2.82
District of Columbia	36,741	1,590	74	.20	4.65	35,151	932	2.54	2.65
Florida	94,792	4,543	441	.47	9.71	90,249	9,701	10.23	10.75
Georgia	260,296	1,383	54	.02	3.90	258,913	13,414	5.15	5.18
Idaho	45,982	4,622	1,270	2.76	27.48	41,360	1,080	2.35	2.61
Illinois	707,962	143,299	9,919	1.40	6.92	564,663	14,670	2.07	2.60
Indiana	283,843	22,751	2,514	.89	11.05	261,092	3,937	1.39	1.51
Iowa	240,934	16,847	1,656	.69	9.83	224,087	4,123	1.71	1.84
Kansas	167,486	5,441	1,176	.70	21.61	162,045	2,251	1.34	1.39
Kentucky	215,936	1,256	199	.09	15.84	214,680	3,665	1.69	1.70
Louisiana	180,226	2,829	607	.34	21.46	177,397	7,605	4.22	4.29
Maine	68,214	9,413	1,406	2.06	14.94	58,801	1,176	1.72	2.00
Maryland	136,552	9,546	895	.66	9.38	127,006	5,346	3.91	4.19
Massachusetts	398,364	139,766	12,070	3.03	8.64	258,598	8,436	2.12	3.26
Michigan	411,596	106,830	11,939	2.90	11.18	304,766	6,298	1.53	2.07
Minnesota	249,937	40,260	5,022	2.01	12.47	209,677	5,707	2.28	2.72
Mississippi	157,607	572	231	.15	40.38	157,035	9,594	6.09	6.11
Missouri	335,012	11,719	1,703	.51	14.53	323,293	10,637	8.18	3.29
Montana	97,762	19,793	4,242	4.34	21.43	77,969	3,767	3.85	4.83
Nebraska	132,458	8,897	1,057	.80	11.88	123,561	1,780	1.34	1.44
Nevada	13,044	4,030	669	5.13	16.60	9,014	726	5.57	8.05
New Hampshire	41,743	10,896	705	1.69	6.47	30,847	726	1.74	2.35
New Jersey	332,895	80,932	7,948	2.39	9.82	251,963	15,699	4.72	6.23
New Mexico	37,300	4,364	1,914	5.13	43.86	32,936	1,343	3.60	4.08
New York	1,120,332	374,308	36,753	3.28	9.82	746,024	24,330	2.17	3.26
North Carolina	228,844	597	62	.03	10.39	228,247	6,050	2.64	2.65
North Dakota	73,341	9,245	1,469	2.00	15.89	64,096	1,070	1.46	1.67
Ohio	617,371	113,000	10,746	1.74	9.51	504,371	16,148	2.62	3.20
Oklahoma	193,236	2,684	773	.40	28.80	190,552	6,310	3.27	3.31
Oregon	70,549	11,048	832	1.18	7.53	59,501	1,209	1.71	2.03
Pennsylvania	902,996	215,070	20,718	2.29	9.63	687,925	17,620	1.96	2.56
Rhode Island	59,059	20,037	1,405	2.38	7.01	39,022	1,186	2.01	3.04
South Carolina	144,701	654	30	.02	4.59	144,047	5,666	3.93	3.93
South Dakota	66,189	4,532	463	70	10.22	61,657	807	1.22	1.31
Tennessee	213,427	745	52	.02	6.98	212,682	7,901	3.70	3.71
Texas	460,326	35,437	7,358	1.60	20.76	424,889	17,239	3.74	4.06
Utah	46,901	7,502	1,107	2.36	14.76	39,399	639	1.36	1.62
Vermont	30,884	2,472	340	1.10	13.75	28,412	354	1.15	1.25
Virginia	206,190	2,500	593	.29	23.72	203,690	7,432	3.60	3.65
Washington	125,708	19,287	3,481	2.77	18.05	106,421	3,810	3.03	3.58
West Virginia	142,174	10,744	2,320	1.63	21.59	131,430	4,487	3.16	3.41
Wisconsin	266,691	35,068	2,376	.89	6.78	231,623	2,360	.88	1.02
Wyoming	25,151	3,090	763	3.03	24.69	22,061	1,034	4.11	4.69
Alaska			469				140		
Hawaii			106				78		
Porto Rico							15		

APPENDIX TABLE 78–A.—*Quota sheet No. 1—Statement of men called under first levy of 687,000 men.*

	Gross quotas.	Enlist-ment credits.	Net quotas.	Fur-nished to Dec. 31, 1917.	Due Jan. 1, 1918.	Date last of these men were called.
United States	1,152,985	465,985	687,000	516,212	170,788	
Alabama	21,300	7,651	13,612	10,926	2,686	Mar. 29, 1918
Arizona	4,478	998	3,472	2,999	473	Mar. 4, 1918
Arkansas	17,452	7,155	10,267	6,521	3,746	Apr. 26, 1918
California	34,907	11,786	23,060	23,079	−19	Nov. 2, 1917
Colorado	9,797	5,027	4,753	4,105	648	Mar. 4, 1918
Connecticut	18,817	7,807	10,977	9,739	1,238	Apr. 30, 1918
Delaware	2,569	1,363	1,202	925	277	Mar. 4, 1918
District of Columbia	3,796	2,860	929	941	−12	Nov. 2, 1917
Florida	10,129	3,786	6,325	2,224	4,101	Apr. 30, 1918
Georgia	27,209	8,825	18,337	8,215	10,122	Apr. 26, 1918
Idaho	4,833	2,538	2,287	2,302	−15	Nov. 2, 1917
Illinois	79,094	27,304	51,653	33,940	17,713	Apr. 26, 1918
Indiana	29,971	12,409	17,510	11,500	6,010	Do.
Iowa	25,465	12,672	12,749	6,456	6,293	Feb. 23, 1918
Kansas	17,795	11,325	6,439	5,712	727	Do.
Kentucky	22,152	7,878	14,236	9,687	4,549	May 1, 1918
Louisiana	18,481	4,867	13,582	8,297	5,285	Apr. 26, 1918
Maine	7,076	5,243	1,821	1,899	−78	May 1, 1918
Maryland	14,139	7,018	7,096	7,118	−22	Nov. 2, 1917
Massachusetts	43,109	22,448	20,586	18,342	2,244	Apr. 30, 1918
Michigan	43,936	13,569	30,291	23,309	6,982	Mar. 29, 1918
Minnesota	26,021	8,198	17,778	9,312	8,466	Feb. 23, 1918
Mississippi	16,429	5,600	10,801	6,103	4,698	Mar. 29, 1918
Missouri	35,461	16,740	18,660	15,664	2,996	Apr. 26, 1918
Montana	10,423	2,533	7,872	7,911	−39	Nov. 2, 1917
Nebraska	13,900	5,691	8,185	7,085	1,100	Mar. 4, 1918
Nevada	1,435	382	1,051	1,053	−2	Nov. 2, 1917
New Hampshire	4,419	3,207	1,204	1,180	24	Apr. 30, 1918
New Jersey	35,623	14,896	20,665	12,740	7,925	Mar. 4, 1918
New Mexico	3,856	1,558	4,102	1,972	320	Do.
New York	122,424	52,971	69,240	57,828	11,413	Apr. 26, 1918
North Carolina	23,486	7,471	15,974	9,992	5,982	Do.
North Dakota	7,737	2,452	5,272	2,652	2,620	Mar. 29, 1918
Ohio	66,474	27,586	38,773	31,754	7,019	Mar. 15, 1918
Oklahoma	19,943	4,344	15,564	12,292	3,272	Apr. 26, 1918
Oregon	7,387	6,657	717	741	−24	Nov. 2, 1917
Pennsylvania	98,277	37,248	60,859	51,081	9,778	Mar. 29, 1918
Rhode Island	6,277	4,055	2,211	2,000	121	Apr. 30, 1918
South Carolina	15,147	5,040	10,081	6,717	3,364	Feb. 23, 1918
South Dakota	6,854	4,125	2,717	2,325	392	Mar. 4, 1918
Tennessee	22,158	7,592	14,528	11,061	3,467	Apr. 26, 1918
Texas	48,116	17,488	30,545	24,451	6,094	Do.
Utah	4,945	2,566	2,370	2,383	−13	Nov. 2, 1917
Vermont	3,243	2,188	1,049	996	53	May 1, 1918
Virginia	21,354	7,522	13,795	13,809	−14	Oct. 27, 1917
Washington	12,768	5,450	7,296	7,327	−31	Nov. 2, 1917
West Virginia	14,848	5,721	9,101	7,613	1,488	Mar. 4, 1918
Wisconsin	28,199	15,274	12,876	9,033	3,843	Apr. 26, 1918
Wyoming	2,683	1,868	810	811	−1	Nov. 2, 1917
Alaska	710	13	696	....	696	June 30, 1918
Hawaii	2,403	4,397	....	....	....	
Porto Rico	13,480	624	12,833	....	12,833	June 20, 1918

APPENDIX TABLE 78-B.—*Quota sheet No. 2—Interim quotas from date of completing respective quotas under first levy of 687,000 to May 31, 1918, on basis of population with credits.*

| | Population. | Proportion. | Gross quotas. | Credits for enlistments from July 1, 1917, to Mar. 31, 1918. | | | | Net quotas. | Furnished under second draft. | Balance due on net quotas. |
				Regular Army.	National Guard.	Enlisted Reserve.	Total credits.			
Total United States...	105,366,056	1.000000	1,036,046	209,895	114,404	157,204	481,503	554,543	254,543	300,000
Alabama	1,946,536	.018474	19,140	2,409	776	2,450	5,635	13,505	4,543	8,962
Arizona	409,203	.003884	4,024	465	144	438	1,047	2,977	961	2,016
Arkansas	1,594,835	.015136	15,682	1,563	1,810	974	4,347	11,335	3,679	7,656
California	3,189,998	.030275	31,366	10,738	5,510	10,052	26,300	5,066	7,879	-2,813
Colorado	895,336	.008497	8,803	2,244	832	1,344	4,420	4,383	2,251	2,132
Connecticut	1,719,623	.016320	16,908	3,730	1,592	2,839	8,161	8,747	4,735	4,012
Delaware	234,710	.002228	2,308	384	453	269	1,106	1,202	575	627
District of Columbia	346,850	.003292	3,411	952	580	1,750	3,282	129	851	-722
Florida	925,641	.008785	9,102	1,639	1,024	1,044	3,707	5,395	2,141	3,254
Georgia	2,486,544	.023599	24,450	3,143	1,169	4,336	8,648	15,802	5,719	10,083
Idaho	441,684	.004192	4,343	1,318	410	794	2,522	1,821	1,012	809
Illinois	7,227,952	.068599	71,072	12,749	8,192	13,599	34,540	36,532	17,253	19,279
Indiana	2,738,893	.025994	26,931	9,107	3,216	3,498	15,821	11,110	7,200	3,910
Iowa	2,327,079	.022086	22,882	6,411	2,055	3,600	12,066	10,816	7,053	3,763
Kansas	1,626,226	.015434	15,990	3,395	1,941	1,714	7,050	8,940	3,827	5,113
Kentucky	2,024,353	.019213	19,906	3,519	1,686	1,218	6,423	13,483	5,211	8,272
Louisiana	1,688,862	.016029	16,607	1,520	628	1,100	3,248	13,359	3,862	9,497
Maine	646,588	.006137	6,358	1,232	985	947	3,164	3,194	1,673	1,521
Maryland	1,292,091	.012263	12,705	2,227	1,649	1,962	5,838	6,867	3,105	3,762
Massachusetts	3,939,561	.037389	38,737	11,687	3,411	11,122	26,220	12,517	9,898	2,619
Michigan	4,015,053	.038106	39,480	8,750	2,311	7,725	18,786	20,694	10,191	10,503
Minnesota	2,377,938	.022568	23,381	5,402	1,409	4,231	11,042	12,339	7,500	4,839
Mississippi	1,501,345	.014249	14,763	1,133	1,467	998	3,598	11,165	3,465	7,700
Missouri	3,240,679	.030756	31,865	6,030	3,751	4,600	14,381	17,484	8,686	8,798
Montana	952,478	.009040	9,366	3,046	555	1,350	4,951	4,415	2,207	2,208
Nebraska	1,270,301	.012056	12,490	4,248	1,868	1,762	7,878	4,612	2,984	1,628
Nevada	131,232	.001245	1,290	751	38	242	1,031	259	300	-41
New Hampshire	403,884	.003833	3,971	1,006	605	649	2,260	1,711	1,084	627
New Jersey	3,255,407	.030896	32,010	6,588	4,207	5,166	15,961	16,049	7,977	8,072
New Mexico	352,392	.003344	3,465	691	500	472	1,663	1,802	806	996
New York	11,187,798	.106180	110,007	20,511	10,766	18,295	49,572	60,435	27,560	32,875
North Carolina	2,146,266	.020370	21,104	1,538	2,758	1,195	5,491	15,613	4,965	10,648
North Dakota	706,992	.006710	6,952	1,440	1,928	646	4,014	2,938	1,678	1,260
Ohio	6,074,771	.057654	59,732	11,081	6,766	6,217	24,064	35,668	14,632	21,036
Oklahoma	1,822,470	.017297	17,920	4,748	1,121	1,103	6,972	10,948	4,253	6,695
Oregon	675,092	.006407	6,638	2,666	812	2,240	5,718	920	1,644	-724
Pennsylvania	8,981,082	.085237	88,309	22,270	9,021	15,114	46,405	41,904	21,725	20,179
Rhode Island	573,583	.005444	5,640	1,250	910	632	2,792	2,848	1,540	1,308
South Carolina	1,384,203	.013137	13,611	1,050	776	1,517	3,343	10,268	2,818	7,450
South Dakota	626,359	.005945	6,159	1,828	504	499	2,831	3,328	1,469	1,859
Tennessee	2,024,893	.019218	19,911	2,613	2,882	2,182	7,677	12,234	5,108	7,126
Texas	4,397,097	.041732	43,236	6,918	9,673	5,251	21,842	21,394	9,415	11,979
Utah	451,932	.004289	4,444	1,401	369	787	2,557	1,887	1,060	897
Vermont	296,426	.002813	2,914	566	560	443	1,569	1,345	743	602
Virginia	1,951,521	.018521	19,189	2,085	2,420	1,755	6,260	12,929	4,725	8,204
Washington	1,160,855	.011074	11,473	3,377	1,278	3,496	8,151	3,322	2,770	552
West Virginia	1,356,907	.012878	13,342	2,443	601	885	3,929	9,413	3,204	6,209
Wisconsin	2,576,931	.024457	25,339	3,192	3,628	2,455	9,275	16,064	6,025	10,039
Wyoming	245,226	.002327	2,411	640	850	166	1,656	755	581	174
Alaska	64,912	.000616	638	47	5	44	96	542		542
Hawaii	219,580	.002084	2,159	70	1,997	21	2,088	71		71
Porto Rico	1,231,880	.011691	12,112	84	5	16	105	12,007		12,007

APPENDIX TABLE 78–C.—*Quota sheet No. 3—Class I quotas as of June 1, 1918.*

(1)	Class I.				Current quotas. (6)		
	Remaining on June 1, 1918, finally classified in Class I and examined physically and accepted for general military service.	Inducted and called for induction since the date of completing quotas, first levy.	Voluntary and individual inductions.	Total of (2), (3) and (4) = quota basis.	Quotas (80 per cent of quota basis.)	Credits (previous inductions).	Net current quotas not called.
	(2)	(3)	(4)	(5)	(a)	(b)	(c)
Total United States.........	1,166,317	255,414	61,095	1,482,826	1,186,262	627,405	559,439
Alabama...................	26,549	4,504	946	31,999	25,599	12,567	13,032
Arizona...................	1,836	961	289	3,086	2,469	3,051	[1] 582
Arkansas.................	23,405	3,679	290	27,374	21,899	8,512	13,387
California................	18,432	7,879	3,870	30,181	24,145	13,348	10,797
Colorado.................	9,441	2,251	624	12,316	9,853	6,783	3,070
Connecticut..............	9,501	4,735	508	14,744	11,795	9,244	2,551
Delaware.................	1,989	575	134	2,698	2,158	1,191	967
District of Columbia........	4,049	851	362	5,262	4,210	1,938	2,272
Florida...................	11,488	2,141	233	13,862	11,090	3,038	8,052
Georgia..................	25,659	5,719	430	31,808	25,447	8,144	17,303
Idaho....................	6,899	1,012	454	8,365	6,692	2,311	4,381
Illinois..................	82,308	17,253	3,470	103,031	82,425	55,608	26,817
Indiana..................	28,417	7,200	2,783	38,400	30,720	17,412	13,308
Iowa....................	36,757	7,053	1,582	45,392	36,314	12,706	23,608
Kansas..................	22,399	3,827	733	26,959	21,567	11,059	10,508
Kentucky................	30,305	5,137	379	35,821	28,657	14,521	14,136
Louisiana................	31,201	3,862	764	35,827	28,662	9,361	19,301
Maine...................	8,977	1,673	230	10,880	8,704	3,960	4,744
Maryland................	13,214	3,105	460	16,779	13,423	6,644	6,779
Massachusetts............	29,634	9,898	1,475	41,007	32,806	17,242	15,564
Michigan................	34,440	10,191	3,255	47,886	38,309	23,957	14,352
Minnesota...............	35,718	7,500	2,238	45,456	36,365	15,011	21,354
Mississippi..............	24,603	3,465	530	28,598	22,878	8,212	14,666
Missouri.................	45,930	8,686	1,319	55,935	44,748	18,225	26,523
Montana.................	12,743	2,207	1,264	16,214	12,971	5,874	7,097
Nebraska................	14,787	2,984	911	18,682	14,946	5,617	9,329
Nevada..................	977	300	215	1,492	1,194	525	669
New Hampshire...........	4,148	1,084	151	5,383	4,306	2,530	1,776
New Jersey..............	27,430	7,977	1,210	36,617	29,294	17,855	11,439
New Mexico.............	3,879	806	192	4,877	3,902	3,087	815
New York...............	102,277	27,560	5,146	134,983	107,985	72,883	35,102
North Carolina...........	25,680	4,965	846	31,491	25,193	14,237	10,956
North Dakota............	8,882	1,678	1,012	11,572	9,258	3,945	5,313
Ohio....................	57,160	14,632	2,881	74,673	59,738	41,277	18,461
Oklahoma...............	27,357	4,253	2,310	33,920	27,136	15,966	11,170
Oregon..................	9,373	1,644	632	11,649	9,319	3,861	5,458
Pennsylvania.............	69,518	21,725	4,817	96,060	76,848	49,359	27,489
Rhode Island.............	6,131	1,540	184	7,855	6,284	3,771	2,513
South Carolina...........	20,665	2,818	137	23,620	18,896	5,459	13,437
South Dakota............	16,028	1,469	388	17,885	14,308	4,553	9,755
Tennessee...............	30,172	5,108	868	36,148	28,918	11,751	17,167
Texas...................	51,140	10,415	2,610	64,165	51,332	23,357	27,975
Utah....................	3,384	1,060	712	5,156	4,125	2,870	1,255
Vermont.................	2,770	743	636	4,149	3,319	2,572	747
Virginia.................	32,215	4,709	459	37,383	29,906	12,199	17,707
Washington..............	9,604	2,770	1,046	13,420	10,736	4,923	5,813
West Virginia............	22,213	3,204	3,071	28,488	22,790	13,710	9,080
Wisconsin...............	38,745	6,025	1,716	46,486	37,189	18,536	18,653
Wyoming................	5,888	581	323	6,792	5,434	2,643	2,791

[1] Excess.

97250°—19——30

APPENDIX TABLE 78-D.—*Quota sheet No. 4—Class I quotas as of Sept. 1, 1918.*

(1)	Class I. Remaining on Sept. 1, 1918, finally classified in Class I and examined physically and accepted for general military service. (2)	Inducted and called for induction since the date of completing quotas on first levy. (3)	Voluntary and individual inductions. (4)	Total of (2), (3), and (4) =quotas. (5)	Current quotas. (6) Credits (previous inductions). (a)	Net current quotas not called. (b)
Total United States....	290,820	1,506,405	85,990	1,883,215	1,744,159	139,056
Alabama................	9,032	33,497	1,289	43,818	40,086	3,732
Arizona................	477	3,374	348	4,199	4,129	70
Arkansas...............	7,116	29,231	414	36,761	33,593	3,168
California.............	4,777	29,617	4,705	39,099	38,530	569
Colorado...............	714	14,677	818	16,209	16,038	171
Connecticut............	2.037	16,929	801	19,767	18,480	1,287
Delaware...............	291	2,884	186	3,361	3,188	173
District of Columbia....	942	6,057	602	7,601	7,159	442
Florida................	1,517	15,426	383	17,326	16,490	836
Georgia................	7,298	37,693	745	45,736	42,434	3,302
Idaho..................	896	7,981	537	9,414	9,230	184
Illinois................	20,994	99,537	5,164	125,695	110,243	15,452
Indiana................	9,212	40,251	3,350	52,813	47,849	4,964
Iowa..................	11,576	41,287	2,197	55,060	51,607	3,453
Kansas................	5,275	27,683	1,203	34,161	33,493	668
Kentucky..............	8,121	39,369	567	48,057	40,636	7,421
Louisiana..............	10,410	29,798	954	41,162	36,570	4,592
Maine.................	1,932	10,768	348	13,048	11,828	1,220
Maryland..............	1,828	21,831	875	24,534	23,364	1,170
Massachusetts..........	5,223	42,191	2,312	49,726	46,611	3,115
Michigan..............	6,095	49,502	4,350	59,947	56,329	3,618
Minnesota.............	9,231	40,418	2,992	52,641	45,945	6,696
Mississippi............	10,681	24,017	747	35,445	30,807	4,638
Missouri..............	10,813	55,408	2,369	68,590	63,627	4,963
Montana..............	2,321	15,653	1,551	19,525	18,222	1,303
Nebraska.............	7,783	17,087	1,188	26,058	19,371	6,687
Nevada...............	128	1,492	252	1,872	1,850	22
New Hampshire.......	658	5,586	342	6,586	5,958	628
New Jersey...........	5,645	37,130	2,296	45,071	43,523	1,548
New Mexico...........	785	5,406	485	6,676	6,502	174
New York.............	14,972	135,090	9,113	159,175	156,722	2,453
North Carolina........	3,809	38,339	1,309	43,457	40,923	2,534
North Dakota.........	3,793	10,104	1,087	14,984	12,401	2,583
Ohio.................	16,250	77,788	3,959	97,997	92,325	5,672
Oklahoma.............	5,957	37,490	2,823	46,270	44,607	1,663
Oregon...............	1,079	11,924	993	13,996	13,817	179
Pennsylvania..........	21,940	105,618	6,937	134,495	123,473	11,022
Rhode Island..........	38	7,852	336	8,226	8,194	32
South Carolina........	4,498	27,534	258	32,290	29,434	2,856
South Dakota.........	1,934	16,264	507	18,705	17,412	1,293
Tennessee.............	11,573	30,676	1,141	43,390	38,847	4,543
Texas................	19,173	66,899	3,813	89,885	80,411	9,474
Utah.................	1,044	5,733	592	7,369	7,230	139
Vermont..............	443	3,918	684	5,045	4,854	191
Virginia..............	4,400	37,012	866	42,278	40,403	1,875
Washington...........	2,396	14,925	1,332	18,653	18,274	379
West Virginia.........	6,073	25,849	3,479	35,401	34,530	871
Wisconsin.............	6,700	45,757	2,045	54,502	50,111	4,391
Wyoming..............	940	5,853	346	7,139	6,499	640

APPENDIX TABLE 78–E.—*Quota sheet No. 5—Class I quotas as of Oct. 1, 1918.*

(1)	Class I.				Current quotas. (6)	
	Remaining on Oct. 1, 1918, finally classified in Class I and examined physically and accepted for general military service.	Inducted and called for induction since the date of completing quotas on first levy.	Voluntary and individual inductions.	Total of (2), (3), and (4) = quotas.	Credits (previous inductions).	Net current quotas not called.
	(2)	(3)	(4)	(5)	(a)	(b)
United States...........	193,712	1,774,381	93,797	2,061,890	2,003,757	58,133
Alabama.................	3,272	42,634	1,225	47,131	45,981	1,150
Arizona.................	328	3,935	410	4,673	4,545	128
Arkansas................	3,026	36,509	455	39,990	38,926	1,064
California..............	4,155	35,367	4,989	44,511	41,903	2,608
Colorado................	858	15,764	878	17,500	17,292	208
Connecticut.............	2,087	18,881	914	21,882	21,021	861
Delaware................	239	3,370	202	3,811	3,732	79
District of Columbia....	575	7,201	787	8,563	8,333	230
Florida.................	1,206	17,438	421	19,065	18,433	632
Georgia.................	5,435	45,220	832	51,487	48,562	2,925
Idaho...................	755	9,097	515	10,367	10,083	284
Illinois................	18,120	113,051	5,509	136,680	133,820	2,860
Indiana.................	7,532	46,303	3,495	57,330	55,774	1,556
Iowa....................	5,893	50,483	2,468	58,844	57,351	1,493
Kansas..................	1,485	33,024	1,181	35,690	34,930	760
Kentucky................	9,449	42,805	732	52,986	51,932	1,054
Louisiana...............	2,180	40,199	989	43,368	42,258	1,110
Maine...................	916	11,990	374	13,280	13,280	....
Maryland................	1,556	24,535	975	27,066	26,296	770
Massachusetts...........	6,733	48,272	2,654	57,659	53,294	4,365
Michigan................	5,931	56,197	4,425	66,553	64,172	2,381
Minnesota...............	8,357	45,133	3,226	56,716	55,109	1,607
Mississippi.............	3,039	34,294	2,453	40,786	39,554	1,232
Missouri................	7,017	64,161	2,669	73,847	71,845	2,002
Montana.................	1,789	17,616	1,089	20,494	20,005	489
Nebraska................	8,630	19,405	1,295	29,330	28,120	1,210
Nevada..................	109	1,719	256	2,084	2,075	9
New Hampshire...........	731	6,215	300	7,246	7,084	162
New Jersey..............	4,294	43,760	2,647	50,701	49,328	1,373
New Mexico..............	600	6,251	252	7,103	6,908	195
New York................	13,361	159,470	10,325	183,156	178,208	4,948
North Carolina..........	2,131	43,186	1,056	46,373	45,787	586
North Dakota............	3,474	11,667	1,072	16,213	15,859	354
Ohio....................	7,645	93,023	4,280	104,948	102,193	2,755
Oklahoma................	4,322	43,280	2,685	50,287	48,945	1,342
Oregon..................	980	13,363	965	15,308	14,964	344
Pennsylvania............	12,749	127,481	7,764	147,994	144,515	3,479
Rhode Island............	453	8,353	274	9,080	8,837	243
South Carolina..........	2,216	32,443	289	34,948	33,838	1,110
South Dakota............	1,783	17,759	520	20,062	19,564	498
Tennessee...............	4,045	41,040	1,131	46,216	45,006	1,210
Texas...................	10,477	82,349	4,023	96,849	94,454	2,395
Utah....................	442	7,136	787	8,365	8,223	142
Vermont.................	425	4,520	705	5,650	5,525	125
Virginia................	1,829	42,312	835	44,976	44,097	879
Washington..............	2,361	17,758	1,331	21,450	20,993	457
West Virginia...........	1,398	32,180	3,391	36,969	36,056	913
Wisconsin...............	6,783	49,681	2,331	58,795	57,447	1,348
Wyoming.................	541	6,551	416	7,508	7,300	208

APPENDIX TABLE 79–A.—*Enlistments and inductions, Apr. 2, 1917, to Oct. 31, 1918, under first and second registrations, compared by States.*

	Total increment, armed forces.	Inductions under first and second registrations.		Enlistments.					
		National Army.	Per cent of increment.	Army.	Per cent of increment.	Navy.	Per cent of increment.	Marine Corps.	Per cent of increment.
United States	4,034,743	2,666,867	66.10	877,458	21.75	437,527	10.84	52,891	1.31
Alabama	73,543	59,755	81.25	9,562	13.00	3,938	5.35	288	.40
Arizona	11,410	8,113	71.10	1,854	16.25	1,269	11.12	174	1.53
Arkansas	65,311	49,312	75.50	11,699	17.91	4,025	6.16	275	.43
California	131,484	67,067	51.00	38,992	29.66	23,058	17.54	2,367	1.80
Colorado	38,751	22,858	58.99	9,670	24.95	5,075	13.10	1,148	2.96
Connecticut	55,218	32,539	58.93	13,151	23.82	9,319	16.88	209	.37
Delaware	7,935	4,993	62.53	2,003	25.08	919	11.51	70	.68
District of Columbia	17,945	9,631	53.67	4,442	24.75	3,500	19.50	372	2.06
Florida	36,211	24,916	68.81	6,834	18.87	4,375	12.08	86	.24
Georgia	86,973	66,841	76.85	14,160	16.28	5,382	6.19	590	.68
Idaho	20,467	12,566	61.40	4,955	24.20	2,450	11.97	496	2.45
Illinois	272,235	177,483	65.19	61,938	22.75	28,264	10.38	4,550	1.66
Indiana	104,973	69,749	66.44	25,847	24.62	8,313	7.92	1,064	1.02
Iowa	101,638	66,864	65.79	26,389	25.96	7,832	7.71	553	.54
Kansas	66,645	41,905	62.88	18,217	27.33	5,907	8.86	616	.93
Kentucky	77,983	58,330	74.80	13,934	17.88	5,163	6.62	556	.70
Louisiana	71,271	56,205	78.86	7,570	10.62	6,782	9.52	714	1.00
Maine	26,602	15,266	57.39	7,290	27.40	4,025	15.13	21	.08
Maryland	51,700	33,867	65.51	10,144	19.62	6,913	13.37	776	1.50
Massachusetts	157,101	76,567	48.74	41,985	26.72	36,884	23.48	1,665	1.06
Michigan	142,397	96,480	67.75	32,403	22.76	11,463	8.05	2,051	1.44
Minnesota	106,918	73,680	68.91	20,272	18.96	10,588	9.90	2,378	2.22
Mississippi	56,740	43,362	76.42	9,044	15.94	4,069	7.17	265	.47
Missouri	140,257	92,843	66.19	29,863	21.29	14,132	10.08	3,419	2.44
Montana	39,049	27,340	70.02	7,331	18.77	3,281	8.40	1,097	2.81
Nebraska	49,614	29,807	60.08	14,416	29.06	4,944	9.96	447	.90
Nevada	5,488	3,164	57.65	1,888	34.40	350	6.38	86	1.57
New Hampshire	14,970	8,404	56.14	4,408	29.45	2,100	14.03	58	.38
New Jersey	118,350	71,390	60.32	28,333	23.94	17,457	14.75	1,170	.99
New Mexico	13,586	8,862	65.23	3,649	26.86	1,050	7.73	25	.18
New York	410,569	253,589	61.77	89,031	21.68	61,779	15.05	6,170	1.50
North Carolina	74,705	58,441	78.23	10,573	14.15	5,250	7.03	441	.59
North Dakota	27,253	18,595	68.23	6,611	24.26	1,838	6.74	209	.77
Ohio	205,852	138,148	67.11	48,885	23.75	14,176	6.89	4,643	2.25
Oklahoma	84,909	64,941	76.49	14,105	16.61	5,513	6.49	350	.41
Oregon	34,430	16,158	46.93	10,626	30.86	6,694	19.44	952	2.77
Pennsylvania	313,297	201,211	64.22	78,671	25.11	29,446	9.40	3,969	1.27
Rhode Island	22,270	11,176	50.18	5,436	24.41	5,600	25.15	58	.26
South Carolina	54,284	44,059	81.16	6,505	11.98	3,675	6.77	45	.09
South Dakota	30,130	21,255	70.54	7,083	23.51	1,663	5.52	129	.43
Tennessee	80,139	59,878	74.72	13,563	16.92	5,425	6.77	1,273	1.59
Texas	174,061	117,395	67.44	37,704	21.66	16,889	9.71	2,073	1.19
Utah	19,421	10,788	55.55	5,335	27.47	2,494	12.84	804	4.14
Vermont	11,223	6,629	59.07	3,088	27.51	1,488	13.26	18	.16
Virginia	78,524	58,337	74.29	10,556	13.45	9,144	11.64	487	.62
Washington	55,433	28,686	51.75	12,761	23.02	12,382	22.34	1,604	2.89
West Virginia	55,895	45,355	81.14	7,359	13.17	2,625	4.70	556	.99
Wisconsin	101,696	70,982	69.80	22,349	21.98	7,569	7.44	796	.78
Wyoming	12,223	7,923	64.82	3,554	29.08	656	5.37	90	.73
Alaska	2,105	1,962	93.21	143	6.79				
Hawaii	5,733	5,466	95.34	267	4.66				
Porto Rico	16,490	15,734	95.42	756	4.58				
Not allocated	1,286			254		394		638	

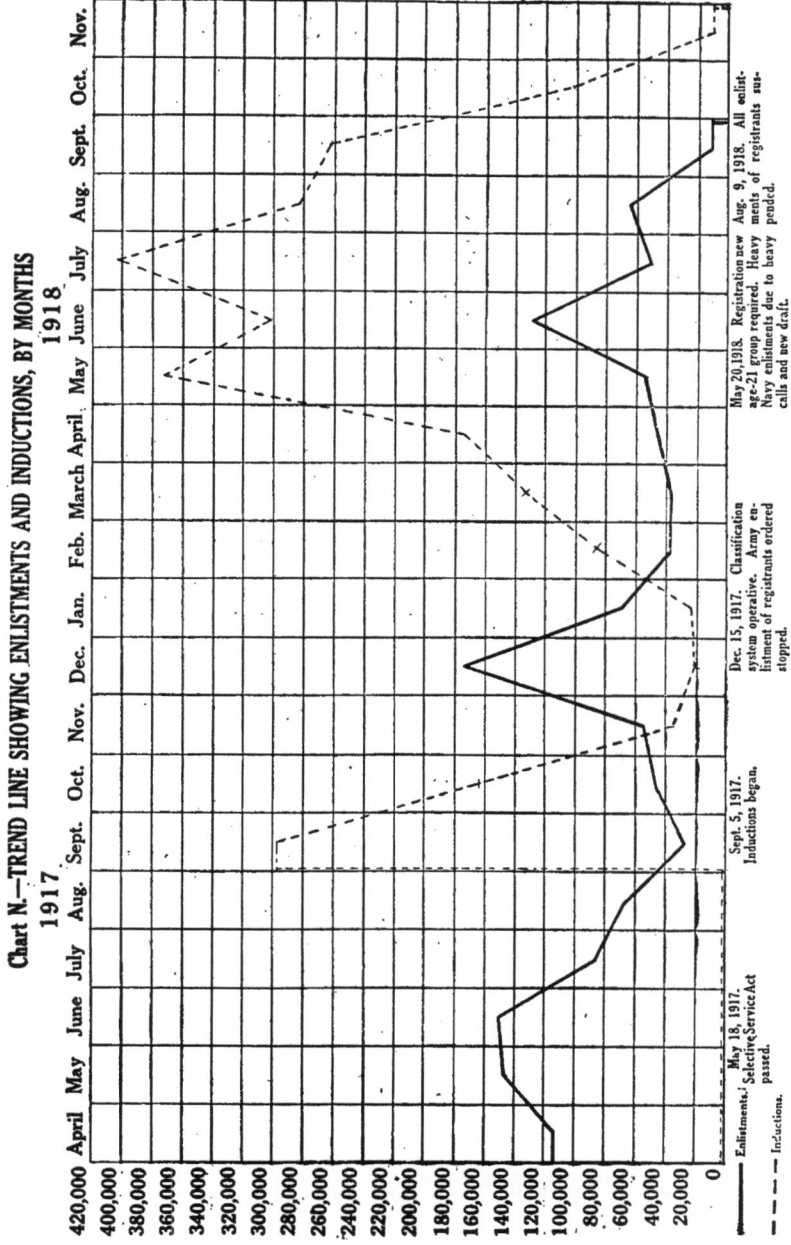

Chart N.—TREND LINE SHOWING ENLISTMENTS AND INDUCTIONS, BY MONTHS

APPENDIX TABLE 81-A.—*List of requisitions for men, received by the Provost Marshal General from The Adjutant General of the Army, Aug. 25, 1917, to Nov. 7, 1918.*

Requisition No.	Date received.	Qualifications.	Number of men.
01	Aug. 25, 1917	Run of the draft to 16 mobilization camps	31,643
02	Aug. 8, 1917	....do	265,035
03	Sept. 22, 1917	Run of the draft to 18 mobilization camps	126,800
04	Oct. 13, 1917	Run of the draft to 12 mobilization camps	31,790
05	....do	Run of the draft to 2 mobilization camps	18,471
06a	Nov. 6, 1917	Run of the draft to 1 mobilization camp	6,454
06b	Nov. 5, 1917	....do	10,796
07	Nov. 21, 1917	....do	8,440
08	Nov. 15, 1917	Run of the draft to 15 mobilization camps	6,408
09	Dec. 8, 1917	Run of the draft to 21 coast defenses	9,000
09a	Dec. 7, 1917	Run of the draft to 1 mobilization camp	1,000
010	Dec. 14, 1917	Run of the draft to 8 mobilization camps	Unlimited.
011	Dec. 29, 1917	Run of the draft to 9 mobilization camps	Unlimited.
012	Dec. 31, 1917	Run of the draft to 3 mobilization camps	Unlimited.
013	Jan. 3, 1918	Run of the draft to 2 mobilization camps	Unlimited.
014	....do	Spruce producers	5,000
015	Jan. 19, 1918	Cost accountants	200
016	Feb. 2, 1918	Run of the draft to 13 mobilization camps	74,116
017	Feb. 11, 1918	Run of the draft to 2 mobilization camps	8,000
018	Feb. 20, 1918	Run of the draft to 5 mobilization camps	Unlimited.
019	Feb. 27, 1918	Run of the draft to 1 mobilization camp	Unlimited.
1	Feb. 28, 1918	1,470 airplane mechanics and assemblers; 972 apprentice gunsmiths, machinists, and instrument makers and repairers; 1,200 engine airplane mechanics or auto mechanics; 978 rigger airplane mechanics, auto mechanics, or general repair men; 240 general auto mechanics; 120 general blacksmiths; 96 journeymen joiner cabinetmakers; 180 boat, carriage, or house carpenters or pattern makers; 1,200 truck chauffeurs; 378 general clerical workers or stenographers; 372 cooks; 108 coppersmiths or tinsmiths; 12 draftsmen; 150 electricians; 12 engine block testers; 66 camera repairmen or engineering, general, mechanical, nautical, or watch and clock instrument makers or repairmen; 150 general machinists; 150 magneto and ignition auto mechanics; 54 general sheet metal workers; 270 motorcyclists; 12 motorcycle repairmen; 12 molders; 24 painters; 12 pattern makers; 72 propeller makers or testers; 108 wireless constructors; 60 wireless operators; 6 saddlers; 108 stock keepers; 186 tailors or awning, tent, or sail makers; 54 truck masters; 54 vulcanizers; 54 welders; 30 telegraphers; 30 wireless telephone operators.	9,000
2	Mar. 1, 1918	Photographers	800
3	Apr. 10, 1918 Mar. 3, 1918	Inspectors for gas defense	40
4	Mar. 12, 1918	Chemists	60
5	Mar. 11, 1918	50 meteorologists; 95 physicists; 90 mechanical engineers; 50 civil engineers; 10 instrument makers or repairmen; 5 clerical workers.	300
7	Mar. 1, 1918	2 lithographers; 31 instrument repairmen; 5 propeller makers; 8 sailmakers; 10 tailors.	56
7a	Apr. 10, 1918	100 surveyors; 15 lithographers	115
8	Mar. 1, 1918	Laborers	1,000
9	Mar. 15, 1918	Photographers	64
9G	Mar. 10, 1918	Run of the draft to 16 mobilization camps	94,808
9aG	Mar. 11, 1918	Run of the draft to 1 coast defense	11,500
10	Apr. 10, 1918	Telephone operators with extensive knowledge of German	75
12	Apr. 18, 1918	442 locomotive engineers; 368 conductors; 1,075 brakemen and flagmen; 326 locomotive firemen; 53 yardmasters; 76 switch tenders; 8 engine house firemen; 6 engine dispatchers; 323 railroad shop mechanics; 84 locomotive inspectors; 149 airbrake inspectors; 58 flue repairmen; 223 boiler makers and helpers; 46 plumbers; 2 electricians; 78 carpenters; 29 stationary engineers and firemen; 58 locomotive hostlers; 4 car inspectors; 23 riveters and helpers; 137 car repairmen; 15 machinist foremen; 8 boiler maker foremen; 32 acetylene welders; 26 pneumatic riveters; 26 hand riveters; 20 buckers up; 40 structural steel rivet heaters; 40 structural steel punchers; 44 tinsmiths; 16 boiler inspectors; 11 railroad shop draftsmen; 28 electric crane operators; 40 steel railroad car workers.	3,914
13	Mar. 22, 1918	Grammar-school education with mechanical experience for 14 schools.	4,509
14	Mar. 30, 1918	Grammar-school education with mechanical experience for 10 schools.	2,825
14G	Apr. 3, 1918	Run of the draft to 16 mobilization camps	150,000
15	Apr. 1, 1918	42 buglers; 40 building construction foremen; 395 carpenters; 48 chauffeurs; 34 clerks; 68 cooks; 300 bricklayers; 24 blacksmiths; 195 levelers; 3,420 laborers.	4,566
16	Apr. 2, 1918	Photographers	400

APPENDIX TABLE 81–A.—*List of requisitions for men, received by the Provost Marshal General from The Adjutant General of the Army, Aug. 25, 1917, to Nov. 7, 1918—Con.*

Requisition No.	Date received.	Qualifications.	Number of men.
17	Apr. 3, 1918	6 steam engineers; 2 quarry foremen; 6 powdermen; 2 gyratory crusher foremen; 4 jaw crusher foremen; 6 firemen; 5 auto truck drivers; 5 bakers; 19 barbers; 49 blacksmiths; 76 carpenters; 22 civil engineers; 2 cobblers; 116 cooks; 18 crusher operators; 8 gas engine men; 3 gunsmiths; 3 horseshoers; 16 plumbers; 30 rock drill runners and helpers; 5 shovel operators; 92 teamsters; 48 railroad construction foremen; 243 railroad section hands; 36 railroad engineers; 24 bridge construction foremen; 120 railroad section foremen; 48 masons; 48 bridge carpenters; 5 level men and transit men; 6 pile drivers; 18 railroad track foremen; 26 bricklayers; 36 bridge foremen; 90 clerks; 4 concrete foremen; 20 concrete workers; 16 draftsmen; 13 earthwork foremen; 6 gas engine repairmen; 14 pipe fitters; 8 pump men; 4 shoemakers; 6 steam shovel runners and cranemen; 51 stenographers; 17 tailors; 6 tinsmiths; 3 water supply foremen; 120 section foremen; 816 section hands; 18 buglers; 36 civil engineers and draftsmen; 104 airbrake inspectors; 860 brakemen and flagmen; 280 conductors; 128 electricians; 368 locomotive engineers; 372 locomotive firemen; 50 locomotive inspectors; 60 switchmen; 12 yardmasters; 144 boiler makers and helpers; 88 car repairmen; 12 engine dispatchers; 24 flue repairmen; 16 locomotive hostlers; 140 railroad machinists; 52 railroad clerks; 1,311 laborers; 8 car inspectors; 12 engine house foremen; 50 electrical engineers; 90 gas engineers; 15 forest rangers; 25 timber cruisers; 10 optical instrument makers; 15 electrical instrument makers; 15 instrument makers; 30 oxyacetylene welders; 20 topographical draftsmen; 30 surveyors; 30 railroad surveyors; 30 topographers; 15 acetylene workers; 15 compressor workers; 15 hydrogen oxygen workers; 15 illuminating gas workers; 15 poison gas workers; 20 construction foremen; 20 steam enginemen; 24 molders; 20 pattern makers; 50 structural steel workers; 50 wagon makers; 20 solderers; 20 map makers; 5 auto chauffeurs; 5 auto mechanics; 6 instrument repairmen; 44 linemen; 10 truck drivers; 2 photographers; 2 store keepers; 12 topographical surveyors; 2 telegraph operators; 12 telephone operators; 10 mathematicians; 10 meteorologists; 10 physicists; 8 ship carpenter foremen; 24 marine gasoline enginemen; 80 steersmen; 4 ship carpenters; 12 hoistmen; 12 ship and boat blacksmiths; 12 ship riggers; 12 sailmakers; 12 saddlers; 200 bargemen or boatmen; 4 pipemen; 924 railroad section hands.	8,535
17G	Apr. 11, 1918	Run of the draft to 11 mobilization camps............................	49,757
18	Apr. 6, 1918	Gunsmiths..	630
18G	Apr. 18, 1918	Run of the draft to 1 mobilization camp................................	696
19	Apr. 8, 1918	3 timekeepers and checkers; 5 storekeepers; 4 overseers of labor; 80 laborers; 8 cooks; 2 buglers; 10 riggers; 13 machinists; 11 machinist helpers; 15 floor hands; 5 auto mechanics; 5 auto mechanic helpers; 6 blacksmiths; 10 blacksmith helpers; 10 angle ironsmiths; 20 boiler makers; 10 riveters; 5 riveter helpers; 10 sheet iron workers; 5 tinsmiths; 5 tinsmith helpers; 7 plumbers; 9 plumber helpers; 10 steam fitters; 9 steam fitter helpers; 16 carpenters and joiners; 10 carpenter helpers; 6 boat builders; 6 boat builder helpers; 5 wood carpenters; 37 painters; 6 sailmakers; 8 electricians, armature winders and wiremen; 5 stenographers and typists.	376
22	Apr. 10, 1918	Chemical engineers...	35
23	.....do........	Gas inspectors..	20
24	.....do........	Chemists...	10
25	Apr. 17, 1918	Grammar-school education with mechanical experience to 5 schools.	1,190
26	Apr. 10, 1918	Stock raisers, veterinarians, hostlers and stablemen.................	1,600
27	Apr. 24, 1918	5 laundry foremen; 25 laundry workers; 50 horseshoers; 80 journeymen teamsters; 50 mule packers; 15 horse trainers; 6 hostlers; 50 journeymen tailors; 20 wheelwrights; 100 journeymen carpenters; 75 apprentice blacksmiths; 75 apprentice electricians; 150 apprentice mechanics.	701
28	Apr. 25, 1918	120 telegraphers; 120 telephone and telegraph linemen; 3 cobblers; 12 buglers; 6 tailors; 6 barbers; 30 telephone operators; 12 wire chiefs; 6 caterers; 15 cooks; 6 general repairmen; 6 wireless operators; 6 motorcycle repairmen; 33 laborers.	381
29	.....do........	Grammar-school education with mechanical experience to 26 schools.	8,985
29G	May 3, 1918	Run of the draft to 27 mobilization camps............................	233,600
33	May 1, 1918	Grammar-school education with mechanical experience to 1 school..	150
33G	May 6, 1918	Run of the draft to 1 mobilization camp...............................	150
34G	May 14, 1918	Run of the draft to 11 mobilization camps............................	51,600
35	May 2, 1918	Grammar-school education with mechanical experience to 72 schools.	25,873
35G	May 15, 1918	Run of the draft to 1 mobilization camp...............................	200
36	May 3, 1918	Grammar-school education with mechanical experience to 19 schools.	6,125
36G	May 22, 1918	Run of the draft to 12 mobilization camps............................	40,000
37	May 10, 1918	Grammar-school education with mechanical experience to 5 schools.	1,980
37G	May 25, 1918	Run of the draft to 22 mobilization camps............................	200,000

APPENDIX TABLE 81–A.—*List of requisitions for men, received by the Provost Marshal* *General from The Adjutant General of the Army, Aug. 25, 1917, to Nov. 7, 1918*—Con.

Requisition No.	Date received.	Qualifications.	Number of men.
40	May 27, 1918	50 locomotive engineers; 50 firemen; 50 railroad grade foremen; 50 railroad track foremen; 100 wooden bridge carpenters; 200 locomotive repairmen; 50 telephone linemen; 50 surveyors; 25 telegraphers; 25 draftsmen; 25 pile driver foremen; 25 stationary engineers for donkey engines; 25 steam shovel operators; 500 carpenters; 50 steam fitters; 100 electricians; 100 auto mechanics; 100 auto drivers; 300 cooks; 250 clerks; 6,625 laborers; 200 railroad brakemen; 50 railroad conductors.	9,000
40G	June 10, 1918	Run of the draft to 1 mobilization camp............................	12,468
41	June 4, 1918	1 clerk; 1 caterer; 2 cooks; 17 butchers; 12 assistant butchers; 23 laborers.	56
41G	June 10, 1918	Run of the draft to 1 mobilization camp............................	4,336
42	June 4, 1918	Grammar-school education with mechanical experience to 1 school..	381
43	June 7, 1918	Grammar-school education with mechanical experience to 3 schools.	803
43G	June 18, 1918	Run of the draft to 14 mobilization camps.........................	54,500
44	June 8, 1918	Grammar-school education with mechanical experience to 34 schools.	13,030
44G	June 20, 1918	Run of the draft to 12 mobilization camps.........................	45,000
45	June 18, 1918	Grammar-school education with mechanical experience to 30 schools.	8,976
45G	June 20, 1918	Run of the draft to 10 mobilization camps.........................	25,000
46	June 19, 1918	Grammar-school education with mechanical experience to 1 school..	500
47	June 21, 1918	Grammar-school education with mechanical experience to 2 schools..	330
48	June 24, 1918	Grammar-school education with mechanical experience to 1 school..	2,800
49	....do.......	....do..	100
50	June 26, 1918	....do..	185
51	....do.......	....do..	258
52	June 27, 1918	108 auto repairmen; 54 axmen; 162 blacksmiths; 108 boatmen; 543 bridge carpenters; 162 cabinetmakers; 54 calkers; 54 concrete foremen; 272 concrete workers; 54 construction foremen; 162 cooks; 108 draftsmen; 54 electricians; 54 gas enginemen; 54 stationary enginemen; 27 farriers; 54 horseshoers; 54 lithographers; 108 machinists; 54 buglers; 54 photographers; 54 plumbers; 12 powdermen; 54 quarrymen; 108 riggers; 27 saddlers; 27 shoemakers; 108 surveyors; 27 tailors; 54 teamsters; 54 telephone operators; 270 timbermen; 108 topographers; 108 clerks; 3,265 laborers.	6,630
52G	July 2, 1918	Run of the draft to 1 mobilization camp............................	300
53	July 3, 1918	Grammar-school education with mechanical experience to 43 schools.	25,575
53G	July 2, 1918	Clerks...	650
54	July 8, 1918	35 general logging superintendents; 35 section bosses; 35 rigging foremen; 35 hook tenders; 35 hook-on men; 35 high climbers; 70 chasers; 70 chokermen; 35 head riggers; 105 donkey engineers; 70 donkey firemen; 195 fallers; 345 buckers; 35 spool tenders; 35 crosscut saw fillers; 50 head buckers; 35 snipers; 35 knotters; 35 blacksmiths; 35 blacksmiths' helpers; 96 carriage men; 24 cooks; 48 assistant cooks; 24 doggers; 24 edgermen; 24 assistant edgermen; 24 chief engineers; 48 engineer helpers; 48 band filers; 24 circular filers; 24 assistant circular filers; 24 head foremen; 75 assistant foremen; 48 general sawmill foremen; 75 graders; 24 log deckers; 24 millwrights; 48 assistant millwrights; 48 offbearers; 48 oilers; 35 camp helpers; 35 pumpmen; 35 head loaders; 35 signal boys; 24 trimmermen; 195 planer feeders; 195 planer trimmermen; 24 resawers; 48 setters; 144 tallymen; 48 assistant trimmermen.	3,000
54G	....do......	Run of the draft to 11 mobilization camps.........................	46,000
55	July 11, 1918	Grammar-school education with mechanical experience to 12 schools.	7,528
55G	....do......	Run of the draft to 1 mobilization camp...........................	10,000
56G	July 12, 1918	Cooks...	400
57G	July 17, 1918	Run of the draft to 15 mobilization camps.........................	50,100
58G	....do......	Physicians...	Unlimited.
59	July 16, 1918	Grammar-school education with mechanical experience to 12 schools.	3,814
62	July 19, 1918	264 laborers; 8 plumbers; 12 electricians; 8 blacksmiths; 8 machinists; 80 clerks; 28 stenographers; 24 foremen; 16 cooks; 8 second cooks; 8 mess sergeants; 8 printers; 24 carpenters; 24 crane operators; 16 painters; 20 motor mechanics; 12 motor truckmasters; 48 chauffeurs.	600
63	July 18, 1918	6 instrument repairmen; 6 mechanical instrument makers; 6 camera repairmen; 6 instrument makers.	24
63G	July 29, 1918	Run of the draft to 1 mobilization camp...........................	6,000
64	July 20, 1918	Grammar-school education with mechanical experience to 19 schools..	4,325
65	July 23, 1918	Grammar-school education with mechanical experience to 5 schools.	1,261
65G	July 27, 1918	Clerks...	10
66	July 26, 1918	Grammar-school education with mechanical experience to 1 school.	309
66G	July 30, 1918	Run of the draft to 1 mobilization camp...........................	1,084
67	Aug. 2, 1918	2 plumbers; 3 electricians; 2 blacksmiths; 2 machinists; 20 clerks; 7 stenographers; 6 foremen; 4 cooks; 2 second cooks; 2 mess sergeants; 2 printers; 6 carpenters; 2 crane operators; 4 painters; 5 motor mechanics; 3 motor truckmasters; 12 chauffeurs; 66 laborers.	150
67G	Aug. 1, 1918	Run of the draft to 13 mobilization camps.........................	30,000
68	Aug. 23, 1918	75 auto repairmen; 19 stenographers.............................	94
68G	Aug. 1, 1918	Run of the draft to 16 mobilization camps.........................	100,000
69G	Aug. 8, 1918	Run of the draft to 3 mobilization camps..........................	12,000

APPENDIX TABLE 81-A.—*List of requisitions for men, received by the Provost Marshal General from The Adjutant General of the Army, Aug. 25, 1917, to Nov. 7, 1918*—Con.

Requisition No.	Date received.	Qualifications.	Number of men.
70	Aug. 3, 1918	25 stenographers; 25 clerks..	50
71	Aug. 5, 1918	Grammar-school education with mechanical experience to 10 schools.	2,339
72	Aug. 15, 1918	Draftsmen...	253
73	.....do.......	Stenographers...	15
74	.....do.......	.....do..	15
75	Aug. 27, 1918	Grammar-school education with mechanical experience to 8 schools.	2,304
75G	Aug. 20, 1918	Run of the draft to 21 mobilization camps.......................	21,200
76	Sept. 30, 1918	Grammar-school education with mechanical experience to 53 schools.	21,329
76G	Aug. 20, 1918	Run of the draft to 11 mobilization camps.......................	40,500
77G	.....do..*.....	Run of the draft to 21 mobilization camps.......................	125,000
79G	Aug. 15. 1918	Photographers...	3
80G	Aug. 22, 1918	Run of the draft to 1 mobilization camp.........................	5,000
81G	.....do.......	.....o..	900
82G	Aug. 29, 1918	Clerks..	6,054
83G	Aug. 28, 1918	Mechanical draftsmen...	200
84G	Sept. 9, 1918	Stenographers and typists..	2,000
85G	Sept. 10, 1918	Run of the draft to 20 mobilization camps.......................	39,750
87G	.....do.......	Telegraphers..	5
88G	Sept. 13, 1918	Run of the draft to 1 mobilization camp.........................	856
89G	Sept. 17, 1918	Run of the draft to 6 mobilization camps........................	13,000
90G	Sept. 25, 1918	Spruce producers...	1,800
91G	Oct. 4, 1918	Run of the draft to 38 mobilization camps.......................	[1] 114,395
92G	Oct. 22, 1918	Run of the draft to 1 mobilization camp.........................	2,000
93G	Oct. 17, 1918	Run of the draft to 56 mobilization camps.......................	[1] 290,773
94G	Nov. 2, 1918	Warehousemen, clerks, stenographers, typists, stationary engineers, and firemen, forestrymen and lumbermen, electricians, and stock-keepers for 10 mobilization camps.	[1] 18,300
95G	Nov. 7, 1918	Photographers for 3 mobilization camps...........................	[1] 900

REQUISITIONS RECEIVED FROM THE NAVY DEPARTMENT.

1	Oct. 3, 1918	Run of the draft to 2 mobilization points.......................	1,000
2	Nov. 1, 1918	Carpenters for 5 mobilization points.............................	300
3	.....do.......	Boiler makers for 6 mobilization points..........................	200
4	.....do.......	Coppersmiths for 5 mobilization points...........................	200
5	.....do.......	Cooks for 2 mobilization points..................................	200
6	.....do.......	Stewards for 4 mobilization points...............................	200
7	Nov. 7, 1918	Bridge riggers for 13 mobilization points........................	[2] 200

[1] Portions of the requisitions so indicated were suspended on account of the influenza epidemic, and such suspended requisitions were subsequently canceled by the President's order of Nov. 11, 1918.
[2] Requisition canceled account suspension of hostilities.

APPENDIX TABLE 87–A.—*Disbursements and expenses, by States, June, 1917, to October 1, 1918.*

Disbursements and expenses.	(1) Totals of columns 2 to 8.	(2) Board members.	(3) Employes and inspectors.	(4) Physical examination to other than board members.	(5) Travel and per diem.	(6) Office rent.	(7) Stationery, printing, and supplies.	(8) Auto hire, livery, drayage, miscellaneous.	(9) Board members compensation, Mar. 1–Aug. 31, 1918.	(10) Total expenses in States (columns 1 and 9).
Disbursements to Sept. 1 from P. M. G. O. appropriations	$15,006,749.15	$4,916,625.55	$7,913,270.09	$427,155.33	$173,521.32	$245,886.00	$877,091.74	$453,198.52	....	....
Alabama	299,994.75	133,200.44	132,719.69	14,965.00	7,378.07	3,639.76	6,914.86	1,176.93	$56,300.00	$356,294.75
Arizona	66,123.85	12,110.69	45,735.88	402.45	808.81	650.75	3,900.05	2,455.22	10,000.00	76,123.85
Arkansas	237,314.80	102,830.73	103,870.69	11,537.75	2,375.28	2,616.98	10,407.69	3,675.68	45,000.00	282,314.80
California	501,449.82	145,525.22	285,704.42	12,612.85	9,034.74	30,115.77	7,746.38	7,839.38	55,000.00	556,449.82
Colorado	114,766.84	21,533.27	77,816.85	789.43	2,015.73	526.50	15,216.72	4,338.68	22,500.00	137,266.84
Connecticut	172,696.11	29,655.04	116,363.51	1,057.80	46.71	5,496.00	3,078.63	4,860.33	25,000.00	197,696.11
Delaware	41,890.14	12,087.80	21,255.74	1,910.60	1,514.90	540.00	28.00	1,502.47	8,000.00	49,890.14
District of Columbia	29,256.17	3,670.00	25,223.47	234.70	....	....	....	....	....	29,256.17
Florida	155,126.52	45,019.14	69,563.28	4,256.60	2,589.77	1,376.77	4,151.19	1,178.77	....	155,126.52
Georgia	367,976.10	157,594.00	196,760.77	8,986.67	2,929.06	2,773.20	7,995.25	937.15	65,000.00	432,976.10
Idaho	32,578.69	7,258.34	20,302.67	386.60	2,272.44	12.50	1,257.45	1,088.69	15,800.00	48,378.69
Illinois	886,987.91	321,349.56	419,747.71	29,069.19	3,467.18	31,832.92	59,675.55	21,845.80	275,000.00	1,161,987.91
Indiana	296,850.63	129,316.59	135,889.44	11,678.86	1,840.91	3,534.33	12,136.86	2,153.64	60,300.00	357,150.63
Iowa	197,664.30	71,301.13	102,514.03	11,139.22	3,027.11	2,233.61	5,502.64	1,946.52	40,000.00	237,664.30
Kansas	191,841.50	57,745.46	112,857.74	6,385.01	4,197.08	1,878.91	6,285.04	2,492.26	51,900.00	243,741.50
Kentucky	288,573.21	126,729.58	140,726.27	10,597.45	15.50	4,858.53	4,233.85	2,412.03	60,000.00	348,573.21
Louisiana	176,838.95	54,466.62	105,290.87	2,593.29	944.04	2,318.35	8,485.20	2,940.58	45,000.00	221,838.95
Maine	90,021.52	29,389.89	43,072.01	3,712.88	3,205.15	1,261.88	5,600.17	3,779.54	20,300.00	110,321.52
Maryland	210,039.60	81,289.88	94,071.65	9,907.43	3,006.94	7,104.74	8,917.91	5,741.65	48,500.00	258,539.60
Massachusetts	549,565.13	193,108.14	270,336.92	19,835.40	1,296.88	21,751.30	34,761.77	8,474.72	63,000.00	612,565.13
Michigan	707,544.20	220,229.73	385,126.76	22,403.86	9,856.95	12,314.27	46,891.56	10,721.07	109,000.00	816,544.20
Minnesota	287,726.22	98,649.01	156,288.64	9,702.05	3,119.56	3,196.33	12,991.91	3,778.72	70,000.00	357,726.22
Mississippi	193,068.34	79,487.58	93,073.42	5,763.36	9,227.69	1,449.51	2,633.07	533.71	62,000.00	255,068.34
Missouri	463,839.22	192,115.77	218,634.51	12,479.98	9,058.35	9,418.29	17,128.28	4,704.04	75,000.00	538,839.22
Montana	111,998.19	25,133.75	66,455.85	1,348.50	5,176.05	905.50	7,297.21	4,681.33	12,600.00	124,598.19
Nebraska	110,048.50	46,242.82	49,733.52	2,027.75	3,036.33	341.00	6,891.45	1,775.63	25,600.00	135,648.50
Nevada	11,010.29	1,301.10	7,670.42	....	591.76	351.50	347.04	94.10	5,000.00	16,010.29
New Hampshire	46,045.04	16,652.21	23,440.92	2,225.25	2,419.13	....	2,507.67	637.27	10,200.00	56,245.04
New Jersey	342,527.75	70,911.59	228,429.30	6,205.35	3,376.32	4,440.59	25,401.06	4,720.13	136,500.00	479,027.75
New Mexico	60,934.90	16,904.00	33,228.98	643.20	4,138.74	671.89	2,411.96	2,936.13	11,400.00	72,334.90
New York	1,869,517.63	584,798.69	1,020,457.24	43,820.16	14,138.74	38,932.75	122,328.43	45,041.63	250,000.00	2,119,517.63
North Carolina	340,054.92	128,775.07	170,052.42	4,800.20	1,516.86	3,347.25	18,442.38	....	72,000.00	412,054.92
North Dakota	67,490.38	18,222.87	43,289.26	1,594.66	....	380.90	1,640.45	875.38	30,000.00	97,490.38
Ohio	810,563.33	244,073.64	448,481.88	18,736.52	6,381.75	12,263.12	56,185.59	24,490.82	178,000.00	988,563.33

Oklahoma	148,313.45	5,000.00	6,357.07	9,210.49	1,773.85	2,132.21	28.00	116,431.78	7,380.05	143,313.45
Oregon	75,154.09	18,000.00	806.56	3,115.00	280.00	473.69	2,864.54	35,316.04	14,298.26	57,154.09
Pennsylvania	1,455,036.29	250,000.00	10,972.13	66,674.90	11,594.09	2,786.17	52,582.36	589,599.34	470,827.30	1,205,036.29
Rhode Island	73,370.99		1,600.93	6,073.23	255.87	442.47	544.90	51,725.62	12,727.97	73,370.99
South Carolina	244,208.12	60,000.00	1,303.54	9,098.30	3,673.30	4,285.43	4,813.09	98,115.38	62,931.08	184,208.12
South Dakota	99,032.68	33,000.00	2,243.59	1,987.50	638.00	422.65	1,792.19	37,021.79	21,928.96	66,032.68
Tennessee	387,907.42	60,000.00	4,431.95	11,862.24	5,289.54	2,738.87	10,197.77	150,874.49	142,512.56	327,907.42
Texas	895,743.97	175,000.00	7,080.16	36,117.34	14,353.21	14,158.79	21,925.77	334,207.87	292,900.88	720,743.97
Utah	44,999.58	5,000.00	1,069.23	1,966.09	90.50	1,045.81	532.40	25,923.61	9,381.34	39,999.58
Vermont	50,718.14	7,300.00	733.81	674.05	5.00	1,924.65	1,995.15	20,078.28	18,007.20	43,418.14
Virginia	349,859.09	55,000.00	3,876.52	11,508.43	2,830.19	576.70	8,802.38	138,528.44	128,736.43	294,859.09
Washington	229,510.15	30,000.00	4,501.91	10,870.02	3,392.83	4,454.05	6,869.71	106,654.30	62,767.33	196,510.15
West Virginia	246,710.68	50,000.00	5,299.36	8,379.51	2,976.55	3,344.65	6,702.30	109,464.31	60,544.00	196,710.68
Wisconsin	365,267.33	61,500.00	4,268.03	13,159.57	3,337.70	4,574.17	6,147.53	150,178.57	122,101.76	303,767.33
Wyoming	39,097.31	7,700.00	1,948.56	1,499.60	262.55	1,019.64	691.00	19,805.16	6,170.80	31,397.31
Alaska	8,567.00	2,000.00	188.40	771.98	450.56	93.20		5,062.86		6,567.00
Hawaii	27,891.22		1,552.92	4,577.25	15.00	1,497.20	227.20	19,798.85	450.00	27,891.22
Porto Rico	38,443.11		2,207.70	8,678.35	1,379.82	188.80	103.80	25,323.70	437.54	38,443.11
Provost Marshal General's Office			203,814.02	111,386.67		1,432.65		426,401.94	354.00	743,493.08
Expenses, additional										3,968,437.31
Telegrams (Quartermaster General appropriation)										273,037.31
Printing (Government Printing Office appropriation)										825,000.00
Board compensation, Mar. 1-Aug. 31 (unliquidated)										12,860,400.00
Disbursements, Sept., 1918 (not itemized)										1,209,466.07
Total expenses for the period										20,174,652.53

Column 9.

APPENDIX TABLE 88–A.—*Total and per capita cost of selective service system. June, 1917, to Oct. 1, 1918.*

	Cost to Sept. 1, 1918.	Cost from Sept. 1, 1918, to Oct. 1, 1918.	Total cost.	Registrants from June 5, 1917, to Sept. 11, 1918.	Cost per registrant.	Inducted June 5, 1917, to Oct. 1, 1918.	Cost per man inducted.
United States..	$18,965,186.46	$1,209,466.07	$20,174,652.53	10,838,315	$1.86	2,552,173	$7.90
Alabama.......	356,294.75	8,968.00	365,262.75	206,248	1.77	57,459	6.36
Arizona........	76,123.85	5,517.13	81,640.98	40,517	2.01	7,777	10.49
Arkansas.......	282,314.80	12,330.09	294,644.89	168,302	1.75	47,221	4.33
California......	556,449.82	31,651.15	588,100.97	332,593	1.77	63,192	9.31
Colorado.......	137,266.84	8,952.88	146,219.72	91,813	1.59	21,381	6.83
Connecticut....	197,696.11	11,563.96	209,260.07	175,026	1.20	30,847	6.78
Delaware.......	49,890.14	2,321.45	52,211.59	24,563	2.13	4,771	10.94
District of Columbia.......	29,256.17	3,138.16	32,394.33	36,741	.88	9,050	3.57
Florida........	155,126.52	9,778.77	164,905.29	94,792	1.74	24,186	2.64
Georgia	432,976.10	25,331.13	458,307.23	260,296	1.76	62,966	7.27
Idaho.........	48,378.69	3,141.23	51,519.92	45,982	1.12	11,747	4.39
Illinois.........	1,161,987.91	18,095.80	1,180,083.71	707,962	1.67	171,109	6.90
Indiana.........	357,150.63	37,172.62	394,323.25	283,843	1.39	67,473	5.84
Iowa...........	237,664.30	29,185.80	266,850.10	240,934	1.11	65,781	4.05
Kansas........	243,741.50	16,425.96	260,167.46	167,486	1.55	40,680	6.39
Kentucky......	348,573.21	21,323.68	369,896.89	215,936	1.71	57,826	6.39
Louisiana.......	221,838.95	49,421.93	271,260.88	180,226	1.51	54,581	4.96
Maine.........	110,321.52	3,385.27	113,706.79	68,214	1.67	14,205	8.00
Maryland......	258,539.60	14,229.62	272,769.79	136,552	2.00	32,668	8.35
Massachusetts..	612,565.13	46,319.72	658,884.85	398,364	1.65	71,856	9.16
Michigan.......	816,544.20	78,230.08	894,774.28	411,596	2.17	91,109	9.82
Minnesota......	357,726.22	21,914.38	379,640.60	249,937	1.52	66,402	5.71
Mississippi.....	255,068.34	23,691.13	278,759.47	157,607	1.77	43,073	6.47
Missouri........	538,839.22	45,591.92	584,431.14	335,012	1.74	85,722	6.81
Montana.......	124,598.19	5,304.32	129,902.51	97,762	1.33	26,731	4.85
Nebraska.......	135,648.50	6,667.02	142,315.52	132,458	1.07	29,019	4.90
Nevada........	16,010.29	990.62	17,000.91	13,044	1.30	2,981	5.70
New Hampshire	56,245.04	2,831.83	59,076.87	41,743	1.42	7,722	7.65
New Jersey.....	479,027.75	23,635.93	502,663.68	332,895	1.51	67,165	7.48
New Mexico.....	72,334.90	4,446.65	76,781.55	37,300	2.06	8,774	8.75
New York......	2,119,517.63	81,525.48	2,201,043.11	1,120,332	1.96	239,499	9.19
North Carolina.	412,054.92	11,817.11	423,872.03	228,844	1.85	57,748	7.34
North Dakota..	97,490.38	6,200.02	103,690.40	73,341	1.41	18,117	5.72
Ohio..........	988,563.33	53,547.28	1,042,110.61	617,371	1.69	136,461	7.63
Oklahoma......	148,313.45	15,079.90	163,393.35	193,236	.85	61,621	2.65
Oregon.........	75,154.09	7,621.31	82,775.40	70,549	1.17	14,916	5.54
Pennsylvania...	1,455,036.29	86,623.01	1,541,659.30	902,996	1.71	194,604	7.92
Rhode Island...	73,370.99	3,641.32	77,012.31	59,059	1.30	10,833	7.11
South Carolina.	244,208.12	12,272.93	256,481.05	144,701	1.77	42,857	5.98
South Dakota..	99,032.68	6,668.45	105,701.13	66,189	1.60	20,938	5.04
Tennessee......	387,907.42	17,565.26	405,472.68	213,427	1.90	55,770	7.27
Texas..........	895,743.97	40,527.54	936,271.51	460,326	2.03	115,724	8.09
Utah..........	44,999.58	8,786.96	53,786.54	46,901	1.15	10,375	5.23
Vermont.......	50,718.14	2,451.14	53,169.28	30,884	1.72	6,275	8.47
Virginia........	349,859.09	16,079.83	365,938.92	206,190	1.77	56,975	6.42
Washington.....	229,510.15	16,951.03	246,461.18	125,708	1.96	25,715	9.58
West Virginia..	246,710.68	14,788.93	261,499.61	142,174	1.84	44,687	5.85
Wisconsin......	365,267.33	13,396.18	378,663.51	266,691	1.42	64,841	5.83
Wyoming......	39,097.31	3,350.91	42,448.22	25,151	1.69	7,709	5.50
Alaska.........	8,567.00	2,092.88	10,659.88	6,851	1.56	1,937	5.50
Hawaii.........	27,891.22	3,472.14	31,363.36	31,200	1.01	5,464	5.74
Porto Rico.....	38,443.11	4,708.16	43,151.27	120,450	.36	13,733	3.14
Not allocated (Table 87–A, col. 1, lines 4, 5,7,from bottom)........	1,841,530.39	208,740.07	2,050,270.46	....	.19	....	.80

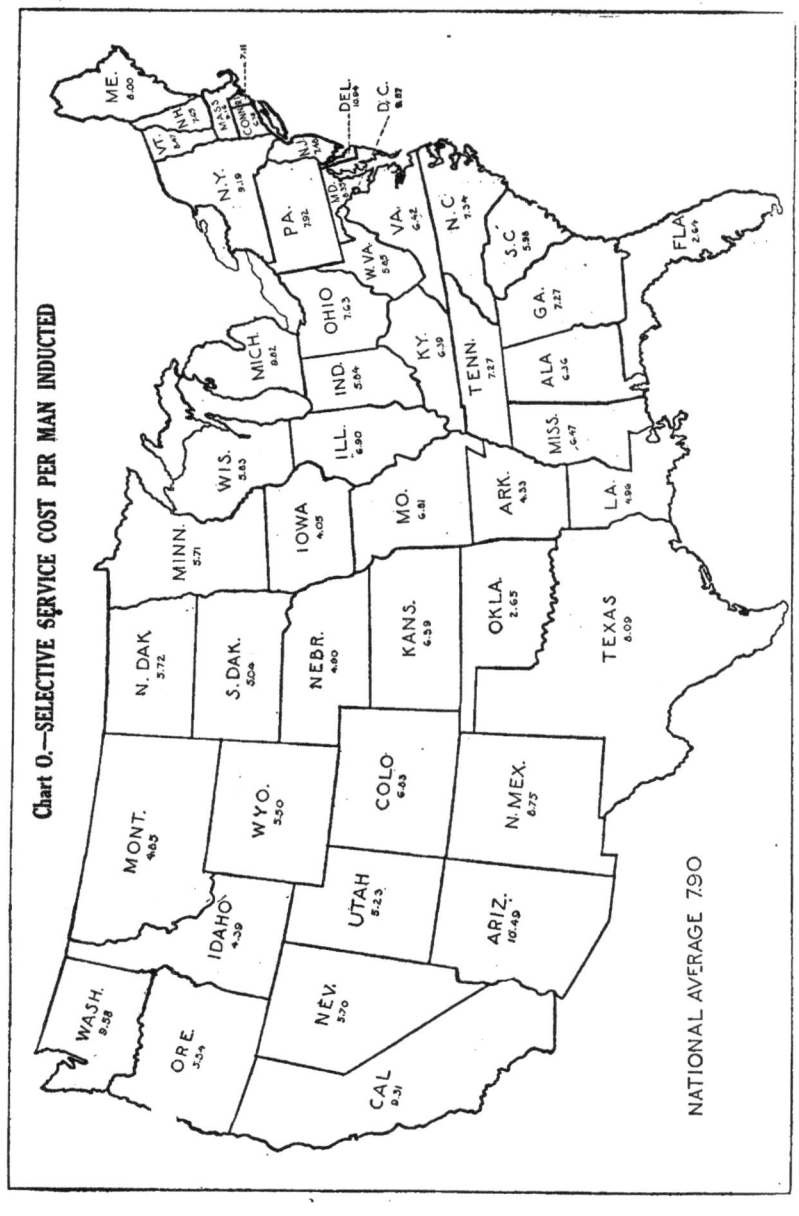

Chart O.—SELECTIVE SERVICE COST PER MAN INDUCTED

NATIONAL AVERAGE 7.90

APPENDIX TABLE 91-A.—*Number of personnel in the selective service administration, April, 1917, to November, 1918.*

	State headquarters						District boards						Local boards						Legal advisory boards			Medical advisory boards				Boards of instruction		
	Governors	Adjutants general	Assistants to adjutants general	Medical aides	Civilian clerks	Enlisted clerks	Number of district boards	Number of members	Additional members	Civilian clerks	Enlisted clerks	Industrial advisers	Number of local boards	Number of members	Civilian clerks	Enlisted clerks	Government appeal agents	Additional examining physicians	Number of legal advisory boards	Number of members	Associate members	Number of medical advisory boards	Number of members	Civilian clerks	Enlisted clerks	Number of boards of instruction	Number of members	Total personnel by States
United States	54	49	49	49	624	174	155	915	124	944	145	411	4,648	14,416	9,227	3,218	4,679	12,039	3,646	10,915	108,367	1,319	9,577	411	246	2,352	16,055	192,688
Alabama	1	1	1	1	9	2	4	20	4	5	3	12	78	234	163	69	73	152	78	234	1,121	22	66	15	9	46	253	2,443
Arizona	1	1	1	1	9	2	4	20	4	5		6	14	46	20	13	14	80	14	42	303	9	59	2		6	23	557
Arkansas	1	1	1	1	13	3	5	14	4	11		15	80	242	169	62	82	250	84	252	2,090	33	177	1	7	69	378	3,558
California	1	1	1	1	27	4	5	25	4	26	8	5	125	375	351	108	125	85	84	164	2,875	11	118	5	3	46	150	4,643
Colorado	1	1	1	1	9		2	10		2		6	75	228	92	50	74	353	58	225	1,356	19	103	5		38	162	2,423
Connecticut	1	1	1	1	6	3	3	15		16		9	44	122	120	61	44	22	75	132	2,230	17	149	14	2	34	89	3,376
Delaware	3	1	1	1	5	1	1	5		6		3	7	21	17	10	7	77	44	21	446	7	37			7	12	617
Dist. of Columbia		1	1	1	11		1	10		19		9	11	36	26	9	11	1	1	3	400	4	51			15		645
Florida	1	1	1	1	5	2	1	15		12	2	3	59	177	121	56	59	177	57	171	958	6	52	3	2	43	91	1,920
Georgia	1	1	1	1	20	3	3	26	28	45	4	9	165	495	220	111	155	165	44	132	3,774	21	139	19	4	11	188	5,478
Idaho	1	1	1	1	15	8	3	10		47	16	9	42	128	38	22	42	3	8	24	449	12	80	25	11	11	39	855
Illinois	1	1	1	1	27	7	8	64		60		24	227	683	460	203	228	1,100	227	681	2,160	34	614	33	16	148	969	7,361
Indiana	1	1	1	1	11		4	20		33		12	124	370	168	108	124	225	100	372	3,500	102	570	8	15	123	624	6,130
Iowa	1	1	1	1	21	4	2	10		27		6	112	336	204	101	112	134	100	299	2,791	33	159	9	8	111	418	4,729
Kansas	1	1	1	1	8	2	3	18		7		6	115	349	231	54	115	203	118	314	1,969	22	147	8		110	512	3,854
Kentucky	1	1	1	1	11		3	19		8		9	131	395	208	72	130	218	62	354	3,013	24	85	5	5	65	266	4,828
Louisiana	1	1	1	1	5		3	10		6		5	78	242	141	42	78	53	24	184	1,055	25	136	6		19	92	2,237
Maine	1	1	1	1	8	3	7	30	3	12	4	7	24	72	53	11	47	61	58	72	2,242	8	171	9		43	71	2,829
Maryland	1	1	1	1	11	2	5	35	4	45	16	18	53	159	107		53	492	69	159	1,465	57	374	21	4	17	71	2,314
Massachusetts	1	1	1	1	37	17	8	39	14	47		20	122	371	75	116	196	135	41	207	4,500	28	288	8	20	100	675	7,045
Michigan	1	1	1	1	19	6	6	30	8	6		16	136	430	216	122	135	109	121	123	792	57	177	7	4	59	3	4,880
Minnesota	1	1	1	1	12	8	7	33	4	12	6	15	121	379	171	59	118	111	83	362	2,783	22	288	21		85	361	2,536
Mississippi	1	1	1	1	12	3	4	10	3	14	2	6	86	259	309	128	84	247	166	249	1,200	112	113	8		144	599	2,903
Missouri	1	1	1	1	14	1	10	33		21	5	16	166	501	81	85	167	150	43	278	2,443	11	645	7		18	683	5,752
Montana	1	1	1	1	4		2	10	8	5	1	6	44	132	80	34	44	21	18	48	480	10	81	2		89	114	1,296
Nebraska	1	1	1	1	5	9	2	10	4	16	3	5	100	299	66	134	100	27	16	48	219	80	330	1	1	89	442	4,134
Nevada	1	1	1	1	6	2	1	5	3	11	1	3	16	48	39	14	16	675	13	69	650	8	34	4	5	16	57	461
New Hampshire	1	1	1	1	5	3	3	15		34	14	9	16	318	281	111	104	37	23	84	2,307	6	84			14	39	987
New Jersey	1	1	1	1	6		1	15		14	1	2	106	84	32	21	26	57	28	84	302	28	325	1	1	14	4,295	4,295
New Mexico	1	1	1	1	3		1	9	2	2			28									23	93			2	17	703

State																				Total
New York	1		1	1	45	3	9	86	16	178	4	4	354	1,002	973	252	380	2,500	58	174	12,000	49	948	42	16	336	3,040	21,722
North Carolina	1	1	1	1	11	3	2	12	2	37	1		109	333	237	40	115		100	299	1,088	18	123	5	4	109	606	2,926
North Dakota	1	1	1	1	5		2	5					53	159	82		53		53	159	90	12						976
Ohio	1	1	1	1	24	2	8	30		40	2	2	155	549	500	109	149	32	154	461	7,500	20	152	22	2	125	1,004	11,218
Oklahoma	1	1	1	1	9	3	3	15		3	4	3	85	256	143	64	87	650	77	231	90	39	68	5	2	66	244	4,800
Oregon	1	1	1	1	8	1	1	16	1	6	1	1	47	142	67	53	57	9	47	141	3,400	25	318	3	1	48	205	2,576
Pennsylvania	1	1	1	1	64	8	8	49	9	70	7		281	846	680	222	281	1,350	282	846	1,728	53	585	30	37	59	415	11,971
Rhode Island	1	1	1	1	12	2	2	10	4	4	2		22	69	62	54	22	111	30	90	6,450	5	63	1	1	21	97	823
South Carolina	1	1	1	1	7	2	1	14		9			56	168	128	12	56	150	48	144	243	10	63	3		51	227	2,739
oSth Dakota	1	1	1	1	1	3	3	4	5	4	1		65	195	71	70	20	3	64	192	1,700	29	148	1	1	24	126	802
Tennessee	1	1	1	1	13	1		15	8	12	3	5	113	341	194	44	114	75	113	339	10	52	297	3	15	83	698	5,879
Texas	1	1	1	1	32	14		20		24	1		280	841	462	23	280	631	274	817	3,651	15	198	12		280	827	11,423
Utah	1	1	1	1	3	16		28		1	2	2	34	112	49	15	31	60	34	102	7,187	4	29	6	2	14	58	667
Vermont	1	1	1	1	1	11		5		5	3		15	45	34	70	15	40	15	45	171	6	42	4	3	7	36	764
Virginia	1	1	1	1	6	4		5		8	6	3	114	352	190	109	106	154	113	339	462	49	356	4		106	364	4,626
Washington	1	1	1	1	9	4		14	4	17	2	6	66	205	164	67	42	58	39	117	2,600	22	135	5	1	67	247	2,310
West Virginia	1	1	1	1	8	5	2	20	5	19	5	1	65	197	180	62	64	70	55	165	1,837	11	68	6	9	68	339	3,048
Wisconsin	1	1	1	1	2	3	1	25	1	40	1	3	104	572	234	66	104	475	71	213	3,755	23	185	12	1	27	126	5,844
Wyoming	1	1	1	1	4			5		1	7		21	63	23	19	21		21	63	174	6	38	1				425
Alaska		1	1	1	7			20		3	2		22	70	11		20	4	4	12	91	4	18	2				252
Hawaii	1	1		1	9			5		9			6	22	31		6		5	15	361	6	18				2	487
Porto Rico	1	1	1	1				5					76	228	76		76	89	7	21	104		29	4				641

APPENDIX TABLE 94-A.—*War Industries Board priorities list*

Key No.	Industry.	W. I. B. priorities rating.	United States.	Alabama.
	Number of district boards reporting..		149	4
	Agricultural implements. *See* Farm implements.			
1	Aircraft: Plants engaged principally in manufacturing aircraft or aircraft supplies and equipment..	I	132	3
2	Ammunition: Plants engaged principally in manufacturing same for the United States Government and the allies......................................	I	138	4
3	Army and Navy: Arsenals and navy yards................................	I	134	4
4	Army and Navy: Cantonments and camps................................	I	118	4
5	Arms (small): Plants engaged principally in manufacturing same for the United States Government and the allies......................................	I	130	4
6	Bags: Hemp, jute, and cotton—plants engaged principally in manufacturing same..	IV	68	1
7	Blast furnaces (producing pig iron)......................................	I	104	3
8	Boots and shoes: Plants engaged exclusively in manufacturing same..........	IV	89	1
9	Brass and copper: Plants engaged principally in rolling and drawing copper, brass, and other copper alloys in the form of sheets, rods, wire, and tubes....	II	97	1
	Buildings. *See* Public institutions and buildings.			
10	Chain: Plants engaged principally in manufacturing iron and steel chain......	III	78	1
11	Chemicals: Plants engaged principally in manufacturing chemicals for the production of military and naval explosives, ammunition, and aircraft, and use in chemical warfare...	I	137	4
12	Chemicals: Plants, not otherwise classified and listed, engaged principally in manufacturing chemicals...	IV	79	1
13	Coke: Plants engaged principally in producing metallurgical coke and byproducts, including toluol...	I	111	4
14	Coke: Plants, not otherwise classified and listed, producing same............	II	74	3
	Copper and brass. *See* Brass and copper.			
15	Cotton: Plants engaged in the compression of cotton.......................	IV	56	......
	Cotton textiles. *See* Textiles.			
16	Cranes: Plants engaged principally in manufacturing locomotive cranes......	II	77	1
17	Cranes: Plants engaged principally in manufacturing traveling cranes.........	II	77	1
18	Domestic consumers: Fuel and electric energy for residential consumption, including homes, apartment houses, residential flats, restaurants, and hotels.	I	93	1
19	Domestic consumers: Fuel and electric energy not otherwise specifically listed.	III	65	......
20	Drugs: Medicines and medical and surgical supplies, plants engaged principally in manufacturing same...	IV	104	1
21	Electrical equipment: Plants engaged principally in manufacturing same.....	III	103	2
22	Explosives: Plants engaged principally in manufacturing same for military and naval purposes for the United States Government and the allies........	I	134	4
23	Explosives: Plants, not otherwise classified or listed, engaged principally in manufacturing same...	III	105	1
24	Farm implements: Plants engaged principally in manufacturing agricultural implements and farm-operating equipment................................	IV	107	......
25	Feed: Plants engaged principally in preparing or manufacturing feed for live stock and poultry..	I	77	
26	Ferro alloys: Plants engaged principally in producing ferrochrome, ferromanganese, ferromolybdenum, ferrosilicon, ferrotungsten, ferrouranium, ferrovanadium, and ferrozirconium..	II	79	1
27	Fertilizers: Plants engaged principally in producing same..................	II	77	......
28	Fire brick: Plants engaged principally in manufacturing same...............	IV	69	......
29	Foods: Plants engaged principally in producing, milling, refining, preserving, refrigerating, wholesaling, or storing food for human consumption embraced within the following description: All cereals and cereal products, meats (including poultry), fish, vegetables, fruit, sugar, sirups, glucose, butter, eggs, cheese, milk and cream, lard, lard compounds, oleomargarine and other substitutes for butter or lard, vegetable oils, beans, salt, coffee, baking powder, soda and yeast; also ammonia for refrigeration............................	I	128	1
30	Foods: Plants engaged principally in pro ucing, milling, preparing, refining, preserving, refrigerating, or storing food for human consumption not otherwise specifically listed; excepting herefrom plants producing confectionery, soft drinks, and chewing gum...	III	103	1
31	Food containers: Plants engaged principally in manufacturing same..........	IV	95	1
32	Foundries (iron): Plants engaged principally in the manufacture of gray iron and malleable iron castings...	IV	119	3
	Fungicides. *See* Insecticides and fungicides.			
	Gas. *See* Oil and gas, also Public utilities.			
33	Guns (large): Plants engaged principally in manufacturing same for the United States Government and the allies......................................	I	127	4
	Hospitals. *See* Public institutions and buildings.			
34	Ice: Plants engaged principally in manufacturing same.....................	III	75	......
35	Insecticides and fungicides: Plants engaged principally in manufacturing same.	IV	45	......
36	Laundries..	IV	37	......
37	Machine tools: Plants engaged principally in manufacturing same............	II	115	3
	Medicines. *See* Drugs and medicines.			
38	Mines: Coal..	I	113	3
39	Mines: Producing metals and ferro-alloy minerals.........................	II	104	3

compared with district board rulings as to necessary industries.

Arizona.	Arkansas.	California.	Colorado.	Connecticut.	Delaware.	District of Columbia.	Florida.	Key No.
1	2	5	2	3	1	1	2	
1	2	5	1	3	1	1	2	1
1	2	5	1	3	1	1	2	2
1	2	5	1	3	1	1	2	3
1	1	5	1	3	1	....	2	4
1	2	5	1	3	1	1	2	5
....	1	4	1	2	1	....	....	6
1	1	5	1	2	1	....	....	7
1	....	4	....	2				8
1	1	4	1	3	....	....	....	9
....	1	2	....	3			1	10
1	2	5	2	3	1	1	2	11
....	....	4	1	2	1	1	1	12
1	1	5	1	2	1	1	....	13
....	....	2	1	2		1	....	14
1	1	2	1	2			2	15
....	1	3	....	2			1	16
....	1	3	1	2			1	17
1	2	3	1	2		1	....	18
....	1	4	1	....			1	19
....	1	3	2	2		1	1	20
....	1	4	2	2	1	1	2	21
1	1	5	2	3	1	1	2	22
....	1	4	1	2	....	1	2	23
....	1	4	2	3		1	2	24
....	1	4	....	2	1	1	1	25
1	1	4	2	....	1	....	1	26
....	2	4	1	2	1	1	2	27
....	1	2	1	....	....	....	....	28
1	2	5	2	3	1	1	1	29
....	1	4	2	2	1	....	1	30
....	1	4	1	3	1	1	1	31
....	1	3	2	3	1	1	2	32
1	1	3	1	3	1	1	2	33
1	1	2	2	2	1	1	2	34
....	2	3	1	1	....	....	1	35
....	1	2	1	1	....	....	....	36
1	2	4	2	3	1	1	1	37
1	2	3	2	3	1	....	2	38
1	1	4	2	1	....	1	1	39

APPENDIX TABLE 94–A.—*War Industries Board priorities list com-*

Key No.	Georgia.	Idaho.	Illinois.	Indiana.	Iowa.	Kansas.	Kentucky.	Louisiana.	Maine.	Maryland.
	3	2	8	4	2	2	3	3	2	3
1	3	1	7	4	2	2	3	2	1	2
2	3	....	8	4	2	2	3	2	2	3
3	3	1	8	4	2	2	3	2	2	2
4	2	....	7	3	2	2	3	2	1	2
5	2	....	7	3	2	2	2	2	1	3
6	2	....	5	2	1	1	1	2	1	2
7	2	....	6	4	1	1	3	2	1	2
8	2	....	6	3	1	1	1	2	1	2
9	2	....	7	4	1	1	1	2	....	2
10	1	1	5	4	1	1	1	2	....	3
11	3	1	8	4	1	2	2	2	2	3
12	2	1	4	3	1	1	2	2	2	2
13	3	....	5	4	1	1	3	2	1	2
14	2	....	4	3	1	1	3	2	....	2
15	2	....	3	2	1	1	1	3	....	2
16	3	....	4	2	1	1	1	2	1	2
17	2	....	4	2	1	1	2	2	....	2
18	2	2	4	2	2	2	2	3	1	3
19	1	1	2	2	2	1	1	3	1	3
20	2	....	5	4	2	2	1	3	1	3
21	3	1	7	3	1	1	2	3	....	2
22	3	1	7	4	1	2	3	2	2	3
23	1	1	6	4	1	2	1	2	2	2
24	3	1	8	3	2	2	2	3	1	2
25	3	1	4	2	2	1	1	2	1	3
26	2	....	5	2	1	....	1	2	....	2
27	2	....	1	2	1	1	1	2	2	2
28	1	....	4	3	2	....	2	2	1	2
29	3	2		4	2	2	3	3	2	3
30	1	2	5	2	2	1	2	3	2	3
31	2	....	5	3	1	2	1	2	2	3
32	3	1	7	4	2	2	2	2	1	2
33	3	1	8	4	1	2	2	2	1	3
34	3	1	1	2	1	2	1	3	....	2
35	2	....	....	2	1	1	2	1	1	2
36	2	....	1	1	2	1	2	2	....	1
37	2	1	8	4	1	1	3	2	1	2
38	2	....	7	4	1	2	3	2	....	2
39	2	2	5	3	2	2		2	1	2

pared with district board rulings as to necessary industries—Continued.

Massachusetts.	Michigan.	Minnesota.	Mississippi.	Missouri.	Montana.	Nebraska.	Nevada.	New Hampshire.	New Jersey.	Key No.
6	7	5	2	5	2	2	1	1	3	
6	7	4	2	5	2	2	1	1	3	1
6	7	5	2	5	2	2	1	1	3	2
6	7	5	2	5	2	2	1	1	3	3
6	6	5	2	5	2	2	1	1	2	4
6	7	5	2	5	2	2	1	1	3	5
3	....	3	1	2	2	2	1	....	1	6
3	5	5	2	2	2	2	1	....	3	7
4	3	5	2	3	2	2	1	1	1	8
5	4	4	2	2	2	2	1	1	3	9
1	1	4	2	2	2	1	1	....	2	10
6	7	4	2	5	2	2	1	1	3	11
3	2	2	2	3	2	2	....	....	2	12
5	5	5	2	3	2	2	1	1	3	13
3	1	4	2	2	2	2	....	....	1	14
2	....	2	1	2	2	1	....	....	1	15
3	4	5	2	3	2	1	1	....	2	16
2	4	5	2	3	2	1	1	1	2	17
5	3	3	1	1	1	1	1	1	2	18
5	2	3	1	1	1	1	....	....	2	19
5	5	5	2	3	1	1	1	....	3	20
5	5	3	2	2	1	1	1	1	3	21
6	7	5	2	5	2	2	1	1	3	22
6	6	4	2	5	1	2	1	1	3	23
5	4	5	2	4	1	1	1	....	2	24
4	....	3	2	2	1	1	1	....	....	25
4	3	4	2	2	2	1	1	....	2	26
4	1	4	2	2	1	1	....	....	1	27
4	1	2	2	4	1	1	1	....	2	28
5	5	5	2	3	1	2	1	1	2	29
5	3	4	2	2	1	1	1	1	2	30
4	3	5	2	2	1	1	1	1	2	31
5	5	5	2	4	1	....	1	....	3	32
6	5	5	2	4	2	1	1	1	3	33
5	....	2	2	2	1	....	1	....	2	34
2	....	1	1	2	1	....	1	....	1	35
3	....	1	1	....	1	....	....	....	....	36
5	6	5	2	3	1	....	....	....	3	37
5	5	4	2	5	2	1	1	....	2	38
4	4	5	2	2	2	....	1	....	2	39

APPENDIX TABLE 94–A.—*War Industries Board priorities list com-*

Key No.	New Mexico.	New York.	North Carolina.	North Dakota.	Ohio.	Oklahoma.	Oregon.	Pennsylvania.	Rhode Island.	South Carolina.
	1	9	2	1	6	2	3	9	2	2
1		9	2	1	6	1	3	0	2	2
2	1	9	2	1	6	2	2	9	2	2
3	1	7	2	1	5	1	3	9	2	2
4	1	6	2	1	3	1	3	9	2	1
5		9	2	1	6	1	1	9	2	2
6		3	1		3		1	4	2	1
7		6	1	1	6			9	1	2
8		3	2	1	4		1	6	2	1
9		7	1	1	4		2	7	2	2
10		4	1	1	6		1	7	1	2
11		9	2	1	6	1	1	9	2	2
12		3	2		3		1	6	2	
13	1	6	2		6			7	2	1
14	1	2	1		4	1		6	1	
15		2	2		2	2		2	1	
16		5	1		4		1	5	1	1
17		4	1		5		1	5	1	1
18	1	5	2		2	1	3	6	2	1
19	1	2	1		1		2	4	2	1
20		8	2		6	1	1	6	2	1
21		8	2		5		1	8	2	1
22		9	2		6	2	1	8	2	2
23		5	1	1	3			8	2	2
24		7	2	1	5	1	1	9	1	1
25	1	6	1		4	1	1	6	2	1
26	1	3	1	1	5			7	1	1
27		4	2		6	1		7	2	1
28		2	2		4			9	1	1
29	1	8	2	1	5	1	3	9	2	1
30	1	7	2	1	4		2	7	2	1
31		4	1	1	4	1	3	7	2	1
32		8	2	1	6	1	3	9	2	2
33		9	1	1	6	1	2	9	2	1
34		4	2		3	1	2	8	1	2
35		3	1		2		1	2	1	1
36		2	2				1	3	1	
37		8	2	1	6		1	9	2	1
38	1	5	2	1	5	2	2	9	2	1
39	1	4	2	1	4	1	2	7	1	2

pared with district board rulings as to necessary industries—Continued.

South Dakota.	Tennessee.	Texas.	Utah.	Vermont.	Virginia.	Washington.	West Virginia.	Wisconsin.	Wyoming.	Key No.
2	3	4	1	2	2	3	2	5	1	
1	3	2	....	1	1	3	2	5	....	1
1	3	2	....	1	2	3	2	5	....	2
1	3	2	....	1	1	3	2	5	....	3
1	2	3	....	1	....	2	2	4	....	4
1	3	2	....	1	2	3	2	5	....	5
....	2	4	....	....	....	2	1	2	....	6
....	3	3	....	1	1	2	2	5	....	7
....	3	3	1	2	1	2	1	5	....	8
....	2	3	....	1	1	3	....	4	....	9
....	2	3	....	1	2	2	....	2	....	10
1	3	4	1	2	2	3	2	4	....	11
....	3	3	....	....	2	3	....	2	....	12
1	3	3	1	2	1	3	2	3	....	13
....	3	3	....	....	1	3	2	2	....	14
....	2	4	....	1	....	2	....	1	....	15
....	1	3	....	1	1	2	....	3	....	16
....	1	3	....	1	1	2	....	3	....	17
....	....	4	1	2	2	3	2	3	....	18
....	....	4	....	....	1	3	1	2	....	19
1	1	3	1	2	1	2	1	5	....	20
1	1	3	....	1	2	3	1	2	....	21
1	3	3	....	1	2	3	2	5	....	22
1	2	3	1	2	2	2	1	4	....	23
1	....	3	....	1	1	3	....	5	....	24
....	1	4	....	....	1	2	....	2	....	25
1	1	2	....	1	1	2	1	3	....	26
....	1	4	1	1	1	2	....	1	....	27
....	2	3	1	....	1	2	....	2	....	28
1	3	4	1	1	2	3	2	5	....	29
1	1	4	1	1	2	3	1	5	....	30
....	2	3	....	1	2	2	1	4	....	31
....	2	3	....	1	2	3	1	5	....	32
2	....	3	....	1	3	3	2	5	....	33
2	....	3	....	1	1	2	....	1	....	34
....	....	3	....	1	....	2	....	....	....	35
....	1	3	1	....	....	1	....	....	....	36
....	3	3	....	1	1	3	1	5	....	37
1	2	3	1	1	1	2	2	2	1	38
1	2	3	1	1	2	3	1	5	....	39

APPENDIX TABLE 94–A.—*War Industries Board priorities list com-*

Key No.	Industry.	W. I. B. priorities rating.	United States.	Alabama.
40	Mines: Plants engaged principally in manufacturing mining tools or equipment.	III	93	3
	Navy. *See* Army and Navy.			
	Navy Department. *See* War and Navy Departments.			
41	Newspapers and periodicals: Plants engaged principally in printing newspapers or periodicals which are entered at the post office as second-class mail matter..	IV	77	·1
42	Oil and gas: Plants engaged principally in producing oil or natural gas for fuel, or for mechanical purposes, including refining or manufacturing oil for fuel, or for mechanical purposes	I	102	1
63	Oil and gas: Pipe lines and pumping stations engaged in transporting oil or natural gas	I	85	1
44	Oil and gas: Plants engaged principally in manufacturing equipment or supplies or producing or transporting oil or natural gas, or for refining and manufacturing oil for fuel or for mechanical purposes	III	81	1
	Paper and pulp. *See* Pulp and paper.			
	Periodicals. *See* Newspapers and periodicals.			
45	Public institutions and buildings (maintenance and operation of) other than hospitals and sanitariums	II	51	....
46	Public institutions and buildings (maintenance and operation of) used as hospitals or sanitariums	I	109	2
47	Public utilities: Gas plants producing toluol	I	103	2
48	Public utilities: Street railways, electric lighting and power companies, gas plants not otherwise classified, telephone and telegraph companies, water-supply companies, and like general utilities	II	129	4
49	Public utilities: Plants engaged principally in manufacturing equipment for railways or other public utilities	II	109	2
50	Pulp and paper: Plants engaged exclusively in manufacturing same	IV	88	....
51	Railways: Operated by United States Railroad Administration	I	141	4
52	Railways: Not operated by United States Railroad Administration (excluding those operated as plant facilities)	II	116	2
	Railways (street). *See* Public utilities.			
	Rope. *See* Twine and rope.			
	Rope wire. *See* Wire rope.			
	Sanitariums. *See* Public institutions and buildings.			
53	Ships (maintenance and operation of): Excluding pleasure craft not common carriers	I	120	3
54	Ships: Plants engaged principally in building ships, excluding (a) pleasure craft not common carriers, (b) ships not built for the United States Government or the allies under license from United States Shipping Board	I	108	3
55	Soap: Plants engaged principally in manufacturing same	IV	72	....
56	Steel-making furnaces: Plants engaged solely in manufacturing ingots and steel castings by the open-hearth, Bessemer, crucible, or electric-furnace process, including blooming mills, billet mills, and slabbing mills for same	I	106	3
57	Steel-plate mills	I	99	3
58	Steel-rail mills: Rolling rails, 50 or more pounds per yard	II	96	3
59	Steel: All plants operating steel rolling and drawing mills exclusive of those taking higher classification	III	107	3
	Surgical supplies. *See* Drugs and medicines.			
60	Tanners: Plants engaged principally in tanning leather	IV	90	1
61	Tanning: Plants engaged principally in manufacturing tanning extracts	IV	73	1
62	Textiles: Plants engaged principally in manufacturing cotton textiles, including spinning, weaving, and finishing	IV	90	3
63	Textiles: Plants engaged principally in manufacturing woolen textiles, including spinners, top makers, and weavers	IV	97	2
64	Textiles: Plants engaged principally in manufacturing cotton or woolen knit goods	IV	93	2
65	Textiles: Plants engaged principally in manufacturing textile machinery	IV	77	1
66	Tin plates: Plants engaged principally in manufacturing same	III	73	1
67	Tobacco: Only for preserving, drying, curing, packing, and storing same—not for manufacturing and marketing	IV	57	1
	Toluol. *See* Coke; also Public utilities.			
68	Tools: Plants engaged principally in manufacturing small or hand tools for working wood or metal	III	93	1
69	Twine (binder and rope): Plants engaged principally in manufacturing same..	IV	80	....
70	War and Navy Departments: Construction work conducted by either the War Department or the Navy Department of the United States, in embarkation ports, harbors, fortified places, flood-protection operations, docks, locks, channels, inland waterways, and in the maintenance and repair of same	II	130	4
71	Wire rope and rope wire: Plants engaged principally in manufacturing same..	II	89	2
	Woolen textiles. *See* Textiles.			

board rulings as to necessary industries—Continued.

s.	California.	Colorado.	Connecti-cut.	Delaware.	District of Columbia.	Florida.	Key No.
1	4	2	2		1	2	40
...	2	2	2		1	2	41
1	4	1	2		1	2	42
2	3	1	2		1		43
1	4	1	2			1	44
...	3		1		1	1	45
2	3	1	3	1	1	1	46
...	4	2	2		1	2	47
2	3		3	1	1	2	48
2	4	2	3		1	2	49
1	2	1	3	1	1	1	50
2	4	2	3	1	1	2	51
2	3	2	1	1	1	2	52
1	4		3	1	1	2	53
1	4	1	2	1		1	54
1	2	2	2			1	55
1	3	1	3	1	1	1	56
1	4	1	3	1	1	1	57
1	4	1	2	1	1	1	58
1	4	1	3	1	1	1	59
1	3	1	2	1	1	1	60
1	3	1	1			1	61
1	4		3	1		1	62
1	4		3	1		1	63
1	3	1	3	1		1	64
1	3	1	3	1		1	65
1	3	1	3			1	66
1	2	1	1				67
1	3	2	3		1	1	68
1	3	1	3			1	69
2	4	2	3	1	1	2	70
1	4	1	3			1	71

APPENDIX TABLE 94-A.—*War Industries Board priorities list com-*

Key No.	Georgia.	Idaho.	Illinois.	Indiana.	Iowa.	Kansas.	Kentucky.	Louisiana.	Maine.	Maryland.
40	2	....	6	3	1	1	3	2		
41	2	1	1	3	2	1	2	3		1
42	3	1	5	4	2	2	2	3		
43	2	....	5	3	1	2	2	3		
44	2	....	5	2	1	2	1	3		
45	2	....	2	1	2	1	1	3		
46	3	1	5	4	2	2	3	3		2
47	2	....	6	4	1	1	1	3		
48	3	2	5	3	2	1	3	3		1
49	2	1	7	3	2	1	1	3		2
50	2	....	4	2	1	1	1	2		1
51	3	2	8	4	2	2	3	3		2
52	3	2	5	3	2	2	2	3		4
53	2	....	5	4	2	1	2	3		
54	1	....	5	4	2	2	3	3		
55	2	....	3	3	2	2	1	2		
56	2	....	6	4	1	2	2	2		
57	2	....	6	4	1	1	1	2		
58	2	....	5	4	1	1	2	2		
59	2	....	6	4	1	1	2	2		
60	2	....	5	3	1	1	2	2		1
61	2	....	5	2	1	1	1	2		1
62		....	4	3			2	2		1
63		....	6	4			1	3		1
64		....	6	4			1	2		1
65		....	5	3			1	2		1
66		....	5	4			2	2		
67		....	4	4			1	2		
68		....	6	2			1	2		1
69		....	6	3				3		1
70		1	8	4				2		2
71		....	6	3				2		

pared with district board rulings as to necessary industries—Continued.

Massa-chusetts.	Michigan.	Minne-sota.	Missis-sippi.	Missouri.	Montana.	Ne-braska.	Nevada.	New Hamp-shire.	New Jersey.	Key No.
3	4	4	2	2	1	.....	1	1	2	40
4	3	4	2	1	1	.....	1	1	1	41
4	2	4	2	4	1	1	1	.....	2	42
3	1	3	2	4	1	.....	1	.....	2	43
4	1	3	2	4	1	.....	1	.....	2	44
3	.....	3	2	1	1	.....	.....	.....	1	45
5	3	4	1	4	1	.....	.....	1	2	46
6	6	4	1	4	1	.....	.....	1	3	47
6	7	5	2	4	1	.....	1	1	2	48
5	4	5	2		1	.....	1	1	2	49
5	2	5	2	3	1	.....	1	1	1	50
6	7	5	2	5	2	1	1	1	2	51
6	6	4	2	5	1	1	1	.....	2	52
	7	5	2	3	2	1	1	1	3	53
6	6	4	2	3	2	1	1	1	2	54
6	.....	3	2	3	1	1	1	.....	2	55
3	6	4	2	4	2	1	1	.....	3	56
4	5	4	2	3	2	.....	1	.....	2	57
3	5	5	2	3	2	.....	1	.....	2	58
4	5	5	2	3	2	.....	1	1	3	59
4	4	4	2	3	1	.....	1	.....	1	60
4	2	4	2	2	1	.....	1	.....	1	61
4	1	4	2	2	1	.....	1	1	2	62
4	3	4	2	3	1	.....	1	1	2	63
4	3	2	2	3	1	.....	1	1	2	64
4	.....	2	2	2	1	.....	1	1	2	65
4	2	1	2	2	1	.....	1	.....	1	66
3	.....	4	2	3	1	.....	.....	.....	.....	67
4	3	5	2	3	1	.....	1	.....	2	68
4	1	5	2	5	1	.....	1	.....	2	69
6	7	5	2	5	2	1	1	1	3	70
4	2	4	2	3	1	1	1	.....	3	71

APPENDIX TABLE 94–A.—*War. Industries · Board priorities list com-*

Key No.	New Mexico.	New York.	North Carolina.	North Dakota.	Ohio.	Oklahoma.	Oregon.	Pennsylvania.	Rhode Island.	South Carolina.
40	....	5	1	1	5	1	1	9	1	1
41	....	3	2	....	2	2	1	5	2	....
42	1	6	1	1	5	2	1	7	2	2
43	....	3	1	1	5	2	....	9	1	2
44	....	3	1	1	4	2	1	7	1	2
45	....	2	1	....	4	....	1	3	....	....
46	1	8	2	1	6	1	1	7	2	2
47	....	7	2	1	5	....	1	7	2	1
48	1	9	2	1	6	1	3	8	2	2
49	1	7	1	1	5	....	2	8	2	2
50	....	6	2	1	6	....	1	8	1	1
51	1	9	2	1	5	3	3	8	2	2
52	1	8	2	1	4	1	1	7	2	1
53	1	8	1	1	4	2	2	7	2	2
54	1	7	2	1	4	2	2	4	2	1
55	....	3	1	....	6	....	1	2	2	1
56	....	7	1	1	6	....	2	8	1	2
57	....	5	1	1	5	....	1	9	2	2
58	....	4	1	1	6	....	....	9	1	2
59	....	6	1	1	6	....	1	9	2	2
60	....	4	2	1	5	1	....	9	2	2
61	....	2	2	1	3	....	....	6	1	2
62	....	6	2	1	3	1	1	5	2	2
63	....	7	2	1	4	2	2	6	2	2
64	....	7	2	1	4	....	2	6	2	2
65	....	3	2	1	6	....	....	6	2	2
66	....	4	2	1	2	....	....	8	1	1
67	....	2	2	1	6	....	1	3	1	....
68	....	7	2	1	5	....	2	8	2	1
69	....	3	2	1	5	1	1	5	2	1
70	1	7	2	1	4	2	3	9	2	2
71	1	4	2	1	4	....	1	8	2	2

pared with district board rulings as to necessary industries—Continued.

South Dakota.	Tennessee.	Texas.	Utah.	Vermont.	Virginia.	Washington.	West Virginia.	Wisconsin.	Wyoming.	Key No.
....	1	3	....	1	1	2	2	3	....	40
2	3	4	1	....	2	1	....	1	....	41
2	1	4	....	1	1	2	2	2	1	42
....	1	4	....	1	1	2	2	1	1	43
....	....	4	....	1	1	2	2	2	....	44
1	2	4	....	....	1	1	....	1	....	45
1	1	4	1	1	2	2	1	2	....	46
1	3	4	....	1	1	2	1	4	....	47
1	1	4	1	1	2	3	2	4	1	48
1	2	3	....	1	2	3	1	3	....	49
1	3	3	....	1	2	2	1	2	....	50
1	1	4	1	1	2	3	2	5	1	51
1	1	3	1	1	2	3	2	5	....	52
1	1	4	....	1·	2	2	2	5	....	53
1	....	4	....	....	1·	3	2	4	....	54
....	3	3	....	1	1	2	....	2	....	55
....	3	3	....	1	1	2	2	3	....	56
....	2	3	....	1	1	2	2	3	....	57
....	2	3	....	1	1	2	2	3	....	58
1	2	3	1	1	1	2	2	3	....	59
....	2	3	....	1	1	2	2	3	....	60
....	3	3	....	1	2	2	2	1	....	61
....	3	4	....	1	2	2	....	4	....	62
....	2	4	....	1	1	3	....	4	....	63
....	2	4	....	1	1	2	....	5	....	64
....	1	3	....	1	1	2	....	2	....	65
....	....	3	....	1	1	2	1	2	....	66
....	1	2	....	1	....	1	....	....	....	67
....	1	4	....	1	....	2	1	4	....	68
....	2	3	....	1	1	2	....	1	....	69
1	1·	4·	....	· 1	1	2	2	2	....	70
....	1	3	....	1·	1	2	....	3	....	71

APPENDIX TABLE 100-A—*Principal statistical data, by local boards.*

ALABAMA.

Local board.	Post-office address.	June 5, 1917.	June and August, 1918.	Sept. 12, 1918.	Total.	Accepted at camp.	General service.	Remediables.	Limited service.	Disqualified.	Dependency.	Agricultural.	Industrial.
Autauga	Prattville	1,317	150	1,681	3,148	514	455	11	19	18	480	9	0
Baldwin	Bay Minette	1,715	139	1,981	3,835	470	593	49	10	13	772	4	0
Barbour	Clayton	2,027	202	2,750	4,979	708	656	9	63	47	858	0	0
Bibb	Centerville	2,014	222	2,468	4,704	559	532	0	24	47	964	7	107
BIRMINGHAM No. 1	Twenty-second floor Jefferson County Bank Building.	2,816	238	4,165	7,219	805	676	20	73	138	1,473	2	65
BIRMINGHAM No. 2	do	3,689	318	4,953	8,960	1,294	999	40	144	293	1,304	1	107
BIRMINGHAM No. 3	do	4,707	372	6,049	11,128	1,498	1,126	55	144	343	1,840	2	109
BIRMINGHAM No. 4	do	4,115	247	3,053	6,185	866	748	35	98	128	1,308	2	118
BIRMINGHAM No. 5	do	2,045	148	2,917	9,001	1,263	1,134	16	134	202	1,914	2	119
BIRMINGHAM No. 6	do	2,182	215	2,532	5,110	605	467	17	60	119	1,071	2	40
Blount	Oneonta	1,360	139	1,831	4,929	447	520	8	24	82	1,209	13	11
Bullock	Union Springs	2,096	236	2,797	3,330	500	478	12	67	6	470	10	1
Butler	Greenville	3,990	534	5,218	5,129	756	814		62	30	1,149	0	1
Calhoun	Anniston	3,454	320	3,518	9,742	1,276	1,244	12	158	32	2,230	16	47
Chambers	Lafayette	1,639	195	2,060	7,292	939	1,056	41	158	347	1,711	3	49
Cherokee	Centre	1,653	148	2,220	3,898	492	77	2	2	23	68		16
Chilton	Clanton	3,000	274	2,012	4,045	535	501		23	70	992	4	
Choctaw	Butler	1,790	209	2,807	3,843	496	989	38	29	31	510		2
Clarke	Grove Hill	1,054	94	1,289	6,141	813	1,050	9	17	87	1,090	3	1
Clay	Ashland	2,256	270	2,678	4,385	578	446	3	20	84	371	4	3
Cleburne	Heflin	2,447	488	4,472	2,437	374	220	30	65	117	1,498	8	10
Coffee	Elba	2,061	183	2,196	5,204	570	505	6	51	41	1,223	36	20
Colbert	Tuscumbia	1,048	134	1,423	7,407	711	604	11	57	40	904	1	0
Conecuh	Evergreen	3,000	303	3,617	4,440	714	693	44	53		565	6	0
Coosa	Rockford	1,921	197	2,215	2,605	365	387	1	109	227	1,514	28	24
Covington	Andalusia	2,439	319	3,465	2,980	1,075	1,117	32	6	138	1,091	18	12
Crenshaw	Luverne	1,695	195	2,121	4,233	740	548	0	40	41	1,357	1	3
Cullman	Cullman	2,994	327	4,808	6,223	424	1,018		23	92	1,080	48	107
Dale	Ozark	2,562	274	3,445	6,011	873	607		67	59	1,589	394	0
Dallas	Selma	2,126	251	2,599	8,129	714	655		83	25	1,555	0	7
DeKalb	Fort Payne	1,868	197	2,339	6,281	700	672	12	110	1	1,166	80	3
Elmore	Wetumpka	4,591	346	5,079	4,976	591	1,003	22	24	200	15	3	50
Escambia	Brewton	1,387	157	1,817	4,404	1,237	415		188	54	2,469	1	4
Etowah	Gadsden	1,823	192	2,069	10,010	519	412	0	46	56	2,810	2	8
Fayette	Fayette				3,361						1,131	0	
Franklin	Russellville				4,064	538		3	64				

County	Place											
Geneva	Geneva	2,106	227	2,778	5,111	664	716	12	67	152	1,109	22	2
Greene	Eutaw	896	92	1,432	2,420	255	28	2	5	127	476	19	1
Hale	Greensboro	1,618	180	1,996	3,794	489	497	2	26	151	1,714	0	0
Henry	Abbeville	1,550	211	1,938	3,699	528	596	6	24	9	1,724	4	0
Hopston	Dothan	2,633	294	3,346	6,263	911	489	6	56	35	1,264	38	12
Jackson	Scottsboro	2,641	280	3,517	6,448	1,038	1,265	18	23	316	1,088	3	6
Jefferson No. 1	Bessemer	6,978	495	6,371	13,844	2,072	1,672	14	192	500	3,021	4	338
Jefferson No. 2	Brookside	2,611	236	3,522	6,369	726	530	18	93	91	736	4	207
Jefferson No. 3	2028 Jefferson County Bank Building, Birmingham	3,600	376	4,257	8,233	986	328	10	78	297	1,817	17	220
Lemar	Vernon	1,432	168	1,872	3,472	472	461	0	15	19	907	0	0
Lauderdale	Florence	2,754	345	3,925	7,024	845	227	10	26	108	1,221	18	3
Lawrence	Moulton	2,074	205	2,340	4,619	510	88	690	40	261	566	4	6
Lee	Opelika	2,322	189	2,756	5,287	758	865	4	135	133	1,244	2	0
Limestone	Athens	2,617	281	3,000	5,898	977	572	3	5	26	820	21	2
Lowndes	Hayneville	1,403	153	1,984	3,540	526	568	2	3	22	374	5	1
Macon	Tuskegee	1,411	164	1,952	3,527	550	1,306	14	51	531	2,226	0	0
Madison	Huntsville	4,266	414	5,023	9,703	1,242	792	2	15	61	1,257	6	3
Marengo	Linden	2,232	230	3,075	5,537	653	635	14	57	45	714	0	0
Marion	Hamilton	1,710	172	2,063	3,965	594	749	2	53	54	991	1	3
Marshall	Guntersville	2,450	325	3,357	6,132	841	825	35	55	53	934	2	0
Mobile No. 1	Old Federal Building	2,672	263	4,190	7,125	711	858	114	53	209	705	1	5
Mobile No. 2	Van Antwerp Building	2,153	185	3,132	5,470	852	1,005	19	56	323	1,289	4	68
Mobile	Old Federal Building, Mobile	2,802	349	4,966	8,187	1,084	717	70	69	204	1,171	19	25
Monroe	Monroeville	3,854	263	2,807	9,796	725	1,277	19	47	423	1,318	3	44
Montgomery	City Building, Montgomery	1,838	350	5,592	4,470	1,297	13	14	42	27	36		3
Montgomery	Courthouse, Montgomery	3,213	228	2,704	4,470	575	470	11	24	10	892	5	54
Morgan	Decatur	1,440	324	4,244	7,781	1,031	516	20	8	182	1,118	13	2
Perry	Marion	2,062	141	2,101	3,691	421	322	1	25	35	641	0	4
Pickens	Carrollton	2,449	204	2,488	4,754	546	818	8	18	112	1,191	0	0
Pike	Troy	2,106	295	2,868	5,612	710	506	18	43	249	946	33	2
Randolph	Wedowee	1,736	226	2,585	4,917	605	797	5	61	74	1,134	1	41
Russell	Seale	2,163	139	2,048	3,923	459	498	5	103	55	1,191	1	9
St. Clair	Asheville	2,037	208	2,339	4,760	632	533	4	17	94	856	48	20
Shelby	Columbiana	1,625	206	2,673	4,916	635	652	28	93	94	254	1	0
Sumter	Livingston	2,947	220	2,358	4,203	450	627	17	28	39	1,208	2	1
Talladega	Talladega	2,154	288	2,640	6,634	891	616	18	52	393	2,449	11	126
Tallapoosa	Dadeville	4,603	273	2,640	5,067	856	577	31	35	172	380	0	232
Tuscaloosa	Tuscaloosa	4,158	465	5,579	10,647	1,283	531	42	74	90	677	4	0
Walker	Jasper	1,326	523	5,916	10,997	1,089	803	0	22	7	982	0	1
Washington	Chatom	1,864	106	1,405	2,837	359	167	3	24	56	124	0	0
Wilcox	Camden	1,864	194	2,551	4,609	660							
Winston	Double Springs	1,065	120	1,604	2,689	259							

ARIZONA.

County	Place											
Apache	St. Johns	478	55	640	1,173	149	175	21	1	39	215	9	0
Cochise	Tombstone	6,830	278	9,288	16,396	1,472	161		74	617	1,515	12	19
Coconino	Flagstaff	1,455	85	1,861	3,401	356	360	0	34	84	258	10	4
Gila	Globe	5,454	269	5,730	11,453	1,078	711	43	80	400	1,292	5	13

APPENDIX TABLES.

Appendix Table 100-A.—*Principal statistical data, by local boards*—Continued.

ARIZONA—Continued.

Local board.	Post-office address.	Registration.				Induction. Accepted at camp.	Physical groups.			Disqualified.	Deferments.		
		June 5, 1917.	June and August, 1918.	Sept. 12, 1918.	Total.		General service.	Remediables.	Limited service.		Dependency.	Agricultural.	Industrial.
Graham	Safford	777	70	1,045	1,892	196	104	8	11	128	330	6	2
Greenlee	Clifton	3,583	123	3,125	6,831	418	365	11	28	50	444	7	6
Maricopa	Phoenix	5,438	501	10,781	16,720	1,608	1,018	45	182	709	1,768	72	4
Mohave	Kingman	1,153	45	962	2,160	292	178	2	66	71	269	4	5
Navajo	Holbrook	976	86	1,336	2,398	289	406	6	6	10	340	8	0
Pima	Tucson	3,491	290	5,239	9,020	731	418	6	23	278	750	50	42
Pinal	Florence	2,902	111	4,016	7,029	305	135	2	35	59	336	1	5
Santa Cruz	Nogales	1,006	42	1,624	2,672	170	104	1	29	41	189	3	0
Yavapai	Prescott	3,509	165	5,933	9,607	1,047	564	18	120	642	654	4	8
Yuma	Yuma	1,256	89	2,213	3,558	406	242	3	49	111	294	10	5

ARKANSAS.

Local board.	Post-office address.	Registration.				Induction. Accepted at camp.	Physical groups.			Disqualified.	Deferments.		
		June 5, 1917.	June and August, 1918.	Sept. 12, 1918.	Total.		General service.	Remediables.	Limited service.		Dependency.	Agricultural.	Industrial.
Arkansas	Stuttgart	2,048	267	2,740	5,055	800	784	0	125	125	1,003	13	5
Ashley	Hamburg	2,215	234	2,724	5,173	943	831	19	175	89	790	11	4
Baxter	Mountain Home	799	93	1,082	1,974	269	255	5	24	79	458	4	0
Benton	Bentonville	2,205	231	3,569	6,005	664	656	47	41	34	973	19	4
Boone	Harrison	1,244	133	1,770	3,147	299	324	3	19	83	817	38	16
Bradley	Warren	1,392	141	1,709	3,242	493	537	0	57	120	765	15	2
Calhoun	Hampton	991	102	1,343	2,436	292	293	54	10	113	578	2	0
Carroll	Berryville	1,170	157	1,907	3,234	292	331	5	58	72	741	14	0
Chicot	Lake Village	1,747	168	2,346	4,261	685	773	18	90	3	632	1	1
Clark	Arkadelphia	2,231	237	2,708	5,176	902	1,112	35	132	62	1,111	23	
Clay	Piggott	2,332	243	3,042	5,617	668	635		22	13	73		
Cleburne	Heber Springs	1,004	149	2,284	5,437	350	343	0	11	103	650	1	0
Cleveland	Rison	1,071	171	1,383	2,625	407	397		89	57	2,028	2	0
Columbia	Magnolia	2,315	230	2,583	6,158	727	501	1	11	8	31		
Conway	Morrilton	1,983	237	2,435	4,535	556	738	22	36	192	1,174	1	0
Craighead	Jonesboro	8,146	313	4,225	7,884	916	578	247	46	168	1,695	7	3
Crawford	Van Buren	2,049	209	2,774	5,032	619	578	2	18	44	1,303	1	0
Crittenden	Marion	3,333	235	4,011	7,579	1,007	1,053		74	928	1,498	1	1
Cross	Wynne	3,170	224	4,712		74			46	37	530	1	0
Dallas	Fordyce	2,175	154	1,640	2,909	488	463	8	34	48	616	2	6
Desha	Arkansas City	1,927	134	2,676	4,437	571	736	24	169	44	691	2	3
Drew	Monticello	1,907	196	2,386	4,479	590	592		86	142	800	0	0

County	Place												
Faulkner	Conway	2,409	277	2,752	5,438	677	669	21	77	274	1,438	37	1
Franklin	Ozark	1,580	203	2,023	3,806	400	519	33	31	35	985	18	3
Fulton	Salem	897	103	1,109	2,109	259	313	3	53	5	653	0	0
Garland	Hot Springs	2,032	208	2,466	5,229	735	662	19	38	155	137	0	2
Grant	Sheridan	955	103	1,147	2,205	312	281	16	8	41	552	0	1
Greene	Paragould	2,347	233	3,966	6,636	545	691	7	83	122	1,546	7	1
Hempstead	Hope	2,564	301	1,875	3,458	832	567		77	52	789	0	0
Hot Springs	Malvern	1,412	171	1,995	3,649	437	340	14	51	24	783	3	2
Howard	Nashville	1,472	182	2,696	5,006	472	475	0	16	94	716	3	1
Independence	Batesville	2,060	250	1,528	2,744	869	679	2	57	238	1,173	0	4
Izard	Melbourne	1,084	132	3,092	5,835	296	206	1	19	40	685	2	1
Jackson	Newport	2,476	267	2,406	4,477	650	257	16	224	268	359	1	0
Jefferson No. 1	Pine Bluff	1,848	163	3,135	8,011	796	447	8	81	29	83	0	3
Jefferson No. 2	do.	3,434	274	4,363	4,274	1,289	1,736	23	111	249	1,138	4	0
Johnson	Clarksville	1,678	226	1,674	3,109	482	506	0	134	54	1,047	1	5
Lafayette	Lewisville	1,273	162	2,400	4,593	549	525	4	51	87	660	0	0
Lawrence	Walnut Ridge	1,993	200	2,867	6,035	612	542	33	112	122	1,230	4	5
Lee	Marianna	2,906	255	2,067	3,198	1,058	1,182	39	84	195	1,153	5	0
Lincoln	Star City	1,845	186	1,768	8,209	543	648		31	44	563	0	0
Little River	Ashdown	1,257	173	8,805	8,200	402	420	26	89	108	766	2	0
Little Rock No. 1	Courthouse, Little Rock	2,885	252	5,338	5,129	1,021	515	14	55	279	1,031	0	0
Little Rock No. 2	714 Southern Trust Building	2,615	256	2,886	6,783	966	880	3	118	50	1,205	1	22
Logan	Paris	1,989	254	8,680	2,740	490	498	25	110	49	359	4	18
Lonoke	Lonoke	2,870	233	1,389	2,196	897	831	6	17	53	1,692	3	2
Madison	Huntsville	1,187	164	1,191	1,607	310	6	5	76	116	831	2	0
Marion	Yellville	909	96	1,607	11,509	210	218	5	34	52	670	1	1
Miller	Texarkana	1,896	225	5,964	4,549	598	560	23	44	87	1,172	10	0
Mississippi	Blytheville	5,070	485	2,492	2,309	1,502	1,316	44	58	84	1,774	3	8
Monroe	Clarendon	1,859	198	1,228	4,036	715	840	0	19	99	938	11	0
Montgomery	Mount Ida	941	140	2,135	2,137	274	237	2		40	538	3	18
Nevada	Prescott	1,696	205	1,180	4,369	471	421	3	11	74	1,142	42	0
Newton	Jasper	867	90	2,235	2,153	226			7			3	0
Ouachita	County Courthouse, Camden	1,900	234	1,108	11,291	693	869	0	59	137	1,008	1	4
Perry	Perryville	897	88	6,619	2,677	264	46	2	21	6	25		2
Phillips	Helena	5,251	421	1,398	5,783	1,681	2,180	4	78	264	3,194	10	0
Pike	Murfreesboro	1,164	115	1,751	3,139	326	221		57	142	964	1	4
Poinsett	Harrisburg	2,398	204	2,972	5,436	834	823	11	81	131	1,015	7	2
Polk	Mena	1,249	139	1,805	3,450	423	387	21	44	19	569	0	3
Pope	Russellville	2,207	257	3,267	5,756	601	681	24	49	152	1,415	1	0
Prairie	Des Arc	1,528	117	2,087	3,637	560	524	3	51	62	809	29	0
Pulaski No. 1	Courthouse, Little Rock	2,262	227	1,979	3,724	716	896	2	14	163	1,288	11	0
Pulaski No. 2	North Little Rock	1,419	131	3,407	6,551	495	600	17	14	77	600	1	22
Randolph	Pocahontas	1,553	192	1,855	3,503	479	489		33	134	918	2	0
St. Frances	Forrest City	2,910	234	1,427	2,701	927	712	5	14	68	2,702	2	2
Saline	Benton	1,480	168	1,633	2,998	509	410	45	82	12	788	1	0
Scott	Waldron	1,148	128	3,408	6,011	353	252	2	39	58	522	0	2
Searcy	Marshall	1,205	100	2,955	5,187	302	316	34		148	796	5	0
Sebastian No. 1	Fort Smith	2,317	226	1,848	3,338	883	320	6	20	48	1,060	5	1
Sebastian No. 2	Greenwood	1,994	238	1,165	2,152	585	661	3	18	53	1,270	21	7
Sevier	De Queen	1,307	183	976	1,820	469		3		13	11		16
Sharp	Eveningshade	884	103			310	290	67	20	86	491	5	0
Stone	Mountain View	755	89			258	177		18	5	409	0	0

APPENDIX TABLE 100-A.—*Principal statistical data, by local boards*—Continued.

ARKANSAS—Continued.

Local board.	Post-office address.	Registration.				Induction.	Physical groups.				Deferments.		
		June 5, 1917.	June and August, 1918.	Sept. 12, 1918.	Total.	Accepted at camp.	General service.	Remediables.	Limited service.	Disqualified.	Dependency.	Agricultural.	Industrial.
Union	El Dorado	2,586	277	3,262	6,125	875	177		16	109	1,463	13	6
Van Buren	Clinton	1,168	129	1,447	2,744	428	301	13	28	25	808	60	3
Washington	Fayetteville	2,752	289	3,854	6,895	780	879		64	122	1,106	84	15
White	Searcy	2,922	337	3,710	6,969	1,036	1,306		58	62	958	0	0
Woodruff	Augusta	2,219	213	2,470	4,902	626	735	12	66	149	1,042	3	0
Yell	Danville	1,971	224	2,748	4,943	545	335	0	28	76		70	26

CALIFORNIA.

Local board.	Post-office address.	Registration.				Induction.	Physical groups.				Deferments.		
		June 5, 1917.	June and August, 1918.	Sept. 12, 1918.	Total.	Accepted at camp.	General service.	Remediables.	Limited service.	Disqualified.	Dependency.	Agricultural.	Industrial.
Alameda No. 1	1434 Park Street, Alameda	2,151	169	3,874	6,194	402	308	16	79	119	840	34	134
Alameda No. 2	Haywards	2,841	237	4,370	7,448	591	476	21	105	124	674	241	46
Alameda No. 3	Emeryville Town Hall, Emeryville	605	35	1,360	2,000	104	86	1	13		228	4	16
Alpine	Markleville	41	3	45	89	9	10	0	1	2	6	0	0
Amador	Jackson	1,117	61	1,217	2,395	309	215	8	60	55	235	2	6
BERKELEY No. 1	304 Telegraph Avenue, South Berkeley	2,061	151	3,490	5,702	578	295	8	88	148	811	5	74
BERKELEY No. 2	2089 Allston Way, Berkeley	2,377	208	3,440	5,995	703	528	6	159	100	662	18	50
Butte	Chico	2,366	194	4,089	6,649	617	23	21	41	22	708	40	21
Calaveras	San Andreas	772	47	903	1,812	225	177	10	32	16	205	23	3
Colusa	Colusa	955	77	1,552	2,584	309	219	9	47	25	247	14	4
Contra Costa No. 1	Martinez	3,600	234	5,890	9,724	915	804	8	98	92	790	34	15
Contra Costa No. 2	Richmond	2,887	163	5,238	8,288	684	514	9	86	51	761	7	54
Del Norte	Cresent City	291	14	455	760	96	118	5	143	30	77	16	1
El Dorado	Placerville	711	63	1,091	1,985	175	111		28	104	153	24	4
FRESNO	209 Holland Building,...	3,784	329	8,011	12,124	884	658	28	198	228	1,301	8	19
Fresno No. 1	308 Cory Building, Fresno	4,167	292	6,106	10,565	1,014	646	23	184	193	1,475	59	20
Fresno No. 2	do.	935	263	1,825	2,850	898	530	24	155	199	1,063	46	20
Glenn	Willows		90			264	185	43	20	25	322	52	6
Humboldt	Federal Building, Eureka	3,788	311	6,148	10,247	1,039	693	37	229	184	1,073	86	25
Imperial	El Centro	6,020	385	7,166	13,571	1,532	933	46	261	333	1,242	131	23
Inyo	Bishop	931	60	1,372	2,372	279	186	8	37	39	241	9	18
Kern No. 1	do.	3,494	218	4,738	8,450	911	721	3	153	126	917	20	5
Kern No. 2	Bakersfield	3,631	198	5,170	8,994	1,019	1,301	1	113	277	1,356	28	50
Kings	Courthouse, Hanford	2,327	183	3,644	6,164	1,023	529	1	113	128	668	60	7
Lake	Lakeport	436	36	634		152	142	6	11	22	77	15	2
Lassen	Susanville	1,157	60	1,501	2,718	275	272	15	68	3	301	10	1
LOS ANGELES No. 1	Branch City Hall, Van Nuys	778	37	1,157	1,972	162	83	0	23	53	221	21	2

Precinct / County	Address												
							3	**1**	**5**	**18**	**80**	**2**	
LOS ANGELES No. 2	7530 Mr Avenue, Palms	243	19	357	619	79	263	14	46	134	644	0	15
LOS ANGELES No. 3	Branch City Hall, San Pedro	1,589	211	4,631	6,431	320	175	5	57	125	776	0	15
LOS ANGELES No. 4	5829 — Ave.	1,146	76	2,075	3,297	214	542		76	125	1,119	6	7
LOS ANGELES No. 5	4726 South Park Avenue	1,374	139	2,510	4,023	305	232	15	99	147	876	1	14
LOS ANGELES No. 6	1201 West Forty-eighth Street, Library Building	1,898	119	3,161	5,178	447	307	10	111	143	99	2	14
LOS ANGELES No. 7	4304 — Avenue	1,617	161	2,624	4,402	377	285	11	94	175	610	5	15
LOS ANGELES No. 8	State — Building, Exposition Park	1,758	160	3,034	4,108	461	372	8	122	371	980	6	11
LOS ANGELES No. 9	3 Berkeley Square	1,487	137	2,481	6,643	387	1,188	29	285	117	1,691	1	41
LOS ANGELES No. 10	1904 South Main Street	2,500	215	3,928	11,148	593	141	10	112	1	66	0	17
LOS ANGELES No. 11	Northwest — Sentons and Piero Streets	4,573	331	6,244	4,880	1,152	555	3	79	88	510	1	
LOS ANGELES No. 12	Corner Pico and El — Streets	1,696	100	2,197	3,263	468	516	14	147	29	759	0	3
LOS ANGELES No. 13	601 West Seventh Street	998	68	3,075	4,822	260	482	35	211	274	1,317	13	22
LOS ANGELES No. 14	6422 Hollywood —	1,661	128	3,033	10,975	467	2,134	6	355	1,297	1,342	16	27
LOS ANGELES No. 15	Echo Park	4,199	331	6,445	14,669	778	522	160	400	178	1,60	19	70
LOS ANGELES No. 16	2015 East First Street	5,610	399	8,660	21,668	902	338	13	130	401	2,174	9	368
LOS ANGELES No. 17	226 South Broadway	8,520	538	12,610	9,195	1,925	346	9	135	157	2,121	36	105
LOS ANGELES No. 18	112 North Workman	3,424	244	5,527	9,137	724	254	0	88	186	70	6	25
Los Angeles No. 1	201 — Bank Building, Long Beach	2,823	339	5,975	6,010	559	337	7	85	145	949	48	20
Los Angeles No. 2	Pomona	2,414	192	3,414	6,299	68	586	5	141	243	682	21	14
Los Angeles No. 3	Tower Room, City Hall, Santa Monica	1,708	130	3,911	5,579	545	291		90	185	1,958	21	31
Los Angeles No. 4	City Hall, Redondo Beach	4,383	141	3,730	13,081	393	239	13	66	102	995		11
Los Angeles No. 5	City Hall, Huntington Park	2,570	280	8,418	7,329	705		35			835		12
Los Angeles No. 6	City Hall, Alhambra	1,950	151	4,608	5,540	571							
Los Angeles No. 7	1015 West Broadway, Glendale	485	117	525	1,033	437					406		6
Los Angeles No. 8	Acton	1,259	23	1,843	3,802	123	187	2	58	75	3	34	
Madera	Madera	2,289	100	3,386	5,794	341	16		90	298	675	1	0
Marin	San Rafael	616	119	502	1,155	463	814	6	77	135	712	29	15
Mariposa	Mariposa	2,473	37	3,692	6,417	185	287	7	47	5	269	126	9
Mendocino	Ukiah	2,811	252	3,553	6,539	710	107	1	14	22	35	21	4
Merced	Merced	608	175	788	1,444	548	66	11	94	71	535	2	2
Modoc	Alturas	256	48	209	484	153	550	4	64	120	381	112	26
Mono	Bridgeport	2,377	19	4,456	7,013	65	417	12	94	167	360	36	7
Monterey	Salinas	1,605	180	5,281	7,024	750	338	17	67	190	910	1	3
Napa	—, Napa	1,302	138	1,847	3,240	463	454	10	64	164	1,001	0	126
Nevada	Nevada City	2,895	91	5,203	8,362	375	187	5	61	157	840	3	61
OAKLAND No. 1	City Hall	2,233	264	4,101	6,479	537	197	21	71	351	624	14	74
OAKLAND No. 2	702 City Hall	1,953	145	4,059	6,138	426	63	9	181	183	879	4	41
OAKLAND No. 3	320 City Hall	1,914	124	4,000	6,045	436	392	8	91	351	1,119	1	186
OAKLAND No. 4	301 City Hall	3,649	131	7,464	11,447	99	53	5	53	183	951	8	34
OAKLAND No. 5	318 City Hall	2,299	34	4,242	6,775	651	188	21	120	83	838	58	53
OAKLAND No. 6	108 City Hall	1,811	234	3,935	5,898	461	351	9	99	53	833	4	7
OAKLAND No. 7	7307 East Fourteenth Street	2,290	152	3,528	5,993	361	295	8	96	74	498	10	48
Orange No. 1	Courthouse, Santa Ana	2,478	175	4,068	6,712	538	174	5	73	130	540	4	11
Orange No. 2	Fullerton	1,282	166	1,800	3,170	358	146	18	75	120	553	5	0
PASADENA No. 1	608 Chamber of Commerce Building	1,309	88	2,005	3,431	323	196	1	44	171	222	6	40
PASADENA No. 2	30 North Raymond Avenue	1,935	117	2,884	4,935	393	147	2	44	36	90		18
Placer	Auburn	1,175	116	1,562	2,781	258	370	4	79	126	694	76	2
Plumas	Quincy	2,019	44	2,513	2,641	394	480	10	66	129	1,110	10	16
Riverside No. 1	Courthouse, Riverside	2,156	109	3,196	4,491	477	477	8		244			61
Riverside No. 2	do	2,618	93	4,628	7,423	721	613	11		291	762		76
SACRAMENTO No. 1	107 State Capitol Building	2,618	177	4,628	7,423	721		14					
SACRAMENTO No. 2	California Trust Building	4,088	283	7,830	12,201	892		43	181			1	

APPENDIX TABLE 100-A.—*Principal statistical data, by local boards*—Continued.

CALIFORNIA—Continued.

Local board.	Post-office address.	Registration: June 5, 1917.	Registration: June and August, 1918.	Registration: Sept. 12, 1918.	Registration: Total.	Induction: Accepted at camp.	Physical groups: General service.	Physical groups: Remediables.	Physical groups: Limited service.	Physical groups: Disqualified.	Deferments: Dependency.	Deferments: Agricultural.	Deferments: Industrial.
Sacramento	202 Courthouse, Sacramento	2,882	205	4,640	7,727	502	332	12	69	78	545	66	19
San Benito	Hollister	986	66	1,611	2,663	273	171	2	15	46	253	0	0
San Bernardino No. 1	Courthouse, San Bernardino	3,933	253	5,388	9,574	745	418	27	149	283	1,372	4	1
San Bernardino No. 2	City Hall, Redlands	1,727	99	2,507	4,333	436	42	13	44	150	508	4	2
San Bernardino No. 3	Barstow	1,676	68	1,994	3,738	356	284		73	21	433	1	2
San Diego	244 Federal Building	3,138	167	3,562	5,603	562	260	3	101	171	781	5	10
San Diego No. 2	239 Federal Building	2,505	288	5,655	9,081	789	651	34	156	266	985	6	36
San Diego	Courthouse, San Diego	3,254	203	4,030	6,738	623	323	4	88	320	769	96	21
San Joaquin	Farmers & Merchants Bank, Stockton	2,953	296	6,819	10,369	705	675	5	54	397	1,107	151	102
San Jose	Twohy Building, San Jose	1,970	231	4,633	7,817	731	782	18	127	103	921	5	20
San Luis Obispo	San Luis Obispo	3,789	167	2,946	5,083	518	450		55	96	576	1	0
San Mateo	San Mateo	6,877	244	6,250	10,283	813	420	25	222	150	895	30	55
San Francisco No. 1	1245 Market Street	2,229	428	12,296	19,591	1,392	1,217	12	244	593	687	3	216
San Francisco No. 2	1676 Newcomb Avenue	3,206	202	4,257	8,781	487	321	5	142	84	868	7	120
San Francisco No. 3	State Armory	2,646	206	5,367	7,546	627	68	2	5	21	33		9
San Francisco No. 4	85 Cerritas Avenue	2,157	181	4,719	10,729	549	480	24	118	203	1,116	3	79
San Francisco No. 5	1284 Valencia Street	3,719	313	5,259	10,293	789	558	4	198	134	1,129	2	79
San Francisco No. 6	216 Scott Street	2,455	259	6,315	10,293	902	488	26	202	291	1,332	0	130
San Francisco No. 7	1411 Ninth Avenue	2,710	145	4,486	7,098	614	144	0	88		1,008	2	46
San Francisco No. 8	Richmond Police Station	4,387	203	5,644	8,557	760	332	18	118	6	1,114	7	47
San Francisco No. 9	State Armory	2,533	264	6,146	11,986	791	855	0	307	252	1,147	2	50
San Francisco No. 10	do.	5,702	256	7,343	6,602	889	227	23	143	474	847	0	10
San Francisco No. 11	250 Sansone Street	12,245	162	3,907	15,442	662	807	55	239	142	1,500	8	109
San Francisco No. 12	City Hall (236)	4,143	355	9,385	29,933	1,378	1,462	52	175	227	1,120	15	64
San Francisco No. 13	Hall of Justice	2,230	884	16,904	6,235	1,395	669	1	298	855	1,223	77	34
Santa Barbara	Santa Barbara	2,408	286	6,628	6,496	1,165	343	3	76	195	444	27	40
Santa Clara No. 1	Second floor, Twohy Building, San Jose	2,101	204	3,801	5,487	635	36		133	220	505	19	2
Santa Clara No. 2	Twohy Building, San Jose	2,017	181	3,907	4,989	605	510	19	96	284	528	45	7
Santa Cruz	Santa Cruz	270	139	3,331	691	537	386	29	46	159	543	33	13
Shasta	Redding	2,804	14	2,792	10,128	545	96	0	7	143	77	27	20
Sierra	Downieville	3,454	192	363	5,612	102	527	12	115	27	910	30	76
Siskiyou	Siskiyou	2,080	373	3,666	4,730	688	670	8	158	176	1,018	29	14
Solano	Fairfield	1,821	168	6,301	10,238	854	455	31	96	121	652	154	6
Sonoma No. 1	Sebastopol	3,972	135	3,364	15,089	573	323	19	38	15	1,491	22	2
Sonoma No. 2	Santa Rosa	1,821	297	2,774	2,431	433	653	21	45	305	1,230	105	17
Stanislau	Modesto		367	5,969		1,064	573	59	306	250	1,406	18	118
Stockton	Belding Building	5,390	68	9,382		1,049	196	6	49	359	282	41	3
Sutter	Yuba City	883		1,500		234				56			

County	Place												
Tehama	Red Bluff	1,60	85	1,605	2,720	271	278	22	36	18	416	35	21
Trinity	Weaverville	309	14	342	665	115	125	0	21	18	80	8	3
Tulare No. 1	Visalia	3,402	275	5,597	9,274	85	548	15	122	148	888	76	13
Tulare No. 2	Lindsay	2,182	55	2,417	4,719	421	336	13	65	116	754	54	37
Tuolumne	Sonora	1,167	210	1,445	2,667	84	220	0	47	33	249	12	8
Ventura	County Courthouse, Ventura	3,005	143	5,043	8,258	708	319	19	120	148	908	62	8
Yolo	Woodland	1,557	76	2,723	4,423	418	339	20	76	11	409	44	12
Yuba	Marysville	1,259		2,134	3,479	56	43	2	4		1		1

COLORADO.

County	Place												
Adams	Brighton	1,139	131	1,897	3,167	327	26	14	9	109	429	128	9
Alamosa	Alamosa	46	39	692	1,227	143	149		11	22	265	22	2
Arapahoe	Littleton	982	100	78	2,760	270	220	12	42	116	390	52	8
Archuleta	Pagosa Springs	313	34	429	776	109	126		14	7	182	0	0
Baca	Springfield	1,094	92	1,118	2,277	470	312		71	75	725	40	1
Bent	Las Animas	85	65	1,118	7,50	293	230		17	85	449	48	3
Boulder	Boulder	2,681	290	4,085	2,026	773	538	7	97	240	1,149	114	30
Chaffee	Salida	789	68	1,169	835	240	248	20	83	30	250	12	4
Cheyenne	Cheyenne Wells	326	25	484	835	97	67	11	18	23	31	22	4
Clear Creek	Georgetown	338	22	523	883	135	130	11	22	24	108	1	
Colorado Springs	City Hall, Colorado Springs	2,102	183	3,275	5,560	583	364	12	99	123	862	23	132
Conejos	Conejos	704	63	851	1,618	178		4	6	42	343	20	2
Costilla	San Luis	415	45	506	966	85	88		10	22	460	6	1
Crowley	Ordway	594	46	850	1,490	169	177		19	40	221	13	2
Custer	Silver Cliff	192	20	303	515	67	50		7	20	79	23	1
Delta	Delta	977	111	1,656	2,744	371	441	7	21	104	432	19	1
Denver No. 1	3607 West Thirty-second Avenue	1,704	130	2,851	4,685	468	376	5	27	145	97	8	19
Denver No. 2	821 West Eighth Avenue	2,345	240	3,667	6,252	624	544	14	61	212	1,138	4	52
Denver No. 3	289 South Broadway	1,858	170	2,943	4,971	455	338	25	29	272	99	3	32
Denver No. 4	Room 31, Courthouse	1,528	124	2,654	4,306	432	251		77	207	715	4	14
Denver No. 5	Capitol Building	1,343	109	2,457	3,909	460	252	18	50	246	504	6	14
Denver No. 6	738 First National Bank	1,699	114	2,396	4,209	481	375		59	266	232	12	26
Denver No. 7	203 City Hall	3,300	242	5,321	8,863	88	28	42	133	528	773	9	38
Denver No. 8	622 Majestic Building	2,371	228	3,904	6,503	69	86	14	91	261	1,004	2	44
Denver No. 9	203 City Hall	2,583	277	3,990	6,850	713	679	28	43	199	1,400	8	78
Dolores	Rico	126	4	167	297	35							
Douglas	Castle Rock	342	34	492	868	91	81	4	21	28	143	47	7
Eagle	Red Cliff	437	40	613	1,090	167	113	8	15	40	35	24	4
Elbert	Kiowa	658	88	949	1,695	214	237	9	8	85	256	86	
El Paso	Courthouse, Colorado Springs	1,102	101	1,772	2,975	283	252	10	85	177	449	78	5
Fremont	Canon City	1,265	148	2,067	3,480	350	301	9	45	23	9	14	21
Garfield	Glenwood Springs	894	84	1,296	2,274	295	246		30	58	184	13	3
Gilpin	Central City	183	15	256	454	62	1		5	35	60		1
Grand	Kremmling	382	26	555	963	126	84	2	11	24	105	9	10
Gunnison	Gunnison	617	45	885	1,547	218	120	3	30	41	183	27	16
Hinsdale	Lake City	43	3	83	129	17	12				20	1	
Huerfano	Walsenburg	1,678	168	2,578	4,424	86	288	96	39	187	712	29	11
Jackson	Walden	199	13	247	439	0.69	28	1	4	11	80	39	1
Jefferson	Golden	1,144	102	1,813	3,59	307	250	7	18	52	409	106	13

APPENDIX TABLE 100-A.—*Principal statistical data, by local boards*—Continued.

COLORADO—Continued.

Local board.	Post-office address.	Registration.				Induction.	Physical groups.				Deferments.		
		June 5, 1917.	June and August 1918.	Sept. 12, 1918.	Total.	Accepted at camp.	General service.	Remediables.	Limited service.	Disqualified.	Dependency.	Agricultural.	Industrial.
Kiowa	Eads	442	26	568	1,036	126	83		10	46	226	16	
Kit Carson	Burlington	707	76	1,160	1,913	260	230	1	16	18	342	20	1
Lake	Leadville	1,211	90	1,469	2,770	380	288	6	27	105	394	1	8
La Plata	Durango	991	100	1,442	2,533	393	341	12	28	32	364	27	12
Larimer	Fort Collins	2,187	266	3,451	5,904	727	543	3	41	176	992	64	
Las Animas	Trinidad	4,471	299	5,953	10,723	1,110	925	5	90	250	1,575	86	91
Lincoln	Hugo	871	62	1,154	2,087	270	182	6	22	30	415	151	7
Logan	Sterling	1,804	170	2,707	4,681	490	512		19	170	760	67	23
Mesa	Grand Junction	1,573	194	2,694	4,461	514	370	9	45	121	673		8
Mineral	Creede	67	10	153	230	23	42		5		14		
Moffat	Craig	636	49	756	1,441	230	208	15	21	50	63	22	2
Montezuma	Cortez	536	50	754	1,340	162	224	3	11	58	231	7	1
Montrose	Montrose	1,010	117	1,610	2,737	399	446	4	17	68	440	77	2
Morgan	Fort Morgan	1,421	152	2,165	3,738	372	322		39	118	560	97	9
Otero	La Junta	2,006	154	3,275	5,435	402	370	11	14	166	881	62	14
Ouray	Ouray	304	25	463	792	122	89		25	5	85	10	
Park	Fairplay	240	22	315	577	95	64	5	5	13	90	10	3
Phillips	Holyoke	398	77	772	1,247	144	120		9	32	208	50	1
Pitkin	Aspen	278	33	432	743	102	19	1	3		3	1	
Prowers	Lamar	1,445	114	1,815	3,374	379	281		40	93	418	1	
PUEBLO No. 1	City Hall	1,906	145	2,950	5,001	534	577	6	95	211	792	5	18
PUEBLO No. 2	302 Federal Building	2,912	189	3,981	7,082	661	370	15	104	161	909	1	20
Pueblo	County Courthouse, Pueblo	1,297	141	1,963	3,401	305	233	15	15	95	470	47	8
Rio Blanco	Meeker	307	31	427	765	112	87	4	15	17	128	27	
Rio Grande	Del Norte	614	73	1,004	1,691	177	105		13	42	315	53	9
Routt	Steamboat Springs	1,022	79	1,530	2,631	255	395	1	22	83	365	26	
Saguache	Saguache	417	43	636	1,096	131	134	2	13	46	210	29	4
San Juan	Silverton	382	23	524	929	118	7	2	6	38	59	0	3
San Miguel	Telluride	791	57	942	1,790	209	200		29	49	240	4	1
Sedgwick	Julesburg	358	37	621	1,016	108	55	8	21	10	149	46	2
Summit	Breckenridge	195	17	395	607	55	82		15	14	84	7	2
Teller	Cripple Creek	1,013	68	1,069	2,150	304	208		37	65	450	3	4
Washington	Akron	1,170	114	1,520	2,804	252	27	15	11	204	677	142	4
Weld No. 1	County Courthouse, Greeley	3,491	311	4,905	8,797	854	694		13		1,246	259	18
Weld No. 2	Eaton	2,131	88	2,909	5,285	613	14	7	35	88	929	156	22
Yuma	Wray	1,291	168	1,783	3,226	345	886	3	22	91	733	138	7

CONNECTICUT.

Precinct	Polling place											
BRIDGEPORT No. 1	309 Old Building, 1188 Main Street	5,587	289	5,624	11,500	1,065	611	59	196	85	886	2	196
BRIDGEPORT No. 2	93 Broad Street	3,086	256	3,279	6,621	741	421	38	169	100	852	9	108
BRIDGEPORT No. 3	886 Main Street	4,648	314	4,866	9,828	1,024	656	21	235	268	1,310	24	115
BRIDGEPORT No. 4	83 Fairfield Avenue	4,773	285	4,297	9,355	968	599	52	190	241	1,204	2	133
BRIDGEPORT No. 5	333 East Main Street	4,356	262	4,245	8,863	794	632	38	106	1,410	694		157
BRIDGEPORT No. 6	Room 209, 886 Main Street	3,980	284	3,942	8,206	809	544	27	126	235	283	4	200
HARTFORD No. 1	Old Halls of Record, 114 Pearl Street	5,008	374	6,103	11,485	1,148	812	54	212	431	1,341	0	211
HARTFORD No. 2	do	6,089	469	7,214	11,772	1,493	1,401	60	234	216	1,889	4	204
HARTFORD No. 3	do	6,059	425	7,160	13,644	1,210	56	32	190	306	1,614	0	166
NEW BRITAIN No. 1	Room 408, City Hall Building	3,849	244	3,949	8,042	862	861	41	111	238	1,253	2	81
NEW BRITAIN No. 2	Room 201, City Hall Building	3,448	233	3,985	7,666	834	661	27	180	129	892	4	109
NEW HAVEN No. 1	Y. M. C. A. Building, 152 Temple Street	3,629	197	3,629	6,455	541	426	21	79	65	505	7	167
NEW HAVEN No. 2	County Courthouse	4,006	283	4,275	8,564	760	385	32	85	16	20	0	25
NEW HAVEN No. 3	224 Orange Street	4,219	364	5,664	10,247	744	515	37	119	185	875	0	246
NEW HAVEN No. 4	185 Church Street	2,339	202	2,918	5,459	437	338	16	105	153	928	1	258
NEW HAVEN No. 5	106 Elm Street	3,406	310	4,355	8,071	724	503	38	138	213	939	2	225
NEW HAVEN No. 6	Room 5, Wright Hall, corner Elm and High Streets	2,838	305	3,827	6,970	709	284	5	106	143	1,057		418
STAMFORD	City Hall	4,503	320	5,851	10,674	1,076	689	27	121	220	503	1	64
WATERBURY No. 1	do	6,132	534	6,708	13,374	891	618	84	179	133	1,455	5	413
WATERBURY No. 2	111 West Main Street	6,909	247	4,008	15,172	581	235	31	122	20	736	2	12
WATERBURY No. 3	County Courthouse	4,267	523	7,740	10,255	1,092	32	29	105	205	1,341	3	827
Hartford No. 1	Wells Hall, East Hartford	5,372	328	5,660	12,598	1,208	985	30	182	355	1,450	33	119
Hartford No. 2	Plainville	3,942	349	5,127	9,418	1,217	864	269	314	61	1,667	64	135
Hartford No. 3	82 Main Street, Thomsonville	3,484	267	4,319	8,924	907	564	64	274	184	1,458	72	51
New Haven No. 4	Branford	3,612	265	2,677	8,196	545	533	23	102	184	1,229	118	195
New Haven No. 5	Meriden	2,295	180	3,752	8,152	715	427	37	172	264	1,248	13	204
New Haven No. 7	Naugatuck	2,781	197	6,820	5,152	502	246	15	81	110	708	61	164
New Haven No. 8	Milford	6,319	404	6,359	6,730	1,169	957	23	102	122	1,155	20	128
New London No. 9	Ansonia	3,397	313	4,103	13,543	593	582	30	178	288	408	34	180
New London No. 10	Municipal Building, New London	3,958	247	4,356	9,069	559	597		70	354	1,325	3	28
New London No. 11	Norwich	2,856	291	3,727	7,308	736	377	26	229	70	739	12	59
Fairfield No. 12	217 Plant Building, New London	2,640	357	4,501	7,503	666	496	23	168	240	1,001	132	91
Fairfield No. 13	Bethel	4,289	273	2,842	10,817	899	574	23	172	224	1,144	42	140
Fairfield No. 14	Courthouse, Bridgeport	3,377	134	2,911	5,211	845	550	28	152	303	1,598	58	39
Fairfield No. 15	Norwalk	3,235	198	3,102	5,083	472	615	51	69	298	1,228	8	16
Windham No. 16	Greenwich	1,974	218	5,648	5,648	455	17	17	61	248	778	8	19
No. 17	Putnam	2,328	68	3,102	8,131	498	347	28	101	78	316	12	114
Litchfield No. 18	Courthouse, Willimantic	3,601	307	4,225	4,350	708	654	63	68	222	1,072	90	79
Litchfield No. 19	Town Clerk's Office, Torrington	1,728	142	3,189	4,350	543	446	64	105	78	620	32	51
Litchfield No. 20	Canaan	2,281	196	2,480	5,666	554	308	30	90	46	730	77	39
Middlesex No. 21	Town Clerk's Office, New Milford	2,168	180	3,189	5,206	554	475	22	100	202	680	49	129
Middlesex No. 22	Municipal Building, Middletown	1,707	137	2,858	4,220	418	232	34	103	35	570	30	48
Tolland No. 23	Deep River	2,053	218	2,376	5,464	611	443	13	96	130	722	70	29
	Rockville			3,193				19				32	

APPENDIX TABLE 100-A.—*Principal statistical data, by local boards*—Continued.

DELAWARE.

Local board.	Post-office address.	Registration.				Induction.	Physical groups.				Deferments.		
		June 5, 1917.	June and August, 1918.	Sept. 12, 1918.	Total.	Accepted at camp.	General service.	Remediables.	Limited service.	Disqualified.	Dependency.	Agricultural.	Industrial.
Kent	314 South State Street, Dover	2,198	261	3,495	5,954	389	447	3	46	84	1,058	581	49
New Castle	Purnell Hall, Newark	2,564	377	5,480	9,421	918	850		263	160	1,406	405	79
Sussex	County Building, Georgetown	3,538	397	5,283	9,218	650	426		132	110	751	144	19
Wilmington No. 1	Old Courthouse, Tenth and Market Streets	3,346	336	5,268	7,950	938	760	11	255	215	1,161	7	253
Wilmington No. 2	do	3,038	319	4,010	7,367	756	757	8	186	159	1,292	6	234
Wilmington No. 3	do	3,582	308	4,283	8,173	635	652	2	334	57	1,412	8	200
Wilmington No. 4	do	3,056	243	3,895	7,194	813	707		257	121	779	3	96

DISTRICT OF COLUMBIA.

Local board.	Post-office address.	June 5, 1917.	June and August, 1918.	Sept. 12, 1918.	Total.	Accepted at camp.	General service.	Remediables.	Limited service.	Disqualified.	Dependency.	Agricultural.	Industrial.
No. 1	Room 314, District Building, Washington	3,478	361	6,055	9,894	1,011	932	45	239	278	789		46
No. 2	Room 201, District Building, Washington	3,772	349	5,651	9,772	1,219	2,672	225	384		26	1	7
No. 3	City Post Office, Washington	2,816	290	4,337	7,443	1,065	1,005	14	55	242	722		21
No. 4	Room 405, District Building, Washington	2,775	319	4,417	7,511	924	727	28	45	267	1,062	1	43
No. 5	Room 426, District Building, Washington	3,217	336	5,171	8,724	848	714	24	126	10	1,204	3	85
No. 6	Room 427, District Building, Washington	3,711	327	5,725	9,763	935	536	25	175	187	1,726	1	36
No. 7	Room 115, District Building, Washington	1,949	190	3,234	5,373	648	1,371	27	103	67	791	4	10
No. 8	Room 5, District Building, Washington	3,770	407	5,834	10,011	1,238	634	40	155	246	1,378		15
No. 9	Room 112, District Building, Washington	2,619	193	4,594	7,406	857	183	26	132	38	920	4	53
No. 10	Room 421, District Building, Washington	3,284	315	5,825	9,424	826	634	15	83	18	1,436	9	54
No. 11	Room 428, District Building, Washington	2,081	182	2,777	5,040	438	296	21	33	96	971	6	49

FLORIDA.

Local board.	Post-office address.	June 5, 1917.	June and August, 1918.	Sept. 12, 1918.	Total.	Accepted at camp.	General service.	Remediables.	Limited service.	Disqualified.	Dependency.	Agricultural.	Industrial.
Alachua	Gainesville	2,789	321	3,809	6,919	983	966	24	54	161	1,288	49	18
Baker	Macclenny	479	55	631	1,165	151	157	1	9	37	32	1	0
Bay	Panama City	1,222	70	1,342	2,634	411	460	1	42	15	531	2	2
Bradford	Starke	1,256	106	1,599	2,961	315	259	7	55	76	730	6	0
Brevard	Titusville	797	56	948	1,801	274	259	9	32	16	309	2	3
Broward	Fort Lauderdale	712	41	656	1,409	165	178	11	34	85	177	1	1
Calhoun	Blountstown	755	72	870	1,697	207	199	5	26	45	395	0	0
Citrus	Inverness	504	66	701	1,271	177	85	3	11	27	134		1

County / Place												
Clay — Green Cove Springs	617	59	688	1,364	221	221	6	68	46	216	1	1
Columbia — Lake City	1,227	163	1,584	2,974	481	514	3	46	92	552	11	2
Dade — Miami	4,310	323	4,849	9,482	880	1,159	41	42	109	1,060	2	6
De Soto — Arcadia	2,275	180	3,074	5,529	797	1,438	8	6	98	636	1	1
Duval — 120 West Bay Street, Jacksonville	2,719	259	4,297	7,275	777	174	20	196	110	1,214	5	35
Escambia — Pensacola	3,632	335	5,531	9,498	868	149	34	7	23	61		1,450
Flagler — Bunnell				325	15	173	17			2	0	5
Franklin — Apalachicola	571	46	681	1,298	146	345	9	21	20	247	7	1
Gadsden — Quincy	1,592	144	2,061	3,797	345	392	1	295	6	848	2	1
Hamilton — Jasper	937	114	1,096	2,147	352	177	0	65	21	464	1	8
Hernando — Brooksville	494	36	640	1,170	180	425	5	40	34	183	0	5
Hillsborough — Courthouse, Tampa	3,134	209	4,471	7,874	814	205	3	220	80	712	6	4
Holmes — Bonifay	1,125	105	1,330	2,560	305	282	4	111	58	675	1	0
Jackson — Marianna	2,252	302	3,113	5,667	583	713		106	38	1,499	0	18
JACKSONVILLE No. 1 — Dyal-Upchurch Building	2,391	234	3,926	6,551	712	851	7	177	137	957	2	33
JACKSONVILLE No. 2 — 120 West Bay Street	3,273	154	3,641	7,068	950	1,191	25	349	253	983	11	10
JACKSONVILLE No. 3 — do	3,764	365	6,907	11,036	1,291	304	103	151	184	633	36	3
Jefferson — Monticello	917	110	1,202	2,229	257	319	4	41	41	539	10	24
Lafayette — Mayo	862	90	924	1,876	298	450	11	22	22	318	0	4
Lake — Tavares	1,164	85	1,201	2,450	469	244	13	61	61	414	2	1
Lee — Fort Myers	842	45	1,039	1,926	307	545	10	69	29	271	27	0
Leon — Tallahassee	1,446	133	1,825	3,404	446	427	21	15	40	621	0	14
Levy — Bronson	1,135	105	1,357	2,627	167	158	18	90	65	423	2	0
Liberty — Bristol	535	39	643	1,217	449	453	0	61	6	218	0	4
Madison — Madison	1,377	148	1,773	3,298	511	625	4	86	29	729	3	11
Manatee — Brandentown	1,714	110	1,751	3,575	597	625	2	3	19	688	0	9
Marion — Ocala	1,908	202	2,717	4,823	241	200	25	95	30	856	2	1
Monroe — Key West	1,888	187	2,725	4,800	199	212	21	270	79	798	0	8
Nassau — Fernandina	632	43	923	1,598	281	327	0	220	1	244	3	7
Okaloosa — Crestview	788	73	971	1,832	8	511	17	7	21	412	0	4
Okeechobee — Okeechobee		71	332	353	423	140	1	22		1	2	6
Orange — Orlando	1,451	106	1,787	3,344	136	505	0	110	67	717		1
Osceola — Kissimmee	560	44	749	1,353	391	328	7	112	13	281	14	7
Palm Beach — West Palm Beach	1,379	71	1,731	3,181	287	255	8	27	35	422	6	4
Pasco — Dade City	782	62	1,070	1,914	565	1,525	11	61	50	267	1	6
Pinellas — Clearwater	1,921	140	2,261	4,322	1,216	487	53	69	61	715	0	1
Polk — Bartow	3,646	248	4,593	8,486	489	477	12	28	125	1,527	2	13
Putnam — Palatka	1,355	98	1,741	3,194	425	212	1	69	61	148	14	45
St. Johns — St. Augustine	1,400	82	1,592	3,074	217	506	0	81	19	571	6	5
St. Lucie — Fort Pierce	883	33	803	1,699	425	341	3	42	21	376	1	10
Santa Rosa — Milton	1,394	112	1,597	3,103	332	119	2	29	23	517	5	1
Seminole — Sanford	1,041	44	1,151	2,236	212	376	3	19	42	458	1	13
Sumter — Bushnell	647	71	919	1,637	372	641	11	10	8	31	5	20
Suwannee — Live Oak	1,602	196	2,013	3,811	577	577		46	72	896	0	0
TAMPA No. 1 — City Hall	2,352	152	3,425	5,929	533	184	20	16	102	602	0	4
TAMPA No. 2 — 1909 Nebraska Avenue	3,063	203	4,043	7,339	621	174	19	109	70	554	9	0
Taylor — Perry	1,573	99	1,550	3,222	163	496	10	179	33	832	1	24
Volusia — De Land	1,932	115	2,331	4,378	384	334	6	61	16	186	2	0
Wakulla — Crawfordville	499	37	541	1,077			10	14	21	343	1	7
Walton — De Funiak Springs	965	97	1,286	2,348			0	45	36	450		1
Washington — Vernon	924	105	1,111	2,140	372							

APPENDIX TABLES.

APPENDIX TABLE 100-A.—*Principal statistical data, by local boards—Continued.*

GEORGIA.

Local board.	Post-office address.	Registration.				Induction.	Physical groups.				Deferments.		
		June 5, 1917.	June and August, 1918.	Sept. 12, 1918.	Total.	Accepted at camp.	General service.	Remediables.	Limited service.	Disqualified.	Dependency.	Agricultural.	Industrial.
Appling	Baxley	869	87	1,099	2,055	245	271	6	55	474	48	4	118
ATLANTA No. 1	63-65 Inman Building	3,715	300	5,131	9,146	1,010	1,774	32	238	322	2,026	64	35
ATLANTA No. 2	317 Central Building	2,437	223	3,191	5,851	519	455	25	64	397	1,156	1	27
ATLANTA No. 3	1794 Grant Street	2,661	220	3,448	6,329	540	484	20	68	397	1,380	2	2
ATLANTA No. 4	3,409	179	3,565	7,153	978	1,117	13	84	173	1,087	14	29
ATLANTA No. 5	Hurt Building	3,035	236	3,539	6,830	655	547	34	96	540	908		1
ATLANTA No. 6	Tenth floor, Flatiron Building	1,974	163	3,024	5,161	506	385		120	32	1,045	4	14
ATLANTA No. 7	Gordon and Lee Streets	2,848	229	4,271	7,348	779	61	22	25	172	1,355	5	47
AUGUSTA No. 1	599 Peachtree Street	2,398	194	2,851	5,443	731	924	33	42	21	921	5	49
AUGUSTA No. 2	414 Leonard Building	2,723	145	3,242	6,110	638	1,060		47	383	1,383		1
Bacon	216 Leonard Building	477	66	660	1,203	110	79		6		307	8	
Baker	Alma	556	65	682	1,303	157	218	3		14	382	2	5
Baldwin	Newton	1,171	62	1,162	2,395	403	420		34	143	497	13	4
Banks	Milledgeville	906	128	1,112	2,146	180	154	3	28	37	645	38	3
Barrow	Homer	1,182	111	1,396	2,689	274	408	8	19	93	656	2	9
Bartow	Courthouse, Winder	2,061	209	2,488	4,758	583	515	15	59	101	1,222	1	9
Ben Hill	Cartersville	1,349	106	1,544	2,999	293	371	21	42	43	761	16	3
Berrien	Fitzgerald	2,230	233	2,481	4,944	503	639	4	35	178	1,207	5	7
Bibb	Nashville	1,156	138	1,738	3,052	381	388	32	34	94	570	19	7
Bleckley	22 Jacques Building, Macon	880	92	996	1,968	296	286	21	9	10	496	37	4
Brooks	Cochran	1,949	139	2,230	4,318	558	607	7	33	234	883		
Bryan	Quitman	493	42	631	1,166	135	190	22	48	21	234	19	
Bulloch	Clyde	2,247	182	2,589	5,018	507	96		126	21	108	2	1
Burke	Statesboro	2,808	182	2,859	5,909	725	986	28	81	55	1,098	3	
Butts	Waynesboro	1,195	85	1,150	2,430	330	384		39	12	547	105	1
Calhoun	Jackson	823	70	996	1,889	201	213		9	32	16		
Camden	Morgan	494	52	715	1,261	147	177	1	17	69	227		1
Campbell	St. Marys	888	118	1,135	2,121	239	190	52	29	51	539	10	1
Candler	Fairburn	782	48	899	1,729	165	247	3	13	76	469	10	
Carroll	Metter	2,668	263	3,501	6,432	429	797	3	2	11	1,693	2	1
Catoosa	Carrollton	471	58	677	1,206	139	133	2	12	205	280	7	1
Charlton	Ringgold	402	31	502	935	118	144		3	12	189	1	1
Chatham	Folkston	1,434	79	1,744	3,257	598	641	25	72	8	225	1	12
Chattahoochee	312 Savannah Bank & Trust Building, Savannah	391	47	450	888	103	112	6	6	171	254	4	
Chattooga	Cusseta	1,037	131	1,378	2,546	269	245	2	10	25	665	16	
Cherokee	Summerville	1,361	162	1,846	3,309	316	222	7	24	78	963	17	1
Clarke	Canton	2,021	128	2,324	4,473	613	607	21	49	153	935	8	9

County	County seat												
Clay	Fort Gaines	474	61	683	1,218	150	155	3	12	14	94	5	7
Clayton	Jonesboro	762	135	972	1,869	209	204	2	22	114	409	4	5
Clinch	Homerville	898	87	844	1,839	313	283	1	48	77	243	12	16
Cobb	Marietta	2,271	234	3,083	5,529	599	537	2	68	24	1,222	10	4
Coffee	Douglas	2,144	224	2,743	5,079	622	628		185	110	1,362	70	
Colquitt	Moultrie	1,096	192	1,107	5,083	478	425	5	47	242	1,296	28	5
Columbia	Appling	687	72	2,618	2,275	334	359	4	10	127	450	2	
Coweta	Newnan	2,608	230	858	5,456	687	707	43	51	242	1,525	35	9
Crawford	Knoxville	1,593	44	1,898	1,589	206	228	31	5	4	349	1	2
Crisp	Cordele	316	82	379	3,573	484	446		18	92	252	16	
Dade	Trenton	345	38	446	727	94	72	1	12	9	119	2	1
Dawson	Dawsonville	2,332	225	2,855	829	85	66		23	26	210	6	12
Decatur	Bainbridge	2,111	199	3,084	5,412	604	489	26	103	9	1,086	1	2
Dekalb	Decatur	1,977	192	2,123	5,394	601	511	13	46	218	1,107	1	2
Dodge	Eastman	2,055	119	1,919	4,292	614	521	29	37	24	1,182	11	23
Dooly	Vienna	1,663	90	1,912	4,083	635	659	43	54		693	1	4
Dougherty	Albany	1,431	105	1,013	3,665	576	691		146	2	684	10	6
Douglas	Douglasville	477	179	1,773	1,891	228	32	6	21	101	464	3	
Early	Blakely	867	29	407	3,383	340	322	9	25	36	713	5	6
Echols	Statenville	1,089	48	1,089	913	163	135	3	17	23	108		
Effingham	Springfield	1,702	147	1,975	2,004	219	224	4	25	54	351		6
Elbert	Elberton	2,222	231	2,647	3,824	319	285	4	56	59	967		
Emanuel	Swainsboro	571	71	665	5,100	519	597	4	68	58	1,407		
Evans	Claxton	1,033	87	1,266	1,307	164	165	2	23	41	309		1
Fannin	Blue Ridge	976	93	1,184	2,386	225	197	1	24	76	673	21	
Fayette	Fayetteville	3,239	310	4,105	2,253	279	245	2	7	6	424		16
Floyd	Rome	1,433	104	1,118	7,654	823	806		109	52	1,511		
Forsyth	Cumming	2,771	192	2,019	2,164	166	224	1	68	41	657	11	64
Franklin	Carnesville	687	302	4,187	3,644	422	684	5	110	163	896		
Fulton	Rooms 401–405 Courthouse, Atlanta	350	58	811	7,260	611	528	2	39	21	1,378		
Gilmer	Ellijay	1,545	30	418	1,556	153	120	1	4		426	26	33
Glascock	Courthouse, Gibson	1,316	142	2,821	798	61	2	23	27	59	234	9	2
Glynn	Brunswick	1,500	158	1,867	4,508	365	443	4	88	108	674	7	2
Gordon	Calhoun	1,401	194	1,995	3,341	379	248	22	78	231	793	7	5
Grady	Cairo	2,100	128	1,586	3,689	427	379	11	28	21	875	2	21
Greene	County Courthouse, Greensboro	910	255	2,972	3,715	408	423	2	152	101	825	3	21
Gwinnett	Lawrenceville	2,048	80	2,088	5,327	564	448		17	75	1,152	36	16
Habersham	Clarkesville	1,436	244	2,602	2,078	176	175	3	70	60	561	5	1
Hall	Gainesville	1,020	114	2,546	3,894	473	542	13	32	108	287	11	5
Hancock	Sparta	1,131	133	1,318	3,096	349	465		60	27	806	1	5
Haralson	Buchanan	1,227	138	1,358	2,471	221	140	2	29	69	667	2	2
Harris	Hamilton	815	168	1,660	3,055	279	302	6	19	22	695		
Hart	Hartwell	1,598	101	1,097	2,013	266	318		50	146	838		
Heard	Franklin	2,038	142	1,868	3,608	259	254	3	24	56	503		2
Henry	McDonough	1,090	155	2,046	4,239	435	587			66	883		1
Houston	Perry	1,830	79	1,235	2,404	452	300	1	53	69	657	3	
Irwin	Ocilla	1,356	225	2,419	4,474	289	450	6	34	168	999	5	
Jackson	Jefferson	627	123	1,575	3,054	519	448	21	68	120	711	20	2
Jasper	Monticello	1,805	58	709	1,334	459	205		18	22	334		1
Jeff Davis	Hazlehurst	1,151	143	1,872	3,820	153	628	3	35	96	1,148		
Jefferson	Louisville		107	1,283	2,543	492	97	6	32	72	534	10	7
Jenkins	Millen					315							

APPENDIX TABLE 100-A.—*Principal statistical data, by local boards*—Continued.

GEORGIA—Continued.

Local board.	Post-office address.	Registration. June 5, 1917.	Registration. June and August, 1918.	Registration. Sept. 12, 1918.	Registration. Total.	Induction. Accepted at camp.	Physical groups. General service.	Physical groups. Remediables.	Physical groups. Limited service.	Physical groups. Disqualified.	Deferments. Dependency.	Deferments. Agricultural.	Deferments. Industrial.
Johnson	Wrightsville	1,286	84	1,342	2,712	350	296	53	98	63	774	2	1
Jones	Gray	1,002	84	1,125	2,271	403	361	16	41	59	443	5	
Laurens	Dublin	3,333	293	3,683	7,309	847	756	9	34	123	1,894	24	5
Lee	Leesburg	1,002	63	926	1,981	321	387	2	50	39	388		
Liberty	Hinesville	931	118	1,257	2,306	228	229	7	29	9	329	6	
Lincoln	Lincolnton	750	102	946	1,798	297	311	22	30	60	367	5	6
Lowndes	Valdosta	2,462	182	2,751	5,395	786	353	9	24	164	781	3	
Lumpkin	Dahlonega	387	38	552	977	125	97		11	40	210		2
McDuffie	Thompson	942	74	940	1,956	331	320	3	30	139	418	2	3
McIntosh	Darien	384	34	526	944	117	11		4	45	176		5
Macon No. 1	415 Georgia Casualty Building	2,696	196	3,505	6,398	625	233	15	81	31	870	2	69
Macon No. 2	918 Georgia Casualty Building	2,244	235	3,170	5,649	439	610	19	53	208	906		1
Macon	Oglethorpe	1,294	150	1,439	2,873	313	348	9	82	29	442	7	7
Madison	Clerk's Office, Superior Court, Danielsville	1,363	161	1,805	3,329	341	287	28	31	113	962		
Marion	Buena Vista	658	79	752	1,489	196	219	2	9	74	360	3	8
Meriwether	Greenville	2,293	203	2,563	5,069	591	555	8	32	224	1,101	18	
Miller	Colquitt	868	64	881	1,813	225	233		41	21	505		8
Milton	Alpharetta	569	61	765	1,395	136			16	12	44		
Mitchell	Camilla	2,321	189	2,346	4,856	444	702	4	62	96	1,314	17	4
Monroe	Forsyth	1,557	138	1,896	3,591	431	457		143	31	811	11	6
Montgomery	Mount Vernon	1,290	134	1,412	2,836	369	399	25	49	65	670	32	4
Morgan	Madison	1,860	158	1,670	3,688	522	159	14	20	117	886	45	6
Murray	Chatsworth	784	73	976	1,833	155	148		35	52	505	2	
Muscogee	Columbus	4,034	349	4,668	9,051	898	907	24	135	368	2,275	20	25
Newton	Covington	1,687	187	2,001	3,875	438	146	1	25	85	978	25	5
Oconee	Watkinsville	941	88	1,116	2,145	294	290	8	22	29	443	1	1
Oglethorpe	Lexington	1,613	149	1,869	3,639	441	185	2	2	158	986	10	7
Paulding	Dallas	967	120	1,392	2,479	211	173	7	5	23	127	4	1
Pickens	Jasper	622	69	830	1,521	130	154	1	6		409		8
Pierce	Blackspear	899	96	1,177	2,172	224	193	6	54	20	551	111	1
Pike	Zebulon	1,639	97	1,913	3,639	499	433	12	50	144	737		12
Polk	Cedartown	1,009	98	2,029	3,842	385	380	14	83	106	952	6	
Pulaski	Hawkinsville	1,167	85		2,198	94	409	4	8	87	421	1	
Putnam	Eatonton		170	1,342	2,594	125	328	3	7	35	626		
Quitman	Georgetown	208	44	264	642		94			12	103		
Rabun	Clayton	387	160	582	1,013		144	4	31	38	224	1	1
Randolph	Clayton	1,227	160	1,376	2,783	347	401	15	45	8	701		1
Richmond	123 Jackson Street, Augusta	860	84	1,072	2,016	237	292	4	17	84	369	8	3

Rockdale	Conyers	701	97	913	1,711	194	168	1	6	96	312	1	1
SAVANNAH No. 1	5 Whitaker Street	3,143	262	4,674	8,089	935	1,103	11	111	143	1,308	1	
SAVANNAH No. 2	49 Citizens' Trust Co. Building	4,557	451	6,340	11,348	1,145	1,629	83	220	30	1,075	2	127
Schley	Ellaville	357	38	513	938	117	118	6	23	45	103	8	3
Screven	Sylvania	2,011	162	2,267	4,025	602	592	2	32	104	1,168	15	1
Spalding	Griffin	1,881	128	2,016	2,198	481	553	14	94	61	926	6	3
Ste phns	boa	912	103	1,183	1,892	242	312	4	32	56	493	1	4
Stewart	Lumpkin	774	109	1,009	4,797	281	258	18	27	47	383	11	15
Sumter	Americus	2,237	137	2,423	1,960	670	750	7	46	18	789	2	2
Talbot	on	859	89	1,012	1,589	288	326	13	33	84	425	1	2
Taliaferro	Crawfordville	729	57	803	2,859	229	281	4	18	81	330	4	
Tall	Reidsville	1,305	110	1,444	1,999	350	484	20	32	80	717	1	3
Taylor	Butler	848	96	1,055	2,927	277	332	5	34	53	464	5	8
Telfair	McRae	1,261	148	1,518	3,139	399	402	3	29	4	714	11	8
Terrell	Dawson	1,447	113	1,579	5,943	361	343	4	66	158	780	2	2
Tift	alle	2,362	299	3,282	2,849	636	816	30	113	63	234	4	1
Tifton		1,267	109	1,473	2,671	384	421	7	64	20	588	2	
Tfts		1,140	111	1,420	688	306	234		24	3	552	1	11
Towns	Hiawassee	295	39	354	7,103	90	100	21	13	65	184	12	2
Troup	La Grange	3,226	276	3,601	2,761	948	944	10	67	30	1,721	18	
Turner	shburn	1,329	91	1,341	1,973	295	305		32	35	694	9	
Twiggs	Jeffersonville	924	82	967	1,131	312	269		25	64	630		
Union	Blairsville	450	57	634	2,546	131	111	5	12	154	256		2
Upson	Thomaston	1,132	116	1,298	4,271	326	17		33	138	522	29	
Walker	La Fayette	166	186	2,378	4,345	531	420	21	73	39	952		54
Walton	Monroe	2,033	172	2,317	4,748	483	13	1	49	997	753		
Ware	Waycross	2,412	191	2,524	2,180	333	381	1	57	112	977	10	2
Warren	Warrenton	1,131	58	1,132	5,149	358	324	2	41	58	449	2	8
Washington	Sandersville	358	213	2,524	2,696	806	246	3	39	93	1,167	10	
Wayne	Jesup	774	132	1,433	1,738	357	217	10	43		587	21	
Webster	Preston	518	87	464	1,203	85				41	411		
Wheeler	Alamo	1,222	51	877	3,087	231	223	3	23	22	275	1	9
White	Cleveland	66	154	1,711	3,105	150	199		29	60	794	20	
Whitfield	Dalton	1,955	51	1,550	4,227	302	282	11	82	46	888	5	
Wilcox	Abbeville	1,031	171	2,101	2,163	364	420	8	29	384	783	2	
Wilkes	Washington	904	77	1,055	4,210	627	780	4	115	20	330	4	
Wilkinson	Irwinton		141	2,165		289	333	6	21	35	1,127	28	5
Worth	Sylvester					60	460	9	27				

IDAHO.

Ada	Boise	982	87	1,545	2,614	309	214	12	50	56	386	44	5
Adams	Council	309	24	414	747	106	89	1	9	43	140	12	0
Bannock	Pocatello	3,831	234	4,586	8,651	991	773	3	81	135	1,612	93	30
Bear Lake	Paris	833	99	974	1,906	259	219	10	27	57	403	32	2
Benewah	St. Maries	867	61	1,283	2,211	431	281	4	39	16	261	1	1
Bingham	Blackfoot	1,026	142	2,241	4,009		136						
Blaine	Hailey	547	43	720	1,310	210		19	34	23	106	10	2
Boise	Boise	1,315	126	2,250	3,691	400	367	0	59	79	589	6	6
Boise	Idaho City	390	13	416	819	114	88		10	16	122	11	0

APPENDIX TABLE 100-A.—*Principal statistical data, by local boards*—Continued.

IDAHO—Continued.

Local board.	Post-office address.	Registration. June 5, 1917.	June and August, 1918.	Sept. 12, 1918.	Total.	Induction. Accepted at camp.	Physical groups. General service.	Remediables.	Limited service.	Disqualified.	Deferments. Dependency.	Agricultural.	Industrial.
Bonner	Sandpoint	1,167	72	1,671	2,910	303	311		31	103	268	1	13
Bonneville	Idaho Falls	1,817	173	2,660	4,650	604					108	9	3
Boundary	Bonners Ferry	425	39	685	1,149	153	103	5	25	25	99	17	1
Butte		331	31	456	819	127		3	2	12	77	37	0
Camas	Fairfield	206	20	273	499	68	61	0	9	5	779	53	2
Canyon		1,543	158	2,975	4,676	470	472	13	58	99	706	39	0
Cassia	Albion	1,400	128	1,902	3,430	404	330	0	49	64	170	8	2
Clearwater		438	44	673	1,155	148	105	7	10	22	156	7	1
Custer	Challis	549	38	693	1,280	199	157	4	6	42	178	8	6
Elmore	Mountain Home	627	47	867	1,541	213	159	8	17	33	184	10	0
Franklin	Preston	625	70	800	1,495	204	230	10	38	41	607	178	6
Fremont	St. Anthony	1,508	129	1,925	3,562	495	399	13	53	90	247	57	1
Gem	Emmett	632	66	790	1,488	166	189	4	17	12	256	17	0
Gooding	Gooding	668	57	970	1,695	322	214	5	7		456	10	1
Idaho	Grangeville	1,087	124	1,091	2,900	250	387	2	19	129	444	93	1
Jefferson	Rigby	852	90	1,589	2,033	445	440	20	63	18	669	1	2
Kootenai	Coeur d'Alene	1,345	141	2,373	3,859	603	409	17	164	79	175	18	1
Latah		1,687	187	2,233	4,107	202	205	14	14	55	261	11	3
Lemhi	Salmon	505	45	821	1,371	180	127	2	7	10	184	35	1
Lewis	Nez Perce	584	53	783	1,420	286	250	9	29	11	219	2	0
Lincoln	Shoshone	865	78	1,276	2,219	262	33	2	15	71	440	25	2
Madison	Rexburg	802	102	1,099	2,003	335	407	14	31	83	505	92	7
Minidoka	Rupert	1,121	99	1,457	2,677	361	357	25	83	189	190	17	1
Nez Perce	Lewiston	1,231	135	1,813	3,179	179	218	2	16	17	216	15	2
Oneida	Malad	684	54	804	1,542	176	109	13	16	30	583	17	3
Owyhee	Silver City	607	32	671	1,310	121				17	174	1	1
Payette	Payette	445	48	654	1,147	185	680	66	206	31	1,158	24	0
Power	American Falls	687	42	816	1,545	874	116	1	12	34	121	103	6
Shoshone	Wallace	3,035	139	3,710	6,884	107	716	22	74	133	453	5	0
Teton	Driggs	371	38	549	958	668	94	3	9	28		57	5
Twin Falls	Twin Falls	2,545	227	4,016	6,788	92	243	17	50	35			
Valley	Cascade	322	38	642	1,002	270							
Washington	Weiser	914	84	1,189	2,187								

ILLINOIS.

Place	Address												
Adams	Liberty	2,056	224	2,827	5,107	694	698	6	27	177	991	153	1
Alexander	Cairo	2,247	196	3,008	5,451	877	997	4	67	14	465	4	3
AURORA	City Hall	3,481	301	4,915	8,697	1,043	917	23	64	253	1,489	12	47
Bond	Greenville	1,252	150	1,783	3,325	434	431	2	13	13	823	143	12
Boone	421 South State Street, Belvidere	1,422	120	1,093	1,924	328	316	4	14	137	700	78	14
Brown	Mount Sterling	749	82	2,663	4,904	787	609	1	47	8	397	24	0
Bureau No. 1	Princeton	2,066	175	2,803	5,109	570	660	2	110	27	867	298	7
Bureau No. 2	City Hall, Spring Valley	2,114	192	953	1,753	295	343	1	32	181	793	93	9
Calhoun	Hamburg	708	92	2,328	4,104	364	324	0	7	36	339	117	0
Carroll	Savanna	1,620	156	2,254	4,229	662	479	2	25	108	203	87	40
Cass	Beardstown	1,813	162	3,202	5,848	652	543	0	62	69	804	2	86
Champaign No. 1	115 West Main Street, Urbana	2,414	232	3,591	6,867	864	94	25	90	135	1,153	0	35
Champaign No. 2	504 First National Bank Building, Champaign	2,979	297	7,659	13,127	550	1,735	4	43	173	1,322	2	45
CHICAGO No. 1	1122 County Building	5,206	262	5,136	9,371	1,370	778	72	325	39	442		35
CHICAGO No. 2	2348 Michigan Avenue	3,908	327	5,408	9,819	1,163	1,111	15	142	355	864		7
CHICAGO No. 3	3193 Indiana Avenue	4,082	329	5,156	9,352	1,005	19	138	310	342	1,087		13
CHICAGO No. 4	3333 South State Street	3,837	389	5,133	8,881	635	1,472	3	4	35	35		
CHICAGO No. 5	Thirty-ninth Street and Prairie Avenue	3,461	287	5,737	7,752	1,025	773	94	159	273	1,348	6	8
CHICAGO No. 7	490 East Forty-third Street	2,019	169	4,414	6,945	808	507	36	263	238	875	3	14
CHICAGO No. 7	431 East Forty-third Street	3,083	255	3,925	7,288	768	736	37	143	184	1,105	1	8
CHICAGO No. 8	4301 Fifth Avenue	2,839	181	3,796	8,870	971	838	26	126	163	1,234	0	15
CHICAGO No. 9	2901 Wallace Street	3,235	257	4,412	7,958	929	673	26	97	1	1,428	0	8
CHICAGO No. 10	3205 South Morgan Street	4,190	268	4,020	12,669	992	1,297	46	164	192	1,251	3	20
CHICAGO No. 11	2040 West Thirty-fifth Street	671	287	4,615	6,589	835	528	22	120	151	1,646	0	25
CHICAGO No. 12	2500 West Thirty-eighth Street	5,674	380	3,906	8,105	958	1,045	9	80	234	754	3	25
CHICAGO No. 13	1510 Hyde Park Boulevard	2,518	165	4,550	7,200	915	858	37	109	244	938	3	57
CHICAGO No. 14	do	3,342	213	4,034	8,104	952	623	16	69	329	1,029	10	41
CHICAGO No. 15	Fifty-seventh Street and Cottage Grove Avenue	2,969	197	4,600	8,446	995	794	27	125	232	1,321	1	47
CHICAGO No. 16	6240 Kimbark Avenue	3,302	202	4,910	7,622	766	482	11	192	313	1,568	1	82
CHICAGO No. 17	1114 East Sixty-third Street	3,298	238	4,346	12,264	1,147	1,090	25	68	225	1,577	2	89
CHICAGO No. 18	6731 Stoney Island Avenue	3,073	203	6,648	12,008	1,063	212	10	117	103	1,645	5	52
CHICAGO No. 19	2924 East Seventy-ninth Street	5,280	347	6,511	11,574	923	759	4	133	244	1,308	3	221
CHICAGO No. 20	Federal Building, South Chicago	5,087	410	6,328	11,811	1,151	47	43	59	140	1,635	2	151
CHICAGO No. 21	Ninety-fifth Street and Cottage Grove Avenue	4,723	325	3,708	7,107	521	413		66	77	1,600	0	29
CHICAGO No. 22	200 East One hundred and fifteenth Street	5,120	241	3,568	7,027	612	574	18	56	222	1,193		27
CHICAGO No. 23	1545 West Twelfth Street	3,153	202	3,823	7,640	681			50	159	736	0	5
CHICAGO No. 24	1801 South Racine Avenue	3,257	222	4,498	9,087	924	791	8	44	120	997	6	23
CHICAGO No. 25	1808 South Ashland Avenue	3,595	224	4,966	10,176	1,055	479	12	132	196	1,102	1	14
CHICAGO No. 26	2334 South Oakley Avenue	4,367	347	3,154	6,299	746	1,141	7	129	169	627	2	33
CHICAGO No. 27	3517 West Twenty-sixth Street	4,863	217	4,059	7,597	890	718	26	91	187	817	0	36
CHICAGO No. 28	2759 West Twenty-second Street	2,919	231	3,086	6,715	963	106	4	86	6	24	1	15
CHICAGO No. 29	218 South Western Avenue	3,307	235	3,644	5,714	836	727	26	111	228	1,794		0
CHICAGO No. 30	Y. M. C. A., 3210 Arthington Street	333	174										
CHICAGO No. 31	3340 Colorado Avenue	2,454	292	3,952	11,122	870							25
CHICAGO No. 32	1601 West Grand Avenue	5,186	194		6,996	880	820	93	192	459	1,441		
CHICAGO No. 33	3233 Fulton Street	2,850	444	5,854	11,462	1,176						6	15
CHICAGO No. 34	1432 North Leavitt Street	5,164	516	6,596	13,985	1,217							
CHICAGO No. 35	915 North Paulina Street	6,873					531	8	91	145	993	1	5
CHICAGO No. 36	1814 North Hermitage Avenue	2,883	197	2,831	6,911	701		35	46	357	1,070	2	7
CHICAGO No. 37	Pulaski Park, Blackhawk and Noble Streets	4,095	294	4,370	8,759	687	570						

APPENDIX TABLE 100-A.—*Principal statistical data, by local boards*—Continued.

ILLINOIS—Continued.

Local board.	Post-office address.	Registration. June 5, 1917.	Registration. June and August, 1918.	Registration. Sept. 12, 1918.	Registration. Total.	Induction. Accepted at camp.	Physical groups. General service.	Physical groups. Remediables.	Physical groups. Limited service.	Physical groups. Disqualified.	Deferments. Dependency.	Deferments. Agricultural.	Deferments. Industrial.
Chicago No. 38	1329 West Augusta Street	3,200	181	3,257	6,638	735	645	12	72	84	890	0	2
Chicago No. 39	949 West Grand Avenue	6,023	340	5,790	12,153	883	635	25	137	202	1,104	0	10
Chicago No. 40	238 Aberdeen Street	5,112	216	7,038	12,366	1,221	1,305	35	130	101	752	6	24
Chicago No. 41	Marquette School, 546 South Wood Street	3,975	287	4,359	8,621	1,096	1,291	11	154	275	1,325	1	23
Chicago No. 42	600 Blue Island Avenue	3,817	259	4,313	8,389	1,221	1,305	35	130	101	1,391	6	24
Chicago No. 43	Andrew Jackson School, 820 South Sholto Street	4,568	288	4,663	9,519	965	729	13	122	294	822	3	5
Chicago No. 44	Fourteenth Place and Union Avenue	4,851	292	4,378	9,521	766	870	14	128	271	401	1	7
Chicago No. 45	2000 Canalport Avenue	2,195	107	2,612	4,914	487	17	15	30	81	1,147	1	3
Chicago No. 46	Newberry Library, Walton Place	4,602	281	6,118	11,001	1,189	860	119	298	463	790	3	36
Chicago No. 47	400 East Chicago Avenue	5,457	287	5,851	11,595	1,174	1,012	66	331	450	732	0	18
Chicago No. 48	659 West North Avenue	2,156	179	3,001	5,336	510	372	7	30	71	1,199	2	7
Chicago No. 49	1544 Larabee Street	3,955	270	4,994	9,219	908	690	37	91	251	28	0	9
Chicago No. 50	1730 Tribune Building	3,799	242	5,335	9,376	1,022	1,676	32	106	14	1,281	8	18
Chicago No. 51	Lincoln School, Kemper Place and Larabee Street	4,231	250	5,127	9,608	1,111	1,428	22	113	469	1,281	2	17
Chicago No. 52	3035 North Hoyne Avenue	3,354	299	3,842	7,495	830	664	26	104	327	1,697	0	15
Chicago No. 53	1200 Belden Avenue	3,697	284	4,152	8,133	879	646	23	66	170	1,278	1	14
Chicago No. 54	4078 Broadway	2,965	179	4,109	7,253	895	873	47	192	231	1,012	1	19
Chicago No. 55	4500 Clarendon Avenue	3,780	216	5,542	9,538	1,114	808	37	190	0	948	14	16
Chicago No. 56	5900 Winthrop Avenue	2,411	141	3,970	6,522	838	507	17	91	178	947	0	35
Chicago No. 57	7075 North Clark Street	2,103	109	3,654	5,866	587	297	10	61	111	807	1	12
Chicago No. 58	4142 Greenview Avenue	3,170	282	3,949	7,401	......	......	......	......	......	......	......	......
Chicago No. 59	1757 Wilson Avenue	3,176	269	4,213	7,658	934	741	29	133	252	817	4	51
Chicago No. 60	1950 Lawrence Avenue	3,073	222	4,219	7,514	920	720	16	102	223	1,362	3	13
Chicago No. 61	3606 Lawrence Avenue	3,288	225	5,131	8,644	767	549	34	64	179	2,803	1	18
Chicago No. 62	3945 North Springfield Avenue	2,991	260	4,148	7,399	871	702	2	77	131	1,261	5	13
Chicago No. 63	Carl Schurz High School, Room 202, Addison Avenue.	3,925	378	5,780	10,083	1,023	961	14	52	259	3,182	5	21
Chicago No. 64	3350 Diversey Avenue	3,472	243	3,396	7,101	912	982	6	140	147	1,861	0	22
Chicago No. 65	Holstein Park Field House, Oakley Avenue	3,420	350	4,833	9,603	1,266	1,422	9	128	351	1,658	4	42
Chicago No. 66	2318 North California Avenue	3,060	251	3,717	7,028	900	715	41	121	287	1,362	3	40
Chicago No. 67	Cornell Square Park Field House, Fifty-first and Wood Streets.	8,688	580	9,124	18,342	1,403	1,655	38	281	239	2,387	2	42
Chicago No. 68	6311 South Saint Louis Avenue	4,333	350	6,249	10,932	1,053	700	40	213	276	2,094	7	34
Chicago No. 69	724 West Forty-seventh Street	3,775	278	4,655	8,708	1,082	1,165	44	107	255	1,299	3	23
Chicago No. 70	Forty-fifth Street and Princeton Avenue	3,066	252	4,077	7,395	1,030	742	55	116	257	1,109	0	20
Chicago No. 71	6238 Princeton Avenue	2,159	171	2,850	5,180	599	566	11	82	177	953	0	37

Precinct	Location											
CHICAGO NO. 72	5507 South Halsted Street	2,330	215	2,755	5,300	768	719	39	95	189	985	0	1
CHICAGO NO. 73	1646 West Sixty-third Street	2,839	233	3,392	6,464	803	497	15	106	173	1,299	0	26
CHICAGO NO. 74	6321 Harvard Avenue	2,468	200	3,149	5,736	843	643	6	100	220	1,576	2	42
CHICAGO NO. 75	6730 Wentworth Avenue	2,588	205		5,942	813	440	14	4	142	997	3	32
CHICAGO NO. 76	7621 South Perry Avenue	3,081	268	4,033	7,372	938			100		1,299		
CHICAGO NO. 77	Ridge Field House, Ninety-seventh Street and Longwood Drive	2,075	164	3,308	5,547	617	440				997		
CHICAGO NO. 78	2532 Milwaukee Avenue	2,985	226	3,747	6,958	771	578	23	197	190	1,412	1	59
CHICAGO NO. 79	816 North Laramie Avenue	5,302	469	7,340	13,111	1,251	1,471	30	182	87	2,406	1	7
CHICAGO NO. 80	5610 West Lake Street	2,545	195	3,321	6,061	860	565	21	129	35	142	1	39
CHICAGO NO. 81	1433 South Ridgeway Avenue	4,926	452	4,957	10,021	1,126	871	30	216	330	2,282	0	13
CHICAGO NO. 82	3844 Ogden Avenue	3,700	347	4,128	8,173	1,039	684	35	86	345	1,453	1	87
CHICAGO NO. 83	2901 South Ridgeway Avenue	3,096	289	3,699	7,084	948	783	58	88	193	1,412	0	62
CHICAGO NO. 84	Humboldt Park Refectory	3,774	324	4,469	8,867	867	803	14	159	254	1,386	0	10
CHICAGO NO. 85	4359 Washington Boulevard	3,387	267	4,393	8,047	951	664	27	61	93	1,148	3	43
CHICAGO NO. 86	227 South Cicero Avenue	2,659	223	3,589	6,501	893	814	38	162	189	878	2	29
Christian	Taylorville	3,167	343	5,067	8,577	1,116	1,000		156	209	1,421	82	31
Clark	Marshall	1,634	191	2,264	1,089	369	389	0	38	20	686	91	5
Clay	Flora	1,373	147	1,811	3,331	361	422	23	41	46	435	28	14
Clinton	Carlyle	1,824	213	2,854	4,891	729	732	17	87	74	814	119	15
Coles	Mattoon	2,799	315	4,164	7,278	812	726	24	53	244	1,364	195	41
Cook No. 1	Des Plaines	2,890	293	4,264	7,023	773	739	7	58	215	933	279	11
Cook No. 2	City Hall, Evanston	2,119	172	4,284	7,642	874	415	17	110	126	1,204		28
Cook No. 3	Brown Building, Wilmette	3,823	150	3,637	906	630	391	17	41	233	754	2	5
Cook No. 4	Municipal Building, Maywood	3,984	312	5,332	9,467	1,048	870	4	103	103	1,691	48	33
Cook No. 5	Municipal Building, Oak Park	6,511	276	6,892	11,152	1,201	936	52	180	202	1,802	14	57
Cook No. 6	5601 West Twenty-second Street, Cicero	2,656	437	8,487	15,435	1,391	1,068	28	101	315	2,618	0	98
Cook No. 7	City Hall, Blue Island	3,609	255	3,233	9,171	848	719	16	96	144	955	19	39
Cook No. 8	City Hall, Harvey	1,812	310	5,252	6,144	950	785	9	51	221	1,467	55	51
Cook No. 9	City Hall, Chicago Heights	1,090	241	4,132	5,252	833	786	7	32	226	1,077	77	36
Crawford	Post Office, Robinson	2,796	186	2,686	4,684	476	405	11	40	178	1,052	97	38
Cumberland	Toledo	3,413	105	4,447	2,548	259	326	16	100	15	529	33	8
DANVILLE	303 Federal Building	3,048	258	5,159	7,501	904	891	25	235	288	1,239	23	1
DECATUR	Courthouse	1,646	301	3,899	8,873	873	673	62	67	288	1,643	7	17
De Kalb	Sycamore	1,489	259	7,206	7,206	846	744	15	35	33	664	0	0
Dewitt	Clinton	3,500	165	2,339	4,144	539	555	22	21	74	940	90	46
Douglas	Tuscola	3,506	322	2,319	3,973	469	473	7	139	157	844	33	11
DuPage	Wheaton	2,296	199	3,769	8,962	994	765	23	119	40	291	50	10
EAST ST. LOUIS No. 1	City Hall	3,209	174	2,948	7,474	904	910	15	95	236	1,185	249	34
EAST ST. LOUIS No. 2	Public Library Building	2,046	218	3,933	5,418	687	528	34	110	247	1,063	1	6
EAST ST. LOUIS No. 3	Elks' Building	711	195	2,987	7,360	874	982	21	63	106	1,193	0	18
Edgar	Paris	1,389	64	1,035	5,228	530	691	1	21	39	1,055	2	31
Edwards	Albion	2,018	163	2,146	1,810	238	209	9	26	57	250	113	21
Effingham	Effingham	1,415	209	2,917	2,146	500	636		47	144	697	76	2
Fayette	Vandalia	5,184	145	1,947	2,917	684	710		29	82	1,069	108	9
Ford	Paxton	1,759	376	3,507	1,947	549	730	37	201	945	578	6	4
Franklin	Benton	2,113	173	13,936	3,507	1,129	2,161	26			2,434	65	2
Fulton No. 1	Lewiston		217	5,742	13,936	588	655	17	84	142	959	0	0
Fulton No. 2	Canton	1,818	93	2,649	5,742	623	277	4	55	128	629	54	18
Gallatin	Shawneetown	2,113	182	2,649	2,649	318	665		35	73	946	2	1
Greene	Carrollton	1,818	173	2,688	4,688	580	665	0	89	82	946	66	24
Grundy	Morris	1,675	199	2,382	4,256	544	705		89		469	385	18

APPENDIX TABLE 100-A.—*Principal statistical data, by local boards*—Continued.

ILLINOIS—Continued.

Local board.	Post-office address.	Registration.				Induction.	Physical groups.				Deferments.		
		June 5, 1917.	June and August, 1918.	Sept. 12, 1918.	Total.	Accepted at camp.	General service.	Remediables.	Limited service.	Disqualified.	Dependency.	Agricultural.	Industrial.
Hamilton	McLeansboro	1,261	137	1,763	3,161	446	437	0	13	155	626	14	11
Hancock	Carthage	2,259	261	3,252	5,772	777	790	16	90	188	1,204	49	3
Hardin	Elizabethtown	614	70	823	1,507	172	154	1	17	57	361	4	5
Henderson	Oquawka	808	85	1,136	2,029	274	257	1	15	1	393	46	0
Henry	Cambridge	4,062	333	5,647	10,002	1,357	1,436	27	191	157	1,671	130	14
Iroquois	Watseka	2,956	311	4,113	7,402	919	1,277	20	55	40	889	135	4
Jackson	Murphysboro	2,914	136	4,263	7,488	760	111	17	74	139	1,474	26	13
Jasper	Newton	1,213	224	1,723	3,072	374	431	1	16	40	547	0	0
Jefferson	Mount Vernon	2,164	93	3,123	5,511	722	442	25	29	27	360	191	29
Jersey	Post Office Building, Jerseyville	1,047	196	1,482	2,622	439	759	40	31	38	779	283	7
Jo Daviess	Galena	1,896	120	2,674	4,766	575					1,794	4	109
Johnson	Vienna	996	386	1,288	2,401	339	1,338	27	93	156	912	175	28
JOLIET	206 Woodruff Building	4,858	231	5,894	11,138	1,335	641	74	111	157	1,402	145	36
Kane No. 1	Room 43, Courthouse, Geneva	2,545	231	3,222	5,998	708	745	35	178	144	1,349	41	26
Kane No. 2	Room 4, Opera House Block, Elgin	2,909	278	3,906	7,093	954	1,237	5	166	79	418	72	3
Kankakee	Courthouse, Kankakee	3,647	354	5,014	9,015	1,018	297	23	26	29	887	140	1
Kendall	Yorkville	948	89	1,228	2,265	308	523	26	42	148	964	7	16
Knox No. 1	161 South Cherry Street, Galesburg	1,830	208	2,626	4,661	560	638	62	88	139	1,010	149	29
Knox No. 2	do.	2,185	194	3,152	5,531	879	806	31	106	133	1,215	2	3
Lake No. 1	Libertyville	3,000	235	3,732	6,967	707	877	79	61	115	1,252	290	7
Lake No. 2	111 North Genessee Street, Waukegan	3,336	277	4,485	8,062	955	1,128	34	79	133	1,262	182	188
La Salle No. 1	407 Central Life Building, Ottawa	3,188	307	4,445	7,910	1,072	694	8	101	159	958	119	13
La Salle No. 2	City Hall, La Salle	3,484	237	4,387	8,178	1,722	489	0	64	151	1,122	36	11
La Salle No. 3	Post Office Building, Streator	2,348	138	3,051	5,636	525	621	8	40	115	1,008	349	16
Lawrence	Lawrenceville	1,881	257	2,541	4,560	734	1,065	31	93	205	1,560	7	5
Lee	Courthouse, Dixon	2,562	241	2,315	6,134	1,072	605	8	20	219	777	270	13
Livingston	Pontiac	3,435	324	4,636	8,395	803	726	2	91	239	1,187	207	2
Logan	Lincoln	2,377	241	3,348	5,966	729	750	154	104	47	1,267	42	20
McDonough	Macomb	2,202	222	3,120	5,544	746	856	13	174	185	1,626	456	14
McHenry	Woodstock	3,050	307	3,966	7,323	912	765	9	136	196	1,289	106	48
McLean No. 1	Bloomington	3,076	316	4,290	7,682	870	358	0	94	230	1,104	21	3
McLean No. 2	do.	2,821	231	3,801	6,853	592	764	23	45	73	763	28	15
Macon	Oakley	1,763	171	2,408	4,342	830	950	7	48	117	840	97	8
Macoupin No. 1	Carlinville	1,957	236	3,378	5,571	886	870	0	63	72	1,027	29	25
Macoupin No. 2	Staunton	2,306	275	4,338	6,919	1,000	264	15	107	202	396	108	125
Madison No. 1	Courthouse, Edwardsville	2,666	286	4,045	6,997	1,263				194		13	
Madison No. 2	Y. M. C. A., Alton	4,255	367	5,200	9,912								

County (district)	Building											
Madison No. 3	City Hall, Madison	4,710	384	7,054	12,148	1,379	1,358	22	149	173	1,862	27	86
Marion	Courthouse, Salem	3,052	281	4,454	7,787	975	154	3	12	30	51	6	8
Marshall	------	1,372	118	2,033	3,368	484	498	16	25	93	539	99	6
Mason	Havana	1,418	143	1,564	3,594	419	617	31	36	16	498	26	1
Massac	Temple Building, Metropolis	1,203	108	1,387	2,465	279	447	2	41	28	577	7	5
Menard	Courthouse, Petersburg	961	117	1,516	3,960	385	381	0	33	47	439	14	5
Mercer	Aledo	1,583	150	5,693	2,757	438	453	15	77	56	842	62	6
Monroe	Waterloo	1,084	157	3,493	9,511	434	461	4	39	142	427	98	4
Montgomery	Hillsboro	3,500	335	3,639	6,136	1,069	214	2	17	233	1,681	23	28
Morgan	200 Ayers Bank Building, Jacksonville	2,397	246	6,181	2,942	927	836	22	66	7	675	133	3
Moultrie	Sullivan	1,191	112	4,930	5,961	361	326	16	71	166	611	121	14
Ogle	Oregon	2,426	230	4,491	8,507	668	481	21	57	314	1,033	413	41
PEORIA No. 1	312 Government Building	4,095	365	2,982	7,678	1,230	1,132	52	298	106	1,723	2	20
PEORIA No. 2	314 Government Building	3,328	249	1,849	5,274	967	891	22	163	43	1,837	5	22
Peoria	Courthouse, Peoria	2,872	315	2,964	3,268	871	881	20	86	140	1,430	119	29
Perry	Pinckneyville	2,111	181	1,150	5,458	578	102	0	44	38	769	13	5
Piatt	Monticello	1,263	156	1,734	2,152	414	407	19	74	93	677	30	3
Pike	Mansion House, Pittsfield	2,266	228	1,036	3,168	632	820	39	40	126	1,147	55	0
Pope	Golconda	902	100	4,264	1,891	266	440	0	23	31	461	27	20
Pulaski	Mound City	1,289	145	3,169	7,612	459	442	4	30	63	672	8	26
Putnam	Granville	800	55	1,617	5,511	228	1,024		325	92	1,306	0	1
QUINCY	Post Office Building	3,082	266	4,459	2,857	1,023	730	8	69	66	759	105	89
Randolph	Chester	2,083	259	4,471	8,656	729	441	2	57	143	515	22	134
Richland	Courthouse, Olney	1,140	100	6,710	11,291	392	998		37	100	982	2	32
ROCKFORD No. 1	Courthouse	3,379	288	8,284	14,203	1,015	756	27	120	214	1,323	15	79
ROCKFORD No. 2	City Hall	3,834	351	5,177	7,905	962	1,458	17	214	359	1,345	58	97
Rock Island No. 1	400 People's National Bank Building	4,153	428	5,023	8,803	1,379	1,593	44	249	130	2,304	33	56
Rock Island No. 2	Room 215, Sohrbeck Building, Moline	5,421	498	5,618	9,504	1,614	869	27	188	104	1,290	336	8
St. Clair No. 1	City Hall, Belle Ille.	2,841	315	1,535	1,845	861	888	24	130	68	1,488	38	2
St. Clair No. 2	Federal Building, Belleville	3,302	324	1,038	5,814	1,046	923	62	103	58	1,810	8	0
Saline	Odd Fellows Building, Harrisburg	3,184	329	3,359	6,409	901	1,074	3	84	86	1,576	107	5
Sangamon	Illiopolis	3,536	350	3,889	6,859	1,087	582	11	82	43	463	1	8
Schuyler	Rushville	1,091	129	4,058	2,087	461	241	5	47	20	369	23	54
Scott	Winchester	713	94	1,106	7,804	711	856		24	134	893	119	0
Shelby	Shelbyville	2,185	270	4,325	8,715	711	598	30	76	15	25	8	14
SPRINGFIELD No. 1	504 Booth Building	2,335	185	4,794	3,740	862	847	20	82	51	1,053	24	53
SPRINGFIELD No. 2	Room 17, Illinois National Bank Building	2,603	198	2,011	5,577	324	358	18	26	46	367	152	0
Stark	Toulon	900	81	2,991	2,971	821	638	6	89	90	1,549	7	14
Stephenson	Freeport	3,165	314	1,640	4,686	971	1,543	32	91	106	958	2	53
Tazewell	Pekin	3,602	319	2,610	3,523	489	418	37	28	149	790	26	0
Union	Room 6, Anna National Bank Building, Anna	1,567	162	2,010	4,449	591	610	13	48	38	1,066	20	10
Vermilion No. 1	Hoopeston	2,255	222	2,449	4,147	622	575	11	14	110	1,009	46	28
Vermilion No. 2	Georgetown	2,094	211	2,335	7,801	320	291	13	37	120	687	126	8
Wabash	Mt Carmel	1,235	96	4,246	6,369	556	503	1	95	158	977	97	10
Warren	Monmouth	1,883	183	3,444	6,104	512	471	3	86	123	542	37	12
Washington	Nashville	1,358	155	3,225	5,516	563	514	24	31	137	899	383	0
Wayne	Fairfield	1,831	189	3,283		550	1,068		97	41	1,553	465	14
White	Carmi	1,644	168			856	649	12	40		239	101	34
Whiteside	10 East Third Street, Sterling	3,242	313			668	80	15	12		903	2	63
Will No. 1	Courthouse, Joliet	2,649	276			570	685	23	74		1,061		4
Will No. 2	Woodruff Building, Joliet	2,689	190			656		1					
Williamson No. 1	201½ Public Square, Marion	2,028	205					0					

APPENDIX TABLE 100-A.—*Principal statistical data, by local boards*—Continued.

ILLINOIS—Continued.

Local board.	Post-office address.	Registration. June 5, 1917.	Registration. June and August, 1918.	Registration. Sept. 12, 1918.	Registration. Total.	Induction. Accepted at camp.	Physical groups. General service.	Physical groups. Remediables.	Physical groups. Limited service.	Physical groups. Disqualified.	Deferments. Dependency.	Deferments. Agricultural.	Deferments. Industrial.
Williamson No. 2	217 North Park Avenue, Herrin	2,760	291	4,933	7,984	824	751	......	211	......	1,782	3	22
Winnebago	Rockford	1,719	185	2,527	4,431	497	450	17	44	69	598	368	34
Woodford	Eureka	1,699	164	2,314	4,177	533	800	21	38	82	861	523	18

INDIANA.

Local board.	Post-office address.	Registration. June 5, 1917.	Registration. June and August, 1918.	Registration. Sept. 12, 1918.	Registration. Total.	Induction. Accepted at camp.	Physical groups. General service.	Physical groups. Remediables.	Physical groups. Limited service.	Physical groups. Disqualified.	Deferments. Dependency.	Deferments. Agricultural.	Deferments. Industrial.
Adams	Decatur	1,633	193	2,240	4,066	418	411	6	67	39	731	162	19
Allen	Grand Jury Room, Courthouse, Fort Wayne	2,619	252	3,647	6,518	547	736	......	115	429	878	689	27
Bartholomew	Columbus	1,821	169	2,835	4,825	609	556	18	67	43	794	16	6
Benton	Fowler	1,085	126	1,375	2,586	346	283	6	32	88	526	100	5
Blackford	Hartford City	1,049	91	1,478	2,618	268	198	0	11	72	523	38	8
Boone	Lebanon	1,935	183	2,685	4,803	629	519	11	49	61	1,067	64	10
Brown	Nashville	459	57	716	1,232	169	204	......	10	39	234	1	2
Carroll	Delphi	1,296	157	1,832	3,285	343	244	......	18	113	556	308	7
Cass	Logansport	3,225	265	4,411	7,901	869	818	5	55	175	1,749	202	134
Clark	306 Spring Street, Jeffersonville	2,060	244	3,351	5,655	760	39	13	61	79	1,014	48	50
Clay	Brazil	2,249	249	3,438	5,936	764	584	0	68	53	1,235	16	3
Clinton	Frankfort	2,164	229	3,149	5,542	601	456	26	78	125	1,212	117	22
Crawford	English	886	75	1,240	2,203	339	362	11	28	19	430	6	3
Daviess	Washington	1,987	245	2,854	5,086	610	503	......	54	125	1,124	93	29
Dearborn	Lawrenceburg	1,548	168	2,269	3,985	652	774	0	0	103	401	63	2
Decatur	Greensburg	1,233	127	2,015	3,375	396	389	3	38	24	623	54	3
Dekalb	Auburn	2,039	194	2,915	5,148	537	484	16	28	99	1,142	80	27
Delaware No. 1	407 Wysor Building, Muncie	3,555	284	4,776	8,615	918	759	9	137	103	1,616	14	81
Delaware No. 2	Muncie	1,344	159	1,945	3,448	341	276	......	50	98	371	38	8
Dubois	Jasper	1,987	201	3,183	5,371	702	93	0	62	105	658	11	16
East Chicago	City Hall, East Chicago	7,013	387	8,962	16,362	1,239	1,387	4	110	61	973	126	214
Elkhart No. 1	424 South Third Street	1,946	192	2,853	4,991	515	408	33	46	68	1,061	19	30
Elkhart No. 2	Elkhart	2,712	248	3,896	6,855	654	570	27	29	271	1,526	2	101
Evansville No. 1	424 South Third Street	2,771	216	3,536	6,523	979	931	40	148	15	1,124	1	29
Evansville No. 2	203 Ewing Avenue	2,209	200	2,668	5,002	627	508	......	121	77	1,154	1	41
Evansville No. 3	Room 10, fourth floor, Courthouse	2,261	174	2,720	5,155	664	633	9	92	75	1,276	70	17
Fayette	Connersville	1,517	141	2,075	3,733	409	331	10	81	49	782	70	38
Floyd	New Albany	2,365	226	3,428	6,019	738	717	37	160	105	901	20	45
Fort Wayne No. 1	Post Office Building	2,514	210	3,057	5,781	687	113	......	10	6	28	......	11

FORT WAYNE No. 2 ... 11 Swinney Block	2,256	172	2,601	5,089	688	678	61	41	92	1,058	9	61
FORT WAYNE No. 3 ... 1615 South Calhoun Street	3,187	260	4,187	734	886	778	63	26	187	446	0	105
Fountain ... Covington	1,655	151	2,203	4,009	429	327	49	9	58	951	162	87
Franklin ... Brookville	1,039	116	1,620	2,781	314	249	50	13	58		134	6
Fulton ... Rochester	1,148	143	1,801	3,092	285	242	16		70	326	104	6
GARY No. 1 ... Room 6, Federal Building	3,866	249	4,031	11,338	876	1,029	180	20	179	.690	1	129
GARY No. 2 ... 112 Broadway	3,303	152	3,864	7,319	717	637	117	43	28	1,294	2	29
GARY N. 3 ... 515 Broadway	3,425	180	3,592	7,197	684	653	94	0	97	612	0	19
6son ... Princeton	2,389	271	3,732	5,932	831	233	66		60	383	53	25
Marion ... Marion	2,667	248	3,272	6,647	657	868	103	0	116	1,309	1	3
Grant No. 1 ... Upland	1,556	183	2,037	3,776	418	410	22	0	103	1,156	81	6
Grant No. 2 ... Bloomfield	2,944	352	4,314	7,610	830	784	105	28	62	884	28	19
Greene ... Noblesville	2,036	227	2,713	4,876	556	563	33	29	719	1,708	214	22
Hamilton ... Greenfield	1,365	145	2,117	3,627	474	406	139	1	34	916	36	6
Hancock ... Corydon	1,266	209	1,937	3,412	453	491	66	7	128	705	20	1
Harrison ... Danville	1,416	158	2,307	3981	457	305	48	1	40	676	198	31
Hendricks ... New Castle	2,930	285	3,876	7,091	763	815	96	33	290	736	140	78
Henry ... Kokomo	3,996	349	3,943	9,288	748	659	40	7	229	1,525	124	50
Howard ... Huntington	2,463	280	3,497	1,240	708	579	64	7	137	2,576	115	60
Huntington ... 2204 East Tenth Street	3,664	224	3,668	6,456	737	680	63	30	216	1,374	2	94
INDIANAPOLIS No. 1 ... 905 City Trust Building	3,359	236	4,299	7,894	708	1,040	108	32	87	1,469	3	74
INDIANAPOLIS No. 2 ... 717 Law Building	3,790	260	5,719	9,769	938	688	92	23	56	1,414	8	52
INDIANAPOLIS No. 3 ... 421 Fletcher American National Bank Building	3,981	254	3,960	8,195	1,366	1,176	131	23	324	2,235	3	32
INDIANAPOLIS No. 4 ... 1340 Lemcke Annex	3,239	244	4,031	7,514	1,928	923	209	28	151	979	0	9
INDIANAPOLIS No. 5 ... Washington and Rural Streets	3,238	225	4,643	8,106	859	644	62	52	5	1,192	0	20
INDIANAPOLIS No. 6 ... 1024 Hume-Mansur Building	2,799	217	6,592	6,592	722	657	60	60	220	1,660	14	114
INDIANAPOLIS No. 7 ... 817 High Street	9,948	239	3,726	6,913	835	863	125	49	54	1,339	0	65
INDIANAPOLIS No. 8 ... 830 State Life Building	2,151	190	2,864	5,205	574	510	112	2	1	1,089	0	40
INDIANAPOLIS No. 9 ... 2810 West Michigan Street	3,856	302	5,125	9,283	897	1,019	141	38	82	1,085	2	82
INDIANAPOLIS No. 10 ... Brownstown	1,772	182	203	4,547	583	454	47	5	417	199	124	17
Jackson ... Rensselaer	1,159	111	1,600	2,870	361	392	16	8	75	801	173	6
Jasper ... Portland	1,982	185	2,537	3,516	510	584	92	0	94	417	136	16
Jay ... Madison	1,306	156	2,054	2,408	362	293	61	16	106	996	4	2
Jefferson ... North Vernon	900	88	1,420	4,253	353	269	37	0	41	628	5	0
Jennings ... Franklin	1,822	189	2,242	9,879	525	537	38		52	470	150	20
Johnson ... Vin mes	3,869	383	5,627	5,312	1,159	947	109	14	38	1,144	154	64
Knox ... Warsaw	2,054	200	3,048	2,722	509	456	48	2	57	2,092	44	7
Kosciusko ... Lagrange	1,082	127	1,513	2,983	294	220	44	4	71	975	207	12
Lagrange ... Whiting	1,821	104	2,058	9,917	310	304	24	11	51	527	0	9
Lake No. 1 ... Hammond	3,975	303	5,639	4,758	931	1,102	136		80	391	38	91
Lake No. 2 ... Crown Point	2,031	169	2,558	5,332	474	507	67	12	123	1,639	176	34
Lake No. 3 ... Michigan City	2,326	183	2,823	5,692	560	603	31	1	233	827	67	65
La Porte No. 1 ... La Porte	2,330	209	2,353	5,635	612	600	131	3	91	996	166	26
La Porte No. 2 ... Bedford	2,305	224	3,106	5,974	508	632	28	9	83	1,089	13	12
Lawrence ... Anderson	3,562	302	4,580	8,444	886	710	45	9	50	230	30	23
Madison No. 1 ... Elwood	2,321	279	3,374	6,327	701	614	94	42	56	1,534	92	33
Madison No. 2 ... 1022 Hume-Mansur, Indianapolis	2,702	239	3,386	5,974	776	630	50	21	117	802	60	44
Marion ... Plymouth	1,868	193	2,565	4,626	428	346	20	4	109	1,406	162	12
Marshall ... Shoals	892	113	1,223	2,228	363	281	28	4	123	1,150	3	0
Martin ... Peru	2,651	243	3,428	6,322	563	470	53	40	41	394	82	16
Miami ... Bloomington	2,056	185	2,569	4,810	564	508	19	2	176	98	20	15
Monroe ... Crawfordsville	2,184	219	3,240	5,643	770	743	76	30	16	1,052	19	7
Montgomery ...										788		

APPENDIX TABLE 100-A.—*Principal statistical data, by local boards*—Continued.

INDIANA—Continued.

Local board.	Post-office address.	Registration.				Induction.	Physical groups.				Deferments.		
		June 5, 1917.	June and August, 1918.	Sept. 12, 1918.	Total.	Accepted at camp.	General service.	Remediables.	Limited service.	Disqualified.	Dependency.	Agricultural.	Industrial.
Morgan		1,512	200	2,239	3,951	533	468	12	27	25	806	38	8
Newton	Kentland	870	99	1,258	2,227	280	225	5	11	23	328	63	4
Noble	Kendallville	1,721	161	2,487	4,369	329	285	19	55	58	1,041	182	14
Ohio	Rising Sun	339	33	441	813	118	230		10	28	119	44	5
Orange	Paoli	1,417	132	1,900	3,449	481	449	0	30	156	714	15	8
Owen	Spencer	956	106	1,372	2,434	366	370	5	16	33	477	7	4
Parke	Rockville	1,633	173	2,130	3,936	512	551	0	26	114	837	64	24
Perry	Cannelton	1,258	149	1,725	3,132	482	471	2	59	51	664	8	3
Pike		1,390	175	2,020	3,585	491	439	14	38	61	825	26	23
Porter	Valparaiso	2,007	220	2,372	4,599	627	545		24		801	44	8
Posey	Mt. Vernon	1,596	149	2,232	3,977	501	670	10	44	116	405	79	8
Pulaski		985	126	1,326	2,437	320	260	1	26	46	487	140	1
Putnam	Greencastle	1,411	166	2,279	3,856	418	69	4	26	5	533	17	1
Randolph	Winchester	2,042	230	3,109	5,381	569	409		70	104	1,176	132	14
Ripley	Versailles	1,268	127	2,051	3,446	486	429	18	46	105	547	81	3
Rush	Rushville	1,471	147	2,246	3,864	346	280		15	38	587	65	2
Scott	Scottsburg	478	46	833	1,357	153	125	0	5	41	281	17	1
Shelby	Shelbyville	2,041	182	3,037	5,260	536	414	6	39	233	1,148	33	7
SOUTH BEND No. 1	Room 261, Farmers' Trust Building	3,154	229	4,588	7,971	635	545	31	95	155	1,630	12	43
SOUTH BEND No. 2	South Bend	3,440	202	4,265	7,907	873	841	37	114	56	202	4	46
Spencer	Rockport	1,443	148	2,054	3,645	629	591		10	153	665	57	3
Starke	Knox	879	100	1,180	2,159	252	191	0	10	122	444	79	10
Steuben	Angola	1,030	90	1,520	2,640	284	248	5	35	52	575	52	9
St. Joseph	South Bend	2,792	272	3,927	6,991	681	633	15	120	126	1,331	199	25
Sullivan	Sullivan	2,477	301	3,807	6,585	789	633	56	90	94	1,373	44	22
Switzerland		683	103	1,076	1,862	241	94	4	9	35	342	6	0
TERRE HAUTE No. 1	116 South Sixth Street	2,517	230	3,017	6,364	922	907	51	116	21	916	1	12
TERRE HAUTE No. 2	Sixth and Cherry, 302 Grand Opera Block	3,835	332	5,470	9,657	1,000	1,229	71	173	25	1,414	9	20
Tippecanoe		3,668	342	4,972	8,982	1,363	625		98	40	1,711	203	33
Tipton	Tipton	1,304	142	1,857	3,303	351	308	6	31	78	652	5	0
Union	Liberty	484	35	687	1,186	147	38	7	4	18	115	219	0
Vanderburgh	Evansville	1,178	137	1,621	2,936	390	422	19	47	18	350	59	4
Vermillion	Newport	2,784	258	4,212	7,254	744	748	21	63	56	1,118	25	5
Vigo	Room 16, Post Office Building, Terre Haute	2,744	298	4,945	7,987	883	942	0	80	86	1,175	0	1
Wabash	Wabash	2,182	206	2,945	5,333	735	753	1	81	13	729	1	0
Warren	Williamsport	839	73	1,215	2,127	244	222	0	18	44	429	55	2
Warrick	**Boonville**	**1,474**	**198**	**2,313**	**3,985**	**406**	**521**		**16**	**205**	**776**	**105**	**45**

17	52	675	40	15	8	332	406	3,127	1,773	133	1,221	Washington
91	29	1,478	51	86	14	593	799	6,782	3,861	207	2,714	Wayne No. 1
7	65	418	50	8	2	292	277	2,936	1,654	111	1,171	Wayne No. 2
17	126	851	203	8	18	313	361	4,062	2,286	172	1,604	Wells
19	195	564	89	3	2	439	381	3,412	1,889	147	1,376	White
9	119	702	35	38	18	245	336	3,245	1,862	130	1,253	Whitley

IOWA.

												County	Location
2	49	662	99	13	10	349	353	3,055	1,612	134	1,309	Adair	Greenfield
2	26	61	45	12	10	313	232	2,271	1,291	85	895	Adams	Corning
28	635	566	72	21	22	508	464	3,715	2,031	175	1,509	Allamakee	Waukon
164	86	1,304	128	28	30	520	633	6,448	3,758	244	2,446	Appanoose	Centerville
13	106	539	103	36	22	431	479	2,986	1,477	132	1,357	Audubon	Audubon
8	25	1,073	162	44	38	680	720	5,292	2,815	232	2,245	Benton	Vinton
2	114	767	76	48	32	673	710	4,314	2,266	186	2,862	Blackhawk	Cedar Rapids
2	10	1,147	125	63	7	973	830	6,326	2,581	259	2,486	Boone	Boone
2	49	688	102	22	6	159	506	3,394	873	145	673	Bremer	Waverly
5	86	695	44	19	16	617	560	3,900	2,070	157	1,932	Buchanan	Independence
5	16	857	47	96	2	770	730	4,377	1,986	196	1,653	Buena Vista	Storm Lake
7	130	713	68	10	26	595	528	3,794	2,112	155	1,686	Butler	Allison
11	129	713	54	33	1	615	605	3,982	2,298	184	2,014	Calhoun	Rockwell City
11	101	879	69	34	14	752	805	4,619	2,136	227	1,769	Carroll	Carroll
4	149	554	85	17	16	548	570	3,918	2,378	170	1,619	Cass	Atlantic
1	53	335	68	79	31	559	629	10,238	60	163	4,236	Cedar	Tipton
79		1,902	370	121	48	1,043	1,085	8,537	4,404	312	1,834	Cedar Rapids	Cedar Rapids
21	198	1,483	147	40	18	1,063	989	3,888	2,076	299	1,649	Cerro Gordo	Mason City
1	9	730	50	23	3	65	534	3,225	1,746	13	1,316	Cherokee	Cherokee
5	196	559	138	17		389	410	2,170	1,243	163	837	Chickasaw	New Hampton
6	51	462	51	58	31	242	232	2,666	1,891	90	1,600	Clarke	Osceola
9	148	622	110	36	16	532	559	5,324	2,932	175	2,133	Clay	Spencer
11	244	889	214	31	11	738	754	4,907	2,694	259	2,025	Clayton	Elkader
25	20	1,022	209	28		832	717	4,333	2,305	188	1,820	Clinton No. 1	208 Wilson Building, Clinton
5	227	90	148	31		672	689	7,628	4,180	208	3,211	Clinton No. 2	De Witt
18		1,496	148	97	6	838	794	4,909	2,473	237	2,227	Council Bluffs	Council Bluffs
2	67	662	125	59	9	610	612	4,959	3,088	209	2,379	Crawford	
12	145	1,142	161	59	34	613	659	5,674	3,525	207	2,292	Dallas	Adel
47	2	1,116	141	94	36	689	715	6,043	4,429	231	2,747	Davenport No. 1	56 Davenport Savings Bank Building
77	7	1,156	185	72		783	836	7,461	1,421	285	1,077	Davenport No. 2	608 Putman Building
9	192	551	27	15		310	251	2,593	1,819	95	1,246	Davis	Bloomfield
3	98	739	82	20	6	41	379	3,201	1,993	86	1,469	Decatur	Leon
7	200	661	49	47		414	458	3,638	4,613	176	3,034	Delaware	Manchester
27	6	1,504	173	68	34	674	925	7,927	4,802	280	3,547	Des Moines No. 1	Courthouse
87	57	1,496	229	89	46	988	978	8,618	3,373	269	2,974	Des Moines No. 2	507 Euclid Avenue
7		78	3	42	11	1,141	754	6,545	2,351	198	1,606	Des Moines No. 3	City Hall
20	4	767	34	31	55	351	351	4,095	4,182	138	3,081	Des Moines No. 4	Phillips School
96	120	1,009	204	104	8	867	1,026	7,566	1,261	303	1,108	Des Moines	Burlington
7	125	232	21	15	16	370	400	2,490	4,437	121	3,421	Dickinson	Spirit Lake
72		1,438	59	167	12	846	1,342	8,177	2,027	319	1,569	Dubuque	Dubuque
4	168	546	155	35		551	537	3,770		174		Dubuque	Epworth

APPENDIX TABLES.

APPENDIX TABLE 100–A—*Principal statistical data, by local boards*—Continued.

IOWA—Continued.

Local board.	Post-office address.	Registration: June 5, 1917.	Registration: June and August, 1918.	Registration: Sept. 12, 1918.	Registration: Total.	Induction: Accepted at camp.	Physical groups: General service.	Physical groups: Remediables.	Physical groups: Limited service.	Physical groups: Disqualified.	Deferments: Dependency.	Deferments: Agricultural.	Deferments: Industrial.
Emmet	Estherville	1,279	122	1,497	2,898	432	479		23	122	309	313	23
Fayette	West Union	2,551	267	3,307	6,125	725	750	31	46	189	1,186	625	47
Floyd	Charles City	1,740	164	2,334	4,233	514	562		48	134	827	121	32
Franklin	Hampton	1,689	163	1,958	3,810	627	607	16	29	110	700	154	6
Fremont	Sidney	1,396	150	1,715	3,261	402	405	7	23	108	725	113	2
Greene	Jefferson	1,669	119	1,935	3,723	536	594	10	37	82	764	111	4
Grundy	Grundy Center	1,398	148	1,750	3,296	468	431	15	41	27	403	180	6
Guthrie	Guthrie Center	1,522	138	2,010	3,670	464	561	2	18	54	838	72	2
Hamilton	Webster City	1,849	208	2,308	4,365	587	888	1	49	58	672	102	6
Hancock	Garner	1,493	186	1,786	3,465	624	627		51	92	598	129	8
Hardin	Eldora	2,108	204	2,573	4,885	733	584	14	72	126	575	495	45
Harrison	Logan	2,227	228	2,899	5,354	740	736	20	24	121	203	72	9
Henry	Mount Pleasant	1,361	133	1,879	3,373	468	571	9	13	50	653	14	1
Howard	Cresco	1,179	124	1,526	2,829	366	308	8	8	174	457	160	2
Humboldt	Dakota City	1,404	132	1,555	3,091	401	411	9	18	16	610	459	8
Ida	Ida Grove	1,458	126	1,433	3,017	483	541	10	25	42	54	230	15
Iowa	Marengo	1,548	179	2,139	3,866	522	510	13	14	28	82	260	4
Jackson	Maquoketa	1,609	174	2,287	4,070	576	562		37	83	675	215	3
Jasper	Newton	2,552	227	2,813	5,986	791	735	1	47	81	1,330	15	16
Jefferson	Fairfield	1,362	139	1,811	3,312	399	350	13	34	85	752	112	2
Johnson	Iowa City	2,476	283	2,942	5,701	780	647	20	37	89	541	223	2
Jones	Anamosa	1,684	171	2,059	3,914	601	533	22	51	95	767	129	18
Keokuk	Sigourney	1,666	167	2,346	4,179	560	513	1	50	128	906	95	82
Kossuth	Algona	2,571	287	3,013	5,871	845	1,014	2	64	208	612	524	8
Lee	Keokuk	3,192	327	4,321	7,840	999	800	31	62	255	1,477	233	4
Linn	Marion	2,327	243	3,297	5,867	798	676	16	49	78	1,093	178	10
Louisa	Wapello	1,066	110	1,375	2,551	270	311	49	27	51	503	75	8
Lucas	Chariton	1,301	141	1,887	3,329	417	285	15	27	25	686	26	
Lyon	Rock Rapids	1,581	174	1,798	3,553	558	504	9	65	94	564	231	95
Madison	Winterset	1,275	137	1,761	3,173	405	378	10	22	166	747	14	20
Mahaska	Oskaloosa	2,234	244	2,635	5,413	711	676		46	141	582	121	20
Marion	Knoxville	1,964	234	2,920	5,118	546	481	25	41	94	1,007	136	3
Marshall	Marshalltown	3,106	249	3,720	7,074	891	948	23	49	14	1,419	103	6
Mills	Glenwood	1,131	113	1,615	2,859	346	376	15	30	103	585	126	8
Mitchell	Osage	1,242	151	1,680	3,073	439	397	24	27	80	509	127	6
Monona	Onawa	1,713	162	2,023	3,898	605	657	18	51		791	105	8
Monroe	Albia	1,950	217	2,982	5,149	456	83	3	2	5	37	33	19

Montgomery	Red Oak	1,609	139	2,035	3,783	452	489	19	38	124	629	135	3
Muscatine	Pine	2,725	229	3,419	6,373	905	939	19	51	60	1,268	202	12
O'Brien	Primghar	1,935	184	2,098	4,217	674	652	22	53	142	787	114	33
Osceola	Sibley	1,006	120	1,189	2,315	371	335	24	25	54	428	54	8
Page	Clarinda	1,922	182	2,623	4,727	551	572	13	47	50	1,055	72	9
Palo Alto	Emmetsburg	1,549	153	1,766	3,468	544	600	59	39	28	345	383	2
Plymouth	Le Mars	2,346	241	2,825	5,412	811	986	11	49	1	938	219	2
Pocahontas	Pocahontas	1,682	151	1,885	3,718	653	686	3	41	110	636	171	19
Polk	Room 7, Courthouse, Des Moines	2,411	206	3,348	5,965	627	685	14	33	128	1,132	84	8
Pottawattamie	Avoca	2,731	266	3,064	6,061	780	726	4	68	133	1,087	224	11
Poweshiek		1,778	99	2,288	2,731	502	465	15	41	87	902	186	0
Ringgold	Mt Ayr	1,065	126	1,540	4,108	331	387	3	6	50	641	87	3
Sac	Sac City	1,828	176	2,104	4,532	600	620	12	69	81	806	64	5
Scott	Davenport	1,936	212	2,384	3,841	537	588	15	70	82	690	209	5
Shelby	Harlan	1,702	187	1,952	7,836	936	610	30	33	187	717	206	54
Sioux City No. 1	Sioux City	3,085	297	4,454	8,369	966	914	54	133	45	1,503	22	76
Sioux City No. 2	do.	3,443	291	4,635	5,760	848	884	4	207	128	1,372	12	11
Sioux	Orange City	2,452	313	2,995	6,060	859	887	21	43	134	1,040	281	231
Story	Nevada	2,791	254	3,015	4,990	683	895	34	67	36	1,238	223	12
Tama	Toledo	2,111	194	1,818	3,223	408	594	34	32	55	972	154	1
Taylor	Bedford	1,268	137	1,923	3,446	320	339		13	30	778	63	1
Union	Creston	1,371	153	1,612	2,732	339	334	2	51	55	293	7	1
Van Buren	Keosauqua	1,006	114	1,671	3,687	1,021	287	1	29	70	548	46	55
Wapello	Ottumwa	3,177	302	4,671	8,150	550	1,056	28	54	58	1,649	52	3
Warren	Indianola	1,671	173	2,265	4,094	511	484	4	25	36	741	103	14
Washington	Washington	3,764	158	4,551	8,579	1,086	517	16	34	185	1,809	67	0
WATERLOO	Black Building, Waterloo	1,270	264	1,746	3,177	405	1,054	16	101	47	624	0	24
Wayne	Corydon	3,665	161	4,698	8,689	1,083	474	2	18	116	1,568	345	28
Webster	Fort Dodge	1,251	326	1,541	2,928	448	220	54	126	85	473	239	5
Winnebago	Forest City	1,856	136	2,502	4,590	604	442	25	25	221	367	238	10
Winneshiek	Decorah	2,098	232	2,511	4,817	621	533	13	32	58	846	330	8
Woodbury	Mor Mart Bui ldg, Sioux City	1,193	208	1,484	2,793	385	680	45	76	70	436	258	8
Worth	Northwood		116				353	7	33	60		198	8
Wright	Clarion	1,985	217	2,388	4,590	636	563	16	24		855	106	19

KANSAS.

Allen	Iola	1,895	201	2,717	4,813	527	659	9	89	33	1,007	130	16
Anderson	Garnett	945	116	1,457	2,518	326	272	4	19	42	201	289	7
Atchison	Atchison	1,947	194	2,780	4,921	689	542	0	57	17	834	85	6
Barber	Medicine Lodge	895	84	1,221	2,200	324	274	5	28	2	304	97	2
Barton	Great Bend	1,581	173	2,225	3,979	549	537	8	24	81	619	198	22
Bourbon	Fort Scott	1,603	194	2,682	4,479	482	446	1	17	101	885	93	19
Brown	Hiawatha	1,987	184	2,467	4,638	497	460	5	37	73	830	187	59
Butler	Eldorado	3,831	510	6,787	11,158	1,292	1,254	16	46	202	1,431	252	75
Chase	Cottonwood Falls	731	64	864	1,659	162	142	0	43	33	271	93	5
Chautauqua	Sedan	984	103	1,498	2,885	389	356	6	41	14	499	74	5
Cherokee	Columbus	2,921	348	4,276	7,545	1,055	811	18	81	94	1,612	60	12
Cheyenne	St. Francis	506	51	646	1,203	135	84	0	5	9	220	218	7
Clark	Ashland	544	60	568	1,162	175	131	8	11	16	251	67	3

APPENDIX TABLE 100-A.—Principal statistical data, by local boards—Continued.

KANSAS—Continued.

Local board	Post-office address	Registration: June 5, 1917	Registration: June and August, 1918	Registration: Sept. 12, 1918	Registration: Total	Induction: Accepted at camp	Physical groups: General service	Physical groups: Remediables	Physical groups: Limited service	Disqualified	Deferments: Dependency	Deferments: Agricultural	Deferments: Industrial
Clay	Clay Center	1,303	154	1,807	3,264	428	352	0	3	60	409	158	4
Cloud	Concordia	1,547	142	2,150	3,839	554	305	18	48	108	707	111	0
Coffey	Burlington	1,108	116	1,655	2,879	311	317	12	13	72	502	179	8
Comanche	Coldwater	591	57	672	1,320	172	132	5	14	9	112	56	0
Cowley	Winfield	2,712	270	4,302	7,284	729	695	17	55	124	1,377	237	29
Crawford No. 1	Girard	3,177	250	4,476	7,903	704	803	12	83		1,455	50	17
Crawford No. 2	Pittsburg	2,507	270	3,773	6,550	918	155	4	12	64	112	1	0
Decatur	Oberlin	803	73	905	1,781	250	170	11	12	28	104		22
Dickenson	Abilene	2,304	221	3,141	5,666	591	526	118	36	26	285	91	0
Doniphan	Troy	1,276	218	1,622	3,016	443	299	5	22	3	577	278	1
Douglas	Lawrence	1,985	218	2,558	4,761	682	659	6	31	72	778	106	8
Edwards	Kinsley	710	57	909	1,676	107	165	1	14		333	3	0
Elk	Howard	738	80	1,079	1,897	209	172	5	13	33	224	124	0
Ellis	Hays	1,265	107	1,388	2,760	383	314	1	24	12	641	16	9
Ellsworth	Ellsworth	1,120	79	1,337	2,538	270	298	9	17	62	330	100	51
Finney	Garden City	740	61	945	1,746	229	194	0	17	10	185	67	14
Ford	Dodge City	1,472	92	1,699	3,263	355	217	8	28	35	721	41	13
Franklin	Ottawa	1,599	146	2,445	4,190	463	735	13	36	43	407	126	151
Geary	Junction City	804	109	1,634	2,547	241	201		31	161	14	495	2
Gove	Gove	517	56	539	1,112	177	140	2	9	3	75	12	0
Graham	Hill City	759	75	819	1,653	227	186	0	5	11	108	132	0
Grant	New Ulysses	122	19	140	281	51	57		6	21	56	85	4
Gray	Cimarron	559	48	545	1,152	148	184	4	11	1	257	9	3
Greeley	Tribune	118	13	140	271	37	24	2	7	10	53	72	3
Greenwood	Eureka	1,145	123	1,814	3,083	307	308	1	13	6	589	9	2
Hamilton	Syracuse	244	32	373	649	87	65	0	7	27	105	176	12
Harper	Anthony	1,287	125	1,656	3,068	369	463	7	30	27	561	12	33
Harvey	Newton	1,826	194	2,440	4,450	534	463	33	24	45	788	487	0
Haskell	Santa Fe	183	12	214	409	64	64		4	37	77	208	0
Hodgeman	Jetmore	407	37	428	872	99	89	1	3	4	174	15	19
Jackson	Holton	1,288	143	1,843	3,272	292	285	0	15	9	590	24	0
Jefferson	Oskaloosa	1,179	119	1,701	2,999	386	393	1	24	91	490	303	0
Jewell		1,463	148	1,923	3,554	459	87	3	2	61	572	75	10
Johnson	Olathe	1,406	141	2,208	3,755	444	468	1	22	114	608	290	0
Kansas City No. 1	City Hall	1,434	99	2,073	3,606	413	436	3	6	11	384	36	6
Kansas City No. 2	do	3,663	321	5,274	9,278	980	468	46	85	81	2,291	0	33
Kansas City No. 3	do	3,838	358	4,902	9,188	966	15	27	37	19	1,655	5	120
Kansas City No. 4	do	1,080	59	1,511	2,650	237	264	1	7	80	1,521	2	31

County	City	1	2	3	4	5	6	7	8	9	10	11	12
Kearny	Lakin	274	22	390	688	76	65	1	9	15	113	17	1
Kingman	Kingman	1,139	138	1,444	2,721	338	239	1	27	68	546	187	7
Kiowa	Greensburg	2,810	68	774	1,465	191	132	7	16	5	325	260	7
Labette	Oswego	319	301	4,469	7,580	845	823	23	71	125	475	149	42
Lane	Dighton	2,491	31	303	653	104	77	5	4	13	159	41	1
Leavenworth	Leavenworth	919	231	3,542	6,264	835	560	27	125	217	922	72	1
Lincoln	Lincoln	1,030	121	1,574	2,817	327	252	0	9	47	417	168	1
Linn	Md Ct.	348	107	397	2,711	258	227	1	7	46	532	31	2
Logan	Russell Springs	2,139	27	3,114	772	116	111		16	14	140	34	3
Lyon	Emporia	1,852	225	2,552	5,478	801	598	19	71	88	956	146	3
McPherson	McPherson	1,760	213	2,419	4,617	639	544	3	36	52	875	349	28
Marion	Marion	1,795	188	2,656	4,367	518	395		25	13	642	127	4
Marshall	Marysville	639	232	630	4,683	561	505	12	29	31	767	129	8
Meade		1,486	65	2,421	1,334	175	103	5	7	21	279	52	9
Miami	Paola	1,254	163	1,608	4,070	498	448	11	40	97	722	160	1
Mitchell	Beloit	2,151	105	3,089	3,027	405	305	6	40	67	556	208	9
Montgomery No. 1	Independence	2,358	214	3,055	5,454	524	511	8	40	214	1,181	53	5
Montgomery No. 2		1,002	185	1,431	5,598	497	715	1	31	146	1,065	160	12
Morris	Grove	276	102	403	2,535	279	10	1	9	43	476	185	44
Morton	Elkhart	1,469	18	2,062	697	94	86		6	26	121	17	8
Nemaha	Seneca	2,039	153	2,893	3,664	445	341	8	24	44	736	232	1
Neosho	Erie	694	215	800	5,147	510	536	16	29	58	1,117	168	1
Ness	Ness City	1,010	80	1,244	1,574	176	178	1	16	30	97	97	26
Norton	Norton	1,434	98	2,141	2,350	290	217	7	9	60	221	127	5
Osage	Lyndon	1,140	150	1,475	3,725	315	214	14	26	42	579	182	2
Osborne	Osborne	992	104	1,334	2,719	317							19
Ottawa	Minneapolis	921	90	1,138	2,416	223	276	8	12	30	316	305	1
Pawnee	Larned	1,176	78	1,440	2,137	298	258	7	19	44	441	118	2
Phillips	Phillipsburg	1,249	132	1,908	2,748	361	268	8	21	14	314	96	0
Potawatomie	Westmoreland	1,166	154	1,567	3,311	417	347	14	25	86	508	200	7
Pratt	Pratt	550	118	749	2,851	370	310	36	25	58	562	104	19
Rawlins		3,461	66	5,146	1,365	221	160	0	13	17	251	91	0
Reno	Hutchinson	1,446	381	2,033	8,978	1,036	859	18	46	208	1,745	252	27
Republic	Belleville	1,373	139	2,156	3,618	531	730	0	80	14	664	177	0
Rice	Lyons	1,422	127	2,132	3,366	441	395	2	15	47	604	221	7
Riley	Manhattan	891	193	948	3,771	414	365	2	25	16	602	2	23
Rooks		826	85	1,272	2,118	306	217	1	15	61	160	88	0
Rush	La Crosse	978	88	3,023	1,800	252	186	5	9	14	452	39	3
Russell	Russell	2,136	110	5,362	2,300	359	294	13	28	96	676	72	6
Saline	Salina	308	203	379	5,362	592	510	1	104	7	90	85	7
Scott	Scott City	1,618	35	2,421	722	105	81	12	14	28	939	333	0
Sedgwick	Courthouse, Wichita	538	167	778	4,206	467	288	6	31	21	697	42	6
Seward		1,539	66	2,433	1,382	157	156	6	16	170	109	124	1
Shawnee	Courthouse, Topeka	532	164	623	4,136	484	306	1	13	38	234	1	1
Sheridan	Hoxie	1,411	57	591	1,220	187	146	12	8	162	726	20	0
Sherman		956	44	1,700	1,191	148	263	6	14	28	447	115	4
Smith	Smith Center	100	122	1,386	1,255	410	323	3	20	10	48	110	3
Stafford	St. John	303	16	145	2,464	362	271	2	11	118	82	11	0
Stanton	Johnson		33	551	261	261	28	0	7	31	1,225	45	0
Stevens	Hugoton	2,392	251	3,585	887	32	100	12	10		237	270	32
Sumner	Wellington	566	57	614	6,228	87	591	15	16			76	3
Thomas					1,237	99	193						

APPENDIX TABLE 100-A.—*Principal statistical data, by local boards*—Continued.

KANSAS—Continued.

Local board.	Post-office address.	Registration. June 5, 1917.	June and August, 1918.	Sept. 12, 1918.	Total.	Induction. Accepted at camp.	Physical groups. General service.	Remediables.	Limited service.	Disqualified.	Deferments. Dependency.	Agricultural.	Industrial.
TOPEKA No. 1	City Hall	1,828	139	2,558	4,525	567	448	16	34	99	909	5	29
TOPEKA No. 2	do	2,448	201	3,011	5,660	703	523	21	31	3	1,084	3	20
Trego	Wakeeney	515	54	665	1,234	162	132	0	19	6	255	55	2
Wabaunsee	Alma	1,016	122	1,432	2,570	374	335	2	25	45	493	138	9
Wallace	Sharon Springs	216	14	318	548	78	64	2	3	......	1	......	1
Washington	Washington	1,646	195	2,071	3,912	501	366	12	21	49	687	385	2
WICHITA No. 1	Suite 1001, Schweiter Building	2,882	278	4,714	7,874	912	790	43	190	35	1,542	8	36
WICHITA No. 2	City Hall	2,693	277	4,574	7,644	872	767	36	178	34	1,498	12	37
Leoti	Leoti	131	14	189	334	67	29	1	7	0	3	40	......
Wilson	Fredonia	1,715	157	2,427	4,299	420	404	10	38	158	657	97	10
Woodson	Yates Center	634	80	1,031	1,745	231	39	......	4	4	4	1	......
Wyandotte	Edwardsville	1,822	141	2,630	4,593	470	527	20	48	171	893	45	18

KENTUCKY.

Local board.	Post-office address.	Registration. June 5, 1917.	June and August, 1918.	Sept. 12, 1918.	Total.	Induction. Accepted at camp.	Physical groups. General service.	Remediables.	Limited service.	Disqualified.	Deferments. Dependency.	Agricultural.	Industrial.
Adair	Columbia	1,403	162	1,829	3,394	402	549	5	99	95	710	1	0
Allen	Scottsville	1,303	174	1,846	3,323	477	450	7	15	90	192	39	7
Anderson	Lawrenceburg	753	83	1,116	1,952	244	214	7	28	68	386	13	8
Ballard	Wickliffe	1,151	125	1,421	2,697	351	61	28	25	32	489	29	0
Barren	Glasgow	1,893	247	2,682	4,822	701	743	12	19	30	540	1	1
Bath	Owingsville	1,060	121	1,361	2,532	276	278	5	6	109	639	0	0
Bell	Middlesboro	2,639	291	3,826	6,756	459	460	6	62	309	1,706	2	33
Boone	Burlington	677	74	1,109	1,860	240	268	1	13	60	295	15	6
Bourbon	Paris	1,550	121	2,256	3,927	580	539	0	24	106	705	10	22
Boyd	Catlettsburg	2,377	238	3,294	5,909	580	643	16	46	105	1,321	3	93
Boyle	Danville	1,196	136	1,692	3,024	424	302	9	47	105	674	10	5
Bracken	Brooksville	912	95	1,218	2,225	256	289	1	13	27	518	17	1
Breathitt	Jackson	1,598	205	2,109	3,912	281	353	5	33	58	5	1	5
Breckenridge	Hardinsburg	1,695	194	2,195	4,054	432	536	12	102	2	873	5	10
Bullitt	Shepherdsville	701	87	1,093	1,881	213	212	0	15	47	328	2	6
Butler	Morgantown	1,217	150	1,718	3,085	357	367	2	5	20	738	24	1
Caldwell	Princeton	1,061	128	1,587	2,761	305	328	1	7	85	575	9	2
Calloway	Murray	1,704	178	2,310	4,192	453	483	1	14	144	920	1	0
Campbell	City Hall, Fort Thomas	2,726	223	3,878	6,836	810	875	64	49	165	1,253	9	6
Carlisle	Bardwell	796	89	1,028	1,913	178	243	0	16	94	424	31	3

County	Place												
Carroll	Carrollton	724	81	923	1,728	180	232	5	21	58	409	8	2
Carter	Grayson	1,756	245	2,433	2,434	446	600	0	20	129	290	55	29
Casey	Liberty	1,240	169	1,729	3,138	340	469		5	3	674	2	0
Christian	Hopkinsville	2,959	313	3,924	7,196	923	424	17	45	128	1,461	22	6
Clark	404 McEldowney Building, Winchester	1,388	164	2,171	3,723	485	535	174	28	15	639	3	3
Clay	Manchester	1,313	147	1,918	3,378	324							
Clinton	Albany	600	93	881	1,574	222	242	1	15	59	147	7	0
Covington No. 1	City Building	2,888	203	3,684	6,475	790	620	18	62	171	266	1	51
Covington No. 2	do	2,888	290	3,588	6,766	799	1,105	35	60	290	358	2	31
Crittenden	Marion	808	141	1,455	2,632	385	326	1	7	84	565	12	0
Cumberland	Burkesville	1,036	105	1,074	1,987	228	256	8	82		372	2	0
Daviess	Owensboro	3,303	337	4,699	8,339	849	1,027	25	89	359	1,831	98	19
Edmonson	Brownsville	787	95	1,127	2,009	205	209	2	83	9	445	0	0
Elliott	Sandy Hook	730	105	899	1,734	208	272	7	23	76	401	0	0
Estill	Irvine	1,183	157	1,562	2,903	266	293	4	9	66	633	6	43
Fayette	Lexington	1,101	116	1,642	2,859	382	415		24	77	531	18	3
Fleming	Flemingsburg	1,228	125	1,641	2,994	367	440	6	19	15	638	0	0
Floyd	Prestonsburg	2,054	269	2,716	5,029	4	495	19	21	38	1,268	1	44
Franklin	Frankfort	1,494	138	2,068	3,630	498	550	13	14	32	669	34	1
Fulton	Hickman	394	128	1,961	3,583	462	446	13	46	53	672	11	1
Gallatin	Warsaw	1,141	138	539	971	107	98	3	25	36	215	39	0
Garrard	Lancaster	766	37	1,459	2,737	266	548	0	8	21	506	10	3
Grant	Williamstown	1,141	99	1,215	2,080	429	284	14	54	59	361		2
Graves	Mayfield	2,635	318	3,660	6,613	266	179	12	17	26	77		
Grayson	Leitchfield	1,643	179	2,158	3,980	823	563	9	13	58	981	0	0
Green	Greensburg	956	125	1,286	2,347	374	257	8	30	28	338	0	0
Greenup	Greenup	1,523	190	2,195	3,908	284	450	1	34	129	871	1	25
Hancock	Hawesville	1,651	81	772	1,404	425	183		26	140	288	11	1
Hardin	Elizabethtown	1,597	193	2,687	4,447	159			9	40			
Harlan	Harlan	1,781	327	3,356	5,474	394	512	1	41	72	1,167	4	29
Harrison	Cynthiana	1,229	162	1,873	3,264	500	458	9	31	42	737	8	10
Hart	Munfordsville	1,428	199	1,972	3,599	410	470	0	52	191	743	18	4
Henderson	Henderson	2,345	268	3,239	3,239	443	824	5	28	133	1,064	140	20
Henry	Newcastle	1,099	118	1,577	2,794	783	377	7	28	26	452	11	2
Hickman	Clinton	908	79	1,168	2,155	405	221		28	92	476	11	2
Hopkins	Madisonville	2,950	332	4,081	7,363	208	1,092	0	10	179	1,699	44	96
Jackson	McKee	819	111	1,263	2,193	939	238	1	24	92	545	0	0
Jefferson	Louisville	3,723	343	5,181	9,247	206	1,191	3	17	221	1,790	51	50
Johnson	Paintsville	996	120	1,389	2,505	1,169	358	0	102	188	400	2	0
Kenton	Covington	1,874	191	2,039	4,104	358	381	0	10	184	1,144	0	11
Knott	Hindman	1,464	177	2,068	3,709	316	581	17	6	93	591	15	33
Knox	Barbourville	921	128	2,117	2,117	555	57		67	19	49		
Larue	Hodgenville	1,556	240	2,502	4,598	220	463	0	2	164	1,251	0	8
Laurel	London	734	89	1,132	1,955	408	274	2	96	54	105	183	9
Lawrence	Louisa	1,294	198	2,092	3,584	293	51	1	16	4	34	16	1
Lee	Beattyville	1,340	166	1,839	3,345	296	137	6	4	92	759	1	2
Leslie	Hyden	740	110	1,196	2,046	399	308	4	12	1	397	1	8
Letcher	Whitesburg	768	92	934	1,794	237	260	fo	9	65	467	0	0
Lewis	Vanceburg	2,443	224	2,856	5,523	210	429	1	31	139	660		6
Lexington	Third floor, Courthouse, Lexington	1,200	153	1,712	3,065	537	461	17	89	116	1,322	2	16
Lincoln	Stanford	3,339	154	4,705	8,327	1,103	394	4	22	138	614	3	1

APPENDIX TABLE 100-A.—*Principal statistical data, by local boards*—Continued.

KENTUCKY—Continued.

Local board	Post-office address	Registration — June 5, 1917	Registration — June and August, 1918	Registration — Sept. 12, 1918	Registration — Total	Induction — Accepted at camp	Physical groups — General service	Physical groups — Remediables	Physical groups — Limited service	Physical groups — Disqualified	Deferments — Dependency	Deferments — Agricultural	Deferments — Industrial
Livingston	Smithland	855	87	1,100	2,042	258	238	7	29	27	478	0	0
Logan	Russellville	970	228	2,660	4,638	516	630	6	19	13	841	4	0
LOUISVILLE No. 1	515 Louisville Trust Building	1,369	123	1,956	3,448	409	321	22	55	90	643	0	22
LOUISVILLE No. 2	501-502 Inter-Southern Building, Louisville	3,856	374	5,731	9,961	1,293	1,300	36	188	81	1,933	2	66
LOUISVILLE No. 3	111 West Chestnut Street	2,679	236	3,887	6,837	1,028	633	20	102	61	895	0	26
LOUISVILLE No. 4	Masonic Temple Building	2,193	169	3,242	5,604	832	836	39	109	98	618	0	60
LOUISVILLE No. 5	Louisville Trust Building	2,115	223	2,987	5,325	782	1,046	15	115	46	522	0	12
LOUISVILLE No. 6	1221 West Market Street	3,908	338	5,770	10,064	1,547	1,079	12	126	260	465	0	59
LOUISVILLE No. 7	408 Inter-Southern Building	4,205	362	6,100	10,667	1,343	1,410	27	191	82	1,633	0	5
Lyon	Eddyville	644	94	867	1,605	206	76	3		84	347	7	0
McCracken	Paducah	3,189	274	4,621	8,084	925	998		50	243	1,201	7	4
McCreary	Stearns	937	108	1,182	2,227	239	228	1	14	63	600	1	23
McLean	Calhoun	992	109	1,465	2,566	250							
Madison	Richmond	2,008	259	2,850	5,117	768	797	6	51	209	214	38	9
Magoffin	Salyersville	1,132	136	1,374	2,662	231	271	10	34	65	814	0	3
Marion	Lebanon	1,117	152	1,366	2,635	393	441	13	32	31	619	10	2
Marshall	Benton	1,252	154	1,617	3,023	141	137						
Martin	Inez	643	85	783	1,511	531		0	6	37	410	0	4
Mason	Maysville	1,445	160	2,110	3,715	211	563	8	29	143	637	47	2
Meade	Brandenburg	754	79	997	1,830	93	263	8	14	17	330	11	1
Menifee	Frenchburg	410	48	644	1,102	304	79	0	16	22	288	1	1
Mercer	Harrodsburg	1,097	111	1,667	2,875	251	329	2	4	33	651	8	5
Metcalfe	Edmonston	694	106	1,103	1,903	358	63		8	9	23		
Monroe	Tompkinsville	1,024	157	1,448	2,629	288	324	0	24	47	81	0	0
Montgomery	Mount Sterling	1,047	123	1,309	2,479	636	365	0	40	78	546	5	5
Morgan	Clerk's office, West Liberty	1,317	154	1,737	3,208	538			30	216	1,453	13	104
Muhlenberg	Greenville	2,397	304	3,717	6,418	827	536	5	18	138	559	49	0
Nelson	Bardstown	1,307	147	1,902	3,356	260	560	2	51	413	1,306	1	26
Newport	Room 21, Courthouse, Newport	2,856	253	3,623	6,732	501	763	20	50	48	399	6	1
Nicholas	Carlisle	783	87	1,124	1,994	198	259	3	16	46	1,006	16	19
Ohio	Hartford	2,059	256	3,087	5,382	289	546	35	22	5	586	32	4
Oldham	La Grange	640	64	857	1,561	160	263	2	9	102	631	5	2
Owen	Owenton	1,044	126	1,469	2,639	336	308	5	11	89	315	0	0
Owsley	Booneville	567	82	821	1,470	283	201	5	27	41	493	27	6
Pendleton	Falmouth	912	111	1,295	2,318		288						
Perry	Hazard	1,931	216	2,667	4,814							1	5
Pike	Pikeville	3,967	441	4,920	9,388	895	808	19	80	86	2,484		

County	City												
Powell	Stanton	476	58	748	1,263	130	121		10	56	266	1	6
Pulaski	Somerset	2,401	302	3,561	6,264	548	646	11	23	104	1,573	5	4
Robertson	Mount Olivet	326	35	446	807	98	87	11	5	12	193	0	1
Rockcastle	Mt Vernon	1,057	147	1,517	2,721	281	278	7	41	13	631	1	7
Rowan	Morehead	708	84	1,030	1,822	166	158	1	10	61	521	0	2
Russell	Jamestown	833	103	1,166	2,102	196	500	7	19	59	584	1	1
Scott	Georgetown	1,348	141	1,778	3,267	518	499	1	10		645	6	2
Shelby	Shelbyville	1,385	174	2,174	3,733	545	669	0	40	57	505	41	4
Simpson	Franklin	905	109	1,232	2,246	228	245	11	19		195	63	1
Spencer		630	93	915	1,638	254	230	7	8	29	509	22	2
Taylor	Campbell	910	149	74	2,333	299	377	2	13	29	723	12	1
Todd	Elkton	1,229	156	1,720	3,105	339	282	2	52	90	24	60	11
Trigg	Cadiz	1,172	138	1,538	2,848	305	78	4	13		278	1	
Trimble	Bedford	532	57	668	1,257	163	214	1	13	11	716	14	0
Union	Morganfield	1,557	179	2,016	3,752	160	588	11	25	127	1,185	46	43
Warren	Bowling Green	2,394	274	3,302	5,970	764	348	14	53	159	616	76	9
Washington	Springfield	1,088	161	1,532	2,781	368	337	43	15	111	1,091	32	6
Wayne	Monticello	1,230	174	1,632	3,036	375	520	7	73	64	1,242	11	11
Webster	Dixon	1,896	216	2,555	4,667	486	885	0	20	183		42	53
Whitley	Williamsburg	2,179	268	2,924	5,371	545	303	1	74	77	379	12	71
Wolfe	Campton	746	92	932	1,770	231	303		20	56	27	0	2
Woodford	Versailles	1,013	103	1,413	2,529	339	332	1	16	474		3	

LOUISIANA.

Parish	City												
Acadia	Crowley	2,833	368	3,736	6,937	828	1,034	9	93	4	1,761	5	4
Allen	Oberlin	2,343	179	2,643	5,165	740	771		34	148	987	1	1
Ascension	Donaldsonville	1,860	232	2,356	4,448	706	11	12	65	200	807	8	3
Assumption	Napoleonville	1,665	201	2,269	4,135	561	491		62	235	923	0	1
Avoyelles	Marksville	3,239	392	3,708	7,359	993	1,402	1	54	316	1,079	2	4
Beauregard	De Ridder	2,528	169	2,495	5,858	932	981		47	19	895	0	0
Bienville	Arcadia	2,034	235	2,185	4,764	609	867	3	51	134	733	6	4
Bossier	Benton	1,765	140	4,844	4,090	1,066	708	14	41	319	1,900	7	2
Caddo	806 City, Commercial Bank Building, Shreveport	3,548	368	5,024	8,760	1,112	1,018	21	64	355	339	12	7
Calcasieu	Lake Charles	3,283	265	1,254	8,572	328	340	25	21	69	455	17	18
Caldwell	Columbia	919	100	418	2,273	98	95		4	34	166	2	0
Cameron	Cameron	279	46	1,422	743	331	80	2	6	14	27	1	2
Catahoula	Harrisonburg	885	118	2,429	2,455	612	784		34	12	1,187	5	1
Claiborne	Homer	2,033	233	1,577	4,696	476	446	28	42	134	353	4	8
Concordia	Vidalia	939	150	3,418	2,666	980	1,225	26	95	34	905	3	0
De Soto	Mansfield	2,753	291	4,859	6,465	1,523	1,192	73	142	5	1,551	4	39
East Baton Rouge	United States Courtroom, Post Office Building, Baton Rouge	3,870	420		9,149					98			
East Carroll	Lake Providence	874	125	1,232	2,231	511	538	29	18	13	282	4	4
East Feliciana	Clinton	1,054	167	1,641	2,862	415	464	0	47	41	547	1	5
Evangeline	Ville Platte	2,311	285	2,525	5,121	560	664	9	59	16	1,676	5	4
Franklin	Winnsboro	1,822	220	2,541	4,583	678	320		13	28	629	3	1
Grant	Colfax	1,324	135	1,835	3,294	473	477		21	22	635	0	0
Iberia	New Iberia	2,430	250	3,200	5,880	891	729	34	57	265	1,171	2	10
Iberville	Plaquemine	2,235	235	2,860	5,330	733	929	16	25	83	948	5	12

APPENDIX TABLE 100-A.—Principal statistical data, by local boards—Continued.

LOUISIANA—Continued.

Local board.	Post-office address.	Registration.				Induction.	Physical groups.				Deferments.		
		June 5, 1917.	June and August, 1918.	Sept. 12, 1918.	Total.	Accepted at camp.	General service.	Remediables.	Limited service.	Disqualified.	Dependency.	Agricultural.	Industrial.
Jackson	Jonesboro	1,096	143	1,550	2,789	358	190	7	25	46	608	2	2
Jefferson	Gretna	2,072	164	2,631	4,867	665	553	46	107	163	882	22	23
Jefferson Davis	Courthouse, Jennings	1,651	192	2,254	4,097	568	586	14	46	0	674	4	0
Le Salle	Jena	1,011	89	1,032	2,132	369	287	7	10	56	520	0	2
Lafayette	Lafayette	2,541	286	3,417	6,244	774	667	0	28	242	1,567	6	14
Lafourche	Thibodaux	2,780	320	3,506	6,606	869	873	1	46	49	1,765	7	12
Lincoln	Ruston	1,570	190	1,913	3,673	707	571	....	6	68	851	9	2
Livingston	Springville	1,029	133	1,326	2,480	379	369	7	23	17	526	1	0
Madison	Tallulah	861	98	1,060	2,019	349	462	....	8	....	346	0	0
Morehouse	Bastrop	1,723	148	2,130	4,001	452	644	....	50	146	747	0	3
Natchitoches	Natchitoches	3,097	374	4,237	7,708	1,074	1,265	0	49	23	1,866	8	9
NEW ORLEANS No. 1	1904 Erato Street	3,820	342	4,741	8,903	1,277	468	65	108	137	1,101	1	34
NEW ORLEANS No. 2	704 Canal Bank Building	4,392	380	5,487	10,259	1,228	442	47	320	471	1,371	1	37
NEW ORLEANS No. 3	1651 Canal Street	1,771	152	2,250	4,173	546	445	37	114	186	508	0	12
NEW ORLEANS No. 4	2101 Dumaine Street	2,940	261	2,977	6,178	898	393	....	....	....	519	0	4
NEW ORLEANS No. 5	2529 Barracks Street	1,557	145	2,105	3,807	662	931	18	61	151	1,536	0	0
NEW ORLEANS No. 6	Rampart and Esplanade	3,266	354	4,060	7,680	1,041	238	123	191	250	666	0	19
NEW ORLEANS No. 7	2601 Urquhart Street	1,396	181	1,946	3,523	394	661	52	54	45	1,218	14	24
NEW ORLEANS No. 8	do.	2,586	240	3,304	6,130	759	728	83	180	167	845	2	17
NEW ORLEANS No. 9	1900 Jackson Avenue	2,228	224	2,990	5,442	790	659	39	105	260	1,119	0	3
NEW ORLEANS No. 10	901 Hibernia Bank	1,622	237	3,585	5,444	787	360	30	91	36	930	1	19
NEW ORLEANS No. 11	2013 Louisiana Avenue	2,304	234	3,158	5,696	829	494	50	60	201	679	3	11
NEW ORLEANS No. 12	Napoleon Avenue and Prytania Street	1,949	170	2,395	4,514	594	940	17	83	15	2,126	19	87
NEW ORLEANS No. 13	Gibson Hall	4,698	441	7,017	12,156	1,311	1,063	25	394	555	1,209	23	19
Ouachita	Monroe	2,597	267	3,558	6,422	997	814	10	117	29	1,209	16	14
Plaquemines	Courthouse, Pointe à la Hache	1,114	90	1,292	2,496	350	356	56	38	111	402	4	1
Pointe Coupee	New Roads	1,881	263	2,706	4,850	700	413	0	15	82	961	18	44
Rapides No. 1	Alexandria	2,360	308	4,281	6,949	989	1,246	....	88	32	971	1	2
Rapides No. 2	do.	2,879	309	3,853	7,041	1,150	455	37	101	25	1,518	1	3
Red River	Coushatta	1,418	119	1,551	3,088	290	858	31	30	78	791	1	2
Richland	Rayville	2,015	251	2,346	4,612	704	510	26	54	90	973	11	1
Sabine	Many	2,251	240	2,520	5,011	714	178	20	88	25	974	1	17
St. Bernard	St. Bernard	560	43	656	1,259	175	133	0	21	26	220	0	10
St. Charles	Hahnville	933	92	901	1,926	339	154	0	14	6	372	8	0
St. Helena	Greensburg	551	52	820	1,423	166	693	....	31	18	312	16	3
St. James	Courthouse, Convent	2,044	186	2,498	4,728	723	693	0	40	121	910	2	0
St. John the Baptist	Edgard	1,273	159	1,484	2,916	509	538	36	34	151	563	13	12

St. Landry	Opelousas	3,822	561	5,239	9,622	1,425	1,219	0	35	240	2,186	7	4
St. Martin	St. Martinsville	1,729	201	2,252	4,212	570	518	9	28	108	976	2	0
St. Mary	Franklin	3,417	338	4,312	8,067	1,161	1,178	74	35	310	1,603	10	2
St. Tammany	Covington	2,203	266	3,024	5,493	1,789	466	27	89	165	889	4	20
SHREVEPORT	City Hall, Shreveport	3,909	298	3,598	9,598	1,456	1,262	39	94	457	321	0	16
Tangipahoa	Courthouse, Amite	3,069	267	3,083	6,934	977	970	3	59	246	1,914	10	4
Tensas	St. Joseph	910	107	2,022	2,605	352	428	4	13	67	396	2	1
Terrebonne	Houma	2,696	258	2,390	6,037	696	844	3	69	168	1,540	7	2
Union	Farmerville	1,661	206	2,897	3,889	507	460	17	30	14	1,049	68	0
Vermilion	Abbeville	2,619	274	3,276	6,283	908	771	6	39	201	1,049	1	0
Vernon	Leesville	2,386	210	2,192	5,493	767	774	13	80	313	1,068	1	9
Washington	Franklinton	2,989	295	1,225	6,560	615	1,056	0	52	18	1,340	3	1
Webster	Minden	1,975	198	1,151	4,365	458	635	48	84	67	729	0	0
West Baton Rouge	Port Allen	1,051	95	1,146	2,371	294	454	8	26	138	486	3	7
West Carroll	Oak Grove	738	91	1,905	1,960	343	268		34	26	•369	1	1
West Feliciana	St. Francisville	110	110		2,014		392	2		40	111	1	2
Winn	Winnfield	1,481	158		3,542	539	297	12	29	54	787	5	7

MAINE.

Androscoggin No. 1	City Building, Lewiston	3,290	266	3,990	7,546	859	684	1	316	464	1,355	14	16
Androscoggin No. 2	Auburn	2,342	208	3,386	5,936	658	602	48	159	346	810	122	32
Aroostook No. 1	Houlton	2,766	386	4,817	9,169	836	798	53	138	674	1,534	231	33
Aroostook No. 2	Fort Fairfield	3,687	379	5,103		995	773	49	210	396	1,796	149	20
Cumberland No. 1	Yarmouthville	1,284	90	2,016	7,148	715	365	18	65	130	548	53	26
Cumberland No. 2	847 Main Street, Westbrook	2,754	250	4,144	6,089	475	704	3	193	200	1,323	46	12
Franklin	Farmington	1,537	165	2,425	6,583	471	78		2	2	13	3	
Hancock	Ellsworth	2,216	222	3,592	5,877	647	105	17	28	1	31	1	2
Kennebec No. 1	Federal Building, Augusta	2,580	231	3,430	6,583	503	495	51	82	192	1,208	50	32
Kennebec No. 2	74 Main Street, Waterville	1,923	210	3,793	5,194	253	686	22	154	82	1,164	52	69
Knox	Rockland	1,027	155	3,116	2,924	780	271	12	161	48	848	31	35
Lincoln	Wiscasset	3,067	106	1,791	8,178	1,093	108	11	32	99	468	19	18
Oxford	South Paris	3,889	322	4,789	9,817	1,034	725	53	213	323	1,434	120	46
Penobscot No. 1	Federal Building, Old Town	3,866	386	5,542	9,801	1,043	1,034	41	148	108	1,831	84	57
Penobscot No. 2	Bangor	1,652	313	5,622			1,143	34	179	41	1,292	33	37
Piscataquis	Dover	3,216	172	2,551	8,058	99	432	35	43	157	727	23	49
PORTLAND No. 1	County Courthouse, Probate Court	2,719	285	4,375	7,171	873	846	0	96	174	1,178	2	21
PORTLAND No. 2	Cumberland County Courthouse	1,634	240	4,547	4,608	786	670	62	233	52	1,195	0	116
Sagadahoc	Bath	3,398	211	4,212	8,545	338	548	10	122	40	558	22	19
Somerset	Skowhegan	1,428	335	2,763	3,976	704	712	8	71	54	1,110	25	14
Waldo	Courthouse, Belfast	3,171	163	4,812	8,287	928	221	17	91	62	692	31	64
Washington	Calais	2,568	358	2,385	7,134	742	797	0	243	34	1,575	14	13
York No. 1	City Building, Saco		293	4,758	6,739	674	603	18	44	376	1,012	27	21
York No. 2	Town Hall, Kennebunk		282	3,944			629		85	38	1,226	23	

APPENDIX TABLE 100-A—*Principal statistical data, by local boards*—Continued.

MARYLAND.

Local board	Post-office address	Registration June 5, 1917	Registration June and August, 1918	Registration Sept. 12, 1918	Total	Induction. Accepted at camp	Physical groups. General service	Physical groups. Remediables	Physical groups. Limited service	Physical groups. Disqualified	Deferments. Dependency	Deferments. Agricultural	Deferments. Industrial
Allegany No. 1	Cumberland	2,569	299	4,176	7,044	853	14	14	88	3	1,484	35	43
Allegany No. 2	Frostburg	3,072	389	4,502	7,963	1,127	20	14	33	164	1,581	139	66
Anne Arundel	Annapolis	3,555	323	5,533	9,411	1,041	735	40	57	0	2,689	0	32
BALTIMORE No. 1	Pulic School, ...hood and Eastern Avenues	3,482	216	3,787	7,532	685	365	32	49	149	1,017	1	16
BALTIMORE No. 2	1704 East Lombard Street	3,446	263	3,512	7,174	460	557	24	76	141	658	0	2
BALTIMORE No. 3	22 South Broadway	2,396	244	3,432	6,072	609	819	35	88	188	465	2	18
BALTIMORE No. 4	733 West Baltimore Street	2,100	193	3,450	5,803	764	570	48	111	70	594	1	3
BALTIMORE No. 5	School 40, ...ons and Aquith Streets	2,112	216	3,154	5,482	653	663	8	115	261	1,452	0	45
BALTIMORE No. 6	220 East Fairmount Avenue	3,018	307	3,734	7,059	709	539	16	40	8	1,759	0	54
BALTIMORE No. 7	2125 East ...eet Street	3,551	321	4,149	8,021	860	538	26	111	333	1,613	2	101
BALTIMORE No. 8	Eastern High School, ...ay and North Avenues	3,114	315	4,446	7,875	795							
BALTIMORE No. 9	724 East ...th Avenue	2,476	197	3,521	6,194	563	22	8	43	302	1,301	1	42
BALTIMORE No. 10	1312 East Eager Street	1,928	164	2,212	4,304	625	520	15	51	326	742	0	26
BALTIMORE No. 11	Northwest ...ner Park ...ue and Hoffman Street	1,877	146	2,791	4,814	619	484	3	96	92	495	3	17
BALTIMORE No. 12	Northwest, ...ner Charles and ...th Streets	2,838	246	4,234	7,318	686	440	26	123	252	1,353	1	76
BALTIMORE No. 13	School 61, Linden Avenue and Konig Street	2,650	259	3,781	6,690	686	467	16	139	235	1,295	0	71
BALTIMORE No. 14	332 ...on ...eet	2,131	174	3,191	5,496	676	542	1	149	305	820	0	15
BALTIMORE No. 15	Public School 64, Garrison and ...die Avenues	3,586	291	6,028	9,905	1,014	810	23	0	194	1,541	1	32
BALTIMORE No. 16	Lafayette and Carrollton ...ues	2,890	265	4,156	7,311	823	664	26	94	64	1,535	2	80
BALTIMORE No. 17	1048 Myrtle Avenue	2,492	254	3,599	6,345	964	886	0	174	91	596	0	3
BALTIMORE No. 18	1031 West Mulberry Street	2,025	184	2,761	4,970	611	591	21	88	193	634	0	45
BALTIMORE No. 19	Y. M. C. A. Building, ...rner Baltimore and ...fey Streets	2,089	223	2,899	5,211	693	540	22	78		1,008	0	53
BALTIMORE No. 20	Pulic Shool No. 20, Mulberry and Payson Streets	3,066	319	4,398	7,783	731	606	1	122	267	1,550	0	60
BALTIMORE No. 21	Public School 22, Scott and Hamburg Streets	2,169	190	2,658	5,017	481	1,009	25	91	87	948	0	20
BALTIMORE No. 22	Public School 4, Hanover and Lee Streets	2,116	224	3,157	5,497	650	717	37	104	2	496	0	31
BALTIMORE No. 23	School 70, ...ue and William Street	1,854	141	3,254	5,249	517	447	0	102	216	712	0	37
BALTIMORE No. 24	121 East Fort Avenue	2,248	240	3,084	5,572	475	434	26	78	124	1,105	3	94
...re No. 1	Lutherville	2,605	248	3,770	6,623	748	505	18	119	192	1,091	241	88
Baltimore No. 2	Masonic Temple Building, Catonsville	2,677	264	4,252	7,193	807	518	5	66	139	781	3	0
Baltimore No. 3	Canton Police Station, Sparrows Point	4,673	547	7,049	12,269	1,155	937	36	172	6	7	16	324
Baltimore No. 4	Courthouse, Towson	2,875	242	3,945	7,062	757	434	3	102	349	1,340	24	111
Calvert	Prince Frederick	808	115	2,003	3,003	294	381	9	56	95	365	41	2
...lie	Courthouse, Denton	1,356	156	2,102	3,614	347	273	8	5	45	485	338	21
...oll	Westminster	2,465	283	4,047	6,706	646	466	30	157	2	1,407	209	27

County	Address	C1	C2	C3	C4	C5	C6	C7	C8	C9	C10	C11	C12
Gil	Courthouse, Elton	1,751	207	2,883	4,841	461	580	24	66	156	616	350	95
Charles	Chase, La Plata	1,298	183	2,033	3,514	341	25	0	29	0	446	0	0
Dorchester	Cambridge	2,236	259	3,135	5,650	622	574	14	21	282	1,177	81	16
Frederick No. 1	29 Market Seet, Frerick	1,080	78	1,313	2,471	1,046	273	6	118	71	511	3	6
Frederick No. 2	Frederick	3,142	387	4,325	7,854	545	781	37	45	46	1,561	311	38
Garrett	Care of E. Z., Oakland	1,522	89	3,951	3,914	366	387	13	88	123	735	39	13
Harford	Amy, Bel r	2,055	268	1,793	6,274	384	583	30	109	217	558	0	0
Howard	Ellicott City	1,202	156	1,687	3,151	796	309	6	22	81	324	109	19
Kent	Che	1,192	146	3,900	3,025	812	304	48	91	31	1,161	181	8
Montgomery	Rockville	2,490	288	4,744	6,678	308	617	13	36	113	1,275	249	19
Prince Georges	ee, Upper Marlboro	2,755	316	1,812	7,815	334	804	6	11	30	609	156	14
Queen Annes	Courthouse, Centerville	1,230	137	1,626	3,179	619	225	6	25	76	346	194	4
St. Marys	Leonardtown	1,155	143	2,924	2,924	463	404	31	70	182	923	14	6
Somerset	Princess Anne	1,921	218	2,730	4,863	739	512	15	23	128	655	41	15
Talbot	Easton	1,482	142	2,064	3,688	663	279	4	80	88	1,420	121	11
Washington No. 1	First National Bank Building, Hagerstown	2,781	255	3,482	6,518	664	463	0	99	156	1,170	7	94
Washington No. 2	1214 Negley Building, Hagerstown	2,447	259	3,047	5,753	528	102	21	60	10	1,217	103	25
Wicomico	Salisbury	2,230	230	3,088	5,548		648	6	79	22	894	0	6
Worcester	Snow Hill	1,630	165	2,337	4,152		482			11		4	1

MASSACHUSETTS.

District	Address	C1	C2	C3	C4	C5	C6	C7	C8	C9	C10	C11	C12
North Adams No. 1	City Hall	2,387	219	3,298	5,934	749	569	8	115	115	723	11	15
Adams No. 2	Fourth District Court Rooms	2,348	211	3,489	6,048	718	495	36	90	102	935	39	9
Lee No. 3	Courthouse	2,384	222	3,022	5,628	668	520	7	131	199	708	54	18
Greenfield No. 4	do	2,961	240	3,717	6,918	715	595	1	194	142	1,103	47	85
Northampton No. 5	Memorial Hall Building	2,917	243	3,440	6,600	771	649	32	213	241	1,318	8	15
Westfield No. 6	22 Elm Street	3,204	261	4,319	7,794	743	407	27	128	115	893	31	62
Ludlow No. 7	Town Hall, Main Street, South Hadley Falls	3,197	249	3,814	7,260	645	376	12	140	165	818	104	25
Amherst No. 8	37 South Pleasant Street	2,388	220	3,307	5,915	787	525	14	102	76	700	57	19
Ware No. 9	Town Hall	2,304	210	3,270	5,784	683	419	17	175	45	723	35	24
Southbridge No. 10	92 Main Street	2,915	284	3,859	7,058	773	647	39	170	269	1,015	2	12
East Brookfield No. 11	District Court Rooms	2,384	255	3,707	6,346	625	439	30	318	208	835	45	45
Athol No. 12	64 Exchange Street	2,566	235	3,332	6,133	712	482	23	137	296	812	23	29
Gardner No. 13	12 Main Street	2,640	225	3,845	6,710	634	372	6	151	25	11	43	29
Leominster No. 14	Town Hall	3,039	255	3,960	7,254	813	811	28	262	172	684	60	41
Ayer No. 15	City Hall	3,607	244	4,024	6,865	785	397	22	237	36	836	28	37
Marlborough No. 16	Town Hall	2,794	203	3,801	6,839	644	896	29	211	83	957	51	59
Uxbridge No. 17	204 Main Set	2,920	209	3,947	7,070	676	449	40	170	230	699	21	32
Milford No. 18	Twn Hall	2,584	214	3,697	6,247	743	548	37	184	176	751	39	26
Newbury No. 19	Juvenile urt Room, 4 den Street	2,351	213	3,421	6,262	522	441	13	111	132	812	4	16
Newburyport No. 20	32 et Main Street	2,674	185	3,341	5,840	576	394	27	158	138	837	8	11
Georgetown No. 21	100 Main Set	2,314	216	3,570	6,112	500	337	32	185	188	1,035	3	24
Gloucester No. 22	City Hall	2,326	204	3,565	6,488	610	326	6	109	196	538	4	23
Beverly No. 23	Town Hall	2,719	76	1,976	3,359	397	356	15	170	88	1,641	19	214
Swampscott No. 24	126 Winthrop Street	1,307	324	3,359	9,567	798	205	7	307	224	768	17	63
Winthrop No. 25	City Hall	3,750	251		8,018	696	426	184	96		952	2	9
Peabody No. 26	Selectmen's Office, Central Square	3,457	158		5,782	485	546	3	135	211	778		61
Sm No. 27	City Hall	2,158	209		5,856	498	296	16	150	216			42
Melrose No. 28	City Hall	2,200					364	27					

APPENDIX TABLE 100-A.—*Principal statistical data, by local boards*—Continued.

MASSACHUSETTS—Continued.

Local board.	Post-office address.	Registration.				Induction.	Physical groups.				Deferments.		
		June 5, 1917.	June and August, 1918.	Sept. 12, 1918.	Total.	Accepted at camp.	General service.	Remediables.	Limited service.	Disqualified.	Dependency.	Agricultural.	Industrial.
....RN No. 29	Old Courthouse	2,595	203	3,641	6,439	651	547	14	173	67	797	17	19
ARLINGTON No. 30	Town Hall	2,130	154	3,379	5,663	515	263	19	152	120	804	14	38
BELMONT No. 31	18 Tremont Street, Boston	3,309	242	4,830	8,381	792	625	19	131	132	1,070	18	41
....AM No. 32	1 Mason Building	2,931	223	4,247	7,411	639	478	5	201	279	876	27	52
NEEDHAM No. 33	Town Hall	2,375	160	3,518	7,083	730	429	2	237	176	690	7	40
NORWOOD No. 34	Selectmen's Office	3,070	223	3,311	7,604	661	571	49	369	85	833	30	159
CANTON No. 35	Memorial Hall, 807 Washington Street	2,357	215	3,568	6,170	659	350	7	138	88	696	17	57
SOUTH ....FREE No. 36	Town Hall	2,411	221	3,796	6,428	576	263	13	102	158	922	13	157
ROCKLAND M. 37	323 Union Street	2,418	200	3,572	6,190	624	953	10	225	136	738	8	42
EAST BRIDGEWATER No. 38	27 Bedford Street	2,297	161	3,828	6,286	553	61	15	78	217	766	0	2
PLYMOUTH No. 39	Town House	2,312	198	3,464	5,974	558	436	5	59	210	929	1	7
ATTLEBORO No. 40	Courthouse	2,443	185	3,625	6,253	388	412	38	152	252	951	20	41
NORTH EASTON No. 41	Town Hall, Mansfield	2,188	221	3,428	5,840	540	288	4	105	69	802	71	70
FAIRHAVEN No. 42	Town Hall	2,190	174	3,643	6,007	544	245	0	69	312	726	29	18
BARNSTABLE No. 43	County Courthouse	2,413	202	3,771	6,380	643	207	18	152	133	1,058	22	20
BOSTON:													
EAST BOSTON No. 1	Library Building, Meridian Street, East Boston	4,291	216	2,938	5,445	483	365	38	138	93	885	3	112
EAST BOSTON No. 2	East Boston District Courthouse	4,669	340	5,070	10,079	709	613	299	175	350	1,912	2	53
CHARLESTOWN No. 3	Charlestown Trust Co. Building, Charlestown	3,326	269	4,449	8,044	836	821	97	142	451	1,087	0	63
BOSTON No. 4	Aldermanic Chamber, City Hall	5,680	405	6,228	12,313	1,092	....	....	....	....	....	....	....
BOSTON No. 5	Room 727, 40 Court Street	5,533	465	7,279	13,277	816	832	60	366	22	961	0	33
BOSTON No. 6	John J. Williams School, Groton Street	4,203	326	5,823	10,351	1,238	788	21	294	372	940	1	30
BOSTON No. 7	177 Huntington Avenue	4,880	329	6,302	11,511	1,231	1,109	35	565	447	912	4	88
BOSTON No. 8	1 Beacon Street, eighth floor	3,870	203	4,644	8,717	851	602	47	210	120	753	1	60
SOUTH BOSTON No. 9	Municipal Building, East Broadway, South Boston	3,597	277	4,146	8,020	750	716	9	191		895	0	69
SOUTH BOSTON No. 10	Talbot Building, 395 Broadway, South Boston	2,415	332	3,246	5,993	547	481	29	179	189	880	0	52
DORCHESTER No. 11	160 East Cottage Street, Edward Everett Square	2,502	196	3,228	5,926	616	458	19	83	100	937	2	24
ROXBURY No. 12	Municipal Building, Dudley Street, Roxbury	2,592	226	3,356	6,174	640	696	8	316	29	651	1	21
ROXBURY No. 13	Roxbury Courthouse, Roxbury	2,990	255	3,966	7,211	826	577	56	328	125	738	1	26
ROXBURY No. 14	Mission Church School, St. Alphonsus Street	2,428	224	3,159	5,811	621	525	35	98	192	709	2	28
BOSTON No. 15	1538 Columbus Avenue, Boston (Roxbury)	2,613	175	3,364	6,152	571	340	31	138	124	901	0	31
....RY No. 16	552 Warren Street, Grove Hall	2,368	254	3,250	5,872	587	365	47	132	174	662	0	27
DORCHESTER No. 17	584 Columbia Road, Dorchester	2,306	256	3,483	6,045	661	366	27	155	77	775	0	13
DORCHESTER No. 18	Courthouse, Arcadia Street, Dorchester	2,693	242	3,310	6,245	733	516	60	140	168	912	4	19
DORCHESTER No. 19	Norfolk Hall, 328 Washington Street, Dorchester	2,015	201	2,983	5,108	494	357	60	58	119	775	0	57
DORCHESTER No. 20	104 Adamont Street, Peabody Square, Boston	1,990	176	3,194	5,300	402	271	28	98		998		

Precinct	Location												
DORCHESTER NO. 21.	Lithgow Building, Codman Square, Dorchester.	2,961	243	4,329	7,533	571	482	157	116	252	1,107	3	25
JAMAICA PLAIN NO. 22	Curtis Hall, Center Street, Jamaica Plain.	2,390	185	3,084	5,659	627	376	7	195	146	1,013	0	74
WEST ROXBURY NO. 23.	West Roxbury Branch Library, West Roxbury.	1,855	146	2,983	4,984	512	325	12	95	137	682	1	30
HYDE PARK NO. 24.	Hyde Park Trust Co. Building, Hyde Park.	2,335	201	3,054	5,590	520	41	0	86	173	687	0	78
BRIGHTON NO. 25.	Brighton District Court, Brighton.	3,780	272	5,508	9,560	885	646	55	195	155	1,303	5	99
BROCKTON NO. 1.	City Hall.	2,880	278	4,071	7,499	773	439	34	272	140	1,169	5	45
BROCKTON NO. 2.	...do...	3,163	216	3,778	7,450	708	335	22	207	26	1,080	0	19
BROOKLINE.	Town Hall.	2,335	160	3,481	6,273	740	374	9	177	183	659	5	42
CAMBRIDGE NO. 1.	391 Cambridge Street.	2,837	218	3,254	6,553	470	348	0	198	156	783	2	63
CAMBRIDGE NO. 2.	Municipal Building, Central Square.	3,603	185	4,018	6,276	916	902	33	140	367	909	43	11
CAMBRIDGE NO. 3.	City Hall, Brattle Square.	2,605	311	3,530	7,932	652	788	0	327	38	816	1	132
CAMBRIDGE NO. 4.	Courthouse.	2,759	236	3,231	6,371	743	557	4	244	139	832	5	56
CHELSEA NO. 1.	City Hall.	2,365	159	2,857	6,149	525	463	2	150	22	736	1	45
CHELSEA NO. 2.	Police Court Room.	4,214	186	4,475	9,022	542	313	41	208	223	1,008	10	23
CHICOPEE.	State Armory, Chelsea Street.	3,636	333	4,674	8,593	727	718	19	132	276	1,354	1	28
EVERETT.	109 South Main Street.	2,910	283	3,858	7,064	790	706	28	189	193	953	1	184
FALL RIVER NO. 1.	1472 South Main Street.	2,622	276	3,276	6,110	740	431	14	249	65	978	0	17
FALL RIVER NO. 2.	10 Basset Street.	2,673	212	3,368	6,286	495	207	14	141	105	843	0	14
FALL RIVER NO. 3.	Room 5, Borden Block.	2,417	255	3,584	6,233	572	346	19	209	156	731	1	4
FALL RIVER NO. 4.	State Armory.	4,163	232	5,601	10,049	648	564	22	175	181	1,435	8	21
FITCHBURG.	Boys' Club Building, 55-57 Emerson Street.	2,457	385	3,100	5,738	970	856	61	190	296	1,251	1	107
HAVERHILL NO. 1.	City Hall.	3,076	181	3,508	6,838	542	472	29	64	292	1,241	4	3
HAVERHILL NO. 2.	...do...	3,221	254	3,701	7,229	673	499	7	127	241	883	1	10
HOLYOKE NO. 1.	424 Bay State Building.	3,208	307	3,836	7,316	720	640	20	115	277	1,011	1	11
HOLYOKE NO. 2.	Courthouse, Appleton Street.	3,313	272	4,265	7,864	724	619	22	149	197	703	2	16
LAWRENCE NO. 1.	Room 18, Meigs Building.	3,795	288	4,452	8,481	637	483	33	95	214	1,023	2	30
LAWRENCE NO. 2.	Room 3, 226 Merrimac Street.	3,001	224	4,084	7,357	623	76	25	89	64	843	2	13
LAWRENCE NO. 3.	City Hall.	3,188	272	4,256	7,722	654	546	29	116	205	790	1	16
LOWELL NO. 1.	Courthouse, Gorham Street.	3,334	278	4,396	7,950	621	635	11	264	188	1,021	2	287
LOWELL NO. 2.	Greenhalge School, Ennell Street.	3,282	260	4,258	7,790	434	71	13	80	143	665	2	98
LOWELL NO. 3.	Courthouse, 578 Essex Street.	1,813	300	2,426	4,445	646	521	0	64	80	851	5	176
LOWELL NO. 4.	7 Central Square.	3,208	206	4,019	7,461	369	295	11	178	298	1,195	0	0
LYNN NO. 1.	Houghton Branch Library, Breed Square, West Lynn.	3,105	234	4,719	8,051	785	733	36	223	202	1,148	7	128
LYNN NO. 2.	District Courthouse.	3,278	227	3,741	7,247	812	843	38	246	75	639	0	67
LYNN NO. 3.	City Hall.	2,156	228	2,721	5,077	610	540	39	188	24	722	1	6
MALDEN NO. 1.		2,200	200	3,066	5,480	539	432	32	154	80	1,519	0	15
MALDEN NO. 2.		3,133	214	4,452	7,840	521	281	3	178	89	902	0	12
MEDFORD.	Room 10, Medford Building.	3,139	235	3,411	6,786	567	480	0	224	122	1,032	3	63
NEW BEDFORD NO. 1.	Fire Engine House, Acushnet Avenue.	3,014	236	4,262	7,513	551	927	13	146	166	809	1	7
NEW BEDFORD NO. 2.	Care of the Evening Standard.	3,210	237	4,345	7,742	608	395	6	210	175	850	1	21
NEW BEDFORD NO. 3.	Third District Court Building.	3,084	187	3,444	6,788	614	388	41	207	299	1,673	1	14
NEW BEDFORD NO. 4.	No. 11 Fire Station, 754 Brock Avenue.	4,320	260	5,622	10,298	461	266	14	109	160	1,527	1	58
PITTSFIELD.	City Hall.	4,619	336				818	16	236	84		0	
QUINCY.	Quincy Courthouse.	4,278	562	4,963	12,375	1,028	756	49	178	140	1,129	7	563
SALEM.	Room 2, Masonic Temple.	2,780	326	3,828	6,868	857	1,031	43	206	117	970	0	144
SOMERVILLE NO. 1.	Police Building, Bow Street.	2,736	260	3,668	6,677	560	369	8	218	219	1,229	0	82
SOMERVILLE NO. 2.	State Armory, Highland Avenue.	2,500	243	3,848	6,553	652	474	23	144	225	1,469	5	52
SOMERVILLE NO. 3.	Branch Library, College Avenue.	5,631	205	3,917	12,001	590	339	21	128	20	1,364	4	28
SPRINGFIELD NO. 1.	299 Main Street.		453	5,959	11,766	1,103	962	30	258	126		3	63
SPRINGFIELD NO. 2.	476 Main Street.	5,398	409			1,190	1,059	62	271	199		1	89

APPENDIX TABLE 100-A.—*Principal statistical data, by local boards*—Continued.

MASSACHUSETTS—Continued.

Local board.	Post-office address.	Registration — June 5, 1917.	Registration — June and August, 1918.	Registration — Sept. 12, 1918.	Registration — Total.	Induction — Accepted at camp.	Physical groups — General service.	Physical groups — Remediables.	Physical groups — Limited service.	Disqualified.	Deferments — Dependency.	Deferments — Agricultural.	Deferments — Industrial.
SPRINGFIELD No. 3	Room 1008, Third National Bank Building	4,404	353	6,387	11,144	922	657	58	366	49	2,004	3	60
TAUNTON	City Hall	3,559	305	4,701	8,565	633	376	33	223	446	991	3	135
WALTHAM	Waltham Public Library	2,723	224	3,575	6,522	561	452	39	169	146	1,063	12	89
WEST NEWTON	District Court Building	3,434	288	5,329	9,049	851	595	23	234	174	1,042	6	101
WORCESTER No. 1	75 Grove Street	3,522	285	4,815	8,622	751	665	44	140	292	789	1	50
WORCESTER No. 2	Fire Department Headquarters, 3 Mercantile St.	4,595	293	4,664	9,552	838	815	55	312		1,216	0	0
WORCESTER No. 3	720 Slater Building	4,047	379	5,028	9,454	838	622	44	313	219	1,328	0	108
WORCESTER No. 4	Boys' Club, Ionic Avenue	4,783	291	5,039	10,113	806	741	24	210	354	1,145	1	152
WORCESTER No. 5	15 Maple Street	4,028	309	5,208	9,545	909							

MICHIGAN.

Local board.	Post-office address.	Registration — June 5, 1917.	Registration — June and August, 1918.	Registration — Sept. 12, 1918.	Registration — Total.	Induction — Accepted at camp.	Physical groups — General service.	Physical groups — Remediables.	Physical groups — Limited service.	Disqualified.	Deferments — Dependency.	Deferments — Agricultural.	Deferments — Industrial.
Alcona	Harrisville	514	54	612	1,180	144	107	0	9	20	226	27	3
Alger	Munising	832	89	1,485	2,456	267	204		25	170	317	6	4
Allegan	Allegan	2,073	321	4,318	7,612	782	512	19	51	299	859	954	36
Alpena	Alpena	1,239	149	1,930	3,318	347	354	9	43	155	602	40	7
Antrim	Bellaire	925	104	1,488	2,517	324	301	2	16	98	421	13	3
Arenac	Standish	803	84	1,042	1,929	210	284		29	73	503	102	3
Baraga	L'Anse	634	62	1,026	1,722	211	238	18	35	14	171	2	0
Barry	Hastings	1,672	65	2,452	4,289	319	229	9	42	151	736	246	14
BATTLE	City Hall	3,229	263	4,672	8,164	981	675	48	126	359	1,248	4	36
BAY CITY No. 1	do.	2,035	196	2,850	5,081	462	410	0	119	215	962	2	65
BAY CITY No. 2	do.	1,511	161	2,384	4,056	413	370	18	52	124	816		59
Bay	Bay City	1,779	222	2,425	4,427	531	425	21	93	186	787	219	3
Benzie	Beulah	632	61	899	1,592	188	130	3	28	62	315	21	1
Berrien No. 1	St. Joseph	2,848	313	3,809	6,970	805	578	34	55	250	1,227	73	37
Berrien No. 2	Buchanan	2,228	317	3,442	5,987	557	411	24	34	105	1,065	151	39
Branch	Coldwater	1,564	161	2,663	4,388	474	390	7	32	152	856	137	3
Calhoun	Marshall	2,857	244	4,200	7,301	748	448	20	30	74	1,422	166	16
Cass	Cassopolis	1,365	135	2,373	3,873	315	180	13	37	154	363	0	0
Cheboygan	Cheboygan	1,216	136	1,736	3,088	426	370	0	97	89	44	27	8
Charlevoix	Charlevoix	1,305	137	1,890	3,332	426	350	5	41	102	624	51	40
Chippewa	Sault Ste. Marie	2,438	261	3,216	5,935	705	723	97	43	177	984	202	2
Clare	Harrison	673	65	930	1,668	225	197	6	5	64	357	24	

County	Location												
Clinton	St. Johns	1,651	186	2,659	4,526	492	485	18	68	172	760	86	7
Crawford	Grayling	434	43	604	1,081	140	88	0	9	11	209	2	4
Delta	Escanaba	2,882	264	4,050	7,215	927	754	34	109	304	903	115	102
DETROIT No. 1	408 County Building	3,944	632	7,283	15,210	2,334	199	150	200	841	1,216	6	181
DETROIT No. 2	Municipal Court Building	6,592	263	4,164	8,371	1,210	730	43	289	343	1,428	2	87
DETROIT No. 3	...do...	8,639	406	6,650	13,648	2,118	1,590	33	412	747	1,239	2	174
DETROIT No. 4	195 East Forest Avenue	6,756	537	7,902	17,078	2,183	1,384	80	483	909	2,422	1	99
DETROIT No. 5	209 Owen Building	10,426	449	7,100	14,305	2,208	143	105	300	845	1,744	1	126
DETROIT No. 6	Municipal Court Building	6,331	740	10,728	21,894	2,144	1,652	113	359	882	2,530	3	78
DETROIT No. 7	Trinity Church House, Myrtle and Trumbull Avenues	5,863	323	6,390	13,044	1,513	949	81	229	565	2,740	3	112
DETROIT No. 8	Municipal Court Building, St. Antoine and Clinton	5,050	269	5,180	11,312	1,286	839	13	80	324	1,063	4	63
DETROIT No. 9	Vermont Hall, Trumbull and Grand River Avenues	4,029	286	5,555	10,881	1,280	752	0	233	563	2,176	9	117
DETROIT No. 10	Atwater and McDougall Avenues	5,918	224	3,512	7,765	881	388	25	92	172	1,048	1	53
DETROIT No. 11	Dom Polski Building	4,773	297	5,039	11,254	1,002	633	74	155	259	1,214	2	52
DETROIT No. 12	945 Grand River Avenue	5,529	348	5,020	10,141	1,264	1,114	7	16	394	1,835	4	194
DETROIT No. 13	Mal Court Building	5,856	340	4,880	10,749	1,119	863	11	183	470	1,569	0	102
DETROIT No. 14	Ward	6,725	344	4,021	12,221	1,393	817	128	246	415	2,351	2	110
DETROIT No. 15	1018 Gratiot Avenue	3,578	448	6,808	13,981	1,594	982	16	229	123	2,188	3	202
DETROIT No. 16	Riverside	2,659	236	3,417	7,231	844	477	4	124	205	1,195	0	26
DETROIT No. 17	284 Wreford Avenue	5,616	155	3,220	6,034	656	348	25	106	379	1,423	1	58
DETROIT No. 18	Eastern High School	6,778	392	5,409	11,417	1,506	979	69	302	361	2,313	8	261
DETROIT No. 19	707 Dix	3,182	428	6,261	13,467	1,319	765	12	84	257	1,754	3	0
DETROIT No. 20	Room 410, County Building	2,461	206	3,154	6,542	682	416	74	98	177	1,485	4	46
DETROIT No. 21	178 Thirty-third Street	3,231	153	2,683	5,307	614	430	74	96	16	1,117	1	98
DETROIT No. 22	1235 Gratiot Avenue	5,621	247	3,522	7,000	785	412	56	204	272	1,586	1	31
DETROIT No. 23	1988 Fort Street west	5,000	313	5,904	11,838	1,079	663	31	74	239	1,439	2	79
DETROIT No. 24	801 Kercheval Avenue	4,700	329	5,681	11,010	1,219	749	32	273	208	2,602	0	132
DETROIT No. 25	331 Ferndale Avenue	6,805	279	5,598	10,577	909	468	26	82	470	1,378	1	45
DETROIT No. 26	2524 East Jefferson	1,743	450	7,135	14,390	1,450	957	73	116	84	3,339	11	58
Iron	Min.	2,268	210	2,455	5,814	638	491	11	49	84	525	11	23
Eaton	Charlotte	1,111	186	3,360	5,814	473	329	5	53	59	808	348	10
Emmet	Petoskey	4,185	118	1,834	3,063	379	279	73	84	4	418	6	5
FLINT No. 1	116 Dryden Building	6,229	312	4,237	8,734	1,265	875	64	139	388	2,051	8	37
FLINT No. 2	...do...	2,329	447	5,896	12,572	1,783	1,068	29	181	354	2,110	1	83
Genesee	City Hall, Flint	730	253	3,611	6,193	642	607	17	64	140	1,153	48	4
Gladwin	Gladwin	4,213	92	971	1,793	212	149	21	23	93	254	123	113
Gogebic	Bessemer	3,960	326	5,181	9,720	1,141	1,020	61	45	99	218	7	36
GRAND RAPIDS No. 1	8½ Monroe Avenue, Monument Park Building	4,041	334	4,728	9,201	1,233	1,066	54	284	241	2,002	1	39
GRAND RAPIDS No. 2	...do...	1,506	294	5,541	9,795	1,062	928	47	247	252	1,842	2	46
GRAND RAPIDS No. 3	...do...	2,632	348	5,631	10,020	880	820	15	132	304	2,374	3	1
Grand Traverse	Traverse City	6,338	121	2,135	3,762	466	539	20	92	67	768	21	15
Gratiot	Alma	2,011	304	3,986	6,922	643	543	69	76	54	1,564	119	106
HIGHLAND PARK	20 Gerald Avenue	2,826	290	6,645	13,273	1,558	1,401	0	361	382	2,417	0	10
Hillsdale	Hillsdale	3,163	205	3,105	5,321	638	364	25	89	191	1,089	148	91
Houghton No. 1	Houghton	2,760	212	3,493	6,531	696	492	31	85	218	714	18	82
Houghton No. 2	Hancock	2,792	255	3,672	7,090	951	672	24	87	193	651	10	6
Houghton No. 3	Laurium	1,773	234	3,312	6,306	770	657	41	81	249	961	2	11
Huron	Bad Axe	2,792	288	3,337	6,915	795	795	3	86	337	1,232	327	
Ingham	Mason	1,773	145	2,647	4,565	461	320		84	115	992	129	

APPENDIX TABLE 100-A.—*Principal statistical data, by local boards*—Continued.

MICHIGAN—Continued.

Local board.	Post-office address.	Registration.				Induction.	Physical groups.				Deferments.		
		June 5, 1917.	June and August, 1918.	Sept. 12, 1918.	Total.	Accepted at camp.	General service.	Remediables.	Limited service.	Disqualified.	Dependency.	Agricultural.	Industrial.
Ionia	Ionia	2,508	247	3,598	6,413	731	659	28	78	197	1,297	158	8
Iosco	Tawas City	703	66	803	1,632	256	294	9	31	56	275	50	4
Iron	Crystal Falls	2,640	155	3,133	5,928	841	703	21	56	124	1,565	16	41
Isabella	Mount Pleasant	1,764	227	2,639	4,630	541	525	19	45	35	529	15	0
JACKSON	City Hall	5,381	369	6,246	12,016	1,157	971	62	153	128	1,812	3	509
Jackson	Jackson	1,822	178	2,765	4,765	471	356	10	40	128	923	170	15
KALAMAZOO No. 1	City Hall	1,898	156	2,575	4,639	426	410	30	75	158	888	5	50
KALAMAZOO No. 2	...do	2,299	263	3,017	5,489	537	403	40	85	307	823	4	45
Kalamazoo	Kalamazoo	1,564	179	2,514	4,257	369	209		48	178	1,134	181	14
Kalkaska	Kalkaska	518	49	717	1,284	184	153	0	19	57	241	24	1
Kent No. 1	Grand Rapids	1,898	173	2,620	4,679	560	521	0	100	36	885	210	4
Kent No. 2	...do	1,819	194	2,735	4,748	585	336	0	121	38	877	131	5
Keweenaw	Mohawk	677	59	879	1,615	182	192	5	18	59	116	0	3
Lake	Baldwin	320	38	559	917	95	83	0	30	18	148	8	0
LANSING	Dodge Building	6,371	439	6,429	13,239	1,674	1,342	14	446	406	2,988	11	137
Lapeer	Lapeer	1,921	210	2,792	4,923	441	255	10	40	274	954	286	5
Leelanau	Leland	817	103	1,023	1,943	273	195	1	57	130	314	122	5
Lenawee No. 1	Adrian	1,675	139	2,653	4,467	396	273	33	48	102	695	212	17
Lenawee No. 2	...do	1,944	184	2,660	4,788	404	407	18	63	79	632	404	1
Livingston	Howell	1,371	129	1,979	3,479	361	306	2	40	39	501	2	13
Luce	Newberry	568	47	799	1,414	174	121	15	23	26	151	40	2
Mackinac	St. Ignace	820	80	1,054	1,960	313	239	31	29	83	305	214	6
Macomb	Mount Clemens	2,822	243	4,226	7,291	734	488	2	92	268	1,325	11	13
Manistee	Manistee	1,844	166	2,297	4,327	530	480	27	84	173	560	8	7
Marquette No. 1	Ishpeming	2,595	191	3,269	6,085	795	633	1	84	257	883	3	83
Marquette No. 2	Marquette	2,151	215	2,915	5,234	647	493	26	82	204	777	115	142
Mason	Ludington	1,595	194	2,270	4,049	609	531	25	111	115	609	70	4
Mecosta	Big Rapids	1,349	152	2,088	3,589	400	353	22	92	40	713	242	6
Menominee	Menominee	2,065	244	2,523	4,832	695	567	9	76	419	732	21	31
Midland	Midland	1,357	146	2,116	3,649	392	271	0	39	118	663	37	16
Missaukee	Lake City	902	105	1,095	2,192	272	215	8	68	35	93	2	1
Monroe	Monroe	3,031	307	4,332	7,870	669	547	0	68	315	1,375	440	19
Montcalm	Stanton	2,378	302	3,415	6,095	694	617	0	38	151	1,184	273	19
Montmorency	Atlanta	281	37	506	924	154	31	0	119	31	147	106	0
Muskegon	Muskegon	6,218	547	7,628	14,391	1,697	1,466	72	388	362	2,704	12	174
Newaygo	White Cloud	1,499	159	2,024	3,682	512	416	9	79	97	666	74	1
Oakland No. 1	Pontiac	4,325	357	4,700	9,382	1,025	724	2	71	107	1,622	106	18

Oakland No. 2 — 413 Washington Avenue, Royal Oak	3,400	218	4,678	8,296	844	521	8	123	82	1,240	33	5
Oceana — Hart	1,322	141	1,830	3,293	432	306	15	45	148	535	182	8
Ogemaw — West Branch	600	76	916	1,592	156	131	7	45	58	238	100	1
Ontonagon — Ontonagon	1,453	116	1,818	3,387	426	317	13	100	58	330	10	15
Osceola — Hersey	1,230	142	1,821	3,193	375	310	0	110	196	607	83	2
Oscoda — Mio	148	19	187	354	51	37	2	17	5	63	8	0
Otsego — Gaylord	501	60	687	1,248	171	179	0	12	25	216	5	1
Ottawa No. 1 — Grand Haven	1,638	185	2,374	4,197	546	415	2	123	122	680	134	8
Ottawa No. 2 — Holland	2,286	231	3,041	5,558	673	468	3	94	133	208	172	8
Presque Isle — Rogers	968	111	1,438	2,517	280	251	4	33	31	518	27	2
Roscommon — Roscommon	174	13	271	458	73	47	.	1	20	83	3	1
Saginaw No. 1 — Armory Building	2,661	205	3,799	6,665	728	555	51	85	231	1,334	1	43
Saginaw No. 2 — 105 ... Building	1,976	183	2,787	4,946	581	446	40	70	148	1,033	0	35
Saginaw — Courthouse, Saginaw	2,976	345	4,401	7,722	849	593	18	108	338	1,147	536	25
St. Clair No. 1 — Port Huron	2,407	248	3,775	6,430	531	313	2	93	90	1,162	112	18
St. Clair No. 2 — St. Clair	1,876	221	2,879	4,976	401	253	7	33	188	532	293	9
St. Joseph — Centerville	2,082	219	2,974	5,275	550	470	19	43	151	1,105	256	35
Sanilac — Sandusky	2,399	278	3,634	6,311	623	471	12	56	78	981	305	4
Schoolcraft — Manistique	779		1,306	2,162	283	268	8	21	42	318	23	20
Shiawassee — Corunna	2,640	277	4,071	6,988	642	529	53	77	200	1,268	164	12
Tuscola — Caro	2,350	262	3,753	6,365	718	547	31	66	190	1,130	144	2
Van Buren — Paw Paw	2,242	231	3,306	5,779	504	491	13	49	71	1,120	156	13
Washtenaw — Ann Arbor	4,735	461	5,793	10,989	1,261	876	26	180	382	1,825	466	50
Wayne No. 1 — Hamtramck	6,925	314	6,348	13,587	1,015	545	5	116	211	1,472	2	29
Wayne No. 2 — 409 ... Building, Detroit	3,966	148	3,163	9,638	757	407	13	74	132	1,377	29	55
Wayne No. 3 — Wyandotte		353	5,319			658	23	25	83	1,585	28	147
Wayne No. 4 — Plymouth	2,471	243	3,777	6,491	674	439	24	61	228	808	145	16
Wd. — Cadillac	1,656	134	2,090	3,880	372	355	25	112	122	674	45	17

MINN.

Aitkin — Aitkin	1,182	133	1,677	2,992	430	443	19	52	104	426	54	6
Anoka — Anoka	1,188	124	1,649	2,961	331	364	16	22	49	467	175	12
Becker — Detroit	1,864	214	2,416	4,494	613	631	1	75	52	769	61	4
Beltrami — Bemidji	2,431	160	3,322	5,913	837	1,129	43	98	119	865	34	9
Benton — Foley	1,223	145	1,467	2,835	446	438	.	25	88	416	219	13
Big Stone — Ortonville	866	101	1,232	2,199	291	375	.	9	41	219	243	20
Blue Earth — Mankato	2,942	255	3,607	6,804	796	927	37	99	135	1,099	220	12
Brown — New Ulm	1,813	236	2,579	4,628	584	546	18	49	49	400	657	16
Carlton — Carlton	1,840	180	2,589	4,609	556	241	4	22	148	618	27	6
Carver — Chaska	1,512	217	1,860	3,589	548	544	12	20	93	525	333	15
Cass — Walker	1,415	131	1,851	3,397	424	374	16	32	236	537	31	5
Chippewa — Montevideo	1,410	143	1,811	3,364	481	421	4	21	74	455	303	31
Chisago — Center City	1,232	130	1,701	3,065	502	469	15	79	73	134	305	7
Clay — Moorhead	2,124	223	2,688	5,035	790	838	13	48	32	413	285	21
Clearwater — Bagley	595	88	849	1,532	248	291	3	17	16	256	10	0
Cook — Grand Marais	197	15	322	534	62	63	0	7	.	.	.	0
Cottonwood — Windom	1,350	171	1,702	3,223	453	453	.	99	41	231	264	15
Crow Wing — Brainerd	2,579	233	3,576	6,388	744	628	2	45	212	942	91	77
Dakota — Hastings	3,149	279	3,762	7,190	861	740	.	174	85	931	431	59

APPENDIX TABLE 100-A.—*Principal statistical data, by local boards*—Continued.

MINNESOTA—Continued.

Local board	Post-office address	Registration June 5, 1917	Registration June and August, 1918	Registration Sept. 12, 1918	Registration Total	Induction Accepted at camp	Physical groups General service	Physical groups Remediables	Physical groups Limited service	Physical groups Disqualified	Deferments Dependency	Deferments Agricultural	Deferments Industrial
Dodge	Mtr's Office, Mtle	1,111	118	1,420	2,649	368	294	0	19	14	502	200	14
Douglas	Alexandria	1,553	201	2,172	3,926	534	504	1	58	137	432	402	6
DULUTH No. 1	Moina Court Building, West Duluth Station	3,289	276	4,021	7,386	766	816	0	80	144	948	4	325
DULUTH No. 2	Room 13, Stan Block	3,502	333	4,263	8,098	959	932	9	127	251	813	2	179
DULUTH No. 3	230 West Superior Steet	2,549	175	3,307	6,031	584	487	25	58	28	894	1	44
DULUTH No. 4	4-5 East Superior Street	1,442	129	2,628	4,199	463	315	16	41	85	631	5	32
Faribault	Blue Earth	1,964	239	2,433	4,636	694	730	8	29	71	773	380	4
Fillmore	Iton	2,213	253	2,961	5,427	799	771		56	156	801	409	14
Freeborn	Abrt Lea	2,172	280	2,942	5,394	822	971	34	224	49	438	687	18
Goodhue	Red Wing	2,599	305	3,847	6,751	938	933	27	60	232	853	432	22
Grant	Ehw Lake	863	121	1,226	2,210	287	310		18	91	238	262	4
Hennepin	Hopkins	3,246	323	4,275	7,844	1,098	1,420	26	81	216	1,170	408	22
Houston	Caledonia	1,198	156	1,641	2,995	366	376	10	31	106	411	307	6
Hubbard	Park Rapids	676	87	1,090	1,853	302	267	10	10	67	254	34	1
Isanti	Cambridge	1,194	190	1,576	2,940	437	460	0	21	117	313	336	5
Itasca	Gand Rapids	2,656	189	4,035	6,880	683	588	3	51	151	668	4	21
Jackson	Jackson	1,590	160	1,846	3,596	541	516	46	45	22	539	327	9
Kanabec	Mia	747	102	1,090	1,939	298	291	0	63	14	275	112	3
Kandiyohi	Willmar	2,153	242	2,681	5,076	663	1,081	1	92	90	553	348	42
Kittson	Hallock	1,006	111	1,228	2,375	364	789	3	22	109	355	225	3
Koochiching	International Falls	1,532	96	2,046	3,674	511	41	15	35	96	56	5	5
Lac qui Parle	Madison	1,519	197	1,952	3,663	498	477	19	19	97	473	432	6
Lake	Two Harbors	974	101	1,291	2,366	243	270	3	7	40	193	2	8
Le Sueur	Le Sueur Center	1,493	207	2,045	3,745	400	381		77	151	79	736	34
Lincoln	Ivanhoe	1,121	124	1,338	2,583	404	406	15	16	55	410	217	3
Lyon	Marshall	1,838	201	2,342	4,381	677	710	7	38	38	693	365	20
McLeod	Glencoe	1,666	210	2,317	4,193	661	623	20	38	101	635	212	1
Mahnomen	Mahnomen	591	62	612	1,295	172	228	5	8	105	217	52	0
Marshall	Warren	1,935	226	2,365	4,646	595	613	7	90	8	522	503	8
Martin	Fairmont	2,058	223	2,169	3,906	642	837	0	38	23	737	317	13
Meeker	Litchfield	1,526	211	1,474	2,627	622	686		50	14	478	317	3
Mille Lacs	Princeton	1,001	149			328	342	10	0	43	679	198	5
MINNEAPOLIS No. 1	301 East Hennepin Avenue	2,295	162	2,493	4,950	694	626	21	74	90	775	4	43
MINNEAPOLIS No. 2	Main Engineering Room, State University	2,640	261	2,318	5,219	992	783	13	121	110	1,501	2	65
MINNEAPOLIS No. 3	North High School, Girard and Seventeenth Avenue north	4,340	349	5,147	9,836	1,693	1,384	31	133	24			78
MINNEAPOLIS No. 4	The Armory, Kenwood Parkway	5,417	343	5,801	11,561	1,936	1,423	95	138	298	920	1	34

MINNEAPOLIS No. 3 — 715 New York Life Building	4,854	289	5,107	10,130	1,656	1,899	14	385	31	1,067	13	83
MINNEAPOLIS No. 6 — Pillsbury Settlement, 320 Sixteenth Avenue south	1,680	86	2,053	3,819	513	401	5	34	114	130	2	27
MINNEAPOLIS No. 7 — Irving School, Twenty-eighth Street and Seventeenth Avenue south	2,684	194	3,327	6,205	981	730	40	113	78	1,185	1	76
MINNEAPOLIS No. 8 — 315 Metropolitan National Bank Building	4,181	227	5,057	9,465	1,375	1,073	23	222	106	1,098	2	24
MINNEAPOLIS No. 9 — 2423 Central Avenue	3,220	223	3,651	7,064	945	776	14	112	179	1,380	2	87
MINNEAPOLIS No. 10 — 3116 Emerson Avenue	2,410	189	3,065	7,664	874	785	0	81	74	1,141	4	42
MINNEAPOLIS No. 11 — Care of Adams School, Sixteenth Avenue south and Frank	2,225	189	2,424	4,838	837	678	5	152	39	747	9	51
MINNEAPOLIS No. 12 — 3002 Twenty-seventh Avenue south	2,881	223	4,100	7,204	764	623	13	74	75	1,533	7	117
MINNEAPOLIS No. 13 — Lake Harriet Commercial Club	2,223	126	4,229	6,578	746	444	5	97	12	1,105	7	33
Morrison — Little Falls	2,085	261	2,598	4,944	752	718	14	131	36	820	421	8
Mer — Austin	2,188	250	2,824	5,262	686	562	28	139	119	896	313	30
Slayton	1,356	146	1,632	3,164	488	539	0	51	93	441	287	4
Nicollet — St. Peter	1,220	139	1,529	2,888	399	319	13	36	128	420	246	4
Nobles — Worthington	1,654	176	2,053	2,883	510	500	22	32	73	654	0	0
N — Ada	1,367	188	1,720	3,275	494	43	1	61	110	353	386	9
Rochester	2,463	266	2,062	4,812	798	798	1	39	135	968	353	12
Otter Tail No. 1 — Fergus Falls	2,318	278	3,163	5,759	892	892	12	40	51	649	335	12
Otter Tail No. 2 — Henning	1,746	227	2,334	4,307	609	647	3	110	51	255	498	5
Pennington — Thief River Falls	908	118	1,390	2,416	342	324	8	27	128	370	334	7
Pine — Pine City	1,577	209	2,352	4,138	622	570	1	95	394	574	124	13
Pipestone — Pipestone	1,085	110	1,361	2,556	356	355	2	31	31	411	130	7
Polk — Crookston	3,537	432	4,292	8,261	1,130	951	1	26	59	994	110	68
Pope — Gld	1,175	127	1,637	2,939	363	344	9	37	44	384	99	16
Ramsey — White Bear Lake	1,080	93	1,286	2,459	415	480	16	47	63	395	340	19
Red Lake — Red Lake Falls	639	63	784	1,486	181	191	0	47	188	285	89	3
Redwood — Redwood Falls	1,933	222	2,535	4,690	718	135	3	4	195	717	131	6
Renville — Ga	2,439	251	2,883	5,573	867	871	0	69	118	636	363	5
Rice — Faribault	2,180	204	2,806	5,190	661	661	19	78	190	803	560	16
Rock — Luverne	1,092	122	1,365	2,579	648	282	0	66	64	417	322	1
Roseau — Roseau	1,200	137	1,543	2,880	399	428	19	28	69	403	145	6
St. Louis No. 1 — 211 Courthouse, Duluth	1,360	180	2,181	3,671	528	616	13	17	57	397	165	60
St. Louis No. 2 — Eveleth	2,566	156	3,811	6,533	298	579	6	36	421	694	16	12
St. Louis No. 3 — Ely	2,656	90	4,403	7,240	483	241	0	69	70	245	0	8
St. Louis No. 4 — Virginia	1,120					76	52	16		922	4	0
St. Louis No. 5 — Chisholm	1,696	88	2,269	4,053	289	0	0	0		366	15	10
St. Louis No. 6 — Hibbing	2,596	134	3,223	5,953	401	300	1	69	182	564	2	52
ST. PAUL No. 1 — Woodman Hall, Payne Avenue and Jenks Street	3,006	266	3,757	6,029	951	821	34	107	281	1,158	4	103
ST. PAUL No. 2 — Daytons Bluff Commercial Club	2,109	208	2,516	4,833	733	659	11	48	154	689	6	62
ST. PAUL No. 3 — 200 Pittsburgh Building	2,511	145	2,982	5,638	1,018	868	26	146	220	393	9	61
ST. PAUL No. 4 — West End Commercial Club	2,406	168	2,655	5,229	619	514	11	57	194	811	1	55
ST. PAUL No. 5 — Corner Humboldt and George Streets	2,143	176	2,746	5,005	717	564	5	87	176	735	0	27
ST. PAUL No. 6 — 300 Germania Life Building	2,077	172	2,779	5,028	895	1,179	42	131	165	729	2	65
ST. PAUL No. 7 — 458 Rice Street	2,818	257	3,309	6,384	876	675	12	146	70	1,394	13	48
ST. PAUL No. 8 — 410 Shubert Building	1,935	199	2,108	4,212	692	652	254	33	208	577	8	54
ST. PAUL No. 9 — Room 407, Hackney Building	1,803	123	2,297	4,223	681	515	33	63	92	685	3	45
ST. PAUL No. 10 — 510 Metropolitan Opera House Building	2,006	147	3,007	5,220	697	461	26	74	34	777	8	30
ST. PAUL No. 11 — Third floor, Old State Capitol	1,396	126	1,850	5,372	387	479	63	42	46	632	5	32
Scott — Shakopee	1,197	157	1,542	2,896	403	154	7	18	78	405	236	7
Sherburne — Elk River	863	69	1,066	1,908	269	278	0	39	35	323	42	3

APPENDIX TABLE 100-A.—*Principal statistical data, by local boards*—Continued.

MINNESOTA—Continued.

Local board.	Post-office address.	Registration.				Induction.	Physical groups.				Deferments.		
		June 5, 1917.	June and August, 1918.	Sept. 12, 1918.	Total.	Accepted at camp.	General service.	Remediables.	Limited service.	Disqualified.	Dependency.	Agricultural.	Industrial.
Sibley	Gaylord	1,434	156	1,850	3,470	455	391	0	59	105	438	395	3
Stearns No. 1	St. Cloud	2,936	402	3,687	7,025	873	947	0	95	220	1,132	473	57
Stearns No. 2	Melrose	1,000	244	2,037	3,891	480	460	46	14	106	650	335	28
Steele		1,583	146	2,016	3,747	551	706	0	3	39	811	0	19
Stevens	Morris	832	104	1,773	2,125	276	261	0	20	68	286	239	7
Swift	Benson	1,211	170	2,840	3,151	475	484	13	40	74	383	147	6
Todd	Long Prairie	2,100	283	907	5,283	712	881	18	102	113	870	535	22
Traverse	Wheaton	762	86	2,194	1,815	228	259	0	37	66	210	296	1
Wabasha		1,554	170	1,125	3,918	573	459	0	29	145	517	295	1
Wadena		810	110	1,688	2,076	319	348	0	40	13	345	104	1
Waseca	Waseca	1,288	130	2,936	3,100	471	413	8	44	89	506	210	5
Washington	Stillwater	1,857	211	1,489	2,775	498	451	1	18	184	654	186	30
Watonwan	St. James	1,158	89	1,255	2,263	400	403	5	8	28	17	290	7
Wilkin	Breckenridge	914	94	3,860	2,114	290	232	0	100	209	294	164	19
Winona		2,964	280	3,170	5,794	915	16	13			1,050	355	76
Wright	Buffalo	2,328	296	3,170		865	808	26	90	65	746	517	15
Yellow Medicine	Granite Falls	1,661	218	2,143	4,022	558	724	6	53	168	867	481	117

MISSISSIPPI.

Local board.	Post-office address.	Registration.				Induction.	Physical groups.				Deferments.		
		June 5, 1917.	June and August, 1918.	Sept. 12, 1918.	Total.	Accepted at camp.	General service.	Remediables.	Limited service.	Disqualified.	Dependency.	Agricultural.	Industrial.
Adams	Natchez	1,436	150	2,284	3,870	619	724	128	46	15	439	11	3
Alcorn	Corinth	1,197	158	2,228	4,083	408	425	3	47	18	1,042	7	2
Amite	Liberty	1,566	168	2,026	3,760	510	715	6	27	14	735	0	5
Attala	Kosciusko	1,575	181	2,399	4,155	508	693	0	10	206	833	1	0
Benton	Ashland	808	80	1,018	1,906	258	45	6	20	34	388	5	0
Bolivar No. 1	Rosedale	2,332	240	2,538	5,410	641	800	30	30	329	1,025		
Bolivar No. 2	Cleveland	3,642	325	4,064	8,031	891							
Calhoun	Pittsboro	1,259	138	1,629	3,026	330	318	14	21	63	803	0	0
Carroll	Carrollton	1,327	155	1,865	3,347	378	410	14	31	55	643	3	1
Chickasaw	Houston	1,554	129	2,040	3,723	318	471	36	78	36	792	4	4
Choctaw	Ackerman	957	119	1,175	2,305	356	361	16	38	136	442	0	1
Claiborne	Port Gibson	1,387	126	1,222	3,371	349	463	4	15	50	460	8	4
Clay	West Point	1,010	161	1,833	2,744	313	63	26	20	30	771	1	5
Coahoma	Clarksdale	4,752	336	5,373	10,461	1,334	1,552	21	41	439	2,228	5	10

County	City												
Copiah	Hazlehurst	0	2	886	15	42	44	808	772	5,187	2,750	222	2,215
Covington	Collins	9	2	576	150	27	7	344	376	2,728	1,492	143	1,088
De Soto		1	4	1,167	72	34	4	609	566	4,752	2,420	216	2,116
Forrest	Hattiesburg	14	4	673	8	22	0	41	735	4,911		257	1,806
Franklin	Meadville	9		626	129	63	13	423	433	2,846	1,475	130	1,241
George	Lucedale	0	1	231	22	9		173	139	1,144	618	55	471
Greene	Leaksville	138	41	432	18	17	1	312	178	1,552	821	71	660
Grenada		3	7	543	138	40	8	276	251	2,531	1,353	80	1,095
Hancock	Bay St. Louis	1	0	493	23	47	0	372	340	2,580	1,307	94	1,179
Harrison	Gulfport	24	8	1,244	130	144	64	755	757	6,526	3,621	236	2,669
Hinds	Jackson	5	13	1,278	107	40	23	700	500	5,346	2,989	251	2,106
Holmes	Lexington	0	11	1,516	26	120		1,005	538	6,592	3,488	276	2,828
	Belzoni	11	6	978	9	34	3	915	512	4,594	2,083	160	2,351
Issaquena	Mayersville	3	2	263	90	13	1	213	173	1,424	793	81	550
Itawamba	Fulton	0	3	749	251	16	0	286	344	2,824	1,539	145	1,140
Jackson	404 Capitol National Bank Building	17	1	763	33	5	43	910	599	4,774	2,550	139	2,083
Jasper	Pascagoula	17	1	597	95	13	6	363	321	3,821	2,340	187	1,294
Jefferson	Bay Springs	4	7	691	45	43	15	491	411	3,251	1,789	185	1,280
Jefferson Davis	Gayetie	3	1	470	83	5	5	258	446	2,822	1,610	148	1,064
Jones	Prentiss	1	2	509	18	38	17	926	209	2,204	1,246	106	852
Kemper	Laurel	11	1	76	57	57	2	602	810	6,372	3,463	319	2,565
Lafayette	De Kalb	0	1	915	34	81	9	293	431	3,455	1,883	172	1,605
Lamar	Oxford	2	3	688	62	37	4	437	425	3,660	1,891	155	1,409
Lauderdale No. 1	Purvis	8	0	569	157	44	0	692	392	2,779	1,500	107	1,172
Lauderdale No. 2	Meridian	59	0	814		83	0	93	604	5,434	3,061	165	2,208
Lawrence	...do...	24	0	350	0	43	11	350	589	4,237	1,243	239	1,761
Leake	...do...	0	0	406	39	24	6	428	249	2,141	1,667	108	790
Lee	Carthage	0	3	669	191	43	3	309	422	3,015	2,923	163	1,185
Leflore	Tupelo	5	8	1,180	94	44	17	1,092	637	5,229	4,433	248	2,058
Lincoln	Greenwood	2	15	1,153	82	32	6	535	840	8,292	2,323	261	3,607
Lowndes	Brookhaven	5	3	910	46	43	17	933	637	4,459	2,345	215	1,721
Madison		16	1	860	111	37	26	845	533	4,334	1,973	146	1,843
Marion	Canton	5	6	1,117	18	37	16	237	802	4,947	2,329	171	2,163
Marshall	Columbia	0	1	765	210	7	0	649	422	3,676	2,918	135	1,568
Monroe	Holly Springs	3	6	1,196	167	50	32	668	727	4,681	1,240	140	2,212
Montgomery		10	1	1,131	21	62	32	363	584	5,218	1,945	229	2,071
Neshoba	Winona	4	5	559	74	96		370	303	2,310	2,034	84	986
Newton	Philadelphia	9	5	923	143	70	16	508	452	3,655	1,971	197	1,513
Noxubee	Decatur	2	4	592	121	30	2	473	441	3,716	1,565	202	1,480
Oktibbeha	Macon	1	2	926	57	57	9	341	404	3,738	2,701	158	1,609
Panola	Starkville	1	7	520	18	18		771	299	2,739	1,562	141	1,033
Pearl River	Batesville	1	18	1,345	29	29	0	437	792	5,373	1,111	195	2,477
Perry	Poplarville	1	2	549	22	22	4	379	389	2,863	2,783	128	1,173
Pike	New Augusta	10	3	424	15	15	15	665	348	2,160	2,024	100	949
Pontotoc	Magnolia	22	2	1,137	51	51	4	262	656	3,596	1,827	179	2,067
Prentiss	Pontotoc	0	0	967	193	112	27	293	418	3,482	2,442	165	1,407
Quitman	Booneville	6	1	931	1	26	12	857	373	4,784	1,993	168	1,497
Rankin	Marks	15	13	939	140	12	0	578	578	3,547	1,775	149	2,193
Scott	Brandon	2	13	465	93	38	13	456	488	3,238		141	1,413
	Forest	0	0	873	238	36	2	381	402		1,775	156	1,307
Sharkey	Rolling Fork	4	2	321	52	21		778	556	2,977	1,490	193	1,288

APPENDIX TABLE 100-A.—*Principal statistical data, by local boards*—Continued.

MISSISSIPPI—Continued.

Local board.	Post-office address.	Registration. June 5, 1917.	Registration. June and August, 1918.	Registration. Sept. 12, 1918.	Registration. Total.	Induction. Accepted at camp.	Physical groups. General service.	Physical groups. Remediables.	Physical groups. Limited service.	Physical groups. Disqualified.	Deferments. Dependency.	Deferments. Agricultural.	Deferments. Industrial.
Simpson	Mendenhall	1,284	158	1,895	3,337	353	391	20	16	129	746	1	4
Smith	Raleigh	1,305	143	1,667	3,115	413	385	3		9	717	0	0
Stone	Wiggins	744	59	821	1,624	223	224	2	10	14	355	2	1
Sunflower	Indianola	4,627	455	5,968	11,050	1,079	1,526	0	121	10	1,629	14	4
Tallahatchie	Charleston	3,439	386	3,918	7,743	913	210	14	96	138	1,751	0	0
Tate	Senatobia	1,854	163	1,907	3,924	546	57	1	26	144	640	0	0
Tippah	Ripley	1,206	148	1,638	2,992	364	258	9	22	123	416	1	0
Tishomingo	Iuka	1,223	139	1,543	2,905	346	296	0	28	59	780	2	3
Tunica	Tunica	2,185	139	2,207	4,331	680	691	54	7	138	990	0	1
Union	New Albany	1,511	179	2,005	3,695	468	384	3	18	24	907	5	0
Walthall	Tylertown	988	106	1,247	2,341	258	244	3	35	61	592	9	3
Warren	Marg.	2,580	223	3,764	6,567	839	1,114	14	31	81	974	9	42
Washington	Greenville	2,428	218	6,096	8,742	703	804	0	109	18	827	19	34
Wayne	Æro	1,292	118	1,526	2,936	488	628	2	53	48	646	3	6
Webster	Walthall	987	123	1,227	2,337	294	232	0	44	131	517	0	0
Wilkinson	Woodville	1,071	130	1,543	2,764	462	537	0	19	59	457	0	2
Winston	Louisville	1,323	139	1,827	3,289	388	312	12	64	124	685	1	3
Yalobusha	Water Valley	1,286	147	1,869	3,302	381	382	22	34	69	711	8	4
Yazoo No. 1	Yazoo City	1,459	114	1,314	2,887	446	477	29	25	129	722	8	0
Yazoo No. 2	...do...	1,546	170	2,043	3,759	456	134	13	20	231	770	9	5

MISSOURI.

Local board.	Post-office address.	Registration. June 5, 1917.	Registration. June and August, 1918.	Registration. Sept. 12, 1918.	Registration. Total.	Induction. Accepted at camp.	Physical groups. General service.	Physical groups. Remediables.	Physical groups. Limited service.	Physical groups. Disqualified.	Deferments. Dependency.	Deferments. Agricultural.	Deferments. Industrial.
Adair	Kirksville	2,041	186	2,490	4,717	515	512	20	77	106	829	117	90
Andrew	Savannah	1,184	137	1,652	2,973	396	291	6	15	91	534	93	2
Atchison	Rockport	1,176	113	1,553	2,847	377	335	7	24	26	616	46	3
Audrain	Mexico	1,712	225	5,479	7,416	526	402	14	35	171	706	272	20
Barry	Cassville	2,066	192	2,675	4,933	592	640	0	30	31	1,126	65	3
Barton	Lamar	1,242	154	1,973	3,369	378	367	19	52	69	603	39	4
Bates	Butler	1,687	189	2,723	4,599	599	514	3	19	91	823	127	3
Benton	Warsaw	1,044	143	1,466	2,653	370	307	5	50	64	500	118	2
Bollinger	Marble Hill	1,062	143	1,537	2,742	401	334	0	39	57	618	19	2
Boone	Columbia	2,911	302	3,414	6,627	887	850	21	73	233	1,536	99	8
Buchanan	St. Joseph	1,290	145	1,938	3,373	413	305	0	16	18	650	36	2
Butler	Poplar Bluff	2,138	174	2,859	5,171	519	427	26	72	41	1,134	16	5

County	City												
Caldwell	Kingston	1,000	124	1,599	2,723	349	340	0	16	71	548	94	1
Callaway	Fulton	1,756	211	2,614	4,581	549	600	2	11	182	852	158	19
Camden	Linn Creek	2,500	83	1,128	2,016	276	298		13	61	16	3	2
Cape Girardeau	Jackson	805	257	3,574	6,331	836	725	11	99	158	1,273	137	2
Carroll	Carrollton	1,662	195	2,421	1,294	453	464	5	55	41	895	137	2
Carter	Van Buren	499	51	744	4,250	136	116	3	6		228	0	0
Cass	Harrisonville	1,648	196	1,846	2,566	530	570		17	82	779	29	6
Cedar	Stockton	962	119	1,485	4,520	272	213	120	6	118	540	51	0
Chariton	Keytesville	1,766	231	2,523	2,419	595	82	17	47	176	773	202	9
Christian	Ozark	1,368	143	1,753	3,264	301	312		81	38	904	7	1
Clark	Kahoka	933	98	1,388	2,419	339	277	15	37	66	330	123	5
Clay	Liberty	1,735	160	2,446	4,341	530	413	6	83	24	514	17	0
Clinton	Plattsburg	1,187	130	1,671	2,988	423	424	8	4	127	563	18	5
Cole	Jefferson City	2,058	194	2,595	4,847	594	512	8	53	187	967	125	0
Cooper	Boonville	1,674	153	1,377	4,022	534	457	6	32	37	603	73	4
Crawford	Steelville	935	142	1,566	2,454	260	297	7	29	91	547	81	3
Dade	Greenfield	1,197	144	1,251	2,907	316	242	6	15	111	603	106	1
Dallas	Buffalo	791	134	2,014	2,176	268	87		54	29	534	9	0
Daviess	Gallatin	1,320	151	2,411	3,485	367	353	7	19	95	804	64	0
Dekalb	Maysville	901	164	1,323	9,385	237	164	0	5	74	503	59	0
Dent	Salem	870	98	1,613	2,332	220	261		2	133	364	32	0
Douglas	Ava	1,087	146	1,323	2,846	373	311	7	21	147	608	7	1
Dunklin	Kennett	3,538	283	4,286	8,109	722	887	0	128	256	1,930	175	0
Franklin	Union	2,304	286	3,276	5,866	751	568	91	47	53	872	57	1
Gasconade	Hermann	996	151	1,450	2,597	341	283	16	27	49	476	119	3
Gentry	Albany	1,263	131	1,756	3,150	466	311		24	22	693	73	5
Greene	Springfield	2,196	233	3,260	5,709	696	354	0	26	153	1,344	85	2
Grundy	Trenton	1,403	144	2,130	3,677	377	535	12	14	47	382	186	3
Harrison	Bethany	1,614	176	2,358	4,148	524	413	6	16	79	967	52	4
Henry	Clinton	1,854	197	9,668	4,719	574	479	3	39	127	1,016	85	77
Hickory	Hermitage	535	82	834	1,451	136	511	9	12	21	288	16	6
Holt	Oregon	1,105	134	1,609	2,938	308	107	4	23	17	610	134	0
Howard	Fayette	1,221	148	1,829	3,191	504	328	3	30	177	503	80	0
Howell	West Plains	1,260	172	2,086	3,318	350	331	22	32	31	754	9	12
Iron	Ironton	714	86	957	1,757	249	422	26	33	21	386	1	3
Jackson	Independence	3,615	333	5,114	9,062	911	193	14	82	255	2,043	112	3
Jasper No. 1	Carthage	1,939	188	2,639	4,766	653	845	0	7	10	1,082	81	0
Jasper No. 2	Web City	4,331	238	3,640	809	790	175	43	134	291	2,461	19	11
Jefferson	Hillsboro	2,710	279	3,226	6,215	610	765	2	76	54	2,179	0	7
Johnson	Warrensburg	1,847	229	2,804	4,880	1,401	409	26	50	34	915	192	9
JOPLIN	Federal Building, Joplin	4,510	367	4,968	9,845	827	1,275	9	99	503	1,677	1	0
KANSAS CITY No. 1	1108 ... to Street	2,522	186	4,062	6,70	827	962	3	98	249	515	2	4
KANSAS CITY No. 2	316 Cumbel ... ing	2,080	176	3,013	5,269	531	344	36					0
KANSAS CITY No. 3	906 Commerce Building	1,744	124	3,473	4,341	510	389	65	71	20	556	0	1
KANSAS CITY No. 4	908 New York Life Building	1,742	138	3,086	4,956	427	590	6	47	104	907	0	5
KANSAS CITY No. 5	702 ...al Boulevard	2,478	183	3,618	6,285	831	1,085	7	30	32	815	0	8
KANSAS CITY No. 6	Care of ...re Hotel	2,501	186	2,357	3,205	925	447	29	92	139	536	2	11
KANSAS CITY No. 7	417 R. A. Long Building	1,755	128	4,064	4,240	509	102	19	30	97	861	0	5
KANSAS CITY No. 8	305-306 New ...ding	2,618	235	2,736	6,917	1,042	516	12	43	2	454	1	7
KANSAS CITY No. 9	3401 East Fifteenth Street	1,851	147	4,734	4,734	520	409-	23	102	65	827	0	6
KANSAS CITY No. 10	...st and Campbell Streets	1,578	129	2,322	4,029	420	683	3	85	108	921	1	4
KANSAS CITY No. 11	3005 Troost ...nue	2,113	152	3,011	5,306	713		14	92	93	878	0	3

APPENDIX TABLE 100-A.—*Principal statistical data, by local boards.*—Continued.

MISSOURI—Continued.

Local board.	Post-office address.	Registration. June 5, 1917.	Registration. June and August 1918.	Registration. Sept. 12, 1918.	Registration. Total.	Induction. Accepted at camp.	Physical groups. General service.	Physical groups. Remediables.	Physical groups. Limited service.	Physical groups. Disqualified.	Deferments. Dependency.	Deferments. Agricultural.	Deferments. Industrial.
KANSAS CITY No. 12	3429 ...st Avenue	1,769	118	2,531	4,418	560	257	4	70	128	647	1	5
KANSAS CITY No. 13	419 Gloyd Building	2,620	188	4,209	7,027	557	472	41	104	107	257	1	2
KANSAS CITY No. 14	...-331 New York Life, Huling	1,544	125	2,547	4,216	448	349	3	24	70	839	0	10
KANSAS CITY No. 15	4301 East Fifteenth Street	1,795	132	2,583	4,510	395	350	17	45	21	1,108	2	6
KANSAS CITY No. 16	107 South ...tty Street	1,950	150	2,952	5,082	435	410	20	90	107	1,067	0	19
Knox	Edina	852	112	1,235	2,299	223	178	16	45	89	379	152	11
Laclede	Lebanon	1,027	159	1,743	2,929	335	299	0	101	4	513	19	10
Lafayette	Lexington	2,815	222	3,654	6,777	888	803	34	0	237	1,176	192	33
Lawrence	Mount Vernon	1,954	118	2,656	4,832	545	704	0	53	66	921	258	11
Lewis	Monticello	1,109	151	1,508	2,735	322	54	1	43	4	12	5	1
Lincoln	Troy	1,481	199	1,859	3,491	450	360	28	30	46	611	64	1
Linn	Linneus	1,986	164	2,841	5,026	443	473	12	42	61	1,023	117	79
Livingston	Chillicothe	1,463	142	2,044	3,661	309	115	0	8	70	800	88	3
McDonald	Pineville	1,020	272	1,576	2,744	702	356	1	20	126	515	241	0
Macon	Macon	2,086	101	3,229	5,597	392	608	14	66	3	84	84	118
Madison	Fredericktown	1,056	110	1,146	2,303	313	324	0	26	94	573	8	6
Maries	Vienna	761	260	1,026	1,897	605	276	2	9	55	412	0	0
Marion	Palmyra	2,817	114	3,728	6,805	433	926	37	64	53	1,446	7	2
Mercer	Princeton	917	149	1,307	2,338	362	295	2	37	90	619	94	1
Miller	Tuscumbia	1,139	115	1,756	3,044	362	302	10	33	22	457	84	1
Mississippi	Charleston	1,331	150	1,784	3,260	455	240	16	53	107	552	245	11
Moniteau	California	1,006	106	1,529	2,650	371	423	8	33	107	414	140	8
Monroe	Paris	1,313	119	1,889	3,362	398	203	5	12	98	540	73	1
Montgomery	Montgomery City	1,131	234	1,648	2,887	292	771		125	155	1,487	28	0
Morgan	Versailles	929	257	1,371	2,419	708	572	11	53	163	1,277	78	17
New Madrid	New Madrid	2,619	110	3,106	5,959	607	443	4	43	30	1,286	131	4
Newton	Neosho	2,173	147	2,975	5,405	619	275	0	32	95	606	19	0
Oregon	Alton	1,019	118	3,193	5,736	306	395	36	43	24	365	145	2
Osage	Linn	1,220	312	1,512	2,494	312	228	12	10	145	592	6	0
Ozark	Gainesville	935	149	1,134	2,879	184	969	8	69	124	17	17	3
Pemiscot	Caruthersville	2,631	328	3,848	6,791	909	374	6	59	112	1,333	105	20
Perry	Perryville	1,006	149	4,271	2,687	457	1,302	17	45	172	450	111	5
Pettis	Sedalia	3,396	328	1,675	2,991	1,006	264		29	46	1,509	32	14
Phelps	Rolla	1,607	149	2,314	2,185	420	851	19	56	102	474	127	0
Pike	Bowling Green	1,317	174	1,765	2,386	454	374	4	17		1,055		
Platte	Platte City		133			385					793	5	

Polk	Bolivar	1,432	188	2,142	3,762	474	438	4	18	89	889	29	0
Pulaski	Waynesville	752	114	1,139	2,005	232	209	4	17	82	441	1	0
Putnam	Unionville	1,027	124	1,548	2,699	300	299	4	12	149	500	178	30
Ralls	New London	914	87	1,419	2,420	223	151	4	17	19	408	49	1
Randolph	Huntsville	2,269	232	3,006	6,107	693	570	12	41	158	1,150	109	87
Ray	Richmond	1,794	231	2,634	4,659	515	447	10	32	77	917	100	15
Reynolds	Centerville	905	103	1,025	2,630	213	241		41	63	528	73	0
Ripley	Doniphan	908	88	1,230	2,223	290	307	10	23	50	468	17	3
St. Charles	St. Charles	2,069	237	2,733	59	701	519	22	119	64	467	167	10
St. Charles		1,080	145	1,655	2,860	348	241	10	23	59	651	78	0
St. Clair		3,316	278	4,606	8,199	922	820	19	95	242	1,745	53	1
St. Francois	Farmington	755	108	1,162	2,025	327	267		20	84	107	106	2
Ste. Genevieve	Ste. Genevieve	1,942	172	2,755	4,809	482	626	3	13	171	981		3
St. Joseph No. 1	Seventh and Felix	2,342	202	3,394	5,938	648	577	26	62	158	1,111	0	21
St. Joseph No. 2	203 Federal Building	2,507	236	3,339	6,499	553	67	41	57	190	1,133	1	19
St. Joseph No. 3	5024½ King Hill Avenue	2,438	181	2,888	6,033	816	945	11	97	186	1,165	4	43
St. Louis No. 1	North Broadway	2,576	184	2,554	5,120	625	597	16	91	172	712	1	19
St. Louis No. 2	Blair Avenue and Salisbury	1,869	300	4,377	4,607	583	488	21	188	135	871	5	20
St. Louis No. 3	1909 St. Louis Avenue	3,291	208	4,388	7,968	733							
St. Louis No. 4	Fourteenth and Cass Avenue	2,877	270	4,837	7,473	887	1,013	14	75	402	637	1	11
St. Louis No. 5	... of Jefferson	3,016	188	2,676	8,123	1,143	1,143	18	80	228	456	1	13
St. Louis No. 6	125 South Fourth Street	1,971	172	3,035	4,835	676	634	0	44	211	708	0	14
St. Louis No. 7	1328 South Broadway	2,349	223	3,078	5,409	531	452	30	66	108	811	0	8
St. Louis No. 8	714 Soulard Street	2,241	263	2,713	5,650	578	544	26	132	121	939	1	1
St. Louis No. 9	Eighteenth and Shenadoah Avenue	2,940	261	2,745	5,217	579	449	25	135	182	937	0	30
St. Louis No. 10	3373 South Seventh Street	2,816	269	3,842	6,946	831	77	6	115	253	1,471	2	31
St. Louis No. 11	3548 South Grand Avenue	4,287	370	6,139	6,927	945	677	32	121	248	1,340	5	36
St. Louis No. 12	6818 Michigan Avenue	2,589	258	3,279	10,796	1,195							
St. Louis No. 13	3155 South	2,334	212	2,990	6,126	780	649	25	111	254	1,231	0	30
St. Louis No. 14	Grand and Magnolia	2,315	227	3,205	5,636	769	792	42	98	209	835	3	33
St. Louis No. 15	... and Mississippi	3,747	331	5,237	5,837	810	69	24	126	207	913	0	19
St. Louis No. 16	3132 Park Avenue	1,931	176	2,460	9,315	1,672	1,615	51	160	42	1,012	2	3
St. Louis No. 17	3088 Olive Street	2,388	238	3,329	4,567	821	544	5	62	300	948	2	6
St. Louis No. 18	1800 North	2,825	266	3,053	5,955	813	564	9	78	167	1,472	4	52
St. Louis No. 19	Jefferson Avenue and Dayton	2,884	296	3,944	5,584	813	687	8	206	41	643	0	14
St. Louis No. 20	Grand and Franklin	2,466	223	3,453	7,094	913	848	13	128	257	1,487	2	39
St. Louis No. 21	3126 North Grand Avenue	2,637	255	3,889	6,081	814	636	31	150	238	1,091	1	28
St. Louis No. 22	4103 Easton Avenue	3,963	359	6,321	6,961	975	722	37	131	209	1,034	0	47
St. Louis No. 23		2,903	212	3,871	10,49	1,046	742	51	78	475	1,934	4	53
St. Louis No. 24	Magnolia and Clifton Avenues	2,194	260	3,119	7,016	967	680	11	129	292	1,098	2	59
St. Louis No. 25	Washington Hotel	4,469	413	6,443	5,513	632	488	27	69	238	1,642	8	15
St. Louis No. 26	503 Page Avenue	3,145	252	5,032	11,265	1,238	967	0	127	335	2,192	7	66
St. Louis No. 27	1902 ... Union Boulevard	2,512	206	3,966	8,430	1,01	625	11	140	307	1,029	13	63
St. Louis No. 28	218 Delmar Building	2,732	312	4,021	6,684	656	445	20	105	236	1,258	98	34
St. Louis No. 1	Clayton	2,623	289	3,711	7,065	856	807	1	53	16	1,167	1,068	82
St. Louis No. 2	Ferguson	2,391	257	3,308	6,614	689	605	2	55	201	901	114	12
St. Louis No. 3	Kirkwood	577	81	1,019	5,956	808	675		65	42	895		
Saline	Lancaster	838	108	1,217	1,677	170							
Schuyler	Memphis	2,117	215	2,912	2,163	234	311	9	48	58	378	95	16
Scotland	Benton	873	89	2,183	5,244	634	538	0	121	98	1,130	33	1
Scott	Eminence	1,024	121	1,532	2,145	285	304	2	31	43	524	2	0
Shannon	Shelbyville				2,687	288	233	1	49	48	461	213	16

APPENDIX TABLE 100-A.—*Principal statistical data, by local boards*—Continued.

MISSOURI—Continued.

Local board.	Post-office address.	Registration.				Induction. Accepted at camp.	Physical groups.				Deferments.		
		June 5, 1917.	June and August, 1918.	Sept. 12, 1918.	Total.		General service.	Remediables.	Limited service.	Disqualified.	Dependency.	Agricultural.	Industrial.
SPRINGFIELD	Springfield	3,509	311	4,690	8,510	1,159	825	37	140	270	1,786	2	36
Stoddard	Bloomfield	2,504	240	3,472	5,216	590	149	1	14	1	86	9	1
Sne	Galena	1,070	114	1,398	2,582	258	481	12	57	24	549	4	2
Sullivan	Milan	1,420	165	2,013	3,598	440	439	1	30		852	76	7
Taney	Forsyth	699	102	996	1,797	231	226	0	19	43	348	1	0
Texas	Houston	1,364	185	2,035	3,584	467	564	0	12	34	733	15	0
Vernon	Nevada	1,907	186	2,741	4,834	538	634	39	42	77	1,007	112	2
Warren	Warrenton	750	94	1,030	1,874	254	54	0	25	107	163	122	7
Washington	Potosi	1,036	127	1,430	2,593	328	392	17	18	110	587	11	1
Wayne	Greenville	1,150	132	1,415	2,697	328	279	2	13	13	630	11	0
Webster	Marshfield	1,201	130	1,798	3,239	395	389		13	33	794	0	1
Worth	Grant City	526	69	852	1,447	160	170	0	9	23	330	25	0
Wright	Hartville	1,181	167	1,850	3,198	392	363	0	12	68	642	27	3
Beaverhead	Dillon	1,277	71	1,884	3,232	498	395	25	57	49	177	40	3
Big Horn	Hardin	739	57	994	1,790	281	275	12	42	34	219	42	0
Blaine	Chinook	1,909	73	1,515	3,497	623	464	29	82	109	593	135	10
Broadwater	Townsend	529	29	557	1,115	178	163		27	7	183	68	3
BUTTE	City Hall, Butte	9,080	501	11,713	21,294	2,256	1,641	79	672	247	2,532	3	45
Carbon	Red Lodge	1,832	117	2,632	4,581	557	414	26	36	171	536	136	17
Carter	Ekalaka	843	55	764	1,662	319	274	11	33	46	280	38	1
Cascade	Great Falls	6,165	351	7,120	13,666	1,620	1,788	5	147	369	1,696	289	188
Chouteau	Ft. Benton	3,126	150	2,703	5,979	976	199	6	74	271	896	249	0
Custer	Miles City	2,769	127	2,721	5,617	981	817	33	121	116	829	107	47
Dawson	Glendive	3,751	170	3,183	7,104	1,251	994	40	77	289	1,260	228	32
Deer Lodge	Anaconda	2,768	146	3,375	6,280	702	635	4	89	160	715	9	41
Fallon	Baker	776	44	836	1,656	233	279	0	18	16	319	26	3
Fergus	Lewiston	5,230	231	5,731	11,192	1,006	1,249	8	362	355	2,098	364	36
Flathead	Kalispell	2,252	146	2,956	5,354	623	542	23	106	131	825	98	77
Gallatin	Bozeman	1,927	159	2,576	4,662	627	641	23	50	45	676	139	33
Granite	Philipsburg	616	48	949	1,613	185	183	0	12	30	139	39	1
Hill	Havre	3,659	183	3,298	7,140	1,003	773	16	70	78	524	438	101
Jefferson	Boulder	652	42	776	1,470	224	219	0	23	69	193	40	16

MONTANA (continued)

County	County seat												
Lewis and Clark	Helena	2,431	151	2,803	5,385	74	551	12	121	68	696	40	18
Lincoln	Libby	856	52	1,257	2,65	199	127	0	32	103	273	4	8
Madison	Virginia City	939	72	1,320	2,331	370	322	11	62	19	348	43	2
Meagher	White Sulphur Springs	564	74	639	1,009	198	266	6	30	6	167	7	0
Mineral	Superior	402	15	592		11	65	4	15	29	00	4	10
Musselshell	Roundup	1,945	10	2,564	4,619	512	441	1	112	91	723	203	27
Missoula	Missoula	2,915	219	3,646		830	680	14	108	108	830	32	43
Park	Livingston	1,765	128	1,977	90	705	602	21	55	69	383	35	41
Phillips	Malta	2,440	92	1,713	45	759	786	0	48	10	684	154	10
Powell	Deer Lodge	823	47	1,198	90	230	161	2	21	80	259	50	15
Prairie	Terry	785	46	666	47	241	236	9	21	73	85	62	0
Ravalli	Hamilton	964	81	1,263	98	297	215	7	62	35	99	40	1
Richland	Sidney	1,773	83	1,816	3,09	508	362	20	63	25	69	97	5
Rosebud	Forsyth	1,885	85	1,741	1,688	643							
Sanders	Thompson Falls	761	55	872	92	275	293	15	70	32	175	13	3
Sheridan	Plentywood	3,505	21	4,146	22	1,96	1,606	0	7	80	81	347	19
Silver Bow	Butte	3,562	188		63	836	1,552	31	201	5	83	3	2
Stillwater	Columbus	1,048	66	1,418		251	166	10	50	116	96	123	2
Sweet Grass	Big Timber	758	53	802		260	164		9	16	83	26	0
Teton	Choteau	2,876	157	2,836	5,869	863	1,134	17	47	251	89	188	17
Toole	Shelby	1,064	64	967	95	309	311		25	27	37	133	8
Valley	Glasgow	3,066	95	2,166	5,335	996	741	14	14	59	185,	420	57
Wheatland	Harlowton	807	52	1,061	1,920	274	225	2	45	10	147	67	0
Wibaux	Wibaux	404	30	512	92	13	92	25	7	9		66	0
Yellowstone	Billings	4,017	256	4,869		1,067	894		170	100	1,368	165	50

NEBRASKA.

County	County seat												
Adams	Hastings	1,99	153	2,94	4,86	481	562	9	37	51	810	247	28
Antelope	Neligh	1,32	162	1,705	3,189	283	276	2	42	100	512	362	5
Arthur	Arthur	04	11	48	48	46	4	0		2	32	67	2
Banner	Harrisburg	60	19	32	40	44	36	0	6	8	69	32	0
Blaine	Brewster	39	14	29	40	42	53	5	11	25	51	30	6
Boone	Albion	31	9	42	42	336	443		6	45	460	218	6
Box Butte	Alliance	82	87	1,65	3,075	187	154		33	69	207	74	57
Boyd	Butte	68	83	1,297	2,276	158	269	0	17	26	232	98	5
Brown	Ainsworth	63	39	84	1,65	150	173	17	7	28	266	9	1
Buffalo	Kearney	85	211	33	1,335	484	543	10	47	24	30	285	20
Burt	Tekamah	1,227	31	2,605	4,861	355	400	0	29	78	483	31	2
Butler	David City	1,371	135	1,86	2,948	325	298	2	21	27	71	71	2
Cass	Plattsmouth	1,707	11	1,749	3	370	425	7	31	61	744	285	26
Cedar	Hartington		143	81	81	381	6		29	13	635	188	1
Chase	Imperial	400	165	29	3,724	127	123	32	13	9	79	151	2
Cherry	Valentine	28	43	95	98	3	421	4	63	56	628	90	1
Cheyenne	Courthouse, Sidney		115	35	64	218	294	8	3	73	353	127	2
Clay	Clay Center	35	118	1	3,04	31	240	10	15	23	537	91	7
Colfax	Schuyler	36	117	93	2,212	178	262	13	18	39	155	91	5
Cuming	West Point	27	73	1,730	3,203	389	100	20	20	34	41	322	6
Custer	Broken Bow	1,313	55	1,613	3,146	558	653	6	25	62	1,222	346	9
Dakota	Dakota City	63	252	98	1,636	192	225		40	21	201	78	

APPENDIX TABLE 100-A.—*Principal statistical data, by local boards*—Continued.

NEBRASKA—Continued.

Local board.	Post-office address.	Registration. June 5, 1917.	Registration. June and August, 1918.	Registration. Sept. 12, 1918.	Registration. Total.	Induction. Accepted at camp.	Physical groups. General service.	Physical groups. Remediables.	Physical groups. Limited service.	Disqualified.	Deferments. Dependency.	Deferments. Agricultural.	Deferments. Industrial.
Dawes	Chadron	833	110	1,118	2,061	229	296	6	9	41	265	97	26
Dawson	Lexington	1,459	139	1,757	3,355	272	373	28	16	62	735	214	7
Deuel	Chappell	346	33	456	865	84	88	2	10	9	167	14	2
Dixon	Ponca	1,060	117	1,388	2,565	289	407	1	20	76	430	183	3
Dodge	Fremont	2,237	187	2,804	5,228	662	907	17	45	139	870	306	29
Douglas	Benson	1,952	174	2,430	4,556	457	464	4	64	75	733	251	20
Dundy	Benkelman	430	61	498	982	103	147	0	4	3	138	79	1
Fillmore	Geneva	1,260	116	1,560	2,966	308	270	10	20		594	180	25
Franklin	Bloomington	836	98	1,118	2,102	206	221	1	24	57	403	124	2
Frontier	Stockville	831	83	962	1,876	158	164	5	6	35	436	129	1
Furnas	Beaver City	938	104	1,274	2,316	252	221	0	9	60	496	41	1
Gage	Beatrice	2,459	238	3,223	5,920	595	696	25	67	13	476	1	0
Garden	Oshkosh	531	45	623	1,199	115	185	16	12	60	246	46	0
Garfield	Burwell	271	39	413	723	76	102	6	4	31	145	9	1
Gosper	Elwood	424	47	544	1,015	121	105	6	11	12	179	81	0
Grant	Hyannis	186	14	173	373	46	71	0	5	6	7*	6	3
Greeley	Greeley Center	784	83	930	1,797	111	209	7	5	56	351	176	40
Hall	Grand Island	2,217	178	2,811	5,206	561	498	5	71	35	975	172	131
Hamilton	Aurora	1,241	121	1,583	2,945	250	348	0	20	49	229	445	3
Harlan	Alma	781	94	1,023	1,898	220	210	1	18	24	130	32	3
Hayes	Hayes Center	325	37	346	708	75	90	1	6	8	0	93	0
Hitchcock	Trenton	403	60	661	1,214	114	178	5	2	40	238	0	0
Holt	O'Neill	1,419	150	1,932	3,501	378	265	2	10	34	599	435	16
Hooker	Mullen	147	18	193	358	37	43	4	11	11	79	0	1
Howard	St. Paul	961	105	1,178	2,244	277	279	6	20	67	329	212	2
Jefferson	Fairbury	1,417	135	1,925	3,477	310	312	5	26	76	692	153	16
Johnson	Tecumseh	850	89	1,035	1,974	206	315	9	18	36	247	203	5
Kearney	Minden	837	92	1,026	1,955	247	219	19	16	67	260	236	8
Keith	Ogallala	477	39	599	1,115	126	189	0	27	1	172	23	8
Keya Paha	Springview	385	43	411	839	108	226	1	11	21	143	40	0
Kimball	Kimball	410	48	605	1,063	139	161	4	28	21	114	61	4
Knox	Center	1,760	223	2,330	4,303	533	616	9	17	202	674	209	7
Lancaster	Courthouse, Lincoln	3,066	304	3,528	6,898	700	208	20	66	64	1,128	168	31
LINCOLN No. 1	City Hall	3,008	216	3,353	6,577	825	663	24	96	104	1,343	14	81
LINCOLN No. 2	...do...	1,827	159	2,591	4,647	564	490	16	74	127	851	11	47
Lincoln	North Platte	1,758	162	2,598	4,618	461	512	2	25	80	696	204	18
Logan	Gandy	207	16	265	488	50	105	0	6	99	90	13	0

Columns below are transcribed left-to-right as printed. No column headers are shown in the source.

Place	Location	(1)	(2)	(3)	(4)	(5)	(6)	(7)	(8)	(9)	(10)	(11)	(12)
Loup	Taylor	170	13	222	405	54	53	1	0	2	28	18	0
McPherson	Tryon	137	15	192	344	23	43	0	0	1	23	71	0
Madison	Madison	1,054	63	2,539	11,684	454	415	19	91	154	83	178	34
Merrick	Central City	879	60	1,136	2,168	254	267	8	15	57	367	94	3
Merrill	Office of County Clerk, Bridgeport	965	87	1,139	2,164	254	243	5	26	25	88	52	6
Nance	Fullerton	820	127	975	1,882	205	192	13	15	71	52	86	7
Nemaha	South Auburn	1,66?	111	1,459	2,622	96	80	4	32	34	97	165	3
Nuckolls	Nelson	1,100	234	1,506	2,717	304	272	4	55	56	506	126	1
OMAHA NO. 1	Fire Engine House, Twenty-second and Ames Avenue	3,167		4,554	7,955	897	796	42	55	179	1,482	12	36
OMAHA NO. 2	Twenty-fourth and O Streets	3,82?	279	4,501	8,212	90	1,204	4	11	185	1,234	8	20
OMAHA NO. 3	City Hall	4,6?	61	5,183	9,545	1,492	1,226	66	241	98	582	4	45
OMAHA NO. 4	Federal Building	4,91?	339	5,452	10,382	31	1,239	41	38	17	2,005	12	66
OMAHA NO. 5	Courthouse	3,91?	305	5,291	9,577	1,273	1,117	42	145	63	1,216	1	13
Otoe	Nebraska City	1,98?	177	2,258	4,233	91	574	13	16	95	65	337	10
Pawnee	Pawnee City	90	97	1,092	2,099	61	91	15	24	45	23	223	2
Perkins	Grant	32	42	454	808	69	89	2	2	8	60	38	1
Phelps	Holdrege	89	90	1,201	2,236	245	245	4	19	50	375	186	3
Pierce	Pierce	94	107	1,284	2,365	255	27	4	24	53	476	147	1
Platte	Gs.	2,92?	91	2,386	4,421	431	89	33	34	19	745	251	4
Polk	Ga, dk.	2,00?	65	1,286	2,391	283	218	5	17	19	253	47	2
Red Willow	ls Gy,	91	102	1,284	2,381	293	94	6	24	57	66	19	18
Richardson	it	95	173	2,077	3,920	84	405	7	41	84	99	86	24
Rock		36	37	448	831	84	57	3	10	24	98	39	2
Saline	Wilber	1,450	88	2,099	3,613	346	272	5	16	81	274	622	29
Sarpy	ln.	34	207	1,076	1,978	213	238	11	26	30	51	107	6
Saunders	Wahoo	1,946	19	2,474	4,627	483	98	13	46	4	570	342	12
Scotts Bluff	Gering	1,403	61	2,064	4,530	44	114	27	50	9	673	13	6
Seward	Wd	91	19	2,094	3,468	352	388	0	9	97	83	170	4
Sheridan	Rushville	91	79	1,679	2,691	228	231	0	40	47	84	61	4
Sherman	lop Gy	79	43	1,014	1,588	30	21	7	7	4	335	41	5
Sioux	ln.	34	89	644	1,121	127	18	1	11	28	617	36	1
Stanton	Sn.	1,22?	128	97	1,825	193	66	0	10	29	45	85	3
Thayer	dn.	68	12	1,632	2,882	38	360	12	17	66	146	15	8
Thomas		91	82	226	406	11	42	0	4	13	30	13	5
Thurston	al	06	106	1,280	2,285	165	29	2	4	13	292	59	0
Valley	Ord	1,05?	132	1,082	2,154	21	112	4	17	21	428	62	6
Washington	Blair	1,06?	127	1,504	2,741	329	31	3	13	23	455	31	2
Wayne	Wayne	95	114	1,226	2,309	314	321	5	24	63	102	152	1
Webster	Icd Gl	85	28	1,256	2,315	245	38	5	18	18		38	7
Wheeler	Bartlett	204		288	530	44	76	0	8	4			0
York	York	1,601	149	1,887	3,637	395	63	1	61	142	732	137	10

NEVADA.

Place	Location	(1)	(2)	(3)	(4)	(5)	(6)	(7)	(8)	(9)	(10)	(11)	(12)
Churchill	Fallon	477	29	745	1,251	133	18	4	10	10	144	30	5
Clark	Las Vegas	758	52	862	1,672	208	277	12	51	28	334	0	1
Douglas	Minden	238	33	334	439	66			2		1	6	
Elko	Elko	1,554	99	2,106	3,759	447	286	57	46	75	61	112	39
Esmeralda	Goldfield	378	21	469	868	120	78		7	28	99	3	3

APPENDIX TABLE 100-A.—*Principal statistical data, by local boards*—Continued.

NEVADA—Continued.

Local board.	Post-office address.	Registration. June 5, 1917.	Registration. June and August, 1918.	Registration. Sept. 12, 1918.	Total.	Induction. Accepted at camp.	Physical groups. General service.	Physical groups. Remediables.	Physical groups. Limited service.	Disqualified.	Deferments. Dependency.	Deferments. Agricultural.	Deferments. Industrial.
Eureka	Eureka	213	13	274	500	49	1					3	
Humboldt	Winnemucca	1,185	59	1,688	2,932	305	203	11	43	14	212	55	16
Lander	Austin	285	25	412	722	80	61	2	27	13	45	21	16
Lincoln	Pioche	369	20	449	838	96	126	1	4	11	124	2	0
Lyon	Yerington	759	40	1,045	1,844	200	133	2	28	52	161	37	1
Mineral	Hawthorne	348	13	486	817	92	112		12	13	59	9	7
Nye	Tonopah	915	33	1,435	2,388	214	182	8	18	24	214		3
Ormsby	Carson City	150	7	282	439	51	3		1				5
Storey	Virginia City	157	5	267	429	53	28	3	6	10	44	0	0
Washoe	Reno	2,409	136	3,733	6,273	615	344	20	86	71	565	50	66
White Pine	Ely	2,124	148	3,157	5,429	482	342	19	44	125	355	22	5

NEW HAMPSHIRE.

Local board.	Post-office address.	Registration. June 5, 1917.	Registration. June and August, 1918.	Registration. Sept. 12, 1918.	Total.	Induction. Accepted at camp.	Physical groups. General service.	Physical groups. Remediables.	Physical groups. Limited service.	Disqualified.	Deferments. Dependency.	Deferments. Agricultural.	Deferments. Industrial.
Belknap	Laconia	1,809	154	2,494	4,457	433	478	25	126	64	606	58	27
Carroll	Ossipee	1,154	140	1,801	3,095	328	197	0	67	126	567	26	19
Cheshire	Keene	2,293	205	3,596	6,094	1,016	603	14	228	27	813	57	43
Coos	Lancaster	3,310	334	4,937	8,581	850	86	1	41	53	1,373	97	29
Grafton	Woodsville	3,435	271	5,113	8,819	636	858	30	217	33	1,239	142	49
Hillsborough No. 1	Nashua	3,136	267	3,553	6,956	524	503	4	89	202	1,124	11	140
Hillsborough No. 2	Milford	2,063	214	3,331	5,608	500	467	31	96	73	839	114	38
Manchester No. 1	Manchester	2,887	208	3,437	6,532	629	522	40	96	23	918	10	35
Manchester No. 2	...do...	3,633	253	3,889	7,775	451	471	42	219	165	995	5	28
Manchester No. 3	...do...	1,936	161	2,279	4,376	385	383	0	165	6	934	2	15
Merrimack No. 1	Concord	1,610	142	2,391	4,143	588	293	13	140	83	711	4	52
Merrimack No. 2	Franklin	2,238	213	3,208	5,659	494	457	11	228	49	1,013	69	28
Rockingham No. 1	Portsmouth	2,090	219	3,607	5,916	454	420	0	218	87	133	26	26
Rockingham No. 2	Exeter	1,779	136	2,619	4,534	086	315	3	10	172	758	70	27
Strafford	Dover	3,090	295	4,524	7,909	686	643	20	238	297	1,333	106	101
Sullivan	Newport	1,892	176	2,576	4,644	475	355	11	83	214	687	57	20

NEW JERSEY.

ATLANTIC CITY No. 1	Room 16, City Hall	2,394	243	3,292	5,929	764	943	31	213	227	810	1	21
[illegible]ic CITY No. 2	Room 15, City Hall	2,923	236	4,192	7,351	821	688	27	210	165	1,094	3	13
Atlantic	Courthouse, Mays Landing	2,198	277	4,568	7,043	657	483	5	65	166	1,092	9	9
BAYONNE No. 1	29 West Eighth Street	5,489	271	6,079	11,839	1,106	857	16	230	185	1,420	0	153
BAYONNE No. 2	734 Broadway	3,436	173	4,763	8,272	1,034	109	2	31	19	8		7
Bergen No. 1	Municipal Building, East Rutherford	3,691	290	5,301	9,282	711	799	3	155	262	1,408	1	2
Bergen No. 2	Courthouse, Hackensack	2,680	341	4,031	7, 52[illegible]	797							
Bergen No. 3	Municipal Building, Edgewater	3,556	211	5,433	9,194	821							
Bergen No. 4	Room 11, Wilsey Building, 3 Broadway, Ridgewood.	2,433	312	3,914	6,659	697	594	103	321	47	1,042	28	31
Bergen No. 5	18 Engle Street, Englewood	2,444	239	4,561	7,244	768	688	16	102	163	1,003	10	27
Bergen No. 6	46 Hudson Street, Hackensack	1,358	195	2,369	3,922	342							
Burlington No. 1	Courthouse, Mount Holly	1,761	191	2,674	4,626	489	392	2	54	25	825	268	12
Burlington No. 2	City Hall, Hackensack	2,322	275	3,123	5,720	632	578	0	244	8	761	21	20
Burlington No. 3	City Hall, Burlington	2,343	149	3,707	6,199	442							
CAMDEN No. 1	Courthouse	3,159	207	4,551	7,917	765	797	31	152	273	1,521	4	123
CAMDEN No. 2	City Hall	2,917	339	4,109	7,365	710	762	0	78	290	1,265	10	69
CAMDEN No. 3	1729 Ferry Avenue	4,233	161	5,009	9,403	653	489	8	47	2	1,723	1	122
CAMDEN No. 4	Library, Twenty-sixth and Federal Streets	1,441	268	2,078	3,787	278	244	6	58	16	818	2	65
[illegible]n No. 1	Courthouse	1,975	366	3,618	5,959	431	371	17	128	37	847	148	34
Camden No. 2	do	2,957	341	5,312	8,610	554	580	3	43	63	1,355	15	168
Cape May	Courthouse, Cape May	1,650	286	2,542	4,478	393	383	25	74	7	698	17	17
Cumberland No. 1	Courthouse, Bridgeton	2,203	199	3,325	5,727	449	401	1	144	129	918	240	107
[illegible]land No. 2	City Hall, Vineland	2,606	152	3,883	6,641	669	643	20	214	207	1,169	32	32
EAST ORANGE	High School, Winans Street	3,613	284	6,305	10,202	790	463	36	227	252	1,600	4	208
ELIZABETH No. 1	City Hall	3,821	172	5,044	9,037	730	592	1	142	120	1,077	0	147
ELIZABETH No. 2	do	3,383	269	4,452	8,104	655	522		84	138	986	2	97
ELIZABETH No. 3	do	2,821	170	4,225	7,216	670	452	7	158	140	1,381	4	179
Essex No. 1	Courthouse, Newark	1,851	166	2,964	4,981	430							
Essex No. 2	Town Hall, Glen Ridge	2,088	239	3,456	5,783	417	286		81	52	876	12	52
Essex No. 3	Town Hall, Montclair	2,301	319	3,759	6,379	622							
Essex No. 4	285 Bloomfield Avenue, Caldwell	2,523	361	3,914	6,798	575	436	40	46	237	1,034	22	47
Essex No. 5	Police Headquarters, Irvington	2,888	149	4,800	7,837	667	572	15	121	225	1,357	10	98
Gloucester No. 1	Courthouse, Woodbury	3,287	198	4,992	8,477	688	647	15	79	114	1,383	148	175
Gloucester No. 2	do	944	243	1,462	2,649	209	145	1	35	72	483	138	9
HOBOKEN No. 1	City Hall	8,314	202	4,300	7,816	795	738	4	162	47	944	1	2
HOBOKEN No. 2	Free Public Library	3,197	367	4,189	7,753	872	715	11	264	104	941	1	2
HOBOKEN No. 3	School 6, Willow and Eleventh Streets	1,678	205	2,189	4,072	502	672	20	110	100	551	0	62
Hudson No. 1	Courthouse, Jersey City	3,769	298	5,014	9,081	965	917	54	278	128	234	0	60
Hudson No. 2	Town Hall, North Bergen	2,582	294	3,790	6,666	803	3	17	89	257	1,030	13	47
Hudson No. 3	City Hall, Union	2,130	123	3,097	5,350	723							
Hudson No. 4	Town Hall, Harrison	3,686	143	4,496	8,325	881	654		247	198	1,157	0	0
Hudson No. 5	Town Hall, Kearney	2,702	311	3,574	6,587	675	513	12	188	100	1,254	0	65
Hunterdon	Courthouse, Flemington	2,366	304	3,851	6,521	715	514	4	122	56	1,073	289	90
JERSEY CITY No. 1	City Hall	4,374	566	5,237	10,177	1,150	1,468	29	306	185	1,386	1	79
JERSEY CITY No. 2	School 32, Coles and Eighth Streets	2,592	223	2,936	5,751	774	697	57	132	32	701	0	17
JERSEY CITY No. 3	School 9, Mercer and Brunswick Streets	4,184	133	5,352	9,669	1,015	880	88	319	71	1,389	1	63
JERSEY CITY No. 4	School 20, Danforth Avenue	3,962	192	5,327	9,481	902	938	21	186	39	1,966	0	90
JERSEY CITY No. 5	School 24, Virginia Avenue	3,688	219	5,396	9, 03	1,079	710	66	149	212	1,393	0	98

APPENDIX TABLE 100-A.—*Principal statistical data, by local boards*—Continued.

NEW JERSEY—Continued.

Local board.	Post-office address.	Registration.				Induction.	Physical groups.				Deferments.		
		June 5, 1917.	June and August, 1918.	Sept. 12, 1918.	Total.	Accepted at camp.	General service.	Remediables.	Limited service.	Disqualified.	Dependency.	Agricultural.	Industrial.
JERSEY CITY No. 6	Bergen Avenue and Mercer Street	2,933	199	3,870	7,002	803	1,092	23	273	138	1,206	1	64
JERSEY CITY No. 7	School 31, Boulevard	2,957	224	3,644	6,825	890	918	21	223	119	1,116	0	35
JERSEY CITY No. 8	Hancock Avenue	2,840	253	3,832	6,925	896	787	0	51	219	1,338	0	56
JERSEY CITY No. 9	Sixth Precinct Police Station	2,834	344	3,867	7,045	816	1,010	8	111	155	1,278	2	57
JERSEY CITY No. 10	School No. 2 Erie and 14th Sts.	2,042	275	2,401	4,718	649	586	25	93	82	660	0	35
Mercer	57 Livingston Ave., New Brunswick	3,275	296	4,893	8,469	766	676	12	83	9	1,700	3	4
Middlesex No. 1	New Brunswick	4,176	158	5,482	9,816	861	558	14	152	199	1,188	1	92
Middlesex No. 2	New Brunswick	3,380	204	4,083	7,680	757	568	16	128	100	1,289	63	101
Middlesex No. 3	Bush Hall, Sayreville	2,941	181	5,016	9,007	715	539	1	124	97	953	100	235
No. 4	Borough Hall, Machen	3,498	207	2,661	8,721	681	470	1	52	74	851	12	89
Monmouth No. 1	Courthouse, Freehold	3,229	78	4,102	5,573	592	458	11	48	155	1,000	251	11
Monmouth No. 2	Borough Hall, Keyport	2,014	293	2,980	4,808	518	558	29	54	95	730	54	39
Monmouth No. 3	Elks' Home, Red Bank	2,022	210	3,769	7,234	831	663	9	112	323	1,270	29	40
Monmouth No. 4	701 Mattison Avenue, Asbury Park	2,121	152	5,193	5,253	537	329	0	83	227	946	13	11
Morris No. 1	Courthouse, Morristown	2,581	288	4,126	6,638	684	450	3	265	293	1,008	56	13
Morris No. 2	Municipal Building	3,907	275	6,958	9,375	859	941	0	96	6	1,167	14	32
Morris No. 3	Town Hall, Boonton	3,789	347	5,852	7,421	384	250	0	18	289	638	44	51
NEWARK No. 1	88 Seventh Avenue	3,165	130	4,126	11,577	750	786	24	39	8	1,465	1	36
NEWARK No. 2	391 Erie Street	4,433	186	6,958	10,426	993	1,093	4	194	461	1,014	46	141
NEWARK No. 3	City Hall	4,380	244		8,039	837							116
NEWARK No. 4	516 Clinton Avenue	3,275	162	4,602	6,608	700	616	29	71	263	1,585	0	27
NEWARK No. 5	136 Van Buren Street	2,744	261	3,603	4,709	477	489	2	57	62	860	0	50
NEWARK No. 6	258 South Seventh Street	1,853	298	2,558	8,831	480	405	21	72	214	726	1	
NEWARK No. 7	51 Bruce Street	3,603	244	4,981	6,554	927							72
NEWARK No. 8	Eliot School	2,516	283	3,750	8,500	587	411	12	125	209	1,348	5	167
NEWARK No. 9	City Hall	3,373	233	4,694	5,663	705	653	52	251	84	1,545	0	38
NEWARK No. 10	do	2,449	229	2,984	4,550	574	624	1	53	139	973	2	80
NEWARK No. 11	205 Orange Street	1,851	123	2,576	7,111	470	373	0	49	152	876	2	79
NEWARK No. 12	School, South Market Street	3,153	170	3,788	9,202	643	635	14	117	9	831	4	115
NEWARK No. 13	Fourth floor, City Hall	3,840	119	5,243	9,869	806	751		164	267	2,034	1	86
NEWARK No. 14	Police Station, Seventeenth Avenue and Livingston Street	4,304	130	5,435		836	845	10	62	398	1,478	0	
Ocean	Courthouse, Toms River	1,755	209	2,712	4,676	445	396	93	74	48	784	45	25
ORANGE	City Hall, 247 Littleton Avenue	2,900	323	3,957	7,180	673	68	6	74	46	848	1	10
PASSAIC No. 1	City Hall	4,341	122	4,241	8,704	605	454	20	82	90	767	0	5
PASSAIC No. 2	do	3,095	259	3,963	7,317	525	709	14	88	210	1,200	13	104
Passaic No. 1	Courthouse, Paterson	3,388	255	4,504	8,147	813							

Precinct	Location												
Passaic No. 2	...do...	3,004	148	3,803	6,955	703	443	1	78	192	1,217	18	21
Paterson No. 1	City Hall.	2,835	326	4,175	7,336	622	384	0	220	177	1,355	5	35
Paterson No. 2	...do...	3,259	234	4,698	8,191	711	554	3	88	489	1,284	1	11
Paterson No. 3	301 Colt Building.	1,300	186	1,844	3,330	399	303	3	50	158	450	0	17
Paterson No. 4	City Hall.	2,242	251	2,479	4,972	532	636	29	89	34	662	0	13
Paterson No. 5	...do...	3,100	227	4,361	7,688	711	632	5	89	319	331	1	38
Perth Amboy	City Hall, Perth Amboy.	5,784	245	6,582	12,611	1,160							
Salem No. 1	Courthouse, Salem.	5,707	324	2,491	8,522	1,036	605	6	179	177	315	315	572
Salem No. 2													
Somerset No. 1	Courthouse, Somerville.	2,790	174	3,773	6,737	610	564	16	85	127	55	55	138
Somerset No. 2	Room 6, Voorhees Building, South Boundbrook.	1,621	331	2,380	4,332	367	269	8	70	84	113	113	36
Sussex	Courthouse, Newton.	2,438	314	3,439	6,191	559	412	2	74	60	87	187	55
Trenton M. 1	Library, Statehouse.	2,786	354	3,883	7,023	809	824	12	216	130	5	5	82
Trenton No. 2	City Hall.	3,162	232	4,185	7,579	712	621	12	171	13	938	1	16
Trenton No. 3	...do...	3,428	254	4,279	7,961	858	791	49	152	70	1,655	0	76
Trenton No. 4	...do...	2,929	237	3,492	6,658	616	532	0	135	114	1,291	2	62
Union No. 1	Courthouse, Elizabeth.	2,869	216	4,657	7,742	663	646	6	113	123	1,151	15	285
Union No. 2	Babcock Building, Plainfield.	2,908	231	4,120	7,319	640	495	13	117	179	984	20	166
Union No. 3	City Hall, Summit.	2,622	178	4,475	7,274	608	421	1	116	84	752	192	54
Warren No. 1	Courthouse, Belvidere.	1,911	160	2,708	4,779	461	311		61	53	1,044	11	37
Warren No. 2	Pennsylvania R. R. Building, Phillipsburg.	2,362	201	3,125	5,688	556	609		73				149
West Hoboken	City Hall, West Hoboken.	3,957	290	5,679	9,926	1,078		33					

NEW MEXICO.

County	Seat												
Bernalillo	...que...	2,398	179	3,327	5,904	671	743	0	68	152	735	23	16
Chaves	Roswell.	1,834	109	1,776	3,719	481	502	0	35	121	695	8	8
Colfax	Raton.	2,581	183	3,442	6,206	615	484	3	75	41	872	64	37
Curry	Clovis.	982	85	1,368	2,425	238	219	6	21	44	553	19	12
De Baca	Fort Sumner.		16	441	457	10	13						
Dona Ana	Las Cruces.	1,250	89	1,743	3,062	254	223	5	24	95	448	21	3
Eddy	Carlsbad.	1,163	99	1,144	2,406	302	366	5	34	65	493	20	16
Grant	Silver City.	4,226	173	4,469	8,868	681	595	59	14	296	935	6	11
Guadalupe	Santa Rosa.	1,109	70	922	2,101	316	381	24	31	31	282	17	9
Lea			32	511	643	0	16						
Lincoln	Carrizozo.	956	58	1,205	2,219	307	366	3	2	16	354	0	7
Luna	Deming.	1,009	87	1,815	2,991	120	200		42	22	176	9	0
McKinley	Gallup.	1,002	58	1,508	2,628	163	252	6	23	5	238	6	22
Mora	Wagon Mound or M.	1,139	127	1,359	2,625	345	427		21	24	984	45	5
Otero	Alamogordo.	863	78	1,115	2,056	237	120	4	19	94	266	5	9
Quay	Tucumcari.	1,160	66	1,325	2,551	259	79	0	2	23	641	10	7
Rio Arriba	Chama.	1,400	147	1,504	3,351	453	347	12	51	196	559	78	8
Roosevelt	Portales.	588	59	873	3,520	159	155	5	11	19	332	8	7
Sandoval	Bernalillo.	490	47	625	1,162	199	89	0	17	22	245	7	5
San Juan	Aztec.	405	35	517	937	143			5	39	163	12	1
San Miguel	Las Vegas.	1,890	116	2,369	4,435	570	705	0	19	25	647	18	3
Santa Fe	Santa Fe.	1,153	88	2,620	2,861	390	362	5	31	91	272	19	15
Sierra	Hillsboro.	405	42	527	974	133	111	2	5	17	165	1	0
Socorro	Socorro.	1,871	175	2,141	4,187	523	524	25	31		757	7	9
Taos	Taos.	857	86	1,140	2,083	389	343		29	111	284	0	0

APPENDIX TABLE 100-A.—*Principal statistical data, by local boards*—Continued.

NEW MEXICO—Continued.

NEW YORK.

Local board.	Post-office address.	Registration.				Induction.	Physical groups.				Deferments.		
		June 5, 1917.	June and August, 1918.	Sept. 12, 1918.	Total.	Accepted at camp.	General service.	Remediables.	Limited service.	Disqualified.	Dependency.	Agricultural.	Industrial.
NEW MEXICO—Continued.													
Torrance	Estancia	1,050	75	1,192	2,317	214	258	3	16	42	152	120	7
Union	Clayton	1,829	133	2,102	4,064	457	704	71	58	1	908	138	3
Valencia	Los Lunas	1,042	88	1,283	2,413	259	311	0	13	128	242	0	0
NEW YORK.													
ALBANY No. 1	County Courthouse, Albany	3,355	247	4,344	7,946	977	773	97	525	176	1,022	3	56
ALBANY No. 2	Arkay Building, Albany	2,561	208	3,137	5,906	725	661	32	119	196	986	3	75
ALBANY No. 3	Room 320, County Courthouse, Albany	2,215	144	3,214	5,573	666	517	40	106	139	672	13	22
ALBANY No. 4	County Courthouse, Albany	2,681	180	4,047	6,908	597	531	48	191	175	1,318	10	123
Albany No. 1	Mayor's Office, City Hall, Cohoes	2,055	203	2,801	5,059	500	430	24	94	184	759	4	31
Albany No. 2	City Hall, Watervliet	2,365	238	3,276	5,879	625	518	29	72	234	904	49	58
Albany No. 3	Room 236, County Courthouse, Albany	1,976	185	2,932	5,093	476	374	26	88	110	780	216	43
Allegany	Courthouse, Belmont	2,860	327	4,183	7,370	673	645	8	115	121	1,370	473	93
AMSTERDAM	Sanford Homestead Building, 1 Market Street	3,435	267	4,026	7,728	884	1,158	14	73	90	1,326	5	103
AUBURN	City Hall	3,264	250	4,251	7,765								
BINGHAMTON No. 1	210, Security Mutual Building	3,633	217	3,701	7,570	774	555		94	237	1,332	7	36
BINGHAMTON No. 2	Basement Courthouse Annex	3,152	236	3,701	7,089	708	811		144	52	1,381	6	32
Broome	606 Press Building, Binghamton	4,413	351	5,437	10,201	904	920	28	119	421	950	203	54
BUFFALO No. 1	739 Seneca Street	3,857	281	4,419	8,557	1,140	989	114	134	33	799	18	132
BUFFALO No. 2	22 Maurice Street	3,425	307	4,738	8,520	794	772	6	164	212	1,677	4	234
BUFFALO No. 3	Room 328, Federal Building	6,656	563	8,781	16,000	1,444	1,785	26	264	121	1,356	1	78
BUFFALO No. 4	495 William Street	3,424	310	3,929	7,663	1,100	845	80	163	275	1,059	5	96
BUFFALO No. 5	761-765 Fillmore Avenue	2,734	209	2,511	5,454	731	698	44	152	143	952	1	38
BUFFALO No. 6	254 Main Street	3,399	291	4,385	8,075	1,064	975	42	187	299	1,717	5	109
BUFFALO No. 7	Benevolent Hall, 17 Walden Avenue	4,337	404	4,545	9,288	1,135	1,212	59	175	661	1,773	1	133
BUFFALO No. 8	595-597 Walden Avenue	2,605	241	3,032	5,878	729	725	32	124	147	1,141	5	178
BUFFALO No. 9	11 East Utica Street	3,018	233	4,156	7,427	893	701	3	96	390	1,402	3	90
BUFFALO No. 10	1152 Bailey Avenue	2,486	250	2,894	5,630	657	945	14	113	143	1,002	0	181
BUFFALO No. 11	174 French Street	2,441	267	3,140	5,848	608	392	26	138	405	1,293	4	152
BUFFALO No. 12	2633 Main Street	2,614	193	4,691	7,498	664	418	16	92	238	1,378	3	86
BUFFALO No. 13	Jubilee Library Building, 1036 Niagara Street	4,545	321	5,570	10,436	1,010	1,052	39	81	245	251	10	128
BUFFALO No. 14	Old Central High School Building, Court and Franklin.	5,664	482	7,479	13,625	1,842	1,530	103	319	440	1,628	4	144

Location	Address	V1	V2	V3	V4	V5	V6	V7	V8	V9	V10	V11	V12
BUFFALO No. 15	376 Connecticut Street	19	4	1,708	466	198	34	719	1,111	9,512	5,311	359	3,842
BUFFALO No. 16	371 Delaware Avenue	148	6	824	464	360	9	576	983	8,254	4,855	223	3,176
...gus No. 1	Federal Building, Olean	108	204	945	132	121	48	28	663	6,133	3,461	243	2,429
...gus No. 2	90 Main Street, Salamanca	100	116	845	70	128	8	581	603	5,436	3,105	296	2,125
...gus No. 3	Town Hall, Gowanda	30	194	744	70	63	15	309	395	4,031	2,282	108	1,581
Cayuga	Federal Building, Auburn	24	463	956	180	72	0	337	442	5,699	3,372	218	2,109
Chautauqua No. 1	Fredonia	87	48	965	184	96	13	747	891	6,476	3,745	269	2,462
...qua No. 2	Care of S. C. Crandall, Westfield	35	205	745	133	62	5	315	435	4,295	2,522	142	1,631
Chautauqua No. 3	Care of J. F. McCarthy, Silver Creek	40	254	936	107	36	11	630	552	5,122	2,803	238	2,081
Chemung	Courthouse Annex, Almira	10	30	32		6	4	51	370	4,089	2,333	166	1,590
Chenango	Box 147, Courthouse, Norwich	60	272	1,236	188	166	20	383	599	6,773	3,380	248	2,540
Clinton No. 1	County Court Building, Margaret Street, Plattsburg	18	102	572	161	95	38	485	618	4,956	2,777	211	1,968
Clinton No. 2	Au Sable Forks	16	149	744	124	76	17	302	418	4,072	2,294	175	1,613
Columbia	Courthouse, Hudson	77	275	1,408	257	83	45	586	753	8,310	4,736	294	3,280
Cortland	15 Court Street, Cortland	44	229	1,076	139	115	51	425	578	6,084	3,471	230	2,383
Delaware No. 1	Delhi	57	225	832	173	87	18	350	423	4,593	2,488	179	1,926
...re No. 2	Walton	24	309	739	130	134	0	289	326	4,387	2,468	80	1,739
...ess No. 1	574 Main Street, Beacon	57	220	96	63	4	25	283	624	5,809	3,271	211	2,327
Dutchess No. 2	Beekman Arms, Rhinebeck	170	13	580	171	96	51	316	505	5,734	3,217	242	2,275
ELMIRA	City Hall	167	17	1,912	276	251	3	1,047	1,213	10,592	5,866	410	4,316
Erie No. 1	City Hall, Lackawanna	106	99	1,110	72	112	15	821	899	12,631	4,045	300	5,404
Erie No. 2	Room 5, Hamburg Bank Building, Hamburg	20	471	31	159	97	20	559	779	7,072	3,410	263	2,764
Erie No. 3	Collins Community House, Collins	60	287	838	128	39	35	366	590	5,980	4,104	251	2,319
Erie No. 4	Town Hall, Lancaster	26	97	974	290	118	33	650	809	7,417	4,369	278	3,035
Essex	County Clerk's Office, Elizabethtown	56	183	1,100	319	143	20	523	846	7,814	2,857	258	3,187
Franklin No. 1	20 Church Street, Malone	25	76	803	306	72	6	661	470	5,155	2,730	254	2,044
Franklin No. 2	County Clerk's Office, Malone	32	9	67	263	89	17	400	448	4,972	2,796	481	1,761
Fulton No. 1	State Armory, Washington Street, Gloversville	34	136	990	85	67	31	8	555	4,836	2,753	183	1,887
Fulton No. 2	County Clerk's Building, Johnstown	48	521	728	152	88	23	12	490	4,727	4,527	179	1,795
Genesee	Courthouse, Batavia	28	149	1,095	157	85	26	622	802	7,846		302	3,017
Greene	Courthouse, Catskill	3	14	896	41	136	10	580	533	5,436		195	2,124
Hamilton	Long Lake	0	0	141	43	29	49	89	141	998	596	371	371
Herkimer No. 1	City Hall, Little Falls	103	287	998	48	111	37	623	868	8,638	4,651	373	3,614
Herkimer No. 2	Courthouse, Herkimer	88	12	1,307	175	153	41	536	796	8,303	4,696	352	3,334
JAMESTOWN	City Hall, East Third Street	130	28	1,069	50	251	25	677	913	9,029	4,764	313	3,913
Jefferson No. 1	Courthouse, Watertown	35	371	1,860	74	238	16	599	209	7,843	4,672	176	2,838
Jefferson No. 2	Continental Hotel, Adams	51	359	1,281	185	108	22	260	789	4,777	2,870	218	1,731
Jefferson No. 3	Strickland Building, Carthage	38	355	641	146	104	13	444	517	5,786	3,259	99	2,309
Lewis	Lewis County Courthouse, Lowville	74	670	816	85	42	27	47	430	4,875	2,858	296	1,818
Livingston	Courthouse, Geneseo	39	270	712	218	162	9	736	704	7,374	4,101	279	2,977
Madison	Courthouse, Wampsville	18	251	1,287	320	98	12	578	808	7,828	4,600	172	2,949
Monroe No. 1	City Hall, Rochester	68	348	1,442	59	48	16	242	388	4,730	2,734	171	1,824
Monroe No. 2	do	78	265	959	48	90	6	349	655	4,803	2,696	188	1,936
Monroe No. 3	do	31	271	1,075	29	123	21	367	466	5,551	3,089	154	2,276
Monroe No. 4	City Hall, Fairport	58	3	905	142	59	20	482	535	5,118	2,855	230	2,109
Montgomery	Courthouse, Fonda	14	42	1,532	173	77	35	617	799	8,160	4,797	226	3,133
MOUNT VERNON	City Hall	12	27	1,035	92	150		666	888	7,713	4,274	181	3,213
Nassau No. 1	Glen Cove Bank Building, Glen Cove			817	14	80		547	775	6,595	3,664	221	2,750
Nassau No. 2	Denton Building, Mineola								657	7,442	4,556	215	2,718
Nassau No. 3	78 Church Street, Freeport										4,513		2,714
Nassau No. 4	Fireman's Hall, Lawrence	31	18	1,137	11	103	35	690	982	7,442	4,513	215	2,714
NEW ROCHELLE	237 Main Street	24	3	1,066	147	132	29	454	762	6,988	4,187	199	2,020

APPENDIX TABLE 100–A.—*Principal statistical data, by local boards—Continued.*

NEW YORK—Continued.

Local board.	Post-office address.	Registration.				Induction.	Physical groups.				Deferments.		
		June 5, 1917.	June and August, 1918.	Sept. 12, 1918.	Total.	Accepted at camp.	General service.	Remediables.	Limited service.	Disqualified.	Dependency.	Agricultural.	Industrial.
NEW YORK No. 1	148 Alexander Avenue, New York	2,669	235	3,562	6,466	622	341	43	149	236	1,084	0	42
NEW YORK No. 2	2720 Third Avenue, New York	3,637	316	4,867	8,820	1,348	1,091	34	182	90	1,209	1	47
NEW YORK No. 3	One hundred and forty-seventh Street and St. Ann's Avenue, New York	2,952	221	4,193	7,366	664	555	46	108	22	1,274	2	27
NEW YORK No. 4	830 Westchester Avenue, New York	3,894	401	4,685	8,990	916	721	50	249	151	1,698	1	20
NEW YORK No. 5	1025 East One hundred and sixty-third Street, New York	4,676	431	5,778	10,885	1,195	800	30	303	273	2,436	8	42
NEW YORK No. 6	1473 Williamsbridge Road, New York	2,451	221	3,916	6,588	704	460	22	108	125	1,116	2	37
NEW YORK No. 7	3777 White Plains Avenue, New York	2,319	203	3,362	5,889	685	701	25	80	115	968	8	63
NEW YORK No. 8	391 East One hundred and forty-ninth Street, New York	3,613	259	4,665	8,537	1,059	1,212	75	169	287	1,494	1	21
NEW YORK No. 9	One hundred and sixty-first Street and St. Ann's Avenue, New York	3,520	228	4,296	8,044	1,002	906	6	150	288	1,493	0	27
NEW YORK No. 10	County Courthouse, One hundred and sixty-first Street and Third Avenue, New York	3,525	265	4,309	8,099	942	696	50	112	239	364	0	44
NEW YORK No. 11	1035 Stebbins Avenue, New York	3,614	280	4,275	8,179	981	747	44	171	282	388	0	28
NEW YORK No. 12	Morris High School, Boston Road and One hundred and sixty-sixth Street, New York	3,059	250	3,462	6,791	769	504	50	146	30	1,437	1	33
NEW YORK No. 13	1319 Boston Road, New York	4,378	399	5,799	10,576	953	696	55	165	320	1,974	2	21
NEW YORK No. 14	1738 Crotona Park, New York	4,079	275	4,213	8,567	829	27	58	110	155	1,969	0	35
NEW YORK No. 15	Public School 4, One hundred and seventy-third Street and Fulton Avenue, New York	3,697	202	4,980	8,879	765	448	51	159	180	1,901	1	25
NEW YORK No. 16	Boro Hall, Tremont and Third Avenue, New York	4,034	356	4,816	9,206	788	496	40	118	208	2,308	1	23
NEW YORK No. 17	Public Schoo. 32, East One hundred and eighty-third Street and Beaumont Avenue, New York	2,802	240	3,628	6,670	871	799	26	121	145	1,423	0	11
NEW YORK No. 18	910 Morris Avenue, New York	3,447	234	4,763	8,444	813	547	42	137	235	1,772	0	44
NEW YORK No. 19	Park Commissioner's Office, Clermont Park, New York	3,142	274	4,014	7,430	612	380	42	162	48	1,192	1	12
NEW YORK No. 20	New York University, Gould Hall, New York	3,331	236	4,507	8,074	653	355	43	98	120	1,476	0	53
NEW YORK No. 21	Public School 33, Jerome Avenue and One hundred and eighty-fourth Street	3,744	253	5,170	9,167	797	220	17	48	207	2,014	21	36
NEW YORK No. 22	do	2,681	218	4,216	7,115	720	603	28	93	208	1,136	2	41
NEW YORK No. 23	124 Schermerhorn Street, Brooklyn	3,423	220	4,060	8,303	827	658	49	177	211	649	4	90
NEW YORK No. 24	99–105 Myrtle Avenue, Brooklyn	3,336	233	4,298	7,867	1,047	1,106	7	225	261	611	0	20
NEW YORK No. 25	153 York Street, Brooklyn	3,259	210	4,195	7,664	1,701	621	33	193	192	766	2	25

No.	Location												
NEW YMK No. 26	174 Nassau Street, Brooklyn.	35	1	1,102	143	56	27	570	703	6,120	3,370	201	2,549
NEW OAK No. 27	Public Library, Clinton and Union Streets, Brooklyn.	13	1	86	313	199	1	643	812	9,849	5,316	333	4,200
NEW OMK No. 28	105 Rapelye Street, Brooklyn.	191	2	1,111	92	206	37	626	779	10,650	5,856	430	4,364
NEW YMK No. 29	Municipal Court, 6 Lee Avenue, Brooklyn.	42	3	1,560	436	186	24	701	909	9,247	4,655	355	4,257
NEW YMK No. 30	Forty-seventh Regiment Armory, Lynch Street and Marcy Avenue, Brooklyn.	15	2	1,147	250	170	50	591	925	7,272	3,824	290	3,158
NEW OMK No. 31	411 Lewis Avenue, Brooklyn.	20	1	888	178	71	35	415	741	5,946	3,333	192	2,421
NEW YMK No. 32	219 Patchen Avenue, Brooklyn.	32	1	1,125	127	122	28	492	770	6,850	3,927	233	2,690
NEW YMK No. 33	115 Stockton Street, Brooklyn.	30	0	996	190	157	34	450	643	5,545	3,019	177	2,349
NEW YMK No. 34	Annex Public School 25, 335 Kosciusko Street, Brooklyn.	22	0	976	308	142	20	488	710	5,760	3,077	240	2,443
NEW YMK No. 35	1104 Broadway, Brooklyn.	4	0	30		24	1	25	696	6,387	3,433	259	2,695
NEW OMK No. 36	261 Prospect Avenue, Brooklyn.	48	0	1,247	310	168	57	1,124	1,019	8,236	4,588	262	3,388
NEW YMK No. 37	Public School 172, Fourth Avenue and Ninth Street, Brooklyn.	69	0	1,248	54	174	40	851	941	9,410	4,821	327	4,262
NEW YMK No. 38	403 Butler Street, Brooklyn.	21	0	1,023	156	71	13	600	908	7,000	3,848	268	2,884
NEW YMK No. 39	307 Ninth Street near Union Street, Brooklyn.	47	0	1,040	277	130	25	782	785	6,752	3,567	252	2,953
NEW OMK No. 40	Public Library, First Street and North Avenue, Brooklyn.	146	0	1,335	41	132	7	873	739	9,004	4,934	257	3,813
NEW OMK No. 41	Public School 40, Fourth Avenue and Sixtieth Street, Brooklyn.	138	2	1,345	245	121	7	567	747	8,054	4,581	233	3,240
NEW YORK No. 42	509 Third Avenue, Brooklyn.	113	0	1,614	92	138	34	474	774	9,337	5,355	269	3,713
NEW YMK No. 43	7824 Fifth Avenue, Brooklyn.	49	2	1,234	161	184	41	444	641	7,138	4,311	241	2,586
NEW YMK No. 44	Public School 111, Sterling Place, corner Vanderbilt Avenue, Brooklyn.	60	0	752	207	117	34	587	828	6,226	3,497	221	2,507
NEW YMK No. 45	55 Hanson Place, Y. M. C. A., Brooklyn.	76	0	701	365	169	31	869	895	7,943	4,241	293	3,409
NEW YMK No. 46	Public School 45, Monroe and Lafayette Avenues, Brooklyn.	42	0	913	225	119	45	598	821	6,349	3,522	210	2,617
NEW YMK No. 47	1210 Bedford Avenue, Brooklyn.	44	2	633	216	103	17	851	846	7,254	4,142	213	2,899
NEW YMK No. 48	Seventh Avenue and Fourth Street Manual Training High School, Brooklyn.	60	0	1,055	278	61	17	14	942	7,236	4,027	266	2,943
NEW YMK No. 49	Public Library, Ninth Street and Sixth Avenue, Brooklyn.	88	0	1,224	288	110	41	25	808	7,733	4,366	329	3,038
NEW OMK No. 50	468 Humboldt Street, Brooklyn.	19	2	1,581	218	73	34	638	773	7,344	4,018	239	3,087
NEW YMK No. 51	144 De Voe Street, Brooklyn.	28	1	1,253	355	134	50	592	957	7,523	3,923	245	3,305
NEW YMK No. 52	Public School 50, 183 South Third Street, Brooklyn.	6	0	726	194	77	24	528	632	6,256	5,008	258	3,010
NEW OMK No. 53	Public School 143, Havemeyer and North Sixth Street, Brooklyn.	23	0	750	149	171	37	442	604	6,208	3,115	189	2,964
NEW YORK No. 54	586 Driggs Avenue, Brooklyn.	30	1	622	153	192	24	418	527	5,335	2,830	181	2,374
NEW YORK No. 55	87 Herbert Street, Brooklyn.	34	0	1,153	125	158	39	540	747	7,089	3,787	265	3,037
NEW YMK No. 56	99 Belle Street, Brooklyn.	47	1	1,249	136	183	32	703	916	8,210	4,160	291	3,739
NEW YORK No. 57	2215 Dey Island Avenue, Brooklyn.	32	1	1,081	23	99	38	675	985	9,113	5,128	314	3,676
NEW OMK No. 58	1770 Eighty-sixth Street, Brooklyn.	65	3	1,296	192	130	42	551	923	7,682	4,818	223	2,641
NEW YMK No. 59	1215 Avenue Q, Brooklyn.	40	0	1,424	291	116	43	421	745	7,154	4,208	220	2,726
NEW YMK No. 60	7024 New Utrecht Avenue, Brooklyn.	42	1	1,832	243	145	29	678	997	8,442	4,965	292	3,135
NEW YORK No. 61	Public School 34, Ocean Parkway and Eighteenth Avenue, Brooklyn.	61	2			127	25	583	672	8,504	4,998	296	3,300
NEW YMK No. 62	Bedford Avenue and Monroe Street, Y. M. C. A., Brooklyn.	42	0	890	224	145	32	441	644	5,814	3,299	211	2,304

APPENDIX TABLE 100-A.—*Principal statistical data, by local boards*—Continued.

NEW YORK—Continued.

Local board.	Post-office address.	Registration. June 5, 1917.	Registration. June and August, 1918.	Registration. Sept. 12, 1918.	Registration. Total.	Induction. Accepted at camp.	Physical groups. General service.	Physical groups. Remediables.	Physical groups. Limited service.	Physical groups. Disqualified.	Deferments. Dependency.	Deferments. Agricultural.	Deferments. Industrial.
NEW YORK No. 63	Public School 44, Throop and Putnam Avenues, Brooklyn.	2,288	225	3,204	5,717	706	371	32	162	152	860	1	24
NEW YORK No. 64	Commercial High School, Bergen Street and Albany Avenue, Brooklyn.	2,422	189	3,732	6,343	693	357	33	94	333	934	0	44
NEW YORK No. 65	852 St. Johns Place, Brooklyn.	3,490	290	5,763	9,503	790	441	26	103	248	1,977	0	58
NEW YORK No. 66	Erasmus High School, Church and Flatbush Avenues, Brooklyn.	2,549	210	3,744	6,503	740	486	33	95	257	1,179	1	40
NEW YORK No. 67	Public School 139, Avenue C and East Thirteenth Street, Brooklyn.	3,072	205	4,607	7,884	760	454	18	99	215	1,470	5	53
NEW YORK No. 68	Public School 124, Avion Place and Beaver Street, Brooklyn.	2,339	193	2,780	5,312	620	377	19	151	182	618	0	12
NEW YORK No. 69	957 Broadway, Brooklyn.	2,239	209	3,048	5,496	563	377	0	148	224	1,051	1	22
NEW YORK No. 70	1019 Hart Street, corner St. Nicholas Ave., Brooklyn.	2,123	236	2,529	4,888	559	384	17	145	141	1,071	0	35
NEW YORK No. 71	Public School 56, Madison Street and Bushwick Avenue, Brooklyn.	2,398	205	3,141	5,744	637	800	0	78	265	958	35	23
NEW YORK No. 72	Public School 75, Evergreen Avenue and Grove Street, Brooklyn.	2,456	218	4,060	6,734	886	738	9	167	131	1,012	0	43
NEW YORK No. 73	290 Graham Avenue, Brooklyn.	3,838	268	3,737	7,843	866	821	250	183	250	1,738	0	29
NEW YORK No. 74	Royal Palace, 16–18 Manhattan Avenue, Brooklyn.	2,411	211	2,950	5,572	649	498	34	165	76	1,140	0	5
NEW YORK No. 75	Public School 141, McKibben and Leonard Streets, Brooklyn.	2,353	199	2,903	5,455	687	509	31	156	159	1,024	0	15
NEW YORK No. 76	Public School 106, Hamburg and Putnam Avenues, Brooklyn.	2,547	238	3,337	6,122	894	597	6	92	285	1,156	0	48
NEW YORK No. 77	2893 Fulton Street, Brooklyn.	2,413	237	3,074	5,724	674	417	57	135	105	991	2	19
NEW YORK No. 78	Brooklyn Waterworks Building, Avenue and Logan Street, Brooklyn.	2,904	260	3,800	6,963	783	492	43	124	130	1,494	0	50
NEW YORK No. 79	Public School 108, Linwood Street and Livington Avenue, Brooklyn.	2,526	220	3,324	6,070	844	535	20	108		1,039	0	41
NEW YORK No. 80	Public School 72, New Lots Road and Schneck Avenue, Brooklyn.	2,810	255	4,206	7,271	518	312	17	98	329	1,227	1	18
NEW YORK No. 81	Belmont Avenue and Berriman Street, Brooklyn.	2,590	251	3,861	6,702	417	290	21	91	352	1,387	0	26
NEW YORK No. 82	343–345 Ralph Avenue, Brooklyn.	2,877	254	3,897	7,028	737	499	30	118	31	1,439	0	29
NEW YORK No. 83	223 Utica Avenue, Brooklyn.	3,420	334	4,642	8,396	835	446	44	172	360	1,630	1	12
NEW YORK No. 84	2613 Atlantic Avenue, Brooklyn.	2,710	219	3,350	6,279	571	280	11	177	156	1,000	3	11
NEW YORK No. 85	111 Watkins Street, Brooklyn.	2,901	222	3,672	6,795	399	169	20	92	218	1,012	2	4
NEW YORK No. 86	461 Rockaway Avenue, Brooklyn.	3,112	327	3,632	7,071	431	370	21	135	277	1,253	2	14

Location	No.	Institution												
New York	No. 87	...do...	3,415	253	4,906	8,574	474	309	44	59	368	1,421	1	33
New York	No. 88	Public School 114, Remsen Avenue and School Lane, Brooklyn.	3,138	208	3,912	7,256	471	320	27	98	245	331	2	13
New York	No. 89	128 Prince Street, New York.	4,708	269	5,601	10,578	1,049	69	76	180	166	857	1	13
New York	No. 90	498 West Broadway, New York.	3,841	307	5,457	9,633	828	129	28	127	266	1,433	0	7
New York	No. 91	33 East Broadway, New York.	6,159	413	7,890	14,462	687	807	46	212	45	976	1	1
New York	No. 92	Public School 2, 116 Henry Street, New York.	3,105	223	3,528	6,856	520	327	33	109	131	854	1	4
New York	No. 93	229–231 East Broadway, New York.	3,902	291	3,787	7,980	671	423	62	307	64	753	0	6
New York	No. 94	143 Baxter Street, New York.	3,304	331	6,061	9,696	623	462	4	63	56	963	0	5
New York	No. 95	Public School 21, 222 Mott Street, New York.	2,861	242	3,683	6,786	735	656	94	207	166	929	1	12
New York	No. 96	8 East Third Street, Y. M. C. A., New York.	4,046	348	4,610	9,004	837	707	61	244	227	1,050	2	11
New York	No. 97	25 Montgomery Street, New York.	3,016	206	3,170	6,302	649	572	43	292	44	837	0	8
New York	No. 98	128 Attorney Street, New York.	3,303	281	3,321	6,905	557	319	87	301	196	747	0	4
New York	No. 99	300 Rivington Street, New York.	2,595	234	3,221	6,050	542	599	14	129	110	871	0	4
New York	No. 100	Public School 3, 490 Hudson Street, New York.	3,641	288	5,028	8,935	742	777	36	101	101	849	0	13
New York	No. 101	29 Horatio Street, New York.	3,012	225	3,781	7,018	784	604	41	152	172	840	4	12
New York	No. 102	388 Houston Street, New York.	3,653	272	3,652	7,577	541	119	63	231	178	691	2	7
New York	No. 103	51 Avenue C, New York.	3,754	354	3,645	7,753	566	587	43	227	150	848	0	15
New York	No. 104	20 Avenue C, New York.	3,640	275	3,504	7,419	593	462	56	171	271	769	2	48
New York	No. 105	Public School 56, 351 West Eighteenth Street, New York.	3,568	239	5,074	8,881	787	669	92	153	231	709	2	27
New York	No. 106	Public School 33, 418 West Twenty-eighth Street, New York.	3,269	272	4,300	7,841	721	776	76	232	62	889	0	7
New York	No. 107	Public School 75, 27 Norfolk Street, New York.	3,712	286	3,641	7,639	804	433	46	175	266	364	0	16
New York	No. 108	Public School 65, Forsythe and Canal Streets, New York.	4,289	292	3,829	8,410	685	377	55	142	259	1,102	0	4
New York	No. 109	Public School 161, Ludlow and Delancey Streets, New York.	3,953	316	3,765	8,034	539	314	49	146	134	819	0	18
New York	No. 110	461 Eighth Avenue, New York.	3,987	329	5,015	9,331	999	1,110	40	268	221	756	2	14
New York	No. 111	711 Eighth Avenue, New York.	3,332	292	4,094	7,718	613	421	54	137	153	903	2	1
New York	No. 112	44 Avenue A, New York.	4,592	337	4,726	9,455	753	690	56	131	48	671	0	9
New York	No. 113	76 Second Avenue, New York.	3,944	274	3,733	7,951	659	520	53	110	173	894	1	13
New York	No. 114	126 Second Avenue, New York.	4,440	347	4,516	9,303	798	670	62	117	332	1,294	3	18
New York	No. 115	1416 Broadway, New York. Public Library.	3,290	237	3,800	7,327	846	571	79	221	262	1,010	1	15
New York	No. 116	Rooms 402–403, New York Public Library. Columbus Branch 742 Tenth Street, near Fifty-first Street, New York.	3,243	267	4,181	7,696	890	686	112	208	301	1,037	0	7
New York	No. 117	288 East Tenth Street, New York.	2,797	148	2,754	5,699	599	521	15	80	45	534	0	14
New York	No. 118	Stuyvesant High School, Fifteenth Street, near First Avenue, New York.	3,430	221	3,614	7,265	622	465	26	128	137	624	4	14
New York	No. 119	228 East Twenty-third Street, New York.	2,892	226	3,716	6,834	694	588	37	189	1	742	1	13
New York	No. 120	318 West Fifty-seventh Street, Y. M. C. A., New York.	2,860	237	3,422	6,519	903	830	8	204	150	770	0	67
New York	No. 121	117 West Sixty-first Street, New York.	3,651	275	4,170	8,096	796	678	102	190	308	975	0	17
New York	No. 122	240 East Thirty-first Street, New York.	3,784	255	4,520	8,559	879	636	57	180	401	849	0	14
New York	No. 123	303 East Thirty-sixth Street, Public Library, New York.	401	258	5,247	9,606	972	880	82	185	187	1,087	0	16
New York	No. 124	190 Amsterdam Avenue, New York.	2,529	114	4,132	6,775	732	591	14	123	26	372	0	52
New York	No. 125	251 West Eightieth Street, New York.	2,245	127	3,845	6,217	672	419	14	178	102	461	1	37
New York	No. 126	692 Amsterdam Avenue and Ninty-third Street, New York.	2,122	133	3,426	5,681	631	332	30	198	173	492	2	

APPENDIX TABLE 100-A.—*Principal statistical data, by local boards*—Continued.

NEW YORK—Continued.

Local board.	Post-office address.	Registration				Induction.	Physical groups.			Disqualified.	Deferments.		
		June 5, 1917.	June and August, 1918.	Sept. 12, 1918.	Total.	Accepted at camp.	General service.	Remediables.	Limited service.		Dependency.	Agricultural.	Industrial.
New York No. 127	Public School 73, 209 East Forty-sixth Street, New York.	3,556	280	4,713	8,549	635	815	5	157	98	915	1	44
New York No. 128	Public School 135, 931 First Avenue, New York.	2,930	223	3,784	6,937	760	640	45	200	291	796	2	15
New York No. 129	American Museum National History, 51 West Fifty-seventh Street, New York.	3,065	191	5,140	8,396	901	520	39	168	186	674	5	71
New York No. 130	2741 Broadway, New York.	3,987	257	5,342	9,586	1,056	734	150	241	251	993	2	62
New York No. 131	777 Lexington Avenue, New York.	2,914	191	3,712	6,817	637	381	25	130	16	934	3	13
New York No. 132	201 East Sixty-ninth Street, New York.	2,538	182	3,505	6,225	550	300	29	72	140	232	0	7
New York No. 133	338 East Sixty-seventh Street, New York.	2,342	184	2,980	5,506	615	639	15	97	108	507	2	4
New York No. 134	2875 Broadway, corner One hundred and twelfth Street, New York.	3,148	197	5,050	8,395	849	437	28	183	234	864	7	257
New York No. 135	One hundred and seventeenth Street and Amsterdam Avenue, East Hall, Columbia University, New York.	3,740	231	4,867	8,833	1,005	611	51	190	171	1,243	1	56
New York No. 136	Public School 81, 212 West One hundred and twentieth Street, New York.	2,989	203	4,357	7,549	829	484	61	180	34	923	6	37
New York No. 137	Public School 117, 1465 Avenue A, New York.	3,101	214	4,128	7,443	700	514	48	116	139	1,103	1	17
New York No. 138	Public School 53, 211 East Seventy-ninth Street, New York.	3,023	287	5,284	9,194	828	669	40	143	62	1,042	0	7
New York No. 139	336 Lenox Avenue, New York.	3,238	253	4,476	7,967	959	699	165	263	173	833	1	35
New York No. 140	St. Phillips Parish House, 215 West One hundred and thirty-third Street, New York.	4,261	423	5,511	10,195	876	897	221	177	94	1,063	3	20
New York No. 141	City College, One hundred and thirty-eighth Street and Amsterdam Avenue, New York.	2,627	183	4,054	6,864	707	454	24	144	159	919	0	27
New York No. 142	451 East Eighty-sixth Street, New York.	2,943	255	3,776	6,874	606	399	38	155	105	927	0	6
New York No. 143	304 East Eighty-seventh Street, New York.	2,165	197	3,084	5,446	592	459	12	185	139	770	1	7
New York No. 144	252 West One hundred and thirty-eighth Street, New York.	4,206	356	6,451	11,013	1,102	963	65	218	146	1,382	0	17
New York No. 145	Room 218, Main ... One hundred and ... and Convent Avenue, City College, New York.	2,849	195	4,406	7,450	789	443	45	125	138	1,186	0	27
New York No. 146	506 West One ... and forty-fifth Street, New York.	2,611	196	4,339	7,146	694	343	44	170	219	906	0	31
New York No. 147	922 St. Nicholas Avenue, New York.	3,084	196	5,178	8,458	676	388	17	183	62	1,333	1	30
New York No. 148	... second Regiment ... Fort Washington Avenue and One ... and sixty-eighth Street, New York.	2,987	182	4,795	7,964	784	599	45	111	195	1,249	6	83

New York No. 149	Library, 535 West One hundred and seventy-ninth Street, New York.	4,541	276	7,029	11,946	384	575	36	107	291	2,120	0	12
New York No. 150	Public School 151, Ninty-first Street and First Avenue, New York.	2,418	207	3,357	5,882	563	552	24	66	98	751	0	10
New York No. 151	240 East One hundred and eighth Street, New York.	2,552	170	3,275	5,997	492	283	11	90	72	559	0	1
New York No. 152	231 East One hundred and fourth Street, New York.	3,076	268	3,883	7,227	531	475	49	120	144	1,051	0	7
New York No. 153	59 South Washington Square, New York.	2,503	152	3,709	6,364	601	441	9	150	110	739	1	34
New York No. 154	60 West Thirteenth Street, New York.	3,306	187	4,055	8,143	691	22	42	227	135	521	1	31
New York No. 155	Public School 86, Ninty-sixth Street and Lexington Avenue, New York.	3,150	252	3,594	6,986	736	452	26	350	15	863	1	18
New York No. 156	72 East One hundred and eighth Street, New York.	3,337	319	3,539	7,195	625	441	47	224	12	1,271	1	25
New York No. 157	83 East One hundred and eighth Street, New York.	3,367	347	3,388	7,102	946	597	48	272	255	511	0	13
New York No. 158	1482 ... way, New York.	4,622	249	6,746	11,617	942	841	94	78	430	675	0	24
New York No. 159	121 East first Street, New York.	2,451	103	4,389	6,943	641	352	40	143	161	366	4	66
New York No. 160	174 East One hundred and eighth Street, New York.	2,634	204	3,602	6,440	655	626	18	78	103	633	374	4
New York No. 161	161 East One hundred and eighth Street, New York.	3,061	253	3,593	6,907	785	652	30	153	66	1,248	0	5
New York No. 162	121 East One hundred and ninth Street, New York.	2,479	240	4,728	7,447	524	412	30	92	298	916	1	5
New York No. 163	Central Park Arsenal, Fifth Avenue and Sixty-fourth Street, New York.	2,877	147	4,472	7,496	828	462	73	197	129	537	7	47
New York No. 164	51 East Eighty-third Street, New York.	2,194	157	3,477	5,828	763	428	52	248	181	455	3	31
New York No. 165	Public School 159, 241 East One hundred and ninth Street, New York.	2,863	237	3,599	6,699	639	477	66	102	113	821	0	9
New York No. 166	165 East One hundred and twenty-first Street, New York.	3,390	246	4,379	8,015	811	788	67	94	153	56	0	18
New York No. 167	57 East One hundred and twenty-fifth Street, New York.	4,900	355	5,467	10,722	1,298	1,021	75	284	190	1,160	2	30
New York No. 168	31 West One hundred and tenth Street, New York.	2,749	296	2,902	5,947	807	651	57	321	186	712	1	32
New York No. 169	144 St. Nicholas Avenue, New York.	3,043	305	3,756	7,104	838	662	54	252	247	951	0	29
New York No. 170	220 Lenox Avenue, New York.	2,758	187	3,622	6,567	794	545	58	275	128	648	0	69
New York No. 171	9 ...ton Avenue, Long Island.	2,880	224	3,842	6,946	787	661	38	280	131	1,272	1	64
New York No. 172	158 Second Avenue, New York.	3,110	247	3,782	7,139	780	1,135	11	162	188	674	0	16
New York No. 173	442 fifth Avenue, Long Island City.	2,799	257	3,737	6,733	695	487	40	173	128	1,290	3	47
New York No. 174	Public School 11, ...le, Long Island.	2,520	182	3,467	6,109	639	557	28	137	75	1,061	8	27
New York No. 175	15 ...ley Avenue, Elmhurst, Long Island.	2,609	249	4,571	7,429	801	656	11	117	180	1,323	5	55
New York No. 176	23A South Eighth Avenue, ...le, Long Island.	2,202	180	3,188	5,576	622	406	20	125	115	935	5	90
New York No. 177	14 ... St, Maspeth, Long Island.	3,443	292	4,281	8,016	918	931	35	203	160	1,413	15	34
New York No. 178	Seneca and Bleeker Streets, Ridgewood, Long Island.	2,781	291	3,727	6,799	919	664	34	108	108	1,343	0	5
New York No. 179	2404 Myrtle Avenue, Ridgewood, Long Island.	3,966	338	4,959	9,293	1,067	620	28	107	162	2,237	0	55
New York No. 180	Glendale, Long Island.	2,900	264	4,111	7,275	692	384	65	198	138	1,711	10	38
New York No. 181	372 Boulevard, Rockaway Beach, Long Island.	2,180	144	3,104	5,438	545	349	18	56	189	779	7	14
New York No. 182	4110 Jamaica Avenue, ...n, Long Island.	2,785	242	4,405	7,423	748	863	15	108	155	1,125	0	43

APPENDIX TABLE 100-A.—*Principal statistical data, by local boards*—Continued.

NEW YORK—Continued.

Local board	Post-office address	Registration				Induction	Physical groups				Deferments		
		June 5, 1917.	June and August, 1918.	Sept. 12, 1918.	Total.	Accepted at camp.	General service.	Remediables.	Limited service.	Disqualified.	Dependency.	Agricultural.	Industrial.
NEW YORK No. 183	4568 Jamaica Avenue, corner Woodhoof Avenue, Richmondville, Long Island.	2,536	228	4,301	7,065	779	558	13	86	127	1,172	2	42
NEW YORK No. 184	Post Office ... Jamaica, Long Island.	2,539	214	4,401	7,454	761	632	11	156	175	1,194	7	39
NEW YORK No. 185	Town Hall, Broadway, ..., Long Island.	2,208	200	4,169	6,577	743	411	24	155	115	807	68	40
NEW YORK No. 186	Curtis High ..., with Brighton, Staten Island.	2,660	210	3,752	6,622	608	385	18	107	230	1,202	0	101
NEW YORK No. 187	Public School 20, Park Avenue, Port Richmond, Staten Island.	2,870	253	4,314	7,437	601	663	13	90	49	158	5	103
NEW YORK No. 188	Public School 14, ... and Wright Streets, ..., Staten Island.	2,345	193	3,249	5,787	509	321	14	90	158	882	42	49
NEW YORK No. 189	Public School 8, Great Kills, Staten Island.	2,349	187	3,686	6,222	616	481	14	89	150	807	11	104
NIA FALLS	..., 413 Gluck Building, Niagara Falls.	7,673	508	9,563	17,744	1,245	1,105	77	335	117	2,019	17	150
Niagara No. 1	13 Main Street, Lockport.	3,452	332	4,861	8,645	982	996	35	174	395	997	19	115
Niagara No. 2	Room 26, ..., Lockport.	2,915	234	2,880	6,029	610	814	19	57	36	1,112	743	46
Oneida No. 1	Y. M. C. A. Building, Rome.	4,449	342	5,254	10,045	813	711	39	217	639	1,288	63	106
Oneida No. 2	Booneville.	1,700	146	2,563	4,409	478	297	17	88	164	685	300	27
Oneida No. 3	New Hartford.	2,373	212	3,427	6,012	698	497	12	125	28	739	150	44
Onondaga No. 1	Village Hall, Solvay.	2,774	219	3,803	6,796	476	403	18	93	107	949	115	101
Onondaga No. 2	410 ..., Syracuse.	1,700	155	2,466	4,321	376	274	18	114	45	716	295	60
Onondaga No. 3	Town Hall, Baldwinsville.	1,894	168	2,938	5,000	371	314	10	51	135	783	261	37
Ontario No. 1	Surrogate's, Canandaigua.	2,281	200	3,067	5,548	565	463	27	42	238	991	127	57
Ontario No. 2	..., Canandaigua.	2,171	215	3,404	5,790	435	316	11	67	88	955	484	45
Ontario No. 3	Town House, Canandaigua.	2,594	270	4,114	6,978	721	675	48	127	209	894	13	57
Orange No. 1	City Hall, Newburgh.	2,434	198	3,088	5,720	526	0	7	98	55	647	65	44
Orange No. 2	... Park.	2,771	250	3,692	6,713	779	688	47	131	210	1,064	85	76
Orange No. 3	City Hall, Middletown.	2,441	219	3,433	6,093	519	490	28	133	263	1,016	186	82
Orange No. 4	..., Goshen.	2,261	232	3,231	5,724	598	591	14	85	99	1,091	322	25
Oswego No. 1	Courthouse, ... Building, Oswego.	2,072	182	2,720	4,974	523	385	1	128	236	1,788	3	69
Oswego No. 2	Fulton.	1,915	195	3,007	5,117	410	30	0	32	239	888	90	24
Oswego No. 3	Courthouse, Pulaski.	1,538	129	2,331	3,998	404	313	14	91	122	722	181	32
Otsego No. 1	Room 8, Oneonta Hotel Building, Oneonta.	1,907	175	2,854	4,936	480	405	27	120	90	926	124	33
Otsego No. 2	Cooperstown.	1,509	148	2,453	4,110	480	226	23	77	121	519	449	21
POUGHKEEPSIE	255 Mill Street.	3,200	248	2,455	5,903	733	463	15	85	263	1,455	8	91
Putnam	County Courthouse Building, Carmel.	1,029	81	1,463	2,573	143	137	7	35	49	409	59	23
Rensselaer No. 1	Broadway and Ferry Streets, Rensselaer.	1,984	163	2,664	4,811	480	497	15	53	109	804	144	77

District	Building												
Rensselaer No. 2	Municipal Building, Hoosick Falls	1,704	176	2,510	4,390	398	367	25	66	70	668	34	5
Rochester No. 1	City Hall	3,706	311	5,122	9,139	1,047	747	47	156	143	1,636	12	34
Rochester No. 2	do.	3,575	324	5,222	8,374	901	1,030	53	168	193	1,488	15	214
Rochester No. 3	do.	3,509	279	4,475	9,010	1,023	825	76	201	171	1,489	12	180
Rochester No. 4	do.	3,410	343	5,302	7,959	801	699	129	108	177	1,615	3	232
Rochester No. 5	do.	4,631	282	4,919	10,276	1,142	887	38	267	200	1,746	7	112
Rochester No. 6	do.	3,637	321	4,939	8,838	1,060	851	102	265	119	1,091	20	130
Rochester No. 7	do.	3,273	238	3,930	8,533	868	610	47	211	110	1,704	10	183
Rochester No. 8	do.	2,479	174	2,372	6,647	744	495	61	181	184	1,058	5	89
Rockland No. 1	Haverstraw, Nyack	1,697	181	2,972	4,243	534	448	33	97	158	581	19	27
Rockland No. 2	Business Men's Club, Broadway and First Avenue, Nyack	2,060	212	3,134	5,213	512	346	37	131	49	838	34	40
St. Lawrence No. 1	State Armory, Ogdensburg	2,078	313	4,809	5,424	687	481	19	69	168	853	221	22
St. Lawrence No. 2	Potsdam	3,410	271	3,482	8,532	836	631	39	158	69	1,000	447	52
St. Lawrence No. 3	107 East Main Street, Gouverneur	2,415	215	3,334	6,168	635	453	27	112	208	1,710	54	28
Saratoga No. 1	Convention Hall, Saratoga Springs	2,103	266	4,426	5,752	536	553	38	78	99	1,276	189	110
Saratoga No. 2	Strong Hose Company, North Third Street, Mechanicsville	2,992	207	3,275	7,684	714	354	19	72	96	992	0	85
Schenectady No. 1	Room 305, County Court-Building, Schenectady	2,232	236	3,634	5,714	459	540	16	98	56	1,025	2	88
Schenectady No. 2	County Courthouse Building, State Street	2,523	156	3,136	6,393	558	215	7	106	158	805	1	133
Schenectady No. 3	Fire Station No. 9, 540 Brandywine Avenue	1,797	242	3,808	5,089	434	455	9	86	27	728	2	136
Schenectady No. 4	County Courthouse, Schenectady	2,732	160	2,794	6,782	702	276	16	40	161	739	66	48
Schenectady	do.	1,513	173	2,313	4,467	279	206	16	60	50	587	367	63
Schoharie	County Clerk's Office, Schoharie	1,544	91	1,538	4,030	348	284	14	101	129	244	101	33
Schuyler	Courthouse Watkins	955	187	2,714	3,584	236	151	21	13	120	647	344	45
Seneca	Courthouse, Waterloo	1,755	246	2,357	4,656	399	419	4	93	219	54	4	6
Steuben No. 1	Courthouse, Corning	2,357	209	3,290	5,978	666	391	35	49	164	1,145	176	99
Steuben No. 2	Courthouse, Cornell	2,292	192	3,036	5,781	572	565	15	209	267	813	197	134
Steuben No. 3	Town Clerk's Office, Addison	2,219	199	2,611	5,447	442	378	41	150	426	880	16	21
Suffolk No. 1	c/o Jeremiah Robbins, Babylon	2,611	233	3,645	6,455	805	530	24	105	189	1,256	28	33
Suffolk No. 2	Bay Shore	2,714	204	5,420	8,367	738	582	34	167	110	1,067	97	34
Suffolk No. 3	Courthouse, Riverhead	2,963	287	4,022	7,189	828	331	61	426	217	895	266	50
Sullivan	Monticello	2,788	274	4,173	7,248	705	556	48	189	259	1,359	4	47
Syracuse No. 1	313 Highland Avenue	3,274	258	4,165	7,713	766	743	46	110	397	1,282	7	75
Syracuse No. 2	107 Educational Building, West Genesee	3,928	274	4,574	8,760	812	628	D4	217	165	1,235	3	159
Syracuse No. 3	Grace School, Grace and Messina Streets	3,716	277	4,546	8,536	820	459	43	259	223	1,280	160	102
Syracuse No. 4	City Hall	4,120	267	5,300	9,697	897	242	39	102	52	1,644	249	115
Syracuse No. 5	The Arena, 1140 South Salina Street	3,259	66	4,617	8,143	737	616	7	70	226	845	1	27
Tioga	Courthouse, Owego	1,625	293	2,615	4,406	368	558	26	150	24	1,069	6	101
Tompkins	Courthouse, Ithaca	3,006	225	4,253	7,552	808	608	14	385	271	813	10	24
Troy No. 1	Courthouse Building, Troy	2,627	212	3,257	6,109	694	271	46	201	140	811	11	44
Troy No. 2	Post Office Building, Troy	2,242	147	3,416	5,870	739	684	15	107	161	738	119	98
Troy No. 3	Fire Headquarters, Fifteenth Street, North Troy	1,490	220	2,175	3,812	349	591	20	66	239	883	216	89
Ulster No. 1	Surrogate's Court, Main and Fair Streets, Kingston	2,152	180	3,138	5,510	668	504	29	59	327	826	6	41
Ulster No. 2	44 Main Street, Kingston	2,093	234	2,528	5,447	514	719	5	92	266	890	4	36
Ulster No. 3	Mechanic's Hall, Napanoch	2,053	251	3,160	8,533	499	529	32	122	201	1,967	35	243
Utica No. 1	Corner Catherine and Genesee Streets	3,763	268	4,519	7,215	788	336	41	174	52	855		0
Utica No. 2	Special Term Room, County Building	2,833	242	4,114	6,956	691	778	6	59	59	1,056		89
Utica No. 3	Home Defense Building	3,026	250	3,688	6,513	557		24	93	93	1,037		32
Warren	Rooms Public Safety Board, Municipal Building, Glen Falls	2,448		3,815		817							

APPENDIX TABLE 100-A.—*Principal statistical data, by local boards*—Continued.

NEW YORK—Continued.

Local board.	Post-office address.	Registration.				Induction.	Physical groups.				Deferments.		
		June 5, 1917.	June and August, 1918.	Sept. 12, 1918.	Total.	Accepted at camp.	General service.	Remediables.	Limited service.	Disqualified.	Dependency.	Agricultural.	Industrial.
Washington No. 1	Church Street Schoolhouse, Granville	1,800	172	2,833	4,805	543	394	29	118	124	584	111	44
Washington No. 2	Electric Light Co.'s Office, Greenwich	1,650	180	2,574	4,404	395	448	9	71	133	642	227	28
Wayne No. 1	Cuyler Building, Palmyra	1,985	209	3,002	5,166	431	309	6	50	22	998	325	80
Wayne No. 2	9 Canal Street, Lyons	1,992	179	2,849	5,020	433	290		30	92	966	229	16
Westchester No. 1	1029 Main Street, Peekskill	2,110	179	3,114	5,310	560	425	35	101	146	900	62	43
Westchester No. 2	17 North Broadway, Tarrytown	2,277	108	2,925	5,403	571	365	23	82	144	585	9	41
Westchester No. 3	Courthouse, White Plains	1,788	117	2,655	5,310	495	333	25	75	113	621	1	13
Westchester No. 4	do	1,457	83	2,635	4,560	400	333	10	81	59	527	6	5
Westchester No. 5	Brier Cliff Manor	2,154	181	2,876	3,813	400	487	21	101	176	791	9	26
Westchester No. 6	465 Main Street, Portchester	4,501	303	6,268	5,211	779	107	28	137	193	1,646	17	89
Wyoming	Main Street, Warsaw	2,468	239	3,531	11,072	1,129	699	11	86	105	1,061	586	84
Yates	County Building, Penn Yan	1,212	120	1,918	6,238	644	255	14	49	89	576	146	6
Yonkers No. 1	City Hall	3,388	226	4,757	3,250	344	412	32	120	227	1,319	0	63
Yonkers No. 2	do	2,175	162	3,319	5,656	481	488	16	100	106	845	3	29
Yonkers No. 3	45 Warburton Avenue	3,268	236	3,992	7,496	618	556	28	117	176	1,400	0	1

NORTH CAROLINA.

Local board.	Post-office address.	June 5, 1917.	June and August, 1918.	Sept. 12, 1918.	Total.	Accepted at camp.	General service.	Remediables.	Limited service.	Disqualified.	Dependency.	Agricultural.	Industrial.
Alamance	Graham	2,400	221	3,107	5,818	616	611	6	77	5	1,368	76	21
Alexander	Taylorsville	800	111	1,172	2,083	227	164	6	34	65	793	20	8
Alleghany	Stratford	473	64	710	1,246	135	94	0	18	36	290	0	14
Anson	Wadesboro	2,126	236	2,580	4,942	649	621	27	51	114	1,206	20	8
Ashe ?	West Jefferson	1,480	168	2,028	3,676	486	106	0	9	12	72	6	1
Avery	Newland	797	103	1027	1,927	235	171	2	5	51	527	0	1
Beaufort	Washington	2,564	284	3,369	6,207	824	713	8	45	320	1,405	7	4
Bertie	Windsor	1,730	191	2,364	4,265	542	577	14	37	134	773	2	18
Bladen	Elizabethtown	1,477	141	1,970	3,588	395	390	4	84	177	818	7	0
Brunswick	Southport	1,218	101	1,490	2,808	296	287	19	22	48	204	1	1
Buncombe No. 1	do	2,068	274	3,776	6,718	749	614	24	88	126	173	3	36
Buncombe No. 2	Asheville	2,519	129	2,249	5,397	688	634	26	118	224	1,775	2	11
Burke	Morgantown	1,726	179	2,089	3,946	481	436	2	64	27	234	3	1
Cabarrus	Concord	3,060	273	3,420	6,773	655	713	32	125	225	1,738	54	2
Caldwell	Lenoir	1,610	160	1,918	3,686	401	326	13	72	64	870	0	
Camden	Camden	473	47	612	1,132	148	149	7	9	29	260	10	2

County	Town
Carteret	Beaufort
Caswell	Yanceyville
Catawba	Hickory
Charlotte City	Charlotte
Chatham	Silver City
Cherokee	Murphy
Chowan	Edenton
Clay	Hayesville
Cleveland	Shelby
Columbus	Whiteville
Craven	Newbern
Cumberland	Fayetteville
Currituck	Poplar Branch
Dare	Manteo
Davidson	Lexington
Davie	Mocksville
Duplin	Warsaw
Durham	Durham
Edgecombe	Tarboro
Forsyth	Winston-Salem
Franklin	Louisburg
Gaston	Gastonia
Gates	Gatesville
Graham	Robbinsville
Granville	Oxford
Greene	Snow Hill
Guilford No. 1	Greensboro
Guilford No. 2	do
Guilford No. 3	High Point
Halifax	Weldon
Harnett	Duke
Haywood	Waynesville
Henderson	Hendersonville
Hertford	Ahoskie
Hoke	Raeford
Hyde	Fairfield
Iredell	Statesville
Jackson	Sylva
Johnston No. 1	Smithfield
Johnston No. 2	Selma
Jones	Trenton
Lee	Sanford
Lenoir	111 East King Street, Kinston
Lincoln	Lincolnton
McDowell	Marion
Macon	Franklin
Madison	Marshall
Martin	Williamston
Mecklenburg	County Courthouse, Charlotte
Mitchell	Bakersville
Montgomery	Mount Gilead
Moore	Carthage

APPENDIX TABLE 100-A.—*Principal statistical data, by local boards*—Continued.

NORTH CAROLINA—Continued.

Local board.	Post-office address.	Registration. June 5, 1917.	Registration. June and August, 1918.	Registration. Sept. 12, 1918.	Registration. Total.	Induction. Accepted at camp.	Physical groups. General service.	Physical groups. Remediables.	Physical groups. Limited service.	Physical groups. Disqualified.	Deferments. Dependency.	Deferments. Agricultural.	Deferments. Industrial.
Nash	Nashville	8,540	316	4,425	13,281	1,296	1,359	60	85	225	1,246	5	17
New Hanover	Wilmington	443	36	661	1,143	131	143	2	23	28	219	2	0
Northampton	Jackson	1,876	175	2,334	4,385	510	245	9	20	20	540	0	0
Onslow	Jacksonville	1,193	138	1,587	2,918	420	35	11	21	235	684	37	9
Orange	Chapel Hill	1,506	130	1,728	3,371	497	209	7	32	43	381	1	0
Pamlico	Bayshoro	734	91	999	1,824	240	437	8	94	20	803	8	6
Pasquotank	Elizabeth City	1,521	108	1,702	3,331	405	295		6	21	488	1	8
Pender	Burgaw	1,047	129	1,624	2,800	328	241	10	27	99	526	10	4
Perquimans	Hertford	945	96	1,187	2,228	255	384	12	65	121	695	4	5
Person	Roxboro	1,375	163	1,696	3,234	402	883	30	105	232	2,309	4	6
Pitt	Greenville	3,636	348	4,519	8,503	874	215	0	13	48	341	0	2
Polk	Tryon	622	62	885	1,569	193	492	32	166	34	1,254	111	27
Randolph	Asheboro	2,084	235	2,958	5,277	546	667	14	62	49	190	4	3
Richmond	Rockingham	2,350	206	2,697	5,253	699	586	10	84	137	1,257	13	11
Robeson No. 1	Lumberton	2,074	247	2,715	5,036	676	588	9	11	118	1,061	19	18
Robeson No. 2	Red Springs	1,993	198	2,446	4,637	581	717	19	340	321	1,792	54	20
Rockingham	Reidsville	2,974	363	4,062	7,399	739	671	19	196	12	2,133	27	70
Rowan	Salisbury	3,500	353	4,098	8,461	1,044	803	0	14	65	1,388	15	4
Rutherford	Rutherfordton	2,119	237	2,789	5,145	610	514	8	48	199	1,708	17	15
Sampson	Clinton	2,768	257	3,376	6,401	735	762	22	33	69	868	10	2
Scotland	Laurinburg	1,450	99	1,578	3,127	408	364						
Stanley	...do	2,801	317	2,877	5,965	933	427	6	30	193	998	32	6
Stokes	R. F. D. No. 1, Danbury	1,723	176	2,018	3,917	380	461	4	177	49	347	10	0
Surry	Mount Airy	2,231	265	3,105	5,601	496	295	0	52	59	647	0	6
Swain	Bryson City	1,001	117	1,262	2,380	286	143	7	38	54	423	0	0
Transylvania	Brevard	852	62	892	1,806	197	116	3	7	32	292	3	0
Tyrrell	...do	512	44	568	1,124	119	92	8	42	207	...	...	12
Union	Monroe	2,729	315	3,427	6,471	762	735	8	92	217	1,630	6	12
Vance	Henderson	1,842	255	2,132	4,229	579	657	11	42	79	980	2	6
Wake No. 1	Raleigh	3,482	406	4,466	8,354	1,025	1,202	38	126	168	1,655	32	16
Wake No. 2	...do	2,699	174	3,065	5,938	659	615	24	75	44	1,390	3	90
Warren	Warrenton	1,696	192	2,149	4,037	600	692	7	32	41	926	5	10
Washington	Plymouth	1,060	66	1,135	2,261	319	417	29	12	130	532	3	1
Watauga	Boone	1,065	100	1,268	2,433	220	217	13	18	41	629	3	0
Wayne	Goldsboro	3,549	346	4,272	8,167	1,110	493	28	87	243	1,945	34	13
Wilkes	Wilkesboro	2,367	282	5,797	5,516	562	471	12	83	248	1,414	28	25
Wilmington	Wilmington	2,760	216	3,708	6,771	757	731	21	84	273	1,197	2	68

County / Place												
Wilson	3,120	294	3,728	7,142	859	863	52	115	76	866	0	5
WINSTON-SALEM	5,161	447	4,756	10,364	1,637	1,191	24	137	17	2,006	2	21
Yadkin	987	145	1,534	2,066	1,228	191	9	53	99	616	14	0
Yancey	1,013	108	1,445	2,566	227	325	25	30	151	829	0	0

NORTH DAKOTA.

Adams (Hettinger)	441	50	876	1,367	151	135	5	25	26	154	56	3
Barnes (Valley City)	2,007	206	2,320	4,533	550	635	4	16	156	645	283	11
Benson (Minnewaukan)	1,293	112	1,794	3,199	445	412		47	96	399	176	6
Billings (Medora)	423	21	482	926	112	103	2	2	17	184	26	0
Bottineau (Bottineau)	1,478	143	1,968	3,589	502	554	5	29	153	457	224	9
Bowman (Bowman)	498	45	891	1,434	182	191	24	23	20	144	67	2
Burke (Bowbells)	906	100	1,527	2,533	290	448	0	12	35	95	251	17
Burleigh (Bismarck)	1,804	124	1,899	3,827	442		1					
Cass (Fargo)	4,333	423	5,583	10,339	1,344	137		10	135	488	319	5
Cavalier (Langdon)	1,505	162	1,921	3,648	375	333	5	47	56	136	149	5
Dickey (Ellendale)	1,111	117	1,438	2,666	265	419	0	27	55	329	169	8
Divide (Crosby)	1,103	65	1,693	2,861	311	337		27	61	489	63	0
Dunn (Dunn Center)	1,078	65	1,311	2,454	288		3					
Eddy (New Rockford)	719	77	985	1,781	161	369	0	34	58	220	195	6
Emmons (Linton)	1,049	110	1,299	2,458	207	182	0	27	59	554	130	0
Foster (Carrington)	725	86	873	1,684	146	194	0	21	29	204	78	2
Golden Valley (Beach)	671	49	867	1,587	139	765	23	87	138	1,003	466	43
Grand Forks (Grand Forks)	2,884	296	3,583	6,763	794	429	0	47	12	111	100	0
Grant (Carson)	944	83	1,391	2,418	198	239	11	38	13	52	75	1
Griggs (Cooperstown)	818	71	988	1,877	251	249	13	12	18	370	48	2
Hettinger (Mott)	743	55	1,103	1,901	189	240	0	20	36	317	101	2
Kidder (Steele)	812	66	1,118	1,996	226	291	0	45	26	430	201	3
La Moure (La Moure)	1,218	117	1,565	2,900	304	147	6	1	76	409	53	1
Logan (Napoleon)	580	73	818	1,471	136	395	3	28	34	516	188	3
McHenry (Towner)	1,446	121	2,078	3,645	431	185	6		141	448	40	2
McIntosh (Ashley)	743	89	845	1,677	190	432		8	40	570	174	2
McKenzie (Schafer)	1,351	68	1,726	3,145	411		4	14	7	319	261	0
McLean (Washburn)	1,825	126	2,479	4,430	556	556		36	120	505	41	1
Mercer (Stanton)	728	64	965	1,757	204	214	10	29	25	780	193	9
Morton (Mandan)	1,749	169	2,164	4,082	482	476	3	20	116	428	376	16
Mountrail (Stanley)	1,765	106	2,142	3,923	542	572	17	45	53	346	293	11
Nelson (Latoka)	1,204	130	1,358	2,692	317	291		35	62	159	82	1
Oliver (Center)	420	44	556	1,020	87	129	3		58	82	340	19
Pembina (Pembina)	1,496	154	1,742	3,392	437	488	4	33	18	373	104	6
Pierce (Rugby)	774	82	1,064	1,920	202	185	1	9	67	322	199	26
Ramsey (Devils Lake)	1,635	165	2,504	4,304	465	473	5	45	128	536	185	7
Ransom (Lisbon)	1,202	98	1,490	2,790	315	404	17	22	54	378	138	47
Renville (Mohall)	820	78	1,165	2,063	220	229		13	78	301	337	8
Richland (Wahpeton)	1,914	227	2,418	4,559	572	649	5	61	118	670	253	1
Rolette (Rolla)	827	92	1,126	2,045	151	226	4	28	65	180	260	0
Sargent (Forman)	1,095	113	1,352	2,560	353	378	6	31	30	204	94	1
Sheridan (McClusky)	653	55	892	1,600	137	183		16	11	239		
Sioux (Fort Yates)	325	15	398	738	106	89	0	9		133	25	

APPENDIX TABLE 100-A.—*Principal statistical data, by local boards*—Continued.

NORTH DAKOTA—Continued.

Local board	Post-office address	Registration June 5, 1917	Registration June and August, 1918	Registration Sept. 12, 1918	Registration Total	Induction. Accepted at camp.	Physical groups. General service.	Physical groups. Remediables.	Physical groups. Limited service.	Disqualified.	Deferments. Dependency.	Deferments. Agricultural.	Deferments. Industrial.
Slope	Amidon	720	54	891	1,665	226	229		18	28	272	40	3
Starke	Dickinson	1,410	111	1,647	3,168	303	79	7	17	143	602	83	8
Steele	Sherbrooke	776	91	1,036	1,903	299	362	11	31	38	207	244	1
Stutsman	Jamestown	2,492	222	3,069	5,783	676	927		39	61	940	252	20
Towner	Cando	899	79	1,250	2,228	293	270	2	39	70	286	101	2
Trail	Hillsboro	1,293	165	1,559	3,017	373	447	4	49	93	315	248	6
Walsh	Grafton	1,954	209	2,151	4,314	511	88	11	36	113	561	573	9
Ward	Minot	3,201	210	4,039	7,450	831	1,000		109	194	702	270	61
Wells	Fessenden	1,409	121	1,684	3,214	359	432	0	33	9	623	175	5
Williams	Williston	1,999	129	2,868	4,996	570							

OHIO.

Local board	Post-office address	Registration June 5, 1917	Registration June and August, 1918	Registration Sept. 12, 1918	Registration Total	Induction. Accepted at camp.	Physical groups. General service.	Physical groups. Remediables.	Physical groups. Limited service.	Disqualified.	Deferments. Dependency.	Deferments. Agricultural.	Deferments. Industrial.
Adams	Manchester	1,537	123	2,525	4,185	328	363	5	40	21	864	106	12
AKRON No. 1	Courthouse, Akron	5,658	428	4,531	10,617	1,735	2,197	45	322	235	2,005	5	30
Akron No. 2	do	7,120	596	6,364	13,990	2,057	1,964	76	134	244	2,563	3	54
Akron No. 3	do	6,383	483	7,124	13,990	2,342	1,117	83	139	164	1,792	1	9
Akron No. 4	do	5,174	379	4,545	10,098	1,407	949	16	79	139	1,847		25
AKRON No. 5	do	8,358	527	7,882	16,767	2,463	1,791	68	175	426	3,187	151	78
Allen	Memorial Hall, Lima	1,384	202	3,018	5,104	652	594	11	47	43	151	585	17
Ashland	Orange and Third Streets, Ashland	1,800	190	2,909	4,899	418	984		52	23	649	24	49
Ashtabula No. 1	Federal Building, Ashtabula	3,620	405	5,282	9,307	719	607	12	187	93	325	146	213
Ashtabula No. 2	Grand Jurors' Rooms, Jefferson	1,799	105	3,032	5,026	360	249	17	70	171	855	39	13
Athens	18 East Washington Street, Athens	3,626	483	5,963	10,082	1,140	1,103	42	142	222	1,886	158	6
Auglaize	Courthouse, Wapakoneta	3,087	241	3,460	5,894	698	543	33	100	23	1,133	158	35
Belmont No. 1	Courthouse, Martins Ferry	3,087	267	4,516	8,120	824	717	0	60	116	1,255	3	10
Belmont No. 2	City Building, Bellaire	3,00	277	4,409	7,706	848	605	12	88	101	1,306	21	35
Belmont No. 3	340 West Main Street, St. Clairsville	2,063	289	4,292	7,244	797	594	11	44	227	1,087	43	4
Brown	Georgetown	1,531	182	2,488	4,201	339	380	2	27	119	732	338	18
Butler	Y. M. C. A. Building, Middletown	4,822	524	6,271	11,617	984	910	31	75	248	1,223	219	121
CANTON No. 1	Courthouse, Canton	5,769	535	8,905	15,200	1,551	1,164	65	333	248	1,826	45	230
CANTON No. 2	Council Chambers, City Hall Building	6210	423	1,814	24,210	1,519	1,116	108	186	108	1,965	68	127
Carroll	Public Square, Carrollton	1,332	143	1,814	3,251	401	431		30	16	495	68	10
Champaign	Urbana	1,819	157	2,525	4,439	473	51	19	23	109	888	179	23

Location	Place	(1)	(2)	(3)	(4)	(5)	(6)	(7)	(8)	(9)	(10)	(11)	(12)
CINCINNATI No. 1	Northwest corner Sixth and Main Streets	3,979	338	5,465	9,782	1,028	771	50	166	399	2,120	12	181
CINCINNATI No. 2	205 Turner Building, 2458 Gilbert Avenue	3,406	293	4,608	8,507	1,373	62	42	92	235	1,092	1	57
CINCINNATI No. 3	328 Government Building	4,451	391½	6,234	11,126	1,423	1,311	13	400	210	1,477	1	48
CINCINNATI No. 4	Shelter House, Inwood Park, Vine and Hollister Streets	4,446	432	5,769	10,647	1,293	888	36	118	116	1,926	3	130
CINCINNATI No. 5	3023 Reading Road, Avondale	3,137	261	4,477	7,875	1,016	810	33	247	292	1,131	3	71
CINCINNATI No. 6	Sands Public School, Poplar and Freeman Streets	3,947	362	5,107	9,416	1,146	1,344	1	258	86	1,244	0	7
CINCINNATI No. 7	First National Bank Building, Fourth and Walnut Streets	6,351	470	7,558	14,379	1,909	1,777	19	130	340	1,748	1	53
CINCINNATI No. 8	931 Harriet Street	4,740	384	5,649	10,773	1,108	1,254	42	277	246	377	6	138
CINCINNATI No. 9	Eighth and Elberon Avenue	3,430	306	4,761	8,497	1,129	1,146	43	229	304	1,532	13	103
CINCINNATI No. 10	Cumminsville Branch Library	3,769	322	5,037	9,28	1,064	908	39	110	22	1,920	11	136
Clark	Springfield	1,478	165	2,285	3,928	433	299	0	57	71	789	128	5
Clermont	Batavia	2,161	226	2,985	5,372	447	66	12	36	167	1,042	317	50
CLEVELAND No. 1	Central Armory	5,279	438	5,237	12,934	1,382	833	67	17	206	2,377	2	91
CLEVELAND No. 2	New Courthouse	3,505	344	4,547	8,396	677	110	—	133	53	53	—	13
CLEVELAND No. 3	Central Armory	5,275	400	6,578	12,253	1,145	771	55	21	290	1,202	1	53
CLEVELAND No. 4	2907 Archwood Avenue	3,203	365	4,821	8,389	742	161	17	89	204	1,633	6	72
CLEVELAND No. 5	Old Courthouse	7,823	533	8,223	16,579	1,611	1,123	25	89	701	2,198	2	92
CLEVELAND No. 6	3200 Franklin Avenue	9,856	617	11,244	21,727	2,197	1,960	10	505	510	1,677	3	95
CLEVELAND No. 7	Central Armory	6,991	492	5,978	15,461	1,539	964	79	334	240	1,866	4	92
CLEVELAND No. 8	do	5,310	447	5,930	14,635	1,571	1,611	57	373	325	1,576	0	78
CLEVELAND No. 9	do	6,606	536	7,043	9,556	1,201	798	52	223	639	1,462	7	13
CLEVELAND No. 10	do	4,873	327	6,356	11,991	1,001	154	110	122	49	1,040	1	56
CLEVELAND No. 11	do	4,942	372	6,677	11,546	1,035	726	86	149	187	2,288	0	108
CLEVELAND No. 12	Broadway Y. M. C. A.	4,776	420	6,350	12,700	871	559	33	86	139	1,576	2	55
CLEVELAND No. 13	2530 East Eightieth Street	5,467	419	6,814	16,097	1,192	744	59	160	193	1,682	3	55
CLEVELAND No. 14	706 Woodland Avenue	5,077	562	8,206	11,026	2,061	2,131	133	467	294	2,629	3	87
CLEVELAND No. 15	Central Armory	4,968	297	5,652	11,040	1,293	860	44	308	224	2,030	10	154
CLEVELAND No. 16	do	5,347	296	5,760	13,105	881	758	58	114	147	898	0	254
CLEVELAND No. 17	Dean School Building	5,785	472	7,286	14,349	1,523	951	131	247	351	2,557	8	51
CLEVELAND No. 18	Central Armory	4,200	425	8,139	4,494	461	178	8	27	—	58	8	173
Clinton	Wilmington		187	2,607	7,058		270		20	125	189	2	28
Columbiana No. 1	City Hall, Wellsville	4,424	515	6,868		1,797	1,299	13	235	148	2,259	310	99
Columbiana No. 2	Chamber of Commerce, Salem	2,819	305	3,934		717	620	32	52	117	2,817	84	12
COLUMBUS No. 1	Memorial Hall	5,593	496	8,094		1,632	3,754	20	525	350	1,372	67	87
COLUMBUS No. 2	do	4,770	430	8,830	12,090	1,463	1,181	62	171	131	1,104	4	19
COLUMBUS No. 3	do	5,908	478	7,623	14,004	1,862	1,746	48	248	288	2,318	5	90
COLUMBUS No. 4	do	5,954	534	7,659	14,147	1,732	1,403	79	324	376	2,314	13	57
Coshocton	111 North Sixth Street, Coshocton	2,430	259	3,483	6,177	611	850	22	97	14	905	38	9
Crawford	Courthouse, Bucyrus	3,031	347	4,674	8,052	903	841	4	103	137	1,176	159	75
Cuyahoga No. 1	Lakewood	5,358	433	9,161	14,942	1,048	706	9	181	48	2,551	295	151
Cuyahoga No. 2	Town Hall, Oland Heights	6,122	470	9,676	16,268	1,163	65	8	31	—	55	13	29
Darke	Courthouse, Greenville	3,115	381	4,833	8,379	781	505	0	58	123	720	2	0
DAYTON No. 1	312 Post Office Building, Dayton	4,978	419	7,564	12,961	1,360	1,083	48	197	70	495	11	148
DAYTON No. 2	205-206 Post Office Building	5,771	627	8,112	14,530	1,181	1,209	74	213	250	2,665	12	264
DAYTON No. 3	222 Federal Building	4,683	426	6,743	11,852	946	639	61	182	306	2,798	8	39
Defiance		1,998	221	2,528	5,047	637	637	25	32	0	987	94	9
Delaware		2,111	244	2,854	5,212	688	653	26	108	67	1,024	163	11
Erie	Courthouse Sandusky	3,394	341	4,831	8,666	886	683	22	92	101	1,493	293	129
Fairfield	West Main Street, Lancaster	2,733	330	4,448	7,511	361	964	45	79	179	1,271	542	17
Fayette	Pavey Building, Washington Court House	1,602	183	2,435	4,220	445	345	12	33	95	936	142	1

APPENDIX TABLE 100-A.—*Principal statistical data, by local boards*—Continued.

OHIO—Continued.

Local board	Post-office address	Registration — June 5, 1917	June and August, 1918	Sept. 12, 1918	Total	Induction — Accepted at camp	Physical groups — General service	Remediables	Limited service	Disqualified	Deferments — Dependency	Agricultural	Industrial
Franklin	Memorial Hall, Columbus	3,837	360	5,820	10,017	1,005	628	1	38	259	1,799	362	30
Fulton	Courthouse, Wauseon	1,748	216	2,660	4,624	640	33	6	16	74	1,037	82	25
Gallia	Courthouse, Gallipolis	1,390	216	2,372	3,978	525	688	25	55	113	659	68	4
Geauga	Court house, Chardon	1,023	95	1,671	2,789	222	140	0	8	92	429	200	11
Greene	Courthouse, Xenia	2,251	260	3,523	6,034	761	482	14	32	177	1,109	262	7
Guernsey	Cambridge	3,523	393	5,477	9,398	1,066	781	50	99	124	107	14	1
Hamilton	Y.M.C.A. Building, Hamilton	3,459	332	5,111	8,902	1,008	559	44	79	276	1,652	1	142
Hamilton No. 1	City Hall, Norwood	3,462	300	4,779	8,541	1,011	687	36	124	13	1,442	0	2
Hamilton No. 2	Third and Walnut Streets, Cincinnati	4,582	492	6,474	11,548	1,174	949	66	198	345	1,598	337	162
Hancock	Municipal Building, Findlay	2,810	320	4,313	7,443	858	690	47	70	155	1,528	134	6
Hardin	Kenton	2,172	253	3,310	5,735	708	697	19	62	20	1,161	118	23
Harrison	Cadiz	1,214	169	2,341	3,724	430	291	10	42	12	564	69	10
Henry	Courthouse, Napoleon	1,944	249	2,666	4,859	601	560	7	36	16	1,027	70	9
Highland	Bell Building, Hillsboro	1,887	224	3,060	5,171	381	462	19	38	78	1,094	223	11
Hocking	Market Street, Logan	1,724	194	2,829	4,747	432	468	0	47	67	986	34	6
Holmes	Millersburg	1,260	173	1,862	3,295	365	286	1	58	49	325	112	1
Huron	Courthouse, Norwalk	2,456	286	3,939	6,681	562	71	14	52	150	2,233	606	158
Jackson	213½ Broadway, Jackson	1,796	242	3,139	5,177	614	692	39	58	99	888	38	5
Jefferson No. 1	Courthouse, Steubenville	4,069	344	5,875	10,288	929	624	30	59	325	1,413	4	52
Jefferson No. 2	do	3,805	375	6,487	10,667	855	608	131	68	207	1,279	73	17
Knox	Strible Building, Mount Vernon	2,162	235	3,454	5,851	566	547	61	41	124	1,266	149	9
Lake	Courthouse, Painesville	2,247	227	3,510	5,984	444	838	17	76	18	1,442	64	40
Lawrence	Fourth and Center Streets, Ironton	2,920	362	4,397	7,679	1,128	1,237	33	134	60	1,164	26	7
Licking	Municipal Building, Granville	2,010	253	3,183	5,446	725	548	13	77	79	2,295	231	0
Lima	Memorial Hall	4,134	380	5,513	10,057	1,092	885	42	130	34	1,204	1	138
Logan	Bellefontaine	2,142	240	3,267	5,649	549	29	46	23	147	1,207	184	23
Lorain	239 Century Building, Lorain	4,208	396	7,351	11,955	889	656	17	129	113	1,977	5	102
Lorain	902 Lorain County Bank Building, Elyria	4,831	456	6,741	12,028	1,205	951	4	102	273	1,440	368	174
Lucas	624 Segur Avenue, Toledo	2,585	267	3,837	6,689	652	526	3	233	137	781	174	34
Madison	Courthouse, London	1,490	168	2,305	3,963	365	314	12	24	28	1,509	16	0
Mahoning	Fourth floor, Courthouse, Youngstown	6,700	501	9,705	16,906	1,124	689	38	99	184	168	130	17
Marion	131½ West Center Street, Marion	3,728	385	5,122	9,235	928	1,008	29	58	117	2,185	108	44
Medina	Wadsworth	2,142	219	3,063	5,424	520	491	15	26	101	491	357	20
Meigs	Courthouse, Pomeroy	1,841	231	3,049	5,121	600	488	12	60	23	1,052	21	6
Mercer	Courthouse, Celina	2,312	280	2,843	5,435	651	827	14	63	9	1,064	197	7
Miami	City Building, Troy	2,609	499	5,944	9,052	879	659	25	112	324	1,065	213	68
Monroe	Monroe Bank Building, Woodsfield	1,458	206	2,303	3,966	617	533		16	149	670	71	4

County / City	Location	1	2	3	4	5	6	7	8	9	10	11	12
Montgomery	203 Federal Building, Dayton	3,663	424	6,331	10,618	902	867	20	53	215	2,207	353	71
Morgan	McConnelsville	983	132	1,577	2,692	334	330	6	43	28	538	63	2
Morrow	Courthouse, Mount Gilead	1,170	150	1,723	3,043	332	241	5	28	54	679	153	3
Muskingum No. 1	Courthouse, Zanesville	2,321	265	3,698	6,284	515	688		35	78	1,391	10	44
Muskingum No. 2	do	2,207	237	3,706	6,496	671	381	13	75	57	1,053	0	11
NEWARK	Second floor, Courthouse, Newark	2,534	256	2,079	5,705	711	500	123	57	1,246	1,246	9	11
Noble	I. O. O. F. Building, Caldwell	1,282	135	3,068	3,328	431	343	6	27	17	660	49	2
Ottawa	Port Clinton	2,081	179	2,146	3,938	511	466	3	93	250	831	141	11
Paulding	Paulding	1,615	177	4,264	7,214	441	598	27	20	71	829	62	3
Perry	Citizens' State Bank Building, Somerset	2,602	348	4,264	5,012	846	818	33	75	233	1,419	88	16
Pickaway	Courthouse, Circleville	1,993	222	2,797	2,658	477	577	9	30	36	1,066	268	1
Pike	Waverly	1,011	131	1,516	7,446	338	391	0	27	44	470	7	0
Portage	111 East Main Street, Ravenna	2,785	284	4,377	4,415	831	853	24	109	84	684	92	40
Preble	Office of H. R. Gilmore, Eaton	1,606	202	2,607	5,499	332	173	4	18	98	1,005	254	12
Putnam	Ottawa	2,105	260	3,134	11,372	634	727		17	104	1,000	12	6
Richland	Mansfield	4,216	464	4,902	8,092	987	904	57	1,098	193	2,227	264	94
Ross	5 Federal Building, Chillicothe	2,843	347	4,482	7,808	818	754	17	55	110	1,590	84	416
Sandusky	Elks Block, Fremont	3,009	317	4,946	13,919	967	763	4	74	165	1,634	156	38
Scioto	Portsmouth	5,426	646	7,847	8,792	1,528	1,578	34	125	194	1,704	66	64
Seneca	Courthouse, Tiffin	3,475	371	2,839	8,150	1,196	1,063	14	62	40	2,713	139	17
Shelby	Courthouse, Sidney	2,078	233	7,802	14,367	515	612	42	30	119	1,140	341	30
SPRINGFIELD	New City Building, Springfield	6,046	519	5,746	9,491	1,891	1,496	29	173	408	2,835	5	40
Stark No. 1	City Hall, Massillon	2,306	439	5,465	9,794	758	564	43	120	330	1,443	44	112
Stark No. 2	9 City Hall, Canton	3,863	466	9,804	17,917	1,099	776	42	137		1,655	125	141
Summit	Akron	7,454	659	7,022	14,442	1,835	1,345	44	183	48	3,132	102	38
TOLEDO No. 1	40 Empire Building	6,937	483	7,461	14,464	1,682	1,491	107	162	356	2,785	4	108
TOLEDO No. 2	763 Nicholas Building	6,592	411	4,800	8,903	1,894	1,460	6	249	386	1,364	4	71
TOLEDO No. 3	408 Produce Exchange Building	3,820	283	5,945	12,067	1,105	745	38	203	224	1,863	3	52
TOLEDO No. 4	432-433 Valentine Building	5,622	500	4,058	7,883	1,507	1,397	33	143	60	2,387	2	13
TOLEDO No. 5	519 Colburn Street	3,576	249	6,568	12,624	946	893	22	61	234	1,761	1	78
TOLEDO No. 6	228 Main Street	5,637	419	7,164	11,560	923	859	17	51	108	2,518	11	186
Trumbull No. 1	Courthouse, Warren	4,007	389	6,442	10,788	911	667	14	96	28	1,623	29	3
Trumbull No. 2	15 East Park Avenue, Niles	3,948	398	4,526	7,872	1,000	787	30	96	140	1,460	44	49
Tuscarawas No. 1	Courthouse, New Philadelphia	2,979	367	3,822	6,506	824	665	10	58	191	2,068	96	63
Tuscarawas No. 2	105½ South Water Street, Uhrichsville	2,383	301	2,334	3,969	714	697	8	41	117	1,213	101	73
Union	127½ West Fifth Street, Marysville	1,467	168	3,129	5,520	401	427		26	22	846	161	2
Van Wert	Van Wert	2,162	229	1,329	2,262	301	263	16	50	46	438	5	2
Vinton	McArthur	828	105	2,837	4,910	355	401	18	41	132	976	170	64
Warren	City Building, Lebanon	1,856	217	4,726	8,319	967	781	30	76	150	1,653	172	51
Washington	Courthouse, Marietta	3,200	393	4,975	8,441	1,098	897	29	142	89	1,540	144	33
Wayne	Courthouse, Wooster	3,137	329	2,925	5,051	611	628	18	87	81	1,164	40	5
Williams	Courthouse, Bryan	1,914	212	5,523	9,736	1,024	557	29	35	161	1,761	690	26
Wood	129 Court Street, Bowling Green	3,821	392	2,172	3,759	462	411	22	29	44	1,313	23	0
Wyandot	Upper Sandusky	1,432	155	6,978	22,577	1,215	888	49	163	174	1,155	4	42
YOUNGSTOWN No. 1	Courthouse, Youngstown	5,191	408	11,844	22,253	1,660	1,532	25	128	263	2,335	8	69
YOUNGSTOWN No. 2	do	9,756	653	6,246	10,972	1,014	757	25	173	162	1,987	1	15
YOUNGSTOWN No. 3	do	4,390	336										

APPENDIX TABLE 100-A.—*Principal statistical data, by local boards*—Continued.

OKLAHOMA.

Local board.	Post-office address.	Registration. June 5, 1917.	June and August, 1918.	Sept. 12, 1918.	Total.	Induction. Accepted at camp.	Physical groups. General service.	Remediables.	Limited service.	Disqualified.	Deferments. Dependency.	Agricultural.	Industrial.
Adair	Stillwell	1,144	121	1,528	2,793	424	465	0	7	10	660	3	2
Alfalfa	Cherokee	1,455	182	1,947	3,484	550	633	5	74	89	340	12	2
Atoka	Atoka	1,720	170	2,595	4,485	547	554	5	30	159	979	10	8
Beaver	Beaver	1,067	113	1,974	3,154	394	75		8	7	19	1	
Beckham	Sayre	1,507	180	2,132	3,819	546	442	5	16	86	835	98	4
Blaine	Watonga	1,410	160	1,870	3,440	513	459	4	27	31	762	60	8
Bryan	Durant	3,269	440	4,700	8,409	1,242	1,009	26	19	157	1,862	37	1
Caddo No. 1	Anadarko	1,824	191	2,344	4,359	637	540	8	52	31	885	39	4
Caddo No. 2	Bridgeport	1,212	131	1,533	2,876	357	9		14	42	670	12	0
Canadian	Elreno	2,035	218	2,720	4,971	847	714	11	63	16	931	57	18
Carter	Ardmore	4,343	447	5,526	10,316	1,566	1,926	6	196	146	2,038	27	12
Cherokee	Tahlequah	1,607	183	2,116	3,906	631	568		12	12	916	2	2
Choctaw	Hugo	2,433	319	3,793	6,545	945	789	17	22	162	1,328	57	21
Cimarron	Boise City	309	24	559	892	115	125	2	4	7	149	3	0
Cleveland	Norman	1,596	235	2,254	4,085	579	799	5	14	101	969	20	4
Coal	Coalgate	1,609	206	2,381	4,193	662	99	4	5	31	745	4	0
Comanche	Lawton	1,925	237	2,982	5,144	798	612	2	62	129	906	21	6
Cotton	Walter	1,127	149	1,423	2,699	461	453	0	24	9	627	3	1
Craig	Vinita	1,446	158	2,283	3,885	567	429	21	20	17	733	3	103
Creek No. 1	Sapulpa	4,968	515	6,184	11,667	2,048	2,410	10	46	50	2,260	2	0
Creek No. 2	Bristow	1,871	185	2,544	4,600	764	659		16	147	1,025	0	0
Custer	Clinton	1,802	197	1,982	4,041	560	794	4	32	142	1,037	15	0
Delaware	Grove	1,086	133	1,545	2,764	392	293		14		595	33	
Dewey	Taloga	1,005	135	1,427	2,567	353	93	1	3	1	23	1	1
Ellis	Shattuck	955	110	1,394	2,461	380	314	1	3	68	480	34	0
Garfield	Enid	2,539	321	4,253	7,113	874	852	5	65	138	1,047	24	3
Garvin	101½ Paul Avenue, Pauls Valley	2,690	306	3,606	6,602	991	772	22	27	18	1,550	28	
Grady No. 1	Chickasha	1,741	167	2,489	4,397	980	781	9	26	177	1,723	92	23
Grady No. 2	do.	1,225	120	1,822	2,940	548	618		3	67	600	30	1
Grant	Medford	1,282	171	1,607	3,273	560	420		25	79	771	11	2
Greer	Mangum	1,369	147	1,607	3,123	296	287	2	12	21	415	21	27
Harmon	Hollis	950	127	1,134	2,211	258	41	1	23	150	945	30	3
Harper	Buffalo	714	74	966	1,764	660	928	0	76	21	1,318	21	8
Haskell	Stigler	1,709	173	2,405	4,242	846	505	0	83	108	1,080	8	0
Hughes	Holdenville	2,351	282	3,105	5,719	714	500		28	0	579		0
Jackson	Altus	2,064	204	2,198	4,453								
Jefferson	Waurika	1,599	191	2,133	3,982	549	491	1	33				

County	Place												
Johnston	Tishomingo	1,678	190	2,416	4,294	607	543	3	49	71	988	19	0
Kay	Newkirk	2,822	359	4,405	7,584	1,128	973	6	48	215	1,335	144	8
Kingfisher	Kingfisher	2,458	195	3,794	3,397	550	414	0	47	18	669	16	0
Kiowa	Hobart	2,065	285	2,531	3,851	781	663	1	35	44	1,004	7	10
Latimer	Wilburton	1,165	148	1,718	3,035	883	829		28	11	612	6	6
Le Flore	Poteau	3,391	398	4,846	6,635	1,116	1,079		51	171	985	8	5
Lincoln	Chandler	2,600	387	3,924	6,891	973	890	3	21	93	1,452	10	8
Logan	Guthrie	1,981	206	2,684	4,871	814	10	19	30	106	919	11	6
Love	Marietta	1,171	159	1,515	2,845	457	383		70	16	780	16	5
McClain	Purcell	1,514	180	2,175	3,869	530	438	28	19	20	843	85	8
McCurtain	Idabell	3,056	364	4,409	7,829	1,189	734	44	21	38	1,358	54	0
McIntosh	Eufaula	2,600	265	2,973	5,828	1,012	155	3	27	90	1,172	1	1
Major	Fairview	934	149	1,399	3,328	366	309		22	88	485	88	0
Marshall	Madill	1,381	166	1,801	3,292	470	13	0	49	98	688	0	5
Mayes	Mayes, Prior	1,190	157	1,945	2,496	534	473	1	31	70	496	13	0
Murray	Sulphur	976	96	1,411	2,972	415	467	8	23	74	388	1	2
Muskogee No. 1	Muskogee City	1,112	121	1,764	4,059	410	307	2	33	50	630	2	22
Muskogee No. 2	...do...	2,494	354	2,444	6,545	620	535	10	57	128	510	1	19
Muskogee	Muskogee, care of Wm. Harrower	2,455	138	3,738		1,132	35	39		123	1,117	26	2
Noble	Perry	1,106	151	1,626	2,870	565	568	6	33	58	790	20	7
Nowata	Nowata	1,665	261	2,047	3,863	586	661	23	56	116	1,121	21	10
Okfuskee	Okemah	1,977	147	3,034	5,272	666	686	8	46	111	741	0	8
Oklahoma Cry No. 1	Oklahoma City	1,917	293	2,955	5,019	706	1,234	7	105	34	1,276	4	12
Oklahoma Cry No. 2	...do...	3,277	205	4,749	8,319	1,273	33	11	102	200	1,157	1	8
Oklahoma Cry No. 3	City Hall, Oklahoma City	2,528	85	3,843	6,576	787	256	0	28	17	375	9	2
Oklahoma No. 1	Choctaw	867	110	2,250	2,207	378	256	2	30	60	441	40	1
Oklahoma No. 2	Okmulgee	850	477	1,290	2,250	319	966	1	65	49	2,425	11	11
Okmulgee	Pawhuska	4,768	293	6,898	13,143	1,784	1,510	19	78	127	2,163	11	3
Osage	Miami	3,602	415	4,313	7,465	1,151	1,137	18	58	3	1,339	43	14
Ottawa	Pawnee	1,995	221	5,657	9,874	1,360	969	17	27	99	935	24	3
Pawnee	Stillwater	2,374	315	2,374	4,590	724	937	7	35	148	333	0	0
Payne	McAlester	2,923	223	3,829	7,067	749	618	12	43	130	1,232	17	17
Pittsburg No. 1	Hartshorne	2,222	205	3,502	5,947	649	563	14	48	82	1,075	23	23
Pittsburg No. 2	Ada	1,983	360	2,843	5,031	927	987	32	28	62	1,455	3	1
Pontotoc	Shawnee	2,688	374	3,701	8,825	1,099	846		72	45	2,074	1	9
Pottawatomie	Antlers	3,460	157	4,991	3,450	562	113	5	15	12	637	0	0
Pushmataha	Cheyenne	1,347	99	1,946	2,192	362	267	0	32	35	536	50	0
Roger Mills	Claremore	863	206	1,230	2,111	738	680	0	78	52	1,010	2	10
Rogers	Seminole	2,284	234	2,752	2,752	715	634	2	24	33	1,145	10	0
Seminole	Sallisaw	2,083	271	2,923	5,309	863	45	8	79	93	1,152	9	9
Sequoyah	Duncan	2,115	242	2,766	5,322	742	973		16	28	1,324	1	1
Stephens	Guymon	2,314	143	1,824	3,056	346	82		9	7	568	29	2
Texas	Frederick	1,089	182	2,090	3,965	563	439	5	247	68	954	59	2
Tillman	Tulsa, Care of J. H. Simmons	1,693	701	5,393	16,753	2,878	2,025	28	66	274	2,779	28	63
TULSA	...do...	3,589	378	9,785	9,785	1,053	998	3	71	132	2,066	12	17
Tulsa	Wagoner	1,544	221	2,238	4,003	678	525	10	61	185	697	61	2
Wagoner	Bartlesville	2,826	271	3,713	6,940	1,091	828	7	91	129	1,342	28	8
Washington	Cordell	2,032	243	2,355	4,630	719	601	3	92	45	1,186	3	0
Washita	Alva	1,342	152	1,848	3,342	548	564	5	17	100	598	2	3
Woods	Woodward	1,191	148	1,662	3,001	585	390	1	24	47	618	14	1

APPENDIX TABLE 100-A.—*Principal statistical data, by local boards—Continued.*

OREGON.

Local board.	Post-office address.	Registration. June 5, 1917.	Registration. June and August, 1918.	Registration. Sept. 12, 1918.	Registration. Total.	Induction. Accepted at camp.	Physical groups. General service.	Physical groups. Removables.	Physical groups. Limited service.	Disqualified.	Deferments. Dependency.	Deferments. Agricultural.	Deferments. Industrial.
Baker	Baker	1,636	134	2,542	4,312	484	85		26	3	6	2	21
Benton	Corvallis	1,102	96	1,363	2,561	331	230	4	52	42	468	88	15
Clackamas	Oregon City	2,665	236	4,213	7,114	762	674	18	118	144	1,079	107	27
Clatsop	Astoria	2,467	205	4,903	7,575	705	877		193	123	593	16	33
Columbia	St. Helens	1,251	106	2,306	3,663	367	321	2	95	88	407	25	197
Coos	Coquille	1,995	226	3,396	5,587	542	538	8	92	179	756	63	1
Crook	Prineville	432	32	612	1,076	147	174	2	14	6	138	26	1
Curry	Gold Beach	303	29	504	836	92	101		10	9	79	3	
Deschutes	Bend	825	51	1,400	2,276	249	182		62	92	288	24	42
Douglas	Roseburg	1,634	156	2,279	4,069	496	494	44	63	20	738	87	45
Gilliam	Condon	518	46	587	1,151	168	140	17	14	41	83	63	9
Grant	Canyon City	630	40	854	1,524	178	205	92	31	12	102	17	3
Harney	Burns	654	39	713	1,406	206	156	0	31	45	225	42	0
Hood River	Hood River	617	33	984	1,634	133	125	0	40	15	208	12	4
Jackson	Jacksonville	1,569	130	2,294	3,993	489	50	22	40	133	462	110	27
Jefferson	Madras	405	19	498	922	111	118		29	34	161	13	1
Josephine	Grants Pass	612	46	922	1,580	174	160	5	7	29	247	21	11
Klamath	Klamath Falls	1,277	99	2,050	3,426	350	523	9	21	85	235	19	9
Lake	Lakeview	710	31	623	1,364	205	176	8	32	38	185	74	5
Lane	Eugene	2,696	243	3,704	6,633	726	674		18	102	984	84	66
Lincoln	Toledo	392	34	799	1,225	133		9	90				34
Linn	Albany	1,841	205	2,576	4,622	514	526		88	67	919	127	6
Malheur	Vale	1,243	98	1,661	3,002	421	379	32	63	25	415	51	22
Marion No. 1	Salem	1,906	174	2,885	5,055	569	514	19	85	209	833	75	6
Marion No. 2	Woodburn	1,076	95	1,636	2,807	303	274	30	47	87	414	93	3
Morrow	Heppner	626	48	836	1,510	186	203	14	21	29	205	115	8
Multnomah	325 Courthouse, Portland	1,233	93	2,233	3,559	316	315	1	60	72	443	49	44
Polk	Dallas	1,197	102	1,622	2,921	325	309	7	29	107	510	71	29
PORTLAND No. 1	359 Morgan Building	2,744	282	6,600	9,716	611	637	9	115	39	493	1	44
PORTLAND No. 2	414 Pittock Block	2,930	261	6,398	9,589	794	859	25	248	183	573	3	13
PORTLAND No. 3	405 Corbett Building	1,862	221	3,802	5,885	515	526	44	102	201	923	2	28
PORTLAND No. 4	408 Stevens Building	1,963	168	4,151	6,282	366	365	36	70	77	1,117	9	2
PORTLAND No. 5	522 Selling Building	1,020	152	3,006	6,676	488	482	15	84	135	994	1	31
PORTLAND No. 6	406 Stevens Building	2,071	215	3,990	6,675	557	385	5	267	144	852	2	13
PORTLAND No. 7	Courthouse	1,555	99	3,989	5,514	431	217	18	74	104	830	3	28
PORTLAND No. 8	...do...	1,555	175	3,112	4,942	387	284	1	97	119	749	5	10
PORTLAND No. 9	406 Stevens Building	1,298	57	1,448	2,783	195	214		63	26	464	1	

PORTLAND No. 10 — 1084 Jersey Street	35	2	973	110	116	20	579	476	7,143	4,827	241	2,075
Sherman — Moro	0	28	184	28	15	3	131	156	1,075	593	31	451
Tillamook — Tillamook	25	39	294	8	53	8	194	237	1,938	1,176	68	744
Umatilla — Clerk's Office, Pendleton	6	112	622	55	33	7	457	598	6,149	3,552	196	2,401
Union — La Grande	26	81	525	41	41	9	401	492	3,827	2,155	124	1,518
Wallowa — Enterprise	6	92	456	14	53	7	354	328	2,685	1,507	70	1,108
Wasco — The Dalles	15	101	449	20	73	7	393	324	3,000	1,718	96	1,186
Washington — Hillsboro	0	137	851	81	124	33	566	599	4,949	2,837	178	1,934
Wheeler — Fossil	7	38	123	24	16	11	116	112	778	392	35	351
Yamhill — McMinnville		123	626	157	76	11	356	391	3,696	2,079	130	1,467

PENNSYLVANIA.

Adams — Law Library, Courthouse, Gettysburg	35	222	1,477	201	125	18	510	567	6,374	3,628	313	2,433
Allegheny 5. 1 — Public Safety Building, Coraopolis	62	48	275	115	19	8	407	695	7,864	4,547	238	3,081
Allegheny No. 2 — Municipal Building, Chartars Avenue, McKeesport.	201	1	753	91	13	11	833	729	8,099	4,627	232	3,240
Allegheny No. 3 — Bridgeville	141	73	726	73	44	26	523	707	6,961	4,178	236	2,547
Allegheny No. 4 — High School Building, Carnegie	294	14	1,361	76	87	11	842	1,000	8,958	5,094	295	3,569
Allegheny No. 5 — Municipal Building, Carrick	62	4	1,248	95	101	0	931	891	8,416	4,978	305	3,133
Allegheny N6. — 808 Sarah Street, West Homestead	232	28	1,077	133	26	2	578	492	7,360	4,284	296	2,780
Allegheny No. 7 — Municipal Building, Homestead	477	2	1,145	148	36	25	529	790	9,422	4,920	325	4,177
Allegheny No. 8 — City Hall, Duquesne	365	1	999	62			661	967	10,677	4,034	385	4,328
Allegheny No. 9 — Glassport Trust Building, Glassport	45	5	877	63	37	12	609	674	7,275	4,034	253	2,988
Allegheny No. 10 — Relief Department Building, W. A. B. Co., Wilmerding.	199	15	1,065	136	57	3	802	867	8,663	5,123	322	3,218
Allegheny No. 11 — 711 Linden Avenue, East Pittsburgh	42	3	1,419	235	47	13	1,994	1,041	10,615	5,736	454	4,425
Allegheny No. 12 — Room 6, second floor, Municipal Building, Braddock.	13	0	951	2	44	32	1,053	857	10,084	5,325	303	4,456
Allegheny No. 13 — 511 Penwood Avenue, Wilkinsburg	418	3	1,537	106	82	62	931	938	8,910	4,902	344	3,664
Allegheny No. 14 — Town Hall, Swissvale	214	33	1,081	187	59	6	631	656	6,532	3,721	194	2,617
Allegheny No. 15 — Borough Building, Tarentum	125	20	1,431	134	37	4	598	817	8,865	4,847	284	3,734
Allegheny No. 16 — 1027 North Canal Street, Sharpsburg	245	69	1,178	176	124	0	799	1,035	9,439	5,351	337	3,751
Allegheny No. 17 — Second Ward Public School Building, Millvale	122	123	1,252	86	33	7	772	793	6,792	3,759	268	2,765
Allegheny No. 18 — Borough Hall, Avalon	122	6	1,002	122	56	18	481	763	6,839	4,223	225	2,391
ALLENTOWN No. 1 — Courthouse, Fifth and Hamilton Street, Allentown.	277	4	1,507	240	141	75	710	726	9,946	5,277	351	4,318
ALLENTOWN No. 2 — New Courthouse, third floor, Allentown	173	2	1,716	165	79	20	690	743	7,412	4,042	285	3,085
ALTOONA No. 1 — Federal Building, Chestnut and Eleventh Streets.	73	3	1,315	143	58	5	559	587	6,373	3,662	222	2,489
ALTOONA No. 2 — 802 Twelfth Street	80	1	1,587	206	62	11	572	633	7,082	3,963	228	2,871
Armstrong No. 1 — Wick Theater Building, Kittanning	25	159	1,383	126	16	0	701	784	8,648	4,975	333	3,340
Armstrong No. 2 — Courthouse, Kittanning	66	117	1,251	212	21	13	741	915	8,910	5,149	380	3,381
Beaver No. 1 — Leaf Building, Rochester	139	46	823	200	87	2	535	1,101	12,263	6,686	393	5,184
Beaver No. 2 — Care of W. H. Boyce, New Brighton	229	62	1,585	124	80	28	500	979	11,193	6,044	355	4,794
Beaver No. 3 — Municipal Building, Woodlawn	161	80	1,041	78	19	14	583	767	10,613	5,410	216	4,957
Bedford — Room 3, Ridenour Block, Bedford	72	309	1,521	193	96	23	584	606	7,315	4,174	325	2,816
Berks No. 1 — Fleetwood	54	201	1,239	188	71	43	734	642	6,457	3,720	211	2,486
Berks No. 2 — Birdsboro	58	195	1,370	284	154	16	729	713	6,897	3,911	322	2,634
Berks No. 3 — Wyomissing	17	222	1,159	184	49	5	421	465	5,461	3,231	228	1,992

APPENDIX TABLE 100-A.—Principal statistical data, by local boards—Continued.

PENNSYLVANIA—Continued.

Local board	Post-office address	Registration				Induction	Physical groups				Deferments		
		June 5, 1917	June and August, 1918	Sept. 12, 1918	Total	Accepted at camp	General service	Remediables	Limited service	Disqualified	Dependency	Agricultural	Industrial
Blair No. 1	324½ Allegheny Street, Hollidaysburg	2,617	259	3,431	6,307	649	615	17	91	2	934	112	38
Blair No. 2	Municipal Building, Tyrone	2,957	232	4,537	7,786	685	561	1	81	91	785	22	68
Bradford No. 1	Sheriff's office, Towanda	1,968	203	3,046	5,217	427	352	19	80	118	1,171	171	22
Bradford No. 2	Towanda	2,014	199	3,157	5,370	781	338	25	144	99	1,003	182	78
Bucks No. 1	Post Office Building, Bristol	2,699	271	4,790	7,760	479	469		200	6	659	116	74
Bucks No. 2	Doylestown	1,678	168	2,534	4,380	357	224	13	53	166	749	299	23
Bucks No. 3	Perkasie	1,850	209	2,814	4,873	411	184	7	103	93	876	94	25
Butler No. 1	County Courthouse, Butler	3,498	304	4,774	8,576	801	694	10	90	17	1,330	10	231
Butler No. 2	Courthouse, Butler	1,713	218	2,688	4,619	577	407	16	40	153	732	161	57
Butler No. 3	do.	1,851	213	2,713	4,777	492	354	23	25	68	759	206	100
Cambria No. 1	Y. M. C. A. Building, Johnstown	3,695	318	5,289	9,202	804	863	1	60	24	1,177	41	92
Cambria No. 2	510 Railroad Street, South Fork	2,977	304	4,738	8,019	738	651	3	56	169	1,180	8	146
Cambria No. 3	Ebensburg	2,436	267	4,768	8,471	894	660	4	103	86	816	113	137
Cambria No. 4	Barnesboro	3,153	209	3,369	5,735	590	459	15	45	200	814	64	26
Cameron No. 1	Emporium	914	92	1,296	2,302	238	233	10	20	91	310	2	55
Carbon No. 1	Room 27, Navigation Building, Mauch Chunk	2,852	216	3,812	6,880	622	490	10	56	134	861	14	99
Carbon No. 2	178 South First Street, Lehighton	3,077	283	4,225	7,585	557	598	18	97	209	1,108	46	105
Center	Bellefonte	3,199	385	4,832	8,416	829	917	0	78	239	1,504	161	62
Chester No. 1	City Hall	3,559	404	5,076	9,725	821	474	46	42	338	113	4	316
Chester No. 2	do.	4,176	450	5,301	9,881	707	291	8	89	324	937	212	201
Chester No. 3	Wyebrooke	2,949	239	4,262	7,450	417	369	23	61	126	1,183	571	94
Chester No. 4	Courthouse, Westchester	3,575	349	4,713	8,637	686	567	10	132	167	1,531	816	210
Chester No. 5	Masonic Building, Oxford	4,625	500	6,235	11,360	723	760	10	67	104	1,038	198	700
Clarion	Clarion	2,619	363	4,089	7,071	859	823	14	50	133	992	44	135
Clearfield No. 1	Murray Building, Clearfield	2,827	310	4,162	7,229	801	731	23	157	102	1,371	90	59
Clearfield No. 2	Dubois	2,068	286	4,015	6,969	702	196	16	63	152	1,286	59	131
Clearfield No. 3	Houtzdale	3,180	302	4,000	7,542	721	850	5	143	89	1,353	59	69
Clinton	Lock Haven	2,836	288	3,706	6,890	763	687	26	19	247	1,347	34	76
Columbia No. 1	Courthouse, Bloomsburg	1,834	265	2,737	4,776	470	472	22	87	158	982	66	90
Columbia No. 2	100A Market Street, Berwick	2,103	229	3,182	5,514	522	386	19	92	142	124	233	33
Crawford No. 1	Titusville	1,940	249	2,971	5,160	471	384	26	50	96	561	30	75
Crawford No. 2	Courthouse, Meadville	3,411	273	3,094	7,068	631	2,612	15	25	73	761	126	15
Cumberland No. 1	Courthouse, Carlisle	2,240	231	3,430	5,907	461	461	4	32	278	1,359	157	98
Cumberland No. 2	Kronenberg Building, Carlisle	2,223	347	2,874	5,097	448	596	28	45	77	1,162	29	57
Dauphin No. 1	49 Front Street, Steelton	2,273	265	2,874	7,501	786	463		64	166	1,149	2	97
Dauphin No. 2	Dauphin Building, Harrisburg	2,076	205	2,350	6,392	524	596	22	64	130	1,355	55	3
Dauphin No. 3	Elizabethtown	1,676	184	2,360	4,280	240	313	15	62	153			84

		128	30	913	161	90	2	334	486	5,580	3,344	192	2,044
Delaware No. 1	Haverford Township Building, Upper Darby. Branch	162	25	1,078	173	132	23	543	504	7,394	4,688	224	2,482
Delaware No. 2	Borough Hall, Swarthmore	210	24	548	160	127	3	361	650	8,081	4,980	239	2,812
Delaware No. 3	Borough Hall, Ridley Park	109	91	1,154	94	61	150	585	580	8,680	3,820	226	2,635
Delaware No. 4	Courthouse, Media	253	2	864	47	194	13	980	940	8,740	4,753	321	3,066
Easton	City Hall, Easton	178	68	1,108	85	80	19	635	632	8,515	4,774	358	3,353
Elk	Ridgway	340	4	1,669	137	180	22	1,004	1,268	10,795	5,987	301	3,417
Erie No. 1	Post Office Building	400	10	1,107	362	104	18	672	827	9,846	5,921	414	3,511
Erie No. 2	907 Marine Bank Building	419	9	1,759	119	82		610	728	8,452	4,867	424	3,161
Erie No. 3	Washington School, Twenty-first and Sassafras Streets	83	272	896	64	56	29	293	430	5,665	3,316	223	2,116
Erie No. 1	City Building, Union City	109	181	1,035	290	58	14	227	440	6,776	4,316	237	2,223
Erie No. 2	Culbertson Block, Girard	74	7	1,149	187	42	0	988	942	8,373	4,753	327	3,263
Fayette No. 1	Uniontown	225	30	459	17	76	16	647	881	8,818	3,825	299	2,694
Fayette No. 2	State Armory, Connellsville	111	81	899	4	84	8	1,018	664	7,727	3,431	237	3,059
Fayette No. 3	61 Market Street, Brownsville	106	25	800	92	25	3	427	412	7,099	3,658	205	2,336
Fayette No. 4	Devlin Building, Point Marion	214	79	699	95	35	0	561	600	5,226	2,949	232	2,045
Fayette No. 5	409 Title & Trust Building, Connellsville	76	35	612	85	41	3	463	541	7,227	4,256	185	2,788
Fayette No. 6	Welfare Hall, Republic	107	8	592	39	5	0	406	371	5,756	3,336	137	2,313
Fayette No. 7	McClellandtown	20	24	280	31	19	30	99	185	1,555	869	74	612
Forest	Tionesta	94	155	1,338	38	90	20	450	568	6,337	3,074	301	2,302
Franklin No. 1	Greencastle	19	55	1,263	274	85	7	283	458	5,409	3,128	246	2,125
Franklin No. 2	Courthouse, Chambersburg	3	109	321	29	40	1	154	181	1,741	980	89	672
Fulton	McConnellsburg	38	213	1,010	133	32	37	534	671	6,370	3,968	273	2,129
Greene	Waynesburg	79	3	468	135	44	17	146	483	4,338	2,519	172	1,695
Harrisburg No. 1	Room A. Courthouse	189	2	1,572	131	58	8	599	680	7,110	4,035	281	2,774
Harrisburg No. 2	Crescent and Mulberry Streets	111	1	1,492	173	87	44	439	507	6,970	4,092	308	2,570
Harrisburg No. 3	222 Market Street	102	224	1,550	273	117	36	496	725	8,828	5,029	349	3,430
Huntingdon	Courthouse, Huntingdon	90	139	1,274	117	112	25	651	884	7,459	4,466	271	2,732
Indiana No. 1	Indiana	83	65	513	125	63	2	574	837	11,363	6,676	359	4,128
Indiana No. 2	Sheriff's Office, Indiana	44	142	1,173	176	33	21	725	645	6,606	3,849	272	2,141
Jefferson No. 1	Brookville	65	77	1,148	95	108	16	633	645	6,833	3,412	280	2,141
Jefferson No. 2	Municipal Building, Punxsutawney	156	9	762	132	93	8	1,309	1,121	9,236	4,936	374	3,926
JOHNSTOWN No. 1	425 Lincoln Street	75	0	810	158	45	0	502	633	8,705	4,057	202	3,786
JOHNSTOWN No. 2	Engine House No. 5, Fairfield Avenue	13	182	540	62	56	6	168	264	2,042	1,496	125	1,041
Juniata	Mifflintown	133	36	1,169	296	68	23	558	614	5,973	3,166	210	2,597
Lackawanna No. 1	Moscow	143	17	727	29	138	4	418	520	6,106	3,516	191	2,399
Lackawanna No. 2	965 Main Street, Dickson City	204	5	802	10	122	26	423	547	6,440	3,598	270	2,572
Lackawanna No. 3	Archbald	134	18	949	80	83	6	554	595	5,979	3,360	244	2,929
Lackawanna No. 4	49 Main Street, Carbondale	85	31	993	56	78	1	525	555	7,406	4,234	243	2,015
Lackawanna No. 5	Borough Hall, Taylor	92	8	1,011	185	42	10	353	399	5,088	2,895	178	2,089
LANCASTER No. 1	City Hall, Lancaster	86	4	1,084	152	84	4	494	444	5,245	2,956	200	2,299
LANCASTER No. 2	Courthouse, Lancaster	81	244	1,339	76	119	26	170	392	5,987	3,433	265	2,353
Lancaster No. 2	Sheriff's Office, Lancaster	74	297	1,405	179	10	6	362	427	5,955	3,321	281	2,331
Lancaster No. 3	Ephrata	64	685	1,346	157	45	10	138	309	5,901	3,272	298	2,055
Lancaster No. 4	Christiana	138	314	963	60	99	4	243	409	5,281	3,024	202	4,352
Lawrence	39 North Duke Street, Lancaster	150	97	1,624	47	89	30	659	811	10,667	5,930	385	2,586
Lebanon No. 1	304 Mercantile Building, Newcastle	88	207	1,406	238	64	14	512	622	7,140	4,266	288	2,674
Lebanon No. 2	Courthouse, Lebanon	39	44	1,420	33	132	22	300	444	6,342	5,137	251	2,820
Lehigh No. 1	North Railroad Street, Annville	135	151	1,681	250	71	4	483	813	9,254	3,957	311	3,622
Lehigh No. 2	Courthouse, Allentown	68		1,454	60		0	373	542	6,907		328	2,622
	do												

APPENDIX TABLE 100-A.—*Principal statistical data, by local boards*—Continued.

PENNSYLVANIA—Continued.

Local board.	Post-office address.	Registration: June 5, 1917.	Registration: June and August, 1918.	Registration: Sept. 12, 1918.	Registration: Total.	Induction: Accepted at camp.	Physical groups: General service.	Physical groups: Remediables.	Physical groups: Limited service.	Physical groups: Disqualified.	Deferments: Dependency.	Deferments: Agricultural.	Deferments: Industrial.
Luzerne No. 1	Old First National Bank Building, Pittston	2,496	199	3,693	6,388	572	535	34	140	19	870	5	245
Luzerne No. 2	Post Office Building, Pittston	2,755	220	3,699	6,674	581	606	40	131	12	1,143	31	206
Luzerne No. 3	Town Hall, Plains	3,131	196	3,810	7,137	755	716	30	27	143	1,042	4	224
Luzerne No. 4	Edward's Hall, Kingston	2,803	241	3,894	6,938	602	559	24	42	248	204	8	128
Luzerne No. 5	Dallas	1,449	130	2,093	3,672	325	294	18	56	64	662	31	42
Luzerne No. 6	State Armory, Plymouth	2,178	215	2,934	5,327	644	493	9	178	97	799	4	184
Luzerne No. 7	Shickshinny	1,521	171	2,267	3,959	282	249	7	41	113	500	14	4
Luzerne No. 8	Town Hall, Ashley	2,479	205	3,374	6,058	551	668	16	106	125	868	10	261
Luzerne No. 9	137 State Street, Nanticoke	2,957	226	3,958	7,141	686	595	18	46	198	1,115	3	169
Luzerne No. 10	Municipal Building, Freeland	2,521	201	3,134	5,856	618	694	17	51	120	778	11	135
Luzerne No. 11	Room 4, City Hall, Hazleton	3,112	383	4,581	8,086	795	669	16	112	219	1,611	1	171
Lycoming No. 1	Courthouse, Williamsport	1,811	180	2,688	4,679	398	335	8	55	194	906	62	36
Lycoming No. 2	Montoursville	1,790	183	2,652	4,625	472	636	13	93	97	827	137	28
McKean No. 1	21 Main Street, Bradford	1,850	193	2,847	4,890	519	528	39	48	160	873	50	87
McKean No. 2	Smethport	2,321	223	3,384	5,928	574	590	11	57	107	854	0	0
McKeesport No. 1	704 Peoples Bank Building	3,721	327	4,768	8,816	917	630	15	80	50	1,275	1	163
McKeesport No. 2	706 Peoples Bank Building	2,069	213	3,014	5,296	637	566	15	35	45	949	1	152
Mercer No. 1	Mercer	1,698	220	2,011	3,929	468	371		27	64	802	219	78
Mercer No. 2	Main and Water Streets, Greenville	4,225	399	6,516	11,140	1,150	799	33	92	157	1,560	41	176
Mercer No. 3	City Building, Farrell	4,557	311	5,842	10,710	681	466	9	19	38	967	69	72
Mifflin	Courthouse, Lewiston	2,940	338	4,656	7,934	501	645	3	59	101	1,083	3	0
Monroe	Stroudsburg	1,829	224	2,784	4,837	426	395	21	182	100	948	111	44
Montgomery No. 1	Merion Title & Trust Building, Ardmore	3,227	253	4,408	7,888	928	456	14	66	259	1,162	28	66
Montgomery No. 2	Willow Grove	2,778	212	4,000	6,990	866	509	1	125	199	783	73	107
Montgomery No. 3	Room 55, Boyer Arcade, Norristown	2,984	268	3,754	7,006	685	585	14	151	91	1,181	107	145
Montgomery No. 4	Tremont House, Lansdale	2,389	237	3,388	6,014	516	243	14	44	188	1,258	249	79
Montgomery No. 5	Y. M. C. A. Building, Pottstown	2,784	282	3,688	6,754	626	301	6	94	56	1,445	96	155
Montour	Courthouse, Danville	947	115	1,409	2,471	270	243	7	22	71	467	54	10
NEWCASTLE	City Building, Newcastle	5,117	406	6,948	12,471	1,014	684	37	68	20	266	1	493
NORRISTOWN	City Hall, Norristown	2,068	240	3,334	6,442	583	457	35	206	180	1,198	7	191
Northampton No. 1	35 Broadway, Bangor	1,012	198	2,881	4,901	575	372	8	56	156	911	103	80
Northampton No. 2	Nazareth	2,306	190	3,478	5,974	547	388	26	136	76	641	17	28
Northampton No. 3	South Bethlehem	8,012	539	9,853	18,404	780	542	35	80	176	1,525	26	343
Northampton No. 4	North Catasauqua	2,098	310	4,028	7,306	664	407	22	102	116	1,222	58	247
Northumberland No. 1	Milton	2,111	238	2,881	5,230	467	408	9	68	173	249	110	89
Northumberland No. 2	Courthouse, Sunbury	2,112	338	3,158	5,498	594	329	9	68	68	1,009	46	24
Northumberland No. 3	High School Building, Shamokin	3,115	356	4,233	7,674	910	1,113	37	262	90	456	2	103

Northumberland No. 4	High School Building, Mount Carmel	2,544	256	3,514	6,314	616	457	59	131	116	1,015	3	283
Perry	New Bloomfield	1,810	194	2,366	4,370	419	504	9	160	231	848	153	39
PHILADELPHIA No. 1	1507 East Moyamensing Street	5,060	448	6,003	11,511	1,629	1,386	49	752	78	1,150	2	15
PHILADELPHIA No. 2	Northwest corner Seventh and Carpenter Streets	4,537	361	5,341	10,239	628	1,388	90	248	449	1,864	7	65
PHILADELPHIA No. 3	Second District Police Station, Second and Glen Streets	3,099	233	3,428	6,760	1,067	777	64	128	115	1,016	0	14
*PHILADELPHIA No. 4	511 South Broad Street	3,279	223	4,598	8,100	659	776	47	192	60	1,188	7	37
PHILADELPHIA No. 5	323 Race Street	5,199	899	14,783	20,881	1,798	580	47	110	300	747	2	25
PHILADELPHIA No. 6	511 South Broad Street	3,349	252	5,240	8,841	971	653	23	112	211	515	0	132
PHILADELPHIA No. 7	253 North Fifteenth Street	4,993	377	7,313	12,663	1,108	920	49	166	275	1,813	3	60
PHILADELPHIA No. 8	1012 Buttonwood Street	4,686	384	6,270	11,340	1,283	1,309	25	218	172	1,247	1	178
PHILADELPHIA No. 9	Southeast near Twentieth and Buttonwood Streets	3,408	285	4,253	7,946	606	650	15	64	207	840	0	12
PHILADELPHIA No. 10	1417 North Front Street	3,150	266	3,409	6,825	540	730	26	82	232	1,071	5	273
PHILADELPHIA No. 11	615 East Girard Street	4,415	413	6,100	10,928	1,231	137	48	142	364	1,392	2	99
PHILADELPHIA No. 12	Front and Diamond Streets	5,267	527	6,926	12,720	1,436	1,094	83	454	6	1,790	3	70
PHILADELPHIA No. 13	1429 North Eighth Street	3,490	269	4,433	8,192	838	685	4	266	201	1,511	7	136
PHILADELPHIA No. 15	4215 Manayunk Avenue / Police Station, Highland Avenue and Shawnee Street	1,588	107	2,556	4,251	543	443	37	65	154	637	1	22
PHILADELPHIA No. 16	43 West Hanes Street, Germantown	2,949	257	3,852	7,058	783	566	31	174	207	295	5	78
PHILADELPHIA No. 17	25 West Pennsylvania Street, Germantown	2,026	173	3,040	5,239	650	325	28	118	10	727	1	110
PHILADELPHIA No. 18	Fifteenth District Police Station, Paul and Ruan Streets	3,768	318	4,886	8,972	1,004	805	16	209	99	1,698	0	98
PHILADELPHIA No. 19	Thirty-ninth and Lancaster Avenue	2,761	243	3,837	6,841	791	604	20	206	15	405	1	80
PHILADELPHIA No. 20	Thirty-ninth and Spring Garden Streets	2,728	273	3,835	6,836	769	550	24	103	268	1,116	10	100
PHILADELPHIA No. 21	Twenty-fourth District Police Station	4,756	462	5,965	11,183	1,251	1,099	109	119	390	2,190	2	403
PHILADELPHIA No. 22	Northwest corner Fifteenth Street and Snyder Avenue	6,506	626	8,274	15,406	1,668	1,631	113	453	21	2,816	7	129
PHILADELPHIA No. 23	3214 Woodland Avenue	2,169	198	3,027	5,394	563	340	4	131	301	546	0	66
PHILADELPHIA No. 24	1428 West Dauphin Street	1,918	183	2,682	4,785	558	500	2	122	117	898	2	34
PHILADELPHIA No. 25	Thirty-first District Police Station, Twenty-sixth and York Streets	2,751	256	3,910	6,917	812	808	37	229	131	1,295	4	79
PHILADELPHIA No. 26	Twenty-eighth and Oxford Streets	3,015	284	3,989	7,288	795	553	28	140	190	1,268	5	64
PHILADELPHIA No. 27	1923 Fitzwater Street	3,829	326	5,231	9,386	1,420	1,315	85	247	249	1,055	3	55
PHILADELPHIA No. 28	Parish House, East Cumberland and Collins Streets	2,650	266	3,421	6,347	837	667	27	191	73	891	1	27
PHILADELPHIA No. 29	1900 North Twentieth Street	3,834	386	5,541	9,761	1,047	882	13	318	141	1,216	0	51
PHILADELPHIA No. 30	539 East Allegheny Avenue	2,932	278	4,119	7,329	655	520	24	178	197	1,567	1	50
PHILADELPHIA No. 31	Bonderot School, D Street and Indiana Avenue	3,166	285	4,013	7,464	738	495	23	255	193	1,453	0	30
PHILADELPHIA No. 32	1145 North Sixty-third Street	2,751	234	4,563	7,548	810	693	2	216	26	1,457	0	31
PHILADELPHIA No. 33	Southeast corner Sixtieth and Market Streets, second floor	3,405	283	4,981	8,669	982	657	20	221	150	1,739	0	2
PHILADELPHIA No. 34	Longshore and State Road, Tacony	2,755	212	8,947	6,914	666	503	97	129	193	198	52	7
PHILADELPHIA No. 35	1210 South Twentieth Street	5,462	528	7,325	13,315	1,801	1,733	15	177	297	2,059	1	163
PHILADELPHIA No. 36	Twenty-second District Police Station, Park and Lehigh Avenues	2,019	99	2,853	5,071	600	395	7	48	79	763	2	40
PHILADELPHIA No. 37	Twenty-second and Hunting Park Avenue	5,409	382	6,770	5,409	1,310	1,238	39	328	244	2,086	5	265
PHILADELPHIA No. 38	do.	2,154	161	2,666	4,981	502	383	45	120	50	1,172	1	54
PHILADELPHIA No. 39	Southwest corner Fourth Street and Snyder Avenue	3,264	266	3,835	7,365	807	748		152	243	707	2	50

*Philadelphia No. 4 combined with Philadelphia No. 6.

APPENDIX TABLE 100-A.—*Principal statistical data, by local boards*—Continued.

PENNSYLVANIA—Continued.

Local board.	Post-office address.	Registration.				Induction.	Physical groups.					Deferments.		
		June 5, 1917.	June and August, 1918.	Sept. 12, 1918.	Total.	Accepted at camp.	General service.	Remediables.	Limited service.	Disqualified.	Dependency.	Agricultural.	Industrial.
PHILADELPHIA No. 40...	Southwest corner Fourth Street and Snyder Avenue.	4,815	394	5,615	10,824	1,347	923	118	310	318	3,051	4	63
PHILADELPHIA No. 41...	Fiftieth Street and Chester Avenue	3,351	284	4,998	8,633	797	469	25	170	8	1,988	0	110
PHILADELPHIA No. 42...	Sixty-fifth and Woodlawn Avenue	3,134	361	4,993	8,488	709	536	35	160	150	1,722	9	181
PHILADELPHIA No. 43...	York Road and Nedro Street	4,438	365	7,199	12,002	1,109	626	17	208	342	2,593	8	98
PHILADELPHIA No. 44...	3967 Germantown Avenue	2,924	227	4,091	7,252	966	531	34	98	47	103	1	79
PHILADELPHIA No. 45...	3447 Germantown Avenue	2,364	215	3,155	5,734	652	519	21	296	30	383	1	31
PHILADELPHIA No. 46...	Forty-eighth Street and Wyalusing Avenue	4,337	424	5,977	10,733	1,105	1,346	0	182	249	1,847	0	116
PHILADELPHIA No. 47...	Richmond and Kirkland Streets	4,450	312	5,807	10,569	923	608	28	161	303	1,761	3	43
PHILADELPHIA No. 48...	Fifty-seventh and Spruce Streets	3,175	203	5,041	8,419	813	508	25	196	303	1,655	3	333
PHILADELPHIA No. 49...	Fifty-fifth and Pine Streets	3,128	236	5,440	8,804	615	402	29	140	191	1,733	1	99
PHILADELPHIA No. 50...	Nineteenth and Oxford Streets	2,794	271	4,084	7,149	877	692	48	148	364	929	0	45
PHILADELPHIA No. 51...	Stephen Girard School, Eighteenth and Snyder Avenue.	2,633	230	4,210	6,073	648	527	40	90	115	1,336	5	68
Pike...	Courthouse, Milford	540	41	793	1,374	175	209	14	22	39	198	37	14
PITTSBURGH No. 1...	515 Smithfield Street	4,054	330	6,090	10,474	1,279	1,185	31	97	258	823	3	85
PITTSBURGH No. 2...	1901 Fifth Avenue	4,594	394	5,592	10,580	1,354	1,533	25	308	113	1,200	0	55
PITTSBURGH No. 3...	515 Smithfield Street	3,912	215	4,653	8,780	989	1,558	5	66	60	955	10	368
PITTSBURGH No. 4...	Centre Avenue and Morgan Street	3,465	326	4,463	8,259	1,021	892	56	128	148	1,629	1	67
PITTSBURGH No. 5...	5 McKee School, Ligonier Street	3,802	252	3,818	7,582	1,038	938	42	93	0	1,111	1	0
PITTSBURGH No. 6...	Elmer and Ivy Streets	3,432	291	4,697	8,423	1,180	1,058	16	78	245	1,097	3	237
PITTSBURGH No. 7...	227 Forty-third Street	2,518	173	2,994	5,685	629	819	1	30	1	777	0	149
PITTSBURGH No. 8...	Peabody High School, Margaretta Street	4,242	357	6,961	10,570	1,325	1,337	33	62	295	1,602	2	200
PITTSBURGH No. 9...	428 Frankstown Avenue	2,970	257	3,614	6,841	1,067	1,474	0	2	81	1,232	0	136
PITTSBURGH No. 10...	Carnegie Library, Hamilton and Long Avenue.	2,894	243	3,995	7,132	728	537	22	80	38	1,459	3	160
PITTSBURGH No. 11...	5870 Northumberland Street	1,434	111	2,620	4,165	534	410	0	41	91	452	0	106
PITTSBURGH No. 12...	Hazlewood Avenue and Lytle Street	8,196	269	4,443	7,908	685	618	3	33	130	1,123	3	391
PITTSBURGH No. 13...	Corner Warrington and Estella Avenue.	4,877	431	5,871	11,179	1,294	1,263	17	95	283	1,990	3	378
PITTSBURGH No. 14...	49 South Fourteenth Street	3,302	273	3,654	7,204	707	701	23	47	173	1,421	0	23
PITTSBURGH No. 15...	Prospect Street School	2,805	219	4,079	7,108	833	684	18	51	171	1,306	7	156
PITTSBURGH No. 16...	Corner Crucible and Lorane Avenue	2,094	182	2,832	5,048	855	577	13	43	21	672	13	466
PITTSBURGH No. 17...	Corner Chestnut and Juniata Streets	2,817	223	2,665	5,705	765	110	8	13	1	43		21
PITTSBURGH No. 18...	Allegheny High School, Arch Street, North Side.	3,786	300	5,535	9,671	1,293	1,293	27	274	30	1,474	1	109
PITTSBURGH No. 19...	Palmer High School	2,345	205	3,323	6,019	1,053	20	38	123	7	849	0	85
PITTSBURGH No. 20...	City Hall, Federal and Ohio Streets, North Side.	2,451	186	3,352	6,113	1,063	85	22	90	81	1,140	8	71
PITTSBURGH No. 21...	Eureka Co., 55 Ohio Street	1,675	119	3,813	4,171	744	478	22	89	42	764	0	67
Potter...	Coudersport	1,675	113	3,352	4,171	742	478	15	29	87	667	0	80
READING No. 1...	City Hall	2,195	145	3,967	4,654	535	314	15	104	150	735	5	25

Station	Location												
Reading No. 2	603 Baer Building	40	1	1,050	242	165	13	571	727	5,961	3,402	194	2,365
Reading No. 3	24 North Eleventh Street	13	0	257	207	115	21	564	633	5,873	3,274	241	2,338
Reading No. 4	24 North Sixth Street	107	2	1,336	10	229	35	710	905	7,615	4,202	285	3,128
Schuylkill No. 1	Shenandoah	673	0	1,843	88	222	10	980	646	8,919	3,550	262	3,709
Schuylkill No. 2	Mahanoy City	345	0	936	67	66	12	684	699	6,308	3,714	202	2,546
Schuylkill No. 3	Ashland	217	26	854	17	49	2	553	511	4,315	2,521	187	1,834
Schuylkill No. 4	Schuylkill Haven	59	64	871	102	65	5	390	414	11,187	6,160	174	1,620
Schuylkill No. 5	Courthouse, Pottsville	597	16	1,182	139	151	18	876	806	6,366	3,713	400	4,627
Schuylkill No. 6	Tamaqua	370	23	1,026	86	29	22	300	488	6,779	3,757	239	2,786
Schuylkill No. 7	Minersville	194	37	1,151	83	67	9	721	676	6,140	3,538	236	2,390
Scranton No. 1	Auditorium, 1821 North Main Avenue	121	0	960	114	55	32	41	542	6,498	3,354	213	2,384
Scranton No. 2	1128 Jackson Street	67	0	797	97	96	12	508	567	5,199	3,016	210	2,294
Scranton No. 3	Corner South Main and Hampton Streets	59	1		3	86	60	597	469	6,060	3,249	189	2,541
Scranton No. 4	414 Cedar Avenue	109	1	1,034	158	125	32	841	686	7,451	4,288	270	2,889
Scranton No. 5	909 Mears Building	20	224	692	71	36	29	265	781	3,089	1,720	294	1,232
Snyder	Courthouse, Middleburg	123	170	1,251	173	39	20	523	279	7,118	6,305	137	2,472
Somerset No. 1	Miller Building, Rockwood	64	88	382	61	30	13	687	732	10,527		326	3,471
Somerset No. 2	Sheriff's Office, Somerset	28	44	289	66	26	3	185	779	1,195		301	757
Sullivan	Laporte	32	304	1,301	90	107	20	338	248	6,825	3,930	82	2,626
Susquehanna	Montrose	42	214	1,357	310	91	15	1,039	568	7,398	4,225	259	2,853
Tioga	Wellsboro	12	36	436	16	17	1	325	837	2,855	1,443	320	1,059
Union	Lewisburg	66	95	1,074	129	120	20	458	246	5,885	3,352	153	2,262
Venango No. 1	Courthouse, Franklin	135	70	1,285	85	74		831	84	7,149	4,054	271	2,784
Venango No. 2	Oil City	104	93	68	145	105	35	746	810	7,825	4,383	332	3,110
Warren	Qrs Post Office, Warren	46	110	1,279	185	42	16	638	833	7,275	6,293	303	9,802
Washington No. 1	Courthouse, Washington	76	141	1,052	185	23	5	781	971	10,048	4,434	288	4,067
Washington No. 2	McDonald	175	139	1,090	123	20	15	522	916	7,882	6,293	279	3,119
Washington No. 3	Public Building, Canonsburg	80	83	1,305	40	20	107	588	681	11,470	6,633	337	4,200
Washington No. 4	Ellsworth				91	15			702	12,171	6,037	388	5,146
Washington No. 5	Post Office Building, Donora	24	143	607	125	86	30	561	1,256	5,152	2,998	232	1,922
Wayne	Honesdale	110	46	1,582	134	78	2	750	382	9,821	5,424	359	4,038
Westmoreland No. 1	Courthouse, Greensburg	173	88	1,449	28	29	38	1,213	935	8,768	5,029	355	3,934
Westmoreland No. 2	Irwin	179	83	1,257	32	34	5	894	973	8,418	4,746	293	3,379
Westmoreland No. 3	New Kensington	110	81	1,073	87	20	3	568	765	7,100	4,103	99	2,788
Westmoreland No. 4	Vandergrift	37	18	46		19		132	589	9,269	5,189	337	3,473
Westmoreland No. 5	High School Building, Latrobe	1,174	102	885	77	19	1	487	816	7,432	4,271	316	2,845
Westmoreland No. 6	Mount Pleasant	113	75	1,082	99	20	16	634	596	7,714	4,416	300	2,998
Westmoreland No. 7	West Newton	133	19	1,033	71	44	18	405	784	10,012	5,516	268	4,128
Westmoreland No. 8	Monessen	91	2	996	204	67	51	678	606	5,650	3,170	216	2,294
Wilkes-Barre No. 1	City Hall	24	2	733	221	85	47	677	530	5,693	3,069	216	2,408
Wilkes-Barre No. 2	do	90	2	825	174	104	39	345	554	5,276	2,921	206	2,149
Wilkes-Barre No. 3	do	55	7	1,472	275	145	25	660	597	7,404	4,124	291	3,019
Williamsport	do	11	69	463	121	19	0	190	800	2,496	1,468	01	997
Wyoming	Tunkhannock	87	4	1,178	186	167	26	316	266	4,777	2,670	207	90
York No. 1	City Hall	67		1,123	122	143	16	441	363	4,980	2,802	212	1,966
York No. 2	25 South Duke Street	30	161	1,236	136	73	8	457	457	5,289	3,038	250	1,991
York No. 1	3 East Market Street	30	242	1,345	125	114	19	308	529	5,299	3,802	272	2,225
York No. 3	Rooms 11a and 12, Security Building	51	242	2,055	147	98	8	609	793	7,635	4,220	329	3,066

APPENDIX TABLE 100-A.—*Principal statistical data, by local boards*—Continued.

RHODE ISLAND.

Local board.	Post-office address.	Registration.				Induction.	Physical groups.			Disqualified.	Deferments.		
		June 5, 1917.	June and August, 1918.	Sept. 12, 1918.	Total.	Accepted at camp.	General service.	Remediables.	Limited service.		Dependency.	Agricultural.	Industrial.
SAUNDERSTOWN No. 1	Town Hall, East Greenwich	2,272	179	3,339	5,790	584	473	17	71	248	1,055	59	49
OPPONAUG No. 2	Town Hall, Apponaug	2,636	231	3,600	6,467	631	606	40	191	291	1,173	15	44
BURRILLVILLE No. 3	Pocasset Mill, Thornton	2,475	224	3,734	6,433	574	471	7	110	209	1,196	55	28
LONSDALE No. 4	Town Hall, do	2,499	191	3,274	5,964	573	455	30	87	256	913	34	35
BARRINGTON No. 5	Town Hall, East Providence	2,666	221	4,099	6,986	496	375	58	37	57	1,533	75	139
BRISTOL No. 6	Federal Building	2,155	127	2,839	5,121	335	233	17	24	185	685	85	17
CENTRAL FALLS No. 7	City Hall, Central Falls	2,485	217	3,162	5,864	532	14	38	80	138	915	2	36
do No. 8	City Hall, do	2,025	161	3,259	5,445	399	345	15	83	228	233	21	42
NEWPORT	City Hall, Newport	3,257	204	3,414	5,906	712	411	42	77	220	1,036	17	10
PAWTUCKET No. 1	Room 209, do	2,257	246	4,311	7,814	730	613	27	167	311	263	2	70
PAWTUCKET No. 2	251 Main Street	2,710	218	3,729	6,657	642	552	22	158	14	1,037	5	61
PROVIDENCE No. 1	Room 15, Statehouse, Providence	2,082	123	2,754	4,959	391	250	10	114	183	390	3	37
PROVIDENCE No. 2	Room 8A, Statehouse, Providence	1,726	160	2,902	4,788	388	239	9	83	213	639	3	56
PROVIDENCE No. 3	113 Smith Street	3,338	294	3,971	7,603	577	546	34	81	257	1,275	2	68
PROVIDENCE No. 4	Court Room, Central Police Station	2,520	163	3,346	6,029	518	376	21	151	297	604	4	86
PROVIDENCE No. 5	do	2,021	132	2,809	4,962	420	288	23	138	211	647	1	88
PROVIDENCE No. 6	Seventh Police Station, Potter Avenue	1,878	175	3,256	5,309	413	297	33	69	183	886	3	74
PROVIDENCE No. 7	205 Benefit Street	1,334	129	2,298	3,761	302	188	10	57	116	582	6	77
PROVIDENCE No. 8	275 Plainfield Street	2,370	216	3,269	5,855	386	345	28	121	236	1,136	2	50
PROVIDENCE No. 9	1134 Westminster Street	3,362	262	3,977	7,601	705	734	47	75	234	1,201	1	78
PROVIDENCE No. 10	103 Smith Street	2,038	217	2,870	5,125	461	410	11	68	32	863	1	80
WOONSOCKET	City Hall, Woonsocket	4,117	345	5,244	9,706	959	53	35	89	295	1,662	9	130

SOUTH CAROLINA.

Local board.	Post-office address.	June 5, 1917.	June and August, 1918.	Sept. 12, 1918.	Total.	Accepted at camp.	General service.	Remediables.	Limited service.	Disqualified.	Dependency.	Agricultural.	Industrial.
Abbeville	Abbeville	1,974	248	2,594	4,816	736	748	6	38	145	959	26	34
Aiken	Aiken	3,853	253	4,385	8,491	1,197	1,293	81	156	69	1,855	104	12
Anderson No. 1	Anderson	2,486	270	2,866	5,622	980	21	1	25	254	875	7	14
Anderson No. 2	Williamston	2,001	223	2,351	4,575	629	782	31	84	209	1,131	21	13
Anderson No. 3	Honea Path	1,632	181	2,011	3,824	544	524	6	69	103	735	11	2
Bamberg	Bamberg	1,777	152	1,866	3,795	503	477	16	29	52	567	47	7
Barnwell	Barnwell	3,429	240	3,507	7,176	1,115	1,073	43	33	32	1,807	12	5
Beaufort	Beaufort	1,545	140	2,012	3,697	741	696	44		44	427	5	2
Berkeley	Moncks Corner	1,453	176	2,263	3,892	397							

Name	Address												
Calhoun	St. Matthews,	1,543	135	1,629	3,307	547	536	3	24	73	824	13	2
CHARLESTON No. 1	Broad Street, Charleston	2,151	194	2,854	5,199	625	481	11	114	412	612	4	37
CHARLESTON No. 2	16 Lucas Street, Charleston	3,726	329	5,088	9,143	923	834	6	137	720	3,531	8	50
Charleston	Vendue Range, Charleston	2,368	186	3,535	6,089	685	705	4	23	209	1,220	24	12
Cherokee	Gaffney	2,070	243	3,211	6,014	787	836	11	39	121	2,004	26	14
Chester	Chester	2,542	261	3,029	5,004	873	818	18	66	188	828	130	31
Chesterfield	Cheraw	2,303	244	3,179	5,066	724	543	22	128	75	1,416	45	37
son	Manning	2,761	240	2,884	6,180	819	748	3	19	117	1,526	7	2
Colleton	Walterboro	2,399	264	4,983	5,547	837	703	1	19	20	889	5	99
COLUMBIA	City Hall,	3,978	346	3,657	9,307	1,410	1,485	0	128	101	1,392	21	3
Darlington	Darlington	3,087	276	2,313	7,020	923	897	6	54	225	1,668	22	5
Dillon	Dillon	1,849	159	1,881	4,321	615	553	67	19	122	824	23	3
Dorchester	St. George	1,341	133	2,112	3,355	423	400	10	22	28	289	23	2
Edgefield	Mo.	1,900	186	2,292	4,198	592	654	12	96	33	978	18	9
Fairfield		873	198	5,114	4,363	658	624	0	49	93	534	17	34
Florence	Florence	3,944	358	2,454	9,416	1,122	96	25	80	350	237	0	1
Georgetown	rn	1,362	162	1,857	3,447	458	454		168	21	150	0	0
Greenville No. 1	Hrs Rest. ville	1,429	161	5,474	4,178	447	470	234	52	64	864	12	58
Greenville No. 2	Box 973, Greenville	4,497	425	2,083	10,396	1,262	1,451	10	281	71	1,580	503	52
Greenville No. 3	Box 504, Greenville	1,699	176	3,390	3,878	552	508	18	39	180	460	8	15
Greenwood	red	2,793	289	2,116	6,472	935	918		45		1,153		
Hampton	Hampton	1,920	215	3,170	4,251	448	809	13	18	1	99	1	5
Horry	Conway	2,415	209		5,794	888	335	7	9	35	373	1	1
Jasper	and	803	76	931	1,810	307	870	2	91	60	1,231	23	10
Kershaw	Camden	2,375	239	2,867	5,481	826	914	37	87	198	1,070	15	3
Lancaster	Lancaster	2,316	200	2,612	5,128	814	1,433	0	85	85	1,398	54	17
Laurens	Laurens	3,316	362	4,047	7,725	1,467	694	10	20	59	1,263	28	1
Lee	Bishopville	1,956	157	2,247	4,360	509	707	14	92	51	1,652	19	21
Lexington	Lexington	2,736	280	3,544	6,560	840	412	1	46	88	747	17	5
McCormick	McCormick	1,284	125	1,510	2,919	381	303	22	50	123	869	17	10
Marion	Marion	1,979	186	2,339	4,504	688	560	12	41	13	1,513	9	4
Marlboro	Bennettsville	2,716	241	2,891	5,848	839	862	39	125	181	1,352	14	20
Newberry	Newberry	2,667	316	3,278	6,261	966	732	28	76	111	1,315	19	17
Oconee	Walhalla	2,201	306	2,946	5,453	721	965	14	42	268	1,614	19	11
Orangeburg No. 1	Orangeburg	2,976	293	3,461	6,730	934	652	7	56	152	1,033	17	2
Orangeburg No. 2	Ellorce	1,987	206	2,242	4,435	656	629	22	27	143	1,208	4	0
Pickens	Rns	2,203	248	2,909	5,360	755	827	0	35	47	1,276	48	8
Richland	1211½ Washington Street, Columbia	2,506	187	3,238	5,931	818	653	39	41	33	1,552	48	3
Saluda	Saluda	2,929	194	2,193	4,380	660	797		86	186	1,370	20	6
Spartanburg No. 1	Spartanburg	1,757	287	3,643	6,859	891	245	4	48	83	640	2	3
Spartanburg No. 2	do	3,176	331	3,363	6,375	621	648	17	40	142	1,814	1	36
Spartanburg No. 3	do	2,372	227	2,735	4,719	913	886	16	54	160	1,245	45	39
Sumter	Sumter	2,596	306	3,733	7,215	808	1,094	8	143	91	1,546	0	1
Union	Union	1,824	244	2,952	5,568	913	830	3	13	183	836	14	2
Williamsburg	Kingstree	1,909	374	3,354	6,324	534	519	2	37	95	938	7	12
York No. 1	Rock Hill		171	2,280	4,275	687	624		60	257		20	4
York No. 2	York		225	2,473	8,882								

APPENDIX TABLE 100-A.—*Principal statistical data, by local boards*—Continued.

SOUTH DAKOTA.

Local board.	Post-office address.	Registration. June 5, 1917.	June and August, 1918.	Sept. 12, 1918.	Total.	Induction. Accepted at camp.	Physical groups. General service.	Remediables.	Limited service.	Disqualified.	Deferments. Dependency.	Agricultural.	Industrial.
Aurora	Plankinton	653	84	894	1,631	241	203	5	31	14	111	103	1
Beadle	Huron	1,851	182	2,653	4,086	577	443	21	57	124	777	100	4
Bennett	Courthouse, Martin	200	15	244	459	62	84		4	23	67	19	1
Bon Homme	Tyndall	1,027	116	1,318	2,461	414	441	62	26	63	384	44	0
Brookings	Brookings	1,506	160	1,863	3,529	610		46	40	139	131	178	64
Brown	Aberdeen	3,310	306	3,873	7,489	873	1,079	63	119	216	945	290	80
Brule	Min.	689	63	859	1,616	214	198	10	13	76	256	112	0
Buffalo	Gann Valley	157	19	171	347	54	57	2	5	1	72	11	4
Butte	Bellefourche	932	55	1,019	2,026	246	101		20		220	34	0
Campbell	Pollock	454	62	339	1,055	162	427	2	13	19	309	86	9
Charles Mix	Lake Andes	1,326	147	2,062	3,335	476	431	20	16	80	455	110	0
Clark	Clark	1,089	107	1,432	2,628	315	494	13	19		0	0	0
Clay	Vermillion	959	91	1,261	2,311	428	541	24	63	59	516	187	8
Codington	Mn.	1,471	139	2,010	3,620	451	380	1	24	86	339	56	5
Corson	Mn.	893	60	1,057	2,010	359	140	17	25	27	113	20	1
Custer	Custer	372	37	528	937	157	71		45	60	472	88	6
Davison	Mitchell	1,234	99	1,715	3,048	374	576	4	17	87	377	408	0
Day	Mr.	1,477	183	1,827	3,487	527	322	1	46	43	249	95	1
Deuel	War Lake	819	100	1,150	2,069	357	229	4	11	17	157	32	0
Dewey	Thor Lake	507	28	805	1,134	178	242	9	7	41	254	97	0
Douglas	Amr.	508	77	892	1,480	230	297	10	7	9	292	63	0
Edmunds	Bis, Ipswich	688	95	985	1,675	239	264	2	15	81	254	43	12
Fall River	Hot Springs	767	73	894	1,825	278	212	4	12	37	217	105	2
Faulk	Faulkton	623	63	1,334	1,880	214	442	10	49	63	310	200	4
Grant	Milbank	987	122	1,468	2,433	348	369	2	19	12	390	75	3
Gregory	Bonesteel	1,000	125	659	2,593	359	206	13	16	24	47	159	0
Haakon	Philip	404	41	1,011	1,104	141	257		21	74	263	169	1
Hamlin	Hayti	812	90	1,121	1,913	284	329	1	22	47	316	101	0
Hand	Miller	877	116	764	1,488	342	214	6	38	29	89	59	0
Hanson	Alexandria	614	60	821	1,409	247	212	1	25	22	221	58	1
Harding	Buffalo	609	39	696	1,077	256	125	9	19	31	163	19	1
Hughes	Pierre	443	88	1,414	2,774	146	405	9	43	35	308	139	0
Hutchinson	Parkston	1,220	181	425	2,780	436	120	2	14	13	96	37	0
Hyde	Highmore	1,299	20	425	585	187	187	3	11	3	96	8	0
Jackson	Kadoka	100	22	744	585	53	120	0	11	53	49	72	0
Jerauld	Wessington Springs	641	71	744	1,366	174	187		10	53	224	72	1
Jones	Murdo	251	27	421	699	101	4		1	26	92	16	1

TENNESSEE.

APPENDIX TABLE 100-A.—*Principal statistical data, by local boards*—Continued.

TENNESSEE—Continued.

Local board	Post-office address	Registration — June 5, 1917	Registration — June and August, 1918	Registration — Sept. 12, 1918	Registration — Total	Induction — Accepted at camp	Physical groups — General service	Physical groups — Remediables	Physical groups — Limited service	Physical groups — Disqualified	Deferments — Dependency	Deferments — Agricultural	Deferments — Industrial
Cumberland	Crossville	704	97	1,038	1,839	182	496	22	54	50	1,013	42	34
Davidson No. 1	American ... Bank Building, Nashville	1,914	313	5,428	7,655	614	310		60	144	677	42	15
Davidson No. 2	605 ... Street, Nashville	1,358	146	2,001	3,505	399	239	1	13	23	460	2	0
Decatur	Decaturville	792	80	1,115	1,987	285	286	9	5	65	256	1	0
Dekalb	...	1,268	145	1,646	3,059	385	361	0	27	50	896	22	17
Dickson	Dickson	1,464	199	2,086	3,749	433	642		43	118	1,324	4	0
Dyer	Dyersburg	2,515	286	3,544	6,345	889	934	25	63	6	1,392	4	3
Fayette	Somerville	2,445	267	2,897	5,609	964	136	0	19	71	297	5	4
Fentress	Jamestown	724	77	1,047	1,848	184	394	4	40		925	0	0
Franklin	Winchester	1,633	172	2,272	4,077	498	1,058	5	142	33	2,085	3	13
Gibson	Trenton	3,619	429	4,597	8,645	1,296	617	42	107	272	1,341	149	12
Giles	Pulaski	2,368	274	3,185	5,827	626	194	16	31	257	490	15	4
Grainger	Rutledge	984	137	1,511	2,632	272	454		81	181	402	60	5
Greene	Greeneville	2,468	333	3,358	6,159	718							
Grundy	Tracy City	654	111	1,022	1,787	197	196	4	13	54	410	2	17
Hamilton No. 1	North Chattanooga	1,392	158	2,080	3,630	458	294	11	48	178	704	11	23
Hamilton No. 2	1115 Hamilton National Bank Building, Chattanooga	2,711	304	3,714	6,729	998	839	10	216	165	1,147	13	37
Hamblen	Morristown	1,185	134	1,566	2,885	302	388	1	14	122	563	110	14
Hancock	Sneedville	765	83	1,070	1,918	180	138	20	3	105	499	60	1
Hardeman	Bolivar	1,798	198	2,191	4,187	622	550	0	86	46	968	10	6
Hardin	Savannah	1,385	162	1,815	3,362	514	417	0	50	23	849	0	0
Hawkins	Rogersville	1,700	228	2,548	4,476	519	556	11	23	289	552	9	7
Haywood	Brownsville	2,208	285	2,653	5,146	723	563	7	47	244	1,292	17	3
Henderson	Lexington	1,431	182	1,986	3,599	448	380	7	19	163	884	0	0
Henry	Paris	2,090	252	2,849	5,191	627	578	10	54	24	1,099	1	3
Hickman	Centerville	1,179	159	1,604	2,942	376	299	0	31	155	674	33	9
Houston	Erin	494	50	670	1,214	191	198	17	26	33	213	19	37
Humphreys	Waverly	1,087	131	1,474	2,692	330	244	3	7	67	630	31	5
Jackson	Gainesboro	1,157	148	1,559	2,864	306	62	3	13	10	45	3	
James	Birchwood	405	42	598	1,045	105	92	2	17	47	220	10	2
Jefferson	Jefferson City	1,300	182	1,945	3,427	349	317	1	29	43	576	51	8
Johnson	Mountain City	520	118	1,526	2,164	229	197	10	95	17	522	6	5
Knox No. 1	Knoxville	1,697	192	2,836	4,725	511	365	11	28	57	933	57	20
Knox No. 2	do	1,098	139	1,639	2,876	249	255	4		59	545	81	15
Knoxville No. 1	**210 Federal Building**	**4,152**	**415**	**5,194**	**9,761**	**1,246**	**898**	**97**	**91**	**153**	**1,791**	**2**	**139**
Knoxville No. 2	**Federal Building**	**3,053**	**345**	**4,065**	**7,463**	**702**	**738**	**25**	**65**	**182**	**1,888**	**4**	**63**

Lake	967	97	1,100	2,164	356	366	2	21	126	306	1	0
Lauderdale	2,420	236	2,546	5,202	675	703	13	21	462	1,231	8	1
Lawrence	1,776	206	2,343	4,325	449	391	—	57	153	1,005	21	8
Lewis	461	56	564	1,081	136	150	6	10	1	284	0	0
Lincoln	2,057	230	2,778	5,565	593	308	3	37	111	1,473	51	3
Loudon	1,331	176	1,661	3,168	369	309	1	35	27	882	71	12
McMinn	1,818	271	2,587	4,076	375	445	12	26	52	783	0	0
McNairy	1,400	153	1,883	3,436	514	140	3	32	74	881	12	0
Macon	1,169	134	1,592	2,895	244	1,478	84	194	31	284	4	2
Madison	3,979	384	4,779	9,142	1,206	470	9	53	64	822	29	30
Marion	1,470	160	1,721	3,351	509	373	8	56	25	767	60	3
Marshall	1,449	177	1,927	3,553	488	698	8	122	212	1,495	159	27
Maury	2,811	338	3,880	7,069	889	143	35	14	18	234	17	0
Meigs	466	55	611	1,132	159		0					
Memphis No. 1 ... 218 East McLemon Avenue	3,303	270	4,865	8,438	1,176	1,328	76	105	342	1,062	3	36
Memphis No. 2 ... 6, Police Station	2,606	160	3,493	6,259	736	833	38	74	290	996	2	55
Memphis No. 3 ... Police Station / 301	3,117	224	4,214	7,555	1,138	366	15	60	155	1,045	145	14
Memphis No. 4 ... 64 ... 6th Second Street	3,413	236	4,008	7,809	1,156	739	44	137	173	1,574	317	31
Memphis No. 5 ... Police Station	2,780	220	4,133	7,008	913	130	4	8	10	207	17	2
Monroe ... Madisonville	1,739	200	3,142	4,133	413	296	10	26	50	434	5	17
Montgomery ... Clarksville	2,552	269	952	5,963	734	722	9	184	180	1,214	4	69
Moore ... burg	386	45	530	1,541	122	894	8	141	22	937	3	50
Morgan ... Oakdale	928	114	1,432	2,474	264	533	10	68	284	1,509	0	60
Nashville No. 1 ... 818 Stahlman Building	2,786	324	4,424	7,548	847	412	24	44	179	1,067	5	24
Nashville No. 2 ... 40 Noel Block / 301	2,802	277	4,469	7,307	982	619	5	58	241	1,331	12	0
Nashville No. 3 ... Eve Building	2,665	283	4,359	5,146	531	446	5	43	171	858	26	9
Nashville No. 4 ... Union City	1,905	208	4,359	5,862	516	152	3	20	55	442	10	1
Obion	2,441	229	3,192	3,366	858	64	16	21	12	258	4	0
Overton ... Livingston	1,355	167	1,847	1,541	324	328	1	29	38	855	53	36
Perry ... Linden	702	80	759	2,838	199	389	1	31	151	1,018	58	13
Pickett ... Byrdstown	386	63	479	4,074	98	206	13	26	56	535	52	7
Polk ... Benton	1,288	122	1,428	4,571	324	490	—	31	166	843	26	23
Putnam ... Cookeville	1,577	215	2,282	5,214	377	601	12	59	1,172	1,397	87	14
Rhea ... Dayton	909	146	1,342	2,391	300	657	7	162	255	563	42	43
Roane ... Harriman	1,776	217	2,578	870	434	227	1	15	54	177	3	16
Robertson ... Springfield	2,178	247	2,789	6,647	672	104	0	8	22	993	2	0
Rutherford ... Murfreesboro	2,634	315	2,348	7,383	832	286	—	24	234		114	8
Scott ... Huntsville	914	111	1,366	3,775	256	994	24	57	10	1,489	4	5
Sequatchie ... Dunlap	311	51	505	2,920	87	321	1	19	119	954	35	2
Sevier ... Sevierville	1,653	237	2,283	6,865	410	314	102	29	103	732	21	1
Shelby No. 1 ... Memphis	3,034	242	3,960	5,341	922	1,063	1	114	48	2,005	229	39
Shelby No. 2 ... Binghampton	1,650	307	4,042	5,998	1,001	495	44	84	27	1,194	67	15
118th ... Carthage	1,210	173	1,952	1,193	424	1,337	6	20	75	1,221	2	0
Smart ... Dover	1,500	150	1,500	1,907	324	120	0	29	39	277	38	17
Summer ... Bristol	2,900	318	3,647	2,064	746	184	—	7	10	432	1	6
Tipton ... Gallatin	2,054	290	3,019	3,356	661	108	1	15	22	494	22	2
Trousdale ... Covington	2,639	340	608		1,107	288		5	154	175	8	0
Unicoi ... Hartsville	521	64	521		1,116					684		
Union ... Erwin	773	90	1,044		225							
Van Buren ... Maynardville	771	96	1,197		164							
Warren ... Spencer	271	24	301		73							
... McMinnville	1,294	174	1,898		433							

APPENDIX TABLE 100-A.—*Principal statistical data, by local boards*—Continued.

TENNESSEE—Continued.

Local board.	Post-office address.	Registration. June 5, 1917.	Registration. June and August, 1918.	Registration. Sept. 12, 1918.	Registration. Total.	Induction. Accepted at camp.	Physical groups. General service.	Physical groups. Remediables.	Physical groups. Limited service.	Disqualified.	Deferments. Dependency.	Deferments. Agricultural.	Deferments. Industrial.
Washington	Johnson City	2,324	274	3,365	5,963	598	483	10	44	260	1,388	103	24
Wayne	Waynesboro	1,100	119	1,355	2,574	237	186			103	645	4	1
Weakley	Dresden	2,654	322	3,513	6,319	843	746	13	103	94	1,285	1	0
White	Sparta	2,190	162	1,683	3,035	361	316		25	100	157	2	0
Williamson	Franklin	1,750	208	2,359	4,317	512	438	15	28	130	891	97	6
Wilson	Lebanon	2,073	219	2,695	4,987	619	390	23	38	184	743	118	6

TEXAS.

Local board.	Post-office address.	June 5, 1917.	June and August, 1918.	Sept. 12, 1918.	Total.	Accepted at camp.	General service.	Remediables.	Limited service.	Disqualified.	Dependency.	Agricultural.	Industrial.
Anderson	Palestine	2,841	366	3,937	7,144	963	628	10	14	60	1,047	2	7
Andrews	Andrews	64	2	53	119	10		0	65	20			
Angelina	Lufkin	1,993	194	2,443	4,630	500	463	0	7	2	1,019	1	14
Aransas	Rockport	113	22	282	417	50	68	10		29	44	30	2
Archer	Archer City	359	53	521	1,126	143	144		25	16	298	73	3
Armstrong	Claude	320	18	354	692	66	94	1	88	44	116	32	4
Atascosa	Pleasanton	1,250	96	1,360	2,700	287	64	31	19	141	575	6	2
Austin	Austin	3,227	317	3,857	7,401	821	844	0	9	102	1,497	25	21
Austin	Belleville	1,755	195	2,117	4,067	744	580	3	0	16	907	1	3
Bandera	Bandera	401	45	462	908	128	129	3	18	135	180	0	0
Bastrop	Bastrop	2,313	218	3,193	5,992	754	629	6	14	34	1,963	8	2
Baylor	Seymour	787	73	653	1,513	256	241	1	11	43	434	11	0
Bee	Beeville	953	81	1,255	2,292	270	169	4	63	77	399	35	5
Bell No. 1	Belton	2,246	252	2,400	4,904	723	508	23	18	67	1,137	29	20
Bell No. 2	Temple	2,784	197	2,546	5,078	654	642	10		123	1,096	85	1
Bexar	San Antonio	386	40	3,777	6,738	561	422			38	1,113	15	0
Blanco	Johnson City	127	13	441	867	98	68	0	1	3	194	12	0
Borden	Gail	1,707	90	90	230	31	30	10	20	9	77	17	3
Bosque	Clifton	3,377	213	1,919	3,839	642	489	38	60	29	1,021	23	8
Bowie	Texarkana	1,657	397	4,551	8,325	1,034	1,023	3	1	141	1,859	7	2
Brazoria	Angleton	2,061	197	2,522	4,370	519	114		0	0	40		
Brazos	Bryan	446	159	2,258	4,418	723				38	140	13	3
Brewster	Alpine	272	30	682	1,147	112	69	2	8	10	34	47	1
Briscoe	Silverton	293	39	332	459	79	80	3	1	8	54	0	0
Brown	Brownwood	1,793	287	2,319	4,513	546	353	12	81	42	944	62	25

County													City
Burleson	3	5	972	60	4	14	661	695	4,430	2,323	225	1,882	Caldwell
Burnet	1	3	494	44	31	9	255	320	2,083	1,001	75	1,009	Burnet
Caldwell	0	0	720	120	30	2	563	441	5,066	2,718	208	2,145	Lockhart
Calhoun	1	1	132	4	8	0	114	101	1,087	1,182	65	357	Port Lavaca
Callahan	4	15	643	53	27	2	314	290	2,433	1,362	113	1,138	Baird
Cameron	0	41	465	27	38	1	160	434	6,215	1,202	218	2,479	Brownsville
Camp	1	44	507	33	22	7	298	335	859	401	128	887	Pittsburg
Carson	3	30	187	34	10	0	84	105	6,789	42	42	416	Panhandle
Cass	0	40	1,418	140	21	28	441	789	529	3,036	327	2,426	Linden
Castro	7		129	9	1	3	125	80	1,006	233	30	256	Dimmit
Chambers			198	21	1	4	127	155	2,150	514	47	443	Mont Belvieu
Cherokee			78	30	14	19	189	985	7,573	4,184	362	3,027	Rusk
Childress	1	20	380	31	30	9	352	269	3,222	1,714	171	1,020	Childress
Clay	2	1	252	18	4	2	149	402	807	527	45	1,337	Henrietta
Coke	8	24	1,035	113	19	19	509	125	8,589	1,398	175	412	Robert Lee
Coleman	3	2	1,497	789	19	8	220	508	6,976	3,754	325	1,816	Coleman
Collin No. 1	0	3	1,222	72	39	4	530	858	4,791	2,727	177	2,897	McKinney
Collin No. 2	3	14	520	33	21	9	144	440	1,871	99		781	Farmersville
Collingsworth	2	13	842	120	9	9	32	174	4,002	1,011	205	1,739	Wellington
Colorado	9	24	323	25	13	2	160	627	1,912	2,118	64	793	Columbus
Comal	3	14	2,176	129	9	21	529	245	4,819	1,035	190	2,214	New Braunfels
Comanche	3	7	321	29	11	1	660	529	1,067	2,426	41	580	Comanche
Concho							134	178	5,863	3,198	309	2,356	Paint Rock
Cooke	0	6	1,089	49	17	20	632	528	4,455	2,171	241	2,043	Gatesville
Cooke	0	12	379	30	0	0	0	191	1,218	527	50	641	Gatesville
Coryell	0	12	74	10	2	0	62	74	485	214	71	200	Paducah
Cottle	1	33	378	30	7	7	180	217	1,470	725	71	738	Ozona
Crosby	1		30	9	2	1	44	56	297	126	46	120	Balls
Culberson	12	6	186	17	3	0	154	149	1,361	618	251	492	Van Horn
Dallam	25	0	1,753	374	100	60	1,801	1,475	9,381	4,888	343	4,445	Dalhart
Dallas No. 1	25	4	1,844	435	141	47	921	1,406	10,384	5,246	326	4,782	Second floor, Junip Building
Dallas No. 2	7	6	2,023	107	73	35	975	1,043	8,878	5,052	170	3,642	323 Slaughter Building
Dallas No. 3	28	4	1,604	113	39	9	453	524	6,162	3,265	550	2,347	Park and Bryan Streets
Dallas No. 4	7	88	604	330	42	33	1,182	1,305	12,298	7,196	39	4,988	214 Linz Building
Dallas	0	4	316	34	7	0	78	103	943	420	47	476	Carrollton
Dawson	0	1	145	7	8	1	99	140	943	438	139	366	Lamesa
Deaf Smith	2	27	670	56	22	12	272	318	3,679	1,952	390	1,337	Hereford
Delta	1	18	635	257	126	0	208	921	7,579	4,244	265	3,070	Cooper
Denton	0	0	633	30	20	16	110	747	6,069	3,420	82	2,567	Denton
De Witt	0	2	322	15	3	0	242	204	1,289	632	30	637	Cuero
Dickens	0	5	130	19	13	1	43	51	1,000	470	20	372	Spur
Dimmit	0	0	262	20	5	0	211	176	1,557	867	158	641	Carrizo Springs
Donley	6	26	30	155	0	0	167	121	1,901	945	49	660	Clarendon
Duval	0	0	980	40	14	1	420	500	5,088	3,434	296	1,647	San Diego
Eastland	0	7	58	10	3	0	103	25	240	93	7	104	Eastland
Ector	13	22	124	20	7	15	74	65	879	253	43	261	Odessa
Edwards	16	10	271	211	59	10	804	979	7,071	3,857	335	2,917	Rock Springs
Ellis No. 1	21	4	486	172	26	14	771	869	8,604	4,220	297	2,780	Waxahachie
Ellis No. 2	2	8	975	191	37	9	323	478	11,077	5,358	236	4,105	Ennis
El Paso No. 1	7	9	699	141	88	0	506	886	4,926	5,643	279	5,643	El Paso
El Paso No. 2	5	19	374	105	13	0	98	219		2,535	325	2,066	do
El Paso													do

APPENDIX TABLE 100-A.—*Principal statistical data, by local boards*—Continued.

TEXAS—Continued.

Local board	Post-office address	Registration — June 5, 1917	Registration — June and August, 1918	Registration — Sept. 12, 1918	Registration — Total	Induction — Accepted at camp	Physical groups — General service	Physical groups — Remediables	Physical groups — Limited service	Physical groups — Disqualified	Deferments — Dependency	Deferments — Agricultural	Deferments — Industrial
Erath	Stephenville	2,424	301	3,050	5,775	596	457	20	19	99	1,373	62	121
Falls	Marlin	3,802	535	3,786	8,123	1,250	1,231	1	60	210	1,837	25	2
Fannin	Bonham	4,084	292	5,921	10,297	1,287	1,291	5	56	378	2,447	3	2
Fayette	Lagrange	2,620	75	3,328	6,023	839	802	42	49	153	1,323	16	4
Fisher	Roby	1,169	106	777	2,052	290	213		18	45	683	14	3
Floyd	Floydada	927	47	970	1,944	259	165	1	18	38	615	157	0
Foard	Crowell	490	235	514	1,239	139	141	1	11	3	293	15	2
Fort Bend	Richmond	2,214	268	3,067	5,549	766	914	1	37	72	801	29	1
Fort Worth No. 1	Stockyards Station	2,272	187	3,241	5,700	548	468	9	43	31	218	2	12
Fort Worth No. 2	Room 20, Post Office Building	2,250	190	3,204	5,644	783	508	6	35	21	739	13	81
Fort Worth No. 3	City Hall	1,944	187	3,659	5,790	572	499	14	53	87	1,095	0	23
Fort Worth No. 4	104½ East Third Street	2,099	110	3,128	5,337	646	696	15	32	165	1,050	4	43
Franklin	Mount Vernon	878	243	1,162	2,283	213	215	1	9	65	569	0	0
Freestone	Fairfield	1,800	243	2,530	4,573	545	430	4	31	96	1,153	13	13
Frio	Pearsall	618	46	1,034	1,698	113	60			22	47	9	0
Gaines	Seminole	128	9	139	276	41	17	0		3		2	15
Galveston	Municipal Building, Galveston	5,154	291	5,677	11,122	1,533	1,433	0	320	155	1,515	1	
Garza	Post City	672	42	975	1,689	190	122		3	31	304	4	1
Gillespie	Fredericksburg	933	98	1,015	2,046	159	281	3	8	66	434	38	1
Glasscock	Garden City	89	3	58	150	29	21	0	9	36	49	0	3
Goliad	Goliad	1,015	87	1,195	2,297	325	266		5	166	414	11	0
Gonzales	Gonzales	2,742	289	3,150	6,181	764	731	31	30	13	1,250	40	0
Gray	Lefors	524	43	591	1,158	110	103		12	308	22	1	3
Grayson No. 1	Sherman	3,140	360	4,549	8,049	930	770	7	16	163	1,814	20	18
Grayson No. 2	Denison	3,100	320	4,481	7,901	886	750	0	63	100	1,838	6	21
Gregg	Longview	1,303	170	1,745	3,218	465	287	0	1	95	675	2	11
Grimes	Navasota	2,043	212	2,544	4,799	713	507	16	14	130	1,111	9	2
Guadalupe	Seguin	2,281	224	2,742	5,247	570	588	12	49	63	65	15	11
Hale	Plainview	1,218	92	1,161	2,471	329	320	11	19	10	518	81	9
Hall	Memphis	989	119	1,250	2,358	235	254	0	33	84	500	27	1
Hamilton	Hamilton	1,224	140	1,492	2,856	321	241		22	3	769	17	
Hansford	Hansford	171	17	168	356	49		3	10	51			
Hardeman	Quanah	**1,230**	**100**	**1,103**	**2,433**	**240**	**289**	**1**	**4**	**27**	**673**	**27**	**15**
Hardin	Kountze	**1,780**	**152**	**2,123**	**4,055**	**508**	**219**	**12**	**63**	**240**	**876**	**0**	**2**
Harris	1012 Union National Bank Building, Houston	**5,731**	**551**	**8,110**	**14,392**	**1,493**	**1,038**	**2**	**121**		**2,394**	**12**	**0**
Harrison	Marshall	**3,318**	**319**	**4,069**	**7,706**	**1,110**	**794**		**53**		**1,989**		**23**

County	Place	Population
Hartley	Channing	132
Haskell	Haskell	1,592
Hays	San Marcos	1,271
Hamphill	Canadian	431
Henderson	Athens	2,355
Hidalgo	Edinburg	1,608
Hill No. 1	Hillsboro	2,497
Hill No. 2	Itasca	2,063
Hood	Granbury	751
Hopkins	Sulphur Springs	2,976
HOUSTON No. 1	201 Main Street	2,051
HOUSTON No. 2	Loraine Street	2,269
HOUSTON No. 3	507 Stewart Building	5,061
HOUSTON No. 4	1204 Union National Bank Building	3,079
Houston	Crockett	2,620
Howard	Big Springs	783
Hudspeth	Sierra Blanca	184
Hunt No. 1		2,738
Hunt No. 2		1,703
Hutchinson	Plemons	116
Irion	Mertzon	157
Jack	Jackboro	955
Jackson	Edna	821
Jasper	Jasper	1,617
Jeff Davis	Fort Davis	197
Jefferson No. 1	Beaumont	4,391
Jefferson No. 2	Port Arthur	4,427
Jim Hogg	Hebbronville	173
Jim Wells	Alice	624
Johnson	Cleburne	3,154
Jones		1,622
Karnes	Kennedy	2,407
Kaufman	Terrell	3,746
Kendall	Boerne	397
Kent		499
Kerr	Kerrville	396
Kimble	Junction	114
King	Guthrie	230
Kinney	Brackettville	674
Kleberg	Kingsville	1,028
Knox	Benjamin	2,534
Lamar No. 1	Paris	2,204
Lamar No. 2	Paris	847
Lamb	Olton	345
Lampasas	Lampasas	2,510
La Salle	Cotulla	164
Lavaca	Halletsville	1,791
Lee	Giddings	1,377
Leon	Marquez	3,563
Liberty	Groesbeck	329
Limestone	Liberty	
Lipscomb	Lipscomb	

APPENDIX TABLE 100-A.—*Principal statistical data, by local boards*—Continued.

TEXAS—Continued.

Local board	Post-office address	Registration — June 5, 1917	Registration — June and August, 1918	Registration — Sept. 12, 1918	Registration — Total	Induction — Accepted at camp	Physical groups — General service	Physical groups — Remediables	Physical groups — Limited service	Physical groups — Disqualified	Deferments — Dependency	Deferments — Agricultural	Deferments — Industrial
Live Oak	Oakville	386	30	427	843	102	71	0	9	16	137	5	0
Llano	Llano	589	61	585	1,235	186	130	4	12	29	0	0	0
Lubbock	Lubbock	1,121	96	1,123	2,340	306	261	10	9	29	622	46	15
Lynn	Tahoka	516	43	409	968	127	160		12	14	293	0	0
McCulloch	Brady	987	81	924	1,992	319	217	6	6	42	544	5	3
McLennan No. 1	West	2,127	208	2,527	4,862	552	902	13	27	59	1,088	19	14
McLennan No. 2	Moody	2,480	237	2,588	5,305	743	694	0	28	124	1,231	22	0
McMullen	Tilden	121	10	100	231	24	40	0			65	0	1
Madison	Madisonville	1,108	113	1,348	2,569	288	280	2	5	53	692	3	2
Marion	Jefferson	824	93	1,074	1,991	335	351	5	16	32	458	0	0
Martin	Stanton	112	7	106	225	30	40	9	1	9	62	1	0
Mason	Mason	507	60	513	1,060	174	256	1	11		271	0	3
Matagorda	Bay City	1,292	164	2,228	3,684	508	577	6	28	94	340	92	7
Maverick	Eagle Pass	613	54	970	1,637	107	119	1	7	35	135	3	1
Medina	Hondo	1,126	75	1,324	2,525	227	181	0	9	66	365	19	1
Menard	Menard	322	39	388	744	114	87	2	5	18	165	7	5
Midland	Midland	322	17	305	644	96	65	.		34	127	1	3
Milam	Cameron	3,746	381	4,094	8,221	1,046	919	31	33	252	1,897	25	4
Mills	Goldthwaite	766	97	882	1,745	187	140	18	15	67	473	15	0
Mitchell	Colorado	743	48	574	1,365	205	133	4	16	46	455	2	0
Montague	Bowie	1,943	277	2,607	4,827	408	373	3	32	163	1,301	26	6
Montgomery	Conroe	1,552	165	2,023	3,740	466	435	4	71	40	787	35	0
Moore	Dumas	86	5	90	181	26	32	0	1	9	20	26	0
Morris	Daingerfield	819	101	1,087	2,007	268	202	0	13	55	502	1	4
Motley	Matador	423	42	435	900	156	136	1	13	11	108	3	15
Nacogdoches	Nacogdoches	2,336	274	3,122	5,732	755	835	16	66	11	1,394	2	11
Navarro No. 1	Corsicana	2,605	294	3,424	6,323	899	828	18	29	169	1,387	15	0
Navarro No. 2	Blooming Grove	2,490	270	2,910	5,670	721	517	4	9	190	1,427	0	4
Newton	Newton	960	87	1,303	2,350	301	273		62	19	439	1	6
Nolan	Sweetwater	1,079	58	837	1,964	203	172	4	11	35	642	5	7
Nueces	Corpus Christi	1,825	178	3,055	5,058	372	385	25	63	85	755	24	0
Ochiltree	Ochiltree	279	20	272	577	66	16	0	2	11	1	7	2
Oldham	Vega	97	9	113	219	39	34	0	2	3	39	7	3
Orange	Orange	1,619	255	2,883	4,757	401	464	5	81	88	766	97	47
Palo Pinto	Mineral Wells	1,641	176	2,374	4,691	452	400	15	49	94	869	7	64
Panola	Carthage	1,980	226	2,405	4,611	551	597	0	90	161	1,217	6	3
Parker	Weatherford	2,069	234	2,648	4,971	586	572	1	48	90	1,075	74	5

County / Place													
Parmer	220	12	222	454	63	4	0		1	5	0	2
Fort Stockton	40	26	608	937	108	136	26	8	9	130		14
Fort ...	1,654	186	2,094	3,899	527	554	5	66	82	735	18	38
Amarillo	1,627	138	2,094	1,771	343	387	9	26	140	822	13	0
Sutk.	614	36	938	1,754	195	164	9	25	135	7	0
Emory	726	98	447	846	130	174	8	11	461	1	0
Canyon City	361	38	48	101	25	25	4	12	161	9	2
Big Lake	46	7	160	318	61	77	4	0	0	0
Lakey	146	12	4,217	7,558	942	843	4	6	7	57	2	1
Red River	2,961	380	513	908	91	54	0	2	221	1,803	10	1
Pecos	2,365	30	685	1,157	105	18	3	14	28	150	10	4
Refugio	444	28	200	464	71	60	0	7	2	157	18	3
Courthouse, Miami	196	8	2,943	5,783	830	882	19	4	5	85	6	0
Franklin	2,560	241	1,240	2,168	316	303	7	3	153	1,293	5	2
Rockwall	822	106	1,423	3,227	562	407	10	30	53	378	16	0
Ballinger	1,649	155	3,212	6,120	819	832	21	3	98	860	2	0
Henderson	2,583	325	6,231	8,759	593	533	21	13	176	1,359	1	1
San Antonio	3,239	289	5,213	9,270	960	069	38	31	216	936	4	11
619 Bedell Building	3,724	333	3,627	6,664	787	43	15	21	297	150	5	8
429 Gunter Building	196	264	4,120	7,311	663	667	22	73	224	371	1	16
City Hall	2,927	93	1,352	2,595	347	374	11	30	196	900	4	0
Hemphill	1,226	141	1,571	2,938	482	440	9	48	27	1,477	5	0
San Augustine	912	162	1,023	2,097	188	205	3	15	28	568	1	1
Cold Springs	808	60	1,307	2,177	189			29	71	549	0	13
Sinton	1,027	122	1,028	1,637	343	224	1	32	50	543	13
San Saba	245	20	202	832	50	45	9	22	587	8	0
Eldorado	922	60	655	5,955	267	9	0	14	57	103	4	0
Snyder	382	30	420	351	122	79	16	10	21	490	4	0
Albany	2,495	310	3,150	9,465	995	904	0	39	101	203	2	1
Center	131	18	202	47	47	44	2	253	1	0
Stratford	3,773	495	5,197	9,465	822	283	0	4	01	1	1
Tyler	340	44	965	764	93	93	0	6	98	0
Glen Rose	544	33	769	1,542	22	15	3	63	45	2
Rio Grande City	557	72	114	1,388	145	117	1	12	17	168	2
Breckenridge	106	10	372	230	84	10	42	75
Sterling City	616	43	265	1,081	118	105	69	4
Aspermont	224	30	589	60	51	5	30	385	3
Sonora	429	51	526	1,006	154	129	0	19	93	4	3
Tulia	3,680	386	5,519	9,485	992	723	0	29	226	2	4
Courthouse, Fort Worth	2,290	210	2,055	4,558	630	53	9	59	246	1,106	52	27
Abilene	194	16	284	474	76	56	5	26	188	549	4	1
Sanderson	316	20	259	565	111	2	0	2	14	6	3
Brownfield	427	46	400	873	131						
Throckmorton	1,439	188	1,913	3,569	504	132	4	10	10	245	8	2
Mount ...	1,542	154	1,681	3,377	439	414	3	8	99	853	8	5
San Angelo	2,341	218	2,644	5,203	553	366	7	34	158	721	21	6
Austin	1,286	179	1,636	3,101	493	442	1	33	53	63	18
Woodville	835	111	1,139	2,105	285	480	22	35	25	1,210	5	6
...	2,006	220	2,043	4,874	624	311	3	11	30	632	3	2
Rankin	18	4	44	66	25	505	0	0	20	0	0
Uvalde	724	86	579	1,689	191	21	1	44	11	1,249	2	0

APPENDIX TABLE 100-A.—*Principal statistical data, by local boards*—Continued.

TEXAS—Continued.

Local board.	Post-office address.	Registration. June 5, 1917.	Registration. June and August, 1918.	Registration. Sept. 12, 1918.	Registration. Total.	Induction. Accepted at camp.	Physical groups. General service.	Physical groups. Remediables.	Physical groups. Limited service.	Physical groups. Disqualified.	Deferments. Dependency.	Deferments. Agricultural.	Deferments. Industrial.
Val Verde	Del Rio	870	83	1,454	2,407	150	139	0	3	68	205	14	0
Van Zandt	Wills Point	2,554	396	3,639	6,589	801	873	30	39	11	1,709	3	5
Victoria	Victoria	1,815	160	2,198	4,173	595	338	14	31	135	441	9	2
Waco	Federal Building, Waco	3,744	407	5,532	9,683	1,063	683	15	79	397	1,761	10	33
Walker	Huntsville	1,361	131	1,723	3,215	401	385			53	726	4	0
Waller	Hempstead	1,161	117	1,401	2,679	502	483	3	13		481	7	3
Ward	Barstow	177	18	285	480	61	42		3		65	4	0
Washington	Brenham	2,357	257	2,837	5,481	853	199	0	58	93	935	5	3
Webb	Laredo	2,244	185	3,769	6,398	215	84	9	20	14	19	0	0
Wharton	Wharton	2,413	258	3,269	5,940	795	1,063	29	33	1	1,131	37	3
Wheeler	Wheeler	689	62	872	1,623	194	183	12	6	50	382	28	2
Wichita	Wichita Falls	3,416	387	4,911	8,714	1,223	1,210	46	48	101	1,641	21	46
Wilbarger	Vernon	1,484	132	1,466	3,082	433	487	14	37	6	798	4	0
Willacy	Sarita	87	18	125	230	113	0	0	1	5	26	16	0
Williamson No. 1	Taylor	4,570	364	2,632	7,566	1,174	1,282	25	48	173	1,751	533	521
Williamson No. 2	Georgetown												
Wilson	Floresville	1,669	163	2,003	3,825	397	411	1	14	81	830	11	0
Winkler	Kermit	13	0	11	24	2	4				2	0	0
Wise	Decatur	2,041	297	2,933	5,271	595	546	16	28	116	1,203	37	3
Wood	Winnsboro	2,297	285	2,935	5,517	632	172	1	4	174	1,496	1	5
Yoakum	Plains	91	10	79	180	180	41	0	2	1	36	4	0
Young	Graham	1,093	128	1,324	2,545	328	72	0	12	3	622	6	4
Zavalla	Crystal City	223	15	302	540	49	78	7	4	20	92	0	1
Zapata	Zapata	190	20	276	486	20				3			

UTAH.

Local board.	Post-office address.	Registration. June 5, 1917.	Registration. June and August, 1918.	Registration. Sept. 12, 1918.	Registration. Total.	Induction. Accepted at camp.	Physical groups. General service.	Physical groups. Remediables.	Physical groups. Limited service.	Physical groups. Disqualified.	Deferments. Dependency.	Deferments. Agricultural.	Deferments. Industrial.
Beaver	Beaver	615	38	717	1,370	170	206	5	16	26	297	3	1
Box Elder	Brigham	1,499	141	2,012	3,652	359	485	19	27	59	791	50	7
Cache	Logan	2,014	236	2,521	4,771	584	487	12	80	63	1,153	83	4
Carbon	Price	2,097	126	3,291	5,514	468	565	5	40		489	25	22
Davis	Farmington	843	98	1,226	2,162	197	158	15	28	28	492	26	9
Duchesne	Duchesne	711	76	1,018	1,804	237		3	55	60	398	3	0
Emery	Castledale	588	54	779	1,421	133	98		16	6	347	0	0
Garfield	Panguitch	438	48	468	984	124	130	0	20		255	3	0

County	Location												
Grand	Moab	224	11	240	475	69	85	1	6	32	60	5	0
Iron	Cedar City	574	62	647	1,283	205	196	4	22	89	279	4	0
Juab	Nephi	1,173	89	1,257	2,519	275	79		10	53	0	0	0
Kane	Kanab	202	20	215	437	77	212	2	57	2	430	12	3
Millard	Fillmore	841	90	1,137	2,068	273	78	2	14	74	93	0	0
Morgan	Morgan	209	23	329	561	80							
Ogden	Ogden	2,940	267	4,069	7,176	768	875	12	112	161	1,415	16	42
Piute	Junction	254	26	296	576	60	38	4	8	7	149	2	0
Rich	Randolph	192	18	227	437	68	50	1			106	6	0
Salt Lake No. 1	Garfield Club, Garfield	4,854	261	4,675	9,790	809	608	39	122	152	1,206	0	8
Salt Lake No. 2	Hillcrest High School, Murray	2,038	182	2,854	5,071	546	360	37	85	256	835	11	10
Salt Lake City No. 1	Room 300 Capitol Building	2,413	180	3,828	6,421	635	370	31	100	150	1,343	5	9
Salt Lake City No. 2	Room 327 Capitol Building	3,203	213	3,924	7,340	749	678	30	133	185	1,089	1	33
Salt Lake City No. 3	Room 308 Capitol Building	2,650	215	3,500	6,455	773	680	27	135	25	1,046	8	19
Salt Lake City No. 4	State Capitol Building	2,839	192	3,334	6,365	736	620	39	152	17	1,081	8	1
San Juan	Monticello	255	9	250	514	74	117			21	93	6	5
Sanpete	Manti	1,190	154	1,813	3,157	379	361	10	34	50	698	46	4
Sevier	Richfield	788	113	1,149	2,070	306	64		24	34	18	6	4
Summit	Park City	1,090	63	1,130	2,283	317	177	8	3	12	326	20	1
Tooele	Tooele	1,139	48	1,385	2,572	305	171	15	47	215	386	31	5
Uinta	Vernal	738	55	956	1,749	188	115	3	47	21	420	17	0
Utah	Provo	2,872	357	4,265	7,494	981	893	20	130	29	1,606	7	0
Wasatch	Heber	329	41	56	956	127	57	4	13	6	179	6	0
Washington	St. George	543	74	633	1,250	209	166	7	34	20	279	77	3
Wayne	Loa	179	18	189	386	55	44	4	6		98		
Weber	Courthouse, Ogden	780	95	1,124	1,999	215	171	2	20		311	137	

VERMONT.

County	Location												
Addison	Middlebury	1,417	160	2,073	3,650	449	236	16	93	150	569	177	17
Bennington	Bennington	1,757	201	2,648	4,606	505	398	9	75	174	744	44	16
Caledonia	St. Johnsbury	1,949	202	3,042	5,193	396	344	12	137	163	950	169	28
Chittenden	Burlington	3,696	353	3,841	7,690	923	1,118	118	388	137	1,375	235	88
Essex	Island Pond	631	76	886	1,593	128							
Franklin	St. Albans	2,431	298	3,533	6,262	471	377	9	115	275	1,276	256	100
Grand Isle	North Hero	320	37	476	833	102	70		25	72	156	29	1
Lamoille	Hyde Park	798	103	1,369	2,270	221	158	6	93	72	394	64	6
Orange	Chelsea	1,869	131	1,990	3,228	350	231		123	169	366	208	25
Orleans	Newport	2,897	210	2,754	4,833	420	279	9	89	298	890	161	11
Rutland No. 1	Rutland	920	225	4,131	7,253	690	406	61	211	312	938	128	153
Rutland No. 2	Fair Haven	3,190	95	1,385	2,400	300	291	21	103	53	346	62	19
Washington	Montpelier	2,059	310	4,867	8,367	820	741	54	176	329	1,294	120	73
Windham	Brattleboro	2,902	182	3,085	5,326	471	444	1	117	157	834	132	72
Windsor	White River Junction		298	4,680	7,780	666	762	31	124	70	1,047	2	7

APPENDIX TABLE 100-A.—*Principal statistical data, by local boards*—Continued.

VIRGINIA.

Local board.	Post-office address.	Registration. June 5, 1917.	Registration. June and August, 1918.	Registration. Sept. 12, 1918.	Registration. Total.	Induction. Accepted at camp.	Physical groups. General service.	Physical groups. Remediables.	Physical groups. Limited service.	Disqualified.	Deferments. Dependency.	Deferments. Agricultural.	Deferments. Industrial.
Accomac	Accomac	3,169	241	4,104	7,514	895	1,156	34	61	199	1,442	353	7
Albemarle	Charlottesville	3,322	290	3,926	7,538	962	916	24	90	11	1,147	435	149
Alexandria	Alexandria	2,500	246	4,508	7,254	646	775	0	32	187	1,227	8	43
Alleghany	Covington	1,865	154	2,492	4,511	237	478	26	106	35	1,036	7	43
Amelia	Amelia	728	57	949	1,734	492	170		28	27	338	37	4
Amherst	Amherst	1,581	156	2,000	3,737	492	468	0	22	289	674	0	136
Appomattox	Appomattox	692	68	987	1,747	209	152	2	6	48	361	63	24
Augusta	Staunton	3,077	333	4,469	7,879	951	835	30	49	204	1,460	196	29
Bath	Hot Springs	557	65	768	1,390	182	138	13	15	2	269	20	10
Bedford	Bedford City	2,111	257	2,996	5,364	762	640	0	52	47	1,000	126	64
Bland	Bland	410	54	543	1,007	141	131	2	21	2	193	17	3
Botetourt	Fincastle	1,311	127	1,712	3,179	516	386	1	80	31	531	24	34
Brunswick	Lawrenceville	1,599	127	2,136	3,862	621	195	0	29	52	785	67	10
Buchanan	Grundy	1,156	138	1,330	2,624	253	253	10	69	150	721	0	6
Buckingham	Buckingham	871	107	1,438	2,416	345	305	6	10	94	389	54	21
Campbell	Rustburg	1,895	158	2,512	4,565	637	450	16	43	95	868	54	55
Caroline	Bowling Green	1,181	114	1,757	3,052	374	252	12	35	25	454	30	5
Carroll	Hillsville	1,513	202	2,129	3,844	565	418	4	45	49	886	9	8
Charles City	Courthouse, Charles City	444	63	545	1,052	138	152	11	4	146	202	9	0
Charlotte	Charlotte Courthouse	1,451	123	1,612	3,186	493	571	43	39	22	584	9	9
Chesterfield	Centralia	1,490	135	2,088	3,713	463	416	14	36	80	688	7	10
Clarke	Berryville	567	73	784	1,424	220	163	3	19	162	211	93	3
Craig	New Castle	361	52	455	868	116	30	4	16	28	190	12	10
Culpepper	Culpepper	881	109	1,203	2,193	270	320	7	8	69	429	104	1
Cumberland	Courthouse, Cumberland	586	70	893	1,549	215	194		15	53	268	20	11
Dickenson	Clintwood	876	99	1,166	2,141	219	202	10	47		535	0	11
Dinwiddie	Petersburg	4,776	436	6,230	11,442	1,404	1,022	49	52	768	2,245	91	0
Elizabeth City	Hampton	1,562	208	2,791	4,561	510	672	1	76	65	741	18	103
Essex	Tappahannock	653	45	764	1,362	157	126	6	8	76	207	82	27
Fairfax	Fairfax	1,476	160	2,201	3,887	502	352	1	50	127	669	60	1
Fauquier	Warrenton	1,704	152	2,278	4,134	553	427	6	38	126	561	82	9
Floyd	Floyd	1,110	139	1,379	2,628	338	323	13	41	132	513	319	9
Fluvanna	Palmyra	548	67	840	1,455	211	197		14	7	200	31	11
Franklin	Rocky Mount	1,683	228	2,465	4,376	581	417	14	14	156	978	21	16
Frederick	Winchester	1,482	164	2,211	3,857	556	482	12	46	112	638	55	26
Giles	Pearisburg	942	94	1,235	2,271	291	220	2	16	91	459	24	25
Gloucester	Gloucester	824	67	1,260	2,151	297	275		22	66	418	21	1

Place	Address												
Goochland	Perkinsville	681	60	847	1,588	184	193	0	13	81	280	71	6
Grayson	Independence	1,392	189	1,899	3,480	450	405	5	47	46	724	11	3
Greene	Standardsville	445	45	359	1,079	136	74		8	31	135	5	5
Greensville	Emporia	1,014	92	1,206	2,402	282	398	14	35	15	109	45	6
Halifax	Houston	2,462	261	3,865	6,588	787	280	8	39	112	611	193	23
Hanover	Courthouse, Hanover	1,370	131	1,967	3,468	398	248	12	31	148	630	92	21
Henrico	Richmond	1,528	108	2,179	3,813	487	341	10	22	194	646	8	16
Henry	Martinsville	1,174	156	1,891	3,221	386	108	5	23	42	157	33	4
Highland	May	350	51	548	952	141	477	20	61	14	551	70	9
Isle of Wight	Isle of Wight	1,320	109	1,580	3,009	375	156	0	4	44	132	38	23
James City	Williamsburg	409	70	584	1,063	168	164	0	1	16	190	22	2
King George	King George	427	33	576	1,063	119	147		16	57	298	38	3
King and Queen	King and Queen Courthouse	641	63	892	1,596	181	147	1	24	61	219	37	0
King William	Lester Manor	682	63	957	1,701	250	194	4	47	123	182	0	62
Lancaster		722	74	965	1,761	243	196	16	94	111	1,198	53	6
Lee	Jonesville	1,995	237	2,719	4,951	452	68	3	47	137	734	284	16
Loudoun	Leesburg	1,654	190	2,250	4,094	477	17	9	23	78	494	144	25
Louisa		1,147	116	1,732	2,985	374	314	13	19	85	75	196	155
Lunenburg		1,314	131	1,627	3,072	436	361	4	33	131	915	0	12
LYNCHBURG		2,703	203	3,224	6,130	894	848		120	79	296	101	
Madison	Courthouse, Madison	681	69	937	1,687	150	266		11		770		2
Mathews	Mathews	626	61	953	1,640	178		3	50	1	242	21	2
Mecklenburg	Boydton	574	225	2,935	5,469	451	841	1	38	73		19	
Middlesex	Saluda	2,309	65	884	1,523	416	137		52	161	1,074	93	15
Montgomery	Christiansburg	1,698	145	2,438	5,501	118	725	33	20	22	608	34	35
Nansemond	Suffolk	2,381	139	2,981	4,281	1,152	221	4	7	8	146	17	1
Nelson	Lovingston	1,337	128	1,725	3,190	816	122	0	75	5	628	0	1
New Kent	New Kent	880	25	489	894	753	1,499		89	224	1,965	0	6
NORFOLK No. 1	913 Bank Building	4,011	531	6,533	11,075	581	725	14	64	169	919	4	33
NORFOLK No. 2	Bank Building	3,989	300	7,463	742	333	338	13	13	515	1,732	87	48
NORFOLK No. 3	505 Law Building	2,674	199	3,346	6,219	446	2,056	1	47	60	663	97	16
Norfolk	1118 Bank of	4,435	511	7,226	3,760	249	542	17	23	51	422	45	5
Northampton	Eastville	1,617	62	2,018	2,760	253	296	2	76	68	473	58	60
Northumberland	Heathsville	915	113	1,308	2,285	370	433	6	73	50	314	110	2
Nottoway		1,208	82	1,510	2,831	1,028	309	16	59	124	339	78	91
Orange	Orange	884	117	1,316	2,282	628	140	3	36	134	662	10	13
Page	Luray	1,104	165	1,536	2,757	888	290	1	152	192	2,150	72	38
Patrick	Stuart	1,164	415	1,731	3,060	170	967	60	88	146	803	3	41
Pittsylvania No. 1	Chatham	4,111	163	5,393	9,919	380	31	25	160	108	1,522	2	27
Pittsylvania No. 2	Danville	2,018	336	2,392	4,573	1,311	1,154	1		43	174	72	33
PORTSMOUTH	Building	3,505	47	5,446	9,287	284	101	0	6	320	314	33	7
Powhatan	Courthouse, Powhatan	466	105	630	1,143	336	146	0	25	86	1,814	81	816
Prince Edward	Farmville	1,103	588	1,442	2,650	337	800	7	52	100	391	103	7
Prince George	Hopewell	5,197	73	6,080	11,865	189	236	2	19	76	386	97	5
Princess Anne	Courthouse, Princess Anne	955	113	1,318	2,345	977	312	11	46	38	704	58	56
Pulaski	Manassas	1,002	161	1,376	2,551	1,274	399	2	20		269	56	3
Rappahannock	Pulaski	1,285	52	1,748	3,194	816	163	7	179	221	1,653	0	89
RICHMOND No. 1	Washington	573	279	786	41	1,019	745	57	319	279	1,165	4	57
RICHMOND No. 2	Grays Armory	3,366	279	4,316	7,961		1,306	10		321	1,208	4	80
RICHMOND No. 3	do	3,861	237	4,606	8,746		698	48	43	321	1,573	2	111
RICHMOND No. 4	Twenty-second and Broad Streets	2,815	255	3,411	6,463		154	34	143				

APPENDIX TABLE 100-A.—*Principal statistical data, by local boards*—Continued.

VIRGINIA—Continued.

Local board.	Post-office address.	Registration.				Induction.	Physical groups.				Deferments.		
		June 5, 1917.	June and August, 1918.	Sept. 12, 1918.	Total.	Accepted at camp.	General service.	Remediables.	Limited service.	Disqualified.	Dependency.	Agricultural.	Industrial.
RICHMOND No. 5	Grays Armory	3,251	248	3,856	7,385	925	826	37	175	322	589	4	54
Richmond	Warsaw	520	60	2,728	1,308	198	185	8	7	29	234	12	1
ROANOKE No. 1	202 Municipal Building, third floor	2,016	179	2,600	4,735	372	384	1	74	91	998	0	240
ROANOKE No. 2	Municipal Building	2,521	241	3,377	6,139	557	575	3	50	92	1,291	3	374
Roanoke	Salem	1,793	165	2,533	4,491	402	313	3	31	179	957	69	94
Rockbridge	Lexington	1,875	180	2,620	4,675	066	421	20	76	84	499	11	12
Rockingham	Harrisburg	2,574	296	3,575	6,445	632	464	16	87	136	1,416	304	35
Russell	Cleland	2,426	235	2,926	5,581	578	591	12	45	157	243	49	99
Scott	Gate City	2,820	209	2,574	5,603	509	398	3	58	92	1,141	13	6
Shenandoah		1,486	184	2,269	3,939	419	299	13	58	124	779	172	32
Smyth	Marion	1,637	173	2,223	4,033	460	289	9	30	146	1,024	28	18
Southampton		2,191	170	2,668	5,629	667	633	23	63	102	897	74	5
Spotsylvania	Fredericksburg	1,222	104	1,692	3,018	432	600		43	51	552	26	18
Stafford		616	57	874	1,547	218	485		12	5	256	58	3
Surry	Surry	913	66	1,102	2,081	273	221	7	24	98	407	37	5
Sussex	Sussex	1,266	97	1,339	2,702	333	259	10	24	140	391	64	5
Tazewell		2,360	290	3,135	5,775	728	468	19	61	171	1,219	49	128
Warren	Front Royal	685	69	956	1,710	170	194	14	22	120	296	41	26
Warwick No. 1 and No. 2	Newport News	4,500	422	7,203	12,125	1,052	1,565	8	173	101	1,671	5	33
Washington	Abingdon	2,996	310	4,121	7,427	714	513	18	84	40	1,447	29	10
Westmoreland	Montross	735	65	1,003	1,803	226	220	7	7	97	312	30	0
Wise	Second floor, Post Office Building, Norton	4,312	420	5,601	10,333	1,192	981		62	251	2,041	211	96
Wythe	Wytheville	1,446	160	2,052	3,658	412	378	10	44	53	573	3	138
York	Yorktown	526	103	2,416	3,045	187	51	5	9	11	6		10

WASHINGTON.

Local board.	Post-office address.	June 5, 1917.	June and August, 1918.	Sept. 12, 1918.	Total.	Accepted at camp.	General service.	Remediables.	Limited service.	Disqualified.	Dependency.	Agricultural.	Industrial.
Adams	Sheriff's Office, Ritzville	1,156	115	1,258	2,529	362	292	14	51	37	415	178	6
Asotin	Sheriff's Office, Asotin	468	45	610	1,123	156	19		17	52	138	33	
Bellingham City	350 Federal Building, Bellingham	2,195	165	3,319	5,679	469	429	24	121	177	840	4	123
Benton	Sheriff's Office, Prosser	748	62	1,173	1,983	245	347	6	28	39	171	17	
Chelan	Sheriff's Office, Wenatchee	1,738	138	2,761	4,637	401	289	2	33	29	264	32	32
Clallam	Port Angeles	1,101	63	2,352	3,516	352	182		33	104	264	25	24
Clarke	Sheriff's Office, Vancouver	2,100	36	4,090	6,385	597	375	34	181	136	604	100	89

County / District	Office / Address												K.
Columbia	Dayton	626	56	718	1,400	190	183	3	15	11	274	8	57
Cowlitz	Kalama	947	80	1,488	2,512	252	205	12	43	129	306	23	2
Douglas	Waterville	1,249	111	1,360	2,720	321	225		131	97	473	162	131
EVERETT	Office of Mayor	2,323	173	3,625	6,121	529	424	39	131	171	693	5	1
Ferry	Republic	411	23	1,360	1,804	46	104	4	16	54	146	5	9
Franklin	Pasco	744	50	1,010	1,038	274	220		30	39	245	28	
Garfield	Pomeroy	652	35	549	2,117	137	104	7	28	40	187	56	10
Grant	Ephrata	454	70	1,138	4,836	233	168	27	29	78	339	148	82
Grays Harbor No. 1	Montesano	909	125	2,782	8,7?	488	252	21	93	202	459	24	9
Grays Harbor No. 2	Hoquiam	1,949	240	5,666	972	534	335	2	161	174	547		3
Island	Coupeville	2,799	29	574	1,370	126	94		25	22	120	24	7
Jefferson	Port Townsend	309	32	802	7,239	167	15	9	46	53	115	5	58
King No. 1	107 County and City Building, Seattle	536	137	4,679	8,498	703	361	47	228	117	729	43	60
King No. 2	117 Public Safety Building, Seattle	2,403	206	5,407	90	834	746	2	144	254	745	16	62
Kitsap	Port Orchard	2,385	214	4,150	4,045	472	336	38	73	24	585	15	17
Kittitas	Ellensburg	1,646	123	1,246	2,171	454	359	1	50	199	593	65	2
Klickitat	Goldendale	1,764	75	90		237	341	26	440	20	325	38	69
Lewis	Chehalis	850	267	4,783	4,227	720	449	16	85	35	731	31	5
Lincoln	Davenport	2,944	151	2,146	1,221	597	372	1	39	166	302	245	7
Mason	Shelton	1,930	34	708	3,799	156	123	6	24	39	141		2
Okanogan	Okanogan	479	103	2,110	4,0?2	435	408	5	100	226	587	126	91
Pacific	South Bend	1,556	132	2,375	1,610	405	326		27	63	517	19	
Pend Oreille	Newport	1,555	53	961	3,369	247	159		67	41	142	1	25
Place No. 1	312 Scandinavian-American Bank Building, Tacoma	596	110	1,968		375	231	14		200	388	12	
Pierce No. 2	302 Bank of California Building, Tacoma	1,291	214	4,086	98	509	376	20	92	93	591	20	81
San Juan	Friday Harbor	2,208	31	453	816	84	16		82	7	111	16	4
SEATTLE No. 1	5411½ Ballard Avenue	332	173	4,163	6,655	477	402	11	194	31	1,097	4	180
SEATTLE No. 2	320 Colman Building	2,319	118	2,958	4,623	407	511	6	71	100	786	1	75
SEATTLE No. 3	3610 Sixth Avenue N E	1,547	140	3,335	5,417	497	460	21	95	153	521	1	99
SEATTLE No. 4	Room 323, Alaska Building	1,942	128	3,416	5,217	40	258	21	87	84	758	3	139
SEATTLE No. 5	1014 Paulson Building	1,673	194	5,956	15,216	768	1,244		338	187	765		18
SEATTLE No. 6	1416 Alaska Building	3,015	460	9,746	5,59	1,594	1,435	62	563	431	494	5	321
SEATTLE No. 7	321 Lyon Building	5,010	144	3,272	6,413	463	290	15	148	142	565	1	118
SEATTLE No. 8	211 Lyon Building	1,669	134	2,789	4,450	413	501	55	121	154	459	1	81
SEATTLE No. 9	116 Public Safety Building	1,527	241	4,207	6,413	446	539	25	96	185	846		34
SEATTLE No. 10	206-207 Transportation Building	1,965	422	13,164	19,102	989	727	8	170	436	651	25	273
SEATTLE No. 11	365 Lyon Building	5,516	142	3,322	6,057	342	268	17	63	75	678	1	112
SEATTLE No. 12	323 Lyon Building	1,438	178	4,280	7,539	352	340	12	56	104	708	95	149
Skagit	Mount Vernon	1,599	206	4,472	65	723	467	8	306	89	74	7	57
Skamania	Stevenson	2,861	16	395	4,471	163	55	7	17	12	508	23	11
Snohomish No. 1	Arlington	254	120	2,571	3,327	553	415	3	103	181	319	29	40
Snohomish No. 2	Snohomish	1,780	168	1,873	4,964	377	315	9	184	14	826		17
SPOKANE No. 1	City Hall, Spokane	1,286	127	3,099	7,2?	377	299	23	100	100	391	1	9
SPOKANE No. 2	do	1,738	116	4,393	24	703	617	20	108	16	406	3	1
SPOKANE No. 3	do	2,619	53	1,527	4,399	317	247	5	64	104	693		5
SPOKANE No. 4	do	1,035	129	2,672	4,681	363	239		61	90	833	2	11
SPOKANE No. 5	1014 Paulson Building, Spokane	1,599	133	2,878	7,743	404	299	10	60	173	1,133	208	11
Spokane	Courthouse, Spokane	1,670	239	4,389	4,658	846	623	20	111	221	652	72	34
Stevens	Colville	3,105	150	2,717	90	587	452	42	76	207	622	2	10
?A No. 1	533 Provident Building	1,821	125	3,297		334	279	99	60	64	523	3	85
?A No. 2	1601 National Realty Building	1,574	267	4,111	6,346	410	402	55	93	258			107

APPENDIX TABLE 100-A.—*Principal statistical data, by local boards*—Continued.

WASHINGTON—Continued.

Local board.	Post-office address.	Registration.				Induction.	Physical groups.			Dis- quali- fied.	Deferments.		
		June 5, 1917.	June and August, 1918.	Sept. 12, 1918.	Total.	Ac- cepted at camp.	Gen- eral serv- ice.	Reme- diables.	Lim- ited serv- ice.		De- pend- ency.	Agri- cul- tural.	Indus- trial.
TACOMA No. 3	1310 National Realty Building	1,922	189	5,207	7,318	401	64		25	13	10		
TACOMA No. 4	5243½ Union Avenue	1,678	178	3,574	5,430	386	325	27	93	173	775	2	120
Thurston	Olympia	1,783	167	2,976	4,929	480	268	16	119	40	549	40	109
Wahkiakum	Cathlamet	510	28	557	1,095	152	95	12	35	25	117	8	25
Walla Walla	Walla Walla	2,259	190	3,305	5,754	656	478	28	162	81	888	92	11
Whatcom	Blaine	2,109	174	2,657	4,940	570	283	5	139	200	642	47	24
Whitman	Colfax	3,366	281	4,024	7,671	931	792	21	131	314	1,186	171	19
Yakima	Yakima	4,653	398	7,392	12,443	1,081	689	6	220	788	1,423	155	23

WEST VIRGINIA.

Local board.	Post-office address.	Registration.				Induction.	Physical groups.			Dis- quali- fied.	Deferments.		
		June 5, 1917.	June and August, 1918.	Sept. 12, 1918.	Total.	Ac- cepted at camp.	Gen- eral serv- ice.	Reme- diables.	Lim- ited serv- ice.		De- pend- ency.	Agri- cul- tural.	Indus- trial.
Barbour	Phillippi	1,225	187	2,181	3,593	43	33	0	32	69	526	4	1
Berkeley	Martinsburg	2,096	224	2,859	5,179	65	80	9	18	25	938	5	5
Boone	Danville	1,120	130	1,925	3,275	399	49	3	25	22	676		21
Braxton		1,23	244	2,673	4,639	65	67		65	164	840	12	19
Brooke	Wellsburg	1,17	143	2,414	4,359	36	32	5	53	130	600	11	11
Cabell		97	121	1,303	2,366	60	36	4	11	93	84	8	3
Calhoun		71	102	1,174	2,017	67	26		7	132	371		2
CHARLESTON	Federal Building, Charleston	3,516	375	5,174	9,065	1,100	1,...	1	14	203	1,503	3	117
Clay		36	104	1,223	2,173	33	33	1	14	81			6
Doddridge		97	140	1,075	2,732	42	31		35	68	468	1	3
Fayette No. 1	Fayetteville	3,44	333	4,898	8,045	1,169	94	14	70	49	1,377	5	109
Fayette No. 2		2,62	260	3,384	6,052	98	87	7	89	227	1,121	3	68
Gilmer		899	111		2,143	47	24	8	26	47	383	14	1
Grant	Petersburg	30	82	999	1,811	89	32	3	12	10	291	75	21
Greenbrier	Lewisburg	2,131	262	2,870	5,259	82	87	3	33	84	828	6	3
Hampshire		1,067	129	1,307	2,503	69	521	3	97	61	444	13	7
Hancock	New	1,988	160	2,652	4,790	43	87		51	110	569	2	2
Hardy		38	85	986	1,819	86	86	13	29	59	409	13	51
Harrison No. 1	404 Goff Building, Clarksburg	4,144	390	5,617	10,151	1,275	1,106	19	84	156	1,774	2	23
Harrison No. 2	311 Goff Building, Clarksburg	2,790	318	4,284	7,392	56	92	2	82	62	440	21	7
HUNTINGTON No. 1	Huntington	1,910	194	2,633	6,400	80	75	5	67	63	705	11	47
HUNTINGTON No. 2	do.	2,339	229	3,502	3,522	58	67		93	10	363	3	0
Jackson	Ripley	1,312	215	1,995	2,957	34	99	0	19	97	714	17	18
Jefferson	Charles Town	1,166	125	1,653		47	42	1	59	64	1,514	50	

County / District	Place												
Kanawha No. 1	212 Union Building, Charleston	3,093	329	4,484	7,900	912	731	11	146	145	1,500	1	97
Kanawha No. 2	2 Federal Building, Charleston	3,220	503	6,462	10,185	1,083	1,144	190	79	101	1,806	7	47
Lewis	Weston	1,530	201	2,242	3,973	674	581	10	15	122	745	17	22
Lincoln	Hamlin	1,523	166	2,106	3,795	475	414		15	175	864	1	6
Logan	Logan	4,094	444	6,641	11,179	1,203	1,066	20	58	308	1,910		117
McDowell No. 1	Welch	4,706	361	5,359	10,428	1,127	1,302		81	207	1,793	1	177
McDowell No. 2	...do	4,274	308	4,810	9,351	628	646		43	181	1,569	1	298
Marion No. 1	Fairmount	1,640	168	2,574	4,382	1,015	999	13	25	19	758	1	12
Marion No. 2	Mannington	3,064	325	4,402	8,380	1,084	908	1	32	125	1,317	16	40
Marshall	Moundsville	3,398	380	2,380	8,199	567	628	63	182	253	1,541	5	25
Mason	Point Pleasant	1,692	211	2,275	4,283	493	509	25	48	83	824	28	26
Mercer No. 1	Bluefield	1,818	152	3,814	4,245	822	821	3	43	81	1,012	6	121
Mercer No. 2	Princeton	2,816	304	2,505	6,934	621	493		98	169	1,455	10	156
Mineral	Keyser	1,659	169	1,680	4,363	773	494		87	146	798	4	21
Mingo	Williamson	2,536	303	2,505	6,209	910	342		11	132	1,225	1	7
Monongalia	Morgantown	2,619	315	4,335	7,269		229						
Monroe	Alderson	1,030	123	1,434	2,587	379		2	85	48	462	31	4
Morgan	Berkeley Springs	654	83	917	1,653			79	12	10			
Nicholas	Richwood	1,998	202	2,589	4,789	253	660	7	110	155	306	22	10
Ohio	Care of Chairman, Wheeling	1,836	175	2,804	4,815	621	318	4	31	86	812	7	6
Pendleton	Franklin	775	108	1,027	1,910	644	165		13	21	327	7	
Pleasants	St. Marys	457	58	825	1,370	331	433		7	18	262		1
Pocahontas	Marlington	1,460	158	1,956	3,574	173	667	15	43	32	531	6	2
Preston	Kingwood	1,887	283	3,364	5,534	522	403	45	41	8	888	0	31
Putnam	Buffalo	1,278	160	1,863	3,301	602	1,106		42	34	748	9	9
Raleigh	Beckley	4,387	447	5,752	10,591	412	705	7	168	127	2,193	2	75
Randolph	Elkins	2,114	241	3,368	5,723	1,309	462	7	36	62	904	4	11
Ritchie	Harrisville	1,260	165	1,953	3,378	814	021	2	37	135	164	6	4
Roane	Spencer	1,536	180	2,098	3,814	558	538	9	17	84	829	10	6
Summers	Hinton	1,544	189	2,063	3,796	643	467	3	16	77	656	20	29
Taylor	Grafton	1,515	162	2,315	3,992	501	421		54	128	699	2	59
Tucker	Parsons	1,519	140	2,065	3,724	529	359		8	133	639	1	2
Tyler	Middlebourne	1,014	151	1,680	2,845	410	470	9	18	176	481	0	2
Upshur	Buckhannon	1,156	182	2,008	3,346	485	626		64	103	604	4	6
Wayne	Kenova	1,891	227	2,720	4,833	563	325	4	4	217	1,060	30	30
Webster	Webster Springs	915	115	1,241	2,271	336	877	7	59	75	544	0	0
Wetzel	New Martinsville	2,033	275	2,423	4,736	700	1,135	0	141	181	907	6	7
WHEELING	Wheeling	4,764	422	6,299	11,485	1,614	313	69	22	366	1,794	0	47
Wirt	Elizabeth	541	83	857	1,481	263	1,110	0	68	47	248	2	1
Wood	Parkersburg	3,114	314	4,652	8,110	1,049		2	304	304	1,718	7	61
Wyoming	Mullens	1,355	151	1,773	3,279	414	0	0	32	32	693	0	4

WISCONSIN.

County	Place												
Adams	County Clerk's Office, Friendship	783	96	1,144	2,013	233	167	13	13	47	302	159	12
Ashland	Ashland	2,660	234	3,361	6,255	766	866	17	83	6	760	49	56
Barron	Barron	2,707	325	3,672	6,704	994	1,274	18	89	38	806	117	9
Bayfield	Washburn	1,677	212	2,529	4,418	496	98	2	57	130	515	90	146
Brown	De Pere	2,327	304	3,334	5,965	770	680	7	58	180	935	427'	13
Buffalo	Alma	1,404	188	1,825	3,420	414	451	14	39	44	554	370'	5

APPENDIX TABLE 100-A.—*Principal statistical data, by local boards*—Continued.

WISCONSIN—Continued.

Local board.	Post-office address.	Registration. June 5, 1917.	June and August, 1918.	Sept. 12, 1918.	Total.	Induction. Accepted at camp.	Physical groups. General service.	Remediables.	Limited service.	Disqualified.	Deferments. Dependency.	Agricultural.	Industrial.
Burnett	City Clk's Office, Grantburg	896	117	1,218	2,231	322	436	0	15	91	312	140	3
Calumet	Mon.	1,623	159	2,047	3,829	414	339	17	33	108	646	110	2
Chippewa	Chippewa Falls	3,184	307	3,858	7,349	951	1,019	45	43	218	989	609	41
Clark	Neillsville	2,566	330	3,876	6,772	847	1,106	38	44	168	718	439	41
Columbia	Portage	2,519	302	3,457	6,278	726	559	1	90	163	965	597	29
Crawford	Prairie du Chien	1,429	149	1,999	3,577	488	422		62	153	551	270	8
Dane No. 1	South Carroll St., Madison	2,132	259	2,943	5,334	610	546	23	35	120	736	644	18
Dane No. 2	Courthouse, Madison	2,488	275	3,328	6,091	825	647	16	42	121	393	490	26
Dodge No. 1	Horicon	2,353	246	2,971	5,540	720	594	34	103	126	890	375	34
Dodge No. 2	Beaver Dam	2,484	223	3,040	5,747	671	572	40	78	112	679	517	23
Door	Sturgeon Bay	1,571	179	2,211	3,961	436	389	0	84	133	435	240	9
Douglas	Superior	742	83	1,099	1,924	248	286	2	15	2	212	239	6
Dunn	Menomonie	2,228	296	2,970	5,494	721	684	46	61	163	465	457	22
Eau Claire	Eau Claire	2,991	343	3,797	7,131	1,028	1,217	25	116	104	1,173	299	57
Florence	Florence	353	43	398	794	170	147	8	13	22	69	39	4
Fond du Lac No. 1	Fond du Lac	2,950	289	3,859	7,098	895	761	17	100	231	1,237	175	58
Fond du Lac No. 2	Ripon	2,035	246	2,599	4,880	635	530	22	63	139	766	392	27
Forest	Crandon	933	60	1,161	2,154	202	211	0	39	42	345	21	3
Grant	Lancaster	3,307	337	4,533	8,177	1,082	909	21	76	241	1,341	502	41
Green	Monroe	2,153	221	2,685	5,059	540	473	13	55	80	306	475	24
Green Bay	City Hall, Green Bay	2,395	193	3,562	6,150	686	723	13	49	223	1,161	6	83
Green Lake	Green Lake	1,184	131	1,691	3,006	391	410	4	22	80	519	163	6
Iron	Hurley	2,134	222	2,592	4,948	669	489	17	74	114	370	387	31
Iowa	Dodgeville	1,247	90	1,073	3,010	253	303	23	44	96	298	19	49
Jackson	Black River Falls	1,460	166	2,041	3,667	374	23	22	44	4	314	556	13
Jefferson	County Clerk's Office, Jefferson	3,015	318	4,088	7,421	874	721	36	98	261	1,185	382	43
Juneau	Mauston	1,434	168	2,127	3,729	401	450	6	65	9	518	302	13
Kenosha	City Hall, Kenosha	4,555	332	6,248	11,135	1,392	1,078	55	199	287	1,457	0	94
Kewaunee	County Courthouse, Kewaunee	1,018	94	1,415	2,527	338	214	7	56	60	199	332	18
La Crosse	City Hall, La Crosse	1,200	147	1,876	3,283	403	374	14	37	29	424	90	20
La Crosse	La Crosse	2,793	291	3,452	6,536	1,198	994	46	171	157	1,170	4	97
Lafayette	Darlington	1,261	142	1,560	2,963	352	392	10	39	84	440	237	13
Langlade	Antigo	2,450	215	2,675	5,340	646	464	56	89	27	532	664	28
Lincoln	Merrill	2,024	180	2,555	4,759	546	681	38	89	51	680	122	20
Madison		1,636	196	2,404	4,236	530	558	44	47	108	654	82	15
MADISON	City Hall, Madison	4,471	384	4,744	9,602	582	973	6	131	314	1,029	24	224
Manitowoc No. 1	Manitowoc	2,110	302	3,147	5,559	669	680	39	79	139	781	196	73

Manitowoc No. 2	Two Rivers	2,181	270	2,793	5,244	713	566	0	58	186	874	287	24
Marathon No. 1	Courthouse, Wausau	2,468	337	3,388	6,193	986	1,082	44	93	19	945	181	13
Marathon No. 2	...do	2,807	307	3,962	7,076	1,053	1,192	20	46	52	977	62	11
Marinette	Marinette	2,879	314	3,716	6,909	1,006	910	9	82	223	1,087	167	22
Marquette	Montello	985	96	1,261	2,342	328	324	0	30	75	323	54	1
MILWAUKEE No. 1	320 Colby-Abbott Building	4,456	376	5,503	10,335	1,380	600	81	98	404	1,238	1	188
MILWAUKEE No. 2	Room 20, Metropolitan Building	2,377	189	3,099	5,665	538	649	20	72	140	455	0	66
MILWAUKEE No. 3	Eighth Street School	4,097	302	5,450	9,849	933	661	41	203	275	870	3	164
MILWAUKEE No. 4	2918 North Avenue	4,478	425	6,234	11,137	1,009	923	44	170	247	2,368	0	159
MILWAUKEE No. 5	Room 1, 322 Reed Street	2,484	169	3,370	6,023	538	405		148	123	532	1	70
MILWAUKEE No. 6	306-308 North Avenue	2,224	189	2,813	5,226	519	436	24	62	179	689	3	78
MILWAUKEE No. 7	1201 North Avenue	3,503	320	4,389	8,212	792	620	19	138	349	1,705	12	151
MILWAUKEE No. 8	Tenth and Forest Home Avenue	2,287	230	2,421	4,938	561	616	42	88	101	938	1	133
MILWAUKEE No. 9	1210 Galena Street	1,976	209	2,553	4,558	468	372	26	52	181	649	3	77
MILWAUKEE No. 10	Third Street School	4,038	407	4,831	9,276	1,036	762	55	240	331	2,004	6	231
MILWAUKEE No. 11	903 Railway Exchange Building	4,164	370	4,886	9,420	956	734	18	211	212	1,898	6	334
MILWAUKEE No. 12	149 Lincoln Avenue	4,151	376	4,861	9,388	1,021	1,152	55	155	295	1,647	2	236
MILWAUKEE No. 13	510-511 Colby-Abbott Building	3,073	282	4,295	7,650	855	660	40	126	211	1,234	7	148
MILWAUKEE No. 14	Fifth Avenue School	3,534	312	4,065	7,911	914	820	42	67	169	1,505	2	199
MILWAUKEE No. 15	Twentieth and Cold Spring Avenue	2,730	253	3,872	6,855	707	496	31	130	199	1,214	9	189
Milwaukee No. 1	Milwaukee	4,034	30	6,202	10,556	837	847	21	44	305	1,590	144	268
Milwaukee No. 2	...do	3,460	358	4,878	8,696	776	510	31	91	145	1,036	296	129
Monroe	Sparta	2,228	254	3,102	5,584	577	550	33	42	144	679	825	16
Oconto	Oconto	2,190	237	3,055	5,482	726	44	24	70	161	775	129	27
Oneida	Rhinelander	1,287	121	1,837	3,245	369	378	37	74	11	397	9	4
OSHKOSH	City Hall, Oshkosh	2,783	273	3,505	6,561	804	713	38	187	6	1,100	5	30
Outagamis No. 1	Appleton	2,369	265	3,013	5,647	776	653	37	66	167	998	203	33
Outagamis No. 2	Kaukauna	2,354	280	3,132	5,766	888	792	28	62	198	922	249	35
Ozaukee	County Clerk's Office, Port Washington	1,372	177	1,896	3,445	375	324	22	64	139	456	312	37
Pepin	Durand	609	93	836	1,538	205	211	8	18	42	115	132	5
Pierce	Ellsworth	1,857	205	2,521	4,583	772	712	14	53	93	529	427	6
Polk	Balsam Lake	2,024	264	2,988	5,276	791	649	32	110	132	600	432	14
Portage	Stevens Point	2,697	325	3,454	6,476	869	929	38	60	30	820	616	44
Price	Phillips	1,530	206	2,337	4,073	475	511	0	78	138	529	40	3
RACINE No. 1	City Hall, Racine	3,363	312	4,014	7,689	988	847	43	170	134	218	4	82
RACINE No. 2	1508 Washington Avenue, Racine	3,098	236	3,518	6,852	1,044	908	35	159	121	1,068	2	57
Racine	Burlington	1,930	90	2,659	4,779	685	537	30	70	116	413	311	10
Richland	Richland Center	1,618	176	2,262	4,056	406	294	0	31	143	811	288	13
Rock No. 1	Janesville	2,387	253	3,324	5,962	769	678	15	78	75	967	247	44
Rock No. 2	Beloit	3,450	337	4,243	8,030	998	136		37	189	1,278	523	68
Rusk	Ladysmith	1,106	124	1,841	3,071	310	40		5		21	9	1
St. Croix	Hudson	2,420	288	2,992	5,700	891	870	54	71	52	648	346	24
Sauk	Baraboo	2,775	339	3,862	6,976	940	902	30	41	193	1,062	431	33
Sawyer	Hayward	634	55	839	1,528	221	168	4	9	15	154	41	5
Shawano	Shawano	2,816	357	3,682	6,855	896	848	47	104	220	702	420	8
Sheboygan No. 1	Sheboygan	3,344	296	4,077	7,717	835	722	19	144	272	333	30	55
Sheboygan No. 2	Plymouth	2,370	297	3,119	5,786	745	567	46	90	160	1,034	376	51
SUPERIOR No. 1	City Hall, Superior	2,293	199	3,575	6,067	763	790	2	29	179	706	4	183
SUPERIOR No. 2	...do	1,410	166	2,533	4,109	402	463	7	30	17	503	2	86
Taylor	Mrd	1,234	164	2,036	3,434	453	389	13	28	29	256	99	5
[illegible]au	Whitehall	2,075	254	2,791	5,120	625	550	5	51	111	760	500	5
Vernon	Viroqua	2,381	286	3,316	5,983	807	731	25	55	189	980	446	9

APPENDIX TABLE 100-A.—*Principal statistical data, by local boards*—Continued.

WISCONSIN—Continued.

Local board.	Post-office address.	Registration.				Induction.	Physical groups.			Dis-qualified.	Deferments.		
		June 5, 1917.	June and August, 1918.	Sept. 12, 1918.	Total.	Accepted at camp.	General service.	Reme-diables.	Limited service.		Depend-ency.	Agri-cul-tural.	Indus-trial.
Vilas	Eagle River	525	47	756	1,328	201	169	4	15	39	190	4	2
Walworth	Elkhorn	2,608	244	3,329	6,181	874	703	39	137	188	696	472	25
Washburn	Shell Lake	862	101	1,164	2,127	215	215	18	29	66	261	41	21
Washington	Courthouse, West Bend	2,457	289	3,104	5,850	890	699	37	57	151	572	273	71
Waukesha	Courthouse, Waukesha	4,010	437	5,130	9,577	1,354	1,078	39	90	289	2,038	1,347	684
Waupaca	Waupaca	2,922	359	3,758	7,039	813	787	15	25	181	1,224	690	95
Waushara	Wautoma	1,410	169	1,967	3,546	294	274	17	55	34	613	267	7
Winnebago	Neenah	2,631	253	3,568	6,452	615	572	6	55	199	1,080	361	27
Wood	Grand Rapids	2,928	310	3,867	7,095	855	1,108	30	121	273	1,265	273	61
WYOMING.													
Albany	Laramie	1,240	86	1,745	3,071	455	48	16	2	17	285	8	2
Big Horn	Basin	1,240	123	1,649	3,012	454	542	0	40	11	451	39	14
Campbell	Gillette	945	41	903	1,889	423	529	23	25	41	292	27	2
Carbon	Rawlins	1,560	106	2,089	3,555	460	383	20	34	64	343	26	15
Converse	Douglas	987	93	1,263	2,343	388	370	2	37	70	257	29	7
Crook	Sundance	611	48	838	1,497	230	290		16	22	244	16	0
Fremont	Lander	1,228	94	2,201	3,524	385	495	3	36	23	306	25	6
Goshen	Torrington	1,011	74	1,220	2,305	384	377		11	67	472	16	1
Hot Springs	Thermopolis	679	56	1,129	1,864	277	324	2	30	7	180	12	6
Johnson	Buffalo	726	41	801	1,568	299	206	0	22	70	185	21	1
Laramie	Cheyenne	2,290	194	3,237	5,721	723	845	5	59	148	735	28	16
Lincoln	Downing Building, Kemmerer	1,096	161	2,600	4,457	575	715		83	79	699	8	6
Natrona	Casper	1,085	196	2,337	5,218	638	719	0	68	72	539	14	22
Niobrara	Lusk	565	40	670	1,275	231	198	8	18	22	201	15	2
Park	Cody	749	44	1,156	1,949	270	310	1	18	9	285	10	2
Platte	Wheatland	944	55	1,181	2,180	201	251	8	35	45	292	35	7
Sheridan	Courthouse, Sheridan	1,774	144	3,120	5,038	567	711	28	30	120	550	2	50
Sweetwater	Courthouse, Green River	1,852	123	3,147	6,122	568	416		33	49	324	8	5
Uinta	Courthouse, Evanston	739	74	1,122	1,935	281	223	15	17	24	315	25	4
Washakie	Courthouse, Worland	436	39	548	1,023	154	171		26	17	113		4
Weston	**Newcastle**	**530**	**42**	**870**	**1,442**	**206**	**185**	**1**	**6**	**41**	**152**	**8**	**3**

INDEX.

[References are to pages.]

Lightning Source UK Ltd.
Milton Keynes UK
UKHW021838140219
337217UK00005B/433/P

9 780266 218388